We've strengthened
our applications.

Steve Robbins and Tim Judge understand the importance of connecting concepts to students' personal lives and real business scenarios. To support your efforts in translating the science to great management practice and facilitating great classroom discussions, the following materials are provided:

- *"He who knows others is clever, he who knows himself is enlightened."*
  —Chinese philosopher, Lao-tzu

Students will benefit from taking self-assessment tests right after they've learned a concept, promoting self-understanding. **Prentice Hall's Self-Assessment Library (S.A.L.)** contains 51 assessments, 18 of which are now tightly integrated into the chapters. See pp. v-vi for more detail.

- *Abusive Customers (p. 291), Backstabbing (p. 497), Generation Gap (p. 462)*

  Students are confronted with vivid problems and issues that managers and employees face on a daily basis. The *new additional* **Case Incidents** at the end of each chapter provide students with the opportunity to analyze and make decisions on real-world events. Each short Case Incident is based on articles from popular business sources and supported with discussion questions.

- *What Customers Don't Know Won't Hurt Them, or Will It? (p. 697)*

  New **Comprehensive Cases** bring together multiple topics, helping students apply what they have learned in the course. All of these two- to three-page-long comprehensive, realistic, and real cases are supported with discussion questions. Many are based on articles from popular business sources. Case notes are provided in the *Instructor Manual.*

- *Is Managing Impressions Unethical? (p. 494)*

  Yes and no, depending on how you look at the issue! There are two sides to each controversy argued in **Point/Counterpoint.** This feature, ideal for use in classroom discussions, shows how students' preconceived notions may be inadequate or even incorrect. Several of these 19 dialogues are new to this edition.

We've strengthened
our research.

Who better to strengthen the research base of this text than Tim Judge? Tim has updated the theory and research throughout this twelfth edition. As the world is seemingly getting smaller, the international influences on organizational behavior become more pertinent. We increased the international coverage in the text and also link OB concepts to diverse countries and cultures in the **International OB** feature in every chapter. The following are highlights of the most significant research updates:

- New section on managing people during the war on terror (Chapter 1)
- New discussion on deviant workplace behavior (Chapter 1)
- Revised discussion of general intelligence (Chapter 2)
- Added section on race when discussing biographical characteristics such as age and gender (Chapter 2)
- Added coverage on Skinner/behaviorism (Chapter 2)
- Added a discussion on affective, normative, and continuance commitment (Chapter 3)
- Expanded discussion of other job attitudes, including perceived organizational support (POS) and employee engagement (Chapter 3)
- New section on critiquing the distinctiveness of these supposedly distinct job attitudes (Chapter 3)
- Added a section on "What Causes Job Satisfaction" (Chapter 3)
- Added a section on "Job Satisfaction and Workplace Deviance" (Chapter 3)
- Expanded material on Hofstede (Chapter 4)
- Expanded coverage of the Big Five model (Chapter 4)
- Integrated material on locus of control and self-esteem into new discussion on "Core Self-Evaluations" (Chapter 4)
- Added section on measuring personality (Chapter 4)
- Expanded material on person-organization fit (Chapter 4)
- ERG theory shortened and moved under Maslow's Theory (Chapter 6)

- Expanded goal-setting theory (Chapter 6)

- Added more material on self-efficacy (Chapter 6)

- New material on equity and justice theory (Chapter 6)

- New chapter on emotions (Chapter 8)

- Expanded material on "Composition: Abilities of Members" and "Composition: Personality" (Chapter 10)

- Expanded LMX coverage of "Leader-Member Exchange" (Chapter 12)

- Updated critique of the path-goal model (Chapter 12)

- Restructured *Contemporary Issues in Leadership* chapter (Chapter 13)

- Increased coverage of "Transformational Leadership" (Chapter 13)

- Updated "Substitutes and Neutralizers to Leadership" material (Chapter 13)

- Updated material on sexual harassment based on recent research (Chapter 14)

- Revised and updated "Spirituality and Organizational Culture" section (Chapter 17)

- Revised and updated material on "Selection Practices" (Chapter 18)

- New discussion on "Evaluating Effectiveness" (Chapter 18)

- New section on how to select people who accept change (Chapter 19)

- Incorporated recent research on change (Chapter 19)

- Added recent research on work and stress (Chapter 19)

Additionally, users of the previous edition will note a few changes in the structure of the book.

- The most important of these are the expansion of emotions to a full chapter (Chapter 8)

- The move of values to Chapter 4 now entitled *Personality and Values*

- The condensing of the MBO coverage and its move to Chapter 6, to bring it closer to the discussion on goal-setting theory; and the move of the job characteristics model coverage to Chapter 7.

We've strengthened our teaching resources.

Organizational Behavior, 12e, is supported with a complete suite of resources for instructors. All materials to support your teaching were thoroughly updated and reviewed to the highest quality.

- **Test Item File** — The completely revamped Test Item File, reviewed and accuracy-checked by a panel of faculty and assessment experts, includes new multiple-choice, true/false, scenario-based, discussion, and comprehensive essay questions. Listening to your feedback, we've updated difficulty levels of test questions and now offer a fifth choice for each multiple-choice question. The Test Item File is available in print and in electronic formats through the Instructor Resource Center. **We now have the best test bank in the industry. You be the judge.**

- **TestGen (test generator software)** — This computerized package allows instructors to custom-design, save, and generate classroom tests. The test program permits instructors to edit, add, or delete questions from the test banks; edit existing graphics and create new graphics; analyze test results; and organize a database of tests and student results. This software allows for greater flexibility and ease of use. It provides many options for organizing and displaying tests, along with a search and sort feature. The software as well as the test banks are available through the Instructor Resource Center.

- **Instructor Manual** — The updated *Instructor Manual* includes learning objectives, chapter overviews, lecture outlines, Web exercises, teaching notes for all end-of-chapter materials, Internet links, activities, supplemental readings, and sample syllabi. In addition, a guide to the *Self-Assessment Library* that guides faculty in interpreting student results and facilitates classroom discussion is provided. The *Instructor Manual* also includes a video guide and a guide to the accompanying PowerPoint slides.

- **PowerPoints** — Two sets of slides are available: instructor and student PowerPoints. Instructor PowerPoint slides include text outlines and figures from the text and are available on both the Instructor Resource Center on CD-ROM and on the Companion Website at www.prenhall.com/robbins. Student PowerPoints are available for download on the Companion Website.

- **Instructor Resource Center** — The Instructor Resource Center (IRC), available on CD, at www.prenhall.com/robbins, or within the OneKey course management course, includes all presentation and classroom resources all in one place for you. All resources can be edited to incorporate into custom classroom lectures or uploaded onto course management systems. The IRC for Robbins/Judge includes the following materials: Instructor Manual; PowerPoints; Test Item File; TestGen test-generating software; converted TestGen software for WebCT, Blackboard, and Course Compass; Instructor Manual for the Self-Assessment Library; and art files from the text.

- **19 *NEW* ABC News Videos** — Professionally edited ABC News videos bring issues covered in *Organizational Behavior, 12e,* to students' attention and draw them into the text materials—*Gender Wage Gap, Fired for Being Fat, "Colorism", Micro "soft" on Gay Rights?, No Smoking Employees, Bullies on the Job, What Stress Does to Your Body.* See pages viii-x for complete list of the videos. Videos are available on DVD only.

We've enhanced the learning experience for students.

Prentice Hall's Self-Assessment Library (S.A.L.)

SELF ASSESSMENT LIBRARY
A hallmark of the Robbins series, S.A.L. is a unique learning tool that allows you to assess your knowledge, beliefs, feelings, and actions in regard to a wide range of personal skills, abilities, and interests. Now tightly integrated into the text, S.A.L. helps students better understand their interpersonal and behavioral skills as they relate to the theoretical concepts presented in each chapter.

Highlights

- **51 research-based self-assessments** — Our entire collection of 51 instruments are from sources such as *Journal of Social Behavior and Personality, Harvard Business Review, Organizational Behavior: Experiences and Cases, Journal of Experimental Education, Journal of Applied Measurement,* and more.

- **Work-life and career focused** — All self-assessments are focused to help individuals better manage their work lives or careers. Organized in three parts—*What About Me? Working with Others,* and *Life in Organizations*—these instruments offer you one source from which to learn more about yourself.

- **Choice of Formats** — The Prentice Hall Self-Assessment Library is available in your choice of format: print, CD-ROM, or online. It is integrated into the Robbins-authored OneKey materials for use within the course-management context for his textbooks.

- **Save Feature** — Students can take the self-assessments an unlimited number of times, save and print their scores for class discussion.

- **Scoring Key** — The self-assessments have been edited by Steve Robbins to allow students to quickly make sense of the results of their score, and relate it to the concepts in the book.

- **Instructor Manual** — An *Instructor Manual* guides instructors in interpreting self-assessments and helps facilitate better classroom discussion.

For the new, twelfth edition, S.A.L. is included on CD-ROM with every new copy of the text. Additionally, faculty can select to ValuePack S.A.L. in the following available formats: print and online (stand-alone site or within your OneKey course management course offered in WebCT, Blackboard, and CourseCompass). S.A.L. is also available for stand-alone purchase in all formats.

I. WHAT ABOUT ME?

A. Personality Insights
1. What's My Basic Personality?
2. What's My Jungian 16-Type Personality?
3. Am I a Type-A?
4. How Well Do I Handle Ambiguity?
5. How Creative Am I?

B. Values and Attitude Insights
1. What Do I Value?
2. How Involved Am I in My Job?
3. How Satisfied Am I with My Job?
4. What Are My Attitudes Toward Workplace Diversity?

Companion Website

This Web site serves as a student study and review site This site—accessible at **www.prenhall.com/robbins**—includes chapter quizzes and Student PowerPoints.

OneKey Online Course Management Materials

 OneKey means all your resources are in one place for maximum convenience, simplicity, and success.

What's Key for Students?

- **Learning Modules** — Every section of all 19 chapters is supported by section level pretest, content summary for review, learning application exercise, and post-test. Learning modules are a great way to study for exams and are not connected to the instructor grade book offering unlimited practice.

- **Prentice Hall's Self-Assessment Library (S.A.L.)**

- **Research Navigator™** — is the easiest way for students to start a research assignment or research paper. Complete with extensive help on the research process and four exclusive databases of credible and reliable source material—including the EBSCO Academic Journal and Abstract Database, *New York Times* Search by Subject Archive, "Best of the Web" Link Library, and *Financial Times* Article Archive and Company Financials. Research Navigator helps students quickly and efficiently make the most of their research time.

What's Key for Instructors?

- **Instructor Resource Center** — Faculty can access all instructor resources in one place.

We've created a brand-new **abc NEWS** video program.

Enhance your classroom presentation with these 19 new, professionally edited ABC News Videos. These clips cover high-interest issues — *Gender Wage Gap, Fired for Being Fat, "Colorism", Micro "soft" on Gay Rights?, No Smoking Employees, Bullies on the Job, What Stress Does to Your Body.*

Recipe for Success College isn't for everyone; some young people just want to get trained for a profession in which they'll be able to get a decent paying job after high school. The "Careers Through Culinary Arts," program takes kids from some of the toughest high schools in America and places them in some of the top kitchens in America. Students, who often start out directionless, come out of the program motivated to become on the best chefs in the United States. (Chapters 3, 4, 6, and 7)

Gender Wage Gap Do women really get paid less than men for equal work? Most Americans believe that a man will be paid more than a woman for the same job. Warren Farrell, author of "Why Men Earn More," challenges this widely held assumption. (Chapter 4)

Fired for Being Fat The Borgata Hotel, Casino, and Spa in Atlantic City, New Jersey, threatens to suspend or fire cocktail servers and bartenders if they put on too much weight. A former female employee describes what it was like to work in an environment in which her body size was constantly monitored. Is this kind of company policy legal and what does it say about the values of the organization? (Chapter 4)

Dilley Six Pack In the nurture vs. nature debate, the notion of personality is often aligned with the nurture side of the equation. Meet the sextuplets of Becki and Keith Dilley and it becomes apparent that personality has a genetic component and is a force all its own. Each of the six children has a very distinct personality and needs to be dealt with differently. How does this experiment in personality apply to the rest of the world? (Chapter 4)

Surfer Girl Makes Comeback Bethany Hamilton was well on her way to becoming a professional surfer when tragedy struck. While waiting to catch a wave one Halloween morning, a shark attacked Bethany and bit off her entire left arm. After this traumatic event, Bethany's attitude helped her heal both emotionally and physically, and it propelled her back in to the water where she still competes as a surfer. (Chapter 3, 5, 6, 7, and 8)

Building Confidence Social interaction is a huge part of many people's jobs and yet many suffer from social anxiety in the workplace and beyond. Ann Demarais Ph.D., author of "First Impressions," helps a woman overcome her fear of talking to strangers, giving her the confidence to hand out her business cards to potential clients. (Chapter 8)

"Colorism" Racism is most commonly understood in terms of white people discriminating against African Americans and other people of color. Racism doesn't stop there. Many African Americans also discriminate against other African Americans based on the shade of their skin. How and why is lighter skin favored over darker shades within the African American community? (Chapter 5)

Age Discrimination (SPC Ruling) The U.S. Supreme Court rules that employees can sue their employers for discrimination based on age, even if the discrimination was not intentional. Company policy is where this unintentional age discrimination might be found. This ruling gives workers age 40 and over protection from being squeezed out by younger, cheaper workers. (Chapter 5)

Micro "soft" on Gay Rights? Historically, Microsoft has been very supportive of gay employees. However, when faced with the decision about whether or not to support a bill in the Washington State Senate outlawing discrimination against gays, the software giant had to answer to many stakeholders. When forced to choose between succumbing to pressure from conservative groups and supporting their gay employees and customers, who should take priority? (Chapter 5)

E-mail Code Text messaging, instant messaging and e-mail have changed the way people communicate with each other. A new shorthand has evolved and most young people are fluent in this abbreviated language. Take a crash course in instant-message speak. (Chapter 11)

Home Shopping Network A group of inventors compete to get a chance to present their products on the Home Shopping Network. The opportunity tests their ability to peddle their products when the stakes are high. Who will win the prize for best communication skills? (Chapter 11)

No Smoking Employees Howard Weyers runs a health-care benefits company, and he is a health nut. One day, he decided his employees at Weyco should be healthy too. So, he gave all the smokers at the company 15 months to quit smoking. He offered to pay for all the smoking cessation treatments, but anyone who was still smoking at the end of the 15 months would be terminated? Some employees claim that he violated their rights. Can a business owner force a healthy corporate culture on his employees? (Chapters 12, 13, and 19)

Nepotism The word "nepotism" usually has a negative connotation for most of us. Mobsters like Tony Soprano practice nepotism. Adam Bellow, author of, "In Praise of Nepotism," says nepotism is often a good thing. (Chapter 14)

Crimson Controversy Harvard President, Larry Summers, spoke at the National Bureau of Economic Research in 2005. He was asked to talk about why there aren't more women mathematicians and scientists at top American universities. He told the audience he wanted to speak unofficially and that he did; his provocative statements about women's innate abilities in math and science are still being discussed today. Should a leader from one of the country's most renowned universities be playing the role of provocateur when discussing the equality of the sexes? (Chapters 12, 13, and 14)

Bullies on the Job Every school has its share of bullies, but it turns out some of the kids grow up to be bullies at work too. About one out of every six people experiences psychological abuse in the workplace. Gary Namie, the author of a book called *The Bully at Work* explains the phenomenon and provides some advice on how to confront the problem. (Chapter 15)

Army Boot Camp One glimpse into army boot camp and it's not too hard to find adjectives to describe its culture. Discipline reigns supreme. Boot camp is designed to slowly break down the recruits until they submit to the highly structured and controlled world of the military. It sounds like torture and yet high-ranking officers assert that this rigorous orientation is essential in order for recruits to graduate from basic training ready to serve. (Chapter 17)

What Stress Does to Your Body An article in the New England Journal of Medicine reveals some disturbing findings about the serious damage that chronic stress does to our body. After a stressful episode the body releases a hormone called cortisol to calm down the nervous system. Although this chemical initially helps the body, it ultimately turns into something that is bad for our health. (Chapter 19)

Ways Men and Women Handle Stress Stress, stress, stress; who isn't stressed—it's an epidemic. Some may fall prey to stereotypes and say that men handle stress better than women. Think again. Researchers at UCLA tell us there's evidence women may actually handle stress better than men. (Chapter 19)

Kraft Changes Obesity is huge problem in the United States. Rather than taking responsibility for their own eating habits, some Americans are blaming restaurants like McDonald's and Burger King for making unhealthy, fattening food. In the wake of the blame game, Kraft has pledged to reduce the calories, fat content and portion size of many of the most popular products on these shelves. (Chapter 19)

Acknowledgments

Getting this book into your hands was a team effort. It took faculty reviewers and a talented group of designers and production specialists, editorial personnel, and marketing and sales staff. Sincere appreciation goes to Anthony Chelte, Midwestern State University, for his skillful and dedicated work on the Instructor Manual; Bryan Bonner, University of Utah, for his tireless work on perfecting the Test Item File; Kate Demarest, Carroll Community College, for her work on the imaginative Online Content; Nick Kaufman Productions for its professional work on the ABC News Videos; Patricia Lanier, University of Louisiana at Lafayette, for her wonderful work on the Video Guide; Brent Scott, University of Florida, for his dedicated work on the Case Teaching Notes; and last but not least Talya Bauer, Portland State University, for her support in chapter review and analysis and the special attention to accuracy of materials presented.

More than 100 instructors reviewed parts or all of the twelfth edition of *Organizational Behavior*. Their comments, compliments, and suggestions have significantly improved the final product. The authors would like to extend their sincerest thank you to the following instructors:

Janet Adams, Kennesaw State University

Cheryl Adkins, Longwood University

David Albritton, Northern Arizona University

Bradley Alge, Purdue University

Anke Arnaud, University of Central Florida

Gary Ballinger, Purdue University

Deborah Balser, University of Missouri at St. Louis

Joy Benson, University of Wisconsin at Green Bay

Gregory Bier, Stephens College

Weldon Blake, Bethune-Cookman College

Bryan Bonner, University of Utah

Peggy Brewer, Eastern Kentucky University

Jim Breaugh, University of Missouri

Deborah Brown, North Carolina State University

Reginald Bruce, University of Louisville

Allen Bures, Radford University

Holly Buttner, University of North Carolina at Greensboro

Kristin Byron, Rochester Institute of Technology

David Carmichael, Oklahoma City University

Suzanne Chan, Tulane University

Carolyn Gardner, Radford University

Evelyn Dadzie, Clark Atlanta University

Emmeline de Pillis, University of Hawaii

Doug Dierking, University of Texas at Austin

Ceasar Douglas, Florida State University

Ken Dunegan, Cleveland State University

Kathy Edwards, University of Texas at Austin

Berrin Erdogan, Portland State University

Sandra Fisher, Clarkson University

Edward Fox, Wilkes University

Alison Fragale, University of North Carolina at Chapel Hill

Dean Frear, Wilkes University

Crissie Frye, Eastern Michigan University

Janice Gates, Western Illinois University

David Glew, University of North Carolina at Wilmington

Ellen Kaye Gehrke, Alliant International University

Joe Gerard, University of Wisconsin at Milwaukee

Donald Gibson, Fairfield University

Mary Giovannini, Truman State University

Jeffrey Goldstein, Adelphi University

Jodi Goodman, University of Connecticut

Wendy Gradwohl, Wittenburg University

Claude Graeff, Illinois State University

W. Lee Grubb III, East Carolina University

Rebecca Guidice, University of Nevada at Las Vegas

Andra Gumbus, Sacred Heart University

Dan Hallock, University of North Alabama

Edward Hampton, University of Central Florida

Vernard Harrington, Radford University

Phyllis Harris, University of Central Florida

Nell Hartley, Robert Morris University

Tom Head, Roosevelt University

Ted Herbert, Rollins College

Ronald Hester, Marymount University

Patricia Hewlin, Georgetown University

Chad Higgins, University of Washington

Kathie Holland, University of Central Florida

Elaine Hollensbe, University of Cincinnati

Kristin Holmberg-Wright, University of Wisconsin at Parkside

Stephen Humphrey, Florida State University

Gazi Islam, Tulane University

Elizabeth Jamison, Radford University

John Jermier, University of South Florida

Ray Jones, University of Pittsburgh

Anthony Jost, University of Delaware

Louis Jourdan, Clayton College

Marsha Katz, Governors State College

Sigrid Khorram, University of Texas at El Paso

Jack Kondrasuk, University of Portland

Glen Kreiner, University of Cincinnati

James Kroeger, Cleveland State University

David Leuser, Plymouth State College

Benyamin Lichtenstein, University of Massachusetts at Boston

Robert Liden, University of Illinois at Chicago

Kathy Lund Dean, Idaho State University

Nora Madjar-Nanouska, University of Connecticut

Paul Maxwell, Saint Thomas University

James McElroy, Iowa State University

Nancy Meyer-Emerick, Cleveland State University

Linda Morable, Richland College

Lori Muse, Western Michigan University

Padmakumar Nair, University of Texas at Dallas

Alison O'Brien, George Mason University

Kelly Ottman, University of Wisconsin at Milwaukee

Peg Padgett, Butler University

Jennifer Palthe, Western Michigan University

Dennis Passovoy, University of Texas at Austin

Karen Paul, Florida International University

Bryan Pesta, Cleveland State University

William Pinchuk, Rutgers University at Camden

Theresa Porter, Franklin University

Paul Preston, University of Montevallo

Scott Quatro, Grand Canyon University

Jere Ramsey, Cal Poly at San Luis Obispo

David Ritchey, University of Texas at Dallas

Christopher Ann Robinson-Easley, Governors State University

Tracey Rockett Hanft, University of Texas at Dallas

Joe Rode, Miami University

Bob Roller, LeTourneau University

Craig Russell, University of Oklahoma at Norman

Andy Schaffer, North Georgia College and State University

Holly Schroth, University of California at Berkeley

Ted Shore, California State University at Long Beach

Randy Sleeth, Virginia Commonwealth University

Kay Snavely, Miami University of Ohio

Shane Spiller, Morehead State University

John Stark, California State University at Bakersfield

Joo-Seng Tan, Cornell University

Tom Tudor, University of Arkansas at Little Rock

Daniel Turban, University of Missouri

Jim Turner, Morehead State University

Leslie Tworoger, Nova Southeastern University

M.A. Viets, University of Vermont

Roger Volkema, American University

John David Watt, University of Central Arkansas

Shirley Wilson, Bryant University

Barry Wisdom, Southeast Missouri State University

Jun Zhao, Governors State University

Laurie Ziegler, University of Texas at Dallas

Gail Zwart, Riverside Community College

Over the last editions this text has grown stronger with the contribution and feedback of the following instructors:

Brad Alge, Purdue University

Lehman Benson III, University of Arizona

Richard Blackburn, University of North Carolina–Chapel Hill

Bongsoon Cho, State University of New York–Buffalo

Savannah Clay, Central Piedmont Community College

Kathleen Edwards, University of Texas at Austin

Ellen Fagenson Eland, George Mason University

Jann Freed, Central College

Barbara Hassell, Indiana University, Kelley School of Business

Abigail Hubbard, University of Houston

Jack Johnson, Consumnes River College

Stephen Jenner, California State University, Dominguez Hills

Robert Key, University of Phoenix

Leslie A. Korb, University of Nebraska at Kearney

Lou Marino, University of Alabama

Timothy A. Matherly, Florida State University

Melony Mead, University of Phoenix

Janice Miller, University of Wisconsin at Milwaukee

Clint Relyea, Arkansas State University

Philip Roth, Clemson University

Daniel Sherman, University of Alabama, Huntsville

Stuart Sidle, DePaul University

William Smith, Emporia State University

Kenneth Solano, Northeastern University

William D. Tudor, Ohio State University

We owe a debt of gratitude to all those at Prentice Hall who have supported this text over the last 30 years and who have worked so hard on the development of this latest edition. On the development and editorial side, we want to thank Development Editor, Erika Rusnak; Director of Development, Steve Deitmer; Marketing Development Manager, Kathleen McLellan; Director of Market Development, Annie Todd; Editorial Assistant, Denise Vaughn; Editor, Michael Ablassmeir; and Editorial Director, Jeff Shelstad. On the design and production side, Creative Director, Maria Lange and Production Editor, Judy Leale did an outstanding job. Last but not least, we would like to thank Marketing Manager, Anke Braun and Director of Marketing, Eric Frank, and their sales staff who have been selling this book over its many editions. Thank you for the attention you've given this book.

BUS 105
PRINCIPLES *of* ORGANIZATIONAL BEHAVIOR

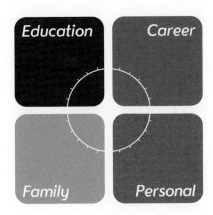

SECOND CUSTOM EDITION

Taken From:
Organizational Behavior, Twelfth Edition
by Stephen A. Judge and Timothy A. Judge

Cover image: courtesy of Digital Vision/Getty Images.

Taken from:

Organizational Behavior, Twelfth Edition
Copyright © 2007, 2005, 2003, 2001, 1998 by Pearson Education, Inc.
Published by Prentice Hall
A Pearson Education Company
Upper Saddle River, New Jersey, 07458

This special edition published in cooperation with Pearson Custom Publishing.

Printed in the United States of America

10 9 8 7 6 5 4 3 2

ISBN 0-536-33930-9

2006160661

SB

Please visit our web site at *www.pearsoncustom.com*

PEARSON CUSTOM PUBLISHING
75 Arlington Street, Suite 300, Boston, MA 02116
A Pearson Education Company

Brief Contents

Contents

Chapter 8   **Emotions and Moods**   258

Organizational Behavior

Twelfth Edition

What Is Organizational Behavior?

After studying this chapter, you should be able to:

1 Describe what managers do.

2 Define organizational behavior (OB).

3 Explain the value of the systematic study of OB.

4 Identify the contributions made to OB by major behavioral science disciplines.

5 List the major challenges and opportunities for managers to use OB concepts.

6 Identify the three levels of analysis in this book's OB model.

7 Explain the need for a contingency approach to the study of OB.

LEARNING OBJECTIVES

CHAPTER 1

What Defines a Successful Manager?

Meet Lakshmi Gopalkrishnan (see photo). She has undergraduate and master's degrees in English from Delhi University and Georgetown University, respectively, and is completing her Ph.D. in English at the University of Washington. In 1995, she began working for Microsoft in Redmond, Washington. Lakshmi currently manages a team of 16 full-time employees and a varying number of contractors in Denmark, North Dakota, and Washington. She oversees a team of Web designers and marketing specialists; and she is responsible for marketing and Web strategy on a range of Microsoft products and solutions.

"My background is basically journalism," says Lakshmi. "But I think I'm effective as a manager because I've developed my skills at managing individuals and teams. I've learned the importance of creating a compelling vision, the need to hire complementary skills, and how to inspire and challenge my team. For instance, I've learned that a clear and compelling vision inspires people to be part of something bigger than themselves. I've also learned that it takes time to understand what motivates each person. Each person brings a highly subjective lens to work every day, and it's important to understand differences. With senior contributors, for instance, my value might be limited to providing appropriate 'air cover' in negotiations. With more junior employees, I need to be much more hands on."

Lakshmi Gopalkrishnan has learned what most managers learn very quickly: A large part of the success in any management job is developing good interpersonal, or people, skills. Managers need to be technically proficient in their area of expertise, but technical knowledge is not enough. Successful managers, entrepreneurs, and employees also need interpersonal skills in order to work with others.[1] ∎

Although practicing managers have long understood the importance of interpersonal skills to managerial effectiveness, business schools have been slower to get the message. Until the late 1980s, business school curricula emphasized the technical aspects of management, specifically focusing on economics, accounting, finance, and quantitative techniques. Course work in human behavior and people skills received minimal attention relative to the technical aspects of management. Over the past two decades, however, business faculty have come to realize the importance that an understanding of human behavior plays in determining a manager's effectiveness, and required courses on people skills have been added to many curricula. As the director of leadership at MIT's Sloan School of Management recently put it, "M.B.A. students may get by on their technical and quantitative skills the first couple of years out of school. But soon, leadership and communication skills come to the fore in distinguishing the managers whose careers really take off."[2]

Recognition of the importance of developing managers' interpersonal skills is closely tied to the need for organizations to get and keep high-performing employees. Regardless of labor market conditions, outstanding employees are always in short supply.[3] Companies with reputations as good places to work—such as Starbucks, Adobe Systems, Cisco, Whole Foods, American Express, Amgen, Goldman Sachs, Pfizer, and Marriott—have a big advantage. A national study of the U.S. workforce found that wages and fringe benefits are not the main reasons people like their jobs or stay with an employer. Far more important is the quality of the employee's job and the supportiveness of the work environment.[4] So having managers with good interpersonal skills is likely to make the workplace more pleasant, which, in turn, makes it easier to hire and keep qualified people. In addition, creating a pleasant workplace appears to make good economic sense. For instance, companies with reputations as good places to work (such as the companies that are included among the "100 Best Companies to Work for in America") have been found to generate superior financial performance.[5]

We have come to understand that technical skills are necessary, but they are not enough to succeed in management. In today's increasingly competitive and demanding workplace, managers can't succeed on their technical skills alone. They also have to have good people skills. This book has been written to help both managers and potential managers develop those people skills.

What Managers Do

Let's begin by briefly defining the terms manager and organization—the place where managers work. Then let's look at the manager's job; specifically, what do managers do?

Managers get things done through other people. They make decisions, allocate resources, and direct the activities of others to attain goals. Managers do their work in an **organization**, which is a consciously coordinated social unit, composed of two or more people, that functions on a relatively continuous basis to achieve a common goal or set of goals. On the basis of this definition, manufacturing and service firms are organizations and so are schools, hospitals, churches, military units, retail stores, police departments, and local, state, and federal government agencies. The people who oversee the activities of others and who are responsible for attaining goals in these organizations are managers (although they're sometimes called *administrators*, especially in not-for-profit organizations).

Reality-show television producer Mark Burnett gets things done through other people. Burnett manages more than 1500 people. He structures each show, from *Survivor* to *Rock Star*, as its own company within his organization, Mark Burnett Productions. Burnett's goal is to produce TV mega hits. To accomplish his goal, he directs the development of his shows before he markets them to the networks, and he even remains on the set for the entire filming of every show. In this photo Burnett is in Borneo for the filming of *Survivor*.

Management Functions

In the early part of the twentieth century, a French industrialist by the name of Henri Fayol wrote that all managers perform five management functions: They plan, organize, command, coordinate, and control.[6] Today, we have condensed these to four: planning, organizing, leading, and controlling.

Because organizations exist to achieve goals, someone has to define those goals and the means for achieving them; management is that someone. The **planning** function encompasses defining an organization's goals, establishing an overall strategy for achieving those goals, and developing a comprehensive set of plans to integrate and coordinate activities.

Managers are also responsible for designing an organization's structure. We call this function **organizing**. It includes determining what tasks are to be done, who is to do them, how the tasks are to be grouped, who reports to whom, and where decisions are to be made.

Every organization contains people, and it is management's job to direct and coordinate those people. This is the **leading** function. When managers motivate employees, direct the activities of others, select the most effective communication channels, or resolve conflicts among members, they're engaging in leading.

The final function managers perform is **controlling**. To ensure that things are going as they should, management must monitor the organization's performance.

managers   *Individuals who achieve goals through other people.*

organization   *A consciously coordinated social unit, composed of two or more people, that functions on a relatively continuous basis to achieve a common goal or set of goals.*

planning   *A process that includes defining goals, establishing strategy, and developing plans to coordinate activities.*

organizing   *Determining what tasks are to be done, who is to do them, how the tasks are to be grouped, who reports to whom, and where decisions are to be made.*

leading   *A function that includes motivating employees, directing others, selecting the most effective communication channels, and resolving conflicts.*

controlling   *Monitoring activities to ensure they are being accomplished as planned and correcting any significant deviations.*

Actual performance is then compared with the previously set goals. If there are any significant deviations, it is management's job to get the organization back on track. This monitoring, comparing, and potential correcting is what is meant by the controlling function.

So, using the functional approach, the answer to the question—"What do managers do?"—is that they plan, organize, lead, and control.

Management Roles

In the late 1960s, Henry Mintzberg, a graduate student at MIT, undertook a careful study of five executives to determine what these managers did on their jobs. On the basis of his observations, Mintzberg concluded that managers perform 10 different, highly interrelated roles—or sets of behaviors—attributable to their jobs.[7] As shown in Exhibit 1-1, these 10 roles can be grouped as being primarily (1) interpersonal, (2) informational, and (3) decisional.

Interpersonal Roles   All managers are required to perform duties that are ceremonial and symbolic in nature. For instance, when the president of a college hands out diplomas at commencement or a factory supervisor gives a group of high school students a tour of the plant, he or she is acting in a *figurehead* role. All managers also have a *leadership* role. This role includes hiring, training, motivating, and disciplining employees. The third role within the interpersonal grouping is the *liaison* role. Mintzberg described this activity as contacting outsiders who provide the manager with information. These may be individuals or groups inside or outside the organization. The sales manager who obtains information from the quality-control manager in his or her own company has an internal liaison relationship. When that sales manager has contacts with other sales executives through a marketing trade association, he or she has an outside liaison relationship.

Exhibit 1-1	Mintzberg's Managerial Roles
Role	**Description**
Interpersonal	
Figurehead	Symbolic head; required to perform a number of routine duties of a legal or social nature
Leader	Responsible for the motivation and direction of employees
Liaison	Maintains a network of outside contacts who provide favors and information
Informational	
Monitor	Receives wide variety of information; serves as nerve center of internal and external information of the organization
Disseminator	Transmits information received from outsiders or from other employees to members of the organization
Spokesperson	Transmits information to outsiders on organization's plans, policies, actions, and results; serves as expert on organization's industry
Decisional	
Entrepreneur	Searches organization and its environment for opportunities and initiates projects to bring about change
Disturbance handler	Responsible for corrective action when organization faces important, unexpected disturbances
Resource allocator	Makes or approves significant organizational decisions
Negotiator	Responsible for representing the organization at major negotiations

Source: Adapted from *The Nature of Managerial Work* by H. Mintzberg. Copyright © 1973 by H. Mintzberg. Reprinted by permission of Pearson Education.

Informational Roles   All managers, to some degree, collect information from outside organizations and institutions. Typically, they obtain it by reading magazines and talking with other people to learn of changes in the public's tastes, what competitors may be planning, and the like. Mintzberg called this the *monitor* role. Managers also act as a conduit to transmit information to organizational members. This is the *disseminator* role. In addition, managers perform a *spokesperson* role when they represent the organization to outsiders.

Decisional Roles   Finally, Mintzberg identified four roles that revolve around making choices. In the *entrepreneur* role, managers initiate and oversee new projects that will improve their organization's performance. As *disturbance handlers*, managers take corrective action in response to unforeseen problems. As *resource allocators*, managers are responsible for allocating human, physical, and monetary resources. Last, managers perform a *negotiator* role, in which they discuss issues and bargain with other units to gain advantages for their own unit.

Management Skills

Still another way of considering what managers do is to look at the skills or competencies they need to achieve their goals. Robert Katz has identified three essential management skills: technical, human, and conceptual.[8]

Technical Skills   **Technical skills** encompass the ability to apply specialized knowledge or expertise. When you think of the skills held by professionals such as civil engineers or oral surgeons, you typically focus on their technical skills. Through extensive formal education, they have learned the special knowledge and practices of their field. Of course, professionals don't have a monopoly on technical skills, and not all technical skills have to be learned in schools or formal training programs. All jobs require some specialized expertise, and many people develop their technical skills on the job.

Human Skills   The ability to work with, understand, and motivate other people, both individually and in groups, defines **human skills**. Many people are technically proficient but interpersonally incompetent. They might be poor listeners, unable to understand the needs of others, or have difficulty managing conflicts. Because managers get things done through other people, they must have good human skills to communicate, motivate, and delegate.

Conceptual Skills   Managers must have the mental ability to analyze and diagnose complex situations. These tasks require **conceptual skills**. Decision making, for instance, requires managers to identify problems, develop alternative solutions to correct those problems, evaluate those alternative solutions, and select the best one. Managers can be technically and interpersonally competent yet still fail because of an inability to rationally process and interpret information.

technical skills   *The ability to apply specialized knowledge or expertise.*

human skills   *The ability to work with, understand, and motivate other people, both individually and in groups.*

conceptual skills   *The mental ability to analyze and diagnose complex situations.*

Effective Versus Successful Managerial Activities

Fred Luthans and his associates looked at the issue of what managers do from a somewhat different perspective.[9] They asked the question: Do managers who move up the quickest in an organization do the same activities and with the same emphasis as managers who do the best job? You would tend to think that the managers who were the most effective in their jobs would also be the ones who were promoted the fastest. But that's not what appears to happen.

Luthans and his associates studied more than 450 managers. What they found was that these managers all engaged in four managerial activities:

1. *Traditional management.* Decision making, planning, and controlling
2. *Communication.* Exchanging routine information and processing paperwork
3. *Human resource management.* Motivating, disciplining, managing conflict, staffing, and training
4. *Networking.* Socializing, politicking, and interacting with outsiders

The "average" manager in the study spent 32 percent of his or her time in traditional management activities, 29 percent communicating, 20 percent in human resource management activities, and 19 percent networking. However, the amount of time and effort that different managers spent on those four activities varied a great deal. Specifically, as shown in Exhibit 1-2, managers who were *successful* (defined in terms of the speed of promotion within their organization) had a very different emphasis than managers who were *effective* (defined in terms of the quantity and quality of their performance and the satisfaction and commitment of their employees). Among successful managers, networking made the largest relative contribution to success, and human resource management activities made the least relative contribution. Among effective managers, communication made the largest relative contribution and networking the least. More recent studies, conducted in a variety of countries (Australia, Israel, Italy, Japan, and the United States), further confirm the link between networking and success within an organization.[10] For example, one study found that

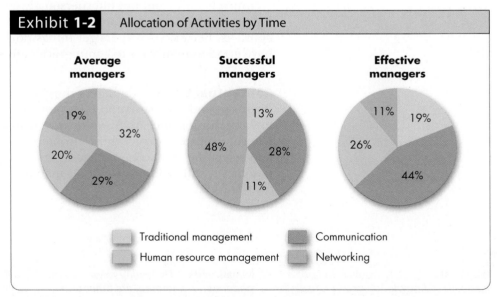

Exhibit 1-2   Allocation of Activities by Time

Source: Based on F. Luthans, R. M. Hodgetts, and S. A. Rosenkrantz, *Real Managers* (Cambridge, MA: Ballinger, 1988).

Australian managers who actively networked received more promotions and enjoyed other rewards associated with career success. And the connection between communication and effective managers is also clear. A study of 410 U.S. managers indicates that managers who seek information from colleagues and employees—even if it's negative—and who explain their decisions are the most effective.[11]

This research adds important insights to our knowledge of what managers do. On average, managers spend approximately 20 to 30 percent of their time on each of the four activities: traditional management, communication, human resource management, and networking. However, successful managers don't give the same emphasis to each of those activities as do effective managers. In fact, their emphases are almost the opposite. This finding challenges the historical assumption that promotions are based on performance, and illustrates the importance of networking and political skills in getting ahead in organizations.

A Review of the Manager's Job

One common thread runs through the functions, roles, skills, activities, and approaches to management: Each recognizes the paramount importance of managing people. Regardless of whether it is called "the leading function," "interpersonal roles," "human skills," or "human resource management, communication, and networking activities," it's clear that managers need to develop their people skills if they're going to be effective and successful.

Enter Organizational Behavior

We've made the case for the importance of people skills. But neither this book nor the discipline on which it is based is called People Skills. The term that is widely used to describe the discipline is *Organizational Behavior*.

Organizational behavior (often abbreviated as OB) is a field of study that investigates the impact that individuals, groups, and structure have on behavior within organizations, for the purpose of applying such knowledge toward improving an organization's effectiveness. That's a mouthful, so let's break it down.

Organizational behavior is a field of study, meaning that it is a distinct area of expertise with a common body of knowledge. What does it study? It studies three determinants of behavior in organizations: individuals, groups, and structure. In addition, OB applies the knowledge gained about individuals, groups, and the effect of structure on behavior in order to make organizations work more effectively.

organizational behavior (OB) *A field of study that investigates the impact that individuals, groups, and structure have on behavior within organizations, for the purpose of applying such knowledge toward improving an organization's effectiveness.*

Starbucks understands how organizational behavior affects an organization's performance. The company builds and maintains good employee relationships by providing a great work environment, stock options, and medical, dental, and vision coverage for all workers, including part-timers. Friendly and well-trained employees, in turn, treat their customers well. Starbucks continues to open new stores worldwide, such as this coffee shop in Lima, Peru, and to increase revenues 20 percent each year.

To sum up our definition, OB is concerned with the study of what people do in an organization and how their behavior affects the organization's performance. And because OB is concerned specifically with employment-related situations, you should not be surprised to find that it emphasizes behavior as related to concerns such as jobs, work, absenteeism, employment turnover, productivity, human performance, and management.

There is increasing agreement as to the components or topics that constitute the subject area of OB. Although there is still considerable debate as to the relative importance of each, there appears to be general agreement that OB includes the core topics of motivation, leader behavior and power, interpersonal communication, group structure and processes, learning, attitude development and perception, change processes, conflict, work design, and work stress.[12]

Complementing Intuition with Systematic Study

Each of us is a student of behavior. Since our earliest years, we've watched the actions of others and have attempted to interpret what we see. Whether or not you've explicitly thought about it before, you've been "reading" people almost all your life. You watch what others do and try to explain to yourself why they have engaged in their behavior. In addition, you've attempted to predict what they might do under different sets of conditions. Unfortunately, your casual or commonsense approach to reading others can often lead to erroneous predictions. However, you can improve your predictive ability by supplementing your intuitive opinions with a more systematic approach.

The systematic approach used in this book will uncover important facts and relationships and will provide a base from which more-accurate predictions of behavior can be made. Underlying this systematic approach is the belief that behavior is not random. Rather, there are certain fundamental consistencies underlying the behavior of all individuals that can be identified and then modified to reflect individual differences.

These fundamental consistencies are very important. Why? Because they allow predictability. When you get into your car, you make some definite and usually highly accurate predictions about how other people will behave. In North America, for instance, you would predict that other drivers will stop at stop signs and red lights, drive on the right side of the road, pass on your left, and not cross the solid double line on mountain roads. Notice that your predictions about the behavior of people behind the wheels of their cars are almost always correct. Obviously, the rules of driving make predictions about driving behavior fairly easy.

What may be less obvious is that there are rules (written and unwritten) in almost every setting. We would argue that it's possible to predict behavior (undoubtedly, not always with 100 percent accuracy) in supermarkets, classrooms, doctors' offices, elevators, and in most structured situations. For instance, do you turn around and face the doors when you get into an elevator? Almost everyone does. But did you ever read that you're supposed to do this? Probably not! Just as we make predictions about automobile drivers (for which there are definite rules of the road), we can make predictions about the behavior of people in elevators (where there are few written rules). In a class of 60 students, if you wanted to ask a question of the instructor, we predict that you would raise your hand. Why don't you clap, stand up, raise your leg, cough, or yell "Hey, dude, over here!"? The reason is that you've learned that raising your hand is appropriate behavior in school. These examples support a major contention in this textbook: Behavior is generally predictable, and the *systematic study* of behavior is a means to making reasonably accurate predictions.

Myth or Science?
"Preconceived Notions Versus Substantive Evidence"

Assume you signed up to take an introductory college course in calculus. On the first day of class your instructor asks you to take out a piece of paper and answer the following question: "Why is the sign of the second derivative negative when the first derivative is set equal to zero, if the function is concave from below?" It's unlikely you'd be able to answer that question. Your reply to that instructor would probably be something like, "How am I supposed to know? That's why I'm taking this course!"

Now, change the scenario. You're in an introductory course in organizational behavior. On the first day of class your instructor asks you to write the answer to the following question: "What's the most effective way to motivate employees at work?" At first you might feel a bit of reluctance, but once you began writing, you'd likely have no problem coming up with suggestions on motivation.

The previous scenarios were meant to demonstrate one of the challenges of teaching a course in OB. You enter an OB course with a lot of *preconceived notions* that you accept as *facts*. You think you already know a lot about human behavior.[13] That's not typically true in calculus, physics, chemistry, or even accounting. So, in contrast to many other disciplines, OB not only introduces you to a comprehensive set of concepts and theories; it has to deal with a lot of commonly accepted "facts" about human behavior and organizations that you've acquired over the years. Some examples might include: "You can't teach an old dog new tricks;" "leaders are born, not made" and "two heads are better than one." But these "facts" aren't necessarily true. So one of the objectives of a course in organizational behavior is to *replace* popularly held notions, often accepted without question, with science-based conclusions.

As you'll see in this book, the field of OB is built on decades of research. This research provides a body of substantive evidence that is able to replace preconceived notions. Throughout this book, we've included boxes entitled "Myth or Science?" They call your attention to some of the more popular of these notions or myths about organizational behavior. We use the boxes to show how OB research has disproved them or, in some cases, shown them to be true. Hopefully, you'll find these boxes interesting. But more importantly, they'll help remind you that the study of human behavior at work is a science and that you need to be vigilant about "seat-of-the-pants" explanations of work-related behaviors. ■

When we use the phrase **systematic study**, we mean looking at relation-ships, attempting to attribute causes and effects, and basing our conclusions on scientific evidence—that is, on data gathered under controlled conditions and measured and interpreted in a reasonably rigorous manner. (See Appendix A for a basic review of research methods used in studies of organiza-tional behavior.)

Systematic study adds to **intuition**, or those "gut feelings" about "why I do what I do" and "what makes others tick." Of course, a systematic approach does not mean that the things you have come to believe in an unsystematic way are necessarily incorrect. Some of the conclusions we make in this text, based on reasonably substantive research findings, will only support what you always knew was true. But you'll also be exposed to research evidence that runs counter to what you may have thought was common sense. One of the objec-tives of this text is to encourage you to enhance your intuitive views of behavior with a systematic analysis, in the belief that such analysis will improve your accu-racy in explaining and predicting behavior.

Contributing Disciplines to the OB Field

Organizational behavior is an applied behavioral science that is built on contri-butions from a number of behavioral disciplines. The predominant areas are psychology and social psychology, sociology, and anthropology. As we shall learn, psychology's contributions have been mainly at the individual or micro level of analysis, while the other disciplines have contributed to our understand-ing of macro concepts such as group processes and organization. Exhibit 1-3 is an overview of the major contributions to the study of organizational behavior.

Psychology

Psychology is the science that seeks to measure, explain, and sometimes change the behavior of humans and other animals. Psychologists concern themselves with studying and attempting to understand individual behavior. Those who have contributed and continue to add to the knowledge of OB are learning theorists, personality theorists, counseling psychologists, and, most important, industrial and organizational psychologists.

Early industrial/organizational psychologists concerned themselves with the problems of fatigue, boredom, and other factors relevant to working conditions that could impede efficient work performance. More recently, their contributions have been expanded to include learning, perception, personality, emotions, training, leadership effectiveness, needs and motiva-tional forces, job satisfaction, decision-making processes, performance appraisals, attitude measurement, employee-selection techniques, work design, and job stress.

Social Psychology

Social psychology blends concepts from both psychology and sociology, though it is generally considered a branch of psychology. It focuses on peoples' influence on one another. One major area receiving considerable investigation from social psy-chologists has been *change*—how to implement it and how to reduce barriers to its acceptance. In addition, we find social psychologists making significant contribu-tions in the areas of measuring, understanding, and changing attitudes; commu-nication patterns; and building trust. Finally, social psychologists have made important contributions to our study of group behavior, power, and conflict.

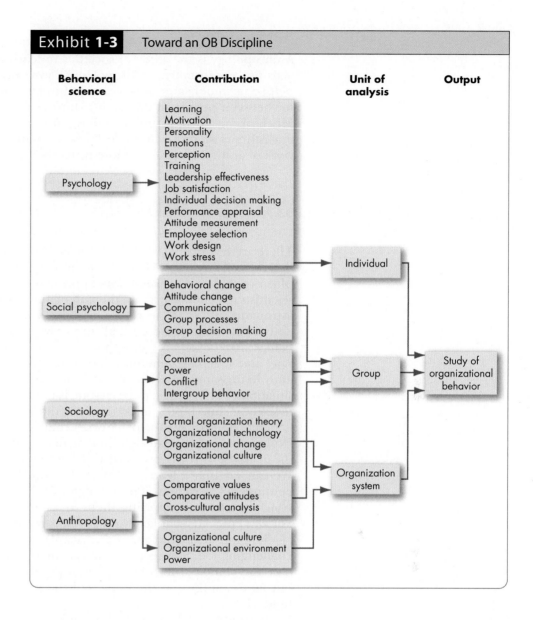

Exhibit 1-3   Toward an OB Discipline

Sociology

While psychology focuses on the individual, **sociology** studies people in relation to their social environment or culture. Sociologists have contributed to OB through their study of group behavior in organizations, particularly formal and complex organizations. Perhaps most importantly, sociology has contributed to research on organizational culture, formal organization theory and structure, organizational technology, communications, power, and conflict.

Anthropology

Anthropology is the study of societies to learn about human beings and their activities. For instance, anthropologists' work on cultures and environments has helped us understand differences in fundamental values, attitudes, and behavior between people in different countries and within different organizations. Much of our current understanding of organizational culture, organizational environments, and differences between national cultures is the result of the work of anthropologists or those using their methods.

There Are Few Absolutes in OB

There are few, if any, simple and universal principles that explain organizational behavior. There are laws in the physical sciences—chemistry, astronomy, physics—that are consistent and apply in a wide range of situations. They allow scientists to generalize about the pull of gravity or to be confident about sending astronauts into space to repair satellites. But as a noted behavioral researcher aptly concluded, "God gave all the easy problems to the physicists." Human beings are complex. Because they are not alike, our ability to make simple, accurate, and sweeping generalizations is limited. Two people often act very differently in the same situation, and the same person's behavior changes in different situations. For instance, not everyone is motivated by money, and you behave differently at church on Sunday than you did at a party the night before.

That doesn't mean, of course, that we can't offer reasonably accurate explanations of human behavior or make valid predictions. However, it does mean that OB concepts must reflect situational, or contingency, conditions. We can say that x leads to y, but only under conditions specified in z—the **contingency variables**. The science of OB was developed by taking general concepts and then applying them to a particular situation, person, or group. For example, OB scholars would avoid stating that everyone likes complex and challenging work (the general concept). Why? Because not everyone wants a challenging job. Some people prefer the routine over the varied or the simple over the complex. In other words, a job that is appealing to one person may not be to another, so the appeal of the job is contingent on the person who holds it.

As you proceed through this book, you'll encounter a wealth of research-based theories about how people behave in organizations. But don't expect to find a lot of straightforward cause-and-effect relationships. There aren't many! Organizational behavior theories mirror the subject matter with which they deal. People are complex and complicated, and so too must be the theories developed to explain their actions.

Challenges and Opportunities for OB

Understanding organizational behavior has never been more important for managers. A quick look at a few of the dramatic changes now taking place in organizations supports this claim. For instance, the typical employee is getting older; more and more women and people of color are in the workplace; corporate downsizing and the heavy use of temporary workers are severing the bonds of loyalty that historically tied many employees to their employers; and global competition is requiring employees to become more flexible and to learn to cope with rapid change. The war on terror has brought to the forefront the challenges of working with and managing people during uncertain times.

In short, there are a lot of challenges and opportunities today for managers to use OB concepts. In this section, we review some of the more critical issues confronting managers for which OB offers solutions—or at least some meaningful insights toward solutions.

Responding to Globalization

Organizations are no longer constrained by national borders. Burger King is owned by a British firm, and McDonald's sells hamburgers in Moscow. ExxonMobil, a so-called American company, receives almost 75 percent of its revenues from sales outside the United States. New employees at Finland-based phone maker Nokia are increasingly being recruited from India, China, and other developing countries—with non-Finns now outnumbering Finns at Nokia's renowned research center in Helsinki. And all major automobile manufacturers now build cars outside their borders; for instance, Honda builds cars in Ohio; Ford in Brazil; Volkswagen in Mexico; and both Mercedes and BMW in South Africa.

These examples illustrate that the world has become a global village. In the process, the manager's job is changing.

Increased Foreign Assignments   If you're a manager, you are increasingly likely to find yourself in a foreign assignment—transferred to your employer's operating division or subsidiary in another country. Once there, you'll have to manage a workforce that is likely to be very different in needs, aspirations, and attitudes from those you were used to back home.

Working with People from Different Cultures   Even in your own country, you're going to find yourself working with bosses, peers, and other employees who were born and raised in different cultures. What motivates you may not motivate them. Or your style of communication may be straightforward and open, but they may find this approach uncomfortable and threatening. To work effectively with people from different cultures, you need to understand how their culture, geography, and religion have shaped them, and how to adapt your management style to their differences.

Coping with Anticapitalism Backlash   Capitalism's focus on efficiency, growth, and profits may be generally accepted in the United States, Australia, and Hong Kong, but these capitalistic values aren't nearly as popular in places like France, the Middle East, and the Scandinavian countries. For instance, because Finland's egalitarian values have created a "soak the rich" mentality among politicians, traffic fines are based on the offender's income rather than the severity of the offense.[14] So when one of Finland's richest men (he is heir to a sausage fortune), who was making close to $9 million a year, was ticketed for doing 80 kilometers per hour through a 40-kilometer zone in central Helsinki, the Finnish court hit him with a fine of $217,000!

Managers at global companies like McDonald's, Disney, and Coca-Cola have come to realize that economic values are not universally transferable. Management practices need to be modified to reflect the values of the different countries in which an organization operates.

anthropology   *The study of societies to learn about human beings and their activities.*

contingency variables   *Situational factors: variables that moderate the relationship between two or more other variables.*

Facing anti-capitalism backlash from human rights and environmental activists, ExxonMobil hired Ellen Brown (left) to work as its anthropologist while building a 660-mile pipeline from Chad to Cameroon Africa. Brown visits hundreds of villages, explaining to locals how the pipeline will affect them. She helps oversee a $1.5 million Exxon initiative to build schools, fund health clinics, dig wells, advise local entrepreneurs, field an AIDS-education van, and distribute anti-malarial mosquito nets.

Overseeing Movement of Jobs to Countries with Low-cost Labor   It's increasingly difficult for managers in advanced nations, where minimum wages are typically $6 or more an hour, to compete against firms who rely on workers from China and other developing nations where labor is available for 30 cents an hour. It's not by chance that a good portion of Americans wear clothes made in China, work on computers whose microchips came from Taiwan, and watch movies that were filmed in Canada. In a global economy, jobs tend to flow to places where lower costs provide business firms with a comparative advantage. Such practices, however, often come with strong criticism from labor groups, politicians, local community leaders, and others who see this exporting of jobs as undermining the job markets in developed countries. Managers must deal with the difficult task of balancing the interests of their organization with their responsibilities to the communities in which they operate.

Managing People During the War on Terror   If you read the paper or watch the evening news, chances are you will find that the war on terror is one of the top stories. But when you think about the war, do you think about the workplace? Probably not. So you might be surprised to learn that the war on terror has had a profound effect on the business world. In fact, surveys suggest that fear of terrorism is the number-one reason business travelers have cut back on their trips. But travel isn't the only concern. Increasingly, organizations need to find ways to deal with employee fears about security precautions (in most cities, you can't get into an office building without passing through several layers of airport-like security) and assignments abroad (how would you feel about an assignment in a country with substantial sentiments against people from your country?).[15] An understanding of OB topics like emotions, motivation, communication, and leadership can help managers to deal more effectively with their employees' fears about terrorism.

Managing Workforce Diversity

One of the most important and broad-based challenges currently facing organizations is adapting to people who are different. The term we use for describing this challenge is workforce diversity. While globalization focuses on differences

How Globalization Is Changing Labor Markets

The movement of manufacturing jobs from the United States, Britain, Germany, and other countries with high labor costs to places like China, Mexico, India, Malaysia, and the Philippines has been going on for two decades. What is often overlooked is that service jobs are increasingly being exported to low-labor-cost countries.

It was recently estimated that between 2003 and 2008, 500,000 jobs in the U.S. financial services industry alone will be moved outside the country. Banks, brokerage firms, insurance companies, and mutual funds will transfer functions such as data entry, transac-

tion processing, and call centers to China, India, the Philippines, Canada, the Czech Republic, Brazil, Ireland, and Russia. Why? A call center employee who would make $20,000 in the United States can be hired in India for about $2,500. Moreover, this movement is not limited to low-skill jobs. U.S. financial-services firms are also transferring professional functions like financial analysis, regulatory reporting, accounting, and graphic design to lower-cost locations. Why pay a U.S.-based stock researcher $250,000 a year when you can get an equally proficient researcher to do the job for $20,000 in India? Executives at BearingPoint (formerly KPMG Consulting) say that the engineers they hire in Shanghai for $500 a month would cost them $4,000 a month in the United States.

Here are some current examples, to give you a preview of what the future may

hold: Massachusetts General Hospital is using radiologists in India to interpret CT scans. Boeing uses aeronautical specialists in Russia to design aircraft parts. Delta Airlines has 6,000 contract workers in India and the Philippines handling airline reservations and customer service. The architectural firm Flour has 700 employees in the Philippines drawing blueprints. Oracle has a staff of 4,000 in India doing software design, customer support, and accounting. And IBM is currently shifting 3,000 programming jobs from the United States to China, India, and Brazil.

Digitalization, the Internet, and global high-speed data networks are allowing organizations to shift knowledge work to low-wage countries. And this trend is likely to continue. Experts predict that at least 3.3 million white-collar jobs will move from the United States to low-cost countries by 2015.

Based on P. Engardio, A. Bernstein, and M. Kripalani, "Is Your Job Next?" *BusinessWeek*, February 3, 2003, pp. 50–60; M. Schroeder, "More Financial Jobs Go Offshore," *Wall Street Journal*, May 1, 2003, p. A2; and B. Davis, "Migration of Skilled Jobs Abroad Unsettles Global-Economy Fans," *Wall Street Journal*, January 26, 2004, p. A1.

between people *from* different countries, workforce diversity addresses differences among people *within* given countries.

Workforce diversity means that organizations are becoming a more heterogeneous mix of people in terms of gender, age, race, ethnicity, and sexual orientation. A diverse workforce, for instance, includes women, people of color, the physically disabled, senior citizens, and gays and lesbians (see Exhibit 1-4). Managing this diversity has become a global concern. It's not just an issue in the United States, but also in Canada, Australia, South Africa, Japan, and Europe. For instance, managers in Canada and Australia are finding it necessary to adjust to large influxes of Asian workers. The "new" South Africa is increasingly characterized by blacks' holding important technical and managerial jobs. Women, long confined to low-paying temporary jobs in Japan, are moving into managerial positions. And the European Union cooperative trade arrangement, which opened up borders throughout much of Western Europe, has increased workforce diversity in organizations that operate in countries such as Germany, Portugal, Italy, and France.

workforce diversity *The concept that organizations are becoming more heterogeneous in terms of gender, age, race, ethnicity, sexual orientation, and inclusion of other diverse groups.*

Exhibit **1-4**	Major Workforce Diversity Categories

Gender

Nearly half of the U.S. workforce is now made up of women, and women are a growing percentage of the workforce in most countries throughout the world. Organizations need to ensure that hiring and employment policies create equal access and opportunities to individuals regardless of gender.

Race

The percentage of Hispanics, blacks, and Asians in the U.S. workforce continues to increase. Organizations need to ensure that policies provide equal access and opportunities regardless of race.

National Origin

A growing percentage of U.S. workers are immigrants or come from homes where English is not the primary language spoken. Because employers in the U.S. have the right to demand that English be spoken at the workplace on job-related activities, communication problems can occur when employees' English-language skills are weak.

Age

The U.S. workforce is aging, and recent polls indicate that an increasing percentage of employees expect to work past the traditional retirement age of 65. Organizations cannot discriminate on the basis of age and need to make accommodations to the needs of older workers.

Disability

Organizations need to ensure that jobs and workplaces are accessible to the mentally and physically challenged, as well as to the health-challenged.

Domestic Partners

An increasing number of gay and lesbian employees, as well as employees with live-in partners of the opposite sex, are demanding the same rights and benefits for their partners that organizations have provided for traditional married couples.

Non-Christian

Organizations need to be sensitive to the customs, rituals, and holidays, as well as the appearance and attire, of individuals of non-Christian faiths such as Judaism, Islam, Hinduism, Buddhism, and Sikhism, and ensure that these individuals suffer no adverse impact as a result of their appearance or practices.

Embracing Diversity   We used to take a melting-pot approach to differences in organizations, assuming people who were different would somehow automatically want to assimilate. But we now recognize that employees don't set aside their cultural values, lifestyle preferences, and differences when they come to work. The challenge for organizations, therefore, is to make themselves more accommodating to diverse groups of people by addressing their different lifestyles, family needs, and work styles. The melting-pot assumption is being replaced by one that recognizes and values differences.[16]

Haven't organizations always included members of diverse groups? Yes, but they were a small percentage of the workforce and were, for the most part, ignored by large organizations. Moreover, it was assumed that these minorities would seek to blend in and assimilate. For instance, the bulk of the pre-1980s U.S. workforce were male Caucasians working full-time to support a nonemployed wife and school-aged children. Now such employees are the true minority![17]

Changing U.S. Demographics   The most significant change in the U.S. labor force during the last half of the twentieth century was the rapid increase in the number of female workers.[18] In 1950, for instance, only 29.6 percent of the workforce was made up of women. By 2003, it was 46.7 percent. So today's workforce is rapidly approaching gender balance. In addition, with women now sig-

With more than 370,000 employees in 200 countries, United Parcel Service embraces the value of diversity. Since 1968, UPS senior managers participate in a four-week Community Internship Program that deepens their responsiveness to the needs of a diverse workforce and customer base while helping with charitable causes in the community. In this photo, UPS managers from Germany and California help a bicycle shop owner reorganize his business.

nificantly outnumbering men on U.S. college campuses, we can expect an increasing number of technical, professional, and managerial jobs to be filled by the expanding pool of qualified female applicants.

In the same way that women dramatically changed the workplace in the latter part of the twentieth century, the first half of the twenty-first century will be notable for changes in racial and ethnic composition and an aging baby-boom generation. By 2050, Hispanics will grow from today's 11 percent of the workforce to 24 percent, blacks will increase from 12 percent to 14 percent, and Asians will increase from 5 percent to 11 percent. Meanwhile, the labor force will be aging in the near-term. The 55-and-older age group, which currently makes up 13 percent of the labor force, will increase to 20 percent by 2014.

Implications Workforce diversity has important implications for management practice. Managers have to shift their philosophy from treating everyone alike to recognizing differences and responding to those differences in ways that ensure employee retention and greater productivity while, at the same time, not discriminating. This shift includes, for instance, providing diversity training and revamping benefits programs to accommodate the different needs of different employees. Diversity, if positively managed, can increase creativity and innovation in organizations as well as improve decision making by providing different perspectives on problems.[19] When diversity is not managed properly, there is a potential for higher turnover, more-difficult communication, and more interpersonal conflicts.

Improving Quality and Productivity

In the 1990s, organizations around the world added capacity in response to increased demand. Companies built new facilities, expanded services, and added staff. The result? Today, almost every industry suffers from excess supply. Retail suffers from too many malls and shopping centers. Automobile factories can build more cars than consumers can afford. The telecom industry is drowning in debt from building capacity that might take 50 years to absorb, and most cities and towns now have far more restaurants than their communities can support.

Excess capacity translates into increased competition. And increased competition is forcing managers to reduce costs and, at the same time, improve their organization's productivity and the quality of the products and services they offer. Management guru Tom Peters says, "Almost all quality improvement comes via simplification of design, manufacturing, layout, processes, and procedures." To achieve these ends, managers are implementing programs such as quality management and process reengineering—programs that require extensive employee involvement.

Today's managers understand that the success of any effort at improving quality and productivity must include their employees. These employees will not only be a major force in carrying out changes but increasingly will actively participate in planning those changes. OB offers important insights into helping managers work through these changes.

Responding to the Coming Labor Shortage

Economic ups and downs are difficult to predict. The world economy in the late 1990s, for instance, was generally quite robust and labor markets were tight. Most employers found it difficult to find skilled workers to fill vacancies. Then, beginning in 2001, most developed countries entered an economic downturn. Layoffs were widespread and the supply of skilled workers became much more plentiful. In contrast, demographic trends are much more predictable, and we're facing one that has direct implications for OB: Barring some unforeseeable economic or political calamity, there will be a labor shortage for at least another 10 to 15 years.[20] This shortage of skilled labor is also likely to be just as prevalent in most of Europe, due to a graying population and a declining birthrate.

The U.S. labor shortage is a function of two factors—birthrates and labor participation rates. From the late 1960s through the late 1980s, American employers benefited from the large number of baby boomers (those born between 1946 and 1965) entering the workforce. Specifically, there are 76 million baby boomers in the workforce. But there are 10 million fewer Gen-Xers to replace them when they retire. The problem becomes serious beginning between 2007 and 2010, when the major exodus of boomers from the workplace begins. Importantly, in spite of continued increases in immigration, new entrants to the workforce from foreign countries will not do much to correct the supply shortage.

The labor shortage problem is compounded by the fact that the latter part of the twentieth century benefited from a huge increase in the number of women entering the workforce. That provided a new supply of talented and skilled workers. This source has now been tapped. Moreover, there has been a declining interest by older workers to stay in the labor force. In 1950, nearly 80 percent of all 62-year-old men were still working; today, it is only slightly more than half. Improved pension plans and expanded Social Security benefits have led many workers to retire early, especially those whose jobs were stressful or unchallenging. While the stock market decline between 2001 and 2003 ate up a good part of many baby boomers' retirement savings, and may result in some older workers postponing retirement,[21] early indications suggest this is unlikely to offset the significantly smaller future labor pool from which employers can hire.

In times of labor shortage, good wages and benefits aren't going to be enough to get and keep skilled employees. Managers will need sophisticated recruitment and retention strategies. In addition, managers will need to modify organizational practices to reflect the needs of an older workforce and consider ways to motivate younger workers who feel stuck when older colleagues don't retire. OB can help managers solve these problems. In tight labor markets, managers who don't understand human behavior and fail to treat their employees properly risk having no one to manage!

Improving Customer Service

American Express recently turned Joan Weinbel's worst nightmare into a non-event. It was 10:00 P.M. Joan was home in New Jersey, packing for a week-long trip, when she suddenly realized she had left her AmEx Gold Card at a restaurant in New York City earlier in the evening. The restaurant was 30 miles away. She had a flight to catch at 7:30 the next morning and she wanted her card for the trip. She called American Express. The phone was quickly answered by a courteous and helpful AmEx customer service representative. He told Ms. Weinbel not to worry. He asked her a few questions and told her "help was on the way." To say Joan was flabbergasted would be an understatement when her doorbell rang at 11:45 P.M.— less than two hours after she had called AmEx. At her door was a courier with a new card. How the company was able to produce the card and get it to her so quickly still puzzles Joan. But she said the experience made her a customer for life.

Today, the majority of employees in developed countries work in service jobs. For instance, 80 percent of the U.S. labor force is employed in service industries. In Australia, 73 percent work in service industries. In the United Kingdom, Germany, and Japan the percentages are 69, 68, and 65, respectively. Examples of these service jobs include technical support representatives, fast-food counter workers, sales clerks, waiters or waitresses, nurses, automobile repair technicians, consultants, credit representatives, financial planners, and flight attendants. The common characteristic of these jobs is that they require substantial interaction with an organization's customers. And because an organization can't exist without customers—whether that organization is DaimlerChrysler, Merrill Lynch, L.L. Bean, a law firm, a museum, a school, or a government agency—management needs to ensure that employees do what it takes to please its customers.[22] For example, at Patagonia—the retail outfitter for climbers, mountain bikers, skiers and boarders, and other outdoor fanatics—managers are held directly responsible for customer service. In fact, customer service is the store manager's most important general responsibility: *Instill in your employees the meaning and importance of customer service as outlined in the retail philosophy, "our store is a place where the word*

It's an annual tradition for Michael Dell to work the phone lines helping customers in Dell, Inc.'s consumer department. Dell models the customer-responsive culture he created in founding Dell Computer Corporation in 1984 with the idea of building relationships directly with customers. He attributes his company's climb to market leadership as the world's top computer systems company to a persistent focus on the customer. Dell employees deliver superior customer service by communicating directly with customers via the Internet or by phone.

'no' does not exist"; Empower staff to "use their best judgment" in all customer service mat-ters.[23] OB can help managers at Patagonia achieve this goal, and more generally can contribute to improving an organization's performance by showing managers how employee attitudes and behavior are associated with customer satisfaction.

Many an organization has failed because its employees failed to please the customer. So management needs to create a customer-responsive culture. OB can provide considerable guidance in helping managers create such cultures—cultures in which employees are friendly and courteous, accessible, knowledge-able, prompt in responding to customer needs, and willing to do what's neces-sary to please the customer.[24]

Improving People Skills

We opened this chapter by demonstrating how important people skills are to managerial effectiveness. We said that "this book has been written to help both managers and potential managers develop those people skills."

As you proceed through the chapters, we'll present relevant concepts and theories that can help you explain and predict the behavior of people at work. In addition, you'll gain insights into specific people skills that you can use on the job. For instance, you'll learn ways to design motivating jobs, tech-niques for improving your listening skills, and how to create more effective teams.

Empowering People

If you pick up any popular business periodical nowadays, you'll read about the reshaping of the relationship between managers and those they are supposedly responsible for managing. You'll find managers being called coaches, advisers, sponsors, or facilitators. In some organizations—for example, Marriott, W.L. Gore, and National Westminster Bank—employees are now called associates.

Exhibit 1-5

© 2000 Ted Goff

"Congratulations! You're now empowered to accept all the blame!"

Source: © 2000 Ted Goff.

There's a blurring between the roles of managers and workers. Decision making is being pushed down to the operating level, where workers are being given the freedom to make choices about schedules and procedures and to solve work-related problems.[25] In the 1980s, managers were encouraged to get their employees to participate in work-related decisions. Now, managers are going considerably further by allowing employees full control of their work. An increasing number of organizations are using self-managed teams, in which workers operate largely without bosses.

What's going on? What's going on is that managers are **empowering employees**. They are putting employees in charge of what they do, and in so doing, managers are being forced to learn how to give up control while employees are being forced to learn how to take responsibility for their work and make appropriate decisions. In later chapters, we'll show how empowerment is changing leadership styles, power relationships, the way work is designed, and the way organizations are structured.

Stimulating Innovation and Change

Whatever happened to Montgomery Ward, Woolworth, Smith Corona, TWA, Bethlehem Steel, and WorldCom? All these giants went bust. Why have other giants, such as Sears, Boeing, and Lucent Technologies implemented huge cost-cutting programs and eliminated thousands of jobs? To avoid going broke.

Today's successful organizations must foster innovation and master the art of change or they'll become candidates for extinction. Victory will go to the organizations that maintain their flexibility, continually improve their quality, and beat their competition to the marketplace with a constant stream of innovative products and services. Domino's single-handedly brought on the demise of thousands of small pizza parlors whose managers thought they could continue doing what they had been doing for years. Amazon.com is putting a lot of independent bookstores out of business as it proves you can successfully sell books from an Internet Web site. Dell has become the world's largest seller of computers by continually reinventing itself and outsmarting its competition.

An organization's employees can be the impetus for innovation and change or they can be a major stumbling block. The challenge for managers is to stimulate their employees' creativity and tolerance for change. The field of OB provides a wealth of ideas and techniques to aid in realizing these goals.

Coping with "Temporariness"

With change comes temporariness. Globalization, expanded capacity, and advances in technology have combined in recent years to make it imperative that organizations be fast and flexible if they are to survive. The result is that most managers and employees today work in a climate best characterized as "temporary."

Evidence of temporariness is everywhere in organizations. Jobs are continually being redesigned; tasks are increasingly being done by flexible teams rather than individuals; companies are relying more on temporary workers; jobs are being subcontracted out to other firms; and pensions are being redesigned to move with people as they change jobs.

Workers need to continually update their knowledge and skills to perform new job requirements. For example, production employees at companies such as Caterpillar, Ford, and Alcoa now need to know how to operate computerized

empowering employees   *Putting employees in charge of what they do.*

Coping with temporariness characterizes Nissan Motor Company's new plant in Canton, Mississippi, where it builds pickup trucks, sport utility vehicles, and minivans on the same assembly line. Designed for flexibility, the plant integrates outside part suppliers in the assembly process, and employees do four different jobs during their shifts. Flexibility gives Nissan a competitive advantage because the plant runs at 100 percent capacity and can adjust quickly to changes in market demand.

production equipment. That was not part of their job descriptions 20 years ago. Work groups are also increasingly in a state of flux. In the past, employees were assigned to a specific work group, and that assignment was relatively permanent. There was a considerable amount of security in working with the same people day in and day out. That predictability has been replaced by temporary work groups, teams that include members from different departments and whose members change all the time, and the increased use of employee rotation to fill constantly changing work assignments. Finally, organizations themselves are in a state of flux. They continually reorganize their various divisions, sell off poor-performing businesses, downsize operations, subcontract noncritical services and operations to other organizations, and replace permanent employees with temporary workers.

Today's managers and employees must learn to cope with temporariness. They have to learn to live with flexibility, spontaneity, and unpredictability. The study of OB can provide important insights into helping you better understand a work world of continual change, how to overcome resistance to change, and how best to create an organizational culture that thrives on change.

Working in Networked Organizations

Computerization, the Internet, and the ability to link computers within organizations and between organizations have created a different workplace for many employees—a networked organization. It allows people to communicate and work together even though they may be thousands of miles apart. It also allows people to become independent contractors, who can telecommute via computer to workplaces around the globe and change employers as the demand for their services changes. Software programmers, graphic designers, systems analysts, technical writers, photo researchers, book editors, and medical transcribers are just a few examples of jobs that people can now perform from home or other nonoffice locations.

The manager's job is different in a networked organization, especially when it comes to managing people. For instance, motivating and leading people and making collaborative decisions "online" requires different techniques than those needed in dealing with individuals who are physically present in a single location.

As more and more employees do their jobs linked to others through networks, managers need to develop new skills. OB can provide valuable insights to help with honing those skills.

Helping Employees Balance Work–Life Conflicts

The typical employee in the 1960s or 1970s showed up at the workplace Monday through Friday and did his or her job in eight- or nine-hour chunks of time. The workplace and hours were clearly specified. That's no longer true for a large segment of today's workforce. Employees are increasingly complaining that the line between work and nonwork time has become blurred, creating personal conflicts and stress.[26] At the same time, however, today's workplace presents opportunities for workers to create and structure their work roles.

A number of forces have contributed to blurring the lines between employees' work life and personal life. First, the creation of global organizations means their world never sleeps. At any time and on any day, for instance, thousands of General Electric employees are working somewhere. The need to consult with colleagues or customers eight or ten time zones away means that many employees of global firms are "on call" 24 hours a day. Second, communication technology allows employees to do their work at home, in their cars, or on the beach in Tahiti. This lets many people in technical and professional jobs do their work any time and from any place. Third, organizations are asking employees to put in longer hours. For instance, over a recent 10-year period, the average American workweek increased from 43 to 47 hours; and the number of people working 50 or more hours a week jumped from 24 percent to 37 percent. Finally, fewer families have only a single breadwinner. Today's married employee is typically part of a dual-career couple. This makes it increasingly difficult for married employees to find the time to fulfill commitments to home, spouse, children, parents, and friends.

Employees are increasingly recognizing that work is infringing on their personal lives, and they're not happy about it. For example, recent studies suggest that employees want jobs that give them flexibility in their work schedules so they can better manage work–life conflicts.[27] In fact, evidence indicates that balancing work and life demands now surpasses job security as an employee priority.[28] In addition, the next generation of employees is likely to show similar concerns.[29] A majority of college and university students say that attaining a balance between personal life and work is a primary career goal. They want "a life" as well as a job. Organizations that don't help their people achieve work–life balance will find it increasingly difficult to attract and retain the most capable and motivated employees.

As you'll see in later chapters, the field of OB offers a number of suggestions to guide managers in designing workplaces and jobs that can help employees deal with work–life conflicts.

Improving Ethical Behavior

In an organizational world characterized by cutbacks, expectations of increasing worker productivity, and tough competition in the marketplace, it's not altogether surprising that many employees feel pressured to cut corners, break rules, and engage in other forms of questionable practices.

Members of organizations are increasingly finding themselves facing **ethical dilemmas**, situations in which they are required to define right and wrong conduct. For example, should they "blow the whistle" if they uncover

ethical dilemmas *Situations in which individuals are required to define right and wrong conduct.*

illegal activities taking place in their company? Should they follow orders with which they don't personally agree? Do they give an inflated performance evaluation to an employee whom they like, knowing that such an evaluation could save that employee's job? Do they allow themselves to "play politics" in the organization if it will help their career advancement?

What constitutes good ethical behavior has never been clearly defined, and, in recent years, the line differentiating right from wrong has become even more blurred. Employees see people all around them engaging in unethical practices—elected officials are indicted for padding their expense accounts or taking bribes; corporate executives inflate their company's profits so they can cash in lucrative stock options; and university administrators "look the other way" when winning coaches encourage scholarship athletes to take easy courses to stay eligible in place of those needed for graduation. When caught, you hear these people giving excuses such as "everyone does it" or "you have to seize every advantage nowadays." Is it any wonder that employees are expressing decreased confidence and trust in management and that they're increasingly uncertain about what constitutes appropriate ethical behavior in their organizations?[30]

Managers and their organizations are responding to this problem from a number of directions.[31] They're writing and distributing codes of ethics to guide employees through ethical dilemmas. They're offering seminars, workshops, and similar training programs to try to improve ethical behaviors. They're providing in-house advisors who can be contacted, in many cases anonymously, for assistance in dealing with ethical issues, and they're creating protection mechanisms for employees who reveal internal unethical practices.

Today's manager needs to create an ethically healthy climate for his or her employees, where they can do their work productively and confront a minimal degree of ambiguity regarding what constitutes right and wrong behaviors. In upcoming chapters, we'll discuss the kinds of actions managers can take to create an ethically healthy climate and help employees sort through ethically ambiguous situations. We'll also present ethical-dilemma exercises at the end of each chapter that will allow you to think through ethical issues and assess how you would handle them.

Coming Attractions: Developing an OB Model

We conclude this chapter by presenting a general model that defines the field of OB, stakes out its parameters, and identifies its primary dependent and independent variables. The end result will be a "coming attraction" of the topics making up the remainder of this book.

An Overview

A **model** is an abstraction of reality, a simplified representation of some real-world phenomenon. A mannequin in a retail store is a model. So, too, is the accountant's formula: Assets + Liabilities = Owners' Equity. Exhibit 1-6 presents the skeleton on which we will construct our OB model. It proposes that there are three levels of analysis in OB and that, as we move from the individual level to the organization systems level, we add systematically to our understanding of behavior in organizations. The three basic levels are analogous to building blocks; each level is constructed on the previous level. Group concepts grow out of the foundation laid in the individual section; we overlay structural constraints on the individual and group in order to arrive at organizational behavior.

Exhibit **1-6**	Basic OB Model, Stage I

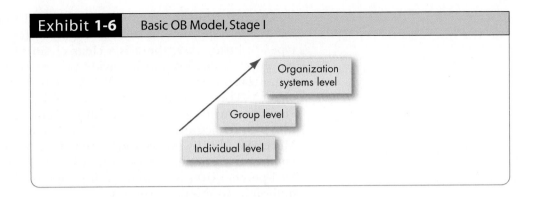

The Dependent Variables

A **dependent variable** is the key factor that you want to explain or predict and that is affected by some other factor. What are the primary dependent variables in OB? Scholars have historically tended to emphasize productivity, absenteeism, turnover, and job satisfaction. More recently, two more variables—deviant workplace behavior and organizational citizenship behavior—have been added to this list. Let's briefly discuss each of these variables to ensure that we understand what they mean and why they have achieved their level of distinction.

Productivity   An organization is productive if it achieves its goals and does so by transferring inputs to outputs at the lowest cost. As such, **productivity** implies a concern for both **effectiveness** and **efficiency**.

A hospital, for example, is *effective* when it successfully meets the needs of its clientele. It is *efficient* when it can do so at a low cost. If a hospital manages to achieve higher output from its present staff by reducing the average number of days a patient is confined to a bed or by increasing the number of staff–patient contacts per day, we say that the hospital has gained productive efficiency. A business firm is effective when it attains its sales or market share goals, but its productivity also depends on achieving those goals efficiently. Popular measures of organizational efficiency include return on investment, profit per dollar of sales, and output per hour of labor.

We can also look at productivity from the perspective of the individual employee. Take the cases of Mike and Al, who are both long-distance truckers. If Mike is supposed to haul his fully loaded rig from New York to Los Angeles in 75 hours or less, he is effective if he makes the 3,000-mile trip within that time period. But measures of productivity must take into account the costs incurred in reaching the goal. That's where efficiency comes in. Let's assume that Mike made the New York to Los Angeles run in 68 hours and averaged 7 miles per gallon. Al, however, made the trip in 68 hours also but averaged 9 miles per gallon (rigs and loads are identical). Both Mike and Al were effective—they accomplished their goal—but Al was more efficient than Mike because his rig consumed less gas and, therefore, he achieved his goal at a lower cost.

model   *An abstraction of reality. A simplified representation of some real-world phenomenon.*

dependent variable   *A response that is affected by an independent variable.*

productivity   *A performance measure that includes effectiveness and efficiency.*

effectiveness   *Achievement of goals.*

efficiency   *The ratio of effective output to the input required to achieve it.*

Organizations in service industries need to include attention to customer needs and requirements in assessing their effectiveness. Why? Because in these types of businesses, there is a clear chain of cause-and-effect running from employee attitudes and behavior to customer attitudes and behavior to an organization's productivity. Sears, in fact, has carefully documented this chain.[32] The company's management found that a 5 percent improvement in employee attitudes leads to a 1.3 percent increase in customer satisfaction, which in turn translated into a 0.5 percent improvement in revenue growth. More specifically, Sears found that by training employees to improve the employee–customer interaction, it was able to improve customer satisfaction by 4 percent over a twelve-month period, which generated an estimated $200 million in additional revenues.

In summary, one of OB's major concerns is productivity. We want to know what factors will influence the effectiveness and efficiency of individuals, of groups, and of the overall organization.

Absenteeism   **Absenteeism** is defined as the failure to report to work. And absenteeism is a huge cost and disruption to employers. For instance, a recent survey found that the average direct cost to U.S. employers of unscheduled absences is $789 a year per employee—and this doesn't include lost productivity or the additional costs for overtime pay or hiring temporary employees to cover for absent workers.[33] Comparable costs in the United Kingdom are also high—approximately $694 a year per employee.[34] In Sweden, an average of 10 percent of the country's workforce is on sick leave at any given time.[35]

It's obviously difficult for an organization to operate smoothly and to attain its objectives if employees fail to report to their jobs. The work flow is disrupted, and often important decisions must be delayed. In organizations that rely heavily on assembly-line production, absenteeism can be considerably more than a disruption; it can result in a drastic reduction in the quality of output, and, in some cases, it can bring about a complete shutdown of the production facility. But levels of absenteeism beyond the normal range in any organization have a direct impact on that organization's effectiveness and efficiency.

Are *all* absences bad? Probably not. Although most absences have a negative impact on the organization, we can conceive of situations in which the organization may benefit by an employee's voluntarily choosing not to come to work. For instance, in jobs in which an employee needs to be alert—consider surgeons and airline pilots, for example—it may be better for the organization if an ill or fatigued employee does *not* report to work. The cost of an accident in such jobs could be disastrous. But these examples are clearly atypical. For the most part, we can assume that organizations benefit when employee absenteeism is low.

Turnover   **Turnover** is the voluntary and involuntary permanent withdrawal from an organization. A high turnover rate results in increased recruiting, selection, and training costs. What are those costs? They're higher than you might think. For instance, the cost for a typical information-technology company in the United States to replace a programmer or systems analyst has been put at $34,100; and the cost for a retail store to replace a lost sales clerk has been calculated at $10,445.[36] In addition, a high rate of turnover can disrupt the efficient running of an organization when knowledgeable and experienced personnel leave and replacements must be found and prepared to assume positions of responsibility.

All organizations, of course, have some turnover. The U.S. national turnover rate averages about 3 percent per month, which is about a 36 percent turnover per year. This average, of course, varies a lot by occupation (for example, the monthly turnover rate for government jobs is less than 1 percent versus 5 to 7 percent in the construction industry).[37] If the "right" people are leaving the organization—the marginal and submarginal employees—turnover can actually be positive. It can create the opportunity to replace an underperforming individual with someone who has higher skills or motivation, open up increased opportunities for promotions, and add new and fresh ideas to the organization.[38] In today's changing world of work, reasonable levels of employee-initiated turnover facilitate organizational flexibility and employee independence, and they can lessen the need for management-initiated layoffs.

But turnover often involves the loss of people the organization doesn't want to lose. For instance, one study covering 900 employees who had resigned from their jobs found that 92 percent earned performance ratings of "satisfactory" or better from their superiors.[39] So when turnover is excessive, or when it involves valuable performers, it can be a disruptive factor, hindering the organization's effectiveness.

Deviant Workplace Behavior   Given the cost of absenteeism and turnover to employers, more and more OB researchers are studying these behaviors as indicators or markers of deviant behavior. Deviance can range from someone playing his music too loud to violence. Managers need to understand this wide range of behaviors to address any form of employee dissatisfaction. If managers don't understand *why* an employee is acting up, the problem will never be solved.

We can define **deviant workplace behavior** (also called *antisocial behavior* or *workplace incivility*) as voluntary behavior that violates significant organizational norms and, in doing so, threatens the well-being of the organization or its members. What are organizational norms in this context? They can be company policies that prohibit certain behaviors like stealing. But they also can be unspoken rules that are widely shared, such as not playing loud music in one's workspace. Consider, for example, an employee who plays Metallica's "St. Anger" at work with the speakers amped up. Yes, he may be showing up at work, but he may not be getting his work done, and he could also be irritating coworkers or customers (unless they are Talli fans themselves). But deviant workplace behaviors can be much more serious than an employee playing loud music. For example, an employee may insult a colleague, steal, gossip excessively, or engage in sabotage, all of which can wreak havoc on an organization.

Managers want to understand the source of workplace deviance in order to avoid a chaotic work environment, and workplace deviance can also have a considerable financial impact. Although the annual costs are hard to quantify, estimates are that deviant behavior costs employers dearly, from $4.2 billion for violence to $200 billion for theft to $7.1 billion for corporate security against cyberattacks.[40]

Deviant workplace behavior is an important concept because it's a response to dissatisfaction, and employees express this dissatisfaction in many ways. Controlling one behavior may be ineffective unless one gets to the root cause. The sophisticated manager will deal with root causes of problems that may result in deviance, rather than solving one surface problem (excessive absence) only to see another one crop up (increased theft or sabotage).

---

absenteeism   *The failure to report to work.*

turnover   *The voluntary and involuntary permanent withdrawal from an organization.*

deviant workplace behavior   *Voluntary behavior that violates significant organizational norms and, in doing so, threatens the well-being of the organization or its members.*

Transfer Pricing and International Corporate Deviance

WORKPLACE DEVIANCE ISN'T LIMITED TO THE harmful behaviors of employees within one location. There are cases of corporate deviance that extend across country borders. Consider transfer pricing, which is the price that one part of a company charges another part of the same company for a product or service. What happens with transfer pricing if various parts of a company are located in different countries, which happens as more and more companies extend their operations across the globe to become multinational businesses?

Tax rates on company profits differ—sometimes greatly—from country to country. Transfer pricing, when used to shift income from high-tax countries to low-tax countries, can be a deviant corporate policy if abused. One way to increase overall profit—that is, the combined profit of the multinational's headquarters and its subsidiaries—is to take profits in the country with the lower taxes.

Take the case of a multinational firm whose headquarters sold toothbrushes to a subsidiary for $5,000—each. The subsidiary, with the higher tax of the two, claimed a loss (after all, it paid $5,000 per toothbrush). The multinational firm, with the lower tax of the two, took the profit and paid the tax on it. Because the two firms were part of the same organization, they combined the results of the transaction, and the company made a staggering profit.

Transfer pricing, according to a survey by the international auditing firm Ernst & Young, has become a heated issue among multinational companies. Why? The U.S. Multistate Tax Commission estimated that states were losing almost a third of their corporate tax income because of tax-sheltering practices by multinational companies—transfer pricing among them. The U.S. Internal Revenue Service is keeping a watchful eye on international transactions.

Source: Based on "Case of the U.S. $5000 Toothbrush," *Finance Week,* April 27, 2005, pp. 45–46.

Organizational Citizenship Behavior   Organizational citizenship behavior **(or OCB)** is discretionary behavior that is not part of an employee's formal job requirements, but that nevertheless promotes the effective functioning of the organization.[41]

Successful organizations need employees who will do more than their usual job duties—who will provide performance that is *beyond* expectations. In today's dynamic workplace, where tasks are increasingly done in teams and where flexibility is critical, organizations need employees who will engage in "good citizenship" behaviors such as helping others on their team, volunteering for extra work, avoiding unnecessary conflicts, respecting the spirit as well as the letter of rules and regulations, and gracefully tolerating the occasional work-related impositions and nuisances.

Organizations want and need employees who will do those things that aren't in any job description. And the evidence indicates that the organizations that have such employees outperform those that don't.[42] As a result, OB is concerned with organizational citizenship behavior (OCB) as a dependent variable.

Job Satisfaction   The final dependent variable we will look at is **job satisfaction**, which we define as a positive feeling about one's job resulting from an evaluation of its characteristics. Unlike the previous five variables, job satisfaction represents an attitude rather than a behavior. Why, then, has it become a

The spirit of good citizenship reigns at brokerage firm Charles Schwab. Generous coworkers transferred 5 1/2 months of their unused sick and vacation days to Curtis Barthold, an accounts payable director, so he could spend time at home to care for his young children and terminally ill wife.

primary dependent variable? For two reasons: its demonstrated relationship to performance factors, and the value preferences held by many OB researchers.

The belief that satisfied employees are more productive than dissatisfied employees has been a basic tenet among managers for years, though only now has research begun to support this theory after decades of questions about the satisfaction–performance relationship.[43] Recently, a study of over 2,500 business units found that units scoring in the top 25 percent on the employee opinion survey were, on average, 4.6 percent *above* their sales budget for the year, while those scoring in the bottom 25 percent were 0.8 percent *below* budget. In real numbers, this was a difference of $104 million in sales per year between the two groups.[44]

Moreover, it can be argued that advanced societies should be concerned not only with the quantity of life—that is, concerns such as higher productivity and material acquisitions—but also with its quality. Those researchers with strong humanistic values argue that satisfaction is a legitimate objective of an organization. Not only is satisfaction negatively related to absenteeism and turnover, but, they argue, organizations have a responsibility to provide employees with jobs that are challenging and intrinsically rewarding. Therefore, although job satisfaction represents an attitude rather than a behavior, OB researchers typically consider it an important dependent variable.

The Independent Variables

What are the major determinants of productivity, absenteeism, turnover, deviant workplace behavior, OCB, and job satisfaction? Our answer to that question brings us to the independent variables. An **independent variable** is the presumed cause of some change in the dependent variable.

organizational citizenship behavior (OCB) *Discretionary behavior that is not part of an employee's formal job requirements, but that nevertheless promotes the effective functioning of the organization.*

job satisfaction *A positive feeling about one's job resulting from an evaluation of its characteristics*

independent variable *The presumed cause of some change in the dependent variable.*

Consistent with our belief that organizational behavior can best be understood when viewed essentially as a set of increasingly complex building blocks, the base, or first level, of our model lies in understanding individual behavior.

Individual-Level Variables   It has been said that "managers, unlike parents, must work with used, not new, human beings—human beings whom others have gotten to first."[45] When individuals enter an organization, they are a bit like used cars. Each is different. Some are "low-mileage"—they have been treated carefully and have had only limited exposure to the realities of the elements. Others are "well-worn," having been driven over some rough roads. This metaphor indicates that people enter organizations with certain intact characteristics that will influence their behavior at work. The more obvious of these are personal or biographical characteristics such as age, gender, and marital status; personality characteristics; an inherent emotional framework; values and attitudes; and basic ability levels. These characteristics are essentially in place when an individual enters the workforce, and, for the most part, there is little management can do to alter them. Yet they have a very real impact on employee behavior. Therefore, each of these factors—biographical characteristics, ability, values, attitudes, personality, and emotions—will be discussed as independent variables in Chapters 2–4 and 8.

There are four other individual-level variables that have been shown to affect employee behavior: perception, individual decision making, learning, and motivation. Those topics will be introduced and discussed in Chapters 2, 5, 6, and 7.

Group-Level Variables   The behavior of people in groups is more than the sum total of all the individuals acting in their own way. The complexity of our model is increased when we acknowledge that people's behavior when they are in groups is different from their behavior when they are alone. Therefore, the next step in the development of an understanding of OB is the study of group behavior.

Chapter 9 lays the foundation for an understanding of the dynamics of group behavior. That chapter discusses how individuals in groups are influenced by the patterns of behavior they are expected to exhibit, what the group considers to be acceptable standards of behavior, and the degree to which group members are attracted to each other. Chapter 10 translates our understanding of groups to the design of effective work teams. Chapters 11 through 15 demonstrate how communication patterns, leadership, power and politics, and levels of conflict affect group behavior.

Organization Systems Level Variables   Organizational behavior reaches its highest level of sophistication when we add formal structure to our previous knowledge of individual and group behavior. Just as groups are more than the sum of their individual members, so are organizations more than the sum of their member groups. The design of the formal organization; the organization's internal culture; and the organization's human resource policies and practices (that is, selection processes, training and development programs, performance evaluation methods) all have an impact on the dependent variables. These are discussed in detail in Chapters 16 through 18.

Toward a Contingency OB Model

Our final model is shown in Exhibit 1-7. It shows the six key dependent variables and a large number of independent variables, organized by level of analysis, that research indicates have varying effects on the former. As complicated as

Exhibit **1-7**	Basic OB Model, Stage II

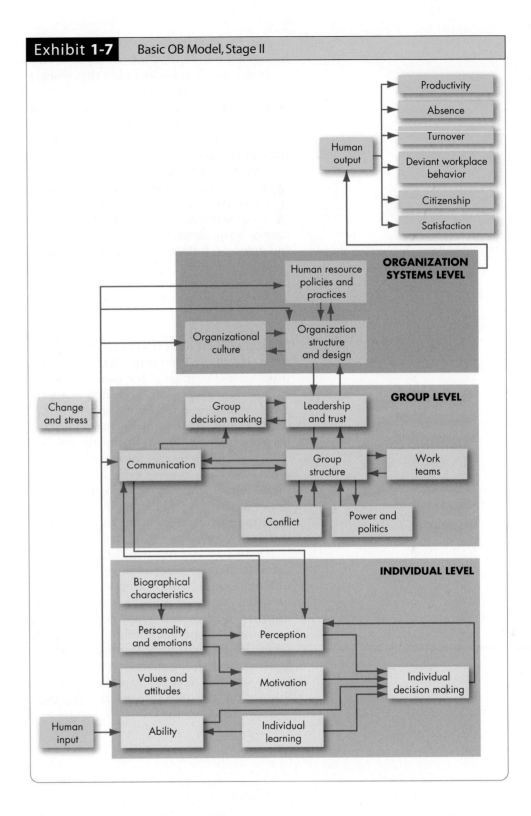

this model is, it still doesn't do justice to the complexity of the OB subject matter. However, it should help explain why the chapters in this book are arranged as they are and help you to explain and predict the behavior of people at work.

For the most part, our model does not explicitly identify the vast number of contingency variables because of the tremendous complexity that would be involved in such a diagram. Rather, throughout this book we will introduce important contingency variables that will improve the explanatory linkage between the independent and dependent variables in our OB model.

Note that we have included the concepts of change and stress in Exhibit 1-7, acknowledging the dynamics of behavior and the fact that work stress is an individual, group, and organizational issue. Specifically, in Chapter 19 we will discuss the change process, ways to manage organizational change, key change issues currently facing managers, consequences of work stress, and techniques for managing stress.

Also note that Exhibit 1-7 includes linkages between the three levels of analysis. For instance, organizational structure is linked to leadership. This link is meant to convey that authority and leadership are related; management exerts its influence on group behavior through leadership. Similarly, communication is the means by which individuals transmit information; thus, it is the link between individual and group behavior.

Summary and Implications for Managers

Managers need to develop their interpersonal or people skills if they are going to be effective in their jobs. Organizational behavior (OB) is a field of study that investigates the impact that individuals, groups, and structure have on behavior within an organization, and then it applies that knowledge to make organizations work more effectively. Specifically, OB focuses on how to improve productivity; reduce absenteeism, turnover, and deviant workplace behavior; and increase organizational citizenship behavior and job satisfaction.

We all hold generalizations about the behavior of people. Some of our generalizations may provide valid insights into human behavior, but many are erroneous. Organizational behavior uses systematic study to improve predictions of behavior that would be made from intuition alone. But, because people are different, we need to look at OB in a contingency framework, using situational variables to moderate cause-and-effect relationships.

Organizational behavior offers both challenges and opportunities for managers. It offers specific insights to improve a manager's people skills. It recognizes differences and helps managers to see the value of workforce diversity and practices that may need to be changed when managing in different countries. It can improve quality and employee productivity by showing managers how to empower their people, design and implement change programs, improve customer service, and help employees balance work–life conflicts. It provides suggestions for helping managers meet chronic labor shortages. It can help managers to cope in a world of temporariness and to learn ways to stimulate innovation. Finally, OB can offer managers guidance in creating an ethically healthy work climate.

Point Counterpoint

In Search of the Quick Fix

Walk into your nearest major bookstore. You'll undoubtedly find a large section of books devoted to management and managing human behavior. A close look at the titles will reveal that there is certainly no shortage of popular books on topics related to organizational behavior. To illustrate the point, consider the following popular book titles that are currently available on the topic of leadership:

- *Catch! A Fishmonger's Guide to Greatness* (Berrett-Koehler, 2003)
- *Leading with the Heart: Coach K's Successful Strategies for Basketball, Business, and Life* (Warner Business Books, 2001)
- *The Art of Leadership by Sun Tzu* (Premier, 2000)
- *Power Plays: Shakespeare's Lessons on Leadership and Management* (Simon & Schuster, 2000)
- *Robert E. Lee on Leadership* (Prima, 2000)
- *The Leadership Teachings of Geronimo* (Sterling House, 2002)
- *Leadership the Eleanor Roosevelt Way* (Prentice Hall, 2002)
- *The Hod Carrier: Leadership Lessons Learned on a Ladder* (Kimbell, 2002)
- *Leadership Wisdom from the Monk Who Sold His Ferrari* (Hay House, 2003)
- *Tony Soprano on Management: Leadership Lessons Inspired by America's Favorite Mobster* (Berkley, 2004)

Organizations are always looking for leaders; and managers and manager-wannabes are continually looking for ways to hone their leadership skills. Publishers respond to this demand by offering hundreds of titles that provide insights into the subject of leadership. Books like these can provide people with the secrets to leadership that others know about.

Beware of the quick fix! We all want to find quick and simplistic solutions to our complex problems. But here's the bad news: On problems related to organizational behavior, the quick and simple solutions are often wrong because they fail to consider the diversity among organizations, situations, and individuals. As Einstein said, "everything should be made as simple as possible, but not simpler."

When it comes to trying to understand people at work, there is no shortage of simplistic ideas and the books and consultants to promote them. And these books aren't just on leadership. Consider three recent bestsellers. *Who Moved My Cheese?* is a metaphor about two mice that is meant to convey the benefits of accepting change. *Fish!* tells how a fish market in Seattle made its jobs motivating. And *Whale Done!* proposes that managers can learn a lot about motivating people from techniques used by whale trainers at Sea World in San Diego. Are the "insights" from these books generalizable to people working in hundreds of different countries, in a thousand different organizations, and doing a million different jobs? It's very unlikely.

Popular books on organizational behavior often have cute titles and are fun to read. But they can be dangerous. They make the job of managing people seem much simpler than it really is. They are also often based on the author's opinions rather than substantive research.

Organizational behavior is a complex subject. There are few, if any, simple statements about human behavior that are generalizable to all people in all situations. Should you really try to apply leadership insights you got from a book on Robert E. Lee or Geronimo to managing software engineers in the twenty-first century?

The capitalistic system ensures that when a need exists, opportunistic individuals will surface to fill that need. When it comes to managing people at work, there is clearly a need for valid and reliable insights to guide managers and those aspiring to managerial positions. However, most of the offerings available at your local bookstore tend to be overly simplistic solutions. To the degree that people buy these books and enthusiastically expect them to provide them with the secrets to effective management, they do a disservice to themselves and those they're trying to manage.

Questions for Review

1. How are OB concepts addressed in management functions, roles, and skills?

2. Define *organizational behavior*. Relate it to *management*.

3. What is an organization? Is the family unit an organization? Explain.

4. Identify and contrast the three general management roles.

5. What is a "contingency approach" to OB?

6. Contrast the contributions of psychology and sociology to OB.

7. "Behavior is generally predictable, so there is no need to formally study OB." Why is that statement wrong?

8. What are the three levels of analysis in our OB model? Are they related? If so, how?

9. If job satisfaction is not a behavior, why is it considered an important dependent variable?

10. What are effectiveness and efficiency, and how are they related to organizational behavior?

Questions for Critical Thinking

1. Contrast the research comparing effective managers with successful managers. What are the implications from the research for practicing managers?

2. Why do you think the subject of OB might be criticized as being "only common sense," when one would rarely hear such a criticism of a course in physics or statistics?

3. Millions of workers have lost their jobs due to downsizing. At the same time, many organizations are complaining that they cannot find qualified people to fill vacancies. How do you explain this apparent contradiction?

4. On a scale of 1 to 10 measuring the sophistication of a scientific discipline in predicting phenomena, mathematical physics would probably be a 10. Where do you think OB would fall on the scale? Why?

5. What do you think is the single most critical "people" problem facing managers today? Give specific support for your position.

Team Exercise

WORKFORCE DIVERSITY

Purpose
To learn about the different needs of a diverse workforce.

Time required
Approximately 40 minutes.

Participants and roles
Divide the class into six groups of approximately equal size. Each group is assigned one of the following roles:

Nancy is 28 years old. She is a divorced mother of three children, aged 3, 5, and 7. She is the department head. She earns $40,000 a year on her job and receives another $3,600 a year in child support from her ex-husband.

Ethel is a 72-year-old widow. She works 25 hours a week to supplement her $8,000 annual pension. Including her hourly wage of $8.50, she earns $19,000 a year.

John is a 34-year-old black male born in Trinidad who is now a U.S. resident. He is married and the father of two small children. John attends college at night and is within a year of earning his bachelor's degree. His salary is $27,000 a year. His wife is an attorney and earns approximately $50,000 a year.

Lu is a 26-year-old physically impaired male Asian American. He is single and has a master's degree in education. Lu is paralyzed and confined to a wheelchair as a result of an auto accident. He earns $32,000 a year.

Maria is a single, 22-year-old Hispanic woman. Born and raised in Mexico, she came to the United States only three months ago. Maria's English needs considerable improvement. She earns $20,000 a year.

Mike is a 16-year-old white male high school sophomore who works 15 hours a week after school and during vacations. He earns $7.20 an hour, or approximately $5,600 a year.

The members of each group are to assume the character consistent with their assigned role.

Background
Our six participants work for a company that has recently installed a flexible benefits program. Instead of the traditional "one benefit package fits all," the company is allo-

cating an additional 25 percent of each employee's annual pay to be used for discretionary benefits. Those benefits and their annual cost are listed below.

- Supplementary health care for employee:
  Plan A (no deductible and pays 90%) = $3,000
  Plan B ($200 deductible and pays 80%) = $2,000
  Plan C ($1,000 deductible and pays 70%) = $500

- Supplementary health care for dependents (same deductibles and percentages as above):
  Plan A = $2,000
  Plan B = $1,500
  Plan C = $500

- Supplementary dental plan = $500

- Life insurance:
  Plan A ($25,000 coverage) = $500
  Plan B ($50,000 coverage) = $1,000
  Plan C ($100,000 coverage) = $2,000
  Plan D ($250,000 coverage) = $3,000

- Mental health plan = $500

- Prepaid legal assistance = $300

- Vacation = 2% of annual pay for each week, up to 6 weeks a year

- Pension at retirement equal to approximately 50% of final annual earnings = $1,500

- Four-day workweek during the three summer months (available only to full-time employees) = 4% of annual pay

- Day-care services (after company contribution) = $2,000 for all of an employee's children, regardless of number

- Company-provided transportation to and from work = $750

- College tuition reimbursement = $1,000

- Language class tuition reimbursement = $500

The Task

1. Each group has 15 minutes to develop a flexible benefits package that consumes 25 percent (and no more!) of their character's pay.

2. After completing step 1, each group appoints a spokesperson who describes to the entire class the benefits package they have arrived at for their character.

3. The entire class then discusses the results. How did the needs, concerns, and problems of each participant influence the group's decision? What do the results suggest for trying to motivate a diverse workforce?

Special thanks to Professor Penny Wright (San Diego State University) for her suggestions during the development of this exercise.

Ethical Dilemma

LYING IN BUSINESS

Do you think it's ever OK to lie? If one was negotiating for the release of hostages, most people would probably agree that if lying would lead to their safety, it's OK. What about in business, where the stakes are rarely life or death? Business executives like Martha Stewart have gone to jail for lying (submitting a false statement to federal investigators). Is misrepresentation or omitting factors okay as long as there is no outright lie?

Consider the negotiation process. A good negotiator never shows all his cards, right? And so omitting certain information is just part of the process. Well, it may surprise you to learn that the law will hold you liable for omitting information if partial disclosure is misleading, or if one side has superior information not accessible to the other.

In one case (*Jordan v. Duff and Phelps*), the company (Duff and Phelps) withheld information from an employee—Jordan—about the impending sale of the company. The problem: Jordan was leaving the organization and therefore sold his shares in the company. Ten days later, those shares became worth much more once the sale of the company became public. Jordan sued his former employer on the argument that it should have disclosed this information. Duff and Phelps countered that it never lied to Jordan. The Court of Appeals argued that in such situations one party cannot take "opportunistic advantage" of the other. In the eyes of the law, sometimes omitting relevant facts can be as bad as lying.

Questions

1. In a business context, is it ever okay to lie?

2. If you answered yes, what are those situations? Why is it okay to lie in these situations?

3. In business, is withholding information for one's advantage the same as lying? Why or why not?

4. In a business context, if someone has something to gain by lying, what percent of the people, do you think, would lie?

Sources: Based on "Brain Scans Detect More Activity in Those Who Lie," Reuters, November 29, 2004; http://www.msnbc.msn.com/id/ 6609019; P. Ekman and E. L. Rosenberg, *What the Fact Reveals: Basic and Applied Studies of Spontaneous Expression Using the Facial Action Coding System (CAPS)*. New York: Oxford University Press. Second expanded edition 2004.

Case Incident 1

HOW A UPS MANAGER CUT TURNOVER

In 1998, Jennifer Shroeger was promoted to district manager for UPS's operations in Buffalo, New York. She was responsible for $225 million in revenue, 2,300 workers, and the processing of some 45,000 packages an hour. When she took over in Buffalo, she faced a serious problem: turnover was out of control. Part-time workers who load, unload, and sort packages and who account for half of Buffalo's workforce—were leaving at the rate of 50 percent a year. Cutting this turnover rate became her highest priority.

The entire UPS organization relies heavily on part-time workers. In fact, it has historically been the primary inroad to becoming a full-time employee. Most of the UPS's current executives, for instance, began as part-timers during their college years, then moved into full-time positions. Additionally, UPS has always treated its part-timers well. They're given high pay, flexible work hours, full benefits, and substantial financial aid for college. Yet these pluses didn't seem to be enough to keep workers at UPS in Buffalo.

Shroeger developed a comprehensive plan to reduce turnover. It focused on improving hiring, communication, the workplace, and supervisory training. She began by modifying the hiring process to screen out people who essentially wanted full-time jobs. She reasoned that unfulfilled expectations were frustrating those hires whose preferences were for full-time work. Given that it typically took new part-timers six years to work up to a full-time job, it made sense to try to identify people who actually preferred part-time work.

Next, Shroeger analyzed the large database of information that UPS had on her district's employees. The data led her to the conclusion that she had five distinct groups working for her—differentiated by age and stages in their careers. And these groups had different needs and interests. In response, Shroeger modified the communication style and motivation techniques she used with each employee to reflect the group to which he or she belonged. For instance, Shroeger found that college students are most interested in building skills that they can apply later in their careers. As long as these employees saw that they were learning new skills, they were content to keep working at UPS. So Shroeger began offering them Saturday classes for computer-skill development and career-planning discussions.

Many new UPS employees in Buffalo were intimidated by the huge warehouse in which they had to work. To lessen that intimidation, Shroeger improved lighting throughout the building and upgraded break rooms to make them more user-friendly. To further help new employees adjust, she turned some of her best shift supervisors into trainers who provided specific guidance during new hires' first week. She also installed more personal computers on the floor, which gave new employees easier access to training materials and human-resource information on UPS's internal network.

Finally, Shroeger expanded training so supervisors had the skills to handle increased empowerment. Recognizing that her supervisors—most of whom were part-timers themselves—were the ones best equipped to understand the needs of part-time employees, supervisors learned how to assess difficult management situations, how to communicate in different ways, and how to identify the different needs of different people. Supervisors learned to demonstrate interest in their workers as individuals. For instance, they were taught to inquire about employees' hobbies, where they went to school, and the like.

By 2002, Shroeger's program was showing impressive results. Her district's attrition rate had dropped from 50 percent to 6 percent. During the first quarter of 2002, not one part-timer left a night shift. Annual savings attributed to reduced turnover, based largely on lower hiring costs, are estimated to be around $1 million. Additional benefits that the Buffalo district has gained from a more stable workforce include a 20 percent reduction in lost workdays due to work-related injuries and a drop from 4 percent to 1 percent in packages delivered on the wrong day or at the wrong time.

Questions

1. In dollars-and-cents terms, why did Jennifer Shroeger want to reduce turnover?

2. In addition to turnover, what other criteria should Ms. Shroeger examine in evaluating the effectiveness of the UPS program? Why is it important to examine multiple criteria in evaluating an OB program?

3. What are the implications from this case for managing in future years when there may be a severe labor shortage?

4. Is it unethical to teach supervisors "to demonstrate interest in their workers as individuals"? Explain.

5. What facts in this case support the argument that OB should be approached from a contingency perspective?

Source: Based on K. H. Hammonds, "Handle With Care," *Fast Company,* August 2002, pp. 103–7.

Case Incident 2

WORKPLACE VIOLENCE

On Wednesday, January 26, 2005, 54-year-old Myles Meyers walked into DaimlerChrysler's Toledo, Ohio, Assembly plant holding a double-barreled shotgun under his coat. Myers, a Jeep repairman, approached Yiesha Martin, a 27-year-old stock supervisor and stated his intentions. He was there to murder three supervisors: Mike Toney, 45, Roy Thacker, 50, and Carrie Woggerman, 24. Afterwards, he said, he would turn the gun on himself. "I was shaking and I started to cry," said Martin. Meyers told her not to cry and to page Toney. Although he was usually eating lunch at his desk around this time, Toney was busy dealing with a problem on the production line. On Martin's second attempt, Toney responded.

Thacker, however, was the first of Meyer's intended victims to approach the former employee. When Thacker asked Meyers why he was at the office, "[Meyers] turned from the partition and just shot him," Martin recalled. "I just saw the shells go. He reloaded in front of me." Martin ran, grabbing a radio in the process. As she ran away, calling into her radio for help, she heard another gunshot. Mike Toney had just arrived and was now the second victim. Carrie Woggerman was able to flee after the first shot, but Paul Medlen, 41, while attempting to come to the aid of Toney, was shot in the chest by Meyers just before Meyers turned the gun on himself, taking his own life. Of the three employees shot by Meyers, two survived. Unfortunately, Thacker died from his wounds.

Regrettably, the shooting at the Toledo Assembly plant was not an isolated incident. Just two years earlier, Doug Williams, an employee at Lockheed Martin, left in the middle of an ethics meeting, went to his car, and came back with several guns. He then shot six coworkers to death and wounded eight others before committing suicide. According to the Bureau of Labor Statistics, 18,104 assaults and 609 homicides occurred at workplaces throughout the United States in 2002. Such violence prompted the Centers for Disease Control to label workplace violence a "national epidemic."

In addition to the obvious devastation workplace violence causes victims and their families, businesses often experience serious repercussions, including legal action. Lockheed Martin is still embroiled in a legal battle over whether the company should assume part of the responsibility for the shooting that took place at its plant. And Paul Medlen has just filed suit against DaimlerChrysler and the plant's security firm, Wackenhut Corp., alleging that both failed to provide adequate security. Given the tremendous damage that companies and employees face following violent episodes, why aren't businesses doing more to curtail workplace violence? According to a recent study by the American Society of Safety Engineers, only 1 percent of U.S. businesses have a formal antiviolence policy.

Advice on how to reduce workplace violence abounds. According to former FBI agent Doug Kane, people who behave violently often announce or hint at their intentions before the violence occurs. Managers, then, need to be aware of at-risk employees who may commit violent acts and should encourage employees to report any threatening or suspicious behavior. Some employees of the DaimlerChrysler plant are even suggesting that metal detectors be installed to prevent future violence. Whatever measures are taken, it is clear that workplace violence is an issue that needs to be addressed for employees to feel safe at work.

Questions

1. How liable should companies be for violent acts that are committed during work by their own employees?

2. Can companies completely prevent workplace violence? If not, what steps can they take to reduce it?

3. Why do you think only 1 percent of companies have a formal antiviolence policy?

4. Some companies are considering the installation of metal detectors to prevent workplace violence. Do you think these measures infringe too much on individual privacy? In other words, can a company take prevention too far?

5. What factors might lead to violent acts in the workplace? Are these acts committed by only a few "sick" individuals, or are many individuals capable of committing acts given certain circumstances?

Source: Based on A. K. Fisher, "How to Prevent Violence at Work," *Fortune*, February 21, 2005, pp. 42, and C. Hall, "Witness Recounts Moments of Horror and Heartbreak," *The Toledo Blade*, January 29, 2005 (toledoblade.com/apps/pbcs.dll/article?AID=/20050129/NEWS03/501290378).

Endnotes

1. See, for instance, G. Marshall, "Nice Guys Can Finish First," *Fast Company*, November 2004, p. 123.; R. Alsop, "Playing Well with Others," *Wall Street Journal*, September 9, 2002, p. R11; and L. A. Witt and G. R. Ferris, "Social Skill as a Moderator of the Conscientiousness–Performance Relationship: Convergent Results Across Four Studies," *Journal of Applied Psychology*, October 2003, pp. 809–21.

2. Cited in R. Alsop, "Playing Well with Others."

3. See, for instance, C. Penttila, "Hiring Hardships," *Entrepreneur*, October 2002, pp. 34–35.

4. *The 2002 National Study of the Changing Workforce* (New York: Families and Work Institute, 2002).

5. I. S. Fulmer, B. Gerhart, and K. S. Scott, "Are the 100 Best Better? An Empirical Investigation of the Relationship Between Being a 'Great Place to Work' and Firm Performance," *Personnel Psychology*, Winter 2003, pp. 965–93.

6. H. Fayol, *Industrial and General Administration* (Paris: Dunod, 1916).

7. H. Mintzberg, *The Nature of Managerial Work* (Upper Saddle River, NJ: Prentice Hall, 1973).

8. R. L. Katz, "Skills of an Effective Administrator," *Harvard Business Review*, September–October 1974, pp. 90–102.

9. F. Luthans, "Successful vs. Effective Real Managers," *Academy of Management Executive*, May 1988, pp. 127–32; and F. Luthans, R. M. Hodgetts, and S. A. Rosenkrantz, *Real Managers* (Cambridge, MA: Ballinger, 1988). See also F. Shipper and J. Davy, "A Model and Investigation of Managerial Skills, Employees' Attitudes, and Managerial Performance," *Leadership Quarterly*, 13, 2002, pp. 95–120.

10. P. H. Langford, "Importance of Relationship Management for the Career Success of Australian Managers," *Australian Journal of Psychology*, December 2000, pp. 163–69; and A. M. Konrad, R. Kashlak, I. Yoshioka, R. Waryszak, and N. Toren, "What Do Managers Like to Do? A Five-Country Study," *Group & Organization Management*, December 2001, pp. 401–33.

11. A. S. Tsui, S. J. Ashford, L. St.Clair, and K. R. Xin, "Dealing with Discrepant Expectations: Response Strategies and Managerial Effectiveness," *Academy of Management Journal*, December 1995, pp. 1515–43.

12. See, for instance, J. E. Garcia and K. S. Keleman, "What Is Organizational Behavior Anyhow?", paper presented at the 16th Annual Organizational Behavior Teaching Conference, Columbia, Missouri, June 1989; and C. Heath and S. B. Sitkin, "Big-B Versus Big-O: What Is *Organizational* about Organizational Behavior?" *Journal of Organizational Behavior*, February 2001, pp. 43–58. For a review of what one eminent researcher believes *should* be included in organizational behavior, based on survey data, see J. B. Miner, "The Rated Importance, Scientific Validity, and Practical Usefulness of Organizational Behavior Theories: A Quantitative Review," *Academy of Management Learning & Education*, September 2003, pp. 250–68.

13. See F. D. Richard, C. F. Bond, Jr., and J. J. Stokes-Zoota, " 'That is Completely Obvious . . . and Important': Lay Judgments of Social Psychological Findings," *Personality and Social Psychological Bulletin*, April 2001, pp. 497–505; and L. A. Burke and J. E. Moore, "A Perennial Dilemma in OB Education: Engaging the Traditional Student," *Academy of Management Learning & Education*, March 2003, pp. 37–52.

14. "In Finland, Fine for Speeding Sets Record," *International Herald Tribune*, February 11, 2004, p. 2.

15. Chris Woodyard, "War, Terrorism Scare off Business Travelers," *USA Today*, March 25, 2003.

16. O. C. Richard, "Racial Diversity, Business Strategy, and Firm Performance: A Resource-Based View," *Academy of Management Journal*, April 2000, pp. 164–77.

17. "Bye-Bye, Ozzie and Harriet," *American Demographics*, December 2000, p. 59.

18. This section is based on M. Toosi, "A Century of Change: The U.S. Labor Force, 1950–2050," *Monthly Labor Review*, May 2002, pp. 15–27; and *CBO's Projections of the Labor Force* (Washington, DC: Congressional Budget Office, September 2004).

19. See M. E. A. Jayne and R. L. Dipboye, "Leveraging Diversity to Improve Business Performance: Research Findings and Recommendations for Organizations," *Human Resource Management*, Winter 2004, pp. 409–24. S. E. Jackson and A. Joshi, "Research on Domestic and International Diversity in Organizations: A Merger that Works?" in N. Anderson et al (eds.), *Handbook of Industrial, Work & Organizational Psychology*, vol. 2 (Thousand Oaks, CA: Sage, 2001), pp. 206–31; and L. Smith, "The Business Case for Diversity," *Fortune*, October 13, 2003, pp. S8–S12.

20. This section is based on P. Francese, "Looming Labor Shortages," *American Demographics*, November 2001, pp. 34–35; A. Bernstein, "Too Many Workers? Not for Long," *Businessweek*, May 20, 2002, pp. 126–30; R. Herman, *Impending Crises: Too Many Jobs, Too Few People* (Winchester, VA: Oakhill Press, 2002); J. S. McClenahen, "The Next Crisis: Too Few Workers," www.industryweek.com, May 1, 2003; and L. Lavelle, "After the Jobless Recovery, A War for Talent," *Businessweek*, September 29, 2003, p. 92.

21. D. Kadlec, "Everyone, Back in the Labor Pool," *Time*, July 29, 2002, pp. 23–31; and K. Greene, "Many Older Workers to Delay Retirement Until After Age 70," *Wall Street Journal*, September 23, 2003, p. D2.

22. See, for instance, S. D. Pugh, J. Dietz, J. W. Wiley, and S. M. Brooks, "Driving Service Effectiveness Through Employee-Customer Linkages," *Academy of Management Executive*, November 2002, pp. 73–84; and H. Liao and A. Chuang, "A Multilevel Investigation of Factors Influencing Employee Service Performance and Customer Outcomes," *Academy of Management Journal*, February 2004, pp. 41–58.

23. See: http://www.patagonia.com/jobs/retail_asst_mgr.shtml; "Patagonia Sets the Pace for Green Business," *Grist Magazine*, October 22, 2004 (www.grist.org).

24. See, for instance,; E. Naumann and D. W. Jackson, Jr., "One More Time: How Do You Satisfy Customers?" *Business Horizons*, 1999, vol. 42(3), pp. 71–76; W-C. Tsai, "Determinants and Consequences of Employee Displayed Positive Emotions," *Journal of Management*, vol. 27, no. 4, 2001, pp. 497–512; S. D. Pugh, "Service with a Smile: Emotional Contagion in the Service Encounter," *Academy of Management Journal*, October 2001, pp. 1018–27; M. K. Brady and J. J.

Cronin Jr., "Customer Orientation: Effects on Customer Service Perceptions and Outcome Behaviors," *Journal of Service Research*, February 2001, pp. 241–51; and M. Workman and W. Bommer, "Redesigning Computer Call Center Work: A Longitudinal Field Experiment," *Journal of Organizational Behavior*, May 2004, pp. 317–37.

25. J. Flaherty, "Suggestions Rise from the Floors of U.S. Factories," *New York Times*, April 18, 2001, p. C1; see also W. M. Greenfield, "Decision Making and Employee Engagement," *Employment Relations Today*, Summer 2004, pp. 13–24.

26. See, for instance, S. Armour, "Workers Put Family First Despite Slow Economy, Jobless Fears," *USA Today*, June 6, 2002, p. 3B; V. S. Major, K. J. Klein, and M. G. Ehrhart, "Work Time, Work Interference with Family, and Psychological Distress," *Journal of Applied Psychology*, June 2002, pp. 427–36; D. Brady, "Rethinking the Rat Race," *Businessweek*, August 26, 2002, pp. 142–43; J. M. Brett and L. K. Stroh, "Working 61 Plus Hours a Week: Why Do Managers Do It?" *Journal of Applied Psychology*, February 2003, pp. 67–78; and T. A. Judge and J. A. Colquitt, "Organizational Justice and Stress: The Mediating Role of Work-Family Conflict," *Journal of Applied Psychology*, June 2004, pp. 395–404.

27. See, for instance, *The 2002 National Study of the Changing Workforce* (New York: Families and Work Institute, 2002).

28. Cited in S. Armour, "Workers Put Family First Despite Slow Economy, Jobless Fears."

29. S. Shellenbarger, "What Job Candidates Really Want to Know: Will I Have a Life?" *Wall Street Journal*, November 17, 1999, p. B1; and "U.S. Employers Polish Image to Woo a Demanding New Generation," *Manpower Argus*, February 2000, p. 2.

30. J. Merritt, "For MBAs, Soul-Searching 101," *Businessweek*, September 16, 2002, pp. 64–66; and S. Greenhouse, "The Mood at Work: Anger and Anxiety," *New York Times*, October 29, 2002, p. E1.

31. See, for instance, G. R. Weaver, L. K. Trevino, and P. L. Cochran, "Corporate Ethics Practices in the Mid-1990's: An Empirical Study of the Fortune 1000," *Journal of Business Ethics*, February 1999, pp. 283–94; and C. De Mesa Graziano, "Promoting Ethical Conduct: A Review of Corporate Practices," *Strategic Investor Relations*, Fall 2002, pp. 29–35.

32. A. J. Rucci, S. P. Kirn, and R. T. Quinn, "The Employee-Customer-Profit Chain at Sears," *Harvard Business Review*, January–February 1998, pp. 83–97.

33. J. Britt, "Workplace No-Shows' Cost to Employers Rise Again," *HRMagazine*, December 2002, pp. 26–29.

34. "Absence-Minded Workers Cost Business Dearly," *Works Management*, June 2001, pp. 10–14.

35. W. Hoge, "Sweden's Crade-to-Grave Welfare Starts to Get Ill," *International Herald Tribune*, September 25, 2002, p. 8.

36. "Employee Turnover Costs in the U.S.," *Manpower Argus*, January 2001, p. 5.

37. See http://data.bls.gov/ (May 11, 2005).

38. See, for example, D. R. Dalton and W. D. Todor, "Functional Turnover: An Empirical Assessment," *Journal of Applied*

Psychology, December 1981, pp. 716–21; G. M. McEvoy and W. F. Cascio, "Do Good or Poor Performers Leave? A Meta-Analysis of the Relationship between Performance and Turnover," *Academy of Management Journal*, December 1987, pp. 744–62; S. Lorge, "When Turnover Isn't So Bad," *Sales & Marketing Management*, September 1999, p. 13; and M. C. Sturman and C. O. Trevor, "The Implications of Linking the Dynamic Performance and Turnover Literatures," *Journal of Applied Psychology*, August 2001, pp. 684–96.

39. Cited in "You Often Lose the Ones You Love," *Industry Week*, November 21, 1988, p. 5.

40. R. J. Bennett and S. L. Robinson, "The Past, Present and Future of Workplace Deviance Research," in J. Greenberg (ed.), *Organizational Behavior: The State of the Science*, 2nd ed., Lawrence Erlbaum Associates, 1994, Hillsdale, New Jersey; R. J. Bennett and S. L. Robinson, "Development of a Measure of Workplace Deviance," *Journal of Applied Psychology*, vol. 85(3), 2000, pp.349–60; A. M. O'Leary-Kelly, M. K. Duffy, and R. W. Griffin, "Construct Confusion in the Study of Antisocial Work Behavior," *Research in Personnel and Human Resources Management*, vol. 18, 2000, pp. 275–303; C. Porath, C. Pearson, and D. L. Shapiro, "Turning the Other Cheek or an Eye for an Eye: Targets' Responses to Incivility," paper interactively presented at the annual meeting of the National Academy of Management, August 1999.

41. D. W. Organ, *Organizational Citizenship Behavior: The Good Soldier Syndrome* (Lexington, MA: Lexington Books, 1988), p. 4. See also W. C. Borman and L. A. Penner, "Citizenship Performance: Its Nature, Antecedents, and Motives," in B. W. Roberts and R. Hogan (eds.), *Personality Psychology in the Workplace* (Washington D.: American Psychological Association, 2001), pp. 45–61; and J. A. LePine, A. Erez, and D. E. Johnson, "The Nature and Dimensionality of Organizational Citizenship Behavior: A Critical Review and Meta-Analysis," *Journal of Applied Psychology*, February 2002, pp. 52–65.

42. P. M. Podsakoff, S. B. MacKenzie, J. B. Paine, and D. G. Bachrach, "Organizational Citizenship Behaviors: A Critical Review of the Theoretical and Empirical Literature and Suggestions for Future Research," *Journal of Management*, vol. 26, no. 3, 2000, pp. 543–48; and M. C. Bolino and W. H. Turnley, "Going the Extra Mile: Cultivating and Managing Employee Citizenship Behavior," *Academy of Management Executive*, August 2003, pp. 60–73.

43. T. A. Judge, C. J. Thoresen, J. E. Bono, and G. R. Patton, "The Job Satisfaction-Job Performance Relationship: A Qualitative and Quantitative Review," *Psychological Bulletin*, vol. 127, 2001, pp. 376–407.

44. M. Buckingham and C. Coffman, *First, Break All the Rules: What the World's Greatest Managers Do Differently* (New York: Simon & Schuster, 1999).

45. H. J. Leavitt, *Managerial Psychology*, rev. ed. (Chicago: University of Chicago Press, 1964), p. 3.

Foundations of Individual Behavior

After studying this chapter, you should be able to:

1 Identify two types of ability.

2 Define the key biographical characteristics.

3 Understand how to shape the behavior of others.

4 Distinguish between the four schedules of reinforcement.

5 Clarify the role of punishment in learning.

LEARNING OBJECTIVES

Do You Know How Many Trees There Are in New York City's Central Park?

Amazon.com and Microsoft have at least three things in common. They both headquarter in the Seattle, Washington area. They're both high-tech success stories. And their executives both emphasize intelligence as the primary factor in hiring new employees.[1]

Most organizations emphasize experience when making employee selection decisions. And experience can be a valid predictor of future job performance. But Amazon and Microsoft prefer to emphasize intelligence. Amazon, for instance, carefully scrutinizes college transcripts and SAT scores of potential customer service reps before making a job offer. Why? The company believes that the key to its success is its ability to innovate, and the smartest people, regardless of their jobs, are the best innovators. So job interviews at Amazon are more likely to focus on an applicant's answers to questions such as "How many windows are in the city of San Francisco?" or "How many trees are in New York City's Central Park?" than "What did you learn from your last job?" Importantly, Amazon interviewers aren't interested in how close an applicant's response is to the correct answer. They're looking at a candidate's reasoning processes. Even for menial jobs, Amazon emphasizes intelligence. Company founder Jeff Bezos defends this approach as a means for fending off mediocrity: "If you start out with A's, you get to keep A's . . . If you start hiring B's, B's hire B's."

Similarly, applicants for a job at Microsoft are likely to be asked questions such as "Why are manhole covers round?" "How many gas stations are there in the United States?" "How much water flows through the Mississippi daily?" Again, the interviewers are concerned with how applicants think rather than their ability to provide a correct answer. Bill Gates, cofounder and CEO of Microsoft, succinctly defends his company's belief that IQ is more important than experience—"you can teach smart people anything."

Amazon and Microsoft believe their greatest asset is the collective intellectual resources of their employees. So they consistently seek out and hire the smartest individuals they can find. ■

Intelligence is but one characteristic that people bring with them when they join an organization. In this chapter, we look at how individual differences in the form of ability (which includes intelligence) and biographical characteristics (such as age, gender, race, and tenure) affect employee performance and satisfaction. Then we show how people learn behaviors and what management can do to shape those behaviors.

People, of course, differ in many ways. Appearance-related differences—such as height, weight, skin, hair, and eye color—are the most obvious. Interestingly, there is evidence that appearance matters in the workplace. For example, tall people—because they are seen as more leader-like—actually earn higher performance evaluations and also earn more money. In fact, each inch in height amounted to $789 more a year in pay. So, someone who is 7 inches taller—say, 6 feet versus 5 feet 5 inches—would be expected to earn $5,525 more annually.[2] Evidence also suggests that physical attractiveness matters in OB. For example, applicants judged as physically attractive are more likely to get the job.[3] Throughout this chapter we look at how basic individual differences affect employee performance and satisfaction.

Now you may wonder: Wouldn't personality be considered a basic individual difference, too? Yes, it would. Personality is so fundamental and important that we devote an entire chapter to it! So, keep this in mind as you read through the chapter. We will cover personality in detail in Chapter 4.

Ability

Contrary to what we were taught in grade school, we weren't all created equal. Most of us are to the left or to the right of the median on some normally distributed ability curve. For example, regardless of how motivated you are, it's unlikely that you can act as well as Scarlett Johansson, play basketball as well as LeBron James, write as well as J. K. Rowling, or play the guitar as well as Pat Matheny. Of course, just because we aren't all equal in abilities does not imply that some individuals are inherently inferior to others. What we are acknowledging is that everyone has strengths and weaknesses in terms of ability that make him or her relatively superior or inferior to others in performing certain tasks or activities.[4] From management's standpoint, the issue is not whether people differ in terms of their abilities. They clearly do. The issue is knowing *how* people differ in abilities and using that knowledge to increase the likelihood that an employee will perform his or her job well.

What does ability mean? As we will use the term, **ability** refers to an individual's capacity to perform the various tasks in a job. It is a current assessment of what one can do. An individual's overall abilities are essentially made up of two sets of factors: intellectual and physical.

Intellectual Abilities

Intellectual abilities are those needed to perform mental activities—for thinking, reasoning, and problem solving. People in most societies place a high value on intelligence, and for good reason. Smart people generally earn more money and attain higher levels of education. Smart people are also more likely to emerge as leaders of groups. Intelligence quotient (IQ) tests, for example, are designed to ascertain one's general intellectual abilities. So, too, are popular college admission tests such as the SAT and ACT and graduate admission tests in business (GMAT), law (LSAT), and medicine (MCAT). These testing firms don't make the argument that their tests assess intelligence, but experts know

Exhibit 2-1	Dimensions of Intellectual Ability	
Dimension	**Description**	**Job Example**
Number aptitude	Ability to do speedy and accurate arithmetic	Accountant: Computing the sales tax on a set of items
Verbal comprehension	Ability to understand what is read or heard and the relationship of words to each other	Plant manager: Following corporate policies on hiring
Perceptual speed	Ability to identify visual similarities and differences quickly and accurately	Fire investigator: Identifying clues to support a charge of arson
Inductive reasoning	Ability to identify a logical sequence in a problem and then solve the problem	Market researcher: Forecasting demand for a product in the next time period
Deductive reasoning	Ability to use logic and assess the implications of an argument	Supervisor: Choosing between two different suggestions offered by employees
Spatial visualization	Ability to imagine how an object would look if its position in space were changed	Interior decorator: Redecorating an office
Memory	Ability to retain and recall past experiences	Salesperson: Remembering the names of customers

that they do.[5] The seven most frequently cited dimensions making up intellectual abilities are number aptitude, verbal comprehension, perceptual speed, inductive reasoning, deductive reasoning, spatial visualization, and memory.[6] Exhibit 2-1 describes those dimensions.

Jobs differ in the demands they place on incumbents to use their intellectual abilities. The more complex a job is in terms of information-processing demands, the more general intelligence and verbal abilities will be necessary to perform the job successfully.[7] Of course, a high IQ is not a requirement for all jobs. For jobs in which employee behavior is highly routine and there are little or no opportunities to exercise discretion, a high IQ is not as important to performing well. However, that does not mean that people with high IQs cannot have an impact on jobs that are traditionally less complex.

For example, do you think a high IQ is important for the job of sanitation worker? It certainly can be. Consider the story of a sanitation worker in Tallahassee, Florida, who proposed the city supply garbage cans. City-supplied garbage cans would allow the collectors to start with an empty garbage can, bring it to house A, pick up that house's garbage can, and bring it to the truck without having to return the can. House A's can would then be placed at house B. This would dramatically improve garbage collection times, allowing the city to cover more territory with fewer people. This example also points to another key reason why intelligent people are better job performers: They are more creative. Smart people learn jobs more quickly, are more adaptable to changing circumstances, and are better at inventing solutions that improve performance.[8] In other words, intelligence is one of the better predictors of performance across all sorts of jobs.[9] This explains why companies like Amazon.com and Microsoft emphasize assessing candidates' intelligence as a key element in their hiring process.

It might surprise you that the most widely used intelligence test in hiring decisions takes only 12 minutes. It's called the Wonderlic Personnel Test. There

ability *An individual's capacity to perform the various tasks in a job.*

intellectual abilities *The capacity to do mental activities—thinking, reasoning, and problem solving.*

The Benefits of Cultural Intelligence

HAVE YOU EVER NOTICED THAT SOME INDIVIDUALS seem to have a knack for relating well to people from different cultures? Some researchers have labeled this skill *cultural intelligence*, which is an outsider's natural ability to interpret an individual's unfamiliar gestures and behaviors in the same way that others from the individual's culture would. Cultural intelligence is important because when conducting business with people from different cultures, misunderstandings can often occur, and as a result, cooperation and productivity may suffer.

Consider the following example. An American manager was meeting with his fellow design team engineers, two of whom were German. As ideas floated around the table, his German colleagues quickly rejected them. The American thought the feedback was harsh and concluded that his German colleagues were rude. However, they were merely critiquing the ideas, not the individual—a distinction that the American was unable to make, perhaps due to a lack of cultural intelligence. As a result, the American became wary of contributing potentially good ideas. Had the American been more culturally intelligent, he likely would have recognized the true motives behind his colleagues' remarks and thus may have been able to use those remarks to improve his ideas.

It is unclear whether the notion of cultural intelligence is separate from other forms of intelligence, such as emotional intelligence, and even whether cultural intelligence is different from cognitive ability. However, it is clear that the ability to interact well with individuals from different cultures is a key asset in today's global business environment.

Source: Based on C. Earley and E. Mosakowski, "Cultural Intelligence," *Harvard Business Review*, October 2004, pp. 139–146.

are different forms of the test, and each form has 50 questions. Here are a few example questions from the Wonderlic:

- When rope is selling at $.10 a foot, how many feet can you buy for $.60?
- Assume the first two statements are true. Is the final one:
  1. true, 2. false, 3. not certain?

  a. The boy plays baseball.
  b. All baseball players wear hats.
  c. The boy wears a hat.

The Wonderlic is both a speed (almost nobody has time to answer every question) and power (questions get harder as you go along) test, so the average score is pretty low—about 21/50. And because it's able to provide valid information at a cheap price ($2–$6/applicant), more and more companies are using the Wonderlic in hiring decisions. For example, the Factory Card and Party Outlet, which has 182 stores nationwide, uses the Wonderlic. So does Subway, Peoples Flowers, Security Alarm, Workforce Employment Solutions, and many others. Most companies that use the Wonderlic don't use it in place of other hiring tools like application forms or the interview. Rather, they add the Wonderlic as another source of information—in this case, because of the Wonderlic's ability to provide valid data on applicants' intelligence levels.

Interestingly, while intelligence is a big help in performing a job well, it doesn't make people happier or more satisfied with their jobs. The correlation between intelligence and job satisfaction is about zero. Why? Research suggests that although intelligent people perform better and tend to have more interesting jobs, they also are more critical in evaluating their job conditions. Thus, smart people have it better, but they also expect more.[10]

In the past decade and a half, researchers have begun to expand the meaning of intelligence beyond mental abilities. Some researchers believe that intelligence can be better understood by breaking it down into four subparts: cognitive, social, emotional, and cultural.[11] Cognitive intelligence encompasses the aptitudes that have long been tapped by traditional intelligence tests. Social intelligence is a person's ability to relate effectively to others. Emotional intelligence is the ability to identify, understand, and manage emotions. And cultural intelligence is awareness of cross-cultural differences and the ability to function successfully in cross-cultural situations. It's important to note that this line of inquiry—toward **multiple intelligences**—is in its infancy, and the claims made don't always match the scientific evidence. Furthermore, measuring intelligences other than cognitive intelligence has not proven to be easy.[12] Of course, there are many cases in which so-called smart people—those with high cognitive intelligence—don't necessarily adapt well to everyday life, work well with others, or succeed when placed in leadership roles.

Physical Abilities

To the same degree that intellectual abilities play a larger role in complex jobs with demanding information-processing requirements, specific **physical abilities** gain importance for successfully doing less-skilled and more-standardized jobs. For example, jobs in which success demands stamina, manual dexterity, leg strength, or similar talents require management to identify an employee's physical capabilities.

Research on the requirements needed in hundreds of jobs has identified nine basic abilities involved in the performance of physical tasks.[13] These are described in Exhibit 2-2. Individuals differ in the extent to which they have each

Exhibit **2-2**	Nine Basic Physical Abilities
Strength Factors	
1. Dynamic strength	Ability to exert muscular force repeatedly or continuously over time
2. Trunk strength	Ability to exert muscular strength using the trunk (particularly abdominal) muscles
3. Static strength	Ability to exert force against external objects
4. Explosive strength	Ability to expend a maximum of energy in one or a series of explosive acts
Flexibility Factors	
5. Extent flexibility	Ability to move the trunk and back muscles as far as possible
6. Dynamic flexibility	Ability to make rapid, repeated flexing movements
Other Factors	
7. Body coordination	Ability to coordinate the simultaneous actions of different parts of the body
8. Balance	Ability to maintain equilibrium despite forces pulling off balance
9. Stamina	Ability to continue maximum effort requiring prolonged effort over time

Source: Adapted from *HRMagazine*, published by the Society for Human Resource Management, Alexandria, VA.

multiple intelligences *Intelligence contains four subparts: cognitive, social, emotional, and cultural.*

physical ability *The capacity to do tasks demanding stamina, dexterity, strength, and similar characteristics.*

of these abilities. Not surprisingly, there is also little relationship among them: A high score on one is no assurance of a high score on others. High employee performance is likely to be achieved when management has ascertained the extent to which a job requires each of the nine abilities and then ensures that employees in that job have those abilities.

The Ability–Job Fit

Our concern is with explaining and predicting the behavior of people at work. We have demonstrated that jobs make differing demands on people and that people differ in their abilities. Therefore, employee performance is enhanced when there is a high ability–job fit.

The specific intellectual or physical abilities required for adequate job performance depend on the ability requirements of the job. So, for example, airline pilots need strong spatial-visualization abilities; beach lifeguards need both strong spatial-visualization abilities and body coordination; senior executives need verbal abilities; high-rise construction workers need balance; and journalists with weak reasoning abilities would likely have difficulty meeting minimum job-performance standards. Directing attention at only the employee's abilities or only the ability requirements of the job ignores the fact that employee performance depends on the interaction of the two.

What predictions can we make when the fit is poor? As alluded to previously, if employees lack the required abilities, they are likely to fail. If you're hired as a word processor and you can't meet the job's basic keyboard typing requirements, your performance is going to be poor irrespective of your positive attitude or your high level of motivation. When the ability–job fit is out of sync because the employee has abilities that far exceed the requirements of the job, our predictions would be very different. Job performance is likely to be adequate, but there will be organizational inefficiencies and possible declines in employee satisfaction. Given that pay tends to reflect the highest skill level that employees possess, if an employee's abilities far exceed those necessary to do the job, management will be paying more than it needs to. Abilities significantly above those required can also reduce the employee's job satisfaction when the employee's desire to use his or her abilities is particularly strong and is frustrated by the limitations of the job.

Biographical Characteristics

As discussed in Chapter 1, this textbook is essentially concerned with finding and analyzing the variables that have an impact on employee productivity, absence, turnover, deviance, citizenship, and satisfaction. The list of those variables—as shown in Exhibit 1-7—is long and contains some complicated concepts. Many of the concepts—motivation, say, or power and politics or organizational culture—are hard to assess. It might be valuable, then, to begin by looking at factors that are easily definable and readily available; data that can be obtained, for the most part, simply from information available in an employee's personnel file. What factors would these be? Obvious characteristics would be an employee's age, gender, race, and length of service with an organization. Fortunately, there is a sizable amount of research that has specifically analyzed many of these **biographical characteristics**.

Age

The relationship between age and job performance is likely to be an issue of increasing importance during the next decade. Why? There are at least three reasons. First, there is a widespread belief that job performance declines with increasing age. Regardless of whether it's true or not, a lot of people believe it and act on it. Second, as noted in Chapter 1, is the reality that the workforce is aging. The third reason is U.S. legislation that, for all intents and purposes, outlaws mandatory retirement. Most U.S. workers today no longer have to retire at the age of 70.

What is the perception of older workers? Evidence indicates that employers hold mixed feelings.[14] They see a number of positive qualities that older workers bring to their jobs: specifically, experience, judgment, a strong work ethic, and commitment to quality. But older workers are also perceived as lacking flexibility and as being resistant to new technology. And in a time when organizations actively seek individuals who are adaptable and open to change, the negatives associated with age clearly hinder the initial hiring of older workers and increase the likelihood that they will be let go during cutbacks. Now let's take a look at the evidence. What effect does age actually have on turnover, absenteeism, productivity, and satisfaction?

The older you get, the less likely you are to quit your job. That conclusion is based on studies of the age–turnover relationship.[15] Of course, this shouldn't be too surprising. As workers get older, they have fewer alternative job opportunities. In addition, older workers are less likely to resign than are younger workers because their long tenure tends to provide them with higher wage rates, longer paid vacations, and more-attractive pension benefits.

It's tempting to assume that age is also inversely related to absenteeism. After all, if older workers are less likely to quit, won't they also demonstrate higher stability by coming to work more regularly? Not necessarily. Most studies do show an inverse relationship, but close examination finds that the age–absence relationship is partially a function of whether the absence is avoidable or unavoidable.[16] In general, older employees have lower rates of avoidable absence than do younger employees. However, they have higher rates of unavoidable absence, probably due to the poorer health associated with aging and the longer recovery period that older workers need when injured.

How does age affect productivity? There is a widespread belief that productivity declines with age. It is often assumed that an individual's skills—particularly speed, agility, strength, and coordination—decay over time and that prolonged job boredom and lack of intellectual stimulation all contribute to reduced productivity. The evidence, however, contradicts that belief and those assumptions. For instance, during a 3-year period, a large hardware chain staffed one of its stores solely with employees over 50 and compared its results with those of five stores with younger employees. The store staffed by the over-50 employees was significantly more productive (measured in terms of sales generated against labor costs) than two of the other stores and held its own with the other three.[17] Other reviews of the research find that age and job perfor-

biographical characteristics *Personal characteristics—such as age, gender, race, and length of tenure—that are objective and easily obtained from personnel records.*

Bonne Bell values the work ethic of older workers who package teen cosmetics. The company gives older workers part-time schedules of four hours a day, five days a week, and a bonus of 50 Bonne Bell products every three months. According to company owner Jesse Bell, older workers at the plant are as productive as younger employees.

mance are unrelated.[18] Moreover, this finding seems to be true for almost all types of jobs, professional and nonprofessional. The natural conclusion is that the demands of most jobs, even those with heavy manual labor requirements, are not extreme enough for any declines in physical skills attributable to age to have an impact on productivity; or, if there is some decay due to age, it is offset by gains due to experience.[19]

Our final concern is the relationship between age and job satisfaction. On this issue, the evidence is mixed. Most studies indicate a positive association between age and satisfaction, at least up to age 60.[20] Other studies, however, have found a U-shaped relationship.[21] Several explanations could clear up these results, the most plausible being that these studies are intermixing professional and nonprofessional employees. When the two types are separated, satisfaction tends to continually increase among professionals as they age, whereas it falls among nonprofessionals during middle age and then rises again in the later years.

Gender

Few issues initiate more debates, misconceptions, and unsupported opinions than whether women perform as well on jobs as men do. In this section, we review the research on that issue.

The evidence suggests that the best place to begin is with the recognition that there are few, if any, important differences between men and women that will affect their job performance. There are, for instance, no consistent male–female differences in problem-solving ability, analytical skills, competitive drive, motivation, sociability, or learning ability.[22] Psychological studies have found that women are more willing to conform to authority and that men are more aggressive and more likely than women to have expectations of success, but those differences are minor. Given the significant changes that have taken place in the past 40 years in terms of increasing female participation rates in the workforce and rethinking what constitutes male and female roles, you should operate on the assumption that there is no significant difference in job productivity between men and women.[23]

JPMorgan Chase, a global banking and financial services firm, believes that women perform as well on jobs as men do. Almost 60 percent of the firm's employees are women, and 50 percent of its managers and professionals are women. The many working moms at JPMorgan appreciate flexible work schedules such as job sharing, compressed workweeks, flextime, and telecommuting. JPMorgan also provides on-site, back-up child care centers for employees whose usual child-care arrangements fall through. Shown here are stockbrokers and traders at company headquarters in New York City.

One issue that does seem to differ between genders, especially when the employee has preschool-age children, is preference for work schedules.[24] Working mothers are more likely to prefer part-time work, flexible work schedules, and telecommuting in order to accommodate their family responsibilities.

But what about absence and turnover rates? Are women less stable employees than men? First, on the question of turnover, the evidence indicates no significant differences.[25] Women's quit rates are similar to those for men. The research on absence, however, consistently indicates that women have higher rates of absenteeism than men do.[26] The most logical explanation for this finding is that the research was conducted in North America, and North American culture has historically placed home and family responsibilities on the woman. When a child is ill or someone needs to stay home to wait for the plumber, it has been the woman who has traditionally taken time off from work. However, this research is undoubtedly time-bound.[27] The historical role of the woman in caring for children and as secondary breadwinner has definitely changed in the past generation, and a large proportion of men nowadays are as interested in day care and the problems associated with child care in general as are women.

Race

Race is a controversial issue. It can be so contentious that it's tempting to avoid the topic. A complete picture of individual differences in OB, however, would be incomplete without a discussion of race.

What is race? Before we can discuss how race matters in OB, first we have to reach some consensus about what race is, and that's not so easily done. Some scholars argue that it's not productive to discuss race for policy reasons (it's a divisive issue), for biological reasons (a large percentage of us are a mixture of races), or for genetic and anthropological reasons (many anthropologists and evolutionary scientists reject the concept of distinct racial categories).

Most people in the United States identify themselves according to a racial group. (However, in some countries, like Brazil, people are less likely to define themselves according to distinct racial categories.) The Department of Education classifies individuals according to five racial categories: African American, Native American (American Indian/Alaskan Native), Asian/Pacific Islander, Hispanic, and White. We'll define race as the biological heritage people use to identify themselves. This definition allows each individual to define his or her race. Tiger Woods, for example, refuses to place himself into a single racial category, emphasizing his multiethnic roots.

Race has been studied quite a bit in OB, particularly as it relates to employment outcomes such as personnel selection decisions, performance evaluations, pay, and workplace discrimination. Doing justice to all of this research isn't possible here, so let's summarize a few points.

First, in employment settings, there is a tendency for individuals to favor colleagues of their own race in performance evaluations, promotion decisions, and pay raises.[28] Second, there are substantial racial differences in attitudes toward affirmative action, with African Americans approving such programs to a greater degree than Whites.[29] Third, African Americans generally fare worse than Whites in employment decisions. For example, African Americans receive lower ratings in employment interviews, are paid less, and are promoted less frequently.[30]

The major dilemma faced by employers who use mental ability tests for selection, promotion, training, and similar personnel decisions is concern that they may have a negative impact on racial and ethnic groups.[31] For instance, some minority groups score, on the average, as much as 1 standard deviation lower than Whites on verbal, numerical, and spatial ability tests, meaning that only 10 percent of minority group members score above the average for Whites. However after reviewing the evidence, researchers have concluded that "despite group differences in mean test performance, there is little convincing evidence that well-constructed tests are more predictive of educational, training, or occupational performance for members of the majority group than for members of minority groups."[32] The issue of racial differences in cognitive ability tests continues to be hotly debated.[33]

Tenure

The last biographical characteristic we'll look at is tenure. With the exception of gender and racial differences, few issues are more subject to misconceptions and speculations than the impact of seniority on job performance.

Extensive reviews of the seniority–productivity relationship have been conducted.[34] If we define seniority as time on a particular job, we can say that the most recent evidence demonstrates a positive relationship between seniority and job productivity. So tenure, expressed as work experience, appears to be a good predictor of employee productivity.

The research relating tenure to absence is quite straightforward. Studies consistently demonstrate seniority to be negatively related to absenteeism.[35] In fact, in terms of both frequency of absence and total days lost at work, tenure is the single most important explanatory variable.[36]

Tenure is also a potent variable in explaining turnover. The longer a person is in a job, the less likely he or she is to quit.[37] Moreover, consistent with research that suggests that past behavior is the best predictor of future behavior,[38] evidence indicates that tenure on an employee's previous job is a powerful predictor of that employee's future turnover.[39]

The evidence indicates that tenure and job satisfaction are positively related.[40] In fact, when age and tenure are treated separately, tenure appears to be a more consistent and stable predictor of job satisfaction than is chronological age.

Learning

All complex behavior is learned. If we want to explain and predict behavior, we need to understand how people learn. In this section, we define learning, present three popular learning theories, and describe how managers can facilitate employee learning.

A Definition of Learning

What is **learning**? A psychologist's definition is considerably broader than the layperson's view that "it's what we did when we went to school." In actuality, each of us is continuously "going to school." Learning occurs all the time. Therefore, a generally accepted definition of learning is *any relatively permanent change in behavior that occurs as a result of experience.*[41] Ironically, we can say that changes in behavior indicate that learning has taken place and that learning is a change in behavior.

The previous definition suggests that we can see changes taking place but not the learning itself. The concept is theoretical and, hence, not directly observable:

> You have seen people in the process of learning, you have seen people who behave in a particular way as a result of learning and some of you (in fact, I guess the majority of you) have "learned" at some time in your life. In other words, we infer that learning has taken place if an individual behaves, reacts, responds as a result of experience in a manner different from the way he formerly behaved.[42]

Our definition has several components that deserve clarification. First, learning involves change. Change may be good or bad from an organizational point of view. People can learn unfavorable behaviors—to hold prejudices or to shirk their responsibilities, for example—as well as favorable behaviors. Second, the change must become ingrained. Immediate changes may be only reflexive or as a result of fatigue (or a sudden burst of energy) and thus may not represent learning. Third, some form of experience is necessary for learning. Experience may be acquired directly through observation or practice, or it may be acquired indirectly, as through reading. The crucial test still remains: Does this experience result in a relatively permanent change in behavior? If the answer is Yes, we can say that learning has taken place.

Theories of Learning

How do we learn? Three theories have been offered to explain the process by which we acquire patterns of behavior. These are classical conditioning, operant conditioning, and social learning.

Classical Conditioning   **Classical conditioning** grew out of experiments to teach dogs to salivate in response to the ringing of a bell, conducted in the early 1900s by Russian physiologist Ivan Pavlov.[43] A simple surgical procedure

---

learning   *Any relatively permanent change in behavior that occurs as a result of experience.*

classical conditioning   *A type of conditioning in which an individual responds to some stimulus that would not ordinarily produce such a response.*

Sabre, a travel services firm, used a board game as a training tool to help its 7,000 employees learn how their work affects the firm's bottom line. Through "Sabre's Financial Success and You," employees learned how to complete an income statement and balance sheet and how to compute return on equity. After the training, employees applied what they learned to their jobs to help Sabre cut costs and increase revenue.

allowed Pavlov to measure accurately the amount of saliva secreted by a dog. When Pavlov presented the dog with a piece of meat, the dog exhibited a noticeable increase in salivation. When Pavlov withheld the presentation of meat and merely rang a bell, the dog did not salivate. Then Pavlov proceeded to link the meat and the ringing of the bell. After repeatedly hearing the bell before getting the food, the dog began to salivate as soon as the bell rang. After a while, the dog would salivate merely at the sound of the bell, even if no food was offered. In effect, the dog had learned to respond—that is, to salivate—to the bell. Let's review this experiment to introduce the key concepts in classical conditioning.

The meat was an *unconditioned stimulus*; it invariably caused the dog to react in a specific way. The reaction that took place whenever the unconditioned stimulus occurred was called the *unconditioned response* (or the noticeable increase in salivation, in this case). The bell was an artificial stimulus, or what we call the *conditioned stimulus*. Although it was originally neutral, after the bell was paired with the meat (an unconditioned stimulus), it eventually produced a response when presented alone. The last key concept is the *conditioned response*. This describes the behavior of the dog; it salivated in reaction to the bell alone.

Using these concepts, we can summarize classical conditioning. Essentially, learning a conditioned response involves building up an association between a conditioned stimulus and an unconditioned stimulus. When the stimuli, one compelling and the other one neutral, are paired, the neutral one becomes a conditioned stimulus and, hence, takes on the properties of the unconditioned stimulus.

Classical conditioning can be used to explain why Christmas carols often bring back pleasant memories of childhood; the songs are associated with the festive holiday spirit and evoke fond memories and feelings of euphoria. In an organizational setting, we can also see classical conditioning operating. For example, at one manufacturing plant, every time the top executives from the head office were scheduled to make a visit, the plant management would clean up the administrative offices and wash the windows. This went on for years. Eventually, employees would turn on their best behavior and look prim and

Exhibit **2-3**	

THE FAR SIDE® BY GARY LARSON

**Unbeknownst to most students of psychology,
Pavlov's first experiment was to ring a bell
and cause his dog to attack Freud's cat.**

proper whenever the windows were cleaned—even in those occasional instances when the cleaning was not paired with a visit from the top brass. People had learned to associate the cleaning of the windows with a visit from the head office.

Classical conditioning is passive. Something happens and we react in a specific way. It is elicited in response to a specific, identifiable event. As such, it can explain simple reflexive behaviors. But most behavior—particularly the complex behavior of individuals in organizations—is emitted rather than elicited. That is, it's voluntary rather than reflexive. For example, employees *choose* to arrive at work on time, ask their boss for help with problems, or "goof off" when no one is watching. The learning of those behaviors is better understood by looking at operant conditioning.

Operant Conditioning   **Operant conditioning** argues that behavior is a function of its consequences. People learn to behave to get something they want or to avoid something they don't want. Operant behavior means voluntary or learned behavior in contrast to reflexive or unlearned behavior. The tendency to repeat such behavior is influenced by the reinforcement or lack of reinforcement

operant conditioning   *A type of conditioning in which desired voluntary behavior leads to a reward or prevents a punishment.*

brought about by the consequences of the behavior. Therefore, reinforcement strengthens a behavior and increases the likelihood that it will be repeated.

What Pavlov did for classical conditioning, the Harvard psychologist B. F. Skinner did for operant conditioning.[44] Skinner argued that creating pleasing consequences to follow specific forms of behavior would increase the frequency of that behavior. He demonstrated that people will most likely engage in desired behaviors if they are positively reinforced for doing so; that rewards are most effective if they immediately follow the desired response; and that behavior that is not rewarded, or is punished, is less likely to be repeated. For example, we know a professor who places a mark by a student's name each time the student makes a contribution to class discussions. Operant conditioning would argue that this practice is motivating because it conditions a student to expect a reward (earning class credit) each time she demonstrates a specific behavior (speaking up in class). The concept of operant conditioning was part of Skinner's broader concept of **behaviorism**, which argues that behavior follows stimuli in a relatively unthinking manner. In Skinner's form of radical behaviorism, concepts such as feelings, thoughts, and other states of mind are rejected as causes of behavior. In short, people learn to associate stimulus and response, but their conscious awareness of this association is irrelevant.[45]

You see apparent illustrations of operant conditioning everywhere. For example, any situation in which it is either explicitly stated or implicitly suggested that reinforcements are contingent on some action on your part involves the use of operant learning. Your instructor says that if you want a high grade in the course you must supply correct answers on the test. A commissioned salesperson wanting to earn a sizable income finds that doing so is contingent on generating high sales in her territory. Of course, the linkage can also work to teach the individual to engage in behaviors that work against the best interests of the organization. Assume that your boss tells you that if you will work overtime during the next 3-week busy season, you'll be compensated for it at your next performance appraisal. However, when performance-appraisal time comes, you find that you are given no positive reinforcement for your overtime work. The next time your boss asks you to work overtime, what will you do? You'll probably decline! Your behavior can be explained by operant conditioning: If a behavior fails to be positively reinforced, the probability that the behavior will be repeated declines.

Social Learning   Individuals can also learn by observing what happens to other people and just by being told about something, as well as by direct experiences. So, for example, much of what we have learned comes from watching models—parents, teachers, peers, motion picture and television performers, bosses, and so forth. This view that we can learn through both observation and direct experience is called **social-learning theory**.[46]

Although social-learning theory is an extension of operant conditioning—that is, it assumes that behavior is a function of consequences—it also acknowledges the existence of observational learning and the importance of perception in learning. People respond to how they perceive and define consequences, not to the objective consequences themselves.

The influence of models is central to the social-learning viewpoint. Four processes have been found to determine the influence that a model will have on an individual:

1. *Attentional processes.* People learn from a model only when they recognize and pay attention to its critical features. We tend to be most influenced by models that are attractive, repeatedly available, important to us, or similar to us in our estimation.

Toyota Motor Corporation applies social learning theory in teaching employees skills they need to meet the company's high standards of quality and efficiency. At its new Global Production Center training facility in Toyota City, Japan, employees from factories around the world learn production techniques through observation and direct experience. Trainees first watch computerized "visual manuals" to learn basic skills. Then, under the tutelage of an experienced production master, they practice the skills. In this photo a trainer (left) models a spray-painting technique while the trainee practices the skill.

2. *Retention processes.* A model's influence will depend on how well the individual remembers the model's action after the model is no longer readily available.
3. *Motor reproduction processes.* After a person has seen a new behavior by observing the model, the watching must be converted to doing. This process then demonstrates that the individual can perform the modeled activities.
4. *Reinforcement processes.* Individuals will be motivated to exhibit the modeled behavior if positive incentives or rewards are provided. Behaviors that are positively reinforced will be given more attention, learned better, and performed more often.

Shaping: A Managerial Tool

Because learning takes place on the job as well as prior to it, managers will be concerned with how they can teach employees to behave in ways that most benefit the organization. When we attempt to mold individuals by guiding their learning in graduated steps, we are **shaping behavior**.

Consider the situation in which an employee's behavior is significantly different from that sought by management. If management rewarded the individual only when he or she showed desirable responses, there might be very little reinforcement taking place. In such a case, shaping offers a logical approach toward achieving the desired behavior.

We *shape* behavior by systematically reinforcing each successive step that moves the individual closer to the desired response. If an employee who has chronically been a half-hour late for work comes in only 20 minutes late, we can reinforce that improvement. Reinforcement would increase as responses more closely approximated the desired behavior.

Myth or Science?

"You Can't Teach an Old Dog New Tricks!"

This statement is false. It reflects the widely held stereotype that older workers have difficulties in adapting to new methods and techniques. Studies consistently demonstrate that older employees are perceived as being relatively inflexible, resistant to change, and less willing and able to be trained than their younger counterparts.[47] But these perceptions are mostly wrong.

Evidence does indicate that older workers (typically defined as people aged 50 and over) are less confident of their learning abilities (perhaps due to acceptance of societal stereotypes). Moreover, older workers do seem to be somewhat less efficient in acquiring complex or demanding skills, and, on average, they are not as fast in terms of reaction time or in solving problems. That is, they may take longer to train. Finally, older employees receive less support from supervisors and coworkers for engaging in learning and developmental activities.[48] However, once trained, research indicates that older workers actually learn more than their younger counterparts, and they are better at transferring what they have learned to the job.[49]

The ability to acquire the skills, knowledge, or behavior necessary to perform a job at a given level—that is, trainability—has been the subject of much research. And the evidence indicates that there are differences between people in their trainability. A number of individual-difference factors (such as low ability and reduced motivation) have been found to impede learning and training outcomes. However, age has not been found to influence these outcomes. In fact, older employees actually benefit more from training. Still, the stereotypes persist.[50] ■

Methods of Shaping Behavior   There are four ways in which to shape behavior: through positive reinforcement, negative reinforcement, punishment, and extinction.

Following a response with something pleasant is called *positive reinforcement.* This would describe, for instance, the boss who praises an employee for a job well done. Following a response by the termination or withdrawal of something unpleasant is called *negative reinforcement.* If your college instructor asks a question and you don't know the answer, looking through your lecture notes is likely to preclude your being called on. This is a negative reinforcement because you have learned that looking busily through your notes prevents the instructor from calling on you. *Punishment* is causing an unpleasant condition in an attempt to eliminate an undesirable behavior. Giving an employee a 2-day suspension from work without pay for showing up drunk is an example of punishment. Eliminating any reinforcement that is maintaining a behavior is called *extinction.* When the behavior is not reinforced, it tends to be gradually extinguished. College instructors who wish to discourage students from asking questions in class can eliminate this behavior in their students by ignoring those who raise their hands to ask questions. Hand-raising will become extinct when it is invariably met with an absence of reinforcement.

Both positive and negative reinforcement result in learning. They strengthen a response and increase the probability of repetition. In the preceding illustrations, praise strengthens and increases the behavior of doing a good job because praise is desired. The behavior of "looking busy" is similarly strengthened and increased by its terminating the undesirable consequence of being called on by the teacher. However, both punishment and extinction weaken behavior and tend to decrease its subsequent frequency. In shaping behavior, a critical issue is the timing of reinforcements. This is an issue we'll consider now.

But before we move on to the next section, check out the Self-Assessment feature on p. 59 where you can assess your disciplining skills. The Self-Assessment feature is a unique learning tool that allows you to assess your knowledge, beliefs, feelings, and actions in regard to a wide range of personal skills, abilities, and interests. You'll find one of these in most chapters.

Learning How To Reward CEOs

Take a look at the compensation of top corporate CEOs from the mid-1990s through 2005. They typically follow a common pattern: Their base salary is less than $1 million but they earn tens-of-millions from cashing in stock options. This pattern is easily explained once you understand the U.S. tax code.

Prior to 1992, most of an executive's compensation was in base salary. But in that year, the U.S. Congress changed the tax code so companies could only deduct, as a business expense, salaries up to $1 million. This was done in response to the public outcry over the huge salaries that CEOs were making.

CEOs and other top executives were not about to take huge cuts in pay. So boards of directors merely changed the way that they paid their top people. Beginning in the mid-1990s, boards lowered base salaries and began handing out large grants of stock options to executives. Importantly, because of arcane accounting rules, these options actually cost the companies nothing and never directly affected profits.

Corporate reformers failed to consider how stock options would change CEO behavior. Options allow recipients to buy company stock at a specific price. So option holders make more money as the price of a company's stock goes up. When the bulk of your compensation becomes tied to options, which are increasingly valuable as a stock's price appreciates, you suddenly have a powerful incentive to drive your stock higher by any means, if only for a short time.

Relying on options as the primary form of executive compensation encourages all kinds of questionable practices that will inflate revenues and cover up costs. One shouldn't be totally surprised, therefore, that Adelphia Communications' executives inflated numbers and hid personal loans; that Xerox executives overstated their company's revenues; that HealthSouth's CEO instructed company officials to circumvent a large write-off that would seriously reduce earnings and batter the company's stock; or that senior managers at Enron grossly manipulated sales and expenses to make their company look highly profitable when it was actually losing money. All these executives' compensation packages were heavy with options. Their actions were consistent with a reward system that provided huge payoffs for executives who could make their companies look profitable for at least long enough for them to execute their stock options and make hundreds of millions of dollars for themselves.

Meanwhile, Krispy Kreme's CEO—Stephen Cooper—is paid by the hour. That's right, he's paid $760 an hour for running the company. You might think that's quite a wage rate, but his $1.52 million salary (based on a 40-hour workweek) pales in comparison to the $475 million Bernie Ebbers or the $325 million Ken Lay earned.

Based on G. Colvin, "Will CEO's Find Their Inner Choirboy?" *Forbes*, April 28, 2003, p. 45; and A. Sloan, "A New Way on CEO Pay," *Newsweek*, February 7, 2005.

SELF ASSESSMENT LIBRARY

HOW GOOD AM I AT DISCIPLINING OTHERS?

In the Self-Assessment Library (available on CD, online, and in print), take assessment II.B.5 (How Good Am I at Disciplining Others) and answer the following questions.

1. *Are you surprised by your results?*
2. *How might you improve your disciplining skills?*

Schedules of Reinforcement The two major types of reinforcement schedules are *continuous* and *intermittent*. A **continuous reinforcement** schedule reinforces the desired behavior each and every time it is demonstrated. Take, for example, the case of someone who historically has had trouble arriving at work on time. Every time he is not tardy his manager might compliment him on his desirable behavior. In an intermittent schedule, on the other hand, not every instance of the desirable behavior is reinforced, but reinforcement is given

continuous reinforcement *Reinforcing a desired behavior each time it is demonstrated.*

often enough to make the behavior worth repeating. This latter schedule can be compared to the workings of a slot machine, which people will continue to play even when they know that it is adjusted to give a considerable return to the casino. The intermittent payoffs occur just often enough to reinforce the behavior of slipping in coins and pulling the handle. Evidence indicates that the intermittent, or varied, form of reinforcement tends to promote more resistance to extinction than does the continuous form.[51]

An **intermittent reinforcement** can be of a ratio or interval type. *Ratio schedules* depend on how many responses the subject makes. The individual is reinforced after giving a certain number of specific types of behavior. *Interval schedules* depend on how much time has passed since the previous reinforcement. With interval schedules, the individual is reinforced on the first appropriate behavior after a particular time has elapsed. A reinforcement can also be classified as fixed or variable.

When rewards are spaced at uniform time intervals, the reinforcement schedule is of the **fixed-interval** type. The critical variable is time, and it is held constant. This is the predominant schedule for most salaried workers in North America. When you get your paycheck on a weekly, semimonthly, monthly, or other predetermined time basis, you're rewarded on a fixed-interval reinforcement schedule.

If rewards are distributed in time so that reinforcements are unpredictable, the schedule is of the **variable-interval** type. When an instructor advises her class that pop quizzes will be given during the term (the exact number of which is unknown to the students) and the quizzes will account for 20 percent of the term grade, she is using a variable-interval schedule. Similarly, a series of randomly timed unannounced visits to a company office by the corporate audit staff is an example of a variable-interval schedule.

In a **fixed-ratio** schedule, after a fixed or constant number of responses are given, a reward is initiated. For example, a piece-rate incentive plan is a fixed-ratio schedule; the employee receives a reward based on the number of work pieces generated. If the piece rate for a zipper installer in a dressmaking factory is $5.00 a dozen, the reinforcement (money in this case) is fixed to the number of zippers sewn into garments. After every dozen is sewn in, the installer has earned another $5.00.

When the reward varies relative to the behavior of the individual, he or she is said to be reinforced on a **variable-ratio** schedule. Salespeople on commission are examples of individuals on such a reinforcement schedule. On some occasions, they may make a sale after only 2 calls on a potential customer. On other occasions, they might need to make 20 or more calls to secure a sale. The reward, then, is variable in relation to the number of successful calls the salesperson makes. Exhibit 2-4 summarizes the schedules of reinforcement.

Exhibit **2-4**	Schedules of Reinforcement		
Reinforcement Schedule	**Nature of Reinforcement**	**Effect on Behavior**	**Example**
Continuous	Reward given after each desired behavior	Fast learning of new behavior but rapid extinction	Compliments
Fixed-interval	Reward given at fixed time intervals	Average and irregular performance with rapid extinction	Weekly paychecks
Variable-interval	Reward given at variable time intervals	Moderately high and stable performance with slow extinction	Pop quizzes
Fixed ratio	Reward given at fixed amounts of output	High and stable performance attained quickly but also with rapid extinction	Piece-rate pay
Variable-ratio	Reward given at variable amounts of output	Very high performance with slow extinction	Commissioned sales

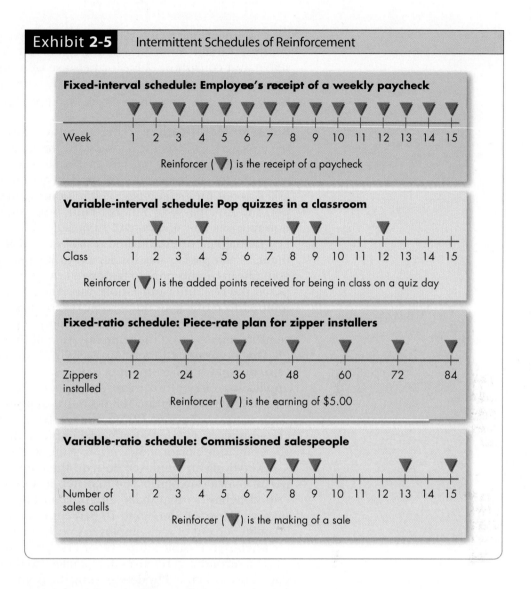

Reinforcement Schedules and Behavior   Continuous reinforcement schedules can lead to early satiation, and under this schedule behavior tends to
weaken rapidly when reinforcers are withheld. However, continuous reinforcers
are appropriate for newly emitted, unstable, or low-frequency responses. In
contrast, intermittent reinforcers preclude early satiation because they don't
follow every response. They are appropriate for stable or high-frequency
responses.

   In general, variable schedules tend to lead to higher performance than
fixed schedules (see Exhibit 2-5). For example, as noted previously, most
employees in organizations are paid on fixed-interval schedules. But such a
schedule does not clearly link performance and rewards. The reward is given

intermittent reinforcement   *Reinforcing a desired behavior often enough to make the behavior worth repeating but not every time it is demonstrated.*

fixed-interval schedule   *Spacing rewards at uniform time intervals.*

variable-interval schedule   *Distributing rewards in time so that reinforcements are unpredictable.*

fixed-ratio schedule   *Initiating rewards after a fixed or constant number of responses.*

variable-ratio schedule   *Varying the reward relative to the behavior of the individual.*

for time spent on the job rather than for a specific response (performance). In contrast, variable-interval schedules generate high rates of response and more stable and consistent behavior because of a high correlation between performance and reward and because of the uncertainty involved—the employee tends to be more alert because there is a surprise factor.

Behavior Modification   There is a now-classic study that took place a number of years ago with freight packers at Emery Air Freight (now part of FedEx).[52] Emery's management wanted packers to use freight containers for shipments whenever possible because of specific economic savings. When packers were asked about the percentage of shipments contained, the standard reply was 90 percent. An analysis by Emery found, however, that the actual container utilization rate was only 45 percent. In order to encourage employees to use containers, management established a program of feedback and positive reinforcements. Each packer was instructed to keep a checklist of daily packings, both containerized and noncontainerized. At the end of each day, the packer computed the container utilization rate. Almost unbelievably, container utilization jumped to more than 90 percent on the first day of the program and held at that level. Emery reported that this simple program of feedback and positive reinforcements saved the company $2 million over a 3-year period.

This program at Emery Air Freight illustrates the use of behavior modification, or what has become more popularly called **OB Mod**.[53] It represents the application of reinforcement concepts to individuals in the work setting. The typical OB Mod program follows a five-step problem-solving model: (1) identifying critical behaviors; (2) developing baseline data; (3) identifying behavioral consequences; (4) developing and implementing an intervention strategy; and (5) evaluating performance improvement.[54]

Everything an employee does on the job is not equally important in terms of performance outcomes. The first step in OB Mod, therefore, is to identify the critical behaviors that make a significant impact on the employee's job performance. These are those 5 to 10 percent of behaviors that may account for up to 70 or 80 percent of each employee's performance. Freight packers using containers whenever possible at Emery Air Freight is an example of a critical behavior.

The second step requires the manager to develop some baseline performance data. This is obtained by determining the number of times the identified behavior is occurring under present conditions. In our freight-packing example at Emery, this would have revealed that 45 percent of all shipments were containerized.

The third step is to perform a functional analysis to identify the behavioral contingencies or consequences of performance. This tells the manager the antecedent cues that emit the behavior and the consequences that are currently maintaining it. At Emery Air Freight, social norms and the greater difficulty in packing containers were the antecedent cues. This encouraged the practice of packing items separately. Moreover, the consequences for continuing the behavior, prior to the OB Mod intervention, were social acceptance and escaping more demanding work.

Once the functional analysis is complete, the manager is ready to develop and implement an intervention strategy to strengthen desirable performance behaviors and weaken undesirable behaviors. The appropriate strategy will entail changing some elements of the performance–reward linkage—structure, processes, technology, groups, or the task—with the goal of making high-level performance more rewarding. In the Emery example, the work technology was altered to require the keeping of a checklist. The checklist plus the computation, at the end of the day, of a container-utilization rate acted to reinforce the desirable behavior of using containers.

The final step in OB Mod is to evaluate performance improvement. In the Emery intervention, the immediate improvement in the container-utilization

British Airways uses OB Mod to strengthen desirable performance behaviors. The airline installed Web-enabled employee performance software as an intervention strategy to monitor and analyze each worker's output in the areas of ticket sales, customer service, and customer complaints. In tracking individual employee's productivity, the new technology identifies top performers and directly applies incentive bonuses into their paychecks.

rate demonstrated that behavioral change took place. That it rose to 90 percent and held at that level further indicates that learning took place. That is, the employees underwent a relatively permanent change in behavior.

OB Mod has been used by a number of organizations to improve employee productivity; to reduce errors, absenteeism, tardiness, and accident rates; and to improve friendliness toward customers.[55] For instance, a clothing manufacturer saved $60,000 in 1 year from fewer absences. A packing firm improved productivity 16 percent, cut errors by 40 percent, and reduced accidents by more than 43 percent—resulting in savings of over $1 million. A bank successfully used OB Mod to increase the friendliness of its tellers, which led to a demonstrable improvement in customer satisfaction.

Problems with OB Mod and Reinforcement Theory   Although the effectiveness of reinforcements in the form of rewards and punishments has a lot of support in the literature, that doesn't necessarily mean that Skinner was right or that OB Mod is the best way to reward people. What if the power of reinforcements isn't due to operant conditioning or behaviorism? One problem with behaviorism is research showing that thoughts and feelings immediately follow environmental stimuli, even those explicitly meant to shape behavior. This is contrary to the assumptions of behaviorism and OB Mod, which assume that people's innermost thoughts and feelings in response to the environment are irrelevant.

Think about praise from a supervisor. For example, assume your course instructor compliments you for asking a good question. A behaviorist would argue that this shapes our behavior because we find the stimulus (the compliment) pleasant and therefore respond by attempting to ask other questions that will generate the same reward. However, imagine, for example, that you had to weigh the pleasant feelings produced by your professor's praise against

OB Mod   *The application of reinforcement concepts to individuals in the work setting.*

the snickers of jealous classmates who whispered "brown noser." Your choice of what to do would likely be dictated by weighing the value of these stimuli, which may be a rather complex mental process involving thinking and feeling.

Also, is it really shaping if the compliment was given without an intention of molding behavior? Isn't it perhaps overly restrictive to view all stimuli as motivated to obtain a particular response? Is the only reason we tell someone we love them because we wish to obtain a reward or to mold their behavior?

Because of these problems, among others, operant conditioning and behaviorism have been superceded by other approaches that emphasize cognitive processes.[56] There is no denying, though, the contribution of these theories to our understanding of human behavior.

Summary and Implications for Managers

This chapter looked at three individual variables—ability, biographical characteristics, and learning. Let's now try to summarize what we found and consider their importance for the manager who is trying to understand organizational behavior.

Ability   Ability directly influences an employee's level of performance and satisfaction through the ability–job fit. Given management's desire to get a compatible fit, what can be done?

First, an effective selection process will improve the fit. A job analysis will provide information about jobs currently being done and the abilities that individuals need to perform the jobs adequately. Applicants can then be tested, interviewed, and evaluated on the degree to which they possess the necessary abilities.

Second, promotion and transfer decisions affecting individuals already in the organization's employ should reflect the abilities of candidates. As with new employees, care should be taken to assess critical abilities that incumbents will need in the job and to match those requirements with the organization's human resources.

Third, the fit can be improved by fine-tuning the job to better match an incumbent's abilities. Often, modifications can be made in the job that, while not having a significant impact on the job's basic activities, better adapts it to the specific talents of a given employee. Examples would be to change some of the equipment used or to reorganize tasks within a group of employees.

Biographical Characteristics   Biographical characteristics are readily observable to managers. However, just because they're observable doesn't mean they should be explicitly used in management decisions.

Learning   Any observable change in behavior is prima facie evidence that learning has taken place.

We found that positive reinforcement is a powerful tool for modifying behavior. By identifying and rewarding performance-enhancing behaviors, management increases the likelihood that they will be repeated. Our knowledge about learning further suggests that reinforcement is a more effective tool than punishment. Although punishment eliminates undesired behavior more quickly than negative reinforcement does, punished behavior tends to be only temporarily suppressed rather than permanently changed. And punishment may produce unpleasant side effects such as lower morale and higher absenteeism or turnover. In addition, the recipients of punishment tend to become resentful of the punisher. Managers, therefore, are advised to use reinforcement rather than punishment.

Point ◄► Counterpoint

All Human Behavior Is Learned[57]

Human beings are essentially blank slates that are shaped by their environment. B. F. Skinner, in fact, summarized his belief in the power of the environment to shape behavior when he said, "Give me a child at birth and I can make him into anything you want."

Following are some of the societal mechanisms that exist because of this belief in the power of learned behavior.

Role of parenting. We place a great deal of importance on the role of mothers and fathers in the raising of children. We believe, for instance, that children raised without fathers will be hindered by their lack of a male role model. And parents who have continual run-ins with the law risk having government authorities take their children from them. The latter action is typically taken because society believes that irresponsible parents don't provide the proper learning environment for their children.

Importance of education. Most advanced societies invest heavily in the education of their young. They typically provide 10 or more years of free education. And in countries such as the United States, going on to college after finishing high school has become the norm rather than the exception. This investment in education is undertaken because it is seen as a way for young people to learn knowledge and skills.

Job training. For individuals who don't go on to college, most will pursue job-training programs to develop specific work-related skills. They'll take courses to become proficient as auto mechanics, medical assistants, and the like. Similarly, people who seek to become skilled trades workers will pursue apprenticeships as carpenters, electricians, or pipe fitters. In addition, business firms invest billions of dollars each year in training and education to keep current employees' skills up-to-date.

Manipulating of rewards. Complex compensation programs are designed by organizations to reward employees fairly for their work performance. But these programs are also designed with the intention to motivate employees. They are designed to encourage employees to engage in behaviors that management desires and to extinguish behaviors that management wants to discourage. Salary levels, for instance, typically reward employee loyalty, encourage the learning of new skills, and motivate individuals to assume greater responsibilities in the organization.

These mechanisms all exist and flourish because organizations and society believe that people can learn and change their behavior.

Although people can learn and can be influenced by their environment, far too little attention has been paid to the role that evolution has played in shaping human behavior. Evolutionary psychology tells us that human beings are basically hardwired at birth. We arrive on Earth with ingrained traits, honed and adapted over millions of years, that shape and limit our behavior.

All living creatures are "designed" by specific combinations of genes. As a result of natural selection, genes that produce faulty design features are eliminated. Characteristics that help a species survive tend to endure and get passed on to future generations. Many of the characteristics that helped early Homo sapiens survive live on today and influence the way we behave. Here are a few examples:

Emotions. Stone Age people, at the mercy of wild predators and natural disasters, learned to trust their instincts. Those with the best instincts survived. Today, emotions remain the first screen to all information we receive. We know we are supposed to act rationally but our emotions can never be fully suppressed.

Risk avoidance. Ancient hunter-gatherers who survived were not big risk takers. They were cautious. Today, when we're comfortable with the status quo, we typically see any change as risky and, thus, tend to resist it.

Stereotyping. To prosper in a clan society, Early Man had to quickly "size up" who he could trust and who he couldn't. Those who could do this quickly were more likely to survive. Today, like our ancestors, we naturally stereotype people based on very small pieces of evidence, mainly their looks and a few readily apparent behaviors.

Male competitiveness. Males in early human societies frequently had to engage in games or battles in which there were clear winners and losers. Winners attained high status, were viewed as more attractive mates, and were more likely to reproduce. The ingrained male desire to do public battle and display virility and competence persists today.

Evolutionary psychology challenges the notion that people are free to change their behavior if trained or motivated. It doesn't say that we can't engage in learning or exercise free will. What it does say is that nature predisposes us to act and interact in particular ways in particular circumstances. As a result, we find that people in organizational settings often behave in ways that don't appear to be beneficial to themselves or their employers.

Questions for Review

1. Assess the validity of using intelligence scores for selecting new employees.

2. Describe the specific steps you would take to ensure that an individual has the appropriate abilities to satisfactorily do a given job.

3. How do age, gender, race, and tenure affect performance at work?

4. Explain classical conditioning.

5. Contrast classical conditioning, operant conditioning, and social learning.

6. How might employees actually learn unethical behaviors on their jobs?

7. Describe the four types of intermittent reinforcers.

8. What are the five steps in behavior modification?

9. If you had to take disciplinary action against an employee, how, specifically, would you do it?

10. Describe the four processes in successful social learning.

Questions for Critical Thinking

1. "All organizations would benefit from hiring the smartest people they can get." Do you agree or disagree with this statement? Support your answer.

2. What do you think is more likely to lead to success on a job—a good ability–job fit or personality–organization fit? Explain.

3. What abilities do you think are especially important for success in senior-level management positions?

4. What have you learned about "learning" that could help you to explain the behavior of students in a classroom if: (a) The instructor gives only one test—a final examination at the end of the course? (b) The instructor gives four exams during the term, all of which are announced on the first day of class? (c) The student's grade is based on the results of numerous exams, none of which are announced by the instructor ahead of time?

Team Exercise

POSITIVE REINFORCEMENT VERSUS PUNISHMENT

Exercise Overview (Steps 1–4)

This 10-step exercise takes approximately 20 minutes.

1. Two volunteers are selected to receive reinforcement or punishment from the class while performing a particular task. The volunteers leave the room.

2. The instructor identifies an object for the student volunteers to locate when they return to the room. (The object should be unobstructed but clearly visible to the class. Examples that have worked well include a small triangular piece of paper that was left behind when a notice was torn off a classroom bulletin board, a smudge on the chalkboard, and a chip in the plaster of a classroom wall.)

3. The instructor specifies the actions that will be in effect when the volunteers return to the room. For punishment, students should hiss or boo when the first volunteer is moving away from the object. For positive reinforcement, they should cheer and applaud when the second volunteer is getting closer to the object.

4. The instructor should assign a student to keep a record of the time it takes each of the volunteers to locate the object.

Volunteer 1 (Steps 5 and 6)

5. Volunteer 1 is brought back into the room and is told, "Your task is to locate and touch a particular object in the room and the class has agreed to help you. You cannot use words or ask questions. Begin."

6. Volunteer 1 continues to look for the object until it is found, while the class engages in the punishing behavior.

Volunteer 2 (Steps 7 and 8)

7. Volunteer 2 is brought back into the room and is told, "Your task is to locate and touch a particular object in the room and the class has agreed to help you. You cannot use words or ask questions. Begin."

8. Volunteer 2 continues to look for the object until it is found, while the class assists by giving positive reinforcement.

Class Review (Steps 9 and 10)

9. The timekeeper will present the results on how long it took each volunteer to find the object.

10. The class will discuss: What was the difference in behavior of the two volunteers? What are the implications of this exercise to shaping behavior in organizations?

Source: Adapted from an exercise developed by Larry Michaelson of the University of Oklahoma. With permission.

Ethical Dilemma

IS OB MOD A FORM OF MANIPULATION?

Two questions: Is OB Mod a form of manipulation? And if it is, is it unethical for managers to manipulate the behavior of employees?

Critics of OB Mod say that it manipulates employees. They argue that when managers purposely select consequences to control employee behavior, they rob workers of their individuality and freedom of choice. For instance, an auto parts plant in Kentucky reinforces safe working conditions through a game called safety bingo. Every day that the plant has no accidents, employees can draw a number for their bingo card. The first employee to fill a bingo card wins a television set. This program, critics might argue, pressures employees to behave in ways they might not otherwise engage in. It makes these human beings little different from the seal at the circus who, every time it does its assigned trick, is given a fish by its trainer. Only instead of getting a fish, some employee walks off with a television.

On the question regarding the ethics of manipulation, the answer typically surrounds what the term "manipulation" means to you. Some people believe the term has a negative connotation. To manipulate is to be devious or conniving. Others, however, would argue that manipulation is merely the thoughtful effort to control outcomes. In fact, one can say that "management is manipulation" because it is concerned with planned efforts to get people to do what management wants them to do.

What do you think?

Case Incident 1

MANAGERS WHO USE PUNISHMENT

As sales manager for a New Jersey auto dealership, Charles Park occasionally relies on punishment to try to improve his employees' performance. For instance, one time he was dealing with a salesman who was having a bad month. Park talked to the employee about what he could do to help him move more cars. But after another week without a sale and a condescending attitude from the employee, Park confronted him. He screamed at the employee, told him his performance was unacceptable, then threw a notebook binder at him. Said Park, "I had talked to him before, said that I would help him out, but that we had to do something about his numbers. The day I tossed my binder at him, he actually sold a couple of cars." And Park is unapologetic about his behavior. "I am always tough on all my salespeople, but they know the reason is that I want them to do better. Do I think it's always effective? No. But if you do it once in a while, it works."

Apparently Charles Park isn't alone. When the pressure for meeting numbers and deadlines is high, some managers rely on punishment to try to motivate employees. Aubrey Daniels, a motivation consultant, says it can backfire on a manager when he or she avoids telling employees that there are negative consequences for poor performance. "Positive reinforcement is something that employees should earn," Daniels says. For instance, Daniels points out cases where a high-performing salesperson refuses to do his paperwork but still gets high praise from his boss because his numbers are good.

Many managers still rely on threats to motivate employees: "Do it or you're fired!" And with some employees, it seems to work. Rick Moyer, a sales manager for TuWay Wireless in Pennsylvania, argues that punishment can sometimes provide a much-needed kick in the pants to salespeople who are slacking or unaware of their poor performance. For instance, he posts individual results at his sales meetings even though he knows that it can be embarrassing for those with lower numbers. For some people, public embarrassment works. He had one of his sales reps come up to him and say, "I'm embarrassed to come to the meetings because I'm always toward the bottom." The employee volunteered that he was going to work extra hard to move up in the rankings. And he did.

Questions

1. What conditions, if any, do you think justify the use of punishment?

2. Do you think most managers use punishment? If so, why?

3. What's the downside of using punishment? Of using positive reinforcement?

4. Have you ever worked for a boss who used punishment? What was your behavioral response?

Source: Based on J. Chang, "Cracking the Whip," *Sales and Marketing Management,* February 2003, pp. 24–29.

Case Incident 2

PROFESSIONAL SPORTS: REWARDING AND PUNISHING THE SAME BEHAVIOR?

Baseball Commissioner Bud Selig is feeling the heat, but not the kind a 90-mile-per-hour fastball brings. He has been facing allegations that many players, including some of Major League Baseball's biggest stars, are using steroids to enhance their performance. When Congress intervened, Selig stated that the league's policy on steroids was "as good as any in professional sports." The policy? Random drug testing, with a 10-day suspension for first-time offenders. Congress and the general public were not satisfied. So, Selig announced that he would attempt to adopt a tougher "three strikes and you're out" policy: a 50-game suspension for the first offense, a 100-game suspension for the second, and a permanent ban from baseball for the third. Players may incur fines as well. Not only does Selig intend on exercising a stricter policy, but other professional sports leagues, such as the NFL and NBA, are promising to improve their drug-testing policies as well.

But here's the problem: The same system that punishes those who take performance-enhancing drugs may also reinforce such behavior. Major League Baseball appears to be genuinely interested in eliminating the use of steroids in professional baseball, but it has yet to implement a stricter policy. And the current repercussions for players may not serve as a strong deterrent. A fine of $10,000 or a 10-day suspension may be a relatively minor setback compared to the millions that can be earned for becoming an all-star power hitter.

Take Rafael Palmeiro as an example. He tested positive for steroids. Though Palmeiro insists that he inadvertently took steroids, the type that was found in his system (stanozolol) is not the kind found in dietary supplements. His punishment? Palmeiro received a 10-day suspension, forfeited $167,000 of his $3 million salary, and a banner celebrating his 3,000th hit was removed from Camden Yards.

Now consider players such as Barry Bonds and Mark McGuire demonstrate the rewards of becoming a power hitter. Both players broke the major league record for the most home runs hit in a single season—first McGuire, then Bonds—eclipsing the record set by Roger Maris in 1961. Although there is speculation that both players had taken performance-enhancing drugs, to date their records are clean (though Bonds admitted to taking steroids without knowing it at the time). In addition to the exorbitant salaries both players received, the players were on the front pages of newspapers across the country. They became larger than life. And the rewards of hitting more than 70 home runs in a single season are not limited to the players. Revenues from increased game attendance and sports merchandise, as well as helping to build the team's popularity and success, to local business revenues are all incentives for players to perform at high levels and for owners to reward these players.

In the NFL, the punishments are stiffer. For a first offense, players face a four-game suspension and a loss of salary for the amount of games missed. However, is this punishment strong enough to deter steroid use? Apparently not. Consider the three members of the Carolina Panthers who reportedly used steroids weeks before their trip to the 2004 Super Bowl. Although a four-game suspension can mean a large loss of income (the average NFL salary tops $1 million), such punishment still may not deter steroid use because the money that can be made from endorsements and winning the Super Bowl can far exceed players' salaries.

It appears that professional sports may be trying to have their cake and eat it too. As we have seen, behavior that may lead individuals and teams to fame and fortune may also be behavior that demands punishment.

Questions

1. What type of reinforcement schedule does random drug testing represent? Is this type of schedule typically effective or ineffective?

2. What are some examples of behaviors in typical organizations that supervisors reward but may actually be detrimental to others or to the organization as a whole? As a manager, what might you do to try to avoid this quandary?

3. If you were the commissioner of baseball, what steps would you take to try to reduce the use of steroids in baseball? Is punishment likely to be the most effective deterrent? Why or why not?

4. Is it ever "okay" to allow potentially unethical behaviors, which on the surface may benefit organizations, to persist? Why or why not?

Source: Based on V. Bernstein, "N.F.L. Seeks Tougher Steroid Policy," *New York Times*, March 30, 2005, p. D4; M. Lewis, "Absolutely, Power Corrupts," *New York Times Magazine*, April 24, 2005, p. 46; and "Fight Against Steroids Just May Be Getting Muscles," *USA Today*, May 6, 2005, p. 12a.

Endnotes

1. Based on F. Vogelstein, "Mighty Amazon," *Fortune*, May 26, 2003; and W. Poundstone, *How Would You Move Mount Fuji? Microsoft's Cult of the Puzzle—How the World's Smartest Company Selects the Most Creative Thinkers* (Boston: Little, Brown, 2003).

2. T. A. Judge and D. M. Cable, "The Effect of Physical Height on Workplace Success and Income: Preliminary Test of a Theoretical Model," *Journal of Applied Psychology*, vol. 89(3), 2004, pp. 428–441.

3. M. Hosoda, E. F. Stone-Romero, and G. Coats, "The Effects of Physical Attractiveness on Job-Related Outcomes: A Meta-Analysis of Experimental Studies," *Personnel Psychology*, vol. 56(2), 2003, pp. 431–462.

4. K. R. Murphy (ed.), *Individual Differences and Behavior in Organizations* (San Francisco: Jossey-Bass, 1996).

5. L. S. Gottfredson, "The Challenge and Promise of Cognitive Career Assessment," *Journal of Career Assessment*, vol. 11(2), 2003, pp. 115–135.

6. M. D. Dunnette, "Aptitudes, Abilities, and Skills," in M. D. Dunnette (ed.), *Handbook of Industrial and Organizational Psychology* (Chicago: Rand McNally, 1976), pp. 478–83.

7. J. F. Salgado, N. Anderson, S. Moscoso, C. Bertua, F. de Fruyt, and J. P. Rolland, "A Meta-Analytic Study of General Mental Ability Validity for Different Occupations in the European Community," *Journal of Applied Psychology*, December 2003, pp. 1068–81; and F. L. Schmidt and J. E. Hunter, "Select on Intelligence," in E. A. Locke (ed.), *Handbook of Principles of Organizational Behavior* (Malden, MA: Blackwell, 2004).

8. J. A. LePine, J. A. Colquitt, and A. Erez, "Adaptability to Changing Task Contexts: Effects of General Cognitive Ability, Conscientiousness, and Openness to Experience," *Personnel Psychology*, vol. 53(3), 2000, pp. 563–593; J. A. Colquitt, J. A. LePine, and R. A. Noe, "Toward an Integrative Theory of Training Motivation: A Meta-Analytic Path Analysis of 20 Years of Research," *Journal of Applied Psychology*, vol. 85(5), 2000, pp. 678–707; and J. A. Harris, "Measured Intelligence, Achievement, Openness to Experience, and Creativity," *Personality and Individual Differences*, vol. 36(4), 2004, pp. 913–929.

9. See, for instance, J. E. Hunter and R. F. Hunter, "Validity and Utility of Alternative Predictors of Job Performance," *Psychological Bulletin*, January 1984, pp. 72–98; J. E. Hunter, "Cognitive Ability, Cognitive Aptitudes, Job Knowledge, and Job Performance," *Journal of Vocational Behavior*, December 1986, pp. 340–62; W. M. Coward and P. R. Sackett, "Linearity of Ability–Performance Relationships: A Reconfirmation," *Journal of Applied Psychology*, June 1990, pp. 297–300; M. J. Ree, J. A. Earles, and M. S. Teachout, "Predicting Job Performance: Not Much More Than *g*," *Journal of Applied Psychology*, August 1994, pp. 518–24; F. L. Schmidt and J. E. Hunter, "The Validity and Utility of Selection Methods in Personnel Psychology: Practical and Theoretical Implications of 85 Years of Research Findings," *Psychological Bulletin*, September 1998, pp. 262–274;" and M. J. Ree, T. R. Carretta, and J. R. Steindl, "Cognitive Ability," in N. Anderson, D. S. Ones, H. K. Sinangil, and C. Viswesvaran, eds., *Handbook of Industrial, Work & Organizational Psychology*, vol. 1 (Thousand Oaks, CA: Sage, 2001), pp. 219–32.

10. Y. Ganzach, "Intelligence and Job Satisfaction," *Academy of Management Journal*, vol. 41(5), 1998, pp. 526–539; and Y. Ganzach, "Intelligence, Education, and Facets of Job Satisfaction," *Work and Occupations*, vol. 30(1), 2003, pp. 97–122.

11. This section is based on R. E. Riggio, S.E. Murphy, and F. J. Pirozzolo (eds.), *Multiple Intelligences and Leadership* (Mahwah, NJ: Lawrence Erlbaum, 2002).

12. D. Lubinski and C. P. Benbow, "An Opportunity for Empiricism," *PsycCRITIQUES*, 2004.

13. E. A. Fleishman, "Evaluating Physical Abilities Required by Jobs," *Personnel Administrator*, June 1979, pp. 82–92.

14. "Valuing Older Workers: A Study of Costs and Productivity," a report prepared for AARP by ICF Inc., 1995; W. C. K. Chiu, A. W. Chan, E. Snape, and T. Redman, "Age Stereotypes and Discriminatory Attitudes towards Older Workers: An East–West Comparison," *Human Relations*, May 2001, pp. 629–61; I. Glover, "Ageism Without Frontiers," in I. Glover and M. Branine (eds.), *Ageism in Work and Employment* (Aldershot, England: Ashgate, 2001), pp. 115–50; K. Greene, "Older Workers Can Get a Raw Deal—Some Employers Admit to Promoting, Challenging Their Workers Less," *Wall Street Journal*, April 10, 2003, p. D2; and K. A. Wrenn and T. J. Maurer, "Beliefs About Older Workers' Learning and Development Behavior in Relation to Beliefs About Malleability of Skills, Age-Related Decline, and Control," *Journal of Applied Social Psychology*, vol. 34(2), 2004, pp. 223–242.

15. S. R. Rhodes, "Age-Related Differences in Work Attitudes and Behavior: A Review and Conceptual Analysis," *Psychological Bulletin*, March 1983, pp. 328–67; J. L. Cotton and J. M. Tuttle, "Employee Turnover: A Meta-Analysis and Review with Implications for Research," *Academy of Management Review*, January 1986, pp. 55–70; and D. R. Davies, G. Matthews, and C. S. K. Wong, "Ageing and Work," in C. L. Cooper and I. T. Robertson (eds.), *International Review of Industrial and Organizational Psychology*, vol. 6 (Chichester, England: Wiley, 1991), pp. 183–87.

16. Rhodes, "Age-Related Differences in Work Attitudes and Behavior," pp. 347–49; R. D. Hackett, "Age, Tenure, and Employee Absenteeism," *Human Relations*, July 1990, pp. 601–19; and Davies, Matthews, and Wong, "Ageing and Work," pp. 183–87.

17. Cited in K. Labich, "The New Unemployed," *Fortune*, March 8, 1993, p. 43.

18. See G. M. McEvoy and W. F. Cascio, "Cumulative Evidence of the Relationship between Employee Age and Job Performance," *Journal of Applied Psychology*, February 1989, pp. 11–17; and F. L. Schmidt and J. E. Hunter, "The Validity and Utility of Selection Methods in Personnel Psychology: Practical and Theoretical Implications of 85 Years of Research Findings," *Psychological Bulletin*, September 1998, pp. 262–74.

19. See, for instance, F. J. Landy, et al, *Alternatives to Chronological Age in Determining Standards of Suitability for Public Safety Jobs* (University Park, PA: Center for Applied Behavioral Sciences, Pennsylvania State University, 1992).

20. A. L. Kalleberg and K. A. Loscocco, "Aging, Values, and Rewards: Explaining Age Differences in Job Satisfaction,"

American Sociological Review, February 1983, pp. 78–90; R. Lee and E. R. Wilbur, "Age, Education, Job Tenure, Salary, Job Characteristics, and Job Satisfaction: A Multivariate Analysis," *Human Relations*, August 1985, pp. 781–91; and Davies, Matthews, and Wong, "Ageing and Work," pp. 176–83.

21. K. M. Kacmar and G. R. Ferris, "Theoretical and Methodological Considerations in the Age-Job Satisfaction Relationship," *Journal of Applied Psychology*, April 1989, pp. 201–07; G. Zeitz, "Age and Work Satisfaction in a Government Agency: A Situational Perspective," *Human Relations*, May 1990, pp. 419–38; and W. A. Hochwarter, G. R. Ferris, P. L. Perrewe, L. A. Witt, and C. Kiewitz, "A Note on the Nonlinearity of the Age-Job Satisfaction Relationship," *Journal of Applied Social Psychology*, June 2001, pp. 1223–37.

22. See, for example, A. H. Eagly and L. L. Carli, "Sex Researchers and Sex-Typed Communications as Determinants of Sex Differences in Influenceability: A Meta-Analysis of Social Influence Studies," *Psychological Bulletin*, August 1981, pp. 1–20; J.S. Hyde, "How Large Are Cognitive Gender Differences?" *American Psychologist*, October 1981, pp. 892–901; P. Chance, "Biology, Destiny, and All That," *Across the Board*, July–August 1988, pp. 19–23; E. M. Weiss, G. Kemmler, E. A. Deisenhammer, W. W. Fleischhacker, and M. Delazer, "Sex Differences in Cognitive Functions," *Personality and Individual Differences*, September 2003, pp. 863–875; and A. F. Jorm, K. J. Anstey, H. Christensen, and B. Rodgers, "Gender Differences in Cognitive Abilities: The Mediating Role of Health State and Health Habits," *Intelligence*, January 2004, pp. 7–23.

23. See, for example, M. M. Black and E. W. Holden, "The Impact of Gender on Productivity and Satisfaction Among Medical School Psychologists," *Journal of Clinical Psychology in Medical Settings*, March 1998, pp. 117–31.

24. See, for example, S. Shellenbarger, "More Job Seekers Put Family Needs First," *Wall Street Journal*, November 15, 1991, p. B1.

25. R. W. Griffeth, P. W. Hom, and S. Gaertner, "A Meta-Analysis of Antecedents and Correlates of Employee Turnover: Update, Moderator Tests, and Research Implications for the Next Millennium," *Journal of Management*, vol. 26, no. 3, 2000, pp. 463–88.

26. See, for instance, K. D. Scott and E. L. McClellan, "Gender Differences in Absenteeism," *Public Personnel Management*, Summer 1990, pp. 229–53; and A. VandenHeuvel and M. Wooden, "Do Explanations of Absenteeism Differ for Men and Women?" *Human Relations*, November 1995, pp. 1309–29.

27. See, for instance, M. Tait, M. Y. Padgett, and T. T. Baldwin, "Job and Life Satisfaction: A Reevaluation of the Strength of the Relationship and Gender Effects as a Function of the Date of the Study," *Journal of Applied Psychology*, June 1989, pp. 502–07; and M. B. Grover, "Daddy Stress," *Forbes*, September 6, 1999, pp. 202–08.

28. J. M. Sacco, C. R. Scheu, A. M. Ryan, and N. Schmitt, "An Investigation of Race and Sex Similarity Effects in Interviews: A Multilevel Approach to Relational Demography," *Journal of Applied Psychology*, vol. 88(5), 2003, pp. 852–865; G. N. Powell and D. A. Butterfield, "Exploring the Influence of Decision Makers' Race and Gender on Actual Promotions to Top Management," *Personnel Psychology*, vol. 55(2), 2002, pp. 397–428; and M. K. Mount, M. R. Sytsma, J. F. Hazucha, and K. E. Holt, "Rater-Ratee Race Effects in Developmental Performance Ratings of Managers," *Personnel Psychology*, vol. 50(1), 1997, pp. 51–69.

29. D. A. Kravitz and S. L. Klineberg, "Reactions to Two Versions of Affirmative Action Among Whites, Blacks, and Hispanics," *Journal of Applied Psychology*, vol. 85(4), 2000. pp. 597–611.

30. G. F. Dreher and T. H. Cox, Jr., "Labor Market Mobility and Cash Compensation: The Moderating Effects of Race and Gender," *Academy of Management Journal*, vol. 43(5), 2000, pp. 890–900; A. I. Huffcutt and P. L. Roth, "Racial Group Differences in Employment Interview Evaluations," *Journal of Applied Psychology*, vol. 83(2), 1998, pp. 179–189; and J. M. Sacco, C. R. Scheu, A. M. Ryan, and N. Schmitt, "An Investigation of Race and Sex Similarity Effects in Interviews: A Multilevel Approach to Relational Demography," *Journal of Applied Psychology*, vol. 88(5), 2003, pp. 852–865.

31. P. Bobko, P. L. Roth, and D. Potosky, "Derivation and Implications of a Meta-Analytic Matrix Incorporating Cognitive Ability, Alternative Predictors, and Job Performance," *Personnel Psychology*, Autumn 1999, pp. 561–89.

32. M. J. Ree, T. R. Carretta, and J. R. Steindl, "Cognitive Ability," p. 228.

33. See Rushton and Jenson, "Thirty Years of Research on Race Differences in Cognitive Ability," *Psychology, Public Policy, and the Law*, vol. 11 (2), 2005, pp. 235–295, and R. E. Nisbett, "Heredity, Environment, and Race Differences in IQ: A Commentary on Rushton and Jensen (2005)," *Psychology, Public Policy, and the Law*, vol. 11 (2), 2005, pp. 302–310.

34. M. E. Gordon and W. J. Fitzgibbons, "Empirical Test of the Validity of Seniority as a Factor in Staffing Decisions," *Journal of Applied Psychology*, June 1982, pp. 311–19; M. E. Gordon and W. A. Johnson, "Seniority: A Review of Its Legal and Scientific Standing," *Personnel Psychology*, Summer 1982, pp. 255–80; M. A. McDaniel, F. L. Schmidt, and J. E. Hunter, "Job Experience Correlates of Job Performance," *Journal of Applied Psychology*, May 1988, pp. 327–30; and M.A. Quinones, J.K. Ford, and M. S. Teachout, "The Relationship between Work Experience and Job Performance: A Conceptual and Meta-Analytic Review," *Personnel Psychology*, Winter 1995, pp. 887–910.

35. Garrison and Muchinsky, "Attitudinal and Biographical Predictors of Incidental Absenteeism"; N. Nicholson, C. A. Brown, and J. K. Chadwick-Jones, "Absence from Work and Personal Characteristics," *Journal of Applied Psychology*, June 1977, pp. 319–27; R.T. Keller, "Predicting Absenteeism from Prior Absenteeism, Attitudinal Factors, and Nonattitudinal Factors," *Journal of Applied Psychology*, August 1983, pp. 536–40; and I. R. Gellatly, "Individual and Group Determinants of Employee Absenteeism: Test of a Causal Model," *Journal of Organizational Behavior*, September 1995, pp. 469–485.

36. P. O. Popp and J. A. Belohlav, "Absenteeism in a Low Status Work Environment," *Academy of Management Journal*, September 1982, p. 681.

37. R. W. Griffeth, P. W. Hom, and S. Gaertner, "A Meta-Analysis of Antecedents and Correlates of Employee Turnover."

38. R. D. Gatewood and H. S. Field, *Human Resource Selection* (Chicago: Dryden Press, 1987).

39. J. A. Breaugh and D. L. Dossett, "The Effectiveness of Biodata for Predicting Turnover," paper presented at the National Academy of Management Conference, New Orleans, August 1987.

40. A. G. Bedeian, G. R. Ferris, and K. M. Kacmar, "Age, Tenure, and Job Satisfaction: A Tale of Two Perspectives," *Journal of Vocational Behavior*, February 1992, pp. 33–48; and W. van Breukelen, R. van der Vlist, and H. Steensma, "Voluntary Employee Turnover: Combining Variables from the 'Traditional' Turnover Literature with the Theory of Planned Behavior," *Journal of Organizational Behavior*, vol. 25(7), 2004, pp. 893–914.

41. See, for instance, H.M. Weiss, "Learning Theory and Industrial and Organizational Psychology," in M. D. Dunnette and L.M. Hough, eds., *Handbook of Industrial & Organizational Psychology*, 2nd ed., vol. 1 (Palo Alto: Consulting Psychologists Press, 1990), pp. 172–73.

42. W. McGehee, "Are We Using What We Know about Training? Learning Theory and Training," *Personnel Psychology*, Spring 1958, p. 2.

43. I. P. Pavlov, *The Work of the Digestive Glands*, trans. W. H. Thompson (London: Charles Griffin, 1902). See also the special issue of *American Psychologist* (September 1997, pp. 933–72) commemorating Pavlov's work.

44. B. F. Skinner, *Contingencies of Reinforcement* (East Norwalk, CT: Appleton-Century-Crofts, 1971).

45. J. A. Mills, *Control: A History of Behavioral Psychology*, New York: New York University Press, 2000.

46. A. Bandura, *Social Learning Theory* (Upper Saddle River, NJ: Prentice Hall, 1977).

47. T. Maurer, K. Wrenn, and E. Weiss, "Toward Understanding and Managing Stereotypical Beliefs about Older Workers' Ability and Desire for Learning and Development," *Research in Personnel and Human Resources Management*, vol. 22, 2003, pp. 253–285.

48. T. J. Maurer, E. M. Weiss, and F. G. Barbeite, "A Model of Involvement in Work-Related Learning and Development Activity: The Effects of Individual, Situational, Motivational, and Age Variables," *Journal of Applied Psychology*, vol. 88(4), 2003, pp. 707–724.

49. J. A. Colquitt, J. A. LePine, and R. A. Noe, "Toward an Integrative Theory of Training Motivation: A Meta-Analytic Path Analysis of 20 Years of Research," *Journal of Applied Psychology*, vol. 85(5), 2000, pp. 678–707.

50. K. A. Wrenn and T. J. Maurer, "Beliefs About Older Workers' Learning and Development Behavior in Relation to Beliefs About Malleability of Skills, Age-Related Decline, and Control," *Journal of Applied Social Psychology*, vol. 34(2), 2004. pp. 223–242.

51. F. Luthans and R. Kreitner, *Organizational Behavior Modification and Beyond*, 2nd ed. (Glenview, IL: Scott, Foresman, 1985); and A. D. Stajkovic and F. Luthans, "A Meta-Analysis of the Effects of Organizational Behavior Modification on Task Performance, 1975–95," *Academy of Management Journal*, October 1997, pp. 1122–49.

52. "At Emery Air Freight: Positive Reinforcement Boosts Performance," *Organizational Dynamics*, Winter 1973, pp. 41–50.

53. F. Luthans and R. Kreitner, *Organizational Behavior Modification and Beyond: An Operant and Social Learning Approach* (Glenview, IL: Scott, Foresman, 1985); A. D. Stajkovic and F. Luthans, "A Meta-Analysis of the Effects of Organizational Behavior Modification on Task Performance, 1975–95," *Academy of Management Journal*, October 1997, pp. 1122–49; and A. D. Stajkovic and F. Luthans, "Behavioral Management and Task Performance in Organizations: Conceptual Background, Meta-Analysis, and Test of Alternative Models," *Personnel Psychology*, Spring 2003, pp. 155–92.

54. A. D. Stajkovic and F. Luthans, "A Meta-Analysis of the Effects of Organizational Behavior Modification on Task Performance," p. 1123.

55. See, for instance, L. W. Frederiksen, *Handbook of Organizational Behavior Management* (New York: Wiley, 1982); B. Sulzer-Azarof, B. Loafman, R. J. Merante, and A.C. Hlavacek, "Improving Occupational Safety in a Large Industrial Plant: A Systematic Replication," *Journal of Organizational Behavior Management*, vol. 11, no. 1, 1990, pp. 99–120; J. C. Landau, "The Impact of a Change in an Attendance Control System on Absenteeism and Tardiness," *Journal of Organizational Behavior Management*, vol. 13, no. 2, 1993, pp. 51–70; C. S. Brown and B. Sulzer-Azaroff, "An Assessment of the Relationship Between Customer Satisfaction and Service Friendliness," *Journal of Organizational Behavior Management*, vol. 14, no. 2 1994, pp. 55–75; F. Luthans and A. D. Stajkovic, "Reinforce for Performance: The Need to Go Beyond Pay and Even Rewards," *Academy of Management Executive*, May 1999, pp. 49–57; and A. D. Stajkovic and F. Luthans, "Differential Effects of Incentive Motivators on Work Performance," *Academy of Management Journal*, vol. 44(3), 2001, pp. 580–590.

56. E. A. Locke, "Beyond Determinism and Materialism, or Isn't It Time We Took Consciousness Seriously?" *Journal of Behavior Therapy & Experimental Psychiatry*, vol. 26(3), 1995, pp. 265–273.

57. Points in this argument are based on N. Nicholson, "How Hardwired Is Human Behavior?" *Harvard Business Review*, July–August 1998, pp. 135–47; and B. D. Pierce and R. White, "The Evolution of Social Structure: Why Biology Matters," *Academy of Management Review*, October 1999, pp. 843–53.

How can I know what I think 'til I see what I say?

— E. M. Forster

Attitudes and Job Satisfaction

After studying this chapter, you should be able to:

1 Contrast the three components of an attitude.

2 Identify the role consistency plays in attitudes.

3 Summarize the relationship between attitudes and behavior.

4 Discuss similarities and differences between job satisfaction and the other job attitudes discussed.

5 Summarize the main causes of job satisfaction.

6 Identify four employee responses to dissatisfaction.

LEARNING OBJECTIVES

VSP: Putting Employees' Job Satisfaction First

VSP is the largest provider of eye care benefits in the United States. It has contracts with 20,000 employers and provides eye care benefits to their 37 million employees and dependents.[1] The majority of VSP's staff is located at the company's headquarters, near Sacramento, California, but it also has people working at a call center in Ohio and at 25 regional offices around the United States.

In spite of increased competition, VSP has grown and prospered. In the past decade, for instance, its workforce has nearly tripled, from 868 to 2,100 employees. To ensure that it's meeting the needs of this growing labor force, VSP relies on regular surveys of employee satisfaction.

VSP's internal human resources group, led by Elaine Leuchars (see photo), annually surveys every employee in the company—one-fourth of the staff each quarter. In addition, the company uses an outside consulting firm to conduct an all-employee survey every other year. Together, these surveys provide Leuchars and the VSP executive team with a reading on the company's "temperature" and insights into areas that can be improved. When these surveys indicate a negative trend in a division or department, focus groups are created to gain more insight

into the problem and to get employee input on suggestions for improvement. VSP's human resource group then offers assistance in creating specific programs to make these improvements.

Leuchars believes that conducting regular surveys of employee attitudes conveys an important message to VSP employees: The company wants to hear what they have to say and values their opinions. Moreover, the fact that the company actively uses this information to improve the workplace has paid dividends. In the past 5 years, overall employee satisfaction responses of good, very good, and excellent have risen from 93 percent to 98 percent. And during this same period, annual turnover has declined from 23 percent to 12 percent. VSP has also recently been on Fortune magazine's list of the "100 Best Companies to Work For" for 3 years in a row. ■

As we see in the case of VSP, it is important that companies monitor employee attitudes. In this chapter, we look at attitudes, their link to behavior, and how employees' satisfaction or dissatisfaction with their jobs impacts the workplace.

Attitudes

Attitudes are evaluative statements—either favorable or unfavorable—concerning objects, people, or events. They reflect how one feels about something. When I say "I like my job," I am expressing my attitude about work.

Attitudes are complex. If you ask people about their attitude toward religion, George W. Bush, or the organization they work for, you may get a simple response, but the reasons underlying the response are probably complex. In order to fully understand attitudes, we need to consider their fundamental properties. In the material that follows, we'll answer six questions about attitudes that will help you understand them better:

1. What are the main components of attitudes?
2. How consistent are attitudes?
3. Does behavior always follow from attitudes?
4. What are the major job attitudes?
5. How are employee attitudes measured?
6. What is the importance of attitudes to workplace diversity?

What Are the Main Components of Attitudes?

Typically, researchers have assumed that attitudes have three components: cognition, affect, and behavior.[2] Let's look at each of these components.

The belief that "discrimination is wrong" is an evaluative statement. Such an opinion is the **cognitive component** of an attitude. It sets the stage for the more critical part of an attitude—its **affective component**. Affect is the emotional or feeling segment of an attitude and is reflected in the statement "I don't like Jon because he discriminates against minorities." Finally, and we'll discuss this issue at considerable length later in this section, affect can lead to behavioral outcomes. The **behavioral component** of an attitude refers to an intention to behave in a certain way toward someone or something. So, to continue our example, I might choose to avoid Jon because of my feelings about him.

Viewing attitudes as made up of three components—cognition, affect, and behavior—is helpful in understanding their complexity and the potential relationship between attitudes and behavior. Keep in mind that these components are closely related. In particular, in many ways cognition and affect are inseparable. For example, imagine that you concluded that someone had just treated you unfairly. Aren't you likely to have feelings about that, occurring virtually instantaneously with the thought? Thus, cognition and affect are intertwined.

Exhibit 3-1 illustrates how the three components of an attitude are related. In this example, an employee didn't get a promotion he thought he deserved; a coworker got it instead. The employee's attitude toward his supervisor is illustrated as follows: cognition (the employee thought he deserved the promotion), affect (the employee strongly dislikes his supervisor), and behavior (the employee is looking for another job). As we previously noted, although we often think that cognition causes affect which then causes behavior, in reality these components are often difficult to separate.

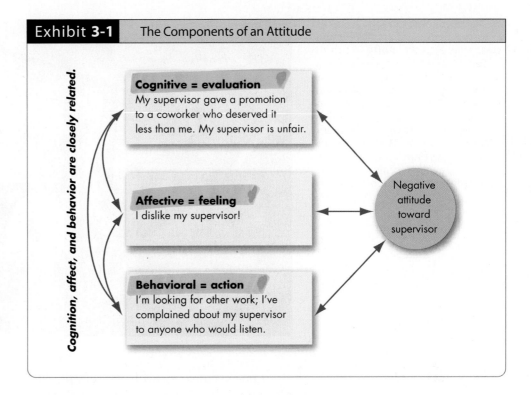

In organizations, attitudes are important because of their behavioral component. If workers believe, for example, that supervisors, auditors, bosses, and time-and-motion engineers are all in conspiracy to make employees work harder for the same or less money, it makes sense to try to understand how these attitudes were formed, their relationship to actual job behavior, and how they might be changed.

How Consistent Are Attitudes?

Did you ever notice how people change what they say so it doesn't contradict what they do? Perhaps a friend of yours has consistently argued that the quality of American cars isn't up to that of the import brands and that he'd never own anything but a Japanese or German car. But his dad gives him a late-model Ford Mustang, and suddenly American cars aren't so bad. Or, when going through sorority rush, a new freshman believes that sororities are good and that pledging a sorority is important. If she fails to make a sorority, however, she may say, "I recognized that sorority life isn't all it's cracked up to be, anyway."

Research has generally concluded that people seek consistency among their attitudes and between their attitudes and their behavior.[3] This means that individuals seek to reconcile divergent attitudes and align their attitudes and behavior so they appear rational and consistent. When there is an inconsistency, forces are initiated to return the individual to an equilibrium state in which attitudes and behavior are again consistent. This can be done by altering either the attitudes or the behavior, or by developing a rationalization for the discrepancy.

attitudes   *Evaluative statements or judgments concerning objects, people, or events.*

cognitive component of an attitude   *The opinion or belief segment of an attitude.*

affective component of an attitude   *The emotional or feeling segment of an attitude.*

behavioral component of an attitude   *An intention to behave in a certain way toward someone or something.*

Marriott Corporation sums up its attitude toward employees and customers with the motto "Spirit to Serve." The hotel chain's CEO Bill Marriott (left in photo) visits employees at more than 200 hotels a year. "I want our associates to know that there really is a guy named Marriott who cares about them," he says. Marriott honors employees with job excellence awards for behavior that exemplifies the attitude of service.

Tobacco executives provide an example.[4] How, you might wonder, do these people cope with the ongoing barrage of data linking cigarette smoking and negative health outcomes? They can deny that any clear causation between smoking and cancer, for instance, has been established. They can brainwash themselves by continually articulating the benefits of tobacco. They can acknowledge the negative consequences of smoking but rationalize that people are going to smoke and that tobacco companies merely promote freedom of choice. They can accept the research evidence and begin actively working to make more healthy cigarettes or at least reduce their availability to more vulnerable groups, such as teenagers. Or they can quit their job because the dissonance is too great.

Can we also assume from this consistency principle that an individual's' behavior can always be predicted if we know their attitude on a subject? If Mr. Jones views the company's pay level as too low, will a substantial increase in his pay change his behavior, that is, make him work harder? The answer to this question is, unfortunately, more complex than merely a "Yes" or "No."

In the late 1950s, Leon Festinger proposed the theory of **cognitive dissonance**.[5] This theory sought to explain the linkage between attitudes and behavior. Dissonance means an inconsistency. *Cognitive dissonance* refers to any incompatibility that an individual might perceive between two or more attitudes, or between behavior and attitudes. Festinger argued that any form of inconsistency is uncomfortable and that individuals will attempt to reduce the dissonance and, hence, the discomfort. Therefore, individuals will seek a stable state, in which there is a minimum of dissonance.

No individual, of course, can completely avoid dissonance. You know that cheating on your income tax is wrong, but you "fudge" the numbers a bit every year and hope you're not audited. Or you tell your children to floss their teeth every day, but *you* don't. So how do people cope? Festinger would propose that the desire to reduce dissonance would be determined by the *importance* of the elements creating the dissonance, the degree of *influence* the individual believes he or she has over the elements, and the *rewards* that may be involved in dissonance.

If the elements creating the dissonance are relatively unimportant, the pressure to correct this imbalance will be low. However, say that a corporate manager—Mrs. Smith—believes strongly that no company should pollute the air or water.

Unfortunately, Mrs. Smith, because of the requirements of her job, is placed in the position of having to make decisions that would trade off her company's profitability against her attitudes on pollution. She knows that dumping the company's sewage into the local river (which we shall assume is legal) is in the best economic interest of her firm. What will she do? Clearly, Mrs. Smith is experiencing a high degree of cognitive dissonance. Because of the importance of the elements in this example, we cannot expect Mrs. Smith to ignore the inconsistency. There are several paths she can follow to deal with her dilemma. She can change her behavior (stop polluting the river). Or she can reduce dissonance by concluding that the dissonant behavior is not so important after all ("I've got to make a living, and in my role as a corporate decision maker, I often have to place the good of my company above that of the environment or society."). A third alternative would be for Mrs. Smith to change her attitude ("There is nothing wrong with polluting the river."). Still another choice would be to seek out more consonant elements to outweigh the dissonant ones ("The benefits to society from manufacturing our products more than offset the cost to society of the resulting water pollution.").

The degree of influence that individuals believe they have over the elements will have an impact on how they will react to the dissonance. If they perceive the dissonance to be due to something over which they have no choice, they are less likely to be receptive to attitude change. If, for example, the dissonance-producing behavior is required as a result of the boss's directive, the pressure to reduce dissonance would be less than if the behavior was performed voluntarily. Though dissonance exists, it can be rationalized and justified.

Rewards also influence the degree to which individuals are motivated to reduce dissonance. High rewards accompanying high dissonance tend to reduce the tension inherent in the dissonance. The rewards act to reduce dissonance by increasing the consistency side of the individual's balance sheet.

These moderating factors suggest that just because individuals experience dissonance they will not necessarily move directly toward reducing it. If the issues underlying the dissonance are of minimal importance, if individuals perceive that the dissonance is externally imposed and is substantially uncontrollable by them, or if rewards are significant enough to offset the dissonance, the individual will not be under great tension to reduce the dissonance.

What are the organizational implications of the theory of cognitive dissonance? It can help to predict the propensity to engage in attitude and behavioral change. For example, if individuals are required by the demands of their job to say or do things that contradict their personal attitude, they will tend to modify their attitude in order to make it compatible with the cognition of what they have said or done. In addition, the greater the dissonance—after it has been moderated by importance, choice, and reward factors—the greater the pressures to reduce it.

Does Behavior Always Follow from Attitudes?

We have maintained that attitudes affect behavior. Early research on attitudes assumed that they were causally related to behavior; that is, the attitudes that people hold determine what they do. Common sense, too, suggests a relationship. Isn't it logical that people watch television programs that they say they like or that employees try to avoid assignments they find distasteful?

cognitive dissonance *Any incompatibility between two or more attitudes or between behavior and attitudes.*

However, in the late 1960s, this assumed relationship between attitudes and behavior was challenged by a review of the research.[6] Based on an evaluation of a number of studies that investigated the attitudes-behavior relationship, the reviewer concluded that attitudes were unrelated to behavior or, at best, only slightly related.[7] More recent research has demonstrated that attitudes significantly predict future behavior and confirmed Festinger's original belief that the relationship can be enhanced by taking moderating variables into account.[8]

Moderating Variables   The most powerful moderators of the attitudes-behavior relationship have been found to be the *importance* of the attitude, its *specificity*, its *accessibility*, whether there exist *social pressures*, and whether a person has *direct experience* with the attitude.[9]

Important attitudes are ones that reflect fundamental values, self-interest, or identification with individuals or groups that a person values. Attitudes that individuals consider important tend to show a strong relationship to behavior. The more specific the attitude and the more specific the behavior, the stronger the link between the two. For instance, asking someone specifically about her intention to stay with the organization for the next 6 months is likely to better predict turnover for that person than if you asked her how satisfied she was with her pay.

Attitudes that are easily remembered are more likely to predict behavior than attitudes that are not accessible in memory. Interestingly, you're more likely to remember attitudes that are frequently expressed. So the more you talk about your attitude on a subject, the more you're likely to remember it, and the more likely it is to shape your behavior.

Discrepancies between attitudes and behavior are more likely to occur when social pressures to behave in certain ways hold exceptional power. This tends to characterize behavior in organizations. This may explain why an employee who holds strong anti-union attitudes attends pro-union organizing meetings; or why tobacco executives, who are not smokers themselves and who tend to believe the research linking smoking and cancer, don't actively discourage others from smoking in their offices.

Finally, the attitude–behavior relationship is likely to be much stronger if an attitude refers to something with which the individual has direct personal experience. Asking college students with no significant work experience how they would respond to working for an authoritarian supervisor is far less likely to predict actual behavior than asking that same question of employees who have actually worked for such an individual.

Self-Perception Theory   Although most attitudes-behavior studies yield positive results, researchers have achieved still higher correlations by pursuing another direction—looking at whether or not behavior influences attitudes. This view, called **self-perception theory**, has generated some encouraging findings. Let's briefly review the theory.[10]

When asked about an attitude toward some object, individuals often recall their behavior relevant to that object and then infer their attitude from their past behavior. So if an employee was asked her feelings about being a training specialist at Marriott, she would likely think, "I've had this same job with Marriott as a trainer for 10 years. Nobody forced me to stay on this job. So I must like it!" Self-perception theory, therefore, argues that attitudes are used, after the fact, to make sense out of an action that has already occurred rather than as devices that precede and guide action. And contrary to cognitive dissonance theory, attitudes are just casual verbal statements. When people are asked about their attitudes and they don't have strong convictions or feelings, self-perception theory says they tend to create plausible answers.

Self-perception theory has been well supported.[11] While the traditional attitude–behavior relationship is generally positive, the behavior–attitude

Jam and jelly maker J.M. Smucker places high importance on the attitude of taking personal responsibility within the company and the community. Smucker encourages its employees to contribute to the community by offering them unlimited paid time off for volunteer work. Brenda Dempsey, Smucker's director of corporate communications, translates her personal commitment to volunteerism into specific behaviors by teaching business ethics, problem-solving, and decision-making classes at a local high school.

relationship is just as strong. This is particularly true when attitudes are vague and ambiguous. When you have had few experiences regarding an attitude issue or have given little previous thought to it, you'll tend to infer your attitudes from your behavior. However, when your attitudes have been established for a while and are well defined, those attitudes are likely to guide your behavior.

What Are the Major Job Attitudes?

A person can have thousands of attitudes, but OB focuses our attention on a very limited number of work-related attitudes. These work-related attitudes tap positive or negative evaluations that employees hold about aspects of their work environment. Most of the research in OB has been concerned with three attitudes: job satisfaction, job involvement, and organizational commitment.[12] A few other attitudes are attracting attention from researchers, including perceived organizational support and employee engagement; we'll also briefly discuss these.

Job Satisfaction   The term **job satisfaction** can be defined as a positive feeling about one's job resulting from an evaluation of its characteristics. A person with a high level of job satisfaction holds positive feelings about the job, while a person who is dissatisfied holds negative feelings about the job. When people speak of employee attitudes, more often than not they mean job satisfaction. In fact, the two are frequently used interchangeably. Because of the high importance OB researchers have given to job satisfaction, we'll review this attitude in considerable detail later in this chapter.

Job Involvement   Although much less studied than job satisfaction, a related concept is **job involvement**.[13] Job involvement measures the degree to which people identify psychologically with their job and consider their perceived performance

Arnold Carbone (center) has a high level of job satisfaction and a positive attitude about his job. Carbone, as Conductor of Bizarre and D at Ben & Jerry's, travels the world and eats as many desserts as he can in his job as developer of new ice-cream flavors for Ben & Jerry's. Carbone created flavors such as Phish Food and Wavy Gravy.

level important to self-worth.[14] Employees with a high level of job involvement strongly identify with and really care about the kind of work they do. A closely related concept is **psychological empowerment**, which is employees' beliefs in the degree to which they impact their work environment, their competence, the meaningfulness of their job, and the perceived autonomy in their work.[15] For example, one study of nursing managers in Singapore found that good leaders empower their employees by involving them in decisions, making them feel that their work is important, and giving them discretion to "do their own thing."[16]

High levels of job involvement and psychological empowerment are positively related to organizational citizenship and job performance.[17] In addition, high job involvement has been found to be related to fewer absences and lower resignation rates.[18]

Organizational Commitment   The third job attitude we will discuss is **organizational commitment**, which is defined as a state in which an employee identifies with a particular organization and its goals and wishes to maintain membership in the organization.[19] So, high job involvement means identifying with one's specific job, while high organizational commitment means identifying with one's employing organization.

There are three separate dimensions to organizational commitment:[20]

1. **Affective Commitment**—an emotional attachment to the organization and a belief in its values. For example, a Petco employee may be affectively committed to the company because of its involvement with animals.
2. **Continuance Commitment**—the perceived economic value of remaining with an organization compared to leaving it. An employee may be committed to an employer because she is paid well and feels it would hurt her family to quit.
3. **Normative Commitment**—an obligation to remain with the organization for moral or ethical reasons. For example, an employee who is spearheading a new initiative may remain with an employer because he feels it would "leave the employer in a lurch" if he left.

Chinese Employees and Organizational Commitment

ARE EMPLOYEES FROM DIFFERENT CULTURES COMmitted to their organizations in similar ways? A 2003 study explored this question and compared the organizational commitment of Chinese employees to the commitment of Canadian and South Korean workers. Although results revealed that the three types of commitment—normative, continuance, and affective—are present in all three cultures, results also showed that there are some differences among the three countries in how important each type of commitment is.

Normative commitment, an obligation to remain with the organization for moral or ethical reasons, was higher in the Chinese sample of employees than in the Canadian and South Korean sample. Affective commitment, an emotional attachment to the organization and a belief in its values, was also stronger in China compared to Canada and South Korea. Chinese culture may explain why. The Chinese emphasize loyalty to one's group, and in this case, one's "group" may be the organization that one works for, so employees may feel a certain loyalty from the start and may become more emotionally attached as their time with the organization grows. To the extent that the Chinese view their organization as part of their group and become emotionally attached to that group, they will be more committed to their organization. Perhaps as a result of this emphasis on loyalty, the normative commitment of Chinese employees strongly predicted intentions to maintain employment with the organization.

Continuance commitment, the perceived economic value of remaining with an organization compared to leaving it, was lower in the Chinese sample than in the Canadian and South Korean sample. One reason for the lower degree of continuance commitment is that Chinese workers value loyalty towards the group more than individual concerns.

It appears that although all three countries experience normative, continuance, and affective commitment, the degree to which each form of commitment is important differs across countries.

Source: Based on Y. Cheng and M. S. Stockdale, "The Validity of the Three-Component Model of Organizational Commitment in a Chinese Context," *Journal of Vocational Behavior*, June 2003, pp. 465–489.

There appears to be a positive relationship between organizational commitment and job productivity, but the relationship is modest.[21] And, as with job involvement, the research evidence demonstrates negative relationships between organizational commitment and both absenteeism and turnover.[22] In general, it seems that affective commitment is more strongly related to organizational outcomes like performance and turnover than the other two commitment dimensions. One study found that affective commitment was a significant

psychological empowerment *Employees' belief in the degree to which they impact their work environment, their competence, the meaningfulness of their job, and the perceived autonomy in their work.*

organizational commitment *The degree to which an employee identifies with a particular organization and its goals and wishes to maintain membership in the organization.*

affective commitment *An emotional attachment to the organization and a belief in its values.*

continuance commitment *The perceived economic value of remaining with an organization compared to leaving it.*

normative commitment *An obligation to remain with the organization for moral or ethical reasons.*

predictor of various outcomes (perception of task characteristics, career satisfaction, intent to leave) in 72 percent of the cases, compared to only 36 percent for normative commitment and 7 percent for continuance commitment.[23] The weak results for continuance commitment make sense in that it really isn't a strong commitment at all. Rather than an allegiance (affective commitment) or an obligation (normative commitment) to an employer, a continuance commitment describes an employee who is "tethered" to an employer simply because there isn't anything better available.

There is reason to believe that the concept of commitment may be less important to employers and employees than it once was. The unwritten loyalty contract that existed 30 years ago between employees and employers has been seriously damaged, and the notion of employees staying with a single organization for most of their career has become increasingly obsolete. As such, "measures of employee–firm attachment, such as commitment, are problematic for new employment relations."[24] This suggests that *organizational commitment* is probably less important as a work-related attitude than it once was. In its place we might expect something akin to *occupational commitment* to become a more relevant variable because it better reflects today's fluid workforce.[25]

Other Job Attitudes   **Perceived organizational support** (POS) is the degree to which employees believe the organization values their contribution and cares about their well-being (for example, an employee believes that his organization would accommodate him if he had a child-care problem or would forgive an honest mistake on his part). Research shows that people perceive their organization as supportive when rewards are deemed fair, when employees have a voice in decisions, and when their supervisors are seen as supportive.[26]

A very new concept is **employee engagement**, which can be defined as individual's involvement with, satisfaction with, and enthusiasm for, the work they do. For example, one might ask employees about the availability of resources and the opportunities to learn new skills, whether they feel their work is important and meaningful, and whether their interactions with their coworkers and supervisors were rewarding.[27] A recent study of nearly 8,000 business units in 36 companies found that business units whose employees had high-average levels of engagement had higher levels of customer satisfaction, were more productive, had higher profits, and had lower levels of turnover and accidents.[28] Because the concept is so new, we don't know how engagement relates to other concepts like job satisfaction, organizational commitment, job involvement, or intrinsic motivation to do one's job well. Engagement may be broad enough that it captures the intersection of these variables. In other words, engagement may be what these attitudes have in common.

Are These Job Attitudes Really All That Distinct?   You might wonder whether these job attitudes are really distinct. After all, if people feel deeply involved in their job (high job involvement), isn't it probable that they like it (high job satisfaction)? Similarly, won't people who think their organization is supportive (high perceived organizational support) also feel committed to it (strong organizational commitment)? Evidence suggests that these attitudes are highly related, perhaps to a troubling degree. For example, the correlation between perceived organizational support and affective commitment is very strong.[29] The problem is that a strong correlation means that the variables may be redundant (so, for example, if you know someone's affective commitment, you basically know her perceived organizational support). But why is this redundancy so troubling? Well, why have two steering wheels on a car when you only need one? Why have two concepts—going by different labels—when you only need one? This redundancy is inefficient and confusing. Although we OB researchers like proposing new attitudes, often we haven't been good at showing how each attitude compares and contrasts to the others. There is some measure of distinctiveness among these attitudes—they are not exactly the same—but they overlap greatly. The overlap may exist for various reasons, including the employee's personality. Some people are predisposed to be positive or negative about almost everything. If someone tells you she loves her company, it may not mean a lot if she is positive about everything else in her life. Or the overlap may mean that some organizations are just all around better places to work than others. This may mean that if you as a manager know someone's level of job satisfaction, you know most of what you need to know about how the person sees the organization.

How Are Employee Attitudes Measured?

As we have seen, knowledge of employee attitudes can be helpful to managers in attempting to predict employee behavior. But how does management get information about employee attitudes? As suggested by the chapter-opening example at VSP, the most popular method is through the use of **attitude surveys**.[30]

The typical attitude survey presents the employee with a set of statements or questions with a rating scale indicating the degree of agreement. Some examples might include: "This organization's wage rates are competitive with those of other organizations';" "My job makes the best use of my abilities';" and "I know what my boss expects of me." Ideally, the items should be tailored to obtain the specific information that management desires. An individual's attitude score is achieved by summing up responses to the questionnaire items. These scores can then be averaged for work groups, teams, departments, divisions, or the organization as a whole.

Results from attitude surveys can frequently surprise management. For instance, managers at the Heavy-Duty Division of Springfield Remanufacturing thought everything was great.[31] Because employees were actively involved in division decisions and profitability was the highest within the entire company, management assumed morale was high. To confirm their beliefs, they conducted a short attitude survey. Employees were asked if they agreed or disagreed with the following statements: (1) At work, your opinions count; (2) Those of you who want to be a leader in this company have the opportunity to become one; and (3) In the past 6 months, someone has talked to you about your personal development. In the survey, 43 percent disagreed with the first statement, 48 percent with the second, and 62 percent with the third. Management was astounded. How could this be? The division had been holding shop floor meetings to review the numbers every week for more than 12 years. And most of the managers had come up through the ranks. Management responded by creating a committee made up of representatives from every department in the division and all three shifts. The committee quickly found that there were lots of little things the division was doing that were alienating employees. Out of this committee came a large number of suggestions that, after implementation, significantly improved employees' perception of their decision-making influence and their career opportunities in the division.

Using attitude surveys on a regular basis provides managers with valuable feedback on how employees perceive their working conditions. Policies and practices that management views as objective and fair may be seen as inequitable

---

perceived organizational support *The degree to which employees believe the organization values their contribution and cares about their well-being.*

employee engagement *An individual's involvement with, satisfaction with, and enthusiasm for the work they do.*

attitude surveys *Eliciting responses from employees through questionnaires on how they feel about their jobs, work groups, supervisors, and the organization.*

After settling a $54 million lawsuit, in which Denny's restaurant chain was accused of discriminating against African-American customers, the company trained all employees to help change their attitudes and increase their diversity awareness and skills. This photo shows employees celebrating Denny's 50 years in business, including Ray Hood-Phillips (front row, right), Denny's chief diversity officer. Today, Denny's ranks high on *Fortune* magazine's list of "Best Companies for Minorities."

by employees in general or by certain groups of employees. If distorted perceptions lead to negative attitudes about the job and organization, it's important for management to know about it. Why? Because, as we'll elaborate on in Chapter 6, employee behaviors are based on perceptions, not reality. The use of regular attitude surveys can alert management to potential problems and employees' intentions early so that action can be taken to prevent negative repercussions.[32]

What Is the Importance of Attitudes to Workplace Diversity?

Managers are increasingly concerned with changing employee attitudes to reflect shifting perspectives on racial, gender, and other diversity issues. A comment to a coworker of the opposite sex that 20 years ago might have been taken as a compliment—for instance, a male telling a female colleague that he thinks her outfit is sexy—can today become a career-limiting episode. As such, organizations are investing in training to help reshape the attitudes of employees.

The majority of large U.S. employers and a substantial proportion of medium-sized and smaller ones sponsor some sort of diversity training.[33] Some examples: Police officers in Escondido, California, receive 36 hours of diversity training each year. The Federal Aviation Administration sponsors a mandatory 8-hour diversity seminar for employees of its Western Pacific region. Denny's restaurants put all its managers through 2 days of intensive diversity training, with each day lasting 7 to 9 hours.

What do these diversity programs look like and how do they address attitude change?[34] They almost all include a self-evaluation phase. People are pressed to examine themselves and to confront ethnic and cultural stereotypes they might hold. Then participants typically take part in group discussions or panels with representatives from diverse groups. So, for instance, a Hmong man might describe his family's life in Southeast Asia and explain why they resettled in California; or a lesbian might describe how she discovered her sexual identity and the reaction of her friends and family when she came out.

Job Satisfaction Hits Record Lows
There is increasing evidence that job satisfaction levels in the United States are dropping. It's hard to know for sure why this is true, but some recent evidence provides some intriguing suggestions. This decline is found among workers of all ages, across all income brackets, and in all regions of the country.

What are the strongest areas of dissatisfaction? Only one in five employees is satisfied with his company's promotions and bonus plans. Surprisingly, satisfaction has dropped the most among those making the highest incomes (although they still have somewhat higher satisfaction than those with relatively low earnings).

But why are so many Americans unhappy at work? One reason may be that many companies are downsizing, leaving the workers overburdened. Downsizing also lowers the morale of layoff survivors. Why? Because not only are the survivors saddled with the duties of their coworkers but they often miss their coworkers and also wonder if they'll be next.

Based on: "Special Consumer Survey Report: Job Satisfaction," The Conference Board—September 2003, Executive Action Report #68; and T. D. Allen, D. M. Freeman, and J. E. A. Russell, "Survivor Reactions to Organizational Downsizing: Does Time Ease the Pain?" *Journal of Occupational and Organizational Psychology*, June 2001, pp. 145–164.

Additional activities designed to change attitudes include arranging for people to do volunteer work in community or social service centers in order to meet face to face with individuals and groups from diverse backgrounds and using exercises that let participants feel what it's like to be different. For example, when people participate in the exercise *Blue Eyes-Brown Eyes*, in which people are segregated and stereotyped according to their eye color, participants see what it's like to be judged by something over which they have no control. Evidence suggests this exercise reduces negative attitudes toward individuals different from participants.[35]

Job Satisfaction

We have already discussed job satisfaction briefly—earlier in this chapter as well as in Chapter 1. In this section, we want to dissect the concept more carefully. How do we measure job satisfaction? How satisfied are employees in their jobs? What causes an employee to have a high level of job satisfaction? How do dissatisfied and satisfied employees affect an organization?

Measuring Job Satisfaction

We've previously defined job satisfaction as a positive feeling about one's job resulting from an evaluation of its characteristics. This definition is clearly a very broad one.[36] Yet this is inherent in the concept. Remember, a person's job is more than just the obvious activities of shuffling papers, writing programming code, waiting on customers, or driving a truck. Jobs require interaction with coworkers and bosses, following organizational rules and policies, meeting performance standards, living with working conditions that are often less than ideal, and the like.[37] This means that an employee's assessment of how satisfied or dissatisfied he or she is with the job is a complex summation of a number of discrete job elements. How, then, do we measure the concept?

The two most widely used approaches are a single global rating and a summation score made up of a number of job facets. The single global rating method is nothing more than asking individuals to respond to one question, such as "All things considered, how satisfied are you with your job?" Respondents then reply by circling a number between 1 and 5 that corresponds to answers from "highly satisfied" to "highly dissatisfied." The other approach—a summation of job facets—is more sophisticated. It identifies key elements in a job and asks for the employee's feelings about each. Typical factors that would be included are the nature of the work, supervision, present pay, promotion opportunities, and relations with coworkers.[38] These factors are rated on a standardized scale and then added up to create an overall job satisfaction score.

Is one of the foregoing approaches superior to the other? Intuitively, it would seem that summing up responses to a number of job factors would achieve a more accurate evaluation of job satisfaction. The research, however, doesn't support this intuition.[39] This is one of those rare instances in which simplicity seems to work as well as complexity. Comparisons of one-question global ratings with the more lengthy summation-of-job-factors method indicate that the former is essentially as valid as the latter. The best explanation for this outcome is that the concept of job satisfaction is inherently so broad that the single question captures its essence. Another explanation may be that some important facets are left out of the summation of job facets. Both methods are helpful. For example, the single global rating method isn't very time consuming, which frees up managers so they can address other workplace issues and problems. And the summation of job facets helps managers zero in on where problems exist, making it easier to deal with unhappy employees and solve problems faster and more accurately.

How Satisfied Are People in Their Jobs?

Are most people satisfied with their jobs? The answer seems to be a qualified "yes" in the United States and in most developed countries. Independent studies, conducted among U.S. workers over the past 30 years, generally indicate that the majority of workers are satisfied with their jobs.[40] Although the percentage range is wide, more people report that they're satisfied than not. Moreover, these results generally apply to other developed countries. For instance, comparable studies among workers in Canada, Mexico, and Europe indicate more positive than negative results.[41]

Research shows that satisfaction levels vary a lot depending on which facet of job satisfaction you're talking about. As shown in Exhibit 3-2, people are on

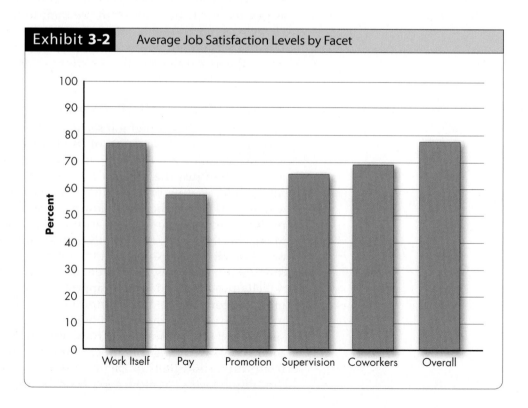

Exhibit 3-2   Average Job Satisfaction Levels by Facet

average satisfied with their jobs overall, with the work itself, and with their supervisors and coworkers. However, they tend to be less satisfied with their pay and with promotion opportunities. It's not really clear why people dislike their pay and promotion possibilities more than other aspects of their jobs.[42]

But what about you? Do you like your job? See the Self-Assessment feature below where you can determine your level of satisfaction with your current or past jobs.

SELF
ASSESSMENT
LIBRARY

HOW SATISFIED AM I WITH MY JOB?

In the Self-Assessment Library (available on CD, online, and in print), take assessment I.B.3. (How Satisfied Am I with My Job?) and answer the following questions. If you currently do not have a job, answer the questions for your most recent job.

1. *How does your job satisfaction compare to others in your class who have taken the assessment?*
2. *Why do you think your satisfaction is higher or lower than average?*

What Causes Job Satisfaction?

Think about the best job you ever had. What made it so? Chances are you probably liked the work you did. In fact, of the major job-satisfaction facets (work itself, pay, advancement opportunities, supervision, coworkers), enjoying the work itself is almost always the facet most strongly correlated with high levels of overall job satisfaction. Interesting jobs that provide training, variety, independence, and control satisfy most employees.[43] In other words, most people prefer work that is challenging and stimulating over work that is predictable and routine.

You have probably noticed that pay comes up often when discussing job satisfaction. Let's explore this topic some more. There is an interesting relationship between salary and job satisfaction. For people who are poor (for example, living below the poverty line), or who live in poor countries, pay does correlate with job satisfaction and with overall happiness. But, once an individual reaches a level of comfortable living (in the United States, that occurs at about $40,000 a year, depending on the region and family size), the relationship virtually disappears. In other words, people who earn $80,000 are, on average, no happier with their jobs than those who earn close to $40,000. Take a look at Exhibit 3-3. It shows the relationship between the average pay for a job and the average level of job satisfaction. As you can see, there isn't much of a relationship there. Jobs that are compensated handsomely have average job satisfaction levels no higher than those that are paid much less. To further illustrate this point, one researcher even found no significant difference when he compared the overall well-being of the richest people on the Forbes 400 list with Maasai herdsmen in East Africa.[44]

Now money does motivate people, as we will discover in Chapter 6. But what motivates us is not necessarily the same as what makes us happy. A recent poll by UCLA and the American Council on Education found that entering freshmen rated becoming "very well off financially" first on a list of 19 goals, ahead of choices such as helping others, raising a family, or becoming proficient in an academic pursuit. Maybe your goal isn't to be happy. But if it is, money's probably not going to do much to get you there.[45]

Job satisfaction is not just about job conditions. Personality also plays a role. For example, some people are predisposed to like almost anything, and others are unhappy even in the seemingly greatest jobs. Research has shown that people who have a negative personality (for example, those who tend to be grumpy, critical, and negative) are usually less satisfied with their jobs. See Exhibit 3-4. The Neutral Objects Satisfaction Questionnaire is a measure for

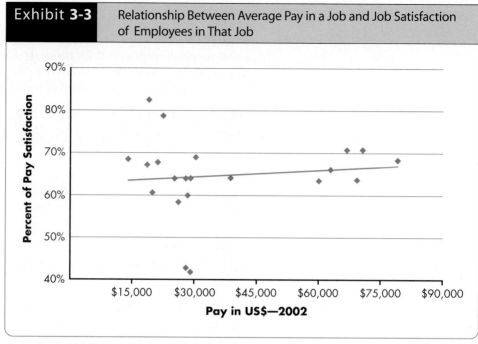

Exhibit 3-3 — Relationship Between Average Pay in a Job and Job Satisfaction of Employees in That Job

Source: T. A. Judge, R. F. Piccolo, N. P. Podsakoff, J. C. Shaw, and B. L. Rich, "Can Happiness Be "Earned"?: The Relationship between Pay and Job Satisfaction," working paper, University of Florida, 2005.

understanding the link between personality and job satisfaction. For example, one study showed that nurses who were dissatisfied with the majority of the items on the list were also dissatisfied with their jobs. This isn't surprising—after all, if someone dislikes his first name, his telephone service, and even 8 ½″ × 11″ paper, you'd expect him to dislike most things in his life—including his job.

Exhibit 3-4 — Neutral Objects Satisfaction Questionnaire

Instructions: Circle whether you are on average satisfied, neutral, or dissatisfied with each item below.

The city in which you live	Satisfied	Neutral	Dissatisfied
The neighbors you have	Satisfied	Neutral	Dissatisfied
The high school you attended	Satisfied	Neutral	Dissatisfied
The climate where you live	Satisfied	Neutral	Dissatisfied
Movies being produced today	Satisfied	Neutral	Dissatisfied
The quality of food you buy	Satisfied	Neutral	Dissatisfied
Today's cars	Satisfied	Neutral	Dissatisfied
Local newspapers	Satisfied	Neutral	Dissatisfied
Your first name	Satisfied	Neutral	Dissatisfied
The people you know	Satisfied	Neutral	Dissatisfied
Telephone service	Satisfied	Neutral	Dissatisfied
8 ½″ × 11″ paper	Satisfied	Neutral	Dissatisfied
Restaurant food	Satisfied	Neutral	Dissatisfied
Modern art	Satisfied	Neutral	Dissatisfied

Source: T. A. Judge and C. L. Hulin, "Job Satisfaction as a Reflection of Disposition: A Multiple-Source Causal Analysis," *Organizational Behavior and Human Decision Processes,* 1993, vol. 56, pp. 388–421.

"Happy Workers Are Productive Workers"

This statement is generally true. The idea that "happy workers are productive workers" developed in the 1930s and 1940s, largely as a result of findings drawn by researchers conducting the Hawthorne studies at Western Electric. Based on those conclusions, managers worked to make their employees happier by focusing on working conditions and the work environment. Then, in the 1980s, an influential review of the research suggested that the relationship between job satisfaction and job performance was not particularly high. The authors of this review even went so far as to label the relationship as "illusory."[46]

More recently, a review of more than 300 studies corrected some errors in this earlier review. It estimated that the correlation between job satisfaction and job performance is moderately strong. This con-clusion also appears to be generalizable across international contexts. The correlation is higher for complex jobs that provide employees with more discretion to act on their attitudes.[47]

It's important to recognize that the reverse causality might be true—productive workers are likely to be happy workers, or productivity leads to satisfaction.[48] In other words, if you do a good job, you intrinsically feel good about it. In addition, your higher productivity should increase your recognition, your pay level, and your probabilities for promotion. Cumulatively, these rewards, in turn, increase your level of satisfaction with the job.

It's probably the case that both arguments are right: That satisfaction can lead to high levels of performance for some people, while for others, high performance may cause them to be satisfied. ■

The Impact of Dissatisfied and Satisfied Employees on the Workplace

There are consequences when employees like their jobs, and there are consequences when employees dislike their jobs. One theoretical framework—the exit-voice-loyalty-neglect framework—is helpful in understanding the consequences of dissatisfaction. Exhibit 3-5 illustrates the framework's four responses, which differ from one another along two dimensions: constructive/destructive and active/passive. The responses are defined as follows:[49]

- **Exit:** Behavior directed toward leaving the organization, including looking for a new position as well as resigning.
- **Voice:** Actively and constructively attempting to improve conditions, including suggesting improvements, discussing problems with superiors, and some forms of union activity.
- **Loyalty:** Passively but optimistically waiting for conditions to improve, including speaking up for the organization in the face of external criticism and trusting the organization and its management to "do the right thing."
- **Neglect:** Passively allowing conditions to worsen, including chronic absenteeism or lateness, reduced effort, and increased error rate.

Exit and neglect behaviors encompass our performance variables—productivity, absenteeism, and turnover. But this model expands employee response to include voice and loyalty—constructive behaviors that allow individuals to tolerate unpleasant situations or to revive satisfactory working conditions. It helps

exit *Dissatisfaction expressed through behavior directed toward leaving the organization.*

voice *Dissatisfaction expressed through active and constructive attempts to improve conditions.*

loyalty *Dissatisfaction expressed by passively waiting for conditions to improve.*

neglect *Dissatisfaction expressed through allowing conditions to worsen.*

Exhibit **3-5**	Responses to Job Dissatisfaction

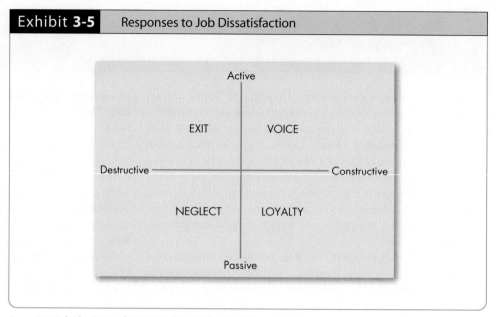

us to understand situations, such as those sometimes found among unionized workers, for whom low job satisfaction is coupled with low turnover.[50] Union members often express dissatisfaction through the grievance procedure or through formal contract negotiations. These voice mechanisms allow union members to continue in their jobs while convincing themselves that they are acting to improve the situation.

As helpful as this framework is in presenting the possible consequences of job dissatisfaction, it's quite general. We now discuss more specific outcomes of job satisfaction and dissatisfaction in the workplace.

Job Satisfaction and Job Performance   As the "Myth or Science?" box concludes, happy workers are more likely to be productive workers, although it's hard to tell which way the causality runs. However, some researchers used to believe that the relationship between job satisfaction and job performance was a management myth. But a review of 300 studies suggested that the correlation is pretty strong.[51] As we move from the individual level to that of the organization, we also find support for the satisfaction–performance relationship.[52] When satisfaction and productivity data are gathered for the organization as a whole, we find that organizations with more satisfied employees tend to be more effective than organizations with fewer satisfied employees.

Job Satisfaction and OCB   It seems logical to assume that job satisfaction should be a major determinant of an employee's organizational citizenship behavior (OCB).[53] Satisfied employees would seem more likely to talk positively about the organization, help others, and go beyond the normal expectations in their job. Moreover, satisfied employees might be more prone to go beyond the call of duty because they want to reciprocate their positive experiences. Consistent with this thinking, early discussions of OCB assumed that it was closely linked with satisfaction.[54] More recent evidence, however, suggests that satisfaction influences OCB, but through perceptions of fairness.

There is a modest overall relationship between job satisfaction and OCB.[55] But satisfaction is unrelated to OCB when fairness is controlled for.[56] What does this mean? Basically, job satisfaction comes down to conceptions of fair outcomes, treatment, and procedures.[57] If you don't feel that your supervisor, the organization's procedures, or pay policies are fair, your job satisfaction is likely to suffer significantly. However, when you perceive organizational processes and outcomes to be fair, trust is developed. And when you trust your employer, you're more willing to voluntarily engage in behaviors that go beyond your formal job requirements.

Job Satisfaction and Customer Satisfaction As we noted in Chapter 1, employees in service jobs often interact with customers. Since the management of service organizations should be concerned with pleasing those customers, it is reasonable to ask: Is employee satisfaction related to positive customer outcomes? For frontline employees who have regular contact with customers, the answer is "Yes."

The evidence indicates that satisfied employees increase customer satisfaction and loyalty.[58] Why? In service organizations, customer retention and defection are highly dependent on how frontline employees deal with customers. Satisfied employees are more likely to be friendly, upbeat, and responsive—which customers appreciate. And because satisfied employees are less prone to turnover, customers are more likely to encounter familiar faces and receive experienced service. These qualities build customer satisfaction and loyalty. In addition, the relationship seems to apply in reverse: Dissatisfied customers can increase an employee's job dissatisfaction. Employees who have regular contact with customers report that rude, thoughtless, or unreasonably demanding customers adversely affect the employees' job satisfaction.[59]

A number of companies are acting on this evidence. Service-oriented businesses such as FedEx, Southwest Airlines, Four Seasons Hotels, American Express, and Office Depot obsess about pleasing their customers. Toward that end, they also focus on building employee satisfaction—recognizing that employee satisfaction will go a long way toward contributing to their goal of having happy customers. These firms seek to hire upbeat and friendly employees, they train employees in the importance of customer service, they reward customer service, they provide positive employee work climates, and they regularly track employee satisfaction through attitude surveys.

Job Satisfaction and Absenteeism We find a consistent negative relationship between satisfaction and absenteeism, but the correlation is moderate to weak.[60] While it certainly makes sense that dissatisfied employees are more likely to miss work, other factors have an impact on the relationship and reduce the correlation coefficient. For example, organizations that provide liberal sick leave benefits are encouraging all their employees—including those who are highly satisfied—to take days off. Assuming that you have a reasonable number of varied interests, you can find work satisfying and yet still take off work to enjoy a 3-day weekend or tan yourself on a warm summer day if those days come free with no penalties.

An excellent illustration of how satisfaction directly leads to attendance, when there is a minimum impact from other factors, is a study done at Sears, Roebuck.[61] Satisfaction data were available on employees at Sears' two headquarters in Chicago and New York. In addition, it is important to note that Sears' policy was not to permit employees to be absent from work for avoidable reasons without penalty. The occurrence of a freak April 2 snowstorm in Chicago created the opportunity to compare employee attendance at the Chicago office with attendance in New York, where the weather was quite nice. The interesting dimension in this study is that the snowstorm gave the Chicago employees a built-in excuse not to come to work. The storm crippled the city's transportation, and individuals knew they could miss work this day with no penalty. This natural experiment permitted the comparison of

Service organizations know that satisfied and loyal customers depend on how front-line employees deal with customers. Singapore Airlines has earned a reputation among world travelers for outstanding customer service. The airline's "putting people first" philosophy applies to both its employees and customers. In recruiting flight attendants, the airline selects people who are warm, hospitable, and happy to serve others. Through extensive training, Singapore molds recruits into attendants focused on complete customer satisfaction.

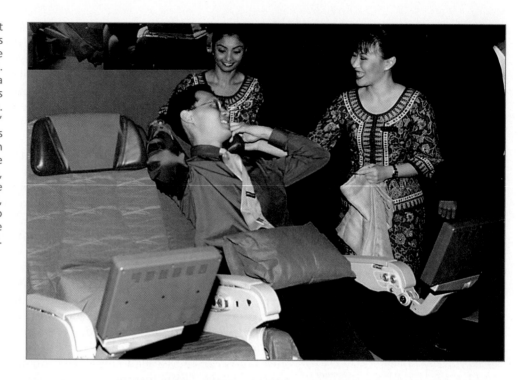

attendance records for satisfied and dissatisfied employees at two locations—one where you were expected to be at work (with normal pressures for attendance) and the other where you were free to choose with no penalty involved. If satisfaction leads to attendance, when there is an absence of outside factors, the more satisfied employees should have come to work in Chicago, while dissatisfied employees should have stayed home. The study found that on this particular April 2, absenteeism rates in New York were just as high for satisfied groups of workers as for dissatisfied groups. But in Chicago, the workers with high satisfaction scores had much higher attendance than did those with lower satisfaction levels. These findings are exactly what we would have expected if satisfaction is negatively correlated with absenteeism.

Job Satisfaction and Turnover   Satisfaction is also negatively related to turnover, but the correlation is stronger than what we found for absenteeism.[62] Yet, again, other factors such as labor-market conditions, expectations about alternative job opportunities, and length of tenure with the organization are important constraints on the actual decision to leave one's current job.[63]

Evidence indicates that an important moderator of the satisfaction-turnover relationship is the employee's level of performance.[64] Specifically, level of satisfaction is less important in predicting turnover for superior performers. Why? The organization typically makes considerable efforts to keep these people. They get pay raises, praise, recognition, increased promotional opportunities, and so forth. Just the opposite tends to apply to poor performers. Few attempts are made by the organization to retain them. There may even be subtle pressures to encourage them to quit. We would expect, therefore, that job satisfaction is more important in influencing poor performers to stay than superior performers. Regardless of level of satisfaction, the latter are more likely to remain with the organization because the receipt of recognition, praise, and other rewards gives them more reasons for staying.

Job Satisfaction and Workplace Deviance   Job dissatisfaction predicts a lot of specific behaviors, including unionization attempts, substance abuse, stealing at work, undue socializing, and tardiness. Researchers argue that these behaviors are indicators of a broader syndrome that we would term deviant behavior in the workplace (or employee withdrawal).[65] The key is that if employees don't like their work environment, they'll respond somehow. It is not always easy to forecast exactly *how* they'll respond. One worker's response might be to quit. But another may respond by taking work time to surf the Internet, taking work supplies home for personal use, and so on. If employers want to control the undesirable consequences of job dissatisfaction, they had best attack the source of the problem—the dissatisfaction—rather than trying to control the different responses.

Summary and Implications for Managers

Managers should be interested in their employees' attitudes because attitudes give warnings of potential problems and because they influence behavior. Satisfied and committed employees, for instance, have lower rates of turnover, absenteeism, and withdrawal behaviors. They also perform better on the job. Given that managers want to keep resignations and absences down—especially among their more productive employees—they will want to do the things that will generate positive job attitudes.

The most important thing managers can do to raise employee satisfaction is to focus on the intrinsic parts of the job, such as making the work challenging and interesting. Although paying employees poorly will likely not attract high-quality employees to the organization, or keep high performers, managers should realize that high pay alone is unlikely to create a satisfying work environment. Managers should also be aware that employees will try to reduce cognitive dissonance. More important, dissonance can be managed. If employees are required to engage in activities that appear inconsistent to them or that are at odds with their attitudes, the pressures to reduce the resulting dissonance are lessened when employees perceive that the dissonance is externally imposed and is beyond their control or if the rewards are significant enough to offset the dissonance.

Managers Can Create Satisfied Employees

A review of the evidence has identified four factors conducive to high levels of employee job satisfaction: mentally challenging work, equitable rewards, supportive working conditions, and supportive colleagues.[66] Importantly, each of these factors is controllable by management.

Mentally challenging work. Generally, people prefer jobs that give them opportunities to use their skills and abilities and offer a variety of tasks, freedom, and feedback on how well they're doing. These characteristics make work mentally challenging.

Equitable rewards. Employees want pay systems that they perceive as being just, unambiguous, and in line with their expectations. When pay is seen as fair, based on job demands, individual skill level, and community pay standards, satisfaction is likely to result.

Supportive working conditions. Employees are concerned with their work environment for both personal comfort and facilitating doing a good job. Studies demonstrate that employees prefer physical surroundings that are not dangerous or uncomfortable. In addition, most employees prefer working relatively close to home, in.clean and relatively modern facilities, and with adequate tools and equipment.

Supportive colleagues. People get more out of work than merely money or tangible achievements. For most employees, work also fulfills the need for social interaction. Not surprisingly, therefore, having friendly and supportive coworkers leads to increased job satisfaction. The behavior of one's boss is also a major determinant of satisfaction. Studies find that employee satisfaction is increased when the immediate supervisor is understanding and friendly, offers praise for good performance, listens to employees' opinions, and shows a personal interest in them.

The notion that managers and organizations can control the level of employee job satisfaction is inherently attractive. It fits nicely with the view that managers directly influence organizational processes and outcomes. Unfortunately, there is a growing body of evidence that challenges the notion that managers control the factors that influence employee job satisfaction. The most recent findings indicate that employee job satisfaction is largely genetically determined.[67]

Whether a person is happy or not is essentially determined by gene structure. Approximately 50–80 percent of people's differences in happiness, or subjective well-being, has been found to be attributable to their genes. Identical twins, for example, tend to have very similar careers, have similar levels of job satisfaction, and change jobs at similar rates.

Analysis of satisfaction data for a selected sample of individuals over a 50-year period found that individual results were consistently stable over time, even when these people changed employers and occupations. This and other research suggests that an individual's disposition toward life—positive or negative—is established by genetic makeup, holds over time, and carries over into a disposition toward work.

Given these findings, there is probably little that most managers can do to influence employee satisfaction. In spite of the fact that managers and organizations go to extensive lengths to try to improve employee job satisfaction through actions such as manipulating job characteristics, working conditions, and rewards, people will inevitably return to their own "set point." A bonus may temporarily increase the satisfaction level of a negatively disposed worker, but it is unlikely to sustain it. Sooner or later, new areas of fault will be found with the job.

The only place where managers will have any significant influence will be through their control of the selection process. If managers want satisfied workers, they need to make sure their selection process screens out negative people who derive little satisfaction from their jobs, irrespective of its conditions.

Questions for Review

1. Contrast the cognitive and affective components of an attitude.

2. What is cognitive dissonance and how is it related to attitudes?

3. What is self-perception theory? How does it increase our ability to predict behavior?

4. What moderating factors can improve the statistical relationship between attitudes and behavior?

5. How can managers get employees to more readily accept working with colleagues who are different than themselves?

6. What explains the recent declines in employee job satisfaction?

7. Do you think job satisfaction means the same thing in all countries? Why or why not?

8. Are happy workers productive workers?

9. Contrast exit, voice, loyalty, and neglect as employee responses to job dissatisfaction.

10. What is the relationship between job satisfaction and absenteeism? Turnover? Which is the stronger relationship?

Questions for Critical Thinking

1. "Managers should do everything they can to enhance the job satisfaction of their employees." Do you agree or disagree? Support your position.

2. Discuss the advantages and disadvantages of using regular attitude surveys to monitor employee job satisfaction.

3. "It doesn't matter how employees say they feel about their employers. What really matters in terms of behavior is whether they have better options out there." Is there any evidence to support or refute this statement?

4. When employees are asked whether they would again choose the same work or whether they would want their children to follow in their footsteps, typically less than half answer in the affirmative. What, if anything, do you think this implies about employee job satisfaction?

5. George Loewenstein, an economist at Carnegie-Mellon University, recently said, "I think it's possible to way overestimate the importance of happiness. Part of the meaning of life is to have highs and lows. A life that was constantly happy was not a good life." Do you agree or disagree with Professor Loewenstein?

Team Exercise

SELF-EMPLOYMENT AND JOB SATISFACTION

Examine the following data, which were taken from a survey of self-employed individuals and regularly employed individuals. (Note: Scores represent average job-satisfaction levels in each country, as rated on a 1 = very dissatisfied to 10 = very satisfied scale):

Nation/Region	Average Job Satisfaction	
	Self-Employed	*Regularly Employed*
Russia	4.95	4.84
Hungary	5.05	4.77
Japan	5.17	4.74
Poland	5.20	5.08
Great Britain	5.40	5.08
Canada	5.44	5.06
Italy	5.45	5.06
France	5.50	5.06
Germany	5.52	5.12
USA	5.63	5.32
Czech Republic	5.63	5.06
Sweden	5.70	5.20
The Philippines	5.71	5.51
Israel (Arabs)	5.72	5.36
Denmark	5.84	5.68
Switzerland	5.87	5.43
Israel (Jews)	5.91	5.24
Cyprus	6.08	5.50

Now gather in teams of 3–4 people and answer the following questions:

1. Can you draw any conclusions about the effect of self-employment on job satisfaction?
2. Do the effects (or noneffects) of self-employment appear to generalize across countries?
3. How might you explain the results for self-employment?
4. Do job-satisfaction levels vary much across countries? Across regions? Are there nations/regions that appear to be particularly happy with their jobs?
5. How might you explain national/regional differences in job satisfaction?

Source of Data: M. Benz and B. S. Frey, "The Value of Autonomy: Evidence from the Self-Employed in 23 Countries," Institute for Empirical Research in Economics, University of Zurich, Working Paper No. 173, November 2003 (http://ssrn.com/abstract= 475140).

Ethical Dilemma

ARE AMERICANS OVERWORKED?

Europeans pride themselves on their quality of life, and rightly so. In a recent worldwide analysis of quality of life, the United States ranked 13th. The 12 nations that finished ahead of the United States were all from Europe. Factors considered in the analysis were material well-being, health, political stability, divorce rates, job security, political freedom, and gender equality, among other factors.

Many Europeans would credit their high quality of life to their nations' free health care, more generous unemployment benefits, and greater emphasis on leisure as opposed to work. Consider that most European nations mandate restricted workweek hours and a month or more of vacation time, but Americans have among the fewest vacation days and longest average workweek in the world. Juliet Schor, a Harvard economist who has written on the subject, argues that the United States "is the world's standout workaholic nation," and that U.S. workers are trapped in a "squirrel cage" of overwork. Some argue that mandated leisure time would force companies to compete within their industry by raising productivity and product quality rather than by requiring workers to put in more hours.

Many European nations also place limits on the hours employers can require employees to work. France, Germany, and other nations limit the workweek to 35 hours. Recently, after much debate, the French parliament voted to do away with the rule that set 35 hours as the maximum workweek. The justification was that more flexible rules would allow French companies to compete more effectively so that, if business required it, they could pay employees for longer hours. Opponents of the new rules argue that it puts the decision of how much to work in the individual's hands. These people argue that it will inevitably detract from quality of life and give employers power to exploit workers. A French union leader said, "They say it's the worker who will choose how much to work, but they're lying because it's always the employer who decides."

Questions

1. Why do you think quality of life is lower in the United States compared to many European nations? Do you think quality of life in the United States would increase if the government required a minimum number of vacation days or limited workweek hours?

2. Do you think the French parliament was right to eliminate the 35-hour workweek limit? Do you think the quality of French life will suffer?

3. Do you think employers have an obligation to watch out for the quality of life of their employees? Could that translate into protecting employees from being overworked?

4. Does it make a difference that the unemployment rate in Europe is roughly double that of the United States and that Europe's gross domestic product (GDP) is about half that of the United States?

Sources: Juliet Schor, *The Overworked American: The Unexpected Decline of Leisure* (New York: Basic Books, 1992). C. S. Smith, "Effort to Extend Workweek Advances in France," *New York Times*, February 10, 2005, p. A9; "The Economist Intelligence Unit's Quality-of-Life Index," *The Economist*, 2005 (http://www.economist.com/media/pdf/QUALITY_OF_LIFE.pdf); E. Olsen, "The Vacation Deficit," *Budget Travel*, October 29, 2004 (http://www.msnbc.msn.com/id/6345416/).

Case Incident 1

ALBERTSONS WORKS ON EMPLOYEE ATTITUDES

Albertsons is a huge grocery and drug company. It has more than 2,400 supermarkets, and its Osco and Sav-on brands make it the fifth-largest drugstore company in the United States. In a typical year, shoppers will make 1.4 billion trips through its stores.

Albertsons competes in tough businesses. Wal-Mart, in particular, has been eating away at its market share. With revenues flat and profits falling, the company hired Larry Johnston to turn the business around.

Johnston came to Albertsons from General Electric. And it was while he was at GE that Johnston met a training specialist named Ed Foreman. Foreman endeared himself to Johnston when the latter hired Foreman to help him with a serious problem. At the time, Johnston had been sent to Paris to fix GE Medical Systems' European division. The division made CT scanners. Over the previous decade, four executives had been brought in to turn the division around and try to make it profitable. All had failed. Johnston responded to the challenge by initiating some important changes—he made a number of acquisitions, he closed down inefficient plants, and he moved factories to Eastern European countries to take advantage of lower labor costs. Then he brought in Ed Foreman to charge up the troops. "After we got Ed in," says Johnston, "people began to live their lives differently. They came to work with a spring in their step." In 3 years, the division was bringing in annual profits of $100 million. Johnston gives a large part of the credit for this turnaround to Foreman.

What is Foreman's secret? He provides motivation and attitude training. Here's an example of Foreman's primary program—called the Successful Life Course. It lasts 3 days and begins each morning at 6 A.M. The first day begins with a chapter from an inspirational handout, followed by 12 minutes of yoga-like stretching. Then participants march up a hill, chanting, "I know I can, I know I can." This is followed by breakfast and then a variety of lectures on attitude, diet, and exercise. But the primary focus of the program is on attitude. Says Foreman, "It's your attitude, not your aptitude, that determines your altitude." Other parts of the program include group hugs, team activities, and mind-control relaxation exercises.

Johnston believes strongly in Foreman's program. "Positive attitude is the single biggest thing that can change a business," says Johnston. He sees Foreman's program as being a critical bridge linking employees with customers: "We're in the business of the maintenance and acquisition of customers." And with so many shoppers going through his stores, Johnston says this "provides a lot of opportunities for customer service. We've got to energize the associates." To prove he's willing to put his money where his mouth is, Johnston has committed $10 million to this training. By year-end 2004, 10,000 managers had taken the course. They, in turn, are training all 190,000 Albertsons "associates," with the help of tapes and books.

Foreman claims his program works. He cites success at companies like Allstate, Milliken & Co., and Abbott Labs. "The goal is to improve mental, physical, and emotional well-being," he says. "We as individuals determine the success of our own lives. Positive thoughts create positive actions."

Questions

1. Explain the logic as to how Foreman's 3-day course could positively influence Albertsons' profitability.

2. Johnston says, "Positive attitude is the single biggest thing that can change a business." How valid and generalizable do you think this statement is?

3. If you were Johnston, what could you do to evaluate the effectiveness of your $10-million investment in Foreman's training program?

4. If you were an Albertsons' employee, how would you feel about going through Foreman's course? Explain your position.

Source: Based on M. Burke, "The Guru in the Vegetable Bin," *Forbes*, March 3, 2003, pp. 56–58.

Case Incident 2

LONG HOURS, HUNDREDS OF E-MAILS, AND NO SLEEP: DOES THIS SOUND LIKE A SATISFYING JOB?

Although the 40-hour workweek is now the exception rather than the norm, some individuals are taking things to the extreme.

- John Bishop, 31, is an investment banker who works for Citigroup's global energy team in New York. A recent workday for Bishop consisted of heading to the office for a conference call at 6:00 P.M. He left the office at 1:30 A.M. and had to be on a plane that same morning for a 9:00 A.M. presentation in Houston. Following the presentation, Bishop returned to New York the same day, and by 7:00 P.M., he was back in his office to work an additional three hours. Says Bishop, "I might be a little skewed to the workaholic, but realistically, expecting 90 to 100 hours a week is not at all unusual."

- Irene Tse, 34, heads the government bond-trading division at Goldman Sachs. For ten years, she has seen the stock market go from all-time highs to recession levels. Such fluctuations can mean millions of dollars in either profits or losses. "There are days when you can make a lot, and other days where you lose so much you're just stunned by what you've done," says Tse. She also states that she hasn't slept completely through the night in years and frequently wakes up several times during the night to check the global market status. Her average workweek? Eighty hours. "I've done this for 10 years, and I can count on the fingers of one hand the number of days in my career when I didn't want to come to work. Every day I wake up and I can't wait to get here."

- Tony Kurtz, 33, is a managing director at Capital Alliance Partners and raises funds for real-estate investments. However, these are not your average properties. He often travels to exotic locations like Costa Rica and Hawaii, wooing prospective clients. He travels more than 300,000 miles a year, often sleeping on planes and dealing with jet lag. Kurtz is not the only one he knows with such a hectic work schedule. His girlfriend, Avery Baker, logs around 400,000 miles a year, working as the senior vice president of marketing for Tommy Hilfiger. "It's not easy to maintain a relationship like this," says Kurz. But do Kurz and Baker like their jobs? You bet.

- David Clark, 35, is the vice president of global marketing for MTV. His job often consists of traveling around the globe to promote the channel, as well as to keep up with the global music scene. If he is not traveling (Clark typically logs 200,000 miles a year), a typical day consists of waking at 6:30 A.M. and immediately responding to numerous messages that have accumulated over the course of the night. He then goes to his office, where throughout the day he will respond to another 500 messages or so from clients around the world. If he's lucky, he gets to spend an hour a day with his son, but then it's back to work until he finally goes to bed around midnight. Says Clark, "there are plenty of people who would love to have this job. They're knocking on the door all the time. So that's motivating."

Many individuals would balk at the prospect of a 60-hour or more workweek with constant traveling and little time for anything else. However, some individuals are exhilarated by such professions. According to the Bureau of Labor Statistics, in 2004, about 17 percent of managers worked more than 60 hours per week. But the demands of such jobs are clearly not for everyone. Many quit, with turnover levels at 55 percent for consultants and 30 percent for investment bankers, according to Vault.com. However, it is clear that such jobs, which are time consuming and often stressful, can be satisfying to some individuals.

Questions

1. Do you think that only certain individuals are attracted to these types of jobs, or is it the characteristics of the jobs themselves that are satisfying?

2. What are some characteristics of these jobs that might contribute to greater levels of job satisfaction?

3. Given that the four individuals we just read about tend to be satisfied with their jobs, how might this satisfaction relate to their job performance, citizenship behavior, and turnover?

4. Recall David Clark's statement, "there are plenty of people who would love to have this job. They're knocking on the door all the time." How might Clark's perceptions of having a job that many others desire contribute to his job satisfaction?

Source: Based on L. Tischler, "Extreme Jobs (And the People Who Love Them)," *Fast Company,* April 2005, pp. 55–60. http://www.glo-jobs.com/article.php?article_no=87.

Endnotes

1. Based on E. Leuchars, S. Harrington, and C. Erickson, "Putting People First: How VSP Achieves High Employee Satisfaction Year After Year," *Journal of Organizational Excellence*, Spring 2003, pp. 33–41.

2. S. J. Breckler, "Empirical Validation of Affect, Behavior, and Cognition as Distinct Components of Attitude," *Journal of Personality and Social Psychology*, May 1984, pp. 1191–1205; and S. L. Crites, Jr., L. R. Fabrigar, and R. E. Petty, "Measuring the Affective and Cognitive Properties of Attitudes: Conceptual and Methodological Issues," *Personality and Social Psychology Bulletin*, December 1994, pp. 619–34.

3. See, for instance, I. R. Newby-Clark, I. McGregor, and M. P. Zanna, "Thinking and Caring About Cognitive Consistency: When and for Whom Does Attitudinal Ambivalence Feel Uncomfortable?" *Journal of Personality & Social Psychology*, February 2002, pp. 157–66; and D. J. Schleicher, J. D. Watt, and G. J. Greguras, "Reexamining the Job Satisfaction-Performance Relationship: The Complexity of Attitudes," *Journal of Applied Psychology* 89. no. 1 (2004), pp. 165–77.

4. See, for instance, M. Geyelin, "Tobacco Executive Has Doubts About Health Risks of Cigarettes," *Wall Street Journal*, March 3, 1998, p. B10; and J. A. Byrne, 'Philip Morris: Inside America's Most Reviled Company,' *U.S. News & World Report*, November 29, 1999, pp. 176–92.

5. L. Festinger, *A Theory of Cognitive Dissonance* (Stanford, CA: Stanford University Press, 1957).

6. A. W. Wicker, "Attitude versus Action: The Relationship of Verbal and Overt Behavioral Responses to Attitude Objects," *Journal of Social Issues*, Autumn 1969, pp. 41–78.

7. Ibid., p. 65.

8. See S. J. Kraus, "Attitudes and the Prediction of Behavior: A Meta-Analysis of the Empirical Literature," *Personality and Social Psychology Bulletin*, January 1995, pp. 58–75; I. Ajzen, "The Directive Influence of Attitudes on Behavior," in M. Gollwitzer and J. A. Bargh (eds.), *The Psychology of Action: Linking Cognition and Motivation to Behavior* (New York: Guilford, 1996), pp. 385–403; S. Sutton, "Predicting and Explaining Intentions and Behavior: How Well Are We Doing?" *Journal of Applied Social Psychology*, August 1998, pp. 1317–38; and I. Ajzen, "Nature and Operation of Attitudes," in S. T. Fiske, D. L. Schacter, and C. Zahn-Waxler (eds.), *Annual Review of Psychology*, vol. 52 (Palo Alto, CA: Annual Reviews, Inc., 2001), pp. 27–58.

9. Ibid.

10. D. J. Bem, "Self-Perception Theory," in L. Berkowitz (ed.), *Advances in Experimental Social Psychology*, vol. 6 (New York: Academic Press, 1972), pp. 1–62.

11. See C. A. Kiesler, R. E. Nisbett, and M. Zanna, "On Inferring One's Belief from One's Behavior," *Journal of Personality and Social Psychology*, April 1969, pp. 321–27; S. E. Taylor, "On Inferring One's Attitudes from One's Behavior: Some Delimiting Conditions," *Journal of Personality and Social Psychology*, January 1975, pp. 126–31; and A. M. Tybout and C. A. Scott, "Availability of Well-Defined Internal Knowledge and the Attitude Formation Process: Information

Aggregation Versus Self-Perception," *Journal of Personality and Social Psychology*, March 1983, pp. 474–91.

12. P. P. Brooke Jr., D. W. Russell, and J. L. Price, "Discriminant Validation of Measures of Job Satisfaction, Job Involvement, and Organizational Commitment," *Journal of Applied Psychology*, May 1988, pp. 139–45; and R. T. Keller, "Job Involvement and Organizational Commitment as Longitudinal Predictors of Job Performance: A Study of Scientists and Engineers," *Journal of Applied Psychology*, August 1997, pp. 539–45.

13. See, for example, S. Rabinowitz and D. T. Hall, "Organizational Research in Job Involvement," *Psychological Bulletin*, March 1977, pp. 265–88; G. J. Blau, "A Multiple Study Investigation of the Dimensionality of Job Involvement," *Journal of Vocational Behavior*, August 1985, pp. 19–36; N. A. Jans, "Organizational Factors and Work Involvement," *Organizational Behavior and Human Decision Processes*, June 1985, pp. 382–96; and I. M. Paullay, G. M. Alliger, and E. F. Stone-Romero, "Construct Validation of Two Instruments Designed to Measure Job Involvement and Work Centrality," *Journal of Applied Psychology* 79, no. 2 (1994), pp. 224–28.

14. Based on G. J. Blau and K. R. Boal, "Conceptualizing How Job Involvement and Organizational Commitment Affect Turnover and Absenteeism," *Academy of Management Review*, April 1987, p. 290.

15. K. W. Thomas and B. A. Velthouse, "Cognitive Elements of Empowerment: An 'Interpretive' Model of Intrinsic Task Motivation," *Academy of Management Review* 15, no. 4 (1990), pp. 666–81; G. M. Spreitzer, "Psychological Empowerment in the Workplace: Dimensions, Measurement, and Validation," *Academy of Management Journal* 38, no. 5 (1995), pp. 1442–65; G. Chen and R. J. Klimoski, "The Impact of Expectations on Newcomer Performance in Teams as Mediated by Work Characteristics, Social Exchanges, and Empowerment," *Academy of Management Journal* 46, no. 5 (2003), pp. 591–607; R. C. Liden, S. J. Wayne, and R. T. Sparrowe, "An Examination of the Mediating Role of Psychological Empowerment on the Relations between the Job, Interpersonal Relationships, and Work Outcomes," *Journal of Applied Psychology* 85, no. 3 (2000), pp. 407–16; and S. E. Seibert, S. R. Silver, and W. A. Randolph, "Taking Empowerment to the Next Level: A Multiple-Level Model of Empowerment, Performance, and Satisfaction," *Academy of Management Journal* 47, no. 3 (2004), pp. 332–49.

16. B. J. Avolio, W. Zhu, W. Koh, and P. Bhatia, "Transformational Leadership and Organizational Commitment: Mediating Role of Psychological Empowerment and Moderating Role of Structural Distance," *Journal of Organizational Behavior*, vol. 25(8), 2004, pp. 951–968.

17. J. M. Diefendorff, D. J. Brown, A. M. Kamin, and R. G. Lord, "Examining the Roles of Job Involvement and Work Centrality in Predicting Organizational Citizenship Behaviors and Job Performance," *Journal of Organizational Behavior*, February 2002, pp. 93–108.

18. G. J. Blau, "Job Involvement and Organizational Commitment as Interactive Predictors of Tardiness and Absenteeism," *Journal of Management*, Winter 1986, pp. 577–84; K. Boal and R. Cidambi, "Attitudinal Correlates of Turnover and Absenteeism: A Meta

Analysis," paper presented at the meeting of the American Psychological Association, Toronto, Canada, 1984; and M. R. Barrick, M. K. Mount, and J. P. Strauss, "Antecedents of Involuntary Turnover Due to A Reduction in Force," *Personnel Psychology* 47, no. 3 (1994), pp. 515–35.

19. Blau and Boal, "Conceptualizing," p. 290.

20. J. P. Meyer, N. J. Allen, and C. A. Smith, "Commitment to Organizations and Occupations: Extension and Test of a Three-Component Conceptualization," *Journal of Applied Psychology* 78, no. 4 (1993), pp. 538–51.

21. M. Riketta, "Attitudinal Organizational Commitment and Job Performance: A Meta-Analysis," *Journal of Organizational Behavior*, March 2002, pp. 257–66.

22. See, for instance, W. Hom, R. Katerberg, and C. L. Hulin, "Comparative Examination of Three Approaches to the Prediction of Turnover," *Journal of Applied Psychology*, June 1979, pp. 280–90; H. Angle and J. Perry, "Organizational Commitment: Individual and Organizational Influence," *Work and Occupations*, May 1983, pp. 123–46; J. L. Pierce and R. B. Dunham, "Organizational Commitment: Pre-Employment Propensity and Initial Work Experiences," *Journal of Management*, Spring 1987, pp. 163–78; and T. Simons and Q. Roberson, "Why Managers Should Care About Fairness: The Effects of Aggregate Justice Perceptions on Organizational Outcomes," *Journal of Applied Psychology* 88, no. 3 (2003), pp. 432–43.

23. R. B. Dunham, J. A. Grube, and M. B. Castañeda, "Organizational Commitment: The Utility of an Integrative Definition," *Journal of Applied Psychology* 79, no. 3(1994), pp. 370–80.

24. D. M. Rousseau, "Organizational Behavior in the New Organizational Era," in J. T. Spence, J. M. Darley, and D. J. Foss (eds.), *Annual Review of Psychology*, vol. 48 (Palo Alto, CA: Annual Reviews, 1997), p. 523.

25. Ibid.; K. Lee, J. J. Carswell, and N. J. Allen, "A Meta-Analytic Review of Occupational Commitment: Relations with Person- and Work-Related Variables" *Journal of Applied Psychology*, October 2000, pp. 799–811; G. Blau, "On Assessing the Construct Validity of Two Multidimensional Constructs: Occupational Commitment and Occupational Entrenchment," *Human Resource Management Review*, Fall 2001, pp. 279–98; and E. Snape and T. Redman, "An Evaluation of a Three-Component Model of Occupational Commitment: Dimensionality and Consequences Among United Kingdom Human Resource Management Specialists," *Journal of Applied Psychology* 88, no. 1 (2003), pp. 152–59.

26. L. Rhoades, R. Eisenberger, and S. Armeli, "Affective Commitment to the Organization: The Contribution of Perceived Organizational Support," *Journal of Applied Psychology* 86, no. 5 (2001), pp. 825–36.

27. D. R. May, R. L. Gilson, and L. M. Harter, "The Psychological Conditions of Meaningfulness, Safety and Availability and the Engagement of the Human Spirit at Work," *Journal of Occupational and Organizational Psychology* 77, no. 1 (2004), pp. 11–37.

28. J. K. Harter, F. L. Schmidt, and T. L. Hayes, "Business-Unit-Level Relationship Between Employee Satisfaction, Employee Engagement, and Business Outcomes: A Meta-Analysis," *Journal of Applied Psychology* 87, no. 2 (2002), pp. 268–79.

29. L. Rhoades and R. Eisenberger, "Perceived Organizational Support: A Review of the Literature," *Journal of Applied Psychology* 87, no. 4 (2002), pp. 698–714; R. L. Payne and D. Morrison, "The Differential Effects of Negative Affectivity on Measures of Well-Being Versus Job Satisfaction and Organizational Commitment," *Anxiety, Stress & Coping: An International Journal* 15, no. 3 (2002), pp. 231–44.

30. See, for example, L. Simpson, "What's Going On in Your Company? If You Don't Ask, You'll Never Know," *Training*, June 2002, pp. 30–34.

31. J. Stack, "Measuring Morale," *INC.*, January 1997, pp. 29–30.

32. See L. Simpson, "What's Going On in Your Company?"

33. See Society for Human Resource Management, "Impact of Diversity on the Bottom Line," www.fortune.com/sections, August 31, 2001, pp. 5–12; M. Bendick, Jr., M. L. Egan, and S. M. Lofhjelm, "Workforce Diversity Training: From Anti-Discrimination Compliance to Organizational Development," *Human Resource Planning* 24, no. 2 (2001), pp. 10–25; and S. T. Brathwaite, "Denny's: A Diversity Success Story," *Franchising World*, July/August 2002, pp. 28–30.

34. This section is based on A. Rossett and T. Bickham, "Diversity Training: Hope, Faith and Cynicism," *Training*, January 1994, pp. 40–46.

35. T. L. Stewart, J. R. LaDuke, C. Bracht, B. A. M. Sweet, and K. E. Gamarel, "Do the 'Eyes' Have It? A Program Evaluation of Jane Elliott's 'Blue-Eyes/Brown-Eyes' Diversity Training Exercise," *Journal of Applied Social Psychology* 33, no. 9 (2003), pp. 1898–1921.

36. For problems with the concept of job satisfaction, see R. Hodson, "Workplace Behaviors," *Work and Occupations*, August 1991, pp. 271–90; and H. M. Weiss and R. Cropanzano, "Affective Events Theory: A Theoretical Discussion of the Structure, Causes and Consequences of Affective Experiences at Work," in B. M. Staw and L. L. Cummings (eds), *Research in Organizational Behavior*, vol. 18 (Greenwich, CT: JAI Press, 1996), pp. 1–3.

37. The Wyatt Company's 1989 national WorkAmerica study identified 12 dimensions of satisfaction: work organization, working conditions, communications, job performance and performance review, coworkers, supervision, company management, pay, benefits, career development and training, job content and satisfaction, and company image and change.

38. See E. Spector, *Job Satisfaction: Application, Assessment, Causes, and Consequences* (Thousand Oaks, CA: Sage, 1997), p. 3.

39. J. Wanous, A. E. Reichers, and M. J. Hudy, "Overall Job Satisfaction: How Good Are Single-Item Measures?" *Journal of Applied Psychology*, April 1997, pp. 247–52.

40. A. F. Chelte, J. Wright, and C. Tausky, "Did Job Satisfaction Really Drop During the 1970s?" *Monthly Labor Review*, November 1982, pp. 33–36; "Job Satisfaction High in America, Says Conference Board Study," *Monthly Labor Review*, February 1985, p. 52; E. Graham, "Work May Be a Rat Race, but It's Not a Daily Grind," *Wall Street Journal*, September 19, 1997, p. R1; and K. Bowman, "Attitudes About Work, Chores, and Leisure in America," *AEI Opinion Studies*; released August 25, 2003.

41. L. Grant, "Unhappy in Japan," *Fortune*, January 13, 1997, p. 142; "Survey Finds Satisfied Workers in Canada," *Manpower*

Argus, January 1997, p. 6; and T. Mudd, "Europeans Generally Happy in the Workplace," *Industry Week*, October 4, 1999, pp. 11–12.

42. W. K. Balzer, J. A. Kihm, P. C. Smith, J. L. Irwin, P. D. Bachiochi, C. Robie, E. F. Sinar, and L. F. Parra, *Users' Manual for the Job Descriptive Index* (JDI; 1997 Revision) and the *Job In General Scales* (Bowling Green, OH: Bowling Green State University, 1997).

43. J. Barling, E. K. Kelloway, and R. D. Iverson, "High-Quality Work, Job Satisfaction, and Occupational Injuries," *Journal of Applied Psychology* 88, no. 2 (2003), pp. 276–83; F. W. Bond and D. Bunce, "The Role of Acceptance and Job Control in Mental Health, Job Satisfaction, and Work Performance," *Journal of Applied Psychology* 88, no. 6 (2003), pp. 1057–67.

44. E. Diener, E. Sandvik, L. Seidlitz, and M. Diener, "The Relationship Between Income and Subjective Well-Being: Relative or Absolute?" *Social Indicators Research* 28 (1993), pp. 195–223.

45. E. Diener and M. E. P. Seligman, "Beyond Money: Toward an Economy of Well-Being" *Psychological Science in the Public Interest* 5, no. 1 (2004), pp. 1–31; A. Grant, "Money=Happiness? That's Rich: Here's the Science Behind the Axiom," *The Sun Herald*, January 8, 2005 (http://www.sunherald.com/mld/thesunherald/news/world/10595331.htm).

46. M. T. Iaffaldano and M. Muchinsky, "Job Satisfaction and Job Performance: A Meta-Analysis," *Psychological Bulletin*, March 1985, pp. 251–73.

47. T. A. Judge, C. J. Thoresen, J. E. Bono, and G. K. Patton, "The Job Satisfaction–Job Performance Relationship: A Qualitative and Quantitative Review," *Psychological Bulletin*, May 2001, pp. 376–407; T. Judge, S. Parker, A. E. Colbert, D. Heller, and R. Ilies, "Job Satisfaction: A Cross-Cultural Review," in N. Anderson, D. S. Ones, H. K. Sinangil, and C. Viswesvaran (eds.), *Handbook of Industrial, Work, & Organizational Psychology*, vol. 2 (Thousand Oaks, CA: Sage, 2001, p. 41).

48. C. N. Greene, "The Satisfaction-Performance Controversy," *Business Horizons*, February 1972, pp. 31–41; E. E. Lawler III, *Motivation in Organizations* (Monterey, CA: Brooks/Cole, 1973); and M. M. Petty, G. W. McGee, and J. W. Cavender, "A Meta-Analysis of the Relationship Between Individual Job Satisfaction and Individual Performance," *Academy of Management Review*, October 1984, pp. 712–21.

49. See D. Farrell, "Exit, Voice, Loyalty, and Neglect as Responses to Job Dissatisfaction: A Multidimensional Scaling Study," *Academy of Management Journal*, December 1983, pp. 596–606; C. E. Rusbult, D. Farrell, G. Rogers, and A. G. Mainous III, "Impact of Exchange Variables on Exit, Voice, Loyalty, and Neglect: An Integrative Model of Responses to Declining Job Satisfaction," *Academy of Management Journal*, September 1988, pp. 599–627; M. J. Withey and W. H. Cooper, "Predicting Exit, Voice, Loyalty, and Neglect," *Administrative Science Quarterly*, December 1989, pp. 521–39; J. Zhou and J. M. George, "When Job Dissatisfaction Leads to Creativity: Encouraging the Expression of Voice," *Academy of Management Journal*, August 2001, pp. 682–96; J. B. Olson-Buchanan and W. R. Boswell, "The Role of Employee Loyalty and Formality in Voicing Discontent," *Journal of Applied Psychology*, December 2002, pp. 1167–74; and A. Davis-Blake, J. P. Broschak, and E. George, "Happy Together? How Using Nonstandard Workers Affects Exit, Voice, and Loyalty Among

Standard Employees," *Academy of Management Journal* 46, no. 4 (2003), pp. 475–85.

50. R. B. Freeman, "Job Satisfaction as an Economic Variable," *American Economic Review*, January 1978, pp. 135–41.

51. T. A. Judge, C. J. Thoresen, J. E. Bono, and G. K. Patton, "The Job Satisfaction–Job Performance Relationship: A Qualitative and Quantitative Review," *Psychological Bulletin*, May 2001, pp. 376–407.

52. C. Ostroff, "The Relationship between Satisfaction, Attitudes, and Performance: An Organizational Level Analysis," *Journal of Applied Psychology*, December 1992, pp. 963–74; A. M. Ryan, M. J. Schmit, and R. Johnson, "Attitudes and Effectiveness: Examining Relations at an Organizational Level," *Personnel Psychology*, Winter 1996, pp. 853–82; and J. K. Harter, F. L. Schmidt, and T. L. Hayes, "Business-Unit Level Relationship Between Employee Satisfaction, Employee Engagement, and Business Outcomes: A Meta-Analysis," *Journal of Applied Psychology*, April 2002, pp. 268–79.

53. P. E. Spector, *Job Satisfaction*, pp. 57–58.

54. See T. S. Bateman and D. W. Organ, "Job Satisfaction and the Good Soldier: The Relationship between Affect and Employee 'Citizenship,' " *Academy of Management Journal*, December 1983, pp. 587–95; C. A. Smith, D. W. Organ, and J. Near, "Organizational Citizenship Behavior: Its Nature and Antecedents," *Journal of Applied Psychology*, October 1983, pp. 653–63; A. P. Brief, *Attitudes in and around Organizations* (Thousand Oaks, CA: Sage, 1998), pp. 44–45; and M. Podsakoff, S. B. MacKenzie, J. B. Paine, and D. G. Bachrach, "Organizational Citizenship Behaviors: A Critical Review of the Theoretical and Empirical Literature and Suggestions for Future Research," *Journal of Management* 26, no. 3 (2000), pp. 513–63.

55. D. W. Organ and K. Ryan, "A Meta-Analytic Review of Attitudinal and Dispositional Predictors of Organizational Citizenship Behavior," *Personnel Psychology*, Winter 1995, p. 791; and J. A. LePine, A. Erez, and D. E. Johnson, "The Nature and Dimensionality of Organizational Citizenship Behavior: A Critical Review and Meta-Analysis," *Journal of Applied Psychology*, February 2002, pp. 52–65.

56. J. Fahr, P. M. Podsakoff, and D. W. Organ, "Accounting for Organizational Citizenship Behavior: Leader Fairness and Task Scope Versus Satisfaction," *Journal of Management*, December 1990, pp. 705–22; R. H. Moorman, "Relationship between Organization Justice and Organizational Citizenship Behaviors: Do Fairness Perceptions Influence Employee Citizenship?" *Journal of Applied Psychology*, December 1991, pp. 845–55; and M. A. Konovsky and D. W. Organ, "Dispositional and Contextual Determinants of Organizational Citizenship Behavior," *Journal of Organizational Behavior*, May 1996, pp. 253–66.

57. D. W. Organ, "Personality and Organizational Citizenship Behavior," *Journal of Management*, Summer 1994, p. 466.

58. See, for instance, B. Schneider and D. E. Bowen, "Employee and Customer Perceptions of Service in Banks: Replication and Extension," *Journal of Applied Psychology*, August 1985, pp. 423–33; W. W. Tornow and J. W. Wiley, "Service Quality and Management Practices: A Look at Employee Attitudes, Customer Satisfaction, and Bottom-line Consequences," *Human Resource Planning* 4, no. 2 (1991), pp. 105–16; J. J. Weaver, "Want Customer Satisfaction? Satisfy Your

Employees First," *HRMagazine*, February 1994, pp. 110–12; E. Naumann and D. W. Jackson, Jr., "One More Time: How Do You Satisfy Customers?" *Business Horizons*, May–June 1999, pp. 71–76; D. J. Koys, "The Effects of Employee Satisfaction, Organizational Citizenship Behavior, and Turnover on Organizational Effectiveness: A Unit-Level, Longitudinal Study," *Personnel Psychology*, Spring 2001, pp. 101–14; and J. Griffith, "Do Satisfied Employees Satisfy Customers? Support-Services Staff Morale and Satisfaction among Public School Administrators, Students, and Parents," *Journal of Applied Social Psychology*, August 2001, pp. 1627–58.

59. M. J. Bitner, B. H. Booms, and L. A. Mohr, "Critical Service Encounters: The Employee's Viewpoint," *Journal of Marketing*, October 1994, pp. 95–106.

60. E. A. Locke, "The Nature and Causes of Job Satisfaction," in M. D. Dunnette (ed.), *Handbook of Industrial and Organizational Psychology* (Chicago: Rand McNally, 1976), p. 1331; S. L. McShane, "Job Satisfaction and Absenteeism: A Meta-Analytic Re-Examination," *Canadian Journal of Administrative Science*, June 1984, pp. 61–77; R. D. Hackett and R. M. Guion, "A Reevaluation of the Absenteeism–Job Satisfaction Relationship," *Organizational Behavior and Human Decision Processes*, June 1985, p. 340–81; K. D. Scott and G. S. Taylor, "An Examination of Conflicting Findings on the Relationship between Job Satisfaction and Absenteeism: A Meta-Analysis," *Academy of Management Journal*, September 1985, pp. 599–612; R. Steel and J. R. Rentsch, "Influence of Cumulation Strategies on the Long-Range Prediction of Absenteeism," *Academy of Management Journal*, December 1995, pp. 1616–34; and G. Johns, "The Psychology of Lateness, Absenteeism, and Turnover," p. 237.

61. F. J. Smith, "Work Attitudes as Predictors of Attendance on a Specific Day," *Journal of Applied Psychology*, February 1977, pp. 16–19.

62. W. Hom and R. W. Griffeth, *Employee Turnover* (Cincinnati, OH: Southwestern, 1995); R. W. Griffeth, P. W. Hom, and S. Gaertner, "A Meta-Analysis of Antecedents and Correlates of Employee Turnover: Update, Moderator Tests, and Research Implications for the Next Millennium," *Journal of Management* 26, no. 3 (2000), p. 479; G. Johns, "The Psychology of Lateness, Absenteeism, and Turnover," p. 237.

63. See, for example, C. L. Hulin, M. Roznowski, and D. Hachiya, "Alternative Opportunities and Withdrawal Decisions: Empirical and Theoretical Discrepancies and an Integration," *Psychological Bulletin*, July 1985, pp. 233–50; and J. M. Carsten and P. E. Spector, "Unemployment, Job Satisfaction, and Employee Turnover: A Meta-Analytic Test of the Muchinsky Model," *Journal of Applied Psychology*, August 1987, pp. 374–81.

64. D. G. Spencer and R. M. Steers, "Performance as a Moderator of the Job Satisfaction–Turnover Relationship," *Journal of Applied Psychology*, August 1981, pp. 511–14.

65. K. A. Hanisch, C. L. Hulin, and M. Roznowski, "The Importance of Individuals' Repertoires of Behaviors: The Scientific Appropriateness of Studying Multiple Behaviors and General Attitudes," *Journal of Organizational Behavior* 19, no. 5 (1998), pp. 463–80; C. L. Hulin, "Adaptation, Persistence, and Commitment in Organizations," in Marvin D. Dunnette, and Leaetta M. Hough (eds.), *Handbook of Industrial and Organizational Psychology*, 2nd ed., vol. 2 (Palo Alto, CA: Consulting Psychologists Press, Inc., 1991), pp. 445–505.

66. T. Judge, S. Parker, A. E. Colbert, D. Heller, and R. Ilies, "Job Satisfaction: A Cross-Cultural Review," in N. Anderson, D. S. Ones, H. K. Sinangil, and C. Viswesvaran (eds.), *Handbook of Industrial, Work, & Organizational Psychology*, vol. 2 (Thousand Oaks, CA: Sage, 2001); T. A. Judge and A. H. Church, "Job Satisfaction: Research and Practice," in C. L. Cooper and E. A. Locke (eds.), *Industrial and Organizational Psychology: Linking Theory with Practice* (Oxford, UK: Blackwell, 2000), pp. 166–98; L. Saari and T. A. Judge, "Employee Attitudes and Job Satisfaction," *Human Resource Management* 43, no. 4 (2004), pp. 395–407.

67. See, for instance, R. D. Arvey, B. McCall, T. J. Bouchard, Jr., and P. Taubman, "Genetic Influences on Job Satisfaction and Work Values," *Personality and Individual Differences*, July 1994, pp. 21–33; D. Lykken and A. Tellegen, "Happiness is a Stochastic Phenomenon," *Psychological Science*, May 1996, pp. 186–89; and D. Lykken and M. Csikszentmihalyi, "Happiness—Stuck With What You've Got?" *Psychologist*, September 2001, pp. 470–72; "Double Take," *UNH Magazine*, Spring 2000 (http://www.unhmagazine.unh.edu/sp00/twinssp00.html).

Creative powers can just as easily turn out to be destructive. It rests solely with the moral personality whether they apply themselves to good things or to bad. And if this is lacking, no teacher can supply it or take its place.

— Carl Jung

Personality and Values

After reading this chapter, you should be able to:

1 Explain the factors that determine an individual's personality.

2 Describe the Myers-Briggs Type Indicator personality framework.

3 Identify the key traits in the Big Five personality model.

4 Explain how the major personality attributes predict behavior at work.

5 Contrast terminal and instrumental values.

6 List the dominant values in today's workforce.

7 Identify Hofstede's five value dimensions of national culture.

LEARNING OBJECTIVES

Overbearing, Insensitive, and Hasty: Is This Your Ideal Boss?

Can a personality test change a person? John Bearden (see photo) thinks it can. He presents himself as evidence.[1]

Bearden had a long and successful career as an executive in the real estate industry. But along the way, he irritated a lot of people. "I was a passionate, driven and nonempathetic leader, inclined to make hasty decisions and to get to the finish line dragging people with me," he says. One day, a consultant told him, "John, you have so much potential, but you're running over everybody. People want to follow you, but you turn people off."

Bearden took the consultant's assessment hard. He decided he needed to better understand his shortcomings. So he hired a personal coach. The first thing this coach did was to give Bearden a personality test. The test confirmed the way Bearden saw himself: He was extraverted, intuitive, and rational rather than emotional. But the test also revealed a side of Bearden that was less flattering—he could be overbearing, insensitive, and hasty.

The results from this personality test led Bearden to rethink the way he managed people. In August 2001, when he took over the job as CEO of GMAC Home Services, a General Motors subsidiary, he put his newfound insights to work. "My whole decision-making and leadership process has been tremendously refined as a result of [the per-

sonality test], which helped me understand the tendencies I had to make hasty decisions." Bearden now considers himself more empathetic and able to listen more carefully to his colleagues' opinions. He displayed his newfound skills at GMAC's national convention during a presentation by his top executive team. "In the past, I would have gotten very much involved in interjecting my own position early on and probably biasing the process. But here I found myself quite content to allow their positions to be articulated . . . All I did was sit and absorb, and it was a very satisfying process."

Bearden may have changed his management style and his workplace behavior, but he is still very much a successful manager. In fact in 2004, franchise sales increased 122 percent and gross commission income was up 271 percent over the same period in 2003. Of course, one never knows what the future may hold, but so far, Bearden and GMAC Home Services have been a successful match. ■

Source: Christopher Berkey/The New York Times

Our personality shapes our behavior. So if we want to better understand the behavior of someone in an organization, it helps if we know something about his or her personality. In the first half of this chapter, we review the research on personality and its relationship to behavior. In the latter half, we look at how values shape many of our work-related behaviors.

Personality

Why are some people quiet and passive, while others are loud and aggressive? Are certain personality types better adapted for certain job types? Before we can answer these questions, we need to address a more basic one: What is personality?

What Is Personality?

When we talk of personality, we don't mean that a person has charm, a positive attitude toward life, a smiling face, or is a finalist for "Happiest and Friendliest" in this year's Miss America contest. When psychologists talk of personality, they mean a dynamic concept describing the growth and development of a person's whole psychological system. Rather than looking at parts of the person, personality looks at some aggregate whole that is greater than the sum of the parts.

The most frequently used definition of personality was produced by Gordon Allport nearly 70 years ago. He said personality is "the dynamic organization within the individual of those psychophysical systems that determine his unique adjustments to his environment."[2] For our purposes, you should think of **personality** as the sum total of ways in which an individual reacts to and interacts with others. It is most often described in terms of measurable traits that a person exhibits.

Personality Determinants

An early debate in personality research centered on whether an individual's personality was the result of heredity or of environment. Was the personality predetermined at birth, or was it the result of the individual's interaction with his or her surroundings? Clearly, there is no simple black-and-white answer. Personality appears to be a result of both hereditary and environmental factors.

Heredity   *Heredity* refers to those factors that were determined at conception. Physical stature, facial attractiveness, gender, temperament, muscle composition and reflexes, energy level, and biological rhythms are characteristics that are generally considered to be either completely or substantially influenced by who your parents are, that is, by their biological, physiological, and inherent psychological makeup. The heredity approach argues that the ultimate explanation of an individual's personality is the molecular structure of the genes, located in the chromosomes.

Three different streams of research lend some credibility to the argument that heredity plays an important part in determining an individual's personality. The first looks at the genetic underpinnings of human behavior and temperament among young children. The second addresses the study of twins who were separated at birth. The third examines the consistency in job satisfaction over time and across situations.

Studies of young children lend strong support to the power of heredity.[3] Evidence demonstrates that traits such as shyness, fear, and aggression can be traced to inherited genetic characteristics. This finding suggests that some per-

The study of identical twins reared apart concluded that heredity plays an important role in determining personality. Dr. Nancy Segal, codirector of the University of Minnesota research project, is shown here with twins separated at birth, reared in different family environments, and reunited after 31 years. Segal and her team of researchers discovered that the sets of twins studied shared more personality characteristics than siblings raised in the same family.

sonality traits may be built into the same genetic code that affects factors such as height and hair color.

Researchers have studied more than 100 sets of identical twins who were separated at birth and raised separately.[4] If heredity played little or no part in determining personality, you would expect to find few similarities between the separated twins. But the researchers found a lot in common. For almost every behavioral trait, a significant part of the variation between the twins turned out to be associated with genetic factors. For instance, one set of twins who had been separated for 39 years and raised 45 miles apart were found to drive the same model and color car, chain-smoked the same brand of cigarette, owned dogs with the same name, and regularly vacationed within three blocks of each other in a beach community 1,500 miles away. Researchers have found that genetics accounts for about 50 percent of the personality differences and more than 30 percent of the variation in occupational and leisure interests.

Interestingly, the twin studies have suggested that the parental environment doesn't add much to our personality development. In other words, the personalities of identical twins raised in different households are more similar to each other than the personalities of the separated twins to the siblings they were actually raised with. Ironically, the most important contribution our parents may have made to our personalities is giving us their genes!

Further support for the importance of heredity can be found in studies of individual job satisfaction. Individual job satisfaction is found to be relatively stable over time. This result is consistent with what you would expect if satisfaction is determined by something inherent in the person rather than by external environmental factors. In fact, research has shown that identical twins reared apart have similar job satisfaction levels, even if their jobs are completely different.[5]

personality *The sum total of ways in which an individual reacts and interacts with others.*

Environment   Among the factors that exert pressures on our personality formation are the culture in which we are raised; the norms among our family, friends, and social groups; and other influences that we experience. These environmental factors play a role in shaping our personalities.

For example, culture establishes the norms, attitudes, and values that are passed along from one generation to the next and create consistencies over time. An ideology that is intensely fostered in one culture may have only moderate influence in another. For instance, North Americans have had the themes of industriousness, success, competition, independence, and the Protestant work ethic constantly instilled in them through books, the school system, family, and friends. North Americans, as a result, tend to be ambitious and aggressive relative to individuals raised in cultures that have emphasized getting along with others, cooperation, and the priority of family over work and career.

There's another way that the environment is relevant to forming personality. An individual's personality, although generally stable and consistent, does change in different situations. Although we've not yet been able to develop a neat classification scheme for these situations, we know that some—for example, church or an employment interview—constrain many behaviors and others—for example, a picnic in a public park—constrain relatively few.[6] In other words, the different demands of different situations call forth different aspects of one's personality. Therefore, we shouldn't look at personality patterns in isolation.[7]

Careful consideration of the arguments favoring either heredity or environment as the primary determinant of personality forces the conclusion that both are important. Heredity provides us with inborn traits and abilities, but our full potential will be determined by how well we adjust to the demands and requirements of the environment.

Personality Traits

The early work in the structure of personality revolved around attempts to identify and label enduring characteristics that describe an individual's behavior. Popular characteristics include shy, aggressive, submissive, lazy, ambitious, loyal, and timid. Those characteristics, when they're exhibited in a large number of situations, are called **personality traits**.[8] The more consistent the characteristic and the more frequently it occurs in diverse situations, the more important that trait is in describing the individual.

Why has so much attention been paid to personality traits? The answer is: Researchers have long believed that these traits could help in employee selection, matching people to jobs, and in guiding career development decisions. For instance, if certain personality types perform better on specific jobs, man-

---

Exhibit 4-1

Source: PEANUTS reprinted with permission of United Features Syndicate, Inc.

agement could use personality tests to screen job candidates and improve employee job performance.

There were a number of early efforts to identify the primary traits that govern behavior.[9] However, for the most part, these efforts resulted in long lists of traits that were difficult to generalize from and provided little practical guidance to organizational decision makers. Two exceptions are the Myers-Briggs Type Indicator and the Big Five Model. Over the past 20 years, these two approaches have become the dominant frameworks for identifying and classifying traits.

The Myers-Briggs Type Indicator The **Myers-Briggs Type Indicator (MBTI®)**[10] is the most widely used personality-assessment instrument in the world.[11] It's a 100-question personality test that asks people how they usually feel or act in particular situations. On the basis of the answers individuals give to the test, they are classified as extraverted or introverted (E or I), sensing or intuitive (S or N), thinking or feeling (T or F), and judging or perceiving (J or P). These terms are defined as follows:

- *Extraverted vs. Introverted* —Extraverted individuals are outgoing, sociable, and assertive. Introverts are quiet and shy.
- *Sensing vs. Intuitive* —Sensing types are practical and prefer routine and order. They focus on details. Intuitives rely on unconscious processes and look at the "big picture."
- *Thinking vs. Feeling* —Thinking types use reason and logic to handle problems. Feeling types rely on their personal values and emotions.
- *Judging vs. Perceiving* —Judging types want control and prefer their world to be ordered and structured. Perceiving types are flexible and spontaneous.

These classifications are then combined into 16 personality types. To illustrate, let's take several examples. INTJs are visionaries. They usually have original minds and great drive for their own ideas and purposes. They are characterized as skeptical, critical, independent, determined, and often stubborn. ESTJs are organizers. They are realistic, logical, analytical, and decisive and have a natural head for business or mechanics. They like to organize and run activities. The ENTP type is a conceptualizer. He or she is innovative, individualistic, versatile, and attracted to entrepreneurial ideas. This person tends to be resourceful in solving challenging problems but may neglect routine assignments. A book that profiled 13 contemporary businesspeople who created supersuccessful firms including Apple Computer, FedEx, Honda Motors, Microsoft, and Sony found that all 13 were intuitive thinkers (NTs).[12] This result is particularly interesting because intuitive thinkers represent only about 5 percent of the population.

As previously noted, the MBTI® is widely used in practice. Some of the organizations using it include Apple Computer, AT&T, Citigroup, GE, 3M Co., plus many hospitals, educational institutions, and even the U.S. Armed Forces. In spite of its popularity, the evidence is mixed as to whether the MBTI® is a valid measure of personality—with most of the evidence suggesting it isn't.[13] One of the problems with the MBTI® is that it forces a person to be categorized as either one type or another (that is, you're either introverted or extraverted). There is no in-between, though people can be both extraverted and introverted

personality traits *Enduring characteristics that describe an individual's behavior.*

Myers-Briggs Type Indicator (MBTI®) *A personality test that taps four characteristics and classifies people into 1 of 16 personality types.*

to some degree. The best we can say is that it can be a valuable tool for increasing self-awareness and for providing career guidance. But because MBTI® results tend to be unrelated to job performance, it probably should not be used as a selection test for choosing among job candidates.

The Big Five Model   The MBTI® may lack for strong supporting evidence, but that can't be said for the five-factor model of personality—more typically called the "Big Five." This is the test John Bearden took, described at the opening of this chapter, and which made him rethink the way he managed people.

In recent years, an impressive body of research supports that five basic dimensions underlie all others and encompass most of the significant variation in human personality.[14] The Big Five factors are:

- **Extraversion** This dimension captures one's comfort level with relationships. Extraverts tend to be gregarious, assertive, and sociable. Introverts tend to be reserved, timid, and quiet.
- **Agreeableness** This dimension refers to an individual's propensity to defer to others. Highly agreeable people are cooperative, warm, and trusting. People who score low on agreeableness are cold, disagreeable, and antagonistic.
- **Conscientiousness** This dimension is a measure of reliability. A highly conscientious person is responsible, organized, dependable, and persistent. Those who score low on this dimension are easily distracted, disorganized, and unreliable.
- **Emotional stability** (often labeled by its converse, neuroticism) This dimension taps a person's ability to withstand stress. People with positive emotional stability tend to be calm, self-confident, and secure. Those with high negative scores tend to be nervous, anxious, depressed, and insecure.
- **Openness to experience** The final dimension addresses one's range of interests and fascination with novelty. Extremely open people are creative, curious, and artistically sensitive. Those at the other end of the openness category are conventional and find comfort in the familiar.

Before we discuss the Big Five factors in more detail, check out the Self-Assessment feature to see how you score on the Big Five.

SELF ASSESSMENT LIBRARY

WHAT'S MY BASIC PERSONALITY?

In the Self-Assessment Library (available on CD, online, and in print), take assessment I.A.1 (What's My Basic Personality?) and answer the following questions.

1. *How did you score on each of the Big Five factors? Did your scores surprise you? Why or why not?*
2. *What was your highest score? Your lowest?*
3. *Do you think this set of scores does a good job describing your basic personality? Why or why not?*

In addition to providing a unifying personality framework, research on the Big Five also has found relationships between these personality dimensions and job performance.[15] A broad spectrum of occupations were looked at: professionals (including engineers, architects, accountants, attorneys), police, managers, salespeople, and semiskilled and skilled employees. Job performance was defined in terms of performance ratings, training proficiency (performance during training programs), and personnel data such as salary level. The results showed that conscientiousness predicted job performance for all occupational groups. "The preponderance of evidence shows that individuals who are dependable, reliable, careful, thorough, able to plan, organized, hardworking,

General Electric CEO Jeffrey Immelt scores high on the extraversion dimension of the Big Five Model. Described as gregarious and adept at building relationships, Immelt spent 20 years at GE in sales and managerial positions, jobs that involve high social interaction, before moving into GE's top management position. As CEO, Immelt travels throughout the world meeting with customers, employees, suppliers, and investors.

persistent, and achievement-oriented tend to have higher job performance in most if not all occupations."[16] In addition, employees who score higher in conscientiousness develop higher levels of job knowledge, probably because highly conscientious people exert greater levels of effort on their jobs. The higher levels of job knowledge then contribute to higher levels of job performance.[17] Consistent with these findings, evidence also finds a relatively strong and consistent relationship between conscientiousness and organizational citizenship behavior.[18] This, however, seems to be the only Big Five personality dimension that predicts OCB.

For the other personality dimensions, predictability depended on both the performance criterion and the occupational group. For instance, extraversion predicted performance in managerial and sales positions. This finding makes sense because those occupations involve high social interaction. Similarly, openness to experience was found to be important in predicting training proficiency, which, too, seems logical. What wasn't so clear was why positive emotional stability wasn't related to job performance. Intuitively, it would seem that people who are calm and secure would do better on almost all jobs than people who are nervous and depressed. The answer might be that some aspects of negative emotional stability—such as nervousness—might actually help job performance. Think about animals. A deer that wasn't easily startled by noises wouldn't last long near a major highway. Consider a stock trader at a Wall Street firm. If she fails to research all of her options thoroughly and is never nervous about making the wrong transaction, she may fail to see the danger in, say, purchasing stock in a volatile young

extraversion *A personality dimension describing someone who is sociable, gregarious, and assertive.*

agreeableness *A personality dimension that describes someone who is good-natured, cooperative, and trusting.*

conscientiousness *A personality dimension that describes someone who is responsible, dependable, persistent, and organized.*

emotional stability *A personality dimension that characterizes someone as calm, self-confident, secure (positive) versus nervous, depressed, and insecure (negative).*

openness to experience *A personality dimension that characterizes someone in terms of imagination, sensitivity, and curiosity.*

company. The other aspect of negative emotional stability—a depressive outlook—is bad for every job. Why? Because when you're depressed, it's difficult to motivate yourself, to make a decision, or to take a risk. So, it may be that negative emotional stability has aspects that both help and hinder performance.[19]

Now that we've dealt with performance, you'll be interested to know that the Big Five have other implications for work and for life. Let's look at the implications of these traits one at a time.

Compared to introverts, extraverts tend to be happier in their jobs and in their lives as a whole. They usually have more friends and spend more time in social situations than introverts. But they also appear to be more impulsive, as evidenced by the fact that extraverts are more likely to be absent from work and engage in risky behavior such as unprotected sex, drinking, and other impulsive or sensation-seeking behavior.[20]

You might expect agreeable people to be happier than disagreeable people, and they are, but only slightly. When people choose romantic partners, friends, or organizational team members, agreeable individuals are usually their first choice. Agreeable children do better in school and as adults are less likely to get involved in drugs or excessive drinking.[21]

Interestingly, conscientious people live longer because they tend to take better care of themselves (eat better, exercise more) and engage in fewer risky behaviors (smoking, drinking/drugs, risky sexual or driving behavior).[22] Still, there are downsides to conscientiousness. It appears that conscientious people, probably because they're so organized and structured, don't adapt as well to changing contexts. Conscientious people are generally performance-oriented. They have more trouble than less conscientious people learning complex skills early on because their focus is on performing well rather than on learning. Finally, conscientious people are often less creative, especially artistically.[23]

People who score high on emotional stability are happier than those who score low on emotional stability. Of the Big Five, emotional stability is most strongly related to life satisfaction, to job satisfaction, and to low stress levels. High scores on emotional stability also are associated with fewer health complaints. One upside for low emotional stability: when in a bad mood, such people make faster and better decisions compared to emotionally stable people in bad moods.[24]

Finally, individuals who score high on openness to experience are more creative in science and in art, tend to be less religious, and are more likely to be politically liberal than those who score lower on openness to experience. Open people cope better with organizational change and are more adaptable in changing contexts.

Measuring Personality

The most important reason managers need to know how to measure personality is because research has shown that personality tests are useful in hiring decisions. Scores on personality tests help managers forecast who the best bet for a job is.[25] And some managers want to know how people score on personality tests to better understand and more effectively manage the people who work for them.

There are three main ways personality is measured:

1. self-report surveys
2. observer-ratings surveys
3. projective measures (Rorschach Inkblot Test and Thematic Apperception Test)

Self-report surveys—which are completed by the individual—are the most common way to measure personality. One concern with self-report surveys, however, is that the individual might lie or practice impression management— that is, the person could "fake good" on the test to create a good impression. This is especially a concern when the survey is the basis for employment.

| Exhibit **4-2** | Thematic Apperception Test |

Source: Reprinted by permission of the publishers from Henry A. Murray, Thematic Apperception Test Plate 12F, Cambridge, Mass.: Harvard University Press, copyright © 1943 by the President and Fellows of Harvard College, © 1971 by Henry A. Murray.

Another concern is accuracy. In other words, a perfectly good candidate could have just been in a bad mood when the survey was taken.

Observer-ratings surveys have been developed to provide an independent assessment of personality. Therefore, instead of an individual taking the survey—as in the case of self-report surveys—perhaps a coworker could do the rating (sometimes with knowledge of the individual, sometimes not). Even though self-report surveys and observer-ratings surveys are strongly correlated, research suggests that observer-ratings surveys are a better predictor of success on the job.[26] However, it is important to realize that both self-report surveys and observer-ratings surveys can tell us something unique about an individual's behavior in the workplace.

Some examples of projective measures are the Rorschach Inkblot Test and the Thematic Apperception Test (TAT). In the Rorschach Inkblot Test, the individual is supposed to state what inkblots seem to resemble. The TAT is a series of pictures (drawings or photos) on cards. (See Exhibit 4-2). The individual being tested writes a story about each picture. With both the Rorschach and the TAT, clinicians then score the responses. However, assessing responses has proven to be a challenge because one clinician often perceives the results differently than another. Therefore, there is no surprise that a recent study suggested that projective measures are not very effective. For this reason they are rarely used.[27]

Major Personality Attributes Influencing OB

In this section, we want to more carefully evaluate specific personality attributes that have been found to be powerful predictors of behavior in organizations. The first attribute is related to one's core self-evaluation. The others are Machiavellianism, narcissism, self-monitoring, propensity for risk taking, and the Type A and proactive personalities.

A positive core self-evaluation helps U.S. Secretary of State Condoleezza Rice meet the daunting challenges and complexity of her job. Confident, skilled in diplomacy, and possessing a relentless work ethic, Rice views the challenges of her job as an opportunity to shape American foreign policy and to take a global leadership role in spreading democracy and constructing a peaceful international climate. Rice works towards these goals by managing relationships with leaders of 191 countries, such as Afghan President Hamid Karzai, shown here.

Core Self-Evaluation   People differ in the degree to which they like or dislike themselves and whether they see themselves as capable and effective. This self-perspective is the concept of **core self-evaluation**. People who have positive core self-evaluations like themselves, see themselves as effective, capable, and in control of their environment. Those with negative core self-evaluations tend to dislike themselves, question their capabilities, and view themselves as powerless over their environment.[28]

An individual's core self-evaluation is determined by two main elements: self-esteem and locus of control. **Self-esteem** is defined as individuals' degree of liking or disliking themselves and the degree to which they think they are worthy or unworthy as a person.[29] It's easy to see why self-esteem is a reflection of core self-evaluation: People who have a positive view of themselves and their capabilities tend to like themselves and see themselves as valuable. People with low self-esteem, however, are more susceptible to external influences, suggesting that low-self-esteem individuals depend on the receipt of positive evaluations from others. As a result, people with low self-esteem are more likely to seek approval from others and are more prone to conform to the beliefs and behaviors of those they respect than are people who believe in themselves. Studies have shown that people with low self-esteem may benefit more from training programs because their self-concept is more influenced by such interventions.[30]

The second element that determines core self-evaluation is **locus of control**. Locus of control is the degree to which people believe that they are masters of their own fate. **Internals** are individuals who believe that they control what happens to them. **Externals** are individuals who believe that what happens to them is controlled by outside forces such as luck or chance.[31] Locus of control is an indicator of core self-evaluation because people who think that they lack control over their lives tend to lack confidence in themselves. For example, if you think your success in school is determined by the whim of the professor or by blind luck, you probably don't have a lot of confidence in your ability to get straight A's. You would have an external locus of control, and most likely this would reflect a negative core self-evaluation.

How is the concept of core self-evaluations related to job satisfaction? People with positive core self-evaluations see more challenge in their job, making it more satisfying to them. Individuals with positive core self-evaluations also tend to obtain more complex and challenging jobs. If you think about it, this makes sense. If I think I'm no good and incapable of performing, why would I take a complicated job? I'd be sure to fail. People with positive core self-evaluations also perceive themselves as having control over their jobs, and they also tend to attribute positive outcomes to their own actions.[32]

But what about job performance? People with positive core self-evaluations perform better because they set more ambitious goals, are more committed to their goals, and persist longer at attempting to reach these goals. For example, one study of life insurance agents found that core self-evaluations were critical predictors of performance. In life insurance sales, 90 percent of sales calls end in rejection, so one has to believe in oneself to persist. In fact, this study showed that the majority of the successful salespersons had positive core self-evaluations.[33]

You might wonder whether someone can be *too* positive. In other words, what happens when someone thinks he is capable, but he is actually incompetent? Surely, one can think of many situations in which an inflated view of oneself is bad. One study of *Fortune* 500 CEOs, for example, showed that many CEOs are overconfident and that this self-perceived infallibility often causes them to make bad decisions.[34] Yes, one might be too confident, but very often we sell ourselves short and are less happy and effective than we could be because of it. If I decide I can't do something, for example, I won't try, and not doing it only reinforces my self-doubts.

Machiavellianism Kuzi is a young bank manager in Taiwan. He's had three promotions in the last 4 years. Kuzi makes no apologies for the aggressive tactics he's used to propel his career upward. "I'm prepared to do whatever I have to do to get ahead," he says. Kuzi would properly be called Machiavellian. Shawna led her St. Louis-based company last year in sales performance. She's assertive and persuasive, and she's effective at manipulating customers to buy her product line. Many of her colleagues, including her boss, also consider Shawna as Machiavellian.

The personality characteristic of **Machiavellianism** (Mach) is named after Niccolo Machiavelli, who wrote in the sixteenth century on how to gain and use power. An individual high in Machiavellianism is pragmatic, maintains emotional distance, and believes that ends can justify means. "If it works, use it" is consistent with a high-Mach perspective. A considerable amount of research has been directed toward relating high- and low-Mach personalities to certain behavioral outcomes.[35] High Machs manipulate more, win more, are persuaded less, and persuade others more than do low Machs.[36] Yet these high-Mach outcomes are moderated by situational factors. It has been found that high Machs flourish (1) when they interact face to face with others rather than indirectly; (2) when the situation has a minimum number of rules and regulations, thus allowing latitude for improvisation; and (3) when emotional involvement with details irrelevant to winning distracts low Machs.[37]

Should we conclude that high Machs make good employees? That answer depends on the type of job and whether you consider ethical implications in evaluating performance. In jobs that require bargaining skills (such as labor negotiation) or that offer substantial rewards for winning (as in commissioned sales), high Machs will be productive. But if ends can't justify the means, if there are absolute standards of behavior, or if the three situational factors noted in the preceding paragraph are not in evidence, our ability to predict a high-Mach's performance will be severely curtailed.

Narcissism Hans likes to be the center of attention. He likes to look at himself in the mirror a lot. He has extravagant dreams and seems to consider himself a person of many talents. Hans is a narcissist. The term is from the Greek myth of Narcissus, the story of a man so vain and proud that he fell in love with his own image. In psychology, **narcissism** describes a person who has a grandiose sense of self-importance, requires excessive admiration, has a sense of entitlement, and is arrogant.[38]

A study found that while narcissists thought they were *better* leaders than their colleagues, their supervisors actually rated them as *worse* leaders. For example, an Oracle executive described that company's CEO Larry Ellison as follows: "The difference between God and Larry is that God does not believe he is Larry."[39] Because narcissists often want to gain the admiration of others and receive affirmation of their superiority, they tend to "talk down" (treating others

---

core self-evaluation *Degree to which individuals like or dislike themselves, whether they see themselves as capable and effective, and whether they feel they are in control of their environment or powerless over their environment.*

self-esteem *Individuals' degree of liking or disliking themselves and the degree to which they think they are worthy or unworthy as a person.*

locus of control *The degree to which people believe that they are masters of their own fate.*

internals *Individuals who believe that they control what happens to them.*

externals *Individuals who believe that what happens to them is controlled by outside forces such as luck or chance.*

Machiavellianism *Degree to which an individual is pragmatic, maintains emotional distance, and believes that ends can justify means.*

narcissism *The tendency to be arrogant, have a grandiose sense of self-importance, require excessive admiration, and have a sense of entitlement.*

as if they were inferior) to those who threaten them. Narcissists also tend to be selfish and exploitive, and they often carry the attitude that others exist for their benefit.[40] Studies indicate that narcissists are rated by their bosses as less effective at their jobs, particularly when it comes to helping other people.[41]

Self-Monitoring   Joyce McIntyre is always in trouble at work. Though she's competent, hardworking, and productive, her performance reviews tend to rate her no better than average and she seems to have made a career of irritating bosses. Joyce's problem is that she's politically inept. She's unable to adjust her behavior to fit changing situations. As she puts it, "I'm true to myself. I don't remake myself to please others." We would be correct to describe Joyce as a low self-monitor.

Self-monitoring refers to an individual's ability to adjust his or her behavior to external, situational factors.[42] Individuals high in self-monitoring show considerable adaptability in adjusting their behavior to external situational factors. They are highly sensitive to external cues and can behave differently in different situations. High self-monitors are capable of presenting striking contradictions between their public persona and their private self. Low self-monitors, like Joyce, can't disguise themselves in that way. They tend to display their true dispositions and attitudes in every situation; hence, there is high behavioral consistency between who they are and what they do.

The evidence indicates that high self-monitors tend to pay closer attention to the behavior of others and are more capable of conforming than are low self-monitors.[43] They also receive better performance ratings, are more likely to emerge as leaders, and show less commitment to their organizations.[44] In addition, high self-monitoring managers tend to be more mobile in their careers, receive more promotions (both internal and cross-organizational), and are more likely to occupy central positions in an organization.[45] We might also hypothesize that high self-monitors will be more successful in managerial positions in which individuals are required to play multiple, and even contradicting, roles. The high self-monitor is capable of putting on different "faces" for different audiences.

Risk Taking   Donald Trump stands out for his willingness to take risks. He started with almost nothing in the 1960s. By the mid-1980s, he had made a fortune by betting on a resurgent New York City real estate market. Then, trying to capitalize on his previous successes, Trump overextended himself. By 1994, he had a *negative* net worth of $850 million. Never fearful of taking chances, "The Donald" leveraged the few assets he had left on several New York, New Jersey, and Caribbean real estate ventures. He hit it big again. In 2004, *Forbes* estimated his net worth at $2.6 billion.

People differ in their willingness to take chances. This propensity to assume or avoid risk has been shown to have an impact on how long it takes managers to make a decision and how much information they require before making their choice. For instance, 79 managers worked on simulated personnel exercises that required them to make hiring decisions.[46] High risk-taking managers made more rapid decisions and used less information in making their choices than did the low risk-taking managers. Interestingly, the decision accuracy was the same for both groups.

Although previous studies have shown managers in large organizations to be more risk averse than growth-oriented entrepreneurs who actively manage small businesses, recent findings suggest that managers in large organizations may actually be more willing to take a risk than entrepreneurs.[47] For the work population as a whole, there are also differences in risk propensity.[48] As a result, it makes sense to recognize these differences and even to consider aligning risk-taking propensity with specific job demands. For instance, a high risk-taking

New York real estate developer Donald Trump is willing to take chances. His risk-taking personality enables him to thrive in situations that others find perilous and stressful. Although his Trump Hotels and Casino Resorts, Inc. filed for bankruptcy in late 2004, Trump continues to build his net worth by developing new real estate projects, starring in *The Apprentice*, and marketing a line of clothing, a fragrance, a board game, and a doll that says "You're fired." Trump is shown here signing copies of his newest book *How to Get Rich*.

propensity may lead to more effective performance for a stock trader in a brokerage firm because that type of job demands rapid decision making. On the other hand, a willingness to take risks might prove a major obstacle to an accountant who performs auditing activities. The latter job might be better filled by someone with a low risk-taking propensity.

Type A Personality   Do you know people who are excessively competitive and always seem to be experiencing a sense of time urgency? If you do, it's a good bet that those people have a **Type A personality**. A person with a Type A personality is "aggressively involved in a chronic, incessant struggle to achieve more and more in less and less time, and, if required to do so, against the opposing efforts of other things or other persons."[49] In the North American culture, such characteristics tend to be highly prized and positively associated with ambition and the successful acquisition of material goods. Type A's:

1. are always moving, walking, and eating rapidly;
2. feel impatient with the rate at which most events take place;
3. strive to think or do two or more things at once;
4. cannot cope with leisure time;
5. are obsessed with numbers, measuring their success in terms of how many or how much of everything they acquire.

In contrast to the Type A personality is the Type B, who is exactly opposite. Type B's are "rarely harried by the desire to obtain a wildly increasing number

self-monitoring *A personality trait that measures an individual's ability to adjust his or her behavior to external, situational factors.*

Type A personality *Aggressive involvement in a chronic, incessant struggle to achieve more and more in less and less time and, if necessary, against the opposing efforts of other things or other people.*

of things or participate in an endless growing series of events in an ever-decreasing amount of time."[50] Type B's:

1. never suffer from a sense of time urgency with its accompanying impatience;
2. feel no need to display or discuss either their achievements or accomplishments unless such exposure is demanded by the situation;
3. play for fun and relaxation, rather than to exhibit their superiority at any cost;
4. can relax without guilt.

Type A's operate under moderate to high levels of stress. They subject themselves to more or less continuous time pressure, creating for themselves a life of deadlines. These characteristics result in some rather specific behavioral outcomes. For example, Type A's are fast workers, because they emphasize quantity over quality. In managerial positions, Type A's demonstrate their competitiveness by working long hours and, not infrequently, making poor decisions because they make them too fast. Type A's are also rarely creative. Because of their concern with quantity and speed, they rely on past experiences when faced with problems. They will not allocate the time necessary to develop unique solutions to new problems. They rarely vary in their responses to specific challenges in their milieu; hence, their behavior is easier to predict than that of Type B's.

Do Type A's differ from Type B's in their ability to get hired? The answer appears to be "yes."[51] Type A's do better in job interviews because they are more likely to be judged as having desirable traits such as high drive, competence, aggressiveness, and success motivation.

Proactive Personality   Did you ever notice that some people actively take the initiative to improve their current circumstances or create new ones while others sit by passively reacting to situations? The former individuals have been described as having a **proactive personality**.[52] Proactives identify opportunities, show initiative, take action, and persevere until meaningful change occurs. They create positive change in their environment, regardless or even in spite of constraints or obstacles.[53] Not surprisingly, proactives have many desirable behaviors that organizations covet. For instance, the evidence indicates that proactives are more likely to be seen as leaders and more likely to act as change agents within the organization.[54] Other actions of proactives can be positive or negative, depending on the organization and the situation. For example, proactives are more likely to challenge the status quo or voice their displeasure when situations aren't to their liking.[55] If an organization requires people with entrepreneurial initiative, proactives make good candidates; however, these are people that are also more likely to leave an organization to start their own business.[56] As individuals, proactives are more likely to achieve career success.[57] This is because they select, create, and influence work situations in their favor. Proactives are more likely to seek out job and organizational information, develop contacts in high places, engage in career planning, and demonstrate persistence in the face of career obstacles.

Personality and National Culture

Do personality frameworks, like the Big Five model, transfer across cultures? Are dimensions like locus of control and the Type A personality relevant in all cultures? Let's try to answer these questions.

The five personality factors identified in the Big Five model appear in almost all cross-cultural studies.[58] This includes a wide variety of diverse cultures—such as China, Israel, Germany, Japan, Spain, Nigeria, Norway, Pakistan, and the United States. Differences tend to surface by the emphasis on dimen-

Myth or Science?

"Deep Down, People Are All Alike"

This statement is essentially false. Only in the broadest sense can we say that "people are all alike." For instance, it's true that people all have values, attitudes, likes and dislikes, feelings, goals, and similar general attributes. But individual differences are far more illuminating.[59] People differ in intelligence, personality, abilities, ambition, motivations, emotional display, values, priorities, expectations, and the like. If we want to understand, explain, or predict human behavior accurately, we need to focus on individual differences. Your ability to predict behavior will be severely limited if you constantly assume that all people are alike or that everyone is like you.

As an illustration, consider the task of selecting among job applicants. Managers regularly use information about a candidate's personality (in addition to experience, knowledge, skill level, and intellectual abilities) to help make their hiring decisions. Recognizing that jobs differ in terms of demands and requirements, managers interview and test applicants to (1) categorize them by specific traits, (2) assess job tasks in terms of the type of personality best suited for effectively completing those tasks, and (3) match applicants and job tasks to find an appropriate fit. So by using an individual-difference variable—in this case, personality—managers improve the likelihood of identifying and hiring high-performing employees. ■

sions and whether countries are predominantly individualistic—meaning that people prefer to act as individuals rather than as members of groups—or collectivistic—where there's a tight social framework in which people expect others in groups of which they are a part to look after them and protect them. Chinese, for example, use the category of conscientiousness more often and use the category of agreeableness less often than do Americans. And the Big Five appear to predict a bit better in individualistic cultures than in collectivist.[60] But there is a surprisingly high amount of agreement, especially among individuals from developed countries. As a case in point, a comprehensive review of studies covering people from the 15-nation European Community found that conscientiousness was a valid predictor of performance across jobs and occupational groups.[61] This is exactly what U.S. studies have found.

There are no common personality types for a given country. You can, for instance, find high and low risk-takers in almost any culture. Yet a country's culture influences the dominant personality characteristics of its population. We can see this by looking at locus of control and the Type A personality.

There is evidence that cultures differ in terms of people's relationship to their environment.[62] In some cultures, such as those in North America, people believe that they can dominate their environment. People in other societies, such as Middle Eastern countries, believe that life is essentially preordained. Note the close parallel to internal and external locus of control.[63] We should expect, therefore, a larger proportion of internals in the American and Canadian workforce than in the Saudi Arabian or Iranian workforce.

The prevalence of Type A personalities will be somewhat influenced by the culture in which a person grows up. There are Type A's in every country, but there will be more in capitalistic countries, where achievement and material success are highly valued. For instance, it is estimated that about 50 percent of the North American population is Type A.[64] This percentage shouldn't be too

proactive personality *People who identify opportunities, show initiative, take action, and persevere until meaningful change occurs.*

A Global Personality

DETERMINING WHICH EMPLOYEES WILL SUCCEED on overseas business assignments is often difficult for an organization's managers because the same qualities that predict success in one culture may not in another. Researchers, however, are naming personality traits that can help managers home in on which employees would be suited for foreign assignments.

Organizational psychologist Robert Hogan, for example, states that emotional maturity, remaining composed under pressure, and being comfortable with uncertainty are traits that breed success in most jobs, and these traits may be especially valuable for the overseas employee to possess. In addition, according to the Center for Global Assignments (CGA), successful global executives tend to be open-minded and imaginative, and they also enjoy talking and networking with others. Other traits that have been linked to overseas employment success include curiosity and risk tolerance.

Viewed from the perspective of the Big Five, characteristics such as open-mindedness and curiosity are similar to the Big Five trait *openness to experience*, while characteristics such as enjoying talking with others and networking resemble the Big Five trait *extraversion*. For the overseas employee, being more open and extraverted may be particularly helpful in breaching communication barriers and cultivating trust, which in turn promotes cooperation.

What is the ultimate upshot for organizations? When it comes to choosing employees for global assignments, personality can make a difference.

Source: Based on J. E. Fernandez, "The Making of a Global Executive," *Journal of Business Strategy* 24, no. 5, (2003), pp. 36–38.

surprising. The United States and Canada both have a high emphasis on time management and efficiency. Both have cultures that stress accomplishments and acquisition of money and material goods. In cultures such as Sweden and France, where materialism is less revered, we would predict a smaller proportion of Type A personalities.

Having discussed personality traits—the enduring characteristics that describe a person's behavior—we now turn to values. Although personality and values are related, they're not the same. Values are often very specific and describe belief systems rather than behavioral tendencies. Some beliefs or values don't say much about a person's personality, and we don't always act in ways consistent with our values.

Values

Is capital punishment right or wrong? If a person likes power, is that good or bad? The answers to these questions are value-laden. Some might argue, for example, that capital punishment is right because it is an appropriate retribution for crimes like murder and treason. However, others might argue, just as strongly, that no government has the right to take anyone's life.

Values represent basic convictions that "a specific mode of conduct or end-state of existence is personally or socially preferable to an opposite or converse mode of conduct or end-state of existence."[65] They contain a judgmental element in that they carry an individual's ideas as to what is right, good, or desirable. Values have both content and intensity attributes. The content attribute says that a mode of conduct or end-state of existence is *important*. The intensity attribute specifies *how important* it is. When we rank an individual's values in terms of their intensity, we obtain that person's **value system**. All of us have a hierarchy of values that forms our value system. This system is identified by the relative importance we assign to values such as freedom, pleasure, self-respect, honesty, obedience, and equality.

Are values fluid and flexible? Generally speaking, no. Values tend to be relatively stable and enduring.[66] A significant portion of the values we hold is established in our early years—from parents, teachers, friends, and others. As children, we are told that certain behaviors or outcomes are *always* desirable or *always* undesirable. There were few gray areas. You were told, for example, that you should be honest and responsible. You were never taught to be just a little bit honest or a little bit responsible. It is this absolute or "black-or-white" learning of values that more or less ensures their stability and endurance. The process of questioning our values, of course, may result in a change. More often, our questioning merely acts to reinforce the values we hold.

Importance of Values

Values are important to the study of organizational behavior because they lay the foundation for the understanding of people's attitudes and motivation, and because they influence our perceptions. Individuals enter an organization with preconceived notions of what "ought" and what "ought not" to be. Of course, these notions are not value free. On the contrary, they contain interpretations of right and wrong. Furthermore, they imply that certain behaviors or outcomes are preferred over others. As a result, values cloud objectivity and rationality.

Values generally influence attitudes and behavior.[67] Suppose that you enter an organization with the view that allocating pay on the basis of performance is right, while allocating pay on the basis of seniority is wrong. How are you going to react if you find that the organization you have just joined rewards seniority and not performance? You're likely to be disappointed—and this can lead to job dissatisfaction and the decision not to exert a high level of effort since "it's probably not going to lead to more money, anyway." Would your attitudes and behavior be different if your values aligned with the organization's pay policies? Most likely.

Types of Values

Can we classify values? The answer is: Yes. In this section, we review two approaches to developing value typologies.

Rokeach Value Survey   Milton Rokeach created the Rokeach Value Survey (RVS).[68] The RVS consists of two sets of values, with each set containing 18 individual value items. One set, called **terminal values**, refers to desirable end-states. These are the goals that a person would like to achieve during his or her lifetime. The other set, called **instrumental values**, refers to preferable modes of behavior, or means of achieving the terminal values. Exhibit 4-3 gives common examples for each of these sets.

---

values   *Basic convictions that a specific mode of conduct or end-state of existence is personally or socially preferable to an opposite or converse mode of conduct or end-state of existence.*

value system   *A hierarchy based on a ranking of an individual's values in terms of their intensity.*

terminal values   *Desirable end-states of existence; the goals that a person would like to achieve during his or her lifetime.*

instrumental values   *Preferable modes of behavior or means of achieving one's terminal values.*

Exhibit 4-3	Terminal and Instrumental Values in Rokeach Value Survey

Terminal Values	Instrumental Values
A comfortable life (a prosperous life)	Ambitious (hardworking, aspiring)
An exciting life (a stimulating, active life)	Broad-minded (open-minded)
A sense of accomplishment (lasting contribution)	Capable (competent, efficient)
A world at peace (free of war and conflict)	Cheerful (lighthearted, joyful)
A world of beauty (beauty of nature and the arts)	Clean (neat, tidy)
Equality (brotherhood, equal opportunity for all)	Courageous (standing up for your beliefs)
Family security (taking care of loved ones)	Forgiving (willing to pardon others)
Freedom (independence, free choice)	Helpful (working for the welfare of others)
Happiness (contentedness)	Honest (sincere, truthful)
Inner harmony (freedom from inner conflict)	Imaginative (daring, creative)
Mature love (sexual and spiritual intimacy)	Independent (self-reliant, self-sufficient)
National security (protection from attack)	Intellectual (intelligent, reflective)
Pleasure (an enjoyable, leisurely life)	Logical (consistent, rational)
Salvation (saved, eternal life)	Loving (affectionate, tender)
Self-respect (self-esteem)	Obedient (dutiful, respectful)
Social recognition (respect, admiration)	Polite (courteous, well-mannered)
True friendship (close companionship)	Responsible (dependable, reliable)
Wisdom (a mature understanding of life)	Self-controlled (restrained, self-disciplined)

Several studies confirm that the RVS values vary among groups.[69] People in the same occupations or categories (for example, corporate managers, union members, parents, students) tend to hold similar values. For instance, one study compared corporate executives, members of the steelworkers' union, and members of a community activist group. Although a good deal of overlap was found among the three groups,[70] there were also some very significant differences (see Exhibit 4-4). The activists had value preferences that were quite different from those of the other two groups. They ranked "equality" as their most important terminal value; executives and union members ranked this value 12 and 13, respectively. Activists ranked "helpful" as their second-highest instrumental value. The other two groups both ranked it 14. These differences are important, because executives, union members, and activists all have a vested interest in what corporations do. These differences make it difficult when these groups have to negotiate with each other and can create serious conflicts when they contend with each other over the organization's economic and social policies.[71]

Exhibit 4-4	Mean Value Ranking of Executives, Union Members, and Activists (Top Five Only)

EXECUTIVES		UNION MEMBERS		ACTIVISTS	
Terminal	Instrumental	Terminal	Instrumental	Terminal	Instrumental
1. Self-respect	1. Honest	1. Family security	1. Responsible	1. Equality	1. Honest
2. Family security	2. Responsible	2. Freedom	2. Honest	2. A world of peace	2. Helpful
3. Freedom	3. Capable	3. Happiness	3. Courageous	3. Family security	3. Courageous
4. A sense of accomplishment	4. Ambitious	4. Self-respect	4. Independent	4. Self-respect	4. Responsible
5. Happiness	5. Independent	5. Mature love	5. Capable	5. Freedom	5. Capable

Contemporary Work Cohorts   We have integrated several recent analyses of work values into four groups that attempt to capture the unique values of different cohorts or generations in the U.S. workforce.[72] Exhibit 4-5 proposes that employees can be segmented by the era in which they entered the workforce. Because most people start work between the ages of 18 and 23, the eras also correlate closely with the chronological age of employees.

Before going any further, let's acknowledge some limitations of this analysis. First, we make no assumption that this framework would apply universally across all cultures. Second, there is very little rigorous research on generational values, so we have to rely on an intuitive framework. Finally, these are imprecise categories. There is no law that someone born in 1985 can't have similar values to someone born in 1955. You may see your values better reflected in other generations than in your own. Despite these limitations, values do change over generations,[73] and there are some useful insights to be gained from analyzing values this way.

Workers who grew up influenced by the Great Depression, World War II, the Andrews Sisters, and the Berlin blockade entered the workforce through the 1950s and early 1960s believing in hard work, the status quo, and authority figures. We call them *Veterans* (some use the label *Traditionalists*). Once hired, Veterans tended to be loyal to their employer and respectful of authority. They tend to be hardworking and practical. These are the people Tom Brokaw wrote about in his book, *The Greatest Generation*. In terms of the terminal values on the RVS, these employees are likely to place the greatest importance on a comfortable life and family security.

Boomers (*Baby Boomers*) are a large cohort who were born after World War II when veterans returned to their families and times were good. Boomers entered the workforce from the mid-1960s through the mid-1980s. This cohort was influenced heavily by the civil rights movement, women's lib, the Beatles, the Vietnam War, and baby-boom competition. They brought with them a large measure of the "hippie ethic" and distrust of authority. But they place a great deal of emphasis on achievement and material success. They work hard and want to enjoy the fruits of their labors. They're pragmatists who believe that ends can justify means. Boomers see the organizations that employ them merely as vehicles for their careers. Terminal values such as a sense of accomplishment and social recognition rank high with them.

Xers (*Generation X*) lives have been shaped by globalization, two-career parents, MTV, AIDS, and computers. They value flexibility, life options, and the achievement of job satisfaction. Family and relationships are very important to this cohort. Unlike Veterans, Xers are skeptical, particularly of

Exhibit **4-5**	Dominant Work Values in Today's Workforce		
Cohort	**Entered the Workforce**	**Approximate Current Age**	**Dominant Work Values**
Veterans	1950s or early 1960s	65+	Hard working, conservative, conforming; loyalty to the organization
Boomers	1965–1985	Early 40s to mid-60s	Success, achievement, ambition, dislike of authority; loyalty to career
Xers	1985–2000	Late 20s to early 40s	Work/life balance, team-oriented, dislike of rules; loyalty to relationships
Nexters	2000 to present	Under 30	Confident, financial success, self-reliant but team-oriented; loyalty to both self and relationships

authority. They also enjoy team-oriented work. Money is important as an indicator of career performance, but Xers are willing to trade off salary increases, titles, security, and promotions for increased leisure time and expanded lifestyle options. In search of balance in their lives, Xers are less willing to make personal sacrifices for the sake of their employer than previous generations were. On the RVS, they rate high on true friendship, happiness, and pleasure.

The most recent entrants to the workforce, the *Nexters* (also called *Neters, Millennials, Generation Y,* and *Generation Next*) grew up during prosperous times but find themselves entering a post-boom economy. Gone are the days of hiring bonuses and abundant jobs. Now they face insecurity about jobs and careers. Yet they have high expectations and seek meaning in their work. Nexters are at ease with diversity and are the first generation to take technology for granted. They've lived much of their lives with ATMs, DVDs, cell phones, laptops, and the Internet. This generation tends to be money-oriented and desirous of the things that money can buy. They seek financial success. Like Xers, they enjoy teamwork but they're also highly self-reliant. They tend to emphasize terminal values such as freedom and a comfortable life.[74]

An understanding that individuals' values differ but tend to reflect the societal values of the period in which they grew up can be a valuable aid in explaining and predicting behavior. Employees in their late 60s, for instance, are more likely to accept authority than their coworkers who are 10 or 15 years younger. And workers in their 30s are more likely than their parents to balk at having to work weekends and more prone to leave a job in mid-career to pursue another that provides more leisure time.

Values, Loyalty, and Ethical Behavior

Has there been a decline in business ethics? Recent corporate scandals involving accounting manipulations, cover-ups, and conflicts of interest certainly suggest such a decline. But is this a recent phenomenon?

Although the issue is debatable, a lot of people think ethical standards began to erode in the late 1970s.[75] If there has been a decline in ethical standards, perhaps we should look to our work cohorts model (see Exhibit 4-5) for a possible explanation. After all, managers consistently report that the action of their bosses is the most important factor influencing ethical and unethical behavior in their organizations.[76] Given this fact, the values of those in middle and upper management should have a significant bearing on the entire ethical climate within an organization.

Through the mid-1970s, the managerial ranks were dominated by Veterans, whose loyalties were to their employers. When faced with ethical dilemmas, their decisions were made in terms of what was best for their organization. Beginning in the mid-to-late 1970s, Boomers began to rise into the upper levels of management. By the early 1990s, a large portion of middle and top management positions in business organizations was held by Boomers. The loyalty of Boomers is to their careers. Their focus is inward and their primary concern is with looking out for "Number One." Such self-centered values would be consistent with a decline in ethical standards. Could this help explain the alleged decline in business ethics beginning in the late 1970s?

The potential good news in this analysis is that Xers are now in the process of moving into middle-management slots and soon will be rising into top management. Since their loyalty is to relationships, they are more likely to consider the ethical implications of their actions on others around them. The result? We might look forward to an uplifting of ethical standards in business over the next decade or two merely as a result of changing values within the managerial ranks.

Since entering the Chinese market in 1984, FedEx has expanded its service to more than 220 cities. The success of FedEx in China, which has a long-term orientation as opposed to a short-term orientation in the United States, stems from the company's understanding of and respect for China's cultural traditions. Doing business in China requires a slow, persistent approach in creating and nurturing relationships built on trust and reliability.

Values Across Cultures

In Chapter 1, we described the new global village and said "managers have to become capable of working with people from different cultures." Because values differ across cultures, an understanding of these differences should be helpful in explaining and predicting behavior of employees from different countries.

Hofstede's Framework for Assessing Cultures   One of the most widely referenced approaches for analyzing variations among cultures was done in the late 1970s by Geert Hofstede.[77] He surveyed more than 116,000 IBM employees in 40 countries about their work-related values. He found that managers and employees vary on five value dimensions of national culture. They are listed and defined as follows:

- **Power distance**: The degree to which people in a country accept that power in institutions and organizations is distributed unequally. A high-power-distance rating means that large inequalities of power and wealth exist and are tolerated in the culture. Such cultures are more likely to follow a class or caste system that discourages upward mobility of its citizens. A low-power-distance ranking indicates the culture discourages differences between power and wealth. These societies stress equality and opportunity.
- **Individualism** versus **collectivism**: Individualism is the degree to which people prefer to act as individuals rather than as members of groups and believe in individual rights above all else. Collectivism emphasizes a tight social framework in which people expect others in groups of which they are a part to look after them and protect them.
- **Masculinity** versus **femininity**: The degree to which the culture favors traditional masculine roles such as achievement, power, and control versus a culture that views men and women as equals. A high-masculinity rating indicates the culture has separate roles for men and women, with men dominating the society. A high-femininity rating means that the culture has little differentiation between male and female roles. To clarify, high femininity does not mean that the culture emphasizes feminine roles; rather, it emphasizes equality between men and women. In such cultures, women are treated as the equals of men in all aspects of the society.
- **Uncertainty avoidance**: The degree to which people in a country prefer structured over unstructured situations. In cultures that score high on uncertainty avoidance, people have an increased level of anxiety about uncertainty and ambiguity. Such cultures tend to emphasize laws, regulations, and controls that are designed to reduce uncertainty. In cultures that score low on uncertainty avoidance, individuals are less dismayed by ambiguity and uncertainty and have a greater tolerance for a variety of opinions. Such cultures are less rule-oriented, take more risks, and more readily accept change.

power distance   *A national culture attribute describing the extent to which a society accepts that power in institutions and organizations is distributed unequally.*

individualism   *A national culture attribute describing the degree to which people prefer to act as individuals rather than as members of groups.*

collectivism   *A national culture attribute that describes a tight social framework in which people expect others in groups of which they are a part to look after them and protect them.*

masculinity   *A national culture attribute describing the extent to which the culture favors traditional masculine work roles of achievement, power, and control. Societal values are characterized by assertiveness and materialism.*

femininity   *A national culture attribute that has little differentiation between male and female roles, where women are treated as the equals of men in all aspects of the society.*

uncertainty avoidance   *A national culture attribute describing the extent to which a society feels threatened by uncertain and ambiguous situations and tries to avoid them.*

● **Long-term** versus **short-term orientation**: This is the newest addition to Hofstede's typology. It focuses on the degree of a society's long-term devotion to traditional values. People in cultures with long-term orientations look to the future and value thrift, persistence, and tradition. In a short-term orientation, people value the here-and-now; change is accepted more readily, and commitments do not represent impediments to change.

How do different countries score on Hofstede's dimensions? Exhibit 4-6 shows the ratings for the countries for which data are available. For example,

Exhibit 4-6	Hofstede's Cultural Values by Nation								
	Power Distance		Individualism versus Collectivism		Masculinity versus Femininity		Uncertainty Avoidance		Long- versus Short-Term Orientation	
Country	Index	Rank	Index	Rank	Index	Rank	Index	Rank	Index	Rank
Argentina	49	35-36	46	22-23	56	20-21	86	10-15		
Australia	36	41	90	2	61	16	51	37	31	22-24
Austria	11	53	55	18	79	2	70	24-25	31	22-24
Belgium	65	20	75	8	54	22	94	5-6	38	18
Brazil	69	14	38	26-27	49	27	76	21-22	65	6
Canada	39	39	80	4-5	52	24	48	41-42	23	30
Chile	63	24-25	23	38	28	46	86	10-15		
Colombia	67	17	13	49	64	11-12	80	20		
Costa Rica	35	42-44	15	46	21	48-49	86	10-15		
Denmark	18	51	74	9	16	50	23	51	46	10
Ecuador	78	8-9	8	52	63	13-14	67	28		
Finland	33	46	63	17	26	47	59	31-32	41	14
France	68	15-16	71	10-11	43	35-36	86	10-15	39	17
Germany	35	42-44	67	15	66	9-10	65	29	31	22-24
Great Britain	35	42-44	89	3	66	9-10	35	47-48	25	28-29
Greece	60	27-28	35	30	57	18-19	112	1		
Guatemala	95	2-3	6	53	37	43	101	3		
Hong Kong	68	15-16	25	37	57	18-19	29	49-50	96	2
Indonesia	78	8-9	14	47-48	46	30-31	48	41-42		
India	77	10-11	48	21	56	20-21	40	45	61	7
Iran	58	29-30	41	24	43	35-36	59	31-32		
Ireland	28	49	70	12	68	7-8	35	47-48	43	13
Israel	13	52	54	19	47	29	81	19		
Italy	50	34	76	7	70	4-5	75	23	34	19
Jamaica	45	37	39	25	68	7-8	13	52		
Japan	54	33	46	22-23	95	1	92	7	80	4
Korea (South)	60	27-28	18	43	39	41	85	16-17	75	5
Malaysia	104	1	26	36	50	25-26	36	46		
Mexico	81	5-6	30	32	69	6	82	18		
Netherlands	38	40	80	4-5	14	51	53	35	44	11-12
Norway	31	47-48	69	13	8	52	50	38	44	11-12
New Zealand	22	50	79	6	58	17	49	39-40	30	25-26
Pakistan	55	32	14	47-48	50	25-26	70	24-25	0	34
Panama	95	2-3	11	51	44	34	86	10-15		
Peru	64	21-23	16	45	42	37-38	87	9		
Philippines	94	4	32	31	64	11-12	44	44	19	31-32
Portugal	63	24-25	27	33-35	31	45	104	2	30	25-26
South Africa	49	35-36	65	16	63	13-14	49	39-40		
Salvador	66	18-19	19	42	40	40	94	5-6		

(continued)

Exhibit **4-6**	Hofstede's Cultural Values by Nation (*cont.*)

Country	Power Distance		Individualism versus Collectivism		Masculinity versus Femininity		Uncertainty Avoidance		Long- versus Short-Term Orientation	
	Index	Rank	Index	Rank	Index	Rank	Index	Rank	Index	Rank
Singapore	74	13	20	39-41	48	28	8	53	48	9
Spain	57	31	51	20	42	37-38	86	10-15	19	31-32
Sweden	31	47-48	71	10-11	5	53	29	49-50	33	20
Switzerland	34	45	68	14	70	4-5	58	33	40	15-16
Taiwan	58	29-30	17	44	45	32-33	69	26	87	3
Thailand	64	21-23	20	39-41	34	44	64	30	56	8
Turkey	66	18-19	37	28	45	32-33	85	16-17		
Uruguay	61	26	36	29	38	42	100	4		
United States	40	38	91	1	62	15	46	43	29	27
Venezuela	81	5-6	12	50	73	3	76	21-22		
Yugoslavia	76	12	27	33-35	21	48-49	88	8		
Regions:										
Arab countries	80	7	38	26-27	53	23	68	27		
East Africa	64	21-23	27	33-35	41	39	52	36	25	28-29
West Africa	77	10-11	20	39-41	46	30-31	54	34	16	33

Scores range from 0 = extremely low on dimension to 100 = extremely high.

NOTE: 1 = highest rank. LTO ranks: 1 = China; 15-16 = Bangladesh; 21 = Poland; 34 = lowest.

Source: Copyright Geert Hofstede BV; hofstede@bovt.nl. Reprinted with permission.

Malaysia has the largest index number in the Power Distance category. This means that Power Distance is higher in Malaysia than in any other country, which gives it its number-one rank. As you can see, the United States is very individualistic. In fact, it's the most individualistic nation of all (closely followed by Australia and Great Britain). The United States also tends to be short-term in its orientation and is low in power distance (people in the United States tend not to accept built-in class differences between people). The United States is also relatively low on uncertainty avoidance, meaning that most Americans are relatively tolerant of uncertainty and ambiguity. The United States scores relatively high on masculinity, meaning that most Americans emphasize traditional gender roles (at least relative to other countries like Denmark, Finland, Norway, and Sweden).

Note that *individualistic* countries like the United States and Great Britain tend to be low-power-distance countries and *collectivistic* countries like Malaysia and Mexico tend to be high-power-distance countries. Also, you'll notice regional differences. Western and Northern nations such as Canada or the Netherlands tend to be more individualistic. Poorer countries like Mexico and the Philippines tend to be higher on power distance. South American nations tend to be higher on uncertainty avoidance, and Asian countries tend to have a long-term orientation.

Hofstede's culture dimensions have been enormously influential on OB researchers and managers. Nevertheless, his research has been criticized. First,

long-term orientation *A national culture attribute that emphasizes the future, thrift, and persistence.*

short-term orientation *A national culture attribute that emphasizes the past and present, respect for tradition, and fulfilling social obligations.*

although the data have since been updated, the original data are from 30 years ago and were based on a single company (IBM). Since these data were originally gathered, a lot has happened on the world scene. Some of the most obvious include the fall of the Soviet Union, the transformation of Central and Eastern Europe, the end of apartheid in South Africa, the spread of Islam throughout the world today, and the rise of China as a global power. Second, few researchers have read the details of Hofstede's methodology closely and therefore are unaware of the many decisions and judgment calls he had to make (for example, reducing the cultural values to just five). Some of the Hofstede results are unexpected. For example, Japan, which is often considered a highly collectivist nation, is considered only average on collectivism under Hofstede's dimensions.[78] Despite these concerns, Hofstede has been one of the most widely cited social scientists ever, and his framework has left a lasting mark on OB.

The GLOBE Framework for Assessing Cultures Begun in 1993, the Global Leadership and Organizational Behavior Effectiveness (GLOBE) research program is an ongoing cross-cultural investigation of leadership and national culture. Using data from 825 organizations in 62 countries, the GLOBE team identified nine dimensions on which national cultures differ (see Exhibit 4-7 for examples of country ratings on each of the dimensions).[79]

Exhibit **4-7**	GLOBE Highlights		
Dimension	**Countries Rating Low**	**Countries Rating Moderate**	**Countries Rating High**
Assertiveness	Sweden	Egypt	Spain
	New Zealand	Ireland	U.S.
	Switzerland	Philippines	Greece
Future orientation	Russia	Slovenia	Denmark
	Argentina	Egypt	Canada
	Poland	Ireland	Netherlands
Gender differentiation	Sweden	Italy	South Korea
	Denmark	Brazil	Egypt
	Slovenia	Argentina	Morocco
Uncertainty avoidance	Russia	Israel	Austria
	Hungary	U.S.	Denmark
	Bolivia	Mexico	Germany
Power distance	Denmark	England	Russia
	Netherlands	France	Spain
	South Africa	Brazil	Thailand
Individualism/collectivism*	Denmark	Hong Kong	Greece
	Singapore	U.S.	Hungary
	Japan	Egypt	Germany
In-group collectivism	Denmark	Japan	Egypt
	Sweden	Israel	China
	New Zealand	Qatar	Morocco
Performance orientation	Russia	Sweden	U.S.
	Argentina	Israel	Taiwan
	Greece	Spain	New Zealand
Humane orientation	Germany	Hong Kong	Indonesia
	Spain	Sweden	Egypt
	France	Taiwan	Malaysia

*A low score is synonymous with collectivism.

Source: M. Javidan and R. J. House, "Cultural Acumen for the Global Manager: Lessons from Project GLOBE," *Organizational Dynamics*, Spring 2001, pp. 289–305. Copyright © 2001. Reprinted with permission from Elsevier.

- *Assertiveness* The extent to which a society encourages people to be tough, confrontational, assertive, and competitive versus modest and tender.
- *Future orientation* The extent to which a society encourages and rewards future-oriented behaviors such as planning, investing in the future, and delaying gratification. This is essentially equivalent to Hofstede's long-term/short-term orientation.
- *Gender differentiation* The extent to which a society maximizes gender role differences. This is equivalent to Hofstede's masculinity-femininity dimension.
- *Uncertainty avoidance* As identified by Hofstede, the GLOBE team defined this term as a society's reliance on social norms and procedures to alleviate the unpredictability of future events.
- *Power distance* As did Hofstede, the GLOBE team defined this as the degree to which members of a society expect power to be unequally shared.
- *Individualism/collectivism* Again, this term was defined as was Hofstede's as the degree to which individuals are encouraged by societal institutions to be integrated into groups within organizations and society.
- *In-group collectivism* In contrast to focusing on societal institutions, this dimension encompasses the extent to which members of a society take pride in membership in small groups, such as their family and circle of close friends, and the organizations in which they are employed.
- *Performance orientation* This refers to the degree to which a society encourages and rewards group members for performance improvement and excellence.
- *Humane orientation* This is defined as the degree to which a society encourages and rewards individuals for being fair, altruistic, generous, caring, and kind to others.

A comparison of the GLOBE dimensions against those identified by Hofstede suggest that the former has extended Hofstede's work rather than replaced it. The GLOBE project confirms that Hofstede's five dimensions are still valid. However, it has added some additional dimensions and provides us with an updated measure of where countries rate on each dimension. As generations evolve and immigrants enter a nation, a country's cultural values can change. For instance, the GLOBE survey suggests that the United States has become somewhat less individualist over time. We can expect future cross-cultural studies of human behavior and organizational practices to increasingly use the GLOBE dimensions to assess differences between countries.

Implications for OB   Twenty years ago, it would have been fair to say that *organizational behavior* had a strong American bias. Most of the concepts had been developed by Americans using American subjects within domestic contexts. For instance, a comprehensive study published in the early 1980s covering more than 11,000 articles published in 24 management and organizational behavior journals over a 10-year period found that approximately 80 percent of the studies were done in the United States and had been conducted by Americans.[80] But times have changed.[81] Although the majority of published findings still focus on Americans, recent research has significantly expanded OB's domain to include European, South American, African, and Asian subjects. Additionally, there has been a marked increase in cross-cultural research by teams of researchers from different countries.[82]

OB has become a global discipline and, as such, its concepts need to reflect the different cultural values of people in different countries. Fortunately, a wealth of research has been published in recent years that

Are Americans' Values Different?

Americans are used to being criticized. After all, it was more than a century ago when the Irish playwright George Barnard Shaw wrote, "Americans adore me and will go on adoring me until I say something nice about them."

But as a result of the Iraq War and the fact that the United States is the world's lone remaining superpower, Americans are taking unprecedented criticism abroad. One critic sneered, "The American pursuit of wealth, size, and abundance—as material surrogates for happiness—is aesthetically unpleasing and ecologically catastrophic." And

many Europeans think that Americans are obsessed with work. Some have even argued that the United States and Europe are becoming increasingly polarized.

Overall, the United States is wealthier than Europe and has higher productivity. But what's wrong with that? Well, some stats are not very positive. For example, compared to Europe, the United States is much more violent; it has 685 prisons for every 100,000 people, compared to 87 in the European Union. Also, the United States has increasingly seemed to reward power with money. For example, in 1980 the average CEO in the United States earned 40 times the annual income of the average manufacturing employee. Today, that ratio is 475:1! By comparison, the ratios are 24:1 in the U.K., 15:1 in France, and 13:1 in

Sweden. Finally, the United States contains 5 percent of the world's population, but it is responsible for 25 percent of the world's greenhouse gas output—which is, many scientists argue, responsible for global warming.

Values may account for some of these differences. For example, in a study of people in 14 countries, Americans were more likely than those from the other nations to see natural resources as elements at their disposal. And compared to Europeans, Americans are more likely to believe that war is often necessary, that it is right to kill to defend property, and that physical punishment of children is necessary.

Do you think American values are an underlying factor behind some of these social phenomena? Or is this academic American bashing?

Source: Based on: T. Judt, "Europe vs. America," *New York Review of Books* (http://www.nybooks.com/articles/17726) (February 20, 2005); P. W. Schultz and L. Zelezny, "Values as Predictors of Environmental Attitudes: Evidence for Consistency Across 14 Countries," *Journal of Environmental Psychology*, September 1999, pp. 255–65; A. McAlister, P. Sandström, P. Puska, A. Veijo, R. Chereches, and L. Heidmets, "Attitudes Towards War, Killing, and Punishment of Children Among Young People in Estonia, Finland, Romania, the Russian Federation, and the USA," *Bulletin of the World Health Organization* 79, no. 5 (2001), pp. 382–87.

allows us to specify where OB concepts are universally applicable across cultures and where they're not. In future chapters, we'll regularly stop to consider the generalizability of OB findings and how they might need to be modified in different countries.

Linking an Individual's Personality and Values to the Workplace

Thirty years ago, organizations were concerned only with personality because their primary focus was to match individuals to specific jobs. That concern still exists. But, in recent years, this interest has expanded to include how well the individual's personality *and* values match the *organization.* Why? Because managers today are less interested in an applicant's ability to perform a *specific* job than with the *flexibility* to meet changing situations and commitment to the organization.

We'll now discuss person–job fit and person–organization fit in more detail.

Person–Job Fit

Matching the job requirements with personality characteristics is best articulated in John Holland's **personality–job fit theory.**[83] The theory is based on the notion of fit between an individual's personality characteristics and

Exhibit **4-8**	Holland's Typology of Personality and Congruent Occupations	
Type	**Personality Characteristics**	**Congruent Occupations**
Realistic: Prefers physical activities that require skill, strength, and coordination	Shy, genuine, persistent, stable, conforming, practical	Mechanic, drill press operator, assembly-line worker, farmer
Investigative: Prefers activities that involve thinking, organizing, and understanding	Analytical, original, curious, independent	Biologist, economist, mathematician, news reporter
Social: Prefers activities that involve helping and developing others	Sociable, friendly, cooperative, understanding	Social worker, teacher, counselor, clinical psychologist
Conventional: Prefers rule-regulated, orderly, and unambiguous activities	Conforming, efficient, practical, unimaginative, inflexible	Accountant, corporate manager, bank teller, file clerk
Enterprising: Prefers verbal activities in which there are opportunities to influence others and attain power	Self-confident, ambitious, energetic, domineering	Lawyer, real estate agent, public relations specialist, small business manager
Artistic: Prefers ambiguous and unsystematic activities that allow creative expression	Imaginative, disorderly, idealistic, emotional, impractical	Painter, musician, writer, interior decorator

the job. Holland presents six personality types and proposes that satisfaction and the propensity to leave a position depend on the degree to which individuals successfully match their personalities to a job. Each one of the six personality types has a congruent occupation. Exhibit 4-8 describes the six types and their personality characteristics and gives examples of congruent occupations.

Holland has developed a Vocational Preference Inventory questionnaire that contains 160 occupational titles. Respondents indicate which of these occupations they like or dislike, and their answers are used to form personality profiles. Using this procedure, research strongly supports the hexagonal diagram shown in Exhibit 4-9.[84] This figure shows that the closer two fields or orientations are in the hexagon, the more compatible they are. Adjacent categories are quite similar, whereas those diagonally opposite are highly dissimilar.

What does all this mean? The theory argues that satisfaction is highest and turnover lowest when personality and occupation are in agreement. Social individuals should be in social jobs, conventional people in conventional jobs, and so forth. A realistic person in a realistic job is in a more congruent situation than is a realistic person in an investigative job. A realistic person in a social job is in the most incongruent situation possible. The key points of this model are that (1) there do appear to be intrinsic differences in personality among individuals, (2) there are different types of jobs, and (3) people in jobs congruent with their personality should be more satisfied and less likely to voluntarily resign than should people in incongruent jobs.

Person–Organization Fit

As previously noted, attention in recent years has expanded to include matching people to *organizations* as well as *jobs*. To the degree that an organization faces a dynamic and changing environment and requires employees who are

personality–job fit theory   *Identifies six personality types and proposes that the fit between personality type and occupational environment determines satisfaction and turnover.*

Exhibit **4-9**	Relationships Among Occupational Personality Types

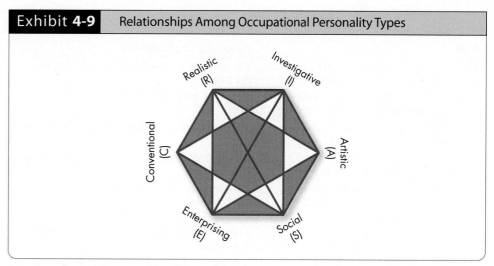

able to readily change tasks and move easily between teams, it's more important that employees' personalities fit with the overall organization's culture than with the characteristics of any specific job.

The person–organization fit essentially argues that people leave organizations that are not compatible with their personalities.[85] Using the Big Five terminology, for instance, we could expect that people high on extraversion fit better with aggressive and team-oriented cultures, that people high on agreeableness match up better with a supportive organizational climate than one that focuses on aggressiveness, and that people high on openness to experience fit better into organizations that emphasize innovation rather than standardization.[86] Following these guidelines at the time of hiring should lead to selecting new employees who fit better with the organization's culture, which, in turn, should result in higher employee satisfaction and reduced turnover.

Research on person–organization fit has also looked at people's values and whether they match the organization's culture. The fit of employees' values with the culture of their organization predicts job satisfaction, commitment to the organization, and low turnover.[87]

The Organizational Culture Profile (OCP) can help assess whether or not an individual's values match the organization's (see Exhibit 4-10).[88] The OCP helps individuals sort their characteristics in terms of importance, which indicates what a person values. The reason individuals sort characteristics—as opposed to just rating them on a scale such as 1 = *this characteristic doesn't matter to me* versus 10 = *this characteristic is extremely important to me*—is that all values are desirable. In other words, who would want to work in an unsupportive organization, or one with a bad reputation? So, if people were using the rating scale, they might rate all the values as extremely important. The forced-choice nature of the OCP makes sense because it's only through having to make hard choices that one's true values become apparent. For example, Motorola emphasizes innovation, tolerance for diversity, and teamwork. These values are assessed in the OCP. So, if these were at the high end of your pyramid, then you'd probably be happy in this type of culture. But you might not be as happy in GE's culture, which emphasizes achievement, performance, results, and individual responsibility.

Exhibit 4-10 Organizational Culture Profile

You will find 40 characteristics that describe people. Please consider each characteristic according to the question: **How well does this characteristic describe me?**

The boxes range from the **most characteristic** to **least characteristic**. Place each characteristic as it describes you in an appropriate box. Each box receives only one attribute. For example, only two items may be "most characteristic" of you and your ideal organization while eight items must be "neither characteristic nor uncharacteristic." You can write the item number in the box rather than the words. It may be easiest to read through the entire list of characteristics looking for extremes first. Although this sorting may appear difficult, it goes quickly if you cross items off as you place them.

Most characteristic ◄──────────► **Neither characteristic** ◄──────────► **Least characteristic**
                                      nor uncharacteristic

The characteristics are

1. Adaptability
2. Stability
3. Being reflective
4. Being innovative
5. Being quick to take advantage of opportunities
6. Taking individual responsibility
7. Risk taking
8. Opportunities for professional growth
9. Autonomy
10. Being rule-oriented
11. Being analytical
12. Paying attention to detail
13. Confronting conflict directly
14. Being team-oriented
15. Sharing information freely
16. Being people-oriented
17. Fairness
18. Not being constrained by many rules
19. Tolerance
20. Informality

21. Decisiveness
22. Being competive
23. Being highly organized
24. Achievement orientation
25. Having a clear guiding philosophy
26. Being results-oriented
27. Having high performance expectations
28. Being aggressive
29. High pay for good performance
30. Security of employment
31. Offers praise for good performance
32. Being supportive
33. Being calm
34. Developing friends at work
35. Being socially responsible
36. Enthusiasm for the job
37. Working long hours
38. Having a good reputation
39. An emphasis on quality
40. Being distinctive/different from others

Summary and Implications for Managers

Personality   What value, if any, does the Big Five provide to managers? From the early 1900s through the mid-1980s, researchers sought to find a link between personality and job performance. "The outcome of those 80-plus years of research was that personality and job performance were not meaningfully related across traits or situations."[89] However, the past 20 years have been more promising, largely due to the findings surrounding the Big Five. Seeking employees who score high on conscientiousness, for instance, is probably sound advice. Similarly, screening candidates for managerial and sales positions to identify those high in extraversion also should pay dividends. In terms of exerting effort at work, there is impressive evidence that people who score high on conscientiousness, extraversion, and emotional stability are likely to be highly motivated employees.[90] Of course, situational factors need to be taken into consideration.[91] Factors such as job demands, the degree of required interaction with others, and the organization's culture are examples of situational variables that moderate the personality–job performance relationship. So you need to evaluate the job, the work group, and the organization to determine the optimum personality fit.

Although the MBTI® has been widely criticized, it may have a place for use in organizations. In training and development, it can help employees to better understand themselves. It can provide aid to teams by helping members better understand each other. And it can open up communication in work groups and possibly reduce conflicts.

Values   Why is it important to know an individual's values? Although they don't have a direct impact on behavior, values strongly influence a person's attitudes, behaviors, and perceptions. So knowledge of an individual's value system can provide insight into what "makes the person tick."

Given that people's values differ, managers can use the Rokeach Value Survey to assess potential employees and determine if their values align with the dominant values of the organization. Employees' performance and satisfaction are likely to be higher if their values fit well with the organization. For instance, the person who places high importance on imagination, independence, and freedom is likely to be poorly matched with an organization that seeks conformity from its employees. Managers are more likely to appreciate, evaluate positively, and allocate rewards to employees who "fit in," and employees are more likely to be satisfied if they perceive that they do fit in. This argues for management to strive during the selection of new employees to find job candidates who not only have the ability, experience, and motivation to perform but also a value system that is compatible with the organization's.

Point ◁▷ Counterpoint

Traits Are Powerful Predictors of Behavior[92]

Point

The essence of trait approaches in OB is that employees possess stable personality characteristics that significantly influence their attitudes toward, and behavioral reactions to, organizational settings. People with particular traits tend to be relatively consistent in their attitudes and behavior over time and across situations.

Of course, trait theorists recognize that all traits are not equally powerful. They tend to put them into one of three categories. *Cardinal traits* are those so strong and generalized that they influence every act a person performs. *Primary traits* are generally consistent influences on behavior, but they may not show up in all situations. Finally, *secondary traits* are attributes that do not form a vital part of the personality but come into play only in particular situations. For the most part, trait theories have focused on the power of primary traits to predict employee behavior.

Trait theorists do a fairly good job of meeting the average person's face-validity test. Think of friends, relatives, and acquaintances you have known for a number of years. Do they have traits that have remained essentially stable over time? Most of us would answer that question in the affirmative. If Cousin Anne was shy and nervous when we last saw her 10 years ago, we would be surprised to find her outgoing and relaxed now.

Managers seem to have a strong belief in the power of traits to predict behavior. If managers believed that situations determined behavior, they would hire people almost at random and structure the situation properly. But the employee selection process in most organizations places a great deal of emphasis on how applicants perform in interviews and on tests. Assume you're an interviewer and ask yourself: What am I looking for in job candidates? If you answered with terms such as *conscientious, hardworking, persistent, confident*, and *dependable*, you're a trait theorist.

Counterpoint

Few people would dispute that there are some stable individual attributes that affect reactions to the workplace. But trait theorists go beyond that generality and argue that individual behavior consistencies are widespread and account for much of the differences in behavior among people.

There are two important problems with using traits to explain a large proportion of behavior in organizations. First, organizational settings are strong situations that have a large impact on employee behavior. Second, individuals are highly adaptive and personality traits change in response to organizational situations.

It has been well known for some time that the effects of traits are likely to be strongest in relatively weak situations and weakest in relatively strong situations. Organizational settings tend to be strong situations because they have rules and other formal regulations that define acceptable behavior and punish deviant behavior; and they have informal norms that dictate appropriate behaviors. These formal and informal constraints minimize the effects of personality traits.

By arguing that employees possess stable traits that lead to cross-situational consistencies in behaviors, trait theorists are implying that individuals don't really adapt to different situations. But there is a growing body of evidence that an individual's traits are changed by the organizations that that individual participates in. If the individual's personality changes as a result of exposure to organizational settings, in what sense can that individual be said to have traits that persistently and consistently affect his or her reactions to those very settings? Moreover, people typically belong to multiple organizations that often include very different kinds of members. And they adapt to those different situations. Instead of being the prisoners of a rigid and stable personality framework as trait theorists propose, people regularly adjust their behavior to reflect the requirements of various situations.

Questions for Review

1. What is *personality*?

2. What is the Myers-Briggs Type Indicator?

3. Describe the factors in the Big Five model. Which factor shows the greatest value in predicting behavior? Why does it?

4. What behavioral predictions might you make if you knew that an employee had (a) low core self-evaluation? (b) a low Mach score? (c) a Type A personality?

5. Do people from the same country have a common personality type? Explain.

6. Contrast the Veteran, Boomers, Xers, and Nexters classifications with the terminal values identified in the Rokeach Value Survey.

7. What are the five value dimensions of national culture as defined by Hofstede? Based on your own national culture, if you were a manager working in Australia, do you think you would find it difficult to lead a team? What about in Japan? How would you create an effective team atmosphere in both countries?

8. What were the six personality types identified by Holland?

9. What is person–job fit, and how is it different from person-organization fit?

10. Why might managers today pay more attention to person–organization fit than to person–job fit?

Questions for Critical Thinking

1. "Heredity determines personality." (a) Build an argument to support this statement. (b) Build an argument against this statement.

2. "The type of job an employee does moderates the relationship between personality and job productivity." Do you agree or disagree with this statement? Discuss.

3. One day your boss comes in and he is nervous, edgy, and argumentative. The next day he is calm and relaxed. Does this behavior suggest that personality traits are not consistent from day to day?

4. "Thirty-five years ago, the young employees we hired were ambitious, conscientious, hardworking, and honest. Today's young workers don't have the same values." Do you agree or disagree with this manager's comments? Support your position.

5. Do you think there might be a positive and significant relationship between the possession of certain personal values and successful career progression in organizations like Merrill Lynch, the AFL-CIO, and the city of Cleveland's police department? Discuss.

Team Exercise

CHALLENGES IN NEGOTIATING WITH CHINESE EXECUTIVES

Form into teams of three to five members each. All your team's members work for a company in the Midwestern part of the United States that manufactures bathroom fixtures such as sinks, toilets, and bathtubs. Your company's senior management has decided to make a serious effort to expand sales of its fixtures into the Chinese market. And to begin the process, your team has been chosen to make a 10-day trip to Beijing and Shanghai to meet with purchasing executives at half-a-dozen Chinese residential and commercial real estate construction developers.

Your team will be leaving for its trip in a week. You will have a translator in both cities, but your team wants to do whatever it can to make a good impression on the Chinese executives they will be meeting. Unfortunately, the members of your team have a relatively limited knowledge of Chinese culture. To help with the trip, one of your team members has found a brochure that summarizes some of the unique characteristics of the Chinese and that might prove valuable in opening negotiations. The highlights of that brochure included:

- Emphasis is placed on trust and mutual connections.
- The Chinese are interested in long-term benefits.
- Chinese seem to have a compelling need to dwell on the subject of friendship.
- Initial business meetings are devoted to pleasantries—such as serving tea and chitchat.
- So as not to lose face, Chinese prefer to negotiate through an intermediary.
- The Chinese are sensitive to national slights and are still addicted to propagandistic slogans and codes.
- The Chinese are well aware of Americans' reputation for impatience. They will often take their time in decision making to gain an advantage in negotiations.
- The Chinese generally believe that foreign businesspersons will be highly qualified technically in their specific area of expertise.
- Chinese posture becomes rigid whenever they feel their goals are being compromised.

- Once Chinese decide upon who and what is the best, they show great steadfastness.
- Foreigners should not focus on the individual Chinese person but rather on the group of individuals who are working for a particular goal.

- In negotiations with the Chinese, nothing should be considered final until it has been actually realized.

Your team has 30 minutes to rough out a strategy for meeting with the Chinese purchasing executives. Be as specific as possible. When finished, be prepared to present your strategy to the entire class.

Source: This exercise is based on information in R. Harris and R. T. Moran, *Managing Cultural Differences*, 5th ed. (Houston, TX: Gulf Publishing, 1999), pp. 286–92.

Ethical Dilemma

HIRING BASED ON GENETIC DATA

The Human Genome Project (HGP) began in 1990. Its goal was to identify the approximately 35,000 genes in human DNA and to map out and sequence the 3 billion chemical base pairs that make up human DNA. As the director of the project said, HGP will allow us to read "our own instruction book."

The project was completed in 2003. And now that it's finished, we're faced with a number of ethical issues as to how the information it developed will be used. From an OB perspective, we should be concerned with how genetic information might be used by employers to screen job applicants and employees.

It is now possible for employers to identify predisposed and presymptomatic genetic conditions. People who are predisposed don't have a disease but have an increased likelihood of developing it. Presymptomatic genetic conditions means a person will develop a disease if they live long enough. For instance, there is a gene that predisposes an individual to breast cancer and another that is presymptomatic of Huntington's disease.

There are federal and state laws in the United States that protect individuals against misuse of genetic data. For instance, the Americans with Disabilities Act protects individuals against genetic discrimination in the workplace. But this applies only to organizations with 15 or more employees. And the law doesn't restrict employers from using genetic testing if it's related to job performance.

Employers and insurance companies argue that genetic information is important to limit potential liability for health and life insurance. Critics respond that employees are entitled to their privacy.

Where it's legal, do you think it's ethical for employers to engage in genetic testing with the intent to screen for diseases or potential diseases? Is it permissible, for example, to use a blood test to perform genetic testing on employees without their consent? What about *with* their consent? Is your answer any different if the genetic information is reasonably related to specific job performance?

Source: This dilemma is based on R. A. Curley Jr. and L. M. Caperna, "The Brave New World Is Here: Privacy Issues and the Human Genome Project," *Defense Counsel Journal*, January 2003, pp. 22–35.

Case Incident 1

THE RISE AND FALL OF CARLY FIORINA

For a long time, Carleton S. ("Carly") Fiorina was one of the best-known CEOs in the world. Brought in as Hewlett-Packard's (HP) CEO in 1999, Fiorina was instantly recognizable for her charisma, visibility, and aggressiveness. Practically every OB book (including this one) featured her. She was even mentioned as a possible cabinet member of the Bush administration or a Senate candidate from California. Widely praised as a change agent and a visionary leader at Lucent Technologies—which she led before joining HP—Fiorina had a way of generating enthusiasm and excitement. Some called her a "rock star" CEO.

However, under Fiorina's leadership, HP struggled as the world's second-largest computer company. Although revenue climbed steadily under her leadership, profits did not. Nor did the stock price—an investor who bought HP stock the day Fiorina was hired would have seen 55 percent of the investment vanish by the time she was fired. Her acquisition of Compaq in 2002, which Walter Hewlett (son of the company's cofounder and one of HP's largest shareholders) was adamantly against, never paid off as promised.

As a result of these struggles, the HP board tried to find a way to limit Fiorina's powers and give more authority to other executives. A month before her firing, Fiorina was told point-blank by three board members that she had to change her style. She adamantly refused. A month later, when informed of the board's decision to fire her, Fiorina was "stunned."

After her firing, there was no shortage of experts to point out her failings. Some felt that Fiorina spent too much time on the road talking to groups and not enough time inside the company. Others felt she overpromised results. One HP executive stated, "There were people inside HP who loved Carly because of her ability to architect a strategy, but then there were the people who thought that she was drawn to all the pomp and circumstance." Another HP observer claimed after Fiorina was ousted, "The stock is up a bit on the fact that nobody liked Carly's leadership all that much." Others argued that HP employees never accepted Fiorina's attempts to change HP culture, or her high-profile ways (she placed her portrait in HP headquarters next to the HP founders, and she frequently rubbed elbows with rock stars like the Edge, Gwen Stefani, and Sheryl Crow).

For someone who was praised for her energy and leadership, how could the tides have turned so dramatically against her? For now, the rock star CEO is without a band.

Questions

1. Why is it that the qualities that seemingly were a great asset to Fiorina and HP—energy, enthusiasm, charisma, vision, tenacity, aggressiveness—became liabilities? Does this case contradict the view that personality is important? Explain.

2. Some have argued that Fiorina failed because her personality was "too big" and that she became more focused on herself than on the nuts-and-bolts of business. Can a person's personality be *too* strong? How so?

3. Some have argued that her firing is an example of the double standard that being aggressive and forceful works for men but backfires for women. Do you think gender had anything to do with Fiorina's firing?

4. Fiorina had to complete a 2-hour, 900-question personality test as part of the process to select her as CEO. Does this suggest that personality testing has little value?

Source: Based on J. Markoff, "When + Adds Up to Minus," *The New York Times*, February 10, 2005, pp. C1, C7; P. R. La Monica, "Fiorina out, HP Stock Soars," *CNN/Money* (http://www.money.cnn.com/2005/02/09/technology/hp_fiorina/) (February 10, 2005)

Case Incident 2

A DIAMOND PERSONALITY

Ask Oscar Rodriguez about the dot-com burst and he may grin at you as if to say, "What burst?" Rodriguez, a 38-year-old entrepreneur, owns an Internet business that sells loose diamonds to various buyers. Business is booming for Rodriguez. In 2004, he had sales of $2.06 million—a 140 percent increase from 2003. Rodriguez's database of almost 60,000 diamonds is one of the largest and is valued, according to Rodriguez, at over $350 million. Needless to say, Oscar Rodriguez is optimistic about his business venture.

The future wasn't always so bright for Rodriguez, however. In 1985, Rodriguez moved from his native country, Puerto Rico, to Gainesville, Florida, with little ability to speak English. There, he attended community college and worked at the local mall to support himself. After graduation, his roommate's girlfriend suggested that he work at a local jeweler. "I thought she was crazy. I didn't know anything about jewelry," says Rodriguez, who took her advice. Though he worked hard and received his Diamonds and Diamonds Grading certification from the Gemological Institute of America, he wasn't satisfied with his progress. "I quickly realized that working there, I was just going to get a salary with a raise here and there. I would never become anything. That drove me to explore other business ventures. I also came to really know diamonds—their pricing and their quality."

In 1997, tired of working for someone else, Rodriguez decided to open his own jewelry store. However, business didn't boom. "Some of my customers were telling me they could find diamonds for less on the Internet. It blew my mind." Rodriguez recognized an opportunity and began contacting well-known diamond dealers to see if they would be interested in selling their gems online. Rodriguez recalls one conversation with a prominent dealer who told him, "You can not sell diamonds on the Internet. You will not survive." Discouraged, Rodriguez then says that he made a mistake. "I stopped working on it. If you have a dream, you have to keep working harder at it."

A year later, Rodriguez did work harder at his dream and found a dealer who agreed to provide him with some diamonds. Says Rodriguez, "Once I had one, I could approach others. Business started to build. The first three months I sold $200,000 worth of diamonds right off the bat. And that was just me. I started to add employees and eventually closed the jewelry store and got out of retail." Although Rodriquez does have some diamonds in inventory, he primarily acts as a connection point between buyers and suppliers, giving his customers an extraordinary selection from which to choose.

Rodriguez is now a savvy entrepreneur, and his company, Abazias.com, went public in October 2003.

Why is Rodriguez successful? Just ask two people who have known Rodriquez over the years. Gary Schneider, a realtor who helped build Rodriguez's building, says, "Oscar is a very ambitious young man. I am not surprised at all how successful he is. He is an entrepreneur in the truest sense of the word." One of Rodriguez's former real-estate instructors, Howard Freeman, concurs. "I am not surprised at all at his success," says Freeman. "Oscar has always been an extremely motivated individual with a lot of resources. He has a wonderful personality and pays close attention to detail. He also has an ability to stick to things. You could tell from the beginning that he was going to persevere, and I am proud of him."

Rodriguez is keeping his success in perspective, but he also realizes his business' potential: "I take a very small salary, and our overhead is $250,000 a year. I am not in debt, and the business is breaking even. I care about the company. I want to keep everything even until we take off, and then it may be another ball game."

Questions

1. What factors do you think attributed to Rodriguez's success? Was he merely "in the right place at the right time," or are there characteristics about him that contribute to his success?

2. How do you believe Rodriguez would score on the Big Five dimensions of personality (extraversion, agreeableness, conscientiousness, emotional stability, openness to experience)? Which ones would he score high on? Which ones might he score low on?

3. Do you believe that Rodriguez is high or low on core self-evaluations? On what information did you base your decision?

4. What information about Rodriguez suggests that he has a proactive personality?

Source: Based on M. Blombert, "Cultivating a Career," *The Gainesville Sun*, May 9, 2005, p. D.1.

Endnotes

1. Based on C. Carr, "Redesigning the Management Psyche," *The New York Times*, May 26, 2002, p. BU-14.

2. G. W. Allport, *Personality: A Psychological Interpretation* (New York: Holt, Rinehart & Winston, 1937), p. 48. For a brief critique of current views on the meaning of personality, see R. T. Hogan and B. W. Roberts, "Introduction: Personality and Industrial and Organizational Psychology," in B. W. Roberts and R. Hogan (eds.), *Personality Psychology in the Workplace* (Washington, DC: American Psychological Association, 2001), pp. 11–12.

3. See, for instance, M. B. Stein, K. L. Jang, and W. J. Livesley, "Heritability of Social Anxiety-Related Concerns and Personality Characteristics: A Twin Study," *Journal of Nervous and Mental Disease*, April 2002, pp. 219–24; and S. Pinker, *The Blank Slate: The Modern Denial of Human Nature* (New York: Viking, 2002).

4. See R. D. Arvey and T. J. Bouchard, Jr., "Genetics, Twins, and Organizational Behavior," in B. M. Staw and L. L. Cummings (eds.), *Research in Organizational Behavior*, vol. 16 (Greenwich, CT: JAI Press, 1994), pp. 65–66; W. Wright, *Born That Way: Genes, Behavior, Personality* (New York: Knopf, 1998); T. J. Bouchard, Jr. and J. C. Loehlin, "Genes, Evolution, and Personality," *Behavior Genetics*, May 2001, pp. 243–73; and G. Lensvelt-Mulders and J. Hettema, "Analysis of Genetic Influences on the Consistency and Variability of the Big Five Across Different Stressful Situations," *European Journal of Personality*, September–October 2001, pp. 355–71.

5. R. Ilies and T. A. Judge, "On the Heritability of Job Satisfaction: The Mediating Role of Personality," *Journal of Applied Psychology* 88, no. 4 (2003), pp. 750–59.

6. W. Mischel, "The Interaction of Person and Situation," in D. Magnusson and N. S. Endler (eds.), *Personality at the Crossroads: Current Issues in Interactional Psychology* (Hillsdale, NJ: Erlbaum, 1977), pp. 166–207.

7. R. C. Carson, "Personality," in M. R. Rosenzweig and L. W. Porter (eds.), *Annual Review of Psychology*, vol. 40 (Palo Alto, CA: Annual Reviews, 1989), pp. 228–29.

8. See A. H. Buss, "Personality as Traits," *American Psychologist*, November 1989, pp. 1378–88; R. R. McCrae, "Trait Psychology and the Revival of Personality and Culture Studies," *American Behavioral Scientist*, September 2000, pp. 10–31; and L. R. James and M. D. Mazerolle, *Personality in Work Organizations* (Thousand Oaks, CA: Sage, 2002).

9. See, for instance, G. W. Allport and H. S. Odbert, "Trait Names, A Psycholexical Study," *Psychological Monographs*, no. 47 (1936); and R. B. Cattell, "Personality Pinned Down," *Psychology Today*, July 1973, pp. 40–46.

10. See R. R. McCrae and T. Costa, Jr., "Reinterpreting the Myers-Briggs Type Indicator from the Perspective of the Five Factor Model of Personality," *Journal of Personality*, March 1989, pp. 17–40; and N. L. Quenk, *Essentials of Myers-Briggs Type Indicator Assessment* (New York: Wiley, 2000).

11. "Identifying How We Think: The Myers-Briggs Type Indicator and Herrmann Brain Dominance Instrument," *Harvard Business Review*, July–August 1997, pp. 114–15.

12. G. N. Landrum, *Profiles of Genius* (New York: Prometheus, 1993).

13. See, for instance, W. L. Gardner and M. L. Martinko, "Using the Myers-Briggs Type Indicator to Study Managers: A Literature Review and Research Agenda," *Journal of Management* 22, no. 1 (1996), pp. 45–83; W. D. Mitchell, "Cautions Regarding Aggregated Data Analyses in Type Research," *Journal of Psychological Type* 53 (2000), pp. 19–30;

T. L. Bess and R. J. Harvey, "Bimodal Score Distributions and the Myers-Briggs Type Indicator: Fact or Artifact?" *Journal of Personality Assessment*, February 2002, pp. 176–86; R. M. Capraro and M. M. Capraro, "Myers-Briggs Type Indicator Score Reliability Across Studies: A Meta-Analytic Reliability Generalization Study," *Educational & Psychological Measurement*, August 2002, pp. 590–602; and R. C. Arnau, B. A. Green, D. H. Rosen, D. H. Gleaves, and J. G. Melancon, "Are Jungian Preferences Really Categorical? An Empirical Investigation Using Taxometric Analysis," *Personality & Individual Differences*, January 2003, pp. 233–51.

14. See, for example, J. M. Digman, "Personality Structure: Emergence of the Five-Factor Model," in M. R. Rosenzweig and L. W. Porter (eds.), *Annual Review of Psychology*, vol. 41 (Palo Alto, CA: Annual Reviews, 1990), pp. 417–40; R. R. McCrae, "Special Issue: The Five-Factor Model: Issues and Applications," *Journal of Personality*, June 1992; D. B. Smith, P. J. Hanges, and M. W. Dickson, "Personnel Selection and the Five-Factor Model: Reexamining the Effects of Applicant's Frame of Reference," *Journal of Applied Psychology*, April 2001, pp. 304–15; and T. A. Judge, D. Heller, and M. K. Mount, "Five-Factor Model of Personality and Job Satisfaction: A Meta-Analysis," *Journal of Applied Psychology*, June 2002, pp. 530–41.

15. See, for instance, M. R. Barrick and M. K. Mount, "The Big Five Personality Dimensions and Job Performance: A Meta-Analysis," *Personnel Psychology*, Spring 1991, pp. 1–26; R. P. Tett, D. N. Jackson, and M. Rothstein, "Personality Measures as Predictors of Job Performance: A Meta-Analytic Review," *Personnel Psychology*, Winter 1991, pp. 703–42; O. Behling, "Employee Selection: Will Intelligence and Conscientiousness Do the Job?" *Academy of Management Executive*, February 1998, pp. 77–86; G. M. Hurtz and J. J. Donovan, "Personality and Job Performance: The Big Five Revisited," *Journal of Applied Psychology*, December 2000, pp. 869–79; T. A. Judge and J. E. Bono, "Relationship of Core Self-Evaluations Traits—Self-Esteem, Generalized Self-Efficacy, Locus of Control, and Emotional Stability—With Job Satisfaction and Job Performance: A Meta-Analysis," *Journal of Applied Psychology*, February 2001, pp. 80–92; J. Hogan and B. Holland, "Using Theory to Evaluate Personality and Job-Performance Relations: A Socioanalytic Perspective," *Journal of Applied Psychology*, February 2003, pp. 100–12; and M. R. Barrick and M. K. Mount, "Select on Conscientiousness and Emotional Stability," in E. A. Locke (ed.), *Handbook of Principles of Organizational Behavior* (Malden, MA: Blackwell, 2004), pp. 15–28.

16. M. K. Mount, M. R. Barrick, and J. P. Strauss, "Validity of Observer Ratings of the Big Five Personality Factors," *Journal of Applied Psychology*, April 1994, p. 272. Additionally confirmed by G. M. Hurtz and J. J. Donovan, "Personality and Job Performance: The Big Five Revisited;" and M. R. Barrick, M. K. Mount, and T. A. Judge, "The FFM Personality Dimensions and Job Performance: Meta-Analysis of Meta-Analyses," *International Journal of Selection and Assessment* 9 (2001), pp. 9–30.

17. F. L. Schmidt and J. E. Hunter, "The Validity and Utility of Selection Methods in Personnel Psychology: Practical and Theoretical Implications of 85 Years of Research Findings," *Psychological Bulletin*, September 1998, p. 272.

18. D. W. Organ, "Personality and Organizational Citizenship Behavior," *Journal of Management*, Summer 1994, pp. 465–78;

D. W. Organ and K. Ryan, "A Meta-Analytic Review of Attitudinal and Dispositional Predictors of Organizational Citizenship Behavior," *Personnel Psychology*, Winter 1995, pp. 775–802; M. A. Konovsky and D. W. Organ, "Dispositional and Contextual Determinants of Organizational Citizenship Behavior," *Journal of Organizational Behavior*, May 1996, pp. 253–66; and P. M. Podsakoff, S. B. MacKenzie, J. B. Paine, and D. G. Bachrach, "Organizational Citizenship Behaviors: A Critical Review of the Theoretical and Empirical Literature and Suggestions for Future Research," *Journal of Management* 6, no. 3 (2000), pp. 513–63.

19. T. A. Judge, A. E. M. Van Vianen, and I. E. De Pater, "Emotional Stability, Core Self-Evaluations, and Job Outcomes: A Review of the Evidence and an Agenda for Future Research," *Human Performance* 17 (2004), pp. 325–46.

20. L. I. Spirling and R. Persaud, "Extraversion as a Risk Factor," *Journal of the American Academy of Child & Adolescent Psychiatry* 42, no. 2 (2003), pp. 130.

21. B. Laursen, L. Pulkkinen, and R. Adams, "The Antecedents and Correlates of Agreeableness in Adulthood," *Developmental Psychology* 38, no. 4 (2002), pp. 591–603.

22. T. Bogg and B. W. Roberts, "Conscientiousness and Health-Related Behaviors: A Meta-Analysis of the Leading Behavioral Contributors to Mortality," *Psychological Bulletin* 130, no. 6 (2004), pp. 887–919.

23. S. Lee and H. J. Klein, "Relationships Between Conscientiousness, Self-Efficacy, Self-Deception, and Learning over Time," *Journal of Applied Psychology* 87, no. 6 (2002), pp. 1175–82; G. J. Feist, "A Meta-Analysis of Personality in Scientific and Artistic Creativity," *Personality and Social Psychology Review* 2, no. 4 (1998), pp. 290–309.

24. M. Tamir and M. D. Robinson, "Knowing Good From Bad: The Paradox of Neuroticism, Negative Affect, and Evaluative Processing," *Journal of Personality & Social Psychology* 87, no. 6 (2004), pp. 913–25.

25. K. I. van der Zee, J. N. Zaal, and J. Piekstra, "Validation of the Multicultural Personality Questionnaire in the Context of Personnel Selection," *European Journal of Personality* 17 (2003), pp. S77–S100.

26. T. A. Judge, C. A. Higgins, C. J. Thoresen, and M. R. Barrick, "The Big Five Personality Traits, General Mental Ability, and Career Success Across the Life Span," *Personnel Psychology* 52, no. 3 (1999), pp. 621–52.

27. J. F. Kihlstrom, "Implicit Methods in Social Psychology," In C. Sansone, C. C. Morf, and A. Panter (eds.), *Handbook of Methods in Social Psychology* (Thousand Oaks, CA: Sage, 2003).

28. T. A. Judge and J. E. Bono, "A Rose by any Other Name. . . Are Self-Esteem, Generalized Self-Efficacy, Neuroticism, and Locus of Control Indicators of a Common Construct?" In B. W. Roberts and R. Hogan (eds.), *Personality Psychology in the Workplace.* (Washington, DC: American Psychological Association), pp. 93–118.

29. See J. Brockner, *Self-Esteem at Work* (Lexington, MA: Lexington Books, 1988); N. Branden, *Self-Esteem at Work* (San Francisco: Jossey-Bass, 1998); and T. J. Owens, S. Stryker, and N. Goodman (eds.), *Extending Self-Esteem Theory and Research: Sociological and Psychological Currents* (New York: Cambridge University Press, 2001).

30. P. A. Creed, T. D. Bloxsome, and K. Johnston, "Self-Esteem and Self-Efficacy Outcomes for Unemployed Individuals

Attending Occupational Skills Training Programs," *Community, Work and Family* 4, no. 3 (2001), pp. 285–303.

31. J. B. Rotter, "Generalized Expectancies for Internal versus External Control of Reinforcement," *Psychological Monographs* 80, no. 609 (1966).

32. T. A. Judge, J. E. Bono, and E. A. Locke, "Personality and Job Satisfaction: The Mediating Role of Job Characteristics," *Journal of Applied Psychology* 85, no. 2 (2000), pp. 237–49.

33. A. Erez and T. A. Judge, "Relationship of Core Self-Evaluations to Goal Setting, Motivation, and Performance," *Journal of Applied Psychology* 86, no. 6 (2001), pp. 1270–79.

34. U. Malmendier and G. Tate, "CEO Overconfidence and Corporate Investment," Research Paper #1799, Stanford Graduate School of Business (http://gobi.stanford.edu/ResearchPapers/detail1.asp?Document_ID=2528) (June 2004).

35. R. G. Vleeming, "Machiavellianism: A Preliminary Review," *Psychological Reports*, February 1979, pp. 295–310.

36. R. Christie and F. L. Geis, *Studies in Machiavellianism* (New York: Academic Press, 1970), p. 312; and N. V. Ramanaiah, A. Byravan, and F. R. J. Detwiler, "Revised Neo Personality Inventory Profiles of Machiavellian and Non-Machiavellian People," *Psychological Reports*, October 1994, pp. 937–38.

37. Christie and Geis, *Studies in Machiavellianism*.

38. R. P. Brown and V. Zeigler-Hall, "Narcissism and the Non-Equivalence of Self-Esteem Measures: A Matter of Dominance?" *Journal of Research in Personality* 38, no. 6 (December 2004), pp. 585–92.

39. M. Maccoby, "Narcissistic Leaders: The Incredible Pros, the Inevitable Cons," *The Harvard Business Review* (www.maccoby.com/Articles/NarLeaders.html) (January–February 2000).

40. W. K. Campbell and C. A. Foster, "Narcissism and Commitment in Romantic Relationships: An Investment Model Analysis," *Personality and Social Psychology Bulletin* 28, no. 4 (2002), pp. 484–95.

41. T. A. Judge, J. A. LePine, and B. L. Rich, "Loving Yourself Abundantly: Relationship of the Narcissistic Personality to Self and Other Perceptions of Workplace Deviance, Leadership, and Task and Contextual Performance," *Journal of Applied Psychology*, in press.

42. See M. Snyder, *Public Appearances/Private Realities: The Psychology of Self-Monitoring* (New York: W. H. Freeman, 1987); and S. W. Gangestad and M. Snyder, "Self-Monitoring: Appraisal and Reappraisal," *Psychological Bulletin*, July 2000, pp. 530–55.

43. Snyder, *Public Appearances/Private Realities*.

44. D. V. Day, D. J. Schleicher, A. L. Unckless, and N. J. Hiller, "Self-Monitoring Personality at Work: A Meta-Analytic Investigation of Construct Validity," *Journal of Applied Psychology*, April 2002, pp. 390–401.

45. M. Kilduff and D. V. Day, "Do Chameleons Get Ahead? The Effects of Self-Monitoring on Managerial Careers," *Academy of Management Journal*, August 1994, pp. 1047–60; and A. Mehra, M. Kilduff, and D. J. Brass, "The Social Networks of High and Low Self-Monitors: Implications for Workplace Performance," *Administrative Science Quarterly*, March 2001, pp. 121–46.

46. R. N. Taylor and M. D. Dunnette, "Influence of Dogmatism, Risk-Taking Propensity, and Intelligence on Decision-Making Strategies for a Sample of Industrial Managers," *Journal of Applied Psychology*, August 1974, pp. 420–23.

47. I. L. Janis and L. Mann, *Decision Making: A Psychological Analysis of Conflict, Choice, and Commitment* (New York: Free Press, 1977); W. H. Stewart, Jr. and L. Roth, "Risk Propensity Differences Between Entrepreneurs and Managers: A Meta-Analytic Review," *Journal of Applied Psychology*, February 2001, pp. 145–53; J. B. Miner and N. S. Raju, "Risk Propensity Differences Between Managers and Entrepreneurs and Between Low- and High-Growth Entrepreneurs: A Reply in a More Conservative Vein," *Journal of Applied Psychology* 89, no. 1 (2004), pp. 3–13; and W. H. Stewart, Jr. and P. L. Roth, "Data Quality Affects Meta-Analytic Conclusions: A Response to Miner and Raju (2004) Concerning Entrepreneurial Risk Propensity," *Journal of Applied Psychology* 89, no. 1 (2004), pp. 14–21.

48. N. Kogan and M. A. Wallach, "Group Risk Taking as a Function of Members' Anxiety and Defensiveness," *Journal of Personality*, March 1967, pp. 50–63.

49. M. Friedman and R. H. Rosenman, *Type A Behavior and Your Heart* (New York: Alfred A. Knopf, 1974), p. 84.

50. Ibid., pp. 84–85.

51. K. W. Cook, C. A. Vance, and E. Spector, "The Relation of Candidate Personality with Selection-Interview Outcomes," *Journal of Applied Social Psychology* 30 (2000), pp. 867–85.

52. J. M. Crant, "Proactive Behavior in Organizations," *Journal of Management* 26, no. 3 (2000), p. 436.

53. S. E. Seibert, M. L. Kraimer, and J. M. Crant, "What Do Proactive People Do? A Longitudinal Model Linking Proactive Personality and Career Success," *Personnel Psychology*, Winter 2001, p. 850.

54. T. S. Bateman and J. M. Crant, "The Proactive Component of Organizational Behavior: A Measure and Correlates," *Journal of Organizational Behavior*, March 1993, pp. 103–18; A. L. Frohman, "Igniting Organizational Change From Below: The Power of Personal Initiative," *Organizational Dynamics*, Winter 1997, pp. 39–53; and J. M. Crant and T. S. Bateman, "Charismatic Leadership Viewed From Above: The Impact of Proactive Personality," *Journal of Organizational Behavior*, February 2000, pp. 63–75.

55. Crant, "Proactive Behavior in Organizations."

56. See, for instance, R. C. Becherer and J. G. Maurer, "The Proactive Personality Disposition and Entrepreneurial Behavior Among Small Company Presidents," *Journal of Small Business Management*, January 1999, pp. 28–36.

57. S. E. Seibert, J. M. Crant, and M. L. Kraimer, "Proactive Personality and Career Success," *Journal of Applied Psychology*, June 1999, pp. 416–27; Seibert, Kraimer, and Crant, "What Do Proactive People Do?"; and J. D. Kammeyer-Mueller, and C. R. Wanberg, "Unwrapping the Organizational Entry Process: Disentangling Multiple Antecedents and Their Pathways to Adjustment," *Journal of Applied Psychology* 88, no. 5 (2003), pp. 779–94.

58. See, for instance, J. E. Williams, J. L. Saiz, D. L. Formy-Duval, M. L. Munick, E. E. Fogle, A. Adom, A. Haque, F. Neto, and J. Yu, "Cross-Cultural Variation in the Importance of Psychological Characteristics: A Seven-Country Study," *International Journal of Psychology*, October 1995, pp. 529–50; R. R. McCrae and P. T. Costa, Jr., "Personality Trait Structure as a Human Universal," *American Psychologist*, 1997, pp. 509–16; R. R. McCrae, "Trait Psychology and the Revival of Personality-and-Culture Studies," *American Behavioral Scientist*, September 2000, pp. 10–31; S. V. Paunonen, M. Zeidner,

H. A. Engvik, P. Oosterveld, and R. Maliphant, "The Nonverbal Assessment of Personality in Five Cultures," *Journal of Cross-Cultural Psychology*, March 2000, pp. 220–39; H. C. Triandis and E. M. Suh, "Cultural Influences on Personality," in S. T. Fiske, D. L. Schacter, and C. Zahn-Waxler (eds.), *Annual Review of Psychology*, vol. 53 (Palo Alto, CA: Annual Reviews, 2002), p. 133–60; R. R. McCrae, and J. Allik, *The Five-Factor Model of Personality Across Cultures* (New York: Kluwer Academic/Plenum, 2002); and R. R. McCrae, P. T. Costa, Jr., T. A. Martin, V. E. Oryol, A. A. Rukavishnikov, I. G. Senin, M. Hrebickova, and T. Urbanek, "Consensual Validation of Personality Traits Across Cultures," *Journal of Research in Personality* 38, no. 2 (2004), pp. 179–201.

59. P. L. Ackerman and L. G. Humphreys, "Individual Differences Theory in Industrial and Organizational Psychology," in M. D. Dunnette and L. M. Hough (eds.), *Handbook of Industrial & Organizational Psychology*, 2nd ed., vol. 1 (Palo Alto: Consulting Psychologists, 1990), pp. 223–82.

60. A. T. Church and M. S. Katigbak, "Trait Psychology in the Philippines," *American Behavioral Scientist*, September 2000, pp. 73–94.

61. J. F. Salgado, "The Five Factor Model of Personality and Job Performance in the European Community," *Journal of Applied Psychology*, February 1997, pp. 30–43.

62. F. Kluckhohn and F. L. Strodtbeck, *Variations in Value Orientations* (Evanston, IL: Row Peterson, 1961).

63. P. B. Smith, F. Trompenaars, and S. Dugan, "The Rotter Locus of Control Scale in 43 Countries: A Test of Cultural Relativity," *International Journal of Psychology*, June 1995, pp. 377–400.

64. Friedman and Rosenman, *Type A Behavior and Your Heart*, p. 86.

65. M. Rokeach, *The Nature of Human Values* (New York: Free Press, 1973), p. 5.

66. M. Rokeach and S. J. Ball-Rokeach, "Stability and Change in American Value Priorities, 1968–1981," *American Psychologist* 44, no. 5 (1989), pp. 775–84; and B. M. Meglino and E. C. Ravlin, "Individual Values in Organizations: Concepts, Controversies, and Research," *Journal of Management* 24, no. 3 (1998), p. 355.

67. See, for instance, Meglino and Ravlin, "Individual Values in Organizations," pp. 351–89.

68. Rokeach, *The Nature of Human Values*, p. 6.

69. J. M. Munson and B. Z. Posner, "The Factorial Validity of a Modified Rokeach Value Survey for Four Diverse Samples," *Educational and Psychological Measurement*, Winter 1980, pp. 1073–79; and W. C. Frederick and J. Weber, "The Values of Corporate Managers and Their Critics: An Empirical Description and Normative Implications," in W. C. Frederick and L. E. Preston (eds.), *Business Ethics: Research Issues and Empirical Studies* (Greenwich, CT: JAI Press, 1990), pp. 123–44.

70. Frederick and Weber, "The Values of Corporate Managers and Their Critics."

71. Ibid., p. 132.

72. See, for example R. Zemke, C. Raines, and B. Filipczak, *Generations at Work: Managing the Clash of Veterans, Boomers, Xers, and Nexters in Your Workplace* (New York: AMACOM, 1999); P. Paul, "Global Generation Gap," *American Demographics*, March 2002, pp. 18–19; L. C. Lancaster and D. Stillman, *When Generations Collide* (San Francisco: Jossey-Bass, 2002); and N. Watson, "Generation Wrecked," *Fortune*, October 14, 2002, pp. 183–90.

73. K. W. Smola and C. D. Sutton, "Generational Differences: Revisiting Generational Work Values for the New Millennium," *Journal of Organizational Behavior* 23 (2002), pp. 363–82; K. Mellahi and C. Guermat, "Does Age Matter? An Empirical Examination of the Effect of Age on Managerial Values and Practices in India," *Journal of World Business* 39, no. 2 (2004), pp. 199–215.

74. M. Dittman, "Generational Differences at Work," *APA Monitor* 36, no. 6, pp. 65–55; S. L. Clausing, D. L. Kurtz, J. Prendeville, and J. L. Walt, "Generational Diversity—The Nexters," *AORN Journal* (www.findarticles.com/p/articles/mi_m0FSL/is_3_78/ai_109352507) (September 2003).

75. R. E. Hattwick, Y. Kathawala, M. Monipullil, and L. Wall, "On the Alleged Decline in Business Ethics," *Journal of Behavioral Economics* 18 (1989), pp. 129–43.

76. B. Z. Posner and W. H. Schmidt, "Values and the American Manager: An Update Updated," *California Management Review* 34, no. 3 (1992), p. 86.

77. G. Hofstede, *Culture's Consequences: International Differences in Work-Related Values* (Beverly Hills, CA: Sage, 1980); G. Hofstede, *Cultures and Organizations: Software of the Mind* (London: McGraw-Hill, 1991); G. Hofstede, "Cultural Constraints in Management Theories," *Academy of Management Executive* 7, no. 1 (1993), pp. 81–94; G. Hofstede and M. F. Peterson, "National Values and Organizational Practices," in N. M. Ashkanasy, C. M. Wilderom, and M. F. Peterson (eds.), *Handbook of Organizational Culture and Climate* (Thousand Oaks, CA: Sage, 2000), pp. 401–16; and G. Hofstede, *Culture's Consequences: Comparing Values, Behaviors, Institutions, and Organizations Across Nations*, 2nd ed. (Thousand Oaks, CA: Sage, 2001). For criticism of this research, see B. McSweeney, "Hofstede's Model of National Cultural Differences and Their Consequences: A Triumph of Faith—a Failure of Analysis," *Human Relations* 55, no. 1 (2002), pp. 89–118.

78. M. H. Bond, "Reclaiming the Individual from Hofstede's Ecological Analysis—A 20-Year Odyssey: Comment on Oyserman et al. (2002). *Psychological Bulletin* 128, no. 1 (2002), pp. 73–77; G. Hofstede, "The Pitfalls of Cross-National Survey Research: A Reply to the Article by Spector et al. on the Psychometric Properties of the Hofstede Values Survey Module 1994," *Applied Psychology: An International Review* 51, no. 1 (2002), pp. 170–78; T. Fang, "A Critique of Hofstede's Fifth National Culture Dimension," *International Journal of Cross-Cultural Management* 3, no. 3 (2003), pp. 347–68.

79. M. Javidan and R. J. House, "Cultural Acumen for the Global Manager: Lessons from Project GLOBE," *Organizational Dynamics* 29, no. 4 (2001), pp. 289–305; and R. J. House, P. J. Hanges, M. Javidan, and P. W. Dorfman (eds.), *Leadership, Culture, and Organizations: The GLOBE Study of 62 Societies* (Thousand Oaks, CA: Sage, 2004).

80. N. J. Adler, "Cross-Cultural Management Research: The Ostrich and the Trend," *Academy of Management Review* 8, no. 2 (1983), pp. 226–32.

81. See, for instance, S. Werner, "Recent Developments in International Management Research: A Review of 20 Top Management Journals," *Journal of Management* 28, no. 3 (2002), pp. 277–305.

82. M. Easterby-Smith and D. Malina, "Cross-Cultural Collaborative Research: Toward Reflexivity," *Academy of*

Management Journal 42, no. 1 (1999), pp. 76–86; and R. House, M. Javidan, and P. Dorfman (eds.), "Project GLOBE: An Introduction," *Leadership, Culture, and Organizations: The GLOBE Study of 62 Societies* (Thousand Oaks, CA: Sage, 2004).

83. J. L. Holland, *Making Vocational Choices: A Theory of Vocational Personalities and Work Environments* (Odessa, FL: Psychological Assessment Resources, 1997).

84. See, for example, A. R. Spokane, "A Review of Research on Person-Environment Congruence in Holland's Theory of Careers," *Journal of Vocational Behavior*, June 1985, pp. 306–43; J. L. Holland and G. D. Gottfredson, "Studies of the Hexagonal Model: An Evaluation (or, The Perils of Stalking the Perfect Hexagon)," *Journal of Vocational Behavior*, April 1992, pp. 158–70; T. J. Tracey and J. Rounds, "Evaluating Holland's and Gati's Vocational-Interest Models: A Structural Meta-Analysis," *Psychological Bulletin*, March 1993, pp. 229–46; J. L. Holland, "Exploring Careers with a Typology: What We Have Learned and Some New Directions," *American Psychologist*, April 1996, pp. 397–406; and S. X. Day and J. Rounds, "Universality of Vocational Interest Structure Among Racial and Ethnic Minorities," *American Psychologist*, July 1998, pp. 728–36.

85. See B. Schneider, "The People Make the Place," *Personnel Psychology*, Autumn 1987, pp. 437–53; D. E. Bowen, G. E. Ledford, Jr., and B. R. Nathan, "Hiring for the Organization, Not the Job," *Academy of Management Executive*, November 1991, pp. 35–51; B. Schneider, H. W. Goldstein, and D. B. Smith, "The ASA Framework: An Update," *Personnel Psychology*, Winter 1995, pp. 747–73; A. L. Kristof, "Person-Organization Fit: An Integrative Review of Its Conceptualizations, Measurement, and Implications," *Personnel Psychology*, Spring 1996, pp. 1–49; B. Schneider, D. B. Smith, S. Taylor, and J. Fleenor, "Personality and Organizations: A Test of the Homogeneity of Personality Hypothesis," *Journal of Applied Psychology*, June 1998, pp. 462–70; A. L. Kristof-Brown, K. J. Jansen, and A. E. Colbert, "A Policy-Capturing Study of the Simultaneous Effects of Fit With Jobs, Groups, and Organization," *Journal of Applied Psychology*, October 2002, pp. 985–93; and J. W. Westerman, and L. A. Cyr, "An Integrative Analysis of Person-Organization Fit Theories"

International Journal of Selection & Assessment 12, no. 4 (2004), pp. 252–61.

86. Based on T. A. Judge and D. M. Cable, "Applicant Personality, Organizational Culture, and Organization Attraction," *Personnel Psychology*, Summer 1997, pp. 359–94.

87. M. L. Verquer, T. A. Beehr, and S. E. Wagner, "A Meta-Analysis of Relations between Person-Organization Fit and Work Attitudes," *Journal of Vocational Behavior* 63, no. 3 (2003), pp. 473–89.

88. B. Adkins and D. Caldwell, "Firm or Subgroup Culture: Where Does Fitting in Matter Most?" *Journal of Organizational Behavior* 25, no. 8 (2004), pp. 969–78; H. D. Cooper-Thomas, A. van Vianen, and N. Anderson, "Changes in Person-Organization Fit: The Impact of Socialization Tactics on Perceived and Actual P-O Fit," *European Journal of Work & Organizational Psychology* 13, no. 1 (2004), pp. 52–78; C. A. O'Reilly, J. Chatman, and D. F. Caldwell, "People and Organizational Culture: A Profile Comparison Approach to Assessing Person-Organization Fit," *Academy of Management Journal* 34, no. 3 (1991), pp. 487–516.

89. L. A. Witt, "The Interactive Effects of Extraversion and Conscientiousness on Performance," *Journal of Management* 28, no. 6 (2002), p. 836.

90. T. A. Judge and R. Ilies, "Relationship of Personality to Performance Motivation: A Meta-Analytic Review," *Journal of Applied Psychology*, August 2002, pp. 797–807.

91. R. P. Tett and D. D. Burnett, "A Personality Trait-Based Interactionist Model of Job Performance," *Journal of Applied Psychology*, June 2003, pp. 500–17.

92. W. Fleeson, "Moving Personality Beyond the Person-Situation Debate: The Challenge and the Opportunity of Within-Person Variability," *Current Directions in Psychological Science* 13, no. 2 (2004), pp. 83–87; R. T. Hogan, and B. W. Roberts, "Introduction: Personality and Industrial and Organizational Psychology," in R. T. Hogan, and B. W. Roberts (eds.), *Personality Psychology in the Workplace* (Washington, DC: American Psychological Association, 2001), pp. 3–16; N. Schmitt, "Beyond the Big Five: Increases in Understanding and Practical Utility," *Human Performance* 17, no. 3 (2004), pp. 347–57.

Esse est percipi (To be is to be perceived).

— George Berkeley

Perception and Individual Decision Making

After studying this chapter, you should be able to:

1 Explain how two people can see the same thing and interpret it differently.

2 List the three determinants of attribution.

3 Describe how shortcuts can assist in or distort our judgment of others.

4 Explain how perception affects the decision-making process.

5 Outline the six steps in the rational decision-making model.

6 Describe the actions of the boundedly rational decision maker.

7 List and explain the common decision biases or errors.

8 Identify the conditions in which individuals are most likely to use intuition in decision making.

9 Contrast the three ethical decision criteria.

LEARNING OBJECTIVES

CHAPTER 5

The Hurtful Power of Stereotypes

Nadia Aman, Mirza Baig, M. Yusuf Mohamed, and Ammar Barghouty have three things in common. They're all young, Muslim, and work for the U.S. federal government. Since September 11, 2001, their lives have changed. And much of this is due to stereotypes that coworkers and the public have of Muslims.

Aman is a project analyst in the U.S. Commerce Department. Baig is a senior network engineer in the executive office of the president. Mohamed is an attorney with the U.S. Labor Department. And Barghouty is a special agent with the FBI. Even though they've all lived in the United States for 20 years or more, each has experienced slights because of their ethnicity and the lack of understanding of their Muslim faith.

Following September 11th, "I find myself constantly having to explain and defend myself," says Aman. She sees "a degree of paranoia among Muslims. [We've become] afraid people will misconstrue what [we] say."

Baig recently was at Reagan National Airport, headed for President Bush's ranch in Texas with a senior government official and holding a plane ticket bought with a government credit card. Although he came to the United States from India when he was 14, the dark-complexioned Baig was the only one on his flight singled out by security officials for a full search.

Mohamed describes problems related to his morning prayers. For instance, he was recently at Reagan National for a 7:20 A.M. flight. He sought out a corner to say his prayers because the airport chapel was closed. But realizing that his behavior could be misconstrued, he did something he never would have done prior to September 11th. "I went over to the gate agent, and I said, 'You know, I'm going to use this corner to make my morning prayers.' They didn't object." Mohamed resented having to give advance notice. "I'm [now] more self-conscious about displays of faith in public," he says.

A few days after September 11th, Barghouty was staking out a Washington, D.C., apartment building and chatting with the FBI manager on duty. "His solution was to ship all the Muslims back home, back where they came from,' "said Barghouty, who came to the United States with his Palestinian parents when he was a year old. Barghouty responded," 'So you can start with me.' He apologized real fast."

Unfortunately, Aman, Baig, Mohamed, and Barghouty aren't alone. Many Muslim women have experienced unfair treatment because of the way people perceive their Muslim dress. For example, US Airways kept a Muslim flight attendant from working after she chose to wear a hijab (a Muslim head scarf), and Dunkin' Donuts fired a Muslim employee after she refused to remove her hijab. Recently, Aicha Baha sued Walt Disney World, alleging that she was fired because she wouldn't remove her hijab at work. Another women, Jennifer Abdelwahed, recently sued her employer—Goodwill Industries—for the same reason.

A San Francisco area journalist started wearing her Muslim head scarf in a less traditional style in the past year. "I was on a bus and some kids got on, and they started calling me a terrorist," says Yasmin, who doesn't want her last name used because of that experience. "They asked if I was going to blow up the bus." Now, she says, "I don't wear a long, flowing head scarf. I wear it in a bun, so it looks more like a wrap or a fashion statement. That allows me to blend in a little more."[1] ■

The terrorist attacks of September 11th brought home to millions of Muslims living in the United States the hurtful power of stereotypes. In this chapter, we'll look at stereotypes as part of our discussion of perception and explain how they shape judgments we make about others. Then we'll link perception to decision making, describe how decisions should be made, and review how decisions are actually made in organizations.

What Is Perception?

Perception is a process by which individuals organize and interpret their sensory impressions in order to give meaning to their environment. However, what one perceives can be substantially different from objective reality. There need not be, but there is often, disagreement. For example, it's possible that all employees in a firm may view it as a great place to work—favorable working conditions, interesting job assignments, good pay, excellent benefits, an understanding and responsible management—but, as most of us know, it's very unusual to find such agreement.

Why is perception important in the study of OB? Simply because people's behavior is based on their perception of what reality is, not on reality itself. *The world as it is perceived is the world that is behaviorally important.*

Factors Influencing Perception

How do we explain that individuals may look at the same thing, yet perceive it differently? A number of factors operate to shape and sometimes distort perception. These factors can reside in the *perceiver*, in the object or *target* being perceived, or in the context of the *situation* in which the perception is made (see Exhibit 5-1).

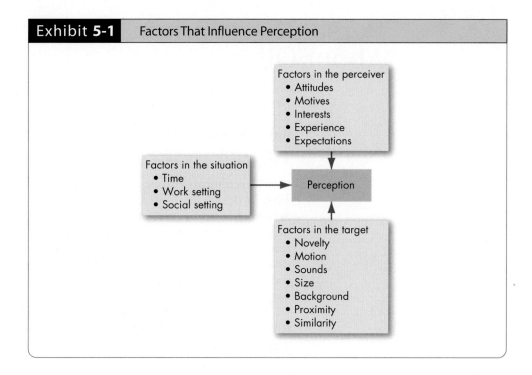

When an individual looks at a target and attempts to interpret what he or she sees, that interpretation is heavily influenced by the personal characteristics of the individual perceiver. Personal characteristics that affect perception include a person's attitudes, personality, motives, interests, past experiences, and expectations. For instance, if you expect police officers to be authoritative, young people to be lazy, or individuals holding public office to be unscrupulous, you may perceive them as such regardless of their actual traits.

Characteristics of the target being observed can affect what is perceived. Loud people are more likely to be noticed in a group than quiet ones. So, too, are extremely attractive or unattractive individuals. Because targets are not looked at in isolation, the relationship of a target to its background also influences perception, as does our tendency to group close things and similar things together. For instance, women, people of color, or members of any other group that has clearly distinguishable characteristics in terms of features or color are often perceived as alike in other, unrelated characteristics as well.

The context in which we see objects or events is also important. The time at which an object or event is seen can influence attention, as can location, light, heat, or any number of situational factors. For example, at a nightclub on Saturday night, you may not notice a 22-year-old female "dressed to the nines." Yet that same woman so attired for your Monday morning management class would certainly catch your attention (and that of the rest of the class). Neither the perceiver nor the target changed between Saturday night and Monday morning, but the situation is different.

perception   *A process by which individuals organize and interpret their sensory impressions in order to give meaning to their environment.*

Person Perception: Making Judgments About Others

Now we turn to the most relevant application of perception concepts to OB. This is the issue of *person perception.* By that, we mean the perceptions people form about each other.

Attribution Theory

Our perceptions of people differ from our perceptions of inanimate objects such as desks, machines, or buildings because we make inferences about the actions of people that we don't make about inanimate objects. Nonliving objects are subject to the laws of nature, but they have no beliefs, motives, or intentions. People do. The result is that when we observe people, we attempt to develop explanations of why they behave in certain ways. Our perception and judgment of a person's actions, therefore, will be significantly influenced by the assumptions we make about that person's internal state.

Attribution theory has been proposed to develop explanations of the ways in which we judge people differently, depending on what meaning we attribute to a given behavior.[2] Basically, the theory suggests that when we observe an individual's behavior, we attempt to determine whether it was internally or externally caused. That determination, however, depends largely on three factors: (1) distinctiveness, (2) consensus, and (3) consistency. First, let's clarify the differences between internal and external causation and then we'll elaborate on each of the three determining factors.

Internally caused behaviors are those that are believed to be under the personal control of the individual. *Externally* caused behavior is seen as resulting from outside causes; that is, the person is seen as having been forced into the behavior by the situation. For example, if one of your employees is late for work, you might attribute his lateness to his partying into the wee hours of the morning and then oversleeping. This would be an internal attribution. But if you attribute his arriving late to an automobile accident that tied up traffic on the road that this employee regularly uses, then you would be making an external attribution.

Now let's discuss each of the three determining factors. *Distinctiveness* refers to whether an individual displays different behaviors in different situations. Is the employee who arrives late today also the source of complaints by coworkers for being someone who regularly "blows off" commitments? What we want to know is whether this behavior is unusual. If it is, the observer is likely to give the behavior an external attribution. If this action is not unusual, it will probably be judged as internal.

If everyone who faces a similar situation responds in the same way, we can say the behavior shows *consensus.* The behavior of the employee discussed above would meet this criterion if all employees who took the same route to work were also late. From an attribution perspective, if consensus is high, you would be expected to give an external attribution to the employee's tardiness, whereas if other employees who took the same route made it to work on time, your conclusion as to causation would be internal.

Finally, an observer looks for *consistency* in a person's actions. Does the person respond the same way over time? Coming in 10 minutes late for work is not perceived in the same way for the employee for whom it is an unusual case (she hasn't been late for several months) as it is for the employee for whom it is part of a routine pattern (she is late two or three times a week). The more consistent the behavior, the more the observer is inclined to attribute it to internal causes.

Exhibit 5-2 summarizes the key elements in attribution theory. It would tell us, for instance, that if your employee—Kim Randolph—generally performs at

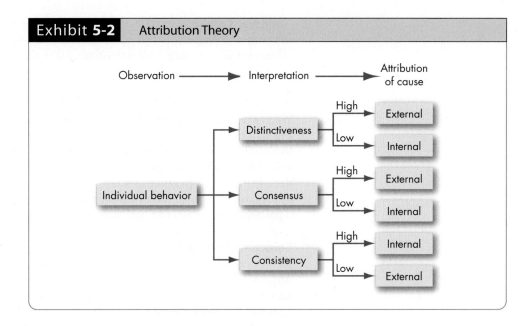

Exhibit **5-2**   Attribution Theory

about the same level on other related tasks as she does on her current task (low distinctiveness), if other employees frequently perform differently—better or worse—than Kim does on that current task (low consensus), and if Kim's performance on this current task is consistent over time (high consistency), you or anyone else who is judging Kim's work is likely to hold her primarily responsible for her task performance (internal attribution).

One of the more interesting findings from attribution theory is that there are errors or biases that distort attributions. For instance, there is substantial evidence that when we make judgments about the behavior of other people, we have a tendency to underestimate the influence of external factors and overestimate the influence of internal or personal factors.[3] This is called the **fundamental attribution error** and can explain why a sales manager is prone to attribute the poor performance of her sales agents to laziness rather than to the innovative product line introduced by a competitor. There is also a tendency for individuals and organizations to attribute their own successes to internal factors such as ability or effort while putting the blame for failure on external factors such as bad luck or unproductive coworkers. This is called the **self-serving bias**.[4] For example, when the Iraq war appeared to go well, the White House declared "Mission Accomplished." But when it became clear that the weapons of mass destruction (WMD) were nowhere to be found and that the fighting was far from over, the White House rushed to blame intelligence failures.

Are these errors or biases that distort attributions universal across different cultures? The evidence is mixed, but most of it suggests that there *are* cultural differences.[5] For instance, a study of Korean managers found that, contrary to the self-serving bias, they tended to accept responsibility for group failure "because I was not a capable leader" instead of attributing it to group members.[6] Attribution theory was developed largely based on experiments with

attribution theory   *An attempt when individuals observe behavior to determine whether it is internally or externally caused.*

fundamental attribution error   *The tendency to underestimate the influence of external factors and overestimate the influence of internal factors when making judgments about the behavior of others.*

self-serving bias   *The tendency for individuals to attribute their own successes to internal factors while putting the blame for failures on external factors.*

Americans and Western Europeans. But the Korean study suggests caution in making attribution theory predictions in non-Western societies, especially in countries with strong collectivist traditions.

Frequently Used Shortcuts in Judging Others

We use a number of shortcuts when we judge others. Perceiving and interpreting what others do is burdensome. As a result, individuals develop techniques for making the task more manageable. These techniques are frequently valuable—they allow us to make accurate perceptions rapidly and provide valid data for making predictions. However, they are not foolproof. They can and do get us into trouble. An understanding of these shortcuts can be helpful in recognizing when they can result in significant distortions.

Selective Perception   Any characteristic that makes a person, object, or event stand out will increase the probability that it will be perceived. Why? Because it is impossible for us to assimilate everything we see—only certain stimuli can be taken in. This tendency explains why you are more likely to notice cars like your own or why some people may be reprimanded by their boss for doing something that, when done by another employee, goes unnoticed. Because we can't observe everything going on about us, we engage in **selective perception**. A classic example shows how vested interests can significantly influence which problems we see.

Dearborn and Simon performed a perceptual study in which 23 business executives read a comprehensive case describing the organization and activities of a steel company.[7] Of the 23 executives, 6 were in sales, 5 in production, 4 in accounting, and 8 in miscellaneous functions. Each manager was asked to write down the most important problem he found in the case. Eighty-three percent of the sales executives rated sales important; only 29 percent of the others did so. This, along with other results of the study, led the researchers to conclude that the participants perceived aspects of a situation that were specifically related to the activities and goals of the unit to which they were attached. A group's perception of organizational activities is selectively altered to align with the vested interests they represent. In other words, when the stimuli are ambiguous, as in the steel company case, perception tends to be influenced more by an individual's base of interpretation (that is, attitudes, interests, and background) than by the stimulus itself.

But how does selectivity work as a shortcut in judging other people? Because we cannot assimilate all that we observe, we take in bits and pieces. But those bits and pieces are not chosen randomly; rather, they are selectively chosen according to our interests, background, experience, and attitudes. Selective perception allows us to "speed-read" others, but not without the risk of drawing an inaccurate picture. Because we see what we want to see, we can draw unwarranted conclusions from an ambiguous situation.

Halo Effect   When we draw a general impression about an individual on the basis of a single characteristic, such as intelligence, sociability, or appearance, a **halo effect** is operating.[8] This phenomenon frequently occurs when students appraise their classroom instructor. Students may give prominence to a single trait such as enthusiasm and allow their entire evaluation to be tainted by how they judge the instructor on that one trait. Thus, an instructor may be quiet, assured, knowledgeable, and highly qualified, but if his or her style lacks zeal, those students would probably give the instructor a low rating.

The reality of the halo effect was confirmed in a classic study in which subjects were given a list of traits such as intelligent, skillful, practical, industrious, determined, and warm and were asked to evaluate the person to whom those traits applied.[9] When those traits were used, the person was judged to be wise,

Can Negative Perceptions Dampen International Business Relations?

JAPAN AND CHINA WOULD SEEM TO BE NATURAL economic partners given that they're so close to each other. However, Japanese companies currently lag behind both the United States and Europe in terms of trade with China. Although the Japanese auto industry has had enormous success in other countries, including the United States, the top-selling foreign cars in China are produced by GM (an American company) and Volkswagen (a German company). Also, Japan's booming electronics industry currently captures only 5 percent of the Chinese market.

But who or what is to blame for the dismal business relationship between Japan and China? The perceptions of the public—in both countries—may be the answer. For example, many Chinese citizens are still angered about a report that employees of a Japanese construction company hired Chinese prostitutes for a corporate party. And many Japanese citizens believe that Chinese immigrants are to blame for many of the violent crimes taking place in Japan. In addition to these recent events, historically, relations between the two countries have been strained. Beijing is still upset about Japan's military invasion of China in the 1930s and 1940s, for which Japan refuses to make amends.

These negative perceptions may be difficult to reverse if one considers perceptual errors such as fundamental attribution error and the halo effect. That is, both countries blame each other for their behaviors (make an internal attribution), and both countries tend to view each other's actions as negative (negative halo effect). Because of these perceptual errors, it is likely that future behaviors, even if they are ambiguous, may be perceived negatively by the other country.

Source: Based on C. Chandler, "Business Is Hot, Relations Are Not," *Fortune (Europe)*, April 19, 2004, pp. 20–21; and "China Urges Japan To Do More To Improve Ties," The Associated Press, March 14, 2005.

humorous, popular, and imaginative. When the same list was modified—cold was substituted for warm—a completely different set of perceptions was obtained. Clearly, the subjects were allowing a single trait to influence their overall impression of the person being judged.

The propensity for the halo effect to operate is not random. Research suggests that it is likely to be most extreme when the traits to be perceived are ambiguous in behavioral terms, when the traits have moral overtones, and when the perceiver is judging traits with which he or she has had limited experience.[10]

Contrast Effects   There is an old adage among entertainers who perform in variety shows: Never follow an act that has kids or animals in it. Why? The common belief is that audiences love children and animals so much that you'll look bad in comparison. This example demonstrates how **contrast effects** can distort perceptions. We don't evaluate a person in isolation. Our reaction to one person is influenced by other persons we have recently encountered.

---

selective perception   *Selectively interpreting what one sees on the basis of one's interests, background, experience, and attitudes.*

halo effect   *Drawing a general impression about an individual on the basis of a single characteristic.*

contrast effects   *Evaluation of a person's characteristics that are affected by comparisons with other people recently encountered who rank higher or lower on the same characteristics.*

An illustration of how contrast effects operate is an interview situation in which an interviewer sees a pool of job applicants. Distortions in any given candidate's evaluation can occur as a result of his or her place in the interview schedule. A candidate is likely to receive a more favorable evaluation if preceded by mediocre applicants and a less favorable evaluation if preceded by strong applicants.

Projection   It's easy to judge others if we assume that they're similar to us. For instance, if you want challenge and responsibility in your job, you assume that others want the same. Or, you're honest and trustworthy, so you take it for granted that other people are equally honest and trustworthy. This tendency to attribute one's own characteristics to other people—which is called **projection**—can distort perceptions made about others.

People who engage in projection tend to perceive others according to what they themselves are like rather than according to what the person being observed is really like. When managers engage in projection, they compromise their ability to respond to individual differences. They tend to see people as more homogeneous than they really are.

Stereotyping   When we judge someone on the basis of our perception of the group to which he or she belongs, we are using the shortcut called **stereotyping**.[11] We saw the problems stereotyping can create at the opening of this chapter: All Muslims are not terrorists!

We rely on generalizations every day because they help us make decisions fast and as accurately as possible. It's a means of simplifying a complex world, and it permits us to maintain consistency. It's less difficult to deal with an unmanageable number of stimuli if we use stereotypes. As an example, assume you're a sales manager looking to fill a sales position in your territory. You want to hire someone who is ambitious and hardworking and who can deal well with adversity. You've had success in the past by hiring individuals who participated in athletics during college. So you focus your search by looking for candidates who participated in collegiate athletics. In so doing, you have cut down con-

Are all business leaders greedy and dishonest? The general public's perception of businesspeople as unethical is shaped by the vast media coverage of corporate corruption and criminal trials of executives like Martha Stewart. Stewart, found guilty of conspiracy, obstructing justice, and lying to the government about a stock sale, is shown here after being sentenced to prison. Stereotyping all business leaders as corrupt is not accurate, but it's a means many people use to simplify their perception of the complexities of the business world.

siderably on your search time. Furthermore, to the extent that athletes are ambitious, hardworking, and able to deal with adversity, the use of this stereotype can improve your decision making. The problem, of course, is when we inaccurately generalize or overgeneralize.[12] In other words, not all college athletes are ambitious, hardworking, or good at dealing with adversity. In organizations, we frequently hear comments that represent stereotypes based on gender, age, race, ethnicity, and even weight:[13] "Women won't relocate for a promotion"; "men aren't interested in child care"; "older workers can't learn new skills"; "Asian immigrants are hardworking and conscientious"; "overweight people lack discipline." From a perceptual standpoint, if people expect to see these stereotypes, that is what they will perceive, whether or not they are accurate.

Obviously, one of the problems of stereotypes is that they *are* widespread and often useful, despite the fact that they may not contain a shred of truth when applied to a particular person or situation. So, we constantly have to check ourselves to make sure we're not unfairly or inaccurately applying a stereotype in our evaluations and decisions. Stereotypes are an example of the saying, "The more useful, the more danger from misuse."

Specific Applications of Shortcuts in Organizations

People in organizations are always judging each other. Managers must appraise their employees' performances. We evaluate how much effort our coworkers are putting into their jobs. When a new person joins a work team, he or she is immediately "sized up" by the other team members. In many cases, these judgments have important consequences for the organization. Let's briefly look at a few of the more obvious applications.

Employment Interview   A major input into who is hired and who is rejected in any organization is the employment interview. It's fair to say that few people are hired without an interview. But the evidence indicates that interviewers make perceptual judgments that are often inaccurate.[14] In addition, agreement among interviewers is often poor; that is, different interviewers see different things in the same candidate and thus arrive at different conclusions about the applicant.

Interviewers generally draw early impressions that become very quickly entrenched. If negative information is exposed early in the interview, it tends to be more heavily weighted than if that same information comes out later.[15] Studies indicate that most interviewers' decisions change very little after the first 4 or 5 minutes of the interview. As a result, information elicited early in the interview carries greater weight than does information elicited later, and a "good applicant" is probably characterized more by the absence of unfavorable characteristics than by the presence of favorable characteristics.

Importantly, who you think is a good candidate and who another thinks is one may differ markedly. Because interviews usually have so little consistent structure and interviewers vary in terms of what they are looking for in a candidate, judgments about the same candidate can vary widely. If the employment interview is an important input into the hiring decision—and it usually is—you should recognize that perceptual factors influence who is hired and eventually the quality of an organization's labor force.

projection   *Attributing one's own characteristics to other people.*

stereotyping   *Judging someone on the basis of one's perception of the group to which that person belongs.*

Performance Expectations   There is an impressive amount of evidence that demonstrates that people will attempt to validate their perceptions of reality, even when those perceptions are faulty.[16] This characteristic is particularly relevant when we consider performance expectations on the job.

The terms **self-fulfilling prophecy**, or *Pygmalion effect*, have evolved to characterize the fact that an individual's behavior is determined by other people's expectations. In other words, if a manager expects big things from his people, they're not likely to let him down. Similarly, if a manager expects people to perform minimally, they'll tend to behave so as to meet those low expectations. The result then is that the expectations become reality.

An interesting illustration of the self-fulfilling prophecy is a study undertaken with 105 soldiers in the Israeli Defense Forces who were taking a 15-week combat command course.[17] The four course instructors were told that one-third of the specific incoming trainees had high potential, one-third had normal potential, and the potential of the rest was unknown. In reality, the trainees were randomly placed into those categories by the researchers. The results confirmed the existence of a self-fulfilling prophecy. The trainees whom instructors were told had high potential scored significantly higher on objective achievement tests, exhibited more positive attitudes, and held their leaders in higher regard than did the other two groups. The instructors of the supposedly high-potential trainees got better results from them because the instructors expected it.

Ethnic Profiling   Following the Japanese attack on Pearl Harbor, 120,000 Americans of Japanese heritage—most living on the west coast—were required to relocate into detention camps. Many of them were forced to stay there throughout World War II. The reason for this action? The U.S. government feared that these Americans might hold pro-Japanese attitudes and spy against the United States. Over time, most Americans came to see this as a terrible mistake and a dark footnote in American history.

The internment of Japanese Americans during World War II is an example of **profiling**—a form of stereotyping in which a group of individuals is singled out—typically on the basis of race or ethnicity—for intensive inquiry, scrutinizing, or investigation. While most Americans look back in shame at the actions the U.S. government took against Japanese Americans some 60 years ago, profiling continues in the United States and in other countries. African American drivers continue to be stopped by police in some U.S. cities merely because of the color of their skin. Middle Easterners are closely scrutinized when they go through security at U.S. airports. In Great Britain, people from Ireland are often singled out as potential terrorists. And in Israel, every Arab is seen as a potential suicide bomber.

But we're interested in organizational behavior. And since September 11th, ethnic profiling has increased implications for OB, specifically as it relates to people of Arab ancestry. Coworkers and managers may look at Arab colleagues through new eyes. They may question why Arab colleagues dress differently or engage in religious practices they don't understand. In fact, Arab Americans' complaints of workplace discrimination grew dramatically after the September 11th attacks, many of whom argued that they felt under constant surveillance at work.[18] The result? This suspicious climate creates distrust and conflicts, undermines motivation, and potentially reduces job satisfaction for ethnic minorities. It's also likely to result in losing quality job candidates when profiling takes place during the employment screening process.

Since September 11th, ethnic profiling has become the subject of much debate.[19] On one side, proponents argue that profiling people of Arab descent is necessary in order to prevent cases of terrorism. After all, a good percentage of the large-scale terrorist attacks that have taken place over the past 30 years have come from Muslim terrorists.[20] On the other side, critics argue that profiling is demeaning, discriminatory, and an ineffective way to find potential terrorists, and that Muslim Americans are as law-abiding as the average American. The debate is important and implies the need to balance the rights of individuals against the greater good of society. Organizations need to sensitize employees and managers to the damage that profiling can create. Diversity training programs, which we discuss in Chapter 18, are increasingly being expanded to particularly address ethnic stereotyping and profiling.

Performance Evaluation Although the impact of performance evaluations on behavior will be discussed fully in Chapter 18, it should be pointed out here that an employee's performance appraisal is very much dependent on the perceptual process.[21] An employee's future is closely tied to the appraisal—promotions, pay raises, and continuation of employment are among the most obvious outcomes. The performance appraisal represents an assessment of an employee's work. Although the appraisal can be objective (for example, a salesperson is appraised on how many dollars of sales she generates in her territory), many jobs are evaluated in subjective terms. Subjective measures are easier to implement, they provide managers with greater discretion, and many jobs do not readily lend themselves to objective measures. Subjective measures are, by definition, judgmental. The evaluator forms a general impression of an employee's work. To the degree that managers use subjective measures in appraising employees, what the evaluator perceives to be good or bad employee characteristics or behaviors will significantly influence the outcome of the appraisal.

The Link Between Perception and Individual Decision Making

Individuals in organizations make **decisions**. That is, they make choices from among two or more alternatives. Top managers, for instance, determine their organization's goals, what products or services to offer, how best to finance operations, or where to locate a new manufacturing plant. Middle- and lower-level managers determine production schedules, select new employees, and decide how pay raises are to be allocated. Of course, making decisions is not the sole province of managers. Nonmanagerial employees also make decisions that affect their jobs and the organizations for which they work. The more obvious of these decisions might include whether or not to come to work on any given day, how much effort to put forth once at work, and whether or not to comply with a request made by the boss. In addition, an increasing number

---

self-fulfilling prophecy *A situation in which one person inaccurately perceives a second person and the resulting expectations cause the second person to behave in ways consistent with the original perception.*

profiling *A form of stereotyping in which a group of individuals is singled out— typically on the basis of race or ethnicity—for intensive inquiry, scrutinizing, or investigation.*

decisions *The choices made from among two or more alternatives.*

Symantec CEO John Thompson made a decision in reaction to the problem of an explosion of Internet viruses. Thompson said, "About every 15 to 18 months, there's a new form of attack that makes old technologies less effective." So he decided to acquire 13 companies that specialize in products such as personal firewalls, intrusion detection, and early warning systems that protect everything from corporate intranets to consumer e-mail inboxes.

of organizations in recent years have been empowering their nonmanagerial employees with job-related decision-making authority that historically was reserved for managers alone. Individual decision making, therefore, is an important part of organizational behavior. But how individuals in organizations make decisions and the quality of their final choices are largely influenced by their perceptions.

Decision making occurs as a reaction to a **problem**.[22] That is, there is a discrepancy between some current state of affairs and some desired state, requiring the consideration of alternative courses of action. So if your car breaks down and you rely on it to get to work, you have a problem that requires a decision on your part. Unfortunately, most problems don't come neatly packaged with a label "problem" clearly displayed on them. One person's *problem* is another person's *satisfactory state of affairs*. One manager may view her division's two percent decline in quarterly sales to be a serious problem requiring immediate action on her part. In contrast, her counterpart in another division of the same company, who also had a two percent sales decrease, may consider that percentage quite acceptable. So the awareness that a problem exists and that a decision needs to be made is a perceptual issue.

Moreover, every decision requires the interpretation and evaluation of information. Data are typically received from multiple sources and they need to be screened, processed, and interpreted. Which data, for instance, are relevant to the decision and which are not? The perceptions of the decision maker will answer that question. Alternatives will be developed, and the strengths and weaknesses of each will need to be evaluated. Again, because alternatives don't come with "red flags" identifying them as such or with their strengths and weaknesses clearly marked, the individual decision maker's perceptual process will have a large bearing on the final outcome. Finally, throughout the entire decision process, perceptual distortions often surface that have the potential to bias analysis and conclusions.

How Should Decisions Be Made?

Let's begin by describing, at least in theory, how individuals should behave in order to maximize or optimize a certain outcome. We call this the rational decision-making process.

The Rational Decision-Making Process

We often think that the best decision maker is **rational**. That is, he or she makes consistent, value-maximizing choices within specified constraints.[23] These choices are made following a six-step **rational decision-making model**.[24] Moreover, specific assumptions underlie this model.

The Rational Model   The six steps in the rational decision-making model are listed in Exhibit 5-3.

The model begins by *defining the problem*. As noted previously, a problem exists when there is a discrepancy between an existing and a desired state of affairs.[25] If you calculate your monthly expenses and find you're spending $100 more than you allocated in your budget, you have defined a problem. Many poor decisions can be traced to the decision maker overlooking a problem or defining the wrong problem.

Exhibit **5-3**	Steps in the Rational Decision-Making Model

1. Define the problem.
2. Identify the decision criteria.
3. Allocate weights to the criteria.
4. Develop the alternatives.
5. Evaluate the alternatives.
6. Select the best alternative.

Once a decision maker has defined the problem, he or she needs to *identify the decision criteria* that will be important in solving the problem. In this step, the decision maker determines what is relevant in making the decision. This step brings the decision maker's interests, values, and similar personal preferences into the process. Identifying criteria is important because what one person thinks is relevant, another person may not. Also keep in mind that any factors not identified in this step are considered irrelevant to the decision maker.

The criteria identified are rarely all equal in importance. So the third step requires the decision maker to *weight the previously identified criteria* in order to give them the correct priority in the decision.

The fourth step requires the decision maker to *generate possible alternatives* that could succeed in resolving the problem. No attempt is made in this step to appraise these alternatives, only to list them.

Once the alternatives have been generated, the decision maker must critically analyze and evaluate each one. This is done by *rating each alternative on each criterion.* The strengths and weaknesses of each alternative become evident as they are compared with the criteria and weights established in the second and third steps.

The final step in this model requires *computing the optimal decision.* This is done by evaluating each alternative against the weighted criteria and selecting the alternative with the higher total score.

Assumptions of the Model   The rational decision-making model we just described contains a number of assumptions.[26] Let's briefly outline those assumptions.

1. *Problem clarity.* The problem is clear and unambiguous. The decision maker is assumed to have complete information regarding the decision situation.
2. *Known options.* It is assumed the decision maker can identify all the relevant criteria and can list all the viable alternatives. Furthermore, the decision maker is aware of all the possible consequences of each alternative.
3. *Clear preferences.* Rationality assumes that the criteria and alternatives can be ranked and weighted to reflect their importance.
4. *Constant preferences.* It's assumed that the specific decision criteria are constant and that the weights assigned to them are stable over time.
5. *No time or cost constraints.* The rational decision maker can obtain full information about criteria and alternatives because it's assumed that there are no time or cost constraints.
6. *Maximum payoff.* The rational decision maker will choose the alternative that yields the highest perceived value.

problem   *A discrepancy between some current state of affairs and some desired state.*

rational   *Making consistent, value-maximizing choices within specified constraints.*

rational decision-making model   *A decision-making model that describes how individuals should behave in order to maximize some outcome.*

Improving Creativity in Decision Making

Although following the steps of the rational decision-making model will often improve decisions, the rational decision maker also needs **creativity**, that is, the ability to produce novel and useful ideas.[27] These are ideas that are different from what's been done before but that are also appropriate to the problem or opportunity presented. Why is creativity important to decision making? It allows the decision maker to more fully appraise and understand the problem, including seeing problems others can't see. However, creativity's most obvious value is in helping the decision maker identify all viable alternatives, or to identify alternatives that aren't readily apparent.

Creative Potential   Most people have creative potential that they can use when confronted with a decision-making problem. But to unleash that potential, they have to get out of the psychological ruts many of us get into and learn how to think about a problem in divergent ways.

People differ in their inherent creativity, and exceptional creativity is scarce. Albert Einstein, Emily Dickinson, Pablo Picasso, and Wolfgang Mozart were individuals of exceptional creativity. But what about the typical individual? People who score high on Openness to Experience (see Chapter 4), for example, are more likely to be creative. Intelligent people also are more likely to be creative.[28] Other traits that have been found to be associated with creative people: independence, self-confidence, risk-taking, an internal locus of control, tolerance for ambiguity, and perseverance in the face of frustration.[29]

A study of the lifetime creativity of 461 men and women found that fewer than 1 percent were exceptionally creative.[30] But 10 percent were highly creative and about 60 percent were somewhat creative. This suggests that most of us have creative potential; we just need to learn to unleash it. See the Self-Assessment feature on p. 159 to assess your level of creativity.

Videogame maker Electronic Arts created an on-site labyrinth to help employees unleash their creative potential. EA encourages video and computer game developers to wander the maze when their creativity levels are running low. While walking the maze, they can think about their challenges in divergent ways for designing innovative products.

HOW CREATIVE AM I?

In the Self-Assessment Library (available on CD, online, and in print), take assessment I.A.5 (How Creative Am I?) and answer the following questions.

1. *Did you score as high as you thought you would?*
2. *What are limitations to self-assessments like this?*
3. *If others [friends, classmates] rated you, would they rate you differently? Why or why not?*
4. *What could you do to increase your creativity?*

Three-Component Model of Creativity   Given that most people have the capacity to be at least somewhat creative, what can individuals and organizations do to stimulate employee creativity? The best answer to this question lies in the **three-component model of creativity**.[31] Based on an extensive body of research, this model proposes that individual creativity essentially requires expertise, creative-thinking skills, and intrinsic task motivation (see Exhibit 5-4). Studies confirm that the higher the level of each of these three components, the higher the creativity.

Expertise is the foundation for all creative work. Many of Eminem's lyrics, for example, were based on his childhood experiences. The film writer, producer, and director Quentin Tarantino spent his youth working in a video rental store, where he built up an encyclopedic knowledge of movies. The potential for creativity is enhanced when individuals have abilities, knowledge, proficiencies, and similar expertise in their field of endeavor. For example, you wouldn't expect someone with a minimal knowledge of programming to be very creative as a software engineer.

Exhibit **5-4**	The Three Components of Creativity

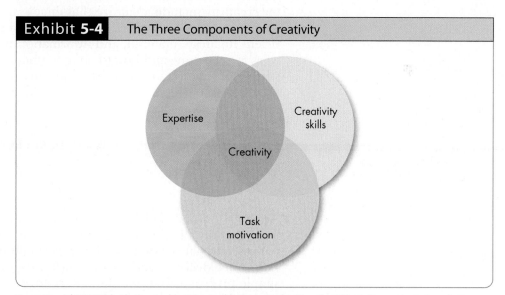

Source: Copyright © 1997, by The Regents of the University of California. Reprinted from *The California Management Review*, vol. 40, no. 1. By permission of The Regents.

---

creativity   *The ability to produce novel and useful ideas.*

three-component model of creativity   *The proposition that individual creativity requires expertise, creative-thinking skills, and intrinsic task motivation.*

The second component is *creative-thinking skills*. This encompasses personality characteristics associated with creativity, the ability to use analogies, as well as the talent to see the familiar in a different light.

Research suggests that we are more creative when we're in good moods, so if we need to be creative we should do things that make us happy. Perhaps that is listening to music we enjoy, eating foods we like, watching funny movies, or socializing with others.[32] There is also evidence that suggests being around others who are creative can actually make us more inspired, especially if we're creatively "stuck."[33]

The effective use of analogies allows decision makers to apply an idea from one context to another. One of the most famous examples in which analogy resulted in a creative breakthrough was Alexander Graham Bell's observation that it might be possible to take concepts of how the ear operates and apply them to his "talking box." He noticed that the bones in the ear are operated by a delicate, thin membrane. He wondered why, then, a thicker and stronger piece of membrane shouldn't be able to move a piece of steel. Out of that analogy, the telephone was conceived.

Some people have developed their creative skills because they are able to see problems in a new way. They're able to make the strange familiar and the familiar strange.[34] For instance, most of us think of hens laying eggs. But how many of us have considered that a hen is only an egg's way of making another egg?

The final component in the three-component model of creativity is *intrinsic task motivation*. This is the desire to work on something because it's interesting, involving, exciting, satisfying, or personally challenging. This motivational component is what turns creativity *potential* into *actual* creative ideas. It determines the extent to which individuals fully engage their expertise and creative skills. So creative people often love their work, to the point of seeming obsessed. Importantly, an individual's work environment can have a significant effect on intrinsic motivation. Work-environment stimulants that have been found to foster creativity include a culture that encourages the flow of ideas, fair and constructive judgment of ideas, and rewards and recognition for creative work; sufficient financial, material, and information resources; freedom to decide what work is to be done and how to do it; a supervisor who communicates effectively, shows confidence in others, and supports the work group; and work-group members who support and trust each other.[35]

How Are Decisions Actually Made in Organizations?

Are decision makers in organizations rational? Do they carefully assess problems, identify all relevant criteria, use their creativity to identify all viable alternatives, and painstakingly evaluate every alternative to find an optimal choice? For novice decision makers with little experience, decision makers faced with simple problems that have few alternative courses of action, or when the cost of searching out and evaluating alternatives is low, the rational model provides a fairly accurate description of the decision process.[36] But such situations are the exception. Most decisions in the real world don't follow the rational model. For instance, people are usually content to find an acceptable or reasonable solution to their problem rather than an optimal one. As such, decision makers generally make limited use of their creativity. Choices tend to be confined to the neighborhood of the problem symptom and to the neighborhood of the current alternative. As one expert in decision making put it: "Most significant decisions are made by judgment, rather than by a defined prescriptive model."[37]

The following discusses a large body of evidence to provide you with a more accurate description of how most decisions in organizations are actually made.[38]

Bounded Rationality

When you considered which college to attend, did you look at every viable alternative? Did you carefully identify all the criteria that were important in your decision? Did you evaluate each alternative against the criteria in order to find the optimal college? We expect the answers to these questions is probably "No." Well, don't feel bad. Few people made their college choice this way. Instead of optimizing, you probably satisficed.

When faced with a complex problem, most people respond by reducing the problem to a level at which it can be readily understood. This is because the limited information-processing capability of human beings makes it impossible to assimilate and understand all the information necessary to optimize.[39] So people *satisfice*; that is, they seek solutions that are satisfactory and sufficient.

Because the capacity of the human mind for formulating and solving complex problems is far too small to meet the requirements for full rationality, individuals operate within the confines of **bounded rationality**. They construct simplified models that extract the essential features from problems without capturing all their complexity.[40] Individuals can then behave rationally within the limits of the simple model.

How does bounded rationality work for the typical individual? Once a problem is identified, the search for criteria and alternatives begins. But the list of criteria is likely to be far from exhaustive. The decision maker will identify a limited list made up of the more conspicuous choices. These are the choices that are easy to find and that tend to be highly visible. In most cases, they will represent familiar criteria and previously tried-and-true solutions. Once this limited set of alternatives is identified, the decision maker will begin reviewing them. But the review will not be comprehensive—not all the alternatives will be carefully evaluated. Instead, the decision maker will begin with alternatives that differ only in a relatively small degree from the choice currently in effect. Following along familiar and well-worn paths, the decision maker proceeds to review alternatives only until he or she identifies an alternative that is "good enough"—one that meets an acceptable level of performance. The first alternative that meets the "good enough" criterion ends the search. So the final solution represents a satisficing choice rather than an optimal one.

One of the more interesting aspects of bounded rationality is that the order in which alternatives are considered is critical in determining which alternative is selected. Remember, in the fully rational decision-making model, all alternatives are eventually listed in a hierarchy of preferred order. Because all alternatives are considered, the initial order in which they are evaluated is irrelevant.

bounded rationality *Making decisions by constructing simplified models that extract the essential features from problems without capturing all their complexity.*

Operating within the confines of bounded rationality, Rose Marie Bravo revitalized the British retailer Burberry Group PLC when she became CEO. Based on her retail experience as president of Saks in the United States, Bravo decided to capitalize on Burberry's quality heritage and trademark plaid design as the solution to the company's stagnant growth. She repositioned Burberry as a global luxury retailer by opening stores around the world, running a celebrity ad campaign with female supermodel Ben Grimes to redefine the brand's image as hip for the younger generation, and by using the plaid design on new lines of swimwear, footwear, and children's clothing.

Every potential solution would get a full and complete evaluation. But this isn't the case with bounded rationality. Assuming that a problem has more than one potential solution, the satisficing choice will be the first *acceptable* one the decision maker encounters. Because decision makers use simple and limited models, they typically begin by identifying alternatives that are obvious, ones with which they are familiar, and those not too far from the status quo. The solutions that depart least from the status quo and meet the decision criteria are those most likely to be selected. A unique and creative alternative may present an optimizing solution to the problem; however, it's unlikely to be chosen because an acceptable solution will be identified well before the decision maker is required to search very far beyond the status quo.

Common Biases and Errors

Decision makers engage in bounded rationality, but an accumulating body of research tells us that decision makers also allow systematic biases and errors to creep into their judgments.[41] These come out of attempts to short-cut the decision process. To minimize effort and avoid difficult trade-offs, people tend to rely too heavily on experience, impulses, gut feelings, and convenient "rules of thumb." In many instances, these shortcuts are helpful. However, they can lead to severe distortions from rationality. The following material highlights the most common distortions.

Overconfidence Bias   It's been said that "no problem in judgment and decision making is more prevalent and more potentially catastrophic than overconfidence."[42] When we're given factual questions and asked to judge the probability that our answers are correct, we tend to be far too optimistic. For instance, studies have found that, when people say they're 65 to 70 percent confident that they're right, they were actually correct only about 50 percent of the time.[43] And when they say they're 100 percent sure, they tended to be 70 to 85 percent correct.[44] Here's another interesting example. In one random-sample national poll, 90 percent of Americans said they expected to go to heaven. But in another random-sample national poll, only 86 percent thought Mother Theresa was in heaven. Talk about an overconfidence bias!

From an organizational standpoint, one of the more interesting findings related to overconfidence is that those individuals whose intellectual and interpersonal abilities are *weakest* are most likely to overestimate their performance and ability.[45] So as managers and employees become more knowledgeable about an issue, the less likely they are to display overconfidence.[46] And overconfidence is most likely to surface when organizational members are considering issues or problems that are outside their area of expertise.[47]

Anchoring Bias   The **anchoring bias** is a tendency to fixate on initial information. Once set, we then fail to adequately adjust for subsequent information.[48] The anchoring bias occurs because our mind appears to give a disproportionate amount of emphasis to the first information it receives. So initial impressions, ideas, prices, and estimates carry undue weight relative to information received later.[49]

Anchors are widely used by people in professions—such as advertising, management, politics, real estate, and law—where persuasion skills are important. For instance, in a mock jury trial, one set of jurors was asked by the plaintiff's attorney to make an award in the range of $15 million to $50 million. Another set of jurors was asked for an award in the range of $50 million to $150 million. Consistent with the anchoring bias, the median awards were $15 million versus $50 million in the two conditions.[50]

Consider the role of anchoring in negotiations and interviews. Any time a negotiation takes place, so does anchoring. As soon as someone states a number, your ability to objectively ignore that number has been compromised. For instance, when a prospective employer asks how much you were making in your prior job, your answer typically anchors the employer's offer. You may want to keep this in mind when you negotiate your salary, but remember to set the anchor only as high as you realistically can (in other words, it probably won't work to ask for as much as Donald Trump makes).

Confirmation Bias   The rational decision-making process assumes that we objectively gather information. But we don't. We *selectively* gather information. The **confirmation bias** represents a specific case of selective perception. We seek out information that reaffirms our past choices, and we discount information that contradicts past judgments.[51] We also tend to accept information at face value that confirms our preconceived views, while being critical and skeptical of information that challenges these views. Therefore, the information we gather is typically biased toward supporting views we already hold. This confirmation bias influences where we go to collect evidence because we tend to seek out places that are more likely to tell us what we want to hear. It also leads us to give too much weight to supporting information and too little to contradictory information.

anchoring bias   *A tendency to fixate on initial information, from which we then fail to adequately adjust for subsequent information.*

confirmation bias   *The tendency to seek out information that reaffirms past choices and to discount information that contradicts past judgments.*

Availability Bias   Many more people suffer from fear of flying than fear of driving in a car. The reason is that many people think flying is more dangerous. It isn't, of course. With apologies ahead of time for this graphic example, if flying on a commercial airline was as dangerous as driving, the equivalent of two 747s filled to capacity would have to crash every week, killing all aboard, to match the risk of being killed in a car accident. But the media gives a lot more attention to air accidents, so we tend to overstate the risk of flying and understate the risk of driving.

This illustrates an example of the **availability bias**, which is the tendency for people to base their judgments on information that is readily available to them.[52] Events that evoke emotions, that are particularly vivid, or that have occurred more recently tend to be more available in our memory. As a result, we tend to be prone to overestimating unlikely events like an airplane crash. The availability bias can also explain why managers, when doing annual performance appraisals, tend to give more weight to recent behaviors of an employee than those behaviors of six or nine months ago.

Representative Bias   Many inner-city African American male teenagers in the United States talk about the goal of playing basketball in the NBA.[53] In reality, these young people have a far better chance of becoming medical doctors than they do of playing in the NBA, but these kids are suffering from a **representative bias**. They tend to assess the likelihood of an occurrence by inappropriately considering the current situation as identical to past ones.[54] They hear about a young man from their neighborhood 10 years ago who went on to play professional basketball. Or they watch NBA games on television and think that those players are like them.

We are all guilty of falling into the representative bias at times. Managers, for example, frequently predict the performance of a new product by relating it to a previous product's success. Or if three graduates from the same college were hired and turned out to be poor performers, managers may predict that a current job applicant from the same college will not be a good employee.

Escalation of Commitment   Another distortion that creeps into decisions in practice is a tendency to escalate commitment when a decision stream represents a series of decisions.[55] **Escalation of commitment** refers to staying with a decision even when there is clear evidence that it's wrong. For example, consider a friend that has been dating his girlfriend for about 4 years. Although he admitted to you that things weren't going too well in the relationship, he said that he was still going to marry her. His justification: "I have a lot invested in the relationship!"

It has been well documented that individuals escalate commitment to a failing course of action when they view themselves as responsible for the failure.[56] That is, they "throw good money after bad" to demonstrate that their initial decision wasn't wrong and to avoid having to admit they made a mistake. Escalation of commitment is also congruent with evidence that people try to appear consistent in what they say and do. Increasing commitment to previous actions conveys consistency.

Escalation of commitment has obvious implications for managerial decisions. Many an organization has suffered large losses because a manager was determined to prove his or her original decision was right by continuing to commit resources to what was a lost cause from the beginning. In addition, consistency is a characteristic often associated with effective leaders. So managers, in an effort to appear effective, may be motivated to be consistent when switching to another course of action may be preferable. In actuality, effective managers are those who are able to differentiate between situations in which persistence will pay off and situations in which it will not.

Research suggests that sports teams give more playing time to highly drafted players even if their recent performance is no better than lower-drafted players. This is an example of escalation of commitment. Dwight Howard of the Orlando Magic, shown here putting up a shot, was the top pick in the 2004 draft. Escalation of commitment predicts that the Orlando Magic will play Dwight more, even if he is no better than a lower-draft pick, as a means of justifying their decision. Of course it's possible that Dwight will fully reward Orlando for picking him.

Randomness Error Human beings have a lot of difficulty dealing with chance. Most of us like to believe we have some control over our world and our destiny. Although we undoubtedly can control a good part of our future by rational decision making, the truth is that the world will always contain random events. Our tendency to believe we can predict the outcome of random events is the **randomness error**.

Consider stock-price movements. In spite of the fact that short-term stock-price changes are essentially random, a large proportion of investors—or their financial advisors—believe they can predict the direction that stock prices will move. For instance, when a group of subjects was given stock prices and trend information, these subjects were approximately 65 percent certain they could predict the direction stocks would change. In actuality, these individuals were correct only 49 percent of the time—about what you'd expect if they were just guessing.[57]

Decision making becomes impaired when we try to create meaning out of random events. One of the most serious impairments caused by random events is when we turn imaginary patterns into superstitions.[58] These can be completely contrived ("I never make important decisions on a Friday the 13th") or evolve from a certain pattern of behavior that has been reinforced previously (Tiger Woods often wears a red shirt during the final round of a golf tournament because he won many junior golf tournaments while wearing red shirts). Although many of us engage in some superstitious behavior, it can

availability bias *The tendency for people to base their judgments on information that is readily available to them.*

representative bias *Assessing the likelihood of an occurrence by inappropriately considering the current situation as identical to ones in the past.*

escalation of commitment *An increased commitment to a previous decision in spite of negative information.*

randomness error *The tendency of individuals to believe that they can predict the outcome of random events.*

be debilitating when it affects daily judgments or biases major decisions. At the extreme, some decision makers become controlled by their superstitions—making it nearly impossible for them to change routines or objectively process new information.

Winner's Curse The **winner's curse** is a decision-making dictum that argues that the winning participants in an auction typically pay too much for the winning item. The winner's curse occurs in competitive bidding. Some buyers will underestimate the value of an item and others will overestimate it, and the highest bidder (the winner) will be the one who overestimated the most. Therefore, unless the bidders dramatically undervalue, there is a good chance that the "winner" paid too much for the item.

Imagine, for example, that all members of your class are bidding on a painting. Obviously, there will be variation in bids, and the person who places the highest bid will receive the painting (in return for the amount that he or she bid). Unless people grossly underestimated the value of the painting, it's likely that the highest bidder will have paid too much. Logic predicts that the winner's curse gets stronger as the number of bidders increases. This is because the more bidders there are, the more likely it is that some of them have greatly overestimated the good's value. So, beware of auctions in which an unexpectedly large number of bidders are involved.

Hindsight Bias The **hindsight bias** is the tendency for us to believe falsely that we'd have accurately predicted the outcome of an event, after that outcome is actually known.[59] When something happens and we have accurate feedback on the outcome, we seem to be pretty good at concluding that this outcome was relatively obvious. For instance, a lot more people seem to have been sure about the inevitability of who would win the Super Bowl on the day *after* the game than they were the day *before*.[60]

What explains the hindsight bias? We apparently aren't very good at recalling the way an uncertain event appeared to us *before* we find out the actual results of that event. However, we seem to be fairly well adept at reconstructing the past by overestimating what we knew beforehand based upon what we learned later. So the hindsight bias seems to be a result of both selective memory and our ability to reconstruct earlier predictions.[61]

The hindsight bias reduces our ability to learn from the past. It permits us to think that we're better at making predictions than we really are and can result in our being more confident about the accuracy of future decisions than we have a right to be. If, for instance, your actual predictive accuracy is only 40 percent, but you think it's 90 percent, you're likely to become falsely overconfident and less vigilant in questioning your predictive skills.

Intuition

Intuitive decision making is an unconscious process created out of distilled experience.[62] It doesn't necessarily operate independently of rational analysis; rather, the two complement each other. And, importantly, intuition can be a powerful force in decision making. For instance, research on chess playing provides an excellent illustration of how intuition works.[63]

Novice chess players and grand masters were shown an actual, but unfamiliar, chess game with about 25 pieces on the board. After 5 or 10 seconds, the pieces were removed and each was asked to reconstruct the pieces by position. On average, the grand master could put 23 or 24 pieces in their correct squares, while the novice was able to replace only 6. Then the exercise

Google and the Winner's Curse

One way the winner's curse is revealed is in Initial Public Offering (IPO) pricing schemes. IPOs occur when a company decides to "go public"—offer itself for sale to investors. In such a case, potential investors need to estimate what the market value of a company's stock will be lest they pay too much for the company's stock. Here's how the winner's curse operated with the pricing of Google.

Google auctioned off a portion of its stock, with the shares sold to those who paid the most per share. Google explicitly warned potential investors of the winner's curse in its SEC registration statement (the company warned: "The auction process for our public offering may result in a phenomenon known as the 'winner's curse,' and, as a result, investors may experience significant losses"). Despite this warning, the winning investors paid more than 10 times the estimated pre-IPO value for Google shares (the estimated value of the Google shares was $2.7 billion before the IPO, compared to the $36 billion that was estimated to be paid for the shares). The winner's curse is hardly confined to Google or other IPOs. Any time auctions or bidding is involved, the potential of the winner's curse is very real. Researchers have argued that companies such as Tyco, MCI-WorldCom, and Bank One overpaid for acquisitions as a result of failing to learn the lessons of the winner's curse.

So, how can the winner's curse be avoided?

Savvy bidders will avoid the winner's curse by bid shading, or placing a bid that is below what they believe the good is worth. This may make it less likely that the bidder will win the auction, but it also will protect them from overpaying in the cases where they do win. Savvy bidders know that they don't want to win if it means they will pay more than a good is worth. For example, assume that before the auction you think a share of Google is worth $100. But you figure that if you end up being a winner in the auction it means that most investors think Google is worth less than $100 (by the way, some investors paid more than $200 for Google stock!). Because fear of the winner's curse can scare away potential bidders, auction sites need to put in place mechanisms that protect novice buyers from accidentally overpaying. Some ideas:

1. Provide lots of information about the items for sale.
2. Draw as many informed bidders to your auction site as possible.
3. Share the risk. Bidders will pay more if the seller or auctioneer provides a warranty.

Sources: Based on J. D. Miller, "Google's 'Winner's Curse'." Published 05/04/2004; G. Anandalingam and Henry C. Lucas, "Beware the Winner's Curse: Victories That Can Sink You and Your Company," November 2004; G. P. Zachary, "Google's Dirty Little Secrets: Investors May Suffer from Winner's Curse," Sunday, August 8, 2004, Page E–3. D. Marasco, "The Winner's Curse," **http://economics.about.com/cs/baseballeconomics/a/winners_curse.htm**.

was changed. This time the pieces were placed randomly on the board. Again, the novice got only about 6 correct, but so did the grand master! The second exercise demonstrated that the grand master didn't have any better memory than the novice. What the grand master did have was the ability, based on the experience of having played thousands of chess games, to recognize patterns and clusters of pieces that occur on chessboards in the course of games. Studies further show that chess professionals can play 50 or more games simultaneously, in which decisions often must be made in only seconds, and exhibit only a moderately lower level of skill than when playing one game under tournament conditions, where decisions take half an hour or longer. The expert's experience allows him or her to recognize the pattern in a situation and draw on previously learned information associated with that pattern to arrive at a decision choice quickly. The result is that the intuitive decision maker can decide rapidly based on what appears to be very limited information.

winner's curse   *A decision-making dictum that argues that the winning participants in an auction typically pay too much for the winning item.*

hindsight bias   *The tendency for us to believe falsely that we'd have accurately predicted the outcome of an event, after that outcome is actually known.*

intuitive decision making   *An unconscious process created out of distilled experience.*

Master chess players Vladimir Kramnik and Garry Kasparov effectively use intuitive decision making during chess tournaments. Based on their expertise from playing thousands of games, these chess champs can quickly choose from among alternative moves while under great pressure to make the right decision.

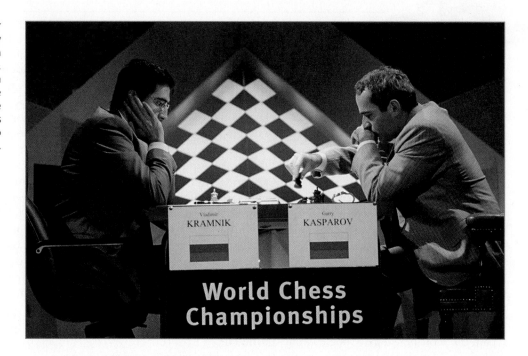

For most of the twentieth century, experts believed that the use of intuition by decision makers was irrational or ineffective. That's no longer the case.[64] There is growing recognition that rational analysis has been overemphasized and that, in certain instances, relying on intuition can improve decision making.

When are people most likely to use intuitive decision making? Eight conditions have been identified: (1) when a high level of uncertainty exists; (2) when there is little precedent to draw on; (3) when variables are less scientifically predictable; (4) when "facts" are limited; (5) when facts don't clearly point the way; (6) when analytical data are of little use; (7) when there are several plausible alternative solutions from which to choose, with good arguments for each; and (8) when time is limited and there is pressure to come up with the right decision.[65]

Although intuitive decision making has gained respectability, don't expect people—especially in North America, Great Britain, and other cultures in which rational analysis is the approved way of making decisions—to readily acknowledge that they're using it. People with strong intuitive abilities don't usually tell their colleagues how they reached their conclusions. And since rational analysis continues to be more socially desirable, intuitive ability is often disguised or hidden. As one top executive commented, "Sometimes one must dress up a gut decision in 'data clothes' to make it acceptable or palatable, but this fine-tuning is usually after the fact of the decision."[66]

Individual Differences

Decision making in practice is characterized by bounded rationality, common biases and errors, and the use of intuition. In addition, there are individual differences that create deviations from the rational model. In this section, we look at two individual-difference variables: personality and gender.

Personality   There hasn't been much research on personality and decision making. One possible reason is that most researchers who conduct decision-making research aren't trained to investigate personality. However, the studies that have been conducted suggest that personality does influence decision making. The research has considered conscientiousness (as you will recall, this is one of the Big Five traits we discussed in Chapter 4) and self-esteem (which we also considered in Chapter 4). Let's discuss each of these.

First, some research has shown that specific facets of conscientiousness—rather than the broad trait itself—affects escalation of commitment (see p. 164).[67] Interestingly, one study revealed that the two facets of conscientiousness—achievement-striving and dutifulness—actually had opposite effects on escalation of commitment. For example, achievement-striving people were more likely to escalate their commitment, whereas dutiful people were less likely to escalate. Why might this be the case? Generally, achievement-oriented people hate to fail, so they escalate their commitment hoping to forestall failure. Dutiful people, however, will be more inclined to do what they see as best for the organization. Second, achievement-striving individuals appear to be more susceptible to the hindsight bias, perhaps because they have a greater need to justify the appropriateness of their actions.[68] Unfortunately, we don't have evidence on whether dutiful people are immune to the hindsight bias.

Finally, people with high self-esteem appear to be especially susceptible to the self-serving bias. Why? Because high self-esteem people are strongly motivated to maintain their self-esteem so they use the self-serving bias to preserve it. That is, they blame others for their failures while taking credit for their successes.[69]

Gender   Recent research on rumination offers insights into gender differences in decision making.[70] Overall, the evidence indicates that women analyze decisions more than men do.

Rumination refers to reflecting at length. In terms of decision making, it means overthinking about problems. And women, in general, are more likely than men to engage in rumination. Twenty years of study find that women spend much more time than men in analyzing the past, present, and future. They're more likely to overanalyze problems before making a decision and rehash the decision once it has been made. On the positive side, this is likely to lead to more careful consideration of problems and choices. However, it can make problems harder to solve, increase regret over past decisions, and increase depression. On this last point, women are nearly twice as likely as men to develop depression.

Why women ruminate more than men is not clear. Several theories have been suggested. One view is that parents encourage and reinforce the expression of sadness and anxiety more in girls than in boys. Another theory is that women, more than men, base their self-esteem and well-being on what others think of them. A third theory is that women are more empathetic and more affected by events in others' lives, so they have more to ruminate about.

This rumination tendency appears to be moderated by age. Gender differences surface early. By age 11, for instance, girls are ruminating more than boys. But this gender difference seems to lessen with age. Differences are largest during young adulthood and smallest after age 65, when both men and women ruminate the least.[71]

Organizational Constraints

Organizations can constrain decision makers, creating deviations from the rational model. Managers, for instance, shape their decisions to reflect the organization's performance evaluation and reward system, to comply with the organization's formal regulations, and to meet organizationally imposed time constraints. Previous organizational decisions also act as precedents to constrain current decisions.

Performance Evaluation   Managers are strongly influenced in their decision making by the criteria on which they are evaluated. If a division manager believes that the manufacturing plants under his responsibility are operating best when he hears nothing negative, we shouldn't be surprised to find his plant managers spending a good part of their time ensuring that negative information doesn't reach the division boss. Similarly, if a college dean believes that an instructor should never fail more than 10 percent of her students—to fail more reflects on the instructor's ability to teach—we should expect that instructors who want to receive favorable evaluations will decide not to fail too many students.

Reward Systems   The organization's reward system influences decision makers by suggesting to them what choices are preferable in terms of personal payoff. For example, if the organization rewards risk aversion, managers are more likely to make conservative decisions. From the 1930s through the mid-1980s, General Motors consistently gave out promotions and bonuses to managers who kept a low profile, avoided controversy, and were good team players. The result was that GM managers became very adept at dodging tough issues and passing controversial decisions on to committees.

Formal regulations shape the decisions of individuals when organizations standardize the behavior of their members. McDonald's, for example, requires that its restaurant crews follow rules and regulations for food preparation and service to meet the company's high standards of food quality and safety and consistent and dependable service.

Formal Regulations   David Gonzalez, a shift manager at a Taco Bell restaurant in San Antonio, Texas, describes constraints he faces on his job: "I've got rules and regulations covering almost every decision I make—from how to make a burrito to how often I need to clean the restrooms. My job doesn't come with much freedom of choice." David's situation is not unique. All but the smallest of organizations create rules, policies, procedures, and other formalized regulations in order to standardize the behavior of their members. By programming decisions, organizations are able to get individuals to achieve high levels of performance without paying for the years of experience that would be necessary in the absence of regulations. And of course, in so doing, they limit the decision maker's choices.

System-Imposed Time Constraints   Organizations impose deadlines on decisions. For instance, department budgets need to be completed by next Friday. Or the report on new-product development has to be ready for the executive committee to review by the first of the month. A host of decisions must be made quickly in order to stay ahead of the competition and keep customers satisfied. And almost all important decisions come with explicit deadlines. These conditions create time pressures on decision makers and often make it difficult, if not impossible, to gather all the information they might like to have before making a final choice.

Historical Precedents   Decisions aren't made in a vacuum. They have a context. In fact, individual decisions are more accurately characterized as points in a stream of decisions.

Decisions made in the past are ghosts that continually haunt current choices—that is, commitments that have already been made constrain current options. To use a social situation as an example, the decision you might make after meeting "Mr. or Ms. Right" is more complicated if you're already married than if you're single. Prior commitments—in this case, having chosen to get married—constrain your options. Consider another example. Government budget decisions also offer an illustration of our point. It's common knowledge that the largest determining factor of the size of any given year's budget is last year's budget.[72] Choices made today, therefore, are largely a result of choices made over the years.

Cultural Differences

The rational model makes no acknowledgment of cultural differences. But Indonesians, for instance, don't necessarily make decisions the same way that Australians do. Therefore, we need to recognize that the cultural background of the decision maker can have significant influence on the selection of problems, depth of analysis, the importance placed on logic and rationality, or whether organizational decisions should be made autocratically by an individual manager or collectively in groups.[73]

Cultures, for example, differ in terms of time orientation, the importance of rationality, their belief in the ability of people to solve problems, and their preference for collective decision making. Differences in time orientation help us understand why managers in Egypt will make decisions at a much slower and more deliberate pace than their American counterparts. Whereas rationality is valued in North America, that's not true everywhere in the world. A North American manager might make an important decision intuitively but knows that it's important to appear to proceed in a rational fashion. This is because rationality is highly valued in the West. In countries such as Iran, where rationality is not deified, efforts to appear rational are not necessary.

Some cultures emphasize solving problems, while others focus on accepting situations as they are. The United States falls in the former category; Thailand and Indonesia are examples of cultures that fall into the latter category. Because problem-solving managers believe they can and should change situations to their benefit, American managers might identify a problem long before their Thai or Indonesian counterparts would choose to recognize it as such.

Decision making by Japanese managers is much more group-oriented than in the United States. The Japanese value conformity and cooperation. So before Japanese CEOs make an important decision, they collect a large amount of information, which is then used in consensus-forming group decisions.

What About Ethics in Decision Making?

No contemporary discussion of decision making would be complete without the inclusion of ethics because ethical considerations should be an important criterion in organizational decision making. This is certainly more true today than at any time in the recent past given the scandals at companies like Enron, WorldCom, Tyco International, Arthur Andersen, Citigroup, Merrill Lynch, ImClone Systems, Adelphia Communications, Sunbeam, and Rite Aid. In this final section, we present three different ways to frame decisions ethically and look at how ethical standards vary across national cultures.

Three Ethical Decision Criteria

An individual can use three different criteria in making ethical choices.[74] The first is the *utilitarian* criterion, in which decisions are made solely on the basis of their outcomes or consequences. The goal of **utilitarianism** is to provide the greatest good for the greatest number. This view tends to dominate business decision making. It is consistent with goals like efficiency, productivity, and high profits. By maximizing profits, for instance, a business executive can argue he is securing the greatest good for the greatest number—as he hands out dismissal notices to 15 percent of his employees.

Another ethical criterion is to focus on *rights*. This calls on individuals to make decisions consistent with fundamental liberties and privileges as set forth in documents like the Bill of Rights. An emphasis on rights in decision making means respecting and protecting the basic rights of individuals, such as the right to privacy, to free speech, and to due process. For instance, use of this criterion would protect **whistle-blowers**—individuals who report unethical or illegal practices by their employer to outsiders—when they reveal unethical practices by their organization to the press or government agencies on the grounds of their right to free speech.

A third criterion is to focus on *justice*. This requires individuals to impose and enforce rules fairly and impartially so that there is an equitable distribution of benefits and costs. Union members typically favor this view. It justifies paying people the same wage for a given job, regardless of performance differences, and using seniority as the primary determination in making layoff decisions.

Each of these three criteria has advantages and liabilities. A focus on utilitarianism promotes efficiency and productivity, but it can result in ignoring the rights of some individuals, particularly those with minority representation in the organization. The use of rights as a criterion protects individuals from injury and is consistent with freedom and privacy, but it can create an overly legalistic work environment that hinders productivity and efficiency. A focus on justice protects the interests of the underrepresented and less powerful, but it can encourage a sense of entitlement that reduces risk taking, innovation, and productivity.

Myth or Science?

"Ethical People Don't Do Unethical Things"

This statement is mostly true. People with high ethical standards are less likely to engage in unethical practices, even in organizations or situations in which there are strong pressures to conform. The essential issue that this statement addresses is whether ethical behavior is more a function of the individual or the situational context. The evidence indicates that people with high ethical principles will follow them in spite of what others do or the dictates of organizational norms.[75] But when an individual's ethical and moral development are not of the highest level, he or she is more likely to be influenced by strong cultures. This is true even when those strong cultures encourage questionable practices.

Because ethical people essentially avoid unethical practices, managers should be encouraged to screen job candidates (through testing and background investigations) to determine their ethical standards. By seeking out people with integrity and strong ethical principles, the organization increases the likelihood that employees will act ethically. Of course, unethical practices can be further minimized by providing individuals with a supportive work climate.[76] This would include clear job descriptions, a written code of ethics, positive management role models, the evaluating and rewarding of means as well as ends, and a culture that encourages individuals to openly challenge questionable practices. ■

Decision makers, particularly in for-profit organizations, tend to feel safe and comfortable when they use utilitarianism. A lot of questionable actions can be justified when framed as being in the best interests of "the organization" and stockholders. But many critics of business decision makers argue that this perspective needs to change.[77] Increased concern in society about individual rights and social justice suggests the need for managers to develop ethical standards based on nonutilitarian criteria. This presents a solid challenge to today's managers because making decisions using criteria such as individual rights and social justice involves far more ambiguities than using utilitarian criteria such as effects on efficiency and profits. This helps to explain why managers are increasingly criticized for their actions. Raising prices, selling products with questionable effects on consumer health, closing down inefficient plants, laying off large numbers of employees, moving production overseas to cut costs, and similar decisions can be justified in utilitarian terms. But that may no longer be the single criterion by which good decisions should be judged.

Ethics and National Culture

What is seen as an ethical decision in China may not be seen as such in Canada. The reason is that there are no global ethical standards.[78] Contrasts between Asia and the West provide an illustration.[79] Because bribery is commonplace in countries such as China, a Canadian working in China might face the dilemma: Should I pay a bribe to secure business if it is an accepted part of that country's culture? Or how about this for a shock? A manager of a large U.S. company operating in China caught an employee stealing. Following company policy, she fired him and turned him over to the local authorities. Later, she was horrified to learn that the employee had been summarily executed.[80]

Although ethical standards may seem ambiguous in the West, criteria defining right and wrong are actually much clearer in the West than in Asia. Few issues are black and white there; most are gray. The need for global organizations to establish ethical principles for decision makers in countries such as India and China, and modifying them to reflect cultural norms, may be critical if high standards are to be upheld and if consistent practices are to be achieved.

Summary and Implications for Managers

Perception   Individuals behave in a given manner based not on the way their external environment actually is but, rather, on what they see or believe it to be. It's the employee's perception of a situation that becomes the basis for behavior. Whether or not a manager successfully plans and organizes the work of employees and actually helps them to structure their work more efficiently and effec-

utilitarianism   *Decisions made to provide the greatest good for the greatest number.*

whistle-blowers   *Individuals who report unethical practices by their employer to outsiders.*

tively is far less important than how employees perceive the manager's efforts. Similarly, issues such as fair pay for work performed, the validity of performance appraisals, and the adequacy of working conditions are not judged by employees in a way that ensures common perceptions; nor can we be assured that individuals will interpret conditions about their jobs in a favorable light. Therefore, to be able to influence productivity, it's necessary to assess how workers perceive their jobs.

Absenteeism, turnover, and job satisfaction are also reactions to the individual's perceptions. Dissatisfaction with working conditions or the belief that there is a lack of promotion opportunities in the organization are judgments based on attempts to create meaning out of one's job. The employee's conclusion that a job is good or bad is an interpretation. Managers must spend time understanding how each individual interprets reality and, when there is a significant difference between what is seen and what exists, try to eliminate the distortions. Failure to deal with the differences when individuals perceive the job in negative terms will result in increased absenteeism and turnover and lower job satisfaction.

Individual Decision Making   Individuals think and reason before they act. It is because of this that an understanding of how people make decisions can be helpful for explaining and predicting their behavior.

Under some decision situations, people follow the rational decision-making model. But for most people, and most nonroutine decisions, this is probably more the exception than the rule. Few important decisions are simple or unambiguous enough for the rational model's assumptions to apply. So we find individuals looking for solutions that satisfice rather than optimize, injecting biases and prejudices into the decision process, and relying on intuition.

Given the evidence we've described on how decisions are actually made in organizations, what can managers do to improve their decision making? We offer five suggestions.

Exhibit 5-5   Toward Reducing Biases and Errors

Focus on goals. Without goals, you can't be rational, you don't know what information you need, you don't know which information is relevant and which is irrelevant, you'll find it difficult to choose between alternatives, and you're far more likely to experience regret over the choices you make. Clear goals make decision making easier and help you to eliminate options that are inconsistent with your interests.

Look for information that disconfirms your beliefs. One of the most effective means for counteracting overconfidence and the confirmation and hindsight biases is to actively look for information that contradicts your beliefs and assumptions. When we overtly consider various ways we could be wrong, we challenge our tendencies to think we're smarter than we actually are.

Don't try to create meaning out of random events. The educated mind has been trained to look for cause-and-effect relationships. When something happens, we ask why. And when we can't find reasons, we often invent them. You have to accept that there are events in life that are outside your control. Ask yourself if patterns can be meaningfully explained or whether they are merely coincidence. Don't attempt to create meaning out of coincidence.

Increase your options. No matter how many options you've identified, your final choice can be no better than the best of the option set you've selected. This argues for increasing your decision alternatives and for using creativity in developing a wide range of diverse choices. The more alternatives you can generate, and the more diverse those alternatives, the greater your chance of finding an outstanding one.

Source: S. P. Robbins, Decide & Conquer: Making Winning Decisions and Taking Control of Your Life (Upper Saddle River, NJ: Financial Times/Prentice Hall, 2004), pp. 164–68.

First, analyze the situation. Adjust your decision-making approach to the national culture you're operating in and to the criteria your organization evaluates and rewards. For instance, if you're in a country that doesn't value rationality, don't feel compelled to follow the rational decision-making model or even to try to make your decisions appear rational. Similarly, organizations differ in terms of the importance they place on risk, the use of groups, and the like. Adjust your decision approach to ensure that it's compatible with the organization's culture.

Second, be aware of biases. Then try to minimize their impact. Exhibit 5-5 offers some suggestions.

Third, combine rational analysis with intuition. These are not conflicting approaches to decision making. By using both, you can actually improve your decision-making effectiveness. As you gain managerial experience, you should feel increasingly confident in imposing your intuitive processes on top of your rational analysis.

Finally, try to enhance your creativity. Overtly look for novel solutions to problems, attempt to see problems in new ways, and use analogies. In addition, try to remove work and organizational barriers that might impede your creativity.

Point ◀▶ Counterpoint

When in Doubt, Do!

Life is full of decisions and choices. The real question is not "To be, or not to be," but rather "To do, or not to do?" For example, should I confront my professor about my midterm grade? Should I buy a new car? Should I accept a new job? Should I choose this major? Very often, we are unsure of our decision. In such cases, it is almost always better to choose action over inaction. In life, people more often regret inaction than action. Take the following simple example:

Act	State	
	Rain	*Shine*
Carry Umbrella	Dry (except your feet!)	Inconvenience
Don't Carry Umbrella	Miserable drenching	Bliss unalloyed

Say you carry an umbrella and it doesn't rain, or you don't carry an umbrella and it does rain. In which situation are you worse off? Would you rather experience the mild inconvenience of the extra weight of the umbrella or get drenched? Chances are you'll regret inaction more than action. Research shows that once a decision has been made, inaction is regretted more than action. Although we often regret actions in their immediate aftermath, over time regrets over actions decline markedly, whereas regrets over missed opportunities increase. For example, you finally decide to take that trip to Europe. You had an amazing time, but a few weeks after you get back, your credit card bill arrives—and it isn't pretty. Unfortunately, you have to work overtime and miss a few dinners out with friends to pay off the bills. A few months down the road, however, you decide to reminisce by looking through your photos from the trip, and sure enough you can't imagine never having gone. So, when in doubt, just do!

It's just silly to think that when in doubt, you should always act. Mistakes will undoubtedly be made when following such simple advice. For example, you're out of work, but you still decide to purchase your dream car—a BMW that is fully loaded. Not the smartest idea. So why is the motto "just do it" dangerous? Because there are two types of regrets that people can have: hot regret, in which an individual kicks herself for having caused something bad, and wistful regret, in which she fantasizes about how things might have turned out. The danger is that actions are more likely to lead to anguish or hot regret and inaction is more likely to lead to wistful regret. So the bottom line is that we can't apply simple credos such as "just do it" to important decisions.[81]

Questions for Review

1. Define *perception*.

2. What is attribution theory? What are its implications for explaining organizational behavior?

3. How are our perceptions of our own actions different from our perceptions of the actions of others?

4. How does selectivity affect perception? Give an example of how selectivity can create perceptual distortion.

5. What is the rational decision-making model? Under what conditions is it applicable?

6. What is the anchoring bias? How does it distort decision making?

7. What is the availability bias? How does it distort decision making?

8. What role does intuition play in effective decision is it likely to be most effective?

9. Describe organizational factors that might constrain decision makers.

10. Are unethical decisions more a function of the individual decision maker or the decision maker's work environment? Explain.

Questions for Critical Thinking

1. How might the differences in the experiences of students and instructors affect their perceptions of students' written work and class comments?

2. An employee does an unsatisfactory job on an assigned project. Explain the attribution process that this person's manager will use to form judgments about this employee's job performance.

3. "For the most part, individual decision making in organizations is an irrational process." Do you agree or disagree? Discuss.

4. What factors do you think differentiate good decision makers from poor ones? Relate your answer to the six-step rational model.

5. Have you ever increased your commitment to a failed course of action? If so, analyze the follow-up decision to increase your commitment and explain why you behaved as you did.

Team Exercise

BIASES IN DECISION MAKING

Step 1

Answer each of the following problems.

1. The following 10 corporations were ranked by *Fortune* magazine to be among the 500 largest United States-based firms according to sales volume for 2005:

    Group A: Apple Computer, Hershey Foods, Hilton Hotels, Mattel, Levi Strauss
    Group B: American International Group, Cardinal Health, Conagra Foods, Ingram Micro, Valero Energy

    Which group of five organizations listed (A or B) had the larger total sales volume? By what percentage (10 percent, 50 percent, 100 percent, or?) do you think the higher group's sales exceeded the lower group's?

2. The best student in your introductory MBA class this past semester writes poetry and is rather shy and small in stature. What was the student's undergraduate major: Chinese studies or psychology?

3. Which of the following causes more deaths in the United States each year?
    (a) Stomach cancer
    (b) Motor vehicle accidents

4. Which would you choose?
    (a) A sure gain of $240
    (b) A 25 percent chance of winning $1,000 and a 75 percent chance of winning nothing.

5. Which would you choose?
    (a) A sure loss of $750
    (b) A 75 percent chance of losing $1,000 and a 25 percent chance of losing nothing.

6. Which would you choose?
    (a) A sure loss of $3,000
    (b) An 80 percent chance of losing $4,000 and a 20 percent chance of losing nothing.

Step 2

Break into groups of 3 to 5. Compare your answers. Explain why you chose the answers that you did.

Step 3

Your instructor will give you the correct answers to each problem. Now discuss the accuracy of your decisions; the biases evident in the decisions you reached; and how you might improve your decision making to make it more accurate.

Source: These problems are based on examples provided in M. H. Bazerman, *Judgment in Managerial Decision Making,* 3rd ed. (New York: Wiley, 1994).

Ethical Dilemma

FIVE ETHICAL DECISIONS: WHAT WOULD YOU DO?

Consider the following ethical decisions. How would you respond to each of the following situations?

1. Assume you're a middle manager in a company with about a thousand employees. You're negotiating a contract with a potentially very large customer whose representative has hinted that you could almost certainly be assured of getting his business if you gave him and his wife an all-expense-paid cruise to the Caribbean. You know the representative's employer wouldn't approve of such a "payoff," but you have the discretion to authorize such an expenditure. What would you do?

2. You have an autographed CD by Snoop Dogg. You have put the CD up for sale on eBay. So far, the highest bid is $44.50. You have a friend who has offered you $75 for the CD, commenting to you that he could get $125 for the CD on eBay in a year. Given the current eBay bid and having followed similar events, you know this is highly unlikely. Should you tell your friend that you have listed your CD on eBay?

3. Assume you work for a company and often have to travel on company business. Your company policy on reimbursement for meals while traveling on company business is that you will be repaid for your out-of-pocket costs, not to exceed $80 a day. You don't need receipts for these expenses—the company will take your word. When traveling, you tend to eat at fast-food places and rarely spend in excess of $20 a day. Most of your colleagues put in reimbursement requests in the range of $55 to $60 a day regardless of

what their actual expenses are. How much would you request for your meal reimbursements?

4. You work for a company that manufactures, markets, and distributes various products, including nutritional supplements, to health food and nutrition stores. One of the company's best-selling products is an herbal supplement called Rosalife. The company advertises that Rosalife "Achieves all the gains of estrogen hormone replacement therapy without any of the side effects." One day a research assistant stops by your office with some troubling information. She tells you that while researching another product, she came across a recent study that suggests that Rosalife does not offer the benefits the company claims it does. You show this study to your supervisor, who says, "We're not responsible for validating non-FDA-controlled products and nobody's hurt anyway." Indeed, you know that this is not the case. What is your ethical responsibility?

5. Assume you're the manager at a gaming company, and you're responsible for hiring a group to outsource the production of a highly anticipated new game. Because your company is a giant in the industry, there are numerous companies trying to get the bid. As the primary contact, one of the outsourcers offers you some kickbacks if you give them the bid, but ultimately it is up to your bosses to decide on the company. So, you don't mention the incentive, but push upper management to give the company that offered you the kickback the bid. In this case, is withholding the truth as bad as lying? Why or why not?

Case Incident 1

J&J AUTOMOTIVE SALES

Joe Baum loves what he does. He just isn't crazy about how others see him. Joe is the owner of J&J Automotive Sales, a used-car dealership in southwest St. Louis with about 30 cars on his lot at any time.

"Used-car dealers deal with a pretty bad reputation," says Joe. Just why, he isn't sure. He didn't realize there was such a stigma attached to used-car dealers until he opened

his dealership in 1997. "At Christmas, when family members would ask what I was doing, I'd tell them, and they'd ask me why I'd want to do that."

Regardless of the public's impression of used-car dealers, Joe loves his business. He enjoys being his own boss. He likes being the sole salesman on his lot. He relishes the diversity of his work—he does everything from buying the vehicles, to fixing them up to sell, to helping buyers arrange financing. And, very importantly, Joe likes the opportunity to work with customers. "There are a thousand guys out there selling cars who are better at selling than I am," Joe says. "I'm more interested in having a relationship."

One of Joe's strengths is that he loves cars. It's in his blood—his father worked for a new-car dealer and frequently traded the family's cars. Joe believes his intimate knowledge of cars makes it easier for him to sell them. "I can tell you whether the car has 75 percent of its brake pad left or if the brake pads are new, because I did it."

To build a meaningful relationship with a customer, Joe has to overcome the stereotype of a used-car salesman. He thinks this might be coming from the hard-sell techniques used by some in his business. "I don't think it would take a customer long to get jaded if they're out shopping for a car. That is a hard thing to overcome."

It's frustrating to Joe when potential customers see him as just another shady salesman. Because he works hard to build a customer's trust, it hurts him when he realizes that he's failed. "If they [customers] question my integrity, that is the hardest thing."

Questions

1. Explain how you think the stereotype of used-car dealers developed.

2. What, if anything, can Joe do to counter this stereotype?

3. In what ways might this stereotype be beneficial to Joe? To potential customers?

4. AutoNation is #93 on the 2003 Fortune 500. It has created a huge business by exploiting the public's perception of used-car dealers. What do you think they have done to change the stereotype?

Source: Based on G. Cancelada, "Used-Car Dealer Sees Bad Rep as a Bum Rap," *St. Louis Post-Dispatch*, March 24, 2003, p. E1.

Case Incident 2

WHISTLE-BLOWERS: SAINTS OR SINNERS?

Corporate whistle-blowers, individuals who report company wrongdoings, are often lauded for their courage and integrity. For example, one famous whistle-blower, former Enron executive Sherron Watkins, was named by *Time* magazine as one of 2002's Persons of the Year. Given that whistle-blowers face unemployment, and, often times, ridicule from their company, many people do not come forward to report illegal activity. To encourage whistle-blowers, the whistle-blower law, adopted in 1986, pays informants as much as 30 percent of legal fines reaped during lawsuits. With settlements often exceeding $100 million, whistle-blowers can sometimes see huge payoffs. Some experts are concerned that these payoffs are creating a culture where employees quickly report wrongdoings instead of trying to rectify the situation internally.

Douglas Durand, for example, was a former vice president of sales at TAP Pharmaceutical Products. In 1995, he began to suspect that TAP was conspiring with doctors to defraud Medicare. Pharmaceutical companies routinely provide doctors with free samples of the latest drugs; however, Durand believed that TAP was working with doctors to bill Medicare for the free drugs, a practice that is against federal law. Later that same year, Durand became more worried when he discovered that TAP had decided to pay a 2 percent fee to individual doctors to cover "administrative costs"—a kickback in Durand's opinion. Durand then began preparing to blow the whistle on TAP and its affiliates. "I wanted to do the right thing," he says. After being referred to attorney Elizabeth Ainslie by one of his colleagues, Durand started keeping notes and collecting company documents, while his lawyer attempted to get the federal government involved.

In February 1996, Durand received a $35,000 bonus from TAP and then quit the company. Three months later, he and Ainslie filed suits against TAP. For the next five years, Durand and Ainslie built their case against TAP. At one point, Durand even obtained some of his former coworkers' home phone numbers and called them while the FBI listened in. During one call to a former TAP colleague, Durand lied, saying that he had been subpoenaed, all in an attempt to get his former colleague to incriminate himself. All in all, over 500 boxes of documents were collected containing evidence against TAP. Although TAP fought the lawsuit, it finally settled in April, 2001. Durand's take was a cool $126 million.

On the day that TAP settled, prosecutors filed criminal fraud charges against the company. One of those prosecutors, Michael Sullivan, said that the charges were filed to send "a very strong signal to the pharmaceutical industry." However, as the trial progressed, holes in Durand's story began to appear. The kickbacks that Durand claimed were paid by TAP to doctors never occurred, the company didn't overcharge Medicare, and a conference that Durand believed TAP used to bribe doctors into using their drugs was actually paid for by the doctors themselves. Finally, in July 2002, a federal jury in Boston cleared TAP of the charges, but not before TAP had incurred over $1 billion in legal fees. Durand is now retired and lives with his wife and daughter in Florida.

Supporters of whistle-blowing, such as Senator Charles Grassley (R-Iowa), say that having informants report on company wrongdoings is the best way to prevent illegal activity. "There can never be enough bureaucrats to discourage fraudulent use of taxpayers' money, but knowing colleagues might squeal can be a deterrent," he states. However, others disagree. According to David Stetler, defense attorney for TAP, "It's absolutely a form of extortion." Whatever position one takes, it seems clear that whistle-blowing is a strong means to deter corporate wrong-doing. However, when this right is abused, whistle-blowers can become as unethical as the companies that they are blowing the whistle on.

Questions

1. Do you believe that whistle-blowing is good for organizations and its members, or is it, as David Stetler believes, often a means to extort large financial gains from companies?

2. How might the self-fulfilling prophecy affect a whistle-blower's search for incriminating evidence against a company?

3. When frivolous lawsuits occur, how might these cases affect future whistle-blowers who have a valid legal claim against their company? Would they be more or less likely to come forward? How might their claims be evaluated? What should companies and the government do to prevent frivolous lawsuits?

4. Do you believe that employees of a company have an ethical obligation to first attempt to report wrongdoing to members of the company itself, or should they go straight to the authorities when they suspect illegal activity? What are some advantages and disadvantages of both actions?

Source: Based on N. Weinberg, "The Dark Side of Whistle-blowing," *Forbes*, March 14, 2005, pp. 90–95.

Endnotes

1. Based on C. Murphy, "Muslim U.S. Workers Hope to Break Image: Start of Ramadan Offers Chance to Reach Out in Faith," *Washington Post*, November 6, 2002, p. B3; J. Curiel, "Muslims Find Bay Area Leans Toward Tolerance: But Even Here, Many Experience 9/11 Backlash," *San Francisco Chronicle*, May 22, 2004, p. A-1; Muslim Woman Sues Goodwill for Alleged Workplace Discrimination," *The NewStandard*, November 24, 2004, http://newstandardnews.net/content/?action=show_item&itemid=1255; T. Chris, "Muslim Woman Sues Disney For Discrimination," September 10, 2004, http://talkleft.com/new_archives/006595.

2. H. H. Kelley, "Attribution in Social Interaction," in E. Jones et al. (eds.), *Attribution: Perceiving the Causes of Behavior* (Morristown, NJ: General Learning Press, 1972).

3. See L. Ross, "The Intuitive Psychologist and His Shortcomings," in L. Berkowitz (ed.), *Advances in Experimental Social Psychology*, vol. 10 (Orlando, FL: Academic Press, 1977), pp. 174–220; and A. G. Miller and T. Lawson, "The Effect of an Informational Option on the Fundamental Attribution Error," *Personality and Social Psychology Bulletin*, June 1989, pp. 194–204.

4. See, for instance, G. Johns, "A Multi-Level Theory of Self-Serving Behavior in and by Organizations," in R. I. Sutton and B. M. Staw (eds.), *Research in Organizational Behavior*, vol. 21 (Stamford, CT: JAI Press, 1999), pp. 1–38; N. Epley and D. Dunning, "Feeling 'Holier Than Thou': Are Self-Serving Assessments Produced by Errors in Self- or Social Prediction?" *Journal of Personality and Social Psychology*, December 2000, pp. 861–75; and M. Goerke, J. Moller, S. Schulz-Hardt, U. Napiersky, and D. Frey, " 'It's Not My Fault—But Only I Can Change It': Counterfactual and Prefactual Thoughts of Managers," *Journal of Applied Psychology*, April 2004, pp. 279–92.

5. See, for instance, G. R. Semin, "A Gloss on Attribution Theory," *British Journal of Social and Clinical Psychology*, November 1980, pp. 291–30; M. W. Morris and K. Peng, "Culture and Cause: American and Chinese Attributions for Social and Physical Events," *Journal of Personality and Social Psychology*, December 1994, pp. 949–71; and D. S. Krull, M. H-M. Loy, J. Lin, C-F. Wang, S. Chen, and X. Zhao, "The Fundamental Attribution Error: Correspondence Bias in Individualistic and Collectivist Cultures," *Personality & Social Psychology Bulletin*, October 1999, pp. 1208–19.

6. S. Nam, "Cultural and Managerial Attributions for Group Performance," unpublished doctoral dissertation; University of Oregon. Cited in R. M. Steers, S. J. Bischoff, and L. H. Higgins, "Cross-Cultural Management Research," *Journal of Management Inquiry*, December 1992, pp. 325–26.

7. D. C. Dearborn and H. A. Simon, "Selective Perception: A Note on the Departmental Identification of Executives," *Sociometry*, June 1958, pp. 140–44. Some of the conclusions in this classic study have recently been challenged in J. Walsh, "Selectivity and Selective Perception: An Investigation of Managers' Belief Structures and Information Processing," *Academy of Management Journal*, December 1988, pp. 873–96; M. J. Waller, G. Huber, and W. H. Glick, "Functional Background as a Determinant of Executives' Selective Perception," *Academy of Management Journal*, August 1995, pp. 943–74; and J. M. Beyer, P. Chattopadhyay, E. George, W. H. Glick, D. T. Ogilvie, and D. Pugliese, "The Selective Perception of Managers Revisited," *Academy of Management Journal*, June 1997, pp. 716–37.

8. See K. R. Murphy and R. L. Anhalt, "Is Halo a Property of the Rater, the Ratees, or the Specific Behaviors Observed?" *Journal of Applied Psychology*, June 1992, pp. 494–500; K. R. Murphy, R. A. Jako, and R. L. Anhalt, "Nature and Consequences of Halo Error: A Critical Analysis," *Journal of Applied Psychology*, April 1993, pp. 218–25; A. L. Solomonson and C. E. Lance, "Examination of the Relationship Between True Halo and Halo Error in

Performance Ratings," *Journal of Applied Psychology*, October 1997, pp. 665–674; and C. E. Naquin and R. O. Tynan, "The Team Halo Effect: Why Teams are not Blamed for their Failures," *Journal of Applied Psychology*, April 2003, pp. 332–340.

9. S. E. Asch, "Forming Impressions of Personality," *Journal of Abnormal and Social Psychology*, July 1946, pp. 258–90.

10. J. S. Bruner and R. Tagiuri, "The Perception of People," in E. Lindzey (ed.), *Handbook of Social Psychology* (Reading, MA: Addison-Wesley, 1954), p. 641.

11. J. L. Hilton and W. von Hippel, "Stereotypes," in J. T. Spence, J. M. Darley, and D. J. Foss (eds.), *Annual Review of Psychology*, vol. 47 (Palo Alto, CA: Annual Reviews Inc., 1996), pp. 237–71.

12. See, for example, C. M. Judd and B. Park, "Definition and Assessment of Accuracy in Social Stereotypes," *Psychological Review*, January 1993, pp. 109–28.

13. See, for example, G. N. Powell, "The Good Manager: Business Students' Stereotypes of Japanese Managers versus Stereotypes of American Managers," *Group & Organizational Management*, March 1992, pp.44–56; W. C. K. Chiu, A. W. Chan, E. Snape, and T. Redman, "Age Stereotypes and Discriminatory Attitudes Towards Older Workers: An East-West Comparison," *Human Relations*, May 2001, pp. 629–61; C. Ostroff and L. E. Atwater, "Does Whom You Work With Matter? Effects of Referent Group Gender and Age Composition on Managers' Compensation," *Journal of Applied Psychology*, August 2003, pp. 725–40; and M. E. Heilman, A. S. Wallen, D. Fuchs, and M. M. Tamkins, "Penalties for Success: Reactions to Women Who Succeed at Male Gender-Typed Tasks," *Journal of Applied Psychology*, June 2004, pp. 416–27.

14. H. G. Heneman III and T. A. Judge, *Staffing Organizations* (Middleton, WI: Mendota House, 2006).

15. See, for example, E. C. Webster, *Decision Making in the Employment Interview* (Montreal: McGill University, Industrial Relations Center, 1964).

16. See, for example, D. Eden, *Pygmalion in Management* (Lexington, MA: Lexington, 1990); D. Eden, "Leadership and Expectations: Pygmalion Effects and Other Self-Fulfilling Prophecies," *Leadership Quarterly*, Winter 1992, pp. 271–305; D. B. McNatt, "Ancient Pygmalion Joins Contemporary Management: A Meta-Analysis of the Result," *Journal of Applied Psychology*, April 2000, pp. 314–22; O. B. Davidson and D. Eden, "Remedial Self-Fulfilling Prophecy: Two Field Experiments to Prevent Golem Effects Among Disadvantaged Women," *Journal of Applied Psychology*, June 2000, pp. 386–98; D. Eden, "Self-Fulfilling Prophecies in Organizations," in J. Greenberg (ed.), *Organizational Behavior: The State of the Science*, 2nd ed. (Mahwah, NJ: 2003), pp. 91–122; and D. B. McNatt and T. A. Judge, "Boundary Conditions of the Galatea Effect: A Field Experiment and Constructive Replication," *Academy of Management Journal*, August 2004, pp. 550–65.

17. D. Eden and A. B. Shani, "Pygmalion Goes to Boot Camp: Expectancy, Leadership, and Trainee Performance," *Journal of Applied Psychology*, April 1982, pp. 194–99.

18. See W. J. Haddad, "Impact of the September 11th Attacks on the Freedoms of Arabs and Muslims," Arab-American Bar Association of Illinois (http://www.arabbar.org/art-sept11impact.asp).

19. See, for example, J. Wilgoren, "Struggling to be Both Arab and American," *New York Times*, November 4, 2001, p. B1; J. Q. Wilson and H. R. Higgins, "Profiles in Courage," *Wall Street Journal*, January 10, 2002, p. A12; and P. R. Sullivan, "Profiling," *America*, March 18, 2002, pp. 12–14.

20. See http://search.localcolorart.com/search/encyclopedia/List_of_terrorist_incidents/.

21. See, for example, R. D. Bretz, Jr., G. T. Milkovich, and W. Read, "The Current State of Performance Appraisal Research and Practice: Concerns, Directions, and Implications," *Journal of Management*, June 1992, pp. 323–24; and S. E. DeVoe and S. S. Iyengar, "Managers' Theories of Subordinates: A Cross-Cultural Examination of Manager Perceptions of Motivation and Appraisal of Performance," *Organizational Behavior and Human Decision Processes*, January 2004, pp. 47–61.

22. R. Sanders, *The Executive Decisionmaking Process: Identifying Problems and Assessing Outcomes* (Westport, CT: Quorum, 1999).

23. See H. A. Simon, "Rationality in Psychology and Economics," *Journal of Business*, October 1986, pp. 209–24; and E. Shafir and R. A. LeBoeuf, "Rationality," in S. T. Fiske, D. L. Schacter, and C. Zahn-Waxler, eds., *Annual Review of Psychology*, vol. 53 (Palo Alto, CA: Annual Reviews, 2002), pp. 491–517.

24. For a review of the rational model, see E. F. Harrison, *The Managerial Decision-Making Process*, 5th ed. (Boston: Houghton Mifflin, 1999), pp. 75–102.

25. W. Pounds, "The Process of Problem Finding," *Industrial Management Review*, Fall 1969, pp. 1–19.

26. J. G. March, *A Primer on Decision Making* (New York: Free Press, 1994), pp. 2–7; and D. Hardman and C. Harries, "How Rational Are We?" *Psychologist*, February 2002, pp. 76–79.

27. T. M. Amabile, "A Model of Creativity and Innovation in Organizations," in B. M. Staw and L. L. Cummings (eds.), *Research in Organizational Behavior*, vol. 10 (Greenwich, CT: JAI Press, 1988), p. 126; and T. M. Amabile, "Motivating Creativity in Organizations," *California Management Review*, Fall 1997, p. 40; and J. E. Perry-Smith and C. E. Shalley, "The Social Side of Creativity: A Static and Dynamic Social Network Perspective" *Academy of Management Review*, January 2003, pp. 89–106.

28. Predicting creativity from early to late adulthood: Intellect, potential, and personality. Feist, Gregory J.; Barron, Frank X.; Journal of Research in Personality, Vol 37(2), April 2003. pp. 62–88.

29. R. W. Woodman, J. E. Sawyer, and R. W. Griffin, "Toward a Theory of Organizational Creativity," *Academy of Management Review*, April 1993, p. 298; and J. M. George and J. Zhou, "When Openness to Experience and Conscientioussness are Related to Creative Behavior: An Interactional Approach," *Journal of Applied Psychology*, June 2001, pp. 513–24.

30. Cited in C. G. Morris, *Psychology: An Introduction*, 9th ed. (Upper Saddle River, NJ: Prentice Hall, 1996), p. 344.

31. This section is based on T. M. Amabile, "Motivating Creativity in Organizations," pp. 42–52.

32. A. M. Isen, "Positive Affect," in *Handbook of Cognition and Emotion*, Tim Dalgleish,and Mick J. Power (eds.) (New York: John Wiley & Sons Ltd., 1999), pp. 521–39.

33. J. Zhou, "When the Presence of Creative Coworkers Is Related to Creativity: Role of Supervisor Close Monitoring, Developmental Feedback, and Creative Personality," *Journal of Applied Psychology* 88, no. 3 (June 2003), pp. 413–22.

34. W. J. J. Gordon, *Synectics* (New York: Harper & Row, 1961).

35. See T .M. Amabile, *KEYS: Assessing the Climate for Creativity* (Greensboro, NC: Center for Creative Leadership, 1995); N. Madjar, G. R. Oldham, and M. G. Pratt, "There's No Place Like Home? The Contributions of Work and Nonwork Creativity Support to Employees' Creative Performance," *Academy of Management Journal*, August 2002, pp. 757–67; and C. E. Shalley, J. Zhou, and G. R. Oldham, "The Effects of Personal and Contextual Characteristics on Creativity: Where Should We Go From Here?" *Journal of Management*, November 2004, pp. 933–58.

36. D. L. Rados, "Selection and Evaluation of Alternatives in Repetitive Decision Making," *Administrative Science Quarterly*, June 1972, pp. 196–206; and G. Klein, *Sources of Power: How People Make Decisions* (Cambridge, MA: MIT Press, 1998).

37. M. Bazerman, *Judgment in Managerial Decision Making*, 3rd ed. (New York: Wiley, 1994), p. 5.

38. See, for instance, L. R. Beach, *The Psychology of Decision Making* (Thousand Oaks, CA: Sage, 1997).

39. D. Kahneman, "Maps of Bounded Rationality: Psychology for Behavioral Economics," *The American Economic Review* 93, no. 5 (2003), pp. 1449–75.

40. See H. A. Simon, *Administrative Behavior*, 4th ed. (New York: Free Press, 1997); and M. Augier, "Simon Says: Bounded Rationality Matters," *Journal of Management Inquiry*, September 2001, pp. 268–75.

41. S. P. Robbins, *Decide & Conquer: Making Winning Decisions and Taking Control of Your Life* (Upper Saddle River, NJ: Financial Times/Prentice Hall, 2004), p. 13.

42. S. Plous, *The Psychology of Judgment and Decision Making* (New York: McGraw Hill, 1993), p. 217.

43. S. Lichtenstein and B. Fischhoff, "Do Those Who Know More Also Know More About How Much They Know?" *Organizational Behavior and Human Performance*, December 1977, pp. 159–83.

44. B. Fischhoff, P. Slovic, and S. Lichtenstein, "Knowing with Certainty: The Appropriateness of Extreme Confidence," *Journal of Experimental Psychology: Human Perception and Performance*, November 1977, pp. 552–64.

45. J. Kruger and D. Dunning, "Unskilled and Unaware of It: How Difficulties in Recognizing One's Own Incompetence Lead to Inflated Self-Assessments," *Journal of Personality and Social Psychology*, November 1999, pp. 1121–34.

46. Fischhoff, Slovic, and Lichtenstein, "Know with Certainty: The Appropriateness of Extreme Confidence."

47. Kruger and Dunning, "Unskilled and Unaware of It: How Difficulties in Recognizing One's Own Incompetence Lead to Inflated Self-Assessments."

48. See, for instance, A. Tversky and D. Kahneman, "Judgment Under Uncertainty: Heuristics and Biases," *Science*, September 1974, pp. 1124–31.

49. J. S. Hammond, R. L. Keeney, and H. Raiffa, *Smart Choices* (Boston: HBS Press, 1999), p. 191.

50. R. Hastie, D. A. Schkade, and J. W. Payne, "Juror Judgments in Civil Cases: Effects of Plaintiff's Requests and Plaintiff's Identity on Punitive Damage Awards," *Law and Human Behavior*, August 1999, pp. 445–70.

51. See R. S. Nickerson, "Confirmation Bias: A Ubiquitous Phenomenon in Many Guises," *Review of General Psychology*, June 1998, pp. 175–220; and E. Jonas, S. Schultz-Hardt, D. Frey, and N. Thelen, "Confirmation Bias in Sequential Information Search After Preliminary Decisions," *Journal of Personality and Social Psychology*, April 2001, pp. 557–71.

52. See A. Tversky and D. Kahneman, "Availability: A Heuristic for Judging Frequency and Probability," in D. Kahneman, P. Slovic, and A. Tversky (eds.), *Judgment Under Uncertainty: Heuristics and Biases* (Cambridge: Cambridge Press, 1982), pp. 163–78; and B. J. Bushman and G. L. Wells, "Narrative Impressions of Literature: The Availability Bias and the Corrective Properties of Meta-Analytic Approaches," *Personality and Social Psychology Bulletin*, September 2001, pp. 1123–30.

53. M. Hutton, "Black Youths All but Ignore Tennis, Golf and Swimming as They Eye NBA," *The Post-Tribune*, February 18, 2002 (http://www.post-trib.com/news/race10.html).

54. See Tversky and Kahneman, "Judgment Under Uncertainty: Heuristics and Biases."

55. See B. M. Staw, "The Escalation of Commitment to a Course of Action," *Academy of Management Review*, October 1981, pp. 577–87; C. R. Greer and G. K. Stephens, "Escalation of Commitment: A Comparison of Differences Between Mexican and U.S. Decision-Makers," *Journal of Management* 27, no. 1 (2001), pp. 51–78; H. Moon. "Looking Forward and Looking Back: Integrating Completion and Sunk-Cost Effects Within an Escalation-of-Commitment Progress Decision," *Journal of Applied Psychology*, February 2001, pp. 104–13; and A. Zardkoohi, "Do Real Options Lead to Escalation of Commitment? Comment," *Academy of Management Review*, January 2004, pp. 111–19.

56. B. M. Staw, "Knee-Deep in the Big Muddy: A Study of Escalating Commitment to a Chosen Course of Action," *Organizational Behavior and Human Performance* 16 (1976), pp. 27–44.

57. B. Fischhoff and P. Slovic, "A Little Learning . . . Confidence in Multicue Judgment Tasks," in R. Nicherson (ed.), *Attention and Performance*, vol. 8 (NJ: Erlbaum, 1980).

58. See, for instance, A. James and A. Wells, "Death Beliefs, Superstitious Beliefs and Health Anxiety," *British Journal of Clinical Psychology*, March 2002, pp. 43–53.

59. R. L. Guilbault, F. B. Bryant, J. H. Brockway, and E. J. Posavac, "A Meta-Analysis of Research on Hindsight Bias," *Basic and Applied Social Psychology*, September 2004, pp. 103–17; and L. Werth, F. Strack, and J. Foerster, "Certainty and Uncertainty: The Two Faces of the Hindsight Bias," *Organizational Behavior and Human Decision Processes*, March 2002, pp. 323–41.

60. J. M. Bonds-Raacke, L. S. Fryer, S. D. Nicks, and R. T. Durr, "Hindsight Biases Demonstrated in the Prediction of a Sporting Event," *Journal of Social Psychology*, June 2001, pp. 349–52.

61. See, for instance, E. Erdfelder and A. Buckner, "Decomposing the Hindsight Bias: A Multinomial Processing Tree Model for Separating Recollection and Reconstruction in Hindsight," *Journal of Experimental Psychology: Learning, Memory, and Cognition*, March 1998, pp. 387–414.

62. See O. Behling and N. L. Eckel, "Making Sense Out of Intuition," *Academy of Management Executive*, February 1991, pp. 46–54; and T. Gilovich, D. Griffin, and D. Kahneman, *Heuristics and Biases: The Psychology of Intuitive Judgment* (New York: Cambridge University Press, 2002).

63. As described in H. A. Simon, "Making Management Decisions: The Role of Intuition and Emotion," *Academy of Management Executive*, February 1987, pp. 59–60.

64. See, for instance, L. A. Burke and M. K. Miller, "Taking the Mystery out of Intuitive Decision Making," *Academy of Management Executive*, November 1999, pp. 91–99; N. Khatri and H. A. Ng, "The Role of Intuition in Strategic Decision Making," *Human Relations*, January 2000, pp. 57–86; J. A. Andersen, "Intuition in Managers: Are Intuitive Managers More Effective?" *Journal of Managerial Psychology* 15, no. 1–2, pp. 46–67; D. Myers, *Intuition: Its Powers and Perils* (New Haven, CT: Yale University Press, 2002); and L. Simpson, "Basic Instincts," *Training*, January 2003, pp. 56–59.

65. See, for instance, W. H. Agor (ed.), *Intuition in Organizations* (Newbury Park, CA: Sage Publications, 1989); L. A. Burke and M. K. Miller, "Taking the Mystery out of Intuitive Decision Making," *Academy of Management Executive*, November 1999, pp. 91–99; N. Khatri and H. A. Ng, "The Role of Intuition in Strategic Decision Making;" J. A. Andersen, "Intuition in Managers: Are Intuitive Managers More Effective?"; D. Myers, *Intuition: Its Powers and Perils*; and L. Simpson, "Basic Instincts," *Training* (January 2003), pp. 56–59.

66. Ibid., p. 15.

67. H. Moon, J. R. Hollenbeck, S. E. Humphrey, and B. Maue, "The Tripartite Model of Neuroticism and the Suppression of Depression and Anxiety within an Escalation of Commitment Dilemma," *Journal of Personality* 71 (2003), pp. 347–68; H. Moon, "The Two Faces of Conscientiousness: Duty and Achievement Striving in Escalation of Commitment Dilemmas," *Journal of Applied Psychology* 86 (2001), pp. 535–40.

68. J. Musch, "Personality Differences in Hindsight Bias," *Memory* 11 (2003), pp. 473–489.

69. W. K. Campbell and C. Sedikides, "Self-Threat Magnifies the Self-Serving Bias: A Meta-Analytic Integration," *Review of General Psychology* 3 (1999), pp. 23–43.

70. This section is based on S. Nolen-Hoeksema, J. Larson, and C. Grayson, "Explaining the Gender Difference in Depressive Symptoms," *Journal of Personality & Social Psychology*, November 1999, pp. 1061–72; S. Nolen-Hoeksema and S. Jackson, "Mediators of the Gender Difference in Rumination," *Psychology of Women Quarterly*, March 2001, pp. 37–47; S. Nolen-Hoeksema, "Gender Differences in Depression," *Current Directions in Psychological Science*, October 2001, pp. 173–76; and S. Nolen-Hoeksema, *Women Who Think Too Much* (New York: Henry Holt, 2003).

71. M. Elias, "Thinking It Over, and Over, and Over," *USA Today*, February 6, 2003, p. 10D.

72. A. Wildavsky, *The Politics of the Budgetary Process* (Boston: Little, Brown, 1964).

73. N. J. Adler, *International Dimensions of Organizational Behavior*, 4th ed. (Cincinnati, OH: Southwestern, 2002), pp. 182–89.

74. G. F. Cavanagh, D. J. Moberg, and M. Valasquez, "The Ethics of Organizational Politics," *Academy of Management Journal*, June 1981, pp. 363–74.

75. L. Kohlberg, "Stage and Sequence: The Cognitive-Developmental Approach to Socialization," in D. A. Goslin (ed.), *Handbook of Socialization Theory and Research* (Chicago: Rand McNally, 1969), pp. 347–480.

76. See, for instance, B. Victor and J. B. Cullen, "The Organizational Bases of Ethical Work Climates," *Administrative Science Quarterly*, March 1988, pp. 101–25; and J. C. Wimbush, "The Effect of Cognitive Moral Development and Supervisory Influence on Subordinates' Ethical Behavior," *Journal of Business Ethics*, February 1999, pp. 383–95; and D. K. Peterson, "Deviant Workplace Behavior and the Organization's Ethical Climate," *Journal of Business and Psychology*, Fall 2002, pp. 47–61.

77. See, for example, T. Machan, ed., *Commerce and Morality* (Totowa, NJ: Rowman and Littlefield, 1988).

78. T. Jackson, "Cultural Values and Management Ethics: A 10-Nation Study," *Human Relations*, October 2001, pp. 1267–302; see also J. B. Cullen, K. P. Parboteeah, and M. Hoegl, "Cross-National Differences in Managers' Willingness to Justify Ethically Suspect Behaviors: A Test of Institutional Anomie Theory," *Academy of Management Journal*, June 2004, pp. 411–21.

79. W. Chow Hou, "To Bribe or Not to Bribe?" *Asia, Inc.*, October 1996, p. 104.

80. P. Digh, "Shades of Gray in the Global Marketplace," *HRMagazine*, April 1997, p. 91.

81. Based on T. Gilovich, V. H. Medvec, and D. Kahneman, "Varieties of Regret: A Debate and Partial Resolution," *Psychological Review*, 105, 1998, pp. 602–05; see also M. Tsiros and V. Mittal, "Regret: A Model of Its Antecedents and Consequences in Consumer Decision Making," *Journal of Consumer Research*, March 2000, pp. 401–17.

*Set me anything to do as a task, and it is inconceivable the
desire I have to do something else.*

— George Bernard Shaw

Motivation Concepts

After studying this chapter, you should be able to:

1 Outline the motivation process.

2 Describe Maslow's needs hierarchy.

3 Differentiate motivators from hygiene factors.

4 List the characteristics that high achievers prefer in a job.

5 Summarize the types of goals that increase performance.

6 Discuss ways self-efficacy can be increased.

7 State the impact of under rewarding employees.

8 Clarify the key relationships in expectancy theory.

9 Explain how the contemporary theories of motivation complement each other.

LEARNING OBJECTIVES

CHAPTER 6

What Makes This Man Tick?

Kim Jong II—or "Dear Leader" as he prefers to be called—is commonly thought to be crazy. After all, he kidnapped a South Korean film director and his wife so they could film his biography. This bizarre behavior is scary for someone who claims to own nuclear weapons. But what motivates Kim Jong II to act in such a way?

Hedonism is one motivator. Kim scoots from palace to palace amidst a convoy of black Mercedes. He has all the latest toys and gadgets. He sends his chef to Tokyo for the world's finest sushi, to Iran for caviar, to Singapore for papayas, and to Copenhagen for bacon. His wine cellar has a collection of 10,000 bottles. His daily rice is inspected grain-by-grain for chipped or defective pieces. Kim also hosts parties that screen the latest Hollywood films, and he is believed to own 20,000 movies. (The producers of *Team America: World Police*, which spoofed Kim, sent him a copy for his collection.)

Kim also appears to be motivated by fear. He moves from palace to palace often, in Saddam Hussein-like fashion, to avoid assassination. He is "desperately worried" about his survival. He is reported to have said, "Without nuclear weapons, we will be attacked." "Kim Jong II does not live in illusion," said Hwang Jang-Yop, a former aide who defected to the United States. "If he thinks he can win, he will never hesitate to attack. He can't stage a war because he knows only too well that he could not win. He will do whatever is best for him." Hedonism and fear. Quite the package of motivators.[1] ■

otivation is one of the most frequently researched topics in OB.[2] One reason for its popularity is revealed in a recent Gallup Poll, which found that a majority of U.S. employees—55 percent to be exact—have no enthusiasm for their work.[3] Clearly, this suggests a problem, at least in the United States. The good news is that all this research provides us with considerable insights into how to improve motivation.

In this chapter, we'll review the basics of motivation, assess a number of motivation theories, and provide an integrative model that shows how the best of these theories fit together.

Defining Motivation

What is motivation? Maybe the place to begin is to say what motivation isn't. Many people incorrectly view motivation as a personal trait—that is, some have it and others don't. In practice, inexperienced managers often label employees who seem to lack motivation as lazy. Such a label assumes that an individual is always lazy or is lacking in motivation. Our knowledge of motivation tells us that this just isn't true. Think about Kim Jong Il. The man is highly motivated, just not motivated in the same direction as you and me. The question, then, is not usually whether someone is motivated, but *what* are they motivated by?

What we know is that motivation is the result of the interaction of the individual and the situation. Certainly, individuals differ in their basic motivational drive. But the same student who finds it difficult to read a textbook for more than 20 minutes may devour a Harry Potter book in one day. For this student, the change in motivation is driven by the situation. So as we analyze the concept of motivation, keep in mind that the level of motivation varies both between individuals and within individuals at different times.

We define **motivation** as the processes that account for an individual's intensity, direction, and persistence of effort toward attaining a goal.[4] While general motivation is concerned with effort toward *any* goal, we'll narrow the focus to *organizational* goals in order to reflect our singular interest in work-related behavior.

The three key elements in our definition are intensity, direction, and persistence. *Intensity* is concerned with how hard a person tries. This is the element most of us focus on when we talk about motivation. However, high intensity is unlikely to lead to favorable job-performance outcomes unless the effort is channeled in a *direction* that benefits the organization. Therefore, we have to consider the quality of effort as well as its intensity. Effort that is directed toward, and consistent with, the organization's goals is the kind of effort that we should be seeking. Finally, motivation has a *persistence* dimension. This is a measure of how long a person can maintain effort. Motivated individuals stay with a task long enough to achieve their goal.

Early Theories of Motivation

The 1950s were a fruitful period in the development of motivation concepts. Three specific theories were formulated during this period, which although heavily attacked and now questionable in terms of validity, are probably still the best-known explanations for employee motivation. These are the hierarchy of needs theory, Theories X and Y, and the two-factor theory. As you'll see later in this chapter, we have since developed more valid explanations of motivation, but you should know these early theories for at least two reasons: (1) They represent a foundation from which contemporary theories have grown, and (2) practicing managers still regularly use these theories and their terminology in explaining employee motivation.

Hierarchy of Needs Theory

It's probably safe to say that the most well-known theory of motivation is Abraham Maslow's **hierarchy of needs**.[5] He hypothesized that within every human being there exists a hierarchy of five needs. These needs are:

1. *Physiological:* Includes hunger, thirst, shelter, sex, and other bodily needs
2. *Safety:* Includes security and protection from physical and emotional harm
3. *Social:* Includes affection, belongingness, acceptance, and friendship
4. *Esteem:* Includes internal esteem factors such as self-respect, autonomy, and achievement; and external esteem factors such as status, recognition, and attention
5. *Self-actualization:* The drive to become what one is capable of becoming; includes growth, achieving one's potential, and self-fulfillment

As each of these needs becomes substantially satisfied, the next need becomes dominant. In terms of Exhibit 6-1, the individual moves up the steps of the hierarchy. From the standpoint of motivation, the theory would say that although no need is ever fully gratified, a substantially satisfied need no longer motivates. So if you want to motivate someone, according to Maslow, you need to understand what level of the hierarchy that person is currently on and focus on satisfying the needs at or above that level.

Maslow separated the five needs into higher and lower orders. Physiological and safety needs were described as **lower-order needs** and social, esteem, and self-actualization as **higher-order needs**. The differentiation between the two

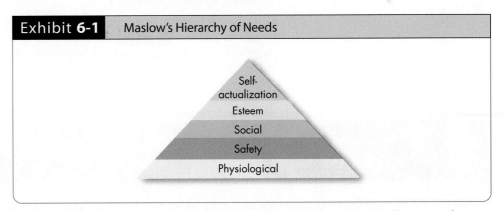

Exhibit 6-1 Maslow's Hierarchy of Needs

Source: A. H. Maslow, *Motivation and Personality*, 3rd ed., R. D. Frager and J. Fadiman (eds.). © 1997. Adapted by permission of Pearson Education, Inc., Upper Saddle River, New Jersey.

motivation *The processes that account for an individual's intensity, direction, and persistence of effort toward attaining a goal.*

hierarchy of needs theory *A hierarchy of five needs—physiological, safety, social, esteem, and self-actualization—exists such that as each need is substantially satisfied, the next need becomes dominant.*

self-actualization *The drive to become what one is capable of becoming.*

lower-order needs *Needs that are satisfied externally; physiological and safety needs.*

higher-order needs *Needs that are satisfied internally; social, esteem, and self-actualization needs.*

orders was made on the premise that higher-order needs are satisfied internally (within the person), whereas lower-order needs are predominantly satisfied externally (by things such as pay, union contracts, and tenure).

Maslow's needs theory has received wide recognition, particularly among practicing managers. This can be attributed to the theory's intuitive logic and ease of understanding. Unfortunately, however, research does not validate the theory. Maslow provided no empirical substantiation, and several studies that sought to validate the theory found no support for it.[6]

Clayton Alderfer attempted to rework Maslow's need hierarchy to align it more closely with empirical research. His revised need hierarchy is labeled **ERG theory**.[7] Alderfer argued that there are three groups of core needs—existence (similar to Maslow's physiological and safety needs), relatedness (similar to Maslow's social and status needs), and growth (similar to Maslow's esteem needs and self-actualization).

Unlike Maslow's theory, ERG does not assume that there exists a rigid hierarchy in which a lower need must be substantially gratified before one can move on. For example, ERG argues that a person can be working on growth needs even though existence or relatedness needs are unsatisfied. An individual could also be focusing on all three need categories simultaneously. Moreover, Alderfer believed that frustration in satisfying a higher-order need might lead to regression to a lower need. Despite these differences, empirical research hasn't been any more supportive of ERG theory than need hierarchy.[8]

Old theories, especially ones that are intuitively logical, apparently die hard. Although the need hierarchy theory and its terminology have remained popular with practicing managers, there is little evidence that need structures are organized along the dimensions proposed by Maslow or Alderfer, that unsatisfied needs motivate, or that a satisfied need activates movement to a new need level.[9]

Theory X and Theory Y

Douglas McGregor proposed two distinct views of human beings: one basically negative, labeled **Theory X**, and the other basically positive, labeled **Theory Y**.[10] After viewing the way in which managers dealt with employees, McGregor con-

---

Myth or Science?

"People Are Inherently Lazy"

This statement is false on two levels. *All* people are not inherently lazy; and "laziness" is more a function of the situation than an inherent individual characteristic.

If this statement is meant to imply that *all* people are inherently lazy, the evidence strongly indicates the contrary.[11] Many people today suffer from the opposite affliction—they're overly busy, overworked, and suffer from overexertion. Whether externally motivated or internally driven, a good portion of the labor force is anything *but* lazy.

Managers frequently draw the conclusion that people are lazy from watching some of their employees, who may be lazy at work.

But these same employees are often quite industrious in one or more activities *off* the job. People have different sets of needs.[12] Unfortunately for employers, work often ranks low in its ability to satisfy individual needs. So the same employee who shirks responsibility on the job may work obsessively on reconditioning an antique car, maintaining an award-winning garden, perfecting bowling skills, or selling Amway products on weekends. Very few people are perpetually lazy. They merely differ in terms of the activities they most enjoy doing. And because work isn't important to everyone, they may appear lazy. ■

cluded that managers' views of the nature of human beings are based on a certain grouping of assumptions and that they tend to mold their behavior toward employees according to these assumptions.

Under Theory X, the four assumptions held by managers are:

1. Employees inherently dislike work and, whenever possible, will attempt to avoid it.
2. Since employees dislike work, they must be coerced, controlled, or threatened with punishment to achieve goals.
3. Employees will avoid responsibilities and seek formal direction whenever possible.
4. Most workers place security above all other factors associated with work and will display little ambition.

In contrast to these negative views about the nature of human beings, McGregor listed the four positive assumptions that he called Theory Y:

1. Employees can view work as being as natural as rest or play.
2. People will exercise self-direction and self-control if they are committed to the objectives.
3. The average person can learn to accept, even seek, responsibility.
4. The ability to make innovative decisions is widely dispersed throughout the population and is not necessarily the sole province of those in management positions.

What are the motivational implications if you accept McGregor's analysis? The answer is best expressed in the framework presented by Maslow. Theory X assumes that lower-order needs dominate individuals. Theory Y assumes that higher-order needs dominate individuals. McGregor himself held to the belief that Theory Y assumptions were more valid than Theory X. Therefore, he proposed such ideas as participative decision making, responsible and challenging jobs, and good group relations as approaches that would maximize an employee's job motivation.

Unfortunately, there is no evidence to confirm that either set of assumptions is valid or that accepting Theory Y assumptions and altering one's actions accordingly will lead to more motivated workers. OB theories need to have empirical support for us to accept them. Similar to the hierarchy of needs theories, such empirical support is lacking for Theory X and Theory Y.

Two-Factor Theory

The **two-factor theory**—also called *motivation-hygiene theory*—was proposed by psychologist Frederick Herzberg.[13] In the belief that an individual's relation to work is basic and that one's attitude toward work can very well determine success or failure, Herzberg investigated the question, "What do people want from their jobs?" He asked people to describe, in detail, situations in which they felt exceptionally *good* or *bad* about their jobs. These responses were then tabulated and categorized.

From the categorized responses, Herzberg concluded that the replies people gave when they felt good about their jobs were significantly different from

ERG theory *A theory that posits three groups of core needs: existence, relatedness, and growth.*

Theory X *The assumption that employees dislike work, are lazy, dislike responsibility, and must be coerced to perform.*

Theory Y *The assumption that employees like work, are creative, seek responsibility, and can exercise self-direction.*

two-factor theory *A theory that relates intrinsic factors to job satisfaction, while associating extrinsic factors with dissatisfaction.*

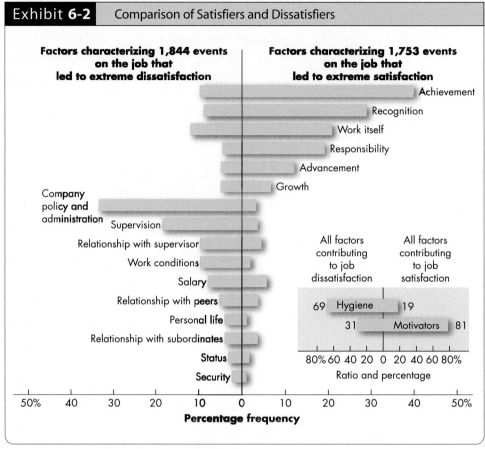

the replies given when they felt bad. As seen in Exhibit 6-2, certain characteristics tend to be consistently related to job satisfaction and others to job dissatisfaction. Intrinsic factors, such as advancement, recognition, responsibility, and achievement seem to be related to job satisfaction. Respondents who felt good about their work tended to attribute these factors to themselves. However, dissatisfied respondents tended to cite extrinsic factors, such as supervision, pay, company policies, and working conditions.

The data suggest, said Herzberg, that the opposite of satisfaction is not dissatisfaction, as was traditionally believed. Removing dissatisfying characteristics from a job does not necessarily make the job satisfying. As illustrated in Exhibit 6-3, Herzberg proposed that his findings indicated the existence of a dual continuum: The opposite of "Satisfaction" is "No Satisfaction," and the opposite of "Dissatisfaction" is "No Dissatisfaction."

According to Herzberg, the factors leading to job satisfaction are separate and distinct from those that lead to job dissatisfaction. Therefore, managers who seek to eliminate factors that can create job dissatisfaction may bring about peace but not necessarily motivation. They will be placating their workforce rather than motivating them. As a result, conditions surrounding the job such as quality of supervision, pay, company policies, physical working conditions, relations with others, and job security were characterized by Herzberg as **hygiene factors**. When they're adequate, people will not be dissatisfied; neither

Exhibit 6-3 Contrasting Views of Satisfaction and Dissatisfaction

Traditional view

Satisfaction — Dissatisfaction

Herzberg's view

Motivators

Satisfaction — No satisfaction

Hygiene factors

No dissatisfaction — Dissatisfaction

will they be satisfied. If we want to motivate people on their jobs, Herzberg suggested emphasizing factors associated with the work itself or to outcomes directly derived from it, such as promotional opportunities, opportunities for personal growth, recognition, responsibility, and achievement. These are the characteristics that people find intrinsically rewarding.

The two-factor theory has not been well supported in the literature, and it has many detractors.[14] The criticisms of the theory include the following:

1. The procedure that Herzberg used is limited by its methodology. When things are going well, people tend to take credit themselves. Contrarily, they blame failure on the extrinsic environment.
2. The reliability of Herzberg's methodology is questioned. Raters have to make interpretations, so they may contaminate the findings by interpreting one response in one manner while treating a similar response differently.
3. No overall measure of satisfaction was utilized. A person may dislike part of a job yet still think the job is acceptable overall.
4. The theory is inconsistent with previous research. The two-factor theory ignores situational variables.
5. Herzberg assumed a relationship between satisfaction and productivity, but the research methodology he used looked only at satisfaction not at productivity. To make such research relevant, one must assume a strong relationship between satisfaction and productivity.

Regardless of criticisms, Herzberg's theory has been widely read and few managers are unfamiliar with his recommendations.

It's important to realize that even though we may intuitively *like* a theory, that does not mean that we should accept it. Many managers find need theories intuitively appealing, but remember, at one time the world seemed intuitively flat. Sometimes science backs up intuition, and sometimes it doesn't. In the case of the two-factor theory—like need hierarchy—it didn't.

hygiene factors *Factors—such as company policy and administration, supervision, and salary—that, when adequate in a job, placate workers. When these factors are adequate, people will not be dissatisfied.*

Contemporary Theories of Motivation

The previous theories are well known but, unfortunately, have not held up well under close examination. However, all is not lost. There are a number of contemporary theories that have one thing in common—each has a reasonable degree of valid supporting documentation. Of course, this doesn't mean that the theories we are about to introduce are unquestionably right. We call them "contemporary theories" not because they necessarily were developed recently, but because they represent the current state of thinking in explaining employee motivation.

McClelland's Theory of Needs

You have one beanbag and there are five targets set up in front of you. Each one is progressively farther away and, hence, more difficult to hit. Target A is a cinch. It sits almost within arm's reach of you. If you hit it, you get $2. Target B is a bit farther out, but about 80 percent of the people who try can hit it. It pays $4. Target C pays $8, and about half the people who try can hit it. Very few people can hit Target D, but the payoff is $16 if you do. Finally, Target E pays $32, but it's almost impossible to achieve. Which target would you try for? If you selected C, you're likely to be a high achiever. Why? Read on.

McClelland's theory of needs was developed by David McClelland and his associates.[15] The theory focuses on three needs: achievement, power, and affiliation. They are defined as follows:

Anne Sweeney is a high achiever. Since joining The Walt Disney Company in 1996, Sweeney led the transition of the struggling Disney Channel from a premium cable service to a basic network, quintupling the channel's subscriber base. As co-chairman of Disney's Media Networks, Sweeney is trying to achieve a turnaround for Disney's ABC Family channel. In addition, when Sweeney became president of ABC Television in 2004, she accepted the challenging goal of lifting the network from its last-place position.

- **Need for achievement**: The drive to excel, to achieve in relation to a set of standards, to strive to succeed
- **Need for power**: The need to make others behave in a way that they would not have behaved otherwise
- **Need for affiliation**: The desire for friendly and close interpersonal relationships

Some people have a compelling drive to succeed. They're striving for personal achievement rather than the rewards of success per se. They have a desire to do something better or more efficiently than it has been done before. This drive is the achievement need (*nAch*). From research into the achievement need, McClelland found that high achievers differentiate themselves from others by their desire to do things better.[16] They seek situations in which they can attain personal responsibility for finding solutions to problems, in which they can receive rapid feedback on their performance so they can determine easily whether they are improving or not, and in which they can set moderately challenging goals. High achievers are not gamblers; they dislike succeeding by chance. They prefer the challenge of working at a problem and accepting the personal responsibility for success or failure rather than leaving the outcome to chance or the actions of others. Importantly, they avoid what they perceive to be very easy or very difficult tasks. They prefer tasks of intermediate difficulty.

High achievers perform best when they perceive their probability of success as being 0.5, that is, when they estimate that they have a 50–50 chance of success. They dislike gambling with high odds because they get no achievement satisfaction from happenstance success. Similarly, they dislike low odds (high probability of success) because then there is no challenge to their skills. They like to set goals that require stretching themselves a little.

The need for power (*nPow*) is the desire to have impact, to be influential, and to control others. Individuals high in nPow enjoy being "in charge," strive for influence over others, prefer to be placed into competitive and status-

What Do Employees Want?

Believe it or not, money is rarely a prime motivator for employees. This was confirmed in a recent survey of 1,500 employees. Here are the top five things that employees considered important:

1. *A learning activity and choice of assignment.* Employees value learning opportunities in which they can gain skills to enhance their mar-

ketability. And they want the ability to choose work assignments whenever possible.

2. *Flexible working hours and time off.* Employees value their time and their time off. Flexibility around their work hours will allow them to better balance personal obligations with work responsibilities.

3. *Personal praise.* People like to feel they're needed and that their work is appreciated. Yet employees report that their bosses rarely thank them for the job they do.

4. *Increased autonomy and authority in their job.* Greater autonomy and

authority tell employees that the organization trusts them to act independently and without the approval of others.

5. *Time with their manager.* When managers spend time with employees, it does two things. First, because a manager's time is valuable, it provides recognition and validation. Second, it provides support through listening to the employees' concerns, answering questions, and offering advice.

Respondents listed money as important, but only after the above items.

Source: B. Nelson, "What Do Employees Want?" *ABA Bank Marketing,* March 2003, pp. 9–10.

oriented situations, and tend to be more concerned with prestige and gaining influence over others than with effective performance.

The third need isolated by McClelland is affiliation (*nAff*). This need has received the least attention from researchers. Individuals with a high affiliation motive strive for friendship, prefer cooperative situations rather than competitive ones, and desire relationships that involve a high degree of mutual understanding.

Relying on an extensive amount of research, some reasonably well-supported predictions can be made based on the relationship between achievement need and job performance. Although less research has been done on power and affiliation needs, there are consistent findings here, too.

First, as shown in Exhibit 6-4, individuals with a high need to achieve prefer job situations with personal responsibility, feedback, and an intermediate degree of risk. When these characteristics are prevalent, high achievers will be strongly

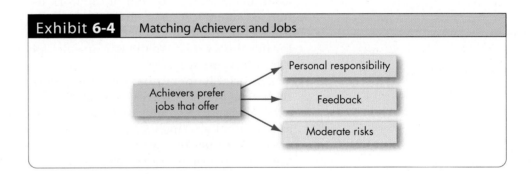

| Exhibit **6-4** | Matching Achievers and Jobs |

McClelland's theory of needs *A theory stating that achievement, power, and affiliation are three important needs that help explain motivation.*

need for achievement *The drive to excel, to achieve in relation to a set of standards, to strive to succeed.*

need for power *The need to make others behave in a way that they would not have behaved otherwise.*

need for affiliation *The desire for friendly and close interpersonal relationships.*

motivated. The evidence consistently demonstrates, for instance, that high achievers are successful in entrepreneurial activities such as running their own businesses and managing a self-contained unit within a large organization.[17]

Second, a high need to achieve does not necessarily lead to being a good manager, especially in large organizations. People with a high achievement need are interested in how well they do personally and not in influencing others to do well. High-nAch salespeople do not necessarily make good sales managers, and the good general manager in a large organization does not typically have a high need to achieve.[18]

Third, the needs for affiliation and power tend to be closely related to managerial success. The best managers are high in their need for power and low in their need for affiliation.[19] In fact, a high power motive may be a requirement for managerial effectiveness.[20] Of course, what the cause is and what the effect is are arguable. It has been suggested that a high power need may occur simply as a function of one's level in a hierarchical organization.[21] The latter argument proposes that the higher the level an individual rises to in the organization, the greater is the incumbent's power motive. As a result, powerful positions would be the stimulus to a high power motive.

Finally, employees have been successfully trained to stimulate their achievement need. Trainers have been effective in teaching individuals to think in terms of accomplishments, winning, and success, and then helping them to learn how to *act* in a high achievement way by preferring situations in which they have personal responsibility, feedback, and moderate risks. So if the job calls for a high achiever, management can select a person with a high nAch or develop its own candidate through achievement training.[22]

Cognitive Evaluation Theory

"It's strange," said Marcia. "I started work at the Humane Society as a volunteer. I put in 15 hours a week helping people adopt pets. And I loved coming to work. Then, three months ago, they hired me full-time at $11 an hour. I'm doing the same work I did before. But I'm not finding it near as much fun."

There's an explanation for Marcia's reaction. It's called **cognitive evaluation theory** and it proposes that the introduction of extrinsic rewards, such as pay, for work effort that was previously intrinsically rewarding due to the pleasure associated with the content of the work itself tends to decrease overall motivation.[23] Cognitive evaluation theory has been extensively researched, and a large number of studies have been supportive.[24] As we'll show, the major implications for this theory relate to the way in which people are paid in organizations, such as reinforcement theory.

Historically, motivation theorists generally assumed that intrinsic motivators such as achievement, responsibility, and competence were independent of extrinsic motivators such as high pay, promotions, good supervisor relations, and pleasant working conditions. But cognitive evaluation theory suggests otherwise. It argues that when extrinsic rewards are used by organizations as payoffs for superior performance, the intrinsic rewards, which are derived from individuals doing what they like, are reduced. In other words, when extrinsic rewards are given to someone for performing an interesting task, it causes intrinsic interest in the task itself to decline.

Why would such an outcome occur? The popular explanation is that the individual experiences a loss of control over his or her own behavior so that the previous intrinsic motivation diminishes. Furthermore, the elimination of extrinsic rewards can produce a shift—from an external to an internal explanation—in an individual's perception of causation of why he or she works on a task. If you're reading a novel a week because your English literature instructor requires you to, you can attribute your reading behavior to an external source. However, after the course is over, if you find yourself continuing to read a novel a week, your natural inclination is to say, "I must enjoy reading novels because I'm still reading one a week."

If the cognitive evaluation theory is valid, it should have major implications for managerial practices. It has been a truism among compensation specialists for years that if pay or other extrinsic rewards are to be effective motivators, they should be made contingent on an individual's performance. But, cognitive evaluation theorists would argue that this will only tend to decrease the internal satisfaction that the individual receives from doing the job. In fact, if cognitive evaluation theory is correct, it would make sense to make an individual's pay *noncontingent* on performance in order to avoid decreasing intrinsic motivation.

We noted earlier that the cognitive evaluation theory has been supported in a number of studies. Yet it has also been met with attacks, specifically on the methodology used in these studies[25] and in the interpretation of the findings.[26] But where does this theory stand today? Can we say that when organizations use extrinsic motivators such as pay and promotions and verbal rewards to stimulate

Exhibit 6-5

"What do you *mean* money isn't everything? This is a bank!"

Source: From the *Wall Street Journal*, February 8, 1995. Reprinted with permission of Cartoon Features Syndicate.

cognitive evaluation theory   *A theory stating that allocating extrinsic rewards for behavior that had been previously intrinsically rewarding tends to decrease the overall level of motivation.*

workers' performance they do so at the expense of reducing intrinsic interest and motivation in the work being done? The answer is not a simple "Yes" or "No."

Extrinsic rewards that are verbal (receiving praise from a supervisor or coworker) or tangible (money) can actually have different effects on people's intrinsic motivation. That is, verbal rewards increase intrinsic motivation, while tangible rewards undermine it. When people are told they will receive a tangible reward, they come to count on it and focus more on the reward than on the task.[27] Verbal rewards, however, seem to keep people focused on the task and encourage them to do it better.

A more recent outgrowth of the cognitive evaluation theory is **self-concordance**, which considers the degree to which peoples' reasons for pursuing goals are consistent with their interests and core values. For example, if individuals pursue goals because of an intrinsic interest, they are more likely to attain their goals and are happy even if they do not attain them. Why? Because the process of striving toward them is fun. In contrast, people who pursue goals for extrinsic reasons (money, status, or other benefits) are less likely to attain their goals and are less happy even when they do achieve them. Why? Because the goals are less meaningful to them.[28] OB research suggests that people who pursue work goals for intrinsic reasons are more satisfied with their jobs, feel like they fit into their organizations better, and may perform better.[29]

How Managers Evaluate Their Employees Depends on Culture

A RECENT STUDY FOUND INTERESTING DIFFERENCES in managers' perceptions of employee motivation. The study examined mangers from three distinct cultural regions: North America, Asia, and Latin America. The results of the study revealed that North American managers perceive their employees as being motivated more by extrinsic factors (for example, pay) than intrinsic factors (for example, doing meaningful work). Asian managers perceive their employees as being motivated by both extrinsic and intrinsic factors, while Latin American managers perceive their employees as being motivated by intrinsic factors.

Even more interesting, these differences affected evaluations of employee performance. As expected, Asian managers focused on both types of motivation when evaluating their employees' performance, and Latin American managers focused on intrinsic motivation. Oddly, North American managers, though believing that employees are motivated primarily by extrinsic factors, actually focused more on *intrinsic* factors when evaluating employee performance. Why the paradox? One explanation is that North Americans value uniqueness, so any deviation from the norm—such as being perceived to be unusually high in intrinsic motivation—is rewarded.

For Latin American managers, their focus on intrinsic motivation when evaluating employees may focus on a cultural norm termed *simpatía*, a tradition that compels employees to display their internal feelings. Consequently, Latin American managers are more sensitized to these displays and can more easily notice their employees' intrinsic motivation.

So, from an employee perspective, the cultural background of your manager can play an important role in how you are evaluated.

Based on S. E. DeVoe and S. S. Iyengar, "Manager's Theories of Subordinates: A Cross-Cultural Examination of Manager Perceptions of Motivation and Appraisal of Performance," *Organizational Behavior and Human Decision Processes*, January 2004, pp. 47–61.

What does all of this mean? It means choose your job carefully. Make sure that you're choosing to do something for reasons other than extrinsic rewards. For organizations, managers need to provide intrinsic rewards in addition to extrinsic incentives. In other words, make the work interesting, provide recognition, and support employee growth and development. Employees who feel that what they do is within their control and a result of free choice are likely to be more motivated by their work and committed to their employers.[30]

Goal-Setting Theory

Gene Broadwater, coach of the Hamilton High School cross-country team, gave his squad these last words before they approached the line for the league championship race: "Each one of you is physically ready. Now, get out there and do your best. No one can ever ask more of you than that."

You've heard the phrase a number of times yourself: "Just do your best. That's all anyone can ask for." But what does "do your best" mean? Do we ever know if we've achieved that vague goal? Would the cross-country runners have recorded faster times if Coach Broadwater had given each a specific goal to shoot for? Might you have done better in your high school English class if your parents had said, "You should strive for 85 percent or higher on all your work in English" rather than telling you to "do your best"? The research on **goal-setting theory** addresses these issues, and the findings, as you'll see, are impressive in terms of the effect that goal specificity, challenge, and feedback have on performance.

In the late 1960s, Edwin Locke proposed that intentions to work toward a goal are a major source of work motivation.[31] That is, goals tell an employee what needs to be done and how much effort will need to be expended.[32] The evidence strongly supports the value of goals. More to the point, we can say that specific goals increase performance; that difficult goals, when accepted, result in higher performance than do easy goals; and that feedback leads to higher performance than does nonfeedback.[33]

Specific goals produce a higher level of output than does the generalized goal of "do your best." Why? The specificity of the goal itself seems to act as an internal stimulus. For instance, when a trucker commits to making 12 round-trip hauls between Toronto and Buffalo, New York, each week, this intention gives him a specific objective to try to attain. We can say that, all things being equal, the trucker with a specific goal will outperform a counterpart operating with no goals or the generalized goal of "do your best."

If factors such as acceptance of the goals are held constant, we can also state that the more difficult the goal, the higher the level of performance. Of course, it's logical to assume that easier goals are more likely to be accepted. But once a hard task is accepted, the employee can be expected to exert a high level of effort to try to achieve it.

But why are people more motivated by difficult goals?[34] First, difficult goals direct our attention to the task at hand and away from irrelevant distractions. Challenging goals get our attention and thus tend to help us focus. Second, difficult goals energize us because we have to work harder to attain them. For example, think of your study habits. Do you study as hard for an easy exam as you do for a difficult one? Probably not. Third, when goals are difficult, people persist in trying to attain them. Finally, difficult goals lead us

---

self-concordance *The degree to which a person's reasons for pursuing a goal is consistent with the person's interests and core values.*

goal-setting theory *The theory that specific and difficult goals, with feedback, lead to higher performance.*

Goal-setting works well for Pat Cavanaugh, CEO and top salesman of his promotional products company. He sets specific goals for himself and his sales team each year and has a long-term company goal of $100 million by 2010. By never missing a goal, the firm has grown 4,000 percent in its first seven years. For Cavanaugh, well-learned tasks are the key to meeting goals. He trains his staff to prepare for client meetings, to listen to the client's needs, and to read people well.

to discover strategies that help us perform the job or task more effectively. If we have to struggle for a way to solve a difficult problem, we often think of a better way to go about it.

People will do better when they get feedback on how well they are progressing toward their goals because feedback helps to identify discrepancies between what they have done and what they want to do; that is, feedback acts to guide behavior. But all feedback is not equally potent. Self-generated feedback—for which employees are able to monitor their own progress—has been shown to be a more powerful motivator than externally generated feedback.[35]

If employees have the opportunity to participate in the setting of their own goals, will they try harder? The evidence is mixed regarding the superiority of participative over assigned goals.[36] In some cases, participatively set goals elicited superior performance, while in other cases, individuals performed best when assigned goals by their boss. But a major advantage of participation may be in increasing acceptance of the goal itself as a desirable one toward which to work.[37] As we'll note shortly, commitment's important. If participation isn't used, then the purpose and importance of the goal needs to be explained clearly by the individual assigning the goal.[38]

Are there any contingencies in goal-setting theory, or can we take it as a universal truth that difficult and specific goals will *always* lead to higher performance? In addition to feedback, three other factors have been found to influence the goals–performance relationship. These are goal commitment, task characteristics, and national culture.

Goal-setting theory presupposes that an individual is committed to the goal; that is, an individual is determined not to lower or abandon the goal. Behaviorally, this means that an individual (a) believes he or she can achieve the goal and (b) wants to achieve it.[39] Goal commitment is most likely to occur when goals are made public, when the individual has an internal locus of control (see Chapter 4), and when the goals are self-set rather than assigned.[40] Research indicates that goal-setting theory doesn't work equally well on all tasks. The evidence suggests that goals seem to have a more substantial effect on performance when tasks are simple rather than complex, well-learned rather than novel, and independent rather than interdependent.[41] On interdependent tasks, group goals are preferable.

Finally, goal-setting theory is culture-bound. It's well adapted to countries like the United States and Canada because its key components align reasonably well with North American cultures. It assumes that employees will be reasonably independent (not too high a score on power distance), that managers and employees will seek challenging goals (low in uncertainty avoidance), and that performance is considered important by both (high in achievement). So don't expect goal setting to necessarily lead to higher employee performance in countries such as Portugal or Chile, where the opposite conditions exist.

Our overall conclusion is that intentions—as articulated in terms of difficult and specific goals—are a potent motivating force. The motivating power of goal-setting theory has been demonstrated on over 100 tasks involving more than 40,000 participants in many different kinds of industries—from lumber, to insurance, to automobiles. Basically, setting specific, challenging goals for employees is the best thing managers can do to improve performance.

When it comes to your courses, what goals do you set for yourself? Do you want to prove yourself to your professor? Are you thinking about furthering your education? See the following Self-Assessment feature, and you can find out what drives you to study.

In the Self-Assessment Library (available on CD, online, and in print), take assessment I.C. 5 (What Are My Course Performance Goals?) and answer the following questions.

1. *After reading the section on goal-setting theory, do you think your course goals are too easy? Or too vague?*
2. *How might you revise your course goals in light of what you've learned about goal-setting theory?*

MBO Programs: Putting Goal-Setting Theory into Practice

Goal-setting theory has an impressive base of research support. But as a manager, how do you make goal setting operational? One answer to that question is: Install a management by objectives (MBO) program. MTW Corp., a provider of software services mainly for insurance companies and state governments, has an MBO-type program.[42] Management attributes this program with helping the company average a 50 percent-a-year growth rate for 5 years in a row and cutting employee turnover to one-fifth of the industry norm.

Management by objectives emphasizes participatively set goals that are tangible, verifiable, and measurable. MBO's appeal undoubtedly lies in its emphasis on converting overall organizational objectives into specific objectives for organizational units and individual members. MBO operationalizes the concept of objectives by devising a process by which objectives cascade down through the organization. As depicted in Exhibit 6-6, the organization's

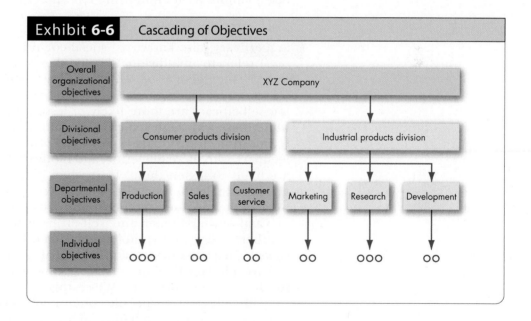

Exhibit 6-6   Cascading of Objectives

management by objectives (MBO) *A program that encompasses specific goals, participatively set, for an explicit time period, with feedback on goal progress.*

overall objectives are translated into specific objectives for each succeeding level (that is, divisional, departmental, individual) in the organization. But because lower-unit managers jointly participate in setting their own goals, MBO works from the "bottom up" as well as from the "top down." The result is a hierarchy that links objectives at one level to those at the next level. And for the individual employee, MBO provides specific personal performance objectives.

There are four ingredients common to MBO programs. These are goal specificity, participation in decision making (including participation in the setting of goals or objectives), an explicit time period, and performance feedback.[43] Many of the elements in MBO programs match goal-setting theory's propositions. For example, having an explicit time period to accomplish objectives matches goal-setting theory's emphasis on goal specificity. Similarly, we noted earlier that feedback about goal progress is a critical element of goal-setting theory. The only area of possible disagreement between MBO and goal-setting theory relates to the issue of participation—MBO strongly advocates it, while goal-setting theory demonstrates that managers assigning goals is usually just as effective.

You'll find MBO programs in many business, health-care, educational, government, and nonprofit organizations.[44] MBO's popularity should not be construed to mean that it always works. There are a number of documented cases in which MBO has been implemented but failed to meet management's expectations.[45] When MBO doesn't work, the culprits tend to be factors such as unrealistic expectations regarding results, lack of commitment by top management, and an inability or unwillingness by management to allocate rewards based on goal accomplishment. Failures can also arise out of cultural incompatibilities. For instance, Fujitsu recently scrapped its MBO-type program because management found it didn't fit well with the Japanese culture's emphasis on minimizing risk and emphasizing long-term goals.

Self-Efficacy Theory

Self-efficacy (also known as "social cognitive theory" or "social learning theory") refers to an individual's belief that he or she is capable of performing a task.[46] The higher your self-efficacy, the more confidence you have in your ability to succeed in a task. So, in difficult situations, we find that people with low self-efficacy are more likely to lessen their effort or give up altogether, while those with high self-efficacy will try harder to master the challenge.[47] In addition, individuals high in self-efficacy seem to respond to negative feedback with increased effort and motivation, while those low in self-efficacy are likely to lessen their effort when given negative feedback.[48] How can managers help their employees achieve high levels of self-efficacy? By bringing together goal-setting theory and self-efficacy theory.

Goal-setting theory and self-efficacy theory don't compete with one another; rather, they complement each other. See Exhibit 6-7. As the exhibit shows, when a manger sets difficult goals for employees, this leads employees to have a higher level of self-efficacy and also leads them to set higher goals for their own performance. Why is this the case? Research has shown that setting difficult goals for people communicates confidence. For example, imagine that your boss sets a high goal for you, and you learn it is higher than the goals she has set for your coworkers. How would you interpret this? As long as you don't feel you're being picked on, you probably would think, "Well, I guess my boss thinks I'm capable of performing better than others." This then sets into motion a psychological process where you're more confident in yourself (higher self-efficacy), and you set higher personal goals, causing you to perform better both in the workplace and outside it.

Exhibit **6-7**   Joint Effects of Goals and Self-Efficacy on Performance

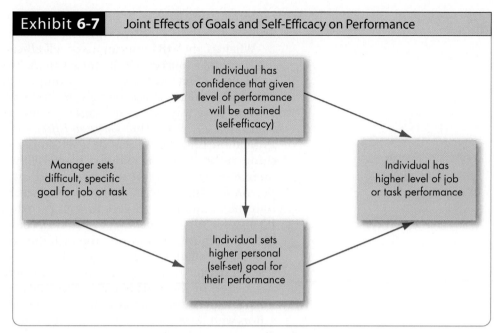

Based on E. A. Locke and G. P. Latham, "Building a Practically Useful Theory of Goal Setting and Task Motivation: A 35-Year Odyssey," *American Psychologist*, September 2002, pp. 705–717.

The researcher who developed self-efficacy theory, Albert Bandura, argues that there are four ways self-efficacy can be increased:[49]

1. enactive mastery
2. vicarious modeling
3. verbal persuasion
4. arousal

According to Bandura, the most important source of increasing self-efficacy is what he calls *enactive* mastery. Enactive mastery is gaining relevant experience with the task or job. If I've been able to do the job successfully in the past, then I'm more confident I'll be able to do it in the future.

The second source is *vicarious modeling*—or becoming more confident because you see someone else doing the task. For example, if my friend loses weight, then it increases my confidence that I can lose weight too. Vicarious modeling is most effective when you see yourself similar to the person you are observing. It doesn't increase my confidence in being able to play a difficult golf shot by watching Tiger Woods do it. But, if I watch a golfer with a handicap similar to mine, it's more persuasive.

The third source is *verbal persuasion*, which is becoming more confident because someone convinces you that you have the skills necessary to be successful. Motivational speakers use this tactic a lot.

Finally, Bandura argues that *arousal* increases self-efficacy. Arousal leads to an energized state, which drives a person to complete the task. The person gets "psyched up" and performs better. But when arousal is not relevant, then arousal hurts performance. In other words, if the task is something that

self-efficacy *The individual's belief that he or she is capable of performing a task.*

requires a steadier, lower-key perspective (say, carefully editing a manuscript), arousal may in fact hurt performance.

What are the OB implications of self-efficacy theory? Well, it's a matter of applying Bandura's sources of self-efficacy to the work setting. Training programs often make use of enactive mastery by having people practice and build their skills. In fact, one of the reasons training works is because it increases self-efficacy.[50]

The best way for a manager to use verbal persuasion is through the *Pygmalion Effect* or the *Galatea Effect*. As we discussed in Chapter 5, the Pygmalion Effect is a form of a self-fulfilling prophecy where believing something to be true can make it true. In the Pygmalion Effect, self-efficacy is increased by communicating to an individual's teacher or supervisor that the person is of high ability. For example, studies were done where teachers were told their students had very high IQ scores (when in fact they had a range of IQs—some high, some low, and some in between). Consistent with a Pygmalion Effect, teachers spent more time with the students they *thought* were smart, gave them more challenging assignments, and expected more of them—all of which lead to higher student self-efficacy and better student grades.[51] This also has been used in the workplace.[52] The Galatea Effect occurs when high performance expectations are communicated directly to the employee. For example, sailors who were told, in a convincing manner, that they would not get seasick in fact were much less likely to get seasick.[53]

Note that intelligence and personality are absent from Bandura's list. A lot of research shows that intelligence and personality (especially conscientiousness and emotional stability) can increase self-efficacy.[54] Those individual traits are so strongly related to self-efficacy (people who are intelligent, conscientiousness, and emotionally stable are much more likely to have high self-efficacy than those who score low on these characteristics) that some researchers would argue self-efficacy does not exist.[55] What this means is that self-efficacy may simply be a byproduct of a smart person with a confident personality and the term *self-efficacy* is superfluous and unnecessary. Although Bandura strongly disagrees with this conclusion, more research on the issue is needed.

Reinforcement Theory

A counterpoint to goal-setting theory is **reinforcement theory.** The former is a cognitive approach, proposing that an individual's purposes direct his or her action. In reinforcement theory, we have a behavioristic approach, which argues that reinforcement conditions behavior. The two are clearly at odds philosophically. Reinforcement theorists see behavior as being environmentally caused. You need not be concerned, they would argue, with internal cognitive events; what controls behavior are reinforcers—any consequence that, when immediately following a response, increases the probability that the behavior will be repeated.

Reinforcement theory ignores the inner state of the individual and concentrates solely on what happens to a person when he or she takes some action. Because it does not concern itself with what initiates behavior, it is not, strictly speaking, a theory of motivation. But it does provide a powerful means of analysis of what controls behavior, and it is for this reason that it is typically considered in discussions of motivation.[56]

We discussed the reinforcement process in detail in Chapter 2. Although it's clear that so-called reinforcers like pay can motivate people, it's just as clear that for people the process is much more complicated than stimulus-response. In its pure form, reinforcement theory ignores feelings, attitudes, expectations, and other cognitive variables that are known to impact behavior. In fact, some researchers look at the same experiments that reinforcement theorists use to support their position and interpret the findings in a cognitive framework.[57]

Reinforcement is undoubtedly an important influence on behavior, but few scholars are prepared to argue that it is the only influence. The behaviors you engage in at work and the amount of effort you allocate to each task are affected by the consequences that follow from your behavior. For instance, if you're consistently reprimanded for outproducing your colleagues, you'll likely reduce your productivity. But your lower productivity may also be explained in terms of goals, inequity, or expectancies.

Equity Theory

Jane Pearson graduated last year from the State University with a degree in accounting. After interviews with a number of organizations on campus, she accepted a position with a top public accounting firm and was assigned to their Boston office. Jane was very pleased with the offer she received: challenging work with a prestigious firm, an excellent opportunity to gain valuable experience, and the highest salary any accounting major at State was offered last year—$4,550 a month. But Jane was the top student in her class; she was articulate and mature and fully expected to receive a commensurate salary.

Twelve months have passed since Jane joined her employer. The work has proved to be as challenging and satisfying as she had hoped. Her employer is extremely pleased with her performance; in fact, she recently received a $200-a-month raise. However, Jane's motivational level has dropped dramatically in the past few weeks. Why? Her employer has just hired a fresh college graduate out of State University, who lacks the 1-year experience Jane has gained, for $4,800 a month—$50 more than Jane now makes! It would be an understatement to describe Jane in any other terms than irate. Jane is even talking about looking for another job.

Jane's situation illustrates the role that equity plays in motivation. Employees make comparisons of their job inputs (for example, effort, experience, education, competence) and outcomes (for example, salary levels, raises, recognition) relative to those of others. We perceive what we get from a job situation (outcomes) in relation to what we put into it (inputs), and then we compare our outcome-input ratio with the outcome-input ratio of relevant others. This is shown in Exhibit 6-8. If we perceive our ratio to be equal to that of the relevant others with whom we compare ourselves, a state of equity is said to exist. We perceive our situation as fair—that justice prevails. When we see the ratio as

| Exhibit **6-8** | Equity Theory |

Ratio Comparisons*	Perception
$\dfrac{O}{I_A} < \dfrac{O}{I_B}$	Inequity due to being underrewarded
$\dfrac{O}{I_A} = \dfrac{O}{I_B}$	Equity
$\dfrac{O}{I_A} > \dfrac{O}{I_B}$	Inequity due to being overrewarded

*Where $\dfrac{O}{I_A}$ represents the employee; and $\dfrac{O}{I_B}$ represents relevant others.

reinforcement theory   *A theory that behavior is a function of its consequences.*

unequal, we experience equity tension. When we see ourselves as underrewarded, the tension creates anger; when overrewarded, the tension creates guilt. J. Stacy Adams has proposed that this negative state of tension provides the motivation to do something to correct it.[58]

The referent that an employee selects adds to the complexity of **equity theory**.[59] There are four referent comparisons that an employee can use:

1. *Self-inside:* An employee's experiences in a different position inside the employee's current organization
2. *Self-outside:* An employee's experiences in a situation or position outside the employee's current organization
3. *Other-inside:* Another individual or group of individuals inside the employee's organization
4. *Other-outside:* Another individual or group of individuals outside the employee's organization

Employees might compare themselves to friends, neighbors, coworkers, or colleagues in other organizations or compare their present job with past jobs they themselves have had. Which referent an employee chooses will be influenced by the information the employee holds about referents as well as by the attractiveness of the referent. This has led to focusing on four moderating variables—gender, length of tenure, level in the organization, and amount of education or professionalism.[60]

Research shows that both men and women prefer same-sex comparisons. The research also demonstrates that women are typically paid less than men in comparable jobs and have lower pay expectations than men for the same work.[61] So a woman who uses another woman as a referent tends to calculate a lower comparative standard. This leads us to conclude that employees in jobs that are not sex segregated will make more cross-sex comparisons than those in jobs that are either male- or female-dominated. This also suggests that if women are tolerant of lower pay, it may be due to the comparative standard they use. Of course, employer's stereotypes about women (for example, the belief that women are less committed to the organization, or that "women's work" is less valuable) also may contribute to the pay gap.[62]

Employees with short tenure in their current organizations tend to have little information about others inside the organization, so they rely on their own personal experiences. However, employees with long tenure rely more heavily on coworkers for comparison. Upper-level employees, those in the professional ranks, and those with higher amounts of education tend to have better information about people in other organizations. Therefore, these types of employees will make more other-outside comparisons.

Based on equity theory, when employees perceive inequity, they can be predicted to make one of six choices[63]:

1. Change their inputs (for example, don't exert as much effort)
2. Change their outcomes (for example, individuals paid on a piece-rate basis can increase their pay by producing a higher quantity of units of lower quality)
3. Distort perceptions of self (for example, "I used to think I worked at a moderate pace but now I realize that I work a lot harder than everyone else.")
4. Distort perceptions of others (for example, "Mike's job isn't as desirable as I previously thought it was.")
5. Choose a different referent (for example, "I may not make as much as my brother-in-law, but I'm doing a lot better than my Dad did when he was my age.")
6. Leave the field (for example, quit the job)

The theory establishes the following propositions relating to inequitable pay:

A. *Given payment by time, overrewarded employees will produce more than will equitably paid employees.* Hourly and salaried employees will generate high quantity or quality of production in order to increase the input side of the ratio and bring about equity.
B. *Given payment by quantity of production, overrewarded employees will produce fewer, but higher-quality, units than will equitably paid employees.* Individuals paid on a piece-rate basis will increase their effort to achieve equity, which can result in greater quality or quantity. However, increases in quantity will only increase inequity, since every unit produced results in further overpayment. Therefore, effort is directed toward increasing quality rather than increasing quantity.
C. *Given payment by time, underrewarded employees will produce less or poorer quality of output.* Effort will be decreased, which will bring about lower productivity or poorer-quality output than equitably paid subjects.
D. *Given payment by quantity of production, underrewarded employees will produce a large number of low-quality units in comparison with equitably paid employees.* Employees on piece-rate pay plans can bring about equity because trading off quality of output for quantity will result in an increase in rewards with little or no increase in contributions.

Some of these propositions have been supported, but other ones haven't.[64] First, inequities created by overpayment do not seem to have a very significant impact on behavior in most work situations. Apparently, people have a great deal more tolerance of overpayment inequities than of underpayment inequities or are better able to rationalize them. It's pretty damaging to a theory when one-half of the equation (how people respond to overreward) falls apart. Second, not all people are equity sensitive.[65] For example, there is a small part of the working population who actually prefer that their outcome-input ratios be less than the referent comparison's. Predictions from equity theory are not likely to be very accurate with these "benevolent types."

It's also important to note that while most research on equity theory has focused on pay, employees seem to look for equity in the distribution of other organizational rewards. For instance, it has been shown that the use of high-status job titles as well as large and lavishly furnished offices may function as outcomes for some employees in their equity equation.[66]

Finally, recent research has been directed at expanding what is meant by equity or fairness.[67] Historically, equity theory focused on **distributive justice**, which is the employee's perceived fairness of the *amount and allocation* of rewards among individuals. But increasingly equity is thought of from the standpoint of **organizational justice**, which we define as an overall perception of what is fair in the workplace. Employees perceive their organizations as just when they believe the outcomes they have received, the way in which the outcomes were received, are fair. One key element of organizational justice is an individual's *perception* of justice. In other words, under organizational justice, fairness or equity can be subjective, and it resides in the perception of the person. What one person may see as unfair another may see as perfectly appropriate. In general, people have an egocentric or self-serving bias. They see allocations or procedure favoring themselves as fair.[68] For example, a recent poll showed that 61 percent of all

equity theory *A theory that individuals compare their job inputs and outcomes with those of others and then respond to eliminate any inequities.*

distributive justice *Perceived fairness of the amount and allocation of rewards among individuals.*

organizational justice *An overall perception of what is fair in the workplace, comprised of distributive, procedural, and interactional justice.*

respondents say that they are personally paying their fair share of taxes, but an almost equal number (54 percent) of those polled feel the system as a whole is unfair, saying that some people skirt the system.[69] Fairness often resides in the eye of the beholder, and we tend to be fairly self-serving about what we see as fair.

Beyond its focus on perceptions of fairness, the other key element of organizational justice is the view that justice is multidimensional. Organizational justice argues that distributive justice is important. For example, how much we get paid, relative to what we think we should be paid (distributive justice), is obviously important. But, according to justice researchers, *how* we get paid is just as important. Exhibit 6-9 shows a model of organizational justice.

Beyond distributive justice, the key addition under organizational justice was **procedural justice**—which is the perceived fairness of the *process* used to determine the distribution of rewards. Two key elements of procedural justice are *process control* and *explanations*. *Process control* is the opportunity to present one's point of view about desired outcomes to decision makers. *Explanations* are clear reasons given to a person by management for the outcome. Thus, for employees to see a process as fair, they need to feel they have some control over the outcome and feel they were given an adequate explanation about why the outcome occurred. Also for procedural fairness, it's important that a manager is *consistent* (across people and over time), is *unbiased*, makes decisions based on *accurate information*, and is *open to appeals*.[70]

Research shows that the effects of procedural justice become more important when distributive justice is lacking. This makes sense. If we don't get what we want, we tend to focus on *why*. For example, if your supervisor gives a cushy office to a coworker instead of you, you're much more focused on your supervisor's treat-

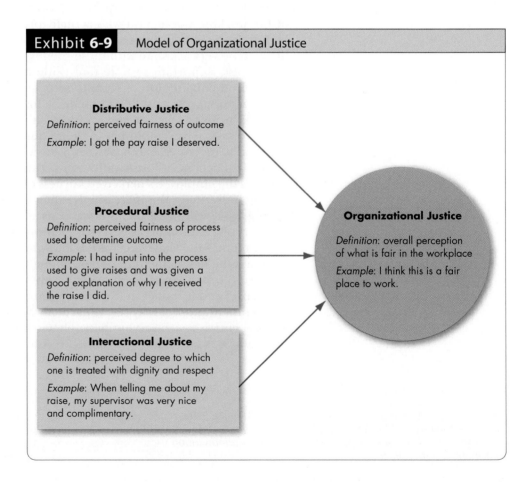

Exhibit 6-9   Model of Organizational Justice

Distributive Justice

Definition: perceived fairness of outcome

Example: I got the pay raise I deserved.

Procedural Justice

Definition: perceived fairness of process used to determine outcome

Example: I had input into the process used to give raises and was given a good explanation of why I received the raise I did.

Interactional Justice

Definition: perceived degree to which one is treated with dignity and respect

Example: When telling me about my raise, my supervisor was very nice and complimentary.

Organizational Justice

Definition: overall perception of what is fair in the workplace

Example: I think this is a fair place to work.

W. L. Gore, maker of Gore-Tex® fabric and Elixir guitar strings, has a compensation and reward system based on procedural justice. At Gore, motivation comes from approval of coworkers. Compensation is determined by employees, who rank their team members each year. Gore openly shares information about how pay decisions are made based on consistent procedures. Procedural fairness helps create a strong organizational commitment among employees.

ment of you than if you had gotten the office. Explanations are beneficial when they take the form of post-hoc excuses (admitting that the act is unfavorable but denying sole responsibility for it) rather than justifications (accepting full responsibility, but denying that the outcome is unfavorable or inappropriate).[71] In the office example, an excuse would be, "I know this is bad. I wanted to give you the office but it was not my decision" and a justification would be, "Yes, I decided to give the office to Sam, but having the corner office is not that big of a deal."

A recent addition to research on organizational justice is **interactional justice**, which is the individual's perception of the degree to which he or she is treated with dignity, concern, and respect. When people are treated in an unjust manner (at least in their own eyes), they respond by retaliating (for example, badmouthing a supervisor).[72] Because interactional justice or injustice is intimately tied to the conveyer of the information (usually one's supervisor), whereas procedural injustice often results from impersonal policies, one would expect perceptions of injustice to be more closely related to one's supervisor. Generally, that's what the evidence suggests.[73]

Of these three forms of justice, distributive justice is most strongly related to satisfaction with outcomes (for example, satisfaction with pay) and organizational commitment. Procedural justice relates most strongly to job satisfaction, employee trust, withdrawal from the organization, job performance, and citizenship behaviors. There is less evidence on interactional justice.[74]

Managers should consider openly sharing information on how allocation decisions are made, following consistent and unbiased procedures, and engaging in similar practices to increase the perception of procedural justice. By having an increased perception of procedural fairness, employees are likely to view their bosses and the organization positively even if they are dissatisfied with pay, promotions, and other personal outcomes.

procedural justice   *The perceived fairness of the process used to determine the distribution of rewards.*

interactional justice   *Perceived degree to which an individual is treated with dignity, concern, and respect.*

In conclusion, equity theory predicts that, for most employees, motivation is influenced significantly by others' rewards as well as by one's own rewards But some key issues are still unclear.[75] For instance, how do employees handle conflicting equity signals, such as when unions point to other employee groups who are substantially *better off*, while management argues the opposite? How do employees define inputs and outcomes? How do they combine and weigh their inputs and outcomes to arrive at a judgment of equity across various outcomes? And when and how does the perception of the inputs and outcomes change over time? Because of these problems, most researchers today tend to focus solely on the perception of what's fair, rather than trying to figure out whether a person's outcome was objectively fair compared to the inputs. This is why, today, most researchers study organizational justice rather than equity theory per se.

Expectancy Theory

Currently, one of the most widely accepted explanations of motivation is Victor Vroom's **expectancy theory**.[76] Although it has its critics, most of the evidence is supportive of the theory.[77]

Expectancy theory argues that the strength of a tendency to act in a certain way depends on the strength of an expectation that the act will be followed by a given outcome and on the attractiveness of that outcome to the individual. In more practical terms, expectancy theory says that employees will be motivated to exert a high level of effort when they believe that effort will lead to a good performance appraisal; that a good appraisal will lead to organizational rewards such as a bonus, a salary increase, or a promotion; and that the rewards will satisfy the employees' personal goals. The theory, therefore, focuses on three relationships (see Exhibit 6-10).

1. *Effort–performance relationship.* The probability perceived by the individual that exerting a given amount of effort will lead to performance.
2. *Performance–reward relationship.* The degree to which the individual believes that performing at a particular level will lead to the attainment of a desired outcome.
3. *Rewards–personal goals relationship.* The degree to which organizational rewards satisfy an individual's personal goals or needs and the attractiveness of those potential rewards for the individual.[78]

Expectancy theory helps explain why a lot of workers aren't motivated on their jobs and do only the minimum necessary to get by. This is evident when we look at the theory's three relationships in a little more detail. We present them as questions employees need to answer in the affirmative if their motivation is to be maximized.

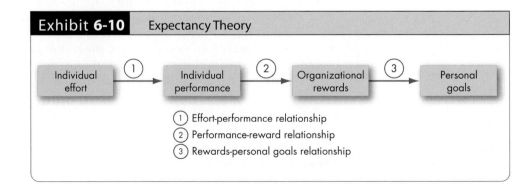

Exhibit **6-10**	Expectancy Theory

① Effort-performance relationship
② Performance-reward relationship
③ Rewards-personal goals relationship

Earl Berg (right) a manager at the Trane division of plumbing-supply manufacturer American Standard, applies the expectancy theory of motivation with team leader Perry Gilbert. Gilbert told Berg about his desire to achieve a promotion. Berg, as shown here, clarifies to Gilbert his performance expectations that will lead to this reward.

First, *if I give a maximum effort, will it be recognized in my performance appraisal?* For a lot of employees, the answer is "No." Why? Their skill level may be deficient, which means that no matter how hard they try, they're not likely to be a high performer. The organization's performance appraisal system may be designed to assess nonperformance factors such as loyalty, initiative, or courage, which means more effort won't necessarily result in a higher evaluation. Still another possibility is that employees, rightly or wrongly, perceives that the boss doesn't like them. As a result, they expect to get a poor appraisal regardless of level of effort. These examples suggest that one possible source of low employee motivation is the belief by employees that no matter how hard they work, the likelihood of getting a good performance appraisal is low.

Second, *if I get a good performance appraisal, will it lead to organizational rewards?* Many employees see the performance–reward relationship in their job as weak. The reason is that organizations reward a lot of things besides just performance. For example, when pay is allocated to employees based on factors such as seniority, being cooperative, or for "kissing up" to the boss, employees are likely to see the performance–reward relationship as being weak and demotivating.

Finally, *if I'm rewarded, are the rewards ones that I find personally attractive?* The employee works hard in hope of getting a promotion but gets a pay raise instead. Or the employee wants a more interesting and challenging job but receives only a few words of praise. Or the employee puts in extra effort to be relocated to the company's Paris office but instead is transferred to Singapore. These examples illustrate the importance of the rewards being tailored to individual employee needs. Unfortunately, many managers are limited in the

expectancy theory   *The strength of a tendency to act in a certain way depends on the strength of an expectation that the act will be followed by a given outcome and on the attractiveness of that outcome to the individual.*

rewards they can distribute, which makes it difficult to individualize rewards. Moreover, some managers incorrectly assume that all employees want the same thing, thus overlooking the motivational effects of differentiating rewards. In either case, employee motivation is submaximized.

In summary, the key to expectancy theory is the understanding of an individual's goals and the linkage between effort and performance, between performance and rewards, and, finally, between the rewards and individual goal satisfaction. As a contingency model, expectancy theory recognizes that there is no universal principle for explaining everyone's motivations. In addition, just because we understand what needs a person seeks to satisfy does not ensure that the individual perceives high performance as necessarily leading to the satisfaction of these needs.

Does expectancy theory work? Attempts to validate the theory have been complicated by methodological, criterion, and measurement problems. As a result, many published studies that purport to support or negate the theory must be viewed with caution. Importantly, most studies have failed to replicate the methodology as it was originally proposed. For example, the theory proposes to explain different levels of effort from the same person under different circumstances, but almost all replication studies have looked at different people. Correcting for this flaw has greatly improved support for the validity of expectancy theory.[79] Some critics suggest that the theory has only limited use, arguing that it tends to be more valid for predicting in situations in which effort–performance and performance–reward linkages are clearly perceived by the individual.[80] Because few individuals perceive a high correlation between performance and rewards in their jobs, the theory tends to be idealistic. If organizations actually rewarded individuals for performance rather than according to such criteria as seniority, effort, skill level, and job difficulty, then the theory's validity might be considerably greater. However, rather than invalidating expectancy theory, this criticism can be used in support of the theory, because it explains why a significant segment of the workforce exerts low levels of effort in carrying out job responsibilities.

Integrating Contemporary Theories of Motivation

We've looked at a lot of motivation theories in this chapter. The fact that a number of these theories have been supported only complicates the matter. How simple it would have been if, after presenting half-a-dozen theories, only one was found valid. But the theories we presented are not all in competition with one another. Because one is valid doesn't automatically make the others invalid. In fact, many of the theories presented in this chapter are complementary. The challenge is now to tie these theories together to help you understand their interrelationships.[81]

Exhibit 6-11 presents a model that integrates much of what we know about motivation. Its basic foundation is the expectancy model shown in Exhibit 6-10. Let's work through Exhibit 6-11. (We will look at job design closely in Chapter 7.)

We begin by explicitly recognizing that opportunities can either aid or hinder individual effort. The individual effort box also has another arrow leading into it. This arrow flows out of the person's goals. Consistent with goal-setting theory, this goals–effort loop is meant to remind us that goals direct behavior.

Expectancy theory predicts that employees will exert a high level of effort if they perceive that there is a strong relationship between effort and perfor-

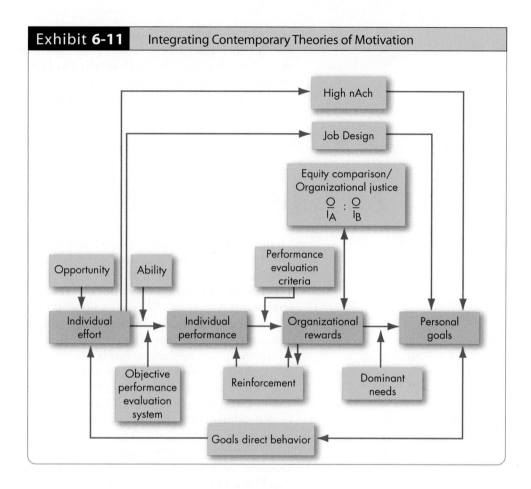

Exhibit 6-11 Integrating Contemporary Theories of Motivation

mance, performance and rewards, and rewards and satisfaction of personal goals. Each of these relationships, in turn, is influenced by certain factors. For effort to lead to good performance, the individual must have the requisite ability to perform, and the performance appraisal system that measures the individual's performance must be perceived as being fair and objective. The performance–reward relationship will be strong if the individual perceives that it is performance (rather than seniority, personal favorites, or other criteria) that is rewarded. If cognitive evaluation theory were fully valid in the actual workplace, we would predict here that basing rewards on performance should decrease the individual's intrinsic motivation. The final link in expectancy theory is the rewards–goals relationship. Motivation would be high to the degree that the rewards an individual received for high performance satisfied the dominant needs consistent with individual goals.

A closer look at Exhibit 6-11 will also reveal that the model considers achievement motivation, job design, reinforcement, and equity theories/organizational justice. The high achiever is not motivated by the organization's assessment of performance or organizational rewards, hence the jump from effort to personal goals for those with a high nAch. Remember, high achievers are internally driven as long as the jobs they are doing provide them with personal responsibility, feedback, and moderate risks. They are not concerned with the effort–performance, performance–rewards, or rewards–goal linkages.

Reinforcement theory enters our model by recognizing that the organization's rewards reinforce the individual's performance. If management has designed a reward system that is seen by employees as "paying off" for good performance, the rewards will reinforce and encourage continued good performance. Rewards also play the key part in organizational justice research. Individuals will judge the favorability of their outcomes (for example, their pay) relative to what others receive, but also with respect to how they are treated—when people are disappointed in their rewards, they are likely to be sensitive to the perceived fairness of the procedures used and the consideration given to them by their supervisor.

Caveat Emptor: Motivation Theories Are Often Culture-Bound

In our discussion of goal setting, we said that care needs to be taken in applying this theory because it assumes cultural characteristics that are not universal. This is true for many of the theories presented in this chapter because most current motivation theories were developed in the United States by Americans and about Americans.[82] For instance, both goal-setting and expectancy theories emphasize goal accomplishment as well as rational and individual thought—characteristics consistent with American culture. Let's take a look at several motivation theories and consider their cross-cultural transferability.

Maslow's needs hierarchy argues that people start at the physiological level and then move progressively up the hierarchy in this order: physiological, safety, social, esteem, and self-actualization. This hierarchy, if it has any application at all, aligns with American culture. In countries like Japan, Greece, and Mexico, where uncertainty avoidance characteristics are strong, security needs would be on top of the need hierarchy. Countries that score high on nurturing characteristics—Denmark, Sweden, Norway, the Netherlands, and Finland—would have social needs on top.[83] We would predict, for instance, that group work will motivate employees more when the country's culture scores high on the nurturing criterion.

Another motivation concept that clearly has an American bias is the achievement need. The view that a high achievement need acts as an internal motivator

U.S. firms expanding their operations in China are learning that motivation concepts that succeed in the United States don't always apply to Chinese employees. For example, compensation for sales people in China is based on seniority, not on performance. And most Chinese firms do not offer any nonmonetary motivation such as employee recognition programs. For the Chinese saleswoman shown here assisting a customer interested in GM's Cadillac CTS, motivation may come from satisfying her physiological and achievement needs.

presupposes two cultural characteristics—a willingness to accept a moderate degree of risk (which excludes countries with strong uncertainty avoidance characteristics) and a concern with performance (which applies almost singularly to countries with strong achievement characteristics). This combination is found in Anglo-American countries like the United States, Canada, and Great Britain.[84] However, these characteristics are relatively absent in countries such as Chile and Portugal.

Equity theory has gained a relatively strong following in the United States. That's not surprising since U.S.-style reward systems are based on the assumption that workers are highly sensitive to equity in reward allocations. And in the United States, equity is meant to closely tie pay to performance. However, evidence suggests that in collectivist cultures, especially in the former socialist countries of Central and Eastern Europe, employees expect rewards to reflect their individual needs as well as their performance.[85] Moreover, consistent with a legacy of communism and centrally planned economies, employees exhibited an entitlement attitude—that is, they expected outcomes to be *greater* than their inputs.[86] These findings suggest that U.S.-style pay practices may need modification, especially in Russia and former communist countries, in order to be perceived as fair by employees.

But don't assume there are *no* cross-cultural consistencies. For instance, the desire for interesting work seems important to almost all workers, regardless of their national culture. In a study of seven countries, employees in Belgium, Britain, Israel, and the United States ranked "interesting work" number one among 11 work goals. And this factor was ranked either second or third in Japan, the Netherlands, and Germany.[87] Similarly, in a study comparing job-preference outcomes among graduate students in the United States, Canada, Australia, and Singapore, growth, achievement, and responsibility were rated the top three and had identical rankings.[88] Both of these studies suggest some universality to the importance of intrinsic factors in the two-factor theory.

Summary and Implications for Managers

The theories we've discussed in this chapter address different outcome variables. Some, for instance, are directed at explaining turnover, while others emphasize productivity. The theories also differ in their predictive strength. In this section, we (1) review the most established motivation theories to determine their relevance in explaining our dependent variables, and (2) assess the predictive power of each.[89]

Need Theories   We introduced four theories that focused on needs. These were Maslow's hierarchy, ERG, McClelland's needs, and the two-factor theory. None of these theories has found widespread support, though the strongest of these is probably McClelland's, particularly regarding the relationship between achievement and productivity. In general, need theories (Maslow and ERG) are not very valid explanations of motivation.

Goal-Setting Theory   There is little dispute that clear and difficult goals lead to higher levels of employee productivity. This evidence leads us to conclude that goal-setting theory provides one of the more powerful explanations of this dependent variable. The theory, however, does not address absenteeism, turnover, or satisfaction.

Reinforcement Theory   This theory has an impressive record for predicting factors like quality and quantity of work, persistence of effort, absenteeism, tardiness, and accident rates. It does not offer much insight into employee satisfaction or the decision to quit.

Equity Theory/Organizational Justice   Equity theory also deals with productivity, satisfaction, absence, and turnover variables. However, its strongest legacy probably is that it provided the spark for research on organizational justice, which has more support in the literature.

Expectancy Theory   Our final theory focused on performance variables. It has proved to offer a relatively powerful explanation of employee productivity, absenteeism, and turnover. But expectancy theory assumes that employees have few constraints on their decision discretion. It makes many of the same assumptions that the rational model makes about individual decision making (see Chapter 5). This acts to restrict its applicability.

For major decisions, like accepting or resigning from a job, expectancy theory works well because people don't rush into decisions of this nature. They're more prone to take the time to carefully consider the costs and benefits of all the alternatives. However, expectancy theory is not a very good explanation for more typical types of work behavior, especially for individuals in lower-level jobs, because such jobs come with considerable limitations imposed by work methods, supervisors, and company policies. We would conclude, therefore, that expectancy theory's power in explaining employee productivity increases when the jobs being performed are more complex and higher in the organization (where discretion is greater).

Point ◀ ▶ Counterpoint

Money Motivates!

Behavioral scientists tend to downplay money as a motivator.[90] They prefer to emphasize the importance of challenging jobs, goals, participative decision making, feedback, recognition, cohesive work teams, and other nonmonetary factors. We argue otherwise here—that is, money is *the* critical incentive to work motivation.

Money is important to employees because it's a medium of exchange. People may not work *only* for money, but take the money away and how many people would come to work? A study of nearly 2,500 employees found that although these people disagreed over what was their number-one motivator, they unanimously chose money as their number two.

As equity theory suggests, money has symbolic value in addition to its exchange value. We use pay as the primary outcome against which we compare our inputs to determine if we are being treated equitably. When an organization pays one executive $80,000 a year and another $95,000, it means more than the latter's earning $15,000 a year more: It's a message, from the organization to both employees, of how much it values the contribution of each.

In addition to equity theory, both reinforcement and expectancy theories attest to the value of money as a motivator. In the former, if pay is contingent on performance, it will encourage workers to generate high levels of effort. Consistent with expectancy theory, money will motivate to the extent that it is seen as being able to satisfy an individual's personal goals and is perceived as being dependent on performance criteria.

However, maybe the best case for money is a review of studies that looked at four methods of motivating employee performance: money, goal setting, participative decision making, and redesigning jobs to give workers more challenge and responsibility. The average improvement from money was consistently higher than with any of the other methods.

Money can motivate *some* people under *some* conditions, so the issue isn't really whether or not money can motivate.[91] The answer to that is: "It can!" The more relevant question is: Does money motivate most employees in the workforce today? The answer to this question, we propose, is "No."

For money to motivate an individual's performance, certain conditions must be met. First, money must be important to the individual. Yet money isn't important to everybody. High achievers, for instance, are intrinsically motivated. Money would have little impact on these people.

Second, money must be perceived by the individual as being a direct reward for performance. Unfortunately, performance and pay are poorly linked in most organizations. Pay increases are far more often determined by nonperformance factors such as experience, community pay standards, or company profitability.

Third, the marginal amount of money offered for the performance must be perceived by the individual as being significant. Research indicates that merit raises must be at least 7 percent of base pay for employees to perceive them as motivating. Unfortunately, data indicates average merit increases in recent years have been typically only in the 3.3 to 4.4 percent range.

Finally, management must have the discretion to reward high performers with more money. Unfortunately, unions and organizational compensation policies constrain managerial discretion. Where unions exist, that discretion is almost zero. In nonunionized environments, traditionally narrow compensation grades create severe restrictions on pay increases. For example, in one organization, a Systems Analyst IV's pay grade ranges from $4,775 to $5,500 a month. No matter how good a job that analyst does, her boss cannot pay more than $5,500 a month. Similarly, no matter how poor the performance, the analyst will not earn less than $4,775. So money might be theoretically capable of motivating employee performance, but most managers aren't given enough flexibility to do much about it.

Questions for Review

1. Does motivation come from within a person or is it a result of the situation? Explain.

2. What are the implications of Theories X and Y for motivation practices?

3. Compare and contrast Maslow's hierarchy of needs theory with (a) Alderfer's ERG theory and (b) Herzberg's two-factor theory.

4. Describe the three needs isolated by McClelland. How are they related to worker behavior?

5. Explain cognitive evaluation theory. How applicable is it to management practice?

6. Relate goal-setting theory to the MBO process. How are they similar? Different?

7. What is the role of self-efficacy in goal setting?

8. Contrast distributive and procedural justice. What implications might they have for designing pay systems in different countries?

9. Identify the variables in expectancy theory.

Questions for Critical Thinking

1. "The cognitive evaluation theory is contradictory to reinforcement and expectancy theories." Do you agree or disagree? Explain.

2. Analyze the application of Maslow's and Herzberg's theories to an African or Caribbean nation where more than a quarter of the population is unemployed.

3. Can an individual be too motivated, so that performance declines as a result of excessive effort? Discuss.

4. Identify three activities you really enjoy (for example, playing tennis, reading a novel, going shopping). Next, identify three activities you really dislike (for example, going to the dentist, cleaning the house, staying on a restricted-calorie diet). Using the expectancy model, analyze each of your answers to assess why some activities stimulate your effort while others do not.

Team Exercise

GOAL-SETTING TASK

Purpose
This exercise will help you learn how to write tangible, verifiable, measurable, and relevant goals that might evolve from an MBO program.

Time
Approximately 20 to 30 minutes.

Instructions
1. Break into groups of three to five.

2. Spend a few minutes discussing your class instructor's job. What does he or she do? What defines good performance? What behaviors will lead to good performance?

3. Each group is to develop a list of five goals that, although not established participatively with your instructor, you believe might be developed in an MBO program at your college. Try to select goals that seem most critical to the effective performance of your instructor's job.

4. Each group will select a leader who will share the group's goals with the entire class. For each group's goals, class discussion should focus on their: (a) specificity, (b) ease of measurement, (c) importance, and (d) motivational properties.

Ethical Dilemma

IS MOTIVATION MANIPULATION?

Managers are interested in the subject of motivation because they're concerned with learning how to get the most effort from their employees. Is this ethical? For example, when managers link rewards to productivity, aren't they manipulating employees?

"To manipulate" is defined as "(1) to handle, manage, or use, especially with skill, in some process of treatment or performance; (2) to manage or influence by artful skill; (3) to adapt or change to suit one's purpose or advan-

tage." Aren't one or more of these definitions compatible with the notion of managers skillfully seeking to influence employee productivity for the benefit of the manager and the organization?

Do managers have the right to seek control over their employees? Does anyone, for that matter, have the right to control others? Does control imply manipulation? And is there anything wrong with managers manipulating employees?

Case Incident 1

FRUSTRATED AT AGE 30

Bob Wood is 30. But if you listened to him, you'd think he was 60 and washed-up. "I graduated college at a great time. It was 1996. I started as an analyst for Accenture, worked as a health-care IT consultant for two other firms, and then became chief technology officer at Claimshop.com, a medical claims processor." By 2001, Bob was making $80,000 a year plus bonus, driving an expensive European sports car, and optimistic about his future. But Bob Wood has become a statistic. He's one of 40 million Americans born between 1966 and 1975 whose peak earnings may be behind them. Bob now makes $44,000 as a technology analyst at a hospital and is trying to adjust to the fact that the go-go years of the late-1990s are history.

Like many of his generation, Bob is mired in debt. He owes $23,000 on his college loans and has run up more than $4,500 on his credit cards. He faces a world very different from the one his father found when he graduated college in the early 1960s.

"The rules have changed. And we Generations Xers are getting hit hard. We had to go to college to get a decent job. But the majority of us graduated with high student debt. The good news was, when we graduated, the job market was great. I got a $5,000 hiring bonus on my first job! The competition by employers for good people drove salaries up. When I was 28, I was making more money than my dad, who had been with the same company for over 20 years. But my dad has job security. And he has a nice retirement plan that will pay him a guaranteed pension when he turns 58. Now look at me. I don't know if I'll ever make

$80 thou again. If I do, it'll be in 20 or more years. I have no job security. I'm paying $350 a month on my college loans. I'm paying another $250 a month on my credit card account. I've got 30 more payments on my BMW. And my girlfriend says it's time for us to settle down and get married. It would be nice to own a house, but how can I commit myself to a 30-year mortgage when I don't know if I'll have a job in six months?

"I'm very frustrated. I feel like my generation got a bad deal. We initially got great jobs with unrealistically high pay. I admit it; we were spoiled. We got used to working one job for six months, quitting, then taking another and getting ourselves a 25 or 30 percent raise. We thought we'd be rich and retired by 40. The truth is that we're now lucky to have a job and, if we do, it probably pays half what we were making a few years ago. We have no job security. The competition for jobs, combined with pressures by business to keep costs down, means a future with minimal salary increases. It's pretty weird to be only 30 years old and to have your best years behind you!"

Questions

1. Analyze Bob using the Maslow need hierarchy.

2. Analyze Bob's lack of motivation using organizational justice and expectancy theory.

3. If you were Bob's boss, what could you do to positively influence his motivation?

4. What are the implications of this case for employers hiring Generation Xers?

Source: Ideas for this case are based on N. Watson, "Generation Wrecked," *Fortune,* October 14, 2002, pp. 183–90.

Case Incident 2

BULLYING BOSSES

"It got to where I was twitching, literally, on the way into work," states Carrie Clark, a 52-year-old retired teacher and administrator. After enduring 10 months of repeated insults and mistreatment from her supervisor, she finally quit her job. "I had to take care of my health."

Though many individuals recall bullies from their elementary school days, some are realizing that bullies can exist in the workplace as well. And these bullies do not just pick on the weakest in the group; rather, any subordinate in their path may fall prey to their torment, according to Dr. Gary Namie, director of the Workplace Bullying and Trauma Institute. Dr. Namie further says workplace bullies are not limited to men—women are at least as likely to be bullies. However, gender discrepancies are found in victims of bullying, as women are more likely to be targets.

What motivates a boss to be a bully? Dr. Harvey Hornstein, a retired professor from Teachers College at Columbia University, suggests that supervisors may use bullying as a means to subdue a subordinate that poses a threat to the supervisor's status. Additionally, supervisors may bully individuals to vent frustrations. Many times, however, the sheer desire to wield power may be the primary reason for bullying.

What is the impact of bullying on employee motivation and behavior? Surprisingly, even though victims of workplace bullies may feel less motivated to go to work every day, it does not appear that they discontinue performing their required job duties. However, it does appear that victims of bullies are less motivated to perform extra-role or citizenship behaviors. Helping others, speaking positively about the organization, and going beyond the call of duty are behaviors that are reduced as a result of bullying. According to Dr. Bennett Tepper of the University of North Carolina, fear may be the reason that many workers continue to perform their job duties. And not all individuals reduce their citizenship behaviors. Some continue to engage in extra-role behaviors to make themselves look better than their colleagues.

What should you do if your boss is bullying you? Don't necessarily expect help from coworkers. As Emelise Aleandri, an actress and producer from New York who left her job after being bullied, stated, "Some people were afraid to do anything. But others didn't mind what was happening at all, because they wanted my job." Moreover, according to Dr. Michelle Duffy of the University of Kentucky, coworkers often blame victims of bullying in order to resolve their guilt. "They do this by wondering whether maybe the person deserved the treatment, that he or she has been annoying, or lazy, they did something to earn it," states Dr. Duffy. One example of an employee who observed this phenomenon firsthand is Sherry Hamby, who was frequently verbally abused by her boss and then eventually fired. She stated, "This was a man who insulted me, who insulted my family, who would lay into me while everyone else in the office just sat there and let it happen. The people in my office eventually started blaming me."

What can a bullied employee do? Dr. Hornstein suggests that employees try to ignore the insults and respond only to the substance of the bully's gripe. "Stick with the substance, not the process, and often it won't escalate," he states. Of course, that is easier said than done.

Questions

1. Of the three types of organizational justice, which one does workplace bullying most closely resemble?

2. What aspects of motivation might workplace bullying reduce? For example, are there likely to be effects on an employee's self-efficacy? If so, what might those effects be?

3. If you were a victim of workplace bullying, what steps would you take to try to reduce its occurrence? What strategies would be most effective? What strategies might be ineffective? What would you do if one of your colleagues was a victim of an abusive supervisor?

4. What factors do you believe contribute to workplace bullying? Are bullies a product of the situation, or are they flawed personalities? What situations and what personality factors might contribute to the presence of bullies?

Source: Based on C. Benedict, "The Bullying Boss," *New York Times,* June 22, 2004, p. F.1

Endnotes

1. M. Hersh and J. Barry, "Nuclear Offense," *Newsweek*, February 21, 2005, pp. 22–27. B. K. Martin, "Kim Jong Il May Be Crazy . . . Like a Fox," *Los Angeles Times* (http://www.latimes.com/news/opinion/commentary/la-oe-martin17feb17,0,147539.story) (February 17, 2005).

2. C. A. O'Reilly III, "Organizational Behavior: Where We've Been, Where We're Going," in M. R. Rosenzweig and L. W. Porter (eds.), *Annual Review of Psychology*, vol. 42 (Palo Alto, CA: Annual Reviews, Inc., 1991), p. 431. See also M. L. Ambrose and C. T. Kulik, "Old Friends, New Faces: Motivation Research in the 1990s," *Journal of Management* 25, no. 3 (1999), pp. 231–92.

3. Cited in D. Jones, "Firms Spend Billions to Fire Up Workers—With Little Luck," *USA Today*, May 10, 2001, p. 1A.

4. See, for instance, T. R. Mitchell, "Matching Motivational Strategies with Organizational Contexts," in L. L. Cummings and B. M. Staw (eds.), *Research in Organizational Behavior*, vol. 19 (Greenwich, CT: JAI Press, 1997), pp. 60–62.

5. A. Maslow, *Motivation and Personality* (New York: Harper & Row, 1954).

6. See, for example, E. E. Lawler III and J. L. Suttle, "A Causal Correlation Test of the Need Hierarchy Concept," *Organizational Behavior and Human Performance*, April 1972, pp. 265–87; D. T. Hall and K. E. Nougaim, "An Examination of Maslow's Need Hierarchy in an Organizational Setting," *Organizational Behavior and Human Performance*, February 1968, pp. 12–35; A. K. Korman, J. H. Greenhaus, and I. J. Badin, "Personnel Attitudes and Motivation," in M. R. Rosenzweig and L. W. Porter (eds.), *Annual Review of Psychology* (Palo Alto, CA: Annual Reviews, 1977), pp. 178–79; and J. Rauschenberger, N. Schmitt, and J. E. Hunter, "A Test of the Need Hierarchy Concept by a Markov Model of Change in Need Strength," *Administrative Science Quarterly*, December 1980, pp. 654–70.

7. C. P. Alderfer, "An Empirical Test of a New Theory of Human Needs," *Organizational Behavior and Human Performance*, May 1969, pp. 142–75.

8. C. P. Schneider and C. P. Alderfer, "Three Studies of Measures of Need Satisfaction in Organizations," *Administrative Science Quarterly*, December 1973, pp. 489–505; and I. Borg and M. Braun, "Work Values in East and West Germany: Different Weights, But Identical Structures," *Journal of Organizational Behavior* 17, special issue (1996), pp. 541–55.

9. M. A. Wahba and L. G. Bridwell, "Maslow Reconsidered: A Review of Research on the Need Hierarchy Theory," *Organizational Behavior and Human Performance*, April 1976, pp. 212–40.

10. D. McGregor, *The Human Side of Enterprise* (New York: McGraw-Hill, 1960). For an updated analysis of Theory X and Theory Y constructs, see R. J. Summers and S. F. Cronshaw, "A Study of McGregor's Theory X, Theory Y and the Influence of Theory X, Theory Y Assumptions on Causal Attributions for Instances of Worker Poor Performance," in S. L. McShane (ed.), Organizational Behavior, *ASAC 1988 Conference Proceedings*, vol. 9, Part 5. Halifax, Nova Scotia, 1988, pp. 115–23.

11. See, for example, E. E. Lawler III, Motivation in Work Organizations (Belmont, CA: Brooks/Cole, 1973); B. Weiner, Human Motivation (New York: Holt, Rinehart, and Winston,

1980); and K. W. Thomas, Intrinsic Motivation at Work (San Francisco: Berrett-Koehler, 2000).

12. See, for instance, K. A. Kovach, "What Motivates Employees? Workers and Supervisors Give Different Answers," Business Horizons, September–October 1987, p. 61. This research was updated in 1995 and reported in a paper by K. A. Kovach, "Employee Motivation: Addressing a Crucial Factor in Your Organization's Performance," Fairfax, VA: George Mason University.

13. F. Herzberg, B. Mausner, and B. Snyderman, *The Motivation to Work* (New York: Wiley, 1959).

14. R. J. House and L. A. Wigdor, "Herzberg's Dual-Factor Theory of Job Satisfaction and Motivations: A Review of the Evidence and Criticism," *Personnel Psychology*, Winter 1967, pp. 369–89; D. P. Schwab and L. L. Cummings, "Theories of Performance and Satisfaction: A Review," *Industrial Relations*, October 1970, pp. 403–30; R. J. Caston and R. Braito, "A Specification Issue in Job Satisfaction Research," *Sociological Perspectives*, April 1985, pp. 175–97; and J. Phillipchuk and J. Whittaker, "An Inquiry into the Continuing Relevance of Herzberg's Motivation Theory," *Engineering Management Journal* 8 (1996), pp. 15–20.

15. D. C. McClelland, *The Achieving Society* (New York: Van Nostrand Reinhold, 1961); J. W. Atkinson and J. O. Raynor, *Motivation and Achievement* (Washington, D.C.: Winston, 1974); D. C. McClelland, *Power: The Inner Experience* (New York: Irvington, 1975); and M. J. Stahl, *Managerial and Technical Motivation: Assessing Needs for Achievement, Power, and Affiliation* (New York: Praeger, 1986).

16. C. McClelland, *The Achieving Society*.

17. D. C. McClelland and D. G. Winter, *Motivating Economic Achievement* (New York: Free Press, 1969); and J. B. Miner, N. R. Smith, and J. S. Bracker, "Role of Entrepreneurial Task Motivation in the Growth of Technologically Innovative Firms: Interpretations from Follow-up Data," *Journal of Applied Psychology*, October 1994, pp. 627–30.

18. D. C. McClelland, *Power;* D. C. McClelland and D. H. Burnham, "Power Is the Great Motivator," *Harvard Business Review*, March–April 1976, pp. 100–10; and R. E. Boyatzis, "The Need for Close Relationships and the Manager's Job," in D. A. Kolb, I. M. Rubin, and J. M. McIntyre, *Organizational Psychology: Readings on Human Behavior in Organizations*, 4th ed. (Upper Saddle River, NJ: Prentice Hall, 1984), pp. 81–86.

19. D. G. Winter, "The Motivational Dimensions of Leadership: Power, Achievement, and Affiliation," in R. E. Riggio, S. E. Murphy, and F. J. Pirozzolo (eds.), *Multiple Intelligences and Leadership* (Mahwah, NJ: Lawrence Erlbaum, 2002), pp. 119–38.

20. J. B. Miner, *Studies in Management Education* (New York: Springer, 1965).

21. D. Kipnis, "The Powerholder," in J. T. Tedeschi (ed.), *Perspectives in Social Power* (Chicago: Aldine, 1974), pp. 82–123.

22. D. McClelland, "Toward a Theory of Motive Acquisition," *American Psychologist*, May 1965, pp. 321–33; and D. Miron and D. C. McClelland, "The Impact of Achievement Motivation Training on Small Businesses," *California Management Review*, Summer 1979, pp. 13–28.

23. R. de Charms, *Personal Causation: The Internal Affective Determinants of Behavior* (New York: Academic Press, 1968).

24. E. L. Deci, *Intrinsic Motivation* (New York: Plenum, 1975); J. Cameron and W. D. Pierce, "Reinforcement, Reward, and Intrinsic Motivation: A Meta-Analysis," *Review of Educational Research*, Fall 1994, pp. 363–423; S. Tang and V. C. Hall, "The Overjustification Effect: A Meta-Analysis," *Applied Cognitive Psychology*, October 1995, pp. 365–404; E. L. Deci, R. Koestner, and R. M. Ryan, "A Meta-Analytic Review of Experiments Examining the Effects of Extrinsic Rewards on Intrinsic Motivation," *Psychological Bulletin* 125, no. 6 (1999), pp. 627–68; R. M. Ryan and E. L. Deci, "Intrinsic and Extrinsic Motivations: Classic Definitions and New Directions," *Contemporary Educational Psychology*, January 2000, pp. 54–67; and N. Houlfort, R. Koestner, M. Joussemet, A. Nantel-Vivier, and N. Lekes, "The Impact of Performance-Contingent Rewards on Perceived Autonomy and Competence," *Motivation & Emotion* 26, no. 4 (2002), pp. 279–95.

25. W. E. Scott, "The Effects of Extrinsic Rewards on 'Intrinsic Motivation': A Critique," *Organizational Behavior and Human Performance*, February 1976, pp. 117–19; B. J. Calder and B. M. Staw, "Interaction of Intrinsic and Extrinsic Motivation: Some Methodological Notes," *Journal of Personality and Social Psychology*, January 1975, pp. 76–80; and K. B. Boal and L. L. Cummings, "Cognitive Evaluation Theory: An Experimental Test of Processes and Outcomes," *Organizational Behavior and Human Performance*, December 1981, pp. 289–310.

26. G. R. Salancik, "Interaction Effects of Performance and Money on Self-Perception of Intrinsic Motivation," *Organizational Behavior and Human Performance*, June 1975, pp. 339–51; and F. Luthans, M. Martinko, and T. Kess, "An Analysis of the Impact of Contingency Monetary Rewards on Intrinsic Motivation," *Proceedings of the Nineteenth Annual Midwest Academy of Management*, St. Louis, 1976, pp. 209–21.

27. Deci, Koestner, and Ryan, "A Meta-Analytic Review of Experiments Examining the Effects of Extrinsic Rewards on Intrinsic Motivation."

28. K. M. Sheldon, A. J. Elliot, and R. M. Ryan, "Self-Concordance and Subjective Well-Being in Four Cultures," *Journal of Cross-Cultural Psychology* 35, no. 2 (2004), pp. 209–23.

29. J. E. Bono and T. A. Judge, "Self-Concordance at Work: Toward Understanding the Motivational Effects of Trans-formational Leaders," *Academy of Management Journal* 46, no. 5 (2003), pp. 554–71.

30. J. P. Meyer, T. E. Becker, and C. Vandenberghe, "Employee Commitment and Motivation: A Conceptual Analysis and Integrative Model," *Journal of Applied Psychology* 89, no. 6 (2004), pp. 991–1007.

31. E. A. Locke, "Toward a Theory of Task Motivation and Incentives," *Organizational Behavior and Human Performance*, May 1968, pp. 157–89.

32. P. C. Earley, P. Wojnaroski, and W. Prest, "Task Planning and Energy Expended: Exploration of How Goals Influence Performance," *Journal of Applied Psychology*, February 1987, pp. 107–14.

33. See, for instance, E. A. Locke, K. N. Shaw, L. M. Saari, and G. P. Latham, "Goal Setting and Task Performance," *Psychological Bulletin*, January 1981, pp. 125–52; A. J. Mento, R. P. Steel, and R. J. Karren, "A Meta-Analytic Study of the Effects of Goal Setting on Task Performance: 1966–1984," *Organizational Behavior and Human Decision Processes*, February 1987, pp. 52–83; M. E. Tubbs "Goal Setting: A Meta-Analytic

Examination of the Empirical Evidence," *Journal of Applied Psychology*, August 1986, pp. 474–83; E. A. Locke and G. P. Latham, *A Theory of Goal Setting and Task Performance* (Upper Saddle River, NJ: Prentice Hall, 1990); E. A. Locke and G. P. Latham, "Building a Practically Useful Theory of Goal Setting and Task Motivation," *American Psychologist*, September 2002, pp. 705–17; and R. P. DeShon, S. W. Kozlowski, A. M. Schmidt, K. R. Milner, and D. Wiechmann, "A Multiple-Goal, Multilevel Model of Feedback Effects on the Regulation of Individual and Team Performance," *Journal of Applied Psychology* 89, no. 6 (2004), pp. 1035–56.

34. E. A. Locke and G. P. Latham, "Building a Practically Useful Theory of Goal Setting and Task Motivation: A 35-Year Odyssey," *American Psychologist* 57, no. 9 (2002), pp. 705–17.

35. J. M. Ivancevich and J. T. McMahon, "The Effects of Goal Setting, External Feedback, and Self-Generated Feedback on Outcome Variables: A Field Experiment," *Academy of Management Journal*, June 1982, pp. 359–72; and E. A. Locke, "Motivation through Conscious Goal Setting," *Applied and Preventive Psychology* 5 (1996), pp. 117–24.

36. See, for example, G. P. Latham, M. Erez, and E. A. Locke, "Resolving Scientific Disputes by the Joint Design of Crucial Experiments by the Antagonists: Application to the Erez-Latham Dispute Regarding Participation in Goal Setting," *Journal of Applied Psychology*, November 1988, pp. 753–72; T. D. Ludwig and E. S. Geller, "Assigned versus Participative Goal Setting and Response Generalization: Managing Injury Control among Professional Pizza Deliverers," *Journal of Applied Psychology*, April 1997, pp. 253–61; and S. G. Harkins and M. D. Lowe, "The Effects of Self-Set Goals on Task Performance," *Journal of Applied Social Psychology*, January 2000, pp. 1–40.

37. M. Erez, P. C. Earley, and C. L. Hulin, "The Impact of Participation on Goal Acceptance and Performance: A Two-Step Model," *Academy of Management Journal*, March 1985, pp. 50–66.

38. E. A. Locke, "The Motivation to Work: What We Know," *Advances in Motivation and Achievement* 10 (1997), pp. 375–412; Latham, Erez, and Locke, "Resolving Scientific Disputes by the Joint Design of Crucial Experiments by the Antagonists," pp. 753–72.

39. H. J. Klein, M. J. Wesson, J. R. Hollenbeck, P. M. Wright, and R. D. DeShon, "The Assessment of Goal Commitment: A Measurement Model Meta-Analysis," *Organizational Behavior and Human Decision Processes* 85, no. 1 (2001), pp. 32–55.

40. J. R. Hollenbeck, C. R. Williams, and H. J. Klein, "An Empirical Examination of the Antecedents of Commitment to Difficult Goals," *Journal of Applied Psychology*, February 1989, pp. 18–23. See also J. C. Wofford, V. L. Goodwin, and S. Premack, "Meta-Analysis of the Antecedents of Personal Goal Level and of the Antecedents and Consequences of Goal Commitment," *Journal of Management*, September 1992, pp. 595–615; M. E. Tubbs, "Commitment as a Moderator of the Goal-Performance Relation: A Case for Clearer Construct Definition," *Journal of Applied Psychology*, February 1993, pp. 86–97; and J. E. Bono and A. E. Colbert, "Understanding Responses to Multi-Source Feedback: The Role of Core Self-Evaluations" *Personnel Psychology*, Spring 2005, pp. 171–203.

41. See R. E. Wood, A. J. Mento, and E. A. Locke, "Task Complexity as a Moderator of Goal Effects: A Meta Analysis," *Journal of*

Applied Psychology, August 1987, pp. 416–25; R. Kanfer and P. L. Ackerman, "Motivation and Cognitive Abilities: An Integrative/Aptitude-Treatment Interaction Approach to Skill Acquisition," *Journal of Applied Psychology (monograph)*, vol. 74, 1989, pp. 657–90; T. R. Mitchell and W. S. Silver, "Individual and Group Goals When Workers Are Interdependent: Effects on Task Strategies and Performance," *Journal of Applied Psychology*, April 1990, pp. 185–93; and A. M. O'Leary-Kelly, J. J. Martocchio, and D. D. Frink, "A Review of the Influence of Group Goals on Group Performance," *Academy of Management Journal*, October 1994, pp. 1285–301.

42. E. O. Welles, "Great Expectations," *INC.*, March 2001, pp. 68–73.

43. See, for instance, S. J. Carroll and H. L. Tosi, *Management by Objectives: Applications and Research* (New York, Macmillan, 1973); and R. Rodgers and J. E. Hunter, "Impact of Management by Objectives on Organizational Productivity," *Journal of Applied Psychology*, April 1991, pp. 322–36.

44. See, for instance, R. C. Ford, F. S. MacLaughlin, and J. Nixdorf, "Ten Questions about MBO," *California Management Review*, Winter 1980, p. 89; T. J. Collamore, "Making MBO Work in the Public Sector," *Bureaucrat*, Fall 1989, pp. 37–40; G. Dabbs, "Nonprofit Businesses in the 1990s: Models for Success," *Business Horizons*, September– October 1991, pp. 68–71; R. Rodgers and J. E. Hunter, "A Foundation of Good Management Practice in Government: Management by Objectives," *Public Administration Review*, January–February 1992, pp. 27–39; T. H. Poister and G. Streib, "MBO in Municipal Government: Variations on a Traditional Management Tool," *Public Administration Review*, January/February 1995, pp. 48–56; and C. Garvey, "Goalsharing Scores," *HRMagazine*, April 2000, pp. 99–106.

45. See, for instance, C. H. Ford, "MBO: An Idea Whose Time Has Gone?" *Business Horizons*, December 1979, p. 49; R. Rodgers and J. E. Hunter, "Impact of Management by Objectives on Organizational Productivity," *Journal of Applied Psychology*, April 1991, pp. 322–36; R. Rodgers, J. E. Hunter, and D. L. Rogers, "Influence of Top Management Commitment on Management Program Success," *Journal of Applied Psychology*, February 1993, pp. 151–55; and M. Tanikawa, "Fujitsu Decides to Backtrack on Performance-Based Pay," *New York Times*, March 22, 2001, p. W1.

46. A. Bandura, *Self-Efficacy: The Exercise of Control* (New York: Freeman, 1997).

47. A. D. Stajkovic and F. Luthans, "Self-Efficacy and Work-Related Performance: A Meta-Analysis," *Psychological Bulletin*, September 1998, pp. 240–61; and A. Bandura, "Cultivate Self-Efficacy for Personal and Organizational Effectiveness," in E. Locke (ed.), *Handbook of Principles of Organizational Behavior* (Malden, MA: Blackwell, 2004), pp. 120–36.

48. A. Bandura and D. Cervone, "Differential Engagement in Self-Reactive Influences in Cognitively-Based Motivation," *Organizational Behavior and Human Decision Processes*, August 1986, pp. 92–113.

49. A. Bandura, *Self-Efficacy: The Exercise of Control* (New York: Freeman, 1997).

50. C. L. Holladay and M. A. Quiñones, "Practice Variability and Transfer of Training: The Role of Self-Efficacy Generality," *Journal of Applied Psychology* 88, no. 6 (2003), pp. 1094–1103.

51. R. C. Rist, "Student Social Class and Teacher Expectations: The Self-Fulfilling Prophecy in Ghetto Education," *Harvard Educational Review* 70, no. 3 (2000), pp. 266–301.

52. D. Eden, "Self-Fulfilling Prophecies in Organizations," in J. Greenberg (ed.), *Organizational Behavior: The State of the Science*, 2nd ed. (Mahwah, NJ: Erlbaum, 2003), pp. 91–122.

53. Ibid.

54. T. A. Judge, C. L. Jackson, J. C. Shaw, B. Scott, and B. L. Rich, "Is the Effect of Self-Efficacy on Job/Task Performance an Epiphenomenon?" 2005, Working paper, University of Florida.

55. Ibid.

56. J. L. Komaki, T. Coombs, and S. Schepman, "Motivational Implications of Reinforcement Theory," in R. M. Steers, L. W. Porter, and G. Bigley (eds.), *Motivation and Work Behavior*, 6th ed. (New York: McGraw-Hill, 1996), pp. 87–107.

57. E. A. Locke, "Latham vs. Komaki: A Tale of Two Paradigms," *Journal of Applied Psychology*, February 1980, pp. 16–23.

58. J. S. Adams, "Inequity in Social Exchanges," in L. Berkowitz (ed.), *Advances in Experimental Social Psychology* (New York: Academic Press, 1965), pp. 267–300.

59. P. S. Goodman, "An Examination of Referents Used in the Evaluation of Pay," *Organizational Behavior and Human Performance*, October 1974, pp. 170–95; S. Ronen, "Equity Perception in Multiple Comparisons: A Field Study," *Human Relations*, April 1986, pp. 333–46; R. W. Scholl, E. A. Cooper, and J. F. McKenna, "Referent Selection in Determining Equity Perception: Differential Effects on Behavioral and Attitudinal Outcomes," *Personnel Psychology*, Spring 1987, pp. 113–27; and T. P. Summers and A. S. DeNisi, "In Search of Adams' Other: Reexamination of Referents Used in the Evaluation of Pay," *Human Relations*, June 1990, pp. 497–511.

60. C. T. Kulik and M. L. Ambrose, "Personal and Situational Determinants of Referent Choice," *Academy of Management Review*, April 1992, pp. 212–37.

61. C. Ostroff and L. E. Atwater, "Does Whom You Work with Matter? Effects of Referent Group Gender and Age Composition on Managers' Compensation," *Journal of Applied Psychology* 88, no. 4 (2003), pp. 725–40.

62. Ibid.

63. See, for example, E. Walster, G. W. Walster, and W. G. Scott, *Equity: Theory and Research* (Boston: Allyn & Bacon, 1978); and J. Greenberg, "Cognitive Reevaluation of Outcomes in Response to Underpayment Inequity," *Academy of Management Journal*, March 1989, pp. 174–84.

64. P. S. Goodman and A. Friedman, "An Examination of Adams' Theory of Inequity," *Administrative Science Quarterly*, September 1971, pp. 271–88; R. P. Vecchio, "An Individual-Differences Interpretation of the Conflicting Predictions Generated by Equity Theory and Expectancy Theory," *Journal of Applied Psychology*, August 1981, pp. 470–81; J. Greenberg, "Approaching Equity and Avoiding Inequity in Groups and Organizations," in J. Greenberg and R. L. Cohen (eds.), *Equity and Justice in Social Behavior* (New York: Academic Press, 1982), pp. 389–435; R. T. Mowday, "Equity Theory Predictions of Behavior in Organizations," in R. Steers, L. W. Porter, and G. Bigley (eds.), *Motivation and Work Behavior*, 6th ed. (New York: McGraw-Hill, 1996), pp. 111–31; S. Werner and N. P. Mero, "Fair or Foul? The Effects of External, Internal, and Employee Equity on Changes in Performance of Major League Baseball Players," *Human Relations*, October 1999, pp. 1291–1312; R. W. Griffeth and

S. Gaertner, "A Role for Equity Theory in the Turnover Process: An Empirical Test," *Journal of Applied Social Psychology*, May 2001, pp. 1017–37; and L. K. Scheer, N. Kumar, and J.-B. E. M. Steenkamp, "Reactions to Perceived Inequity in U.S. and Dutch Interorganizational Relationships," *Academy of Management 46*, no. 3 (2003), pp. 303–16.

65. See, for example, R. C. Huseman, J. D. Hatfield, and E. W. Miles, "A New Perspective on Equity Theory: The Equity Sensitivity Construct" *Academy of Management Journal*, April 1987, pp. 222–34; K. S. Sauley and A. G. Bedeian, "Equity Sensitivity: Construction of a Measure and Examination of Its Psychometric Properties," *Journal of Management 26*, no. 5 (2000), pp. 885–910; M. N. Bing and S. M. Burroughs, "The Predictive and Interactive Effects of Equity Sensitivity in Teamwork-Oriented Organizations," *Journal of Organizational Behavior*, May 2001, pp. 271–90; and J. A. Colquitt, "Does the Justice of One Interact With the Justice of Many? Reactions to Procedural Justice in Teams," *Journal of Applied Psychology 89*, no. 4 (2004), pp. 633–46.

66. J. Greenberg and S. Ornstein, "High Status Job Title as Compensation for Underpayment: A Test of Equity Theory," *Journal of Applied Psychology*, May 1983, pp. 285–97; and J. Greenberg, "Equity and Workplace Status: A Field Experiment," *Journal of Applied Psychology*, November 1988, pp. 606–13.

67. See, for instance, J. Greenberg, *The Quest for Justice on the Job* (Thousand Oaks, CA: Sage, 1996); R. Cropanzano and J. Greenberg, "Progress in Organizational Justice: Tunneling through the Maze," in C. L. Cooper and I. T. Robertson (eds.), *International Review of Industrial and Organizational Psychology*, vol. 12 (New York: Wiley, 1997); J. A. Colquitt, D. E. Conlon, M. J. Wesson, C. O. L. H. Porter, and K. Y. Ng, "Justice at the Millennium: A Meta-Analytic Review of the 25 Years of Organizational Justice Research," *Journal of Applied Psychology*, June 2001, pp. 425–45; T. Simons and Q. Roberson, "Why Managers Should Care About Fairness: The Effects of Aggregate Justice Perceptions on Organizational Outcomes," *Journal of Applied Psychology*, June 2003, pp. 432–43; and G. P. Latham and C. C. Pinder, "Work Motivation Theory and Research at the Dawn of the Twenty-First Century," *Annual Review of Psychology 56* (2005), pp. 485–516.

68. K. Leung, K. Tong, and S. S. Ho, "Effects of Interactional Justice on Egocentric Bias in Resource Allocation Decisions," *Journal of Applied Psychology 89*, no. 3 (2004), pp. 405–15.

69. "Americans Feel They Pay Fair Share of Taxes, Says Poll," *NewsTarget.com*, May 2, 2005 (http://www.newstarget.com/007297.html).

70. G. S. Leventhal, "What Should Be Done with Equity Theory? New Approaches to the Study of Fairness in Social Relationships," in K. Gergen, M. Greenberg, and R. Willis (eds.), *Social Exchange: Advances in Theory and Research* (New York: Plenum, 1980), pp. 27–55.

71. J. C. Shaw, E. Wild, and J. A. Colquitt, "To Justify or Excuse?: A Meta-Analytic Review of the Effects of Explanations," *Journal of Applied Psychology 88*, no. 3 (2003), pp. 444–58.

72. D. P. Skarlicki and R. Folger, "Retaliation in the Workplace: The Roles of Distributive, Procedural, and Interactional Justice," *Journal of Applied Psychology 82*, no. 3 (1997), pp. 434–43.

73. R. Cropanzano, C. A. Prehar, and P. Y. Chen, "Using Social Exchange Theory to Distinguish Procedural from Interactional

Justice," *Group & Organization Management 27*, no. 3 (2002), pp. 324–51.

74. J. A. Colquitt, D. E. Conlon, M. J. Wesson, C. O. L. H. Porter, and K. Y. Ng, "Justice at the Millennium: A Meta-Analytic Review of the 25 Years of Organizational Justice Research," *Journal of Applied Psychology 86*, no. 3 (2001), pp. 425–45.

75. P. S. Goodman, "Social Comparison Process in Organizations," in B. M. Staw and G. R. Salancik (eds.), *New Directions in Organizational Behavior* (Chicago: St. Clair, 1977), pp. 97–132; and J. Greenberg, "A Taxonomy of Organizational Justice Theories," *Academy of Management Review*, January 1987, pp. 9–22.

76. V. H. Vroom, *Work and Motivation* (New York: John Wiley, 1964).

77. For criticism, see H. G. Heneman III and D. P. Schwab, "Evaluation of Research on Expectancy Theory Prediction of Employee Performance," *Psychological Bulletin*, July 1972, pp. 1–9; T. R. Mitchell, "Expectancy Models of Job Satisfaction, Occupational Preference and Effort: A Theoretical, Methodological and Empirical Appraisal," *Psychological Bulletin*, November 1974, pp. 1053–77; L. Reinharth and M. A. Wahba, "Expectancy Theory as a Predictor of Work Motivation, Effort Expenditure, and Job Performance," *Academy of Management Journal*, September 1975, pp. 502–37; and W. Van Eerde and H. Thierry, "Vroom's Expectancy Models and Work-Related Criteria: A Meta-Analysis," *Journal of Applied Psychology*, October 1996, pp. 575–86. For support, see L. W. Porter and E. E. Lawler III, *Managerial Attitudes and Performance* (Homewood, IL: Irwin, 1968); D. F. Parker and L. Dyer, "Expectancy Theory as a Within-Person Behavioral Choice Model: An Empirical Test of Some Conceptual and Methodological Refinements," *Organizational Behavior and Human Performance*, October 1976, pp. 97–117; H. J. Arnold, "A Test of the Multiplicative Hypothesis of Expectancy-Valence Theories of Work Motivation," *Academy of Management Journal*, April 1981, pp. 128–41; and J. J. Donovan, "Work Motivation," in N. Anderson et al (eds.), *Handbook of Industrial, Work & Organizational Psychology*, vol. 2 (Thousand Oaks, CA: Sage, 2001), pp. 56–59.

78. Vroom refers to these three variables as expectancy, instrumentality, and valence, respectively.

79. P. M. Muchinsky, "A Comparison of Within- and Across-Subjects Analyses of the Expectancy-Valence Model for Predicting Effort," *Academy of Management Journal*, March 1977, pp. 154–58; and C. W. Kennedy, J. A. Fossum, and B. J. White, "An Empirical Comparison of Within-Subjects and Between-Subjects Expectancy Theory Models," *Organizational Behavior and Human Decision Process*, August 1983, pp. 124–43.

80. R. J. House, H. J. Shapiro, and M. A. Wahba, "Expectancy Theory as a Predictor of Work Behavior and Attitudes: A Reevaluation of Empirical Evidence," *Decision Sciences*, January 1974, pp. 481–506.

81. For other examples of models that seek to integrate motivation theories, see H. J. Klein, "An Integrated Control Theory Model of Work Motivation," *Academy of Management Review*, April 1989, pp. 150–72; E. A. Locke, "The Motivation Sequence, the Motivation Hub, and the Motivation Core," *Organizational Behavior and Human Decision Processes*, December 1991, pp. 288–99; and T. R. Mitchell, "Matching

Motivational Strategies with Organizational Contexts," in *Research in Organizational Behavior.*

82. N. J. Adler, *International Dimensions of Organizational Behavior,* 4th ed. (Cincinnati, OH: Southwestern, 2002), p. 174.

83. G. Hofstede, "Motivation, Leadership, and Organization: Do American Theories Apply Abroad?" *Organizational Dynamics,* Summer 1980, p. 55.

84. Ibid.

85. J. K. Giacobbe-Miller, D. J. Miller, and V. I. Victorov, "A Comparison of Russian and U.S. Pay Allocation Decisions, Distributive Justice Judgments, and Productivity under Different Payment Conditions," *Personnel Psychology,* Spring 1998, pp. 137–63.

86. S. L. Mueller and L. D. Clarke, "Political-Economic Context and Sensitivity to Equity: Differences between the United States and the Transition Economies of Central and Eastern Europe," *Academy of Management Journal,* June 1998, pp. 319–29.

87. I. Harpaz, "The Importance of Work Goals: An International Perspective," *Journal of International Business Studies,* First Quarter 1990, pp. 75–93.

88. G. E. Popp, H. J. Davis, and T. T. Herbert, "An International Study of Intrinsic Motivation Composition," *Management International Review,* January 1986, pp. 28–35.

89. This section is based on F. J. Landy and W. S. Becker, "Motivation Theory Reconsidered," in L. L. Cummings and B. M. Staw (eds.), *Research in Organizational Behavior,* vol. 9 (Greenwich, CT: JAI Press, 1987), pp. 24–35.

90. S. Caudron, "Motivation? Money's Only No. 2," *Industry Week,* November 15, 1993, p. 33; T. R. Mitchell and A. E. Mickel, "The Meaning of Money: An Individual-Difference Perspective," *Academy of Management Review* 24 (1999), pp. 568–78; E. A. Locke et al., "The Relative Effectiveness of Four Methods of Motivating Employee Performance," in K. D. Duncan, M. M. Gruenberg, and D. Wallis (eds.), *Changes in Working Life* (London: Wiley, 1980), pp. 363–83.

91. A. Mitra, N. Gupta, and G. D. Jenkins, Jr., "The Case of the Invisible Merit Raise: How People See Their Pay Raises," *Compensation & Benefits Review,* May–June 1995, pp. 71–76; Hewitt Associates Salary Survey, 2000; and "Workers Have Little to Cheer With Pay Raises of Only 3.5%," *The Wall Street Journal,* July 30, 2003, p. D2.

Motivation is everything. You can do the work of two people, but you can't be two people. Instead, you have to inspire the next guy down the line and get him to inspire his people.

— Lee Iacocca

Motivation: From Concepts to Applications

After studying this chapter, you should be able to:

1 Discuss the ways in which employees can be motivated by changing the work environment.

2 Explain why managers might want to use employee involvement programs.

3 Discuss how the different types of variable-pay programs can increase employee motivation.

4 Describe the link between skill-based pay plans and motivation theories.

5 Explain how flexible benefits turn benefits into motivators.

L E A R N I N G   O B J E C T I V E S

CHAPTER 7

Performance Pays

It's no longer "business as usual" at the New Jersey accounting firm of J. H. Cohn.[1] Along with an increasing number of professional organizations, Cohn has changed the way it compensates its partners. It now allocates around 30 percent of the partners' total compensation pool on the basis of each partner's contribution to the firm in the previous year.

Accounting firms historically followed a seniority model for paying its partners. Once a person made partner, which means being a part owner in the firm, annual compensation tended to follow length of tenure. Those partners with the greatest seniority received the highest pay. This rewarded loyalty to the firm but did little to motivate key behaviors like generating billable client hours or bringing in new business. So J. H. Cohn modified its compensation program to reflect pay-for-performance.

Cohn's CEO, Tom Marino (see photo) sees performance-based pay as undermining complacency and helping motivate younger partners to build the business. It provides incentive and rewards performance. "It's 100 percent better than it used to be, as far as allowing the young, aggressive partners to move up in the firm without the politics," says Marino. ■

P ay-for-performance is the practical application of a theory we discussed in the previous chapter: Consistent with expectancy theory, motivation should be enhanced when employees see that rewards are allocated on performance criteria. In this chapter, we focus on applying motivation concepts. We link motivation theories to practices such as employee involvement and skill-based pay. Why? Because it's one thing to be able to know specific motivation theories; it's quite another to see how, as a manager, you can use them.

Motivating by Changing the Nature of the Work Environment

Increasingly, research on motivation is focused on approaches that link motivational concepts to changes in the way work is structured.

Research in **job design** provides stronger evidence that the way the elements in a job are organized can act to increase or decrease effort. This research also offers detailed insights into just what those elements are. We'll first review the job characteristics model and then discuss some ways jobs can be redesigned. Finally, we'll explore some alternative work arrangements.

The Job Characteristics Model

Developed by J. Richard Hackman and Greg Oldham, the **job characteristics model (JCM)** proposes that any job can be described in terms of five core job dimensions:[2]

1. **Skill variety**: The degree to which the job requires a variety of different activities so the worker can use a number of different skills and talent. For instance, an example of a job scoring high on skill variety would be the owner-operator of a garage who does electrical repairs, rebuilds engines, does body work, and interacts with customers. A job scoring low on this dimension would be a body shop worker who sprays paint eight hours a day.
2. **Task identity**: The degree to which the job requires completion of a whole and identifiable piece of work. An example of a job scoring high on identity would be a cabinetmaker who designs a piece of furniture, selects the wood, builds the object, and finishes it to perfection. A job scoring low on this dimension would be a worker in a furniture factory who operates a lathe solely to make table legs.
3. **Task significance**: The degree to which the job has a substantial impact on the lives or work of other people. An example of a job scoring high on significance would be a nurse handling the diverse needs of patients in a hospital intensive care unit. A job scoring low on this dimension would be a janitor sweeping floors in the same hospital.
4. **Autonomy**: The degree to which the job provides substantial freedom, independence, and discretion to the individual in scheduling the work and in determining the procedures to be used in carrying it out. An example of a job scoring high on autonomy is a salesperson who schedules his or her own work each day and decides on the most effective sales approach for each customer without supervision. A job scoring low on this dimension would be a salesperson who is given a set of leads each day and is required to follow a standardized sales script with each potential customer.
5. **Feedback**: The degree to which carrying out the work activities required by the job results in the individual obtaining direct and clear information about the effectiveness of his or her performance. An example of a job with high feedback is a factory worker who assembles iPods and then tests them to see if they operate properly. A job scoring low on feedback would be that same factory worker

who, after assembling the iPod, is required to route it to a quality-control inspector who tests it for proper operation and makes needed adjustments.

Exhibit 7-1 presents the job characteristics model. Note how the first three dimensions—skill variety, task identity, and task significance—combine to create meaningful work. That is, if these three characteristics exist in a job, the model predicts that the incumbent will view the job as being important, valuable, and worthwhile. Note, too, that jobs that possess autonomy give job incumbents a feeling of personal responsibility for the results and that, if a job provides feedback, employees will know how effectively they are performing. From a motivational standpoint, the JCM says that internal rewards are obtained by individuals when they learn (knowledge of results) that they personally (experienced responsibility) have performed well on a task that they care about (experienced meaningfulness).[3] The more that these three psychological states are present, the greater will be employees' motivation, performance, and satisfaction, and the lower their absenteeism and likelihood of leaving the organization. As Exhibit 7-1 shows, the links between the job dimensions and the outcomes are moderated or adjusted by the strength of the individual's growth need—that is, by the employee's desire for self-esteem and self-actualization. This means that individuals with a high growth need are more likely to experience the psychological states when their jobs are enriched than are their counterparts with a low

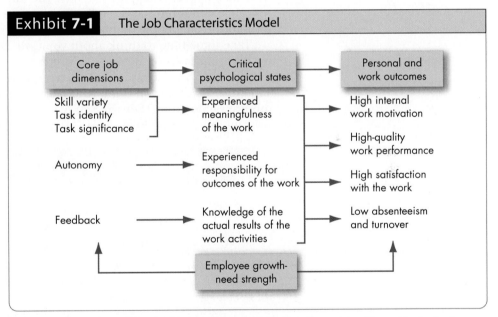

Exhibit 7-1   The Job Characteristics Model

Source: J. R. Hackman and G. R. Oldham, *Work Redesign* © 1980; pp. 78–80. Adapted by permission of Pearson Education, Inc. Upper Saddle River, New Jersey.

job design *The way the elements in a job are organized.*

job characteristics model (JCM) *A model that proposes that any job can be described in terms of five core job dimensions: skill variety, task identity, task significance, autonomy, and feedback.*

skill variety *The degree to which the job requires a variety of different activities.*

task identity *The degree to which the job requires completion of a whole and identifiable piece of work.*

task significance *The degree to which the job has a substantial impact on the lives or work of other people.*

autonomy *The degree to which the job provides substantial freedom and discretion to the individual in scheduling the work and in determining the procedures to be used in carrying it out.*

feedback *The degree to which carrying out the work activities required by the job results in the individual obtaining direct and clear information about the effectiveness of his or her performance.*

growth need. Moreover, they will respond more positively to the psychological states when they are present than will individuals with a low growth need.

The core dimensions can be combined into a single predictive index, called the **motivating potential score (MPS)**. It's calculated as follows:

$$MPS = \frac{\text{Skill variety} + \text{Task identity} + \text{Task significance}}{3} \times \text{Autonomy} \times \text{Feedback}$$

Jobs that are high on motivating potential must be high on at least one of the three factors that lead to experienced meaningfulness, and they must be high on both autonomy and feedback. If jobs score high on motivating potential, the model predicts that motivation, performance, and satisfaction will be positively affected and that the likelihood of absence and turnover will be lessened.

The JCM has been well researched. And most of the evidence supports the general framework of the theory—that is, there is a multiple set of job characteristics and these characteristics affect behavioral outcomes.[4] But it does appear that the MPS model doesn't work—that is, one can better derive motivating potential by adding the characteristics rather than using the complex MPS formula.[5] Beyond employee growth-need strength, other variables, such as the employee's perception of his or her workload compared to others, may also moderate the link between the core job dimensions and personal and work outcomes.[6] Overall, though, it appears that jobs that have the intrinsic elements of variety, identity, significance, autonomy, and feedback are more satisfying and generate higher performance from people than jobs that lack these characteristics.

Take some time to think about your job. Do you have the opportunity to work on different tasks or is your day pretty routine? Are you able to work independently or do you constantly have a supervisor or coworker looking over your shoulder? What do you think your answers to these questions say about your job's motivating potential? See the Self-Assessment feature below and you can calculate your motivating potential score (MPS) from the job characteristics model.

WHAT'S MY JOB'S MOTIVATING POTENTIAL?

In the Self-Assessment Library (available on CD, online, and in print), take assessment I.C.9 (What's My Job's Motivating Potential?) and answer the following questions. If you currently do not have a job, answer the questions for your most recent job.

1. *How did you score relative to your classmates?*
2. *Did your score surprise you? Why or why not?*
3. *How might your results affect your career path?*

How Can Jobs Be Redesigned?

"Every day was the same thing," Frank Greer said. "Stand on that assembly line. Wait for an instrument panel to be moved into place. Unlock the mechanism and drop the panel into the Jeep Liberty as it moved by on the line. Then I plugged in the harnessing wires. I repeated that for eight hours a day. I don't care that they were paying me $24 an hour. I was going crazy. I did it for almost a year and a half. Finally, I just said to my wife that this isn't going to be the way I'm going to spend the rest of my life. My brain was turning to Jell-O on that Jeep assembly line. So I quit. Now I work in a print shop and I make less than $15 an hour. But let me tell you, the work I do is really interesting. The job changes all the time, I'm continually learning new things, and the work really challenges me! I look forward every morning to going to work again."

Frank Greer's job at the Jeep plant was made up of repetitive tasks that provided him with little variety, autonomy, or motivation. In contrast, his job in the print shop is challenging and stimulating. Let's look at some of the ways that the JCM can be put into practice to make jobs more motivating.

Job Rotation If employees suffer from overroutinization of their work, one alternative is to use **job rotation** (or what many now call *cross-training*). We define this practice as the periodic shifting of an employee from one task to another. When an activity is no longer challenging, the employee is rotated to another job, usually at the same level, that has similar skill requirements. Singapore Airlines, one of the best-rated airlines in the world, uses job rotation extensively. For example, a ticket agent may take on the duties of a baggage handler. Job rotation is one of the reasons Singapore Airlines is rated as a highly desirable place to work. Job rotation has also been adopted by many manufacturing firms as a means of increasing flexibility and avoiding layoffs.[7] For instance, managers at Apex Precision Technologies, a custom-machine shop in Indiana, continually train workers on all of the company's equipment so they can be moved around in response to the requirements of incoming orders. During the 2001 recession, Cleveland-based Lincoln Electric moved some salaried workers to hourly clerical jobs and rotated production workers among various machines. This manufacturer of welding and cutting parts was able to minimize layoffs because of its commitment to continual cross-training and moving workers wherever they're needed.

The strengths of job rotation are that it reduces boredom, increases motivation through diversifying the employee's activities, and helps employees better

Job rotation adds variety to routine assembly tasks at the Autoliv automobile airbag manufacturing plant. Autoliv replaced its assembly line with U-shaped production cells that consist of a group of workstations staffed by a handful of employees. Workers change their jobs every 24 minutes when Autoliv announces a job rotation by piping rock music from the 1970s group Steam through the company's public address system: "Na, na, na, na, hey, hey, hey, good-bye."

motivating potential score (MPS) *A predictive index suggesting the motivating potential in a job.*

job rotation *The periodic shifting of an employee from one task to another.*

understand how their work contributes to the organization. Job rotation also has indirect benefits for the organization because employees with a wider range of skills give management more flexibility in scheduling work, adapting to changes, and filling vacancies.[8] However, job rotation is not without its drawbacks. Training costs are increased, and productivity is reduced by moving a worker into a new position just when efficiency at the prior job is creating organizational economies. Job rotation also creates disruptions. Members of the work group have to adjust to the new employee. And supervisors may also have to spend more time answering questions and monitoring the work of recently rotated employees.

Job Enlargement   More than 35 years ago, the idea of expanding jobs horizontally, or what we call **job enlargement**, grew in popularity. Increasing the number and variety of tasks that an individual performed resulted in jobs with more diversity. Instead of only sorting the incoming mail by department, for instance, a mail sorter's job could be enlarged to include physically delivering the mail to the various departments or running outgoing letters through the postage meter. The difference between job rotation and job enlargement may seem subtle. However, in job rotation, jobs are not redesigned. Employees simply move from one job to another, but the nature of the work does not change. Job enlargement, however, involves actually changing the job.

Efforts at job enlargement met with less than enthusiastic results.[9] As one employee who experienced such a redesign on his job remarked, "Before I had one lousy job. Now, through enlargement, I have three!" However, there have been some successful applications of job enlargement. The job of housekeeper in some smaller hotels, for example, includes not only cleaning bathrooms, making beds, and vacuuming but also replacing burned out light bulbs, providing turn-down service, and restocking mini-bars.

Job Enrichment   **Job enrichment** refers to the vertical expansion of jobs. It increases the degree to which the worker controls the planning, execution, and evaluation of the work. An enriched job organizes tasks so as to allow the

Myth or Science?   *"Everyone Wants a Challenging Job"*

This statement is false. In spite of all the attention focused by the media, academicians, and social scientists on human potential and the needs of individuals, there is no evidence to support that the vast majority of workers want challenging jobs.[10] Some individuals prefer highly complex and challenging jobs; others prosper in simple, routinized work.

The individual-difference variable that seems to gain the greatest support for explaining who prefers a challenging job and who doesn't is the strength of an individual's higher-order needs.[11] Individuals with high growth needs are more responsive to challenging work. But what percentage of rank-and-file workers actually desires higher-order need satisfactions and will respond positively to challenging jobs? No current data are available, but a study from the 1970s estimated the figure at about 15 percent.[12] Even after adjusting for changing work attitudes and the growth in white-collar jobs, it seems unlikely that the number today exceeds 40 percent.

The strongest voice advocating challenging jobs has *not* been workers—it's been professors, social-science researchers, and journalists. Professors, researchers, and journalists undoubtedly made their career choices, to some degree, because they wanted jobs that gave them autonomy, identity, and challenge. That, of course, is their choice. But for them to project their needs onto the workforce in general is presumptuous.

Not every employee is looking for a challenging job. Many workers meet their higher-order needs *off* the job. There are 168 hours in every individual's week. Work rarely consumes more than 30 percent of this time. That leaves considerable opportunity, even for individuals with strong growth needs, to find higher-order need satisfaction outside the workplace. ■

worker to do a complete activity, increases the employee's freedom and independence, increases responsibility, and provides feedback, so individuals will be able to assess and correct their own performance.[13] The enrichment of jobs can be traced to Herzberg's two-factor theory. Following this theory, by increasing the intrinsic factors in a job—such as achievement, responsibility, and growth—employees are more likely to be satisfied with the job and motivated to perform it.

How does management enrich an employee's job? Exhibit 7-2 offers suggested guidelines based on the job characteristics model. *Combining tasks* takes existing and fractionalized tasks and puts them back together to form a new and larger module of work. *Forming natural work units* means that the tasks an employee does create an identifiable and meaningful whole. *Establishing client relationships* increases the direct relationships between workers and their clients (these may be an internal customer as well as someone outside the organization). *Expanding jobs vertically* gives employees responsibilities and control that were formerly reserved for management. *Opening feedback channels* lets employees know how well they are performing their jobs and whether their performance is improving, deteriorating, or remaining at a constant level.

To illustrate job enrichment, let's look at what management at Bank One in Chicago did with its international trade banking department.[14] The department's chief product is commercial letters of credit—essentially a bank guarantee to stand behind huge import and export transactions. Prior to enriching jobs, the department's 300 employees processed documents in an assembly-line fashion, with errors creeping in at each handoff. Meanwhile, employees did little to hide the boredom they were experiencing from doing narrow and specialized tasks. Management enriched these jobs by making each clerk a trade expert who was able to handle a customer

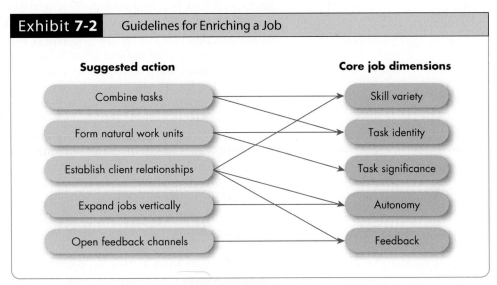

Exhibit 7-2 Guidelines for Enriching a Job

Source: J. R. Hackman and J. L. Suttle (eds.), *Improving Life at Work* (Glenview, IL: Scott Foresman, 1977), p. 138. Reprinted by permission of Richard Hackman and J. Lloyd Suttle.

job enlargement *Increasing the number and variety of tasks that an individual performs results in jobs with more diversity.*

job enrichment *The vertical expansion of jobs, increasing the degree to which the worker controls the planning, execution, and evaluation of the work.*

from start to finish. After 200 hours of training in finance and law, the clerks became full-service advisers who could turn around documents in a day while advising clients on such arcane matters as bank procedures in Turkey and U.S. munitions' export controls. And the results? Department productivity more than tripled, employee satisfaction soared, and transaction volume rose more than 10 percent a year.

The overall evidence on job enrichment generally shows that it reduces absenteeism and turnover costs and increases satisfaction, but on the critical issue of productivity, the evidence is inconclusive.[15] In some situations, job enrichment increases productivity; in others, it decreases it. However, even when productivity goes down, there does seem to be consistently more conscientious use of resources and a higher quality of product or service.

Alternative Work Arrangements

Beyond redesigning the nature of the work itself, and involving employees in decisions, another approach to making the work environment more motivating is to alter work arrangements. We'll discuss three alternative work arrangements: flextime, job sharing, and telecommuting. With the increasing advances in technology, all of these alternative work arrangements have become more popular.

Flextime   Susan Ross is your classic "morning person." She rises each day at 5 A.M. sharp, full of energy. However, as she puts it, "I'm usually ready for bed right after the 7 P.M. news."

Susan's work schedule as a claims processor at The Hartford Financial Services Group is flexible. It allows her some degree of freedom as to when she comes to work and when she leaves. Her office opens at 6 A.M. and closes at 7 P.M. It's up to her how she schedules her 8-hour day within this 13-hour period. Because Susan is a morning person and also has a seven-year-old son who gets out of school at 3 P.M. every day, she opts to work from 6 A.M. to 3 P.M. "My work hours are perfect. I'm at the job when I'm mentally most alert, and I can be home to take care of my son after he gets out of school."

Susan Ross's work schedule at The Hartford is an example of **flextime**. The term is short for "flexible work hours." It allows employees some discretion over when they arrive at work and when they leave. Employees have to work a specific number of hours a week, but they are free to vary the hours of work within certain limits. As shown in Exhibit 7-3, each day consists of a common core, usually six hours, with a flexibility band surrounding the core. For example, exclusive of a one-hour lunch break, the core may be 9 A.M. to 3 P.M., with the office actually opening at 6 A.M. and closing at 6 P.M. All employees are required to be at their jobs during the common core period, but they are allowed to accumulate their other two hours before and/or after the core time. Some flextime programs allow extra hours to be accumulated and turned into a free day off each month.

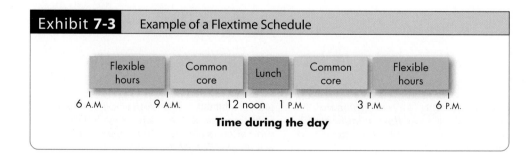

Exhibit 7-3	Example of a Flextime Schedule

Flexible hours | Common core | Lunch | Common core | Flexible hours

6 A.M.   9 A.M.   12 noon   1 P.M.   3 P.M.   6 P.M.

Time during the day

The growing number of firms offering flexible work schedules recognize that this work option is a popular motivational reward. At Sun Microsystems, 95 percent of employees take advantage of the company's flextime by scheduling their own work hours.

Flextime has become an extremely popular scheduling option. The proportion of full-time U.S. employees on flextime more than doubled between the late 1980s and 2005. Approximately 43 percent of the U.S. full-time workforce now has flexibility in their daily arrival and departure times.[16] And this is not just a U.S. phenomenon. In Germany, for instance, 29 percent of businesses have flextime for their employees.[17]

The benefits claimed for flextime are numerous. They include reduced absenteeism, increased productivity, reduced overtime expenses, a lessening in hostility toward management, reduced traffic congestion around work sites, elimination of tardiness, and increased autonomy and responsibility for employees that may increase employee job satisfaction.[18] But beyond the claims, what's flextime's record?

Most of the performance evidence stacks up favorably. Flextime tends to reduce absenteeism and frequently improves worker productivity,[19] probably for several reasons. Employees can schedule their work hours to align with personal demands, thus reducing tardiness and absences, and employees can adjust their work activities to those hours in which they are individually more productive.

Flextime's major drawback is that it's not applicable to every job. It works well with clerical tasks for which an employee's interaction with people outside his or her department is limited. It is not a viable option for receptionists, sales personnel in retail stores, or similar jobs for which comprehensive service demands that people be at their work stations at predetermined times.

Job Sharing A recent work scheduling innovation is **job sharing**. It allows two or more individuals to split a traditional 40-hour-a-week job. So, for example, one person might perform the job from 8 A.M. to noon, while another performs the same job from 1 P.M. to 5 P.M.; or the two could work full, but alternate, days. As a case in point, Sue Manix and Charlotte Schutzman share the title of vice president of employee communications in the Philadelphia office of Verizon.[20] Schutzman works Monday and Tuesday; Manix works Thursday and Friday; and they alternate Wednesdays. The two women have job-shared for 10 years, acquiring promotions, numerous bonuses, and a 20-person staff along the way. With each having children at home, this arrangement allows them the flexibility to better balance their work and family responsibilities.

Approximately 31 percent of large organizations now offer their employees job sharing.[21] However, in spite of its availability, it doesn't seem to be widely adopted by employees. This is probably because of the difficulty of finding compatible partners to share a job and the negative perceptions historically held of individuals not completely committed to their job and employer.

Job sharing allows the organization to draw on the talents of more than one individual in a given job. A bank manager who oversees two job sharers describes it as an opportunity to get two heads but "pay for one."[22] It also opens up the opportunity to acquire skilled workers—for instance, women with young children and retirees—who might not be available on a full-time basis.[23] Many Japanese firms are increasingly considering job sharing—but for a very different reason.[24] Because Japanese executives are extremely reluctant to fire people, job sharing is seen as a potentially humanitarian means for avoiding layoffs due to overstaffing.

flextime *Flexible work hours.*

job sharing *An arrangement that allows two or more individuals to split a traditional 40-hour-a-week job.*

From the employee's perspective, job sharing increases flexibility. As such, it can increase motivation and satisfaction for those to whom a 40-hour-a-week job is just not practical. But the major drawback from management's perspective is finding compatible pairs of employees who can successfully coordinate the intricacies of one job.[25]

Telecommuting   It might be close to the ideal job for many people. No commuting, flexible hours, freedom to dress as you please, and few or no interruptions from colleagues. It's called **telecommuting** and refers to employees who do their work at home at least two days a week on a computer that is linked to their office.[26] (A closely related term—*the virtual office*—is increasingly being used to describe employees who work out of their home on a relatively permanent basis.)

Recent estimates indicate that between 9 million and 24 million people telecommute in the United States, depending on exactly how the term is defined.[27] This translates to about 10 percent or more of the workforce. Well-known organizations that actively encourage telecommuting include AT&T, IBM, Merrill Lynch, American Express, Hewlett-Packard, and a number of U.S. government agencies.[28] The concept is also catching on worldwide. In Finland, Sweden, Britain, and Germany, telecommuters represent 17, 15, 8, and 6 percent of their workforces, respectively.[29]

What kinds of jobs lend themselves to telecommuting? Three categories have been identified as most appropriate: routine information-handling tasks, mobile activities, and professional and other knowledge-related tasks.[30] Writers, attorneys, analysts, and employees who spend the majority of their time on computers or the telephone are natural candidates for telecommuting. For instance, telemarketers, customer-service representatives, reservation agents, and product-support specialists spend most of their time on the phone. As telecommuters, they can access information on their computer screens at home as easily as in the company's office.

There are numerous stories of telecommuting's success.[31] For instance, 3,500 Merrill Lynch employees telecommute. And after the program was in place just a year, management reported an increase in productivity of between 15 and 20 percent among their telecommuters, 3.5 fewer sick days a year, and a 6 percent decrease in turnover. Putnam Investments, located in Boston, has found telecommuting to be an attractive recruitment tool. The company was having difficulty attracting new hires. But after introducing telecommuting, the number of its applicants grew by 20-fold. And Putnam's management calculates that the 12 percent of its employees who telecommute have substantially higher productivity than in-office staff and about one-tenth the attrition rate.

The potential pluses for management of telecommuting include a larger labor pool from which to select, higher productivity, less turnover, improved morale, and reduced office-space costs. The major downside for management is less direct supervision of employees. In addition, in today's team-focused workplace, telecommuting may make it more difficult for management to coordinate teamwork.[32] From the employee's standpoint, telecommuting offers a considerable increase in flexibility. But not without costs. For employees with a high social need, telecommuting can increase feelings of isolation and reduce job satisfaction. And all telecommuters potentially suffer from the "out of sight, out of mind" effect. Employees who aren't at their desks, who miss meetings, and who don't share in day-to-day informal workplace interactions may be at a disadvantage when it comes to raises and promotions. It's easy for bosses to overlook or undervalue the contribution of employees whom they see less regularly.

Telecommuting is appropriate for the knowledge-based tasks performed by employees of Miller Consultants, an organizational performance consulting firm. Company owner Kathleen Miller, shown here, and an assistant work from a traditional office in Louisville, Kentucky, but her employees work from their home offices in states from Texas to Connecticut. Telecommuting enables Miller to hire employees with the best expertise to serve clients in different geographic areas. Employees communicate with each other through the firm's Web site and teleconferencing system.

Don't Forget Ability and Opportunity

Robin and Chris both graduated from college a couple of years ago with their degrees in elementary education. They each took jobs as first-grade teachers but in different school districts. Robin immediately confronted a number of obstacles on the job: a large class (42 students), a small and dingy classroom, and inadequate supplies. Chris's situation couldn't have been more different. He had only 15 students in his class, plus a teaching aide for 15 hours each week, a modern and well-lighted room, a well-stocked supply cabinet, an iMac computer for every student, and a highly supportive principal. Not surprisingly, at the end of their first school year, Chris had been considerably more effective as a teacher than had Robin.

The preceding episode illustrates an obvious but often overlooked fact. Success on a job is facilitated or hindered by the existence or absence of support resources.

A popular, although arguably simplistic, way of thinking about employee performance is as a function (f) of the interaction of ability (A) and motivation (M); that is, performance = $f(A \times M)$. If either is inadequate, performance will be negatively affected. This helps to explain, for instance, the hard-working athlete or student with modest abilities who consistently outperforms a more gifted, but lazy, rival. So, as we noted in Chapter 2, an individual's intelligence and skills (subsumed under the label *ability*) must be considered in addition to motivation if we are to be able to accurately explain and predict employee performance. But a piece of the puzzle is still missing. We need to add **opportunity to perform** (O) to our equation: performance = $f(A \times M \times O)$.[33] Even though an individual may be willing and able, there may be obstacles that constrain performance.

When you attempt to assess why an employee may not be performing to the level that you believe he or she is capable, take a look at the work environment to see if it's supportive. Does the employee have adequate tools, equipment, materials, and supplies? Does the employee have favorable working conditions, helpful coworkers, supportive work rules and procedures, sufficient information to make job-related decisions, adequate time to do a good job, and the like? If not, performance will suffer.

Employee Involvement

What specifically do we mean by **employee involvement**? We define it as a participative process that uses the input of employees to increase their commitment to the organization's success. The underlying logic is that by involving workers in the decisions that affect them and by increasing their autonomy and control over their work lives, employees will become more motivated, more committed to the organization, more productive, and more satisfied with their jobs.[34]

Employee involvement programs differ among countries.[35] For instance, a study comparing the acceptance of employee involvement programs in four countries, including the United States and India, confirmed the importance of modifying practices to reflect national culture.[36] Specifically, while American

---

telecommuting   *Refers to employees who do their work at home at least two days a week on a computer that is linked to their office.*

opportunity to perform   *High levels of performance are partially a function of an absence of obstacles that constrain the employee.*

employee involvement   *A participative process that uses the input of employees and is intended to increase employee commitment to the organization's success.*

employees readily accepted these programs, managers in India who tried to empower their employees through employee involvement programs were rated low by those employees. In these Indian cases, employee satisfaction also decreased. These reactions are consistent with India's high power–distance culture, which accepts and expects differences in authority.

Examples of Employee Involvement Programs

Now let's look at the three major forms of employee involvement—participative management, representative participation, and quality circles—in more detail.

Participative Management   The distinct characteristic common to all **participative management** programs is the use of joint decision making. That is, subordinates actually share a significant degree of decision-making power with their immediate superiors. Participative management has, at times, been promoted as a panacea for poor morale and low productivity. But for it to work, the issues in which employees get involved must be relevant to their interests so they'll be motivated, employees must have the competence and knowledge to make a useful contribution, and there must be trust and confidence between all parties involved.[37]

Dozens of studies have been conducted on the participation–performance relationship. The findings, however, are mixed.[38] When the research is reviewed carefully, it appears that participation typically has only a modest influence on variables such as employee productivity, motivation, and job satisfaction. Of course, that doesn't mean that the use of participative management can't be beneficial under the right conditions. What it says, however, is that the use of participation is not a sure means for improving employee performance.

Representative Participation   Almost every country in Western Europe has some type of legislation requiring companies to practice **representative participation**. That is, rather than participating directly in decisions, workers are represented by a small group of employees who actually participate. Representative participation has been called "the most widely legislated form of employee involvement around the world."[39] The goal of representative participation is to redistribute power within an organization, putting labor on a more equal footing with the interests of management and stockholders.

The two most common forms which representative participation takes are works councils and board representatives.[40] Works councils are groups of nominated or elected employees who must be consulted when management makes decisions involving personnel. Board representatives are employees who sit on a company's board of directors and represent the interests of the firm's employees.

The overall influence of representative participation on working employees seems to be minimal.[41] For instance, the evidence suggests that works councils are dominated by management and have little impact on employees or the organization. And although this form of employee involvement might increase the motivation and satisfaction of the individuals who are doing the representing, there is little evidence that this trickles down to the operating employees whom they represent. Overall, "the greatest value of representative participation is symbolic. If one is interested in changing employee attitudes or in improving organizational performance, representative participation would be a poor choice."[42]

Quality Circles   **Quality circles** became popular in North America and Europe during the 1980s.[43] Companies such as Hewlett-Packard, General Electric, Xerox, Procter & Gamble, IBM, Motorola, and American Airlines used quality circles. Quality circles are defined as a work group of 8 to 10 employees and supervisors who have a shared area of responsibility and who

Wegmans grocery stores involve their employees in making decisions that affect their work and please their customers. For example, Wegmans bakery employee Maria Benjamin, shown here, persuaded the company president to sell her chocolate meatball cookies from a recipe passed down from Italian ancestors. Wegmans encourages employees to make on-the-spot decisions without consulting their immediate supervisors. That could include an employee's decision to cook customers' Thanksgiving turkeys because the ones they bought were too big for their home ovens.

meet regularly—typically once a week, on company time and on company premises—to discuss their quality problems, investigate causes of the problems, recommend solutions, and take corrective actions.

A review of the evidence on quality circles indicates that they tend to show little or no effect on employee satisfaction, and although many studies report positive results from quality circles on productivity, these results are by no means guaranteed.[44] The failure of many quality circle programs to produce measurable benefits has also led to a large number of them being discontinued. One of the reasons for their failure is that managers deal with employee involvement in only a limited way. "At most, these programs operate for one hour per week, with the remaining 39 hours unchanged. Why should changes in 2.5 percent of a person's job have a major impact?"[45] Basically, quality circles were an easy way for management to get on the employee involvement bandwagon without really involving employees.

Linking Employee Involvement Programs and Motivation Theories

Employee involvement draws on a number of the motivation theories discussed in the previous chapter. For instance, Theory Y is consistent with participative management, while Theory X aligns with the more traditional autocratic style of managing people. In terms of two-factor theory, employee involvement programs could provide employees with intrinsic motivation by increasing opportunities for growth, responsibility, and involvement in the work itself. Similarly, the opportunity to make and implement decisions, and then seeing them work out, can help satisfy an employee's needs for responsibility, achievement, recognition, growth, and enhanced self-esteem. So employee involvement is compatible with ERG theory and efforts to stimulate the achievement need. And extensive employee involvement programs clearly have the potential to increase employee intrinsic motivation in work tasks.

Rewarding Employees

In deciding what to pay employees, and how to pay them, management must make some strategic decisions. Will the organization lead, match, or lag the market in pay? How will individual contributions be recognized? In this section, we consider four major strategic rewards decisions that need to be made: (1) what to pay employees (which is decided by establishing a pay structure); (2) how to pay individual employees (which is decided through variable pay plans and skill-based pay plans); (3) what benefits to offer, especially whether to offer employees choice in benefits (flexible benefits); and (4) how to construct employee recognition programs.

What to Pay: Establishing a Pay Structure

There are many ways to pay employees. The process of initially setting pay levels can be rather complex and entails balancing *internal equity*—the worth of the job to the organization (usually established through a technical process called

---

participative management   *A process in which subordinates share a significant degree of decision-making power with their immediate superiors.*

representative participation   *Workers participate in organizational decision making through a small group of representative employees.*

quality circle   *A work group of employees who meet regularly to discuss their quality problems, investigate causes, recommend solutions, and take corrective actions.*

job evaluation)—and *external equity*—the external competitiveness of an organization's pay relative to pay elsewhere in its industry (usually established through pay surveys). Obviously, the best pay system pays the job what it is worth (internal equity) while also paying competitively relative to the labor market.

But some organizations prefer to be pay leaders by paying above the market, while some may lag the market because they can't afford to pay market rates, or they are willing to bear the costs of paying below market (namely, higher turnover as people are lured to better-paying jobs). Wal-Mart, for example, pays less than its competitors and often outsources jobs overseas. Chinese workers in Shenzhen earn $120 a month (that's $1,440 per year) to make stereos for Wal-Mart. Of the 6,000 factories that are worldwide suppliers to Wal-Mart, 80 percent are located in China. In fact, one-eighth of all Chinese exports to the United States go to Wal-Mart.[46]

Pay more, and you may get better qualified, more highly motivated employees who will stay with the organization longer. But pay is often the highest single operating cost for an organization, which means that paying too much can make the organization's products or services too expensive. It's a strategic decision an organization must make, with clear trade-offs.

How to Pay: Rewarding Individual Employees Through Variable-Pay Programs

"Why should I put any extra effort into this job?" asked Anne Garcia, a fourth-grade elementary schoolteacher in Denver, Colorado. "I can excel or I can do the bare minimum. It makes no difference. I get paid the same. Why do anything above the minimum to get by?"

Comments similar to Anne's have been voiced by schoolteachers for decades because pay increases were tied to seniority. Recently, however, a number of schools have begun revamping their compensation systems to motivate people like Anne to strive for excellence in their jobs. For instance, Arizona, Florida, Iowa, and Kentucky have introduced state programs that tie teacher pay to the performance of the students in their classrooms.[47] In California, some teachers are now eligible for performance bonuses as high as $25,000 a year.[48]

A number of organizations—business firms as well as school districts and other government agencies—are moving away from paying people based solely on credentials or length of service and toward using variable-pay programs. Piece-rate plans, merit-based pay, bonuses, profit-sharing, gainsharing, and employee stock ownership plans are all forms of **variable-pay programs**. Instead of paying a person only for time on the job or seniority, a variable-pay program bases a portion of an employee's pay on some individual and/or organizational measure of performance. Earnings therefore fluctuate up and down with the measure of performance.[49] Variable-pay plans have long been used for compensating salespeople and executives. Recently they have begun to be applied to all employees. IBM, Wal-Mart, Pizza Hut, Cigna Corp., and John Deere are just a few examples of companies using variable pay with rank-and-file employees.[50] Today, more than 70 percent of U.S. companies have some form of variable-pay plan, up from only about 5 percent in 1970.[51] Unfortunately, recent survey data indicate that most employees still don't see a strong connection between pay and performance. Only 29 percent say that when they do a good job, their performance is rewarded.[52]

It is precisely the fluctuation in variable pay that has made these programs attractive to management. It turns part of an organization's fixed labor costs into a variable cost, thus reducing expenses when performance declines. So when the U.S. economy encountered a recession in 2001, companies with variable pay were able to reduce their labor costs much faster than companies that had maintained

Minnesota high school English teacher Chris Sandy participates in an experiment of motivating teachers to strive for excellence by paying teachers based on their performance rather than on their seniority. This move toward rewarding teachers for their individual performance in the classroom follows the adoption of variable-pay plans in many businesses and government agencies.

non-performance-based compensation systems.[53] In addition, when pay is tied to performance, the employee's earnings recognize contribution rather than being a form of entitlement. Low performers find, over time, that their pay stagnates, while high performers enjoy pay increases commensurate with their contribution.

Let's examine the different types of variable-pay programs in more detail.

Piece-Rate Pay   Piece-rate wages have been popular for more than a century as a means of compensating production workers. In **piece-rate pay plans** workers are paid a fixed sum for each unit of production completed. When an employee gets no base salary and is paid only for what he or she produces, this is a pure piece-rate plan. People who work in ballparks selling peanuts and soda pop frequently are paid this way. If they sell only 40 bags, their take is only $40. The harder they work and the more peanuts they sell, the more they earn. Many organizations use a modified piece-rate plan, in which employees earn a base hourly wage plus a piece-rate differential. So a medical transcriber might be paid $7 an hour plus 20 cents per page. Such modified plans provide a floor under an employee's earnings while still offering a productivity incentive.

Merit-Based Pay   Merit-based pay plans also pay for individual performance. However, unlike piece-rate plans, which pay based on objective output, **merit-based pay plans** are based on performance appraisal ratings. A main advantage of merit pay plans is that they allow employers to differentiate pay based on performance, so that those people thought to be high performers are given bigger raises. The plans can be motivating because, if they are designed correctly, individuals perceive a strong relationship between their performance and the rewards they receive. The evidence supports the importance of this linkage.[54]

Moreover, unlike organization-based compensation (such as profit-sharing and gainsharing plans which we will discuss), merit pay plans pay for individual performance, which presumably is more directly under the individual's control. Thus, because most individuals desire control over their pay, employees tend to like merit pay plans. Finally, merit pay plans allow organizations to compensate for external factors that may have reduced objective performance measures due to no fault of the employee (such as, sales being down nationwide).

Most large organizations have merit pay plans, especially for salaried employees. IBM's merit pay plan, for example, provides increases to employees' base salary based on their annual performance evaluation. Since the 1990s, when the economy stumbled badly, an increasing number of Japanese companies have abandoned seniority-based pay in favor of merit-based pay. Koichi Yanashita, of Takeda Chemical Industries, commented, "The merit-based salary system is an important means to achieve goals set by the company's top management, not just a way to change wages."[55]

Despite the intuitive appeal of pay for performance, merit pay plans have several limitations. One of them is that, typically, such plans are based on an annual performance appraisal. Thus, the merit pay is as valid or invalid as the performance ratings on which it is based. Another limitation of merit pay is that sometimes the pay raise pool fluctuates based on economic conditions or other factors that have little to do with an individual employee's performance. A colleague at a top university who performed very well in teaching and research was

variable-pay program   *A pay plan that bases a portion of an employee's pay on some individual and/or organizational measure of performance.*

piece-rate pay plan   *A pay plan in which workers are paid a fixed sum for each unit of production completed.*

merit-based pay plan   *A pay plan based on performance appraisal ratings.*

given a pay raise of $300 one year. Why? Because the pay raise pool was very small. Yet that is hardly pay-for-performance.

Finally, unions typically resist merit pay plans. The vast majority of primary and secondary schoolteachers are paid on seniority rather than performance. Recently, California Governor Arnold Schwarzenegger proposed "that teacher pay be tied to merit, not tenure, and I propose that teacher employment be tied to performance, not to just showing up." This proposal drew a swift reaction. Terry Pesta, president of the San Diego teacher's union, commented, "It's a crazy idea . . . just another blast at teachers."[56]

Bonuses   Annual bonuses in the tens of millions of dollars are not uncommon in U.S. corporations. Apple Computer's CEO Steve Jobs, for example, received a $90 million bonus in 2002 for his success in reenergizing the company.[57] Increasingly, bonus plans are casting a larger net within organizations to include lower-ranking employees.[58] Many companies now routinely reward production employees with bonuses in the thousands of dollars when company profits improve. One advantage of bonuses over merit pay is that **bonuses** reward employees for recent performance rather than historical performance.

Profit-Sharing Plans   **Profit-sharing plans** are organizationwide programs that distribute compensation based on some established formula designed around a company's profitability. These can be direct cash outlays or, particularly in the case of top managers, allocations of stock options. When you read about executives like Reuben Mark, the CEO at Colgate-Palmolive, earning $148 million in one year, almost all this comes from cashing in stock options previously granted based on company profit performance.

Gainsharing   A variable-pay program that has gotten a great deal of attention in recent years is **gainsharing**.[59] This is a formula-based group incentive plan. Improvements in group productivity—from one period to another—determine the total amount of money that is to be allocated. The division of productivity savings can be split between the company and employees in any number of ways, but 50–50 is typical. Gainsharing's popularity seems to be narrowly

Both profit-sharing and gainsharing are part of the incentive programs for team members at Whole Foods Market, a chain specializing in natural and organic food. The profit-sharing plan adds another 6 percent to employee wages. The gainsharing plan rewards work teams that help reduce costs by sharing the savings with team members. With these plans, Whole Foods' employees benefit from the success of their company and from their teamwork efforts.

focused among large manufacturing companies such as American Safety Razor, Champion Spark Plug, Cincinnati Milacron, Hooker Chemical, and Mead Paper. For instance, approximately 45 percent of *Fortune* 1000 firms have implemented gainsharing plans.[60]

How is gainsharing different from profit sharing? By focusing on productivity gains rather than on profits, gainsharing rewards specific behaviors that are less influenced by external factors. Employees in a gainsharing plan can receive incentive awards even when the organization isn't profitable.

Employee Stock Ownership Plans   Employee stock ownership plans **(ESOPs)** can mean any number of things, from employees owning some stock in the company at which they work to their owning and personally operating the firm. Employee stock ownership plans are company-established benefit plans in which employees acquire stock, often at below-market prices, as part of their benefits. Companies as varied as Publix Supermarkets, Graybar Electric, and W.L. Gore & Associates are now over 50 percent employee-owned.[61] But most of the 10,000 or so ESOPs in the United States are in small, privately held companies.[62]

In the typical ESOP, an employee stock ownership trust is created. Companies contribute either stock or cash to buy stock for the trust and allocate the stock to employees. Employees usually cannot take physical possession of their shares or sell them as long as they're still employed at the company. The research on ESOPs indicates that they increase employee satisfaction.[63] But their impact on performance is less clear. For instance, one study compared 45 ESOPs against 238 conventional companies.[64] The ESOPs outperformed the conventional firms both in terms of employment and sales growth. Another study found that ESOPs had total shareholder returns that averaged 6.9 percentage points higher over the four years after the ESOP was set up than market returns of similar companies without an ESOP.[65] But other studies have shown disappointing results.[66]

ESOPs have the potential to increase employee job satisfaction and work motivation. But for this potential to be realized, employees need to psychologically experience ownership.[67] That is, in addition to merely having a financial stake in the company, employees need to be kept regularly informed of the status of the business and also have the opportunity to exercise influence over it. The evidence consistently indicates that it takes ownership and a participative style of management to achieve significant improvements in an organization's performance.[68]

Do variable-pay programs increase motivation and productivity? The answer is a qualified "Yes." For example, studies generally support the idea that organizations with profit-sharing plans have higher levels of profitability than those without them.[69] Similarly, gainsharing has been found to improve productivity in a majority of cases and often has a positive impact on employee attitudes.[70] The downside of variable pay, from an employee's perspective, is its unpredictability. With a straight base salary, employees know what they'll be earning. They can finance cars and homes based on reasonably solid assumptions. That's more difficult to do with

---

bonus   *Pay program that rewards employees for recent performance rather than historical performance.*

profit-sharing plan   *An organizationwide program that distributes compensation based on some established formula designed around a company's profitability.*

gainsharing   *A formula-based group incentive plan.*

employee stock ownership plan (ESOP)   *Company-established benefit plans in which employees acquire stock, often at below-market prices, as part of their benefits.*

The Rise and Fall of Stock Options

The 1990s saw stock options become the favored way to reward executives. But the heyday of stock options appears to be over.

Stock options give employees the right, but not the obligation, to purchase a company's stock shares at a specified price. When a stock is rising rapidly, stock options can be a powerful motivator. For instance, in the 1990s, technology companies like Cisco, Sun, and Microsoft relied heavily on the issuance of stock options to hire and to build loyalty among employees and executives. Microsoft could hire the brightest programmers for only $40,000 or $50,000 a year because their real compensation would come from stock options. In 2000, for instance, Microsoft employees *averaged* an incredible $416,353 in stock-based compensation!

At their peak, stock options weren't handed out by all companies nor to all employees. They were most popular among small, start-up companies, which relied on options to encourage talented people to incur the risk of joining a new firm. In spite of all the attention directed at stock options, a limited number of employees actually got them. About 2 percent of the workforce at publicly traded companies held stock options in 1992. In 2003, that figure was up to only 15 percent. And these numbers hide the fact that the vast majority of stock options, among the 1,500 largest U.S. companies, were issued to just the top five executive officers.

Stock options can be powerful motivators to executives. The problem is they can also encourage the wrong behavior. Consistent with reinforcement theory, options encourage executives to focus on increasing the stock price—in the short term—rather than building the business for the long term. And executives are motivated to

do whatever is necessary to increase their stock price, even if it means fabricating revenues, hiding expenses, and engaging in similar manipulative accounting practices. The eventual collapses of Enron, Global Crossing, and WorldCom were largely due to executives misrepresenting financial data in order to enrich themselves by cashing in large stock-option grants.

The use of stock options as compensation is declining. The biggest impact of the decline is likely to be felt among middle managers. But senior executives will probably continue to receive the bulk of their compensation through stock-option grants. And start-up companies are likely to continue to rely on stock options as a major incentive to attract and keep employees. Microsoft's recent decision to eliminate stock options and pay its 54,000 employees with actual stock that can be gradually sold off over a 5-year period may encourage other firms to compensate workers with real stock rather than options.

Based on R. Buckman and D. Bank, "For Silicon Valley, Stocks' Fall Upsets Culture of Options," *The Wall Street Journal*, July 18, 2002, p. A1; A. Bernstein, "Options: Middle Managers Will Take the Hit," *Business Week*, December 9, 2002, p. 120; P. Elias, "Start-Ups Still Favor Stock Options," *Seattle Post-Intelligencer*, July 10, 2003, p. C6; and J. Greene, "Will Stock Options Lose Their Sex Appeal?" *Business Week*, July 21, 2003, pp. 23-35.

variable pay. Your group's performance might slip this year or a recession might undermine your company's profits. Depending on how your variable pay is determined, these can cut your income. Moreover, people begin to take repeated annual performance bonuses for granted. A 15 or 20 percent bonus, received 3 years in a row, begins to become expected in the fourth year. If it doesn't materialize, management will find itself with some disgruntled employees on its hands.

How to Pay: Rewarding Individual Employees Through Skill-Based Pay Plans

Organizations hire people for their skills, then typically put them in jobs and pay them based on their job title or rank. But if organizations hire people because of their competencies, why don't they pay them for those same competencies? Some organizations do.[71] For instance, employees at American Steel & Wire can boost their annual salaries by up to $12,480 by acquiring as many as 10 new skills. Frito-Lay Corporation ties its compensation for front-line operations managers to developing their skills in leadership, workforce development, and functional excellence. **Skill-based pay** is an alternative to job-based pay. Rather than having an individual's job title define his or her pay category, skill-based pay (also called *competency-based* or *knowledge-based pay*) sets pay levels on the basis of how many skills employees have or how many jobs they can do.[72]

What's the appeal of skill-based pay plans? From management's perspective: flexibility. Filling staffing needs is easier when employee skills are interchange-

At its Minneapolis plant, Turck Manufacturing needs highly skilled employees to satisfy an increased global demand for the firm's sensor products. Turck started a training program for production workers so they can learn more complicated tasks. During weekly training classes, Turck encourages employees to acquire new skills such as reading engineers' blueprints and soldering, shown here. A skill-based pay plan compensates employees who learn new skills. For example, learning new skills may move employees from Assembler 1 to Assembler 2 and increase their pay up to 50 percent.

able. This is particularly true today, as many organizations cut the size of their workforce. Downsized organizations require more generalists and fewer specialists. Skill-based pay also facilitates communication across the organization because people gain a better understanding of each others' jobs. Where skill-based pay exists, you're less likely to hear the phrase "It's not my job!" In addition, skill-based pay helps meet the needs of ambitious employees who confront minimal advancement opportunities. These people can increase their earnings and knowledge without a promotion in job title.

What about the downside of skill-based pay? People can "top out"—learning all the skills the program calls for them to learn. This can frustrate employees after they've become challenged by an environment of learning, growth, and continual pay raises. And skills can become obsolete. When this happens, what should management do? Cut employee pay or continue to pay for skills that are no longer relevant? There is also the problem created by paying people for acquiring skills for which there may be no immediate need. This happened at IDS Financial Services.[73] The company found itself paying people more money even though there was little immediate use for their new skills. IDS eventually dropped its skill-based pay plan and replaced it with one that equally balances individual contribution and gains in work-team productivity. Finally, skill-based plans don't address the level of performance. They deal only with the issue of whether or not someone can perform the skill.

Linking Skill-Based Pay Plans to Motivation Theories

Skill-based pay plans are consistent with several motivation theories. Because they encourage employees to learn, expand their skills, and grow, they are consistent with ERG theory. Among employees whose lower-order needs are substantially satisfied, the opportunity to experience growth can be a motivator.

Paying people to expand their skill levels is also consistent with research on the achievement need. High achievers have a compelling drive to do things better or more efficiently. By learning new skills or improving the skills they already hold, high achievers will find their jobs more challenging.

There is also a link between reinforcement theory and skill-based pay. Skill-based pay encourages employees to develop their flexibility, to continue to learn, to cross-train, to be generalists rather than specialists, and to work cooperatively with others in the organization. To the degree that management wants employees to demonstrate such behaviors, skill-based pay should act as a reinforcer.

In addition, skill-based pay may have equity implications. When employees make their input-outcome comparisons, skills may provide a fairer input criterion for determining pay than factors such as seniority or education. To the degree that employees perceive skills as the critical variable in job performance, the use of skill-based pay may increase the perception of equity and help optimize employee motivation.

Skill-Based Pay in Practice

A number of studies have investigated the use and effectiveness of skill-based pay. The overall conclusion, based on these studies, is that skill-based pay is expanding and that it generally leads to higher employee performance, satisfaction, and perceptions of fairness in pay systems.[74]

skill-based pay   *A pay plan that sets pay levels on the basis of how many skills employees have or how many jobs they can do.*

Research has also identified some interesting trends. The increased use of skills as a basis for pay appears particularly strong among organizations facing aggressive global competition and companies with shorter product life cycles and speed-to-market concerns.[75] Also, skill-based pay is moving from the shop floor to the white-collar workforce, and sometimes as far as the executive suite.[76]

Skilled-based pay appears to be an idea whose time has come. As one expert noted, "Slowly, but surely, we're becoming a skill-based society where your market value is tied to what you can do and what your skill set is. In this new world where skills and knowledge are what really counts, it doesn't make sense to treat people as jobholders. It makes sense to treat them as people with specific skills and to pay them for those skills."[77]

Flexible Benefits: Developing a Benefits Package

Todd Evans and Allison Murphy both work for Citigroup, but they have very different needs in terms of employee benefits. Todd is married and has three young children and a wife who is at home full time. Allison, too, is married, but her husband has a high-paying job with the federal government, and they have no children. Todd is concerned about having a good medical plan and enough life insurance to support his family if he weren't around. In contrast, Allison's husband already has her medical needs covered on his plan, and life insurance is a low priority for both her and her husband. Allison is more interested in extra vacation time and long-term financial benefits such as a tax-deferred savings plan.

A standardized benefit package for all employees at Citigroup would be unlikely to satisfactorily meet the needs of both Todd and Allison. Citigroup could, however, cover both sets of needs if it offered flexible benefits.

Flexible benefits allow each employee to put together a benefit package individually tailored to his or her own needs and situation. It replaces the traditional "one-benefit-plan-fits-all" programs that dominated organizations for more than 50 years.[78] Consistent with expectancy theory's thesis that organizational rewards should be linked to each individual employee's goals, flexible benefits individualize rewards by allowing each employee to choose the compensation package that best satisfies his or her current needs. The average organization provides fringe benefits worth approximately 40 percent of an employee's salary. Traditional benefit programs were designed for the typical employee of the 1950s—a male with a wife and two children at home. Less than 10 percent of employees now fit this stereotype. About 25 percent of today's employees are single, and a third are part of two-income families with no children. Traditional programs don't meet their diverse needs, but flexible benefits do. They can be uniquely tailored to accommodate differences in employee needs based on age, marital status, spouses' benefit status, number and age of dependents, and the like.

The three most popular types of benefit plans are modular plans, core-plus options, and flexible spending accounts.[79] *Modular plans* are predesigned packages of benefits, with each module put together to meet the needs of a specific group of employees. So a module designed for single employees with no dependents might include only essential benefits. Another, designed for single parents, might have additional life insurance, disability insurance, and expanded health coverage. *Core-plus plans* consist of a core of essential benefits and a menulike selection of other benefit options from which employees can select and add to the core. Typically, each employee is given "benefit credits," which allow the "purchase" of additional benefits that uniquely meet his or her needs. *Flexible spending plans* allow employees to set aside up to the dollar amount offered in the plan to pay for particular services. It's a convenient way, for example, for employees to pay for health-care and dental premiums. Flexible spending accounts can increase employee take-home pay because employees don't have to pay taxes on the dollars they spend out of these accounts.

Today, almost all major corporations in the United States offer flexible benefits. And they're becoming the norm in other countries too. For instance, a recent survey of 136 Canadian organizations found that 93 percent have adopted or will adopt flexible benefits in the near term.[80] And a similar survey of 307 firms in the United Kingdom found that while only 16 percent have flexible benefit programs in place, another 60 percent are either in the process of implementing them or are seriously considering it.[81]

Intrinsic Rewards: Employee Recognition Programs

Laura Schendell makes only $8.50 an hour working at her fast-food job in Pensacola, Florida, and the job isn't very challenging or interesting. Yet Laura talks enthusiastically about her job, her boss, and the company that employs her. "What I like is the fact that Guy [her supervisor] appreciates the effort I make. He compliments me regularly in front of the other people on my shift, and I've been chosen "Employee of the Month" twice in the past six months. Did you see my picture on that plaque on the wall?"

Organizations are increasingly recognizing what Laura Schendell knows: Important work rewards can be both intrinsic and extrinsic. Rewards are intrinsic in the form of employee recognition programs and extrinsic in the form of compensation systems. In this section, we deal with ways in which managers can reward and motivate employee performance.

Employee recognition programs range from a spontaneous and private "thank you" up to widely publicized formal programs where specific types of behavior are encouraged and the procedures for attaining recognition are clearly identified.[82]

Exhibit 7-4

Source: From *The Wall Street Journal*, October 21, 1997. Reprinted by permission of Cartoon Features Syndicate.

flexible benefits   *A benefits plan that allows each employee to put together a benefit package individually tailored to his or her own needs and situation.*

Nichols Foods Ltd., a British bottler of soft drinks and syrups, has a comprehensive recognition program.[83] The central hallway in its production area is lined with "bragging boards," where the accomplishments of various individuals and teams are regularly updated. Monthly awards are presented to people who have been nominated by peers for extraordinary effort on the job. And monthly award winners are eligible for further recognition at an annual off-site meeting for all employees. In contrast, most managers use a far more informal approach. Julia Stewart, president of Applebee's restaurants, frequently leaves sealed notes on the chairs of employees after everyone has gone home.[84] These notes explain how critical Stewart thinks the person's work is or how much she appreciates the completion of a recent project. Stewart also relies heavily on voice mail messages left after office hours to tell employees how appreciative she is for a job well done.

A few years ago, 1,500 employees were surveyed in a variety of work settings to find out what they considered to be the most powerful workplace motivator. Their response? Recognition, recognition, and more recognition.[85] As illustrated in Exhibit 7-5, Phoenix Inn, a west-coast chain of small hotels, encourages employees to smile by letting customers identify this desirable behavior and then recognizing those employees who are identified most often with rewards and publicity.

An obvious advantage of recognition programs is that they are inexpensive (praise, of course, is free!).[86] It shouldn't be surprising, therefore, to find that employee recognition programs have grown in popularity. A 2002 survey of 391 companies found that 84 percent had some program to recognize worker achievements and that 4 in 10 said they were doing more to foster employee recognition than they were just a year earlier.[87]

Exhibit 7-5

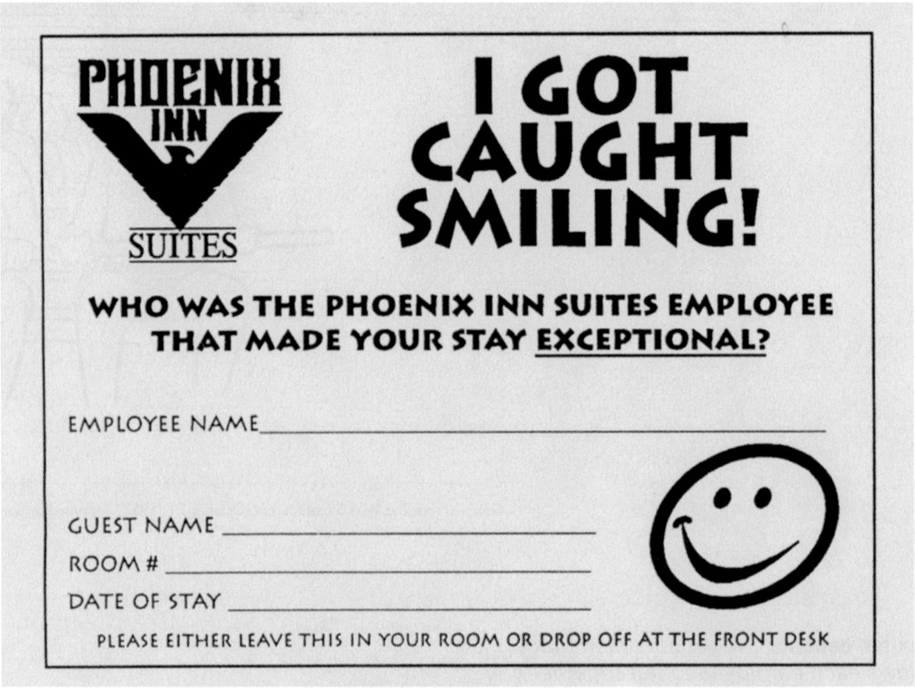

PHOENIX INN SUITES

I GOT CAUGHT SMILING!

WHO WAS THE PHOENIX INN SUITES EMPLOYEE THAT MADE YOUR STAY EXCEPTIONAL?

EMPLOYEE NAME_____

GUEST NAME _____
ROOM # _____
DATE OF STAY _____

PLEASE EITHER LEAVE THIS IN YOUR ROOM OR DROP OFF AT THE FRONT DESK

Cultural Differences in Job Characteristics and Job Satisfaction

HOW DO VARIOUS FACTORS OF ONE'S JOB CONtribute to satisfaction in different cultures? A recent study attempted to answer this question in a survey of over 49 countries. The authors of the study distinguished between intrinsic job characteristics (having a job that allows one to use one's skills, frequently receiving recognition from one's supervisor) and extrinsic job characteristics (receiving pay that is competitive within a given industry, working in an environment that has comfortable physical conditions) and assessed differences between the two in predicting employee job satisfaction.

The study found that, across all countries, extrinsic job characteristics were consistently and positively related to satisfaction with one's job. However, countries differed in the extent to which intrinsic job characteristics predicted job satisfaction. Richer countries, countries with stronger social security, countries that stress individualism rather than collectivism, and countries with a smaller power distance (those that value a more equal distribution of power in organizations and institutions) showed a stronger relationship between the presence of intrinsic job characteristics and job satisfaction.

What explains these findings? One explanation is that in countries with greater wealth and social security, concerns over survival are taken for granted, and thus employees have the freedom to place greater importance on intrinsic aspects of the job. Another explanation is that cultural norms emphasizing the individual and less power asymmetry socialize individuals to focus on the intrinsic aspects of their job. In other words, such norms tell individuals that it is okay to want jobs that are intrinsically rewarding.

Based on X. Huang and E. Van De Vliert, "Where Intrinsic Job Satisfaction Fails to Work: National Moderators of Intrinsic Motivation," *Journal of Organizational Behavior*, 2003, pp. 159–179.

Despite the increased popularity, critics argue that employee recognition programs are highly susceptible to political manipulation by management.[88] When applied to jobs where performance factors are relatively objective like sales, recognition programs are likely to be perceived by employees as fair. However, in most jobs, the criteria for good performance aren't self-evident, which allows managers to manipulate the system and recognize their favorite employees. When abused, this can undermine the value of recognition programs and lead to demoralizing employees.

Summary and Implications for Managers

We've presented a number of motivation theories and applications in this and the previous chapter. Although it's always dangerous to synthesize a large number of complex ideas into a few simple guidelines, the following suggestions summarize the essence of what we know about motivating employees in organizations.

Recognize Individual Differences   Managers should be sensitive to individual differences. For example, employees from Asian cultures prefer not to be singled out as special because it makes them uncomfortable.

Employees have different needs. Don't treat them all alike. Moreover, spend the time necessary to understand what's important to each employee. This will allow you to individualize goals, level of involvement, and rewards to align with individual needs. Also, design jobs to align with individual needs and therefore maximize the motivation potential in jobs.

Use Goals and Feedback   Employees should have hard, specific goals, as well as feedback on how well they are faring in pursuit of those goals.

Allow Employees to Participate in Decisions That Affect Them
Employees can contribute to a number of decisions that affect them: setting work goals, choosing their own benefits packages, solving productivity and quality problems, and the like. This can increase employee productivity, commitment to work goals, motivation, and job satisfaction.

Link Rewards to Performance   Rewards should be contingent on performance. Importantly, employees must perceive a clear linkage. Regardless of how closely rewards are actually correlated to performance criteria, if individuals perceive this relationship to be low, the results will be low performance, a decrease in job satisfaction, and an increase in turnover and absenteeism.

Check the System for Equity   Rewards should also be perceived by employees as equating with the inputs they bring to the job. At a simplistic level, this should mean that experience, skills, abilities, effort, and other obvious inputs should explain differences in performance and, hence, pay, job assignments, and other obvious rewards.

Point ◄► Counterpoint

Professional Employees Are More Difficult to Motivate

Professional employees are different from your average employee. And they're more difficult to motivate. Why? Because professionals don't respond to the same stimuli that nonprofessionals do. Professionals like engineers, accountants, lawyers, nurses, and software designers are different from nonprofessionals. They have a strong and long-term commitment to their field of expertise. Their loyalty is more often to their profession than to their employer. And typical rewards, like money and promotions, are rarely effective in encouraging professionals to exert high levels of effort.

Professionals see their allegiance to their profession, not to the organization that employs them. A nurse, for instance, may work for Mercy Hospital but she reads nursing journals, belongs to nursing associations, attends nursing conferences, and hangs around with other nurses during her breaks at work. When asked what she does for a living, she's more apt to respond, "I'm a registered nurse" than "I work at Mercy Hospital."

Money and promotions are typically low on the professional's priority list. Why? Because they tend to be well paid already and they enjoy what they do. For instance, professionals are not typically anxious to give up their work to take on managerial responsibilities. They've invested a great deal of time and effort in developing their professional skills. They've typically gone to professional schools for several years and undergone specialized training to build their proficiencies. They also invest regularly—in terms of reading, taking courses, attending conferences, and the like—to keep their skills current. Moving into management often means cutting off their ties to their profession, losing touch with the latest advances in their field, and having to let the skills that they've spent years developing become obsolete.

This loyalty to the profession and less interest in typical organizational rewards makes motivating professionals more challenging and complex. They don't respond to traditional rewards. And because they tend to give their primary allegiance to their profession rather than to their employer, they're more likely to quit if they're dissatisfied. As an employer, you might be justified in deciding not to exert the effort to develop and keep professionals because they're unlikely to reciprocate loyalty efforts you make.

Let's first address the question of whether professionals with advanced degrees are really that different from nonprofessionals. One of the differences often cited regarding professionals is their allegiance to their profession. But this isn't unique to the so-called degreed professionals. For instance, plumbers, electricians, and similar tradespeople aren't considered professionals but they typically see themselves as affiliated to their trade or union rather than their employer. Similarly, many autoworkers at Ford and GM give their primary allegiance to the United Auto Workers union.

Even if you accept that professionals are different from nonprofessionals, these differences may make it easier to motivate professionals rather than harder. For a large proportion of professionals, their work is their life. They rarely define their workweek in terms of 8 to 5 and five days a week. Working 60 hours a week or more is often common. They love what they do and often prefer to be working rather than doing anything else. So as long as they enjoy their work, they're likely to be self-motivated.

What factors are likely to determine if they enjoy their work? Job challenge tends to be ranked high. They like to tackle problems and find solutions. They prefer jobs that score high on the job characteristics model; that is, they want jobs that provide variety, identity, significance, autonomy, and feedback. Professionals also value support, recognition, and opportunities to improve and expand their professional expertise.

So how do you motivate professionals? Provide them with ongoing challenging projects. Give them autonomy to follow their interests and allow them to structure their work in ways that they find productive. Provide them with lateral moves that allow them to broaden their experience. Reward them with educational opportunities—training, workshops, attending conferences—that allow them to keep current in their field. In addition, reward them with recognition. And consider creating alternative career paths that allow them to earn more money and status without assuming managerial responsibilities. At Merck, IBM, and AT&T, for instance, the best scientists, engineers, and researchers gain titles such as fellow and senior scientist. They carry pay and prestige comparable to those of managers but without the corresponding authority or responsibility.

Questions for Review

1. What are the advantages of flextime from an employee's perspective? From management's perspective?

2. What are the advantages of job sharing from an employee's perspective? From management's perspective?

3. Explain the formula: Performance = f (A × M × O) and give an example.

4. Explain the roles of employees and management in quality circles.

5. What is gainsharing? What explains its recent popularity?

6. What is an ESOP? How might it positively influence employee motivation?

7. What are the pluses of variable-pay programs from an employee's viewpoint? From management's viewpoint?

8. Contrast job-based and skill-based pay.

9. What role, if any, does money play in employee recognition, job redesign, and skill-based pay?

10. What can you do, as a manager, to increase the likelihood that your employees will exert a high level of effort?

Questions for Critical Thinking

1. Identify five different criteria by which organizations can compensate employees. Based on your knowledge and experience, do you think performance is the criterion most used in practice? Discuss.

2. "Recognition may be motivational for the moment but it doesn't have any staying power. It's an empty reinforcer. Why? Because when you go to the grocery store, they don't take recognition as a form of payment!" Do you agree or disagree? Discuss.

3. "Performance can't be measured, so any effort to link pay with performance is a fantasy. Differences in performance are often caused by the system, which means the organization ends up rewarding the circumstances.

It's the same thing as rewarding the weather forecaster for a pleasant day." Do you agree or disagree with this statement? Support your position.

4. It's an indisputable fact that there has been an explosive increase in the difference between the average U.S. worker's income and those of senior executives. In 1980 the average CEO made 42 times the average blue-collar worker's pay. In 1990 it was 85 times. In 2000 it had risen to 531 times. What are the implications of this trend for motivation in organizations?

5. This book argues for recognizing individual differences. It also suggests paying attention to members of diversity groups. Is this contradictory? Discuss.

Team Exercise

ASSESSING EMPLOYEE MOTIVATION AND SATISFACTION USING THE JOB CHARACTERISTICS MODEL

Purpose
To examine outcomes of the Job Characteristics Model for different professions.

Time
Approximately 30–45 minutes.

Background
Data were collected on 6,930 employees in 56 different organizations in the United States using the Job Diagnostic Survey. The following table contains data on

the five core job dimensions of the Job Characteristics Model for several professions. Also included are growth needs strength, internal motivation, and pay satisfaction for each profession. The values are averages based on a 7-point scale.

Job Characteristics Averages for Six Professions

Profession

Variable	Professional/ Technical	Managerial	Sales	Service	Clerical	Machine Trades
Skill Variety	5.4	5.6	4.8	5.0	4.0	5.1
Task Identity	5.1	4.7	4.4	4.7	4.7	4.9
Task Significance	5.6	5.8	5.5	5.7	5.3	5.6
Autonomy	5.4	5.4	4.8	5.0	4.5	4.9
Feedback	5.1	5.2	5.4	5.1	4.6	4.9
Growth Needs Strength	5.6	5.3	5.7	5.4	5.0	4.8
Internal Motivation	5.8	5.8	5.7	5.7	5.4	5.6
Pay Satisfaction	4.4	4.6	4.2	4.1	4.0	4.2

Step 1
Break into groups of three to five.

Step 2
Calculate the MPS score for each of the professions and compare them. Discuss whether or not you think these scores accurately reflect your perceptions of the motivating potential of these professions.

Step 3
Graph the relationship between each profession's core job dimensions and its corresponding value for internal motivation and for pay satisfaction, using the core job dimensions as independent variables. What conclusions can you draw about motivation and satisfaction of employees in these professions?

Source of data: Hackman, J. R. & Oldham, G. R. (1980). *Work Redesign.* Reading, MA: Addison-Wesley.

Ethical Dilemma

ARE AMERICAN CEOS PAID TOO MUCH?

Critics have described the astronomical pay packages given to American CEO's as "rampant greed." They note, for instance, that between 1980 and 2002, average annual CEO pay has skyrocketed 442 percent, adjusting for inflation—from $1.4 million to $7.4 million. Meanwhile, during this same period, average worker pay inched up just 1.6 percent—from $30,344 to $30,722. To put this in perspective, if average worker pay had grown at the same pace as the CEOs, your typical American worker would be making $164,018 today!

High levels of executive compensation seem to be widely spread in the United States. Between 2000 and 2002, for instance, Larry Ellison of Oracle took home $781.4 million; Cendant's Henry Silverman was paid $184.5 million; and Cisco Systems CEO John Chambers earned $157.6 million. And don't assume that Oracle, Cendant, and Cisco's stock prices did well during this 3-year period. Shareholder return at these companies all actually declined 60 percent or more between 2000 and 2002! Twenty-five years ago, an executive who earned a million dollars a year made headlines. Now it's "routine" for a senior executive at a large U.S. corporation to earn more than $1 million in compensation—whether the company makes money or not and regardless of the company's stock performance.

How do you explain such astronomical pay? Some say this represents a classic economic response to a situation in which the demand is great for high-quality top executive talent and the supply is low. Ira Kay, a compensation consultant, says: "It's not fair to compare [executives] with hourly workers. Their market is the global market for executives." Other arguments in favor of paying executives $1 million a year or more are the need to compensate people for the responsibilities and stress that go with such jobs, the motivating potential that seven- and eight-figure annual incomes provide to senior executives and those who might aspire to be, the need to keep the best and the brightest in the corporate world rather than being enticed into investment banking or other high-paying fields, and the influence that senior executives have on a company's bottom line.

Contrary to the global argument, executive pay is considerably higher in the United States than in most other countries. U.S. CEOs are paid more than twice as much as Canadian CEOs, nearly three times as much as British CEOs, and four times as much as German CEOs. This difference is even greater when compared to what average workers make. American CEOs make 531 times the pay of their average hourly employees. In contrast, British CEOs made 25 times as much as their workers, Canadians 21 times as much, and Germans 11 times as much.

Critics of executive pay practices in the United States argue that CEOs choose board members whom they can count on to support ever-increasing pay (including lucrative bonus and stock-option plans) for top management. If board members fail to "play along," they risk losing their positions, their fees, and the prestige and power inherent in board membership.

Is high compensation of U.S. executives a problem? If so, does the blame for the problem lie with CEOs or with the shareholders and boards that knowingly allow the practice? Are American CEOs greedy? Are these CEOs acting unethically? What do you think?

Source: Pay data from H. Sklar, "CEO Pay Still Outrageous," (www.raisethefloor.org) (April 24, 2003); and G. Moregenson, "Explaining (or Not) Why the Boss Is Paid So Much," *New York Times*, January 25, 2004, p. 1BU.

Case Incident 1

WHEN THE PERKS FADE

Sean Neale is facing a dilemma. And he's not alone. Like many managers, Sean is struggling to find creative ways to keep his employees motivated.

Sean is CEO of a robotics' manufacturing firm located in the Midwestern United States. The company prospered in the 1990s—sales revenue nearly tripled and the company's workforce doubled. The price of the company's stock rose from under $8 a share to more than $60. And his employees prospered because the firm had a pay-for-performance compensation system. Specifically, every year, 20 percent of the company's profits were set aside in a bonus pool and used to reward employees. Profit sharing provided the typical employee with an extra $7,800 in 1998 and $9,400 in 1999. Then it dropped to just $2,750 in 2000. The company lost money in 2001 and 2002, so there were no profits to share. Meanwhile, Sean's executive team was not spared from watching their profit-sharing bonuses disappear. The average executive bonus in 1999 was over $150,000. Like the company's operating employees, in 2001 and 2002, executives got nothing over and above their basic salaries.

Sean's situation seems to be common among many firms. While employees in 2002 and 2003 were often glad to just have a job, the incentives they enjoyed in the 1990s were eroding. For instance, Ford Motor Company suspended contributions to salaried employees' 401(k) retirement plans and merit raises for about 2,200 senior executives; media company Tribune Co. in Chicago froze wages and cut 140 senior managers' pay by 5 percent; and Hewlett-Packard eliminated profit sharing in 2001. A 2002 survey of 391 companies found that 48 percent planned to lower performance-based rewards for both managers and workers in the next 12 months.

Questions

1. What implications can you draw from this case regarding pay-for-performance?

2. If you were Sean Neale, what can you offer employees as an alternative to compensation that will not place an undue hardship on your organization's bottom line? Be specific.

Source: This case is based on S. Jones, "When the Perks Fade," *The Wall Street Journal*, April 11, 2002, p. B12.

Case Incident 2

THANKS FOR NOTHING

Though it may seem fairly obvious that receiving praise and recognition from one's company is a motivating experience, sadly many companies are failing miserably when it comes to saying "thanks" to their employees. According to Curt Coffman, global practice leader at Gallup, 71 percent of U.S. workers are "disengaged," essentially meaning that they could care less about their organization. Coffman states, "We're operating at one-quarter of the capacity in terms of managing human capital. It's alarming." Employee recognition programs, which became more popular as the U.S. economy shifted from industrial to knowledge-based, can be an effective way to motivate employees and make them feel valued. In many cases, however, recognition programs are doing "more harm than good" according to Coffman.

Take Ko, a 50-year-old former employee of a dot-com in California. Her company proudly instituted a rewards program designed to motivate employees. What were the rewards for a job well-done? Employees would receive a badge which read "U Done Good" and, each year, would receive a T-shirt as a means of annual recognition. Once an employee received 10 "U Done Good" badges, he or she could trade them in for something bigger and better—a paperweight. Ko states that she would have preferred a raise. "It was patronizing. There wasn't any deep thought involved in any of this." To make matters worse, she says, the badges were handed out arbitrarily and were not tied to performance. And what about those T-shirts? Ko states that the company instilled a strict dress code, so employees couldn't even wear the shirts if they wanted to. Needless to say, the employee recognition program seemed like an empty gesture rather than a motivator.

Even programs that provide employees with more expensive rewards can backfire, especially if the rewards are given insincerely. Eric Lange, an employee of a trucking company, recalls the time when one of the company's vice presidents achieved a major financial goal for the company. The vice president, who worked in an office next to Lange, received a Cadillac Seville as his company car and a new Rolex wristwatch that cost the company

$10,000. Both were lavish gifts, but the way they were distributed left a sour taste in the vice president's mouth. He entered his office to find the Rolex in a cheap cardboard box sitting on his desk, along with a brief letter explaining that he would be receiving a 1099 tax form in order to pay taxes on the watch. Lange states of the vice president, "He came into my office, which was right next door, and said, 'Can you believe this?'" A mere 2 months later, the vice president pawned the watch. Lange explains, "It had absolutely no meaning for him."

Such experiences resonate with employees who may find more value in a sincere pat on the back than gifts from management that either are meaningless or aren't conveyed with respect or sincerity. However, sincere pats on the back may be hard to come by. Gallup's poll found that 61 percent of employees stated that they haven't received a sincere "thank you" from management in the past year. Findings such as these are troubling, as verbal rewards are not only inexpensive for companies to hand out but also are quick and easy to distribute. Of course, verbal rewards do need to be paired sometimes with tangible benefits that employees value—after all, money talks. In addition, when praising employees for a job well-done, managers need to ensure that the praise is given in conjunction with the specific accomplishment. In this way, employees may not only feel valued by their organization but will also know what actions to take to be rewarded in the future.

Questions

1. If praising employees for doing a good job seems to be a fairly easy and obvious motivational tool, why do you think companies and managers don't often do it?

2. As a manager, what steps would you take to motivate your employees after observing them perform well?

3. Are there any downsides to giving employees too much verbal praise? What might these downsides be and how could you alleviate them as a manager?

4. As a manager, how would you ensure that recognition given to employees is distributed fairly and justly?

Source: Based on J. Sandberg, "Been Here 25 Years and All I Got Was This Lousy T-Shirt," *The Wall Street Journal,* January 28, 2004, p. B.1.

Endnotes

1. Based on J. Stimpson, "Paying for Performance," The Practical Accountant, May 2003, pp. 32–34.

2. J. R. Hackman and G. R. Oldham, "Motivation through the Design of Work: Test of a Theory," *Organizational Behavior and Human Performance*, August 1976, pp. 250–79; and J. R. Hackman and G. R. Oldham, *Work Redesign* (Reading, MA: Addison-Wesley, 1980).

3. J. R. Hackman, "Work Design," in J. R. Hackman and J. L. Suttle (eds.), *Improving Life at Work* (Santa Monica, CA: Goodyear, 1977), p. 129.

4. See "Job Characteristics Theory of Work Redesign," in J. B. Miner, *Theories of Organizational Behavior* (Hinsdale, IL: Dryden Press, 1980), pp. 231–66; B. T. Loher, R. A. Noe, N. L. Moeller, and M. P. Fitzgerald, "A Meta-Analysis of the Relation of Job Characteristics to Job Satisfaction," *Journal of Applied Psychology*, May 1985, pp. 280–89; W. H. Glick, G. D. Jenkins, Jr., and N. Gupta, "Method versus Substance: How Strong Are Underlying Relationships between Job Characteristics and Attitudinal Outcomes?" *Academy of Management Journal*, September 1986, pp. 441–64; Y. Fried and G. R. Ferris, "The Validity of the Job Characteristics Model: A Review and Meta-Analysis," *Personnel Psychology*, Summer 1987, pp. 287–322; S. J. Zaccaro and E. F. Stone, "Incremental Validity of an Empirically Based Measure of Job Characteristics," *Journal of Applied Psychology*, May 1988, pp. 245–52; J. R. Rentsch and R. P. Steel, "Testing the Durability of Job Characteristics as Predictors of Absenteeism over a Six-Year Period," *Personnel Psychology*, Spring 1998, pp. 165–90; S. J. Behson, E. R. Eddy, and S. J. Lorenzet, "The Importance of the Critical Psychological States in the Job Characteristics Model: A Meta-Analytic and Structural Equations Modeling Examination," *Current Research in Social Psychology*, May 2000, pp. 170–89; and T. A. Judge, "Promote Job Satisfaction Through Mental Challenge," in E. A. Locke (ed.), *Handbook of Principles of Organizational Behavior*, pp. 75–89.

5. T. A. Judge, S. K. Parker, A. E. Colbert, D. Heller, and R. Ilies, "Job Satisfaction: A Cross-Cultural Review," In N. Anderson, D. S. Ones (eds.), *Handbook of Industrial, Work and Organizational Psychology*, vol. 2 (Thousand Oaks, CA: Sage Publications, 2002), pp. 25–52.

6. C. A. O'Reilly and D. F. Caldwell, "Informational Influence as a Determinant of Perceived Task Characteristics and Job Satisfaction," *Journal of Applied Psychology*, April 1979, pp. 157–65; R. V. Montagno, "The Effects of Comparison Others and Prior Experience on Responses to Task Design," *Academy of Management Journal*, June 1985, pp. 491–98; and P. C. Bottger and I. K.-H. Chew, "The Job Characteristics Model and Growth Satisfaction: Main Effects of Assimilation of Work Experience and Context Satisfaction," *Human Relations*, June 1986, pp. 575–94.

7. C. Ansberry, "In the New Workplace, Jobs Morph to Suit Rapid Pace of Change," *The Wall Street Journal*, March 22, 2002, p. A1.

8. J. Ortega, "Job Rotation as a Learning Mechanism," *Management Science*, October 2001, pp. 1361–70.

9. See, for instance, data on job enlargement described in M. A. Campion and C. L. McClelland, "Follow-up and Extension of the Interdisciplinary Costs and Benefits of Enlarged Jobs," *Journal of Applied Psychology*, June 1993, pp. 339–51.

10. J. R. Hackman, "Work Design," in J. R. Hackman and J. L. Suttle (eds.), Improving Life at Work (Santa Monica, CA: Goodyear, 1977), pp. 115–20.

11. J. P. Wanous, "Individual Differences and Reactions to Job Characteristics," *Journal of Applied Psychology*, October 1974, pp. 616–22; and H. P. Sims and A. D. Szilagyi, "Job Characteristic Relationships: Individual and Structural Moderators," *Organizational Behavior and Human Performance*, June 1976, pp. 211–30.

12. M. Fein, "The Real Needs and Goals of Blue-Collar Workers," The Conference Board Record, February 1972, pp. 26–33.

13. J. R. Hackman and G. R. Oldham, *Work Redesign* (Reading, MA: Addison Wesley, 1980).

14. Cited in *U.S. News & World Report*, May 31, 1993, p. 63.

15. See, for example, J. R. Hackman and G. R. Oldham, *Work Redesign*; J. B. Miner, *Theories of Organizational Behavior* (Hinsdale, IL: Dryden Press, 1980), pp. 231–66; R. W. Griffin, "Effects of Work Redesign on Employee Perceptions, Attitudes, and Behaviors: A Long-Term Investigation," *Academy of Management Journal* 34, no. 2 (1991), pp. 425–35; and J. L. Cotton, *Employee Involvement* (Newbury Park, CA: Sage, 1993), pp. 141–72.

16. From the National Study of the Changing Workforce cited in S. Shellenbarger, "Number of Women Managers Rise," *The Wall Street Journal*, September 30, 2003, p. D2.

17. Cited in "Flextime Gains in Popularity in Germany," *Manpower Argus*, September 2000, p. 4.

18. D. R. Dalton and D. J. Mesch, "The Impact of Flexible Scheduling on Employee Attendance and Turnover," *Administrative Science Quarterly*, June 1990, pp. 370–87; K. S. Kush and L. K. Stroh, "Flextime: Myth or Reality," *Business Horizons*, September–October 1994, p. 53; and L. Golden, "Flexible Work Schedules: What Are We Trading Off to Get Them?" *Monthly Labor Review*, March 2001, pp. 50–55.

19. See, for example, D. A. Ralston and M. F. Flanagan, "The Effect of Flextime on Absenteeism and Turnover for Male and Female Employees," *Journal of Vocational Behavior*, April 1985, pp. 206–17; D. A. Ralston, W. P. Anthony, and D. J. Gustafson, "Employees May Love Flextime, But What Does It Do to the Organization's Productivity?" *Journal of Applied Psychology*, May 1985, pp. 272–79; J. B. McGuire and J. R. Liro, "Flexible Work Schedules, Work Attitudes, and Perceptions of Productivity," *Public Personnel Management*, Spring 1986, pp. 65–73; P. Bernstein, "The Ultimate in Flextime: From Sweden, by Way of Volvo," *Personnel*, June 1988, pp. 70–74; and D. R. Dalton and D. J. Mesch, "The Impact of Flexible Scheduling on Employee Attendance and Turnover," *Administrative Science Quarterly*, June 1990, pp. 370–87; and B. B. Baltes, T. E. Briggs, J. W. Huff, J. A. Wright, and G. A. Neuman, "Flexible and Compressed Workweek Schedules: A Meta-Analysis of Their Effects on Work-Related Criteria," *Journal of Applied Psychology*, Vol. 84(4), 1999, pp. 496-513.

20. Cited in S. Caminiti, "Fair Shares," *Working Woman*, November 1999, pp. 52–54.

21. Cited in S. Caminiti, "Fair Shares," *Working Woman*, November 1999, p. 54.

22. S. Shellenbarger, "Two People, One Job: It Can Really Work," *The Wall Street Journal*, December 7, 1994, p. B1.

23. "Job-Sharing: Widely Offered, Little Used," *Training*, November 1994, p. 12.

24. C. Dawson, "Japan: Work-Sharing Will Prolong the Pain," *Business Week*, December 24, 2001, p. 46.

25. Shellenbarger, "Two People, One Job."

26. See, for example, T. H. Davenport and K. Pearlson, "Two Cheers for the Virtual Office," *Sloan Management Review*, Summer 1998, pp. 61–65; E. J. Hill, B. C. Miller, S. P. Weiner, and J. Colihan, "Influences of the Virtual Office on Aspects of Work and Work/Life Balance," *Personnel Psychology*, Autumn 1998, pp. 667–83; K. E. Pearlson and C. S. Saunders, "There's No Place Like Home: Managing Telecommuting Paradoxes," *Academy of Management Executive*, May 2001, pp. 117–28; S. J. Wells, "Making Telecommuting Work," *HRMagazine*, October 2001, pp. 34–45; and E. J. Hill, M. Ferris, and V. Martinson, "Does it Matter Where You Work? A Comparison of How Three Work Venues (Traditional Office, Virtual Office, and Home Office) Influence Aspects of Work and Personal/Family Life," *Journal of Vocational Behavior* 63, no. 2 (2003), pp. 220–41.

27. N. B. Kurland and D. E. Bailey, "Telework: The Advantages and Challenges of Working Here, There, Anywhere, and Anytime," *Organizational Dynamics*, Autumn 1999, pp. 53–68; and Wells, "Making Telecommuting Work," p. 34.

28. See, for instance, J. D. Glater, "Telecommuting's Big Experiment," *New York Times*, May 9, 2001, p. C1; and S. Shellenbarger, "Telework Is on the Rise, But It Isn't Just Done from Home Anymore," *The Wall Street Journal*, January 23, 2001, p. B1.

29. U. Huws, "Wired in the Country," *People Management*, November 1999, pp. 46–47.

30. Cited in R. W. Judy and C. D'Amico, *Workforce 2020* (Indianapolis: Hudson Institute, 1997), p. 58.

31. Cited in Wells, "Making Telecommuting Work."

32. J. M. Stanton and J. L. Barnes-Farrell, "Effects of Electronic Performance Monitoring on Personal Control, Task Satisfaction, and Task Performance," *Journal of Applied Psychology*, December 1996, pp. 738–45; B. Pappas, "They Spy," *Forbes*, February 8, 1999, p. 47; S. Armour, "More Bosses Keep Tabs on Telecommuters," *USA Today*, July 24, 2001, p. 1B; and D. Buss, "Spies Like Us," *Training*, December 2001, pp. 44–48.

33. L. H. Peters, E. J. O'Connor, and C. J. Rudolf, "The Behavioral and Affective Consequences of Performance-Relevant Situational Variables," *Organizational Behavior and Human Performance*, February 1980, pp. 79–96; M. Blumberg and C. D. Pringle, "The Missing Opportunity in Organizational Research: Some Implications for a Theory of Work Performance," *Academy of Management Review*, October 1982, pp. 560–69; D. A. Waldman and W. D. Spangler, "Putting Together the Pieces: A Closer Look at the Determinants of Job Performance," *Human Performance* 2 (1989), pp. 29–59; and J. Hall, "Americans Know How to Be Productive If Managers Will Let Them," *Organizational Dynamics*, Winter 1994, pp. 33–46.

34. See, for example, the increasing body of literature on empowerment, such as W. A. Randolph, "Re-Thinking Empowerment: Why Is It So Hard to Achieve?" *Organizational Dynamics*, 29, no. 2 (2000), pp. 94–107; K. Blanchard, J. P. Carlos, and W. A. Randolph, *Empowerment Takes More Than a Minute*, 2nd ed. (San Francisco: Berrett-Koehler, 2001); D. P. Ashmos, D. Duchon, R. R. McDaniel, Jr., and J. W. Huonker, "What a Mess! Participation as a Simple Managerial Rule to 'Complexify' Organizations," *Journal of Management Studies*, March 2002, pp. 189–206; and S. E. Seibert, S. R. Silver, and W. A. Randolph, "Taking Empowerment to the Next Level: A Multiple-Level Model of Empowerment, Performance, and Satisfaction" *Academy of Management Journal* 47, no. 3 (2004), pp. 332–49.

35. See, for instance, A. Sagie and Z. Aycan, "A Cross-Cultural Analysis of Participative Decision-Making in Organizations," *Human Relations*, April 2003, pp. 453-73; and J. Brockner, "Unpacking Country Effects: On the Need to Operationalize the Psychological Determinants of Cross-National Differences," in R. M. Kramer and B. M. Staw (eds.), *Research in Organizational Behavior*, vol. 25 (Oxford, UK: Elsevier, 2003), pp. 336-40.

36. C. Robert, T. M. Probst, J. J. Martocchio, R. Drasgow, and J. J. Lawler, "Empowerment and Continuous Improvement in the United States, Mexico, Poland, and India: Predicting Fit on the Basis of the Dimensions of Power Distance and Individualism," *Journal of Applied Psychology*, October 2000, pp. 643–58.

37. F. Heller, E. Pusic, G. Strauss, and B. Wilpert, *Organizational Participation: Myth and Reality* (Oxford: Oxford University Press, 1998).

38. See, for instance, K. L. Miller and P. R. Monge, "Participation, Satisfaction, and Productivity: A Meta-Analytic Review," *Academy of Management Journal*, December 1986, pp. 727–53; J. A. Wagner III and R. Z. Gooding, "Shared Influence and Organizational Behavior: A Meta-Analysis of Situational Variables Expected to Moderate Participation–Outcome Relationships," *Academy of Management Journal*, September 1987, pp. 524–41; J. A. Wagner III, "Participation's Effects on Performance and Satisfaction: A Reconsideration of Research Evidence," *Academy of Management Review*, April 1994, pp. 312–30; C. Doucouliagos, "Worker Participation and Productivity in Labor-Managed and Participatory Capitalist Firms: A Meta-Analysis," *Industrial and Labor Relations Review*, October 1995, pp. 58–77; J. A. Wagner III, C. R. Leana, E. A. Locke, and D. M. Schweiger, "Cognitive and Motivational Frameworks in U.S. Research on Participation: A Meta-Analysis of Primary Effects," *Journal of Organizational Behavior* 18 (1997), pp. 49–65; J. S. Black and H. B. Gregersen, "Participative Decision-Making: An Integration of Multiple Dimensions," *Human Relations*, July 1997, pp. 859–78; E. A. Locke, M. Alavi, and J. A. Wagner III, "Participation in Decision Making: An Information Exchange Perspective," in G. R. Ferris (ed.), *Research in Personnel and Human Resource Management*, vol. 15 (Greenwich, CT: JAI Press, 1997), pp. 293–331; and J. A. Wagner III and J. A. LePine, "Effects of Participation on Performance and Satisfaction: Additional Meta-Analytic Evidence," *Psychological Reports*, June 1999, pp. 719–25.

39. Cotton, *Employee Involvement*, p. 114.

40. See, for example, M. Gilman and P. Marginson, "Negotiating European Works Council: Contours of Constrained Choice," *Industrial Relations Journal*, March 2002, pp. 36–51; J. T. Addison and C. R. Belfield, "What Do We Know About the New European Works Council? Some Preliminary Evidence From Britain," *Scottish Journal of Political Economy*, September 2002, pp. 418–44; and B. Keller, "The European Company Statute: Employee Involvement—and Beyond," *Industrial Relations Journal*, December 2002, pp. 424–45.

41. Cotton, *Employee Involvement*, pp. 129–30, 139–40.

42. Ibid., p. 140.

43. See, for example, G. W. Meyer and R. G. Stott, "Quality Circles: Panacea or Pandora's Box?" *Organizational Dynamics*, Spring 1985, pp. 34–50; E. E. Lawler III and S. A. Mohrman, "Quality Circles: After the Honeymoon," *Organizational Dynamics*, Spring 1987, pp. 42–54; T. R. Miller, "The Quality Circle Phenomenon: A Review and Appraisal," *SAM Advanced Management Journal*, Winter 1989, pp. 4–7; K. Buch and R. Spangler, "The Effects of Quality Circles on Performance and Promotions," *Human Relations*, June 1990, pp. 573–82; P. R. Liverpool, "Employee Participation in Decision-Making: An Analysis of the Perceptions of Members and Nonmembers of Quality Circles," *Journal of Business and Psychology*, Summer 1990, pp. 411–22, E. E. Adams, Jr., "Quality Circle Performance," *Journal of Management*, March 1991, pp. 25–39; and L. I. Glassop, "The Organizational Benefits of Teams," *Human Relations* 55, no. 2 (2002), pp. 225–49.

44. T. L. Tang and E. A. Butler, "Attributions of Quality Circles' Problem-Solving Failure: Differences Among Management, Supporting Staff, and Quality Circle Members," *Public Personnel Management*, Summer 1997, pp. 203–25; G. Hammersley and A. Pinnington, "Quality Circles Reach End of the Line at Land Rover," *Human Resource Management International Digest*, May/June 1999, pp. 4–5; and D. Nagar and M. Takore, "Effectiveness of Quality Circles in a Large Public Sector," *Psychological Studies*, January–July 2001, pp. 63–68.

45. Cotton, *Employee Involvement*, p. 87.

46. P. S. Goodman and P. P. Pan, "Chinese Workers Pay for Wal-Mart's Low Prices," *The Washington Post*, February 8, 2004; p. A01.

47. See T. Henry, "States to Tie Teacher Pay to Results," *USA Today*, September 30, 1999, p. 1A.

48. D. Kollars, "Some Educators Win $25,000 Bonus as Test Scores Rise," *The Sacramento Bee*, January 8, 2001, p. 1.

49. Based on J. R. Schuster and P. K. Zingheim, "The New Variable Pay: Key Design Issues," *Compensation & Benefits Review*, March–April 1993, p. 28; K. S. Abosch, "Variable Pay: Do We Have the Basics in Place?" *Compensation & Benefits Review*, July–August 1998, pp. 12–22; and K. M. Kuhn, and M. D. Yockey, "Variable Pay as a Risky Choice: Determinants of the Relative Attractiveness of Incentive Plans," *Organizational Behavior and Human Decision Processes*, March 2003, pp. 323–41.

50. W. Zellner, "Trickle-Down Is Trickling Down at Work," *Business Week*, March 18, 1996, p. 34; and "Linking Pay to Performance is Becoming a Norm in the Workplace," *The Wall Street Journal*, April 6, 1999, p. A1.

51. L. Wiener, "Paycheck Plus," *U.S. News & World Report*, February 24/March 3, 2003, p. 58.

52. Cited in "Pay Programs: Few Employees See the Pay-for-Performance Connection," *Compensation & Benefits Report*, June 2003, p. 1.

53. B. Wysocki, Jr., "Chilling Reality Awaits Even the Employed," *The Wall Street Journal*, November 5, 2001, p. A1.

54. M. Fein, "Work Measurement and Wage Incentives," *Industrial Engineering*, September 1973, pp. 49–51. For updated reviews of the effect of pay on performance, see G. D. Jenkins, Jr., N. Gupta, A. Mitra, and J. D. Shaw, "Are Financial Incentives Related to Performance? A Meta-Analytic Review of Empirical Research," *Journal of Applied Psychology*, October 1998, pp. 777–87; and S. L. Rynes, B. Gerhart, and L. Parks, "Personnel Psychology: Performance Evaluation and Pay for Performance," *Annual Review of Psychology* 56, no. 1 (2005), pp. 571–600.

55. E. Arita, "Teething Troubles Aside, Merit-Based Pay Catching On," *The Japan Times* (http://www.202.221.217.59/print/business/nb04-2004/nb20040423a3.htm) (April 23, 2004).

56. C. M. DiMassa and J. Rubin, "Teachers Unions Blast Governor's Merit Pay Plan," *Los Angeles Times* (http://www.latimes.com/news/local/la-me-merit10jan10.story) (January 10, 2005).

57. L. Lavelle, "Executive Pay," *BusinessWeek*, April 16, 2001, p. 77.

58. R. Balu, "Bonuses Aren't Just for the Bosses," *Fast Company*, December 2000, pp. 74–76; and M. Conlin, "A Little Less in the Envelope This Week," *Business Week*, February 18, 2002, pp. 64–66.

59. See, for instance, D-O. Kim, "Determinants of the Survival of Gainsharing Programs," *Industrial & Labor Relations Review*, October 1999, pp. 21–42; "Why Gainsharing Works Even Better Today Than in the Past," *HR Focus*, April 2000, pp. 3–5; L. R. Gomez-Mejia, T. M. Welbourne, and R. M. Wiseman, "The Role of Risk Sharing and Risk Taking Under Gainsharing," *Academy of Management Review*, July 2000, pp. 492–507; W. Atkinson, "Incentive Pay Programs That Work in Textile," *Textile World*, February 2001, pp. 55–57; M. Reynolds, "A Cost-Reduction Strategy That May Be Back," *Healthcare Financial Management*, January 2002, pp. 58–64; and M. R. Dixon, L. J. Hayes, and J. Stack, "Changing Conceptions of Employee Compensation," *Journal of Organizational Behavior Management* 23, no. 2–3 (2003), pp. 95–116.

60. "U.S. Wage and Productivity Growth Attainable Through Gainsharing," Employment Policy Foundation; (http://www.epf.org) (May 10, 2000).

61. "The Employee Ownership 100," (http://www.nceo.org) (July 2003).

62. Cited in K. Frieswick, "ESOPs: Split Personality," *CFO*, July 7, 2003, p. 1.

63. A. A. Buchko, "The Effects of Employee Ownership on Employee Attitudes.

64. C. M. Rosen and M. Quarrey, "How Well Is Employee Ownership Working?" *Harvard Business Review*, September–October 1987, pp. 126–32.

65. Cited in "ESOP Benefits Are No Fables," *BusinessWeek*, September 6, 1999, p. 26.

66. W. N. Davidson and D. L. Worrell, "ESOP's Fables: The Influence of Employee Stock Ownership Plans on Corporate Stock Prices and Subsequent Operating Performance," *Human Resource Planning*, January 1994, pp. 69–85.

67. Pierce and Furo, "Employee Ownership."

68. See data in D. Stamps, "A Piece of the Action," *Training*, March 1996, p. 66.

69. C. G. Hanson and W. D. Bell, *Profit Sharing and Profitability: How Profit Sharing Promotes Business Success* (London: Kogan Page, 1987); M. Magnan and S. St-Onge, "Profit-Sharing and Firm Performance: A Comparative and Longitudinal Analysis," paper presented at the 58th annual meeting of the Academy of Management, San Diego, August 1998; and D. D'Art, and T. Turner, "Profit Sharing, Firm Performance, and Union Influence in Selected European Countries," *Personnel Review* 33, no. 3 (2004), pp. 335–50.

70. T. M. Welbourne and L. R. Gomez-Mejia, "Gainsharing: A Critical Review and a Future Research Agenda," *Journal of Management* 21, no. 3 (1995), pp. 559–609.

71. See "Skill-Based Pay Program" (http://www.bmpoc.org) (June 29, 2001).

72. G. E. Ledford, Jr., "Paying for the Skills, Knowledge, and Competencies of Knowledge Workers," *Compensation & Benefits Review*, July–August 1995, pp. 55–62; B. Murray and B. Gerhart, "An Empirical Analysis of a Skill-Based Pay Program and Plant Performance Outcomes," *Academy of Management Journal*, February 1998, pp. 68–78; J. R. Thompson and C. W. LeHew, "Skill-Based Pay as an Organizational Innovation," *Review of Public Personnel Administration*, Winter 2000, pp. 20–40; and J. D. Shaw, N. Gupta, A. Mitra, and G. E. Ledford, Jr. "Success and Survival of Skill-Based Pay Plans," *Journal of Management*, February 2005, pp. 28–49.

73. "Tensions of a New Pay Plan," *New York Times*, May 17, 1992, p. F5.

74. E. E. Lawler III, S. A. Mohrman, and G. E. Ledford, Jr., Creating High Performance Organizations: Practices and Results in the Fortune 1000 (San Francisco: Jossey-Bass, 1995); C. Lee, K. S. Law, and P. Bobko, "The Importance of Justice Perceptions on Pay Effectiveness: A Two-Year Study of a Skill-Based Pay Plan," Journal of Management, vol. 25, no. 6, 1999, pp. 851–73; A. Podolske, "Seven-Year Update on Skill-Based Pay Plans," www.ioma.com, July 1999.

75. Lawler, Ledford, and Chang, "Who Uses Skill-Based Pay, and Why."

76. M. Rowland, "It's What You Can Do That Counts," New York Times, June 6, 1993, p. F17.

77. Ibid.

78. See, for instance, M. W. Barringer and G. T. Milkovich, "A Theoretical Exploration of the Adoption and Design of Flexible Benefit Plans: A Case of Human Resource Innovation," *Academy of Management Review*, April 1998, pp. 305–24; D. Brown, "Everybody Loves Flex," *Canadian HR Reporter*, November 18, 2002, p. 1; J. Taggart, "Putting Flex Benefits Through Their Paces," *Canadian HR Reporter*, December 2, 2002, p. G3; and N. D. Cole, and D. H. Flint, "Perceptions of Distributive and Procedural Justice in Employee Benefits: Flexible Versus Traditional Benefit Plans," *Journal of Managerial Psychology* 19, no. 1 (2004), pp. 19–40.

79. D. A. DeCenzo and S. P. Robbins, *Human Resource Management*, 7th ed. (New York: Wiley, 2002), pp. 346–48.

80. Brown, "Everybody Loves Flex."

81. E. Unsworth, "U. K. Employers Find Flex Benefits Helpful: Survey," *Business Insurance*, May 21, 2001, pp. 19–20.

82. Our definition of a formal recognition system is based on S. E. Markham, K. D. Scott, and G. H. McKee, "Recognizing Good Attendance: A Longitudinal, Quasi-Experimental Field Study," *Personnel Psychology*, Autumn 2002, p. 641.

83. D. Drickhamer, "Best Plant Winners: Nichols Foods Ltd.," *Industry Week*, October 1, 2001, pp. 17–19.

84. M. Littman, "Best Bosses Tell All," *Working Woman*, October 2000, p. 54.

85. Cited in S. Caudron, "The Top 20 Ways to Motivate Employees," *Industry Week*, April 3, 1995, pp. 15–16. See also B. Nelson, "Try Praise," *INC.*, September 1996, p. 115.

86. A. D. Stajkovic and F. Luthans, "Differential Effects of Incentive Motivators on Work Performance," *Academy of Management Journal*, June 2001, p. 587. See also F. Luthans and A. D. Stajkovic, "Provide Recognition for Performance Improvement," in E. A. Locke (ed.), *Handbook of Principles of Organizational Behavior* (Malden, MA: Blackwell, 2004), pp. 166–80.

87. Cited in K. J. Dunham, "Amid Shrinking Workplace Morale, Employers Turn to Recognition," *The Wall Street Journal*, November 19, 2002, p. B8.

88. Ibid.

Emotions and Moods

After reading this chapter, you should be able to:

1 Differentiate emotions from moods.

2 Discuss the different aspects of emotions.

3 Identify the sources of emotions and moods.

4 Describe external constraints on emotions.

5 Discuss the impact emotional labor has on employees.

6 Discuss the case for and the case against emotional intelligence.

7 Apply concepts on emotions and moods to OB issues.

LEARNING OBJECTIVES

CHAPTER 8

Emotions Can Be Powerful

Steve Wynn, the famous hotel mogul, is an emotional person.[1] He is known for his infectious enthusiasm, as well as his temper. He once shot off his index finger in his office. And when describing his new $2.7 billion hotel, which he named after himself, he broke into a song from a musical. When have you ever seen a CEO do that? Wynn's also given to making outlandish statements. He said of his new hotel, "This building is more complex than any other structure in the history of the world." He also once commented, smiling, that "Las Vegas is sort of like how God would do it if he had money."

Many regard Wynn as the most powerful man in Nevada, largely because he can both inspire and scare people. One politician stated, "Steve Wynn's control over politicians is all-encompassing. It's overwhelming. Either you work for him or he tries to get you out of office."

Those who know Wynn say his temper can erupt as fiercely as the volcano he put on the grounds of his flagship hotel and casino, The Mirage. At the same time, while Wynn was in charge of the Mirage, it was high on *Fortune's* list of *America's Most Admired Companies*.

Interestingly, in contrast to Wynn's volatile personality, his new hotel is meant to appeal to people's desire for calmness. Gone are the exotic public displays, such as volcanoes and caged tigers, that graced his earlier hotels. He even says that he'd get rid of the casinos if he could. No casinos in a Las Vegas hotel? Could Steve Wynn be bluffing? ■

I t's probably safe to assume that most of us are not as given to emotional extremes as Steve Wynn. If we were, could we be as successful as he in our professions? Given the obvious role that emotions play in our work and everyday lives, it might surprise you to learn that, until recently, the field of OB has given the topic of emotions little or no attention.[2] How could this be? We can offer two possible explanations.

The first is the *myth of rationality*.[3] Since the late nineteenth century and the rise of scientific management, the protocol of the work world has been to keep a damper on emotions. A well-run organization was one that didn't allow employees to express frustration, fear, anger, love, hate, joy, grief, and similar feelings. The prevailing thought was that such emotions were the antithesis of rationality. Even though researchers and managers knew that emotions were an inseparable part of everyday life, they tried to create organizations that were emotion-free. That, of course, wasn't possible.

The second explanation was the belief that emotions of any kind are disruptive.[4] When researchers considered emotions, they looked at strong, negative emotions—especially anger—that interfered with an employee's ability to work effectively. They rarely viewed emotions as constructive or able to enhance performance.

Certainly some emotions, particularly when exhibited at the wrong time, can reduce employee performance. But this doesn't change the fact that employees bring their emotional sides with them to work every day and that no study of OB could be comprehensive without considering the role of emotions in workplace behavior.

What Are Emotions and Moods?

Although we don't want to obsess over definitions, before we can proceed with our analysis, we need to clarify three terms that are closely intertwined: *affect, emotions,* and *moods.*

Affect is a generic term that covers a broad range of feelings that people experience. It's an umbrella concept that encompasses both emotions and moods.[5] **Emotions** are intense feelings that are directed at someone or something.[6] **Moods** are feelings that tend to be less intense than emotions and that often (though not always) lack a contextual stimulus.[7]

Most experts believe that emotions are more fleeting than moods.[8] For example, if someone is rude to you, you'll feel angry. That intense feeling of anger probably comes and goes fairly quickly, maybe even in a matter of seconds. When you're in a bad mood, though, you can feel bad for several hours.

Emotions are reactions to a person (seeing a friend at work may make you feel glad) or event (dealing with a rude client may make you feel angry). You show your emotions when you're "happy about something, angry at someone, afraid of something."[9] Moods, in contrast, aren't usually directed at a person or event. But emotions can turn into moods when you lose focus on the event or object that started the feeling. And, by the same token, good or bad moods can make you more emotional in response to an event. So when a colleague criticizes how you spoke to a client, you might become angry at him. That is, you show emotion (anger) toward a specific object (your colleague). But as the specific emotion dissipates, you might just feel generally dispirited. You can't attribute this feeling to any single event; you're just not your normal self. You might then overreact to other events. This affect state describes a mood. Exhibit 8-1 shows the relationships among affect, emotions, and mood.

First, as the exhibit shows, affect is a broad term that encompasses emotions and moods. Second, there are differences between emotions and moods. Some

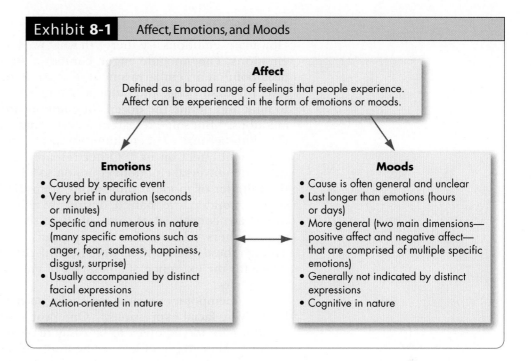

Exhibit 8-1   Affect, Emotions, and Moods

Affect
Defined as a broad range of feelings that people experience.
Affect can be experienced in the form of emotions or moods.

Emotions
- Caused by specific event
- Very brief in duration (seconds or minutes)
- Specific and numerous in nature (many specific emotions such as anger, fear, sadness, happiness, disgust, surprise)
- Usually accompanied by distinct facial expressions
- Action-oriented in nature

Moods
- Cause is often general and unclear
- Last longer than emotions (hours or days)
- More general (two main dimensions—positive affect and negative affect—that are comprised of multiple specific emotions)
- Generally not indicated by distinct expressions
- Cognitive in nature

of these differences—that emotions are more likely to be caused by a specific event, and emotions are more fleeting than moods—we just discussed. Other differences are subtler. For example, unlike moods, emotions tend to be more clearly revealed with facial expressions (anger, disgust). Also, some researchers speculate that emotions may be more action-oriented—they may lead us to some immediate action—while moods may be more cognitive, meaning they may cause us to think or brood for a while.[10]

Finally, the exhibit shows that emotions and moods can mutually influence each other. For example, an emotion, if it's strong and deep enough, can turn into a mood: Getting your dream job may generate the emotion of joy, but it also can put you in a good mood for several days. Similarly, if you're in a good or bad mood, it might make you experience a more intense positive or negative emotion than would otherwise be the case. For example, if you're in a bad mood, you might "blow up" in response to a coworker's comment when normally it would have just generated a mild reaction. Because emotions and moods can mutually influence each other, there will be many points throughout the chapter where emotions and moods will be closely connected.

Although affect, emotions, and moods are separable in theory, in practice the distinction isn't always crystal clear. In fact, in some areas, researchers have studied mostly moods, and in other areas, mainly emotions. So, when we review the OB topics on emotions and moods, you may see more information on emotions in one area and moods in another. This is simply the state of the research.

Also, the terminology can be confusing. For example, the two main mood dimensions are positive affect and negative affect, yet we have defined affect more broadly than mood. So, although the topic can be fairly dense in places, hang in there. The material is interesting—and applicable to OB.

affect *A broad range of feelings that people experience.*

emotions *Intense feelings that are directed at someone or something.*

moods *Feelings that tend to be less intense than emotions and that lack a contextual stimulus.*

A Basic Set of Emotions

How many emotions are there? In what ways do they vary? There are dozens of emotions. They include anger, contempt, enthusiasm, envy, fear, frustration, disappointment, embarrassment, disgust, happiness, hate, hope, jealousy, joy, love, pride, surprise, and sadness. There have been numerous research efforts to limit and define the dozens of emotions into a fundamental or basic set of emotions.[11] But some researchers argue that it makes no sense to think of basic emotions because even emotions we rarely experience, such as shock, can have a powerful effect on us.[12] Other researchers, even philosophers, argue that there are universal emotions common to all of us. René Descartes, often called the founder of modern philosophy, identified six "simple and primitive passions"—wonder, love, hatred, desire, joy, and sadness—and argued that "all the others are composed of some of these six or are species of them."[13] Other philosophers (Hume, Hobbes, Spinoza) identified categories of emotions. Though these philosophers were helpful, the burden to provide conclusive evidence for the existence of a basic set of emotions still rests with contemporary researchers.

In contemporary research, psychologists have tried to identify basic emotions by studying facial expressions.[14] One problem with this approach is that some emotions are too complex to be easily represented on our faces. Take love, for example. Many think of love as the most universal of all emotions,[15] yet it's not easy to express a loving emotion with one's face only. Also, cultures have norms that govern emotional expression, so how we *experience* an emotion isn't always the same as how we *show* it. And many companies today offer anger-management programs to teach people to contain or even hide their inner feelings.[16]

It's unlikely psychologists or philosophers will ever completely agree on a set of basic emotions, or even whether it makes sense to think of basic emotions. Still, enough researchers have agreed on six essentially universal emotions—anger, fear, sadness, happiness, disgust, and surprise—with most other emotions subsumed under one of these six categories.[17] Some researchers even plot these six emotions along a continuum: happiness—surprise—fear—sadness—anger—disgust.[18] The closer any two emotions are to each other on this continuum, the more likely it is that people will confuse them. For instance, we sometimes mistake happiness for surprise, but rarely do we confuse happiness and disgust. In addition, as we'll see later on, cultural factors can also influence interpretations.

Some Aspects of Emotions

There are some other fundamental aspects of emotions that we need to consider. These aspects include the biology of emotions, the intensity of emotions, their frequency and duration, the relationship between rationality and emotions, and the functions of emotions. Let's deal with each of these aspects in turn.

The Biology of Emotions   All emotions originate in the brain's limbic system, which is about the size of a walnut and near our brain stem.[19] People tend to be happiest (report more positive than negative emotions) when their limbic system is relatively inactive. When the limbic system "heats up," negative emotions such as anger and guilt dominate over positive ones such as joy and happiness. Overall, the limbic system provides a lens through which you interpret events. When it's active, you see things in a negative light. When it's inactive, you interpret information more positively.

Not everyone's limbic system is the same. Moderately depressed people have more active limbic systems, particularly when they encounter negative information.[20] And women tend to have more active limbic systems than men, which,

Joanna Hayes expressed the emotion of joy after winning the gold medal in the women's 100m hurdle during track and field competition at the 2004 Summer Olympic Games in Athens, Greece. Joy is one of the dozens of basic emotions that originate in our brain's limbic system to help us interpret events. As a positive emotion, joy expresses a favorable evaluation or feeling.

some argue, explains why women are more susceptible to depression than men and are more likely to emotionally bond with children.[21] Of course, as always, these are average differences—women are more likely to be depressed than men, but naturally that doesn't mean that all depressed people are women, or that men are incapable of bonding with their kids.

Intensity   People give different responses to identical emotion-provoking stimuli. In some cases, personality is responsible for the difference. Other times, it's a result of the job requirements.

People vary in their inherent ability to express emotional intensity. You may know people who almost never show their feelings. They rarely get angry. They never show rage. In contrast, you probably also know people who seem to be on an emotional roller coaster. When they're happy, they're ecstatic. When they're sad, they're deeply depressed. We'll explore the impact personality has on an individual's emotions in more detail later on in the chapter.

Jobs make different demands on our emotions. For instance, air traffic controllers, surgeons, and trial judges are expected to be calm and controlled, even in stressful situations. Conversely, the effectiveness of television evangelists, public-address announcers at sporting events, and lawyers can depend on their ability to alter their emotional intensity as the need arises.

Frequency and Duration   Sean Wolfson is basically a quiet and reserved person. He loves his job as a financial planner. He doesn't enjoy, however, having to give speeches to increase his visibility and to promote his programs. But he still has to give speeches occasionally. "If I had to speak to large audiences every day, I'd quit this business," he says. "I think this works for me because I can fake excitement and enthusiasm for an hour, a couple of times a month."

Whether an employee can successfully meet the emotional demands of a given job depends not only on what emotions need to be displayed and their intensity but also on how frequently and for how long they need to make the effort.

Do Emotions Make Us Irrational?   How often have you heard someone say, "Oh, you're just being emotional"? You might have been offended. The famous astronomer Carl Sagan once wrote, "Where we have strong emotions, we're liable to fool ourselves." These observations suggest that rationality and emotion are in conflict with one another and that if you exhibit emotion, you are likely to act irrationally. One team of authors argue that displaying emotions like sadness, to the point of crying, is so toxic to a career that we should leave the room rather than allow others to witness our emotional display.[22] The author Lois Frankel advises that women should avoid being emotional at work because it will undermine how others rate their competence.[23] These perspectives suggest that the demonstration or even experience of emotions is likely to make us seem weak, brittle, or irrational. However, the research disagrees and is increasingly showing that emotions are actually critical to rational thinking.[24] In fact, there has been evidence of such a link for a long time.

Take the example of Phineas Gage. Gage was a railroad worker in Vermont. One September day in 1848, while setting an explosive charge at work, a 3'7" iron bar flew into Gage's lower left jaw and out through the top of his skull. Remarkably, Gage survived his injury. He was still able to read and speak, and he performed well above average on cognitive ability tests. However, it became clear that Gage had lost his ability to experience emotion. He was emotionless at even the saddest misfortunes or happiest occasions. Gage's inability to express emotion eventually took away his ability to reason. He started making irrational choices about his life, often behaving erratically and against his self-interests. Despite being an intelligent man whose intellectual abilities were

By studying the skull of Phineas Gage, shown here, and other brain injuries, researchers discovered an important link between emotions and rational thinking. They found that losing the ability to emote led to the loss of the ability to reason. From this discovery, researchers learned that our emotions provide us with valuable information that helps our thinking process.

unharmed by the accident, Gage drifted from job to job, eventually taking up with a circus. In commenting on Gage's condition, one expert noted, "Reason may not be as pure as most of us think it is or wish it were . . . emotions and feelings may not be intruders in the bastion of reason at all: they may be enmeshed in its networks, for worse *and* for better."[25]

The example of Phineas Gage and many other brain injury studies, show us that emotions are critical to rational thinking. We must have the ability to experience emotions to be rational. Why? Because our emotions provide important information about how we understand the world around us. Although we might think of a computer as intellectually superior, a human so void of emotion would be unable to function. Think about a manager making a decision to fire an employee. Would you really want the manager to make the decision without regarding either his or the employee's emotions? The key to good decision making is to employ both thinking *and* feeling in one's decisions.

What Functions Do Emotions Serve?   Why do we have emotions? What role do they serve? We just discussed one function—that we need them to think rationally. Charles Darwin, however, took a broader approach. In *The Expression of the Emotions in Man and Animals*, Darwin argued that emotions developed over time to help humans solve problems. Emotions are useful, he said, because they motivate people to engage in actions important for survival—actions such as foraging for food, seeking shelter, choosing mates, guarding against predators, and predicting others' behaviors. For example, disgust (an emotion) motivates us to avoid dangerous or harmful things (such as rotten foods). Excitement (also an emotion) motivates us to take on situations in which we require energy and initiative (for example, tackling a new career).

Drawing from Darwin are researchers who focus on **evolutionary psychology**. This field of study says we must experience emotions—whether they are positive or negative—because they serve a purpose.[26] For example, you would probably consider jealousy to be a negative emotion. Evolutionary psychologists would argue that it exists in people because it has a useful purpose. Mates may feel jealousy to increase the chance that their genes, rather than a rival's genes, are passed on to the next generation.[27] Although we tend to think of anger as being "bad," it actually can help us protect our rights when we feel they're being violated. For example, a person showing anger when she's double-crossed by a colleague is serving a warning for others not to repeat the same behavior. Consider another example. Rena Weeks was a secretary at a prominent law firm. Her boss wouldn't stop touching and grabbing her. His treatment made her angry. So she did more than quit—she sued, and won a multimillion-dollar case.[28] It's not that anger is always good. But as with all other emotions, it exists because it serves a useful purpose. Positive emotions also serve a purpose. For example, a service employee who feels empathy for a customer may provide better customer service.

But some researchers are not firm believers of evolutionary psychology. Why? Think about fear (an emotion). It's just as easy to think of the harmful effects of fear as it is the beneficial effects. For example, running in fear from a predator increases the likelihood of survival. But what benefit does freezing in fear serve? Evolutionary psychology provides an interesting perspective on the functions of emotions, but it's hard to know whether or not this perspective is valid all the time.[29]

Mood as Positive and Negative Affect

One way to classify emotions is by whether they are positive or negative.[30] Positive emotions—like joy and gratitude—express a favorable evaluation or feeling. Negative emotions—like anger or guilt—express the opposite. Keep in mind that emotions can't be neutral. Being neutral is being nonemotional.[31]

When we group emotions into positive and negative categories, they become mood states because we are now looking at them more generally instead of isolating one particular emotion. See Exhibit 8-2. In this exhibit, excited is a specific emotion that is a pure marker of high positive affect, while boredom is a pure marker of low positive affect. Similarly, nervous is a pure marker of high negative affect, while relaxed is a pure marker of low negative affect. Finally, some emotions—like contentment (a mixture of high positive affect and low negative affect) or sadness (a mixture of low positive affect and high negative affect)—are in between. You'll notice that this model does not include all emotions. There are two reasons why. First, we can fit other emotions like enthusiasm or depression into the model, but we're short on space. Second, some emotions, like surprise, don't fit well because they're not as clearly positive or negative.

So, we can think of **positive affect** as a mood dimension consisting of positive emotions such as excitement, self-assurance, and cheerfulness at the high end, and boredom, sluggishness, and tiredness at the low end. **Negative affect** is a mood dimension consisting of nervousness, stress, and anxiety at the high end, and relaxation, tranquility, and poise at the low end. (Note that positive and negative affect *are* moods. We're using these labels, rather than positive and negative mood, because that's how researchers label them.)

Positive affect and negative affect play out at work (and beyond work, of course) in that they color our perceptions, and these perceptions can become their own reality. For example, one flight attendant posted an anonymous blog on the Web that said: "I work in a pressurized aluminum tube and the

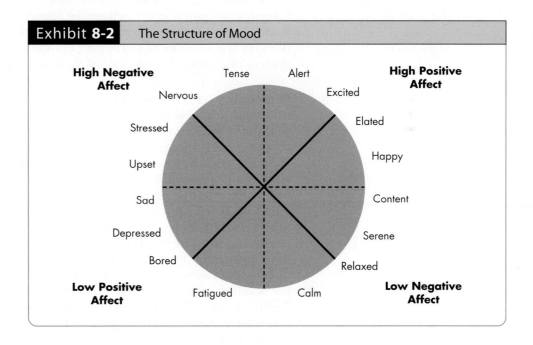

Exhibit 8-2   The Structure of Mood

High Negative Affect · Tense · Alert · **High Positive Affect** · Nervous · Excited · Elated · Stressed · Happy · Upset · Content · Sad · Depressed · Serene · Bored · Relaxed · **Low Positive Affect** · Fatigued · Calm · **Low Negative Affect**

evolutionary psychology   *An area of inquiry that argues that we must experience the emotions that we do because they serve a purpose.*

positive affect   *A mood dimension consisting of specific positive emotions like excitement, self-assurance, and cheerfulness at the high end, and boredom, sluggishness, and tiredness at the low end.*

negative affect   *A mood dimension consisting of nervousness, stress, and anxiety at the high end, and relaxation, tranquility, and poise at the low end.*

environment outside my 'office' cannot sustain human life. That being said, the human life inside is not worth sustaining sometimes . . . in fact, the passengers can be jerks, and idiots. I am often treated with no respect, nobody listens to me . . . until I threaten to kick them off the plane . . . "[32] Clearly, if a flight attendant is in a bad mood, it's going to influence his perceptions of passengers, which will influence his behavior in turn.

Importantly, negative emotions are more likely to translate into negative moods. People think about events that created strong negative emotions five times as long as they do about events that created strong positive ones.[33] So, we should expect people to recall negative experiences more readily than positive ones. Perhaps one of the reasons is that, for most of us, they're also more unusual. Indeed research shows that there is a **positivity offset**, meaning that at zero input (when nothing in particular is going on), most individuals experience a mildly positive mood.[34] So for most people, positive moods are somewhat more common than negative moods. The positivity offset also appears to operate at work. For example, one study of customer service representatives in a British call center (probably a job where it's pretty hard to feel positive) revealed that people reported experiencing positive moods 58 percent of the time.[35]

Sources of Emotions and Moods

Have you ever said to yourself, "I got up on the wrong side of the bed today"? Have you ever snapped at a coworker or family member for no particular reason? If you have, it probably makes you wonder where emotions and moods come from. Here, we pick up the discussion of moods again because, even though emotions are thought to be more influenced by events than moods, ironically, researchers have conducted more studies on the sources of moods than on the sources of particular emotions. So, now we'll turn to the main sources of moods, though a lot of these sources also affect emotions.

Personality   Do you scream at the TV when your team is losing a big game while your friend seems like she could care less that her team has no chance of winning? Consider another situation. Noel and Jose are coworkers. Noel has a tendency to get angry when a colleague criticizes her ideas during a brainstorming session. Jose, however, is quite calm and relaxed, viewing such criticism as an opportunity for improvement. What explains these different reactions? Personality predisposes people to experience certain moods and emotions. For example, some people feel guilt and anger more readily than others do. Others may feel calm and relaxed no matter the situation. In other words, moods and emotions have a trait component to them—most people have built-in tendencies to experience certain moods and emotions more frequently than others do. Consider Texas Tech basketball coach Bobby Knight. He is infamous for his tirades against players, officials, fans, and the media. Clearly, he is easily moved to experience anger. But take Microsoft CEO Bill Gates, who is known for his relatively distant, unemotional, analytical nature. He rarely displays anger.

So Bobby Knight and Bill Gates have tendencies to *experience* a particular mood or emotion. But, as we mentioned earlier, some people are predisposed to experience *any* emotion more intensely. Such people are high on **affect intensity**, or "individual differences in the strength with which individuals experience their emotions."[36] While most people might feel slightly sad at one movie or be mildly amused at another, someone high on affect intensity would cry like a baby at a sad movie and laugh uncontrollably at a comedy. We might describe such people as "emotional" or "intense." So, emotions differ in their intensity, but people also differ in how predisposed they are to experience emotions intensely. If a person gets really mad at a coworker, he would be experiencing an emotion intensely. But if that person gets mad, or excited, really easily, then he would be high on the personality trait of affect intensity.

Also, positive events are more likely to affect the positive mood and positive emotions of extraverts, and negative events are more likely to influence the negative mood and negative emotions of those scoring low on emotional stability.[37] To illustrate, let's say there are two friends who work together—Paul and Alex. Paul scores high on extraversion and emotional stability. Alex scores low on both. One day at work, Paul and Alex learn they're going to earn a commission for a sale their work group made. Later the same day, their boss stops by and yells at them for no apparent reason. In this situation, you'd expect Paul's positive affect to increase more than Alex's because Paul is more extraverted and attends more to the good news of the day. Conversely, you'd expect Alex's negative affect to increase more than Paul's because Alex scores lower on emotional stability and therefore tends to dwell on the negative event that day.

Day of the Week and Time of the Day   Most people are at work or school Monday through Friday. For most of us, that means the weekend is a time of relaxation and leisure. Does that suggest that people are in their best moods on the weekends? Well, actually, yes. As Exhibit 8-3 shows, people tend to be in

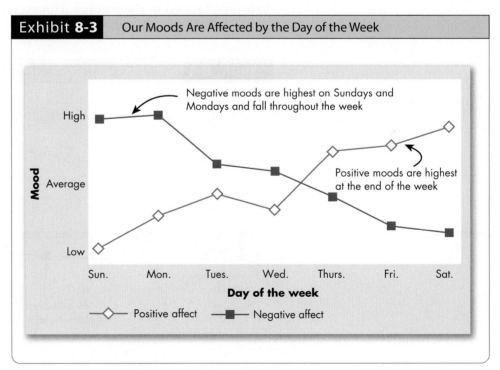

Exhibit **8-3**	Our Moods Are Affected by the Day of the Week

Source: D. Watson, *Mood and Temperament,* New York, Guilford Publications, 2000.

positivity offset   *Tendency of most individuals to experience a mildly positive mood at zero input (when nothing in particular is going on).*

affect intensity   *Individual differences in the strength with which individuals experience their emotions.*

their worst moods (highest negative affect and lowest positive affect) early in the week and in their best moods (highest positive affect and lowest negative affect) late in the week.[38]

What about time of the day? When are you usually in your best mood? Your worst? We often think that people differ, depending on whether they are "morning" or "evening" people. However, the vast majority of us follow a similar pattern. People are generally in lower spirits early in the morning. During the course of the day, our moods tend to improve and then decline in the evening. Exhibit 8-4 shows this pattern. Interestingly, regardless of what time people go to bed at night or get up in the morning, levels of positive affect tend to peak around the halfway point between waking and sleeping. Negative affect, however, shows little fluctuation throughout the day.[39]

What does this mean for organizational behavior? Asking someone for a favor, or conveying bad news, is probably not a good idea on Monday morning. Our workplace interactions will probably be more positive from mid-morning onward, and also later in the week.

It does seem that people who describe themselves as morning people are more alert early in the morning.[40] However, these morning people experience only slightly better moods (more positive affect) in the morning compared to those who describe themselves as evening people (and vice-versa).[41]

Weather   When do you think you would be in a better mood? When it's 70 degrees and sunny or when it's a gloomy, cold, rainy day? Many people believe their mood is tied to the weather. However, evidence suggests that weather has

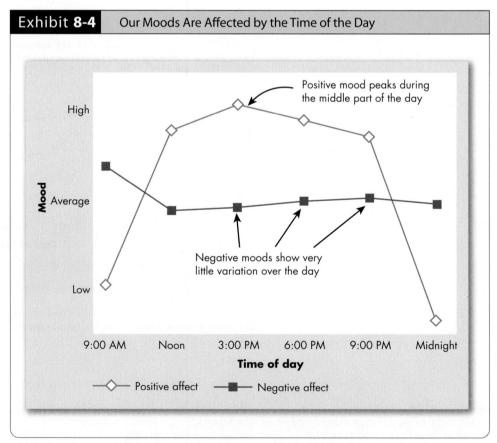

Exhibit 8-4   Our Moods Are Affected by the Time of the Day

Source: D. Watson, *Mood and Temperament*, New York, Guilford Publications, 2000.

little effect on mood. One expert concluded, "Contrary to the prevailing cultural view, these data indicate that people do not report a better mood on bright and sunny days (or, conversely, a worse mood on dark and rainy days)."[42] *Illusory correlation* explains why people tend to *think* that nice weather improves their mood. **Illusory correlation** occurs when people associate two events but in reality there is no connection.

For example, over time, there has been a positive correlation between the length of women's skirts and the Standard and Poor's 500 stock market price. When the length goes up in the fashion world, so does the S&P 500. Does this mean that if we could convince women to shorten their skirts, it would cause a stock market boom? Of course not. There are all sorts of correlations that aren't causal (another example—the salaries of Presbyterian ministers in Massachusetts and the price of rum in Havana). People often associate things as causal when in fact there's no true relationship. That appears to be the case with weather and moods.

Stress   As you might imagine, stress affects emotions and moods. For example, students have higher levels of fear before an exam, but their fear dissipates once the exam is over.[43] At work, stressful daily events (a nasty email, an impending deadline, the loss of a big sale, being reprimanded by your boss, and so on) negatively affect employees' moods. Also, the effects of stress build over time. As the authors of one study note, "a constant diet of even low-level stressful events has the potential to cause workers to experience gradually increasing levels of strain over time."[44] Such mounting levels of stress and strain at work can worsen our moods, and we experience more negative emotions. Consider the following entry from a worker's blog: "i'm in a bit of a blah mood today . . . physically, i feel funky, though and the weather out combined with the amount of personal and work i need to get done are getting to me." Although sometimes we thrive on stress, for most of us, like this blogger, stress begins to take its toll on our mood.[45]

Social Activities   Do you tend to be happiest when you are at a barbeque with friends or out to dinner to celebrate a family member's birthday? For most people, social activities increase positive mood and have little effect on negative mood. But do people in positive moods seek out social interactions, or do social interactions cause people to be in good moods? It seems that both are true.[46] And, does the *type* of social activity matter? Indeed it does. Research suggests that physical (skiing or hiking with friends), informal (going to a party), or Epicurean (eating with others) activities are more strongly associated with increases in positive mood than formal (attending a meeting) or sedentary (watching TV with friends) events.[47]

Social interactions even have long-term health benefits. One study of longevity found that being in the company of others (as opposed to social isolation) was one of *the* best predictors of how long someone lives—more important than gender, or even blood pressure or cholesterol levels.[48] One of the reasons for this is positive affect. A study of nuns 75–95 years old showed that the degree to which the nuns experienced positive moods in their 20s predicted how long they lived six decades later.[49]

illusory correlation   *The tendency of people to associate two events when in reality there is no connection.*

"Does Sharing Good News Affect Our Mood?"

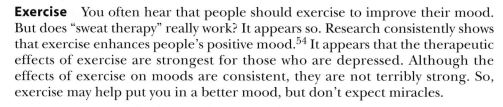

When good things happen to you, do you immediately call a friend or run over to your coworker's office to share the joy? If this isn't your style, you might reconsider. A study shows that those who sought out others when good things happened to them were consistently happier than those who did not share their good news. Additionally, this "capitalizing" effect held irrespective of the events themselves, meaning that if two people both had positive things happen to them, the happier person would be the one who shared the good news. The study ruled out alternative explanations for these findings. For example, personality did not play a role, given that the results were not due to high levels of extraversion in the study's participants.

Peoples' responses to an individual's good news are also important. Only when others reacted with genuine enthusiasm (as opposed to indifference or feigned happiness) did sharing make people happier. So happiness is not just the result of sharing joy, rather, it is also a result of sharing good news with the right people.

But how does capitalizing on positive events affect an individual's job satisfaction? Sharing news about a promotion, a new hire, or a closed sale—contributed to positive moods at work and satisfaction with one's work. Again, the type of response mattered—that is, employees were happiest when they shared positive events with others who were truly happy for them. ■

To keep employees in shape and in touch with coworkers, Ford Motor Company provides fitness centers and fitness challenges for employees. Ford believes that exercise increases positive moods, resulting in happier, healthier, and more productive employees. The company also sponsors recreational clubs for activities such as bowling, racquetball, skiing, and softball that allow employees to get a good physical workout while interacting socially with other employees. Shown here is an employee with Ford's fitness director at an assembly plant in Hazelwood, Missouri.

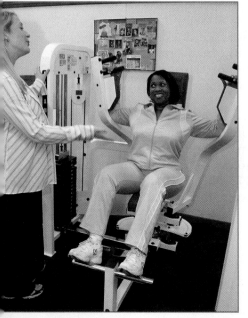

Sleep   According to a recent poll, people are getting less and less sleep. On average, Americans sleep less than seven hours per weekday night—below the eight-hour recommendation. And the number of people who actually sleep eight or more hours a night has steadily decreased over the past few years to about one in four. Roughly 75 percent of those polled reported having at least one symptom of a sleep problem a few nights a week or more within the past year.[50]

As you might imagine, sleep quality affects mood. Undergraduates and adult workers who are sleep-deprived report greater feelings of fatigue, anger, and hostility.[51] One of the reasons why less sleep, or poor sleep quality, puts people in a bad mood is because it impairs decision making and makes it difficult to control emotions.[52] A recent study suggests that poor sleep the previous night also impairs people's job satisfaction the next day, mostly because people feel fatigued, irritable, and less alert.[53]

Exercise   You often hear that people should exercise to improve their mood. But does "sweat therapy" really work? It appears so. Research consistently shows that exercise enhances people's positive mood.[54] It appears that the therapeutic effects of exercise are strongest for those who are depressed. Although the effects of exercise on moods are consistent, they are not terribly strong. So, exercise may help put you in a better mood, but don't expect miracles.

Age   Do you think that young people experience more extreme, positive emotions (so-called "youthful exuberance") than older people do? If you answered yes, you were wrong. One study of people aged 18 to 94 years revealed negative emotions seem to occur less as people get older. Periods of highly positive moods lasted longer for older individuals and bad moods faded more quickly.[55] The study implies that emotional experience tends to improve with age so that as we get older, we experience fewer negative emotions.

Gender   The common belief is that women are more in touch with their feelings than men are—that they react more emotionally and are better able to read emotions in others. Is there any truth to these assumptions?

The evidence does confirm differences between men and women when it comes to emotional reactions and the ability to read others. In contrasting the genders, women show greater emotional expression than men;[56] they experience emotions more intensely; and they display more frequent expressions of both positive and negative emotions, except anger.[57] In contrast to men, women also report more comfort in expressing emotions. Finally, women are better at reading nonverbal and paralinguistic cues than are men.[58]

What explains these differences? Researchers have suggested three possible explanations. One explanation is the different ways men and women have been socialized.[59] Men are taught to be tough and brave. Showing emotion is inconsistent with this image. Women, in contrast, are socialized to be nurturing. This may account for the perception that women are generally warmer and friendlier than men. For instance, women are expected to express more positive emotions on the job (shown by smiling) than men, and they do.[60] A second explanation is that women may have more innate ability to read others and present their emotions than do men.[61] Third, women may have a greater need for social approval and, so, a higher propensity to show positive emotions, such as happiness.

External Constraints on Emotions

An emotion that is acceptable on the athletic playing field may be totally unacceptable when exhibited at the workplace. Similarly, what's appropriate in one country is often inappropriate in another. These two factors play a role in determining what emotions we'll display. Every organization defines boundaries that identify which emotions are acceptable and the degree to which employees may express them. Cultures set boundaries, too. In this section, we look at organizational and cultural influences on emotions.

Organizational Influences   If you can't smile and appear happy, you're unlikely to have much of a career working at a Disney amusement park. And a manual produced by McDonald's states that its counter personnel "must display traits such as sincerity, enthusiasm, confidence, and a sense of humor."[62] There is no single emotional "set" that all organizations worldwide

When it comes to expressing positive emotions, Southwest Airlines imposes few external constraints on employee behavior. It encourages employees to be passionate about their work and gives them freedom in expressing their passion. Southwest's emotional "set" of appropriate behaviors among employees includes caring, nurturing, and fun loving. Displaying these emotions on the job delights Southwest's passengers, as the flight attendant shown here readies to embrace a tiny traveler.

seek in their employees. However, in the United States, the evidence indicates that there's a bias against negative and intense emotions. Expressions of negative emotions such as fear, anxiety, and anger tend to be unacceptable except under fairly specific conditions.[63] For instance, one such condition might be a high-status member of a group conveying impatience with a low-status member.[64] Moreover, expressions of intense emotion, whether negative or positive, tend to be unacceptable because management regards them as undermining routine task performance.[65] Again, there are instances when such expressions are acceptable—for example, a brief grieving over the sudden death of a company's CEO or the celebration of a record year of profits. But for the most part, the climate in well-managed American organizations is one that strives to be emotion-free.

Cultural Influences   Does the degree to which people *experience* emotions vary across cultures? Do people's *interpretations* of emotions vary across cultures? Finally, do the norms for the *expression* of emotions differ across cultures? Let's tackle each of these questions.

Does the degree to which people experience emotions vary across cultures? Yes. In China, for example, people report that they experience fewer positive and negative emotions than those in other cultures, and whatever emotions they do experience are less intense than what other cultures report. Compared to Mainland Chinese, Taiwanese are more like Americans in their experience of emotions: On average Taiwanese report more positive and fewer negative emotions than their Chinese counterparts.[66] In general, people in most cultures appear to experience certain positive and negative emotions, but the frequency of their experience and their intensity does vary to some degree.[67]

Do people's interpretations of emotions vary across cultures? In general, people from all over the world interpret negative and positive emotions the same way. We all view negative emotions, such as hate, terror, and rage, as dangerous and destructive. And we all desire positive emotions—such as joy, love, and happiness. However, some cultures value certain emotions more than others. For example, Americans value enthusiasm while Chinese consider negative emotions to be

In expanding their stores to other countries, Wal-Mart has learned that cultural norms govern emotional expression. The Chinese people, for example, are accustomed to vendors hawking their goods in street markets. When Wal-Mart employees in China shout out special prices for products, customers view the emotional expressions in a positive way as showing excitement and enthusiasm. But these expressions would not be acceptable in countries like Sweden where people place a low value on assertiveness.

Emotional Recognition: Universal or Culture-Specific?

EARLY RESEARCHERS STUDYING HOW WE UNDERstand emotions based on others' expressions believed that all individuals, regardless of their culture, could recognize the same emotion. So, for example, a frown would be recognized as indicating the emotion of sadness, no matter where one was from. However, more recent research suggests that this universal approach to the study of emotions is incorrect because there are subtle differences in the degree to which we can tell what emotions people from different cultures are feeling based on their facial expressions.

One study examined how quickly and accurately we can read the facial expressions of people of different cultural backgrounds. Although individuals were at first faster at recognizing the emotional expression of others from their own culture, when living in a different culture, the speed and accuracy at which they recognized others' emotions increased as they became more familiar with the culture. For example, as Chinese residing in the United States adapted to their surroundings they were able to recognize the emotions of U.S. citizens more quickly. In fact, foreigners are sometimes better at recognizing emotions among the citizens in their non-native country than are those citizens themselves.

Interestingly, these effects begin to occur relatively quickly. For example, Chinese students living in the United States for an average of 2.4 years were better at recognizing the facial expressions of U.S. citizens than the facial expressions of Chinese citizens. Why is this the case? According to the authors of the study, it could be that they, limited in speaking the language, rely more on nonverbal communication. What is the upshot for OB? When conducting business in a foreign country, the ability to correctly recognize others' emotions can facilitate interactions and lead to less miscommunication. Otherwise, a slight smile that is intended to communicate disinterest may be mistaken for happiness.

Based on H. A. Elfenbein and N. Ambady, "When Familiarity Breeds Accuracy: Cultural Exposure and Facial Emotion Recognition," *Journal of Personality and Social Psychology,* August 2003, pp. 276–290.

---

more useful and constructive than do Americans. In general, pride is seen as a positive emotion in Western, individualistic cultures such as the United States, but Eastern cultures such as China and Japan tend to view pride as undesirable.[68]

Do the norms for the expression of emotions differ across cultures? Absolutely. For example, Muslims see smiling as a sign of sexual attraction, so women have learned not to smile at men.[69] And research has shown that in collectivist countries people are more likely to believe that emotional displays have something to do with their own relationship with the person expressing the emotion, while people in individualistic cultures do not think that another's emotional expressions are directed at them.[70]

For example, in Venezuela (a highly collectivistic culture), someone seeing an angry expression on a friend's face would think that the friend is mad at her, but in America (a very individualistic culture), a person would generally not attribute an angry friend's expression to something she had done. Such norms play a role in *emotional labor,* which we'll learn about in the next section.

In general, it's easier for people to accurately recognize emotions within their own culture than in those of other cultures. For example, a Chinese businessperson is more likely to accurately label the emotions underlying the facial expressions of a fellow Chinese colleague than those of an American colleague.[71]

Interestingly, some cultures lack words for standard American emotional terms such as *anxiety, depression,* and *guilt.* Tahitians, as a case in point, don't have a word directly equivalent to *sadness.* When Tahitians are sad, their peers attribute their state to a physical illness.[72] Our discussion illustrates the need to consider cultural factors as influencing what managers consider emotionally appropriate.[73] What's acceptable in one culture may seem extremely unusual or even dysfunctional in another. Managers need to know the emotional norms in each culture they do business in so they don't send unintended signals or misread the reactions of locals. For example, an American manager in Japan should know that while Americans tend to view smiling positively, Japanese are apt to attribute frequent smiling to a lack of intelligence.[74]

Emotional Labor

If you ever had a job working in retail sales or waiting on tables in a restaurant, you know the importance of projecting a friendly demeanor and a smile. Even though there were days when you didn't feel cheerful, you knew management expected you to be upbeat when dealing with customers. So you faked it, and in so doing, you expressed emotional labor.

Every employee expends physical and mental labor when they put their bodies and cognitive capabilities, respectively, into their job. But jobs also require **emotional labor**. Emotional labor is an employee's expression of organizationally desired emotions during interpersonal transactions at work.[75]

The concept of emotional labor emerged from studies of service jobs. Think about it. Airlines expect their flight attendants, for instance, to be cheerful, we expect funeral directors to be sad, and doctors to be emotionally neutral. But really, emotional labor is relevant to almost every job. Your managers expect you, for example, to be courteous, not hostile, in interactions with coworkers. The true challenge is when employees have to project one emotion while simultaneously feeling another.[76] This disparity is **emotional dissonance**, and it can take a heavy toll on employees. Left untreated, bottled-up feelings of frustration, anger, and resentment can eventually lead to emotional exhaustion and burnout.[77] It's from the increasing importance of emotional labor as a key component of effective job performance that an understanding of emotion has gained heightened relevance within the field of OB.

Felt Versus Displayed Emotions

Emotional labor creates dilemmas for employees. There are people with whom you have to work that you just plain don't like. Maybe you consider their personality abrasive. Maybe you know they've said negative things about you behind your back. Regardless, your job requires you to interact with these people on a regular basis. So you're forced to feign friendliness.

It can help you, on the job especially, if you separate emotions into *felt* or *displayed.*[78] **Felt emotions** are an individual's actual emotions. In contrast, **displayed emotions** are those that the organization requires workers to show and considers appropriate in a given job. They're not innate; they're learned. "The ritual look of delight on the face of the first runner-up as the new Miss America is announced is a product of the display rule that losers should mask their sadness with an expression of joy for the winner."[79] Similarly, most of us know that we're expected to act sad at funerals regardless of whether we consider the person's death to be a loss and to pretend to be happy at weddings even if we don't feel like celebrating.[80]

Effective managers have learned to be serious when giving an employee a negative performance evaluation and to hide their anger when they've been passed over for promotion. And the salesperson who hasn't learned to smile and appear friendly, regardless of his true feelings at the moment, isn't typically going to last long on most sales jobs. How we *experience* an emotion isn't always the same as how we *show* it.[81]

The key point here is that felt and displayed emotions are often different. Many people have problems working with others because they naïvely assume that the emotions they see others display is what those others actually feel. This is particularly true in organizations, where role demands and situations often require people to exhibit emotional behaviors that mask their true feelings. In addition, jobs today increasingly require employees to interact with customers. And customers aren't always easy to deal with. They often complain, behave rudely, and make unrealistic demands. In such instances, an employee's felt emotions may need to be disguised. Employees who aren't able to project a friendly and helpful demeanor in such situations are likely to alienate customers and are unlikely to be effective in their jobs.

Yet another point is that displaying fake emotions requires us to suppress the emotions we really feel (not showing anger toward a customer, for example). In other words, the individual has to "act" to keep her job. **Surface acting** is hiding one's inner feelings and forgoing emotional expressions in response to display rules. For example, when a worker smiles at a customer even when he doesn't feel like it, he is surface acting. **Deep acting** is trying to modify one's true inner feelings based on display rules. A health-care provider trying to genuinely feel more empathy for her patients is deep acting.[82] Surface acting deals with one's *displayed* emotions, and deep acting deals with one's *felt* emotions. Research shows that surface acting is more stressful to employees because it entails feigning one's true emotions.[83]

As we've noted, emotional norms vary across cultures. Cultural norms in the United States dictate that employees in service organizations should smile and act friendly when interacting with customers.[84] But this norm doesn't apply worldwide. In Israel, customers see smiling supermarket cashiers as inexperienced, so managers encourage cashiers to look somber.[85] Employees in France are likely to experience a minimal degree of emotional dissonance because they make little effort to hide their true feelings. French retail clerks are infamous for being surly toward customers. (A report from the French government itself confirmed this.)[86] And Wal-Mart has found that its emphasis on employee friendliness, which has won them a loyal following among U.S. shoppers, doesn't work in Germany. Accustomed to a culture where the customer traditionally comes last, serious German shoppers have been turned off by Wal-Mart's friendly greeters and helpful personnel.[87]

And what about gender differences? Do you think society expects women to display different emotions than men, even in the same job? This is a difficult question to answer, but there is some evidence that upper management does expect men and women to display different emotions even in the same

---

emotional labor   *A situation in which an employee expresses organizationally desired emotions during interpersonal transactions at work.*

emotional dissonance   *Inconsistencies between the emotions we feel and the emotions we project.*

felt emotions   *An individual's actual emotions.*

displayed emotions   *Emotions that are organizationally required and considered appropriate in a given job.*

surface acting   *Hiding one's inner feelings and forgoing emotional expressions in response to display rules.*

deep acting   *Trying to modify one's true inner feelings based on display rules.*

job. In professional and managerial jobs, for example, women report having to suppress negative feelings and display more positive feelings than men to conform to what they say their bosses and colleagues expect.[88]

Are Emotionally Demanding Jobs Rewarded with Better Pay?

You may wonder how well the labor market rewards jobs that are emotionally demanding. You might think, for example, that the job of funeral director, which may include mortician duties and arranging funerals with grieving families, should pay well. But it seems that jobs that are emotionally demanding (jobs that are taxing or require an employee to "put on a good face") may be rewarded less well than jobs that are cognitively demanding (ones that require a lot of thinking and that demand a complex set of skills).

A recent study examined this issue across a wide range of jobs.[89] The authors of the study found that the relationship between cognitive demands and pay was quite strong, while the relationship between emotional demands and pay was not. They did find that emotional demands matter, but only when jobs already were cognitively demanding—jobs such as lawyers and nurses. But, for instance, child-care workers and waiters (jobs with high emotional demands but relatively low cognitive demands), receive little compensation for emotional demands.

Exhibit 8-5 shows the relationship between cognitive and emotional demands and pay. For jobs that are cognitively demanding, increasing emotional demands lead to better pay. However, for jobs that are not cognitively demanding, increasing emotional demands lead to *worse* pay. The model doesn't seem to depict a fair state of affairs. After all, why should emotional demands be rewarded in only cognitively complex jobs? One explanation may be that it's hard to find qualified people who are willing and able to work in such jobs.

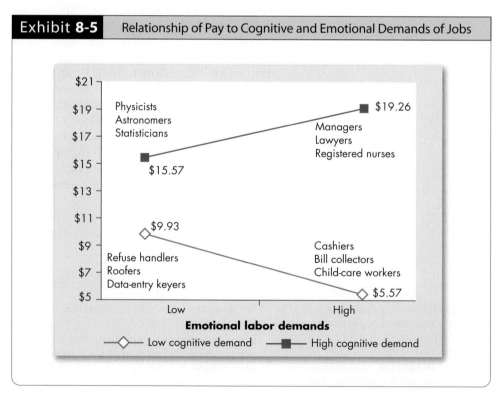

Exhibit 8-5   Relationship of Pay to Cognitive and Emotional Demands of Jobs

Source: Based on: T. M. Glomb, J. D. Kammeyer-Mueller, and M. Rotundo, "Emotional Labor Demands and Compensating Wage Differentials," *Journal of Applied Psychology,* Vol 89(4), Aug 2004, pp. 700–714.

Affective Events Theory

As we have seen, emotions and moods are an important part of our lives, especially our work lives. But how do our emotions and moods influence our job performance and satisfaction? A model called **affective events theory (AET)** has increased our understanding of the links.[90] AET demonstrates that employees react emotionally to things that happen to them at work and that this reaction influences their job performance and satisfaction.

Exhibit 8-6 summarizes AET. The theory begins by recognizing that emotions are a response to an event in the work environment. The work environment includes everything surrounding the job—the variety of tasks and degree of autonomy, job demands, and requirements for expressing emotional labor. This environment creates work events that can be hassles, uplifts, or both. Examples of hassles are colleagues who refuse to carry their share of work, conflicting directions by different managers, and excessive time pressures. Examples of uplifting events include meeting a goal, getting support from a colleague, and receiving recognition for an accomplishment.[91]

These work events trigger positive or negative emotional reactions. But employees' personalities and moods predisposes them to respond with greater or lesser intensity to the event. For instance, people who score low on emotional stability are more likely to react strongly to negative events. And their mood introduces the reality that their general affect cycle creates fluctuations. So a person's emotional response to a given event can change depending on mood. Finally, emotions influence a number of performance and satisfaction variables such as organizational citizenship behavior, organizational commitment, level of effort, intentions to quit, and workplace deviance.

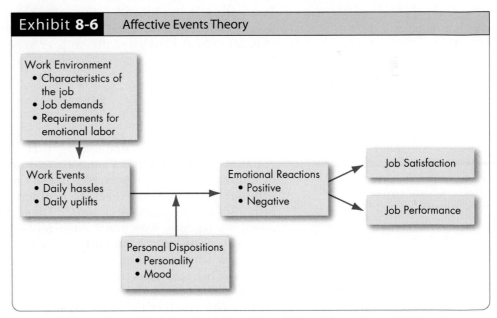

Exhibit 8-6 Affective Events Theory

Source: Based on N. M. Ashkanasy and C. S. Daus, "Emotion in the Workplace: The New Challenge for Managers," *Academy of Management Executive,* February 2002, p. 77.

affective events theory *A model which suggests that workplace events cause emotional reactions on the part of employees, which then influence workplace attitudes and behaviors.*

In addition, tests of the theory suggest that (1) an emotional episode is actually a series of emotional experiences precipitated by a single event. It contains elements of both emotions and mood cycles. (2) Current emotions influence job satisfaction at any given time, along with the history of emotions surrounding the event. (3) Because moods and emotions fluctuate over time, their effect on performance also fluctuates. (4) Emotion-driven behaviors are typically short in duration and of high variability. (5) Because emotions, even positive ones, tend to be incompatible with behaviors required to do a job, they typically have a negative influence on job performance.[92]

An example might help better explain AET.[93] You work as an aeronautical engineer for Boeing. Because of the downturn in the demand for commercial jets, you've just learned that the company is considering laying off 10,000 employees. This layoff could include you. This event is likely to make you feel negative emotions, especially fear that you might lose your job and primary source of income. And because you're prone to worry a lot and obsess about problems, this event increases your feelings of insecurity.

It also puts into place a series of smaller events that create an episode: You talk with your boss and he assures you that your job is safe; you hear rumors that your department is high on the list to be eliminated; you run into a former colleague who was laid off six months ago and still hasn't found work. These events, in turn, create emotional ups and downs. One day you're feeling more upbeat and that you'll survive the cuts. The next day, you might be depressed and anxious. These emotional swings take your attention away from your work and lower your job performance and satisfaction. Finally, your response is magnified because this is the fourth largest layoff that Boeing has initiated in the last three years.

In summary, AET offers two important messages.[94] First, emotions provide valuable insights into understanding employee behavior. The model demonstrates how workplace hassles and uplifts influence employee performance and satisfaction. Second, employees and managers shouldn't ignore emotions and the events that cause them, even when they appear to be minor, because they accumulate.

Emotional Intelligence

Diane Marshall is an office manager. Her awareness of her own and others' emotions is almost nil. She's moody and unable to generate much enthusiasm or interest in her employees. She doesn't understand why employees get upset with her. She often overreacts to problems and chooses the most ineffectual responses to emotional situations.[95] Diane Marshall is someone with low emotional intelligence. **Emotional intelligence (EI)** is one's ability to detect and to manage emotional cues and information.

People who know their own emotions and are good at reading others' emotions may be more effective in their jobs. That, in essence, is the theme underlying recent EI research.[96]

EI is composed of five dimensions:

- *Self-awareness*—being aware of what you're feeling
- *Self-management*—the ability to manage your own emotions and impulses
- *Self-motivation*—the ability to persist in the face of setbacks and failures
- *Empathy*—the ability to sense how others are feeling
- *Social skills*—the ability to handle the emotions of others

Several studies suggest that EI plays an important role in job performance. One study looked at the characteristics of Lucent Technologies' engineers who

Meg Whitman, CEO of eBay, is a leader with high emotional intelligence. Since eBay founder Pierre Omidyar selected Whitman to transform his startup into a global enterprise, she has emerged as a star performer in a job that demands interacting socially with employees, customers, and political leaders throughout the world. Whitman is described as self-confident yet humble, trustworthy, culturally sensitive, and expert at building teams and leading change. Shown here, Whitman welcomes Gloria Arroyo, president of the Philippine Islands where eBay has an auction site, to eBay headquarters.

were rated as stars by their peers. The researchers concluded that stars were better at relating to others. That is, it was EI, not IQ, that characterized high performers. Another illuminating study looked at the successes and failures of 11 American presidents—from Franklin Roosevelt to Bill Clinton. They were evaluated on six qualities—communication, organization, political skill, vision, cognitive style, and emotional intelligence. It was found that the key quality that differentiated the successful (like Roosevelt, Kennedy, and Reagan) from the unsuccessful (like Johnson, Carter, and Nixon) was emotional intelligence.[97]

The Case for EI

EI has been a controversial concept in OB. It has its supporters and detractors. In the upcoming sections, we'll review the arguments for, and against, the viability of EI in OB.

Intuitive Appeal   There's a lot of intuitive appeal to the EI concept. Most everyone would agree that it is good to possess street smarts and social intelligence. Those people who can detect emotions in others, control their own emotions, and handle social interactions well will have a powerful leg up in the business world, so the thinking goes. As just one example, partners in a multinational consulting firm who scored above the median on an EI measure delivered $1.2 million more in business than did the other partners.[98]

EI Predicts Criteria That Matter   Evidence is mounting that suggests a high level of EI means a person will perform well on the job. One study found that EI predicted the performance of employees in a cigarette factory in China.[99]

emotional intelligence   *The ability to detect and to manage emotional cues and information.*

Another study found that being able to recognize emotions in others' facial expressions and to emotionally "eavesdrop" (pick up subtle signals about people's emotions) predicted peer ratings of how valuable these people were to their organization.[100] Finally, a review of 59 studies indicated that, overall, EI correlated moderately with job performance.[101]

EI Is Biologically Based   One study has shown that people with damage to the part of the brain that governs emotional processing (lesions in an area of the prefrontal cortex) score significantly lower on EI tests. Even though these brain-damaged people scored no lower on standard measures of intelligence than people without the same brain damage, they were still impaired in normal decision making. Specifically, when people were playing a card game in which there is a reward (money) for picking certain types of cards and a punishment (a loss of money) for picking other types of cards, the participants with no brain damage learned to succeed in the game, while the performance of the brain-damaged group worsened over time. This study suggests that EI is neurologically based in a way that's unrelated to standard measures of intelligence, and that people who suffer neurological damage score lower on EI and make poorer decisions than people who are healthier in this regard.[102]

The Case against EI

For all its supporters, EI has just as many critics.

EI Is Too Vague a Concept   To many researchers, it's not clear what EI is. Is it a form of intelligence? Most of us wouldn't think that being self-aware or self-motivated or having empathy is a matter of intellect. So, is EI a misnomer? Moreover, many times different researchers focus on different skills, making it difficult to get a definition of EI. One researcher may study self-discipline. Another may study empathy. Another may look at self-awareness. As one reviewer noted, "The concept of EI has now become so broad and the components so variegated that . . . it is no longer even an intelligible concept."[103]

EI Can't Be Measured   Many critics have raised questions about measuring EI. Because EI is a form of intelligence, for instance, then there must be right and wrong answers about it on tests, they argue. Some tests do have right and wrong answers, although the validity of some of the questions on these measures is questionable. For example, one measure asks you to associate particular feelings with specific colors, as if purple always makes us feel cool not warm. Other measures are self-reported, meaning there is no right or wrong answer. For example, an EI test question might ask you to respond to the statement, "I'm good at 'reading' other people." In general, the measures of EI are diverse, and researchers have not subjected them to as much rigorous study as they have measures of personality and general intelligence.[104]

The Validity of EI Is Suspect   Some critics argue that because EI is so closely related to intelligence and personality, once you control for these factors, EI has nothing unique to offer. There is some foundation to this argument. EI appears to be highly correlated with measures of personality, especially emotional stability.[105] But there hasn't been enough research on whether EI adds insight beyond measures of personality and general intelligence in predicting job performance. Still, among consulting firms and in the popular press, EI is wildly popular. For example, one company's promotional materials for an EI measure claimed, "EI accounts for more than 85 percent of star performance in top leaders."[106] To say the least, it's hard to validate this statement with the research literature.

Whatever your view of EI, one thing's for sure: The concept is here to stay.

Now that you know more about emotional intelligence, do you think you are a good judge of people? Do you think you can determine what makes someone tick? Check out the Self-Assessment feature to determine your EI.

SELF ASSESSMENT LIBRARY

WHAT'S MY EMOTIONAL INTELLIGENCE SCORE?

In the Self-Assessment Library (available on CD, online, and in print), take assessment I.E.1 (What's My Emotional Intelligence Score?) and answer the following questions.

1. *How did you score relative to your classmates?*
2. *Did your score surprise you? Why or why not?*
3. *What might you do to improve your ability to read others' emotions?*

OB Applications of Emotions and Moods

We conclude our discussion of emotions and moods by considering their specific application to OB. In this section, we assess how an understanding of emotions and moods can improve our ability to explain and predict the selection process in organizations, decision making, creativity, motivation, leadership, interpersonal conflict, negotiation, customer service, job attitudes, and deviant workplace behaviors. We also look at how managers can influence our moods.

Selection

One implication from the evidence to date on EI is that employers should consider it a factor in hiring employees, especially in jobs that demand a high degree of social interaction. In fact, more and more employers are starting to use EI measures to hire people. A study of U.S. Air Force recruiters showed that top-performing recruiters exhibited high levels of EI. Using these findings, the Air Force revamped its selection criteria. A follow-up investigation found that future hires who had high EI scores were 2.6 times more successful than those who didn't. By using EI in selection, the Air Force was able to cut turnover rates among new recruiters in one year by more than 90 percent and save nearly $3 million in hiring and training costs. At L'Oreal, salespersons selected on EI scores outsold those hired using the company's old selection procedure. On an annual basis, salespeople selected on the basis of emotional competence sold $91,370 more than other salespeople did, for a net revenue increase of $2,558,360.[107]

Decision Making

As you saw in Chapter 5, traditional approaches to the study of decision making in organizations have emphasized rationality. They have downplayed, or even ignored, the role of sadness, anxiety, fear, frustration, happiness, envy, and similar emotions. Yet it's naive to assume that feelings don't influence our decisions.[108] Given the same objective data, we should expect that people may make different choices when they're angry and stressed out than when they're calm and collected.

OB researchers continue to debate the role of negative emotions and moods in decision making. One well-cited article suggested that depressed people (those who chronically experience bad moods or negative emotions such as sadness) make more accurate judgments than nondepressed people.[109] This suggestion led some researchers to argue that the saying "sadder but wiser" is true. However, more recent evidence has suggested that people who are depressed make poorer decisions than happy people. Why? Because depressed people are slower at processing information and tend to weigh all possible options rather than the most likely ones.[110] Although it would seem that weighing all possible options is a good thing, the problem is that depressed people search for the perfect solution when rarely is any solution perfect.

Positive people, in contrast, know when a solution is good enough. Indeed, positive emotions seem to help decision making. Positive emotions can increase problem-solving skills and help us understand and analyze new information. For example, someone in a positive mood may be better able to infer that a subordinate's performance problems were due to some nonwork problems.[111] People in good moods or those experiencing positive emotions are more likely to use heuristics, or rules of thumb,[112] to help them make good decisions quickly. Sometimes, however, these heuristics can be wrong and can lead to stereotyping. So people need to make sure that their positive moods don't cause them to rely on dangerous stereotypes, like women are less dedicated, Muslims are violent people, and so on.

People use their heart as well as their head when making decisions. Therefore, failure to incorporate emotions and moods into the study of decision making will result in an incomplete, and often inaccurate, view of the process.

Creativity

People who are in good moods are more creative than people in bad moods, say some researchers.[113] They produce more ideas, others think their ideas are original, and they tend to identify more creative options to problems.[114] It seems that people who are experiencing positive moods or emotions are more flexible and open in their thinking, which may explain why they're more creative.[115] Supervisors should actively try to keep employees happy because this will create more good moods (employees like their leaders to encourage them and provide positive feedback on a job well done), which in turn leads people to be more creative.[116]

Some researchers, however, do not believe that a positive mood makes people more creative. They argue that when people are in positive moods, they may relax ("if I'm in a good mood, things must be going OK, and I must not need to think of new ideas") and not engage in the critical thinking necessary for some forms of creativity.[117] However, this view is controversial.[118] Until there are more studies on the subject, we can safely conclude that for many tasks, positive moods increase our creativity.

Motivation

As we saw in Chapter 6, motivation theories propose that individuals "are motivated to the extent that their behavior is expected to lead to desired outcomes . . . the employee essentially trades effort for pay, security, promotions, and so forth."[119] But as the Affective Events Theory demonstrated, people aren't cold, unfeeling machines. Their perceptions and calculations of work events are filled with emotional content that significantly influences how much effort they exert. Moreover, when you see people who are highly motivated in their jobs, they're emotionally committed. People who are engaged in their work "become physically, cognitively, *and* emotionally immersed in the experience of activity, in the pursuit of a goal."[120]

Are all people emotionally engaged in their work? No. But many are. So if we focus only on those who are not, we won't be able to explain behaviors such as the biologist who forgets to have dinner and works late into the night, lost in the thrill of her work.[121]

Two studies have highlighted the importance of moods and emotions on motivation. The first study had two groups of people solve a number of word puzzles. One group saw a funny video clip, which was intended to put the group in a good mood before having to solve the puzzles. The other group was not shown the clip and just started working on solving the word puzzles right away. The results? The positive-mood group reported higher expectations of being able to solve the puzzles, worked harder at them, and solved more puzzles as a result.[122]

The second study found that giving people feedback—whether real or fake—about their performance influenced their mood, which then influenced their motivation.[123] So, a cycle can exist in which positive moods cause people to be more creative, which leads to positive feedback from those observing their work. This positive feedback then further reinforces their positive mood, which may then make them perform even better, and so on.

Both of these studies highlight the effects of mood and emotions on motivation and suggest that organizations that promote positive moods at work are likely to have a more motivated workforce.

Leadership

The ability to lead others is a fundamental quality that organizations look for in employees.

When Carlos Ghosn took over as president and CEO of the nearly bankrupt Nissan Motor Corporation, he used emotionally charged speeches in presenting his plan to revive the company. In communicating his vision of returning Nissan to profitability, Ghosn convinced managers and employees to accept the changes of reducing the number of Nissan suppliers, eliminating 20,000 jobs, closing five plants, meeting new performance goals, adding new car models, and entering new markets. Under Ghosn's leadership, Nissan achieved a dramatic turnaround to profitability and revenue growth.

Effective leaders rely on emotional appeals to help convey their messages.[124] In fact, the expression of emotions in speeches is often the critical element that makes us accept or reject a leader's message. "When leaders feel excited, enthusiastic, and active, they may be more likely to energize their subordinates and convey a sense of efficacy, competence, optimism, and enjoyment."[125] Politicians, as a case in point, have learned to show enthusiasm when talking about their chances of winning an election, even when polls suggest otherwise.

Corporate executives know that emotional content is critical if employees are to buy into their vision of their company's future and accept change. When higher-ups offer new visions, especially when the visions contain distant or vague goals, it is often difficult for employees to accept those visions and the changes they'll bring. So when effective leaders want to implement significant changes, they rely on "the evocation, framing, and mobilization of *emotions*."[126] By arousing emotions and linking them to an appealing vision, leaders increase the likelihood that managers and employees alike will accept change.

Interpersonal Conflict

Few issues are more intertwined with emotions than the topic of interpersonal conflict. Whenever conflicts arise between coworkers, you can be fairly certain that emotions are surfacing. A manager's success in trying to resolve conflicts, in fact, is often largely attributable to an ability to identify the emotional elements in the conflict and to get the parties to work through their emotions. The manager who ignores the emotional elements in conflicts, focusing singularly on rational and task-focused concerns, is unlikely to resolve those conflicts.

Negotiation

Negotiation is an emotional process; however, we often say a skilled negotiator has a "poker face." The founder of Britain's Poker Channel, Crispin Nieboer, stated, "It is a game of bluff and there is fantastic human emotion and tension, seeing who can bluff the longest."[127] Several studies have shown that negotiators who feign anger have an advantage over their opponent. Why? Because when a negotiator shows anger, the opponent concludes that the negotiator has conceded all that she can, and so the opponent gives in.[128]

Displaying a negative emotion (such as anger) can be effective, but feeling bad about your performance appears to impair future negotiations. Negotiators who do poorly experience negative emotions, develop negative perceptions of their counterpart, and are less willing to share information or be cooperative in future negotiations.[129] Interestingly, then, while moods and emotions have their benefits at work, in negotiation, unless we're putting up a false front (feigning anger), it seems that emotions may impair negotiator performance. In fact, one 2005 study found that people who suffered damage to the emotional centers of their brains (damage to the same part of the brain as Phineas Gage) may be the *best* negotiators, because they're not likely to overcorrect when faced with negative outcomes.[130] Consider another example. When Northwest Airlines faced a strike from the mechanics union, the company coolly prepared for the strike by hiring replacement workers in advance, and when the union struck, hired replacement workers and calmly asked for even more concessions.[131]

Customer Service

A worker's emotional state influences customer service, which influences levels of repeat business and levels of customer satisfaction.[132] Providing quality customer service makes demands on employees because it often puts them in a state of emotional dissonance. Over time, this state can lead to job burnout, declines in job performance, and lower job satisfaction.[133]

In addition, employees' emotions may also transfer to the customer. Studies indicate a matching effect between employee and customer emotions, an effect that OB practitioners call **emotional contagion**, the "catching" of emotions from others.[134] How does emotional contagion work? The primary explanation is that when someone experiences positive emotions and laughs and smiles at you, you begin to copy that person's behavior. So when employees express positive emotions, customers tend to respond positively. Emotional contagion is important because when customers catch the positive moods or emotions of employees, they shop longer.[135] But what about negative emotions and moods? Are they contagious too? Absolutely. When an employee is cranky or nasty, these negative emotions tend to have negative effects on customers.

Job Attitudes

Ever hear the advice "Never take your work home with you," meaning that people should forget about their work once they go home? As it turns out, that's easier said than done. Several studies have shown that people who had a good day at work tend to be in a better mood at home that evening. And people who had a bad day tend to be in a bad mood once they're at home.[136] Evidence also suggests that people who have a stressful day at work have trouble relaxing once they get off work.[137]

Even though people do emotionally take their work home with them, by the next day, the effect is usually gone.[138] So, though it may be hard or even unnatural to "never take your work home with you," it doesn't appear that, for most people, a negative mood resulting from a bad day at work carries over to the next day.

Deviant Workplace Behaviors

Negative emotions also can lead to a number of deviant workplace behaviors.

Anyone who has spent much time in an organization realizes that people often behave in ways that violate established norms and that threaten the organization, its members, or both. As we saw in Chapter 1, these actions are called workplace deviant behaviors.[139] Many of these deviant behaviors can be traced to negative emotions.

For instance, envy is an emotion that occurs when you resent someone for having something that you don't have but that you strongly desire—such as a better work assignment, larger office, or higher salary.[140] It can lead to malicious deviant behaviors. An envious employee, for example, could then act hostilely by backstabbing another employee, negatively distorting others' successes, and positively distorting his own accomplishments.[141] Evidence suggests that people who feel negative emotions, particularly those who feel angry or hostile, are more likely than people who don't feel negative emotions to engage in deviant behavior at work.[142]

How Managers Can Influence Moods

In general, you can improve peoples' moods by showing them a funny video clip, giving them a small bag of candy, or even having them taste a pleasant beverage.[143] But what can companies do to improve their employees' moods?

emotional contagion *The process by which people's emotions are caused by the emotions of others.*

Managers can use humor and give their employees small tokens of appreciation for work well done. Also, research indicates that when leaders are in good moods, group members are more positive, and as a result the members cooperate more.[144]

Finally, selecting positive team members can have a contagion effect as positive moods transmit from team member to team member. One study of professional cricket teams (cricket is a sport played in countries such as Great Britain and India that's a little like baseball) found that players' happy moods affected the moods of their team members and also positively influenced their performance.[145] It makes sense, then, for managers to select team members who are predisposed to experience positive moods.

Summary and Implications for Managers

Emotions and moods are similar in that both are affective in nature. But they're also different—moods are more general and less contextual than emotions. And, events do matter. The time of day and day of the week, stressful events, social activities, and sleep patterns are all factors that influence emotions and moods.

Can managers control their colleagues' and employees' emotions and moods? Certainly there are limits, practically and ethically. Emotions and moods are a natural part of an individual's makeup. Where managers err is if they ignore their coworkers' emotions and assess others' behavior as if it were completely rational. As one consultant aptly put it, "You can't divorce emotions from the workplace because you can't divorce emotions from people."[146] Managers who understand the role of emotions and moods will significantly improve their ability to explain and predict their coworkers' behavior.

Do emotions and moods affect job performance? Yes. They can *hinder* performance, especially negative emotions. That's probably why organizations, for the most part, try to extract emotions out of the workplace. But emotions and moods can also *enhance* performance. How? Two ways.[147] First, emotions and moods can increase arousal levels, and motivate employees to work better. Second, emotional labor recognizes that certain feelings can be part of a job's requirements. So, for instance, the ability to effectively manage emotions in leadership, sales, and customer service positions may be critical to success in those positions. At the same time, organizations that shun the display of positive emotions, or encourage employees to suppress negative emotions, may find that both take a toll on their workforces.

What differentiates functional from dysfunctional emotions and moods at work? Although there is no precise answer to this, some analysts have suggested that the critical moderating variable is the complexity of the individual's task.[148] The more complex a task, the less emotional a worker can be before interfering with performance. While a minimal level of emotional arousal is probably necessary for good performance, high levels interfere with the ability to function, especially if the job requires calculative and detailed cognitive processes. Given that the trend is toward jobs becoming more complex, you can see why organizations are likely to become more concerned with the role of emotions—especially intense ones—in the workplace.

Point ◁▷ Counterpoint

The Costs and Benefits of Organizational Display Rules

Organizations today realize that good customer service means good business. After all, who wants to end a shopping trip at the grocery store with a surly checker? Research clearly shows that organizations that provide good customer service have higher profits.[149] An integral part of customer service training is to set forth display rules to teach employees to interact with customers in a friendly, helpful, professional way.

As one Starbucks manager says, "What makes Starbucks different is our passion for what we do. We're trying to provide a great experience for people, with a great product. That's what we all care about."[150] Starbucks may have good coffee, but a big part of the company's growth has been the customer experience. For instance, the cashiers are friendly and will get to know you by name if you are a repeat customer.

Asking employees to act friendly is good for them, too. "Forced" smiles can actually make people feel better.[151] And, if someone feels that being asked to smile is bad for him, he doesn't belong in the service industry in the first place.

Organizations have no business trying to regulate the emotions of their employees. Companies should not be "the thought police" and force employees to feel and act in ways that serve only organizational needs. Service employees should be professional and courteous, yes, but many companies expect them to take abuse and refrain from defending themselves. That's wrong. As the philosopher Jean Paul Sartre wrote, we have a responsibility to be authentic—true to ourselves—and within reasonable limits organizations have no right to ask us to be otherwise.

Service industries have no business teaching their employees to be smiling punching bags. Most customers might even prefer that employees be themselves. Employees shouldn't be openly nasty or hostile, of course, but who appreciates a fake smile? Think about trying on an outfit in a store and the clerk automatically says that looks "absolutely wonderful" when you know it doesn't and you sense the clerk is lying. Most customers would rather talk with a "real" person than someone enslaved to an organization's display rules. Furthermore, if an employee doesn't feel like slapping on an artificial smile, then it's only going to create dissonance between her and her employer.[152]

Finally, research shows that forcing display rules on employees takes a heavy emotional toll.[153] It's unnatural to expect someone to smile all the time or to passively take abuse from customers, clients, or fellow employees. Organizations can improve their employees' psychological health by encouraging them to be themselves, within reasonable limits.

Questions for Review

1. What are the differences and similarities between emotions and moods?

2. How does the time of the day, the day of the week, and the weather influence peoples' moods?

3. Are there differences in the degree to which men and women show emotions in the workplace? What types of workplace situations might bring to light these different emotional reactions?

4. Are there cultural differences in the degree to which people experience emotions? What about in the expression of emotions?

5. What is emotional labor, and why is it important to understanding OB?

6. If you were a manager at a busy clothing store, how would you balance increasing positive customer experiences with preventing the loss of good employees who might be worn down by nasty or hostile customers?

7. Explain Affective Events Theory. What are its implications for managing emotions?

8. What is emotional intelligence and why is it important?

9. As a manager, what steps would you take to improve your employees' moods? Explain your answer.

Questions for Critical Thinking

1. In your opinion—and drawing from the arguments in the chapter—are there core or fundamental emotions that everyone experiences? If so, what are they?

2. What has research shown on the relationship between emotions and rational thinking? Do these findings surprise you? Why or why not?

3. Do emotions and moods matter in explaining behavior in organizations? How so?

4. What, if anything, can managers do to *manage* their employees' emotions? Are their ethical implications in any of these actions? If so, what are they?

5. Give some examples of situations in which the overt expression of emotions might enhance job performance.

Team Exercise

WHO CAN CATCH A LIAR?

Earlier in the chapter we discussed how people determine emotions from facial expressions. There has been research on whether people can tell whether someone is lying based on facial expression. Let's see who is good at catching liars.

Split up into teams, and follow these instructions:

1. Randomly choose someone to be the team organizer. Have this person write down on a piece of paper "T" for truth and "L" for lie. If there are, say, six people in the group (other than the organizer), then three people will get a slip with a "T" and three a slip with an "L." It's important that all team members keep what's on their paper a secret.

2. Each team member needs to come up with a true or false statement depending on whether he or she

holds a T or an L slip. Try not to make the statement so outrageous that no one would believe it (for example, "I have flown to the moon").

3. The organizer will have each member make his statement. Group members should then examine the person making the statement closely to try to determine whether he is telling the truth or lying. Once each person has made his statement, the organizer will ask for a vote and record the tallies.

4. Each person should now indicate whether the statement was the truth or a lie.

5. How good was your group at catching the liars? Were some people good "liars"? What did you look for to determine if someone was lying?

Ethical Dilemma

ARE WORKPLACE ROMANCES UNETHICAL?

A large percentage of married individuals first met in the workplace. A 2005 survey revealed that 58 percent of all employees have been in an office romance. Given the amount of time people spend at work, this isn't terribly surprising. Yet office romances pose sensitive ethical issues for organizations and employees. What rights and responsibilities do organizations have to regulate the romantic lives of their employees?

Take the case of former General Electric CEO Jack Welch and Suzy Wetlaufer. The two met while Wetlaufer was interviewing Welch for a *Harvard Business Review* article, and Welch was still married. Once their relationship was out in the open, some accused Wetlaufer of being unethical for refusing to disclose the relationship while working on the article. She eventually left the journal. Others accused Welch of letting his personal life get in the way of the interest of GE and its shareholders. Some even blamed the scandal for a drop in GE stock.

Welch and Wetlaufer didn't even work for the same company. What about when two people work together in the same work unit? For example, Tasha, an account executive at a Chicago advertising firm, started dating Kevin, one of her account supervisors. Their innocent banter turned into going out for drinks, and then dinner, and soon they were dating. Kevin and Tasha's bosses were in-house competitors. The problem: Sometimes in meetings Kevin would make it seem that Tasha and Kevin were on the same side of important issues even when they weren't. In response, Tasha's boss began to isolate her from key projects. Tasha broke up with Kevin, who then tried to have her fired. Tasha said, "I remember times when I would be there all night photocopying hundreds of pages of my work to show that [Kevin's] allegations [of her incompetence] were unfounded. It was just embarrassing because it became a question of my professional judgment."

These examples show that while workplace romances are personal matters, it's hard to keep them out of the political complexities of organizational life.

Questions

1. Do you think organizations should have policies governing workplace romances? What would such policies stipulate?

2. Do you think romantic relationships would distract two employees from performing their jobs? Why or why not?

3. Is it ever appropriate for a supervisor to romantically pursue a subordinate under his or her supervision? Why or why not?

4. Some companies like Nike and Southwest Airlines openly try to recruit couples. Do you think this is a good idea? How would you feel working in a department with a "couple"?

Sources: "Cupid in the Cubicle, Says New Vault Survey," *Vault, Inc.* (www.vault.com); S. Shellenbarger, "The Nasty Downside of Office Romances," *The Wall Street Journal* (www.wsj.com) (2005); J. Amber, "Office Romance" (www.yourpurelife.com).

Case Incident 1

THE UPSIDE OF ANGER?

A researcher doing a case study on emotions in organizations interviewed Laura, a 22-year-old customer service representative in Australia. Below is a summary of the interview (with some paraphrasing of the interviewer questions):

Interviewer: How would you describe your workplace?

Laura: *Very cold, unproductive, [a] very, umm, cold environment, atmosphere.*

Interviewer: What kinds of emotions are prevalent in your organization?

Laura: *Anger, hatred towards other people, other staff members.*

Interviewer: So it seems that managers keep employees in line using fear tactics?

Laura: *Yeah. [The General Manager's] favorite saying is, "Nobody's indispensable." So, it's like, "I can't do that because I'll get sacked!"*

Interviewer: How do you survive in this situation?

Laura: *You have to cater your emotions to the sort of situation, the specific situation . . . because it's just such a hostile environment, this is sort of the only way you can survive.*

Interviewer: Are there emotions you have to hide?

Laura: Managers don't like you to show your emotions . . . They don't like to show that there is anything wrong or anything emotional in the working environment.

Interviewer: Why do you go along?

Laura: I feel I have to put on an act because . . . to show your true emotions, especially towards my managers [Laura names two of her senior managers], it would be hatred sometimes. So, you just can't afford to do that because it's your job and you need the money.

Interviewer: Do you ever rebel against this system?

Laura: You sort of put on a happy face just so you can annoy [the managers]. I find that they don't like people being happy, so you just annoy them by being happy. So, yeah. It just makes you laugh. You just "put it on" just because you know it annoys [management]. It's pretty vindictive and manipulative but you just need to do that.

Interviewer: Do you ever find that this gets to you?

Laura: I did care in the beginning and I think it just got me into more trouble. So now I just tell myself, "I don't care." If you tell yourself something for long enough, eventually you believe it. Yeah, so now I just go "Oh well."

Interviewer: Do you intend to keep working here?

Laura: It's a means to an end now. So every time I go [to work] and every week I just go, "Well, one week down, one week less until I go away." But if I knew that I didn't have this goal, I don't know if I could handle it, or if I would even be there now.

Interviewer: Is there an upside to working here?

Laura: I'm so much better at telling people off now than I ever used to be. I can put people in place in about three sentences. Like, instead of, before I would walk away from it. But now I just stand there and fight . . . I don't know if that's a good thing or a bad thing.

Questions

1. Do you think Laura is justified in her responses to her organization's culture? Why or why not?

2. Do you think Laura's strategic use and display of emotions serve to protect her?

3. Assuming Laura's description is accurate, how would *you* react to the organization's culture?

4. Research shows that acts of coworkers (37 percent) and management (22 percent) cause more negative emotions for employees than do acts of customers (7 percent).[154] What can Laura's company do to change its emotional climate?

Source: J. Perrone and M. H. Vickers, "Emotions as Strategic Game in a Hostile Workplace: An Exemplar Case," *Employee Responsibilities and Rights Journal* 16, no. 3 (2004), pp. 167–78.

Case Incident 2

ABUSIVE CUSTOMERS CAUSE EMOTIONS TO RUN HIGH

Telephone customer-service representatives have a tough time these days. With automated telephone systems that create a labyrinth for customers, result in long hold times, and make it difficult for them to speak to an actual human being, a customer's frustration often settles in before the representative has had time to say "hello." Says Donna Earl, an owner of a customer-service consulting firm in San Francisco, "By the time you get to the person you need to talk to, you're mad."

Erin Calabrese knows all too well just how mad customers can get. A customer-service representative at a financial services company, she still vividly recalls one of her worst experiences—with a customer named Jane. Jane called Calabrese over some charges on her credit card and began "ranting and raving." "Your #%#% company, who do you think you are?" yelled Jane. Though Calabrese tried to console the irate customer by offering a refund, Jane only called Calabrese an "idiot." The heated conversation

continued for almost 10 minutes before Calabrese, shaking, handed the phone to her supervisor and left her desk.

Sometimes customers can be downright racist. One customer-service representative finally quit her job at a New Jersey company because she constantly heard racial remarks from customers after, she contends, they heard her Spanish accent. "By the time you leave, your head is spinning with all the complaints," she said.

Unfortunately, these employees have little choice but to take the abuse. Many companies require customer-service employees to keep positive emotions at all times to maintain satisfied customers. But the result could be an emotional nightmare that doesn't necessarily end once the calls stop. Calabrese stated that she would frequently take her negative emotions home. The day after she received the abusive call from Jane, Calabrese went home and started a fight with her roommate. It was "an all-out battle," recalls Calabrese, "I just blew up." The former customer-service representative who worked in New Jersey also recalls the effects of the abusive calls on her family. "My children would say, 'Mom, stop talking about your work. You're home.' My husband would say the same thing," she said.

Emma Parsons, who quit her job as a customer-service representative for the travel industry, was frustrated by the inability to do anything about abusive customers and the mood they'd put her in. "Sometimes you'd finish a call and you'd want to smash somebody's face. I had no escape, no way of releasing." She said that if she did retaliate toward an abusive customer, her boss would punish her.

Some companies train their representatives to defuse a customer's anger and to avoid taking abuse personally, but the effort isn't enough. Liz Aherarn of Radclyffe Group, a consulting firm in Lincoln Park, New Jersey, says customer-service employees who work the phones are absent more frequently, are more prone to illness, and are more likely to make stress-related disability claims than other employees. Thus, it is apparent that in the world of customer service, particularly when interactions take place over the phone, emotions can run high, and the effects can be damaging. Although the adage "the customer comes first" has been heard by many, companies should empower employees to decide when it is appropriate to put the customer second. Otherwise, employees are forced to deal with abusive customers, the effects of which can be detrimental to both the individual and the company.

Questions

1. From an emotional labor perspective, how does dealing with an abusive customer lead to stress and burnout?

2. If you were a recruiter for a customer-service call center, what personality types would you prefer to hire and why? In other words, what individual differences are likely to affect whether an employee can handle customer abuse on a day-to-day basis?

3. Emotional intelligence is one's ability to detect and to manage emotional cues and information. How might emotional intelligence play a role in responding to abusive customers? What facets of emotional intelligence might employees possess who are able to handle abusive customers?

4. What steps should companies take to ensure that their employees are not the victims of customer abuse? Should companies allow a certain degree of abuse if that abuse results in satisfied customers and perhaps greater profit? What are the ethical implications of this?

Source: Based on S. Shellenbarger, "Domino Effect: The Unintended Results of Telling Off Customer-Service Staff," *The Wall Street Journal*, February 5, 2004, p. D.1.

Endnotes

1. Based on J. Stein, "Wynn's Big Bet," *Time*, May 9, 2005, pp. 43–46.
2. See, for instance, C. D. Fisher and N. M. Ashkanasy, "The Emerging Role of Emotions in Work Life: An Introduction," *Journal of Organizational Behavior*, Special Issue 2000, pp. 123–29; N. M. Ashkanasy, C. E. J. Hartel, and W. J. Zerbe (eds.), *Emotions in the Workplace: Research, Theory, and Practice* (Westport, CT: Quorum Books, 2000); N. M. Ashkanasy and C. S. Daus, "Emotion in the Workplace: The New Challenge for Managers," *Academy of Management Executive*, February 2002, pp. 76–86; and N. M. Ashkanasy, C. E. J. Hartel, and C. S. Daus, "Diversity and Emotion: The New Frontiers in Organizational Behavior Research," *Journal of Management* 28, no. 3 (2002), pp. 307–38.
3. See, for example, L. L. Putnam and D. K. Mumby, "Organizations, Emotion and the Myth of Rationality," in S. Fineman (ed.), *Emotion in Organizations* (Thousand Oaks, CA: Sage, 1993), pp. 36–57; and J. Martin, K. Knopoff, and C. Beckman, "An Alternative to Bureaucratic Impersonality and Emotional Labor: Bounded Emotionality at the Body Shop," *Administrative Science Quarterly*, June 1998, pp. 429–69.
4. B. E. Ashforth and R. H. Humphrey, "Emotion in the Workplace: A Reappraisal," *Human Relations*, February 1995, pp. 97–125.
5. J. M. George, "Trait and State Affect," in K. R. Murphy (ed.), *Individual Differences and Behavior in Organizations* (San Francisco: Jossey-Bass, 1996), p. 145.
6. See N. H. Frijda, "Moods, Emotion Episodes and Emotions," in M. Lewis and J. M. Haviland (eds.), *Handbook of Emotions* (New York: Guilford Press, 1993), pp. 381–403.
7. H. M. Weiss and R. Cropanzano, "Affective Events Theory: A Theoretical Discussion of the Structure, Causes and Consequences of Affective Experiences at Work," in B. M. Staw and L. L. Cummings (eds.), *Research in Organizational Behavior*, vol. 18 (Greenwich, CT: JAI Press, 1996), pp. 17–19.
8. See P. Ekman and R. J. Davidson (eds.), *The Nature of Emotions: Fundamental Questions* (Oxford, UK: Oxford University Press, 1994).
9. Frijda, "Moods, Emotion Episodes and Emotions," p. 381.
10. See Ekman and Davidson (eds.), *The Nature of Emotions: Fundamental Question.*
11. See, for example, P. Shaver, J. Schwartz, D. Kirson, and C. O'Connor, "Emotion Knowledge: Further Exploration of a Prototype Approach," *Journal of Personality and Social Psychology*, June 1987, pp. 1061–86; P. Ekman, "An Argument for Basic Emotions," *Cognition and Emotion*, May/July 1992, pp. 169–200; C. E. Izard, "Basic Emotions, Relations among Emotions, and

Emotion–Cognition Relations," *Psychological Bulletin*, November 1992, pp. 561–65; and R. Plutchik, *The Psychology and Biology of Emotion* (New York: HarperCollins, 1994).

12. R. C. Solomon, "Back to Basics: On the Very Idea of "Basic Emotions," *Journal for the Theory of Social Behaviour* 32, no. 2 (June 2002), pp. 115–44.

13. R. Descartes, *The Passions of the Soul*, 1649 (Indianapolis, IN: Hackett, 1989).

14. P. Ekman, *Emotions Revealed: Recognizing Faces and Feelings to Improve Communication and Emotional Life* (New York: Times Books/Henry Holt and Co., 2003).

15. P. R. Shaver, H. J. Morgan, and S. J. Wu, "Is Love a "Basic" Emotion?" *Personal Relationships* 3, no. 1 (March 1996), pp. 81–96.

16. R. C. Solomon, "Back to Basics: On the Very Idea of 'Basic Emotions,' " *Journal for the Theory of Social Behaviour* 32, no. 2 (June 2002), pp. 115–44.

17. Weiss and Cropanzano, "Affective Events Theory," pp. 20–22.

18. Cited in R. D. Woodworth, *Experimental Psychology* (New York: Holt, 1938).

19. J. Nolte, *The Human Brain*, 5th ed. (St. Louis: Mosby, 2002).

20. D. M. Tucker, P. Luu, G. Frishkoff, J. Quiring, and C. Poulsen, "Frontolimbic Response to Negative Feedback in Clinical Depression," *Journal of Abnormal Psychology* 112, no. 4 (November 2003), pp. 667–78.

21. R. C. Gur, F. Gunning-Dixon, W. B. Bilker, and R. E. Gur, "Sex Differences in Temporo-Limbic and Frontal Brain Volumes of Healthy Adults," *Cerebral Cortex* 12, no. 9 September 2002), pp. 998–1003.

22. L. M. Poverny and S. Picascia, "There is No Crying in Business" (http://www.womensmedia.com/new/Crying-at-Work.shtml).

23. L. P. Frankel, *Nice Girls Don't Get the Corner Office* (New York: Warner Book, 2004).

24. A. R. Damasio, *Descartes' Error: Emotion, Reason, and the Human Brain* (New York: Quill, 1994).

25. Ibid.

26. L. Cosmides and J. Tooby, "Evolutionary Psychology and the Emotions," In M. Lewis and J. M. Haviland-Jones (eds.), *Handbook of Emotions*, 2nd ed. (New York: Guilford Press, 2000), pp. 91–115.

27. D. M. Buss, "Cognitive Biases and Emotional Wisdom in the Evolution of Conflict Between the Sexes," *Current Directions in Psychological Science* 10, no. 6 (December 2001), pp. 219–23.

28. K. Hundley, "An Unspoken Problem—Two-Thirds of Female Lawyers Say They Have Experienced or Seen Harassment at Work. But Few Want to Talk about It," *St. Petersburg Times* (http://www.sptimes.com/2005/04/24/Business/An_unspoken_problem.shtml) (April 25, 2004).

29. K. N. Laland and G. R. Brown, *Sense and Nonsense: Evolutionary Perspectives on Human Behaviour* (Oxford, UK: Oxford University Press, 2002).

30. D. Watson, L. A. Clark, and A. Tellegen, "Development and Validation of Brief Measures of Positive and Negative Affect: The PANAS Scales," *Journal of Personality and Social Psychology*, 1988, pp. 1063–70.

31. A. Ben-Ze'ev, *The Subtlety of Emotions* (Cambridge, MA: MIT Press, 2000), p. 94.

32. "Flight Attendant War Stories. . . . Stewardess" (http://www.aboutmyjob.com/main.php3?action=displayarticle&artid=2111).

33. Cited in Ibid., p. 99.

34. J. T. Cacioppo and W. L. Gardner, "Emotion," *Annual Review of Psychology* 50 (1999), pp. 191–214.

35. D. Holman, "Call Centres," in D. Holman, T. D. Wall, C. Clegg, P. Sparrow, and A. Howard (eds), *The Essentials of the New Work Place: A Guide to the Human Impact of Modern Working Practices* (Chichester, UK: John Wiley and Sons, 2005), pp. 111–32.

36. R. J. Larsen and E. Diener, "Affect Intensity as an Individual Difference Characteristic: A Review," *Journal of Research in Personality* 21 (1987), pp. 1–39.

37. M. Tamir and M. D. Robinson, "Knowing Good from Bad: The Paradox of Neuroticism, Negative Affect, and Evaluative Processing," *Journal of Personality and Social Psychology* 87, no. 6 (2004), pp. 913–25; S. H. Hemenover, "Individual Differences in Rate of Affect Change: Studies in Affective Chronometry," *Journal of Personality and Social Psychology* 85, no. 1 (2003), pp. 121–31.

38. D. Watson, *Mood and Temperament* (New York: Guilford Publications, 2000).

39. Ibid.

40. G. Matthews, "Morningness-Eveningness as a Dimension of Personality: Trait, State, and Psychophysiological Correlates," *European Journal of Personality* 2, no. 4 (December 1988), pp. 277–93; V. Natale and P. Cicogna, "Morningness-Eveningness Dimension: Is It Really a Continuum?" *Personality & Individual Differences*, 32, no. 5 (April 2002), pp. 809–16.

41. Watson, *Mood and Temperament* (2000).

42. Ibid., p. 100.

43. Ibid., p. 73.

44. J. A. Fuller, J. M. Stanton, G. G. Fisher, C. Spitzmüller, S. S. Russell, and P. C. Smith, "A Lengthy Look at the Daily Grind: Time Series Analysis of Events, Mood, Stress, and Satisfaction," *Journal of Applied Psychology* 88, no. 6 (December 2003), pp. 1019–33.

45. See "Monday Blahs, May 16, 2005 (http://www.ashidome.com/blogger/housearrest.asp?c=809&m=5&y=2005) (May 16, 2005).

46. A. M. Isen, "Positive Affect as a Source of Human Strength," in L.G. Aspinwall and U. Staudinger (eds.), *The Psychology of Human Strengths*, (Washington, DC: American Psychological Association, 2003), pp. 179–195.

47. Watson, *Mood and Temperament* (2000).

48. H. S. Friedman, J. S. Tucker, J. E. Schwartz, C. Tomlinson-Keasey et al., "Psychosocial and Behavioral Predictors of Longevity: The Aging and Death of the 'Termites'," *American Psychologist* 50, no. 2 (February 1995), pp. 69–78.

49. D. D. Danner, D. A. Snowdon, and W. V. Friesen, "Positive Emotions in Early Life and Longevity: Findings from the Nun Study," *Journal of Personality and Social Psychology* 80, no. 5 (2001), pp. 804–13.

50. *Sleep in America Poll* (Washington, DC: National Sleep Foundation, 2005).

51. M. Lavidor, A. Weller, and H. Babkoff, "How Sleep Is Related to Fatigue," *British Journal of Health Psychology* 8 (2003), pp. 95–105; J. J. Pilcher and E. Ott, "The Relationships between Sleep and Measures of Health and Well-Being in College Students: A Repeated Measures Approach," *Behavioral Medicine* 23 (1998), pp. 170–78.

52. E. K. Miller and J. D. Cohen, "An Integrative Theory of Prefrontal Cortex Function," *Annual Review of Neuroscience* 24 (2001), pp. 167–202.

53. B. A. Scott and T. A. Judge, "Tired and Cranky?: The Effects of Sleep Quality on Employee Emotions and Job Satisfaction," Working paper, Department of Management, University of Florida, 2005.

54. P. R. Giacobbi, H. A. Hausenblas, and N. Frye, "A Naturalistic Assessment of the Relationship Between Personality, Daily Life Events, Leisure-Time Exercise, and Mood," *Psychology of Sport & Exercise* 6, no. 1 (January 2005), pp. 67–81.

55. L. L. Carstensen, M. Pasupathi, M. Ulrich, and J. R. Nesselroade, "Emotional Experience in Everyday Life Across the Adult Life Span," *Journal of Personality and Social Psychology* 79, no. 4 (2000), pp. 644–55.

56. K. Deaux, "Sex Differences," in M. R. Rosenzweig and L. W. Porter (eds.), *Annual Review of Psychology*, vol. 26 (Palo Alto, CA: Annual Reviews, 1985), pp. 48–82; M. LaFrance and M. Banaji, "Toward a Reconsideration of the Gender-Emotion Relationship," in M. Clark (ed.), *Review of Personality and Social Psychology*, vol. 14 (Newbury Park, CA: Sage, 1992), pp. 178–97; and A. M. Kring and A. H. Gordon, "Sex Differences in Emotion: Expression, Experience, and Physiology," *Journal of Personality and Social Psychology*, March 1998, pp. 686–703.

57. L. R. Brody and J. A. Hall, "Gender and Emotion," in M. Lewis and J. M. Haviland (eds.), *Handbook of Emotions* (New York: Guilford Press, 1993), pp. 447–60; and M. Grossman and W. Wood, "Sex Differences in Intensity of Emotional Experience: A Social Role Interpretation," *Journal of Personality and Social Psychology*, November 1992, pp. 1010–22.

58. J. A. Hall, *Nonverbal Sex Differences: Communication Accuracy and Expressive Style* (Baltimore, MD: Johns Hopkins Press, 1984).

59. N. James, "Emotional Labour: Skill and Work in the Social Regulations of Feelings," *Sociological Review*, February 1989, pp. 15–42; A. Hochschild, *The Second Shift* (New York: Viking, 1989); and F. M. Deutsch, "Status, Sex, and Smiling: The Effect of Role on Smiling in Men and Women," *Personality and Social Psychology Bulletin*, September 1990, pp. 531–40.

60. A. Rafaeli, "When Clerks Meet Customers: A Test of Variables Related to Emotional Expression on the Job," *Journal of Applied Psychology*, June 1989, pp. 385–93; and LaFrance and Banaji, "Toward a Reconsideration of the Gender-Emotion Relationship."

61. L. W. Hoffman, "Early Childhood Experiences and Women's Achievement Motives," *Journal of Social Issues* 28, no. 2 (1972), pp. 129–55.

62. M. Boas and S. Chain, *Big Mac: The Unauthorized Story of McDonald's* (New York: Dutton, 1976), p. 84.

63. Ashforth and Humphrey, "Emotion in the Workplace," p. 104.

64. G. L. Flett, K. R. Blankstein, P. Pliner, and C. Bator, "Impression-Management and Self-Deception Components of Appraised Emotional Experience," *British Journal of Social Psychology*, January 1988, pp. 67–77.

65. B. E. Ashforth and R. H. Humphrey, "Emotion in the Workplace: A Reappraisal," Human Relations, Vol. 48, No. 2, 1995, pp. 97–125.

66. M. Eid and E. Diener, "Norms for Experiencing Emotions in Different Cultures: Inter- and Intranational Differences," *Journal of Personality & Social Psychology* 81, no. 5, 2001, pp. 869–85.

67. S. Oishi, E. Diener, and C. Napa Scollon, "Cross-Situational Consistency of Affective Experiences Across Cultures," *Journal of Personality & Social Psychology* 86, no. 3 (2004), pp. 460–72.

68. Eid and Diener, "Norms for Experiencing Emotions in Different Cultures."

69. Ibid.

70. B. Mesquita, "Emotions in Collectivist and Individualist Contexts," *Journal of Personality and Social Psychology* 80, no. 1 (2001), pp. 68–74.

71. H. A. Elfenbein and N. Ambady, "When Familiarity Breeds Accuracy: Cultural Exposure and Facial Emotional Recognition," *Journal of Personality and Social Psychology* 85, no. 2 (2003), pp. 276–90.

72. R. I. Levy, *Tahitians: Mind and Experience in the Society Islands* (Chicago: University of Chicago Press, 1973).

73. B. Mesquita and N. H. Frijda, "Cultural Variations in Emotions: A Review," *Psychological Bulletin*, September 1992, pp. 179–204; and B. Mesquita, "Emotions in Collectivist and Individualist Contexts," *Journal of Personality and Social Psychology*, January 2001, pp. 68–74.

74. D. Matsumoto, "Cross-Cultural Psychology in the 21st Century" (http://teachpsych.lemoyne.edu/teachpsych/faces/script/Ch05.htm).

75. See J. A. Morris and D. C. Feldman, "Managing Emotions in the Workplace," *Journal of Managerial Issues* 9, no. 3 (1997), pp. 257–74; S. Mann, *Hiding What We Feel, Faking What We Don't: Understanding the Role of Your Emotions at Work* (New York: HarperCollins, 1999); S. M. Kruml and D. Geddes, "Catching Fire Without Burning Out: Is There an Ideal Way to Perform Emotion Labor?" in N. M. Ashkansay, C. E. J. Hartel, and W. J. Zerbe, *Emotions in the Workplace*, (New York: Quorum Books, 2000), pp. 177–88.

76. P. Ekman, W. V. Friesen, and M. O'Sullivan, "Smiles When Lying," In P. Ekman and E. L. Rosenberg (eds.), *What the Face Reveals: Basic and Applied Studies of Spontaneous Expression Using the Facial Action Coding System (FACS)* (London: Oxford University Press, 1997), pp. 201–16.

77. A. Grandey, "Emotion Regulation in the Workplace: A New Way to Conceptualize Emotional Labor," *Journal of Occupational Health Psychology* 5, no. 1 (2000), pp. 95–110; and R. Cropanzano, D. E. Rupp, and Z. S. Byrne, "The Relationship of Emotional Exhaustion to Work Attitudes, Job Performance, and Organizational Citizenship Behavior," *Journal of Applied Psychology*, February 2003, pp. 160–69.

78. A. R. Hochschild, "Emotion Work, Feeling Rules, and Social Structure," *American Journal of Sociology*, November 1979, pp. 551–75; W-C. Tsai, "Determinants and Consequences of Employee Displayed Positive Emotions," *Journal of Management* 27, no. 4 (2001), pp. 497–512; M. W. Kramer and J. A. Hess, "Communication Rules for the Display of Emotions in Organizational Settings," *Management Communication Quarterly*, August 2002, pp. 66–80; and J. M. Diefendorff and E. M. Richard, "Antecedents and Consequences of Emotional Display Rule Perceptions," *Journal of Applied Psychology*, April 2003, pp. 284–94.

79. B. M. DePaulo, "Nonverbal Behavior and Self-Presentation," *Psychological Bulletin*, March 1992, pp. 203–43.

80. C. S. Hunt, "Although I Might Be Laughing Loud and Hearty, Deep Inside I'm Blue: Individual Perceptions Regarding Feeling and Displaying Emotions at Work," paper

presented at the Academy of Management Conference; Cincinnati, August 1996, p. 3.

81. R. C. Solomon, "Back to Basics: On the Very Idea of Basic Emotions," *Journal for the Theory of Social Behaviour* 32, no. 2 (June 2002), pp. 115–44.

82. C. M. Brotheridge and R. T. Lee, "Development and Validation of the Emotional Labour Scale," *Journal of Occupational & Organizational Psychology* 76, no. 3 (September 2003), pp. 365–79.

83. A. A. Grandey, "When 'the show Must Go On': Surface Acting and Deep Acting as Determinants of Emotional Exhaustion and Peer-Rated Service Delivery," *Academy of Management Journal*, February 2003, pp. 86–96; A. A. Grandey, D. N. Dickter, and H. Sin, "The Customer Is not Always Right: Customer Aggression and Emotion Regulation of Service Employees," *Journal of Organizational Behavior* 25, no. 3 (May 2004), pp. 397–418.

84. A. Rafaeli and R. I. Sutton, "The Expression of Emotion in Organizational Life," in L. L. Cummings and B. M. Staw (eds.), *Research in Organizational Behavior*, vol. 11 (Greenwich, CT: JAI Press, 1989), p. 8.

85. A. Rafaeli, "When Cashiers Meet Customers: An Analysis of Supermarket Cashiers," *Academy of Management Journal*, June 1989, pp. 245–73.

86. B. Plasait, "Accueil des Touristes Dans les Grands Centres de Transit Paris," Rapport du Premier Ministre (http://www.tourisme.gouv.fr/fr/navd/presse/dossiers/att00005767/dp_plasait.pdf) (le 4 octobre 2004).

87. D. Rubin, "Grumpy German Shoppers Distrust the Wal-Mart Style," *Seattle Times*, December 30, 2001, p. A15.

88. P. A. Simpson and L. K. Stroh, "Gender Differences: Emotional Expression and Feelings of Personal Inauthenticity," *Journal of Applied Psychology* 89, no. 4 (August 2004), pp. 715–21.

89. T. M. Glomb, J. D. Kammeyer-Mueller, and M. Rotundo, "Emotional Labor Demands and Compensating Wage Differentials," *Journal of Applied Psychology* 89, no. 4 (August 2004), pp. 700–14.

90. H. M. Weiss, and R. Cropanzano, "An Affective Events Approach to Job Satisfaction," *Research in Organizational Behavior, 18,* (1996), pp. 1–74.

91. J. Basch and C. D. Fisher, "Affective Events–Emotions Matrix: A Classification of Work Events and Associated Emotions," in N. M. Ashkanasy, C. E. J. Hartel, and W. J. Zerbe, (eds.), *Emotions in the Workplace* (Westport, CT: Quorum Books, 2000), pp. 36–48.

92. See, for example, H. M. Weiss and R. Cropanzano, "Affective Events Theory"; and C. D. Fisher, "Antecedents and Consequences of Real-Time Affective Reactions at Work," *Motivation and Emotion*, March 2002, pp. 3–30.

93. Based on H. M. Weiss and R. Cropanzano, "Affective Events Theory," p. 42.

94. N. M. Ashkanasy, C. E. J. Hartel, and C. S. Daus, "Diversity and Emotion: The New Frontiers in Organizational Behavior Research," *Journal of Management* 28, no. 3 (2002), p. 324.

95. Based on D. R. Caruso, J. D. Mayer, and P. Salovey, "Emotional Intelligence and Emotional Leadership," in R. E. Riggio, S. E. Murphy, and F. J. Pirozzolo (eds.), *Multiple Intelligences and Leadership* (Mahwah, NJ: Lawrence Erlbaum, 2002), p. 70.

96. This section is based on Daniel Goleman, *Emotional Intelligence* (New York: Bantam, 1995); J. D. Mayer and P. Salovey, "What is Emotional Intelligence?" in P. Salovey and D. J. Sluyter (eds.), *Emotional Development and Emotional Intelligence: Educational Implications* (New York: Basic Books, 1997), pp. 3–31; R. K. Cooper, "Applying Emotional Intelligence in the Workplace," *Training & Development*, December 1997, pp. 31–38; M. Davies, L. Stankov, and R. D. Roberts, "Emotional Intelligence: In Search of an Elusive Construct," *Journal of Personality and Social Psychology*, October 1998, pp. 989–1015; D. Goleman, *Working with Emotional Intelligence* (New York: Bantam, 1999); R. Bar-On and J. D. A. Parker (eds.), *The Handbook of Emotional Intelligence: Theory, Development, Assessment, and Application at Home, School, and in the Workplace* (San Francisco: Jossey-Bass, 2000); J. Ciarrochi, J. P. Forgas, and J. D. Mayer (eds.), *Emotional Intelligence in Everyday Life* (Philadelphia: Psychology Press, 2001).

97. F. I. Greenstein, *The Presidential Difference: Leadership Style from FDR to Clinton* (Princeton, NJ: Princeton University Press, 2001).

98. C. Cherniss, "The Business Case for Emotional Intelligence," Consortium for Research on Emotional Intelligence in Organizations (http://www.eiconsortium.org/research/business_case_for_ei.pdf).

99. K. S. Law, C. Wong, and L. J. Song, "The Construct and Criterion Validity of Emotional Intelligence and Its Potential Utility for Management Studies," *Journal of Applied Psychology* 89, no. 3 (2004), pp. 483–96.

100. H. A. Elfenbein and N. Ambady, "Predicting Workplace Outcomes from the Ability to Eavesdrop on Feelings," *Journal of Applied Psychology* 87, no. 5 (October 2002), pp. 963–71.

101. D. L. Van Rooy and C. Viswesvaran, "Emotional Intelligence: A Meta-Analytic Investigation of Predictive Validity and Nomological Net," *Journal of Vocational Behavior*, 65, no. 1 (August 2004), pp. 71–95.

102. R. Bar-On, D. Tranel, N. L. Denburg, and A. Bechara, "Exploring the Neurological Substrate of Emotional and Social Intelligence," *Brain* 126, no. 8 (August 2003), pp. 1790–1800.

103. E. A. Locke, "Why Emotional Intelligence Is an Invalid Concept," *Journal of Organizational Behavior* 26, no. 4 (June 2005), pp. 425–31.

104. J. M. Conte, "A Review and Critique of Emotional Intelligence Measures," *Journal of Organizational Behavior* 26, no. 4 (June 2005), pp. 433–40; M. Davies, L. Stankov, and R. D. Roberts, "Emotional Intelligence: In Search of an Elusive Construct," *Journal of Personality and Social Psychology* 75, no. 4 (1998), pp. 989–1015.

105. T. Decker, "Is Emotional Intelligence a Viable Concept?" *Academy of Management Review*, 28, no. 2 (April 2003), pp. 433–40; Davies, Stankov, and Roberts, "Emotional Intelligence: In Search of an Elusive Construct."

106. F. J. Landy, "Some Historical and Scientific Issues Related to Research on Emotional Intelligence," *Journal of Organizational Behavior* 26, no. 4 (June 2005), pp. 411–24.

107. L. M. J. Spencer, D. C. McClelland, and S. Kelner, *Competency Assessment Methods: History and State of the Art* (Boston: Hay/McBer, 1997).

108. S. Fineman, "Emotional Arenas Revisited," in S. Fineman (ed.), *Emotion in Organizations*, 2nd ed. (Thousand Oaks, CA: Sage, 2000), p. 11.

109. L. B. Alloy and L. Y. Abramson, "Judgement of Contingency in Depressed and Nondepressed Students: Sadder but Wiser?" *Journal of Experimental Psychology: General* 108 (1979), pp. 441–85.

110. N. Ambady and H. M. Gray, "On Being Sad and Mistaken: Mood Effects on the Accuracy of Thin-Slice Judgments," *Journal of Personality and Social Psychology* 83, no. 4 (2002), pp. 947–61.

111. See, for example, K. Fiedler, "Emotional Mood, Cognitive Style, and Behavioral Regulation," in K. Fiedler and J. Forgas (eds.), *Affect, Cognition, and Social Behavior* (Toronto: Hogrefe International, 1988), pp. 100–19; M. Luce, J. Bettman, and J. W. Payne, "Choice Processing in Difficult Decisions," *Journal of Experimental Psychology: Learning, Memory, and Cognition* 23 (1997), pp. 384–405; and A. M. Isen, "Positive Affect and Decision Making," in M. Lewis and J. M. Haviland-Jones (eds.), *Handbook of Emotions*, 2nd ed. (New York: Guilford, 2000), pp. 261–77.

112. J. Park and M. R. Banaji, "Mood and Heuristics: The Influence of Happy and Sad States on Sensitivity and Bias in Stereotyping," *Journal of Personality and Social Psychology* 78, no. 6 (2000), pp. 1005–23.

113. A. M. Isen, "On the Relationship Between Affect and Creative Problem Solving," in S. W. Russ (ed.), *Affect, Creative Experience and Psychological Adjustment* (Philadelphia, PA: Brunner/Mazel, 1999), pp. 3–17; M. A. Mumford, "Where Have We Been, Where Are We Going? Taking Stock in Creativity Research," *Creativity Research Journal* 15 (2003), pp. 107–20.

114. M. J. Grawitch, D. C. Munz, and E. K. Elliott, "Promoting Creativity in Temporary Problem-Solving Groups: The Effects of Positive Mood and Autonomy in Problem Definition on Idea-Generating Performance," *Group Dynamics* 7, no. 3 (September 2003), pp. 200–13.

115. S. Lyubomirsky, L. King, and E. Diener, "The Benefits of Frequent Positive Affect: Does Happiness Lead to Success?" *Psychological Bulletin*, in press.

116. N. Madjar, G. R. Oldham, and M. G. Pratt, "There's No Place Like Home? The Contributions of Work and Nonwork Creativity Support to Employees' Creative Performance," *Academy of Management Journal* 45, no. 4 (2002), pp. 757–67.

117. J. M. George and J. Zhou, "Understanding When Bad Moods Foster Creativity and Good Ones Don't: The Role of Context and Clarity of Feelings," *Journal of Applied Psychology* 87, no. 4 (August 2002), pp. 687–97; J. P. Forgas and J. M. George, "Affective Influences on Judgments and Behavior in Organizations: An Information Processing Perspective," *Organizational Behavior and Human Decision Processes* 86, no. 1 (2001), pp. 3–34.

118. L. L. Martin, "Mood as Input: A Configural View of Mood Effects," in L. L. Martin and G. L. Clore (eds.), *Theories of Mood and Cognition: A User's Guidebook* (Mahwah, NJ: Lawrence Erlbaum Associates, Publishers, 2001), pp. 135–57.

119. Ashforth and Humphrey, "Emotion in the Workplace," p. 109.

120. Ibid., p. 110.

121. Ibid.

122. A. Erez and A. M. Isen, "The Influence of Positive Affect on the Components of Expectancy Motivation," *Journal of Applied Psychology* 87, no. 6 (2002), pp. 1055–67.

123. Remus Ilies and T. A. Judge, "Goal Regulation Across Time: The Effect of Feedback and Affect," *Journal of Applied Psychology* 90, no, 3 (May 2005), pp. 453-467.

124. K. M. Lewis, "When Leaders Display Emotion: How Followers Respond to Negative Emotional Expression of Male and Female Leaders," *Journal of Organizational Behavior*, March 2000, pp. 221–34; and J. M. George, "Emotions and Leadership: The Role of Emotional Intelligence," *Human Relations*, August 2000, pp. 1027–55.

125. George, "Trait and State Affect," 162.

126. Ashforth and Humphrey, "Emotion in the Workplace," p. 116.

127. N. Reynolds, "Whiz-Kids Gamble on TV Channel for Poker," *news.telegraph* (http://www.telegraph.co.uk) (April 16, 2005).

128. G. A. Van Kleef, C. K. W. De Dreu, and A. S. R. Manstead, "The Interpersonal Effects of Emotions in Negotiations: A Motivated Information Processing Approach," *Journal of Personality and Social Psychology* 87, no. 4 (2004), pp. 510–28; G. A. Van Kleef, C. K. W. De Dreu, and A. S. R. Manstead, "The Interpersonal Effects of Anger and Happiness in Negotiations," *Journal of Personality and Social Psychology* 86, no. 1 (2004), pp. 57–76.

129. K. M. O'Connor and J. A. Arnold, "Distributive Spirals: Negotiation Impasses and the Moderating Role of Disputant Self-Efficacy," *Organizational Behavior and Human Decision Processes* 84, no. 1 (2001), pp. 148–76.

130. B. Shiv, G. Loewenstein, A. Bechara, H. Damasio, and A. R. Damasio, "Investment Behavior and the Negative Side of Emotion," *Psychological Science* 16, no. 6 (2005), pp. 435–439.

131. G. F. Will, "Solidarity Isn't Forever," *The Washington Post*, September 16, 2005, p. A31.

132. W-C. Tsai and Y-M. Huang, "Mechanisms Linking Employee Affective Delivery and Customer Behavioral Intentions," *Journal of Applied Psychology*, October 2002, pp. 1001–08.

133. A. A. Grandey, "When 'the Show Must Go On': Surface Acting and Deep Acting as Determinants of Emotional Exhaustion and Peer-Rated Service Delivery," *Academy of Management Journal*, February 2003, pp. 86–96.

134. See E. Hatfield, J. T. Cacioppo, and R. L. Rapson, *Emotional Contagion* (Cambridge, UK: Cambridge University Press, 1994); and S. D. Pugh, "Service with a Smile: Emotional Contagion in the Service Encounter," *Academy of Management Journal*, October 2001, pp. 1018–27.

135. W. Tasi and Y. Huang, "Mechanisms Linking Employee Affective Delivery and Customer Behavioral Intentions," *Journal of Applied Psychology* 87, no. 5 (2002), pp. 1001–08.

136. R. Ilies and T. A. Judge, "Understanding the Dynamic Relationships among Personality, Mood, and Job Satisfaction: A Field Experience Sampling Study," *Organizational Behavior and Human Decision Processes* 89 (2002), pp. 1119–39.

137. R. Rau, "Job Strain or Healthy Work: A Question of Task Design," *Journal of Occupational Health Psychology* 9, no. 4 (October 2004), pp. 322–38; R. Rau and A. Triemer, "Overtime in Relation to Blood Pressure and Mood During Work, Leisure, and Night Time," *Social Indicators Research* 67, no. 1–2 (June 2004), pp. 51–73.

138. T. A. Judge and R. Ilies, "Affect and Job Satisfaction: A Study of Their Relationship at Work and at Home," *Journal of Applied Psychology* 89 (2004), pp. 661–73.

139. See S. L. Robinson and R. J. Bennett, "A Typology of Deviant Workplace Behaviors: A Multidimensional Scaling Study," *Academy of Management Journal*, April 1995, p. 556; and R. J. Bennett and S. L. Robinson, "Development of a Measure of Workplace Deviance," *Journal of Applied*

Psychology, June 2000, pp. 349–60. See also P. R. Sackett and C. J. DeVore, "Counterproductive Behaviors at Work," in N. Anderson, D. S. Ones, H. K. Sinangil, and C. Viswesvaran (eds.), *Handbook of Industrial, Work & Organizational Psychology*, vol. 1 (Thousand Oaks, CA: Sage, 2001), pp. 145–64.

140. A. G. Bedeian, "Workplace Envy," *Organizational Dynamics*, Spring 1995, p. 50; and A. Ben-Ze'ev, *The Subtlety of Emotions* (Cambridge, MA: MIT Press, 2000), pp. 281–326.

141. Bedeian, "Workplace Envy," p. 54.

142. K. Lee and N. J. Allen, "Organizational Citizenship Behavior and Workplace Deviance: The Role of Affect and Cognition," *Journal of Applied Psychology* 87, no. 1 (2002), pp. 131–42; T. A. Judge, B. A. Scott, and R. Ilies, "Hostility, Job Attitudes, and Workplace Deviance: Test of a Multilevel Model," *Journal of Applied Psychology*, in press.

143. A. M. Isen, A. A. Labroo, and P. Durlach, "An Influence of Product and Brand Name on Positive Affect: Implicit and Explicit Measures," *Motivation & Emotion* 28, no. 1 (March 2004), pp. 43–63.

144. T. Sy, S. Côté, and R. Saavedra, "The Contagious Leader: Impact of the Leader's Mood on the Mood of Group Members, Group Affective Tone, and Group Processes," *Journal of Applied Psychology* 90, no. 2 (2005), pp. 295–305.

145. P. Totterdell, "Catching Moods and Hitting Runs: Mood Linkage and Subjective Performance in Professional Sports Teams," *Journal of Applied Psychology* 85, no. 6 (2000), pp. 848–59.

146. S. Nelton, "Emotions in the Workplace," *Nation's Business*, February 1996, p. 25.

147. Weiss and Cropanzano, "Affective Events Theory," p. 55.

148. See the Yerkes–Dodson law cited in D. O. Hebb, "Drives and the CNS (Conceptual Nervous System)," *Psychological Review*, July 1955, pp. 243–54.

149. H. Liao and A. Chuang, "A Multilevel Investigation of Factors Influencing Employee Service Performance and Customer Outcomes," *Academy of Management Journal* 47, no. 1 (2004), pp. 41–58.

150. Quote from Starbucks.com Web site, May 16, 2005.

151. F. Strack, L. L. Stepper, and S. Martin, "Inhibiting and Facilitating Conditions of the Human Smile: A Nonobstrusive Test of the Facial-Feedback Hypothesis," *Journal of Personality and Social Psychology* 54 (1988), pp. 768–77.

152. D. Zapf, "Emotion Work and Psychological Well-Being: A Review of the Literature and Some Conceptual Considerations," *Human Resource Management Review* 12, no. 2 (2002), pp. 237–68.

153. J. E. Bono and M. A. Vey, "Toward Understanding Emotional Management at Work: A Quantitative Review of Emotional Labor Research," in C. E. Härtel and W. J. Zerbe (eds.), *Emotions in Organizational Behavior* (Mahwah, NJ: Lawrence Erlbaum Associates, Publishers, 2005), pp. 213–33.

154. S. M. Kruml and D. Geddes, "Catching Fire Without Burning Out: Is There an Ideal Way to Perform Emotional Labor?" in N. M. Ashkanasy, C. E. J. Hartel, and W. J. Zerbe (eds.), *Emotions in the Workplace: Research Theory and Practice* (Westport, CT: Quorum Books, 2000), pp. 177–88.

Foundations of Group Behavior

After studying this chapter, you should be able to:

1 Differentiate between formal and informal groups.

2 Compare two models of group development.

3 Explain how role requirements change in different situations.

4 Describe how norms exert influence on an individual's behavior.

5 Explain what determines status.

6 Define social loafing and its effect on group performance.

7 Identify the benefits and disadvantages of cohesive groups.

8 List the strengths and weaknesses of group decision making.

9 Contrast the effectiveness of interacting, brainstorming, nominal, and electronic meeting groups.

LEARNING OBJECTIVES

The Danger of Not Speaking Up

Smart people, working collectively, sometimes do dumb things.[1] Those "dumb things," in fact, may have contributed to the 2003 *Columbia* shuttle disaster. At least that's one of the conclusions provided by the Columbia Accident Investigation Board (CAIB), which was highly critical of NASA's team decision-making process.

NASA has a long history of stifling differences among personnel, especially when those differences threaten the image of the agency or affect its launching schedule. For instance, the investigation of the *Challenger* explosion in 1986 revealed that a number of engineers had been worried for months about the potential for a malfunction of an O-ring seal during launches in cold weather.[2] But NASA internal processes stifled these people from speaking up. The official inquiry concluded that the direct cause of the *Challenger* explosion was the malfunction of the O-ring seal on the right solid-rocket booster just 73 seconds after launch on a cold January day.

The *Columbia* inquiry revealed that NASA engineers decided early in the mission that falling foam (see photo) didn't endanger the shuttle or the crew, although it's now generally accepted that this was the single factor that led to the shuttle's demise. However, the inquiry also revealed that some engineers continued to discuss situations involving possible problems related to tile damage and falling foam underneath the tiles. Yet, because the engineers directly connected to the decision process were satisfied that the foam was not a risk, they didn't pass the results of their discussions up the line, even though other engineers suggested that the material could potentially cause catastrophic damage. In other words, there were engineers closely involved in the *Columbia* mission who felt strongly that the falling foam was a threat to the mission but who chose not to speak out.

Why did these engineers keep quiet and not take their concerns to their superiors? The probable answer is that group pressures for agreement at NASA were so strong that they stifled dissent. The final CAIB report concluded, "Over time, slowly and unintentionally, independent checks and balances intended to increase safety have been eroded in favor of detailed processes that produce massive amounts of data and unwarranted consensus, but little effective communication."[3] In this chapter, we'll address the pressures that groups can place on individuals when we discuss norms and groupthink. ∎

The objectives of this and the following chapter are to introduce you to basic group concepts, provide you with a foundation for understanding how groups work, and to show you how to create effective teams. Let's begin by defining groups and explaining why people join them.

Defining and Classifying Groups

A **group** is defined as two or more individuals, interacting and interdependent, who have come together to achieve particular objectives. Groups can be either formal or informal. By **formal groups**, we mean those defined by the organization's structure, with designated work assignments establishing tasks. In formal groups, the behaviors that one should engage in are stipulated by and directed toward organizational goals. The six members making up an airline flight crew are an example of a formal group. In contrast, **informal groups** are alliances that are neither formally structured nor organizationally determined. These groups are natural formations in the work environment that appear in response to the need for social contact. Three employees from different departments who regularly eat lunch together are an example of an informal group.

It's possible to further subclassify groups as command, task, interest, or friendship groups.[4] Command and task groups are dictated by the formal organization, whereas interest and friendship groups are informal alliances.

A **command group** is determined by the organization chart. It is composed of the individuals who report directly to a given manager. An elementary school principal and her 18 teachers form a command group, as do the director of postal audits and his five inspectors.

Task groups, also organizationally determined, represent those working together to complete a job task. However, a task group's boundaries are not limited to its immediate hierarchical superior. It can cross command relationships. For instance, if a college student is accused of a campus crime, it may require communication and coordination among the dean of academic affairs, the dean of students, the registrar, the director of security, and the student's advisor. Such a formation would constitute a task group. It should be noted that all command groups are also task groups, but because task groups can cut across the organization, the reverse need not be true.

People who may or may not be aligned into common command or task groups may affiliate to attain a specific objective with which each is concerned. This is an **interest group**. Employees who band together to have their vacation schedules altered, to support a peer who has been fired, or to seek improved working conditions represent the formation of a united body to further their common interest.

Groups often develop because the individual members have one or more common characteristics. We call these formations **friendship groups**. Social alliances, which frequently extend outside the work situation, can be based on similar age or ethnic heritage, support for Notre Dame football, interest in the same alternative rock band, or the holding of similar political views, to name just a few such characteristics.

Informal groups provide a very important service by satisfying their members' social needs. Because of interactions that result from the close proximity of workstations or task interactions, we find that workers often do things together—like play golf, commute to work, take lunch, and chat during coffee breaks. We must recognize that these types of interactions among individuals, even though informal, deeply affect their behavior and performance.

There is no single reason why individuals join groups. Because most people belong to a number of groups, it's obvious that different groups provide different benefits to their members. Exhibit 9-1 summarizes the most popular reasons people have for joining groups.

Working in groups requires a certain amount of trust. Are you a trusting person? The Self-Assessment feature will tell you.

DO I TRUST OTHERS?

In the Self-Assessment Library (available on CD, online, and in print), take assessment II.B.3 (Do I Trust Others?) and answer the following questions.

1. *Are you surprised by your results? If yes, why? If not, why not?*
2. *Do you think it is important to always trust your group members? Or do you think a smart group member is one who keeps his guard up at all times?*

You can also check out assessment 11.B.4. (Do Others See Me as Trustworthy?)

Exhibit **9-1**	Why Do People Join Groups?

Security. By joining a group, individuals can reduce the insecurity of "standing alone." People feel stronger, have fewer self-doubts, and are more resistant to threats when they are part of a group.

Status. Inclusion in a group that is viewed as important by others provides recognition and status for its members.

Self-esteem. Groups can provide people with feelings of self-worth. That is, in addition to conveying status to those outside the group, membership can also give increased feelings of worth to the group members themselves.

Affiliation. Groups can fulfill social needs. People enjoy the regular interaction that comes with group membership. For many people, these on-the-job interactions are their primary source for fulfilling their needs for affiliation.

Power. What cannot be achieved individually often becomes possible through group action. There is power in numbers.

Goal Achievement. There are times when it takes more than one person to accomplish a particular task—there is a need to pool talents, knowledge, or power in order to complete a job. In such instances, management will rely on the use of a formal group.

---

group *Two or more individuals, interacting and interdependent, who have come together to achieve particular objectives.*

formal group *A designated work group defined by the organization's structure.*

informal group *A group that is neither formally structured nor organizationally determined; appears in response to the need for social contact.*

command group *A group composed of the individuals who report directly to a given manager.*

task group *Those working together to complete a job task.*

interest group *Those working together to attain a specific objective with which each is concerned.*

friendship group *Those brought together because they share one or more common characteristics.*

Stages of Group Development

Groups generally pass through a standardized sequence in their evolution. We call this sequence the five-stage model of group development. Although research indicates that not all groups follow this pattern,[5] it is a useful framework to understand group development. In this section, we describe the five-stage general model and an alternative model for temporary groups with deadlines.

The Five-Stage Model

As shown in Exhibit 9-2, the **five-stage group-development model** characterizes groups as proceeding through five distinct stages: forming, storming, norming, performing, and adjourning.[6]

The first stage, **forming**, is characterized by a great deal of uncertainty about the group's purpose, structure, and leadership. Members are "testing the waters" to determine what types of behaviors are acceptable. This stage is complete when members have begun to think of themselves as part of a group.

The **storming stage** is one of intragroup conflict. Members accept the existence of the group, but there is resistance to the constraints that the group imposes on individuality. Furthermore, there is conflict over who will control the group. When this stage is complete, there will be a relatively clear hierarchy of leadership within the group.

The third stage is one in which close relationships develop and the group demonstrates cohesiveness. There is now a strong sense of group identity and camaraderie. This **norming stage** is complete when the group structure solidifies and the group has assimilated a common set of expectations of what defines correct member behavior.

The fourth stage is **performing**. The structure at this point is fully functional and accepted. Group energy has moved from getting to know and understand each other to performing the task at hand.

For permanent work groups, performing is the last stage in their development. However, for temporary committees, teams, task forces, and similar groups that have a limited task to perform, there is an **adjourning stage**. In this stage, the group prepares for its disbandment. High task performance is no longer the group's top priority. Instead, attention is directed toward wrapping up activities. Responses of group members vary in this stage. Some are upbeat, basking in the group's accomplishments. Others may be depressed over the loss of camaraderie and friendships gained during the work group's life.

Many interpreters of the five-stage model have assumed that a group becomes more effective as it progresses through the first four stages. Although this assumption may be generally true, what makes a group effective is more

---

Exhibit 9-2   Stages of Group Development

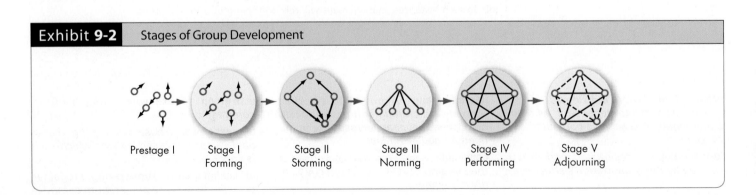

Prestage I   Stage I   Stage II   Stage III   Stage IV   Stage V
Forming   Storming   Norming   Performing   Adjourning

complex than this model acknowledges.[7] Under some conditions, high levels of conflict may be conducive to high group performance. So we might expect to find situations in which groups in Stage II outperform those in Stage III or IV. Similarly, groups do not always proceed clearly from one stage to the next. Sometimes, in fact, several stages go on simultaneously, as when groups are storming and performing at the same time. Groups even occasionally regress to previous stages. Therefore, even the strongest proponents of this model do not assume that all groups follow its five-stage process precisely or that Stage IV is always the most preferable.

Another problem with the five-stage model, in terms of understanding work-related behavior, is that it ignores organizational context.[8] For instance, a study of a cockpit crew in an airliner found that, within 10 minutes, three strangers assigned to fly together for the first time had become a high-performing group. What allowed for this speedy group development was the strong organizational context surrounding the tasks of the cockpit crew. This context provided the rules, task definitions, information, and resources needed for the group to perform. They didn't need to develop plans, assign roles, determine and allocate resources, resolve conflicts, and set norms the way the five-stage model predicts.

An Alternative Model: For Temporary Groups with Deadlines

Temporary groups with deadlines don't seem to follow the previous model. Studies indicate that they have their own unique sequencing of actions (or inaction): (1) Their first meeting sets the group's direction; (2) this first phase of group activity is one of inertia; (3) a transition takes place at the end of this first phase, which occurs exactly when the group has used up half its allotted time; (4) a transition initiates major changes; (5) a second phase of inertia follows the transition; and (6) the group's last meeting is characterized by markedly accelerated activity.[9] This pattern is called the **punctuated-equilibrium model** and is shown in Exhibit 9-3.

The first meeting sets the group's direction. A framework of behavioral patterns and assumptions through which the group will approach its project emerges in this first meeting. These lasting patterns can appear as early as the first few seconds of the group's life. Once set, the group's direction becomes "written in stone" and is unlikely to be reexamined throughout the first half of the group's life. This is a period of inertia—that is, the group tends to stand still or become locked into a fixed course of action. Even if it gains new insights that challenge initial patterns and assumptions, the group is incapable of acting on these new insights in Phase 1.

One of the more interesting discoveries made in these studies[10] was that each group experienced its transition at the same point in its calendar—precisely halfway between its first meeting and its official deadline—despite the fact that some groups spent as little as an hour on their project while others spent

---

five-stage group-development model *The five distinct stages groups go through: forming, storming, norming, performing, and adjourning.*

forming stage *The first stage in group development, characterized by much uncertainty.*

storming stage *The second stage in group development, characterized by intragroup conflict.*

norming stage *The third stage in group development, characterized by close relationships and cohesiveness.*

performing stage *The fourth stage in group development, when the group is fully functional.*

adjourning stage *The final stage in group development for temporary groups, characterized by concern with wrapping up activities rather than task performance.*

punctuated-equilibrium model *Transitions temporary groups go through between inertia and activity.*

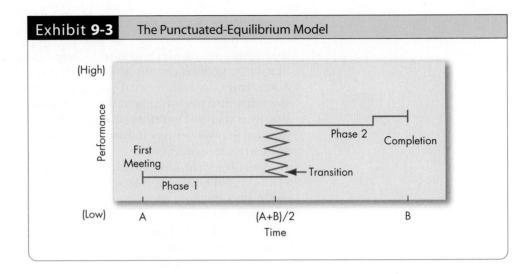

| Exhibit **9-3** | The Punctuated-Equilibrium Model |

6 months. It was as if the groups universally experienced a midlife crisis at this point. The midpoint appears to work like an alarm clock, heightening members' awareness that their time is limited and that they need to "get moving." This transition ends Phase 1 and is characterized by a concentrated burst of changes, dropping of old patterns, and adoption of new perspectives. The transition sets a revised direction for Phase 2. Phase 2 is a new equilibrium or period of inertia. In this phase, the group executes plans created during the transition period.

The group's last meeting is characterized by a final burst of activity to finish its work. In summary, the punctuated-equilibrium model characterizes groups as exhibiting long periods of inertia interspersed with brief revolutionary changes triggered primarily by their members' awareness of time and deadlines. Keep in mind, however, that this model doesn't apply to all groups. It's essentially limited to temporary task groups who are working under a time-constrained completion deadline.[11]

Group Properties: Roles, Norms, Status, Size, and Cohesiveness

Work groups are not unorganized mobs. Work groups have properties that shape the behavior of members and make it possible to explain and predict a large portion of individual behavior within the group as well as the performance of the group itself. What are some of these properties? They include roles, norms, status, group size, and the degree of group cohesiveness.

Roles

Shakespeare said, "All the world's a stage, and all the men and women merely players." Using the same metaphor, all group members are actors, each playing a **role**. By this term, we mean a set of expected behavior patterns attributed to someone occupying a given position in a social unit. The understanding of role behavior would be dramatically simplified if each of us chose one role and "played it out" regularly and consistently. Unfortunately, we are required to play a number of diverse roles, both on and off our jobs. As we'll see, one of the tasks in understanding behavior is grasping the role that a person is currently playing.

Soccer player David Beckham, a husband and father of two young children, plays different roles in several jobs. Beckham is a key player as central midfielder for Spain's Real Madrid soccer team and the English National Team. He plays the role of an actor in advertising campaigns for Gillette, Adidas, and Pepsi. In this photo, Beckham teaches a youngster soccer skills at The David Beckham Academy, soccer training centers he launched for children in England and the United States. Beckham's behavior varies with the roles he plays on and off the job.

For example, Bill Patterson is a plant manager with EMM Industries, a large electrical equipment manufacturer in Phoenix. He has a number of roles that he fulfills on that job—for instance, an EMM employee, member of middle management, electrical engineer, and the primary company spokesperson in the community. Off the job, Bill Patterson finds himself in still more roles: husband, father, Catholic, Rotarian, tennis player, member of the Thunderbird Country Club, and president of his homeowners' association. Many of these roles are compatible; some create conflicts. For instance, how does his religious involvement influence his managerial decisions regarding layoffs, expense account padding, and providing accurate information to government agencies? A recent offer of promotion requires Bill to relocate, yet his family very much wants to stay in Phoenix. Can the role demands of his job be reconciled with the demands of his husband and father roles?

The issue should be clear: Like Bill Patterson, we all are required to play a number of roles, and our behavior varies with the role we are playing. Bill's behavior when he attends church on Sunday morning is different from his behavior on the golf course later that same day. So different groups impose different role requirements on individuals.

Role Identity   There are certain attitudes and actual behaviors consistent with a role, and they create the **role identity**. People have the ability to shift roles rapidly when they recognize that the situation and its demands clearly require major changes. For instance, when union stewards were promoted to supervisory positions, it was found that their attitudes changed from pro-union to pro-management within a few months of their promotion. When these promotions had to be rescinded later because of economic difficulties in the firm, it was found that the demoted supervisors had once again adopted their pro-union attitudes.[12]

Role Perception   Our view of how we're supposed to act in a given situation is a **role perception**. Based on an interpretation of how we believe we are supposed to behave, we engage in certain types of behavior.

Where do we get these perceptions? We get them from stimuli all around us—friends, books, movies, television. For example, many current law enforcement officers may have learned their roles from reading Joseph Wambaugh novels; many of tomorrow's lawyers might be influenced by watching the actions of attorneys in *Law & Order*; and the role of crime investigators, as portrayed on the television program *CSI*, could direct people into careers in criminology. Of course, the primary reason that apprenticeship programs exist in many trades and professions is to allow beginners to watch an "expert" so that they can learn to act as they are supposed to.

Role Expectations   **Role expectations** are defined as how others believe you should act in a given situation. How you behave is determined to a large extent by the role defined in the context in which you are acting. For instance, the role of a U.S. federal judge is viewed as having propriety and dignity, while a football coach is seen as aggressive, dynamic, and inspiring to his players.

role   *A set of expected behavior patterns attributed to someone occupying a given position in a social unit.*

role identity   *Certain attitudes and behaviors consistent with a role.*

role perception   *An individual's view of how he or she is supposed to act in a given situation.*

role expectations   *How others believe a person should act in a given situation.*

In the workplace, it can be helpful to look at the topic of role expectations through the perspective of the **psychological contract**. There is an unwritten agreement that exists between employees and their employer. This psychological contract sets out mutual expectations—what management expects from workers, and vice versa.[13] In effect, this contract defines the behavioral expectations that go with every role. For instance, management is expected to treat employees justly, provide acceptable working conditions, clearly communicate what is a fair day's work, and give feedback on how well the employee is doing. Employees are expected to respond by demonstrating a good attitude, following directions, and showing loyalty to the organization.

What happens when role expectations as implied in the psychological contract are not met? If management is derelict in keeping up its part of the bargain, we can expect negative repercussions on employee performance and satisfaction. When employees fail to live up to expectations, the result is usually some form of disciplinary action up to and including firing.

Role Conflict   When an individual is confronted by divergent role expectations, the result is **role conflict**. It exists when an individual finds that compliance with one role requirement may make it more difficult to comply with another.[14] At the extreme, it would include situations in which two or more role expectations are mutually contradictory.

Our previous discussion of the many roles Bill Patterson had to deal with included several role conflicts—for instance, Bill's attempt to reconcile the expectations placed on him as a husband and father with those placed on him as an executive with EMM Industries. The former, as you will remember, emphasizes stability and concern for the desire of his wife and children to remain in Phoenix. EMM, on the other hand, expects its employees to be responsive to the needs and requirements of the company. Although it might be in Bill's financial and career interests to accept a relocation, the conflict comes down to choosing between family and career role expectations.

An Experiment: Zimbardo's Prison Experiment   One of the more illuminating role experiments was done a number of years ago by Stanford University psychologist Philip Zimbardo and his associates.[15] They created a "prison" in the basement of the Stanford psychology building, hired at $15 a day two dozen emotionally stable, physically healthy, law-abiding students who scored "normal average" on extensive personality tests, randomly assigned them the role of either "guard" or "prisoner," and established some basic rules.

To get the experiment off to a "realistic" start, Zimbardo got the cooperation of the local police department. They went, unannounced, to each future prisoners' home, arrested and handcuffed them, put them in a squad car in front of friends and neighbors, and took them to police headquarters, where they were booked and fingerprinted. From there, they were taken to the Stanford prison.

At the start of the planned 2-week experiment, there were no measurable differences between the individuals assigned to be guards and those chosen to be prisoners. In addition, the guards received no special training in how to be prison guards. They were told only to "maintain law and order" in the prison and not to take any nonsense from the prisoners. Physical violence was forbidden. To simulate further the realities of prison life, the prisoners were allowed visits from relatives and friends. And although the mock guards worked 8-hour shifts, the mock prisoners were kept in their cells around the clock and were allowed out only for meals, exercise, toilet privileges, head-count lineups, and work details.

It took the "prisoners" little time to accept the authority positions of the guards, or the mock guards to adjust to their new authority roles. After the guards crushed a rebellion attempt on the second day, the prisoners became

Students at Stanford University played roles of "guard" and "prisoner" in a simulated prison experiment. The experiment demonstrated how quickly individuals can learn new roles different from their personalities and without any special training.

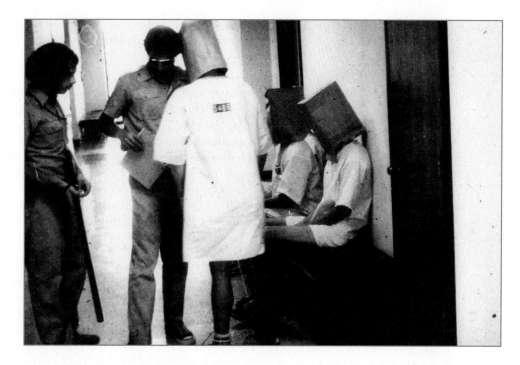

increasingly passive. Whatever the guards "dished out," the prisoners took. The prisoners actually began to believe and act as if they were, as the guards constantly reminded them, inferior and powerless. And every guard, at some time during the simulation, engaged in abusive, authoritative behavior. For example, one guard said, "I was surprised at myself . . . I made them call each other names and clean the toilets out with their bare hands. I practically considered the prisoners cattle, and I kept thinking: 'I have to watch out for them in case they try something.' " Another guard added, "I was tired of seeing the prisoners in their rags and smelling the strong odors of their bodies that filled the cells. I watched them tear at each other on orders given by us. They didn't see it as an experiment. It was real and they were fighting to keep their identity. But we were always there to show them who was boss." Surprisingly, during the entire experiment—even after days of abuse—not one prisoner said, "Stop this. I'm a student like you. This is just an experiment!"

The simulation actually proved *too successful* in demonstrating how quickly individuals learn new roles. The researchers had to stop the experiment after only 6 days because of the participants' pathological reactions. And remember, these were individuals chosen precisely for their normalcy and emotional stability.

What should you conclude from this prison simulation? The participants in this experiment had, like the rest of us, learned stereotyped conceptions of guard and prisoner roles from the mass media and their own personal experiences in power and powerlessness relationships gained at home (parent–child), in school (teacher–student), and in other situations. This, then, allowed them easily and rapidly to assume roles that were very different from their inherent personalities. In this case, we saw that people with no prior personality pathology

psychological contract   *An unwritten agreement that sets out what management expects from the employee, and vice versa.*

role conflict   *A situation in which an individual is confronted by divergent role expectations.*

or training in their roles could execute extreme forms of behavior consistent with the roles they were playing.

Norms

Did you ever notice that golfers don't speak while their partners are putting on the green or that employees don't criticize their bosses in public? Why? The answer is: "Norms!"

All groups have established **norms**, that is, acceptable standards of behavior that are shared by the group's members. Norms tell members what they ought and ought not to do under certain circumstances. From an individual's standpoint, they tell what is expected of you in certain situations. When agreed to and accepted by the group, norms act as a means of influencing the behavior of group members with a minimum of external controls. Norms differ among groups, communities, and societies, but they all have them.[16]

The Hawthorne Studies   It's generally agreed among behavioral scientists that full-scale appreciation of the importance norms play in influencing worker behavior did not occur until the early 1930s. This enlightenment grew out of a series of studies undertaken at Western Electric Company's Hawthorne Works in Chicago between 1924 and 1932.[17] Originally initiated by Western Electric officials and later overseen by Harvard professor Elton Mayo, the Hawthorne studies concluded that a worker's behavior and sentiments were closely related, that group influences were significant in affecting individual behavior, that group standards were highly effective in establishing individual worker output, and that money was less a factor in determining worker output than were group standards, sentiments, and security. Let us briefly discuss the Hawthorne investigations and demonstrate the importance of these findings in explaining group behavior.

The Hawthorne researchers began by examining the relation between the physical environment and productivity. Illumination and other working conditions were selected to represent this physical environment. The researchers' initial findings contradicted their anticipated results.

They began with illumination experiments with various groups of workers. The researchers manipulated the intensity of illumination upward and downward, while at the same time noting changes in group output. Results varied, but one thing was clear: In no case was the increase or decrease in output in proportion to the increase or decrease in illumination. So the researchers introduced a control group: An experimental group was presented with varying intensity of illumination, while the controlled unit worked under a constant illumination intensity. Again, the results were bewildering to the Hawthorne researchers. As the light level was increased in the experimental unit, output rose for both the control and the experimental group. But to the surprise of the researchers, as the light level was dropped in the experimental group, productivity continued to increase in both groups. In fact, a productivity decrease was observed in the experimental group only when the light intensity had been reduced to that of moonlight. The Hawthorne researchers concluded that illumination intensity was only a minor influence among the many influences that affected an employee's productivity, but they could not explain the behavior they had witnessed.

As a follow-up to the illumination experiments, the researchers began a second set of experiments in the relay assembly test room at Western Electric. A small group of women was isolated from the main work group so that their behavior could be more carefully observed. They went about their job of assembling small telephone relays in a room laid out similarly to their normal department. The only significant difference was the placement in the room of a

From the Hawthorne studies, observers gained valuable insights into how individual behavior is influenced by group norms. The group of workers determined the level of fair output and established norms for individual work rates that conformed to the output. To enforce the group norms, workers used sarcasm, ridicule, and even physical force to influence individual behaviors that were not acceptable to the group.

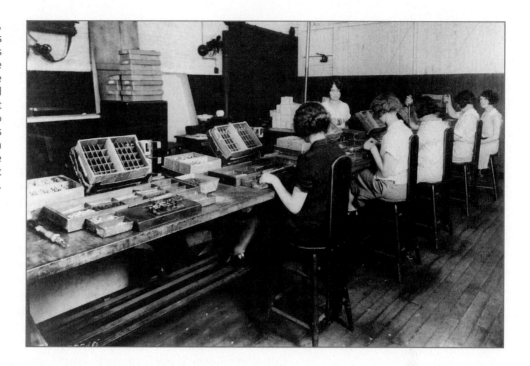

research assistant who acted as an observer—keeping records of output, rejects, working conditions, and a daily log sheet describing everything that happened. Observations covering a multiyear period found that this small group's output increased steadily. The number of personal absences and those due to sickness was approximately one-third of those recorded by women in the regular production department. What became evident was that this group's performance was significantly influenced by its status of being a "special" group. The women in the test room thought that being in the experimental group was fun, that they were in sort of an elite group, and that management was concerned with their interest by engaging in such experimentation. In essence, workers in both the illumination and assembly-test-room experiments were reacting to the increased attention they were receiving.

A third study in the bank wiring observation room was introduced to ascertain the effect of a sophisticated wage incentive plan. The assumption was that individual workers would maximize their productivity when they saw that it was directly related to economic rewards. The most important finding coming out of this study was that employees did not individually maximize their outputs. Rather, their output became controlled by a group norm that determined what was a proper day's work. Output was not only being restricted, but individual workers were giving erroneous reports. The total for a week would check with the total week's output, but the daily reports showed a steady level of output regardless of actual daily production. What was going on?

Interviews determined that the group was operating well below its capability and was leveling output in order to protect itself. Members were afraid that if they significantly increased their output, the unit incentive rate would be cut, the expected daily output would be increased, layoffs might occur, or slower

norms   *Acceptable standards of behavior within a group that are shared by the group's members.*

workers would be reprimanded. So the group established its idea of a fair output—neither too much nor too little. They helped each other out to ensure their reports were nearly level.

The norms the group established included a number of "don'ts." *Don't* be a rate-buster, turning out too much work. *Don't* be a chiseler, turning out too little work. *Don't* be a squealer on any of your peers. How did the group enforce these norms? Their methods were neither gentle nor subtle. They included sarcasm, name-calling, ridicule, and even physical punches to the upper arm of members who violated the group's norms. Members would also ostracize individuals whose behavior was against the group's interest.

The Hawthorne studies made an important contribution to our understanding of group behavior—particularly the significant place that norms have in determining individual work behavior.

Common Classes of Norms   A work group's norms are like an individual's fingerprints—each is unique. Yet there are still some common classes of norms that appear in most work groups.[18]

Probably the most common class of norms is *performance norms*. Work groups typically provide their members with explicit cues on how hard they should work, how to get the job done, their level of output, appropriate levels of tardiness, and the like.[19] These norms are extremely powerful in affecting an individual employee's performance—they are capable of significantly modifying a performance prediction that was based solely on the employee's ability and level of personal motivation.

A second category encompasses *appearance norms*. This includes things like appropriate dress, loyalty to the work group or organization, when to look busy, and when it's acceptable to goof off. Some organizations have formal dress codes. However, even in their absence, norms frequently develop to dictate the kind of clothing that should be worn to work. Similarly, presenting the appearance of loyalty is important, especially among professional employees and those in the executive ranks. So it's often considered inappropriate to be openly looking for another job.

Another category concerns *social arrangement norms*. These norms come from informal work groups and primarily regulate social interactions within the group. With whom group members eat lunch, friendships on and off the job, social games, and the like are influenced by these norms.

A final category relates to *allocation of resources norms*. These norms can originate in the group or in the organization and cover things like pay, assignment of difficult jobs, and allocation of new tools and equipment.

Conformity   As a member of a group, you desire acceptance by the group. Because of your desire for acceptance, you are susceptible to conforming to the group's norms. There is considerable evidence that groups can place strong pressures on individual members to change their attitudes and behaviors to conform to the group's standard.[20]

Do individuals conform to the pressures of all the groups to which they belong? Obviously not, because people belong to many groups and their norms vary. In some cases, they may even have contradictory norms. So what do people do? They conform to the important groups to which they belong or hope to belong. The important groups have been called **reference groups**, and they're characterized as ones in which a person is aware of other members; defines himself or herself as a member, or would like to be a member; and feels that the group members are significant to him or her.[21] The implication, then, is that all groups do not impose equal conformity pressures on their members.

The impact that group pressures for **conformity** can have on an individual member's judgment and attitudes was demonstrated in the now-classic studies by Solomon Asch.[22] Asch made up groups of seven or eight people, who sat around a table and were asked to compare two cards held by the experimenter. One card had one line, the other had three lines of varying length. As shown in Exhibit 9-4, one of the lines on the three-line card was identical to the line on the one-line card. Also as shown in Exhibit 9-4, the difference in line length was quite obvious; in fact, under ordinary conditions, subjects made fewer than 1 percent errors. The object was to announce aloud which of the three lines matched the single line. But what happens if the members in the group begin to give incorrect answers? Will the pressures to conform result in an unsuspecting subject (USS) altering an answer to align with the others? That was what Asch wanted to know. So he arranged the group so that only the USS was unaware that the experiment was "fixed." The seating was prearranged: The USS was placed so as to be one of the last to announce a decision.

The experiment began with several sets of matching exercises. All the subjects gave the right answers. On the third set, however, the first subject gave an obviously wrong answer—for example, saying "C" in Exhibit 9-4. The next subject gave the same wrong answer, and so did the others until it got to the unknowing subject. He knew "B" was the same as "X," yet everyone had said "C." The decision confronting the USS was this: Do you publicly state a perception that differs from the preannounced position of the others in your group? Or do you give an answer that you strongly believe is incorrect in order to have your response agree with that of the other group members?

The results obtained by Asch demonstrated that over many experiments and many trials, 75 percent of the subjects gave at least one answer that conformed—that is, that they knew was wrong but that was consistent with the replies of other group members—and the average for conformers was 37 percent. What meaning can we draw from these results? They suggest that there are group norms that press us toward conformity. That is, we desire to be one of the group and avoid being visibly different.

The preceding conclusions are based on research that was conducted 50 years ago. Has time altered their validity? And should we consider these findings

---

Exhibit 9-4   Examples of Cards Used in Asch's Study

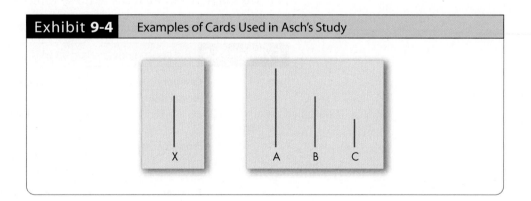

---

generalizable across cultures? The evidence indicates that there have been changes in the level of conformity over time; and Asch's findings are culture-bound.[23] Specifically, levels of conformity have steadily declined since Asch's studies in the early 1950s. In addition, conformity to social norms is higher in collectivist cultures than in individualistic cultures. Nevertheless, even in individualistic countries, you should consider conformity to norms to still be a powerful force in groups.

Deviant Workplace Behavior   Ted Vowinkel is frustrated by a coworker who constantly spreads malicious and unsubstantiated rumors about him. Debra Hundley is tired of a member of her work team who, when confronted with a problem, takes out his frustration by yelling and screaming at her and other work team members. And Rhonda Lieberman recently quit her job as a dental hygienist after being constantly sexually harassed by her employer.

What do these three episodes have in common? They represent employees being exposed to acts of *deviant workplace behavior*.[24] **Deviant workplace behavior** (also called *antisocial behavior* or *workplace incivility*) is voluntary behavior that violates significant organizational norms and, in doing so, threatens the well-being of the organization or its members. Exhibit 9-5 provides a typology of deviant workplace behaviors with examples of each.

Few organizations will admit to creating or condoning conditions that encourage and maintain deviant norms. Yet they exist. Employees report, for example, an increase in rudeness and disregard toward others by bosses and coworkers in recent years. And nearly half of employees who have suffered this incivility report that it has led them to think about changing jobs, with 12 percent actually quitting because of it.[25]

As with norms in general, individual employees' antisocial actions are shaped by the group context within which they work. Evidence demonstrates that the antisocial behavior exhibited by a work group is a significant predictor of an individual's antisocial behavior at work.[26] In other words, deviant workplace behavior is likely to flourish where it's supported by group norms. What this means for managers is that when deviant workplace norms surface, employee cooperation, commitment, and motivation are likely to suffer. This, in turn, can lead to reduced employee productivity and job satisfaction and increased turnover.

Additionally, just being part of a group can increase an individual's deviant behavior. In other words, someone who ordinarily wouldn't engage in deviant behavior might be more likely to do so when working in a group. In fact, a recent

Exhibit **9-5**	Typology of Deviant Workplace Behavior

Category	Examples
Production	Leaving early Intentionally working slowly Wasting resources
Property	Sabotage Lying about hours worked Stealing from the organization
Political	Showing favoritism Gossiping and spreading rumors Blaming coworkers
Personal aggression	Sexual harassment Verbal abuse Stealing from coworkers

Source: Adapted from S. L. Robinson and R. J. Bennett, "A Typology of Deviant Workplace Behaviors: A Multidimensional Scaling Study," *Academy of Management Journal*, April 1995, p. 565.

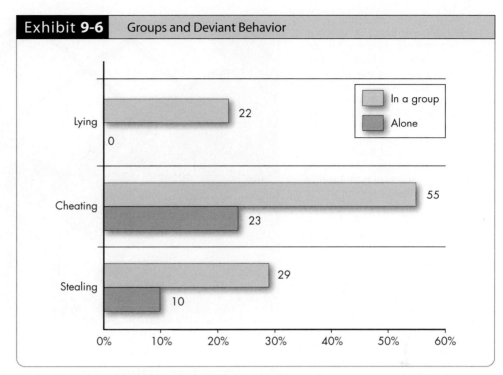

| Exhibit **9-6** | Groups and Deviant Behavior |

Source: A. Erez, H. Elms, and E. Fong, "Lying, Cheating, Stealing: Groups and the Ring of Gyges," paper presented at the Academy of Management Annual Meeting, Honolulu, HI, August 8, 2005.

study suggests that, compared to individuals working alone, those working in a group were more likely to lie, cheat, and steal. As shown in Exhibit 9-6, in this study no individual working alone lied, but 22 percent of those working in groups did. Moreover, individuals working in groups also were more likely to cheat (55 percent of individuals working in a group cheated on a task versus 23 percent of individuals working alone) and steal (29 percent of individuals working in a group stole, compared to only 10 percent working alone).[27] Groups provide a shield of anonymity so that someone who ordinarily might be afraid of getting caught for stealing can rely on the fact that other group members had the same opportunity or reason to steal. This creates a false sense of confidence that may result in more aggressive behavior. Thus, deviant behavior depends on the accepted norms of the group—or even whether an individual is part of a group.[28]

Status

Status—that is, a socially defined position or rank given to groups or group members by others—permeates every society. Despite many attempts, we have made little progress toward a classless society. Even the smallest group will develop roles, rights, and rituals to differentiate its members. Status is an important factor in understanding human behavior because it is a significant motivator and has major behavioral consequences when individuals perceive a disparity between what they believe their status to be and what others perceive it to be.

deviant workplace behavior *Voluntary behavior that violates significant organizational norms and, in doing so, threatens the well-being of the organization or its members.*

status *A socially defined position or rank given to groups or group members by others.*

This group of 70 designers has a high status at BenQ, a consumer electronics company in Taiwan. BenQ designs products for other companies, but it also manufactures and markets its own brand of thin-screen TVs, computer monitors, MP3 players, and cell phones. Working from the BenQ design center, these men and women play an important role in the future of BenQ because the company's success depends on their innovations in developing a constant flow of new products.

What Determines Status?   According to **status characteristics theory**, differences in status characteristics create status hierarchies within groups.[29] Moreover, status tends to be derived from one of three sources: the power a person wields over others; a person's ability to contribute to a group's goals; and an individual's personal characteristics.[30]

People who control the outcomes of a group through their power tend to be perceived as high status. This is largely due to their ability to control the group's resources. So a group's formal leader or manager is likely to be perceived as high status when he or she can allocate resources like preferred assignments, desirable schedules, and pay increases. People whose contributions are critical to the group's success also tend to have high status. The outstanding performers on sports teams, for example, typically have greater status on the team than do average players. Finally, someone who has personal characteristics that are positively valued by the group—such as good looks, intelligence, money, or a friendly personality—will typically have higher status than someone who has fewer valued attributes. This tends to explain why attractive people are often the most popular in high school. Note, of course, that a characteristic valued by one group may mean nothing in another. So high intelligence may give you status at your monthly Mensa meetings, but it may provide no benefit at all to you at your Tuesday bowling league.

Status and Norms   Status has been shown to have some interesting effects on the power of norms and pressures to conform. For instance, high-status members of groups often are given more freedom to deviate from norms than are other group members.[31] High-status people also are better able to resist conformity pressures than their lower-status peers. An individual who is highly valued by a group but who doesn't much need or care about the social rewards the group provides is particularly able to pay minimal attention to conformity norms.[32]

The previous findings explain why many star athletes, celebrities, top-performing salespeople, and outstanding academics seem oblivious to appearance or social norms that constrain their peers. As high-status individuals, they're given a wider range of discretion. But this is true only as long as the high-status person's activities aren't severely detrimental to group goal achievement.[33]

Status and Group Interaction   Interaction among members of groups is influenced by status. We find, for instance, that high-status people tend to be more assertive.[34] They speak out more often, criticize more, state more commands, and interrupt others more often. But status differences actually inhibit diversity of ideas and creativity in groups because lower-status members tend to be less active participants in group discussions. In situations in which lower-status members possess expertise and insights that could aid the group, their expertise and insights are not likely to be fully utilized, thus reducing the group's overall performance.

Status Inequity   It is important for group members to believe that the status hierarchy is equitable. When inequity is perceived, it creates disequilibrium, which results in various types of corrective behavior.[35]

The concept of equity presented in Chapter 6 applies to status. People expect rewards to be proportionate to costs incurred. If Dana and Anne are the two finalists for the head nurse position in a hospital, and it is clear that Dana has more seniority and better preparation for assuming the promotion, Anne will view the selection of Dana to be equitable. However, if Anne is chosen because she is the daughter-in-law of the hospital director, Dana will believe an injustice has been committed.

The trappings that go with formal positions are also important elements in maintaining equity. When we believe there is an inequity between the perceived ranking of an individual and the status accouterments that person is given by the organization, we are experiencing status incongruence. An example of this kind of incongruence is the more desirable office location being held by a lower-ranking individual. Pay incongruence has long been a problem in the insurance industry, where top sales agents often earn two to five times more than senior corporate executives. The result is that it is very hard for insurance companies to entice successful agents into management positions. Our point is that employees expect the things individuals have and receive to be congruent with their status.

Groups generally agree within themselves on status criteria and, hence, there is usually high concurrence in group rankings of individuals. However, individuals can find themselves in a conflict situation when they move between groups whose status criteria are different or when they join groups whose members have heterogeneous backgrounds. For instance, business executives may use personal income or the growth rate of their companies as determinants of status. Government bureaucrats may use the size of their budgets. Blue-collar workers may use years of seniority. In groups made up of heterogeneous individuals or when heterogeneous groups are forced to be interdependent, status differences may initiate conflict as the group attempts to reconcile and align the differing hierarchies. As we'll see in the next chapter, this can be a particular problem when management creates teams made up of employees from across varied functions within the organization.

status characteristics theory   *Theory stating that differences in status characteristics create status hierarchies within groups.*

Status and Culture   Before we leave the topic of status, we should briefly address the issue of cross-culture transferability. Do cultural differences affect status? The answer is a resounding Yes.[36]

The importance of status does vary between cultures. The French, for example, are highly status conscious. Also, countries differ on the criteria that create status. For instance, status for Latin Americans and Asians tends to be derived from family position and formal roles held in organizations. In contrast, although status is still important in countries like the United States and Australia, it tends to be less "in your face." And it tends to be bestowed more on accomplishments than on titles and family trees.[37]

The message here is to make sure you understand who and what holds status when interacting with people from a culture different from your own. An American manager who doesn't understand that office size is not a measure of a Japanese executive's position or who fails to grasp the importance that the British place on family genealogy and social class is likely to unintentionally offend his Japanese or British counterpart and, in so doing, lessen his interpersonal effectiveness.

Size

Does the size of a group affect the group's overall behavior? The answer to this question is a definite Yes, but the effect is contingent on what dependent variables you look at.[38] The evidence indicates, for instance, that smaller groups are faster at completing tasks than are larger ones, and that individuals perform better in smaller groups.[39] However, if the group is engaged in problem solving, large groups consistently get better marks than their smaller counterparts.[40] Translating these results into specific numbers is a bit more hazardous, but we can offer some parameters. Large groups—with a dozen or more members— are good for gaining diverse input. So if the goal of the group is fact-finding, larger groups should be more effective. On the other hand, smaller groups are better at doing something productive with that input. Groups of approximately seven members, therefore, tend to be more effective for taking action.

One of the most important findings related to the size of a group has been labeled **social loafing**. Social loafing is the tendency for individuals to expend less effort when working collectively than when working individually.[41] It directly challenges the logic that the productivity of the group as a whole should at least equal the sum of the productivity of each individual in that group.

A common stereotype about groups is that the sense of team spirit spurs individual effort and enhances the group's overall productivity. But that stereotype may be wrong. In the late 1920s, a German psychologist named Max Ringelmann compared the results of individual and group performance on a rope-pulling task.[42] He expected that the group's effort would be equal to the sum of the efforts of individuals within the group. That is, three people pulling together should exert three times as much pull on the rope as one person, and eight people should exert eight times as much pull. Ringelmann's results, however, didn't confirm his expectations. One person pulling on a rope alone exerted an average of 63 kilograms of force. In groups of three, the per-person force dropped to 53 kilograms. And in groups of eight, it fell to only 31 kilograms per person.

Replications of Ringelmann's research with similar tasks have generally supported his findings.[43] Group performance increases with group size, but the addition of new members to the group has diminishing returns on productivity. So more may be better in the sense that the total productivity of a group of four is greater than that of three people, but the individual productivity of each group member declines.

Goofing-Off in the Twenty-first Century: Cyberloafing

Although the Internet has created a valuable mechanism for speeding communication within and between organizations and for helping employees quickly access information, it has also created a potential source for reducing employee productivity through cyberloafing. *Cyberloafing* is the act of employees using their organization's Internet access for personal purposes during work hours. When employees surf the Web for entertainment, do online stock trading, shop online, or engage in other non-job-related Internet activities while at work, they're cyberloafing.

Survey data indicate that 64 percent of U.S. workers surf the Internet for personal interest during working hours. Moreover, estimates indicate that nearly one-third of employees' Internet use at work is recreational and that cyberloafing is costing U.S. employers approximately $3 million a year for every 1,000 employees with Internet access. In spite of recent efforts by management to monitor employee Internet access, cyberloafing remains a threat to employee productivity. Some forms of Internet abuse can be filed under harassment. Maxine Morse, for example, quit her job after male coworkers repeatedly bombarded her e-mail inbox with pornographic images downloaded from the Internet (she later sued, and won).

Characteristics of the workplace can increase cyberloafing. For example, if the work itself isn't interesting, if it creates stress, or if employees believe they aren't being treated fairly, they will be more motivated to use cyberloafing as a means of distraction or to compensate for perceived mistreatment by the organization.

Sources: Based on M. Griffiths, "Internet Abuse in the Workplace: Issues and Concerns for Employers and Employment Counselors," *Journal of Employment Counseling* 40, no. 2 (2003), pp. 87–96; V. K. G. Lim, "The IT Way of Loafing on the Job: Cyberloafing, Neutralizing and Organizational Justice," *Journal of Organizational Behavior* 23, no. 5 (2002), pp. 675–94; R. W. Kubey, M. J. Lavin, and J. R. Barrows, "Internet Use and Collegiate Academic Performance Decrements: Early Findings," *Journal of Communication* 51, no. 2 (2001), pp. 366–82; and "Internet Usage Statistics," www.n2h2.com, March 27, 2002.

What causes this social loafing effect? It may be due to a belief that others in the group are not carrying their fair share. If you see others as lazy or inept, you can reestablish equity by reducing your effort. Another explanation is the dispersion of responsibility. Because the results of the group cannot be attributed to any single person, the relationship between an individual's input and the group's output is clouded. In such situations, individuals may be tempted to become "free riders" and coast on the group's efforts. In other words, there will be a reduction in efficiency when individuals think that their contribution cannot be measured.

The implications for OB of this effect on work groups are significant. When managers use collective work situations to enhance morale and teamwork, they must also provide means by which individual efforts can be identified. If this isn't done, management must weigh the potential losses in productivity from using groups against any possible gains in worker satisfaction.[44] However, this conclusion has a Western bias. It's consistent with individualistic cultures, like the United States and Canada, that are dominated by self-interest. It is not consistent with collective societies, in which individuals are motivated by in-group goals. For instance, in studies comparing employees from the United States with employees from the People's Republic of China and Israel (both collectivist societies), the Chinese and Israelis showed no propensity to engage in social loafing. In fact, the Chinese and Israelis actually performed better in a group than when working alone.[45]

social loafing *The tendency for individuals to expend less effort when working collectively than when working individually.*

The research on group size leads us to two additional conclusions: (1) Groups with an odd number of members tend to be preferable to those with an even number; and (2) groups made up of five or seven members do a pretty good job of exercising the best elements of both small and large groups.[46] Having an odd number of members eliminates the possibility of ties when votes are taken. And groups made up of five or seven members are large enough to form a majority and allow for diverse input yet small enough to avoid the negative outcomes often associated with large groups, such as domination by a few members, development of subgroups, inhibited participation by some members, and excessive time taken to reach a decision.

Cohesiveness

Groups differ in their **cohesiveness**, that is, the degree to which members are attracted to each other and are motivated to stay in the group.[47] For instance, some work groups are cohesive because the members have spent a great deal of time together, or the group's small size facilitates high interaction, or the group has experienced external threats that have brought members close together. Cohesiveness is important because it has been found to be related to the group's productivity.[48]

Studies consistently show that the relationship of cohesiveness and productivity depends on the performance-related norms established by the group.[49] If performance-related norms are high (for example, high output, quality work, cooperation with individuals outside the group), a cohesive group will be more productive than will a less cohesive group. But if cohesiveness is high and performance norms are low, productivity will be low. If cohesiveness is low and performance norms are high, productivity increases, but less than in the high-cohesiveness/high-norms situation. When cohesiveness and performance-related norms are both low, productivity will tend to fall into the low-to-moderate range. These conclusions are summarized in Exhibit 9-7.

What can you do to encourage group cohesiveness? You might try one or more of the following suggestions: (1) Make the group smaller. (2) Encourage agreement with group goals. (3) Increase the time members spend together. (4) Increase the status of the group and the perceived difficulty of attaining membership in the group. (5) Stimulate competition with other groups. (6) Give rewards to the group rather than to individual members. (7) Physically isolate the group.[50]

Exhibit 9-7	Relationship Between Group Cohesiveness, Performance Norms, and Productivity

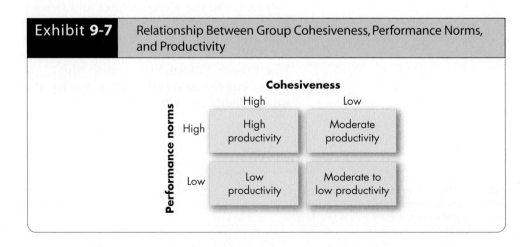

Group Cohesiveness Across Cultures

A RECENT STUDY ATTEMPTED TO DETERMINE whether motivating work groups by giving them more complex tasks and greater autonomy resulted in increased group cohesiveness. Researchers studied bank teams in the United States, an individualist culture, and in Hong Kong, a collectivist culture. Both teams were composed of individuals from each respective country. The results showed, regardless of what culture the teams were from, giving teams difficult tasks and more freedom to accomplish those tasks created a more tight-knit group. Consequently, team performance was enhanced.

However, the teams did differ in the extent to which increases in task complexity and autonomy resulted in greater group cohesiveness. Teams in individualist cultures responded more strongly than did teams in collectivist cultures, became more united and committed, and, as a result, received higher performance ratings from their supervisors than teams from collectivist cultures. Why do these cultural differences exist? One explanation is that collectivist teams already have a strong predisposition to work together as a group so there's less need for increased teamwork. What's the lesson? Managers in individualist cultures may need to work harder to increase team cohesiveness. One way to do this is to give teams more challenging assignments and provide them with more independence.

Source: Based on D. Man and S. S. K. Lam, "The Effects of Job Complexity and Autonomy on Cohesiveness in Collectivist and Individualistic Work Groups: A Cross-Cultural Analysis," *Journal of Organizational Behavior,* December 2003, pp. 979–1001.

Group Decision Making

The belief—characterized by juries—that two heads are better than one has long been accepted as a basic component of North American and many other countries' legal systems. This belief has expanded to the point that, today, many decisions in organizations are made by groups, teams, or committees.[51] In this section, we discuss group decision making.

Groups Versus the Individual

Decision-making groups may be widely used in organizations, but does that imply that group decisions are preferable to those made by an individual alone? The answer to this question depends on a number of factors. Let's begin by looking at the strengths and weaknesses of group decision making.[52]

Strengths of Group Decision Making Groups generate *more complete information and knowledge.* By aggregating the resources of several individuals, groups bring more input into the decision process. In addition to more input, groups can bring heterogeneity to the decision process. They offer *increased diversity of views.* This opens up the opportunity for more approaches and alternatives to

cohesiveness *Degree to which group members are attracted to each other and are motivated to stay in the group.*

The three founders of Blue Man Group use group decision making to generate high-quality decisions. From deciding what material to use in shows and how to manage 500 employees, to expanding their business in other countries, all decisions are made by unanimous agreement of the creators of the show. Group decision making helps Blue Man Group grow without losing focus of the founders' original vision.

be considered. Finally, groups lead to increased *acceptance of a solution*. Many decisions fail after the final choice is made because people don't accept the solution. Group members who participated in making a decision are likely to enthusiastically support the decision and encourage others to accept it.

Weaknesses of Group Decision Making   In spite of the pluses noted, group decisions have their drawbacks. They're time-consuming because groups typically take more time to reach a solution than would be the case if an individual were making the decision. There are *conformity pressures in groups*. The desire by group members to be accepted and considered an asset to the group can result in squashing any overt disagreement. Group discussion can be *dominated by one or a few members*. If this dominant coalition is composed of low- and medium-ability members, the group's overall effectiveness will suffer. Finally, group decisions suffer from *ambiguous responsibility*. In an individual decision, it's clear who is accountable for the final outcome. In a group decision, the responsibility of any single member is watered down.

Effectiveness and Efficiency   Whether groups are more effective than individuals depends on the criteria you use for defining effectiveness. In terms of *accuracy*, group decisions are generally more accurate than the decisions of the average individual in a group but less accurate than the judgments of the most accurate group member.[53] If decision effectiveness is defined in terms of *speed*, individuals are superior. If *creativity* is important, groups tend to be more effective than individuals. And if effectiveness means the degree of *acceptance* the final solution achieves, the nod again goes to the group.[54]

But effectiveness cannot be considered without also assessing efficiency. In terms of efficiency, groups almost always stack up as a poor second to the individual decision maker. With few exceptions, group decision making consumes more work hours than if an individual were to tackle the same problem alone. The exceptions tend to be the instances in which, to achieve comparable quantities of diverse input, the single decision maker must spend a great deal of time reviewing files and talking to people. Because groups can include members from diverse areas, the time spent searching for information can be

Two heads are not necessarily always better than one. In fact, the evidence generally confirms the superiority of individuals over groups when brainstorming. The best individual in a group also makes better decisions than groups as a whole, though groups do tend to do better than the average group member.[55]

Research also indicates that groups are superior only when they meet certain criteria.[56] These criteria include: (1) Diversity among members. The benefits of "two heads" requires that they differ in relevant skills and abilities. (2) The group members must be able to communicate their ideas freely and openly. This requires an absence of hostility and intimidation. (3) The task being undertaken is complex. Relative to individuals, groups do better on complex rather than simple tasks. ■

reduced. However, as we noted, these advantages in efficiency tend to be the exception. Groups are generally less efficient than individuals. In deciding whether to use groups, then, consideration should be given to assessing whether increases in effectiveness are more than enough to offset the losses in efficiency.

Summary   In summary, groups offer an excellent vehicle for performing many of the steps in the decision-making process. They are a source of both breadth and depth of input for information gathering. If the group is composed of individuals with diverse backgrounds, the alternatives generated should be more extensive and the analysis more critical. When the final solution is agreed on, there are more people in a group decision to support and implement it. These pluses, however, can be more than offset by the time consumed by group decisions, the internal conflicts they create, and the pressures they generate toward conformity. Therefore, in some cases, individuals can be expected to make better decisions than groups.

Groupthink and Groupshift

Two byproducts of group decision making have received a considerable amount of attention by researchers in OB. As we'll show, these two phenomena have the potential to affect the group's ability to appraise alternatives objectively and to arrive at quality decision solutions.

The first phenomenon, called **groupthink**, is related to norms. It describes situations in which group pressures for conformity deter the group from critically appraising unusual, minority, or unpopular views. Groupthink is a disease that attacks many groups and can dramatically hinder their performance. The second phenomenon we shall discuss is called **groupshift**. It indicates that in discussing a given set of alternatives and arriving at a solution, group members tend to exaggerate the initial positions that they hold. In some situations, caution dominates, and there is a conservative shift. More often, however, the evidence

groupthink   *Phenomenon in which the norm for consensus overrides the realistic appraisal of alternative courses of action.*

groupshift   *A change in decision risk between the group's decision and the individual decision that members within the group would make; can be either toward conservatism or greater risk.*

indicates that groups tend toward a risky shift. Let's look at each of these phenomena in more detail.

Groupthink   Have you ever felt like speaking up in a meeting, classroom, or informal group but decided against it? One reason may have been shyness. On the other hand, you may have been a victim of groupthink, the phenomenon that occurs when group members become so enamored of seeking concurrence that the norm for consensus overrides the realistic appraisal of alternative courses of action and the full expression of deviant, minority, or unpopular views. It describes a deterioration in an individual's mental efficiency, reality testing, and moral judgment as a result of group pressures.[57]

We have all seen the symptoms of the groupthink phenomenon:

1. Group members rationalize any resistance to the assumptions they have made. No matter how strongly the evidence may contradict their basic assumptions, members behave so as to reinforce those assumptions continually.
2. Members apply direct pressures on those who momentarily express doubts about any of the group's shared views or who question the validity of arguments supporting the alternative favored by the majority.
3. Members who have doubts or hold differing points of view seek to avoid deviating from what appears to be group consensus by keeping silent about misgivings and even minimizing to themselves the importance of their doubts.
4. There appears to be an illusion of unanimity. If someone doesn't speak, it's assumed that he or she is in full accord. In other words, abstention becomes viewed as a Yes vote.[58]

In studies of historic American foreign policy decisions, these symptoms were found to prevail when government policy-making groups failed—unpreparedness at Pearl Harbor in 1941, the U.S. invasion of North Korea, the Bay of Pigs fiasco, and the escalation of the Vietnam War.[59] More recently, the *Challenger* and *Columbia* space shuttle disasters and the failure of the main mirror on the *Hubble* telescope have been linked to decision processes at NASA in which groupthink symptoms were evident.[60] And groupthink was found to be a primary factor leading to setbacks at both British Airways and retailer Marks & Spencer as they tried to implement globalization strategies.[61]

Groupthink appears to be closely aligned with the conclusions Asch drew in his experiments with a lone dissenter. Individuals who hold a position that is different from that of the dominant majority are under pressure to suppress, withhold, or modify their true feelings and beliefs. As members of a group, we find it more pleasant to be in agreement—to be a positive part of the group—than to be a disruptive force, even if disruption is necessary to improve the effectiveness of the group's decisions.

Does groupthink attack all groups? No. It seems to occur most often when there is a clear group identity, when members hold a positive image of their group that they want to protect, and when the group perceives a collective threat to this positive image.[62] So groupthink is not a dissenter-suppression mechanism as much as it's a means for a group to protect its positive image. For NASA, its problems stem from its attempt to confirm its identity as "the elite organization that could do no wrong."[63]

What can managers do to minimize groupthink?[64] One thing is to monitor group size. People grow more intimidated and hesitant as group size increases and, although there is no magic number that will eliminate groupthink, individuals are likely to feel less personal responsibility when groups get larger than about 10. Managers should also encourage group leaders to play an impartial role. Leaders should actively seek input from all members and avoid expressing their own opinions, especially in the early stages of deliberation. Another thing is to appoint one group member to play the role of devil's advocate. This member's role is to overtly challenge the majority position and offer divergent perspectives. Still another suggestion is to use exercises that stimulate active discussion of diverse alternatives without threatening the group and intensifying identity protection. One such exercise is to have group members talk about dangers or risks involved in a decision and delaying discussion of any potential gains. By requiring members to first focus on the negatives of a decision alternative, the group is less likely to stifle dissenting views and more likely to gain an objective evaluation.

Groupshift   In comparing group decisions with the individual decisions of members within the group, evidence suggests that there are differences.[65] In some cases, the group decisions are more conservative than the individual decisions. More often, the shift is toward greater risk.[66]

What appears to happen in groups is that the discussion leads to a significant shift in the positions of members toward a more extreme position in the direction in which they were already leaning before the discussion. So conservative types become more cautious and the more aggressive types take on more risk. The group discussion tends to exaggerate the initial position of the group.

Groupshift can be viewed as actually a special case of groupthink. The decision of the group reflects the dominant decision-making norm that develops during the group's discussion. Whether the shift in the group's decision is toward greater caution or more risk depends on the dominant prediscussion norm.

The greater occurrence of the shift toward risk has generated several explanations for the phenomenon.[67] It's been argued, for instance, that the discussion creates familiarization among the members. As they become more comfortable with each other, they also become more bold and daring. Another argument is that most first-world societies value risk, that we admire individuals who are willing to take risks, and that group discussion motivates members to show that they are at least as willing as their peers to take risks. The most plausible explanation of the shift toward risk, however, seems to be that the group diffuses responsibility. Group decisions free any single member from accountability for the group's final choice. Greater risk can be taken because even if the decision fails, no one member can be held wholly responsible.

So how should you use the findings on groupshift? You should recognize that group decisions exaggerate the initial position of the individual members, that the shift has been shown more often to be toward greater risk, and that whether or not a group will shift toward greater risk or caution is a function of the members' prediscussion inclinations.

Having discussed group decision making and its pros and cons, we now turn to the techniques by which groups make decisions. These techniques reduce some of the dysfunctional aspects of group decision making.

Group Decision-Making Techniques

The most common form of group decision making takes place in **interacting groups**. In these groups, members meet face-to-face and rely on both verbal and nonverbal interaction to communicate with each other. But as our discussion of

interacting groups   *Typical groups, in which members interact with each other face-to-face.*

Exhibit 9-8

S. Adams, *Build a Better Life by Stealing Office Supplies* (Kansas City, MO: Andrews & McMeal, 1991), p. 31. Dilbert reprinted with permission of United Features Syndicate, Inc.

groupthink demonstrated, interacting groups often censor themselves and pressure individual members toward conformity of opinion. Brainstorming, the nominal group technique, and electronic meetings have been proposed as ways to reduce many of the problems inherent in the traditional interacting group.

Brainstorming is meant to overcome pressures for conformity in the interacting group that retard the development of creative alternatives.[68] It does this by utilizing an idea-generation process that specifically encourages any and all alternatives while withholding any criticism of those alternatives.

In a typical brainstorming session, a half-dozen to a dozen people sit around a table. The group leader states the problem in a clear manner so that it is understood by all participants. Members then "freewheel" as many alternatives as they can in a given length of time. No criticism is allowed, and all the alternatives are recorded for later discussion and analysis. That one idea stimulates others and that judgments of even the most bizarre suggestions are withheld until later encourage group members to "think the unusual."

Brainstorming may indeed generate ideas, but not in a very efficient manner. Research consistently shows that individuals working alone will generate more ideas than a group will in a brainstorming session. Why? One of the primary reasons is because of "production blocking." In other words, when people are generating ideas in a group, there are many people talking at once, which blocks the thought process and eventually impedes the sharing of ideas.[69] The following two techniques go further than brainstorming by offering methods that help groups arrive at a preferred solution.[70]

The **nominal group technique** restricts discussion or interpersonal communication during the decision-making process, hence, the term *nominal*. Group members are all physically present, as in a traditional committee meeting, but members operate independently. Specifically, a problem is presented and then the following steps take place:

1. Members meet as a group but before any discussion takes place, each member independently writes down ideas on the problem.
2. After this silent period, each member presents one idea to the group. Each member takes a turn, presenting a single idea until all ideas have been presented and recorded. No discussion takes place until all ideas have been recorded.
3. The group now discusses the ideas for clarity and evaluates them.
4. Each group member silently and independently rank-orders the ideas. The idea with the highest aggregate ranking determines the final decision.

The chief advantage of the nominal group technique is that it permits the group to meet formally but does not restrict independent thinking, as does the interacting group. Research generally shows that nominal groups outperform brainstorming groups.[71]

The most recent approach to group decision making blends the nominal group technique with sophisticated computer technology.[72] It's called the computer-assisted group or **electronic meeting**. Once the technology is in place, the concept is simple. Up to 50 people sit around a horseshoe-shaped table, empty except for a series of computer terminals. Issues are presented to participants and they type their responses onto their computer screen. Individual comments, as well as aggregate votes, are displayed on a projection screen. The proposed advantages of electronic meetings are anonymity, honesty, and speed. Participants can anonymously type any message they want and it flashes on the screen for all to see at the push of a participant's board key. It also allows people to be brutally honest without penalty. And it's supposedly fast because chitchat is eliminated, discussions don't digress, and many participants can "talk" at once without stepping on one another's toes. The early evidence, however, indicates that electronic meetings don't achieve most of their proposed benefits. Evaluations of numerous studies found that electronic meetings actually led to *decreased* group effectiveness, required *more* time to complete tasks, and resulted in *reduced* member satisfaction when compared to face-to-face groups.[73] Nevertheless, current enthusiasm for computer-mediated communications suggests that this technology is here to stay and is only likely to increase in popularity in the future.

Each of these four group decision techniques has its own set of strengths and weaknesses. The choice of one technique over another will depend on what criteria you want to emphasize and the cost–benefit trade-off. For instance, as Exhibit 9-9 indicates, the interacting group is good for achieving commitment to a solution, brainstorming develops group cohesiveness, the nominal group technique is an inexpensive means for generating a large number of ideas, and electronic meetings minimize social pressures and conflicts.

brainstorming *An idea-generation process that specifically encourages any and all alternatives, while withholding any criticism of those alternatives.*

nominal group technique *A group decision-making method in which individual members meet face-to-face to pool their judgments in a systematic but independent fashion.*

electronic meeting *A meeting in which members interact on computers, allowing for anonymity of comments and aggregation of votes.*

| Exhibit **9-9** | Evaluating Group Effectiveness | | | |

Effectiveness Criteria	Type of Group			
	Interacting	Brainstorming	Nominal	Electronic
Number and quality of ideas	Low	Moderate	High	High
Social pressure	High	Low	Moderate	Low
Money costs	Low	Low	Low	High
Speed	Moderate	Moderate	Moderate	Moderate
Task orientation	Low	High	High	High
Potential for interpersonal conflict	High	Low	Moderate	Low
Commitment to solution	High	Not applicable	Moderate	Moderate
Development of group cohesiveness	High	High	Moderate	Low

Summary and Implications for Managers

Performance   A number of group properties show a relationship to performance. Among the more prominent are role perception, norms, status differences, the size of the group, and cohesiveness.

There is a positive relationship between role perception and an employee's performance evaluation.[74] The degree of congruence that exists between an employee and the boss in the perception of the employee's job influences the degree to which that employee will be judged as an effective performer by the boss. To the extent that the employee's role perception fulfills the boss's role expectations, the employee will receive a higher performance evaluation.

Norms control group-member behavior by establishing standards of right and wrong. The norms of a given group can help to explain the behaviors of its members for managers. When norms support high output, managers can expect individual performance to be markedly higher than when group norms aim to restrict output. Similarly, norms that support antisocial behavior increase the likelihood that individuals will engage in deviant workplace activities.

Status inequities create frustration and can adversely influence productivity and the willingness to remain with an organization. Among individuals who are equity-sensitive, incongruence is likely to lead to reduced motivation and an increased search for ways to bring about fairness (that is, taking another job). In addition, because lower-status people tend to participate less in group discussions, groups characterized by high status differences among members are likely to inhibit input from the lower-status members and to underperform their potential.

The impact of size on a group's performance depends on the type of task in which the group is engaged. Larger groups are more effective at fact-finding activities. Smaller groups are more effective at action-taking tasks. Our knowledge of social loafing suggests that if management uses larger groups, efforts should be made to provide measures of individual performance within the group.

We found that cohesiveness can play an important function in influencing a group's level of productivity. Whether or not it does depends on the group's performance-related norms.

Satisfaction   As with the role perception–performance relationship, high congruence between a boss and employee as to the perception of the employee's job shows a significant association with high employee satisfaction.[75] Similarly, role conflict is associated with job-induced tension and job dissatisfaction.[76]

Most people prefer to communicate with others at their own status level or a higher one rather than with those below them.[77] As a result, we should expect satisfaction to be greater among employees whose job minimizes interaction with individuals who are lower in status than themselves.

The group size–satisfaction relationship is what one would intuitively expect: Larger groups are associated with lower satisfaction.[78] As size increases, opportunities for participation and social interaction decrease, as does the ability of members to identify with the group's accomplishments. At the same time, having more members also prompts dissension, conflict, and the formation of subgroups, which all act to make the group a less pleasant entity of which to be a part.

All Jobs Should Be Designed Around Groups

Groups, not individuals, are the ideal building blocks for an organization. There are at least six reasons for designing all jobs around groups.[79]

First, small groups are good for people. They can satisfy social needs and they can provide support for employees in times of stress and crisis.

Second, groups are good problem-finding tools. They are better than individuals in promoting creativity and innovation.

Third, in a wide variety of decision situations, groups make better decisions than individuals do.

Fourth, groups are very effective tools for implementation. Groups gain commitment from their members so that group decisions are likely to be willingly and more successfully carried out.

Fifth, groups can control and discipline individual members in ways that are often extremely difficult through impersonal quasi-legal disciplinary systems. Group norms are powerful control devices.

Sixth, groups are a means by which large organizations can fend off many of the negative effects of increased size. Groups help to prevent communication lines from growing too long, the hierarchy from growing too steep, and the individual from getting lost in the crowd.

Given these arguments for the value of group-based job design, what would an organization look like that was truly designed around group functions? This might best be considered by merely taking the things that organizations do with individuals and applying them to groups. Instead of hiring individuals, they'd hire groups. Similarly, they'd train groups rather than individuals, pay groups rather than individuals, promote groups rather than individuals, fire groups rather than individuals, and so on.

The rapid growth of team-based organizations in recent years suggests we may well be on our way toward the day when almost all jobs are designed around groups.

Capitalistic countries like the United States, Canada, Australia, and the United Kingdom value the individual. Designing jobs around groups is inconsistent with the economic values of these countries. Moreover, as capitalism and entrepreneurship have spread throughout Eastern Europe, we should expect to see *less* emphasis on groups and *more* on the individual in workplaces throughout the world. Let's look at the United States to see how cultural and economic values shape employee attitudes toward groups.

America was built on the ethic of the individual. Americans strongly value individual achievement. They praise competition. Even in team sports, they want to identify individuals for recognition. Americans enjoy being part of a group in which they can maintain a strong individual identity. They don't enjoy sublimating their identity to that of the group. When Americans are assigned to groups, all sorts of bad things happen, including conflict, groupthink, social loafing, and deviant behavior.

The American worker likes a clear link between individual effort and a visible outcome. It is not by chance that the United States, as a nation, has a considerably larger proportion of high achievers than exists in most of the world. America breeds achievers, and achievers seek personal responsibility. They would be frustrated in job situations in which their contribution is commingled and homogenized with the contributions of others.

Americans want to be hired, evaluated, and rewarded on their individual achievements. Americans believe in an authority and status hierarchy. They accept a system in which there are bosses and subordinates. They are not likely to accept a group's decision on such issues as their job assignments and wage increases. It's harder yet to imagine that they would be comfortable in a system in which the sole basis for their promotion or termination would be the performance of their group.

Though teams have grown in popularity as a device for employers to organize people and tasks, we should expect resistance to any effort to treat individuals solely as members of a group—especially among workers raised in capitalistic economies.

Questions for Review

1. Compare and contrast command, task, interest, and friendship groups.

2. What might motivate you to join a group?

3. Describe the five-stage group-development model.

4. What are the Hawthorne studies? What did they tell us about group behavior?

5. What are the implications of Zimbardo's prison experiment for OB?

6. Explain the implications from the Asch experiments.

7. How are status and norms related?

8. When do groups make better decisions than individuals?

9. What is groupthink? What is its effect on decision-making quality?

10. How effective are electronic meetings?

Questions for Critical Thinking

1. How could you use the punctuated-equilibrium model to better understand group behavior?

2. Identify five roles you play. What behaviors do they require? Are any of these roles in conflict? If so, in what way? How do you resolve these conflicts?

3. "High cohesiveness in a group leads to higher group productivity." Do you agree or disagree? Explain.

4. What effect, if any, do you expect that workforce diversity has on a group's performance and satisfaction?

5. If you need to generate a lot of ideas in a short period of time, would you have a bunch of individuals generate ideas on their own, or would you band them together in groups? Explain.

Team Exercise

WILDNESS SURVIVAL

You are a member of a hiking party. After reaching base camp on the first day, you decide to take a quick sunset hike by yourself. After hiking a few exhilarating miles, you decide to return to camp. On your way back, you soon realize that you are lost. It is now dark. And cold.

Your Task

Without communicating with anyone else in your group, read the following scenarios and choose the best answer. Keep track of your answers on a sheet of paper. You have 10 minutes to answer the 10 questions.

1. The first thing you decide to do is to build a fire. However, you have no matches, so you use the bow-and-drill method. What is the bow-and-drill method?
   (a) A dry, soft stick is rubbed between one's hands against a board of supple, green wood.
   (b) A green, soft stick is rubbed between one's hands against a hardwood board.
   (c) A straight stick of wood is quickly rubbed back-and-forth against a dead tree.
   (d) Two sticks (one being the bow, the other the drill) are struck to create a spark.

2. It occurs to you that you can also use the fire as a distress signal. When signaling with fire, how do you form the international distress signal?
   (a) 2 fires.
   (b) 4 fires in a square.

   (c) 4 fires in a cross.
   (d) 3 fires in a line.

3. You are very thirsty. You go to a nearby stream and collect some water in the small metal cup you have in you backpack. How long should you boil the water?
   (a) 15 minutes.
   (b) A few seconds.
   (c) 1 hour.
   (d) Depends on the altitude.

4. You are also very hungry, so you decide to eat what appear to be edible berries. When performing the Universal Edibility Test what should you do?
   (a) Do not eat for 2 hours before the test.
   (b) If the plant stings your lip, confirm the sting by holding it under your tongue for 15 minutes.
   (c) If nothing bad has happened 2 hours after digestion, eat half a cup of the plant and wait again.
   (d) Separate the plant into its basic components and eat each component one at a time.

5. Next, you decide to build a shelter for the evening. In selecting a site, what do you not have to consider?
   (a) It must contain material to make the type of shelter you need.
   (b) It must be free from insects, reptiles, and poisonous plants.
   (c) It must be large enough and level enough for you to lie down comfortably.

(d) It must be on a hill so you can signal rescuers and keep an eye on your surroundings.

6. In the shelter that you built, you notice a spider. You heard from a fellow hiker that black widow spiders populate the area. How do you identify a black widow spider?
   (a) Its head and abdomen is black; its thorax is red.
   (b) It is attracted to light.
   (c) It runs away from light.
   (d) It is a dark spider with a red or orange marking on the female's abdomen.

7. After getting some sleep, you notice that the night sky has cleared, and so you decide to try and find your way back to base camp. You believe you should travel north and can use the North Star for navigation. How do you locate the North Star?
   (a) Hold your right hand up as far as you can and look between your index and middle fingers.
   (b) Find Sirius and look 60 degrees above it and to the right.
   (c) Look for the Big Dipper and follow the line created by its cup end.
   (d) Follow the line of Orion's belt.

8. You come across a fast-moving stream. What is the best way to cross it?
   (a) Find a spot downstream from a sandbar where the water will be calmer.
   (b) Build a bridge.
   (c) Find a rocky area, as the water will be shallow and you will have hand- and footholds.
   (d) Find a level stretch where it breaks into a few channels.

9. After walking for about an hour, you feel several spiders in your clothes. You don't feel any pain, but you know some spider bites are painless. Which of these spider bites is painless?
   (a) Black Widow
   (b) Brown Recluse
   (c) Wolf Spider
   (d) Harvestman (Daddy Longlegs)

10. You decide to eat some insects. Which insects should you avoid?

(a) Adults that sting or bite.
(b) Caterpillars and insects that have a pungent odor.
(c) Hairy or brightly colored ones.
(d) All of the above.

Group Task

Break into groups of 5–6 people. Now imagine that your whole group is lost. Answer each question as a group, employing a consensus approach to reach each decision. Once the group comes to an agreement, write the decision down on the same sheet of paper that you used for your individual answers. You will have approximately 20 minutes for the group task.

Scoring Your Answers

Your instructor will provide you with the correct answers, which are based on expert judgments in these situations. Once you have received the answers, calculate: (A) your individual score; (B) your group's score; (C) the average individual score in the group; (D) the best individual score in the group. Write these down, and consult with your group to ensure that these scores are accurate.

(A) Your individual score _____
(B) Your group's score _____
(C) Average individual score in group _____
(D) Best individual score in group _____

Discussion Questions

1. How did your group (B) perform relative to yourself (A)?

2. How did your group (B) perform relative to the average individual score in the group (C)?

3. How did your group (B) perform relative to the best individual score in the group (D)?

4. Compare your results with those of other groups. Did some groups do a better job of outperforming individuals than did others?

5. What do these results tell you about the effectiveness of group decision making?

6. What can groups do to make group decision-making more effective?

Ethical Dilemma

ARAB DISCRIMINATION

Suicide bombers and terrorist attacks have been commonplace for decades in much of the Middle East. But not so for North America. The attacks on the World Trade Center and Pentagon buildings on September 11, 2001 opened North American eyes to the reality that terrorism is a worldwide phenomenon and that no place is completely safe from terrorist attacks.

Some Americans allowed the actions of a few Arab extremists on September 11th to shape their attitudes toward all Arabs. The result has created new challenges for managers leading diverse groups containing individuals of Middle Eastern backgrounds.

Jeff O'Connell is one of those managers. Jeff oversees a team of five computer chip designers. They work exclusively on defense contracts—designing and building high-powered chips for use by the U.S. military.

Jeff's five-person team is a textbook example of diversity. They've got a woman from Texas, an African American from New York, two Russians, and an Arab American who was born in California but whose parents both immigrated from Iran. Jeff, himself, was born in Canada but raised in the United States.

In the months following the September 11th attack and again in 2003 following widely publicized suicide bombings at the U.N. building in Baghdad and on a bus in Jerusalem—both killing dozens of innocent people,

including children—Jeff became aware that several of his team members were making openly disparaging remarks to Nicholas, their Iranian coworker. They questioned his Arab friends, his religious practices, and his loyalty to America. Nicholas's colleagues understood little about his Islam religion.

It's illegal in the United States for employers to discriminate. But that doesn't stop employees from discriminating against their colleagues. Jeff sees himself in an ethical dilemma. What, if anything, should he do when he sees team members discriminating against Nicholas because of his ethnicity?

Case Incident 1

ROLE CONFLICT AMONG TELEPHONE SERVICE EMPLOYEES

All supervisory jobs aren't alike. Maggie Beckhard is just learning this fact. After having spent 3 years as a production-scheduling supervisor at a Procter & Gamble manufacturing plant, she recently took a position as manager of telephone services at Ohio Provident Insurance. In her new job, Maggie supervises 20 telephone service employees. These people have direct contact with customers—providing quotes, answering questions, following up on claims, and the like.

At P&G, Maggie's employees knew they had only one constituency to please. That was management. But Maggie is finding that her employees at OPI have it more difficult. As service employees, they have to serve two masters—management and the customer. And at least from comments her employees have made, they seem to think there's a discrepancy between what they believe customers want them to do and what they believe management wants them to do. A frequent complaint, for instance, is that customers want the telephone rep's undivided attention and to spend as much time as necessary to solve their problem. But the reps see management as wanting them to handle as many calls as possible per day and to keep each call as short as possible.

This morning, a rep came into Maggie's office complaining of severe headaches. "The more I try to please our customers, the more stress I feel," the rep told Maggie. "I want to do the best job I can for our customers but I don't feel like I can devote the time that's necessary. You

constantly remind us that 'it's the customers that provide our paychecks' and how important it is to give reliable, courteous, and responsive service, but then we feel the pressure to handle more calls per hour."

Maggie is well aware of studies that have shown that role conflict is related to reduced job satisfaction, increased turnover and absenteeism, and fewer organizational citizenship behaviors. And severe role conflict is also likely to lead to poor customer service—the antithesis of her department's goals.

After talking with her staff, Maggie concluded that regardless of whether their perceptions were accurate, her people certainly believed them to be. They were reading one set of expectations through their interactions with customers; and another set through what the company conveyed during the selection process, in training sessions, and through the behaviors that management rewarded.

Questions

1. What's the source of role conflict here?
2. Are there functional benefits to management from role conflict? Explain.
3. Should role conflict among these telephone service employees be any greater than a typical employee who works as part of a team and has to meet the expectations of a boss as well as team members? Explain.
4. What can Maggie do to manage this role conflict?

Source: This case is based on information included in B. G. Chung and B. Schneider, "Serving Multiple Masters: Role Conflict Experienced By Service Employees," *The Journal of Service Marketing* 16, no. 1 (2002), pp. 70–88.

Case Incident 2

THE DANGERS OF GROUPTHINK

Sometimes, the desire to maintain group harmony overrides the importance of making sound decisions. When that occurs, team members are said to engage in "groupthink."

- A civilian worker at a large Air Force base recalls the time that groupthink overcame her team's decision-making ability. She was a member of a process improvement team that an air force general formed to develop a better way to handle the base's mail, which included important letters from high-ranking military individuals. The team was composed mostly of civilians, and it took almost a month to come up with a plan. The problem: The plan was not a process improvement. Recalls the civilian worker, "I was horrified. What used to be 8 steps; now there were 19." The team had devised a new system that resulted in each piece of mail being read by several middle managers before reaching its intended recipient. The team's new plan slowed the mail down considerably, with an average delay of two weeks. Even though the team members all knew that the new system was worse than its predecessor, no one wanted to question the team's solidarity. The problems lasted for almost an entire year. It wasn't until the general who formed the team complained about the mail that the system was changed.

- During the dot-com boom of the late 1990s, Virginia Turezyn, managing director of Infinity Capital, states that she was a victim of groupthink. At first, Turezyn was skeptical about the stability of the boom. But after continually reading about startups turning into multimillion-dollar payoffs, she felt different. Turezyn decided to invest millions into several dot-coms, including I-drive, a company that provided electronic data storage. The problem was that I-drive was giving the storage away for free, and as a result the company was losing money. Turezyn recalls one board meeting at I-drive where she spoke up to no avail. "We're spending way too much money," she screamed. The younger executives shook their heads and replied that if they charged for storage, they would lose their customers. Says Turezyn, "I started to think, 'Maybe I'm just too old. Maybe I really don't get it.'" Unfortunately, Turezyn did get it. I-drive later filed for bankruptcy.

- Steve Blank, an entrepreneur, also fell victim to groupthink. Blank was a dot-com investor, and he participated on advisory boards of several Internet startups. During meetings for one such startup, a Web photo finisher, Blank tried to persuade his fellow board members to change the business model to be more traditional. Recalls Blank, "I went to those meetings and starting saying things like 'Maybe you should spend that $10 million you just raised on acquiring a customer base rather than building a brand.' The CEO told me, 'Steve, you just don't get it—all the rules have changed.'" The team didn't take Blank's advice, and Blank says that he lost hundreds of thousands of dollars on the deal.

According to Michael Useem, a professor at the University of Pennsylvania's Wharton College of Business, one of the main reasons that groupthink occurs is a lack of conflict. "A single devil's advocate or whistle-blower faces a really uphill struggle," he states. "But if you [the naysayer] have one ally that is enormously strengthening."

Questions

1. What are some factors that lead to groupthink in the above cases? What can teams do to attempt to reduce groupthink from occurring?

2. How might differences in status among group members contribute to groupthink? For example, how might lower-status members react to a group's decision? Are lower-status members more or less likely to be dissenters? Why might higher-status group members be more effective dissenters?

3. How do group norms contribute to groupthink? Could group norms guard against the occurrence of groupthink? As a manager, how would you try to cultivate norms that prevent groupthink?

4. How might group characteristics such as size and cohesiveness affect groupthink?

Source: Based on C. Hawn, "Fear and Posing," *Forbes*, March 25, 2002, pp. 22-25, and J. Sandberg, "Some Ideas Are So Bad That Only Team Efforts Can Account for Them," *Wall Street Journal*, September 29, 2004, p. B.1.

Endnotes

1. This is based on J. Schwartz and M. L. Wald, "Groupthink is 30 Years Old, And Still Going Strong," *New York Times*, March 9, 2003, p. WK5; and J. Schwartz and M. L. Wald, "Complacency Seen: 'Broken Safety Culture' Must Be Reformed, Investigators Find," *New York Times*, August 27, 2003, p. A1.

2. See, for instance, M. Maier, "Ten Years After *A Major Malfunction* . . . Reflections on 'The *Challenger* Syndrome,'" *Journal of Management Inquiry*, September 2002, pp. 282–92.

3. The CAIB Report-Volume 1 (August 2003) (http://www.caib.us/news/report/volume1/default.html).

4. L. R. Sayles, "Work Group Behavior and the Larger Organization," in C. Arensburg, et al. (eds.), *Research in Industrial Relations* (New York: Harper & Row, 1957), pp. 131–45.

5. J. F. McGrew, J. G. Bilotta, and J. M. Deeney, "Software Team Formation and Decay: Extending the Standard Model for Small Groups," *Small Group Research* 30, no. 2, (1999), pp. 209–34.

6. B. W. Tuckman, "Developmental Sequences in Small Groups," *Psychological Bulletin*, June 1965, pp. 384–99; B. W. Tuckman and M. C. Jensen, "Stages of Small-Group Development Revisited," *Group and Organizational Studies*, December 1977, pp. 419–27; and M. F. Maples, "Group Development: Extending Tuckman's Theory," *Journal for Specialists in Group Work*, Fall 1988, pp. 17–23; and K. Vroman and J. Kovacich, "Computer-Mediated Interdisciplinary Teams: Theory and Reality," *Journal of Interprofessional Care* 16, no. 2 (2002), pp. 159–70.

7. J. F. George and L. M. Jessup, "Groups over Time: What Are We Really Studying?" *International Journal of Human-Computer Studies* 47, no. 3 (1997), pp. 497–511.

8. R. C. Ginnett, "The Airline Cockpit Crew," in J. R. Hackman (ed.), *Groups That Work (and Those That Don't)* (San Francisco: Jossey-Bass, 1990).

9. C. J. G. Gersick, "Time and Transition in Work Teams: Toward a New Model of Group Development," *Academy of Management Journal*, March 1988, pp. 9–41; C. J. G. Gersick, "Marking Time: Predictable Transitions in Task Groups," *Academy of Management Journal*, June 1989, pp. 274–309; M. J. Waller, J. M. Conte, C. B. Gibson, and M. A. Carpenter, "The Effect of Individual Perceptions of Deadlines on Team Performance," *Academy of Management Review*, October 2001, pp. 586–600; and A. Chang, P. Bordia, and J. Duck, "Punctuated Equilibrium and Linear Progression: Toward a New Understanding of Group Development," *Academy of Management Journal*, February 2003, pp. 106–17; see also H. Arrow, M. S. Poole, K. B. Henry, S. Wheelan, and R. Moreland, "Time, Change, and Development: The Temporal Perspective on Groups," *Small Group Research*, February 2004, pp. 73–105.

10. Gersick, "Time and Transition in Work Teams: Toward a New Model of Group Development;" and Gersick, "Marking Time: Predictable Transitions in Task Groups."

11. A. Seers and S. Woodruff, "Temporal Pacing in Task Forces: Group Development or Deadline Pressure?" *Journal of Management* 23, no. 2 (1997), pp. 169–87.

12. S. Lieberman, "The Effects of Changes in Roles on the Attitudes of Role Occupants," *Human Relations*, November 1956, pp. 385–402.

13. See D. M. Rousseau, *Psychological Contracts in Organizations: Understanding Written and Unwritten Agreements* (Thousand Oaks, CA: Sage, 1995); E. W. Morrison and S. L. Robinson, "When Employees Feel Betrayed: A Model of How Psychological Contract Violation Develops," *Academy of Management Review*, April 1997, pp. 226–56; D. Rousseau and R. Schalk (eds.), *Psychological Contracts in Employment: Cross-Cultural Perspectives* (San Francisco: Jossey-Bass, 2000); L. Sels, M. Janssens, and I. Van den Brande, "Assessing the Nature of Psychological Contracts: A Validation of Six Dimensions," *Journal of Organizational Behavior*, June 2004, pp. 461–88; and C. Hui, C. Lee, and D. M. Rousseau, "Psychological Contract And Organizational Citizenship Behavior in China: Investigating Generalizability and Instrumentality," *Journal of Applied Psychology*, April 2004, pp. 311–21.

14. See M. F. Peterson et al., "Role Conflict, Ambiguity, and Overload: A 21-Nation Study," *Academy of Management Journal*, April 1995, pp. 429–52; and I. H. Settles, R. M. Sellers, and A. Damas, Jr., "One Role or Two? The Function of Psychological Separation in Role Conflict," *Journal of Applied Psychology*, June 2002, pp. 574–82.

15. P. G. Zimbardo, C. Haney, W. C. Banks, and D. Jaffe, "The Mind Is a Formidable Jailer: A Pirandellian Prison," *New York Times*, April 8, 1973, pp. 38–60; and C. Haney and P. G. Zimbardo, "Social Roles and Role-Playing: Observations from the Stanford Prison Study," *Behavioral and Social Science Teacher*, January 1973, pp. 25–45.

16. For a review of the research on group norms, see J. R. Hackman, "Group Influences on Individuals in Organizations," in M. D. Dunnette and L. M. Hough (eds.), *Handbook of Industrial & Organizational Psychology*, 2nd ed., vol. 3 (Palo Alto, CA: Consulting Psychologists Press, 1992), pp. 235–50. For a more recent discussion, see M. G. Ehrhart and S. E. Naumann, "Organizational Citizenship Behavior in Work Groups: A Group Norms Approach," *Journal of Applied Psychology*, December 2004, pp. 960–74.

17. E. Mayo, *The Human Problems of an Industrial Civilization* (New York: Macmillan, 1933); and F. J. Roethlisberger and W. J. Dickson, *Management and the Worker* (Cambridge, MA: Harvard University Press, 1939).

18. Adapted from P. S. Goodman, E. Ravlin, and M. Schminke, "Understanding Groups in Organizations," in L. L. Cummings and B. M. Staw (eds.), *Research in Organizational Behavior*, vol. 9 (Greenwich, CT: JAI Press, 1987), p. 159.

19. See, for instance, G. Blau, "Influence of Group Lateness on Individual Lateness: A Cross-Level Examination," *Academy of Management Journal*, October 1995, pp. 1483–96; and D. F. Caldwell and C. A. O'Reilly, III, "The Determinants of Team-Based Innovation in Organizations: The Role of Social Influence," *Small Group Research*, August 2003, pp. 497–517.

20. C. A. Kiesler and S. B. Kiesler, *Conformity* (Reading, MA: Addison-Wesley, 1969).

21. Ibid., p. 27.

22. S. E. Asch, "Effects of Group Pressure upon the Modification and Distortion of Judgments," in H. Guetzkow (ed.), *Groups, Leadership and Men* (Pittsburgh, PA: Carnegie Press, 1951), pp. 177–90; and S. E. Asch, "Studies of Independence and Conformity: A Minority of One Against a Unanimous Majority," *Psychological Monographs: General and Applied* 70, no. 9 (1956), pp. 1–70.

23. R. Bond and P. B. Smith, "Culture and Conformity: A Meta-Analysis of Studies Using Asch's (1952, 1956) Line Judgment Task," *Psychological Bulletin*, January 1996, pp. 111–37.

24. See S. L. Robinson and R. J. Bennett, "A Typology of Deviant Workplace Behaviors: A Multidimensional Scaling Study," *Academy of Management Journal*, April 1995, pp. 555–72; S. L. Robinson and J. Greenberg, "Employees Behaving Badly: Dimensions, Determinants, and Dilemmas in the Study of Workplace Deviance," in D. M. Rousseau and C. Cooper (eds.), *Trends in Organizational Behavior*, vol. 5 (New York: Wiley, 1998); S. L. Robinson and A. M. O'Leary-Kelly, "Monkey See, Monkey Do: The Influence of Work Groups on the Antisocial Behavior of Employees," *Academy of Management Journal*, December 1998, pp. 658–72; and R. J. Bennett, and S. L. Robinson, "The Past, Present, and Future of Workplace Deviance," in J. Greenberg (ed.), *Organizational Behavior: The State of the Science*, 2nd ed. (Mahwah, NJ: Lawrence Erlbaum Associates, 2003), pp. 237–71.

25. C. M. Pearson, L. M. Andersson, and C. L. Porath, "Assessing and Attacking Workplace Civility," *Organizational Dynamics* 29, no. 2 (2000), p. 130; see also C. Pearson, L. M. Andersson, and C. L. Porath, "Workplace Incivility," in S. Fox and P. E. Spector (eds.), *Counterproductive Work Behavior: Investigations of Actors and Targets* (Washington, D.C.: American Psychological Association, 2005), pp. 177–200.

26. S. L. Robinson and A. M. O'Leary-Kelly, "Monkey See, Monkey Do."

27. A. Erez, H. Elms, and E. Fong, "Lying, Cheating, Stealing: It Happens More in Groups," Paper presented at the European Business Ethics Network Annual Conference, Budapest, August 30, 2003.

28. S. L. Robinson and M. S. Kraatz, "Constructing the Reality of Normative Behavior: The Use of Neutralization Strategies by Organizational Deviants," in R. W. Griffin and A. O'Leary-Kelly (eds.), *Dysfunctional Behavior in Organizations: Violent*

and Deviant Behavio, (Elsevier Science/JAI Press, 1998), pp. 203–20.

29. See, for instance, D. G. Wagner and J. Berger, "Status Characteristics Theory: The Growth of a Program," in J. Berger and M. Zelditch (eds.), *Theoretical Research Programs: Studies in the Growth of a Theory* (Stanford, CA: Stanford University Press, 1993), pp. 23–63; J. Berger, C. L. Ridgeway, and M. Zelditch, "Construction of Status and Referential Structures," *Sociological Theory*, July 2002, pp. 157–79; and J. S. Bunderson, "Recognizing and Utilizing Expertise in Work Groups: A Status Characteristics Perspective," *Administrative Science Quarterly*, December 2003, pp. 557–91.

30. See R. S. Feldman, *Social Psychology*, 3rd ed. (Upper Saddle River, NJ: Prentice Hall, 2001), pp. 464–65.

31. Cited in Hackman, "Group Influences on Individuals in Organizations," p. 236.

32. O. J. Harvey and C. Consalvi, "Status and Conformity to Pressures in Informal Groups," *Journal of Abnormal and Social Psychology*, Spring 1960, pp. 182–87.

33. J. A. Wiggins, F. Dill, and R. D. Schwartz, "On 'Status-Liability,'" *Sociometry*, April–May 1965, pp. 197–209.

34. See J. M. Levine and R. L. Moreland, "Progress in Small Group Research," in J. T. Spence, J. M. Darley, and D. J. Foss (eds.), *Annual Review of Psychology*, vol. 41 (Palo Alto, CA: Annual Reviews Inc., 1990), pp. 585–634; S. D. Silver, B. P. Cohen, and J. H. Crutchfield, "Status Differentiation and Information Exchange in Face-to-Face and Computer-Mediated Idea Generation," *Social Psychology Quarterly*, 1994, pp. 108–23; and J. M. Twenge, "Changes in Women's Assertiveness in Response to Status and Roles: A Cross-Temporal Meta-Analysis, 1931–1993," *Journal of Personality and Social Psychology*, July 2001, pp. 133–45.

35. J. Greenberg, "Equity and Workplace Status: A Field Experiment," *Journal of Applied Psychology*, November 1988, pp. 606–13.

36. See G. Hofstede, *Cultures and Organizations: Software of the Mind* (New York, McGraw-Hill, 1991).

37. This section is based on P. R. Harris and R. T. Moran, *Managing Cultural Differences*, 5th ed. (Houston: Gulf Publishing, 1999).

38. E. J. Thomas and C. F. Fink, "Effects of Group Size," *Psychological Bulletin*, July 1963, pp. 371–84; A. P. Hare, *Handbook of Small Group Research* (New York: Free Press, 1976); and M. E. Shaw, *Group Dynamics: The Psychology of Small Group Behavior*, 3rd ed. (New York: McGraw-Hill, 1981).

39. G. H. Seijts and G. P. Latham, "The Effects of Goal Setting and Group Size on Performance in a Social Dilemma," *Canadian Journal of Behavioural Science* 32, no. 2 (2000), pp. 104–16.

40. Shaw, *Group Dynamics: The Psychology of Small Group Behavior*.

41. See, for instance, D. R. Comer, "A Model of Social Loafing in Real Work Groups," *Human Relations*, June 1995, pp. 647–67; S. M. Murphy, S. J. Wayne, R. C. Liden, and B. Erdogan, "Understanding Social Loafing: The Role of Justice Perceptions and Exchange Relationships," *Human Relations*, January 2003, pp. 61–84; R. C. Liden, S. J. Wayne, R. A. Jaworski, and N. Bennett, "Social Loafing: A Field Investigation," *Journal of Management*, April 2004, pp. 285–304.

42. W. Moede, "Die Richtlinien der Leistungs-Psychologie," *Industrielle Psychotechnik* 4 (1927), pp. 193–207. See also D. A. Kravitz and B. Martin, "Ringelmann Rediscovered: The Original Article," *Journal of Personality and Social Psychology*, May 1986, pp. 936–41.

43. See, for example, J. A. Shepperd, "Productivity Loss in Performance Groups: A Motivation Analysis," *Psychological Bulletin*, January 1993, pp. 67–81; and S. J. Karau and K. D. Williams, "Social Loafing: A Meta-Analytic Review and Theoretical Integration," *Journal of Personality and Social Psychology*, October 1993, pp. 681–706.

44. S. G. Harkins and K. Szymanski, "Social Loafing and Group Evaluation," *Journal of Personality and Social Psychology*, December 1989, pp. 934–41.

45. See P. C. Earley, "Social Loafing and Collectivism: A Comparison of the United States and the People's Republic of China," *Administrative Science Quarterly*, December 1989, pp. 565–81; and P. C. Earley, "East Meets West Meets Mideast: Further Explorations of Collectivistic and Individualistic Work Groups," *Academy of Management Journal*, April 1993, pp. 319–48.

46. Thomas and Fink, "Effects of Group Size"; Hare, *Handbook*; Shaw, *Group Dynamics*; and P. Yetton and P. Bottger, "The Relationships Among Group Size, Member Ability, Social Decision Schemes, and Performance," *Organizational Behavior and Human Performance*, October 1983, pp. 145–59.

47. For some of the controversy surrounding the definition of cohesion, see J. Keyton and J. Springston, "Redefining Cohesiveness in Groups," *Small Group Research*, May 1990, pp. 234–54.

48. B. Mullen and C. Cooper, "The Relation between Group Cohesiveness and Performance: An Integration," *Psychological Bulletin*, March 1994, pp. 210–27; P. M. Podsakoff, S. B. MacKenzie, and M. Ahearne, "Moderating Effects of Goal Acceptance on the Relationship Between Group Cohesiveness and Productivity," *Journal of Applied Psychology*, December 1997, pp. 974–83; and D. J. Beal, R. R. Cohen, M. J. Burke, and C. L. McLendon, "Cohesion and Performance in Groups: A Meta-Analytic Clarification of Construct Relations," *Journal of Applied Psychology*, December 2003, pp. 989–1004.

49. Ibid.

50. Based on J. L. Gibson, J. M. Ivancevich, and J. H. Donnelly, Jr., *Organizations*, 8th ed. (Burr Ridge, IL: Irwin, 1994), p. 323.

51. N. Foote, E. Matson, L. Weiss, and E. Wenger, "Leveraging Group Knowledge for High-Performance Decision-Making," *Organizational Dynamics* 31, no. 2 (2002), pp. 280–95.

52. See N. R. F. Maier, "Assets and Liabilities in Group Problem Solving: The Need for an Integrative Function," *Psychological Review*, April 1967, pp. 239–49; G. W. Hill, "Group Versus Individual Performance: Are $N+1$ Heads Better Than One?" *Psychological Bulletin*, May 1982, pp. 517–39; A. E. Schwartz and J. Levin, "Better Group Decision Making," *Supervisory Management*, June 1990, p. 4; and R. F. Martell and M. R. Borg, "A Comparison of the Behavioral Rating Accuracy of Groups and Individuals," *Journal of Applied Psychology*, February 1993, pp. 43–50.

53. D. Gigone and R. Hastie, "Proper Analysis of the Accuracy of Group Judgments," *Psychological Bulletin*, January 1997, pp. 149–67.

54. See, for example, W. C. Swap and Associates, *Group Decision Making* (Newbury Park, CA: Sage, 1984).

55. D. D. Henningsen, M. G. Cruz, and M. L. Miller, "Role of Social Loafing in Predeliberation Decision Making," *Group Dynamics: Theory, Research, and Practice* 4, no. 2 (June 2000), pp. 168–75.

56. J. H. Davis, *Group Performance* (Reading, MA: Addison-Wesley, 1969); J. P. Wanous and M. A. Youtz, "Solution Diversity and the Quality of Group Decisions," *Academy of Management*

Journal, March 1986, pp. 149–59; and R. Libby, K. T. Trotman, and I. Zimmer, "Member Variation, Recognition of Expertise, and Group Performance," *Journal of Applied Psychology*, February 1987, pp. 81–87.

57. I. L. Janis, *Groupthink* (Boston: Houghton Mifflin, 1982); W. Park, "A Review of Research on Groupthink," *Journal of Behavioral Decision Making*, July 1990, pp. 229–45; C. P. Neck and G. Moorhead, "Groupthink Remodeled: The Importance of Leadership, Time Pressure, and Methodical Decision-Making Procedures," *Human Relations*, May 1995, pp. 537–58; J. N. Choi and M. U. Kim, "The Organizational Application of Groupthink and Its Limits in Organizations," *Journal of Applied Psychology*, April 1999, pp. 297–306; and W. W. Park, "A Comprehensive Empirical Investigation of the Relationships Among Variables of the Groupthink Model," *Journal of Organizational Behavior*, December 2000, pp. 873–87.

58. Janis, *Groupthink*.

59. Ibid.

60. G. Moorhead, R. Ference, and C. P. Neck, "Group Decision Fiascos Continue: Space Shuttle Challenger and a Revised Groupthink Framework," *Human Relations*, May 1991, pp. 539–50; E. J. Chisson, *The Hubble Wars* (New York: HarperPerennial, 1994); and C. Covault, "Columbia Revelations Alarming E-Mails Speak for Themselves. But Administrator O'Keefe Is More Concerned About Board Findings on NASA Decision-Making," *Aviation Week & Space Technology*, March 3, 2003, p. 26.

61. J. Eaton, "Management Communication: The Threat of Groupthink," *Corporate Communication* 6, no. 4 (2001), pp. 183–92.

62. M. E. Turner and A. R. Pratkanis, "Mitigating Groupthink by Stimulating Constructive Conflict," in C. De Dreu and E. Van de Vliert (eds.), *Using Conflict in Organizations* (London: Sage, 1997), pp. 53–71.

63. Ibid., p. 68.

64. See N. R. F. Maier, *Principles of Human Relations* (New York: Wiley, 1952); I. L. Janis, *Groupthink: Psychological Studies of Policy Decisions and Fiascoes*, 2nd ed. (Boston: Houghton Mifflin, 1982); C. R. Leana, "A Partial Test of Janis' Groupthink Model: Effects of Group Cohesiveness and Leader Behavior on Defective Decision Making," *Journal of Management*, Spring 1985, pp. 5–17; L. Thompson, *Making the Team: A Guide for Managers* (Upper Saddle River, NJ: Prentice Hall, 2000), pp. 116–18; and N. Richardson Ahlfinger and J. K. Esser, "Testing the Groupthink Model: Effects of Promotional Leadership and Conformity Predisposition," *Social Behavior & Personality* 29, no. 1 (2001), pp. 31–41.

65. See D. J. Isenberg, "Group Polarization: A Critical Review and Meta-Analysis," *Journal of Personality and Social Psychology*, December 1986, pp. 1141–51; J. L. Hale and F. J. Boster, "Comparing Effect Coded Models of Choice Shifts," *Communication Research Reports*, April 1988, pp. 180–86; and P. W. Paese, M. Bieser, and M. E. Tubbs, "Framing Effects and Choice Shifts in Group Decision Making," *Organizational Behavior and Human Decision Processes*, October 1993, pp. 149–65.

66. See, for example, N. Kogan and M. A. Wallach, "Risk Taking as a Function of the Situation, the Person, and the Group," in *New Directions in Psychology*, vol. 3 (New York: Holt, Rinehart and Winston, 1967); and M. A. Wallach, N. Kogan, and D. J. Bem, "Group Influence on Individual Risk

Taking," *Journal of Abnormal and Social Psychology* 65 (1962), pp. 75–86.

67. R. D. Clark III, "Group-Induced Shift Toward Risk: A Critical Appraisal," *Psychological Bulletin*, October 1971, pp. 251–70.

68. A. F. Osborn, *Applied Imagination: Principles and Procedures of Creative Thinking*, 3rd ed. (New York: Scribner, 1963). See also T. Rickards, "Brainstorming Revisited: A Question of Context," *International Journal of Management Reviews*, March 1999, pp. 91–110; K. L. Dugosh, P. B. Paulus, E. J. Roland, and H-C. Yang, "Cognitive Stimulation in Brainstorming," *Journal of Personality & Social Psychology*, November 2000, pp. 722–35; and R. P. McGlynn, D. McGurk, V. S. Effland, N. L. Johll, and D. J. Harding, "Brainstorming and Task Performance in Groups Constrained by Evidence," *Organizational Behavior and Human Decision Processes*, January 2004, pp. 75–87.

69. N. L. Kerr and R. S. Tindale, "Group Performance and Decision-Making," *Annual Review of Psychology* 55 (2004), pp. 623–55.

70. See A. L. Delbecq, A. H. Van deVen, and D. H. Gustafson, *Group Techniques for Program Planning: A Guide to Nominal and Delphi Processes* (Glenview, IL: Scott, Foresman, 1975); and P. B. Paulus and H.-C. Yang, "Idea Generation in Groups: A Basis for Creativity in Organizations," *Organizational Behavior and Human Decision Processing*, May 2000, pp. 76–87.

71. C. Faure, "Beyond Brainstorming: Effects of Different Group Procedures on Selection of Ideas and Satisfaction with the Process," *Journal of Creative Behavior* 38 (2004), pp. 13–34.

72. See, for instance, A. B. Hollingshead and J. E. McGrath, "Computer-Assisted Groups: A Critical Review of the Empirical Research," in R. A. Guzzo and E. Salas (eds.), *Team Effectiveness and Decision Making in Organizations*, (San Francisco: Jossey-Bass, 1995), pp. 46–78.

73. B. B. Baltes, M. W. Dickson, M. P. Sherman, C. C. Bauer, and J. LaGanke, "Computer-Mediated Communication and Group Decision Making: A Meta-Analysis," *Organizational Behavior and Human Decision Processes*, January 2002, pp. 156–79.

74. T. P. Verney, "Role Perception Congruence, Performance, and Satisfaction," in D. J. Vredenburgh and R. S. Schuler (eds.), *Effective Management: Research and Application*, Proceedings of the 20th Annual Eastern Academy of Management, Pittsburgh, PA, May 1983, pp. 24–27.

75. Ibid.

76. M. Van Sell, A. P. Brief, and R. S. Schuler, "Role Conflict and Role Ambiguity: Integration of the Literature and Directions for Future Research," *Human Relations*, January 1981, pp. 43–71; A. G. Bedeian and A. A. Armenakis, "A Path-Analytic Study of the Consequences of Role Conflict and Ambiguity," *Academy of Management Journal*, June 1981, pp. 417–24; and P. L. Perrewe, K. L. Zellars, G. R. Ferris, A. M. Rossi, C. J. Kacmar, and D. A. Ralston, "Neutralizing Job Stressors: Political Skill as an Antidote to the Dysfunctional Consequences of Role Conflict," *Academy of Management Journal*, February 2004, pp. 141–152.

77. Shaw, *Group Dynamics*.

78. B. Mullen, C. Symons, L. Hu, and E. Salas, "Group Size, Leadership Behavior, and Subordinate Satisfaction," *Journal of General Psychology*, April 1989, pp. 155–70.

79. Based on H. J. Leavitt, "Suppose We Took Groups Seriously," in E. L. Cass and F. G. Zimmer (eds.), *Man and Work in Society* (New York: Van Nostrand Reinhold, 1975), pp. 67–77.

A team effort is a lot of people doing what I say.

— Michael Winner

Understanding Work Teams

After studying this chapter, you should be able to:

1 Explain the growing popularity of teams in organizations.

2 Contrast teams with groups.

3 Identify four types of teams.

4 Specify the characteristics of effective teams.

5 Explain how organizations can create team players.

6 Describe conditions when individuals are preferred over teams.

CHAPTER 10

Team Work for the Greater Good

In 2004, four graduate students at UC Berkeley's Haas School of Business headed to Cameroon to "crack" the kola nut business. The students—Mike Cipresso, Loic Comolli, Steve Hardgrave, and Jonathan Piazza (see picture)—went as part of their International Business Development class, which sends teams of four MBA students to a country outside the United States to work with a client on business issues.

Their client was the World Agroforestry Centre, a private organization headquartered in Nairobi, Kenya. The organization promotes environmentally sound land uses by combining the growth of forest products (such as fruits and nuts) with agricultural crops. Working with their local contact, Zac Tchoundjeu, the students worked as a team to develop a business plan for the production and marketing of indigenous fruits and plants. The business plan's goals were to increase farmers' revenue, while at the same time moving farmers away from cash crops—such as coffee and cocoa—that were resulting in the slash-and-burn deforestation activities common throughout Cameroon and the rest of West Africa. The plan was created around the marketing of an indigenous product, the kola nut, which is similar to a Brazil nut, only smaller (by the way, the kola nut was one of the original ingredients used to make Coca-Cola).

In order to produce their business plan, team members interviewed numerous farmers to understand their business; they also consulted businesspeople involved in the kola nut business. Because the plan was complex, the team members had to coordinate extensively with one another. Team members had to work with farmers, government officials, wholesalers, and environmental organizational representatives, many of whom were in fairly inaccessible locations. Together, they even had to bribe a local guard—who had told the students that their passports were invalid and they were going to jail—and a road worker to get out of the country. By the end of their visit, though, the team produced several deliverables that have the potential not only to help the kola nut cooperative but also to prevent the deforestation problem in West Africa.[1] ■

Teams are increasingly becoming the primary means for organizing work in contemporary business firms. In fact, this trend is so widespread that business students—like Mike Cipresso, Loic Comolli, Steve Hardgrave, and Jonathan Piazza—are learning about teams through first-hand experience.

Why Have Teams Become So Popular?

Decades ago, when companies like W. L. Gore, Volvo, and General Foods introduced teams into their production processes, it made news because no one else was doing it. Today, it's just the opposite. It's the organization that *doesn't* use teams that has become newsworthy. Approximately 80 percent of Fortune 500 companies now have half or more of their employees on teams. And 68 percent of small U.S. manufacturers are using teams in their production areas.[2]

How do we explain the current popularity of teams? The evidence suggests that teams typically outperform individuals when the tasks being done require multiple skills, judgment, and experience.[3] As organizations have restructured themselves to compete more effectively and efficiently, they have turned to teams as a better way to use employee talents. Management has found that teams are more flexible and responsive to changing events than are traditional departments or other forms of permanent groupings. Teams have the capability to quickly assemble, deploy, refocus, and disband.

OB IN THE NEWS

Teams Work to Save Lives in Tsunami-Stricken Asia

When one of the most powerful earthquakes in history struck deep beneath the Indian Ocean on December 26, 2004, more than 225,000 people were killed in the flooding that the resulting tsunami unleashed. Almost immediately, teams of relief workers from around the world were on their way to Indonesia, Sri Lanka, India, Thailand, and other areas in southern Asia. Beyond the immediate need of providing food, water, and shelter to the more than 5 million individuals left homeless, help was needed in identifying and disposing of bodies and providing health care services to the wounded and vulnerable.

In such immediate response situations, a common problem is team coordination—both within and between teams. For example, in the Indonesian province of Aceh, 175 tons of supplies waited at the airport for distribution because the proper equipment wasn't there. In addition, food distribution experts were lacking, and there was even confusion about where the food should be sent. "The aid is here but we are having trouble coordinating it," said Kace Kaihulu, a worker in a medical relief agency. Anticipating such problems in India, IBM installed a complex computer system to coordinate aid among relief centers. The system used police radio sets to gather calls and then log the information onto software for tracking purposes. This system helped set priorities so relief workers could respond quickly to the most needy sites.

Even world leaders had to learn to be team players. When the tsunami first hit, many nations obviously wanted to send help. President Bush wanted a "core group" of countries—India, the United States, Australia, and Japan—to coordinate the relief work. France said it would oversee aid to Sri Lanka, and British Prime Minister Tony Blair proposed that the U.K., since it was chair of the G8 group of industrialized nations, coordinate the relief effort. But to be truly effective, these nations and their leaders had to work together as a team.

This tragedy illustrates both the necessity of teamwork (obviously, no one individual, organization, or even nation could provide all the help needed) and the challenges of coordinating within and between teams.

Sources: Anton La Guardia, "World Launches Mercy Mission as Tsunami Toll Rises Towards 100,000," *news.telegraph*, December 30, 2004, (www.telegraph.co.uk/news/main. jhtml?xml=/news/2004/12/30/wtsu30.xml&sSheet=/news/2004/12/30/ixnewstop.html); "Indian PM in the Frontline as Massive Tsunami Relief Effort Under Way," *TurkishPress.com*, Thursday, December 30, 2004 (www.turkishpress.com/world/news.asp?id=041230172343.2dc6xc0v.xml); S. Kern, "The Geopolitics of Tsunami Relief," USA-Transatlantic Dialogue-ARI N 8/2005, 01/20/2005 (www.realinstitutoelcano.org/analisis/666/Kern666.pdf).

But don't overlook the motivational properties of teams. Consistent with our discussion in Chapter 7 of the role of employee involvement as a motivator, teams facilitate employee participation in operating decisions. For instance, some assembly-line workers at John Deere are part of sales teams that call on customers.[4] These workers know the products better than any traditional salesperson; and by traveling and speaking with farmers, these hourly workers develop new skills and become more involved in their jobs. So another explanation for the popularity of teams is that they are an effective means for management to democratize their organizations and increase employee motivation.

Differences Between Groups and Teams

Groups and teams are not the same thing. In this section, we want to define and clarify the difference between a work group and a work team.[5]

In the previous chapter, we defined a *group* as two or more individuals, interacting and interdependent, who have come together to achieve particular objectives. A **work group** is a group that interacts primarily to share information and to make decisions to help each member perform within his or her area of responsibility.

Work groups have no need or opportunity to engage in collective work that requires joint effort. So their performance is merely the summation of each group member's individual contribution. There is no positive synergy that would create an overall level of performance that is greater than the sum of the inputs.

A **work team** generates positive synergy through coordinated effort. Their individual efforts result in a level of performance that is greater than the sum of those individual inputs. Exhibit 10-1 highlights the differences between work groups and work teams.

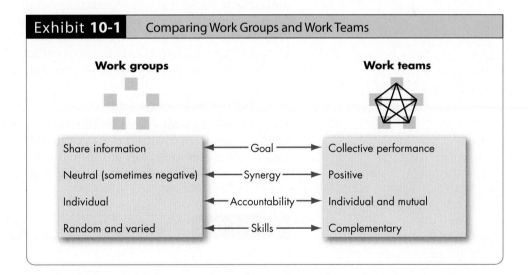

| Exhibit **10-1** | Comparing Work Groups and Work Teams |

Work groups		Work teams
Share information	←— Goal —→	Collective performance
Neutral (sometimes negative)	←— Synergy —→	Positive
Individual	←— Accountability —→	Individual and mutual
Random and varied	←— Skills —→	Complementary

work group   *A group that interacts primarily to share information and to make decisions to help each group member perform within his or her area of responsibility.*

work team   *A group whose individual efforts result in a performance that is greater than the sum of the individual inputs.*

These definitions help clarify why so many organizations have recently restructured work processes around teams. Management is looking for that positive synergy that will allow their organizations to increase performance. The extensive use of teams creates the *potential* for an organization to generate greater outputs with no increase in inputs. Notice, however, we said "potential." There is nothing inherently magical in the creation of teams that ensures the achievement of this positive synergy. Merely calling a *group* a *team* doesn't automatically increase its performance. As we show later in this chapter, effective teams have certain common characteristics. If management hopes to gain increases in organizational performance through the use of teams, it will need to ensure that its teams possess these characteristics.

Types of Teams

Teams can do a variety of things. They can make products, provide services, negotiate deals, coordinate projects, offer advice, and make decisions.[6] In this section we'll describe the four most common types of teams you're likely to find in an organization: *problem-solving teams, self-managed work teams, cross-functional teams*, and *virtual teams* (see Exhibit 10-2).

Problem-Solving Teams

If we look back 20 years or so, teams were just beginning to grow in popularity, and most of those teams took similar form. They were typically composed of 5 to 12 hourly employees from the same department who met for a few hours each week to discuss ways of improving quality, efficiency, and the work environment.[7] We call these **problem-solving teams**.

In problem-solving teams, members share ideas or offer suggestions on how work processes and methods can be improved; although they rarely have the authority to unilaterally implement any of their suggested actions. For instance, Merrill Lynch created a problem-solving team to specifically figure out ways to reduce the number of days it took to open up a new cash management account.[8] By suggesting cuts in the number of steps in the process from 46 to 36, the team was able to reduce the average number of days from 15 to 8.

Self-Managed Work Teams

Problem-solving teams were on the right track but they didn't go far enough in getting employees involved in work-related decisions and processes. This led to experimentation with truly autonomous teams that could not only solve problems but implement solutions and take full responsibility for outcomes.

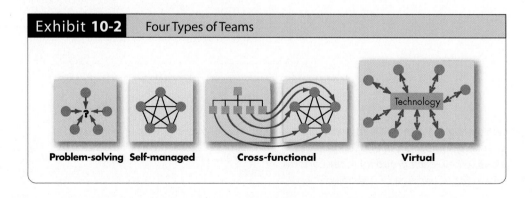

| Exhibit **10-2** | Four Types of Teams |

Problem-solving   Self-managed   Cross-functional   Virtual

Self-managed work teams are groups of employees (typically 10 to 15 in number) who perform highly related or interdependent jobs and take on many of the responsibilities of their former supervisors.[9] Typically, this includes planning and scheduling of work, assigning tasks to members, collective control over the pace of work, making operating decisions, taking action on problems, and working with suppliers and customers. Fully self-managed work teams even select their own members and have the members evaluate each other's performance. As a result, supervisory positions take on decreased importance and may even be eliminated.

A factory at Eaton Corp's Aeroquip Global Hose Division provides an example of how self-managed teams are being used in industry.[10] Located in the heart of Arkansas' Ozark Mountains, this factory makes hydraulic hose that is used in trucks, tractors, and other heavy equipment. In 1994, to improve quality and productivity, Eaton-Aeroquip's management threw out the assembly line and organized the plant's 285 workers into more than 50 self-managed teams. Workers were suddenly free to participate in decisions that were previously reserved solely for management—for instance, the teams set their own schedules, selected new members, negotiated with suppliers, made calls on customers, and disciplined members who created problems. And the results? Between 1993 and 1999, response time to customer concerns improved 99 percent; productivity and manufacturing output both increased by more than 50 percent; and accident rates dropped by more than half.

Business periodicals have been chock-full of articles describing successful applications of self-managed teams. But a word of caution needs to be offered. Some organizations have been disappointed with the results from self-managed teams. For instance, they don't seem to work well during organizational downsizing. Employees often view cooperating with the team concept as an exercise in assisting one's own executioner.[11] The overall research on the effectiveness of self-managed work teams has not been uniformly positive.[12] Moreover, although individuals on these teams do tend to report higher levels of job satisfaction, they also sometimes have higher absenteeism and turnover rates. Inconsistency in findings suggests that the effectiveness of self-managed teams is situationally dependent.[13] In addition to downsizing, factors such as the strength and make-up of team norms, the type of tasks the team undertakes, and the reward structure can significantly influence how well the team performs. Finally, care needs to be taken when introducing self-managed teams globally. For instance, evidence suggests that these types of teams have not fared well in Mexico largely due to that culture's low tolerance of ambiguity and uncertainty and employees' strong respect for hierarchical authority.[14]

Cross-Functional Teams

The Boeing Company created a team made up of employees from production, planning, quality, tooling, design engineering, and information systems to automate shims on the company's C-17 program. The team's suggestions resulted in drastically reduced cycle time, cost, and improved quality on the C-17 program.[15]

This Boeing example illustrates the use of **cross-functional teams**. These are teams made up of employees from about the same hierarchical level, but from different work areas, who come together to accomplish a task.

problem-solving teams *Groups of 5 to 12 employees from the same department who meet for a few hours each week to discuss ways of improving quality, efficiency, and the work environment.*

self-managed work teams *Groups of 10 to 15 people who take on responsibilities of their former supervisors.*

cross-functional teams *Employees from about the same hierarchical level, but from different work areas, who come together to accomplish a task.*

Many organizations have used horizontal, boundary-spanning groups for decades. For example, IBM created a large task force in the 1960s—made up of employees from across departments in the company—to develop its highly successful System 360. And a *task force* is really nothing other than a temporary cross-functional team. Similarly, *committees* composed of members from across departmental lines are another example of cross-functional teams. But the popularity of cross-discipline work teams exploded in the late 1980s. For instance, all the major automobile manufacturers—including Toyota, Honda, Nissan, BMW, GM, Ford, and DaimlerChrysler—currently use this form of team to coordinate complex projects. And Harley-Davidson relies on specific cross-functional teams to manage each line of its motorcycles. These teams include Harley employees from design, manufacturing, and purchasing, as well as representatives from key outside suppliers.[16]

Cross-functional teams are an effective means for allowing people from diverse areas within an organization (or even between organizations) to exchange information, develop new ideas and solve problems, and coordinate complex projects. Of course, cross-functional teams are no picnic to manage. Their early stages of development are often very time-consuming as members learn to work with diversity and complexity. It takes time to build trust and teamwork, especially among people from different backgrounds with different experiences and perspectives.

Virtual Teams

The previous types of teams do their work face-to-face. **Virtual teams** use computer technology to tie together physically dispersed members in order to achieve a common goal.[17] They allow people to collaborate online—using communication links like wide-area networks, video conferencing, or e-mail—whether they're only a room away or continents apart.

Virtual teams can do all the things that other teams do—share information, make decisions, complete tasks. And they can include members from the same organization or link an organization's members with employees from other organizations (such as suppliers and joint partners). They can convene

Virtual teams at computer-chip maker Intel use computer and communications technology to share information and make decisions. Intel equips about 40,000 virtual team employees with laptop computers, pagers, and cell phones so they can work on team projects from anywhere in the world.

Global Virtual Teams

YEARS AGO, BEFORE THE VAST WORKING PUBLIC ever dreamed of e-mail, instant messaging, or live videoconferencing, work teams used to be in the same locations, with possibly one or two members a train or plane ride away. Today, however, the reach of corporations spans many countries, so the need for teams to work together across international lines has increased. To deal with this challenge, multinationals use global virtual teams to gain a competitive advantage.

Global virtual teams have their advantages and disadvantages. On the positive side, because team members come from different countries with different knowledge and points of view, they may develop creative ideas and solutions to problems that work for multiple cultures. On the negative side, global virtual teams face more challenges than traditional teams that meet face-to-face. For one thing, miscommunication can lead to misunderstandings, which can create stress and conflict among team members. Also, members who do not accept individuals from different cultures may hesitate to share information openly, creating problems of trust.

To create and implement effective global virtual teams, managers must carefully select employees who they believe will thrive in such an environment. Employees must be comfortable with communicating electronically with others, and they must be open to different ideas. When dealing with team members in other countries, speaking multiple languages may also be necessary. Team members also must realize that the values they hold may be vastly different from their teammates' values. For instance, an individual from a country that values relationships and sensitivity, such as Sweden, might face a challenge when interacting with someone from Spain, which values assertiveness and competitiveness.

Though there are many challenges facing global virtual teams, companies that implement them effectively can realize tremendous rewards through the diverse knowledge they gain.

Source: Based on N. Zakaria, A. Amelinckx, and D. Wilemon, "Working Together Apart? Building a Knowledge-Sharing Culture for Global Virtual Teams," *Creativity and Innovation Management*, March 2004, pp. 15-29.

for a few days to solve a problem, a few months to complete a project, or exist permanently.[18]

The three primary factors that differentiate virtual teams from face-to-face teams are: (1) the absence of paraverbal and nonverbal cues; (2) limited social context; and (3) the ability to overcome time and space constraints. In face-to-face conversation, people use paraverbal (tone of voice, inflection, voice volume) and nonverbal (eye movement, facial expression, hand gestures, and other body language) cues. These help clarify communication by providing increased meaning but aren't available in online interactions. Virtual teams often suffer from less social rapport and less direct interaction among members. They aren't able to duplicate the normal give-and-take of face-to-face discussion. Especially when members haven't personally met, virtual teams tend to be more task-oriented and exchange less social–emotional information. Not surprisingly, virtual team members report

virtual teams *Teams that use computer technology to tie together physically dispersed members in order to achieve a common goal.*

less satisfaction with the group interaction process than do face-to-face teams. Finally, virtual teams are able to do their work even if members are thousands of miles apart and separated by a dozen or more time zones. It allows people to work together who might otherwise never be able to collaborate.

Companies like Hewlett-Packard, Boeing, Ford, Motorola, GE, Lockheed Martin, VeriFone, and Royal Dutch/Shell have become heavy users of virtual teams. Lockheed Martin, for instance, has put together a virtual team to build a new stealth fighter plane for the U.S. military. The team consists of engineers and designers from around the globe who will be working, simultaneously, on the $225 billion project. The company expects this team structure to save $250 million over the decade it will take to create the jet.[19]

Creating Effective Teams

There is no shortage of efforts at trying to identify factors related to team effectiveness.[20] However, recent studies have taken what was once a "veritable laundry list of characteristics"[21] and organized them into a relatively focused model.[22] Exhibit 10-3 summarizes what we currently know about what makes teams effective. As you'll see, it builds on many of the group concepts introduced in the previous chapter.

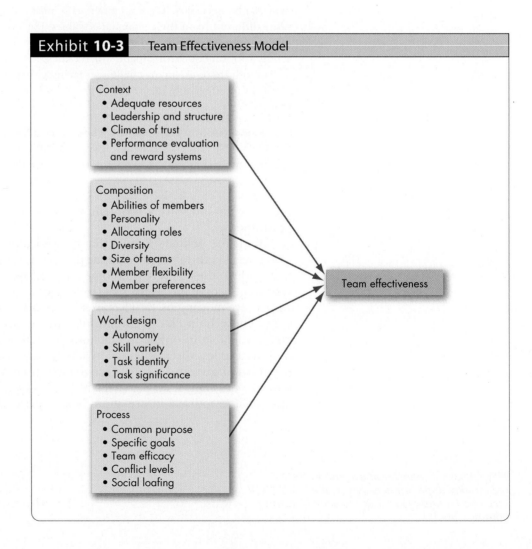

Exhibit 10-3 | Team Effectiveness Model

Context
- Adequate resources
- Leadership and structure
- Climate of trust
- Performance evaluation and reward systems

Composition
- Abilities of members
- Personality
- Allocating roles
- Diversity
- Size of teams
- Member flexibility
- Member preferences

Work design
- Autonomy
- Skill variety
- Task identity
- Task significance

Process
- Common purpose
- Specific goals
- Team efficacy
- Conflict levels
- Social loafing

Team effectiveness

The following discussion is based on the model in Exhibit 10-3. Keep in mind two caveats before we proceed. First, teams differ in form and structure. Since the model we present attempts to generalize across all varieties of teams, you need to be careful not to rigidly apply the model's predictions to all teams.[23] The model should be used as a guide, not as an inflexible prescription. Second, the model assumes that it's already been determined that teamwork is preferable over individual work. Creating "effective" teams in situations in which individuals can do the job better is equivalent to solving the wrong problem perfectly.

The key components making up effective teams can be subsumed into four general categories. First are the resources and other *contextual* influences that make teams effective. The second relates to the team's composition. The third category is *work design*. Finally, *process* variables reflect those things that go on in the team that influences effectiveness. What does *team effectiveness* mean in this model? Typically, this has included objective measures of the team's productivity, managers' ratings of the team's performance, and aggregate measures of member satisfaction.

Context

The four contextual factors that appear to be most significantly related to team performance are the presence of adequate resources, effective leadership, a climate of trust, and a performance evaluation and reward system that reflects team contributions.

Adequate Resources Teams are part of a larger organization system. A research team in Dow's plastic products division, for instance, must live within the budgets, policies, and practices set by Dow's corporate offices. As such, all work teams rely on resources outside the group to sustain it.[24] And a scarcity of resources directly reduces the ability of the team to perform its job effectively. As one set of researchers concluded, after looking at 13 factors potentially related to group performance, "perhaps one of the most important characteristics of an effective work group is the support the group receives from the organization."[25] This support includes timely information, proper equipment, adequate staffing, encouragement, and administrative assistance. Teams must receive the necessary support from management and the larger organization if they are going to succeed in achieving their goals.

Leadership and Structure Team members must agree on who is to do what and ensure that all members contribute equally in sharing the work load. In addition, the team needs to determine how schedules will be set, what skills need to be developed, how the group will resolve conflicts, and how the group will make and modify decisions.[26] Agreeing on the specifics of work and how they fit together to integrate individual skills requires team leadership and structure. This can be provided directly by management or by the team members themselves. Leadership, of course, isn't always needed. For instance, the evidence indicates that self-managed work teams often perform better than teams with formally appointed leaders.[27] And leaders can obstruct high performance when they interfere with self-managing teams.[28] On self-managed teams, team members absorb many of the duties typically assumed by managers.

On traditionally managed teams, we find that two factors seem to be important in influencing team performance—the leader's expectations and his or her mood. Leaders who expect good things from their team are more likely to get them. For instance, military platoons under leaders who held high expectations performed significantly better in training than control platoons.[29] In addition, studies have found that leaders who exhibit a positive mood get better team performance and lower turnover.[30]

Climate of Trust   Members of effective teams trust each other. And they also exhibit trust in their leaders.[31] Interpersonal trust among team members facilitates cooperation, reduces the need to monitor each others' behavior, and bonds members around the belief that others on the team won't take advantage of them. Team members, for instance, are more likely to take risks and expose vulnerabilities when they believe they can trust others on their team. Similarly, as we'll show in Chapter 13, trust is the foundation of leadership. Trust in leadership is important in that it allows the team to be willing to accept and commit to their leader's goals and decisions.

Performance Evaluation and Reward Systems   How do you get team members to be both individually and jointly accountable? The traditional, individually oriented evaluation and reward system must be modified to reflect team performance.[32]

Individual performance evaluations, fixed hourly wages, individual incentives, and the like are not consistent with the development of high-performance teams. So in addition to evaluating and rewarding employees for their individual contributions, management should consider group-based appraisals, profit sharing, gain sharing, small-group incentives, and other system modifications that will reinforce team effort and commitment.

Composition

This category includes variables that relate to how teams should be staffed. In this section, we'll address the ability and personality of team members, allocating roles and diversity, size of the team, member flexibility, and members' preference for team work.

Abilities of Members   Part of a team's performance depends on the knowledge, skills, and abilities of its individual members. It's true that we occasionally read about the athletic team composed of mediocre players who, because of excellent coaching, determination, and precision teamwork, beats a far more talented group of players. But such cases make the news precisely because they represent an aberration. As the old saying goes, "The race doesn't always go to the swiftest nor the battle to the strongest, but that's the way to bet." A team's performance is not merely the summation of its individual members' abilities. However, these abilities set parameters for what members can do and how effectively they will perform on a team.

To perform effectively, a team requires three different types of skills. First, it needs people with *technical expertise*. Second, it needs people with the *problem-solving and decision-making skills* to be able to identify problems, generate alternatives, evaluate those alternatives, and make competent choices. Finally, teams need people with good listening, feedback, conflict resolution, and other *interpersonal skills*.[33] No team can achieve its performance potential without developing all three types of skills. The right mix is crucial. Too much of one at the expense of others will result in lower team performance. But teams don't need to have all the complementary skills in place at their beginning. It's not uncommon for one or more members to take responsibility to learn the skills in which the group is deficient, thereby allowing the team to reach its full potential.

Research on the abilities of team members has revealed some interesting insights into team composition and performance. First, when the task entails considerable thought (for example, solving a complex problem like re-engineering an assembly line), high-ability teams (teams composed of mostly intelligent members) do better, especially when the work load is distributed evenly. (That way, team performance does not depend on the weakest link.) High-ability teams are

The top management team of Pursuit, a Canadian consulting firm, performs effectively because it has the right mix of technical, problem-solving, and interpersonal skills. With backgrounds in different marketing disciplines and training in personal awareness, each team member brings a particular technical skill to the team and a unique approach for solving clients' problems. "As a team, we collaborate like no other that I know," says Wayne Clark (left), "and I've worked with a lot of teams."

also more adaptable to changing situations in that they can more effectively adapt prior knowledge to suit a set of new problems.

Second, although high-ability teams generally have an advantage over lower-ability teams, this is not always the case. For example, when tasks are simple (tasks that individual team members might be able to solve on their own), high-ability teams do not perform as well, perhaps because, in such tasks, high-ability teams become bored and turn their attention to other activities that are more stimulating, whereas low-ability teams stay on task. High-ability teams should be "saved" to tackle the tough problems. So matching team ability to the task is important. Finally, the ability of the team's leader also matters. Research shows that smart team leaders help less intelligent team members when they struggle with a task. But a less intelligent leader can neutralize the effect of a high-ability team.[34]

Personality   We demonstrated in Chapter 4 that personality has a significant influence on individual employee behavior. This can also be extended to team behavior. Many of the dimensions identified in the Big Five personality model have been shown to be relevant to team effectiveness. Specifically, teams that rate higher in mean levels of extraversion, agreeableness, conscientiousness, openness to experience, and emotional stability tend to receive higher managerial ratings for team performance.[35]

Interestingly, the evidence indicates that the *variance* in personality characteristics may be more important than the mean.[36] So, for example, while higher mean levels of conscientiousness on a team are desirable, mixing both conscientious and not-so-conscientious members tends to lower performance. "This may be because, in such teams, members who are highly conscientious not only must perform their own tasks but also must perform or re-do the tasks of low-conscientious members. It may also be because such diversity leads to feelings of contribution inequity."[37] Another interesting finding related to personality is that "one bad apple can spoil the barrel." A single team member who lacks a minimal level of, say, agreeableness, can negatively affect the whole team's performance. So including just one person who is low on agreeableness, conscientiousness, or extraversion can result in strained internal processes and decreased overall performance.[38]

Increasingly, we are learning why these traits are important to team performance.[39] For example, conscientious people are valuable because they're good at "backing up" fellow team members, and they're also good at sensing when that support is truly needed. Extraverts are better at training and motivating team members who are struggling. If a team is confronted with a poor fit between how their team is configured and their work environment (for example, when a team is loosely structured but needs to closely coordinate on a project), emotionally stable team members are critical because they are better at adapting and helping others to adapt. Teams comprised of open people make better use of computer technology in making decisions. Open people better communicate with one another and throw out more ideas, which leads teams comprised of open people to be more creative and innovative. When an unforeseen change happens, teams comprised of conscientious, emotionally stable, and open members cope and adapt better. Personality also influences how teams respond to their surroundings. For example, extraverted teams and agreeable teams respond negatively to individual competitive rewards. Why? Because such individualistic incentives tend to run counter to the social nature of extraverted and agreeable teams.

Personality composition is important to team success. It's best to staff teams with people who are extraverted, agreeable, conscientious, emotionally stable, and open. Management should also minimize the variability within teams on these traits.

Allocating Roles   Teams have different needs, and people should be selected for a team to ensure that all various roles are filled.

We can identify nine potential team roles (see Exhibit 10-4). Successful work teams have people to fill all these roles and have selected people to play these

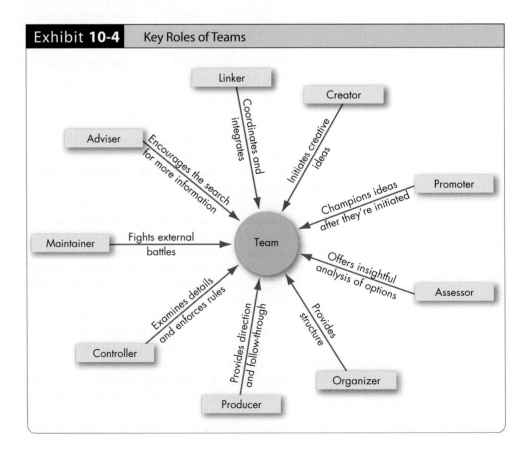

Exhibit 10-4   Key Roles of Teams

Linker — Coordinates and integrates
Creator — Initiates creative ideas
Adviser — Encourages the search for more information
Promoter — Champions ideas after they're initiated
Maintainer — Fights external battles
Assessor — Offers insightful analysis of options
Controller — Examines details and enforces rules
Organizer — Provides structure
Producer — Provides direction and follow-through
Team

roles based on their skills and preferences.[40] (On many teams, individuals will play multiple roles.) Managers need to understand the individual strengths that each person can bring to a team, select members with their strengths in mind, and allocate work assignments that fit with members' preferred styles. By matching individual preferences with team role demands, managers increase the likelihood that the team members will work well together.

Diversity   As previously noted, most team activities require a variety of skills and knowledge. Given this requirement, it would be reasonable to conclude that heterogeneous teams—those composed of dissimilar individuals—would be more likely to have diverse abilities and information and should be more effective. Research studies generally substantiate this conclusion, especially on cognitive, creativity-demanding tasks.[41]

When a team is diverse in terms of personality, gender, age, education, functional specialization, and experience, there is an increased probability that the team will possess the needed characteristics to complete its tasks effectively.[42] The team may be more conflict-laden and less expedient as varied positions are introduced and assimilated, but the evidence generally supports the conclusion that heterogeneous teams perform more effectively than do those that are homogeneous. Essentially, diversity promotes conflict, which stimulates creativity, which leads to improved decision making. One study found that, on a cognitive task, homogenous groups of white males performed the worst relative to mixed race and gender teams or teams of only females. The authors (who were all men) concluded that this was true because male-only teams were overly aggressive and therefore prone to decision-making errors.[43]

But what about diversity created by racial or national differences? The evidence indicates that these elements of diversity interfere with team processes, at least in the short term.[44] Cultural diversity seems to be an asset for tasks that call for a variety of viewpoints. But culturally heterogeneous teams have more difficulty in learning to work with each other and in solving problems. The good news is that these difficulties seem to dissipate with time. Although newly formed culturally diverse teams underperform newly formed culturally homogeneous teams, the differences disappear after about 3 months.[45] The reason is that it takes culturally diverse teams a while to learn how to work through disagreements and different approaches to solving problems.

An offshoot of the diversity issue has received a great deal of attention by group and team researchers. This is the degree to which members of a group share a common demographic attribute, such as age, sex, race, educational level, or length of service in the organization, and the impact of this attribute on turnover. We call this variable **group demography**.

We discussed individual demographic factors in Chapter 2. Here we consider the same type of factors, but in a group context. That is, it's not whether a person is male or female or has been employed with the organization for a year rather than 10 years that concerns us now, but rather the individual's attribute in relationship to the attributes of others with whom he or she works. Let's work

group demography   *The degree to which members of a group share a common demographic attribute, such as age, sex, race, educational level, or length of service in an organization, and the impact of this attribute on turnover.*

The term *cohorts* fits many product-development team members at Microsoft Corporation. Well-educated, young, and results-driven, much of Microsoft's workforce grew up during the information revolution. Sharing these attributes contribute to low turnover among team members working on software development projects such as eBooks shown here.

through the logic of group demography, review the evidence, and then consider the implications.

Groups, teams, and organizations are composed of **cohorts**, which we define as individuals who hold a common attribute. For instance, everyone born in 1960 is of the same age. This means they also have shared common experiences. People born in 1970 have experienced the information revolution, but not the Korean conflict. People born in 1945 shared the Vietnam war, but not the Great Depression. Women in U.S. organizations today who were born before 1945 matured prior to the women's movement and have had substantially different experiences from women born after 1960. Group demography, therefore, suggests that attributes such as age or the date that someone joins a specific work team or organization should help us to predict turnover. Essentially, the logic goes like this: Turnover will be greater among those with dissimilar experiences because communication is more difficult. Conflict and power struggles are more likely and more severe when they occur. The increased conflict makes group membership less attractive, so employees are more likely to quit. Similarly, the losers in a power struggle are more apt to leave voluntarily or to be forced out.

A number of studies have sought to test this thesis, and the evidence is quite encouraging.[46] For example, in departments or separate work groups in which a large portion of members entered at the same time, there is considerably more turnover among those outside this cohort. Also, when there are large gaps between cohorts, turnover is higher. People who enter a group or an organization together, or at approximately the same time, are more likely to associate with one another, have a similar perspective on the group or organization, and thus be more likely to stay. On the other hand, discontinuities or bulges in the group's date-of-entry distribution are likely to result in a higher turnover rate within that group.[47]

The implication of this line of inquiry is that the composition of a team may be an important predictor of turnover. Differences per se may not predict turnover. But large differences within a single team will lead to turnover. If everyone is moderately dissimilar from everyone else in a team, the feelings of being an outsider are reduced. So, it's the degree of dispersion on an attribute, rather than the level, that matters most.

Size of Teams   The president of AOL Technologies says the secret to a great team is "Think small. Ideally, your team should have seven to nine people."[48] His advice is supported by evidence.[49] Generally speaking, the most effective teams have fewer than 10 members. And experts suggest using the smallest number of people who can do the task. Unfortunately, there is a pervasive tendency for managers to err on the side of making teams too large. While a minimum of 4 or 5 may be necessary to develop diversity of views and skills, managers seem to seriously underestimate how coordination problems can geometrically increase as team members are added. When teams have excess members, cohesiveness and mutual accountability declines, social loafing increases, and more and more people do less talking relative to others. Moreover, large teams have trouble coordinating with one another, especially when time pressure is present. So in designing effective teams, managers should try to keep them under 10. If a natural working unit is larger and you want a team effort, consider breaking the group into subteams.[50]

Member Flexibility   Teams made up of flexible individuals have members who can complete each other's tasks. This is an obvious plus to a team because it greatly improves its adaptability and makes it less reliant on any single member.[51] So selecting members who themselves value flexibility, then cross-training them to be able to do each other's jobs, should lead to higher team performance over time.

Member Preferences   Not every employee is a team player. Given the option, many employees will select themselves *out* of team participation. When people who would prefer to work alone are required to team up, there is a direct threat to the team's morale and to individual member satisfaction.[52] This suggests that, when selecting team members, individual preferences should be considered as well as abilities, personalities, and skills. High-performing teams are likely to be composed of people who prefer working as part of a group.

Work Design

Effective teams need to work together and take collective responsibility to complete significant tasks. They must be more than a "team in name only."[53] Based on terminology we introduced in Chapter 7, the work-design category includes variables like freedom and autonomy, the opportunity to use different skills and talents (skill variety), the ability to complete a whole and identifiable task or product (task identity), and working on a task or project that has a substantial impact on others (task significance). The evidence indicates that these characteristics enhance member motivation and increase team effectiveness.[54] These work-design characteristics motivate because they increase members' sense of responsibility and ownership over the work and because they make the work more interesting to perform.[55]

Process

The final category related to team effectiveness is process variables. These include member commitment to a common purpose, establishment of specific team goals, team efficacy, a managed level of conflict, and minimizing social loafing.

Why are processes important to team effectiveness? One way to answer this question is to return to the topic of social loafing. We found that 1 + 1 + 1 doesn't

cohorts   *Individuals who, as part of a group, hold a common attribute.*

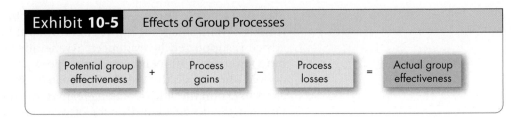

Exhibit 10-5   Effects of Group Processes

Potential group effectiveness   +   Process gains   −   Process losses   =   Actual group effectiveness

Team efficacy applies to this *Halo* video game team at Bungie Studios. Led by Jason Jones (center), the team includes art director Marcus Lehto (left) and physics-programmer Charlie Gough. Confident after the success of their first *Halo* game, the team collaborated on the *Halo 2* sequel. During the first 10 weeks after the release of *Halo 2*, gamers spent 91 million man-hours playing the game online. The *Halo* team's successful performance increases their collective beliefs that future efforts will also lead to success.

necessarily add up to 3. In team tasks for which each member's contribution is not clearly visible, there is a tendency for individuals to decrease their effort. Social loafing, in other words, illustrates a process loss as a result of using teams. But team processes should produce positive results. That is, teams should create outputs greater than the sum of their inputs. The development of creative alternatives by a diverse group would be one such instance. Exhibit 10-5 illustrates how group processes can have an impact on a group's actual effectiveness.[56]

Social loafing, for instance, represents negative synergy. The whole is less than the sum of its parts. On the other hand, research teams are often used in research laboratories because they can draw on the diverse skills of various individuals to produce more meaningful research as a team than could be generated by all of the researchers working independently. That is, they produce positive synergy. Their process gains exceed their process losses.

Common Purpose   Effective teams have a common and meaningful purpose that provides direction, momentum, and commitment for members.[57] This purpose is a vision. It's broader than specific goals.

Members of successful teams put a tremendous amount of time and effort into discussing, shaping, and agreeing on a purpose that belongs to them both collectively and individually. This common purpose, when accepted by the team, becomes the equivalent of what celestial navigation is to a ship captain—it provides direction and guidance under any and all conditions.

Specific Goals   Successful teams translate their common purpose into specific, measurable, and realistic performance goals. Just as we demonstrated in Chapter 6 how goals lead individuals to higher performance, goals also energize teams. These specific goals facilitate clear communication. They also help teams maintain their focus on getting results.

Also, consistent with the research on individual goals, team goals should be challenging. Difficult goals have been found to raise team performance on those criteria for which they're set. So, for instance, goals for quantity tend to raise quantity, goals for speed tend to raise speed, goals for accuracy raise accuracy, and so on.[58]

Team Efficacy   Effective teams have confidence in themselves. They believe they can succeed. We call this *team efficacy*.[59] Success breeds success. Teams that have been successful raise their beliefs about future success, which, in turn, motivates them to work harder. What, if anything, can management do to increase team efficacy? Two possible options are helping the team to achieve small successes and providing skill training. Small successes build team confidence. As a team develops an increasingly stronger performance record, it also increases the collective belief that future efforts will lead to success. In addition, managers should consider providing training to improve members' technical and interpersonal skills. The greater the abilities of team members, the greater the likelihood that the team will develop confidence and the capability to deliver on that confidence.

Conflict Levels   Conflict on a team isn't necessarily bad. As we'll elaborate in Chapter 15, teams that are completely void of conflict are likely to become apathetic and stagnant. So conflict can actually improve team effectiveness.[60] But not all types of conflict. Relationship conflicts—those based on interpersonal incompatibilities, tension, and animosity toward others—are almost always dysfunctional. However, on teams performing nonroutine activities, disagreements among members about task content (called *task conflicts*) is not detrimental. In fact, it is often beneficial because it lessens the likelihood of groupthink. Task conflicts stimulate discussion, promote critical assessment of problems and options, and can lead to better team decisions. So effective teams will be characterized by an appropriate level of conflict.

Social Loafing   We learned in the previous chapter that individuals can hide inside a group. They can engage in social loafing and coast on the group's effort because their individual contributions can't be identified. Effective teams undermine this tendency by holding themselves accountable at both the individual and team level. Successful teams make members individually and jointly accountable for the team's purpose, goals, and approach.[61] Therefore, members should be clear on what they are individually responsible for and what they are jointly responsible for.

Do you think you would be a good team leader? Could you build a successful team from the ground up? The Self-Assessment feature will help you determine whether or not you need to work on your leadership and team-building skills.

HOW GOOD AM I AT BUILDING AND LEADING A TEAM?

In the *Self-Assessment Library* (available on CD, online, and in print), take assessment II.B.6 (How Good Am I At Building and Leading a Team?) and answer the following questions.

1. Did you score as high as you thought you would? Why or why not?
2. Do you think your score can be improved? If so, how? If not, why not?
3. Do you think there are team players? If yes, what are their behaviors?

Turning Individuals into Team Players

To this point, we've made a strong case for the value and growing popularity of teams. But many people are not inherently team players. There are also many organizations that have historically nurtured individual accomplishments. They have created competitive work environments in which only the strong survive. If these organizations adopt teams, what do they do about the selfish, "I've-got-to-look-out-for-me" employees that they've created? Finally, countries differ in terms of how they rate on individualism and collectivism. Teams fit well with countries that score high on collectivism.[62] But what if an organization wants to introduce teams into a work population that is made up largely of individuals born and raised in an individualistic society? As one writer so aptly put it, in describing the role of teams in the United States: "Americans don't grow up learning how to function in teams. In school we never receive a team report card or learn the names of the team of sailors who traveled with Columbus to America."[63] This limitation would obviously be just as true of Canadians, British, Australians, and others from individualistic societies.

The Challenge

The previous points are meant to dramatize that one substantial barrier to using work teams is individual resistance. An employee's success is no longer defined in terms of individual performance. To perform well as team members, individuals must be able to communicate openly and honestly, to confront differences and resolve conflicts, and to sublimate personal goals for the good of the team. For many employees, this is a difficult—sometimes impossible—task. The challenge of creating team players will be greatest when (1) the national culture is highly individualistic and (2) the teams are being introduced into an established organization that has historically valued individual achievement. This describes, for instance, what faced managers at AT&T, Ford, Motorola, and other large U.S.-based companies. These firms prospered by hiring and rewarding corporate stars, and they bred a competitive climate that encouraged individual achievement and recognition. Employees in these types of firms can be jolted by this sudden shift to the importance of team play.[64] A veteran employee of a large company, who had done well working alone, described the experience of joining a team: "I'm learning my lesson. I just had my first negative performance appraisal in 20 years."[65]

On the other hand, the challenge for management is less demanding when teams are introduced where employees have strong collectivist values—such as in Japan or Mexico—or in new organizations that use teams as their initial form for structuring work. Saturn Corp., for instance, is an American organization owned by General Motors. The company was designed around teams from its inception. Everyone at Saturn was hired with the knowledge that they would be working in teams. The ability to be a good team player was a basic hiring qualification that had to be met by all new employees.

Shaping Team Players

The following summarizes the primary options managers have for trying to turn individuals into team players.

Selection   Some people already possess the interpersonal skills to be effective team players. When hiring team members, in addition to the technical skills required to fill the job, care should be taken to ensure that candidates can fulfill their team roles as well as technical requirements.[66]

Many job candidates don't have team skills. This is especially true for those socialized around individual contributions. When faced with such candidates, managers basically have three options. The candidates can undergo training to "make them into team players." If this isn't possible or doesn't work, the other two options are to transfer the individual to another unit within the organization, without teams (if this possibility exists); or don't hire the candidate. In established organizations that decide to redesign jobs around teams, it should be expected that some employees will resist being team players and may be untrainable. Unfortunately, such people typically become casualties of the team approach.

Training   On a more optimistic note, a large proportion of people raised on the importance of individual accomplishments can be trained to become team players. Training specialists conduct exercises that allow employees to experience the satisfaction that teamwork can provide. They typically offer workshops to help employees improve their problem-solving, communication, negotiation, conflict-management, and coaching skills. Employees also learn the five-stage group development model described in Chapter 9. At Verizon, for example, trainers focus on how a team goes through various stages before it finally gels. And employees are reminded of the importance of patience—because teams take longer to make decisions than do employees acting alone.[67]

Outward Bound training programs provide organizations with the ability to develop team players. Training experiences, such as participating in a sailing exercise, teach employees the value of teamwork and give them the practical skills for working in teams.

Emerson Electric's Specialty Motor Division in Missouri, for instance, has achieved remarkable success in getting its 650-member workforce not only to accept but to welcome team training.[68] Outside consultants were brought in to give workers practical skills for working in teams. After less than a year, employees were enthusiastically accepting the value of teamwork.

Rewards   The reward system needs to be reworked to encourage cooperative efforts rather than competitive ones.[69] For instance, Hallmark Cards, Inc., added an annual bonus based on achievement of team goals to its basic individual-incentive system. Trigon Blue Cross Blue Shield changed its system to reward an even split between individual goals and teamlike behaviors.[70]

Promotions, pay raises, and other forms of recognition should be given to individuals for how effective they are as a collaborative team member. This doesn't mean individual contributions are ignored; rather, they are balanced with selfless contributions to the team. Examples of behaviors that should be rewarded include training new colleagues, sharing information with teammates, helping to resolve team conflicts, and mastering new skills that the team needs but in which it is deficient.

Lastly, don't forget the intrinsic rewards that employees can receive from teamwork. Teams provide camaraderie. It's exciting and satisfying to be an integral part of a successful team. The opportunity to engage in personal development and to help teammates grow can be a very satisfying and rewarding experience for employees.

Teams and Quality Management

As discussed in Chapter 1, the issue of "improving quality" has garnered increased attention from management in recent years. In this section, we want to demonstrate the important role that teams play in quality management (QM) programs.

A team approach for quality improvement reigns at New Balance Athletic Shoe, Inc. The company's entire manufacturing process is based on a team structure. New Balance empowers employees to continuously improve their work processes. Shown here is the New Balance stitching department, where the six members of team CS-39 devised a cross-training program so all members learned each other's job skills.

The essence of QM is process improvement, and employee involvement is the linchpin of process improvement. In other words, QM requires management to give employees the encouragement to share ideas and act on what they suggest. As one author put it, "None of the various [quality management] processes and techniques will catch on and be applied except in work teams. All such techniques and processes require high levels of communication and contact, response and adaptation, and coordination and sequencing. They require, in short, the environment that can be supplied only by superior work teams."[71]

Teams provide the natural vehicle for employees to share ideas and to implement improvements. As stated by Gil Mosard, a QM specialist at Boeing: "When your measurement system tells you your process is out of control, you need teamwork for structured problem solving. Not everyone needs to know how to do all kinds of fancy control charts for performance tracking, but everybody does need to know where their process stands so they can judge if it is improving."[72]

Beware! Teams Aren't Always the Answer

Teamwork takes more time and often more resources than individual work. Teams, for instance, have increased communication demands, conflicts to be managed, and meetings to be run. So the benefits of using teams have to exceed the costs. And that's not always the case.[73] In the excitement to enjoy the benefits of teams, some managers have introduced them into situations in which the work is better done by individuals. So before you rush to implement teams, you should carefully assess whether the work requires or will benefit from a collective effort.

How do you know if the work of your group would be better done in teams? It's been suggested that three tests be applied to see if a team fits the situation.[74] First, can the work be done better by more than one person? A good indicator is the complexity of the work and the need for different perspectives. Simple tasks that don't require diverse input are probably better left to individuals. Second, does the work create a common purpose or set of goals for the people in the group that is more than the aggregate of individual goals? For instance, many new-car dealer service departments have introduced teams that link customer service personnel, mechanics, parts specialists, and sales representatives. Such teams can better manage collective responsibility for ensuring that customer needs are properly met. The final test to assess whether teams fit the situation is: Are the members of the group interdependent? Teams make sense when there is interdependence between tasks; when the success of the whole depends on the success of each one *and* the success of each one depends on the success of the others. Soccer, for instance, is an obvious *team* sport. Success requires a great deal of coordination between interdependent players. Conversely, except possibly for relays, swim teams are not really teams. They're groups of individuals, performing individually, whose total performance is merely the aggregate summation of their individual performances.

Summary and Implications for Managers

Few trends have influenced employee jobs as much as the massive movement to introduce teams into the workplace. The shift from working alone to working on teams requires employees to cooperate with others, share information, confront differences, and sublimate personal interests for the greater good of the team.

Effective teams have been found to have common characteristics. They have adequate resources, effective leadership, a climate of trust, and a performance evaluation and reward system that reflects team contributions. The teams have individuals with technical expertise, as well as problem-solving, decision-making, and interpersonal skills; and high scores on the personality characteristics of extraversion, agreeableness, conscientiousness, and emotional stability. Effective teams also tend to be small—with fewer than 10 people—preferably made up of individuals with diverse backgrounds. They have members who fill role demands, are flexible, and who prefer to be part of a group. And the work that members do provides freedom and autonomy, the opportunity to use different skills and talents, the ability to complete a whole and identifiable task or product, and work that has a substantial impact on others. Finally, effective teams have members committed to a common purpose, specific team goals, members who believe in the team's capabilities, a manageable level of conflict, and a minimal degree of social loafing.

Because individualistic organizations and societies attract and reward individual accomplishments, it is more difficult to create team players in these environments. To make the conversion, management should try to select individuals with the interpersonal skills to be effective team players, provide training to develop teamwork skills, and reward individuals for cooperative efforts.

Point ◁▷ Counterpoint

Sports Teams Are Good Models for Workplace Teams

Studies from football, soccer, basketball, hockey, and baseball have found a number of elements that successful sports teams have that can be extrapolated to successful work teams.

Successful teams integrate cooperation and competition. Sports teams with the best win–loss record had coaches who promoted a strong spirit of cooperation and a high level of healthy competition among their players.

Successful teams score early wins. Early successes build teammates' faith in themselves and their capacity as a team. Research on hockey teams of relatively equal ability found that 72 percent of the time the team that was ahead at the end of the first period went on to win. So managers should provide teams with early tasks that are simple and provide "easy wins."

Successful teams avoid losing streaks. A couple of failures can lead to a downward spiral if a team becomes demoralized. Managers need to instill confidence in team members that they can turn things around when they encounter setbacks.

Practice makes perfect. Successful sport teams execute on game day but learn from their mistakes in practice. Practice should be used to try new things and fail. A wise manager encourages work teams to experiment and learn.

Successful teams use half-time breaks. The best coaches in basketball and football use half-time during a game to reassess what is working and what isn't. Managers of work teams should similarly build in assessments at the approximate halfway point in a team project to evaluate what it can do to improve.

Winning teams have a stable membership. Stability improves performance. Studies of professional basketball teams have found that when teammates have more time together, the more able they are to anticipate one another's moves and the clearer they are about one another's roles.

Successful teams debrief after failures and successes. The best sports teams study the game video. Similarly, work teams should routinely assess their successes and failures and should learn from them.

Sports metaphors are useful. For example, a recent *Harvard Business Review* issue had as the lead story "Playing to Win . . . Five Killer Strategies for Trouncing the Competition". The article argues that winners in business play hardball, which means they pick their shots, seek out competitive encounters, set the pace of innovation, and test the edges of the possible. Like sports teams, in business you have to play hardball, which means playing to win. That is what the sports model can teach us.

There are flaws in using sports as a model for developing effective work teams. Here are just four caveats.

All sport teams aren't alike. In baseball, for instance, there is little interaction among teammates. Rarely are more than two or three players directly involved in a play. The performance of the team is largely the sum of the performance of its individual players. In contrast, basketball has much more interdependence among players. Geographic distribution is dense. Usually all players are involved in every play, team members have to be able to switch from offense to defense at a moment's notice, and there is continuous movement by all, not just the player with the ball. The performance of the team is more than the sum of its individual players. So when using sports teams as a model for work teams, you have to make sure you're making the correct comparison. As one expert noted, "The problem with sports metaphors is that the meaning you extract from a sports metaphor is entirely dependent on the sport you pick."

Work teams are more varied and complex. In an athletic league, the design of the task, the design of the team, and the team's context vary relatively little from team to team. But these variables can vary tremendously between work teams. As a result, coaching plays a much more significant part of a sports team's performance than a work team. Performance of work teams is more a function of getting the team's structural and design variables right. So, in contrast to sports, managers of work teams should focus more on getting the team set up for success than coaching.

A lot of employees can't relate to sports metaphors. Not everyone on work teams is conversant in sports. Some people aren't as interested in sports as "sports hounds" and aren't as savvy about sports terminology. And team members from different cultures may not know the sports metaphors you're using. Most Americans, for instance, are unfamiliar with the rules and terminology of Australian Rules football.

Work team outcomes aren't easily defined in terms of wins and losses. Sports teams typically measure success in terms of wins and losses. Such measures of success are rarely as clear for work teams. When managers try to define success in wins and losses it tends to infer that the workplace is ethically no more complex than the playing field, which is rarely true.

Source: See N. Katz, "Sports Teams as a Model for Workplace Teams: Lessons and Liabilities," *Academy of Management Executive*, August 2001, pp. 56–67; "Talent Inc.," *The New Yorker Online Only*, July 22, 2002 (www.newyorker.com/online); D. Batstone, HBR Goes CG?," Worthwhile.com, April 14, 2004 (www.worthwhilemag.com).

Questions for Review

1. Contrast self-managed and cross-functional teams.
2. Contrast virtual and face-to-face teams.
3. List and describe nine team roles.
4. Contrast the pros and cons of having diverse teams.
5. What's group demography and why is it important?
6. List and describe the process variables associated with effective team performance.
7. How do effective teams minimize groupthink?
8. How do effective teams minimize social loafing?
9. Under what conditions will the challenge of creating team players be greatest?
10. What role do teams play in quality management?

Questions for Critical Thinking

1. Don't teams create conflict? Isn't conflict bad? Why, then, would management support the concept of teams?
2. Are there factors in Japanese society that make teams more acceptable in the workplace than in the United States or Canada? Explain.
3. What problems might surface in teams at each stage in the five-stage group development model?
4. How do you think member expectations might affect team performance?
5. Would you prefer to work alone or as part of a team? Why? How do you think your answer compares with others in your class?
6. Do you think there is such a thing as a "team player"? What are the behaviors of such a person?

Team Exercise

FIXED VERSUS VARIABLE FLIGHT CREWS

Break into teams of five. Your team is a panel appointed by the U.S. Federal Aviation Agency to consider the pros and cons of variable flight crews and to arrive at a recommendation on whether to continue this practice.

Almost all commercial airlines now operate with variable flight crews. Pilots, copilots, and flight attendants typically bid for schedules on specific planes (for instance, Boeing 737s, 757s, or 767s) based on seniority. Then they're given a monthly schedule made up of 1- to 4-day trips. So any given flight crew on a plane is rarely together for more than a few days at a time. A complicated system is required to complete the schedules; it's so complicated, in fact, that IBM recently designed a complex software system for El Al Airlines that works through billions of possible combinations to find the best algorithmic solution for crew assignments. Because of this system, it's not unusual for a senior pilot at a large airline to fly with a different copilot on every trip during any given month. And a pilot and copilot that work together for 3 days in January may never work together again the rest of the year.

Arguments can be made in support of the current system. However, it also has serious drawbacks. Each team is to carefully consider the advantages and disadvantages to the current system, consider its effect on airline performance and safety, then be prepared to present to the class its recommendation and justification.

Ethical Dilemma

PRESSURE TO BE A TEAM PLAYER

"O.K., I admit it. I'm not a team player. I work best when I work alone and am left alone," says Zachery Sanders.

Zach's employer, an office furniture manufacturer, recently reorganized around teams. All production in the company's Michigan factory is now done in teams. And Zach's design department has been broken up into three design teams.

"I've worked here for 4 years. I'm very good at what I do. And my performance reviews confirm that. I've scored 96 percent or higher on my evaluations every year I've been here. But now everything is changing. I'm expected to be part of our modular-office design team. My evaluations and pay raises are going to depend on how well the team does. And, get this, 50 percent of my evaluation will be on how well I facilitate the performance of the team. I'm really frustrated and demoralized. They hired me for my design skills. They knew I wasn't a social type. Now they're forcing me to be a team player. This doesn't play to my strengths at all."

Is it unethical for Zach's employer to force him to be a team player? Is his firm breaking an implied contract that it made with him at the time he was hired? Does this employer have any responsibility to provide Zach with an alternative that would allow him to continue to work independently?

Case Incident 1

A VIRTUAL TEAM AT T. A. STEARNS

T. A. Stearns is a national tax accounting firm whose main business is tax preparation services for individuals. Stearns' superior reputation is based on the high quality of its advice and the excellence of its service. Key to the achievement of its reputation is the state-of-the-art computer databases and analysis tools that its people use when counseling clients. These programs were developed by highly trained individuals.

The programs that these individuals produce are highly technical, both in terms of the tax laws they cover and the code in which they are written. Perfecting them requires high levels of programming skill as well as the ability to understand the law. New laws and interpretations of existing laws have to be integrated quickly and flawlessly into the existing regulations and analysis tools.

The creation of these programs is carried out in a virtual environment by four programmers in the greater Boston area. The four work at home and are connected to each other and to the company by e-mail, telephone, and conference software. Formal, onsite meetings among all of the programmers take place only a few times a year, although the workers sometimes meet informally outside of these scheduled occasions. Here's some background on the four:

Tom Andrews is a tax lawyer, a graduate of the University of Maine, and a former hockey player there. At 35, Tom has worked on the programs for 6 years and is the longest-standing member of the team. Along with his design responsibilities, Tom is the primary liaison with Stearns. He is also responsible for training new team members. Single, Tom works out of his farm in Southern New Hampshire, where, in his spare time, he enjoys hunting and fishing.

Cy Crane, a tax accountant and computer science graduate of the University of Massachusetts, is 32 years old, married, with two children ages 4 and 6. His wife works full-time in a law firm in downtown Boston. In his spare time, Cy enjoys biking and fishing.

Marge Dector, a tax lawyer, graduated from Penn State University, is 38 years old, married, with two children ages 8 and 10. Her husband works full-time as an electrical engineer at a local defense contractor. Marge's hobbies include golf and skiing.

Megan Harris, tax accountant and graduate of Indiana University, is 26 years old and single. She recently relocated to Boston and works out of her apartment in the Back Bay area. These four people exchange e-mail messages many times every day. In fact, it's not unusual for them to step away from guests or family to log on and check in with the others. Often, their e-mails are amusing as well as work-related. Sometimes, for instance, when they were facing a deadline and one of Marge's kids is home sick, they help each other with the work. Tom has occasionally invited the others to visit his farm; and Marge and Cy have gotten their families together several times for dinner. About once a month the whole group gets together for lunch.

All four of these Stearns employees are on salary, which, consistent with company custom, is negotiated separately and secretly with management. Although each is required to check in regularly during every workday, they were told when they were hired they could work wherever they wanted. Clearly, flexibility is one of the pluses of these jobs. When the four get together, they often joke about the managers and workers who are tied to the office, referring to them as "face timers" and to themselves as "free agents."

When the programmers were asked to make a major program change, they often developed programming tools called macros that would help them to do their work more efficiently. These macros greatly enhanced the speed at which a change could be written into the programs. Cy, in particular, really enjoyed hacking around with macros. On one recent project, for instance, he became obsessed with the prospect of creating a shortcut that could save him a huge amount of time. One week after he turned in his code and his release notes to the company, Cy bragged to Tom that he created a new macro that had saved him 8 hours of work that week. Tom was skeptical of the shortcut, but after trying it out, he found that it actually saved him many hours too.

Stearns has an employee suggestion program that rewards employees for innovations that save the company money. The program gives an employee 5 percent of the savings generated by their innovation over a period of 3 months. The company also has a profit-sharing plan. Tom and Cy felt that the small amount of money that would be generated by a company reward would not offset the free time that they gained using their new macro. They wanted the time for leisure or consulting work. They also feared their group might suffer if management learned about the innovation. It would allow three people to do the work of four, which could mean one might lose their job. So they didn't share their innovative macro with management.

Although Tom and Cy wouldn't share the innovation with management, they were concerned that they were entering their busy season and knew everyone on the team would be stressed by the heavy work load. They decided to distribute the macro to the other members of their team and swore them to secrecy.

Over lunch one day, the team set for itself a level of production that it felt would not arouse management's suspicion. Several months passed and they used some of their extra time to push the quality of their work even higher. But they also now had more time to pursue their own personal interests.

Dave Regan, the in-house manager of the work team, picked up on the innovation several weeks after it was first implemented. He had wondered why production time had gone down a bit while quality had shot up, and he got his first inkling of an answer when he saw an e-mail from Marge to Cy thanking him for saving her so much time with his "brilliant mind." Not wanting to embarrass his group of employees, the manager hinted to Tom that he wanted to know what was happening, but he got nowhere. He did not tell his own manager about

his suspicions, reasoning that since both quality and productivity were up he did not really need to pursue the matter further.

Dave has just learned that Cy has boasted about his trick to a member of another virtual work team in the company. Suddenly, the situation seems to have gotten out of control. Dave decided to take Cy to lunch. During the meal, Dave asked Cy to explain what was happening. Cy told him about the innovation, but he insisted the team's actions had been justified to protect itself. Dave knew that his own boss would soon hear of the situation and that he would be looking for answers—from him.

Questions

1. Why is this group a team?

2. Has anyone in this case acted unethically?

3. What, if any, characteristics of groupthink are manifested in the work team?

4. Has Dave been an effective team leader? Explain your position.

5. What should Dave do now?

Source: Adapted from "The Virtual Environment Work Team," a case prepared by R. Andre, professor, Northeastern University. With permission.

Case Incident 2

TEAM-BUILDING RETREATS

Some companies are taking team building outside the walls of the office. Corporate retreats, where team members participate in activities ranging from mountain climbing to trust-building exercises (where team members let themselves fall backwards into their colleagues' arms), are used by companies to foster effective teamwork. But why do organizations have teammates participate in activities that seem irrelevant to the organization's primary activities? Howard Atkins, chief financial officer at Wells Fargo, believes that corporate retreats aid in team building, which in turn improves company performance. At a luxury hotel in Sonoma, California, Atkins—along with several other corporate executives—participated in an exercise where he and his team had to build a bridge out of boxes and unstable wooden planks. To the delight of his colleagues, Atkins was able to make it across the bridge. The team succeeded. According to Atkins, "What I have been trying to do is get them to see the power of acting more like a team. It's really a terrific success."

Part of the success that Atkins is referring to is the double-digit gains in earnings by Wells Fargo—gains that he says are one of the effects of the corporate retreats. "Success more often than not is a function of execution, and execution is really about people, so we invest pretty heavily into our people." How heavy is the investment? Wells Fargo paid

$50,000 for the retreat in Sonoma. Given the large expense, some companies are discontinuing their team-building activities outside the organization. According to Susan Harper, a business psychologist, "team-building has definitely gone down. People are reluctant to spend money on what they think is not an absolute necessity." Atkins believes otherwise: "I know intuitively the payback here is huge. It's a very small investment to make for the payback we are going to get."

Sometimes, however, corporate retreats can have unintended consequences. In 2001, a dozen Burger King employees burned themselves while participating in a "fire walk"—a team-building exercise that requires teammates to walk barefoot across an 8-foot pit of burning-hot coals. The results were injured employees and some very negative publicity for Burger King. According to author Joseph Grenny, "Steer away from ridiculous physical challenges. Physical challenges are sometimes based on this notion that if we all experience humiliation together, we'll feel bonded." Grenny states that solving actual problems at work is the best way to build teamwork. Physical challenges may not only result in injuries to employees, but they may also isolate those who lack athletic ability. As an additional example, many companies sponsor golf outings to build teamwork, but such outings may put pressure on employees who are not up to "par" with their colleagues.

Though it is questionable whether team-building exercises such as mountain climbing and fire walks result in improved company financial performance, it may be better to think of such activities as morale boosters. According to Merianne Liteman, a professional corporate retreat organizer, "Where good retreats have a quantifiable effect is on retention, on morale, on productivity." Daryl Jesperson, CEO of RE/MAX International, says, "There is a productivity boost anytime you have one of these. People feel better about themselves, they feel better about the company, and as a result will do a better job."

Questions

1. Do you believe that team-building activities such as mountain climbing increase productivity? Why or why not? What other factors might be responsible for increases in profitability following a corporate retreat?

2. What are some other ways to build effective teams and increase teamwork among company employees? How might these alternatives be better or worse than corporate retreats?

3. What should companies do about employees who lack athletic talent but are still pressured to participate in physical activities with their colleagues? How might poor performance by those with low athletic ability affect their status within the organization?

4. How might you increase teamwork when team members are not often in direct contact with one another? Can you think of any "electronic" team building exercises?

Source: Based on C. Dahle, How to Avoid a Rout at the Company Retreat. *The New York Times,* October 31, 2004, p. 10, and Shuit, D. P. Sound the Retreat, *Workforce Management,* September 2003, vol. 82(9), pp. 38–44.

Endnotes

1. M. Cipresso, L. Comolli, S. Hardgrave, and J. Piazza, "Cracking into the Kola Nut Business: Mission to Cameroon," *UC Berkeley News,* September 10, 2004 (From: w.berkeley.edu/news/media/releases/2004/09/10_kola1.shtml).

2. Cited in C. Joinson, "Teams at Work," *HRMagazine,* May 1999, p. 30; and P. Strozniak, "Teams at Work," *Industry Week,* September 18, 2000, p. 47.

3. See, for example, P. MacMillan, *The Performance Factor: Unlocking the Secrets of Teamwork* (Nashville, TN: Broadman & Holman, 2001); E. Salas, C. A. Bowers, and E. Edens (eds.), *Improving Teamwork in Organizations: Applications of Resource Management Training* (Mahwah, NJ: Lawrence Erlbaum, 2002); and L. I. Glassop, "The Organizational Benefits of Teams," *Human Relations,* February 2002, pp. 225–50.

4. K. Kelly, "The New Soul of John Deere," *Business Week,* January 31, 1994, pp. 64–66.

5. This section is based on J. R. Katzenbach and D. K. Smith, *The Wisdom of Teams* (Cambridge, MA: Harvard University Press, 1993), pp. 21, 45, and 85; and D. C. Kinlaw, *Developing Superior Work Teams* (Lexington, MA: Lexington Books, 1991), pp. 3–21.

6. See, for instance, E. Sunstrom, K. DeMeuse, and D. Futrell, "Work Teams: Applications and Effectiveness," *American Psychologist,* February 1990, pp. 120–33.

7. J. H. Shonk, *Team-Based Organizations* (Homewood, IL: Business One Irwin, 1992); and M. A. Verespej, "When Workers Get New Roles," *Industry Week,* February 3, 1992, p. 11.

8. G. Bodinson and R. Bunch, "AQP's National Team Excellence Award: Its Purpose, Value and Process," *The Journal for Quality and Participation,* Spring 2003, pp. 37–42.

9. See, for example, S. G. Cohen, G. E. Ledford, Jr., and G. M. Spreitzer, "A Predictive Model of Self-Managing Work Team Effectiveness," *Human Relations,* May 1996, pp. 643–76; D. E. Yeats and C. Hyten, *High-Performing Self-Managed Work Teams: A Comparison of Theory to Practice* (Thousand Oaks, CA: Sage, 1998); C. E. Nicholls, H. W. Lane, and M. Brehm Brechu, "Taking Self-Managed Teams to Mexico," *Academy of Management Executive,* August 1999, pp. 15–27; and A. Erez, J. A. LePine, and H. Elms, "Effects of Rotated Leadership and Peer Evaluation on the Functioning and Effectiveness of Self-Managed Teams: A Quasi-experiment," *Personnel Psychology,* Winter 2002, pp. 929–48.

10. W. Royal, "Team-Centered Success," *Industry Week,* October 18, 1999, pp. 56–58.

11. R. Zemke, "Rethinking the Rush to Team Up," *Training,* November 1993, pp. 55–61.

12. See, for instance, T. D. Wall, N. J. Kemp, P. R. Jackson, and C. W. Clegg, "Outcomes of Autonomous Workgroups: A Long-Term Field Experiment," *Academy of Management Journal,* June 1986, pp. 280–304; J. L. Cordery, W. S. Mueller, and L. M. Smith, "Attitudinal and Behavioral Effects of Autonomous Group Working: A Longitudinal Field Study," *Academy of Management Journal,* June 1991, pp. 464–76; R. A. Cook and J. L. Goff, "Coming of Age With Self-Managed Teams: Dealing With a Problem Employee," *Journal of Business and Psychology,* Spring 2002, pp. 485–496; and C. W. Langfred, "To Much of A Good Thing? Negative Effects of High Trust and Individual Autonomy in Self-Managing Teams," *Academy of Management Journal,* June 2004, pp. 385–399.

13. J. R. Barker, "Tightening the Iron Cage: Concertive Control in Self-Managing Teams," *Administrative Science Quarterly,* September 1993, pp. 408–37; S. G. Cohen and G. E. Ledford Jr., "The Effectiveness of Self-Managing Teams: A Field Experiment, *Human Relations,* January 1994, pp. 13–43; and C. Smith and D. Comer, "Self-Organization in Small Groups: A Study of Group Effectiveness Within Non-Equilibrium Conditions," *Human Relations,* May 1994, pp. 553–81.

14. Nicholls, Lane, and Brehm Brechu, "Taking Self-Managed Teams to Mexico."

15. Bodinson and Bunch, "AQP's National Team Excellence Award."

16. M. Brunelli, "How Harley-Davidson Uses Cross-Functional Teams," *Purchasing Online*, November 4, 1999; www.manufacturing.net/magazine/purchasing/archives/1999.

17. See, for example, J. Lipnack and J. Stamps, *Virtual Teams: People Working Across Boundaries and Technology*, 2nd ed. (New York: Wiley, 2000); C. B. Gibson and S. G. Cohen (eds.), *Virtual Teams That Work* (San Francisco: Jossey-Bass, 2003); and L. L. Martins, L. L. Gilson, and M. T. Maynard, "Virtual Teams: What Do We Know and Where Do We Go From Here?" *Journal of Management*, November 2004, pp. 805–35.

18. K. Kiser, "Working on World Time," *Training*, March 1999, p. 30.

19. S. Crock, "Collaboration: Lockheed Martin," *Business Week*, November 24, 2003, p. 85.

20. See, for instance, D. L. Gladstein, "Groups in Context: A Model of Task Group Effectiveness," *Administrative Science Quarterly*, December 1984, pp. 499–517; J. R. Hackman, "The Design of Work Teams," in J. W. Lorsch (ed.), *Handbook of Organizational Behavior* (Upper Saddle River, NJ: Prentice Hall, 1987), pp. 315–42; M. A. Campion, G. J. Medsker, and C. A. Higgs, "Relations Between Work Group Characteristics and Effectiveness: Implications for Designing Effective Work Groups," *Personnel Psychology*, Winter 1993, pp. 823–50; and R. A. Guzzo and M. W. Dickson, "Teams in Organizations: Recent Research on Performance and Effectiveness," in J. T. Spence, J. M. Darley, and D. J. Foss (eds.), *Annual Review of Psychology*, vol. 47, pp. 307–38.

21. D. E. Hyatt and T. M. Ruddy, "An Examination of the Relationship between Work Group Characteristics and Performance: Once More into the Breech," *Personnel Psychology*, Autumn 1997, p. 555.

22. This model is based on M. A. Campion, E. M. Papper, and G. J. Medsker, "Relations between Work Team Characteristics and Effectiveness: A Replication and Extension," *Personnel Psychology*, Summer 1996, pp. 429–52; D. E. Hyatt and T. M. Ruddy, "An Examination of the Relationship between Work Group Characteristics and Performance," pp. 553–85; S. G. Cohen and D. E. Bailey, "What Makes Teams Work: Group Effectiveness Research from the Shop Floor to the Executive Suite," *Journal of Management* 23, no. 3 (1997), pp. 239–90; L. Thompson, *Making the Team* (Upper Saddle River, NJ: Prentice Hall, 2000), pp. 18–33; and J. R. Hackman, *Leading Teams: Setting the Stage for Great Performance* (Boston: Harvard Business School Press, 2002).

23. See M. Mattson, T. V. Mumford, and G. S. Sintay, "Taking Teams to Task: A Normative Model for Designing or Recalibrating Work Teams," paper presented at the National Academy of Management Conference; Chicago, August 1999; and G. L. Stewart and M. R. Barrick, "Team Structure and Performance: Assessing the Mediating Role of Intrateam Process and the Moderating Role of Task Type," *Academy of Management Journal*, April 2000, pp. 135–48.

24. J. W. Bishop, K. D. Scott, and S. M. Burroughs, "Support, Commitment, and Employee Outcomes in a Team Environment," *Journal of Management* 26, no. 6 (2000), pp. 1113–32; and C. L. Pearce and R. A. Giacalone, "Teams Behaving Badly: Factors Associated With Anti-Citizenship Behavior in Teams," *Journal of Applied Social Psychology*, January 2003, pp. 53–75.

25. Hyatt and Ruddy, "An Examination of the Relationship between Work Group Characteristics and Performance," p. 577.

26. F. LaFasto and C. Larson, *When Teams Work Best: 6,000 Team Members and Leaders Tell What It Takes to Succeed* (Thousand Oaks, CA: Sage, 2002).

27. R. I. Beekun, "Assessing the Effectiveness of Sociotechnical Interventions: Antidote or Fad?" *Human Relations*, August 1989, pp. 877–97.

28. S. G. Cohen, G. E. Ledford, and G. M. Spreitzer, "A Predictive Model of Self-Managing Work Team Effectiveness," *Human Relations*, May, 1996, pp. 643–76; see also V. U. Druskat and J. V. Wheeler, "Managing From the Boundary: The Effective Leadership of Self-Managing Work Teams," *Academy of Management Journal*, August 2003, pp. 435–57.

29. D. Eden, "Pygmalion without Interpersonal Contrast Effects: Whole Groups Gain from Raising Manager Expectations," *Journal of Applied Psychology*, August 1990, pp. 394–98.

30. J. M. George and K. Bettenhausen, "Understanding Prosocial Behavior, Sales, Performance, and Turnover: A Group-Level Analysis in a Service Context," *Journal of Applied Psychology*, October 1990, pp. 698–709; J. M. George, "Leader Positive Mood and Group Performance: The Case of Customer Service," *Journal of Applied Social Psychology*, December 1995, pp. 778–94; and A. P. Brief and H. M. Weiss, "Organizational Behavior: Affect in the Workplace," *Annual Review of Psychology*, 2002, pp. 279–307.

31. K. T. Dirks, "Trust in Leadership and Team Performance: Evidence from NCAA Basketball," *Journal of Applied Psychology*, December 2000, pp. 1004–12; and M. Williams, "In Whom We Trust: Group Membership as an Affective Context for Trust Development," *Academy of Management Review*, July 2001, pp. 377–96.

32. See S. T. Johnson, "Work Teams: What's Ahead in Work Design and Rewards Management," *Compensation & Benefits Review*, March–April 1993, pp. 35–41; and L. N. McClurg, "Team Rewards: How Far Have We Come?" *Human Resource Management*, Spring 2001, pp. 73–86.

33. For a more detailed breakdown on team skills, see M. J. Stevens and M. A. Campion, "The Knowledge, Skill, and Ability Requirements for Teamwork: Implications for Human Resource Management," *Journal of Management*, Summer 1994, pp. 503–30.

34. H. Moon, J. R. Hollenbeck, and S. E. Humphrey, "Asymmetric Adaptability: Dynamic Team Structures as One-Way Streets," *Academy of Management Journal* 47, no.5 (October 2004), pp. 681–95; A. P. J. Ellis, J. R. Hollenbeck, and D. R. Ilgen, "Team Learning: Collectively Connecting the Dots," *Journal of Applied Psychology* 88, no. 5 (October 2003), pp. 821–35; J. A. LePine, J. R. Hollenbeck, and D. R. Ilgen, "Effects of Individual Differences on the Performance of Hierarchical Decision-Making Teams: Much More than g," *Journal of Applied Psychology* 82, no. 5 (October 1997), pp. 803–11; C. L. Jackson and J. A. LePine, "Peer Responses to a Team's Weakest Link: A Test and Extension of LePine and Van Dyne's Model," *Journal of Applied Psychology* 88, no. 3 (June 2003), pp. 459–75; J. A. LePine, "Team Adaptation and Postchange Performance: Effects of Team Composition in Terms of Members' Cognitive Ability and Personality," *Journal of Applied Psychology* 88, no. 1 (February 2003), pp. 27–39.

35. M. R. Barrick, G. L. Stewart, M. J. Neubert, and M. K. Mount, "Relating Member Ability and Personality to Work-Team Processes and Team Effectiveness," *Journal of Applied*

Psychology, June 1998, pp. 377–91; G. A. Neuman and J. Wright, "Team Effectiveness: Beyond Skills and Cognitive Ability," *Journal of Applied Psychology*, June 1999, pp. 376–89; and L. M. Moynihan and R. S. Peterson, "A Contingent Configuration Approach to Understanding the Role of Personality in Organizational Groups," in B. M. Staw and R. I. Sutton (eds.), *Research in Organizational Behavior*, vol. 23 (Oxford: JAI/Elsevier, 2001), pp. 332–38.

36. Barrick, Stewart, Neubert, and Mount, "Relating Member Ability and Personality to Work-Team Processes and Team Effectiveness."

37. Ibid., p. 388.

38. Ibid.

39. B. Beersma, J. R. Hollenbeck, and S. E. Humphrey, "Cooperation, Competition, and Team Performance: Toward a Contingency Approach," *Academy of Management Journal* 46, no. 5 (October 2003), pp. 572–90; Ellis, Hollenbeck, and Ilgen, "Team Learning: Collectively Connecting the Dots," pp. 821–35; C. O. L. H. Porter, J. R. Hollenbeck, and D. R. Ilgen, "Backing Up Behaviors in Teams: The Role of Personality and Legitimacy of Need," *Journal of Applied Psychology* 88, no. 3 (June 2003), pp. 391–403; J. R. Hollenbeck, H. Moon, and A. P. J. Ellis, "Structural Contingency Theory and Individual Differences: Examination of External and Internal Person-Team Fit," *Journal of Applied Psychology* 87, no. 3 (June 2002), pp. 599–606; J. A. Colquitt, J. R. Hollenbeck, and D. R. Ilgen, "Computer-Assisted Communication and Team Decision-Making Performance: The Moderating Effect of Openness to Experience," *Journal of Applied Psychology* 87, no. 2 (April 2002), pp. 402–10; LePine, Hollenbeck, and Ilgen, "Effects of Individual Differences on the Performance of Hierarchical Decision-Making Teams: Much More than g," pp. 803–11; Jackson and. LePine, "Peer Responses to a Team's Weakest Link: A Test and Extension of LePine and Van Dyne's Model," pp. 459–75. LePine, "Team Adaptation and Postchange Performance: Effects of Team Composition in Terms of Members' Cognitive Ability and Personality," pp. 27–39.

40. C. Margerison and D. McCann, *Team Management: Practical New Approaches* (London: Mercury Books, 1990).

41. See, for example, R. A. Guzzo and G. P. Shea, "Group Performance and Intergroup Relations in Organizations," in M. D. Dunnette and L. M. Hough (eds.), *Handbook of Industrial & Organizational Psychology*, 2nd ed., vol. 3 (Palo Alto, CA: Consulting Psychologists Press, 1992), pp. 288–90; S. E. Jackson, K. E. May, and K. Whitney, "Understanding the Dynamics of Diversity in Decision-Making Teams," in R. A. Guzzo and E. Salas (eds.), *Team Effectiveness and Decision Making in Organizations* (San Francisco: Jossey-Bass, 1995), pp. 204–61; K. Y. Williams and C. A. O'Reilly III, "Demography and Diversity in Organizations: A Review of 40 Years of Research," in B. M. Staw and L. L. Cummings (eds.), *Research in Organizational Behavior*, vol. 20 (Greenwich, CT: JAI Press, 1998), pp. 77–140; F. Linnehan and A. M. Konrad, "Diluting Diversity: Implications for Intergroup Inequality in Organizations," *Journal of Management Inquiry*, December 1999, pp. 399–414; S. E. Jackson, A. Joshi, and N. L. Erhardt, "Recent Research on Team and Organizational Diversity: SWOT Analysis and Implications," *Journal of Management* 29, no. 6 (2003), pp. 801–30; and D. van Knippenberg, C. K. W. De Dreu, and A. C. Homan, "Work Group Diversity and

Group Performance: An Integrative Model and Research Agenda," *Journal of Applied Psychology*, December 2004, pp. 1008–22.

42. Shaw, *Contemporary Topics*, p. 356.

43. J. A. LePine, J. R. Hollenbeck, and D. R. Ilgen, "Gender Composition, Situational Strength, and Team Decision-Making Accuracy: A Criterion Decomposition Approach," *Organizational Behavior & Human Decision Processes* 88, no. 1 (May 2002), pp. 445–75.

44. W. E. Watson, K. Kumar, and L. K. Michaelsen, "Cultural Diversity's Impact on Interaction Process and Performance: Comparing Homogeneous and Diverse Task Groups," *Academy of Management Journal*, June 1993, pp. 590–602; P. C. Earley and E. Mosakowski, "Creating Hybrid Team Cultures: An Empirical Test of Transnational Team Functioning," *Academy of Management Journal*, February 2000, pp. 26–49; and S. Mohammed and L. C. Angell, "Surface- and Deep-Level Diversity in Workgroups: Examining the Moderating Effects of Team Orientation and Team Process on Relationship Conflict," *Journal of Organizational Behavior*, December 2004, pp. 1015–39.

45. Watson, Kumar, and Michaelsen, "Cultural Diversity's Impact on Interaction Process and Performance: Comparing Homogeneous and Diverse Task Groups."

46. C. A. O'Reilly III, D. F. Caldwell, and W. P. Barnett, "Work Group Demography, Social Integration, and Turnover," *Administrative Science Quarterly*, March 1989, 21–37; S. E. Jackson, J. F. Brett, V. I. Sessa, D. M. Cooper, J. A. Julin, and K. Peyronnin, "Some Differences Make a Difference: Individual Dissimilarity and Group Heterogeneity as Correlates of Recruitment, Promotions, and Turnover," *Journal of Applied Psychology*, August 1991, pp. 675–89; M. F. Wiersema and A. Bird, "Organizational Demography in Japanese Firms: Group Heterogeneity, Individual Dissimilarity, and Top Management Team Turnover," *Academy of Management Journal*, October 1993, pp. 996–1025; F. J. Milliken and L. L. Martins, "Searching for Common Threads: Understanding the Multiple Effects of Diversity in Organizational Groups," *Academy of Management Review*, April 1996, pp. 402–33; B. Lawrence, "The Black Box of Organizational Demography," *Organizational Science*, February 1997, pp. 1–22; and K. Y. Williams and C. A. O'Reilly III, "Demography and Diversity in Organizations: A Review of 40 Years of Research," in B. M. Staw and L. L. Cummings (eds.), *Research in Organizational Behavior*, vol. 20, pp. 77–140.

47. W. G. Wagner, J. Pfeffer, and C. A. O'Reilly, "Organizational Demography and Turnover in Top-Management Groups," *Administrative Science Quarterly* 29, no. 1 (1984), pp. 74–92.

48. J. Katzenbach, "What Makes Teams Work?" *Fast Company*, November 2000, p. 110.

49. The evidence in this section is described in Thompson, *Making the Team*, pp. 65–67. See also L. A. Curral, R. H. Forrester, and J. F. Dawson, "It's What You Do and the Way that You Do It: Team Task, Team Size, and Innovation-Related Group Processes," *European Journal of Work & Organizational Psychology* 10, no. 2 (June 2001), pp. 187–204; R. C. Liden, S. J. Wayne, and R. A. Jaworski, "Social Loafing: A Field Investigation," *Journal of Management* 30, no. 2 (2004), pp. 285–304; J. A. Wagner, "Studies of Individualism-Collectivism: Effects on Cooperation in Groups," *Academy of Management Journal* 38, no. 1 (February 1995).

50. L. A. Curral, R. H. Forrester, J. F. Dawson, and M. A. West, "It's What You Do and the Way that You Do It: Team Task, Team Size, and Innovation-Related Group Processes," *European Journal of Work & Organizational Psychology* 10, no. 2 (2001), pp. 187–204.

51. E. Sundstrom, K. P. Meuse, and D. Futrell, "Work Teams: Applications and Effectiveness," *American Psychologist*, February 1990, pp. 120–33.

52. Hyatt and Ruddy, "An Examination of the Relationship between Work Group Characteristics and Performance"; J. D. Shaw, M. K. Duffy, and E. M. Stark, "Interdependence and Preference for Group Work: Main and Congruence Effects on the Satisfaction and Performance of Group Members," *Journal of Management* 26, no. 2 (2000), pp. 259–79; and S. A. Kiffin-Peterson and J. L. Cordery, "Trust, Individualism, and Job Characteristics of Employee Preference for Teamwork," *International Journal of Human Resource Management*, February 2003, pp. 93–116.

53. R. Wageman, "Critical Success Factors for Creating Superb Self-Managing Teams," *Organizational Dynamics*, Summer 1997, p. 55.

54. Campion, Papper, and Medsker, "Relations between Work Team Characteristics and Effectiveness," p. 430; B. L. Kirkman and B. Rosen, "Powering Up Teams," *Organizational Dynamics*, Winter 2000, pp. 48–66; and D. C. Man and S. S. K. Lam, "The Effects of Job Complexity and Autonomy on Cohesiveness in Collectivist and Individualist Work Groups: A Cross-Cultural Analysis," *Journal of Organizational Behavior*, December 2003, pp. 979–1001.

55. Campion, Papper, and Medsker, "Relations between Work Team Characteristics and Effectiveness," p. 430.

56. I. D. Steiner, *Group Processes and Productivity* (New York: Academic Press, 1972).

57. K. Hess, *Creating the High-Performance Team* (New York: Wiley, 1987); Katzenbach and Smith, *The Wisdom of Teams*, pp. 43–64; K. D. Scott and A. Townsend, "Teams: Why Some Succeed and Others Fail," *HRMagazine*, August 1994, pp. 62–67; and K. Blanchard, D. Carew, and E. Parisi-Carew, "How To Get Your Group To Perform Like a Team," *Training and Development*, September 1996, pp. 34–37.

58. E. Weldon and L. R. Weingart, "Group Goals and Group Performance," *British Journal of Social Psychology*, Spring 1993, pp. 307–34; see also R. P. DeShon, S. W. J. Kozlowski, A. M. Schmidt, K. R. Milner, and D. Wiechmann, "A Multiple-Goal, Multilevel Model of Feeback Effects on the Regulation of Individual and Team Performance," *Journal of Applied Psychology*, December 2004, pp. 1035–56.

59. C. B. Gibson, A. Randel, and P. C. Earley, "Understanding Group Efficacy: An Empirical Test of Multiple Assessment Methods," *Group & Organization Management*, 2000, pp. 67–97; and S. M. Gully, K. A. Incalcaterra, A. Joshi, and J. M. Beaubien, "A Meta-Analysis of Team-Efficacy, Potency, and Performance: Interdependence and Level of Analysis as Moderators of Observed Relationships," *Journal of Applied Psychology*, October 2002, pp. 819–32; C. B. Gibson, "The Efficacy Advantage: Factors Related to the Formation of Group Efficacy," *Journal of Applied Social Psychology*, October 2003, pp. 2153–86; and D. I. Jung and J. J. Sosik, "Group Potency and Collective Efficacy: Examining Their Predictive Validity, Level of Analysis, and Effects of Performance Feedback on Future Group Performance," *Group & Organization Management*, September 2003, pp. 366–91.

60. K. A. Jehn, "A Qualitative Analysis of Conflict Types and Dimensions in Organizational Groups," *Administrative Science Quarterly*, September 1997, pp. 530–57; see also R. S. Peterson and K. J. Behfar, "The Dynamic Relationship Between Performance Feedback, Trust, and Conflict in Groups: A Longitudinal Study," *Organizational Behavior and Human Decision Processes*, September–November 2003, pp. 102–12.

61. Hess, *Creating the High-Performance Team*.

62. See, for instance, B. L. Kirkman and D. L. Shapiro, "The Impact of Cultural Values on Employee Resistance to Teams: Toward a Model of Globalized Self-Managing Work Team Effectiveness," *Academy of Management Review*, July 1997, pp. 730–57; and B. L. Kirkman, C. B. Gibson, and D. L. Shapiro, "'Exporting' Teams: Enhancing the Implementation and Effectiveness of Work Teams in Global Affiliates," *Organizational Dynamics* 30, no. 1 (2001), pp. 12–29.

63. D. Harrington-Mackin, *The Team Building Tool Kit* (New York: AMACOM, 1994), p. 53.

64. T. D. Schellhardt, "To Be a Star among Equals, Be a Team Player," *Wall Street Journal*, April 20, 1994, p. B1.

65. Ibid.

66. See, for instance, J. Prieto, "The Team Perspective in Selection and Assessment," in H. Schuler, J. L. Farr, and M. Smith (eds.), *Personnel Selection and Assessment: Industrial and Organizational Perspectives* (Hillsdale, NJ: Erlbaum, 1994); R. Klimoski and R. G. Jones, "Staffing for Effective Group Decision Making: Key Issues in Matching People and Teams," in R. A. Guzzo and E. Salas (eds.), *Team Effectiveness and Decision Making in Organizations* (San Francisco: Jossey-Bass, 1995), pp. 307–26; and C. Hymowitz, "How to Avoid Hiring the Prima Donnas Who Hate Teamwork," *Wall Street Journal*, February 15, 2000, p. B1.

67. Schellhardt, "To Be a Star among Equals, Be a Team Player."

68. "Teaming Up for Success," *Training*, January 1994, p. S41.

69. J. S. DeMatteo, L. T. Eby, and E. Sundstrom, "Team-Based Rewards: Current Empirical Evidence and Directions for Future Research," in B. M. Staw and L. L. Cummings (eds.), *Research in Organizational Behavior*, vol. 20, pp. 141–83.

70. B. Geber, "The Bugaboo of Team Pay," *Training*, August 1995, pp. 27, 34.

71. Kinlaw, *Developing Superior Work Teams*, p. 43.

72. B. Krone, "Total Quality Management: An American Odyssey," *The Bureaucrat*, Fall 1990, p. 37.

73. C. E. Naquin and R. O. Tynan, "The Team Halo Effect: Why Teams Are Not Blamed for Their Failures," *Journal of Applied Psychology*, April 2003, pp. 332–40.

74. A. B. Drexler and R. Forrester, "Teamwork—Not Necessarily the Answer," *HRMagazine*, January 1998, pp. 55–58. See also R. Saavedra, P. C. Earley, and L. Van Dyne, "Complex Interdependence in Task-Performing Groups," *Journal of Applied Psychology*, February 1993, pp. 61–72; and K. A. Jehn, G. B. Northcraft, and M. A. Neale, "Why Differences Make a Difference: A Field Study of Diversity, Conflict, and Performance in Workgroups," *Administrative Science Quarterly*, December 1999, pp. 741–63.

If you want to make peace, you don't talk to your friends.
You talk to your enemies.

— Moshe Dayan

Communication

After studying this chapter, you should be able to:

1 Describe the communication process.

2 Contrast the advantages and disadvantages of oral versus written communication.

3 Compare the effectiveness of the chain, wheel, and all-channel networks.

4 Identify the factors affecting the use of the grapevine.

5 Discuss how computer-aided technology is changing organizational communication.

6 Explain the importance of channel richness to improving communication effectiveness.

7 Identify common barriers to effective communication.

8 Describe the potential problems in cross-cultural communication.

LEARNING OBJECTIVES

CHAPTER 11

Clear Communication Is Vital

Can the misunderstanding of a few words literally mean the difference between life and death? They can in the airline business. A number of aviation disasters have been largely attributed to problems in communication.[1] Consider the following:

History's worst aviation disaster occurred in 1977 at foggy Tenerife in the Canary Islands. The captain of a KLM flight thought the air traffic controller had cleared him to take off. But the controller intended only to give departure instructions. Although the language spoken between the Dutch KLM captain and the Spanish controller was English, confusion was created by heavy accents and improper terminology. The KLM Boeing 747 hit a Pan Am 747 at full throttle on the runway, killing 583 people.

In 1990, Colombian Avianca pilots, after several holding patterns caused by bad weather, told controllers as they neared New York Kennedy Airport that their Boeing 707 was "running low on fuel." Controllers hear those words all the time, so they took no special action. While the pilots knew there was a serious problem, they failed to use a key phrase—"fuel emergency"—which would have obligated controllers to direct the Avianca flight ahead of all others and clear it to land as soon as possible. The people at Kennedy never understood the true nature of the

pilots' problem. The jet ran out of fuel and crashed 16 miles from Kennedy. Seventy-three people died.

In 1993, Chinese pilots flying a U.S.-built MD-80 tried to land in heavy fog at Urumqi, in northwest China. They were baffled by an audio alarm from the jet's ground proximity warning system. Just before impact, the cockpit recorder picked up one crew member saying to the other in Chinese: "What does 'pull up' mean?" The plane hit power lines and crashed, killing 12.

In September 1997, a Garuda Airlines jetliner crashed into a jungle, just 20 miles south of the Medan Airport on the island of Sumatra. All 234 aboard were killed. The cause of this disaster was the pilot and the air traffic controller confusing the words "left" and "right" as the plane approached the airport under poor visibility conditions.

On October 31, 2000, visibility was very poor at Taipei-Chiang Kai-shek Airport because a major typhoon was in the Taiwan area. The pilots of a Singapore

Airlines 747, stopping in Taipei en route from Singapore to Los Angeles, had not read a report issued 60 days earlier by Taiwan's Civil Aviation Administration informing pilots that runway 05R would be closed for construction from September 13 to November 22. Told by the control tower to use 05L for their takeoff, the Singapore pilots taxied onto 05R, which ran parallel. Less than 4 seconds after beginning their takeoff, their plane plowed into concrete barriers, excavators, and other equipment on the runway. The plane broke apart and 83 people died.

Bad weather and poor communication paired up again to create another disaster in October 2001, this time at Milano-Linae Airport in Italy. Visibility was poor and tower controllers were not able to establish visual or radar contact with planes. Miscommunications between the controllers and pilots of an SAS commercial jet and a small Citation business jet, combined with the poor visibility, led to the two planes colliding on the runway. One hundred and ten people died. ■

The preceding examples tragically illustrate how miscommunication can have deadly consequences. In this chapter, we'll show (obviously not in as dramatic a fashion) that good communication is essential to any group's or organization's effectiveness. Research indicates that poor communication is probably the most frequently cited source of interpersonal conflict.[2] Because individuals spend nearly 70 percent of their waking hours communicating—writing, reading, speaking, listening—it seems reasonable to conclude that one of the most inhibiting forces to successful group performance is a lack of effective communication.

No group can exist without communication: the transference of meaning among its members. It is only through transmitting meaning from one person to another that information and ideas can be conveyed. Communication, however, is more than merely imparting meaning. It must also be understood. In a group in which one member speaks only German and the others do not know German, the individual speaking German will not be fully understood. Therefore, **communication** must include both the *transference and the understanding of meaning*.

An idea, no matter how great, is useless until it is transmitted and understood by others. Perfect communication, if there were such a thing, would exist when a thought or an idea was transmitted so that the mental picture perceived by the receiver was exactly the same as that envisioned by the sender. Although elementary in theory, perfect communication is never achieved in practice, for reasons we shall expand on later in the chapter.

Before making too many generalizations concerning communication and problems in communicating effectively, we need to review briefly the functions that communication performs and describe the communication process.

Functions of Communication

Communication serves four major functions within a group or organization: control, motivation, emotional expression, and information.[3]

Communication acts to *control* member behavior in several ways. Organizations have authority hierarchies and formal guidelines that employees are required to follow. When employees, for instance, are required to first communicate any job-related grievance to their immediate boss, to follow their job description, or to comply with company policies, communication is performing a control function. But informal communication also controls behavior. When work groups tease or harass a member who produces too much (and makes the rest of the group look bad), they are informally communicating with, and controlling, the member's behavior.

Communication fosters *motivation* by clarifying to employees what is to be done, how well they are doing, and what can be done to improve performance if it's subpar. We saw this operating in our review of goal-setting and reinforcement theories in Chapter 6. The formation of specific goals, feedback on progress toward the goals, and reinforcement of desired behavior all stimulate motivation and require communication.

For many employees, their work group is a primary source for social interaction. The communication that takes place within the group is a fundamental mechanism by which members show their frustrations and feelings of satisfaction. Communication, therefore, provides a release for the *emotional expression* of feelings and for fulfillment of social needs.

The final function that communication performs relates to its role in facilitating decision making. It provides the *information* that individuals and groups need to make decisions by transmitting the data to identify and evaluate alternative choices.

No one of these four functions should be seen as being more important than the others. For groups to perform effectively, they need to maintain some form of control over members, stimulate members to perform, provide a means for emotional expression, and make decision choices. You can assume that almost every communication interaction that takes place in a group or organization performs one or more of these four functions.

The Communication Process

Before communication can take place, a purpose, expressed as a message to be conveyed, is needed. It passes between a sender and a receiver. The message is encoded (converted to a symbolic form) and passed by way of some medium (channel) to the receiver, who retranslates (decodes) the message initiated by the sender. The result is transference of meaning from one person to another.[4]

Exhibit 11-1 depicts this **communication process**. The key parts of this model are: (1) the sender, (2) encoding, (3) the message, (4) the channel, (5) decoding, (6) the receiver, (7) noise, and (8) feedback.

The *sender* initiates a message by encoding a thought. The *message* is the actual physical product from the sender's *encoding*. When we speak, the speech is the message. When we write, the writing is the message. When we gesture, the movements of our arms and the expressions on our faces are the message. The *channel* is the medium through which the message travels. It is selected by the sender, who must determine whether to use a formal or informal channel. **Formal channels** are established by the organization and transmit messages that

communication *The transference and understanding of meaning.*

communication process *The steps between a source and a receiver that result in the transference and understanding of meaning.*

formal channels *Communication channels established by an organization to transmit messages related to the professional activities of members.*

Exhibit **11-1**	The Communication Process

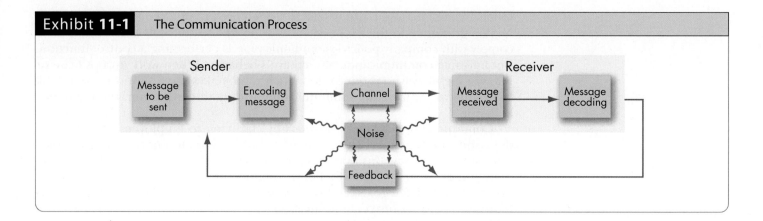

are related to the professional activities of members. They traditionally follow the authority chain within the organization. Other forms of messages, such as personal or social, follow the **informal channels** in the organization. These informal channels are spontaneous and emerge as a response to individual choices.[5] The *receiver* is the object to whom the message is directed. But before the message can be received, the symbols in it must be translated into a form that can be understood by the receiver. This step is the *decoding* of the message. *Noise* represents communication barriers that distort the clarity of the message. Examples of possible noise sources include perceptual problems, information overload, semantic difficulties, or cultural differences. The final link in the communication process is a feedback loop. *Feedback* is the check on how successful we have been in transferring our messages as originally intended. It determines whether understanding has been achieved.

Direction of Communication

Communication can flow vertically or laterally. The vertical dimension can be further divided into downward and upward directions.[6]

Downward

Communication that flows from one level of a group or organization to a lower level is downward communication. When we think of managers communicating with employees, the downward pattern is the one we are usually thinking of. It's used by group leaders and managers to assign goals, provide job instructions, inform employees of policies and procedures, point out problems that need attention, and offer feedback about performance. But downward communication doesn't have to be oral or face-to-face contact. When management sends letters to employees' homes to advise them of the organization's new sick leave policy, it's using downward communication. So is an e-mail from a team leader to the members of her team, reminding them of an upcoming deadline.

Upward

Upward communication flows to a higher level in the group or organization. It's used to provide feedback to higher-ups, inform them of progress toward goals, and relay current problems. Upward communication keeps managers aware of how employees feel about their jobs, coworkers, and the organization in general. Managers also rely on upward communication for ideas on how things can be improved.

Some organizational examples of upward communication are performance reports prepared by lower management for review by middle and top management, suggestion boxes, employee attitude surveys, grievance procedures, superior–subordinate discussions, and informal "gripe" sessions in which employees have the opportunity to identify and discuss problems with their boss or representatives of higher management. For example, FedEx prides itself on its computerized upward communication program. All its employees annually complete climate surveys and reviews of management. This program was cited as a key human resources strength by the Malcolm Baldrige National Quality Award examiners when FedEx won the honor.

Lateral

When communication takes place among members of the same work group, among members of work groups at the same level, among managers at the same level, or among any horizontally equivalent personnel, we describe it as lateral communications.

Why would there be a need for horizontal communications if a group or organization's vertical communications are effective? The answer is that horizontal communications are often necessary to save time and facilitate coordination. In some cases, these lateral relationships are formally sanctioned. More often, they are informally created to short-circuit the vertical hierarchy and expedite action. So lateral communications can, from management's viewpoint, be good or bad. Because strict adherence to the formal vertical structure for all communications can impede the efficient and accurate transfer of information, lateral communications can be beneficial. In such cases, they occur with the knowledge and support of superiors. But they can create dysfunctional conflicts when the formal vertical channels are breached, when members go above or around their superiors to get things done, or when bosses find out that actions have been taken or decisions made without their knowledge.

Interpersonal Communication

How do group members transfer meaning between and among each other? There are three basic methods. People essentially rely on oral, written, and nonverbal communication.

Oral Communication

The chief means of conveying messages is oral communication. Speeches, formal one-on-one and group discussions, and the informal rumor mill or grapevine are popular forms of oral communication.

The advantages of oral communication are speed and feedback. A verbal message can be conveyed and a response received in a minimal amount of time. If the receiver is unsure of the message, rapid feedback allows for early detection by the sender and, hence, allows for early correction.

informal channels *Communication channels that are created spontaneously and that emerge as responses to individual choices.*

As executive VP and chief operating officer for Toyota Motor Sales USA, Jim Press relies on oral communication in guiding the car company's operations in its most important market. Shown here, Press motivates employees with regular pep talks. He frequently visits Toyota dealers, talking to everyone from receptionists to mechanics, to get feedback about U.S. car buyers' preferences and problems.

The major disadvantage of oral communication surfaces in organizations or whenever the message has to be passed through a number of people. The more people a message must pass through, the greater the potential distortion. If you ever played the game "telephone" at a party, you know the problem. Each person interprets the message in his or her own way. The message's content, when it reaches its destination, is often very different from that of the original. In an organization, where decisions and other communiqués are verbally passed up and down the authority hierarchy, there are considerable opportunities for messages to become distorted.

Written Communication

Written communications include memos, letters, fax transmissions, electronic mail, instant messaging, organizational periodicals, notices placed on bulletin boards, or any other device that is transmitted via written words or symbols.

Why would a sender choose to use written communications? They're often tangible and verifiable. When printed, both the sender and receiver have a record of the communication; and the message can be stored for an indefinite period. If there are questions concerning the content of the message, it is physically available for later reference. This feature is particularly important for complex and lengthy communications. The marketing plan for a new product, for instance, is likely to contain a number of tasks spread out over several months. By putting it in writing, those who have to initiate the plan can readily refer to it over the life of the plan. A final benefit of all written communication comes from the process itself. You're usually more careful with the written word than the oral word. You're forced to think more thoroughly about what you want to convey in a written message than in a spoken one. Thus, written communications are more likely to be well thought out, logical, and clear.

Of course, written messages have their drawbacks. They're time-consuming. You could convey far more information to a college instructor in a 1-hour oral exam than in a 1-hour written exam. In fact, you could probably say the same thing in 10 to 15 minutes that it would take you an hour to write. So, although writing may be more precise, it also consumes a great deal of time. The other major disadvantage is feedback, or lack of it. Oral communication allows the receiver to respond rapidly to what he thinks he hears. Written communication, however, does not have a built-in feedback mechanism. The result is that the mailing of a memo is no assurance it has been received, and, if received, there is no guarantee the recipient will interpret it as the sender intended. The latter point is also relevant in oral communiqués, except it's easy in such cases merely to ask the receiver to summarize what you've said. An accurate summary presents feedback evidence that the message has been received and understood.

Nonverbal Communication

Every time we verbally give a message to someone, we also impart a nonverbal message.[7] In some instances, the nonverbal component may stand alone. For example, in a singles bar, a glance, a stare, a smile, a frown, and a provocative body movement all convey meaning. As such, no discussion of communication would be complete without consideration of *nonverbal communication*—which includes body movements, the intonations or emphasis we give to words, facial expressions, and the physical distance between the sender and receiver.

It can be argued that every *body movement* has a meaning and no movement is accidental. For example, through body language we say, "Help me, I'm lonely"; "Take me, I'm available"; "Leave me alone, I'm depressed." And rarely do we send our messages consciously. We act out our state of being with nonverbal body language. We lift one eyebrow for disbelief. We rub our noses for puzzlement. We clasp our arms to isolate ourselves or to protect ourselves. We shrug our shoulders for indifference, wink one eye for intimacy, tap our fingers for impatience, slap our forehead for forgetfulness.[8]

The two most important messages that body language conveys are (1) the extent to which an individual likes another and is interested in his or her views and (2) the relative perceived status between a sender and receiver.[9] For instance, we're more likely to position ourselves closer to people we like and touch them more often. Similarly, if you feel that you're a higher status than another, you're more likely to display body movements—such as crossed legs or a slouched seating position—that reflect a casual and relaxed manner.[10]

Body language adds to, and often complicates, verbal communication. A body position or movement does not by itself have a precise or universal meaning, but when it is linked with spoken language, it gives fuller meaning to a sender's message.

If you read the verbatim minutes of a meeting, you wouldn't grasp the impact of what was said in the same way you would if you had been there or saw the meeting on video. Why? There is no record of nonverbal communication. The emphasis given to words or phrases is missing. Exhibit 11-2 illustrates how *intonations* can change the meaning of a message. *Facial expressions* also convey meaning. A snarling face says something different from a smile. Facial expressions, along with intonations, can show arrogance, aggressiveness, fear, shyness, and other characteristics that would never be communicated if you read a transcript of what had been said.

The way individuals space themselves in terms of *physical distance* also has meaning. What is considered proper spacing is largely dependent on cultural norms. For example, what is considered a businesslike distance in some European countries would be viewed as intimate in many parts of North America. If someone stands closer to you than is considered appropriate, it may indicate aggressiveness or sexual interest; if farther away than usual, it may mean disinterest or displeasure with what is being said.

Exhibit 11-2	Intonations: It's the Way You Say It!

Change your tone and you change your meaning:

Placement of the emphasis	What it means
Why don't I take **you** to dinner tonight?	I was going to take someone else.
Why don't **I** take you to dinner tonight?	Instead of the guy you were going with.
Why **don't** I take you to dinner tonight?	I'm trying to find a reason why I shouldn't take you.
Why don't I take you to dinner tonight?	Do you have a problem with me?
Why don't I **take** you to dinner tonight?	Instead of going on your own.
Why don't I take you to **dinner** tonight?	Instead of lunch tomorrow.
Why don't I take you to dinner **tonight**?	Not tomorrow night.

Source: Based on M. Kiely, "When 'No' Means 'Yes,' " *Marketing*, October 1993, pp. 7–9. Reproduced in A. Huczynski and D. Buchanan, *Organizational Behavior*, 4th ed. (Essex, England: Pearson Education, 2001), p. 194.

It's important for the receiver to be alert to these nonverbal aspects of communication. You should look for nonverbal cues as well as listen to the literal meaning of a sender's words. You should particularly be aware of contradictions between the messages. Your boss may say she is free to talk to you about a pressing budget problem, but you may see nonverbal signals suggesting that this is not the time to discuss the subject. Regardless of what is being said, an individual who frequently glances at her wristwatch is giving the message that she would prefer to terminate the conversation. We misinform others when we express one message verbally, such as trust, but nonverbally communicate a contradictory message that reads, "I don't have confidence in you."

Organizational Communication

In this section, we move from interpersonal communication to organizational communication. Our focus here will be on formal networks, the grapevine, computer-aided mechanisms used by organizations to facilitate communication, and the evolving topic of knowledge management.

Formal Small-Group Networks

Formal organizational networks can be very complicated. They can, for instance, include hundreds of people and a half-dozen or more hierarchical levels. To simplify our discussion, we've condensed these networks into three common small groups of five people each (see Exhibit 11-3). These three networks are the chain, wheel, and all-channel. Although these three networks have been extremely simplified, they do allow us to describe the unique qualities of each.

The *chain* rigidly follows the formal chain of command. This network approximates the communication channels you might find in a rigid three-level organization. The *wheel* relies on a central figure to act as the conduit for all of the group's communication. It simulates the communication network you would find on a team with a strong leader. The *all-channel* network permits all group members to actively communicate with each other. The all-channel network is most often characterized in practice by self-managed teams, in which all group members are free to contribute and no one person takes on a leadership role.

As Exhibit 11-4 demonstrates, the effectiveness of each network depends on the dependent variable you're concerned about. For instance, the structure of

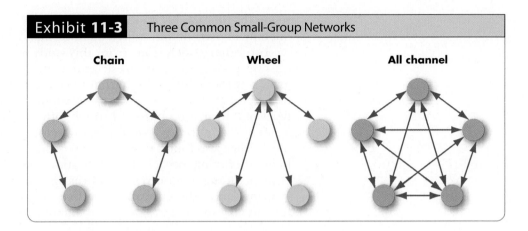

Exhibit 11-3 | Three Common Small-Group Networks

Chain   Wheel   All channel

the wheel facilitates the emergence of a leader, the all-channel network is best if you are concerned with having high member satisfaction, and the chain is best if accuracy is most important. Exhibit 11-4 leads us to the conclusion that no single network will be best for all occasions.

The Grapevine

The formal system is not the only communication network in a group or organization. There is also an informal one, which is called the **grapevine**.[11] And although the grapevine may be informal, this doesn't mean it's not an important source of information. For instance, a survey found that 75 percent of employees hear about matters first through rumors on the grapevine.[12]

The grapevine has three main characteristics.[13] First, it is not controlled by management. Second, it is perceived by most employees as being more believable and reliable than formal communiqués issued by top management. And third, it is largely used to serve the self-interests of the people within it.

One of the most famous studies of the grapevine investigated the communication pattern among 67 managerial personnel in a small manufacturing firm.[14] The basic approach used was to learn from each communication recipient how he or she first received a given piece of information and then trace it back to its source. It was found that, while the grapevine was an important source of information, only 10 percent of the executives acted as liaison individuals, that is, passed the information on to more than one other person. For example, when one executive decided to

Exhibit 11-4 | Small-Group Networks and Effective Criteria

| | Networks | | |
Criteria	Chain	Wheel	All Channel
Speed	Moderate	Fast	Fast
Accuracy	High	High	Moderate
Emergence of a leader	Moderate	High	None
Member satisfaction	Moderate	Low	High

grapevine   *The organization's informal communication network.*

resign to enter the insurance business, 81 percent of the executives knew about it, but only 11 percent transmitted this information to others.

Two other conclusions from this study are also worth noting. Information on events of general interest tended to flow between the major functional groups (production, sales) rather than within them. Also, no evidence surfaced to suggest that any one group consistently acted as liaisons; rather, different types of information passed through different liaison persons.

An attempt to replicate this study among employees in a small state government office also found that only 10 percent act as liaison individuals.[15] This finding is interesting, because the replication contained a wider spectrum of employees, including operative as well as managerial personnel. But the flow of information in the government office took place within, rather than between, functional groups. It was proposed that this discrepancy might be due to comparing an executive-only sample against one that also included operative workers. Managers, for example, might feel greater pressure to stay informed and thus cultivate others outside their immediate functional group. Also, in contrast to the findings of the original study, the replication found that a consistent group of individuals acted as liaisons by transmitting information in the government office.

Is the information that flows along the grapevine accurate? The evidence indicates that about 75 percent of what is carried is accurate.[16] But what conditions foster an active grapevine? What gets the rumor mill rolling?

It's frequently assumed that rumors start because they make titillating gossip. This is rarely the case. Rumors emerge as a response to situations that are *important* to us, when there is *ambiguity*, and under conditions that arouse *anxiety*.[17] The fact that work situations frequently contain these three elements explains why rumors flourish in organizations. The secrecy and competition that typically prevail in large organizations—around issues such as the appointment of new bosses, the relocation of offices, downsizing decisions, and the realignment of work assignments—create conditions that encourage and sustain rumors on the grapevine. A rumor will persist either until the wants and expectations creating the uncertainty underlying the rumor are fulfilled or until the anxiety is reduced.

What can we conclude from the preceding discussion? Certainly the grapevine is an important part of any group or organization communication network and is well worth understanding.[18] It gives managers a feel for the morale of their organization, identifies issues that employees consider important, and helps tap into employee anxieties. It acts, therefore, as both a filter and a feedback mechanism, picking up the issues that employees consider relevant. For employees, the grapevine is particularly valuable for translating formal communications into their group's own jargon. Maybe more important, again from a managerial perspective, it seems possible to analyze grapevine information and to predict its flow, given that only a small set of individuals (approximately 10 percent) actively pass on information to more than one other person. By assessing which liaison individuals will consider a given piece of information to be relevant, we can improve our ability to explain and predict the pattern of the grapevine.

Can management entirely eliminate rumors? No. What management should do, however, is minimize the negative consequences of rumors by limiting their range and impact. Exhibit 11-5 offers a few suggestions for minimizing those negative consequences.

Computer-Aided Communication

Communication in today's organizations is enhanced and enriched by computer-aided technologies. These include electronic mail, instant messaging, intranet and extranet links, and videoconferencing. Electronic mail, for instance, has dramatically reduced the number of memos, letters, and phone

Exhibit **11-5**	Suggestions for Reducing the Negative Consequences of Rumors

1. Announce timetables for making important decisions.
2. Explain decisions and behaviors that may appear inconsistent or secretive.
3. Emphasize the downside, as well as the upside, of current decisions and future plans.
4. Openly discuss worse-case possibilities—it is almost never as anxiety-provoking as the unspoken fantasy.

Source: Adapted from L. Hirschhorn, "Managing Rumors," in L. Hirschhorn (ed.), *Cutting Back* (San Francisco: Jossey-Bass, 1983), pp. 54–56. With permission.

calls that employees historically used to communicate among themselves and with suppliers, customers, or other outside stakeholders.

E-Mail Electronic mail (or e-mail) uses the Internet to transmit and receive computer-generated text and documents. Its growth has been spectacular. In fact, over 100 million adults in the United States use e-mail regularly (at least once a day), and it's estimated that nearly 1 trillion e-mails are sent *daily* worldwide. A good percentage (up to 70 percent—depending on the quality of one's spam filter) of this e-mail comes in the form of spam (unsolicited e-mail ads or other unwanted material) and phishing e-mails (Internet scams initiated with a spoof e-mail message). Nevertheless, the reason we put up with junk e-mail is because, for many of us, e-mail is an indispensable way of communicating.

As a communication tool, e-mail has a long list of benefits. E-mail messages can be quickly written, edited, and stored. They can be distributed to one person or thousands with a click of a mouse. They can be read, in their entirety, at the convenience of the recipient. And the cost of sending formal e-mail messages to employees is a fraction of what it would cost to print, duplicate, and distribute a comparable letter or brochure.

E-mail, of course, is not without its drawbacks.[19] It can be a distraction from work activities when employees use it for personal purposes. And it can be

Computer-aided communication allows Carole Levin to work from her home. Levin is a sales manager with Taconic, a medical research supplier. She manages a team of remote salespeople by using cell phones, handheld PDA devices, and a laptop computer.

impersonal, detracting from special attention to customers or coworkers. John Caudwell—one of Great Britian's richest tycoons and CEO of Caudwell Group—felt e-mail was so distracting that he banned all employees from using it at work, commenting, "Management and staff at HQ and in the stores were beginning to show signs of being constrained by e-mail proliferation. . . . " Although employees have had mixed reactions to the ban on e-mail, Caudwell claims that customer service has improved.[20] We don't know, however, whether Caudwell's claims about improved customer service—due to eliminating e-mail—are in fact true. A recent study, though, revealed that most e-mails from customers are ignored. In this study, the researchers posed as customers and used e-mail to inquire about purchasing a product or service from 147 retail companies in various industries. In 51 percent of the cases, a reply to the e-mail was never received.[21] Perhaps e-mail does hurt customer service, as Caudwell claims.

E-mails also lack emotional content. The nonverbal cues in a face-to-face message or the tone of voice from a phone call convey important information that doesn't come across in e-mail. Additionally, e-mails tend to be cold and impersonal. As such, they're not the ideal means to convey information like layoffs, plant closings, or other messages that might evoke emotional responses and require empathy or social support. Finally, the remote nature of e-mail fuels "conflict spirals" that have been found to escalate ill feelings at double the rate of face-to-face communiqués. Many people seem to be able to say things in e-mails that they would never say to someone face-to-face.

Instant Messaging   It's not just for teenagers anymore. Instant messaging (IM), which has been popular among teens for more than a decade, is now rapidly moving into business.[22]

Instant messaging is essentially real-time e-mail. Employees create a list of colleagues and friends with whom they want to communicate. Then they just click on a name displayed in a small box on their computer screen, type in a message, and the message instantaneously pops up onto the recipient's screen. Increasingly, people are using handheld IM devices, such as cell phones, palm pilots, or Blackberries. The growth of IM has been spectacular. In 2001, for instance, just 8 percent of American employees were using it. In 2003, it was up to 18 percent. And experts estimate that by 2006, more people will be using IM than e-mail as their primary communication tool at work.[23]

IM is a fast and inexpensive means for managers to stay in touch with employees and for employees to stay in touch with each other. For instance, furniture retailer Jennifer Convertibles uses IM to communicate with managers in its 200-plus stores nationwide.[24] Jeff Wenger, vice president at tax preparation and software company Tax Technologies Inc., uses IM to manage a team of software developers and testers who are scattered all over the United States. Wenger says IM has cut his daily telephone time from 3 hours to less than 30 minutes.[25] IM isn't going to replace e-mail. E-mail is still probably a better device for conveying long messages that need to be saved. IM is preferred for sending one- or two-line messages that would just clutter up an e-mail inbox. On the downside, some IM users find the technology intrusive and distracting. IM's continual online presence can make it hard for employees to concentrate and stay focused. Managers also indicate concern that IM will be used by employees to chat with friends and colleagues about nonwork issues. Finally, because instant messages are easily broken into, many organizations are concerned about IM security.[26]

Intranet and Extranet Links   *Intranets* are private, organization-wide information networks that look and act like a Web site but to which only people in an organization have access. Intranets are rapidly becoming a popular means for employees within companies to communicate with each other. IBM, as a case in

At Overlake Hospital Medical Center in Bellevue, Washington, Wi-Fi facilitates communication among medical staff members. For the nurses and doctors at Overlake, who are usually away from a computer or phone, Wi-Fi provides instant access to patients' medical records and drug-safety data. The Overlake medical staff uses Wi-Fi networks to do bedside admittance on laptops, and nurses carry wireless phones to call doctors. The hospital is also replacing paper charts with electronic tablets and PDAs.

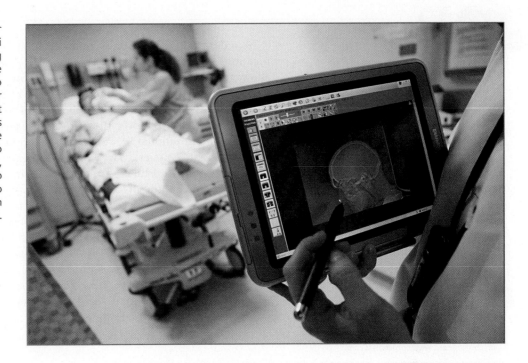

point, recently brought together 52,000 of its employees online for what it called WorldJam.[27] Using the company's intranet, IBMers everywhere swapped ideas on everything from how to retain employees to how to work faster without undermining quality.

The latest development in intranets is using high-speed wireless Internet access (Wi-Fi) for telephone calls within an organization.[28] This voice over Wi-Fi allows employees to make and receive phone calls on the same wireless broadband network that an organization uses for Internet access. BJ's Wholesale Club, for instance, is using voice over Wi-Fi to make it easier for employees and managers to talk with each other as well as customers and suppliers. With stores that average more than 100,000 square feet, voice over Wi-Fi makes BJ's employees readily accessible regardless of where they are in a store.

In addition, organizations are creating *extranet* links that connect internal employees with selected suppliers, customers, and strategic partners. For instance, an extranet allows GM employees to send electronic messages and documents to its steel and rubber suppliers as well as to communicate with its dealers. Similarly, all Wal-Mart vendors are linked into its extranet system, allowing Wal-Mart buyers to easily communicate with its suppliers and for suppliers to monitor the inventory status of its products at Wal-Mart stores.

Videoconferencing *Videoconferencing* is an extension of intranet or extranet systems. It permits employees in an organization to have meetings with people at different locations. Live audio and video images of members allow them to see, hear, and talk with each other. Videoconferencing technology, in effect, allows employees to conduct interactive meetings without the necessity of all being physically in the same location.

In the late 1990s, videoconferencing was basically conducted from special rooms equipped with television cameras, located at company facilities. More recently, cameras and microphones are being attached to individual computers, allowing people to participate in videoconferences without leaving their desks. As the cost of this technology drops in price, videoconferencing is likely to be increasingly seen as an alternative to expensive and time-consuming travel.

Internet Gripe Sites: A Challenge for Management?

Internet gripe sites are the new electronic grapevines. Employees and ex-employees at hundreds of companies—including JPMorgan Chase, Microsoft, BankAmerica, The Limited, Merck, MTV Networks, and Goldman Sachs—are using computer-aided communication to vent their anger and frustration by posting uncensored messages at VaultReports.com Electronic Water-Cooler.

So a downside to electronic communications is that Internet gripe sites allow employees a unilateral (and often anonymous) platform to air their grievances. For instance, an analysis of messages found that they cover the entire gamut of organizational life, including organizational policies, pay worries, internal morale, and hiring practices. Although some comments address the benefits of working at a particular organization, most are complaints.

What makes these sites particularly frustrating to management is that there are no checks-and-balances to ensure that grievances expressed on these sites are accurate. Here is a situation where the adage that "a few bad apples can spoil the barrel" seems entirely appropriate. A few disgruntled employees can go a long way in undermining an entire workforce's morale. And because these sites are accessible to the public, they can also tarnish an organization's image.

Some organizations are turning a negative into a positive by monitoring their gripe sites to instantly uncover "hot-button" issues among employees, the mood of the workforce, and the perception of internal justice procedures—then using this information to identify areas where they need to improve. Still, most employers undoubtedly see these gripe sites as a downside of the Internet age.

Source: Based on "Internet Gripe Sites a Tool for Management," www.uninews.unimelb.edu/au, March 19, 2003; and C. J. Moebius, " 'I Can Top That!' Inside the World of Employee Complaint Sites," www.bordercross.com

Summary   Computer-aided communications are reshaping the way we communicate in organizations. Specifically, it's no longer necessary for employees to be at their work station or desk to be "available." Pagers, cellular phones, personal communicators, and phone messaging allow employees to be reached when they're in a meeting, during a lunch break, while visiting a customer across town, or during a golf game on Saturday morning. The line between an employee's work and nonwork life is no longer distinct. In the electronic age, all employees can theoretically be "on call" 24 hours a day, 7 days a week.

Organizational boundaries become less relevant as a result of computer-aided communications. Networked computers allow employees to jump vertical levels within the organization, work full-time at home or someplace other than an organizationally operated facility, and conduct ongoing communications with people in other organizations. The market researcher who wants to discuss an issue with the vice president of marketing (who is three levels up in the hierarchy) can bypass the people in between and send an e-mail message directly. And in so doing, the traditional status hierarchy, largely determined by level and access, becomes essentially negated. Or that same market researcher may choose to live in the Cayman Islands and work at home via telecommuting rather than do the job in the company's Chicago office. And when an employee's computer is linked to suppliers' and customers' computers, the boundaries separating organizations become further blurred. As a case in point, because Levi Strauss's and Wal-Mart's computers are linked, Levi is able to monitor Wal-Mart's inventory of its jeans and to replace merchandise as needed, clouding the distinction between Levi and Wal-Mart employees.

Knowledge Management

Our final topic under organizational communication is **knowledge management** (KM). This is a process of organizing and distributing an organization's collective wisdom so the right information gets to the right people at the right time.[29] When

With the average age of its aerospace engineers at 54, defense contractor Northrop Grumman has developed a knowledge-based system to transfer knowledge from older to younger employees. Northrop has created a culture of knowledge sharing by forming "communities of practice," groups from different divisions that meet in person and online to share information. Aerospace engineer Tamra Johnson, shown here, started a community of practice for new engineers so they can learn from retired project managers and older employees.

done properly, KM provides an organization with both a competitive edge and improved organizational performance because it makes its employees smarter.

Siemens, the global telecommunications giant, recently won a $460,000 contract to build a telecommunications network for two hospitals in Switzerland in spite of the fact that its bid was 30 percent higher than the competition's. The secret to Siemens's success was its knowledge-management system.[30] This system allowed Siemens's people in the Netherlands to draw on their experience and provide the Swiss sales reps with technical data that proved that the Siemens's network would be substantially more reliable than the competition's.

Siemens is one of a growing number of companies—including Cisco Systems, Ford, British Telecom, Johnson & Johnson, IBM, Whirlpool, Intel, Volkswagen, ChevronTexaco, and Royal Bank of Canada—that have realized the value of knowledge management. In fact, a recent survey found that 81 percent of the leading organizations in Europe and the United States say they have, or are at least considering adopting, some kind of KM system.[31]

Knowledge management is increasingly important today for at least three reasons.[32] First, in many organizations, intellectual assets are now as important as physical or financial assets. Organizations that can quickly and efficiently tap into their employees' collective experience and wisdom are more likely to "outsmart" their competition. Second, as baby boomers begin to leave the workforce, there's an increasing awareness that they represent a wealth of knowledge that will be lost if there are no attempts to capture it. And third, a well-designed KM system will reduce redundancy and make the organization more efficient. For instance, when employees in a large organization undertake a new project, they needn't start from scratch. A knowledge-management system can allow them to access what previous employees have learned and cut wasteful time retracing a path that has already been traveled.

How does an organization record the knowledge and expertise of its employees and make that information easily accessible? It needs to develop computer databases of pertinent information that employees can readily access; it needs to create a culture that supports and rewards sharing; and it has to develop mechanisms that allow employees who have developed valuable expertise and insights to share them with others.

KM begins by identifying what knowledge matters to the organization.[33] Management needs to review processes to identify those that provide the most value. Then it can develop computer networks and databases that can make that information readily available to the people who need it the most. But KM won't work unless the culture supports sharing of information.[34] As we'll show in Chapter 14, information that is important and scarce can be a potent source of power. And people who hold that power are often reluctant to share it with others. So KM requires an organizational culture that promotes, values, and rewards sharing knowledge. Finally, KM must provide the mechanisms and the motivation for employees to share knowledge that employees find useful on the job and enables them to achieve better performance.[35] *More* knowledge isn't necessarily *better* knowledge. Information overload needs to be avoided by designing the system to capture only pertinent information and then organizing it so it can be quickly accessed by the people whom it can help. Royal Bank of Canada, for instance, has

knowledge management   *The process of organizing and distributing an organization's collective wisdom so the right information gets to the right people at the right time.*

created a KM system with customized e-mail distribution lists carefully broken down by employees' specialty, title, and area of interest; set aside a dedicated site on the company's intranet that serves as a central information repository; and created separate in-house Web sites featuring "lessons learned" summaries, where employees with various expertise can share new information with others.[36]

Choice of Communication Channel

Neal L. Patterson, CEO at medical-software maker Cerner Corp., likes e-mail. Maybe too much so. Upset with his staff's work ethic, he recently sent a seething e-mail to his firm's 400 managers.[37] Here are some of that e-mail's highlights:

"Hell will freeze over before this CEO implements ANOTHER EMPLOYEE benefit in this Culture . . . We are getting less than 40 hours of work from a large number of our Kansas City-based employees. The parking lot is sparsely used at 8 A.M.; likewise at 5 P.M. As managers—you either do not know what your EMPLOYEES are doing; or YOU do not CARE . . . You have a problem and you will fix it or I will replace you . . . What you are doing, as managers, with this company makes me SICK."

Patterson's e-mail additionally suggested that managers schedule meetings at 7 A.M., 6 P.M., and Saturday mornings; promised a staff reduction of 5 percent and institution of a time-clock system; and Patterson's intention to charge unapproved absences to employees' vacation time.

Within hours of this e-mail, copies of it had made its way onto a Yahoo! Web site. And within 3 days, Cerner's stock price had plummeted 22 percent. Although one can argue about whether such harsh criticism should be communicated at all, one thing is certainly clear: Patterson erred by selecting the wrong channel for his message. Such an emotional and sensitive message would likely have been better received in a face-to-face meeting.

Why do people choose one channel of communication over another—for instance, a phone call instead of a face-to-face talk? Is there any general insight we might be able to provide regarding choice of communication channel? The answer to the latter question is a qualified "Yes." A model of media richness has been developed to explain channel selection among managers.[38]

Research has found that channels differ in their capacity to convey information. Some are rich in that they have the ability to (1) handle multiple cues simultaneously, (2) facilitate rapid feedback, and (3) be very personal. Others are lean in that they score low on these three factors. As Exhibit 11-6 illustrates, face-to-face conversation scores highest in terms of **channel richness** because it provides for the maximum amount of information to be transmitted during a communication episode. That is, it offers multiple information cues (words, postures, facial expressions, gestures, intonations), immediate feedback (both verbal and nonverbal), and the personal touch of "being there." Impersonal written media such as formal reports and bulletins rate lowest in richness.

The choice of one channel over another depends on whether the message is routine or nonroutine. The former types of messages tend to be straightforward and have a minimum of ambiguity. The latter are likely to be complicated and have the potential for misunderstanding. Managers can communicate routine messages efficiently through channels that are lower in richness. However, they can communicate nonroutine messages effectively only by selecting rich channels. Referring back to the Cerner Corp. example, it appears that Neal Patterson's problem was using a channel relatively low in richness (e-mail) to convey a message that, because of its nonroutine nature and complexity, should have been conveyed using a rich communication medium.

Exhibit **11-6**	Information Richness of Communication Channels

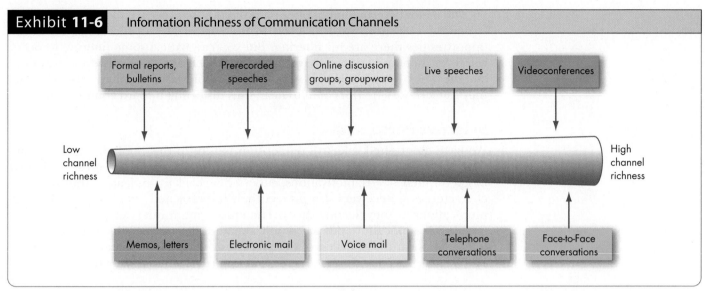

Source: Based on R. H. Lengel and R. L. Daft, "The Selection of Communication Media as an Executive Skill," *Academy of Management Executive,* August 1988, pp. 225–32; and R. L. Daft and R. H. Lengel, "Organizational Information Requirements, Media Richness, and Structural Design," *Managerial Science,* May 1996, pp. 554–72. Reproduced from R. L. Daft and R. A. Noe, *Organizational Behavior,* (Fort Worth, TX: Harcourt, 2001), p. 311.

Evidence indicates that high-performing managers tend to be more media-sensitive than low-performing managers.[39] That is, they're better able to match appropriate media richness with the ambiguity involved in the communication.

The media richness model is consistent with organizational trends and practices during the past decade. It is not just coincidence that more and more senior managers have been using meetings to facilitate communication and regularly leaving the isolated sanctuary of their executive offices to manage by walking around. These executives are relying on richer channels of communication to transmit the more ambiguous messages they need to convey. The past decade has been characterized by organizations closing facilities, imposing large layoffs, restructuring, merging, consolidating, and introducing new products and services at an accelerated pace—all nonroutine messages high in ambiguity and requiring the use of channels that can convey a large amount of information. It is not surprising, therefore, to see the most effective managers expanding their use of rich channels.

Barriers to Effective Communication

A number of barriers can retard or distort effective communication. In this section, we highlight the more important of these barriers.

Filtering

Filtering refers to a sender's purposely manipulating information so it will be seen more favorably by the receiver. For example, when a manager tells his boss what he feels his boss wants to hear, he is filtering information.

---

channel richness *The amount of information that can be transmitted during a communication episode.*

filtering *A sender's manipulation of information so that it will be seen more favorably by the receiver.*

The major determinant of filtering is the number of levels in an organization's structure. The more vertical levels in the organization's hierarchy, the more opportunities there are for filtering. But you can expect some filtering to occur wherever there are status differences. Factors such as fear of conveying bad news and the desire to please one's boss often lead employees to tell their superiors what they think those superiors want to hear, thus distorting upward communications.

Selective Perception

We have mentioned selective perception before in this book. It appears again here because the receivers in the communication process selectively see and hear based on their needs, motivations, experience, background, and other personal characteristics. Receivers also project their interests and expectations into communications as they decode them. The employment interviewer who expects a female job applicant to put her family ahead of her career is likely to see that in female applicants, regardless of whether the applicants feel that way or not. As we said in Chapter 5, we don't see reality; we interpret what we see and call it reality.

Information Overload

Individuals have a finite capacity for processing data. When the information we have to work with exceeds our processing capacity, the result is **information overload**. And with e-mails, instant messaging, phone calls, faxes, meetings, and the need to keep current in one's field, the potential for today's managers and professionals to suffer from information overload is high.

What happens when individuals have more information than they can sort out and use? They tend to select out, ignore, pass over, or forget information. Or they may put off further processing until the overload situation is over. Regardless, the result is lost information and less effective communication.

Emotions

How the receiver feels at the time of receipt of a communication will influence how he or she interprets it. The same message received when you're angry or distraught is often interpreted differently from when you're happy. Extreme emotions such as jubilation or depression are most likely to hinder effective communication. In such instances, we are most prone to disregard our rational and objective thinking processes and substitute emotional judgments.

Language

Words mean different things to different people. Age, education, and cultural background are three of the more obvious variables that influence the language a person uses and the definitions he or she gives to words.

In an organization, employees usually come from diverse backgrounds. Further, the grouping of employees into departments creates specialists who develop their own "buzzwords," or technical jargon. In large organizations, members are also frequently widely dispersed geographically—even operating in different countries—and individuals in each locale will use terms and phrases that are unique to their area. The existence of vertical levels can also cause language problems. For instance, differences in meaning with regard to words such as *incentives* and *quotas* have been found at different levels in management. Top managers often speak about the need for incentives and quotas, yet these terms imply manipulation and create resentment among many lower managers.

The point is that although you and I probably speak a common language—English—our use of that language is far from uniform. If we knew how each of us modified the language, communication difficulties would be minimized.

The problem is that members in an organization usually don't know how those with whom they interact have modified the language. Senders tend to assume that the words and terms they use mean the same to the receiver as they do to them. This assumption is often incorrect.

Communication Apprehension

Another major barrier to effective communication is that some people—an estimated 5 to 20 percent of the population[40]—suffer from debilitating **communication apprehension** or anxiety. Although lots of people dread speaking in front of a group, communication apprehension is a more serious problem because it affects a whole category of communication techniques. People who suffer from it experience undue tension and anxiety in oral communication, written communication, or both.[41] For example, oral apprehensives may find it extremely difficult to talk with others face-to-face or become extremely anxious when they have to use the telephone. As a result, they may rely on memos or faxes to convey messages when a phone call would be not only faster but more appropriate.

Studies demonstrate that oral-communication apprehensives avoid situations that require them to engage in oral communication.[42] We should expect to find some self-selection in jobs so that such individuals don't take positions, such as teacher, for which oral communication is a dominant requirement.[43] But almost all jobs require some oral communication. And of greater concern is the evidence that high-oral-communication apprehensives distort the communication

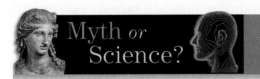

Myth or Science? "People Are Good at Catching Liars at Work"

This statement is essentially false. The core purpose of communication in the workplace may be to convey business-related information. However, the workplace also is a place where we communicate in order to manage impressions others form of us. Some of this impression management is unintentional and harmless (for example, complimenting your boss on his clothing). However, sometimes people manage impressions through outright lies, like making up an excuse for missing work and failing to make a deadline.

One of the reasons that people lie, in the workplace and otherwise, is that it's hard to catch. Although most of us think we're good at detecting a lie, research shows that most people perform no better than chance at detecting whether someone is lying or telling the truth.

Lying is also hard to prove. For example, research shows that negotiators often lie during negotiations. A seller may claim to have another buyer waiting in the wings when in fact no such buyer is out there. Research shows that this "cheap talk" can be an effective tactic in negotiation.

Consider Richard Scrushy, former CEO of HealthSouth, who was acquitted on 36 charges of false reporting, conspiracy, fraud, and money laundering, even though 15 people who worked for Scrushy told the jury that he lied about HealthSouth's earnings in order to inflate his own compensation (which was tied to HealthSouth's performance). Clearly, it was hard for the jury to separate out who was telling the truth. In some cases, we may never know the truth.

The point? Don't believe everything you hear, and don't place too much weight on your ability to catch a liar based just on your intuition. When someone makes a claim that's reasonable to doubt, ask her to back it up with evidence. ■

Sources: N. I. Etcoff, P. Ekman, J. J. Magee, and N. G. Franks, "Lie Detection and Language Comprehension," *Nature*, May 2000 145, p. 139; R. Croson, T. Boles and J. K. Murnighan, "Cheap Talk in Bargaining Experiments: Lying and Threats in Ultimatum Games," *Journal of Economic Behavior & Organization* 51 (2003), pp. 143–59; "Cases of Scrushy's Aides Still Pending," *The Los Angeles Times*, July 5, 2005, www.latimes.com.

information overload *A condition in which information inflow exceeds an individual's processing capacity.*

communication apprehension *Undue tension and anxiety about oral communication, written communication, or both.*

demands of their jobs in order to minimize the need for communication.[44] So we need to be aware that there is a set of people in organizations who severely limit their oral communication and rationalize this practice by telling themselves that more communication isn't necessary for them to do their job effectively.

Current Issues in Communication

In this section, we discuss four current issues related to communication in organizations: Why do men and women often have difficulty communicating with each other? What role does silence play in communication? What are the implications of the "politically correct" movement on communications in organizations? And how can individuals improve their cross-cultural communications?

Communication Barriers Between Women and Men

The classic studies by Deborah Tannen provide us with some important insights into the differences between men and women in terms of their conversational styles.[45] In particular, Tannen has been able to explain why gender often creates oral communication barriers. The essence of Tannen's research is that men use talk to emphasize status, whereas women use it to create connection. Her conclusion, of course, doesn't apply to *every* man or *every* woman. As she puts it, her generalization means "a larger percentage of women or men *as a group* talk in a particular way, or individual women and men *are more likely* to talk one way or the other."[46]

Tannen states that communication is a continual balancing act, juggling the conflicting needs for intimacy and independence. Intimacy emphasizes closeness and commonalities. Independence emphasizes separateness and differences. But here's the kick: Women speak and hear a language of connection and intimacy; men speak and hear a language of status, power, and independence. So, for many men, conversations are primarily a means to preserve independence and maintain status in a hierarchical social order. For many women, conversations are negotiations for closeness in which people try to seek and give confirmation and support. A few examples will illustrate Tannen's thesis.

Men frequently complain that women talk on and on about their problems. Women criticize men for not listening. What's happening is that when men hear a problem, they frequently assert their desire for independence and control by offering solutions. Many women, on the other hand, view telling a problem as a means to promote closeness. The women present the problem to gain support and connection, not to get the man's advice. Mutual understanding is symmetrical. But giving advice is asymmetrical—it sets up the advice giver as more knowledgeable, more reasonable, and more in control. This contributes to distancing men and women in their efforts to communicate.

Men are often more direct than women in conversation. A man might say, "I think you're wrong on that point." A woman might say, "Have you looked at the marketing department's research report on that point?" (the implication being that the report will show the error). Men frequently see female indirectness as "covert" or "sneaky," but women are not as concerned as men with the status and one-upmanship that directness often creates.

Women tend to be less boastful than men.[47] They often downplay their authority or accomplishments to avoid appearing as braggarts and to take the other person's feelings into account. However, men can frequently misinterpret this and incorrectly conclude that a woman is less confident and competent than she really is.

Research indicates that most women use language to create connection while most men use language to emphasize status, power, and independence. These differences in conversational styles may create oral communication barriers between men and women. The businesswomen communicating in this photo illustrate that women generally speak and hear a language of intimacy. But for men, conversations are a way to preserve their independence.

Finally, men often criticize women for seeming to apologize all the time. Women do apologize more than men.[48] Men tend to see the phrase "I'm sorry" as a weakness because they interpret the phrase to mean the woman is accepting blame, when he knows she's not to blame. The woman also knows she's not to blame. The problem is that women frequently use "I'm sorry" to express regret and restore balance to a conversation: "I know you must feel bad about this; I do, too." For many women, "I'm sorry" is an expression of understanding and caring about the other person's feelings rather than an apology.

Silence as Communication

Sherlock Holmes once solved a murder mystery based not on what happened but on what *didn't* happen. Holmes remarked to his assistant, Dr. Watson, about "the curious incident of the dog in the nighttime." Watson, surprised, responds, "But the dog did nothing in the nighttime." To which Holmes replied, "That was the curious incident." Holmes concluded the crime had to be committed by someone with whom the dog was familiar because the watchdog didn't bark.

The dog that didn't bark in the night is often used as a metaphor for an event that is significant by reason of its absence. That story is also an excellent illustration of the importance of silence in communication. Silence—defined here as an absence of speech or noise—has been generally ignored as a form of communication in OB because it represents inaction or nonbehavior. But it's not necessarily inaction. Nor is silence, as many believe, a failure to communicate. It can, in fact, be a powerful form of communication.[49] It can mean someone is thinking or contemplating a response to a question. It can mean a person is anxious and fearful of speaking. It can signal agreement, dissent, frustration, or anger.

In terms of OB, we can see several links between silence and work-related behavior. For instance, silence is a critical element of groupthink, in which it implies agreement with the majority. It can be a way for employees to express dissatisfaction, as when they "suffer in silence." It can be a sign that someone is upset, as when a typically talkative person suddenly says nothing—"What's the matter with him? Is he all right?" It's a powerful tool used by managers to signal disfavor by shunning or ignoring employees with "silent insults." And, of course, it's a crucial element of group decision making, allowing individuals to think over and contemplate what others have said.

Failing to pay close attention to the silent portion of a conversation can result in missing a vital part of the message. Astute communicators watch for gaps, pauses, and hesitations. They hear and interpret silence. They treat pauses, for instance, as analogous to a flashing yellow light at an intersection—they pay attention to what comes next. Is the person thinking, deciding how to frame an answer? Is the person suffering from communication apprehension? Sometimes the real message in a communication is buried in the silence.

"Politically Correct" Communication

What words do you use to describe a colleague who is wheelchair-bound? What terms do you use in addressing a female customer? How do you communicate with a brand-new client who is not like you? Your answers can mean the difference between losing a client, an employee, a lawsuit, a harassment claim, or a job.[50]

Most of us are acutely aware of how our vocabulary has been modified to reflect political correctness. For instance, most of us have cleansed the words *handicapped, blind,* and *elderly* from our vocabulary—and replaced them with terms like *physically challenged, visually impaired,* and *senior.* The *Los Angeles Times,* for instance, allows its journalists to use the term *old age* but cautions that the onset of old age varies from "person to person," so a group of 75-year-olds aren't necessarily all old.[51]

We must be sensitive to others' feelings. Certain words can and do stereotype, intimidate, and insult individuals. In an increasingly diverse workforce, we must be sensitive to how words might offend others. But there's a downside to political correctness. It can complicate our vocabulary, making it more difficult for people to communicate. To illustrate, you probably know what these three terms mean: *garbage, quotas,* and *women.* But each of these words also has been found to offend one or more groups. They've been replaced with terms like *postconsumer waste materials, educational equity,* and *people of gender.* The problem is that this latter group of terms is much less likely to convey a uniform message than the words they replaced.

Words are the primary means by which people communicate. When we eliminate words from use because they're politically incorrect, we reduce our options for conveying messages in the clearest and most accurate form. For the most part, the larger the vocabulary used by a sender and a receiver, the greater the opportunity to accurately transmit messages. By removing certain words from our vocabulary, we make it harder to communicate accurately. When we further replace these words with new terms whose meanings are less well understood, we have reduced the likelihood that our messages will be received as we had intended them.

We must be sensitive to how our choice of words might offend others. But we also have to be careful not to sanitize our language to the point at which it clearly restricts clarity of communication. There is no simple solution to this dilemma. However, you should be aware of the trade-offs and the need to find a proper balance.

Exhibit 11-7

THE FAR SIDE® BY GARY LARSON

"Well, actually, Doreen, I rather resent being called a 'swamp thing.' ... I prefer the term 'wetlands-challenged-mutant.'"

Cross-Cultural Communication

Effective communication is difficult under the best of conditions. Cross-cultural factors clearly create the potential for increased communication problems. This is illustrated in Exhibit 11-8. A gesture that is well understood and acceptable in one culture can be meaningless or lewd in another.[52]

Cultural Barriers One author has identified four specific problems related to language difficulties in cross-cultural communications.[53]

First, there are *barriers caused by semantics.* As we've noted previously, words mean different things to different people. This is particularly true for people from different national cultures. Some words, for instance, don't translate between cultures. Understanding the word *sisu* will help you in communicating with people from Finland, but this word is untranslatable into English. It means something akin to "guts" or "dogged persistence." Similarly, the new capitalists in Russia may have difficulty communicating with their British or Canadian counterparts because English terms such as *efficiency, free market,* and *regulation* are not directly translatable into Russian.

Second, there are *barriers caused by word connotations.* Words imply different things in different languages. Negotiations between Americans and Japanese executives, for instance, are made more difficult because the Japanese word *hai* translates as "yes," but its connotation may be "yes, I'm listening," rather than "yes, I agree."

Exhibit **11-8**	Hand Gestures Mean Different Things in Different Countries

The A-OK Sign

In the United States, this is just a friendly sign for "All right!" or "Good going." In Australia and Islamic countries, it is equivalent to what generations of high school students know as "flipping the bird."

The "Hook'em Horns" Sign

This sign encourages University of Texas athletes, and it's a good luck gesture in Brazil and Venezuela. In parts of Africa it is a curse. In Italy, it is signaling to another that "your spouse is being unfaithful."

"V" for Victory Sign

In many parts of the world, this means "victory" or "peace." In England, if the palm and fingers face inward, it means "Up yours!" especially if executed with an upward jerk of the fingers.

Finger-Beckoning Sign

This sign means "come here" in the United States. In Malaysia, it is used only for calling animals. In Indonesia and Australia, it is used for beckoning "ladies of the night."

Source: "What's A-O-K in the U.S.A. Is Lewd and Worthless Beyond," *New York Times,* August 18, 1996, p. E7. From Roger E. Axtell, *GESTURES: The Do's and Taboos of Body Language Around the World.* Copyright © 1991. This material is used by permission of John Wiley & Sons, Inc.

Third are *barriers caused by tone differences*. In some cultures, language is formal, in others it's informal. In some cultures, the tone changes depending on the context: People speak differently at home, in social situations, and at work. Using a personal, informal style in a situation in which a more formal style is expected can be embarrassing and off-putting.

Fourth, there are *barriers caused by differences among perceptions*. People who speak different languages actually view the world in different ways. Eskimos perceive snow differently because they have many words for it. Thais perceive "no" differently than do Americans because the former have no such word in their vocabulary.

Cultural Context   A better understanding of these cultural barriers and their implications for communicating across cultures can be achieved by considering the concepts of high- and low-context cultures.[54]

Cultures tend to differ in the importance to which context influences the meaning that individuals take from what is actually said or written in light of who the other person is. Countries like China, Korea, Japan, and Vietnam are **high-context cultures**. They rely heavily on nonverbal and subtle situational cues when communicating with others. What is *not* said may be more significant than what *is* said. A person's official status, place in society, and reputation carry considerable weight in communications. In contrast, people from Europe and North America reflect their **low-context cultures**. They rely essentially on words to convey meaning. Body language or formal titles are secondary to spoken and written words (see Exhibit 11-9).

What do these contextual differences mean in terms of communication? Actually, quite a lot. Communication in high-context cultures implies considerably more trust by both parties. What may appear, to an outsider, as casual and insignificant conversation is important because it reflects the desire to build a relationship and create trust. Oral agreements imply strong commitments in high-context cultures. And who you are—your age, seniority, rank in the organization—is highly valued and heavily influences your credibility. But in low-context cultures, enforceable contracts will tend to be in writing, precisely worded, and highly legalistic. Similarly, low-context cultures value directness. Managers are expected to be explicit and precise in conveying intended meaning. It's quite different in high-context cultures, in which managers tend to "make suggestions" rather than give orders.

A Cultural Guide   When communicating with people from a different culture, what can you do to reduce misperceptions, misinterpretations, and misevaluations? You can begin by trying to assess the cultural context. You're likely to have fewer difficulties if people come from a similar cultural context to you. In addition, the following four rules can be helpful.[55]

1. *Assume differences until similarity is proven.* Most of us assume that others are more similar to us than they actually are. But people from different countries often are very different from us. So you are far less likely to make an error if you assume others are different from you rather than assuming similarity until difference is proven.

2. *Emphasize description rather than interpretation or evaluation.* Interpreting or evaluating what someone has said or done, in contrast to description, is based more on the observer's culture and background than on the observed situation. As a result, delay judgment until you've had sufficient time to observe and interpret the situation from the differing perspectives of all the cultures involved.

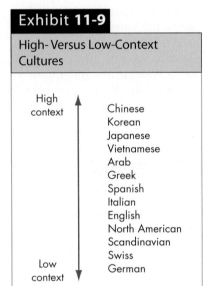

Exhibit 11-9

High- Versus Low-Context Cultures

High context

Chinese
Korean
Japanese
Vietnamese
Arab
Greek
Spanish
Italian
English
North American
Scandinavian
Swiss
German

Low context

"Are East Asians More Responsive to Indirect Communication?"

This statement is mostly true. Because people from East Asia (for example, Japan, China, Korea) place a high value on interpersonal harmony, they tend to communicate less directly than Americans. For example, assume you are responsible for creating a marketing plan. An Asian colleague might respond to your proposal with, "The strategic rationale underlying your marketing plan needs some tightening, and the writing can be rough in places, but otherwise you have some very interesting ideas." It is possible that she is telling you, in an indirect way, that your proposal is of limited value.[56] Americans, however, are more direct in their communications. So an American colleague may respond with, "This marketing plan is way off base. It seems like it was thrown together at the last minute. Please get me a revision by the end of the day today."

What explains these different communication techniques? In the workplace, Americans are generally guided by norms of short-term task accomplishment, and so they believe communication should be designed to get the job at hand done as quickly and as effectively as possible. East Asians, however, are more likely to communicate indirectly due to their desire to foster long-term relationships that are polite and respectful.[57]

So how can managers reduce miscommunication between the two cultures? Americans need to be sensitive to the fact that seemingly "soft" statements from East Asians may contain stronger messages. East Asians need to realize that the blunt communication styles of Americans are generally not personal or intended as a threat to their status or position. ■

3. *Practice empathy.* Before sending a message, put yourself in the recipient's shoes. What are his or her values, experiences, and frames of reference? What do you know about his or her education, upbringing, and background that can give you added insight? Try to see the other person as he or she really is.

4. *Treat your interpretations as a working hypothesis.* Once you've developed an explanation for a new situation or think you empathize with someone from a foreign culture, treat your interpretation as a hypothesis that needs further testing rather than as a certainty. Carefully assess the feedback provided by recipients to see if it confirms your hypothesis. For important decisions or communiqués, you can also check with other foreign and home-country colleagues to make sure that your interpretations are on target.

In this chapter, you have learned a lot about how communication plays out in the workplace. Possessing good listening skills is also critical to effective communication. See the Self-Assessment feature below, which will provide you with some insights into your listening skills.

HOW GOOD ARE MY LISTENING SKILLS?

In the Self-Assessment Library (available on CD, online, and in print), take assessment II.A.2 (How Good Are My Listening Skills?) and answer the following questions.

1. *How did you score relative to your classmates?*
2. *How might you improve your listening skills?*

high-context cultures *Cultures that rely heavily on nonverbal and subtle situational cues in communication.*

low-context cultures *Cultures that rely heavily on words to convey meaning in communication.*

Lost in Translation?

IN GLOBAL COMMERCE, LANGUAGE CAN BE A BAR-
rier to conducting business effectively. Many U.S. companies
have overseas parents, including DaimlerChrysler AG,
Bertelsmann, Diageo PLC, and Anglo-Dutch Unilever PLC. Similarly, U.S. companies
have an overseas presence—for example, Ford has manufacturing plants in Belgium,
Germany, Spain, Sweden, Turkey, and the United Kingdom. To make matters more complicated, as a result of mergers and acquisitions, companies are often owned by multiple
overseas parents, creating an even greater strain on communication. Although English is
the dominant language at many multinational companies, failing to speak a host country's
language can make it tougher for managers to do their jobs well, especially if they are mis-
interpreted or misinterpret what others are saying. Such communication problems make
it tougher to conduct business effectively and efficiently, and may result in lost business
opportunities.

To avoid communication problems, many companies require their managers to learn the
local language. For example, German-based Siemens requires its managers to learn the language of their host country. Ernst Behrens, the head of Siemens's China operations, learned
to speak Mandarin fluently. Robert Kimmett, a former Siemens's board member, believes
that learning a host country's language gives managers "a better grasp of what is going on
inside a company . . . not just the facts and figures but also texture and nuance."

However, learning a foreign language can be difficult for managers. The difficulty for
North Americans in learning a foreign language is often deepened when the language is
Eastern, such as Japanese or Chinese Mandarin, because the language is so different. To
compensate, U.S. managers sometimes rely solely on body language and facial expressions
to communicate. The problem? That there are cultural differences in these nonverbal
forms of communication that may result in serious misunderstandings. To avoid this pit-
fall, one solution would be for managers to familiarize themselves with their host country's
culture.

Source: Based on K. Kanhold, D. Bilefsky, M. Karnitschnig, and G. Parker, "Lost in Translation? Managers at Multinationals May Miss
the Job's Nuances if They Speak Only English," *The Wall Street Journal,* May 18, 2004, p. B.1.

Summary and Implications for Managers

A careful review of this chapter finds a common theme regarding the relationship between communication and employee satisfaction: the less the uncertainty, the greater the satisfaction. Distortions, ambiguities, and incongruities in
communications all increase uncertainty and, hence, they have a negative
impact on satisfaction.[58]

The less distortion that occurs in communication, the more that goals, feedback, and other management messages to employees will be received as they
were intended.[59] This, in turn, should reduce ambiguities and clarify the
group's task. Extensive use of vertical, lateral, and informal channels will
increase communication flow, reduce uncertainty, and improve group performance and satisfaction. We should also expect incongruities between verbal
and nonverbal communiqués to increase uncertainty and to reduce satisfaction.

Findings in the chapter further suggest that the goal of perfect communication is unattainable. Yet, there is evidence that demonstrates a positive relationship between effective communication (which includes factors such as perceived
trust, perceived accuracy, desire for interaction, top-management receptiveness,

and upward information requirements) and worker productivity.[60] Choosing the correct channel, being an effective listener, and using feedback may, therefore, make for more effective communication. But the human factor generates distortions that can never be fully eliminated. The communication process represents an exchange of messages, but the outcome is meanings that may or may not approximate those that the sender intended. Whatever the sender's expectations, the decoded message in the mind of the receiver represents his or her reality. And it is this "reality" that will determine performance, along with the individual's level of motivation and degree of satisfaction. The issue of motivation is critical, so we should briefly review how communication is central in determining an individual's degree of motivation.

You will remember from expectancy theory (see Chapter 6) that the degree of effort an individual exerts depends on his or her perception of the effort–performance, performance–reward, and reward–goal satisfaction links. If individuals are not given the data necessary to make the perceived probability of these links high, motivation will suffer. If rewards are not made clear, if the criteria for determining and measuring performance are ambiguous, or if individuals are not relatively certain that their effort will lead to satisfactory performance, then effort will be reduced. So communication plays a significant role in determining the level of employee motivation.

A final implication from the communication literature relates to predicting turnover. The use of realistic job previews acts as a communication device for clarifying role expectations. Employees who have been exposed to a realistic job preview have more accurate information about that job. Comparisons of turnover rates between organizations that use the realistic job preview versus either no preview or presentation of only positive job information show that those not using the realistic preview have, on average, almost 29 percent higher turnover.[61] This makes a strong case for managers to convey honest and accurate information about a job to applicants during the recruiting and selection process.

Open-Book Management Improves the Bottom Line

Open-book management (OBM) seeks to get every employee to think and behave like an owner.[62] It throws out the notion that bosses run things and employees do what they're told. In the open-book approach, employees are given the information that historically was strictly kept within the management ranks.

There are three key elements to any OBM program. First, management opens the company's books and shares detailed financial and operating information with employees. If employees don't know how the company makes money, how can they be expected to make the firm more successful? Second, employees need to be taught to understand the company's financial statements. This means management must provide employees with a "basic course" in how to read and interpret income statements, balance sheets, and cash flow statements. And third, management needs to show employees how their work influences financial results. Showing employees the impact of their jobs on the bottom line makes financial-statement analysis relevant.

Who is using OBM? More than 3,500 organizations, including Wal-Mart, Allstate Insurance, Amoco Canada, Rhino Foods, and Sprint's Government Systems division.

Why should it work? Access to detailed financial information, and the ability to understand that information, makes employees think like owners. And this leads to them making decisions that are best for the organization, not just for themselves.

Does it work? Most firms that have introduced OBM offer evidence that it has significantly helped the business. For instance, Springfield Remanufacturing was losing $61,000 on sales of $16 million. Management attributes much of the company's current success—profits of $12 million a year on sales of $160 million—to OBM. Similarly, Allstate's Business Insurance Group used OBM to boost return-on-equity from 2.9 percent to 16.5 percent in just 3 years.

The owners of Optics 1 Inc., an optical-engineering company in southern California with 23 employees and sales of less than $10 million a year, implemented an OBM program. After a short time, the program was discontinued. Said one of the co-owners, "Employees used the information against me. When we made a profit, they demanded bigger bonuses and new computers. When I used profits to finance a new product line, everybody said, 'That's nice, but what's in it for me?' . . . If your employees misinterpret financial information, it's more damaging than their not having access at all. I gave them general and administrative rates. Next thing I knew they were backing out everyone's salaries, and I'd hear, 'You're paying that guy $86,000? I contribute more.' "

As the preceding illustrates, part of the downside to OBM is that employees may misuse or misinterpret the information they get against management, especially as it relates to the perceived fairness of their compensation.[63] Another potential problem is leaking of confidential information to competitors. In the hands of the competition, detailed information on the company's operations and financial position may undermine a firm's competitive advantage.

When OBM succeeds, two factors seem to exist. First, the organization or unit in which it's implemented tends to be small. It's a lot easier to introduce OBM in a small, start-up company than in a large, geographically dispersed company that has operated for years with closed books and little employee involvement. Second, there needs to be a mutually trusting relationship between management and workers. In organizational cultures in which management doesn't trust employees to act selflessly or in which managers and accountants have been trained to keep information under lock and key, OBM isn't likely to work. Nor will it succeed when employees believe any new change program is only likely to further manipulate or exploit them for management's advantage.

Questions for Review

1. Describe the functions that communication provides within a group or organization. Give an example of each.

2. Contrast encoding and decoding.

3. Contrast downward with upward communication.

4. What is nonverbal communication? Does it aid or hinder verbal communication?

5. What are the advantages and disadvantages of e-mail? Of instant messaging?

6. What are knowledge-management systems? How do they affect communication?

7. How do the communication styles of men and women differ?

8. What does the phrase "sometimes the real message in a communication is buried in the silence" mean?

9. Describe how political correctness can hinder effective communication.

10. Contrast high- and low-context cultures. What do these differences mean for communication?

Questions for Critical Thinking

1. "Ineffective communication is the fault of the sender." Do you agree or disagree? Discuss.

2. What can you do to improve the likelihood that your communiqués will be received and understood as you intend?

3. How might managers use the grapevine for their benefit?

4. Using the concept of channel richness, give examples of messages best conveyed by e-mail, by face-to-face communication, and on the company bulletin board.

5. "Most people are poor listeners." Do you agree or disagree. Defend your position.

Team Exercise

AN ABSENCE OF NONVERBAL COMMUNICATION

This exercise will help you to see the value of nonverbal communication to interpersonal relations.

1. The class is to split up into pairs (Party A and Party B).

2. Party A is to select a topic from the following list:
   (a) Managing in the Middle East is significantly different from managing in North America.
   (b) Employee turnover in an organization can be functional.
   (c) Some conflict in an organization is good.
   (d) Whistle-blowers do more harm than good for an organization.
   (e) An employer has a responsibility to provide every employee with an interesting and challenging job.
   (f) Everyone should register to vote.
   (g) Organizations should require all employees to undergo regular drug tests.
   (h) Individuals who have majored in business or economics make better employees than those who have majored in history or English.
   (i) The place where you get your college degree is more important in determining your career success than what you learn while you're there.
   (j) It's unethical for a manager to purposely distort communications to get a favorable outcome.

3. Party B is to choose a position on this topic (for example, arguing *against* the view that "some conflict in an organization is good"). Party A now must automatically take the opposite position.

4. The two parties have 10 minutes in which to debate their topic. The catch is that the individuals can only communicate verbally. They may *not* use gestures, facial movements, body movements, or any other nonverbal communication. It may help for each party to sit on their hands to remind them of their restrictions and to maintain an expressionless look.

5. After the debate is over, form groups of six to eight and spend 15 minutes discussing the following:
   (a) How effective was communication during these debates?
   (b) What barriers to communication existed?
   (c) What purposes does nonverbal communication serve?
   (d) Relate the lessons learned in this exercise to problems that might occur when communicating on the telephone or through e-mail.

Ethical Dilemma

DEFINING THE BOUNDARIES OF TECHNOLOGY

You work for a company that has no specific policies regarding non-work-related uses of computers and the Internet. They also have no electronic monitoring devices to determine what employees are doing on their computers. Are any of the following actions unethical? Explain your position on each:

a. Using the company's e-mail system for personal reasons during the workday.

b. Playing computer games during the workday.

c. Using your office computer to do Internet shopping during the workday.

d. Looking for a mate on an Internet dating-service Web site during the workday.

e. Visiting "adult" Web sites on your office computer during the workday.

f. All of the above activities conducted before or after normal work hours.

g. For telecommuters working from home, using a computer and Internet-access line paid for by your employer to visit Internet shopping or dating-service sites during normal working hours.

Case Incident 1

JAMES W. CARUSO HAS COMMUNICATION PROBLEMS

James W. Caruso only has four employees at his public relations firm—MediaFirst PR-Atlanta. But he seems to have done a pretty good job of alienating them.

According to his employees, Caruso, 47, is a brilliant guy who has a lot to learn in terms of being a better communicator. His communication style appears to be a regular source of conflict in his firm. Caruso admits he has a problem. "I'm probably not as verbally reinforcing [as I could be] when someone is doing a good job. I'm a very self-confident person. I don't need to be told I'm doing a good job—but there are people who do."

Caruso's employees had no problem listing things that he does that bother them. He doesn't meet deadlines; he does a poor job of communicating with clients (which often puts the employees in an uncomfortable position);

he doesn't listen fully to employee ideas before dismissing them; his voice tone is frequently condescending; and he's often quick to criticize employees and stingy with praise.

Questions

1. A lot of bosses are accused of being "poor communicators." Why do you think this is?

2. What does this case suggest regarding the relationship between reinforcement theory and communication?

3. *What,* specifically, do you think Caruso needs to do to improve his communication skills?

4. Assuming Caruso wants to improve, *how* would you suggest he go about learning to be a better communicator?

Source: This case is based on N. L. Torres, "Playing Well With Others," *Entrepreneur,* February 2003, p. 30.

Case Incident 2

THE BUSINESS OF BLOGS

As of July 2005 there were 9 million blogs on the Internet, with, estimates say, 40,000 new blogs appearing each day. What are blogs? Blogs are short for "Web logs" You can think of them as online diaries. The content of blogs ranges from daily business happenings and news events to a recap of the homerun that someone's niece hit during a softball game—in other words anyone with a computer and an Internet connection can post a blog. Blogs can include photos, audio clips, and video clips. And blogs are dynamic in nature, changing each day with every addi-

tional posting (For example, check out one popular blogging site, www.blogger.com).

Some analysts believe that blogs are the biggest innovation in communication since the Internet itself in that they are taking power away from the mass media, which traditionally has decided on what news is worthy of reporting. However, a Pew Research Center survey suggests that many people have yet to catch on—only 27 percent of Internet users in America read blogs—though this number is expected to increase dramatically.

The implications of blogs for businesses are numerous. On the positive side, corporations such as IBM can monitor blogs to see what people are saying about the company. Such blogs can be posted by employees, customers, or the general public. Movie studios can track blogs to determine which films are generating positive public opinion and which are not. And advertisers can use blogs to evaluate the success of advertising campaigns. Says Jeff Weiner, senior vice president of Yahoo!, "I'm amazed people don't get it yet. Never in the history of market research has there been a tool like this." Blogs present an unobtrusive and inexpensive means of collecting data. By simply monitoring blogs, companies can determine what products people are talking about.

Blogs are a valuable business tool, but they have their downsides. Many employees use blogs to post proprietary company information or to complain about company practices. Hundreds, if not thousands, of individuals external to the company can read private company information on a blog if it is divulged, regardless of whether the information is credible.

But companies are fighting back. Mark Jen, once a programmer at Google, found this out. In January of 2005, Jen posted a blog complaining that Google's health plan was worse than that of Microsoft's, his former employer. He also wrote that one of Google's touted perks, free dinner prepared daily by an in-house chef, was a Google ploy to get its employees to work past dinner. Google fired Jen shortly after reading his blog. A barrage of blogs in response to Jen's firing led Google to publicly comment on its blogging policy. A spokesperson for the company stated that if the information is such that you wouldn't e-mail it to strangers, don't blog it. Jen says that he understands Google's decision and should have been more sensitive to the company's goals. Fortunately for Jen, his 15 minutes of fame landed him a job at Plaxo, an Internet contact-management company. His job at Plaxo? Coordinating blogging efforts to promote the company.

Blogs are likely to change the way that business information, as well as information in general, is gathered and disseminated. In contrast to the contents of chat rooms and e-mails, which tend to be temporary, a blog can last for as long as the person who posted it desires. Those that blast a company for mistreatment may spread like a wildfire, which leaves companies in a sticky position. What once was thought to be private information may not be so private anymore.

Questions

1. What aspects of the communication process are blogs most likely to influence and how?

2. Although the grapevine typically is thought of as occurring within a given organization, blogging is a form of gossip that can reach beyond an organization's borders. How might blogging change the way that companies are affected by gossip? What can companies do to guard against this?

3. Although companies would prefer to reduce blogs that speak negatively about them, what about blogs that detail mistreatment of employees or illegal work practices by upper management? Should employees post these types of blogs even though they may be reprimanded or terminated as a result?

4. Is it ethical for companies to actively monitor blogs to gain marketing information? In other words, is the monitoring of blogs an invasion of privacy, or are bloggers inviting corporations to gather information because of the public nature of the postings?

Source: Based on S. Baker and H. Green, "Blogs Will Change Your Business," *Business Week*, May 2, 2005, pp. 57-67, and *The Pew Research Center*, 2005.

Endnotes

1. This opening section is based on S. Cushing, *Fatal Words: Communication Clashes and Aircraft Crashes* (Chicago: University of Chicago Press, 1997); "Pilot Communication Risks Flight Safety," www.abc.net.au, March 21, 2001; and www.aviation-safety.net/database, September 5, 2003.

2. See, for example, K. W. Thomas and W. H. Schmidt, "A Survey of Managerial Interests with Respect to Conflict," *Academy of Management Journal*, June 1976, p. 317.

3. W. G. Scott and T. R. Mitchell, *Organization Theory: A Structural and Behavioral Analysis* (Homewood, IL: Richard D. Irwin, 1976).

4. D. K. Berlo, *The Process of Communication* (New York: Holt, Rinehart & Winston, 1960), pp. 30–32.

5. J. Langan-Fox, "Communication in Organizations: Speed, Diversity, Networks, and Influence on Organizational Effectiveness, Human Health, and Relationships," in N. Anderson, D. S. Ones, H. K. Sinangil, and C. Viswesvaran (eds.), *Handbook of Industrial, Work and Organizational Psychology*, vol. 2 (Thousand Oaks, CA: Sage, 2001), p. 190.

6. R. L. Simpson, "Vertical and Horizontal Communication in Formal Organizations," *Administrative Science Quarterly*, September 1959, pp. 188–96; B. Harriman, "Up and Down the Communications Ladder," *Harvard Business Review*, September–October 1974, pp. 143–51; A. G. Walker and J. W. Smither, "A Five-Year Study of Upward Feedback: What Managers Do With Their Results Matter," *Personnel Psychology*,

Summer 1999, pp. 393–424; and J. W. Smither and A. G. Walker, "Are the Characteristics of Narrative Comments Related to Improvement in Multirater Feedback Ratings Over Time?" *Journal of Applied Psychology* 89, no. 3 (June 2004), pp. 575–81.

7. L. S. Rashotte, "What Does That Smile Mean? The Meaning of Nonverbal Behaviors in Social Interaction," *Social Psychology Quarterly*, March 2002, pp. 92–102.

8. J. Fast, *Body Language* (Philadelphia: M. Evan, 1970), p. 7.

9. A. Mehrabian, *Nonverbal Communication* (Chicago: Aldine-Atherton, 1972).

10. N. M. Henley, "Body Politics Revisited: What Do We Know Today?" In P. J. Kalbfleisch and M. J. Cody (eds.), *Gender, Power, and Communication in Human Relationships* (Hillsdale, NJ: Erlbaum, 1995), pp. 27–61.

11. See, for example, N. B. Kurland and L. H. Pelled, "Passing the Word: Toward a Model of Gossip and Power in the Workplace," *Academy of Management Review*, April 2000, pp. 428–38; and N. Nicholson, "The New Word on Gossip," *Psychology Today*, June 2001, pp. 41–45.

12. Cited in "Heard It Through the Grapevine," *Forbes*, February 10, 1997, p. 22.

13. See, for instance, J. W. Newstrom, R. E. Monczka, and W. E. Reif, "Perceptions of the Grapevine: Its Value and Influence," *Journal of Business Communication*, Spring 1974, pp. 12–20; and S. J. Modic, "Grapevine Rated Most Believable," *Industry Week*, May 15, 1989, p. 14.

14. K. Davis, "Management Communication and the Grapevine," *Harvard Business Review*, September–October 1953, pp. 43–49.

15. H. Sutton and L. W. Porter, "A Study of the Grapevine in a Governmental Organization," *Personnel Psychology*, Summer 1968, pp. 223–30.

16. K. Davis, cited in R. Rowan, "Where Did That Rumor Come From?" *Fortune*, August 13, 1979, p. 134.

17. R. L. Rosnow and G. A. Fine, *Rumor and Gossip: The Social Psychology of Hearsay* (New York: Elsevier, 1976).

18. L. Sierra, "Tell It to the Grapevine," *Communication World*, June/July 2002, pp. 28–29.

19. See, for instance, M. Conlin, "Watch What You Put in That Office E-Mail," *Business Week*, September 30, 2002, pp. 114–15; and A. Lantz, "Does the Use of E-Mail Change Over Time?" *International Journal of Human-Computer Interaction* 15, no. 3 (2003), pp. 419–31.

20. "Firm Bans E-mail at Work," Friday, September 19, 2003, www.cnn.com/2003/TECH/internet/09/19/e-mail.ban/.

21. E. Morphy, "Study: Online Customer Service Is Dismal," June 8, 2005, *Yahoo! News*. http://news.yahoo.com/s/nf/36133.

22. See, for instance, A. Harmon, "Appeal of Instant Messaging Extends Into the Workplace," *New York Times*, March 11, 2003, p. A1.

23. Cited in C. Y. Chen, "The IM Invasion," *Fortune*, May 26, 2003, pp. 135–38.

24. A. Stuart, "IM Is Here. RU Ready 2 Try It?" *INC.*, July 2003, pp. 76–81.

25. Ibid., p. 79.

26. R. O. Crockett, "The Office Gossips' New Water Cooler," *Business Week*, June 24, 2002, p. 14.

27. G. Anders, "Inside Job," *Fast Company*, September 2001, p. 178.

28. S. N. Mehta, "This Is Not a Cellphone," *Fortune*, May 26, 2003, pp. 141–42.

29. See S. A. Mohrman, D. Finegold, and J. A. Klein, "Designing the Knowledge Enterprise: Beyond Programs and Tools," *Organizational Dynamics* 31, no. 2 (2002), pp. 134–50; H. Dolezalek, "Collaborating in Cyberspace," *Training* (April 2003), pp. 32–37; and P. R. Carlile, "Transferring, Translating, and Transforming: An Integrative Framework for Managing Knowledge Across Boundaries," *Organization Science* 15, no. 5 (September–October 2004), pp. 555–68.

30. See J. Ewing, "Sharing the Wealth," *BusinessWeek e.biz*, March 19, 2001, pp. EB36–40; and D. Tapscott, D. Ticoll, and A. Lowy, *Digital Capital: Harnessing the Power of Business Webs* (Boston: Harvard Business School Press, 2000).

31. Cited in A. Cabrera and E. F. Cabrera, "Knowledge-Sharing Dilemmas," *Organization Studies* 5 (2002), p. 687.

32. B. Roberts, "Pick Employees' Brains," *HRMagzine*, February 2000, pp. 115–16; B. Fryer, "Get Smart," *INC. Technology 1999* no. 3, p. 65; and D. Zielinski, "Have You Shared a Bright Idea Today?" *Training*, July 2000, p. 65.

33. B. Fryer, "Get Smart," p. 63.

34. E. Truch, "Managing Personal Knowledge: The Key to Tomorrow's Employability," *Journal of Change Management*, December 2001, pp. 102–05; and D. Mason and D. J. Pauleen, "Perceptions of Knowledge Management: A Qualitative Analysis," *Journal of Knowledge Management* 7, no. 4 (2003), pp. 38–48.

35. J. Gordon, "Intellectual Capital and You," *Training*, September 1999, p. 33.

36. D. Zielinski, "Have You Shared a Bright Idea Today?" pp. 65–67.

37. T. M. Burton and R. E. Silverman, "Lots of Empty Spaces in Cerner Parking Lot Get CEO Riled Up," *Wall Street Journal*, March 30, 2001, p. B3; and E. Wong, "A Stinging Office Memo Boomerangs," *The New York Times*, April 5, 2001, p. C1.

38. See R. L. Daft and R. H. Lengel, "Information Richness: A New Approach to Managerial Behavior and Organization Design," in B. M. Staw and L. L. Cummings (eds.), *Research in Organizational Behavior*, vol. 6 (Greenwich, CT: JAI Press, 1984), pp. 191–233; R. L. Daft and R. H. Lengel, "Organizational Information Requirements, Media Richness, and Structural Design," *Managerial Science*, May 1986, pp. 554–72; R. E. Rice, "Task Analyzability, Use of New Media, and Effectiveness," *Organization Science*, November 1992, pp. 475–500; S. G. Straus and J. E. McGrath, "Does the Medium Matter? The Interaction of Task Type and Technology on Group Performance and Member Reaction," *Journal of Applied Psychology*, February 1994, pp. 87–97; L. K. Trevino, J. Webster, and E. W. Stein, "Making Connections: Complementary Influences on Communication Media Choices, Attitudes, and Use," *Organization Science*, March–April 2000, pp. 163–82; and N. Kock, "The Psychobiological Model: Towards a new Theory of Computer-Mediated Communication Based on Darwinian Evolution," *Organization Science* 15, no. 3 (May–June 2004), pp. 327–48.

39. R. L. Daft, R. H. Lengel, and L. K. Trevino, "Message Equivocality, Media Selection, and Manager Performance: Implications for Information Systems," *MIS Quarterly*, September 1987, pp. 355–68.

40. J. C. McCroskey, J. A. Daly, and G. Sorenson, "Personality Correlates of Communication Apprehension," *Human Communication Research*, Spring 1976, pp. 376–80.

41. See, for instance, B. H. Spitzberg and M. L. Hecht, "A Competent Model of Relational Competence," *Human*

Communication Research, Summer 1984, pp. 575–99; and S. K. Opt and D. A. Loffredo, "Rethinking Communication Apprehension: A Myers-Briggs Perspective," *Journal of Psychology*, September 2000, pp. 556–70.

42. See, for example, L. Stafford and J. A. Daly, "Conversational Memory: The Effects of Instructional Set and Recall Mode on Memory for Natural Conversations," *Human Communication Research*, Spring 1984, pp. 379–402; and T. L. Rodebaugh, "I Might Look OK, But I'm Still Doubtful, Anxious, and Avoidant: The Mixed Effects of Enhanced Video Feedback on Social Anxiety Symptoms," *Behaviour Research & Therapy* 42, no. 12 (December 2004), pp. 1435–51.

43. J. A. Daly and J. C. McCroskey, "Occupational Desirability and Choice as a Function of Communication Apprehension," *Journal of Counseling Psychology*, Vol. 22(4), 1975, pp. 309–313.

44. J. A. Daly and M. D. Miller, "The Empirical Development of an Instrument of Writing Apprehension," *Research in the Teaching of English*, Winter 1975, pp. 242–49.

45. See D. Tannen, *You Just Don't Understand: Women and Men in Conversation* (New York: Ballantine Books, 1991); and D. Tannen, *Talking from 9 to 5* (New York: William Morrow, 1995).

46. D. Tannen, *Talking from 9 to 5*, p. 15.

47. L. M. Kyl-Heku and D. M. Buss, "Tactics as Units of Analysis in Personality Psychology: An Illustration Using Tactics of Hierarchy Negotiation," *Personality & Individual Differences* 21, no. 4 (October 1996), pp. 497–517.

48. D. Tannen, "Talking Past one one Another: 'But What Do You Mean?' Women and Men in Conversation," in J. M. Henslin (ed.), *Down to Earth Sociology: Introductory Readings*, 12th ed.. (New York: Free Press, 2003), pp. 175–81.

49. This section is largely based on C. C. Pinder and K. P. Harlos, "Silent Organizational Behavior," paper presented at the Western Academy of Management Conference; March 2000; P. Mornell, "The Sounds of Silence," *INC.*, February 2001, pp. 117–18; C. C. Pinder and K. P. Harlos, "Employee Silence: Quiescence and Acquiescence as Responses to Perceived Injustice," in G. R. Ferris (ed.), *Research in Personnel and Human Resources Management*, vol. 21 (Greenwich, CT: JAI Press, 2001); and F. J. Milliken, E. W. Morrison, and P. F. Hewlin, "An Exploratory Study of Employee Silence: Issues that Employees Don't Communicate Upward and Why," *Journal of Management Studies*, September 2003, pp. 1453–76.

50. M. L. LaGanga, "Are There Words That Neither Offend Nor Bore?" *Los Angeles Times*, May 18, 1994, p. II–27; and J. Leo, "Put on a Sappy Face," *U.S. News & World Report*, November 25, 2002, p. 52.

51. Cited in J. Leo, "Falling for Sensitivity," *U.S. News & World Report*, December 13, 1993, p. 27.

52. R. E. Axtell, *Gestures: The Do's and Taboos of Body Language Around the World* (New York: Wiley, 1991).

53. See M. Munter, "Cross-Cultural Communication for Managers," *Business Horizons*, May–June 1993, pp. 75–76.

54. See E. T. Hall, *Beyond Culture* (Garden City, NY: Anchor Press/Doubleday, 1976); E. T. Hall, "How Cultures Collide," *Psychology Today*, July 1976, pp. 67–74; E. T. Hall and M. R.

Hall, *Understanding Cultural Differences* (Yarmouth, ME: Intercultural Press, 1990); R. E. Dulek, J. S. Fielden, and J. S. Hill, "International Communication: An Executive Primer," *Business Horizons*, January–February 1991, pp. 20–25; D. Kim, Y Pan, and H. S. Park, "High- Versus Low-Context Culture: A Comparison of Chinese, Korean, and American Cultures," *Psychology and Marketing*, September 1998, pp. 507–21; M. J. Martinko and S. C. Douglas, "Culture and Expatriate Failure: An Attributional Explication," *International Journal of Organizational Analysis*, July 1999, pp. 265–93; and W. L. Adair, "Integrative Sequences and Negotiation Outcome in Same- and Mixed-Culture Negotiations," *International Journal of Conflict Management* 14, no. 3–4 (2003), pp. 1359–92.

55. N. Adler, *International Dimensions of Organizational Behavior*, 4th ed. (Cincinnati, OH: Southwestern, 2002), p. 94.

56. J. Sanchez-Burks, "Protestant Relational Ideology and (in)attention to Relational Cues in Work Settings," *Journal of Personality and Social Psychology* 83 (2002), pp. 919–29.

57. J. Sanchez-Burks, F. Lee, I. Choi, R. Nisbett, S. Zhao, and J. Koo, "Conversing Across Cultures: East–West Communication Styles in Work and Nonwork Contexts," *Journal of Personality and Social Psychology* 85 (2003), pp. 363–72.

58. See, for example. R. S. Schuler, "A Role Perception Transactional Process Model for Organizational Communication-Outcome Relationships," *Organizational Behavior and Human Performance*, April 1979, pp. 268–91.

59. J. P. Walsh, S. J. Ashford, and T. E. Hill, "Feedback Obstruction: The Influence of the Information Environment on Employee Turnover Intentions," *Human Relations*, January 1985, pp. 23–46.

60. S. A. Hellweg and S. L. Phillips, "Communication and Productivity in Organizations: A State-of-the-Art Review," in *Proceedings of the 40th Annual Academy of Management Conference*, Detroit, 1980, pp. 188–92; see also B. A. Bechky, "Sharing Meaning Across Occupational Communities: The Transformation of Understanding on a Production Floor," *Organization Science* 14, no. 3 (May–June 2003), pp. 312–30.

61. R. R. Reilly, B. Brown, M. R. Blood, and C. Z. Malatesta, "The Effects of Realistic Previews: A Study and Discussion of the Literature," *Personnel Psychology*, Winter 1981, pp. 823–34; see also J. M. Phillips, "Effects of Realistic Job Previews on Multiple Organizational Outcomes: A Meta-Analysis," *Academy of Management Journal* 41, no. 6, (December 1998), pp. 673–90.

62. Based on J. P. Schuster, J. Carpenter, and M. P. Kane, *The Power of Open-Book Management* (New York: John Wiley, 1996); R. Aggarwal and B. J. Simkins, "Open Book Management—Optimizing Human Capital," *Business Horizons*, September–October 2001, pp. 5–13; and D. Drickhamer, "Open Books to Elevate Performance," *Industry Week*, November 2002, p. 16.

63. Based on M. R. Dixon, L. J. Hayes, and J. Stack, "Changing Conceptions of Employee Compensation," *Journal of Organizational Behavior Management* 23, no. 2–3 (2003), pp. 95–116; S. L. Gruner, "Why Open the Books?" *INC.*, November 1996, p. 95; and T. R. V. Davis, "Open-Book Management: Its Promise and Pitfalls," *Organizational Dynamics* 25, no. 3 (Winter 1997), pp. 7–20.

Basic Approaches to Leadership

After studying this chapter, you should be able to:

1 Contrast leadership and management.

2 Summarize the conclusions of trait theories.

3 Identify the limitations of behavioral theories.

4 Describe Fiedler's contingency model.

5 Explain Hersey and Blanchard's situational theory.

6 Summarize leader-member exchange theory.

7 Describe the path-goal theory.

8 Identify the situational variables in the leader-participation model.

LEARNING OBJECTIVES

CHAPTER 12

Andrea Jung: Giving Avon a Much Needed Makeover

Can one person make a difference in an organization's performance? Andrea Jung, chairman and CEO of Avon Products Inc. (see photo), is proving one can.[1] Jung joined Avon in 1994 after working for retailers such as Neiman Marcus and Bloomingdale's. Her original task at Avon was to create a global brand. And that's what she did. Jung integrated and standardized the company's logo, packaging, and ads to create a uniform image; and she pushed for the current corporate slogan, "The company for women." Based on her success in improving Avon's marketing focus, the company's board appointed her chairman and CEO in November 1999.

The company that Jung took over was in deep trouble. The day of the "Avon Lady" seemed to have passed. Fewer women were signing on as Avon reps and sales were sagging. But after only 4 weeks in her new job, Jung had a turnaround plan worked out. Avon would launch an entirely new line of businesses, develop blockbuster products, begin selling Avon products in retail stores, and significantly expand international sales. She added 46 percent to Avon's research-and-development budget to get blockbusters to market faster. This led to the launching of Retroactive, an antiaging skin cream that has become a runaway hit, and new lines of vitamins and therapy oils. She breathed new life into the ranks of the "Avon Ladies." To rebuild the company's salesforce, she created a multilevel marketing program that rewards current salespeople for signing up new reps. The number of sales reps is now increasing for the first time in years. Finally, by aggressively moving into international markets, Avon now gets almost two-thirds of its $6.2 billion in sales from outside the United States.

After 6 years on the job, Jung's leadership has truly made a difference in Avon's performance. Since Jung took over as CEO, profits have grown by an average of 21.5 percent per year. And Avon's stock price has increased 142 percent, compared to a mediocre performance of the S&P-500 stock index over the same time period. ■

s Andrea Jung is demonstrating at Avon, leaders can make a difference. In this chapter, we'll look at the basic approaches to determining what makes an effective leader and what differentiates leaders from nonleaders. First, we'll present trait theories. They dominated the study of leadership up to the late 1940s. Then we'll discuss behavioral theories, which were popular until the late 1960s. Finally, we'll introduce contingency theories, which are currently the dominant approach to the field of leadership. But before we review these three approaches, let's first clarify what we mean by the term *leadership*.

What Is Leadership?

Leadership and *management* are two terms that are often confused. What's the difference between them?

John Kotter of the Harvard Business School argues that management is about coping with complexity.[2] Good management brings about order and consistency by drawing up formal plans, designing rigid organization structures, and monitoring results against the plans. Leadership, in contrast, is about coping with change. Leaders establish direction by developing a vision of the future; then they align people by communicating this vision and inspiring them to overcome hurdles.

Robert House of the Wharton School at the University of Pennsylvania basically concurs when he says that managers use the authority inherent in their designated formal rank to obtain compliance from organizational members.[3] Management consists of implementing the vision and strategy provided by leaders, coordinating and staffing the organization, and handling day-to-day problems.

Although Kotter and House provide separate definitions of the two terms, both researchers and practicing managers frequently make no such distinctions. So we need to present leadership in a way that can capture how it is used in theory and practice.

We define **leadership** as the ability to influence a group toward the achievement of a vision or set of goals. The source of this influence may be formal, such as that provided by the possession of managerial rank in an organization. Because management positions come with some degree of formally designated authority, a person may assume a leadership role simply because of the position he or she holds in the organization. But not all leaders are managers, nor, for that matter, are all managers leaders. Just because an organization provides its managers with certain formal rights is no assurance that they will be able to lead effectively. We find that nonsanctioned leadership—that is, the ability to influence that arises outside the formal structure of the organization—is often as important or more important than formal influence. In other words, leaders can emerge from within a group as well as by formal appointment to lead a group.

One last comment before we move on: Organizations need strong leadership *and* strong management for optimal effectiveness. In today's dynamic world, we need leaders to challenge the status quo, to create visions of the future, and to inspire organizational members to want to achieve the visions. We also need managers to formulate detailed plans, create efficient organizational structures, and oversee day-to-day operations.

Trait Theories

Throughout history, strong leaders—Buddha, Napoleon, Mao, Churchill, Thatcher, Reagan—have all been described in terms of their traits. For example, when Margaret Thatcher was prime minister of Great Britain, she was regularly described as confident, iron-willed, determined, and decisive.

The trait theories of leadership focus on personal characteristics of the leader. For example, in describing the leadership of American Express CEO Kenneth Chenault, the media use terms such as intelligent, sociable, self-confident, straightforward, responsible, articulate, energetic, and ethical.

Trait theories of leadership differentiate leaders from nonleaders by focusing on personal qualities and characteristics. Individuals like Margaret Thatcher, South Africa's Nelson Mandela, Virgin Group CEO Richard Branson, Apple cofounder Steve Jobs, former New York City mayor Rudolph Giuliani, and American Express chairman Ken Chenault are recognized as leaders and described in terms such as *charismatic, enthusiastic,* and *courageous.* The search for personality, social, physical, or intellectual attributes that would describe leaders and differentiate them from nonleaders goes back to the earliest stages of leadership research.

Research efforts at isolating leadership traits resulted in a number of dead ends. For instance, a review in the late 1960s of 20 different studies identified nearly 80 leadership traits, but only 5 of these traits were common to 4 or more of the investigations.[4] By the 1990s, after numerous studies and analyses, about the best thing that could be said was that most "leaders are not like other people," but the particular traits that were isolated varied a great deal from review to review.[5] It was a pretty confusing state of affairs.

A breakthrough, of sorts, came when researchers began organizing traits around the Big Five personality framework (see Chapter 4).[6] What became clear was that most of the dozens of traits that emerged in various leadership reviews could be subsumed under one of the Big Five and that this approach resulted in consistent and strong support for traits as predictors of leadership. For instance, ambition and energy—two common traits of leaders—are part of extraversion. Rather than focusing on these two specific traits, it is better to think of them in terms of the more general trait of extraversion.

A comprehensive review of the leadership literature, when organized around the Big Five, has found that extraversion is the most important trait of effective leaders.[7] But results show that extraversion is more strongly related to leader emergence than to leader effectiveness. This is not totally surprising since sociable and dominant people are more likely to assert themselves in group situations. Conscientiousness and openness to experience also showed strong and consistent relationships to leadership, though not quite as strong as extraversion. The traits of agreeableness and emotional stability weren't as strongly correlated with leadership. Overall, it does appear that the trait approach does have something to offer. Leaders who are extraverted (individuals who like being around people and are able to assert themselves), conscientious (individuals who are disciplined and keep commitments they make), and open (individuals who are creative and flexible) do seem to have an advantage when it comes to leadership, suggesting that good leaders do have key traits in common.

Recent studies are indicating that another trait that may indicate effective leadership is emotional intelligence (EI), which we discussed in Chapter 8. Advocates of EI argue that without it, a person can have outstanding training, a highly analytical mind, a compelling vision, and an endless supply of terrific ideas but still not make a great leader. This may be especially true as individuals move up in an organization.[8] But why is EI so critical to effective leadership? A core component of EI is empathy. Empathetic leaders can sense others' needs, listen to what followers say (and don't say), and are able to read the reactions of others. As one leader noted, "The caring part of empathy, especially for the

leadership   *The ability to influence a group toward the achievement of a vision or set of goals.*

trait theories of leadership   *Theories that consider personal qualities and characteristics that differentiate leaders from nonleaders.*

Managers Speak Out on Leadership Competencies

Training magazine and The Center for Creative Leadership surveyed more than 250 managers to identify what leadership competencies they thought are most important for success today. Respondents were 54 percent male and 46 percent female. And they covered all levels of management: For instance, 28 percent were senior managers and 48 percent were either in beginning or middle-level management positions.

The survey found that these managers all considered ethics, integrity, and values near the top of their competency requirements. This shouldn't have been surprising given that the survey took place very soon after national headlines were revealing unethical (and, in some cases, illegal) practices by executives at companies like Enron, Tyco, WorldCom, and Arthur Andersen. Respondents believed that for leaders at the top of organizations to be effective, they must command respect. They need to be perceived as honest and reliable. Hence the importance of ethics, integrity, and values. On a 5-point scale, with 5 as most important, this competency received a mean score of 4.7.

Certain leadership competencies were viewed as more valuable, depending on the respondent's level in the organization. For mid-level managers, the survey found that communication (4.7) was just ahead of ethics (4.69) on the importance scale. At senior management levels, the highest importance went to the ability to construct and articulate a clear vision (4.89), with ethics receiving a mean rating of 4.8. Ninety percent of senior-level managers placed developing a vision as highest in importance, but only 19 percent of mid-level managers included vision among their most important competencies.

Source: Based on J. Schettler, "Leadership in Corporate America," *Training,* September 2002, pp. 66–77.

people with whom you work, is what inspires people to stay with a leader when the going gets rough. The mere fact that someone cares is more often than not rewarded with loyalty."[9]

Indeed, at the highest levels of leadership, EI is critical. For example, presidential historian Fred Greenstein argues that EI is the most important predictor of presidential greatness. Greenstein argues that the lack of EI was the undoing of Presidents Johnson, Nixon, Carter, and, to some degree, Clinton. He warns, "Beware the presidential contender who lacks emotional intelligence. In its absence all else may turn to ashes."[10] Emotional intelligence may have also played a key role in the 2004 presidential election. Though John Kerry was believed by many Americans to be smarter, more knowledgeable, and likely to do a better job on the key issues compared to George W. Bush, he lost the election. Why? Some believe that Kerry had lower EI than Bush. As one commentator put it, "In 2004 Kerry had more policy smarts. But Bush had more people smarts. He ran the more emotionally resonant campaign—speaking clearly, simply, and passionately. And he won."[11]

Despite these claims for its importance, the link between EI and leadership effectiveness is much less investigated compared to other traits. One reviewer noted, "Speculating about the practical utility of the EI construct might be premature. Despite such warnings, EI is being viewed as a panacea for many organizational malaises with recent suggestions that EI is essential for leadership effectiveness."[12] But until more rigorous evidence accumulates, we can't be confident about the connection.

Based on the latest findings, we offer two conclusions. First, traits can predict leadership. Twenty years ago, the evidence suggested otherwise. But this was probably due to the lack of a valid framework for classifying and organizing traits. The Big Five seems to have rectified that. Second, traits do a better job at predicting the emergence of leaders and the appearance of leadership than in actually distinguishing between *effective* and *ineffective* leaders.[13] The fact that an individual exhibits the traits and others consider that person to be a leader does not necessarily mean that the leader is successful at getting his or her group to achieve its goals.

Behavioral Theories

The failures of early trait studies led researchers in the late 1940s through the 1960s to go in a different direction. They began looking at the behaviors exhibited by specific leaders. They wondered if there was something unique in the way that effective leaders behave. To use contemporary examples, Siebel Systems Chairman Tom Siebel and Oracle CEO Larry Ellison have been very successful in leading their companies through difficult times.[14] And they both rely on a common leadership style—tough-talking, intense, autocratic. Does this suggest that autocratic behavior is a preferred style for all leaders? In this section, we look at three different **behavioral theories of leadership** to answer that question. First, however, let's consider the practical implications of the behavioral approach.

If the behavioral approach to leadership were successful, it would have implications quite different from those of the trait approach. Trait research provides a basis for *selecting* the "right" persons to assume formal positions in groups and organizations requiring leadership. In contrast, if behavioral studies were to turn up critical behavioral determinants of leadership, we could *train* people to be leaders. The difference between trait and behavioral theories, in terms of application, lies in their underlying assumptions. Trait theories assume leaders are born rather than made. However, if there were specific behaviors that identified leaders, then we could teach leadership—we could design programs that implanted these behavioral patterns in individuals who desired to be effective leaders. This was surely a more exciting avenue, for it meant that the supply of leaders could be expanded. If training worked, we could have an infinite supply of effective leaders.

Ohio State Studies

The most comprehensive and replicated of the behavioral theories resulted from research that began at Ohio State University in the late 1940s.[15] Researchers at Ohio State sought to identify independent dimensions of leader behavior. Beginning with over a thousand dimensions, they eventually narrowed the list to two categories that substantially accounted for most of the leadership behavior described by employees. They called these two dimensions *initiating structure* and *consideration.*

Initiating structure refers to the extent to which a leader is likely to define and structure his or her role and those of employees in the search for goal attainment. It includes behavior that attempts to organize work, work relationships, and goals. The leader characterized as high in initiating structure could be described as someone who "assigns group members to particular tasks," "expects workers to maintain definite standards of performance," and "emphasizes the meeting of deadlines." Larry Ellison and Tom Siebel exhibit high initiating structure behavior.

Consideration is described as the extent to which a person is likely to have job relationships that are characterized by mutual trust, respect for employees' ideas, and regard for their feelings. The person shows concern for followers' comfort, well-being, status, and satisfaction. A leader high in consideration could be described as one who helps employees with personal problems, is friendly

---

behavioral theories of leadership
Theories proposing that specific behaviors differentiate leaders from nonleaders.

initiating structure   *The extent to which a leader is likely to define and structure his or her role and those of subordinates in the search for goal attainment.*

consideration   *The extent to which a leader is likely to have job relationships characterized by mutual trust, respect for subordinates' ideas, and regard for their feelings.*

Thomas Siebel, chairman and CEO of Siebel Systems, ranks high in initiating structure. After forecasting a shrinking market for his firm's software, Siebel quickly devised a new budget and cost-cutting plan. He laid off 10 percent of employees, cut travel spending in half, and pared recruiting costs from $8 million to $1 million. Siebel's leadership style emphasizes cutting costs in order to meet his company's profitability goals.

and approachable, and treats all employees as equals. AOL Time Warner's CEO Richard Parsons rates high on consideration behavior. His leadership style is very people-oriented, emphasizing cooperation and consensus-building.[16]

At one time, the results of the Ohio State studies were thought to be disappointing. One 1992 review concluded, "Overall, the research based on a two-factor conceptualization of leadership behavior has added little to our knowledge about effective leadership."[17] However, a more recent review suggests that this two-factor conceptualization was given a premature burial. A review of 160 studies found that both initiating structure and consideration were associated with effective leadership. Specifically, consideration was more strongly related to the individual. In other words, the followers of leaders who were high in consideration were more satisfied with their jobs and more motivated and also had more respect for their leader. Initiating structure, however, was more strongly related to higher levels of group and organization productivity and more positive performance evaluations.

University of Michigan Studies

Leadership studies undertaken at the University of Michigan's Survey Research Center, at about the same time as those being done at Ohio State, had similar research objectives: to locate behavioral characteristics of leaders that appeared to be related to measures of performance effectiveness.

The Michigan group also came up with two dimensions of leadership behavior that they labeled **employee-oriented** and **production-oriented**.[18] Leaders who were employee-oriented were described as emphasizing interpersonal relations; they took a personal interest in the needs of their employees and accepted individual differences among members. The production-oriented leaders, in contrast, tended to emphasize the technical or task aspects of the job—their main concern was in accomplishing their group's tasks, and the group members were a means to that end. These dimensions—employee-oriented and production-oriented—are closely related to the Ohio State dimensions. Employee-oriented leadership is similar to consideration, and production-oriented leadership is similar to initiating structure. In fact, most leadership researchers use the terms synonymously.[19]

The conclusions arrived at by the Michigan researchers strongly favored the leaders who were employee-oriented in their behavior. Employee-oriented leaders were associated with higher group productivity and higher job satisfaction. Production-oriented leaders tended to be associated with low group productivity and lower job satisfaction. Although the Michigan studies emphasized employee-oriented leadership (or consideration) over production-oriented leadership (or initiating structure), the Ohio State studies garnered more research attention and suggested that *both* consideration and initiating structure are important to effective leadership.

The Managerial Grid

A graphic portrayal of a two-dimensional view of leadership style was developed by Blake and Mouton.[20] They proposed a **managerial grid** (sometimes also now called the *leadership grid*) based on the styles of "concern for people" and "concern for production," which essentially represent the Ohio State dimensions of consideration and initiating structure or the Michigan dimensions of employee-oriented and production-oriented.

The grid, depicted in Exhibit 12-1, has 9 possible positions along each axis, creating 81 different positions in which the leader's style may fall. The grid does not show results produced, but, rather, the dominating factors in a leader's thinking in regard to getting results. Based on the findings of Blake and Mouton, managers were found to perform best under a 9,9 style, as contrasted, for example, with a 9,1 (authority type) or 1,9 (laissez-faire type) style.[21] Unfortunately, the grid offers a better framework for conceptualizing leadership style than for presenting any tangible new information in clarifying the

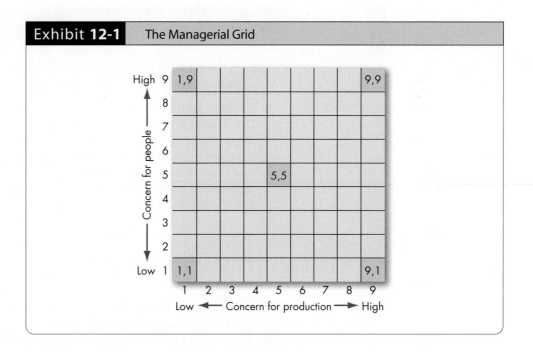

Exhibit 12-1   The Managerial Grid

employee-oriented leader   *Emphasizing interpersonal relations; taking a personal interest in the needs of employees, and accepting individual differences among members.*

production-oriented leader   *One who emphasizes technical or task aspects of the job.*

managerial grid   *A nine-by-nine matrix outlining 81 different leadership styles.*

leadership quandary, because it doesn't really convey any new information in addition to the Ohio State and the University of Michigan research.[22]

Summary of Trait Theories and Behavioral Theories

Judging from the evidence, the behavioral theories, like the trait theories, add to our understanding of leadership effectiveness. Leaders who have certain traits, and who display consideration and structuring behaviors, do appear to be more effective. Perhaps trait theories and behavioral theories should be integrated. For example, you would think that conscientious leaders (conscientiousness is a trait) are more likely to be structuring (structuring is a behavior). And maybe extraverted leaders (extraversion is a trait) are more likely to be considerate (consideration is a behavior). Unfortunately, we can't be sure there is a connection. Future research is needed to integrate these approaches.

Trait theories and behavioral theories aren't the last word on leadership. Missing is consideration of the situational factors that influence success or failure. For example, it seems unlikely that Martin Luther King, Jr., would have been a great civil rights leader at the turn of the twentieth century, yet he was in the 1950s and 1960s. Would Ralph Nader have risen to lead a consumer activist group had he been born in 1834 rather than 1934, or in Costa Rica rather than Connecticut? As important as trait theories and behavioral theories are in determining effective versus ineffective leaders, they do not guarantee a leader's success. The context matters too.

Before you move on to the next section, think about the type of leader you are aspiring to be. The Self-Assessment feature will help you identify your leadership style.

WHAT'S MY LEADERSHIP STYLE?

In the Self-Assessment Library (available on CD, online, and in print) take assessment II.B.1 (What's My Leadership Style?) and answer the following questions.

1. *Did you score as task-oriented (task-oriented is the same as initiating structure under the Ohio State studies and production-oriented under the University of Michigan studies) or people-oriented (people-oriented is the same as consideration under the Ohio State studies and employee-oriented under the University of Michigan studies)?*
2. *Do you think a leader can be both task-oriented and people-oriented? Do you think there are situations in which a leader has to make a choice between the two styles?*
3. *Do you think your leadership style will change over time? Why or why not?*

Contingency Theories

Linda Wachner had a reputation as being a very tough boss. And for a number of years, this style worked. In 1987, Wachner became CEO of Warnaco, a struggling $425-million-a-year apparel company. Over a 14-year period, she transformed Warnaco into a $2.2 billion company whose products ranged from Calvin Klein jeans to Speedo swimsuits. In spite of an abrasive style that included frequently humiliating employees in front of their peers and led to rapid turnover among top managers, Wachner's style worked for most of the 1990s. In fact, in 1993, *Fortune* magazine anointed her "America's most successful businesswoman." But times change and Wachner didn't.[23] Beginning in 1998, the company's business began to unravel, hurt by a reduction in demand

After leading Hewlett-Packard as CEO for 6 years, Carly Fiorina was asked by HP's board of directors to resign, stating that she lacked the leadership skills needed to move the company forward. Although Fiorina brought to HP experience and expertise in marketing and sales, she failed to execute HP's strategy and deliver on promises to improve the company's profits and stock price. Fiorina's failure in leading HP illustrates the premise of contingency theories that leadership effectiveness is dependent on situational influences.

for its products and a fast-eroding market share. Wachner's headstrong approach and brash tactics, which had driven off many competent executives, was now alienating creditors and licensers as well as employees. In June 2001, Warnaco was forced to file for bankruptcy protection. Five months later, the restructuring committee of Warnaco's board of directors fired Wachner. The story doesn't quite end there, though. Wachner sued Warnaco for $25 million in severance pay. They eventually settled for $452,000. Then, the SEC charged Wachner for securities fraud for issuing a false and misleading press release about Warnaco's earnings. In 2004, Wachner settled, agreeing to pay a total of $1,328,444 in fines and disgorged earnings.[24]

Linda Wachner's rise and fall illustrates that predicting leadership success is more complex than isolating a few traits or preferable behaviors. In Wachner's case, what worked in 1990 didn't work in 2000. The failure by researchers in the mid-twentieth century to obtain consistent results led to a focus on situational influences. The relationship between leadership style and effectiveness suggested that under condition *a*, style *x* would be appropriate, whereas style *y* would be more suitable for condition *b*, and style *z* for condition *c*. But what were the conditions *a*, *b*, *c*, and so forth? It was one thing to say that leadership effectiveness was dependent on the situation and another to be able to isolate those situational conditions. Several approaches to isolating key situational variables have proven more successful than others and, as a result, have gained wider recognition. We shall consider five of these: the Fiedler model, Hersey and Blanchard's situational theory, leader-member exchange theory, and the path-goal and leader-participation models.

Fiedler Model

The first comprehensive contingency model for leadership was developed by Fred Fiedler.[25] The **Fiedler contingency model** proposes that effective group performance depends on the proper match between the leader's style and the degree to which the situation gives control to the leader.

Identifying Leadership Style   Fiedler believes a key factor in leadership success is the individual's basic leadership style. So he begins by trying to find out what that basic style is. Fiedler created the **least preferred coworker (LPC) questionnaire** for this purpose; it purports to measure whether a person is task- or relationship-oriented. The LPC questionnaire contains sets of 16 contrasting adjectives (such as pleasant–unpleasant, efficient–inefficient, open–guarded, supportive–hostile). It asks respondents to think of all the coworkers they have ever had and to describe the one person they *least enjoyed* working with by rating that person on a scale of 1 to 8 for each of the 16 sets of contrasting adjectives. Fiedler believes that based on the respondents' answers to this LPC questionnaire, he can determine their basic leadership style. If the least preferred coworker is described in relatively positive terms (a high LPC score), then the respondent is primarily interested in good personal relations with this coworker. That is, if you essentially describe the person you are least able to work with in favorable terms, Fiedler would label you *relationship-oriented*. In

Fiedler contingency model   *The theory that effective groups depend on a proper match between a leader's style of interacting with subordinates and the degree to which the situation gives control and influence to the leader.*

least preferred coworker (LPC) questionnaire   *An instrument that purports to measure whether a person is task- or relationship-oriented.*

contrast, if the least preferred coworker is seen in relatively unfavorable terms (a low LPC score), the respondent is primarily interested in productivity and thus would be labeled *task-oriented.* About 16 percent of respondents score in the middle range.[26] Such individuals cannot be classified as either relationship-oriented or task-oriented and thus fall outside the theory's predictions. The rest of our discussion, therefore, relates to the 84 percent who score in either the high or low range of the LPC.

Fiedler assumes that an individual's leadership style is fixed. As we'll show, this is important because it means that if a situation requires a task-oriented leader and the person in that leadership position is relationship-oriented, either the situation has to be modified or the leader replaced if optimal effectiveness is to be achieved.

Defining the Situation   After an individual's basic leadership style has been assessed through the LPC, it is necessary to match the leader with the situation. Fiedler has identified three contingency dimensions that, he argues, define the key situational factors that determine leadership effectiveness. These are leader-member relations, task structure, and position power. They are defined as follows:

1. **Leader-member relations**: The degree of confidence, trust, and respect members have in their leader
2. **Task structure**: The degree to which the job assignments are procedurized (that is, structured or unstructured)
3. **Position power**: The degree of influence a leader has over power variables such as hiring, firing, discipline, promotions, and salary increases

The next step in the Fiedler model is to evaluate the situation in terms of these three contingency variables. Leader-member relations are either good or poor, task structure is either high or low, and position power is either strong or weak.

Fiedler states the better the leader-member relations, the more highly structured the job, and the stronger the position power, the more control the leader has. For example, a very favorable situation (in which the leader would have a great deal of control) might involve a payroll manager who is well respected and whose employees have confidence in her (good leader-member relations), for which the activities to be done—such as wage computation, check writing, report filing—are specific and clear (high task structure), and the job provides considerable freedom for her to reward and punish her employees (strong position power). However, an unfavorable situation might be the disliked chairperson of a voluntary United Way fund-raising team. In this job, the leader has very little control. Altogether, by mixing the three contingency dimensions, there are potentially eight different situations or categories in which leaders could find themselves (see Exhibit 12-2).

Matching Leaders and Situations   With knowledge of an individual's LPC and an assessment of the three contingency dimensions, the Fiedler model proposes matching them up to achieve maximum leadership effectiveness.[27] Based on his research, Fiedler concluded that task-oriented leaders tend to perform better in situations that were very favorable to them and in situations that were very unfavorable (see Exhibit 12-2). So Fiedler would predict that when faced with a category I, II, III, VII, or VIII situation, task-oriented leaders perform better. Relationship-oriented leaders, however, perform better in moderately favorable situations—categories IV through VI. In recent years, Fiedler has condensed these eight situations down to three.[28] He now says that task-oriented leaders perform best in situations of high and low control, while relationship-oriented leaders perform best in moderate control situations.

| Exhibit **12-2** | Findings from the Fiedler Model |

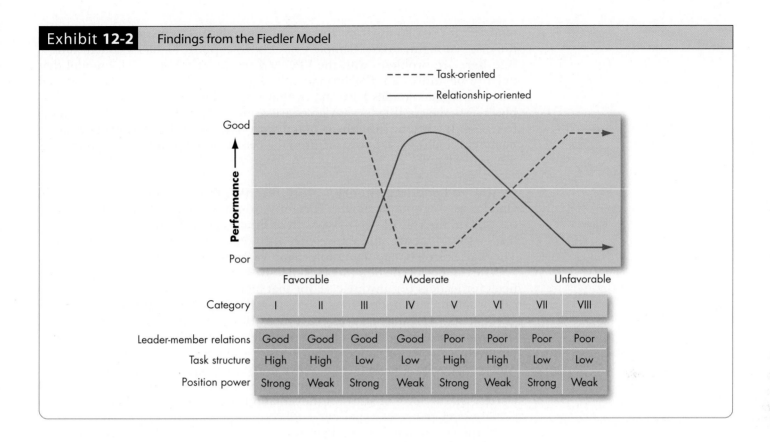

Given Fiedler's findings, how would you apply them? You would seek to match leaders and situations. Individuals' LPC scores would determine the type of situation for which they were best suited. That "situation" would be defined by evaluating the three contingency factors of leader-member relations, task structure, and position power. But remember that Fiedler views an individual's leadership style as being fixed. Therefore, there are really only two ways in which to improve leader effectiveness.

First, you can change the leader to fit the situation—as in a baseball game, a manager can put a right-handed pitcher or a left-handed pitcher into the game, depending on the situational characteristics of the hitter. So, for example, if a group situation rates as highly unfavorable but is currently led by a relationship-oriented manager, the group's performance could be improved by replacing that manager with one who is task-oriented. The second alternative would be to change the situation to fit the leader. That could be done by restructuring tasks or increasing or decreasing the power that the leader has to control factors such as salary increases, promotions, and disciplinary actions.

Evaluation   As a whole, reviews of the major studies that tested the overall validity of the Fiedler model lead to a generally positive conclusion. That is, there is considerable evidence to support at least substantial parts of the

---

leader-member relations   *The degree of confidence, trust, and respect subordinates have in their leader.*

task structure   *The degree to which the job assignments are procedurized.*

position power   *Influence derived from one's formal structural position in the organization; includes power to hire, fire, discipline, promote, and give salary increases.*

model.[29] If predictions from the model use only three categories rather than the original eight, there is ample evidence to support Fiedler's conclusions.[30] But there are problems with the LPC and the practical use of the model that need to be addressed. For instance, the logic underlying the LPC is not well understood and studies have shown that respondents' LPC scores are not stable.[31] Also, the contingency variables are complex and difficult for practitioners to assess. It's often difficult in practice to determine how good the leader-member relations are, how structured the task is, and how much position power the leader has.[32]

Cognitive Resource Theory   More recently, Fiedler and an associate, Joe Garcia, reconceptualized the former's original theory.[33] Specifically, they focused on the role of stress as a form of situational unfavorableness and how a leader's intelligence and experience influence his or her reaction to stress. They call this reconceptualization **cognitive resource theory**.

The essence of the new theory is that stress is the enemy of rationality. It's difficult for leaders (or anyone else, for that matter) to think logically and analytically when they're under stress. Moreover, the importance of a leader's intelligence and experience to effectiveness differs under low- and high-stress situations. Fiedler and Garcia found that a leader's intellectual abilities correlate positively with performance under low stress but negatively under high stress. And, conversely, a leader's experience correlates negatively with performance under low stress but positively under high stress. So, according to Fiedler and Garcia, it's the level of stress in the situation that determines whether an individual's intelligence or experience will contribute to leadership performance.

In spite of its newness, cognitive resource theory is developing a solid body of research support.[34] In fact, a study confirmed that when the stress level was low and the leader was directive (that is, when the leader was willing to tell people what to do), intelligence was important to a leader's effectiveness.[35] And in high-stress situations, intelligence was of little help because the leader was too cognitively

Myth or Science?

"It's Experience That Counts!"

The belief in the value of experience as a predictor of leadership effectiveness is very strong and widespread. Unfortunately, experience alone is generally a poor predictor of leadership.[36]

Organizations carefully screen outside candidates for senior management positions on the basis of their experience. Similarly, organizations usually require several years of experience at one managerial level before a person can be considered for promotion. For that matter, have you ever filled out an employment application that *didn't* ask about previous experience or job history? Clearly, management believes that experience counts. But the evidence doesn't support this view. Studies of military officers, research and development teams, shop supervisors, post office administrators, and school principals tell us that experienced managers tend to be no more effective than the managers with little experience.

One flaw in the "experience counts" logic is the assumption that length of time on a job is actually a measure of experience. This says nothing about the quality of experience. The fact that one person has 20 years' experience while another has 2 years' doesn't necessarily mean that the former has had 10 times as many meaningful experiences. Too often, 20 years of experience is nothing more than 1 year of experience repeated 20 times! In even the most complex jobs, real learning typically ends after about 2 years. By then, almost all new and unique situations have been experienced. So one problem with trying to link experience with leadership effectiveness is not paying attention to the quality and diversity of the experience.

A second problem is that there is variability between situations that influence the transferability or relevance of experience. Situations in which experience is obtained is rarely comparable to new situations. Jobs differ, support resources differ, organizational cultures differ, follower characteristics differ, and so on. So another reason that leadership experience isn't strongly related to leadership performance is undoubtedly due to variability of situations. ■

taxed to put smarts to good use. Similarly, if a leader is nondirective, intelligence is of little help because the leader is afraid to put these smarts to use to tell people what to do. These results are exactly what cognitive resource theory predicts.

Hersey and Blanchard's Situational Theory

Paul Hersey and Ken Blanchard have developed a leadership model that has gained a strong following among management development specialists.[37] This model—called **situational leadership theory (SLT)**—has been incorporated into leadership training programs at over 400 of the *Fortune* 500 companies; and over one million managers a year from a wide variety of organizations are being taught its basic elements.[38]

Situational leadership is a contingency theory that focuses on the followers. Successful leadership is achieved by selecting the right leadership style, which Hersey and Blanchard argue is contingent on the level of the followers' readiness. Before we proceed, we should clarify two points: Why focus on the followers? and What do they mean by the term *readiness*?

The emphasis on the followers in leadership effectiveness reflects the reality that it is the followers who accept or reject the leader. Regardless of what the leader does, effectiveness depends on the actions of the followers. This is an important dimension that has been overlooked or underemphasized in most leadership theories. The term *readiness*, as defined by Hersey and Blanchard, refers to the extent to which people have the ability and willingness to accomplish a specific task.

Kristen Cardwell is an infectious diseases researcher at St. Jude's Children's Research Hospital in Memphis, Tennessee. Cardwell and other medical researchers at the hospital have a high level of follower readiness. As responsible, experienced, and mature employees, they are both able and willing to complete their tasks under leadership that gives them freedom to make and implement decisions. This leader-follower relationship is consistent with Hersey and Blanchard's situational leadership theory.

cognitive resource theory   *A theory of leadership that states that stress unfavorably affects a situation and that intelligence and experience can lessen the influence of stress on the leader.*

situational leadership theory (SLT)   *A contingency theory that focuses on followers' readiness.*

SLT essentially views the leader-follower relationship as analogous to that between a parent and a child. Just as a parent needs to relinquish control as a child becomes more mature and responsible, so too should leaders. Hersey and Blanchard identify four specific leader behaviors—from highly directive to highly laissez-faire. The most effective behavior depends on a follower's ability and motivation. So SLT says if a follower is *unable* and *unwilling* to do a task, the leader needs to give clear and specific directions; if followers are *unable* and *willing*, the leader needs to display high task orientation to compensate for the followers' lack of ability and high relationship orientation to get the followers to "buy into" the leader's desires; if followers are *able* and *unwilling*, the leader needs to use a supportive and participative style; and if the employee is both *able* and *willing*, the leader doesn't need to do much.

SLT has an intuitive appeal. It acknowledges the importance of followers and builds on the logic that leaders can compensate for ability and motivational limitations in their followers. Yet research efforts to test and support the theory have generally been disappointing.[39] Why? Possible explanations include internal ambiguities and inconsistencies in the model itself as well as problems with research methodology in tests of the theory. So in spite of its intuitive appeal and wide popularity, any enthusiastic endorsement, at least at this time, has to be cautioned against.

Leader-Member Exchange Theory

For the most part, the leadership theories we've covered to this point have largely assumed that leaders treat all their followers in the same manner. That is, they assume leaders use a fairly homogeneous style with all of the people in their work unit. But think about your experiences in groups. Did you notice that leaders often act very differently toward different people? Did the leader tend to have favorites who made up his or her "in-group"? If you answered "Yes" to both these questions, you're acknowledging the foundation of leader-member exchange theory.[40] The **leader-member exchange (LMX) theory** argues that because of time pressures, leaders establish a special relationship with a small group of their followers. These individuals make up the in-group—they are trusted, get a disproportionate amount of the leader's attention, and are more likely to receive special privileges. Other followers fall into the out-group. They get less of the leader's time, fewer of the preferred rewards that the leader controls, and have leader-follower relations based on formal authority interactions.

The theory proposes that early in the history of the interaction between a leader and a given follower, the leader implicitly categorizes the follower as an "in" or an "out" and that relationship is relatively stable over time. Leaders induce LMX by rewarding those employees with whom they want a closer linkage and punishing those with whom they do not.[41] But for the LMX relationship to remain intact, the leader and the follower must invest in the relationship.

Just precisely how the leader chooses who falls into each category is unclear, but there is evidence that leaders tend to choose in-group members because they have attitude and personality characteristics that are similar to the leader's or a higher level of competence than out-group members[42] (see Exhibit 12-3). For example, followers who have a mastery orientation develop closer leader-member exchanges because such employees turn to their supervisors for sources of valuable information and experience that can provide employees with prospects for skill development and self-improvement that can further benefit the company.[43] However, communicating frequently with a supervisor appears to be helpful only for high LMX employees, probably because supervi-

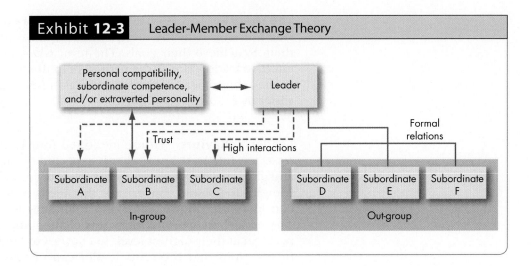

Exhibit 12-3 Leader-Member Exchange Theory

sors perceive frequent communication from low LMX employees as annoying and a waste of their time.[44] The key point to note here is that even though it is the leader who is doing the choosing, it is the follower's characteristics that are driving the leader's categorizing decision.

Few followers would want to be outside a leader's inner circle. There is a danger to being part of the inner circle, though. As part of the inner circle, your fortunes may rise and fall with your leader. When CEOs are ousted, for example, their inner circle usually goes with them. When Tyco CEO Dennis Kozlowski was given the boot, eventually his closest associate, CFO Mark Swartz, was also forced to resign, although he was well regarded on Wall Street and was thought to be one of the executives who best understood the intricacies of Tyco's business.[45]

Research to test LMX theory has been generally supportive. More specifically, the theory and research surrounding it provide substantive evidence that leaders do differentiate among followers; that these disparities are far from random; and that followers with in-group status will have higher performance ratings, lower turnover intentions, greater satisfaction with their superior, and higher overall satisfaction than will the out-group.[46] These positive findings for in-group members shouldn't be totally surprising given our knowledge of the self-fulfilling prophecy (see Chapter 5). Leaders invest their resources with those they expect to perform best. And "knowing" that in-group members are the most competent, leaders treat them as such and unwittingly fulfill their prophecy.[47]

Path-Goal Theory

Developed by Robert House, path-goal theory extracts elements from the Ohio State leadership research on initiating structure and consideration and the expectancy theory of motivation.[48]

leader-member exchange (LMX) theory
The creation by leaders of in-groups and out-groups; subordinates with in-group status will have higher performance ratings, less turnover, and greater job satisfaction.

The Theory   The essence of **path-goal theory** is that it's the leader's job to provide followers with the information, support, or other resources necessary for them to achieve their goals. The term *path-goal* is derived from the belief that effective leaders clarify the path to help their followers get from where they are to the achievement of their work goals and to make the journey along the path easier by reducing roadblocks.

Leader Behaviors   House identified four leadership behaviors. The *directive leader* lets followers know what is expected of them, schedules work to be done, and gives specific guidance as to how to accomplish tasks. The *supportive leader* is friendly and shows concern for the needs of followers. The *participative leader* consults with followers and uses their suggestions before making a decision. The *achievement-oriented leader* sets challenging goals and expects followers to perform at their highest level. In contrast to Fiedler, House assumes leaders are flexible and that the same leader can display any or all of these behaviors depending on the situation.

Contingency Variables and Predictions

As Exhibit 12-4 illustrates, path-goal theory proposes two classes of contingency variables that moderate the leadership behavior–outcome relationship—those in the environment that are outside the control of the employee (task structure, the formal authority system, and the work group) and those that are part of the personal characteristics of the employee (locus of control, experience, and perceived ability). Environmental factors determine the type of leader behavior required as a complement if follower outcomes are to be maximized, while personal characteristics of the employee determine how the environment and leader behavior are interpreted. So the theory proposes that leader behavior will be ineffective when it is redundant with sources of environmental structure or incongruent with employee characteristics. For example, the following are illustrations of predictions based on path-goal theory:

- Directive leadership leads to greater satisfaction when tasks are ambiguous or stressful than when they are highly structured and well laid out.

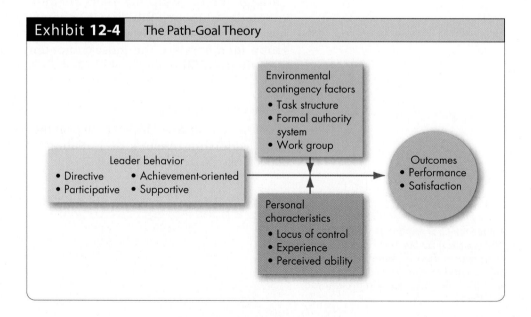

Exhibit **12-4**   The Path-Goal Theory

- Supportive leadership results in high employee performance and satisfaction when employees are performing structured tasks.
- Directive leadership is likely to be perceived as redundant among employees with high perceived ability or with considerable experience.
- Employees with an internal locus of control will be more satisfied with a participative style.
- Achievement-oriented leadership will increase employees' expectancies that effort will lead to high performance when tasks are ambiguously structured.

Evaluation   Due to its complexity, testing path-goal theory has not proven to be easy. A review of the evidence suggests mixed support. As the authors of this review commented, "These results suggest that either effective leadership does not rest in the removal of roadblocks and pitfalls to employee path instrumentalities as path-goal theories propose or that the nature of these hindrances is not in accord with the proposition of the theories." Another review concluded that the lack of support was "shocking and disappointing."[49] These conclusions have been challenged by others who argue that adequate tests of the theory have yet to be conducted.[50] Thus, it is safe to say that the jury is still out regarding the validity of path-goal theory. Because it is so complex to test, that may remain the case for some time to come.

Leader-Participation Model

Victor Vroom and Phillip Yetton developed a **leader-participation model** that related leadership behavior and participation in decision making.[51] Recognizing that task structures have varying demands for routine and non-routine activities, these researchers argued that leader behavior must adjust to reflect the task structure. Vroom and Yetton's model was normative—it provided a sequential set of rules that should be followed in determining the form and amount of participation in decision making, as determined by different types of situations. The model was a decision tree incorporating seven contingencies (whose relevance could be identified by making "yes" or "no" choices) and five alternative leadership styles. More recent work by Vroom and Arthur Jago has resulted in a revision of this model.[52] The revised model retains the same five alternative leadership styles—from the leader's making the decision completely alone to sharing the problem with the group and developing a consensus decision—but adds a set of problem types and expands the contingency variables to 12. The 12 contingency variables are listed in Exhibit 12-5.

Research testing both the original and revised leader-participation models has not been encouraging, although the revised model rates higher in effectiveness.[53] Criticism has tended to focus on variables that have been omitted and on the model's overall complexity.[54] Other contingency theories demonstrate that stress, intelligence, and experience are important situational variables. Yet the

---

path-goal theory   *The theory that it is the leader's job to assist followers in attaining their goals and to provide the necessary direction and/or support to ensure that their goals are compatible with the overall objectives of the group or organization.*

leader-participation model   *A leadership theory that provides a set of rules to determine the form and amount of participative decision making in different situations.*

David Neeleman, founder and CEO of JetBlue Airlines, is an achievement-oriented leader. Neeleman's goal is to make JetBlue the most cost-efficient airline with the best customer service. To achieve this goal, he fosters a sense of ownership in JetBlue's success by sending monthly e-mails to each employee about the company's finances and competitor rankings, and he rewards employees by sharing profits with them. Neeleman shows how vital each employee's work is to JetBlue's success by helping pass out snacks, unload luggage, and clean planes.

leader-participation model fails to include them. But more important, at least from a practical point of view, is the fact that the model is far too complicated for the typical manager to use on a regular basis. Although Vroom and Jago have developed a computer program to guide managers through all the decision branches in the revised model, it's not very realistic to expect practicing managers to consider 12 contingency variables, eight problem types, and five leadership styles in trying to select the appropriate decision process for a specific problem.

We obviously haven't done justice in this discussion to the model's sophistication. So what can you gain from this brief review? Additional insights into relevant contingency variables. Vroom and his associates have provided us with some specific, empirically supported contingency variables that you should consider when choosing your leadership style.

Exhibit 12-5	Contingency Variables in the Revised Leader-Participation Model

1. Importance of the decision
2. Importance of obtaining follower commitment to the decision
3. Whether the leader has sufficient information to make a good decision
4. How well structured the problem is
5. Whether an autocratic decision would receive follower commitment
6. Whether followers "buy into" the organization's goals
7. Whether there is likely to be conflict among follower over solution alternatives
8. Whether followers have the necessary information to make a good decision
9. Time constraints on the leader that may limit follower involvement
10. Whether costs to bring geographically dispersed members together is justified
11. Importance to the leader of minimizing the time it takes to make the decision
12. Importance of using participation as a tool for developing follower decision skills

Cultivating an International Perspective: A Necessity for Leaders

ACCOUNTING AND CONSULTING FIRM PRICEWATER- houseCoopers (PwC) is serious about expanding the world- view of its up-and-coming leaders. So the company started the Ulysses Program, which sends the company's potential leaders to foreign countries to gain knowledge and experience in cultural diversity.

For example, PwC sent one group of managers on an 8-week consulting assignment in the Namibian outback. Their job? To help village leaders deal with the growing AIDS crisis. Without PowerPoint presentations and e-mail, the managers quickly learned to communicate in a more traditional way—face-to-face. The managers were forced to rely less on quick technologies and more on forging connections by cultivating relationships with diverse clients. By experiencing diversity first-hand at what is perhaps its extreme, PwC hopes that its managers will be better-equipped to handle issues in any culture in which they conduct business. The company says that the program gives its future leaders a broad, international perspective on business issues and makes it more likely that they will find creative, unconventional solutions to complex problems. In addition, participants can realize what they are able to accomplish when they do not have access to their usual resources. In essence, they are forced to become leaders.

The jury is still out on whether the program is effective at increasing the global leadership skills of those who participate. Nevertheless, participants of the Ulysses Program tout its benefits, and other companies have taken notice—Johnson & Johnson and Cisco Systems are just two of several companies that have adopted similar programs.

Source: Based on J. Hempel, and S. Porges, "It Takes a Village—And a Consultant," *Business Week*, September 6, 2004, p. 76.

Summary and Implications for Managers

Leadership plays a central part in understanding group behavior, for it's the leader who usually provides the direction toward goal attainment. Therefore, a more accurate predictive capability should be valuable in improving group performance.

The early search for a set of universal leadership traits failed. However, recent efforts using the Big Five personality framework has generated much more encouraging results. Specifically, the traits of extraversion, conscientiousness, and openness to experience show strong and consistent relationships to leadership.

The behavioral approach's major contribution was narrowing leadership into task-oriented and people-oriented styles.

A major breakthrough in our understanding of leadership came when we recognized the need to develop contingency theories that included situational factors. At present, the evidence indicates that relevant situational variables would include the task structure of the job; level of situational stress; level of group support; the leader's intelligence and experience; and follower characteristics such as personality, experience, ability, and motivation.

Point ◀▷ Counterpoint

The Perils of Leadership Training

Organizations spend billions of dollars on leadership training every year. They send managers and manager-wannabes to a wide range of leadership training activities—formal MBA programs, leadership seminars, weekend retreats, and even outward-bound adventures. They appoint mentors. They establish "fast tracks" for high-potential individuals for them to gain a variety of the "right kinds of experience." We propose that much of this effort to train leaders is probably a waste of money. And we base our position by looking at two very basic assumptions that underlie leadership training.[55]

The first assumption is that we know what leadership is. We don't. Experts can't agree if it's a trait, a characteristic, a behavior, a role, a style, or an ability. They further can't even agree on whether leaders really make a difference in organizational outcomes. For instance, some experts have persuasively argued that leadership is merely an attribution made to explain organizational successes and failures, which themselves occur by chance. Leaders are the people who get credit for successes and take the blame for failures, but they may actually have little influence over organizational outcomes.

The second basic assumption is that we can train people to lead. The evidence here is not very encouraging. We do seem to be able to teach individuals *about leadership*. Unfortunately, findings indicate we aren't so good at teaching people *to lead*. There are several possible explanations. To the degree that personality is a critical element in leadership effectiveness, some people may not have been born with the right personality traits. In fact, there is evidence that leadership is, at least in part, inherited.[56] A second explanation is that there is no evidence that individuals can substantially alter their basic leadership style.[57] A third possibility is that, even if certain theories could actually guide individuals in leadership situations and even if individuals could alter their style, the complexity of those theories make it nearly impossible for any normal human being to assimilate all the variables and be capable of enacting the right behaviors in every situation.

Leadership training exists, and is a multi-billion-dollar industry, because it works. Decision makers are, for the most part, rational. Would a company like General Electric spend literally tens of millions of dollars each year on leadership training if it didn't expect a handsome return? We don't think so! And the ability to lead successfully is why a company like Forest Laboratories willingly paid its CEO, Howard Solomon, more than $92 million in 2004. Under Solomon's leadership, the company has experienced spectacular growth—including shareholder gains of 54.20 percent over the past 5 years alone.

Although there are certainly disagreements over the exact definition of leadership, most academics and business-people agree that leadership is an influence process whereby an individual, by his or her actions, facilitates the movement of a group of people toward the achievement of a common goal.

Do leaders affect organizational outcomes? Of course they do. Successful leaders anticipate change, vigorously exploit opportunities, motivate their followers to higher levels of productivity, correct poor performance, and lead the organization toward its objectives. A review of the leadership literature, in fact, led two academics to conclude that the research shows "a consistent effect for leadership explaining 20 to 45 percent of the variance on relevant organizational outcomes."[58]

What about the effectiveness of leadership programs? They vary. But more and more evidence is accumulating from the best management journals, showing that we *can* train people to be better leaders.[59] Many of these studies have used rigorous experimental designs and objective outcomes. Thus, it simply isn't credible to argue that we can't teach people to lead.

Questions for Review

1. Trace the development of leadership research.
2. What traits predict leadership?
3. What is *initiating structure*? *Consideration*?
4. Do initiating structure and consideration predict a leader's effectiveness?
5. What is the managerial grid? Contrast its approach to leadership with the approaches of the Ohio State and Michigan groups.
6. What are Fiedler's three contingency variables?
7. What contribution does cognitive resource theory make to leadership?
8. What are its implications of LMX theory for leadership practice?
9. What are the contingency variables in the path-goal theory?
10. What are the implications if leaders are inflexible in adjusting their style?

Questions for Critical Thinking

1. Review trait theories in the context of the "nature versus nurture" debate.
2. Develop an example in which you operationalize the Fiedler model.
3. Develop an example in which you operationalize the path-goal theory.
4. Develop an example in which you operationalize SLT.

Team Exercise

DEBATE: DO LEADERS REALLY MATTER?

Break the class into groups of two. One group member will argue "Leaders are the primary determinant of an organization's success or failure." The other group member will argue "Leaders don't really matter because most of the things that affect an organization's success or failure are outside a leader's control." Take 10 minutes to develop your arguments; then you have 10 minutes to conduct your debate.

After the dyad debates, form into teams of six. Three from each of these groups should have taken the "pro" argument on leadership and three should have taken the "con" side. The teams have 15 minutes to reconcile their arguments and to develop a unified position. When the 15 minutes are up, each team should be prepared to make a brief presentation to the class, summarizing its unified position.

Ethical Dilemma

DO ENDS JUSTIFY THE MEANS?

The power that comes from being a leader can be used for evil as well as for good. When you assume the benefits of leadership, you also assume ethical burdens. But many highly successful leaders have relied on questionable tactics to achieve their ends. These include manipulation, verbal attacks, physical intimidation, lying, fear, and control. Consider a few examples:

Bill Clinton successfully led the United States through 8 years of economic expansion. Those close to him were committed and loyal followers. Yet he lied under oath (causing him to lose his law license) and "managed" the truth.

Jack Welch, former head of General Electric, provided the leadership that made GE the most valuable company in America. He also ruthlessly preached firing the lowest-performing 10 percent of the company's employees every year.

Cisco Systems CEO John Chambers laid off nearly 20 percent of his workforce and commented that the tough times were "likely to be just a speed bump." Tell that to the 17,000 workers he laid off. And yet, Cisco has returned to profitability.

Few U.S. presidents understood foreign relations or made as much progress in building international cooperation than did Richard Nixon. But his accomplishments are largely overshadowed by the meanness, dirty tricks, and duplicity he exhibited during his tenure in the White House.

Should leaders be judged solely on their end achievements? Or do the means they choose also reflect on their leadership qualities? Are employees, shareholders, and society too quick to excuse leaders who use questionable means if they are successful in achieving their goals? Is it impossible for leaders to be ethical *and* successful?

Source: Based on C. E. Johnson, *Meeting the Ethical Challenges in Leadership* (Thousand Oaks, CA: Sage, 2001), pp. 4–5.

Case Incident 1

MOVING FROM COLLEAGUE TO SUPERVISOR

Cheryl Kahn, Rob Carstons, and Linda McGee have something in common. They all were promoted within their organizations into management positions. And each found the transition a challenge.

Cheryl Kahn was promoted to director of catering for the Glazier Group of restaurants in New York City. With the promotion, she realized that things would never be the same again. No longer would she be able to participate in water-cooler gossip or shrug off an employee's chronic lateness. She says she found her new role to be daunting. "At first I was like a bulldozer knocking everyone over, and that was not well received. I was saying, 'It's my way or the highway.' And was forgetting that my friends were also in transition." She admits that this style alienated just about everyone with whom she worked.

Rob Carstons, a technical manager at IBM in California, talks about the uncertainty he felt after being promoted to a manager from a junior programmer. "It was a little bit challenging to be suddenly giving directives to peers, when just the day before you were one of them. You try to be careful not to offend anyone. It's strange walking into a room and the whole conversation changes."

People don't want to be as open with you when you become the boss."

Linda McGee is now president of Medex Insurance Services in Baltimore, Maryland. She started as a customer service representative with the company, then leapfrogged over colleagues in a series of promotions. Her fast rise created problems. Colleagues "would say, 'Oh, here comes the big cheese now.' God only knows what they talked about behind my back."

Questions

1. A lot of new managers err in selecting the right leadership style when they move into management. Why do you think this happens?

2. What does this say about leadership and leadership training?

3. Which leadership theories, if any, could help new leaders deal with this transition?

4. Do you think it's easier or harder to be promoted internally into a formal leadership position than to come into it as an outsider? Explain.

Source: Based on D. Koeppel, "A Tough Transition: Friend to Supervisor," *The New York Times*, March 16, 2003, p. BU-12.

Case Incident 2

BARACK OBAMA

Political analysts and the media have compared Illinois State Senator Barack Obama to historical figures such as Abraham Lincoln, Martin Luther King, Jr., and Bill Clinton. In January 2005, the 43-year-old Obama, a Democrat, became the only African American in the current U.S. Senate. The Democratic Party is already debating Obama's prospects of becoming president, and they aren't debating whether or not he should run but whether he should run in 2012 or 2016.

How did Obama, the self-proclaimed "skinny kid with a funny name" become one of the most popular political candidates in the Democratic Party today? Ask people who've watched him and they might say he possesses certain personality traits, as well as a keen intellect, and that these have quickly propelled him to the upper political ranks of government.

Obama's early years were a mix of struggles, but he seized opportunities as they arose. His mother was a white native of Kansas, his father a black immigrant from Kenya. Though his father has had a tremendous effect on Obama's astute cultural awareness, he left the family when Obama was two and rarely saw Obama throughout his childhood. His father later died in a car accident in Kenya when Obama was 21. After growing up in Honolulu, except during the ages of 6 to 10, when he and his mother lived in Indonesia, Obama attended Columbia University in New York. Four years after graduating from Columbia and working as a community organizer in Chicago, Obama attended Harvard Law School. There, he was chosen by famous attorney Laurence Tribe to be Tribe's research assistant. Tribe, who also teaches constitutional law, said of Obama, "I've known senators, presidents. I've never known anyone with what seems to me more raw political talent. He just seems to have the surest way of calmly reaching across what are impenetrable barriers to many people."

Obama continued on a path into politics. In 1990, as a result of his successes, he was elected president of the *Harvard Law Review*, the first African American to have accomplished such a feat. Following law school, Obama joined a small civil rights firm in Chicago. But working there was not enough for Obama—politics was where his true aspirations lie. He left the Chicago firm, and, in 1996, Obama ran for the Illinois state senate and won. On the fast track, Obama attempted to run for the U.S. Congress against Bobby Rush, a four-term former member of the activist group the Black Panthers. Obama lost, but his persistence led him to the 2004 senate election, in which he won by a large margin against prominent African American Republican Alan Keyes.

Obama's whirlwind ride to the U.S. Senate has left even him a bit surprised by his tremendous popularity. "What's going on? I'm not entirely sure," he said. "I think what people are most hungry for in politics right now is authenticity."

Obama has a knack for rousing people's attention. Many say that he is extremely charismatic, and his speech at the 2004 Democratic National Convention was an example of that quality. On July 27th, Obama took the podium and began speaking about his idea of a country without racism and fear, a country not led by politicians who are born into wealth. Speaking of his background, which exemplifies diversity in many ways, Obama stated, "In no other country on earth is my story even possible." Obama has been described by political analysts as very self-aware, as evidenced by his ability to tie his own experiences into an engaging political speech in which he portrayed himself as an ordinary citizen, speaking for the general public. Though it may be difficult to say exactly what separates Obama from other political figures, many say that he "just has that something."

So far, Obama's fame is continuing to grow. Stated Congresswoman Gwen Moore during a rally for Senator Russ Feingold, "This young man has set Illinois on fire and set America on fire. He's the future of the Democratic Party!" Former Virginia Governor L. Douglas Wilder concurs. "Obama could be president. There's nothing to stop him."

Questions

1. What traits might Barack Obama possess that contribute to his strong leadership ability? Does Obama's case support a trait perspective of leadership? Why or why not?

2. From a behavioral perspective of leadership, what does Obama do to strengthen his success as a leader?

3. Is Obama's popularity and success a result of "nature," "nurture," or both? What factors can you think of to support your answer?

Source: Based on P. Bacon, Jr. "Barack Obama," *Time*, April 18, 2005, p. 60–61, and A. Ripley, D. E. Thigpen, and J. McCabe, "Obama's Ascent," *Time*, November 11, 2004, pp. 74–78.

Endnotes

1. Based on G. Levine, "Jung: Avon CEO Lauds Global Portfolio," *Forbes.* (www.Forbes.com) (October 29, 2004); "Avon gaining a profile in China," *The Age.*, (www.theage.com.au) (December 30, 2004); N. Byrnes, "Avon Calling—Lots of New Reps," *Business Week*, June 2, 2003, p. 53; "The Best Managers," *Business Week,* January 13, 2003, p. 60.

2. J. P. Kotter, "What Leaders Really Do," *Harvard Business Review*, May–June 1990, pp. 103–11; and J. P. Kotter, *A Force for Change: How Leadership Differs from Management* (New York: Free Press, 1990).

3. R. J. House and R. N. Aditya, "The Social Scientific Study of Leadership: Quo Vadis?" *Journal of Management* 23, no. 3 (1997), p. 445.

4. J. G. Geier, "A Trait Approach to the Study of Leadership in Small Groups," *Journal of Communication*, December 1967, pp. 316–23.

5. S. A. Kirkpatrick and E. A. Locke, "Leadership: Do Traits Matter?" *Academy of Management Executive*, May 1991, pp. 48–60; and S. J. Zaccaro, R. J. Foti, and D. A. Kenny, "Self-Monitoring and Trait-Based Variance in Leadership: An Investigation of Leader Flexibility across Multiple Group Situations," *Journal of Applied Psychology*, April 1991, pp. 308–15.

6. See T. A. Judge, J. E. Bono, R. Ilies, and M. Werner, "Personality and Leadership: A Review," paper presented at the 15th Annual Conference of the Society for Industrial and Organizational Psychology, New Orleans, 2000; and T. A. Judge, J. E. Bono, R. Ilies, and M. W. Gerhardt, "Personality and Leadership: A Qualitative and Quantitative Review," *Journal of Applied Psychology*, August 2002, pp. 765–80.

7. Judge, Bono, Ilies, and Gerhardt, "Personality and Leadership."

8. This section is based on D. Goleman, *Working with Emotional Intelligence* (New York: Bantam, 1998); D. Goleman, "What Makes a Leader?" *Harvard Business Review*, November–December 1998, pp. 93–102; J. M. George, "Emotions and Leadership: The Role of Emotional Intelligence," *Human Relations*, August 2000, pp. 1027–55; D. R. Caruso, J. D. Mayer, and P. Salovey, "Emotional Intelligence and Emotional Leadership," in R. E. Riggio, S. E. Murphy, and F. J. Pirozzolo (eds.), *Multiple Intelligences and Leadership* (Mahwah, NJ: Lawrence Erlbaum, 2002), pp. 55–74; D. Goleman, R. E. Boyatzis, and A. McKee, *Primal Leadership: Realizing the Power of Emotional Intelligence* (Boston: Harvard Business School Press, 2002); C-S. Wong and K. S. Law, "The Effects of Leader and Follower Emotional Intelligence on Performance and Attitude: An Exploratory Study," *Leadership Quarterly*, June 2002, pp. 243–74; and D. R. Caruso, and C. J. Wolfe, "Emotional Intelligence and Leadership Development" in D. David and S. J. Zaccaro (eds.), *Leader Development for Transforming Organizations: Growing Leaders for Tomorrow* (Mahwah, NJ: Lawrence Erlbaum, 2004) pp. 237–63.

9. J. Champy, "The Hidden Qualities Of Great Leaders," *Fast Company* 76 (November 2003), p. 135.

10. F. I. Greenstein, *The Presidential Difference: Leadership Style from FDR to George W. Bush'* (Princeton, NJ: Princeton University Press, 2004).

11. V. Jones, "Emotions Vs Intelligence How It Impacts Elections," *The World from A Hip Hop Perspective.* (http://p076.ezboard.com/fpoliticalpalacefrm21.showMessage?topicID=549.topic) (December 12, 2004).

12. J. Antonakis, "Why 'Emotional Intelligence' Does Not Predict Leadership Effectiveness: A Comment on Prati, Douglas, Ferris, Ammeter, and Buckley (2003)," *International Journal of Organizational Analysis*, 11, 2003. pp. 355–361; see also M. Zeidner, G. Matthews, and R. D. Roberts, "Emotional Intelligence in the Workplace: A Critical Review," *Applied Psychology: An International Review*, Vol 53, 2004. pp. 371–399.

13. Ibid.; Ibid 7; R. G. Lord, C. L. DeVader, and G. M. Alliger, "A Meta-Analysis of the Relation between Personality Traits and Leadership Perceptions: An Application of Validity Generalization Procedures," *Journal of Applied Psychology*, August 1986, pp. 402–10; and J. A. Smith and R. J. Foti, "A Pattern Approach to the Study of Leader Emergence," *Leadership Quarterly*, Summer 1998, pp. 147–60.

14. See S. Hansen, "Stings Like a Bee," *INC.*, November 2002, pp. 56–64; J. Greenbaum, "Is Ghengis On the Hunt Again?" *internetnews.com.* (www.internetnews.com/commentary/article.php/3459771) (January 14, 2005).

15. R. M. Stogdill and A. E. Coons (eds.), *Leader Behavior: Its Description and Measurement*, Research Monograph no. 88 (Columbus: Ohio State University, Bureau of Business Research, 1951). This research is updated in C. A. Schriesheim, C. C. Cogliser, and L. L. Neider, "Is It 'Trustworthy'? A Multiple-Levels-of-Analysis Reexamination of an Ohio State Leadership Study, with Implications for Future Research," *Leadership Quarterly*, Summer 1995, pp. 111–45; and T. A. Judge, R. F. Piccolo, and R. Ilies, "The Forgotten Ones? The Validity of Consideration and Initiating Structure in Leadership Research," *Journal of Applied Psychology*, February 2004, pp. 36–51.

16. H. Yen, "Richard Parsons, AOL Time Warner's New CEO, Known as Consensus-Builder" (www.tbo.com) (December 6, 2001).

17. G. Yukl, and D. D. Van Fleet, "Theory and Research on Leadership in Organizations," in M. D. Dunnette and L. M. Hough (eds.), *Handbook of Industrial and Organizational Psychology*, vol. 2 (Palo Alto, CA: Consulting Psychologists Press, 1992), pp. 147–97.

18. R. Kahn and D. Katz, "Leadership Practices in Relation to Productivity and Morale," in D. Cartwright and A. Zander (eds.), *Group Dynamics: Research and Theory*, 2nd ed. (Elmsford, NY: Row, Paterson, 1960).

19. Judge, Piccolo, and Ilies, "The Forgotten Ones? The Validity of Consideration and Initiating Structure in Leadership Research."

20. R. R. Blake and J. S. Mouton, *The Managerial Grid* (Houston: Gulf, 1964).

21. See, for example, R. R. Blake and J. S. Mouton, "A Comparative Analysis of Situationalism and 9,9 Management by Principle," *Organizational Dynamics*, Spring 1982, pp. 20–43.

22. See, for example, L. L. Larson, J. G. Hunt, and R. N. Osborn, "The Great Hi-Hi Leader Behavior Myth: A Lesson from

Occam's Razor," *Academy of Management Journal*, December 1976, pp. 628–41; and P. C. Nystrom, "Managers and the Hi-Hi Leader Myth," *Academy of Management Journal*, June 1978, pp. 325–31.

23. M. McDonald, "Lingerie's Iron Maiden Is Undone," *U.S. News & World Report*, June 25, 2001, p. 37; and A. D'Innocenzio, "Wachner Ousted as CEO, Chairman at Warnaco," *The Detroit News*, November 17, 2001, p. D1.

24. "SEC Announces Settlement with Warnaco, Former Warnaco Executives, and PwC for Financial Disclosure Violations." (www.sec.gov/news/press/2004-62.htm) (May 11, 2004); D. Leonhardt, "Boards Aim to Pull Back CEO Salary," *The New York Times*. (www.uni-muenster.de/PeaCon/global-texte/g-w/n/ceosalary.htm) (September 16, 2002).

25. F. E. Fiedler, *A Theory of Leadership Effectiveness* (New York: McGraw-Hill, 1967).

26. S. Shiflett, "Is There a Problem with the LPC Score in LEADER MATCH?" *Personnel Psychology*, Winter 1981, pp. 765–69.

27. F. E. Fiedler, M. M. Chemers, and L. Mahar, *Improving Leadership Effectiveness: The Leader Match Concept* (New York: John Wiley, 1977).

28. Cited in R. J. House and R. N. Aditya, "The Social Scientific Study of Leadership," p. 422.

29. L. H. Peters, D. D. Hartke, and J. T. Pohlmann, "Fiedler's Contingency Theory of Leadership: An Application of the Meta-Analysis Procedures of Schmidt and Hunter," *Psychological Bulletin*, March 1985, pp. 274–85; C. A. Schriesheim, B. J. Tepper, and L. A. Tetrault, "Least Preferred coworker Score, Situational Control, and Leadership Effectiveness: A Meta-Analysis of Contingency Model Performance Predictions," *Journal of Applied Psychology*, August 1994, pp. 561–73; and R. Ayman, M. M. Chemers, and F. Fiedler, "The Contingency Model of Leadership Effectiveness: Its Levels of Analysis," *Leadership Quarterly*, Summer 1995, pp. 147–67.

30. House and Aditya, "The Social Scientific Study of Leadership," p. 422.

31. See, for instance, R. W. Rice, "Psychometric Properties of the Esteem for the Least Preferred coworker (LPC) Scale," *Academy of Management Review*, January 1978, pp. 106–18; C. A. Schriesheim, B. D. Bannister, and W. H. Money, "Psychometric Properties of the LPC Scale: An Extension of Rice's Review," *Academy of Management Review*, April 1979, pp. 287–90; and J. K. Kennedy, J. M. Houston, M. A. Korgaard, and D. D. Gallo, "Construct Space of the Least Preferred coworker (LPC) Scale," *Educational & Psychological Measurement*, Fall 1987, pp. 807–14.

32. See E. H. Schein, *Organizational Psychology*, 3rd ed. (Upper Saddle River, NJ: Prentice Hall, 1980), pp. 116–17; and B. Kabanoff, "A Critique of Leader Match and Its Implications for Leadership Research," *Personnel Psychology*, Winter 1981, pp. 749–64.

33. F. E. Fiedler and J. E. Garcia, *New Approaches to Effective Leadership: Cognitive Resources and Organizational Performance* (New York: Wiley, 1987).

34. See F. W. Gibson, F. E. Fiedler, and K. M. Barrett, "Stress, Babble, and the Utilization of the Leader's Intellectual Abilities," *Leadership Quarterly*, Summer 1993, pp. 189–208; F. E. Fiedler and T. G. Link, "Leader Intelligence, Inter-personal Stress, and Task Performance," in R. J. Sternberg and R. K. Wagner (eds.), *Mind in Context: Interactionist Perspectives on Human Intelligence* (London: Cambridge University Press, 1994), pp. 152–67; F. E. Fiedler, "Cognitive Resources and Leadership Performance," *Applied Psychology—An International Review*, January 1995, pp. 5–28; and F. E. Fiedler, "The Curious Role of Cognitive Resources in Leadership," in R. E. Riggio, S. E. Murphy, F. J. Pirozzolo (eds.), *Multiple Intelligences and Leadership* (Mahwah, NJ: Lawrence Erlbaum, 2002), pp. 91–104.

35. T. A. Judge, A. E. Colbert, and R. Ilies, "Intelligence and Leadership: A Quantitative Review and Test of Theoretical Propositions," *Journal of Applied Psychology*, June 2004, pp. 542–52.

36. F. E. Fiedler, "Leadership Experience and Leadership Performance: Another Hypothesis Shot to Hell," *Organizational Behavior and Human Performance*, January 1970, pp. 1–14; F. E. Fiedler, "Time-Based Measures of Leadership Experience and Organizational Performance: A Review of Research and a Preliminary Model," *Leadership Quarterly*, Spring 1992, pp. 5–23; and M. A. Quinones, J. K. Ford, and M. S. Teachout, "The Relationship between Work Experience and Job Performance: A Conceptual and Meta-Analytic Review," *Personnel Psychology*, Winter 1995, pp. 887–910.

37. P. Hersey and K. H. Blanchard, "So You Want to Know Your Leadership Style?" *Training and Development Journal*, February 1974, pp. 1–15; and P. Hersey, K. H. Blanchard, and D. E. Johnson, *Management of Organizational Behavior: Leading Human Resources*, 8th ed. (Upper Saddle River, NJ: Prentice Hall, 2001).

38. Cited in C. F. Fernandez and R. P. Vecchio, "Situational Leadership Theory Revisited: A Test of an Across-Jobs Perspective," *Leadership Quarterly* 8, no. 1 (1997), p. 67.

39. See, for instance, *Ibid.*, pp. 67–84; C. L. Graeff, "Evolution of Situational Leadership Theory: A Critical Review," *Leadership Quarterly* 8, no. 2 (1997), pp. 153–70; and R. P. Vecchio and K. J. Boatwright, "Preferences for Idealized Styles of Supervision," *Leadership Quarterly*, August 2002, pp. 327–42.

40. R. M. Dienesch and R. C. Liden, "Leader-Member Exchange Model of Leadership: A Critique and Further Development," *Academy of Management Review*, July 1986, pp. 618–34; G. B. Graen and M. Uhl-Bien, "Relationship-Based Approach to Leadership: Development of Leader-Member Exchange (LMX) Theory of Leadership Over 25 Years: Applying a Multi-Domain Perspective," *Leadership Quarterly*, Summer 1995, pp. 219–47; R. C. Liden, R. T. Sparrowe, and S. J. Wayne, "Leader-Member Exchange Theory: The Past and Potential for the Future," in G. R. Ferris (ed.), *Research in Personnel and Human Resource Management*, vol. 15 (Greenwich, CT: JAI Press, 1997), pp. 47–119; and C. A. Schriesheim, S. L. Castro, X. Zhou, and F. J. Yammarino, "The Folly of Theorizing 'A' but Testing 'B': A Selective Level-of-Analysis Review of the Field and a Detailed Leader-Member Exchange Illustration," *Leadership Quarterly*, Winter 2001, pp. 515–51.

41. R. Liden and G. Graen, "Generalizability of the Vertical Dyad Linkage Model of Leadership," *Academy of Management*

Journal, September 1980, pp. 451–65; R. C. Liden, S. J. Wayne, and D. Stilwell, "A Longitudinal Study of the Early Development of Leader-Member Exchanges," *Journal of Applied Psychology*, August 1993, pp. 662–74; S. J. Wayne, L. M. Shore, W. H. Bommer, and L. E. Tetrick, "The Role of Fair Treatment and Rewards in Perceptions of Organizational Support and Leader-Member Exchange," *Journal of Applied Psychology* 87, no. 3 (June 2002), pp. 590–98; S. S. Masterson, K. Lewis, and B. M. Goldman, "Integrating Justice and Social Exchange: The Differing Effects of Fair Procedures and Treatment on Work Relationships," *Academy of Management Journal* 43, no. 4 (August 2000), pp. 738–48.

42. D. Duchon, S. G. Green, and T. D. Taber, "Vertical Dyad Linkage: A Longitudinal Assessment of Antecedents, Measures, and Consequences," *Journal of Applied Psychology*, February 1986, pp. 56–60; Liden, Wayne, and Stilwell, "A Longitudinal Study on the Early Development of Leader-Member Exchanges"; R. J. Deluga and J. T. Perry, "The Role of Subordinate Performance and Ingratiation in Leader-Member Exchanges," *Group & Organization Management*, March 1994, pp. 67–86; T. N. Bauer and S. G. Green, "Development of Leader-Member Exchange: A Longitudinal Test," *Academy of Management Journal*, December 1996, pp. 1538–67; S. J. Wayne, L. M. Shore, and R. C. Liden, "Perceived Organizational Support and Leader-Member Exchange: A Social Exchange Perspective," *Academy of Management Journal*, February 1997, pp. 82–111; and M. Uhl-Bien, "Relationship Development as a Key Ingredient for Leadership Development" in S. E. Murphy and R. E. Riggio (eds.), *Future of Leadership Development* (Mahwah, NJ: Lawrence Erlbaum, 2003) pp. 129–47.

43. O. Janssen and N. W. Van Yperen, "Employees' Goal Orientations, the Quality of Leader-Member Exchange, and the Outcomes of Job Performance and Job Satisfaction," *Academy of Management Journal*, Vol 47(3), June 2004, pp. 368–384.

44. K. M. Kacmar, L. A. Witt, and S. Zivnuska, "The Interactive Effect of Leader-Member Exchange and Communication Frequency on Performance Ratings," *Journal of Applied Psychology* 88, no. 4 (August 2003), pp. 764–72.

45. A. Stensgaard, "What Happens to the Inner Circle of the Ousted CEO?" AME Info. (http://www.ameinfo.com/news/Detailed/23359.html) (April 27, 2003).

46. See, for instance, C. R. Gerstner and D. V. Day, "Meta-Analytic Review of Leader-Member Exchange Theory: Correlates and Construct Issues," *Journal of Applied Psychology*, December 1997, pp. 827–44; C. Gomez and B. Rosen, "The Leader-Member Exchange as a Link Between Managerial Trust and Employee Empowerment," *Group & Organization Management*, March 2001, pp. 53–69; J. M. Maslyn and M. Uhl-Bien, "Leader-Member Exchange and Its Dimensions: Effects of Self-Effort and Other's Effort on Relationship Quality," *Journal of Applied Psychology*, August 2001, pp. 697–708; M. L. Kraimer, S. J. Wayne, and R. A. Jaworski, "Sources of Support and Expatriate Performance: The Mediating Role of Expatriate Adjustment," *Personnel Psychology* 54 (Spring 2001), pp. 71–99; and note 42.

47. D. Eden, "Leadership and Expectations: Pygmalion Effects and Other Self-Fulfilling Prophecies in Organizations," *Leadership Quarterly*, Winter 1992, pp. 278–79.

48. R. J. House, "A Path-Goal Theory of Leader Effectiveness," *Administrative Science Quarterly*, September 1971, pp. 321–38; R. J. House and T. R. Mitchell, "Path-Goal Theory of Leadership," *Journal of Contemporary Business*, Autumn 1974, pp. 81–97; and R. J. House, "Path-Goal Theory of Leadership: Lessons, Legacy, and a Reformulated Theory," *Leadership Quarterly*, Fall 1996, pp. 323–52.

49. J. C. Wofford and L. Z. Liska, "Path-Goal Theories of Leadership: A Meta-Analysis," *Journal of Management*, Winter 1993, pp. 857–76; P. M. Podsakoff, S. B. MacKenzie, and M. Ahearne, "Searching for a Needle in a Haystack: Trying to Identify the Illusive Moderators of Leadership Behaviors," *Journal of Management* 21 (1995), pp. 423–70.

50. J. R. Villa, J. P. Howell, and P. W. Dorfman, "Problems with Detecting Moderators in Leadership Research Using Moderated Multiple Regression," *Leadership Quarterly* 14 (2003), pp. 3–23; C. A. Schriesheim, and L. Neider, "Path-Goal Leadership Theory: The Long and Winding Road," *Leadership Quarterly* 7 (1996), pp. 317–21; M. G. Evans, "R. J. House's 'A Path-Goal Theory of Leader Effectiveness.' " *Leadership Quarterly* 7 (1996), pp. 305–09.

51. V. H. Vroom and P. W. Yetton, *Leadership and Decision-Making* (Pittsburgh: University of Pittsburgh Press, 1973).

52. V. H. Vroom and A. G. Jago, *The New Leadership: Managing Participation in Organizations* (Englewood Cliffs, NJ: Prentice Hall, 1988). See also V. H. Vroom and A. G. Jago, "Situation Effects and Levels of Analysis in the Study of Leader Participation," *Leadership Quarterly*, Summer 1995, pp. 169–81.

53. See, for example, R. H. G. Field, "A Test of the Vroom-Yetton Normative Model of Leadership," *Journal of Applied Psychology*, October 1982, pp. 523–32; C. R. Leana, "Power Relinquishment versus Power Sharing: Theoretical Clarification and Empirical Comparison of Delegation and Participation," *Journal of Applied Psychology*, May 1987, pp. 228–33; J. T. Ettling and A. G. Jago, "Participation Under Conditions of Conflict: More on the Validity of the Vroom-Yetton Model," *Journal of Management Studies*, January 1988, pp. 73–83; R. H. G. Field and R. J. House, "A Test of the Vroom-Yetton Model Using Manager and Subordinate Reports," *Journal of Applied Psychology*, June 1990, pp. 362–66; and R. H. G. Field and J. P. Andrews, "Testing the Incremental Validity of the Vroom-Jago Versus Vroom-Yetton Models of Participation in Decision Making," *Journal of Behavioral Decision Making*, December 1998, pp. 251–61.

54. House and Aditya, "The Social Scientific Study of Leadership: Quo Vadis?" p. 428.

55. See R. A. Barker, "How Can We Train Leaders If We Do Not Know What Leadership Is?" *Human Relations*, April 1997, pp. 343–62.

56. N. Nicholson, *Executive Instinct* (New York: Crown, 2001).

57. House and Aditya, "The Social Scientific Study of Leadership: Quo Vadis?" pp. 460–61.

58. D. V. Day and R. G. Lord, "Executive Leadership and Organizational Performance: Suggestions for a New Theory and Methodology," *Journal of Management*, Fall 1988, pp. 453–64.

59. M. Frese, S. Beimel, and S. Schoenborn, "Action Training for Charismatic Leadership: Two Evaluations of Studies of a Commercial Training Module on Inspirational Communication of a Vision," *Personnel Psychology* 56 (2003), pp. 671–97; T. Dvir, D. Eden, and B. J. Avolio, "Impact of Transformational Leadership on Follower Development and Performance: A Field Experiment," *Academy of Management Journal* 45 (2002), pp. 735–44; A. J. Towler, "Effects of Charismatic Influence Training on Attitudes, Behavior, and Performance," *Personnel Psychology* 56 (2003), pp. 363–81; J. Barling, T. Weber, and E. K. Kelloway, "Effects of Transformational Leadership Training on Attitudinal and Financial Outcomes: A Field Experiment," *Journal of Applied Psychology* 81 (1996), pp. 827–32.

Leadership is a combination of strategy and character. If you must be without one, be without the strategy.

— General H. Norman Schwarzkopf

Contemporary Issues in Leadership

After studying this chapter, you should be able to:

1 Explain how framing influences leadership effectiveness.

2 Define the qualities of a charismatic leader.

3 Contrast transformational with transactional leadership.

4 Identify the five dimensions of trust.

5 Identify the four roles that team leaders perform.

6 Explain the role of a mentor.

7 Describe how online leadership differs from face-to-face leadership.

8 Identify when leadership may not be necessary.

9 Explain how to find and create effective leaders.

LEARNING OBJECTIVES

CHAPTER 13

The FBI's Vision Lady

In 2003, Maureen Baginski was given a tremendous task: reorganizing intelligence at the FBI to avoid a repeat of the September 11, 2001, terrorist attacks. Baginski has been described as the FBI's "Vision Lady." Her strong leadership qualities explain why FBI Director Robert Mueller appointed her to be the new directorate for domestic intelligence.

Reorganizing intelligence at the FBI is a daunting task. Prior to the 9/11 attacks, the FBI caught and prosecuted offenders after a crime was committed. However, in a world of increased terror threats, the FBI needs to collect, analyze, and disseminate intelligence in a preemptive manner. Baginski noted, "I wouldn't even begin to claim that it's not hard."

But Baginski is a leader with a vision. Rather than bury herself in details or hide behind her former expertise (most of her career was spent as a Russian linguist and Soviet expert), Baginski has been given credit for her toughness and her vision in avoiding a quick fix.

In her efforts to transform the FBI, Baginski has encountered some opposition, mostly from the 56 field office chiefs who may be entrenched in the old way of doing things. But Mueller, and members of the 9/11 Commission, have backed her. 9/11 commissioner Jamie Gorelick told Baginski, "Many times, we have asked the question: How is X going to get fixed? Who's going to do Y? And often, very often, maybe too often for your comfort level, Mo Baginski is the answer."

Because of her job and influence, Baginski is already regarded as one of the most powerful people in Washington. She admits, though, that it will take at least 5 years to turn the FBI's domestic intelligence group around into a forward-looking unit. In the meantime, as many argue that Al Qaeda is planning another massive attack, Bagainski and her team strive to prevent it. As one reviewer commented, "Baginski seems unfailingly upbeat and optimistic. She needs to be, in the face of never-ending threats from outside and uncertainties from within the FBI."[1] ■

Maureen Baginski embodies the qualities of a transformational leader—that is, she is a leader who inspires followers to transcend their own self-interests and who is capable of having a profound and extraordinary effect on followers. It's true that Baginski faced some challenges, especially with the 56 field office chiefs. But it is not uncommon for transformational leaders to encounter such opposition, especially during the early stages of their leadership role. We'll discuss transformational leadership in more detail later on in the chapter. In addition to transformational leadership, we will also explore charismatic leadership, the role of ethics and trust in leadership, contemporary leadership roles, challenges to the leadership construct, and finally, how companies find and create effective leaders. But first, let's explore how effective leaders use framing to inspire and influence their followers.

Framing: Using Words to Shape Meaning and Inspire Others

Martin Luther King, Jr.'s influential "I Have a Dream" speech, delivered on the steps of the Lincoln Memorial in 1963, succeeded in putting the civil rights movements into vivid and moving terms that all could understand. King's framing statements had a profound effect on the way people saw the struggle for justice in the years that followed.

Martin Luther King, Jr.'s "I Have a Dream" speech largely shaped the civil rights movement. His words created an imagery of what a country would be like where racial prejudice no longer existed. What King did was *frame* the civil rights movement in a way so that others would see it the way he saw it.

Framing is a way to use language to manage meaning.[2] It's a way for leaders to influence how events are seen and understood. It involves the selection and highlighting of one or more aspects of a subject while excluding others.

Framing is analogous to what a photographer does. The visual world that exists is essentially ambiguous. When the photographer aims a camera and focuses on a specific shot, she frames the photo. Others then see what she wanted them to see. They see her point of view. That is precisely what leaders do when they frame an issue. They choose which aspects or portion of the subject they want others to focus on and which portions they want to be excluded.

Trial lawyers make their living by framing issues. Defense attorneys, for instance, shape their arguments so as to get the jury to see their client in the most favorable terms. They include "facts" that might help the jury find their client "not guilty." They exclude facts that might reflect unfavorably on their client. And they try to provide alternative interpretations to the "facts" that the prosecution argues makes their client guilty.

Lobbying groups also provide rich illustrations of the framing concept. The leadership of the National Rifle Association (NRA) has historically been very successful in limiting gun controls in the United States. They've done this not by focusing on shootings, deaths, or even self-defense. They've succeeded by framing gun control as a second amendment "freedom" issue. To the degree that the NRA can shape public opinion to think of gun controls as taking away a citizen's right to bear arms, it has been able to minimize gun control regulations.

So why is framing relevant to leadership today? Because in the complex and chaotic environment in which an increasing number of leaders work, there is typically considerable maneuverability with respect to "the facts." What is real is often what the leader says is real. What's important is what he or she chooses to say is important. Leaders can use language to influence followers' perceptions of the world, the meaning of events, beliefs about causes and consequences, and visions of the future. It's through framing that leaders determine whether people notice problems, how they understand and remember problems, and how they react to problems.[3] Thus, framing is a powerful tool by which leaders influence how others see and interpret reality.

War and the Art of Framing

During World War II, most military operations didn't have names or if they did, they were not for public consumption—such as a landing operation called "Operation Sledgehammer." But in more recent years, political and military leaders have learned how to use language to frame war terminology so as to maximize public support and minimize opposition.

The war against Iraq, which began in the spring of 2003, was called "Operation Iraqi Freedom" by the Bush administration. That label was not chosen arbitrarily. It was carefully selected to give the war an image of helping, instead of hurting, the Iraqi people. And when it came to listing the countries supporting the U.S. invasion of Iraq, the name selected was "The Coalition of the Willing." This label helped in distinguishing the "willing" (the British, for example) from the "unwilling" (the French, for example). Additional phrases like "weapons of mass destruction" and "shock and awe" were carefully chosen to shape the public's image of the Iraqi threat and the U.S. ability to win the war. The selection of the wrong label can undermine a military effort. For instance, the U.S. invasion in Afghanistan was originally called "Infinite Justice." But it soon became obvious to military leaders that this label carried religious connotations and that the United States was trying to claim God was on its side. So the effort was quickly renamed "Enduring Freedom."

The administration of George W. Bush has no monopoly on this game. Take a look at some of the other names given to some U.S. military operations. The Pentagon, for instance, used the term "Just Cause" to describe its 1989–90 operation in Panama, "Desert Shield" for the 1990–91 Gulf War conflict, and "Restore Hope" for its intervention in Somalia.

Source: Based on R. Blumenstein and M. Rose, "Name That Op: How U.S. Coins Phrases of War," *The Wall Street Journal*, March 24, 2003, p. B1; and M. Barone, "A Knack For Framing," *U.S. News & World Report*, September 8, 2003, p. 23.

Inspirational Approaches to Leadership

In this section, we present two contemporary leadership theories with a common theme. They view leaders as individuals who inspire followers through their words, ideas, and behaviors. These theories are charismatic leadership and transformational leadership.

Charismatic Leadership

John F. Kennedy, Martin Luther King, Jr., Ronald Reagan, Bill Clinton, Mary Kay Ash (founder of Mary Kay Cosmetics), Steve Jobs (cofounder of Apple Computer), and former New York City mayor Rudy Giuliani are individuals frequently cited as being charismatic leaders. So what do they have in common?

What Is Charismatic Leadership?   Max Weber, a sociologist, was the first scholar to discuss charismatic leadership. More than a century ago, he defined *charisma* (from the Greek for "gift") as "a certain quality of an individual personality, by virtue of which he or she is set apart from ordinary people and treated as endowed with supernatural, superhuman, or at least specifically exceptional powers or qualities. These are not accessible to the ordinary person, but are regarded as of divine origin or as exemplary, and on the basis of them the individual concerned is treated as a leader."[4] Weber argued that charismatic leadership was one of several ideal types of authority.

The first researcher to consider charismatic leadership in terms of OB was Robert House. According to House's **charismatic leadership theory**, followers

---

framing   *A way to use language to manage meaning.*

charismatic leadership theory   *Followers make attributions of heroic or extraordinary leadership abilities when they observe certain behaviors.*

make attributions of heroic or extraordinary leadership abilities when they observe certain behaviors.[5] There have been a number of studies that have attempted to identify the characteristics of the charismatic leader. One of the best reviews of the literature has documented four—they have a vision, they are willing to take personal risks to achieve that vision, they are sensitive to follower needs, and they exhibit behaviors that are out of the ordinary.[6] These characteristics are described in Exhibit 13-1.

Are Charismatic Leaders Born or Made?   Are charismatic leaders born with their qualities? Or can people actually learn how to be charismatic leaders? The answer to both questions is yes.

It is true that individuals are born with traits that make them charismatic. In fact, studies of identical twins have found that they score similarly on charismatic leadership measures, even if they were raised in different households and had never met. Research suggests that personality is also related to charismatic leadership. Charismatic leaders are likely to be extraverted, self-confident, and achievement-oriented.[7] Consider CNN cofounder Ted Turner. When referring to himself, he has said, "A full moon blanks out all the stars around it" and "If I only had humility, I'd be perfect." Although not all charismatic leaders are as bold or colorful as Turner, most of them do have an alluring, interesting, and dynamic nature.

Although a small minority thinks that charisma is inherited and therefore cannot be learned, most experts believe that individuals also can be trained to exhibit charismatic behaviors and can thus enjoy the benefits that accrue to being labeled "a charismatic leader."[8] After all, just because we inherit certain tendencies doesn't mean that we can't learn to change. Think about weight— it's true that some people are born with predispositions to be overweight, but it would be unreasonable to think that our weight is unaffected by the food we eat. Predispositions exist, and can be powerful, but that doesn't mean people can't change. One set of authors proposes that a person can learn to become charismatic by following a three-step process.[9]

First, an individual needs to develop the aura of charisma by maintaining an optimistic view; using passion as a catalyst for generating enthusiasm; and communicating with the whole body, not just with words. Second, an individual draws others in by creating a bond that inspires others to follow. And third, the individual brings out the potential in followers by tapping into their emotions. This approach seems to work, as evidenced by researchers who've succeeded in actually scripting undergraduate business students to "play" charismatic.[10] The students were taught to articulate an overarching goal, communicate high performance expectations, exhibit confidence in the ability of followers to meet these expectations, and empathize with the needs of their followers; they learned to project a powerful, confident, and dynamic presence; and they prac-

---

Exhibit **13-1**	Key Characteristics of Charismatic Leaders

1. *Vision and articulation.* Has a vision—expressed as an idealized goal—that proposes a future better than the status quo; and is able to clarify the importance of the vision in terms that are understandable to others.
2. *Personal risk.* Willing to take on high personal risk, incur high costs and engage in self-sacrifice to achieve the vision.
3. *Sensitivity to follower needs.* Perceptive of others' abilities and responsive to their needs and feelings.
4. *Unconventional behavior.* Engages in behaviors that are perceived as novel and counter to norms.

Source: Based on J. A. Conger and R. N. Kanungo, *Charismatic Leadership in Organizations* (Thousand Oaks, CA: Sage, 1998), p. 94.

Steve Jobs, the charismatic leader of Apple Computer, reinvented the company by inventing a new market with the iPod digital music player. Jobs's vision was to create a portable music player that could hold digital music so people could listen to it anywhere. Confident of his innovation, Jobs inspired his team to design and build the iPod in less than a year. Since launching iPod, Apple has sold more than 10 million music players, adding $6.2 billion to Apple's revenues.

ticed using a captivating and engaging voice tone. To further capture the dynamics and energy of charisma, the leaders were trained to evoke charismatic nonverbal characteristics: They alternated between pacing and sitting on the edges of their desks, leaned toward the subjects, maintained direct eye contact, and had relaxed postures and animated facial expressions. These researchers found that these students could learn how to project charisma. Moreover, followers of these leaders had higher task performance, task adjustment, and adjustment to the leader and to the group than did followers who worked under groups led by noncharismatic leaders.

How Charismatic Leaders Influence Followers   How do charismatic leaders actually influence followers? The evidence suggests a four-step process.[11] It begins by the leader articulating an appealing **vision**. A vision is a long-term strategy on how to attain a goal or goals. This vision provides a sense of continuity for followers by linking the present with a better future for the organization. For example, at Apple, Steve Jobs championed the iPod, noting, "It's as Apple as anything Apple has ever done." The creation of the iPod achieved Apple's goal of offering groundbreaking and easy-to-use-technology. Apple's strategy was to create a product that had a user-friendly interface where songs could be quickly uploaded and easily organized. It was the first major-market device to link data storage capabilities with music downloading.

A vision is incomplete unless it has an accompanying vision statement. A **vision statement** is a formal articulation of an organization's vision or mission. Charismatic leaders may use vision statements to "imprint" on followers an overarching goal and purpose. PepsiCo, for example, has the following mission statement on its Web site: "To be the world's premier consumer products company focused on convenient foods and beverages. We seek to produce healthy financial rewards to investors as we provide opportunities for growth and enrichment to our employees, our business partners and the communities in which we operate. And in everything we do, we strive for honesty, fairness and integrity."

Once a vision and vision statement are established, the leader then communicates high performance expectations and expresses confidence that followers can attain them. This enhances follower self-esteem and self-confidence. Centra Software CEO Paul Gudonis says that conveying confidence is a central tool in a manager's toolbox.[12]

Next, the leader conveys, through words and actions, a new set of values and, by his or her behavior, sets an example for followers to imitate. One study of Israeli bank employees showed, for example, that charismatic leaders were more effective because their employees personally identified with their leaders. Finally, the charismatic leader engages in emotion-inducing and often unconventional behavior to demonstrate courage and convictions about the vision. There is an emotional contagion in charismatic leadership where followers "catch" the emotions their leader is conveying.[13] The next time you see Martin Luther King's "I Have a Dream" speech, focus on the reactions of the crowd, and it will bring to light how a charismatic leader can spread his emotion to his followers.

Because the vision is such a critical component of charismatic leadership, we should clarify exactly what we mean by the term, identify specific qualities of an effective vision, and offer some examples.[14]

A review of various definitions finds that a vision differs from other forms of direction setting in several ways: "A vision has clear and compelling imagery

vision   *A long-term strategy on how to attain a goal or goals.*

vision statement   *A formal articulation of an organization's vision or mission.*

that offers an innovative way to improve, which recognizes and draws on traditions, and connects to actions that people can take to realize change. Vision taps people's emotions and energy. Properly articulated, a vision creates the enthusiasm that people have for sporting events and other leisure-time activities, bringing this energy and commitment to the workplace."[15]

The key properties of a vision seem to be inspirational possibilities that are value-centered, realizable, with superior imagery and articulation.[16] Visions should be able to create possibilities that are inspirational and unique and that offer a new order that can produce organizational distinction. A vision is likely to fail if it doesn't offer a view of the future that is clearly and demonstrably better for the organization and its members. Desirable visions fit the times and circumstances and reflect the uniqueness of the organization. People in the organization must also believe that the vision is attainable. It should be perceived as challenging yet doable. Also, visions that have clear articulation and powerful imagery are more easily grasped and accepted.

What are some examples of visions? Rupert Murdoch had a vision of the future of the communication industry by combining entertainment and media. Through News Corporation, Murdoch has successfully integrated a broadcast network, TV stations, movie studio, publishing, and global satellite distribution. John Malone of Liberty Media calls News Corporation "the best run, most strategically positioned vertically integrated media company in the world."[17] The late Mary Kay Ash's vision of women as entrepreneurs selling products that improved their self-image gave impetus to her cosmetics company. And Michael Dell has created a vision of a business that allows Dell Computer to sell and deliver a finished PC directly to a customer in fewer than 8 days.

Does Effective Charismatic Leadership Depend on the Situation? There is an increasing body of research that shows impressive correlations between charismatic leadership and high performance and satisfaction among followers.[18] People working for charismatic leaders are motivated to exert extra work effort and, because they like and respect their leader, express greater satisfaction. It also appears that organizations with charismatic CEOs are more profitable. And charismatic college professors enjoy higher course evaluations.[19] However, there is a growing body of evidence indicating that charisma may not always be generalizable; that is, its effectiveness may depend on the situation. Charisma appears to be most successful when the follower's task has an ideological component or when the environment involves a high degree of stress and uncertainty.[20] This may explain why, when charismatic leaders surface, it's more likely to be in politics, religion, wartime, or when a business firm is in its infancy or facing a life-threatening crisis. For example, in the 1930s, Franklin D. Roosevelt offered a vision to get Americans out of the Great Depression. In the early 1970s, when Chrysler Corp. was on the brink of bankruptcy, it needed a charismatic leader with unconventional ideas like Lee Iacocca to reinvent the company. In 1997, when Apple Computer was floundering and lacking direction, the board persuaded charismatic cofounder Steve Jobs to return as interim CEO and to inspire the company to return to its innovative roots.

In addition to ideology and uncertainty, another situational factor limiting charisma appears to be level in the organization. Remember, the creation of a vision is a key component of charisma. But visions typically apply to entire organizations or major divisions. They tend to be created by top executives. As such, charisma probably has more direct relevance to explaining the success and failures of chief executives than of lower-level managers. So even though individuals may have an inspiring personality, it's more difficult to utilize their charismatic leadership qualities in lower-level management jobs. Lower-level managers *can* create visions to lead their units. It's just harder to define such visions and align them with the larger goals of the organization as a whole.

Finally, charismatic leadership may affect some followers more than others. Research suggests, for example, that people are especially receptive to charismatic leadership when they sense a crisis, when they are under stress, or when they fear for their lives. More generally, some peoples' personalities are more susceptible to charismatic leadership.[21] Consider self-esteem. If an individual lacks self-esteem and questions his self-worth, he is more likely to absorb a leader's direction rather than establish his own way of leading or thinking.

The Dark Side of Charismatic Leadership   Charismatic business leaders like Enron's Jeffrey Skilling, GE's Jack Welch, Tyco's Dennis Kozlowski, Southwest Air's Herb Kelleher, Disney's Michael Eisner, WorldCom's Bernie Ebbers, and HealthSouth's Richard Scrushy became no less of a celebrity than Shaquille O'Neal or Madonna. Every company wanted a charismatic CEO. And to attract these people, they were given unprecedented autonomy and resources. They had private jets at their beck and call, use of $30 million penthouses, interest-free loans to buy beach homes and artwork, security staffs provided by their companies, and similar benefits befitting royalty. One study showed that charismatic CEOs were able to use their charisma to leverage higher salaries even when their performance was mediocre.[22]

Unfortunately, charismatic leaders who are larger-than-life don't necessarily act in the best interests of their organizations.[23] Many of these leaders used their power to remake their companies in their own image. These leaders often completely blurred the boundary separating their personal interests from their organization's interests. At its worst, the perils of this ego-driven charisma are leaders who allow their self-interest and personal goals to override the goals of the organization. Intolerant of criticism, they surround themselves with yes-people who are rewarded for pleasing the leader and create a climate where people are afraid to question or challenge the "king" or "queen" when they think he or she is making a mistake. The results at companies such as Enron, Tyco, WorldCom, and HealthSouth were leaders who recklessly used organizational resources for their personal benefit and executives who broke laws and crossed ethical lines to generate financial numbers that temporarily inflated stock prices and allowed leaders to cash in millions of dollars in stock options.

A study of 29 companies that went from good to great (their cumulative stock returns were all at least three times better than the general stock market

Dennis Kozlowski represents the dark side of charismatic leadership. The former charismatic CEO of Tyco International was accused and found guilty of misusing company funds to finance his lavish personal lifestyle. Kozlowski was found guilty of grand larceny, securities fraud, conspiracy, and other charges for stealing more than $150 million in bonuses from Tyco. He also defrauded shareholders by selling $430 million in Tyco stock while misrepresenting the company's financial health.

over 15 years) found an *absence* of ego-driven charismatic leaders. Although the leaders of these firms were fiercely ambitious and driven, their ambition was directed toward their company rather than themselves. They generated extraordinary results, but with little fanfare or hoopla. They took responsibility for mistakes and poor results and gave credit for successes to other people. They prided themselves on developing strong leaders inside the firm who could direct the company to greater heights after they were gone. These individuals have been called **level-5 leaders** because they have four basic leadership qualities—individual capability, team skills, managerial competence, and the ability to stimulate others to high performance—plus a fifth dimension: a paradoxical blend of personal humility and professional will. Level-5 leaders channel their ego needs away from themselves and into the goal of building a great company. So while level-5 leaders are highly effective, they tend to be people you've never heard of and who get little notoriety in the business press—people like Orin Smith at Starbucks, Kristine McDivitt of Patagonia, John Whitehead of Goldman Sachs, and Jack Brennan of Vanguard. This study is important because it confirms that leaders don't necessarily need to be charismatic to be effective, especially where charisma is enmeshed with an outsized ego.[24]

Finally, charisma can reach beyond the walls of the workplace. And because of their power to captivate others, charismatic leaders can be very dangerous. Some of the most oppressive leaders in history were highly charismatic. Consider Hitler. He was the leader of the Nazi Party and responsible for policies that resulted in the Holocaust and the deaths of approximately 6 million Jews. Robespierre was also considered charismatic. He has been credited as one of the leaders of the French Revolution and the Reign of Terror. In fact, he often used the guillotine to control the country and get rid of his political enemies. Cults are also often headed by charismatic leaders. For example, Jim Jones—the founder of the People's Temple church—convinced more than 900 of his followers to commit suicide by drinking poison. And Charles Manson—the leader of "The Family"—convinced his followers to commit mass murder. And, more recently, Osama bin Laden inspired his followers to sacrifice their lives, and the lives of thousands of others, in the name of religion.

We don't mean to suggest that charismatic leadership isn't effective. Overall, its effectiveness is well supported. The point is a charismatic leader isn't always the answer. Yes, an organization with a charismatic leader at the helm is more likely to be successful, but that success depends, to some extent, on the situation and on the leader's vision. Some charismatic leaders like Hitler are all too successful at convincing their followers to pursue a vision that can be disastrous.

Now that you know more about charismatic leadership, are you wondering if you have what it takes to join the ranks of charismatic leaders? The Self-Assessment feature will tell you.

HOW CHARISMATIC AM I?

In the Self-Assessment Library (available on CD, online, and in print), take assessment II.B.2 (How Charismatic Am I?) and answer the following questions.

1. *How did you score compared to your classmates? Do you think your score is accurate?*
2. *Why do you think you scored as you did? Do you think it's because of your genes? Are your parents charismatic? Or do you think your score has to do with your environment? Were there factors in your upbringing or early life experiences that affected your charisma?*
3. *Based on the material presented in the chapter, do you think you could become more charismatic? If yes, how might you go about becoming more charismatic?*

Transformational Leadership

Another stream of research has focused on differentiating transformational leaders from transactional leaders.[25] Most of the leadership theories presented in the previous chapter—for instance, the Ohio State studies, Fiedler's model, and path-goal theory—have concerned **transactional leaders**. These kinds of leaders guide or motivate their followers in the direction of established goals by clarifying role and task requirements. **Transformational leaders** inspire followers to transcend their own self-interests for the good of the organization and are capable of having a profound and extraordinary effect on their followers. Andrea Jung at Avon, Richard Branson of the Virgin Group, and Maureen Baginski are all examples of transformational leaders. They pay attention to the concerns and developmental needs of individual followers; they change followers' awareness of issues by helping them to look at old problems in new ways; and they are able to excite, arouse, and inspire followers to put out extra effort to achieve group goals. Exhibit 13-2 briefly identifies and defines the characteristics that differentiate these two types of leaders.

Transactional and transformational leadership shouldn't be viewed as opposing approaches to getting things done.[26] Transformational and transactional leadership complement each other, but that doesn't mean they're equally important. Transformational leadership builds *on top of* transactional leadership and produces levels of follower effort and performance that go beyond what would occur with a transactional approach alone. But the reverse isn't true. So if you are a good transactional leader but do not have transformational qualities, you'll likely only be a mediocre leader. The best leaders are transactional *and* transformational.

Exhibit **13-2**	Characteristics of Transactional and Transformational Leaders

Transactional Leader

Contingent Reward: Contracts exchange of rewards for effort, promises rewards for good performance, recognizes accomplishments.

Management by Exception (active): Watches and searches for deviations from rules and standards, takes correct action.

Management by Exception (passive): Intervenes only if standards are not met.

Laissez-Faire: Abdicates responsibilities, avoids making decisions.

Transformational Leader

Idealized Influence: Provides vision and sense of mission, instills pride, gains respect and trust.

Inspirational Motivation: Communicates high expectations, uses symbols to focus efforts, expresses important purposes in simple ways.

Intellectual Stimulation: Promotes intelligence, rationality, and careful problem solving.

Individualized Consideration: Gives personal attention, treats each employee individually, coaches, advises.

Source: B. M. Bass, "From Transactional to Transformational Leadership: Learning to Share the Vision," *Organizational Dynamics*, Winter 1990, p. 22. Reprinted by permission of the publisher. American Management Association, New York. All rights reserved.

---

level-5 leaders   *Leaders who are fiercely ambitious and driven, but whose ambition is directed toward their company rather than themselves.*

transactional leaders   *Leaders who guide or motivate their followers in the direction of established goals by clarifying role and task requirements.*

transformational leaders   *Leaders who inspire followers to transcend their own self-interests and who are capable of having a profound and extraordinary effect on followers.*

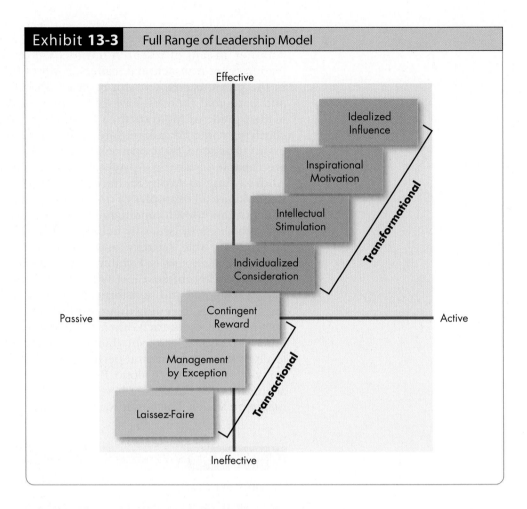

Exhibit 13-3 | Full Range of Leadership Model

Full Range of Leadership Model   Exhibit 13-3 shows the full range of leadership model. Laissez-faire is the most passive and therefore the least effective of the leader behaviors. Leaders using this style are rarely viewed as effective. Management by exception—regardless of whether it is active or passive—is slightly better than laissez-faire, but it's still considered ineffective leadership. Leaders who practice management by exception leadership tend to be available only when there is a problem, which is often too late. Contingent reward leadership can be an effective style of leadership. However, leaders will not get their employees to go above and beyond the call of duty when practicing this style of leadership. Only with the four remaining leadership styles—which are all aspects of transformational leadership—are leaders able to motivate followers to perform above expectations and transcend their own self-interest for the sake of the organization. Individualized consideration, intellectual stimulation, inspirational motivation, and idealized influence all result in extra effort from workers, higher productivity, higher morale and satisfaction, higher organizational effectiveness, lower turnover, lower absenteeism, and greater organizational adaptability. Based on this model, leaders are generally most effective when they regularly use each of the four transformational behaviors.

How Transformational Leadership Works   In the past few years, a great deal of research has been conducted to explain how transformational leadership works. Transformational leaders encourage their followers to be more innovative and creative.[27] For example, Army Colonel Leonard Wong found that, in the Iraq war, the Army was encouraging "reactive instead of proactive thought,

A.G. Lafley is a transformational leader. Since becoming CEO of Procter & Gamble in 2000, Lafley has brought creativity and flexibility to a slow-growing company. He inspired employees to take responsibility for executing his vision of changing P&G by expanding core brands such as Crest toothpaste to innovations like teeth whiteners and toothbrushes. Lafley's changes have raised P&G's revenues, profits, and stock price. Shown here with Iams pet-food mascot Euka, Lafley helped move the brand from the No. 5 to the No.1 position in the United States and doubled Iams worldwide sales.

compliance instead of creativity, and adherence instead of audacity." In response, Colonel Leonard Wong is working to empower junior officers to be creative and to take more risks.[28] Transformational leaders are more effective because they themselves are more creative, but they're also more effective because they encourage those who follow them to be creative too.

Goals are another key mechanism that explains how transformational leadership works. Followers of transformational leaders are more likely to pursue ambitious goals, be familiar with and agree on the strategic goals of the organization, and believe that the goals they are pursuing are personally important.[29] VeriSign's CEO, Stratton Sclavos, says, "It comes down to charting a course—having the ability to articulate for your employees where you're headed and how you're going to get there. Even more important is choosing people to work with who have that same level of passion, commitment, fear, and competitiveness to drive toward those same goals."

Sclavos's remark about goals brings up vision. Just as research has shown that vision is important in explaining how charismatic leadership works, research has also shown that vision explains part of the effect of transformational leadership. Indeed, one study found that vision was even more important than a charismatic (effusive, dynamic, lively) communication style in explaining the success of entrepreneurial firms.[30] Finally, transformational leadership also engenders commitment on the part of followers and instills in them a greater sense of trust in the leader.[31]

Evaluation of Transformational Leadership   The evidence supporting the superiority of transformational leadership over transactional leadership is impressive. Transformational leadership has been supported in different countries (Korea, Russia, Israel, India, Kenya, Norway, Taiwan), in disparate occupations (school principals, marine commanders, ministers, presidents of MBA associations, military cadets, union shop stewards, school teachers, sales reps), and at various job levels. For example, a number of studies with U.S., Canadian, and German military officers found, at every level, that transformational leaders were evaluated as more effective than their transactional counterparts.[32] And a review of 87 studies testing transformational leadership found that it was related to the motivation and satisfaction of followers and to the higher performance and perceived effectiveness of leaders.[33]

Transformational leadership theory is not perfect. There are concerns about whether contingent reward leadership is strictly a characteristic of transactional leaders only. And contrary to the full range of leadership model, contingent reward leadership is sometimes more effective than transformational leadership.

In summary, the overall evidence indicates that transformational leadership is more strongly correlated than transactional leadership with lower turnover rates, higher productivity, and higher employee satisfaction.[34] Like charisma, it appears that transformational leadership can be learned. One study of Canadian bank managers found that those managers who underwent transformational leadership training had bank branches that performed significantly better than branches with managers who did not undergo training. Other studies show similar results.[35]

Transformational Leadership Versus Charismatic Leadership   There is some debate about whether transformational leadership and charismatic leadership are the same. The researcher most responsible for introducing charismatic leadership to OB, Robert House, considers them synonymous, calling the differences "modest" and "minor." However, the individual who first researched transformational leadership, Bernard Bass, considers charisma to be part of transformational leadership but argues that transformational leadership is broader than charisma, suggesting that charisma is, by itself, insufficient to "account for the transformational process."[36] Another researcher commented, "The purely charismatic [leader] may want followers to adopt the charismatic's world view and go no further; the transformational leader will attempt to instill in followers the ability to question not only established views but eventually those established by the leader."[37] Although many researchers believe that transformational leadership is broader than charismatic leadership, studies show that in reality a leader who scores high on transformational leadership is also likely to score high on charisma. Therefore, in practice, measures of charisma and transformational leadership may be roughly equivalent.

Authentic Leadership: Ethics and Trust Are the Foundation of Leadership

Although charismatic leadership theories and transformational leadership theories have added greatly to our understanding of effective leadership, they do not explicitly deal with the role of ethics and trust. Some scholars have argued that a consideration of ethics and trust is essential to complete the picture of effective leadership. Here we consider these two concepts under the rubric of authentic leadership.[38]

What Is Authentic Leadership?

The philosopher Jean Paul Sartre wrote a lot about authenticity, arguing that to be an authentic person, an individual needs to be honest with oneself and avoid self-deception. Although this might be good advice for anyone, it may be especially critical for leaders.

Authentic leaders know who they are, know what they believe in and value, and act on those values and beliefs openly and candidly. Their followers would consider them to be ethical people. The primary quality, therefore, produced by authentic leadership is trust. How does authentic leadership build trust? Authentic leaders share information, encourage open communication, and stick to their ideals. The result: People come to have faith in authentic leaders.

Because the concept is so recent, there hasn't been a lot of research on authentic leadership. However, we believe it's a promising way to think about ethics and trust in leadership because it focuses on the moral aspects of being a leader. Transformational or charismatic leaders can have a vision, and communicate it persuasively, but sometimes the vision is wrong (as in the case of Hitler), or the leader is more concerned with his own needs or pleasures, as in the case with business leaders Dennis Kozlowski (ex-CEO of Tyco) and Jeff Skilling (ex-CEO of Enron).[39]

Ethics and Leadership

The topic of ethics and leadership has received surprisingly little attention. Only recently have ethicists and leadership researchers begun to consider the ethical implications in leadership.[40] Why now? One reason may be the growing general interest in ethics throughout the field of management. Another reason may be the discovery by probing biographers that many of our past leaders— such as Martin Luther King, Jr., John F. Kennedy, and Thomas Jefferson— suffered from ethical shortcomings. Certainly the impeachment hearings of American President Bill Clinton on grounds of perjury and other charges did nothing to lessen concern about ethical leadership. And the unethical practices by executives at organizations like Enron, WorldCom, HealthSouth, Arthur Andersen, Merrill Lynch, Adelphia, and Tyco have increased the public's and politician's concerns about ethical standards in American business.

Ethics touches on leadership at a number of junctures. Transformational leaders, for instance, have been described by one authority as fostering moral virtue when they try to change the attitudes and behaviors of followers.[41] Charisma, too, has an ethical component. Unethical leaders are more likely to use their charisma to enhance *power over* followers, directed toward self-serving ends. Ethical leaders are considered to use their charisma in a socially constructive way to serve others.[42] There is also the issue of abuse of power by leaders, for example, when they give themselves large salaries, bonuses, and stock options while, at the same time, they seek to cut costs by laying off long-time employees. Because top executives set the moral tone for an organization, they need to set high ethical standards, demonstrate those standards through their own behavior, and encourage and reward integrity in others.

Leadership effectiveness needs to address the *means* that a leader uses in trying to achieve goals as well as the content of those goals. For instance, Bill Gates's success in leading Microsoft to domination of the world's software business has been achieved by means of an extremely aggressive work culture. Microsoft's competitors and U.S. government regulators have pinpointed this competitive culture as the source of numerous unethical practices—from using its control of its Windows operating system to favor Microsoft's partners and subsidiaries to

authentic leaders   *Leaders who know who they are, know what they believe in and value, and act on those values and beliefs openly and candidly. Their followers would consider them to be ethical people.*

encouraging its salesforce to "crush" its rivals. Importantly, Microsoft's culture mirrors the personality of its chairman and cofounder, Gates. In addition, ethical leadership must address the content of a leader's goals. Are the changes that the leader seeks for the organization morally acceptable? Is a business leader effective if he or she builds an organization's success by selling products that damage the health of its users? This question, for example, might be asked of executives in the tobacco and junk-food industries. Or is a military leader successful by winning a war that should not have been fought in the first place?

Leadership is not value-free. Before we judge any leader to be effective, we should consider both the means used by the leader to achieve goals and the moral content of those goals.

Now let's examine the issue of trust and its role in shaping strong leaders.

What Is Trust?

Trust, or lack of trust, is an increasingly important leadership issue in today's organizations.[43] In this section, we define *trust* and provide you with some guidelines for helping build credibility and trust.

Trust is a positive expectation that another will not—through words, actions, or decisions—act opportunistically.[44] The two most important elements of our definition are that it implies familiarity and risk.

The phrase *positive expectation* in our definition assumes knowledge and familiarity about the other party. Trust is a history-dependent process based on relevant but limited samples of experience.[45] It takes time to form, building incrementally and accumulating. Most of us find it hard, if not impossible, to trust someone immediately if we don't know anything about them. At the extreme, in the case of total ignorance, we can gamble but we can't trust.[46] But as we get to know someone, and the relationship matures, we gain confidence in our ability to form a positive expectation.

The term *opportunistically* refers to the inherent risk and vulnerability in any trusting relationship. Trust involves making oneself vulnerable as when, for example, we disclose intimate information or rely on another's promises.[47] By its very nature, trust provides the opportunity for disappointment or to be taken advantage of.[48] But trust is not taking risk per se; rather, it is a *willingness* to take risk.[49] So when I trust someone, I expect that they will not take advantage of me. This willingness to take risks is common to all trust situations.[50]

What are the key dimensions that underlie the concept of trust? Evidence has identified five: integrity, competence, consistency, loyalty, and openness[51] (see Exhibit 13-4).

Integrity refers to honesty and truthfulness. Of all five dimensions, this one seems to be most critical when someone assesses another's trustworthiness.[52] For instance, when 570 white-collar employees were recently given a list of 28 attributes related to leadership, honesty was rated the most important by far.[53]

Competence encompasses an individual's technical and interpersonal knowledge and skills. Does the person know what he or she is talking about? You're unlikely to listen to or depend on someone whose abilities you don't respect. You need to believe that the person has the skills and abilities to carry out what he or she says they will do.

Consistency relates to an individual's reliability, predictability, and good judgment in handling situations. "Inconsistencies between words and action decrease trust."[54] This dimension is particularly relevant for managers. "Nothing is noticed more quickly . . . than a discrepancy between what executives preach and what they expect their associates to practice."[55]

Loyalty is the willingness to protect and save face for another person. Trust requires that you can depend on someone not to act opportunistically.

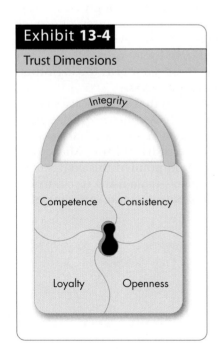

Exhibit 13-4

Trust Dimensions

Integrity

Competence   Consistency

Loyalty   Openness

The final dimension of trust is *openness*. Can you rely on the person to give you the full truth?

Trust and Leadership

Trust is a primary attribute associated with leadership; and when this trust is broken, it can have serious adverse effects on a group's performance.[56] As one author noted: "Part of the leader's task has been, and continues to be, working with people to find and solve problems, but whether leaders gain access to the knowledge and creative thinking they need to solve problems depends on how much people trust them. Trust and trust-worthiness modulate the leader's access to knowledge and cooperation."[57]

When followers trust a leader, they are willing to be vulnerable to the leader's actions—confident that their rights and interests will not be abused.[58] People are unlikely to look up to or follow someone whom they perceive as dishonest or who is likely to take advantage of them. Honesty, for instance, consistently ranks at the top of most people's list of characteristics they admire in their leaders. "Honesty is absolutely essential to leadership. If people are going to follow someone willingly, whether it be into battle or into the boardroom, they first want to assure themselves that the person is worthy of their trust."[59]

Three Types of Trust

There are three types of trust in organizational relationships: *deterrence*-based, *knowledge*-based, and *identification*-based.[60]

Deterrence-Based Trust   The most fragile relationships are contained in **deterrence-based trust**. One violation or inconsistency can destroy the relationship. This form of trust is based on fear of reprisal if the trust is violated. Individuals who are in this type of relationship do what they say because they fear the consequences from not following through on their obligations.

Deterrence-based trust will work only to the degree that punishment is possible, consequences are clear, and the punishment is actually imposed if the trust is violated. To be sustained, the potential loss of future interaction with the other party must outweigh the profit potential that comes from violating expectations. Moreover, the potentially harmed party must be willing to introduce harm (for example, I have no qualms about speaking badly of you if you betray my trust) to the person acting distrustingly.

Most new relationships begin on a base of deterrence. Take, as an illustration, a situation where you're selling your car to a friend of a friend. You don't know the buyer. You might be motivated to refrain from telling this buyer all the problems with the car that you know about. Such behavior would increase your chances of selling the car and securing the highest price. But you don't withhold information. You openly share the car's flaws. Why? Probably because of fear of reprisal. If the buyer later thinks you deceived him, he is likely to share this with your mutual friend. If you knew that the buyer would never say anything to the mutual friend, you might be tempted to take advantage of the opportunity. If it's clear that the buyer would tell and that your mutual friend would think considerably less of you for taking advantage of this buyer-friend, your honesty could be explained in deterrence terms.

Another example of deterrence-based trust is a new manager-employee relationship. As an employee, you typically trust a new boss even though there is little experience to base that trust on. The bond that creates this trust lies in the

---

trust   *A positive expectation that another will not act opportunistically.*

deterrence-based trust   *Trust based on fear of reprisal if the trust is violated.*

Organizational relationships with Xerox CEO Anne Mulcahy are founded on knowledge-based trust. In her 30 years with Xerox, Mulcahy has earned a reputation for being honest, smart, hardworking, and loyal. Confident in her ability and trustworthiness, the Xerox board chose Mulcahy to lead Xerox from the brink of bankruptcy in 2001. Since then, she has greatly reduced Xerox's $14 billion debt, reduced costs, and introduced new products. Under her leadership, Xerox is rebuilding credibility with employees, customers, and shareholders and gaining market share from competitors.

authority held by the boss and the punishment he or she can impose if you fail to fulfill your job-related obligations.

Knowledge-Based Trust   Most organizational relationships are rooted in **knowledge-based trust**. That is, trust is based on the behavioral predictability that comes from a history of interaction. It exists when you have adequate information about someone to understand them well enough to be able to accurately predict his or her behavior.

Knowledge-based trust relies on information rather than deterrence. Knowledge of the other party and predictability of his or her behavior replaces the contracts, penalties, and legal arrangements more typical of deterrence-based trust. This knowledge develops over time, largely as a function of experience that builds confidence of trustworthiness and predictability. The better you know someone, the more accurately you can predict what he or she will do. Predictability enhances trust—even if the other is predictably untrustworthy—because the ways that the other will violate the trust can be predicted! The more communication and regular interaction you have with someone else, the more this form of trust can be developed and depended on.

Interestingly, at the knowledge-based level, trust is not necessarily broken by inconsistent behavior. If you believe you can adequately explain or understand another's apparent violation, you can accept it, forgive the person, and move on in the relationship. However, the same inconsistency at the deterrence level is likely to irrevocably break the trust.

In an organizational context, most manager-employee relationships are knowledge-based. Both parties have enough experience working with each other that they know what to expect. A long history of consistently open and honest interactions, for instance, is not likely to be permanently destroyed by a single violation.

Identification-Based Trust   The highest level of trust is achieved when there is an emotional connection between the parties. It allows one party to act as an agent for the other and substitute for that person in interpersonal transactions. This is called **identification-based trust**. Trust exists because the parties understand each other's intentions and appreciate the other's wants and desires. This mutual understanding is developed to the point that each can effectively act for the other. Controls are minimal at this level. You don't need to monitor the other party because there exists unquestioned loyalty.

The best example of identification-based trust is a long-term, happily married couple. A husband comes to learn what's important to his wife and anticipates those actions. She, in turn, trusts that he will anticipate what's important to her without having to ask. Increased identification enables each to think like the other, feel like the other, and respond like the other.

You see identification-based trust occasionally in organizations among people who have worked together for long periods of time and have a depth of experience that allows them to know each other inside and out. This is also the type of trust that managers ideally seek in teams. Team members are so comfortable and trusting of each other that they can anticipate each other and act freely in each other's absence. In the current work world, it's probably accurate to say that most large corporations have broken the bonds of identification trust that were built with long-term employees. Broken promises have led to a breakdown in what was, at one time, a bond of unquestioned loyalty. It's likely to have been replaced with knowledge-based trust.

Basic Principles of Trust

Research allows us to offer some principles for better understanding the creating of both trust and mistrust.[61]

Mistrust drives out trust. People who are trusting demonstrate their trust by increasing their openness to others, disclosing relevant information, and expressing their true intentions. People who mistrust do not reciprocate. They conceal information and act opportunistically to take advantage of others. To defend against repeated exploitation, trusting people are driven to mistrust. A few mistrusting people can poison an entire organization.

Trust begets trust. In the same way that mistrust drives out trust, exhibiting trust in others tends to encourage reciprocity. Effective leaders increase trust in small increments and allow others to respond in kind. By offering trust in only small increments, leaders limit penalty or loss that might occur if their trust is exploited.

Growth often masks mistrust. Growth gives leaders opportunities for rapid promotion and for increased power and responsibility. In this environment, leaders tend to solve problems with quick fixes that elude immediate detection by higher management and leave the problems arising from mistrust to their successors. Leaders can take a short-term perspective because they are not likely to be around to have to deal with the long-term consequences of their decisions. The lingering effects of mistrust become apparent to the successors when the growth slows.

Decline or downsizing tests the highest levels of trust. The corollary to the previous growth principle is that decline or downsizing tends to undermine even the most trusting environment. Layoffs are threatening. Even after layoffs have been completed, those who survive feel less secure in their jobs. When employers break the loyalty bond by laying off employees, there is less willingness among workers to trust what management says.

Trust increases cohesion. Trust holds people together. Trust means people have confidence that they can rely on each other. If one person needs help or falters, that person knows that the others will be there to fill in. When faced with adversity, group members who display trust in each other will work together and exert high levels of effort to achieve the group's goals.

Mistrusting groups self-destruct. The corollary to the previous principle is that when group members mistrust each other, they repel and separate. They pursue their own interests rather than the group's. Members of mistrusting groups tend to be suspicious of each other, are constantly on guard against exploitation, and restrict communication with others in the group. These actions tend to undermine and eventually destroy the group.

Mistrust generally reduces productivity. Although we cannot say that trust necessarily *increases* productivity, though it usually does, mistrust almost always *reduces* productivity. Mistrust focuses attention on the differences in member interests, making it difficult for people to visualize common goals. People respond by concealing information and secretly pursuing their own interests. When employees encounter problems, they avoid calling on others, fearing that those others will take advantage of them. A climate of mistrust tends to stimulate dysfunctional forms of conflict and retard cooperation.

Is Trust in Our Leaders in Decline?

A strong case can be made that today, more than ever, organizational leadership requires trust. Events of recent years have certainly brought the issue of trust into the headlines: WorldCom fakes nearly $4 billion in operating cash flow.

knowledge-based trust *Trust based on behavioral predictability that comes from a history of interaction.*

identification-based trust *Trust based on a mutual understanding of each other's intentions and appreciation of the other's wants and desires.*

Enron executives manipulate their financial statements. Tyco International's CEO is charged with cheating on sales taxes. Merrill Lynch pays $100 million in fines for misleading investors. Stanley Works tries to evade taxes by setting up sham headquarters in Bermuda. Martha Stewart is jailed for obstructing justice.[62] In addition, reengineering, downsizing, and the increased use of temporary employees have undermined a lot of employees' trust in management. These events, then, beg the question: Is trust on the decline?

A number of recent studies have been conducted in the United States looking at this question.[63] On a positive note, Americans seem to have faith in each other. For instance, in 2000, 35 percent of Americans said "most people" could be trusted. In 2002, that number was up to 41 percent. But when it comes to trusting big business and executives, the results differ depending on whether you ask employees or the general public. The general public holds corporate leaders in pretty low regard. The public's confidence in them as a group peaked in 2000 at only 28 percent. By 2003, that number had dropped to a dismal 13 percent. To put this in perspective, firefighters are considered seven times more trustworthy than CEOs and Americans say they trust CEOs even less than they trust lawyers. But this distrust seems to be directed at executives at large companies. The same polls show that 75 percent of the general public has strong trust in small business owners.

Corporate employees, however, show considerably more trust in their own senior management. From 1995 through 1999, the percentage of workers who said they believe in the senior management at their companies held steady at about 36 percent. By 2003, it had increased to 43 percent (see Exhibit 13-5). Exactly why these numbers are significantly higher than those of the general public or why they have recently increased is not clear. Part of the answer may be explained in terms of cognitive dissonance: Employees want to believe that their own bosses are more trustworthy than senior executives in general. And in

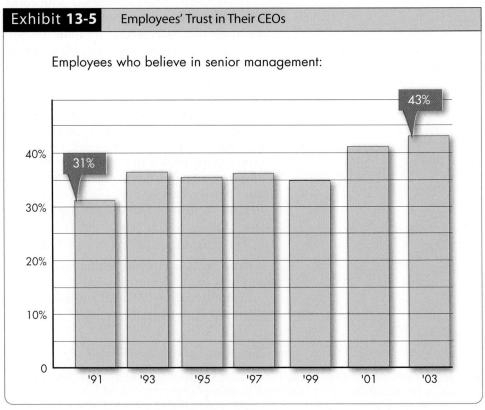

| Exhibit **13-5** | Employees' Trust in Their CEOs |

Source: Gantz Wiley Research. Reproduced in *USA Today*, February 12, 2003, p. 7B.

a time when jobs are hard to get, as they were between 2001 and 2003, employees may be more willing to give their bosses the benefit of the doubt. Additionally, the publicity given to corporate scandals has undoubtedly raised the importance of trust in executive suites and may have made more senior executives more trustworthy.

Contemporary Leadership Roles

What unique demands do teams place on leaders? Why are many effective leaders also active mentors? How can leaders develop self-leadership skills in their employees? And how does leadership work when face-to-face interaction is gone? In this section, we briefly address these four leadership-role issues.

Providing Team Leadership

Leadership is increasingly taking place within a team context. As teams grow in popularity, the role of the leader in guiding team members takes on heightened importance.[64] And the role of team leader is different from the traditional leadership role performed by first-line supervisors. J. D. Bryant, a supervisor at Texas Instruments' Forest Lane plant in Dallas, found that out.[65] One day he was happily overseeing a staff of 15 circuit-board assemblers. The next day he was informed the company was moving to teams and that he was to become a "facilitator." "I'm supposed to teach the teams everything I know and then let them make their own decisions," he said. Confused about his new role, he admitted, "there was no clear plan on what I was supposed to do." In this section, we consider the challenge of being a team leader and review the new roles that team leaders take on.

Many leaders, who came of age when individualism ruled, are not equipped to handle the change to teams. As one prominent consultant noted, "even the most capable managers have trouble making the transition because all the command-and-control type things they were encouraged to do before are no longer appropriate. There's no reason to have any skill or sense of this."[66] This same consultant estimated that "probably 15 percent of managers are natural team leaders; another 15 percent could never lead a team because it runs counter to their personality. [They're unable to sublimate their dominating style for the good of the team.] Then there's that huge group in the middle: Team leadership doesn't come naturally to them, but they can learn it."[67]

The challenge for most managers, then, is to learn how to become an effective team leader. They have to learn skills such as the patience to share information, to trust others, to give up authority, and to understand when to intervene. Effective leaders have mastered the difficult balancing act of knowing when to leave their teams alone and when to intercede. New team leaders may try to retain too much control at a time when team members need more autonomy, or they may abandon their teams at times when the teams need support and help.[68]

A study of 20 organizations that had reorganized themselves around teams found certain common responsibilities that all leaders had to assume. These included coaching, facilitating, handling disciplinary problems, reviewing team/individual performance, training, and communication.[69] Many of these responsibilities apply to managers in general. A more meaningful way to describe the team leader's job is to focus on two priorities: managing the team's external boundary and facilitating the team process.[70] We've broken these priorities down into four specific roles.

First, team leaders are *liaisons with external constituencies*. These include upper management, other internal teams, customers, and suppliers. The leader

Exhibit **13-6**

"So, does anyone in the group feel like responding to what Richard has just shared with us?"

represents the team to other constituencies, secures needed resources, clarifies others' expectations of the team, gathers information from the outside, and shares this information with team members.

Second, team leaders are *troubleshooters*. When the team has problems and asks for assistance, team leaders sit in on meetings and help try to resolve the problems. This rarely relates to technical or operation issues because the team members typically know more about the tasks being done than does the team leader. The leader is most likely to contribute by asking penetrating questions, by helping the team talk through problems, and by getting needed resources from external constituencies. For instance, when a team in an aerospace firm found itself short-handed, its team leader took responsibility for getting more staff. He presented the team's case to upper management and got the approval through the company's human resources department.

Third, team leaders are *conflict managers*. When disagreements surface, they help process the conflict. What's the source of the conflict? Who is involved? What are the issues? What resolution options are available? What are the advantages and disadvantages of each? By getting team members to address questions such as these, the leader minimizes the disruptive aspects of intrateam conflicts.

Finally, team leaders are *coaches*. They clarify expectations and roles, teach, offer support, cheerlead, and do whatever else is necessary to help team members improve their work performance.

Mentoring

Many leaders create mentoring relationships. A **mentor** is a senior employee who sponsors and supports a less-experienced employee (a protégé). Successful mentors are good teachers. They can present ideas clearly, listen well, and empathize with the problems of their protégés. Mentoring relationships have been described in terms of two broad categories of functions—career functions and psychosocial functions.

Career functions

- lobbying to get the protégé challenging and visible assignments
- coaching the protégé to help develop her skills and achieve work objectives
- assisting the protégé by providing exposure to influential individuals within the organization
- protecting the protégé from possible risks to her reputation
- sponsoring the protégé by nominating her for potential advances or promotions
- acting as a sounding board for ideas that the protégé might be hesitant to share with her direct supervisor

Psychosocial functions

- counseling the protégé about anxieties and uncertainty to help bolster her self-confidence
- sharing personal experiences with the protégé
- providing friendship and acceptance
- acting as a role model[71]

Some organizations have formal mentoring programs where mentors are officially assigned to new or high-potential employees. For instance, at Edward Jones, a financial services firm with 24,000 employees, mentors are assigned to new employees after recruits have completed the company's initial 2-month home study program and 5-day customer service seminar.[72] The new employees shadow their mentor for 3 weeks to specifically learn the company's way of doing business. However, in contrast to Edward Jones's formal system, most organizations rely on informal mentoring—with senior managers personally selecting an employee and taking that employee on as a protégé. Informal mentoring is the most effective mentoring relationship outside the immediate boss-subordinate interface.[73] The boss-subordinate context has an inherent conflict of interest and tension, mostly attributable to managers' directly evaluating the performance of subordinates, limiting openness and meaningful communication.

Why would a leader want to be a mentor? There are personal benefits to the leader as well as benefits for the organization. The mentor-protégé relationship gives the mentor unfiltered access to the attitudes and feelings of lower-ranking employees. Protégés can be an excellent source of identifying potential problems by providing early warning signals. They provide timely information to upper managers that short-circuits the formal channels. So the mentor-protégé relationship is a valuable communication channel that allows mentors to have news of problems before they become common knowledge to others in upper management. In addition, in terms of leader self-interest, mentoring can provide personal satisfaction to senior executives. It gives them the opportunity to share with others the knowledge and experience that they've developed over many years.

Are all employees in an organization equally likely to participate in a mentoring relationship? Unfortunately, the answer is no.[74] Evidence indicates that minorities and women are less likely to be chosen as protégés than are white males and thus are less likely to accrue the benefits of mentorship. Mentors tend to select protégés who are similar to themselves on criteria

mentor *A senior employee who sponsors and supports a less-experienced employee.*

such as background, education, gender, race, ethnicity, and religion. "People naturally move to mentor and can more easily communicate with those with whom they most closely identify."[75] In the United States, for instance, upper-management positions in most organizations have been traditionally staffed by white males, so it is hard for minorities and women to be selected as protégés. In addition, in terms of cross-gender mentoring, senior male managers may select male protégés to minimize problems such as sexual attraction or gossip. Organizations have responded to this dilemma by increasing formal mentoring programs and providing training and coaching for potential mentors of special groups such as minorities and women.[76]

You might assume that mentoring is important, but the research has been fairly disappointing. Two large-scale reviews suggest that the benefits are primarily psychological rather than tangible. Based on these reviews, it appears that the objective outcomes of mentoring, in terms of career success (compensation, job performance), are very small. One of these reviews concluded, "Though mentoring may not be properly labeled an utterly useless concept to careers, neither can it be argued to be as important as the main effects of other influences on career success such as ability and personality."[77] It may *feel* nice to have a mentor, but it does not appear that having a mentor, or even having a good mentor who provides both support and advice, is important to one's career.

Self-Leadership

Is it possible for people to lead themselves? An increasing body of research suggests that many can.[78] Proponents of **self-leadership** propose that there are a set of processes through which individuals control their own behavior. And effective leaders (or what advocates like to call *superleaders*) help their followers to lead themselves. They do this by developing leadership capacity in others and nurturing followers so they no longer need to depend on formal leaders for direction and motivation.

Myth or Science?

"Men Make Better Leaders Than Women"

This statement is false. There is no evidence to support the myth that men make better leaders than women, and there is evidence suggesting just the opposite.

Through the late 1980s, the common belief regarding gender and leadership effectiveness was that men made better leaders than women. This stereotype was predicated on the belief that men were inherently better skilled for leadership due to a stronger task focus, lower emotionality, and a greater propensity to be directive.

In the 1990s, this "male advantage" stereotype was replaced with one arguing that there was a "female advantage." This view evolved from studies that showed that female leaders, when rated by their peers, underlings, and bosses, scored higher than their male counterparts on key dimensions of leadership—including goal setting, motivating others, fostering communication, producing high-quality work, listening to others, and mentoring. Moreover, it was argued that

women rely more on a democratic leadership style—they encourage participation, share power and information, nurture followers, and lead through inclusion; and that this style matched up well with the contemporary organization's need for flexibility, teamwork, trust, and information sharing. Males, it was argued, were more likely to use a directive command-and-control style that worked better when organizations emphasized rigid structures, individualism, control, and secrecy.

The most recent assessment of the evidence concludes that women actually have a leadership advantage. Although the differences are fairly small, meaning that there is a great deal of overlap between males and females in their leadership styles, women do have, on average, a slight advantage. A recent review of 45 companies found that female leaders were more transformational than male leaders. These authors concluded, "These data attest to the ability of women to perform very well in leadership roles in contemporary organizations."[79] ■

How do leaders create self-leaders? The following have been suggested:[80]

1. *Model self-leadership* Practice self-observation, setting challenging personal goals, self-direction, and self-reinforcement. Then display these behaviors and encourage others to rehearse and then produce them.
2. *Encourage employees to create self-set goals* Having quantitative, specific goals is the most important part of self-leadership.
3. *Encourage the use of self-rewards to strengthen and increase desirable behaviors* In contrast, self-punishment should be limited only to occasions when the employee has been dishonest or destructive.
4. *Create positive thought patterns* Encourage employees to use mental imagery and self-talk to further stimulate self-motivation.
5. *Create a climate of self-leadership* Redesign the work to increase the natural rewards of a job and focus on these naturally rewarding features of work to increase motivation.
6. *Encourage self-criticism.* Encourage individuals to be critical of their own performance.

The underlying assumptions behind self-leadership are that people are responsible, capable, and able to exercise initiative without the external constraints of bosses, rules, or regulations. Given the proper support, individuals can monitor and control their own behavior.

The importance of self-leadership has increased with the expanded popularity of teams. Empowered, self-managed teams need individuals who are themselves self-directed. Management can't expect individuals who have spent their organizational lives under boss-centered leadership to suddenly adjust to self-managed teams. Therefore, training in self-leadership is an excellent means to help employees make the transition from dependence to autonomy.

Online Leadership

How do you lead people who are physically separated from you and with whom your interactions are basically reduced to written digital communications? This is a question that, to date, has received minimal attention from OB researchers.[81] Leadership research has been directed almost exclusively to face-to-face and verbal situations. But we can't ignore the reality that today's managers and their employees are increasingly being linked by networks rather than geographical proximity. Obvious examples include managers who regularly use e-mail to communicate with their staff, managers overseeing virtual projects or teams, and managers whose telecommuting employees are linked to the office by a computer and modem.

If leadership is important for inspiring and motivating dispersed employees, we need to offer some guidance as to how leadership might function in this context. Keep in mind, however, that there is limited research on this topic. So our intention here is not to provide you with definitive guidelines for leading online. Rather, it's to introduce you to an increasingly important issue and get you to think about how leadership changes when relationships are defined by network interactions.

In face-to-face communications, harsh *words* can be softened by nonverbal action. A smile and comforting gesture, for instance, can lessen the blow behind strong words like *disappointed, unsatisfactory, inadequate,* or *below expectations.* That nonverbal component doesn't exist with online interactions. The

self-leadership *A set of processes through which individuals control their own behavior.*

structure of words in a digital communication also has the power to motivate or demotivate the receiver. Is the message made up of full sentences or phrases? The latter, for instance, is likely to be seen as curt and more threatening. Similarly, a message in all caps is the equivalent of shouting. The manager who inadvertently sends her message in short phrases and in all caps may get a very different response than if she had sent that same message in full sentences using uppercase and lowercase letters.

Leaders need to be sure the *tone* of their message correctly reflects the emotions they want to send. Is the message formal or informal? Does it match the verbal style of the sender? Does it convey the appropriate level of importance or urgency? The fact that many people's writing style is very different from their interpersonal style is certainly a potential problem. Your author, for instance, has observed a number of very warm and charismatic leaders who aren't comfortable with the written word and tend to make their written communications much more formal than their verbal style. This not only creates confusion for employees, it undoubtedly also hinders the leaders' overall effectiveness.

Finally, online leaders must choose a *style.* Do they use emoticons, abbreviations, jargon, and the like? Do they adapt their style to their audience? Observation suggests that some managers are having difficulty adjusting to computer-related communications. For instance, they're using the same style with their bosses that they're using with their staff, with unfortunate consequences. Or they're selectively using digital communications to "hide" when delivering bad news.

We know that messages convey more than surface information. From a leadership standpoint, messages can convey trust or lack of trust, status, task directives, or emotional warmth. Concepts such as task structure, supportive behavior, and vision can be conveyed in written form as well as verbally. It may even be possible for leaders to convey charisma through the written word. But to effectively convey online leadership, managers must recognize that they have choices in the words, structure, tone, and style of their digital communications. They also need to develop the skills of "reading between the lines" in the messages they receive. In the same way that emotional intelligence taps an individual's ability to monitor and assess others' emotions, effective online leaders need to develop the skill of deciphering the emotional components of messages.

Any discussion of online leadership needs to also consider the possibility that the digital age can turn nonleaders into leaders. Some managers whose face-to-face leadership skills are less than satisfactory may shine online. Their talents may lie in their writing skills and ability to read the messages behind written communiqués. Nothing in the mainstream leadership literature addresses this unique situation.

We propose that online leaders have to think carefully about what actions they want their digital messages to initiate. Networked communication is a powerful channel. When used properly, it can build and enhance an individual's leadership effectiveness. But when misused, it has the potential to undermine a great deal of what a leader has been able to achieve through his or her verbal actions.

Additionally, online leaders confront unique challenges, the greatest of which appears to be developing and maintaining trust. Identification-based trust, for instance, is particularly difficult to achieve when there is a lack of intimacy and face-to-face interaction.[82] And online negotiations have also been found to be hindered because parties express lower levels of trust.[83] At this time, it's not clear whether it's even possible for employees to identify with or trust leaders with whom they only communicate electronically.[84]

This discussion leads us to the tentative conclusion that, for an increasing number of managers, good interpersonal skills may include the abilities to communicate support and leadership through written words on a computer screen and to read emotions in others' messages. In this "new world" of communications, writing skills are likely to become an extension of interpersonal skills.

Challenges to the Leadership Construct

A noted management expert takes issue with the omnipotent role that academicians, practicing managers, and the general public have given to the concept of leadership. He says, "In the 1500s, people ascribed all events they didn't understand to God. Why did the crops fail? God. Why did someone die? God. Now our all-purpose explanation is leadership."[85] He notes that when a company succeeds, people need someone to give the credit to. And that's typically the firm's CEO. Similarly, when a company does poorly, they need someone to blame. CEOs also play this role. But much of an organization's success or failure is due to factors outside the influence of leadership. In many cases, success or failure is just a matter of being in the right or wrong place at a given time. This point was illustrated in California during the summer of 2003.[86] California's economy was in bad shape and the state faced a $28 billion deficit. Angry and frustrated, Californians wanted someone to blame and that someone was the state's governor, Gray Davis. With Davis's popularity ratings dropping as low as 21 percent, citizens petitioned for a recall vote on the governor. He was voted out in October 2003 and replaced by actor, turned politician, Arnold Schwarzenegger. In reality, Davis had little to do with the budget deficit. Most of it was due to the collapse of the dot.com craze, which had powered the state's economy in the 1990s, and the stock market decline of 2000–02. In 2001–02, for instance, state revenues declined by nearly 17 percent. But Californians wanted a target for their fiscal pain and frustration, and Davis played that role. The key leadership question should have been: How is ousting Gray Davis going to close California's budget deficit? The answer is: It won't. One may or may not think Schwarzenegger is a good governor, but the point is that leaders cannot do everything. There are limits.

In this section, we present two perspectives that challenge the widely accepted belief in the importance of leadership. The first argument proposes that leadership is more about appearances than reality. You don't have to *be* an effective leader as long as you *look* like one. The second argument directly attacks the notion that some leadership *will always be effective* regardless of the

Californians blamed former governor Gray Davis for budget deficit problems he did not create and that were outside the influence of his leadership. But voters held Gray responsible for the state's economic problems and elected a new leader, Arnold Schwarzenegger, in a recall election. Believing that he can fix the state's financial problems, the California governor is shown here presenting his budget plan that includes huge spending cuts to control a $9 billion deficit. Soon, though, Schwarzenegger himself came under attack and likely faces difficult reelection prospects.

situation. This argument contends that in many situations, whatever actions leaders exhibit are irrelevant.

Leadership as an Attribution

We introduced attribution theory in Chapter 5. As you may remember, it deals with the ways in which people try to make sense out of cause-and-effect relationships. We said when something happens, we want to attribute it to something else. The **attribution theory of leadership** says that leadership is merely an attribution that people make about other individuals.[87] The attribution theory has shown that people characterize leaders as having such traits as intelligence, outgoing personality, strong verbal skills, aggressiveness, understanding, and industriousness.[88] At the organizational level, the attribution framework accounts for the conditions under which people use leadership to explain organizational outcomes. Those conditions are extremes in organizational performance. When an organization has either extremely negative or extremely positive performance, people are prone to make leadership attributions to explain the performance.[89] As noted earlier, this tendency helps to account for the vulnerability of CEOs (and high-ranking state officials) when their organizations suffer a major financial setback, regardless of whether they had much to do with it, and also accounts for why CEOs tend to be given credit for extremely positive financial results—again, regardless of how much or how little they contributed.

One of the more interesting findings in the attribution theory of leadership literature is the perception that effective leaders are generally considered consistent or unwavering in their decisions.[90] One of the explanations for why Ronald Reagan (during his first term as U.S. president) was perceived as a leader was that he was fully committed, steadfast, and consistent in the decisions he made

Cultural Variation in Charismatic Attributions

DO PEOPLE FROM DIFFERENT CULTURES MAKE DIFferent attributions about their leaders' charisma? That's what one recent study attempted to answer.

A team of researchers conducted a study in which individuals from the United States and Turkey read short stories about a hypothetical leader. Each story portrayed the leader's behaviors and the performance of the leader's company differently. In both cultures, individuals believed that the leader possessed more charisma when displaying behaviors such as promoting the company's vision and involving subordinates *and* when the leader's company performed well. However, the participants from the United States, who are more individualist, focused on the leader's behaviors when attributing charisma. In contrast, the participants from Turkey, who are more collectivist, focused on the company's performance when attributing charisma.

Why do these differences exist? The researchers speculated that people from individualist cultures place more emphasis on the person than on the situation and so they attribute charisma when a leader displays certain traits. People from collectivist cultures, in contrast, place more emphasis on the situation and assume that the leader is charismatic when the company performs well. So, whether others see you as charismatic may, in part, depend on what culture you work in.

Source: Based on N. Ensari and S. E. Murphy, "Cross-Cultural Variations in Leadership Perceptions and Attribution of Charisma to the Leader," *Organizational Behavior and Human Decision Processes,* September 2003, pp. 52–66.

and the goals he set. Former U.S. President George Herbert Bush, in contrast, undermined the public's perception of his leadership by increasing income taxes after stating categorically during his campaign: "Read my lips. No new taxes."

Following the attribution theory of leadership, we'd say that what's important in being characterized as an "effective leader" is projecting the *appearance* of being a leader rather than focusing on *actual accomplishments.* Leader-wannabes can attempt to shape the perception that they're smart, personable, verbally adept, aggressive, hardworking, and consistent in their style. And by doing so, they increase the probability that their bosses, colleagues, and employees will *view* them *as* an effective leader.

Substitutes and Neutralizers to Leadership

Contrary to the arguments made throughout this and the previous chapter, leadership may not always be important. A theory of leadership suggests that, in many situations, whatever actions leaders exhibit are irrelevant. Certain individual, job, and organizational variables can act as *substitutes* for leadership or *neutralize* the leader's influence on his or her followers.[91]

Neutralizers make it impossible for leader behavior to make any difference to follower outcomes. They negate the leader's influence. Substitutes, however, make a leader's influence not only impossible but also unnecessary. They act as a replacement for the leader's influence. For instance, characteristics of employees such as their experience, training, "professional" orientation, or indifference toward organizational rewards can substitute for, or neutralize the effect of, leadership. Experience and training can replace the need for a leader's support or ability to create structure and reduce task ambiguity. Jobs that are inherently unambiguous and routine or that are intrinsically satisfying may place fewer demands on the leadership variable. Organizational characteristics like explicit, formalized goals, rigid rules and procedures, and cohesive work groups can also replace formal leadership (see Exhibit 13-7).

Exhibit 13-7	Substitutes and Neutralizers for Leadership	
Defining Characteristics	**Relationship-Oriented Leadership**	**Task-Oriented Leadership**
Individual		
Experience/training	No effect on	Substitutes for
Professionalism	Substitutes for	Substitutes for
Indifference to rewards	Neutralizes	Neutralizes
Job		
Highly structured task	No effect on	Substitutes for
Provides its own feedback	No effect on	Substitutes for
Intrinsically satisfying	Substitutes for	No effect on
Organization		
Explicit formalized goals	No effect on	Substitutes for
Rigid rules and procedures	No effect on	Substitutes for
Cohesive work groups	Substitutes for	Substitutes for

Source: Based on S. Kerr and J. M. Jermier, "Substitutes for Leadership: Their Meaning and Measurement," *Organizational Behavior and Human Performance*, December 1978, p. 378.

attribution theory of leadership   *The idea that leadership is merely an attribution that people make about other individuals.*

This recognition that leaders don't always have an impact on follower outcomes should not be that surprising. After all, we have introduced a number of variables in this text—attitudes, personality, ability, and group norms, to name but a few—that have been documented as having an effect on employee performance and satisfaction. Yet supporters of the leadership concept place an undue burden on this variable for explaining and predicting behavior. It's too simplistic to consider employees as guided to goal accomplishments solely by the actions of their leader. It's important, therefore, to recognize explicitly that leadership is merely another independent variable in our overall OB model. In some situations, it may contribute a lot to explaining employee productivity, absence, turnover, satisfaction, and citizenship behavior, but in other situations, it may contribute little toward that end.

The validity of substitutes and neutralizers is controversial. One of the problems is that the theory is very complicated—there are many possible substitutes for and neutralizers of many different types of leader behaviors across many different situations. Moreover, sometimes the difference between substitutes and neutralizers is fuzzy. For example, if I'm working on a task that's intrinsically enjoyable, the theory predicts that leadership will be less important because the task itself provides enough motivation. But, does that mean that intrinsically enjoyable tasks neutralize leadership effects, or substitute for them, or both? Another problem that this review points out is that substitutes for leadership (like employee characteristics, the nature of the task, and so forth) matter, but it does not appear that they substitute for or neutralize leadership.[92]

Finding and Creating Effective Leaders

We have covered a lot of ground in these two chapters on leadership. But the ultimate goal of our review is to answer this question: How can organizations find or create effective leaders? Let's try to answer that question.

Selection

The entire process that organizations go through to fill management positions is essentially an exercise in trying to identify individuals who will be effective leaders. Your search might begin by reviewing the specific requirements for the position to be filled. What knowledge, skills, and abilities are needed to do the job effectively? You should try to analyze the situation to find candidates who will make a proper match.

Testing is useful for identifying and selecting leaders. Personality tests can be used to look for traits associated with leadership—extraversion, conscientiousness, and openness to experience. Testing to find a leadership-candidate's score on self-monitoring also makes sense. High self-monitors are likely to outperform their low-scoring counterparts because the former are better at reading situations and adjusting their behavior accordingly. You can additionally assess candidates for emotional intelligence. Given the importance of social skills to managerial effectiveness, candidates with a high EI should have an advantage, especially in situations requiring transformational leadership.[93]

Interviews also provide an opportunity to evaluate leadership candidates. For instance, we know that experience is a poor predictor of leader effectiveness, but situation-specific experience is relevant. You can use the interview to determine if a candidate's prior experience fits with the situation you're trying to fill. Similarly, the interview is a reasonably good vehicle for identifying the degree to which a candidate has leadership traits such as extraversion, self-confidence, a vision, the verbal skills to frame issues, or a charismatic physical presence.

A classical music event helps leaders of Verizon, Unilever, Starbucks, Deutsche Bank, and other major firms from around the world shape their behavior and effectiveness. Called "The Music Paradigm," the training program offered by The Stamford Symphony uses the orchestra as a metaphor for an organization and involves the audience in learning about mission statements, business strategy, communication, teamwork, innovation, and change. Shown here in training are real estate brokers from REMAX International.

We know the importance of situational factors in leadership success. And we should use this knowledge to match leaders to situations. Does the situation require a change-focused leader? If so, look for transformational qualities. If not, look for transactional qualities. You might also ask: Is leadership actually important in this specific position? There may be situational factors that substitute for or neutralize leadership. If there are, then the leader essentially performs a figurehead or symbolic role, and the importance of selecting the "right" person is not particularly crucial.

Training

Organizations, in aggregate, spend billions of dollars, yen, and euros on leadership training and development.[94] These efforts take many forms—from $50,000 executive leadership programs offered by universities such as Harvard to sailing experiences at the Outward Bound School. Although much of the money spent on training may provide dubious benefits, our review suggests that there are some things management can do to get the maximum effect from their leadership-training budgets.[95]

First, let's recognize the obvious. People are not equally trainable. Leadership training of any kind is likely to be more successful with individuals who are high self-monitors than with low self-monitors. Such individuals have the flexibility to change their behavior.

What kinds of things can individuals learn that might be related to higher leader effectiveness? It may be a bit optimistic to believe that we can teach "vision creation," but we can teach implementation skills. We can train people to develop "an understanding about content themes critical to effective visions."[96] We also can teach skills such as trust building and mentoring. And leaders can be taught situational-analysis skills. They can learn how to evaluate situations, how to modify situations to make them fit better with their style, and how to assess which leader behaviors might be most effective in given situations. A number of companies have recently turned to executive coaches to help senior managers improve their leadership skills.[97] For instance, Charles Schwab, eBay, Pfizer, Unilever, and American Express have hired executive coaches to provide specific one-on-one training for their company's top executives to help them improve their interpersonal skills and to learn to act less autocratically.[98]

On an optimistic note, there is evidence suggesting that behavioral training through modeling exercises can increase an individual's ability to exhibit charismatic leadership qualities. The success of the researchers mentioned earlier (see "Are Charismatic Leaders Born or Made?") in actually scripting undergraduate business students to "play" charismatic is a case in point.[99] Finally, there is accumulating research showing that leaders can be trained in transformational leadership skills. Once learned, these skills have bottom-line results, whether it is in the financial performance of Canadian banks or the training effectiveness of soldiers in the Israeli Defense Forces.[100]

Summary and Implications for Managers

Organizations are increasingly searching for managers who can exhibit transformational leadership qualities. They want leaders with visions and the charisma to carry those visions out. And although true leadership effectiveness may be a result of exhibiting the right behaviors at the right time, the evidence is quite strong that people have a relatively uniform perception of what a leader should look like. They attribute "leadership" to people who are smart, personable, verbally adept, and the like. To the degree that managers project these qualities, others are likely to deem them leaders.

Effective managers today must develop trusting relationships with those whom they seek to lead. Why? Because as organizations have become less stable and predictable, strong bonds of trust are likely to be replacing bureaucratic rules in defining expectations and relationships. Managers who aren't trusted aren't likely to be effective leaders.

For managers concerned with how to fill key positions in their organization with effective leaders, we have shown that tests and interviews help to identify people with leadership qualities. In addition to focusing on leadership selection, managers should also consider investing in leadership training. Many individuals with leadership potential can enhance their skills through formal courses, workshops, rotating job responsibilities, coaching, and mentoring.

Point ◀▶ Counterpoint

Leadership Is Culturally Bound

Leaders must adapt their style to different national cultures. What works in the United States, for instance, isn't likely to work in France or Indonesia. Fred Hassan, chairman and CEO of Schering-Plough, a pharmaceutical company, argues that a "global attitude" is a critical skill for today's leaders—that is, to be effective, you need to have a curiosity about the world, accept what different cultures have to offer, and adapt yourself to the cultural environment.[101] A GE executive recalls when he used his American leadership style in Japan: "Nothing happened. I quickly realized that I had to adapt my approach, to act more as a consultant to my colleagues and to adopt a team-based motivational decision-making process rather than the more vocal style which tends to be common in the West. In Japan the silence of a leader means far more than a thousand words uttered by somebody else."[102]

Leaders are also constrained by the cultural conditions that their followers have come to expect. For instance, American leaders are expected to empower followers. However, followers in Mexico and some Asian countries look to their leaders to provide structure and direction. For example, a study in Hong Kong found that leaders were expected to be relatively autocratic.[103]

Consistent with the contingency approach, leaders need to adjust their style to the unique cultural aspects of a country. For example, a manipulative or autocratic style is compatible with high-power distance, and we find high-power distance scores in Russia, Spain, Arab, Far Eastern, and most Latin countries. Power distance rankings should also be good indicators of employee willingness to accept participative leadership. Participation is likely to be most effective in low-power distance cultures as exist in Norway, Finland, Denmark, and Sweden.

The GLOBE research program, which we introduced in Chapter 4, has gathered data on approximately 18,000 middle managers in 825 organizations, covering 62 countries. It's the most comprehensive cross-cultural study of leadership ever undertaken. So its findings should not be quickly dismissed. It's illuminating that one of the results coming from the GLOBE program is that there are some universal aspects to leadership. Specifically, a number of the elements making up transformational leadership appear to be associated with effective leadership regardless of what country the leader is in.[104] This conclusion is very important because it flies in the face of the contingency view that leadership style needs to adapt to cultural differences.

What elements of transformational leadership appear universal? Vision, foresight, providing encouragement, trustworthiness, dynamism, positiveness, and proactiveness. The results led two members of the GLOBE team to conclude that "effective business leaders in any country are expected by their subordinates to provide a powerful and proactive vision to guide the company into the future, strong motivational skills to stimulate all employees to fulfill the vision, and excellent planning skills to assist in implementing the vision."[105]

What might explain the universal appeal of these transformational leader attributes? It's been suggested that pressures toward common technologies and management practices, as a result of global competition and multinational influences, may make some aspects of leadership universally accepted. If true, we may be able to select and train leaders in a universal style and thus significantly raise the quality of leadership worldwide.

Questions for Review

1. What could you do if you wanted others to perceive you as a charismatic leader?

2. When can charisma be a liability?

3. Do you believe that transformational leaders are born or trained? Explain your response.

4. How are ethics involved in leadership?

5. Contrast the three types of trust. Relate them to your experience in personal relationships.

6. How does one become an effective team leader?

7. Why would a leader want to be a mentor?

8. How does a leader increase self-leadership among his or her followers?

9. How is leadership an attribution?

10. Contrast substitutes and neutralizers for leadership.

Questions for Critical Thinking

1. What role do you think training plays in an individual's ability to trust others? For instance, does the training of lawyers, accountants, law-enforcement personnel, and social workers take different approaches toward trusting others? Explain.

2. "It's not possible to be both a trusting boss and a politically astute leader. One requires openness and the other requires concealment." Do you agree or disagree with this statement? Explain.

3. As a new employee in an organization, why might you want to acquire a mentor? Why might women and minorities have more difficulty in finding a mentor than would white males?

4. Is there an ethical problem if leaders focus more on looking like a leader than actually being one? Discuss.

5. "Leaders make a real difference in an organization's performance." Build an argument in support of this statement. Then build an argument against this statement.

Team Exercise

YOU BE THE JUDGE: WHICH VISION STATEMENT IS EFFECTIVE?

There is a lot of research about what makes an effective vision statement. A good vision statement is said to have the following qualities:

1. Identifies values and beliefs.

2. Is idealistic or utopian.

3. Represents broad and overarching (versus narrow and specific) goals.

4. Is inspiring.

5. Is future-oriented.

6. Is bold and ambitious.

7. Reflects the uniqueness of the organization.

8. Is well articulated and easily understood.

Now that you know what makes a good vision statement, you can rate vision statements from actual companies.

(a) Break into groups of 4–5 people.

(b) Each group member should rate each vision statement—based on the 8 qualities we list here— on a scale of 1 = very poor to 10 = excellent.

(c) Compare your ratings. Did your group agree or disagree?

(d) What do you think caused the agreement or disagreement?

(e) How would you improve these vision statements?

Vision Statements

- DuPont—Our vision is to be the world's most dynamic science company, creating sustainable solutions essential to a better, safer and healthier life for people everywhere.

- U.S. Army—Our Nation, the Joint Force, and our Army are engaged in one of the most challenging periods in our history. Failure in the current fight is unthinkable. To defeat the enemies who threaten our freedoms, we cannot remain static, trapped in a web of our own no longer relevant policies, procedures, and processes. Transformation during a time of sustained campaigning will not be easy; but it is a practice that appears many times in the history of our great Army. We must examine, design, and develop new solutions for a new and dangerous world, as we have done so successfully in our past. This will require the deep and personal commitment of every member of the Army team—every leader, every Soldier, every civilian, and every family member.

- Cutco Cutlery—To become the largest, most respected and widely recognized cutlery company in the world.

- Bowling Green State University—Bowling Green State University aspires to be the premier learning community in Ohio, and one of the best in the nation. Through the interdependence of teaching, learning, scholarship, and service we will create an academic environment grounded in intellectual discovery and guided by rational discourse and civility.

- Nissan—Call us zealous, even overzealous, but at Nissan we know that settling for just any solution is just that. Settling. And, not to mention, the fastest

way to go from being an automotive company fueled by imagination to just another automotive company, period. That's why we think beyond the answer. And ask. Because only through this process of constant challenge can real change occur. One question at a time.

Source: The vision attributes are based on S. A. Kirkpatrick, E. A. Locke, and G. P. Latham, "Implementing the Vision: How Is It Done?" *Polish Psychological Bulletin* 27, 1996, pp. 93–106.

Ethical Dilemma

ETHICAL LEADERSHIP OR WOULD YOU WORK HERE?

Would you accept a senior leadership position at a major tobacco company like Phillip Morris or R. J. Reynolds? I've asked that question to students over the years and typically 80 percent or more answer "no."

The content of goals is said to have ethical ramifications. Does that mean that certain types of businesses are inherently unethical? For instance, many students defend their position not to work at a tobacco company because they believe the product the company sells is unhealthy. But where do *you* draw the line? Would *you* take a managerial position at Phillip Morris? Would your answer be different if the pay was $300,000 a year rather than $75,000?

Tobacco companies, of course, are not the only firms that produce products that have questionable health consequences. Would you work for Anheuser-Busch, the maker of Budweiser beer? The first response from most of my students is "yes." But many begin to question that

response when told that drunk drivers kill more than 16,000 people a year in the United States alone and injure half-a-million more. Most of these drivers have become intoxicated on beer, and Anheuser-Busch has 45 percent of the U.S. beer market. So thousands of people die each year as a result of Anheuser-Busch products. Is this a fair conclusion? Does it alter your view of working at Anheuser-Busch?

Cookies, fast food (ever see the movie *Super Size Me?*), and ice cream are also products that are hard to argue are good for people's health. High in sugar and fats, they contribute to health problems such as obesity, high blood pressure, and high cholesterol. Could you ethically be a manager at Keebler, Frito-Lay, or Ben & Jerry's?

What companies, if any, wouldn't you be willing to work for and hold a leadership position in because you find their products or services to be unsavory or unethical?

Case Incident 1

WILL GEORGE W. BUSH BE A GREAT PRESIDENT?

What does it take to be a great U.S. president? A survey of 78 history, political science, and law scholars rated the U.S. presidents from George Washington to Bill Clinton. Here are the presidents who were rated "Great" and "Near Great."

Great
George Washington
Abraham Lincoln
Franklin D. Roosevelt (FDR)

Near Great
Thomas Jefferson
Andrew Jackson
James Polk
Theodore Roosevelt
Harry Truman
Dwight Eisenhower
Ronald Reagan

Among recent presidents, Presidents Nixon, Ford, and Carter were ranked "Below Average" and Presidents G. H. W. Bush (the first President Bush) and Clinton were ranked "Average."

So what explains these ratings? The following are some qualities of presidents who have stood the test of time.

1. Great presidents are transformational leaders who engender strong emotions—that is, you either love them or you hate them (it's hard to hate someone who made little difference). And great presidents enact a vision that may not respond to popular opinion. Lincoln and FDR were beloved, and hated, by millions.

2. Great presidents are bold and take risks, and almost all great presidents emerge successfully from a crisis. A great president is perceived as "being there" when a crisis emerges and taking bold action to lead the nation out of the crisis—for example, Lincoln in the Civil War and Roosevelt in WWII.

3. Great presidents are associated with a vision. Most people, for example, are able to associate the great presidents with a defining moment where a clear set of principles was articulated—for example, FDR's speech to Congress after the attacks on Pearl Harbor, and Lincoln's Gettysburg Address.

4. Great presidents are charismatic. They are engaging, articulate, and expressive, which helps capture the public's attention and rallies people around a president's cause. One leadership expert argues that the best presidents create colorful personas with their language by using words with basic emotions—for example, good versus evil or love versus hate.

So what about President George W. Bush (the second President Bush)? Shortly after his second inauguration, President Bush embarked on an ambitious agenda of legal reform, transforming the Social Security system, tax reform, and revising immigration laws. One writer commented, "Bush has always thought big, and always believed you earn political capital by expending it." However, the closeness of the 2004 election (Bush received 51 percent of the vote and Kerry received 48 percent) suggests that Bush may not have overwhelming support.

Questions

1. How would you rate President George W. Bush on the four characteristics outlined at the beginning of the case? How would you contrast his reaction to Hurricane Katrina with his reaction to the terrorist attacks of September 11, 2001? What do you think his handling of these two events says about his leadership?

2. Do you think leaders in other contexts (business, sports, religious) exhibit the same qualities of great or near-great U.S. presidents?

3. Do you think being in the right place at the right time could influence presidential greatness?

Sources: "Federalist Society—The Wall Street Journal Survey on Presidents," *Opinion Journal* (www.opinionjournal.com/hail/rankings.html) (November 16, 2000); M. Greer, "The Science of Savoir Faire," *Monitor on Psychology*, January 2005, pp. 28–30; R. Wolffe, "Window of Opportunity," *Newsweek*, January 24, 2005, pp. 25–30; J. Meacham, "A Road Map to Making History," *Newsweek*, January 24, 2005, pp. 42–43.

Case Incident 2

GENERATION GAP: MENTORS AND PROTÉGÉS

As the baby boomer generation nears retirement, many Boomers are mentoring their future work replacements—Generation Xers. Some Boomers have found the process difficult. William Slater, a 47-year-old computer engineer who participates in his company's formal mentoring program, has had negative experiences with three protégés. He recalls that one tried, unsuccessfully, to take his job, while another repeatedly spoke badly about him to his boss. "I have an ax to grind with Generation X. They're stabbing aging Baby Boomers in the back," says Slater.

It is not only Baby Boomers who have had bad experiences. Joel Bershok, a 24-year-old, was optimistic about the prospects of having a mentor. However, his mentor dissolved the relationship after only 3 weeks. Says Bershok: "He just wanted it for his resume." To Bershok, one of the major problems with a mentoring relationship is a lack of trust. With an uncertain economy and companies making frequent layoff announcements, Boomers are wary of teaching their younger counterparts too much for fear that those counterparts, who usually make less – and so cost the company less than Boomers—may replace them.

The fear may be justified. For example, Janet Wheeler, a 49-year-old broker, saw her job replaced by two younger workers after her company let her go. Wheeler thinks that other Boomers are beginning to notice the risks of mentoring and are responding by not teaching their protégés as much as they could. "You see young people being brought along just enough to get the job done, but not so much that they'll take your job," she states.

Given that some studies have demonstrated the beneficial effects of mentoring on employee outcomes such as performance, job satisfaction, and employee retention, many analysts are concerned that baby boomers are failing to see mentoring as a responsibility. According to a study by Menttium Corporation, a firm that aids companies in installing mentoring programs, almost 90 percent of formal mentoring relationships end prematurely. The primary reasons include poor matching of mentors to protégés and a lack of effort to keep the relationship going.

But some workers have strongly benefited from mentoring programs and are trying to maintain mentoring programs in their companies. Three years after joining Dell, Lynn Tyson, 41, helped start a formal mentoring program open to all of Dell's 42,000 employees. "I never had a formal mentor in my entire career. Most of the time I was shaking in my shoes," says Tyson. Her program has been successful so far—and she mentors 40 protégés. "I'm not trying to make this sound sappy, but I have the ability to make a difference in somebody's career, and that excites me every day." The benefits are especially apparent for women and minorities who, historically, have had greater difficulty than white males in climbing to top management positions. According to a study by Harvard University professor David A. Thomas, the most successful racial minorities at three different corporations had a strong network of mentors. Additionally, research has shown that women also benefit from having positive mentoring experiences in that they have greater career success and career satisfaction.

With the right amount of effort, protégés, mentors, and the companies that sponsor such relationships can realize tremendous benefits. However, individuals in mentoring relationships may need to look past generational and other individual differences to achieve such benefits. Though Slater has had his share of bad mentoring experiences, he is still optimistic. "Mentoring is a time-honored concept. Those of us who've been mentored should mentor others. Otherwise, we've short-circuited the process and the future," he says.

Questions

1. What factors do you believe lead to successful mentoring programs? If you were designing a mentoring program, what might it look like?

2. In what ways might a protégé benefit from having a mentor? In what ways might a mentor benefit from having a protégé?

3. Of the three types of trust discussed in the chapter, which one may be the primary type in mentoring relationships and why?

4. What types of leaders, in terms of personality traits and behavioral tendencies, would most likely be good mentors? What types of leaders might be poor mentors?

Source: Based on J. Zaslow, "Moving On: Don't Trust Anyone Under 30: Boomers Struggle With Their New Role as Mentors, *The Wall Street Journal,* June 5, 2003, p. D.1, P. Garfinkel, "Putting a Formal Stamp on Mentoring," *The New York Times,* January 18, 2004, p. 3.10, and J. E. Wallace, "The Benefits of Mentoring for Female Lawyers," *Journal of Vocational Behavior,* June, 2001, pp. 366–391.

Endnotes

1. E. Walsh, "Learning to Spy: Can Maureen Baginski Save the F.B.I.?" *The New Yorker,* November 8, 2004; D. K. Thompson, "The Toughest Job in Washington," *Capital Hill Blue* (www.capitolhillblue.com/artman/publish/article_4583.shtml) (May 23, 2004); C. Ragavan, "The FBI's 'Vision Lady' " *U.S. News & World Report,* September 27, 2004, pp. 38–40.

2. See R. M. Entman, "Framing: Toward Clarification of a Fractured Paradigm," *Journal of Communication,* Autumn 1993, pp. 51–58; and G. T. Fairhurst and R. A. Starr, *The Art of Framing: Managing the Language of Leadership* (San Francisco: Jossey-Bass, 1996), p. 21.

3. Fairhurst and Starr, *The Art of Framing,* p. 4.

4. M. Weber, *Max Weber: The Theory of Social and Economic Organization,* A. M. Henderson and T. Parsons (trans.) (New York: Free, Press, 1947).

5. J. A. Conger and R. N. Kanungo, "Behavioral Dimensions of Charismatic Leadership," in J. A. Conger, R. N. Kanungo and Associates (eds.), *Charismatic Leadership* (San Francisco: Jossey-Bass, 1988), p. 79.

6. J. A. Conger and R. N. Kanungo, *Charismatic Leadership in Organizations* (Thousand Oaks, CA: Sage, 1998); and R. Awamleh and W. L. Gardner, "Perceptions of Leader Charisma and Effectiveness: The Effects of Vision Content, Delivery, and Organizational Performance," *Leadership Quarterly,* Fall 1999, pp. 345–73.

7. R. J. House and J. M. Howell, "Personality and Charismatic Leadership," *Leadership Quarterly,* 3 (1992), pp. 81–108; D. N. Den Hartog and P. L., "Leadership in Organizations," in N. Anderson and D. S. Ones (eds.), *Handbook of Industrial, Work and Organizational Psychology,* vol. 2 (Thousand Oaks, CA: Sage Publications, 2002), pp. 166–87.

8. See J. A. Conger and R. N. Kanungo, "Training Charismatic Leadership: A Risky and Critical Task," *Charismatic Leadership,* (San Francisco: Jossey-Bass, 1988), pp. 309–23; A. J. Towler, "Effects of Charismatic Influence Training on Attitudes, Behavior, and Performance," *Personnel Psychology,* Summer 2003, pp. 363–81; and M. Frese, S. Beimel, and S. Schoenborn, "Action Training for Charismatic Leadership: Two Evaluations of Studies of a Commercial Training Module on Inspirational Communication of a Vision," *Personnel Psychology,* Autumn 2003, pp. 671–97.

9. R. J. Richardson and S. K. Thayer, *The Charisma Factor: How to Develop Your Natural Leadership Ability* (Upper Saddle River, NJ: Prentice Hall, 1993).

10. J. M. Howell and P. J. Frost, "A Laboratory Study of Charismatic Leadership," *Organizational Behavior and Human Decision Processes,* April 1989, pp. 243–69. See also M. Frese, S. Beimel, and S. Schoenborn, "Action Training for Charismatic Leadership: Two Evaluations of Studies of a Commercial Training Module on Inspirational Communication of a Vision," *Personnel Psychology,* Fall 2003, pp. 671–97.

11. B. Shamir, R. J. House, and M. B. Arthur, "The Motivational Effects of Charismatic Leadership: A Self-Concept Theory," *Organization Science,* November 1993, pp. 577–94.

12. C. H. Schmitt, "The Confidence Game," *U.S. News and World Report,* September 13, 2004, pp. EE4–EE8; S. Levy, "iPod, Therefore i Am," *Newsweek,* July 26, 2004, pp. 44–50.

13. B. Kark, R. Gan, and B. Shamir, "The Two Faces of Transformational Leadership: Empowerment and Dependency," *Journal of Applied Psychology,* April 2003, pp. 246–55; and P. D. Cherlunik, K. A. Donley, T. S. R. Wiewel, and S. R. Miller, "Charisma is Contagious: The Effect of Leaders' Charisma on Observers' Affect," *Journal of Applied Social Psychology,* October 2001, pp. 2149–59.

14. For reviews on the role of vision in leadership, see S. J. Zaccaro, "Visionary and Inspirational Models of Executive Leadership: Empirical Review and Evaluation," in S. J. Zaccaro (ed.), *The Nature of Executive Leadership: A Conceptual and Empirical Analysis of Success* (Washington, DC: American Psychological Assoc., 2001), pp. 259–78; and M. Hauser and R. J. House, "Lead Through Vision and Values," in E. A. Locke (ed.), *Handbook of Principles of Organizational Behavior* (Malden, MA: Blackwell, 2004), pp. 257–73.

15. P. C. Nutt and R. W. Backoff, "Crafting Vision," *Journal of Management Inquiry,* December 1997, p. 309.

16. Ibid., pp. 312–14.

17. J. L. Roberts, "A Mogul's Migraine," *Newsweek,* November 29, 2004, pp. 38–40.

18. R. J. House, J. Woycke, and E. M. Fodor, "Charismatic and Noncharismatic Leaders: Differences in Behavior and Effectiveness," in Conger and Kanungo, *Charismatic Leadership,* pp. 103–104; D. A. Waldman, B. M. Bass, and F.J. Yammarino, "Adding to Contingent-Reward Behavior: The Augmenting

Effect of Charismatic Leadership," *Group & Organization Studies*, December 1990, pp. 381–94; S. A. Kirkpatrick and E. A. Locke, "Direct and Indirect Effects of Three Core Charismatic Leadership Components on Performance and Attitudes," *Journal of Applied Psychology*, February 1996, pp. 36–51; and R. J. Deluga, "American Presidential Machiavellianism: Implications for Charismatic Leadership and Rated Performance," *Leadership Quarterly*, Fall 2001, pp. 339–63.

19. A. H. B. de Hoogh, D. N. den Hartog, P. L. Koopman, H. Thierry, P. T. van den Berg, and J. G. van der Weide, "Charismatic Leadership, Environmental Dynamism, and Performance," *European Journal of Work & Organizational Psychology*, December 2004, pp. 447–71; S. Harvey, M. Martin, and D. Stout, "Instructor's Transformational Leadership: University Student Attitudes and Ratings," *Psychological Reports*, April 2003, pp. 395–402; D. A. Waldman, M. Javidan, and P. Varella, "Charismatic Leadership at the Strategic Level: A New Application of Upper Echelons Theory," *Leadership Quarterly*, June 2004, pp. 355–80.

20. R. J. House, "A 1976 Theory of Charismatic Leadership," in J. G. Hunt and L. L. Larson (eds.), *Leadership: The Cutting Edge* (Carbondale, IL: Southern Illinois University Press, 1977), pp. 189–207; and Robert J. House and Ram N. Aditya, "The Social Scientific Study of Leadership," *Journal of Management*, 23, no. 3 (1997) p. 441.

21. F. Cohen, S. Solomon, M. Maxfield, T. Pyszczynski, and J. Greenberg, "Fatal Attraction: The Effects of Mortality Salience on Evaluations of Charismatic, Task-Oriented, and Relationship-Oriented Leaders," *Psychological Science*, December 2004, pp. 846–51; and M. G. Ehrhart and K. J. Klein "Predicting Followers' Preferences for Charismatic Leadership: The Influence of Follower Values and Personality," *Leadership Quarterly*, Summer 2001, pp. 153–79.

22. H. L. Tosi, V. Misangyi, A. Fanelli, D. A. Waldman, and F. J. Yammarino, "CEO Charisma, Compensation, and Firm Performance," *Leadership Quarterly*, June 2004, pp. 405–20.

23. See, for instance, R. Khurana, *Searching for a Corporate Savior: The Irrational Quest for Charismatic CEOs* (Princeton, NJ: Princeton University Press, 2002); and J. A. Raelin, "The Myth of Charismatic Leaders," *Training & Development*, March 2003, pp. 47–54.

24. J. Collins, "Level 5 Leadership: The Triumph of Humility and Fierce Resolve," *Harvard Business Review*, January 2001, pp. 67–76; J. Collins, "Good to Great," *Fast Company*, October 2001, pp. 90–104; and J. Collins, "The Misguided Mix-Up," *Executive Excellence*, December 2002, pp. 3–4; H. L. Tosi, V. Misangyi, A. Fanelli, D. A. Waldman, and F. J. Yammarino, "CEO Charisma, Compensation, and Firm Performance," *Leadership Quarterly*, June 2004, pp. 405–20.

25. See, for instance, B. M. Bass, *Leadership and Performance Beyond Expectations* (New York: Free Press, 1985); B. M. Bass, "From Transactional to Transformational Leadership: Learning to Share the Vision," *Organizational Dynamics*, Winter 1990, pp. 19–31; F. J. Yammarino, W. D. Spangler, and B.M. Bass, "Transformational Leadership and Performance: A Longitudinal Investigation," *Leadership Quarterly*, Spring 1993, pp. 81–102; J. C. Wofford, V. L. Goodwin, and J. L. Whittington, "A Field Study of a Cognitive Approach to Understanding Transformational and Transactional Leadership," *Leadership Quarterly* 9, no. 1 (1998), pp. 55–84; B. M. Bass, B. J. Avolio, D. I. Jung, and Y. Berson, "Predicting Unit Performance by Assessing Transformational and Transactional Leadership," *Journal of Applied Psychology*, April 2003, pp. 207–18; J. Antonakis, B. J. Avolio, and N. Sivasubramaniam, "Context and Leadership: An Examination of the Nine-Factor Full-Range Leadership Theory Using the Multifactor Leadership Questionnaire," *Leadership Quarterly*, June 2003, pp. 261–95; and T. A. Judge, and R. F. Piccolo, "Transformational and Transactional Leadership: A Meta-Analytic Test of Their Relative Validity," *Journal of Applied Psychology*, October 2004, pp. 755–68.

26. B. M. Bass, "Leadership: Good, Better, Best," *Organizational Dynamics*, Winter 1985, pp. 26–40; and J. Seltzer and B. M. Bass, "Transformational Leadership: Beyond Initiation and Consideration," *Journal of Management*, December 1990, pp. 693–703.

27. D. I. Jung, C. Chow, and A. Wu, "The Role of Transformational Leadership in Enhancing Organizational Innovation: Hypotheses and Some Preliminary Findings," *Leadership Quarterly*, August–October 2003, pp. 525–44; D. I. Jung, "Transformational and Transactional Leadership and Their Effects on Creativity in Groups," *Creativity Research Journal* 13, no. 2 (2001), pp. 185–95; S. J. Shin and J. Zhou, "Transformational Leadership, Conservation, and Creativity: Evidence from Korea," *Academy of Management Journal*, December 2003, pp. 703–14.

28. D. Baum, "Battle Lessons: What the Generals Don't Know," *The New Yorker*, January 17, 2005, pp. 42–48.

29. J. E. Bono and T. A. Judge, "Self-Concordance at Work: Toward Understanding the Motivational Effects of Transformational Leaders," *Academy of Management Journal*, October 2003, pp. 554–71; Y. Berson and B. J. Avolio, "Transformational Leadership and the Dissemination of Organizational Goals: A Case Study of a Telecommunication Firm," *Leadership Quarterly*, October 2004, pp. 625–46; and S. Shinn, "21st-Century Engineer," *BizEd*, January/February, 2005, pp. 18–23.

30. J. R. Baum, E. A. Locke, and S. A. Kirkpatrick, "A Longitudinal Study of the Relation of Vision and Vision Communication to Venture Growth in Entrepreneurial Firms," *Journal of Applied Psychology*, February 2000, pp. 43–54.

31. B. J. Avolio, W. Zhu, W. Koh, and P. Bhatia, "Transformational Leadership and Organizational Commitment: Mediating Role of Psychological Empowerment and Moderating Role of Structural Distance," *Journal of Organizational Behavior*, December 2004, pp. 951–68; T. Dvir, Taly, N. Kass, and B. Shamir, "The Emotional Bond: Vision and Organizational Commitment Among High-Tech Employees," *Journal of Organizational Change Management* 17, no. 2 (2004), pp. 126–43; and D. I. Jung and B. J. Avolio, "Opening the Black Box: An Experimental Investigation of the Mediating Effects of Trust and Value Congruence on Transformational and Transactional Leadership," *Journal of Organizational Behavior*, December 2000, pp. 949–64.

32. Cited in B. M. Bass and B. J. Avolio, "Developing Transformational Leadership: 1992 and Beyond," *Journal of European Industrial Training*, January 1990, p. 23.

33. T. A. Judge and R. F. Piccolo, "Transformational and Transactional Leadership: A Meta-Analytic Test of their Relative Validity," *Journal of Applied Psychology*, October 2004, pp. 755–68.

34. Bass and Avolio, "Developing Transformational Leadership"; K. B. Lowe, K. G. Kroeck, and N. Sivasubramaniam, "Effectiveness Correlates of Transformational and Transactional

Leadership: A Meta-Analytic Review of the MLQ Literature," *Leadership Quarterly*, Fall 1996, pp. 385–425; and T. A. Judge and J. E. Bono, "Five-Factor Model of Personality and Transformational Leadership," *Journal of Applied Psychology*, October 2000, pp. 751–65.

35. See, for instance, J. Barling, T. Weber, and E. K. Kelloway, "Effects of Transformational Leadership Training on Attitudinal and Financial Outcomes: A Field Experiment," *Journal of Applied Psychology*, December 1996, pp. 827–32; T. Dvir, D. Eden, and B. J. Avolio, "Impact of Transformational Leadership on Follower Development and Performance: A Field Experiment," *Academy of Management Journal*, August 2002, pp. 735–44.

36. R. J. House and P. M. Podsakoff, "Leadership Effectiveness: Past Perspectives and Future Directions for Research," in J. Greenberg (ed.), *Organizational Behavior: The State of the Science* (Hillsdale, NJ: Erlbaum, 1994), pp. 45–82; B. M. Bass, *Leadership and Performance Beyond Expectations* (New York: Free Press, 1985).

37. B. J. Avolio and B. M. Bass, "Transformational Leadership, Charisma and Beyond," working paper, School of Management, State University of New York, Binghamton, 1985, p. 14.

38. See B. J. Avolio, W. L. Gardner, F. O. Walumbwa, F. Luthans, and D. R. May, "Unlocking the Mask: A Look at the Process by Which Authentic Impact Follower Attitudes and Behaviors," *Leadership Quarterly*, December 2004, pp. 801–23; W. L. Gardner and J. R. Schermerhorn, Jr., "Performance Gains Through Positive Organizational Behavior and Authentic Leadership," *Organizational Dynamics*, August 2004, pp. 270–81; and D. R. May, A. Y. L. Chan, T. D. Hodges, and B. J. Avolio, "Developing the Moral Component of Authentic Leadership," *Organizational Dynamics*, August 2003, pp. 247–60.

39. R. Ilies, F. P. Morgeson, and J. D. Nahrgang, "Authentic Leadership and Eudaemonic Well-Being and Understanding Leader-Follower Outcomes," in press, *Leadership Quarterly*.

40. This section is based on E. P. Hollander, "Ethical Challenges in the Leader–Follower Relationship," *Business Ethics Quarterly*, January 1995, pp. 55–65; J. C. Rost, "Leadership: A Discussion About Ethics," *Business Ethics Quarterly*, January 1995, pp. 129–42; J. B. Ciulla (ed.), *Ethics: The Heart of Leadership* (New York: Praeger Publications, 1998); J. D. Costa, *The Ethical Imperative: Why Moral Leadership Is Good Business* (Cambridge, MA: Perseus Press, 1999); C. E. Johnson, *Meeting the Ethical Challenges of Leadership* (Thousand Oaks, CA: Sage, 2001); L. K. Trevino, M. Brown, and L. P. Hartman, "A Qualitative Investigation of Perceived Executive Ethical Leadership: Perceptions from Inside and Outside the Executive Suite," *Human Relations*, January 2003, pp. 5–37; and R. M. Fulmer, "The Challenge of Ethical Leadership," *Organizational Dynamics* 33, no. 3 (2004), pp. 307–17.

41. J. M. Burns, *Leadership* (New York: Harper & Row, 1978).

42. J. M. Howell and B. J. Avolio, "The Ethics of Charismatic Leadership: Submission or Liberation?" *Academy of Management Executive*, May 1992, pp. 43–55.

43. See, for example, K. T. Dirks and D. L. Ferrin, "Trust in Leadership: Meta-Analytic Findings and Implications for Research and Practice," *Journal of Applied Psychology*, August 2002, pp. 611–28; the special issue on trust in an organizational context, B. McEvily, V. Perrone, A. Zaheer, guest editors, *Organization Science*, January–February 2003; and R. Galford and A. S. Drapeau, *The Trusted Leader* (New York: Free Press, 2003).

44. Based on S. D. Boon and J. G. Holmes, "The Dynamics of Interpersonal Trust: Resolving Uncertainty in the Face of Risk," in R. A. Hinde and J. Groebel (eds.), *Cooperation and Prosocial Behavior* (Cambridge, UK: Cambridge University Press, 1991), p. 194; D. J. McAllister, "Affect- and Cognition-Based Trust as Foundations for Interpersonal Cooperation in Organizations," *Academy of Management Journal*, February 1995, p. 25; and D. M. Rousseau, S. B. Sitkin, R. S. Burt, and C. Camerer, "Not So Different After All: A Cross-Discipline View of Trust," *Academy of Management Review*, July 1998, pp. 393–404.

45. J. B. Rotter, "Interpersonal Trust, Trustworthiness, and Gullibility," *American Psychologist*, January 1980, pp. 1–7.

46. J. D. Lewis and A. Weigert, "Trust as a Social Reality," *Social Forces*, June 1985, p. 970.

47. J. K. Rempel, J. G. Holmes, and M. P. Zanna, "Trust in Close Relationships," *Journal of Personality and Social Psychology*, July 1985, p. 96.

48. M. Granovetter, "Economic Action and Social Structure: The Problem of Embeddedness," *American Journal of Sociology*, November 1985, p. 491.

49. R. C. Mayer, J. H. Davis, and F. D. Schoorman, "An Integrative Model of Organizational Trust," *Academy of Management Review*, July 1995, p. 712.

50. C. Johnson-George and W. Swap, "Measurement of Specific Interpersonal Trust: Construction and Validation of a Scale to Assess Trust in a Specific Other," *Journal of Personality and Social Psychology*, September 1982, p. 1306.

51. P. L. Schindler and C. C. Thomas, "The Structure of Interpersonal Trust in the Workplace," *Psychological Reports*, October 1993, pp. 563–73.

52. H. H. Tan and C. S. F. Tan, "Toward the Differentiation of Trust in Supervisor and Trust in Organization," *Genetic, Social, and General Psychology Monographs*, May 2000, pp. 241–60.

53. Cited in D. Jones, "Do You Trust Your CEO?" *USA Today*, February 12, 2003, p. 7B.

54. D. McGregor, *The Professional Manager* (New York: McGraw-Hill, 1967), p. 164.

55. B. Nanus, *The Leader's Edge: The Seven Keys to Leadership in a Turbulent World* (Chicago: Contemporary Books, 1989), p. 102.

56. See, for instance, K. T. Dirks and D. L. Ferrin, "Trust in Leadership: Meta-Analytic Findings and Implications for Research and Practice," *Journal of Applied Psychology*, August 2002, pp. 611–28; J. B. Cunningham and J. MacGregor, "Trust and the Design of Work: Complementary Constructs in Satisfaction and Performance," *Human Relations*, December 2000, pp. 1575–91; D. I. Jung and B. J. Avolio, "Opening the Black Box: An Experimental Investigation of the Mediating Effects of Trust and Value Congruence on Transformational and Transactional Leadership," *Journal of Organizational Behavior*, December 2000, pp. 949–64; and A. Zacharatos, J. Barling, and R. D. Iverson, "High-Performance Work Systems and Occupational Safety," *Journal of Applied Psychology*, January 2005, pp. 77–93.

57. D. E. Zand, *The Leadership Triad: Knowledge, Trust, and Power* (New York: Oxford Press, 1997), p. 89.

58. Based on L. T. Hosmer, "Trust: The Connecting Link between Organizational Theory and Philosophical Ethics," *Academy of Management Review*, April 1995, p. 393; and R. C. Mayer, J. H. Davis, and F. D. Schoorman, "An Integrative Model of Organizational Trust," *Academy of Management Review*, July 1995, p. 712.

59. J. M. Kouzes and B. Z. Posner, *Credibility: How Leaders Gain and Lose It, and Why People Demand It* (San Francisco: Jossey-Bass, 1993), p. 14.

60. This section is based on D. Shapiro, B. H. Sheppard, and L. Cheraskin, "Business on a Handshake," *Negotiation Journal*, October 1992, pp. 365–77; R. J. Lewicki and B. B. Bunker, "Developing and Maintaining Trust in Work Relationships," in R. M. Kramer and T. R. Tyler (eds.), *Trust in Organizations* (Thousand Oaks, CA: Sage, 1996), pp. 119–24; and J. Child, "Trust—The Fundamental Bond in Global Collaboration," *Organizational Dynamics* 29, no. 4 (2001), pp. 274–88.

61. This section is based on D. E. Zand, *The Leadership Triad: Knowledge, Trust, and Power* (New York: Oxford University Press, 1997), pp. 122–34; and A. M. Zak, J. A. Gold, R. M. Ryckman, and E. Lenney, "Assessments of Trust in Intimate Relationships and the Self-Perception Process," *Journal of Social Psychology*, April 1998, pp. 217–28.

62. J. Scott, "Once Bitten, Twice Shy: A World of Eroding Trust," *The New York Times*, April 21, 2002, p. WK5; J. A. Byrne, "Restoring Trust in Corporate America," *Business Week*, June 24, 2002, pp. 30–35; B. Nussbaum, "Can Trust Be Rebuilt?" *Business Week*, July 8, 2002, pp. 32–34; and C. Sandlund, "Trust Is a Must," *Entrepreneur*, October 2002, pp. 70–75.

63. The following results are cited in B. Horovitz, "Trust," *USA Today*, July 16, 2002, p. 1A; and D. Jones, "Do You Trust Your CEO?" *USA Today*, February 12, 2003, p. 7B.

64. See, for instance, J. H. Zenger, E. Musselwhite, K. Hurson, and C. Perrin, *Leading Teams: Mastering the New Role* (Homewood, IL: Business One Irwin, 1994); M. Frohman, "Nothing Kills Teams Like Ill-Prepared Leaders," *Industry Week*, October 2, 1995, pp. 72–76; S. J. Zaccaro, A. L. Rittman, and M. A. Marks, "Team Leadership," *Leadership Quarterly*, Winter 2001, pp. 451–83; and B.-C. Lim and R. E. Ployhart, "Transformational Leadership: Relations to the Five-Factor Model and Team Performance in Typical and Maximum Contexts," *Journal of Applied Psychology*, August 2004, pp. 610–21.

65. S. Caminiti, "What Team Leaders Need to Know," *Fortune*, February 20, 1995, pp. 93–100.

66. Ibid., p. 93.

67. Ibid., p. 100.

68. N. Steckler and N. Fondas, "Building Team Leader Effectiveness: A Diagnostic Tool," *Organizational Dynamics*, Winter 1995, p. 20.

69. R. S. Wellins, W. C. Byham, and G. R. Dixon, *Inside Teams* (San Francisco: Jossey-Bass, 1994), p. 318.

70. Steckler and Fondas, "Building Team Leader Effectiveness," p. 21.

71. See, for example, L. J. Zachary, *The Mentor's Guide: Facilitating Effective Learning Relationships* (San Francisco: Jossey-Bass, 2000); M. Murray, *Beyond the Myths and Magic of Mentoring: How to Facilitate an Effective Mentoring Process*, rev. ed. (New York: Wiley, 2001); and F. Warner, "Inside Intel's Mentoring Movement," *Fast Company*, April 2002, pp. 116–20; and K. E. Kram, "Phases of the Mentor Relationship," *Academy of Management Journal*, December 1983, pp. 608-625; R. A. Noe, "An Investigation of the Determinants of Successful Assigned Mentoring Relationships," *Personnel Psychology*, Fall 1988, pp. 559-580; and L. Eby, M. Butts, and A. Lockwood, "Protégés' Negative Mentoring Experiences: Construct Development and Nomological Validation," *Personnel Psychology*, Summer 2004, pp. 411–447.

72. K. McLaughlin, "Training Top 50: Edward Jones," *Training*, March 2001, pp. 78–79.

73. J. A. Wilson and N. S. Elman, "Organizational Benefits of Mentoring," *Academy of Management Executive*, November 1990, p. 90; and J. Reingold, "Want to Grow as a Leader? Get a Mentor?" *Fast Company*, January 2001, pp. 58–60.

74. See, for example, D. A. Thomas, "The Impact of Race on Managers' Experiences of Developmental Relationships: An Intra-Organizational Study," *Journal of Organizational Behavior*, November 1990, pp. 479–92; K. E. Kram and D. T. Hall, "Mentoring in a Context of Diversity and Turbulence," in E. E. Kossek and S. A. Lobel (eds.), *Managing Diversity* (Cambridge, MA: Blackwell, 1996), pp. 108–36; M. N. Ruderman and M. W. Hughes-James, "Leadership Development Across Race and Gender," in C. D. McCauley, R. S. Moxley, and E. Van Velsor (eds.), *The Center for Creative Leadership Handbook of Leadership Development* (San Francisco: Jossey-Bass, 1998), pp. 291–335; B. R. Ragins and J. L. Cotton, "Mentor Functions and Outcomes: A Comparison of Men and Women in Formal and Informal Mentoring Relationships," *Journal of Applied Psychology*, August 1999, pp. 529–50; and D. B. Turban, T. W. Dougherty, and F. K. Lee, "Gender, Race, and Perceived Similarity Effects in Developmental Relationships: The Moderating Role of Relationship Duration," *Journal of Vocational Behavior*, October 2002, pp. 240–62.

75. Wilson and Elman, "Organizational Benefits of Mentoring," p. 90.

76. See, for instance, K. Houston-Philpot, "Leadership Development Partnerships at Dow Corning Corporation," *Journal of Organizational Excellence*, Winter 2002, pp. 13–27.

77. T. D. Allen, L. T. Eby, M. L. Poteet, Mark L., E. Lentz, and L. Lizzette, "Career Benefits Associated With Mentoring for Protégés: A Meta-Analysis," *Journal of Applied Psychology*, February 2004, pp. 127–36; J. D. Kammeyer-Mueller and T. A. Judge, "A Quantitative Review of the Mentoring Literature: Test of a Model," Working paper, University of Florida, 2005.

78. See C. C. Manz, "Self-Leadership: Toward an Expanded Theory of Self-Influence Processes in Organizations," *Academy of Management Review*, July 1986, pp. 585–600; C. C. Manz and H. P. Sims, Jr., "Superleadership: Beyond the Myth of Heroic Leadership," *Organizational Dynamics*, Spring 1991, pp. 18–35; H. P. Sims, Jr. and C. C. Manz, *Company of Heroes: Unleashing the Power of Self-Leadership* (New York: Wiley, 1996); C. C. Manz and H. P. Sims, Jr., *The New Superleadership: Leading Others to Lead Themselves* (San Francisco: Berrett-Koehler, 2001); C. L. Dolbier, M. Soderstrom, M. A. Steinhardt, "The Relationships Between Self-Leadership and Enhanced Psychological, Health, and Work Outcomes," *Journal of Psychology*, September 2001, pp. 469–85; and J. D. Houghton, T. W. Bonham, C. P. Neck, and K. Singh, "The Relationship Between Self-Leadership and Personality: A Comparison of Hierarchical Factor Structures," *Journal of Managerial Psychology* 19, no. 4 (2004), pp. 427–41.

79. A. H. Eagly, M. C. Johannesen-Schmidt, and M. L. van Engen, "Transformational, Transactional, and Laissez-Faire Leadership Styles: A Meta-Analysis Comparing Women and Men," *Psychological Bulletin*, July 2003, pp. 569–91.

80. Based on Manz and Sims, Jr., "Superleadership."

81. B. J. Avolio, S. Kahai, and G. E. Dodge, "E-Leadership: Implications for Theory, Research, and Practice," *Leadership Quarterly*, Winter 2000, pp. 615–68; and B. J. Avolio and S. S. Kahai, "Adding the "E" to E-Leadership: How it May Impact

Your Leadership," *Organizational Dynamics* 31, no. 4 (2003), pp. 325–38.

82. S. J. Zaccaro and P. Bader, "E-Leadership and the Challenges of Leading E-Teams: Minimizing the Bad and Maximizing the Good," *Organizational Dynamics* 31, no. 4 (2003), pp. 381–85.

83. C. E. Naquin and G. D. Paulson, "Online Bargaining and Interpersonal Trust," *Journal of Applied Psychology*, February 2003, pp. 113–20.

84. B. Shamir, "Leadership in Boundaryless Organizations: Disposable or Indispensable? *European Journal of Work and Organizational Psychology* 8, no. 1 (1999), pp. 49–71.

85. Comment by Jim Collins and cited in J. Useem, "Conquering Vertical Limits," *Fortune*, February 19, 2001, p. 94.

86. T. McCarthy, "Can the Terminator Save California?" *Time*, July 14, 2003, pp. 38–39; and L. D. Tyson, "A New Governor Won't Fix What Ails California," *Business Week*, September 22, 2003, p. 24.

87. See, for instance, J. C. McElroy, "A Typology of Attribution Leadership Research," *Academy of Management Review*, July 1982, pp. 413–17; J. R. Meindl and S. B. Ehrlich, "The Romance of Leadership and the Evaluation of Organizational Performance," *Academy of Management Journal*, March 1987, pp. 91–109; R. G. Lord and K. J. Maher, *Leadership and Information Processing: Linking Perception and Performance* (Boston: Unwin Hyman, 1991); B. Shamir, "Attribution of Influence and Charisma to the Leader: The Romance of Leadership Revisited," *Journal of Applied Social Psychology*, March 1992, pp. 386–407; J. R. Meindl, "The Romance of Leadership as a Follower-Centric Theory: A Social Constructionist Approach," *Leadership Quarterly*, Fall 1995, pp. 329–41; and S. A. Haslam, M. J. Platow, J. C. Turner, K. J. Reynolds, C. McGarty, P. J. Oakes, S. Johnson, M. K. Ryan, and K. Veenstra, "Social Identity and the Romance of Leadership: The Importance of Being Seen to be 'Doing it for Us,' " *Group Processes & Intergroup Relations*, July 2001, pp. 191–205.

88. R. G. Lord, C. L. DeVader, and G. M. Alliger, "A Meta-Analysis of the Relation Between Personality Traits and Leadership Perceptions: An Application of Validity Generalization Procedures," *Journal of Applied Psychology*, August 1986, pp. 402–10.

89. J. R. Meindl, S. B. Ehrlich, and J. M. Dukerich, "The Romance of Leadership," *Administrative Science Quarterly*, March 1985, pp. 78–102.

90. B. M. Staw and J. Ross, "Commitment in an Experimenting Society: A Study of the Attribution of Leadership from Administrative Scenarios," *Journal of Applied Psychology*, June 1980, pp. 249–60; and J. Pfeffer, *Managing with Power* (Boston: Harvard Business School Press, 1992), p. 194.

91. S. Kerr and J. M. Jermier, "Substitutes for Leadership: Their Meaning and Measurement," *Organizational Behavior and Human Performance*, December 1978, pp. 375–403; J.M. Jermier and S. Kerr, "Substitutes for Leadership: Their Meaning and Measurement—Contextual Recollections and Current Observations," *Leadership Quarterly*, vol. 8, no. 2, 1997, pp. 95–101; and E. de Vries Reinout, R. A. Roe, and T. C. B. Taillieu, "Need for Leadership as a Moderator of the Relationships Between Leadership and Individual Outcomes," *Leadership Quarterly*, April 2002, pp. 121-38.

92. S. D. Dionne, F. J. Yamarino, L. E. Atwater, and L. R. James, "Neutralizing Substitutes for Leadership Theory: Leadership Effects and Common-Source Bias," *Journal of Applied Psychology*, 87, 2002, pp. 454–64; J. R. Villa, J. P. Howell, P. W. Dorfman, and D. L. Daniel, "Problems with Detecting Moderators in Leadership Research Using Moderated Multiple Regression," *Leadership Quarterly*, 14, 2002, pp. 3–23.

93. B. M. Bass, "Cognitive, Social, and Emotional Intelligence of Transformational Leaders," in R. E. Riggio, S. E. Murphy, and F. J. Pirozzolo (eds.), *Multiple Intelligences and Leadership* (Mahwah, NJ: Erlbaum, 2002), pp. 113–114.

94. See, for instance, R. Lofthouse, "Herding the Cats," *EuroBusiness*, February 2001, pp. 64–65; M. Delahoussaye, "Leadership in the 21st Century," *Training*, September 2001, pp. 60–72; and K. Ellis, "Making Waves," *Training*, June 2003, pp. 16–21.

95. See, for instance, J. Barling, T. Weber, and E. K. Kelloway, "Effects of Transformational Leadership Training on Attitudinal and Financial Outcomes: A Field Experiment," *Journal of Applied Psychology*, December 1996, pp. 827–32; and D. V. Day, "Leadership Development: A Review in Context," *Leadership Quarterly*, Winter 2000, pp. 581–613.

96. M. Sashkin, "The Visionary Leader," in J. A. Conger, R. N. Kanungo and Associates (eds.), *Charismatic Leadership* (San Francisco: Jossey-Bass, 1988), p. 150.

97. D. V. Day, "Leadership Development: A Review in Context," *Leadership Quarterly*, Winter 2000, pp. 590–93.

98. M. Conlin, "CEO Coaches," *Business Week*, November 11, 2002, pp. 98–104.

99. Howell and Frost, "A Laboratory Study of Charismatic Leadership."

100. T. Dvir, D. Eden, and B. J. Avolio, "Impact of Transformational Leadership on Follower Development and Performance: A Field Experiment," *Academy of Management Journal*, August 2002. pp. 735–44; B. J. Avolio and B. M. Bass, *Developing Potential Across a Full Range of Leadership: Cases on Transactional and Transformational Leadership* (Mahwah, NJ: Lawrence Erlbaum Associates, Publishers, 2002); A. J. Towler, "Effects of Charismatic Influence Training on Attitudes, Behavior, and Performance," *Personnel Psychology*, Summer 2003, pp. 363–81; Barling et al., "Effects of Transformational Leadership Training on Attitudinal and Financial Outcomes."

101. P. Rosinski, "Developing Global Leaders with Coaching Across Cultures," *MCE Newsletter*, Management Centre Europe (http://www.mce.be/knowledge/400/27) (May 2004).

102. N. Beccalli, "European Business Forum Asks: Do Companies Get the Leaders They Deserve?," *European Business Forum* (http://www.pwcglobal.com/extweb/pwcpublications.nsf/DocID/D1EC3380F589844585256D7300346A1B) (2003).

103. J. Li, P. Ping, I. Chow, and T. K. P. I-Shou, "Reconsider Cross-Cultural Differences in Leadership Behaviours: A Perspective of Institutional Symbiosis," Working paper, Hong Kong Baptist University, June, 2004.

104. R. J. House, M. Javidan, P. Hanges, and P. Dorfman, "Understanding Cultures and Implicit Leadership Theories Across the Globe: An Introduction to Project GLOBE," *Journal of World Business*, Spring 2002, pp. 3–10.

105. D. E. Carl and M. Javidan, "Universality of Charismatic Leadership: A Multi-Nation Study," paper presented at the National Academy of Management Conference, Washington, DC, August 2001, p. 29.

Power and Politics

After studying this chapter, you should be able to:

1 Contrast leadership and power.

2 Define the five bases of power.

3 Clarify what creates dependency in power relationships.

4 List nine influence tactics and their contingencies.

5 Explain how sexual harassment is about the abuse of power.

6 Describe the importance of a political perspective.

7 List the individual and organizational factors that stimulate political behavior.

8 Explain how defensive behaviors can protect an individual's self-interest.

9 Identify seven techniques for managing the impression one makes on others.

10 List the three questions that can help determine if a political action is ethical.

LEARNING OBJECTIVES

CHAPTER 14

Don't Mess with This CEO

At Merrill Lynch, the huge securities firm, the message is clear: Don't try to usurp the boss's authority. Two high-level executives—Thomas Patrick and Arshad Zakaria—tried it and found themselves out on the street.[1]

The boss in this case is Stan O'Neal (see photo), chairman and CEO at Merrill Lynch. And what makes these actions newsworthy is that Patrick and Zakaria were two of O'Neal's closest confidants. Patrick was executive vice chairman and the second most senior executive in the firm. Zakaria was chairman of global markets and investment banking and a protégé of Patrick. Both Patrick and Zakaria played an active role in persuading Merrill's board of directors that the firm needed major cost cutting and that O'Neal was the best person to do it. O'Neal was named president—and chief-executive-in-waiting—in July 2001. He soon began purging the company of top executives he saw as potential threats. Patrick and Zakaria were major players in helping O'Neal cut 23,000 jobs and dramatically improving the firm's profitability. His success led to his official appointment as CEO and chairman in December 2002.

According to insiders, Patrick and Zakaria's fatal mistake was secretly lobbying board members in the summer of 2003 to have 41-year-old Zakaria made successor-designate to the 51-year-old O'Neal. O'Neal had been CEO less than a year and thought the appointment of a successor premature. When Patrick told O'Neal that he thought Zakaria should be installed as president and heir-apparent, O'Neal had had enough. He forced the 60-year-old Patrick to retire. A week later, he fired Zakaria. The message this sent throughout Merrill Lynch was loud and clear: O'Neal was in power and he was not going to tolerate any challenges to his authority.

In 2004, *Fortune* magazine noted that O'Neal may be the "toughest—some say the most ruthless—CEO in America" while also commenting that he has done much to enhance Merrill Lynch's reputation and financial standing. ■

*P*ower has been described as the last dirty word. It is easier for most of us to talk about sex or money than it is to talk about power. People who have it deny it, people who want it try not to appear to be seeking it, and those who are good at getting it are secretive about how they got it.[2]

A major theme of this chapter is that power is a natural process in any group or organization. As such, you need to know how it's acquired and exercised if you're going to fully understand organizational behavior. Although you may have heard the phrase that "power corrupts, and absolute power corrupts absolutely," power is not always bad. As one author has noted, most medicines can kill if taken in the wrong amount and thousands die each year in automobile accidents, but we don't abandon chemicals or cars because of the dangers associated with them. Rather, we consider danger an incentive to get training and information that will help us to use these forces productively.[3] The same applies to power. It's a reality of organizational life and it's not going to go away. Moreover, by learning how power works in organizations, you'll be better able to use your knowledge to help you be a more effective manager.

A Definition of Power

Power refers to a capacity that *A* has to influence the behavior of *B* so that *B* acts in accordance with *A*'s wishes.[4] This definition implies a *potential* that need not be actualized to be effective and a *dependency* relationship.

Power may exist but not be used. It is, therefore, a capacity or potential. One can have power but not impose it. Probably the most important aspect of power is that it is a function of **dependency**. The greater *B*'s dependence on *A*, the greater is *A*'s power in the relationship. Dependence, in turn, is based on alternatives that *B* perceives and the importance that *B* places on the alternative(s) that *A* controls. A person can have power over you only if he or she controls something you desire. If you want a college degree and have to pass a certain course to get it, and your current instructor is the only faculty member in the college who teaches that course, he or she has power over you. Your alternatives are highly limited and you place a high degree of importance on obtaining a passing grade. Similarly, if you're attending college on funds totally provided by your parents, you probably recognize the power that they hold over you. You're dependent on them for financial support. But once you're out of school, have a job, and are making a good income, your parents' power is reduced significantly. Who among us, though, has not known or heard of the rich relative who is able to control a large number of family members merely through the implicit or explicit threat of "writing them out of the will"?

Contrasting Leadership and Power

A careful comparison of our description of power with our description of leadership in the previous two chapters reveals that the concepts are closely intertwined. Leaders use power as a means of attaining group goals. Leaders achieve goals, and power is a means of facilitating their achievement.

What differences are there between the two terms? One difference relates to goal compatibility. Power does not require goal compatibility, merely dependence. Leadership, on the other hand, requires some congruence between the goals of the leader and those being led. A second difference relates to the direction of influence. Leadership focuses on the downward influence on one's followers. It minimizes the importance of lateral and upward influence patterns. Power does not. Still another difference deals with research emphasis. Leadership research, for the most part, emphasizes style. It seeks answers to questions such as: How supportive should a leader be? How much decision making should be shared with followers? In contrast, the research on power has tended to encompass a broader area and to focus on tactics for gaining compliance. It has gone beyond the individual as the exerciser of power because power can be used by groups as well as by individuals to control other individuals or groups.

Bases of Power

Where does power come from? What is it that gives an individual or a group influence over others? We answer these questions by dividing the bases or sources of power into two general groupings—formal and personal—and then breaking each of these down into more specific categories.[5]

Formal Power

Formal power is based on an individual's position in an organization. Formal power can come from the ability to coerce or reward, or from formal authority.

Coercive Power   The **coercive power** base is dependent on fear. One reacts to this power out of fear of the negative results that might occur if one failed to comply. It rests on the application, or the threat of application, of physical sanctions such as the infliction of pain, the generation of frustration through restriction of movement, or the controlling by force of basic physiological or safety needs.

At the organizational level, A has coercive power over B if A can dismiss, suspend, or demote B, assuming that B values his or her job. Similarly, if A can assign B work activities that B finds unpleasant or treat B in a manner that B finds embarrassing, A possesses coercive power over B. Coercive power also can come from withholding key information. People in an organization who have data or knowledge that others need can make those others dependent on them.

Reward Power   The opposite of coercive power is **reward power**. People comply with the wishes or directives of another because doing so produces positive benefits; therefore, one who can distribute rewards that others view as valuable will have power over those others. These rewards can be either financial—such as controlling pay rates, raises, and bonuses; or nonfinancial—including recognition,

---

power   *A capacity that A has to influence the behavior of B so that B acts in accordance with A's wishes.*

dependency   *B's relationship to A when A possesses something that B requires.*

coercive power   *A power base dependent on fear.*

reward power   *Compliance achieved based on the ability to distribute rewards that others view as valuable.*

In India, Naina Lal Kidwai is a powerful woman in the banking industry. She derives her power as managing director and vice chairman of HSBC Securities and Capital Markets, a group within the Hong Kong and Shanghai Banking Corporation. Kidwai's formal power is an example of legitimate power, as it is based on her structural position at the bank. This power gives Kidwai the authority to control and use organizational resources.

promotions, interesting work assignments, friendly colleagues, and preferred work shifts or sales territories.[6]

Coercive power and reward power are actually counterparts of each other. If you can remove something of positive value from another or inflict something of negative value, you have coercive power over that person. If you can give someone something of positive value or remove something of negative value, you have reward power over that person.

Legitimate Power   In formal groups and organizations, probably the most frequent access to one or more of the power bases is one's structural position. This is called **legitimate power**. It represents the formal authority to control and use organizational resources.

Positions of authority include coercive and reward powers. Legitimate power, however, is broader than the power to coerce and reward. Specifically, it includes acceptance by members in an organization of the authority of a position. When school principals, bank presidents, or army captains speak (assuming that their directives are viewed to be within the authority of their positions), teachers, tellers, and first lieutenants listen and usually comply.

Personal Power

You don't have to have a formal position in an organization to have power. Many of the most competent and productive chip designers at Intel, for instance, have power, but they aren't managers and have no formal power. What they have is personal power—power that comes from an individual's unique characteristics. In this section, we look at two bases of personal power—expertise and the respect and admiration of others.

Expert Power   **Expert power** is influence wielded as a result of expertise, special skill, or knowledge. Expertise has become one of the most powerful sources of influence as the world has become more technologically oriented. As jobs become more specialized, we become increasingly dependent on experts to achieve goals. So, although it is generally acknowledged that physicians have expertise and hence expert power—most of us follow the advice that our doctor gives us—you should also recognize that computer specialists, tax accountants, economists, industrial psychologists, and other specialists are able to wield power as a result of their expertise.

Referent Power   **Referent power** is based on identification with a person who has desirable resources or personal traits. If I like, respect, and admire you, you can exercise power over me because I want to please you.

Referent power develops out of admiration of another and a desire to be like that person. It helps explain, for instance, why celebrities are paid millions of dollars to endorse products in commercials. Marketing research shows that people like LeBron James and Tom Brady have the power to influence your choice of athletic shoes and credit cards. With a little practice, you and I could probably deliver as smooth a sales pitch as these celebrities, but the buying public doesn't identify with you and me. One of the ways in which individuals acquire referent power is through charisma. Some people have referent power who, while not in formal leadership positions, nevertheless are able to exert influence over others because of their charismatic dynamism, likeability, and emotional effects on us.

Exhibit **14-1**

"*I was just going to say 'Well, I don't make the rules.' But, of course, I do make the rules.*"

Source: Drawing by Leo Cullum in *The New Yorker*, copyright © 1986 *The New Yorker Magazine*. Reprinted by permission.

Which Bases of Power Are Most Effective?

Of the three bases of formal power (coercive, reward, legitimate) and two bases of personal power (expert, referent), which is most important to have? Interestingly, research suggests pretty clearly that the personal sources of power are most effective. Both expert and referent power are positively related to employees' satisfaction with supervision, their organizational commitment, and their performance, whereas reward and legitimate power seem to be unrelated to these outcomes. Moreover, one source of formal power—coercive power—actually can backfire in that it is negatively related to employee satisfaction and commitment.[7]

Consider Steve Stoute's company, Translation, which matches pop-star spokespersons with corporations that want to promote their brands. Stoute has paired Gwen Stefani with HP, Justin Timberlake with McDonald's, Beyoncé Knowles with Tommy Hilfiger, and Jay-Z with Reebok. Stoute's business seems to be all about referent power—as one record company executive commented when reflecting on Stoute's successes, "He's the right guy for guiding brands in using the record industry to reach youth culture in a credible way."[8] In other words, using pop stars to market products works because of referent power— people buy products associated with cool figures because they wish to identify with these figures and emulate them.

legitimate power   *The power a person receives as a result of his or her position in the formal hierarchy of an organization.*

expert power   *Influence based on special skills or knowledge.*

referent power   *Influence based on possession by an individual of desirable resources or personal traits.*

Dependency: The Key to Power

Earlier in this chapter it was said that probably the most important aspect of power is that it is a function of dependence. In this section, we show how an understanding of dependency is central to furthering your understanding of power itself.

The General Dependency Postulate

Let's begin with a general postulate: *The greater B's dependency on A, the greater the power A has over B.* When you possess anything that others require but that you alone control, you make them dependent on you and, therefore, you gain power over them.[9] Dependency, then, is inversely proportional to the alternative sources of supply. If something is plentiful, possession of it will not increase your power. If everyone is intelligent, intelligence gives no special advantage. Similarly, among the superrich, money is no longer power. But, as the old saying goes, "In the land of the blind, the one-eyed man is king!" If you can create a monopoly by controlling information, prestige, or anything that others crave, they become dependent on you. Conversely, the more that you can expand your options, the less power you place in the hands of others. This explains, for example, why most organizations develop multiple suppliers rather than give their business to only one. It also explains why so many of us aspire to financial independence. Financial independence reduces the power that others can have over us.

What Creates Dependency?

Dependency is increased when the resource you control is important, scarce, and nonsubstitutable.[10]

Importance   If nobody wants what you've got, it's not going to create dependency. To create dependency, therefore, the thing(s) you control must be perceived as being important. Organizations, for instance, actively seek to avoid uncertainty.[11] We should, therefore, expect that the individuals or groups who can absorb an organization's uncertainty will be perceived as controlling an important resource. For instance, a study of industrial organizations found that the marketing departments in these firms were consistently rated as the most powerful.[12] It was concluded by the researcher that the most critical uncertainty facing these firms was selling their products. This might suggest that engineers, as a group, would be more powerful at Matsushita than at Procter & Gamble. These inferences appear to be generally valid. An organization such as Matsushita, which is heavily technologically oriented, is highly dependent on its engineers to maintain its products' technical advantages and quality. And, at Matsushita, engineers are clearly a powerful group. At Procter & Gamble, marketing is the name of the game, and marketers are the most powerful occupational group.

Scarcity   As noted previously, if something is plentiful, possession of it will not increase your power. A resource needs to be perceived as scarce to create dependency. This can help to explain how low-ranking members in an organization who have important knowledge not available to high-ranking members gain power over the high-ranking members. Possession of a scarce resource—in this case, important knowledge—makes the high-ranking member dependent on the low-ranking member. This also helps to make sense out of behaviors of low-ranking members that otherwise might seem illogical, such as destroying the procedure manuals that describe how a job is done, refusing to train people

Ken Kutaragi is important at Sony Corporation. He is the founder and president of Sony Computer Entertainment, which developed the PlayStation videogame machine. Within a few years, PlayStation generated 40 percent of Sony's operating profit. This success gave Kutaragi the power to persuade Sony to invest $2.5 billion in PlayStation 2, which captured 70 percent of the market. In this photo, Kutaragi displays a disk on a new PlayStation 2 model with a DVD recorder, TV tuner, and capability to download music and movies. Kutaragi continues to wield power at Sony by introducing successful new products such as PlayStation Portable and PlayStation 3.

At University of Kansas: Coach Gets Boss Fired?

You know you have power when you can get your boss fired. That's what apparently happened at the University of Kansas in the spring of 2003.

Roy Williams had been KU's head men's basketball coach for 15 years. During those years, he built a strong following. He averaged nearly 28 wins a season and graduated his athletes. Fans and alumni loved the guy. But Williams was a graduate of the University of North Carolina, and in the spring of 2003, UNC was looking for a new coach for its men's basketball program. Born and raised in North Carolina, and a former assistant coach at UNC, Williams was an obvious candidate for the position. KU's administration was determined to try to keep him. Kansas Chancellor Robert Hemenway promised to "do whatever we can to encourage (Williams) to remain." That included firing his boss—athletic director Al Bohl.

Bohl had been hired in 2001 to replace the longtime athletic director, Bob Frederick, who was a close friend of Williams. But Bohl and Williams never hit it off well and had had numerous clashes. So KU's administration decided to let Bohl go in the hope that this would make Williams's job at KU more comfortable and make it easier for him to turn down any offer from UNC.

Bohl was frank in his assessment, "I believe the Kansas basketball coach had the power to hold his athletic director in his hand like a dove. And he had a choice to either crush me with his power of influence or let me fly with my vision for a better total program. He chose to crush me."

Incidentally, KU's actions didn't get the desired response. Williams was offered the UNC position and, after considerable deliberation, decided to return to North Carolina. After a rough season in his first year at UNC, Williams's Tarheels won the National Championship. Meanwhile, Kansas hired Illinois coach Bill Self to replace Williams. Williams and Self have had their ups and downs at UNC and Kansas, respectively, and at the start of the 2005–2006 season, neither team was ranked in the top 25. And what is Al Bohl up to? He is penning a novel—about basketball.

Source: Based on "Kansas Athletic Director Blames Basketball Coach for His Dismissal," *The New York Times,* April 10, 2003, p. C17; and S. Wieberg, "Williams, N. Carolina Still Talking," *USA Today,* April 11, 2003, p. 1C.

---

in their jobs or even to show others exactly what they do, creating specialized language and terminology that inhibit others from understanding their jobs, or operating in secrecy so an activity will appear more complex and difficult than it really is. Ferruccio Lamborghini, the guy who created the exotic supercars that continue to carry his name, understood the importance of scarcity and used it to his advantage during World War II. Lamborghini was in Rhodes with the Italian army. His superiors were impressed with his mechanical skills, as he demonstrated an almost uncanny ability to repair tanks and cars that no one else could fix. After the war he admitted that his ability was largely due to having been the first person on the island to receive the repair manuals, which he memorized and then destroyed so as to become indispensable.[13]

The scarcity-dependency relationship can further be seen in the power of occupational categories. Individuals in occupations in which the supply of personnel is low relative to demand can negotiate compensation and benefit packages that are far more attractive than can those in occupations for which there is an abundance of candidates. College administrators have no problem today finding English instructors. The market for computer-engineering teachers, in contrast, is extremely tight, with the demand high and the supply limited. The result is that the bargaining power of computer-engineering faculty allows them to negotiate higher salaries, lighter teaching loads, and other benefits.

Nonsubstitutability The fewer viable substitutes for a resource, the more power the control over that resource provides. Higher education again provides an excellent example. At universities in which there are strong pressures for the faculty to publish, we can say that a department head's power over a faculty member is inversely related to that member's publication record. The more recognition the faculty member receives through publication, the more mobile he or she is. That is, since other universities want faculty who are highly published and visible, there is an increased demand for that person's services. Although the concept of tenure can act to alter this relationship by restricting the department head's alternatives, faculty members who have few or no publications have the least mobility and are subject to the greatest influence from their superiors.

Power Tactics

What **power tactics** do people use to translate power bases into specific action? That is, what options do individuals have for influencing their bosses, co-workers, or employees? And are some of these options more effective than others? In this section, we review popular tactical options and the conditions under which one may be more effective than another.

Research has identified nine distinct influence tactics:[14]

- *Legitimacy.* Relying on one's authority position or stressing that a request is in accordance with organizational policies or rules.
- *Rational persuasion.* Presenting logical arguments and factual evidence to demonstrate that a request is reasonable.
- *Inspirational appeals.* Developing emotional commitment by appealing to a target's values, needs, hopes, and aspirations.
- *Consultation.* Increasing the target's motivation and support by involving him or her in deciding how the plan or change will be done.
- *Exchange.* Rewarding the target with benefits or favors in exchange for following a request.
- *Personal appeals.* Asking for compliance based on friendship or loyalty.
- *Ingratiation.* Using flattery, praise, or friendly behavior prior to making a request.
- *Pressure.* Using warnings, repeated demands, and threats.
- *Coalitions.* Enlisting the aid of other people to persuade the target or using the support of others as a reason for the target to agree.

Some tactics are usually more effective than others. Specifically, evidence indicates that rational persuasion, inspirational appeals, and consultation tend to be the most effective. On the other hand, pressure tends to frequently backfire and is typically the least effective of the nine tactics.[15] You can also increase your chance of success by using more than one type of tactic at the same time or sequentially, as long as your choices are compatible.[16] For instance, using both ingratiation and legitimacy can lessen the negative reactions that might come from the appearance of being "dictated to" by the boss.

But some influence tactics work better depending on the direction of influence.[17] As shown in Exhibit 14-2, studies have found that rational persuasion is

Exhibit **14-2**	Preferred Power Tactics by Influence Direction	
Upward Influence	**Downward Influence**	**Lateral Influence**
Rational persuasion	Rational persuasion	Rational persuasion
	Inspirational appeals	Consultation
	Pressure	Ingratiation
	Consultation	Exchange
	Ingratiation	Legitimacy
	Exchange	Personal appeals
	Legitimacy	Coalitions

Influence Tactics in China

RESEARCHERS USUALLY EXAMINE CROSS-CULTURAL influences in business by comparing two very different cultures, such as those from Eastern and Western societies. However, it is also important to examine differences within a given culture, as those differences can sometimes be greater than differences between cultures.

For example, although we might view all Chinese people as being alike due to their shared heritage and appearance, China is a big country housing different cultures and traditions. A recent study examining Mainland Chinese, Taiwanese, and Hong Kong managers explored how the three cultural subgroups differ according to the influence tactics they prefer to use.

Though managers from all three places believe that rational persuasion and exchange are the most effective influence tactics, managers in Taiwan tend to use inspirational appeals and ingratiation more than managers from either Mainland China or Hong Kong. The study also found that managers from Hong Kong rate pressure as more effective in influencing others than do managers in Taiwan or Mainland China. Such differences have implications for business relationships. For example, Taiwanese or Mainland Chinese managers may be taken aback by the use of pressure tactics by the Hong Kong manager. Likewise, managers from Hong Kong may not be persuaded by managers from Taiwan, who tend to use ingratiating tactics. Such differences in influence tactics may make business dealings difficult. Companies should address these issues, perhaps making their managers aware of the differences within cultures.

So, managers need to know what variations exist within their local cultures so they can be better prepared to deal with others. Managers who fail to realize these differences may miss out on opportunities to deal effectively with others.

Source: Based on P. P. Fu, T. K. Peng, J. C. Kennedy, and G. Yukl, "A Comparison of Chinese Managers in Hong Kong, Taiwan, and Mainland China," *Organizational Dynamics*, February, 2004, pp. 32–46.

the only tactic that is effective across organizational levels. Inspirational appeals work best as a downward-influencing tactic with subordinates. When pressure works, it's almost only to achieve downward influence. And the use of personal appeals and coalitions are most effective with lateral influence attempts. In addition to the direction of influence, a number of other factors have been found to affect which tactics work best. These include the sequencing of tactics, a person's skill in using the tactic, a person's relative power, the type of request and how the request is perceived, the culture of the organization, and country-specific cultural factors.

You're more likely to be effective if you begin with "softer" tactics that rely on personal power such as personal and inspirational appeals, rational persuasion, and consultation. If these fail, you can move to "harder" tactics (which emphasize formal power and involve greater costs and risks), such as exchange, coalitions, and pressure.[18] Interestingly, it's been found that using a single soft

power tactics *Ways in which individuals translate power bases into specific actions.*

tactic is more effective than a single hard tactic; and that combining two soft tactics, or a soft tactic and rational persuasion, is more effective than any single tactic or a combination of hard tactics.[19]

Studies confirm that a tactic is "more likely to be successful if the target perceives it to be a socially acceptable form of influence behavior, if the agent has sufficient position and personal power to use the tactic, if the tactic can affect target attitudes about the desirability of the request, if it is used in a skillful way, if it is used for a request that is legitimate, and if it is consistent with the target person's values and needs."[20]

We know that cultures within organizations differ markedly—for example, some are warm, relaxed, and supportive; others are formal and conservative. The organizational culture in which a person works, therefore, will have a bearing on defining which tactics are considered appropriate. Some cultures encourage the use of participation and consultation, some encourage reason, and still others rely on pressure. So the organization itself will influence which subset of power tactics is viewed as acceptable for use.

Finally, evidence indicates that people in different countries tend to prefer different power tactics.[21] For instance, a study comparing managers in the United States and China found that the Americans perceived reason to be most effective, whereas Chinese managers preferred coalition tactics.[22] These differences tend to be consistent with the values in these two countries. Reason is consistent with the preference of Americans for direct confrontation and the use of rational persuasion to influence others and resolve differences. Similarly, coalition tactics are consistent with the Chinese preference for using indirect approaches for difficult or controversial requests.

Power in Groups: Coalitions

Those "out of power" and seeking to be "in" will first try to increase their power individually. Why share the spoils if one doesn't have to? But if this proves ineffective, the alternative is to form a **coalition**—an informal group bound together by the active pursuit of a single issue.[23] The logic of a coalition? There's strength in numbers.

The natural way to gain influence is to become a powerholder. Therefore, those who want power will attempt to build a personal power base. But, in many instances, this may be difficult, risky, costly, or impossible. In such cases, efforts will be made to form a coalition of two or more "outs" who, by joining together, can combine their resources to increase rewards for themselves.[24] Successful coalitions have been found to contain fluid membership and are able to form swiftly, achieve their target issue, and quickly disappear.[25]

What predictions can we make about coalition formation?[26] First, coalitions in organizations often seek to maximize their size. In political science theory, coalitions move the other way—they try to minimize their size. They tend to be just large enough to exert the power necessary to achieve their objectives. But legislatures are different from organizations. Specifically, decision making in organizations does not end just with selection from among a set of alternatives. The decision must also be implemented. In organizations, the implementation of and commitment to the decision is at least as important as the decision itself. It's necessary, therefore, for coalitions in organizations to seek a broad constituency to support the coalition's objectives. This means expanding the coalition to encompass as many interests as possible.

Another prediction about coalitions relates to the degree of interdependence within the organization. More coalitions will likely be created when there is a great deal of task and resource interdependence. In contrast, there will be less interdependence among subunits and less coalition formation activity when subunits are largely self-contained or resources are abundant.

Finally, coalition formation will be influenced by the actual tasks that workers do. The more routine the task of a group, the greater the likelihood that coalitions will form. The more routine the work that people do, the greater their substitutability for each other and, thus, the greater their dependence. To offset this dependence, they can be expected to resort to a coalition. This helps to explain the historical appeal of labor unions, especially among low-skilled workers. Such employees are better able to negotiate improved wages, benefits, and working conditions as a united coalition than if they acted individually. A one-person "strike" has little power over management. However, if a firm's entire workforce goes on strike, management has a serious problem.

Sexual Harassment: Unequal Power in the Workplace

Sexual harassment is wrong. It can also be costly to employers. Just ask executives at Philip Morris, Dial, and UPS.[27] A Kentucky jury awarded $2 million to a Philip Morris plant supervisor who suffered through more than a year of sexual harassment by men she supervised. Dial agreed to pay $10 million to resolve widespread sexual harassment practices at its soap factory in Aurora, Illinois. And a former UPS manager won an $80 million suit against UPS for fostering a hostile work environment when it failed to listen to her complaints of sexual harassment.

Not only are there legal dangers to sexual harassment, it obviously can have a negative impact on the work environment too. Research shows that sexual harassment negatively affects job attitudes and leads those who feel harassed to withdraw from the organization. Moreover, in many cases, reporting sexual harassment doesn't improve the situation because the organization responds in a negative or unhelpful way. When organizational leaders make honest efforts to stop the harassment, the outcomes are much more positive.[28]

Sexual harassment is defined as any unwanted activity of a sexual nature that affects an individual's employment and creates a hostile work environment. The U.S. Supreme Court helped to clarify this definition by adding that the key test for determining if sexual harassment has occurred is whether comments or behavior in a work environment "would reasonably be perceived, and is perceived, as hostile or abusive."[29] But there continues to be disagreement as to what *specifically* constitutes sexual harassment. Organizations have generally made considerable progress in the past decade toward limiting overt forms of sexual harassment. This includes unwanted physical touching, recurring requests for dates when it is made clear the person isn't interested, and coercive threats that a person will lose the job if he or she refuses a sexual proposition. The problems today are likely to surface around more subtle forms of sexual

coalition   *An informal group bound together by the active pursuit of a single issue.*

sexual harassment   *Any unwanted activity of a sexual nature that affects an individual's employment and creates a hostile work environment.*

A federal jury awarded $3.2 million to Marion Shaub, a former tractor-trailer driver for Federal Express Corp., a unit of FedEx, after finding the company guilty of sexual harassment. The only female driver at her workplace, Shaub said coworkers sexually harassed her with antifemale remarks and intimidated her by tampering with the brakes on her truck. She complained to her supervisor but nothing was done to resolve the problem. The jury found the company liable for maintaining a hostile work environment.

harassment—unwanted looks or comments, off-color jokes, sexual artifacts like pin-ups posted in the workplace, or misinterpretations of where the line between "being friendly" ends and "harassment" begins.

A recent review concluded that 58 percent of women report having experienced potentially harassing behaviors and 24 percent report having experienced sexual harassment at work.[30] One problem with sexual harassment is that it is, to some degree, in the eye of the beholder. For example, women are more likely to see a given behavior or sets of behaviors as constituting sexual harassment. Men are less likely to see as harassment such behaviors as kissing someone, asking for a date, or making sex-stereotyped jokes. As the authors of this study note, "Although progress has been made at defining sexual harassment, it is still unclear as to whose perspective should be taken."[31] Thus, although some behaviors indisputably constitute harassment, men and women continue to differ to some degree on what constitutes harassment. For you, the best approach is to be careful—refrain from any behavior that may be taken as harassing even if that was not your intent. Realize that what you see as an innocent joke or hug may be seen as harassment by the other party.

Most studies confirm that the concept of power is central to understanding sexual harassment.[32] This seems to be true whether the harassment comes from a supervisor, a coworker, or an employee. And, sexual harassment is more likely to occur when there are large power differentials. The supervisor-employee dyad best characterizes an unequal power relationship, where formal power gives the supervisor the capacity to reward and coerce. Supervisors give employees their assignments, evaluate their performance, make recommendations for salary adjustments and promotions, and even decide whether or not an employee retains his or her job. These decisions give a supervisor power. Because employees want favorable performance reviews, salary increases, and the like, it's clear supervisors control resources that most employees consider important and scarce. It's also worth noting that individuals who occupy high-status roles (like management positions) sometimes believe that sexually harassing employees is merely an extension of their right to make demands on lower-status individuals. Because of power inequities, sexual harassment by one's boss typically creates the greatest difficulty for those who are being harassed. If there are no witnesses, it is the victim's word against the harasser's. Are there others this boss has harassed and, if so, will they come forward? Because of the supervisor's control over resources, many of those who are harassed are afraid of speaking out for fear of retaliation by the supervisor.

Although coworkers don't have legitimate power, they can have influence and use it to sexually harass peers. In fact, although coworkers appear to engage in somewhat less severe forms of harassment than do supervisors, coworkers are the most frequent perpetrators of sexual harassment in organizations. How do coworkers exercise power? Most often it's by providing or withholding information, cooperation, and support. For example, the effective performance of most jobs requires interaction and support from coworkers. This is especially true nowadays because work is often assigned to teams. By threatening to withhold or delay providing information that's necessary for the successful achievement of your work goals, coworkers can exert power over you.

Although it doesn't get nearly the attention that harassment by a supervisor does, as seen in the lawsuit against Philip Morris, women in positions of power can be subjected to sexual harassment from males who occupy less powerful positions within the organization. This is usually achieved by the employee devaluing the woman through highlighting traditional gender stereotypes (such as helplessness, passivity, lack of career commitment) that reflect negatively on the woman in power. An employee may engage in such practices to attempt to gain some power over the higher-ranking female or to minimize power differentials. Increasingly, too, there are cases of women in positions of power harassing male employees.

The topic of sexual harassment is about power. It's about an individual controlling or threatening another individual. It's wrong. And whether perpetrated against women or men, it's illegal. But you can understand how sexual harassment surfaces in organizations if you analyze it in terms of power.

We have seen how sexual harassment can wreak havoc on an organization, but it can be avoided. A manager's role in preventing sexual harassment is critical. Some ways managers can protect themselves and their employees from sexual harassment follow:

1. Make sure a policy is in place that defines what constitutes sexual harassment, that informs employees that they can be fired for sexually harassing another employee, and that establishes procedures for how complaints can be made.
2. Ensure employees that they will not encounter retaliation if they issue a complaint.
3. Investigate every complaint and include the legal and human resource departments.
4. Make sure that offenders are disciplined or terminated.
5. Set up in-house seminars to raise employee awareness of the issues surrounding sexual harassment.

The bottom line is that managers have a responsibility to protect their employees from a hostile work environment, but they also need to protect themselves. Managers may be unaware that one of their employees is being sexually harassed. But being unaware does not protect them or their organization. If investigators believe a manager could have known about the harassment, both the manager and the company can be held liable.

Politics: Power in Action

When people get together in groups, power will be exerted. People want to carve out a niche from which to exert influence, to earn rewards, and to advance their careers.[33] When employees in organizations convert their power into action, we describe them as being engaged in politics. Those with good political skills have the ability to use their bases of power effectively.[34]

Definition

There has been no shortage of definitions for organizational politics. Essentially, however, they have focused on the use of power to affect decision making in the organization or on behaviors by members that are self-serving and organizationally nonsanctioned.[35] For our purposes, we shall define **political behavior** in organizations as activities that are not required as part

political behavior   *Activities that are not required as part of one's formal role in the organization, but that influence, or attempt to influence, the distribution of advantages and disadvantages within the organization.*

Whistle-blowing is considered an illegitimate political behavior that often results in job loss. That's what happened to David Welch, chief financial officer of Bank of Floyd in Virginia. Welch blew the whistle on the bank's president, alleging that he engaged in the unethical business practice of buying stocks before the announcement of a bank merger. As a result, Welch was fired. Shown here with documents supporting his allegation, Welch hopes his evidence is powerful enough to vindicate his political behavior.

of one's formal role in the organization, but that influence, or attempt to influence, the distribution of advantages and disadvantages within the organization.[36] This definition encompasses key elements from what most people mean when they talk about organizational politics. Political behavior is outside one's specified job requirements. The behavior requires some attempt to use one's power bases. In addition, our definition encompasses efforts to influence the goals, criteria, or processes used for *decision making* when we state that politics is concerned with "the distribution of advantages and disadvantages within the organization." Our definition is broad enough to include varied political behaviors such as withholding key information from decision makers, joining a coalition, whistle-blowing, spreading rumors, leaking confidential information about organizational activities to the media, exchanging favors with others in the organization for mutual benefit, and lobbying on behalf of or against a particular individual or decision alternative.

A final comment relates to what has been referred to as the "legitimate–illegitimate" dimension in political behavior.[37] **Legitimate political behavior** refers to normal everyday politics—complaining to your supervisor, bypassing the chain of command, forming coalitions, obstructing organizational policies or decisions through inaction or excessive adherence to rules, and developing contacts outside the organization through one's professional activities. On the other hand, there are also **illegitimate political behaviors** that violate the implied rules of the game. Those who pursue such extreme activities are often described as individuals who "play hardball." Illegitimate activities include sabotage, whistle-blowing, and symbolic protests such as wearing unorthodox dress or protest buttons, and groups of employees simultaneously calling in sick.

The vast majority of all organizational political actions are of the legitimate variety. The reasons are pragmatic: The extreme illegitimate forms of political behavior pose a very real risk of loss of organizational membership or extreme sanctions against those who use them and then fall short in having enough power to ensure that they work.

The Reality of Politics

Politics is a fact of life in organizations. People who ignore this fact of life do so at their own peril. But why, you may wonder, must politics exist? Isn't it possible for an organization to be politics-free? It's *possible*, but most unlikely.

Organizations are made up of individuals and groups with different values, goals, and interests.[38] This sets up the potential for conflict over resources. Departmental budgets, space allocations, project responsibilities, and salary adjustments are just a few examples of the resources about whose allocation organizational members will disagree.

Resources in organizations are also limited, which often turns potential conflict into real conflict.[39] If resources were abundant, then all the various constituencies within the organization could satisfy their goals. But because they are limited, not everyone's interests can be provided for. Furthermore, whether true or not, gains by one individual or group are often *perceived* as being at the expense of others within the organization. These forces create competition among members for the organization's limited resources.

Maybe the most important factor leading to politics within organizations is the realization that most of the "facts" that are used to allocate the limited resources are open to interpretation. What, for instance, is *good* performance? What's an *adequate* improvement? What constitutes an *unsatisfactory* job? One person's view that an act is a "selfless effort to benefit the organization" is seen by another as a "blatant attempt to further one's interest."[40] The manager of any major league baseball team knows a .400 hitter is a high performer and a .125 hitter is a poor performer. You don't need to be a baseball genius to know you should play your .400 hitter and send the .125 hitter back to the minors. But what if you have to choose between players who hit .280 and .290? Then other factors—less objective ones—come into play: fielding expertise, attitude, potential, ability to perform in a clutch, loyalty to the team, and so on. More managerial decisions resemble choosing between a .280 and a .290 hitter than deciding between a .125 hitter and a .400 hitter. It is in this large and ambiguous middle ground of organizational life—where the facts *don't* speak for themselves—that politics flourish (see Exhibit 14-3).

Finally, because most decisions have to be made in a climate of ambiguity—where facts are rarely fully objective, and thus are open to interpretation—people within organizations will use whatever influence they can to taint the facts to support their goals and interests. That, of course, creates the activities we call *politicking*.

Therefore, to answer the earlier question of whether it is possible for an organization to be politics-free, we can say: "Yes," if all members of that organization hold the same goals and interests, if organizational resources are not scarce, and if performance outcomes are completely clear and objective. But that doesn't describe the organizational world that most of us live in.

Exhibit **14-3**	Politics Is in the Eye of the Beholder

A behavior that one person labels as "organizational politics" is very likely to be characterized as an instance of "effective management" by another. The fact is not that effective management is necessarily political, although in some cases it might be. Rather, a person's reference point determines what he or she classifies as organizational politics. Take a look at the following labels used to describe the same phenomenon. These suggest that politics, like beauty, is in the eye of the beholder.

"Political" Label		"Effective Management" Label
1. Blaming others	vs.	Fixing responsibility
2. "Kissing up"	vs.	Developing working relationships
3. Apple polishing	vs.	Demonstrating loyalty
4. Passing the buck	vs.	Delegating authority
5. Covering your rear	vs.	Documenting decisions
6. Creating conflict	vs.	Encouraging change and innovation
7. Forming coalitions	vs.	Facilitating teamwork
8. Whistle-blowing	vs.	Improving efficiency
9. Scheming	vs.	Planning ahead
10. Overachieving	vs.	Competent and capable
11. Ambitious	vs.	Career-minded
12. Opportunistic	vs.	Astute
13. Cunning	vs.	Practical-minded
14. Arrogant	vs.	Confident
15. Perfectionist	vs.	Attentive to detail

Source: Based on T. C. Krell, M. E. Mendenhall, and J. Sendry, "Doing Research in the Conceptual Morass of Organizational Politics," paper presented at the Western Academy of Management Conference, Hollywood, CA April 1987.

legitimate political behavior   *Normal everyday politics.*

illegitimate political behavior   *Extreme political behavior that violates the implied rules of the game.*

"It's Not What You Know, It's Who You Know"

This statement is somewhat true. While knowledge of *facts* is an increasingly important source of power in an information-based society, knowing the *right people* increases your chances of getting ahead.

Networking is the term for establishing effective relationships with key people inside and/or outside the organization. And networking has been found to be the most important activity performed by managers who were promoted the fastest.[41]

A study of general managers found that they fully understood the importance of networking.[42] They established a wide political network of key people from both inside and outside their organizations. This network provided these managers with information and established cooperative relationships that could enhance their careers. The managers did favors for these contacts, stressed the contacts' obligations to them, and "called in" those obligations when they needed support.

Research also indicates that a person's location within an organization is an important determinant of his or her influence.[43] Being in the right place increases your ability to know "the right people." This further supports the importance of contacts over knowledge of facts in gaining influence.

You should not interpret the preceding evidence to mean that job-relevant expertise is not important. Rather, it means that "who you know" is an important *additional* factor in organizational life. And for people who want to get ahead or build their political power within an organization, spending time and effort developing a network of contacts will be a wise investment. ■

Factors Contributing to Political Behavior

Not all groups or organizations are equally political. In some organizations, for instance, politicking is overt and rampant, while in others, politics plays a small role in influencing outcomes. Why is there this variation? Recent research and observation have identified a number of factors that appear to encourage political behavior. Some are individual characteristics, derived from the unique qualities of the people the organization employs; others are a result of the organization's culture or internal environment. Exhibit 14-4 illustrates how both individual and organizational factors can increase political behavior and provide favorable outcomes (increased rewards and averted punishments) for both individuals and groups in the organization.

Individual Factors   At the individual level, researchers have identified certain personality traits, needs, and other factors that are likely to be related to political behavior. In terms of traits, we find that employees who are high self-monitors, possess an internal locus of control, and have a high need for power are more likely to engage in political behavior.[44] The high self-monitor is more sensitive to social cues, exhibits higher levels of social conformity, and is more likely to be skilled in political behavior than the low self-monitor. Individuals with an internal locus of control, because they believe they can control their environment, are more prone to take a proactive stance and attempt to manipulate situations in their favor. Not surprisingly, the Machiavellian personality—which is characterized by the will to manipulate and the desire for power—is comfortable using politics as a means to further his or her self-interest.

In addition, an individual's investment in the organization, perceived alternatives, and expectations of success will influence the degree to which he or she will pursue illegitimate means of political action.[45] The more a person has invested in the organization in terms of expectations of increased future benefits, the more that person has to lose if forced out and the less likely he or she is to use illegitimate means. The more alternative job opportunities an individual has—due to a favorable job market or the possession of scarce skills or knowledge, a prominent reputation, or influential contacts outside the organization—the more likely that individual is to risk illegitimate political actions. Finally, if

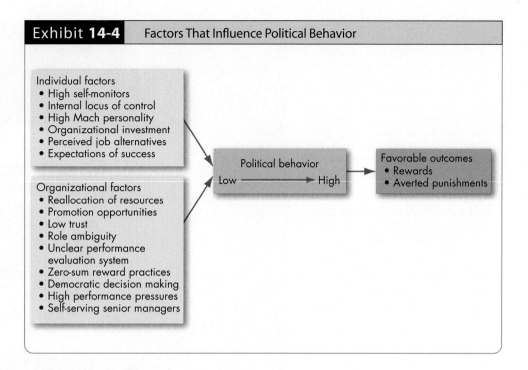

Exhibit 14-4   Factors That Influence Political Behavior

Individual factors
• High self-monitors
• Internal locus of control
• High Mach personality
• Organizational investment
• Perceived job alternatives
• Expectations of success

Organizational factors
• Reallocation of resources
• Promotion opportunities
• Low trust
• Role ambiguity
• Unclear performance
  evaluation system
• Zero-sum reward practices
• Democratic decision making
• High performance pressures
• Self-serving senior managers

Political behavior
Low ———→ High

Favorable outcomes
• Rewards
• Averted punishments

an individual has a low expectation of success in using illegitimate means, it is unlikely that he or she will attempt to do so. High expectations of success in the use of illegitimate means are most likely to be the province of both experienced and powerful individuals with polished political skills and inexperienced and naive employees who misjudge their chances.

Organizational Factors   Political activity is probably more a function of the organization's characteristics than of individual difference variables. Why? Because many organizations have a large number of employees with the individual characteristics we listed, yet the extent of political behavior varies widely.

Although we acknowledge the role that individual differences can play in fostering politicking, the evidence more strongly supports that certain situations and cultures promote politics. More specifically, when an organization's resources are declining, when the existing pattern of resources is changing, and when there is opportunity for promotions, politicking is more likely to surface.[46] In addition, cultures characterized by low trust, role ambiguity, unclear performance evaluation systems, zero-sum reward allocation practices, democratic decision making, high pressures for performance, and self-serving senior managers will create breeding grounds for politicking.[47]

When organizations downsize to improve efficiency, reductions in resources have to be made. Threatened with the loss of resources, people may engage in political actions to safeguard what they have. But any changes, especially those that imply significant reallocation of resources within the organization, are likely to stimulate conflict and increase politicking.

Promotion decisions have consistently been found to be one of the most political actions in organizations. The opportunity for promotions or advancement encourages people to compete for a limited resource and to try to positively influence the decision outcome.

The less trust there is within the organization, the higher the level of political behavior and the more likely that the political behavior will be of the illegitimate kind. So high trust should suppress the level of political behavior in general and inhibit illegitimate actions in particular.

The slogan and graphic on this employee's shirt portray an obvious lack of trust. Union workers shown here at a General Electric plant protested the company's plan to increase their health insurance copayment from 20 to 30 percent. GE's commitment of resources has changed due to the soaring costs of employee health insurance. GE and many other companies argue that the high cost of health insurance is hurting their profits and competitiveness. In fact, the major sticking point in GM's 2005 negotiations with the UAW was also over health care costs (in the past, GM has paid 100 percent of employees' premiums and there were no copayments). Employees, however, want to safeguard their current low copayments.

Role ambiguity means that the prescribed behaviors of the employee are not clear. There are fewer limits, therefore, to the scope and functions of the employee's political actions. Because political activities are defined as those not required as part of one's formal role, the greater the role ambiguity, the more one can engage in political activity with little chance of it being visible.

The practice of performance evaluation is far from a perfect science. The more that organizations use subjective criteria in the appraisal, emphasize a single outcome measure, or allow significant time to pass between the time of an action and its appraisal, the greater the likelihood that an employee can get away with politicking. Subjective performance criteria create ambiguity. The use of a single outcome measure encourages individuals to do whatever is necessary to "look good" on that measure, but often at the expense of performing well on other important parts of the job that are not being appraised. The amount of time that elapses between an action and its appraisal is also a relevant factor. The longer the time, the more unlikely that the employee will be held accountable for his or her political behaviors.

The more that an organization's culture emphasizes the zero-sum or win-lose approach to reward allocations, the more employees will be motivated to engage in politicking. The zero-sum approach treats the reward "pie" as fixed so that any gain one person or group achieves has to come at the expense of another person or group. If I win, you must lose! If $15,000 in annual raises is to be distributed among five employees, then any employee who gets more than $3,000 takes money away from one or more of the others. Such a practice encourages making others look bad and increasing the visibility of what you do.

In the past 25 years, there has been a general move in North America and among most developed nations toward making organizations less autocratic. Managers in these organizations are being asked to behave more democratically. They're told that they should allow employees to advise them on decisions and that they should rely to a greater extent on group input into the decision process. Such moves toward democracy, however, are not necessarily embraced by all individual managers. Many managers sought their positions in order to have legitimate power so as to be able to make unilateral decisions. They fought hard and often paid high personal costs to achieve their influential positions. Sharing their power with others runs directly against their desires. The result is that managers, especially those who began their careers in the 1960s and 1970s, may use the required committees, conferences, and group meetings in a superficial way, as arenas for maneuvering and manipulating.

The more pressure that employees feel to perform well, the more likely they are to engage in politicking. When people are held strictly accountable for outcomes, this puts great pressure on them to "look good." If a person perceives that his or her entire career is riding on next quarter's sales figures or next month's plant productivity report, there is motivation to do whatever is necessary to make sure the numbers come out favorably.

Finally, when employees see the people on top engaging in political behavior, especially when they do so successfully and are rewarded for it, a climate is created that supports politicking. Politicking by top management, in a sense, gives permission to those lower in the organization to play politics by implying that such behavior is acceptable.

How Do People Respond to Organizational Politics?

Trish O'Donnell loves her job as a writer on a weekly television comedy series but hates the internal politics. "A couple of the writers here spend more time kissing up to the executive producer than doing any work. And our head writer clearly has his favorites. While they pay me a lot and I get to really use my creativity, I'm sick of having to be on alert for backstabbers and constantly having to self-promote my contributions. I'm tired of doing most of the work and getting little of the credit." Are Trish O'Donnell's comments typical of people who work in highly politicized workplaces? We all know of friends or relatives who regularly complain about the politics at their job. But how do people in general react to organizational politics? Let's look at the evidence.

In our discussion earlier in this chapter of factors that contribute to political behavior, we focused on the favorable outcomes for individuals who successfully engage in politicking. But for most people—who have modest political skills or are unwilling to play the politics game—outcomes tend to be predominantly negative. Exhibit 14-5 summarizes the extensive research on the relationship between organizational politics and individual outcomes.[48] There is, for instance, very strong evidence indicating that perceptions of organizational politics are negatively related to job satisfaction.[49] The perception of politics also tends to increase job anxiety and stress. This seems to be due to the perception that, by not engaging in politics, a person may be losing ground to others who are active politickers; or, conversely, because of the additional pressures individuals feel because of having entered into and competing in the political arena.[50] Not surprisingly, when politicking becomes too much to handle, it can lead to employees quitting.[51] Finally, there is preliminary evidence suggesting that politics leads to self-reported declines in employee performance. This may occur because employees perceive political environments to be unfair, which demotivates them.[52]

In addition to these conclusions, several interesting qualifiers have been noted. First, the politics–performance relationship appears to be moderated by an individual's understanding of the "hows" and "whys" of organizational politics. "An individual who has a clear understanding of who is responsible for making decisions and why they were selected to be the decision makers would have a better understanding of how and why things happen the way they do than someone who does not understand the decision-making process in the organization."[53] When both politics and understanding are high, performance

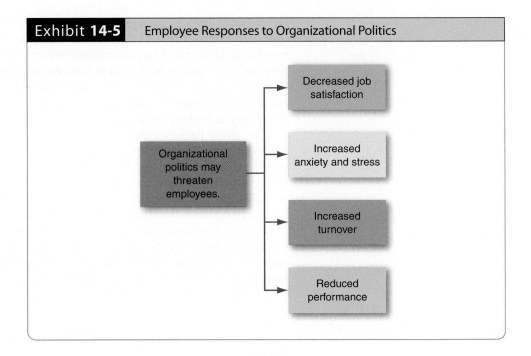

Exhibit 14-5   Employee Responses to Organizational Politics

is likely to increase because the individual will see political actions as an opportunity. This is consistent with what you might expect among individuals with well-honed political skills. But when understanding is low, individuals are more likely to see politics as a threat, which would have a negative effect on job performance.[54] Second, when politics is seen as a threat and consistently responded to with defensiveness, negative outcomes are almost sure to surface eventually. When people perceive politics as a threat rather than as an opportunity, they often respond with **defensive behaviors**—reactive and protective behaviors to avoid action, blame, or change[55] (Exhibit 14-6 provides some examples of these defensive behaviors). And defensive behaviors are often associated with negative feelings toward the job and work environment.[56] In the short run, employees may find that defensiveness protects their self-interest. But in the long run, it wears them down. People who consistently rely on defensiveness find that, eventually, it is the only way they know how to behave. At that point, they lose the trust and support of their peers, bosses, employees, and clients.

Are our conclusions about responses to politics globally valid? Should we expect employees in Israel, for instance, to respond the same way to workplace politics that employees in the United States do? Almost all our conclusions on employee reactions to organizational politics are based on studies conducted in North America. The few studies that have included other countries suggest some minor modifications.[57] Israelis and Brits, for instance, seem to generally respond as do North Americans. That is, the perception of organizational politics among employees in these countries is related to decreased job satisfaction and increased turnover.[58] But in countries that are more politically unstable, like Israel, employees seem to demonstrate greater tolerance of intense political processes in the workplace. This is likely to be because people in these countries are used to power struggles and have more experience in coping with them.[59] This suggests that people from politically turbulent countries in the Middle East or Latin America might be more accepting of organizational politics, and even more willing to use aggressive political tactics in the workplace, than people from countries such as Great Britain or Switzerland.

Exhibit **14-6**	Defensive Behaviors

Avoiding Action

Overconforming. Strictly interpreting your responsibility by saying things like, "The rules clearly state . . . " or "This is the way we've always done it."

Buck passing. Transferring responsibility for the execution of a task or decision to someone else.

Playing dumb. Avoiding an unwanted task by falsely pleading ignorance or inability.

Stretching. Prolonging a task so that one person appears to be occupied—for example, turning a two-week task into a four-month job.

Stalling. Appearing to be more or less supportive publicly while doing little or nothing privately.

Avoiding Blame

Buffing. This is a nice way to refer to "covering your rear." It describes the practice of rigorously documenting activity to project an image of competence and thoroughness.

Playing safe. Evading situations that may reflect unfavorably. It includes taking on only projects with a high probability of success, having risky decisions approved by superiors, qualifying expressions of judgment, and taking neutral positions in conflicts.

Justifying. Developing explanations that lessen one's responsibility for a negative outcome and/or apologizing to demonstrate remorse.

Scapegoating. Placing the blame for a negative outcome on external factors that are not entirely blameworthy.

Misrepresenting. Manipulation of information by distortion, embellishment, deception, selective presentation, or obfuscation.

Avoiding Change

Prevention. Trying to prevent a threatening change from occurring.

Self-protection. Acting in ways to protect one's self-interest during change by guarding information or other resources.

Impression Management

We know that people have an ongoing interest in how others perceive and evaluate them. For example, North Americans spend billions of dollars on diets, health club memberships, cosmetics, and plastic surgery—all intended to make them more attractive to others.[60] Being perceived positively by others should have benefits for people in organizations. It might, for instance, help them initially to get the jobs they want in an organization and, once hired, to get favorable evaluations, superior salary increases, and more rapid promotions. In a political context, it might help sway the distribution of advantages in their favor. The process by which individuals attempt to control the impression others form of them is called **impression management**.[61] It's a subject that has gained the attention of OB researchers only recently.[62]

Is everyone concerned with impression management (IM)? No! Who, then, might we predict to engage in IM? No surprise here! It's our old friend, the high self-monitor.[63] Low self-monitors tend to present images of themselves that are consistent with their personalities, regardless of the beneficial or detrimental effects for them. In contrast, high self-monitors are good at reading situations and molding their appearances and behavior to fit each situation. Given that you want to control the impression others form of you, what techniques could you

defensive behaviors   *Reactive and protective behaviors to avoid action, blame, or change.*

impression management   *The process by which individuals attempt to control the impression others form of them.*

use? Exhibit 14-7 summarizes some of the more popular IM techniques and provides an example of each.

Keep in mind that IM does not imply that the impressions people convey are necessarily false (although, of course, they sometimes are).[64] Excuses, for instance, may be offered with sincerity. Referring to the example used in Exhibit 14-7, you can *actually* believe that ads contribute little to sales in your region. But misrepresentation can have a high cost. If the image claimed is false, you may be discredited.[65] If you "cry wolf" once too often, no one is likely to believe you when the wolf really comes. So the impression manager must be cautious not to be perceived as insincere or manipulative.[66]

Are there *situations* in which individuals are more likely to misrepresent themselves or more likely to get away with it? Yes—situations that are characterized by

---

Exhibit 14-7 | Impression Management (IM) Techniques

Conformity

Agreeing with someone else's opinion in order to gain his or her approval.

Example: A manager tells his boss, "You're absolutely right on your reorganization plan for the western regional office. I couldn't agree with you more."

Excuses

Explanations of a predicament-creating event aimed at minimizing the apparent severity of the predicament.

Example: Sales manager to boss, "We failed to get the ad in the paper on time, but no one responds to those ads anyway."

Apologies

Admitting responsibility for an undesirable event and simultaneously seeking to get a pardon for the action.

Example: Employee to boss, "I'm sorry I made a mistake on the report. Please forgive me."

Self-Promotion

Highlighting one's best qualities, downplaying one's deficits, and calling attention to one's achievements.

Example: A salesperson tells his boss: "Matt worked unsuccessfully for three years to try to get that account. I sewed it up in six weeks. I'm the best closer this company has."

Flattery

Complimenting others about their virtues in an effort to make oneself appear perceptive and likeable.

Example: New sales trainee to peer, "You handled that client's complaint so tactfully! I could never have handled that as well as you did."

Favors

Doing something nice for someone to gain that person's approval.

Example: Salesperson to prospective client, "I've got two tickets to the theater tonight that I can't use. Take them. Consider it a thank-you for taking the time to talk with me."

Association

Enhancing or protecting one's image by managing information about people and things with which one is associated.

Example: A job applicant says to an interviewer, "What a coincidence. Your boss and I were roommates in college."

Source: Based on B. R. Schlenker, *Impression Management* (Monterey, CA: Brooks/Cole, 1980); W. L. Gardner and M. J. Martinko, "Impression Management in Organizations," *Journal of Management*, June 1988, p. 332; and R. B. Cialdini, "Indirect Tactics of Image Management Beyond Basking," in R. A. Giacalone and P. Rosenfeld (eds.), *Impression Management in the Organization* (Hillsdale, NJ: Lawrence Erlbaum Associates, 1989), pp. 45–71.

high uncertainty or ambiguity provide relatively little information for challenging a fraudulent claim and reduce the risks associated with misrepresentation.[67]

Most of the studies undertaken to test the effectiveness of IM techniques have related it to two criteria: (1) interview success; and (2) performance evaluations. Let's consider each of these.

The evidence indicates that most job applicants use IM techniques in interviews[68] and that, when IM behavior is used, it works.[69] In one study, for instance, interviewers felt that applicants for a position as a customer service representative who used IM techniques performed better in the interview, and they seemed somewhat more inclined to hire these people.[70] Moreover, when the researchers considered applicants' credentials, they concluded that it was the IM techniques alone that influenced the interviewers. That is, it didn't seem to matter if applicants were well or poorly qualified. If they used IM techniques, they did better in the interview.

Research indicates that some IM techniques work better than others in the interview. Researchers have compared applicants who used IM techniques that focused on promoting one's accomplishments (called *self-promotion*) to applicants who used techniques that focused on complimenting the interviewer and finding areas of agreement (referred to as *ingratiation*). In general, applicants appear to use self-promotion more than ingratiation.[71] What's more, self-promotion tactics may be more important to interviewing success. Applicants who work to create an appearance of competence by enhancing their accomplishments, taking credit for successes, and explaining away failures do better in interviews. These effects reach beyond the interview—applicants who use more self-promotion tactics also seem to get more follow-up job-site visits, even after adjusting for grade-point average, gender, and job type. Ingratiation also works well in the interview, meaning that applicants who compliment the interviewer, agree with his or her opinions, and emphasize areas of fit do better than those who don't.[72]

In terms of performance ratings, the picture is quite different. Ingratiation is positively related to performance ratings, meaning that those who ingratiate with their supervisors get higher performance evaluations. However, self-promotion appears to backfire—those who self-promote actually seem to receive *lower* performance evaluations.[73]

What explains these results? If you think about them, they make sense. Ingratiating always works because everyone likes to be treated nicely, whether it be the interviewer or the supervisor. However, self-promotion may work only in interviews and backfire on the job because whereas the interviewer has little idea whether you're blowing smoke about your accomplishments, the supervisor knows because it's his or her job to observe you. Thus, if you're going to self-promote, remember that what works in the interview will not always work once you're on the job.

The Ethics of Behaving Politically

We conclude our discussion of politics by providing some ethical guidelines for political behavior. Although there are no clear-cut ways to differentiate ethical from unethical politicking, there are some questions you should consider. Ask yourself: what is the utility of engaging in the behavior? Sometimes we engage in political behaviors for little good reason. For example, Major League Baseball player Al Martin claimed he played football at USC when in fact he never did. Because Martin was playing baseball, not football, there was little to be gained by his lie. Outright lies like this may be a rather extreme example of impression management, but many of us have distorted information to make a favorable impression. The point is that before we do so, one thing to keep in mind is whether it's really worth the risk. Another question to ask is an ethical one—how does the utility of engaging in the political behavior balance out any harm (or potential harm) it will do to others? For example, complimenting a supervisor on his or her appearance to curry favor is probably much less harmful than grabbing credit for a project that is deserved by others.

The final question that needs to be addressed is whether the political activity conforms to standards of equity and justice. Sometimes it is hard to weigh the costs and benefits of a political action, but its ethicality is clear. The department head who inflates the performance evaluation of a favored employee and deflates the evaluation of a disfavored employee—and then uses these evaluations to justify giving the former a big raise and nothing to the latter—has treated the disfavored employee unfairly.

Unfortunately, the answers to these questions are often argued in ways to make unethical practices seem ethical. Powerful people, for example, can become very good at explaining self-serving behaviors in terms of the organization's best interests. Similarly, they can persuasively argue that unfair actions are really fair and just. Our point is that immoral people can justify almost any behavior. Those who are powerful, articulate, and persuasive are most vulnerable because they are likely to be able to get away with unethical practices successfully. When faced with an ethical dilemma regarding organizational politics, try to consider the preceding issues (is playing politics worth the risk and will others be harmed in the process). If you have a strong power base, recognize the ability of power to corrupt. Remember, it's a lot easier for the powerless to act ethically, if for no other reason than they typically have very little political discretion to exploit.

Finally, we've talked a lot about political behavior in organizations. But what about your political skills? Are you comfortable playing politics at work? Or do you think your political skills might need some work? See the self-assessment feature to find out.

HOW GOOD AM I AT PLAYING POLITICS?

In the Self-Assessment Library (available on CD, online, and in print), take assessment II.C.3 (How Good Am I at Playing Politics?) and answer the following questions.

1. *How did you score relative to your classmates? Do you think your score is accurate? Why or why not?*
2. *Do you think political skills are important in the workplace? If yes, why? If no, why not?*
3. *Would you want to be known for your political skills? If yes, why? If no, why not?*

Summary and Implications for Managers

If you want to get things done in a group or organization, it helps to have power. As a manager who wants to maximize your power, you will want to increase others' dependence on you. You can, for instance, increase your power in relation to your boss by developing knowledge or a skill that she needs and for which she perceives no ready substitute. But power is a two-way street. You will not be alone in attempting to build your power bases. Others, particularly employees and peers, will be seeking to make you dependent on them. The result is a continual battle. While you seek to maximize others' dependence on you, you will be seeking to minimize your dependence on others. And, of course, others you work with will be trying to do the same.

Few employees relish being powerless in their job and organization. It's been argued, for instance, that when people in organizations are difficult, argumentative, and temperamental, it may be because they are in positions of powerlessness; positions in which the performance expectations placed on them exceed their resources and capabilities.[74]

There is evidence that people respond differently to the various power bases.[75] Expert and referent power are derived from an individual's personal qualities. In contrast, coercion, reward, and legitimate power are essentially organizationally derived. Because people are more likely to enthusiastically accept and commit to an individual whom they admire or whose knowledge they respect (rather than someone who relies on his or her position for influence), the effective use of expert and referent power should lead to higher employee motivation, performance, commitment, and satisfaction.[76] Competence especially appears to offer wide appeal, and its use as a power base results in high performance by group members. The message for managers seems to be: Develop and use your expert power base!

The power of your boss may also play a role in determining your job satisfaction. "One of the reasons many of us like to work for and with people who are powerful is that they are generally more pleasant—not because it is their native disposition, but because the reputation and reality of being powerful permits them more discretion and more ability to delegate to others."[77]

The effective manager accepts the political nature of organizations. By assessing behavior in a political framework, you can better predict the actions of others and use this information to formulate political strategies that will gain advantages for you and your work unit.

Some people are significantly more "politically astute" than others, meaning that they are aware of the underlying politics and can manage impressions. Those who are good at playing politics can be expected to get higher performance evaluations and, hence, larger salary increases and more promotions than the politically naive or inept.[78] The politically astute are also likely to exhibit higher job satisfaction and be better able to neutralize job stressors.[79] For employees with poor political skills or who are unwilling to play the politics game, the perception of organizational politics is generally related to lower job satisfaction and self-reported performance, increased anxiety, and higher turnover.

Point ◄► *Counterpoint*

Managing Impressions Is Unethical

Managing impressions is wrong for both ethical and practical reasons.

First, managing impressions is just another name for lying. Don't we have a responsibility, both to ourselves and to others, to present ourselves as we really are? The Australian philosopher Tony Coady wrote, "Dishonesty has always been perceived in our culture, and in all cultures but the most bizarre, as a central human vice." Immanuel Kant's Categorical Imperative asks us to consider the following: If you want to know whether telling a lie on a particular occasion is justifiable, you must try to imagine what would happen if everyone were to lie. Surely you would agree that a world in which no one lies is preferable to one in which lying is common, because in such a world we could never trust anyone. Thus, we should try to present the truth as best we can. Impression management goes against this virtue.

Practically speaking, impression management generally backfires in the long run. Remember Sir Walter Scott's quote, "Oh what a tangled web we weave, when first we practice to deceive!" Once we start to distort the facts, where do we stop? When George O'Leary was hired as Notre Dame's football coach, he said on his résumé that 30 years before he had obtained a degree from Stony Brook University that he never earned. Obviously, this information was unimportant to his football accomplishments, and ironically, he had written it on his resume 20 years earlier when hired for a job at Syracuse University; he had simply never corrected the inaccuracies. But when the truth came out, O'Leary was finished.

At Indiana University's Kelley School of Business, the code of ethics instructs students to provide only truthful information on their résumés and obligates them to be honest in interviews.

People are most satisfied with their jobs when their values match the culture of the organizations. If either side misrepresents itself in the interview process, then odds are people won't fit in the organizations they choose. What's the benefit in this?

This doesn't imply that a person shouldn't put his or her best foot forward. But that means exhibiting qualities that are good no matter the context—being friendly, being positive and self-confident, being qualified and competent, while still being honest.

Oh, come on. Get off your high horse. *Everybody* fudges to some degree in the process of applying for a job. If you really told the interviewer what your greatest weakness or worst mistake was, you'd never get hired. What if you answered, "I find it hard to get up in the morning and get to work"?

These sorts of "white lies" are expected and act as a kind of social lubricant in society. If we really knew what people where thinking, we'd go crazy. Moreover, you can quote all the philosophy you want, but sometimes it's necessary to lie. You mean you wouldn't lie to save the life of your family? It's naïve to think we can live in a world without lying.

Sometimes a bit of deception is necessary to get a job. I know a gay applicant who was rejected from a job he really wanted because he told the interviewer he had written two articles for gay magazines. What if he had told the interviewer a little lie? Would harm really have been done? At least he'd have a job.

As another example, when an interviewer asks you what you earned on your previous job, that information will be used against you, to pay you a salary lower than you deserve. Is it wrong to boost your salary a bit? Or would it be better to disclose your actual salary and be taken advantage of?

The same goes for complimenting interviewers, or agreeing with their opinions, and so forth. If an interviewer tells you, "We believe in community involvement," you're supposed to tell the interviewer that you have never volunteered for anything?

Of course one can go too far. We are not advocating that people totally fabricate their backgrounds. What we are talking about here is a reasonable amount of enhancement. If we can help ourselves without doing any real harm, then impression management is not the same as lying, and actually is something we should teach others.

Questions for Review

1. What is power? How do you get it?

2. Which power bases lie with the individual? Which are derived from the organization?

3. State the general dependency postulate. What does it mean?

4. What creates dependency? Give an applied example.

5. Contrast power tactics with power bases. What are some of the key contingency variables that determine which tactic a powerholder is likely to use?

6. What is a coalition? When is it likely to develop?

7. How are power and politics related?

8. Define *political behavior*. Why is politics a fact of life in organizations?

9. What factors contribute to political activity?

10. What is impression management? What types of people are most likely to engage in IM?

Questions for Critical Thinking

1. Based on the information presented in this chapter, what would you do as a recent college graduate entering a new job to maximize your power and accelerate your career progress?

2. "Politics isn't inherently bad. It's merely a way to get things accomplished within organizations." Do you agree or disagree? Defend your position.

3. You're a sales representative for an international software company. After 4 excellent years, sales in your territory are off 30 percent this year. Describe three defensive responses you might use to reduce the potential negative consequences of this decline in sales.

4. "Sexual harassment should not be tolerated at the workplace." "Workplace romances are a natural occurrence in organizations." Are both of these statements true? Can they be reconciled?

5. Which impression management techniques have you used? What ethical implications are there, if any, in using impression management?

Team Exercise

UNDERSTANDING POWER DYNAMICS

1. *Creation of groups* Each student is to turn in a dollar bill (or similar value of currency) to the instructor and students are then divided into three groups based on criteria given by the instructor, assigned to their workplaces, and instructed to read the following rules and tasks. The money is divided into thirds, giving two-thirds of it to the top group, one-third to the middle group, and none to the bottom group.

2. *Conduct exercise* Groups go to their assigned workplaces and have 30 minutes to complete their tasks.

   Rules

   (a) Members of the top group are free to enter the space of either of the other groups and to communicate whatever they wish, whenever they wish. Members of the middle group may enter the space of the lower group when they wish but must request permission to enter the top group's space (which the top group can refuse). Members of the lower group may not disturb the top group in any way unless specifically invited by the top. The lower group does have the right to knock on the door of the middle group and request permission to communicate with them (which can also be refused).

   (b) The members of the top group have the authority to make any change in the rules that they wish, at any time, with or without notice.

   Tasks

   (a) *Top group.* To be responsible for the overall effectiveness and learning from the exercise and to decide how to use its money.

   (b) *Middle group.* To assist the top group in providing for the overall welfare of the organization and to decide how to use its money.

   (c) *Bottom group.* To identify its resources and to decide how best to provide for learning and the overall effectiveness of the organization.

3. *Debriefing* Each of the three groups chooses two representatives to go to the front of the class and discuss the following questions:

   (a) Summarize what occurred within and among the three groups.

(b) What are some of the differences between being in the top group and being in the bottom group?

(c) What can we learn about power from this experience?

(d) How accurate do you think this exercise is in reflecting the reality of resource allocation decisions in large organizations?

Source: This exercise is adapted from L. Bolman and T. E. Deal, *Exchange* 3, no. 4 (1979), pp. 38–42. Reprinted by permission of Sage Publications, Inc.

Ethical Dilemma

SWAPPING PERSONAL FAVORS?

Jack Grubman was a powerful man on Wall Street. As a star analyst of telecom companies for the Salomon Smith Barney unit of Citigroup, he made recommendations that carried a lot of weight with investors.

For years, Grubman had been negative on the stock of AT&T. But in November 1999, he changed his opinion. Based on e-mail evidence, it appears that Grubman's decision to upgrade AT&T wasn't based on the stock's fundamentals. There were other factors involved.

At the time, his boss at Citigroup, Sanford "Sandy" Weill, was in the midst of a power struggle with co-CEO John Reed to become the single head of the company. Meanwhile, Salomon was looking for additional business to increase its revenues. Getting investment banking business fees from AT&T would be a big plus. And Salomon's chances of getting that AT&T business would definitely be improved if Grubman would upgrade his opinion on the stock. Furthermore, Weill sought Grubman's upgrade to win favor with AT&T CEO Michael Armstrong, who sat on Citigroup's board. Weill wanted Armstrong's backing in his efforts to oust Reed.

Grubman had his own concerns. Though earning tens of millions a year in his job, as the son of a city worker in Philadelphia he was a man of modest background. He wanted the best for his twin daughters, which included entry to an exclusive New York City nursery school (The posh 92nd Street Y [http://www.92y.org/])—a school that a year earlier had reportedly turned down Madonna's daughter. Weill made a call to the school on Grubman's behalf and pledged a $1 million donation from Citigroup. At approximately the same time, Weill also asked Grubman to "take a fresh look" at his neutral rating on AT&T. Shortly after being asked to review his rating, Grubman raised it, and AT&T awarded Salomon an investment-banking job worth nearly $45 million. Shares of AT&T soared.

Did Sandy Weill do anything unethical? How about Jack Grubman? What do you think?

Source: Based on C. Gasparino, "Out of School," *Newsweek*, January 17, 2005, pp. 38–39.

Case Incident 1

BILL FOWLER AT BLACKMER/DOVER RESOURCES INC.

Blackmer/Dover Resources' plant, in Grand Rapids Michigan, makes heavy-duty pumps designed to move commodities such as refined oil and chocolate. The plant employs 160 workers.

Historically, management assigned employees to operate the same machine for months or even years at a time. In this way, each worker became intimately familiar with a narrow task. And workers used their expertise to earn more money. Until 1997, about half the workers at the plant earned a premium, on top of their hourly wage, based on the number of pumps or pump parts they produced. The system gave them a strong incentive to conceal output-enhancing tricks they had learned, even from coworkers.

Today, the plant's workers receive a straight hourly wage. To make the plant more flexible, management encourages workers to learn a variety of jobs and accept moves to different parts of the factory floor. Many of the plant's older workers, however, haven't welcomed the change. One of those is Bill Fowler.

Fowler is 56 years old and has worked at the Blackmer plant for 24 years. Fowler doesn't like changing jobs and he doesn't like telling anyone anything about what he does. "I don't want to move around," he says, "because I love my routine—it helps me get through the day."

Fowler's job is cutting metal shafts for industrial pumps. It's a precision task: A minor error could render a pump useless. And Fowler is outstanding at what he does. He is known for the accuracy of his cuts. His bosses also say he can be hours faster than anyone else in readying his giant cutting machines to shift from making one type of pump shaft to another. Management would love to incorporate Fowler's know-how into the manufacturing process, but he refuses to share his secrets even with fellow workers. "If I gave away my tricks, management could use [them] to speed things up and keep me at a flat-out pace all day long," says Fowler.

Employees like Fowler worry when they read about companies soliciting workers' expert advice in the name of making their plants more competitive, and then turn around and move jobs to lower-wage locations in the United States or abroad. Blakmer's top management, however, says it has no plans to relocate jobs or otherwise hurt workers. It wants merely to pool workers' knowledge to make the plant stronger. "We've realized that to get competitive, we need to start asking these guys what they know," says Blackmer's president.

Questions

1. Explain Bill Fowler's behavior in power terms.

2. What, if anything, does this case say about trust and power?

3. What does this case say regarding implementing knowledge-management systems?

4. What, if anything, can management do to change Fowler's behavior?

Source: This case is based on T. Aeppel, "On Factory Floors, Top Workers Hide Secrets to Success," *The Wall Street Journal,* July 1, 2002, p. A1.

Case Incident 2

THE POLITICS OF BACKSTABBING

Scott Rosen believed that he was making progress as an assistant manager of a financial-services company—until he noticed that his colleague, another assistant manager, was attempting to push him aside. On repeated occasions, Mr. Rosen would observe his colleague speaking with their manager behind closed doors. During these conversations, Mr. Rosen's colleague would attempt to persuade the supervisor that Mr. Rosen was incompetent and mismanaging his job, a practice that Mr. Rosen found out after the fact. Mr. Rosen recounts one specific instance of his colleague's backstabbing efforts: When asked a question by his subordinates to which Mr. Rosen did not know the answer, his colleague would state to their supervisor, "I can't believe he didn't know something like that." On other occasions, after instructing a subordinate to complete a specific task, Mr. Rosen's colleague would say, "I wouldn't make you do something like that." What was the end result of such illegitimate political tactics? Mr. Rosen was demoted, an action that led him to resign shortly after, while his colleague was promoted. "Whatever I did, I lost," recounts Mr. Rosen.

What leads individuals to behave this way? According to Judith Briles, a management consultant who has extensively studied the practice of backstabbing, a tight job market is often a contributing factor. Fred Nader, another management consultant, believes that backstabbing is the result of "some kind of character disorder."

One executive at a technology company in Seattle admits that blind ambition was responsible for his backstabbing. In 1999, he was assigned as an external sales representative, partnered with a colleague who worked internally at their client's office. The executive wanted the internal sales position for himself. To reach this goal, he systematically engaged in backstabbing to shatter his colleague's credibility. Each time he heard a complaint, however small, from the client, he would ask for it in an e-mail and then forward the information to his boss. He'd include a short message about his colleague such as: "I'm powerless to deal with this. She's not being responsive and the customer is beating on me." In addition, he would fail to share important information with her before presentations with their boss to convey the impression that she did not know what she was talking about. He even took backstabbing so far as to schedule meetings with their boss on an electronic calendar but then altered her version so that she was late. Eventually, he convinced his boss that she was overworked. He was transferred to the client's office, while his colleague was moved back to the main office.

Incidents such as these may not be uncommon in the workplace. Given today's competitive work environment, employees may be using political games to move ahead. To guard against backstabbing, Bob McDonald, a management consultant, recommends telling supervisors and other key personnel that the backstabber is not a friend. He states that this may be effective because backstabbers often claim to be friends of their victims and then act as if they are hesitant about sharing negative information with others because of this professed friendship. In any event, it is clear that employees in organizations need to be aware of illegitimate political behavior. Companies may need to adopt formal policies to safeguard employees against such behavior; however, it may be the case that behaviors such as backstabbing and spreading negative rumors are difficult to detect. Thus, both employees and managers should try to verify information to avoid the negative repercussions that can come from backstabbing and other illegitimate behaviors.

Questions

1. What factors, in addition to those cited, do you believe lead to illegitimate political behaviors such as backstabbing?

2. Imagine that a colleague is engaging in illegitimate political behavior toward you. What steps might you take to reduce or eliminate this behavior?

3. Do you believe that it is ever justifiable to engage in illegitimate political behaviors such as backstabbing? If so, what are some conditions that might justify such behavior?

4. In addition to the obvious negative effects of illegitimate political behavior on victims, such as those described in the above case, what might be some negative effects on the perpetrators? On the organization as a whole?

Source: Based on J. Sandberg, "Sabotage 101: The Sinister Art of Backstabbing," *The Wall Street Journal,* February 11, 2004, p. B.1.

Endnotes

1. Based on A. Davis and R. Smith, "Merrill Officer Quits, Firming O'Neal's Grip," *The Wall Street Journal,* August 7, 2003, p. C1; and L. Thomas, Jr., "Another Departure as Merrill Chief Tightens Hold," *The New York Times,* August 7, 2003, p. C1.
2. R. M. Kanter, "Power Failure in Management Circuits," *Harvard Business Review,* July–August 1979, p. 65.
3. J. Pfeffer, "Understanding Power in Organizations," *California Management Review,* Winter 1992, p. 35.
4. Based on B. M. Bass, *Bass & Stogdill's Handbook of Leadership,* 3rd ed. (New York: Free Press, 1990).
5. J. R. P. French, Jr., and B. Raven, "The Bases of Social Power," in D. Cartwright (ed.), *Studies in Social Power* (Ann Arbor: University of Michigan, Institute for Social Research, 1959), pp. 150–67; B. J. Raven, "The Bases of Power: Origins and Recent Developments," *Journal of Social Issues,* Winter 1993, pp. 227–51; and G. Yukl, "Use Power Effectively," in E. A. Locke (ed.), *Handbook of Principles of Organizational Behavior* (Malden, MA: Blackwell, 2004), pp. 242–47.
6. E. A. Ward, "Social Power Bases of Managers: Emergence of a New Factor," *Journal of Social Psychology,* February 2001, pp. 144–47.
7. P. M. Podsakoff and C. A. Schriesheim, "Field Studies of French and Raven's Bases of Power: Critique, Reanalysis, and Suggestions for Future Research," *Psychological Bulletin,* May 1985, pp. 387–411; T. R. Hinkin and C. A. Schriesheim, "Development and Application of New Scales to Measure the French and Raven (1959) Bases of Social Power," *Journal of Applied Psychology,* August 1989, pp. 561–67; and P. P. Carson, K. D. Carson, and C. W. Roe, "Social Power Bases: A Meta-Analytic Examination of Interrelationships and Outcomes" *Journal of Applied Social Psychology* 23, no. 14 (1993), pp. 1150–69.
8. J. L. Roberts, "Striking a Hot Match," *Newsweek,* January 24, 2005, pp. 54–55.
9. R. E. Emerson, "Power–Dependence Relations," *American Sociological Review,* February 1962, pp. 31–41.
10. H. Mintzberg, *Power In and Around Organizations* (Upper Saddle River, NJ: Prentice Hall, 1983), p. 24.
11. R. M. Cyert and J. G. March, *A Behavioral Theory of the Firm* (Upper Saddle River, NJ: Prentice Hall, 1963).
12. C. Perrow, "Departmental Power and Perspective in Industrial Firms," in M. N. Zald (ed.), *Power in Organizations* (Nashville, TN: Vanderbilt University Press, 1970).
13. N. Foulkes, "Tractor Boy," *High Life,* October 2002, p. 90.
14. See, for example, D. Kipnis, S. M. Schmidt, C. Swaffin-Smith, and I. Wilkinson, "Patterns of Managerial Influence: Shotgun Managers, Tacticians, and Bystanders," *Organizational Dynamics,* Winter 1984, pp. 58–67; D. Kipnis and S. M. Schmidt, "Upward-Influence Styles: Relationship with Performance Evaluations, Salary, and Stress," *Administrative Science Quarterly,* December 1988, pp. 528–42; G. Yukl and J. B. Tracey, "Consequences of Influence Tactics Used with Subordinates, Peers, and the Boss," *Journal of Applied Psychology,* August 1992, pp. 525–35; G. Blickle, "Influence Tactics Used by Subordinates: An Empirical Analysis of the Kipnis and Schmidt Subscales," *Psychological Reports,* February 2000, pp. 143–54; and G. Yukl, "Use Power Effectively," pp. 249–52.
15. G. Yukl, *Leadership in Organizations,* 5th ed. (Upper Saddle River, NJ: Prentice Hall, 2002), pp. 141–74; G. R. Ferris, W. A. Hochwarter, C. Douglas, F. R. Blass, R. W. Kolodinsky, and D. C. Treadway, "Social Influence Processes in Organizations and Human Resource Systems," in G. R. Ferris and J. J. Martocchio (eds.), *Research in Personnel and Human Resources Management,* vol. 21 (Oxford, UK: JAI Press/Elsevier, 2003), pp. 65–127; and C. A. Higgins, T. A. Judge, and G. R. Ferris, "Influence Tactics and Work Outcomes: A Meta-Analysis," *Journal of Organizational Behavior,* March 2003, pp. 89–106.
16. C. M. Falbe and G. Yukl, "Consequences for Managers of Using Single Influence Tactics and Combinations of Tactics," *Academy of Management Journal,* July 1992, pp. 638–53.
17. Yukl, *Leadership in Organizations.*
18. Ibid.
19. Falbe and Yukl, "Consequences for Managers of Using Single Influence Tactics and Combinations of Tactics."
20. Yukl, "Use Power Effectively," p. 254.
21. P. P. Fu and G. Yukl, "Perceived Effectiveness of Influence Tactics in the United States and China," *Leadership Quarterly,* Summer 2000, pp. 251–66; O. Branzei, "Cultural Explanations of Individual Preferences for Influence Tactics in Cross-Cultural Encounters," *International Journal of Cross Cultural Management,* August 2002, pp. 203–18; G. Yukl, P. P. Fu, and R. McDonald, "Cross-Cultural Differences in Perceived Effectiveness of Influence Tactics for Initiating or Resisting Change," *Applied Psychology: An International Review,* January 2003, pp. 66–82; and P. P. Fu, T. K. Peng, J. C. Kennedy, and G. Yukl, "Examining the Preferences of Influence Tactics in Chinese Societies: A Comparison of Chinese Managers in Hong Kong, Taiwan, and Mainland China," *Organizational Dynamics* 33, no. 1 (2004), pp. 32–46.
22. Fu and Yukl, "Perceived Effectiveness of Influence Tactics in the United States and China."
23. Based on W. B. Stevenson, J. L. Pearce, and L. W. Porter, "The Concept of 'Coalition' in Organization Theory and Research," *Academy of Management Review,* April 1985, pp. 261–63.
24. S. B. Bacharach and E. J. Lawler, "Political Alignments in Organizations," in R. M. Kramer and M. A. Neale (eds.), *Power and Influence in Organizations* (Thousand Oaks, CA: Sage, 1998), pp. 75–77.

25. J. K. Murnighan and D. J. Brass, "Intraorganizational Coalitions," in M. H. Bazerman, R. J. Lewicki, and B. H. Sheppard (eds.), *Research on Negotiation in Organizations* (Greenwich, CT: JAI Press, 1991).

26. See J. Pfeffer, *Power in Organizations* (Marshfield, MA: Pitman, 1981), pp. 155–57.

27. www.chicagolegalnet.com; and S. Ellison and J. S. Lublin, "Dial to Pay $10 Million to Settle a Sexual-Harassment Lawsuit," *The Wall Street Journal*, April 30, 2003, p. B4.

28. L. J. Munson, C. Hulin, and F. Drasgow, "Longitudinal Analysis of Dispositional Influences and Sexual Harassment: Effects on Job and Psychological Outcomes," *Personnel Psychology*, Spring 2000. pp. 21–46; T. M. Glomb, L. J. Munson, C. L. Hulin, M. E. Bergman, and F. Drasgow, "Structural Equation Models of Sexual Harassment: Longitudinal Explorations and Cross-Sectional Generalizations," *Journal of Applied Psychology*, February 1999, pp. 14–28; M. E. Bergman, R. D. Langhout, P. A. Palmieri, L. M. Cortina, and L. F. Fitzgerald, "The (Un)reasonableness of Reporting: Antecedents and Consequences of Reporting Sexual Harassment," *Journal of Applied Psychology*, April 2002, pp. 230–42; L. R. Offermann and A. B. Malamut, "When Leaders Harass: The Impact of Target Perceptions of Organizational Leadership and Climate on Harassment Reporting and Outcomes," *Journal of Applied Psychology*, October 2002, pp. 885–93.

29. S. Silverstein and S. Christian, "Harassment Ruling Raises Free-Speech Issues," *Los Angeles Times*, November 11, 1993, p. D2.

30. R. Ilies, N. Hauserman, S. Schwochau, and J. Stibal, "Reported Incidence Rates of Work-Related Sexual Harassment in the United States: Using Meta-Analysis to Explain Reported Rate Disparities," *Personnel Psychology*, Fall 2003, pp. 607–31

31. M. Rotundo, D. Nguyen, and P. R. Sackett, "A Meta-Analytic Review of Gender Differences in Perceptions of Sexual Harassment," *Journal of Applied Psychology*, October 2001, pp. 914–22.

32. Ilies, Hauserman, Schwochau, and Stibal, "Reported Incidence Rates of Work-Related Sexual Harassment in the United States; A. B. Malamut and L. R. Offermann, "Coping with Sexual Harassment: Personal, Environmental, and Cognitive Determinants," *Journal of Applied Psychology*, December 2001, pp. 1152–66; L. M. Cortina and S. A. Wasti, "Profiles in Coping: Responses to Sexual Harassment Across Persons, Organizations, and Cultures," *Journal of Applied Psychology*, February 2005, pp. 182–92; J. H. Wayne, "Disentangling the Power Bases of Sexual Harassment: Comparing Gender, Age, and Position Power," *Journal of Vocational Behavior*, December 2000, pp. 301–25; and F. Wilson and P. Thompson, "Sexual Harassment as an Exercise of Power," *Gender, Work & Organization*, January 2001, pp. 61–83.

33. S. A. Culbert and J. J. McDonough, *The Invisible War: Pursuing Self-Interest at Work* (New York: John Wiley, 1980), p. 6.

34. Mintzberg, *Power In and Around Organizations*, p. 26. See also K. M. Kacmar and R. A. Baron, "Organizational Politics: The State of the Field, Links to Related Processes, and an Agenda for Future Research," in G. R. Ferris (ed.), *Research in Personnel and Human Resources Management*, vol. 17 (Greenwich, CT: JAI Press, 1999), pp. 1–39; and G. R. Ferris, D. C. Treadway, R. W. Kolokinsky, W. A. Hochwarter, C. J. Kacmar, and D. D. Frink, "Development and Validation of the Political Skill Inventory," *Journal of Management*, February 2005, pp. 126–52.

35. S. B. Bacharach and E. J. Lawler, "Political Alignments in Organizations," in R. M. Kramer and M. A. Neale (eds.), *Power and Influence in Organizations*, pp. 68–69.

36. D. Farrell and J. C. Petersen, "Patterns of Political Behavior in Organizations," *Academy of Management Review*, July 1982, p. 405. For analyses of the controversies underlying the definition of organizational politics, see A. Drory and T. Romm, "The Definition of Organizational Politics: A Review," *Human Relations*, November 1990, pp. 1133–54; and R. S. Cropanzano, K. M. Kacmar, and D. P. Bozeman, "Organizational Politics, Justice, and Support: Their Differences and Similarities," in R. S. Cropanzano and K. M. Kacmar (eds.), *Organizational Politics, Justice and Support: Managing Social Climate at Work* (Westport, CT: Quorum Books, 1995), pp. 1–18.

37. Farrell and Peterson, "Patterns of Political Behavior," pp. 406–407; and A. Drory, "Politics in Organization and Its Perception Within the Organization," *Organization Studies*, vol. 9, no. 2, 1988, pp. 165–79.

38. Pfeffer, *Power in Organizations*.

39. Drory and Romm, "The Definition of Organizational Politics."

40. K. K. Eastman, "In the Eyes of the Beholder: An Attributional Approach to Ingratiation and Organizational Citizenship Behavior," *Academy of Management Journal*, October 1994, pp. 1379–91; M. C. Bolino, "Citizenship and Impression Management: Good Soldiers or Good Actors?" *Academy of Management Review*, January 1999, pp. 82–98; S. M. Rioux and L. A. Penner, "The Causes of Organizational Citizenship Behavior: A Motivational Analysis," *Journal of Applied Psychology*, December 2001, pp. 1306–14; and M. A. Finkelstein and L. A. Penner, "Predicting Organizational Citizenship Behavior: Integrating the Functional and Role Identity Approaches," *Social Behavior & Personality* 32, no. 4 (2004), pp. 383–98.

41. F. Luthans, R. M. Hodgetts, and S.A. Rosenkrantz, *Real Managers* (Cambridge, MA: Allinger, 1988).

42. J. P. Kotter, *The General Managers* (New York: The Free Press, 1982).

43. D. J. Brass, "Being in the Right Place: A Structural Analysis of Individual Influence in an Organization," *Administrative Science Quarterly*, December 1984, pp. 518–39; and N. E. Friedkin, "Structural Bases of Interpersonal Influence in Groups: A Longitudinal Case Study," *American Sociological Review*, December 1993, pp. 861–72.

44. See, for example, G. Biberman, "Personality and Characteristic Work Attitudes of Persons with High, Moderate, and Low Political Tendencies," *Psychological Reports*, October 1985, pp. 1303–10; R. J. House, "Power and Personality in Complex Organizations," in B. M. Staw and L. L. Cummings (eds.), *Research in Organizational Behavior*, vol. 10 (Greenwich, CT: JAI Press, 1988), pp. 305–57; G. R. Ferris, G. S. Russ, and P. M. Fandt, "Politics in Organizations," in R. A. Giacalone and P. Rosenfeld (eds.), *Impression Management in the Organization* (Hillsdale, NJ: Lawrence Erlbaum Associates, 1989), pp. 155–56; and W. E. O'Connor and T. G. Morrison, "A Comparison of Situational and Dispositional Predictors of Perceptions of Organizational Politics," *Journal of Psychology*, May 2001, pp. 301–12.

45. Farrell and Petersen, "Patterns of Political Behavior," p. 408.

46. S. C. Goh and A. R. Doucet, "Antecedent Situational Conditions of Organizational Politics: An Empirical Investigation," paper

presented at the Annual Administrative Sciences Association of Canada Conference, Whistler, B.C., May 1986; C. Hardy, "The Contribution of Political Science to Organizational Behavior," in J. W. Lorsch (ed.), *Handbook of Organizational Behavior* (Englewood Cliffs, NJ: Prentice Hall, 1987), p. 103; and G. R. Ferris and K. M. Kacmar, "Perceptions of Organizational Politics," *Journal of Management*, March 1992, pp. 93–116.

47. See, for example, Farrell and Petersen, "Patterns of Political Behavior," p. 409; P. M. Fandt and G. R. Ferris, "The Management of Information and Impressions: When Employees Behave Opportunistically," *Organizational Behavior and Human Decision Processes*, February 1990, pp. 140–58; Ferris, Russ, and Fandt, "Politics in Organizations," p. 147; and J. M. L. Poon, "Situational Antecedents and Outcomes of Organizational Politics Perceptions," *Journal of Managerial Psychology* 18, no. 2 (2003), pp. 138–55.

48. G. R. Ferris, G. S. Russ, and P. M. Fandt, "Politics in Organizations," in R. A. Giacalone and P. Rosenfeld (eds.), *Impression Management in Organizations* (Newbury Park, CA: Sage, 1989), pp. 143–70; and K. M. Kacmar, D. P. Bozeman, D. S. Carlson, and W. P. Anthony, "An Examination of the Perceptions of Organizational Politics Model: Replication and Extension," *Human Relations*, March 1999, pp. 383–416.

49. K. M. Kacmar and R. A. Baron, "Organizational Politics"; M. Valle and L. A. Witt, "The Moderating Effect of Teamwork Perceptions on the Organizational Politics-Job Satisfaction Relationship," *Journal of Social Psychology*, June 2001, pp. 379–88; and W. A. Hochwarter, C. Kiewitz, S. L. Castro, P. L. Perrewe, and G. R. Ferris, "Positive Affectivity and Collective Efficacy as Moderators of the Relationship Between Perceived Politics and Job Satisfaction," *Journal of Applied Social Psychology*, May 2003, pp. 1009–35.

50. G. R. Ferris, D. D. Frink, M. C. Galang, J. Zhou, K. M. Kacmar, and J. L. Howard, "Perceptions of Organizational Politics: Prediction, Stress-Related Implications, and Outcomes," *Human Relations*, February 1996, pp. 233–66; E. Vigoda, "Stress-Related Aftermaths to Workplace Politics: The Relationships Among Politics, Job Distress, and Aggressive Behavior in Organizations," *Journal of Organizational Behavior*, August 2002, pp. 571–91.

51. C. Kiewitz, W. A. Hochwarter, G. R. Ferris, and S. L. Castro, "The Role of Psychological Climate in Neutralizing the Effects of Organizational Politics on Work Outcomes," *Journal of Applied Social Psychology*, June 2002, pp. 1189–1207; J. M. L. Poon, "Situational Antecedents and Outcomes of Organizational Politics Perceptions"; and M. C. Andrews, L. A. Witt, and K. M. Kacmar, "The Interactive Effects of Organizational Politics and Exchange Ideology on Manager Ratings of Retention," *Journal of Vocational Behavior*, April 2003, pp. 357–69.

52. S. Aryee, Z. Chen, and P. S. Budhwar, "Exchange Fairness and Employee Performance: An Examination of the Relationship Between Organizational Politics and Procedural Justice," *Organizational Behavior & Human Decision Processes*, May 2004, pp. 1–14; and Kacmar, Bozeman, Carlson, and Anthony, "An Examination of the Perceptions of Organizational Politics Model."

53. Ibid., p. 389.

54. Ibid., p. 409.

55. B. E. Ashforth and R. T. Lee, "Defensive Behavior in Organizations: A Preliminary Model," *Human Relations*, July 1990, pp. 621–48.

56. M. Valle and P. L. Perrewe, "Do Politics Perceptions Relate to Political Behaviors? Tests of an Implicit Assumption and Expanded Model," *Human Relations*, March 2000, pp. 359–86.

57. See T. Romm and A. Drory, "Political Behavior in Organizations: A Cross-Cultural Comparison," *International Journal of Value Based Management* 1 (1988), pp. 97–113; and E. Vigoda, "Reactions to Organizational Politics: A Cross-Cultural Examination in Israel and Britain," *Human Relations*, November 2001, pp. 1483–1518.

58. E. Vigoda, "Reactions to Organizational Politics," p. 1512.

59. Ibid., p. 1510.

60. M. R. Leary and R. M. Kowalski, "Impression Management: A Literature Review and Two-Component Model," *Psychological Bulletin*, January 1990, pp. 34–47.

61. Ibid., p. 34.

62. See, for instance, B. R. Schlenker, *Impression Management: The Self-Concept, Social Identity, and Interpersonal Relations* (Monterey, CA: Brooks/Cole, 1980); W. L. Gardner and M. J. Martinko, "Impression Management in Organizations," *Journal of Management*, June 1988, pp. 321–38; Leary and Kowalski, "Impression Management: A Literature Review and Two-Component Model," pp. 34–47; P. R. Rosenfeld, R. A. Giacalone, and C. A. Riordan, *Impression Management in Organizations: Theory, Measurement, and Practice* (New York: Routledge, 1995); C. K. Stevens and A. L. Kristof, "Making the Right Impression: A Field Study of Applicant Impression Management During Job Interviews," *Journal of Applied Psychology*, October 1995, pp. 587–606; D. P. Bozeman and K. M. Kacmar, "A Cybernetic Model of Impression Management Processes in Organizations," *Organizational Behavior and Human Decision Processes*, January 1997, pp. 9–30; M. C. Bolino and W. H. Turnley, "More Than One Way to Make an Impression: Exploring Profiles of Impression Management," *Journal of Management* 29, no. 2 (2003), pp. 141–60; S. Zivnuska, K. M. Kacmar, L. A. Witt, D. S. Carlson, and V. K. Bratton, "Interactive Effects of Impression Management and Organizational Politics on Job Performance," *Journal of Organizational Behavior*, August 2004, pp. 627–40; and W.-C. Tsai, C.-C. Chen, and S.-F. Chiu, "Exploring Boundaries of the Effects of Applicant Impression Management Tactics in Job Interviews," *Journal of Management*, February 2005, pp. 108–25.

63. M. Snyder and J. Copeland, "Self-Monitoring Processes in Organizational Settings," in Giacalone and Rosenfeld (eds.), *Impression Management in the Organization*, p. 11; E. D. Long and G. H. Dobbins, "Self-Monitoring, Impression Management, and Interview Ratings: A Field and Laboratory Study," in J. L. Wall and L. R. Jauch (eds.), *Proceedings of the 52nd Annual Academy of Management Conference*, Las Vegas, August 1992, pp. 274–78; A. Montagliani and R. A. Giacalone, "Impression Management and Cross-Cultural Adaptation," *Journal of Social Psychology*, October 1998, pp. 598–608; and W. H. Turnley and M. C. Bolino, "Achieved Desired Images While Avoiding Undesired Images: Exploring the Role of Self-Monitoring in Impression Management," *Journal of Applied Psychology*, April 2001, pp. 351–60.

64. Leary and Kowalski, "Impression Management," p. 40.

65. Gardner and Martinko, "Impression Management in Organizations," p. 333.

66. R. A. Baron, "Impression Management by Applicants During Employment Interviews: The 'Too Much of a Good Thing'

Effect," in R. W. Eder and G. R. Ferris (eds.), *The Employment Interview: Theory, Research, and Practice* (Newbury Park, CA: Sage Publishers, 1989), pp. 204–15.

67. Ferris, Russ, and Fandt, "Politics in Organizations."

68. A. P. J. Ellis, B. J. West, A. M. Ryan, and R. P. DeShon, "The Use of Impression Management Tactics in Structural Interviews: A Function of Question Type?" *Journal of Applied Psychology*, December 2002, pp. 1200–08.

69. Baron, "Impression Management by Applicants During Employment Interviews"; D. C. Gilmore and G. R. Ferris, "The Effects of Applicant Impression Management Tactics on Interviewer Judgments," *Journal of Management*, December 1989, pp. 557–64; Stevens and Kristof, "Making the Right Impression: A Field Study of Applicant Impression Management During Job Interviews"; and L. A. McFarland, A. M. Ryan, and S. D. Kriska, "Impression Management Use and Effectiveness Across Assessment Methods," *Journal of Management* 29, no. 5 (2003), pp. 641–61; and W.-C. Tsai, C.-C. Chen, and S.-F. Chiu, "Exploring Boundaries of the Effects of Applicant Impression Management Tactics in Job Interviews."

70. Gilmore and Ferris, "The Effects of Applicant Impression Management Tactics on Interviewer Judgments."

71. Stevens and Kristof, "Making the Right Impression: A Field Study of Applicant Impression Management During Job Interviews."

72. C. A. Higgins, T. A. Judge, and G. R. Ferris, "Influence Tactics and Work Outcomes: A Meta-Analysis," *Journal of Organizational Behavior*, March 2003, pp. 89–106.

73. Ibid.

74. R. M. Kanter, *Men and Women of the Corporation* (New York: Basic Books, 1977).

75. See, for instance, C. M. Falbe and G. Yukl, "Consequences for Managers of Using Single Influence Tactics and Combinations of Tactics," *Academy of Management Journal*, August 1992, pp. 638–52.

76. See J. G. Bachman, D. G. Bowers, and P. M. Marcus, "Bases of Supervisory Power: A Comparative Study in Five Organizational Settings," in A. S. Tannenbaum (ed.), *Control in Organizations* (New York: McGraw-Hill, 1968), p. 236; M. A. Rahim, "Relationships of Leader Power to Compliance and Satisfaction with Supervision: Evidence from a National Sample of Managers," *Journal of Management*, December 1989, pp. 545–56; P. A. Wilson, "The Effects of Politics and Power on the Organizational Commitment of Federal Executives," *Journal of Management*, Spring 1995, pp. 101–18; and A. R. Elangovan and J. L. Xie, "Effects of Perceived Power of Supervisor on Subordinate Stress and Motivation: The Moderating Role of Subordinate Characteristics," *Journal of Organizational Behavior*, May 1999, pp. 359–73.

77. J. Pfeffer, *Managing with Power*, p. 137.

78. G. R. Ferris, P. L. Perrewé, W. P. Anthony, and D. C. Gilmore, "Political Skill at Work," *Organizational Dynamics*, Spring 2000, pp. 25–37; K. K. Ahearn, G. R. Ferris, W. A. Hochwarter, C. Douglas, and A. P. Ammeter, "Leader Political Skill and Team Performance," *Journal of Management* 30, no. 3 (2004), pp. 309–27; and S. E. Seibert, M. L. Kraimer, and J. M. Crant, "What Do Proactive People Do? A Longitudinal Model Linking Proactive Personality and Career Success," *Personnel Psychology*, Winter 2001, pp. 845–74.

79. R. W. Kolodinsky, W. A. Hochwarter, and G. R. Ferris, "Nonlinearity in the Relationship Between Political Skill and Work Outcomes: Convergent Evidence from Three Studies," *Journal of Vocational Behavior*, October 2004, pp. 294–308; W. Hochwarter, "The Interactive Effects of Pro-Political Behavior and Politics Perceptions on Job Satisfaction and Affective Commitment," *Journal of Applied Social Psychology*, July 2003, pp. 1360–78; and P. L. Perrewé, K. L. Zellars, G. R. Ferris, A. Rossi, C. J. Kacmar, and D. A. Ralston, "Neutralizing Job Stressors: Political Skill as an Antidote to the Dysfunctional Consequences of Role Conflict," *Academy of Management Journal*, February 2004, pp. 141–52.

Our first and most pressing problem is how to do away with warfare as a method of solving conflicts between national groups within a society who have different views about how the society is to run.

— Margaret Mead

Conflict and Negotiation

After studying this chapter, you should be able to:

1 Define conflict.

2 Differentiate between the traditional, human relations, and interactionist views of conflict.

3 Contrast task, relationship, and process conflict.

4 Outline the conflict process.

5 Describe the five conflict-handling intentions.

6 Contrast distributive and integrative bargaining.

7 Identify the five steps in the negotiation process.

8 Describe cultural differences in negotiations.

LEARNING OBJECTIVES

CHAPTER 15

Conflict at Disney

Through the leadership of Michael Eisner, Frank Wells, Jeffrey Katzenberg, and Roy Disney, the Walt Disney Company became a powerhouse and a Wall Street favorite, but as you will see, conflict at Disney caused much turmoil for the company and its executives.

In 1995, Eisner—Disney's CEO—announced that he was hiring his longtime friend and one of the world's most successful celebrity agents, Michael Ovitz (see photo: Ovitz on left; Eisner on right), to become the company's new president. The two were so close that their families often spent the holidays together in Aspen. In fact, during one of their holidays together, Eisner gave Ovitz a note that concluded with, "We are going to be a great team . . . Every day I am thankful we are together." But a scant 14 months later, Eisner fired Ovitz, wanting him out of Disney so bad that Eisner paid him $140 million to leave. As a result, Disney shareholders sued, alleging that Eisner had breached his fiduciary duty. In October 2004, the lawsuit went to trial, forcing Eisner and Ovitz to reveal details about their partnership.

The seeds of the conflict between the two men were sown from the beginning. Ovitz accepted the position as Disney president without knowing his formal areas of authority. At one point, he told Eisner, "I'm putting myself in your hands." The problem? Even in the midst of hiring Ovitz, Eisner routinely backed those who he knew were hostile to Ovitz's hiring. In fact, the day before Ovitz's hiring was announced, two of Disney's senior executives told Ovitz that they would not work for him because of his relative lack of experience. One said, "Welcome to the company. I just want you to know that I'll never work for you." Eisner sat silent. Privately, Ovitz asked Eisner to back him. "I can't do that," Eisner responded.

Eisner and Ovitz also had conflicting styles. Ovitz liked glitz and glamour. Shortly after starting work at Disney, Ovitz hosted a party where Tom Hanks, Steven Spielberg, and other celebrities were guests. The party cost Disney $90,000, which Ovitz considered a bargain. Eisner considered it lavish. Ovitz also had a habit of canceling meetings at the last minute, which was common for Hollywood agents but offended many at Disney. At the trial, Eisner admitted to wanting to fire Ovitz only 5 weeks after he hired him. According to one of Eisner's associates, the only reason he didn't was the belief that Ovitz would commit suicide. But, a few months later, Eisner was actively trying to remove Ovitz. He wrote to two Disney board members, "I hate saying this but his strength of personality together with his erratic behavior and pathological problems (and I hate saying that) is a mixture leading to disaster for this company." The following week, Eisner sent a Disney executive to fire Ovitz, only to write Ovitz, "I am committed to making this a win-win situation, to keep our friendship intact, to be positive. . . You still are the only one who came to my hospital bed (when Eisner had emergency heart surgery)—and I do remember."

The career of a person once described as Hollywood's most powerful was in ashes. At one point, David Geffen, a successful record executive and producer, said to Ovitz, "This isn't the old you. You could close anything. You could get it done. Now you have no credibility." Meanwhile, Eisner never really recovered from the Ovitz incident. In 2005, 45 percent of Disney shareholders gave Eisner a "no-confidence" vote. Although Disney won the suit filed over Ovitz's $140 million severance package in late 2005, Eisner stepped down as Chairman, and resigned from the board of directors, severing all ties with the company he had led for more than two decades. As one observer put it at the conclusion of the trial in 2005, "It was a no-win, no-win."[1] What started out as friendship ended in a firing and a lawsuit, with both men's careers irreparably damaged. The situation at Disney shows us how conflict can destroy careers and harm companies. ■

As we see in the Disney example, conflict can be a serious problem in an organization. It can create chaotic conditions that make it nearly impossible for employees to work together. However, conflict also has a less-well-known positive side. We'll explain the difference between negative and positive conflicts in this chapter and provide a guide to help you understand how conflicts develop. We'll also present a topic closely akin to conflict—negotiation. But first, let's clarify what we mean by conflict.

A Definition of Conflict

There has been no shortage of definitions of conflict.[2] Despite the divergent meanings the term has acquired, several common themes underlie most definitions. Conflict must be perceived by the parties to it; whether or not conflict exists is a perception issue. If no one is aware of a conflict, then it is generally agreed that no conflict exists. Additional commonalities in the definitions are opposition or incompatibility and some form of interaction.[3] These factors set the conditions that determine the beginning point of the conflict process.

We can define **conflict**, then, as a process that begins when one party perceives that another party has negatively affected, or is about to negatively affect, something that the first party cares about.[4] This definition is purposely broad. It describes that point in any ongoing activity when an interaction "crosses over" to become an interparty conflict. It encompasses the wide range of conflicts that people experience in organizations—incompatibility of goals, differences over interpretations of facts, disagreements based on behavioral expectations, and the like. Finally, our definition is flexible enough to cover the full range of conflict levels—from overt and violent acts to subtle forms of disagreement.

Transitions in Conflict Thought

It is entirely appropriate to say that there has been "conflict" over the role of conflict in groups and organizations. One school of thought has argued that conflict must be avoided—that it indicates a malfunctioning within the group. We call this the *traditional* view. Another school of thought, the *human relations* view, argues that conflict is a natural and inevitable outcome in any group and that it need not be evil, but rather has the potential to be a positive force in determining group performance. The third, and most recent, perspective proposes not only that conflict can be a positive force in a group but explicitly argues that some conflict is *absolutely necessary* for a group to perform effectively. We label this third school the *interactionist* view. Let's take a closer look at each of these views.

The Traditional View

The early approach to conflict assumed that all conflict was bad. Conflict was viewed negatively, and it was used synonymously with such terms as *violence, destruction,* and *irrationality* to reinforce its negative connotation. Conflict, by definition, was harmful and was to be avoided. The **traditional** view was consistent with the attitudes that prevailed about group behavior in the 1930s and 1940s. Conflict was seen as a dysfunctional outcome resulting from poor communication, a lack of openness and trust between people, and the failure of managers to be responsive to the needs and aspirations of their employees.

The view that all conflict is bad certainly offers a simple approach to looking at the behavior of people who create conflict. Because all conflict is to be avoided, we need merely direct our attention to the causes of conflict and correct these malfunctionings to improve group and organizational performance. Although research studies now provide strong evidence to dispute that this approach to conflict reduction results in high group performance, many of us still evaluate conflict situations using this outmoded standard.

The Human Relations View

The **human relations** view argued that conflict was a natural occurrence in all groups and organizations. Because conflict was inevitable, the human relations school advocated acceptance of conflict. Proponents rationalized its existence: It cannot be eliminated, and there are even times when conflict may benefit a group's performance. The human relations view dominated conflict theory from the late 1940s through the mid-1970s.

The Interactionist View

While the human relations view accepted conflict, the **interactionist** view encourages conflict on the grounds that a harmonious, peaceful, tranquil, and cooperative group is prone to becoming static, apathetic, and nonresponsive to needs for change and innovation.[5] The major contribution of the interactionist

---

conflict *A process that begins when one party perceives that another party has negatively affected, or is about to negatively affect, something that the first party cares about.*

traditional view of conflict *The belief that all conflict is harmful and must be avoided.*

human relations view of conflict *The belief that conflict is a natural and inevitable outcome in any group.*

interactionist view of conflict *The belief that conflict is not only a positive force in a group but that it is also an absolute necessity for a group to perform effectively.*

view, therefore, is encouraging group leaders to maintain an ongoing minimum level of conflict—enough to keep the group viable, self-critical, and creative.

The interactionist view does not propose that all conflicts are good. Rather, some conflicts support the goals of the group and improve its performance; these are **functional**, constructive forms of conflict. In addition, there are conflicts that hinder group performance; these are **dysfunctional** or destructive forms of conflict. What differentiates functional from dysfunctional conflict? The evidence indicates that you need to look at the *type* of conflict.[6] Specifically, there are three types: task, relationship, and process.

Task conflict relates to the content and goals of the work. **Relationship conflict** focuses on interpersonal relationships. **Process conflict** relates to how the work gets done. Studies demonstrate that relationship conflicts are almost always dysfunctional.[7] Why? It appears that the friction and interpersonal hostilities inherent in relationship conflicts increases personality clashes and decreases mutual understanding, which hinders the completion of organizational tasks. However, low levels of process conflict and low-to-moderate levels of task conflict are functional. For process conflict to be productive, it must be kept low. Intense arguments about who should do what become dysfunctional when they create uncertainty about task roles, increase the time to complete tasks, and lead to members working at cross purposes. Low-to-moderate levels of task conflict consistently demonstrate a positive effect on group performance because it stimulates discussion of ideas that helps groups perform better.

The Conflict Process

The **conflict process** can be seen as comprising five stages: potential opposition or incompatibility, cognition and personalization, intentions, behavior, and outcomes. The process is diagrammed in Exhibit 15-1.

Stage I: Potential Opposition or Incompatibility

The first step in the conflict process is the presence of conditions that create opportunities for conflict to arise. They *need not* lead directly to conflict, but one of these conditions is necessary if conflict is to surface. For simplicity's sake, these conditions (which also may be looked at as causes or sources of conflict) have been condensed into three general categories: communication, structure, and personal variables.[8]

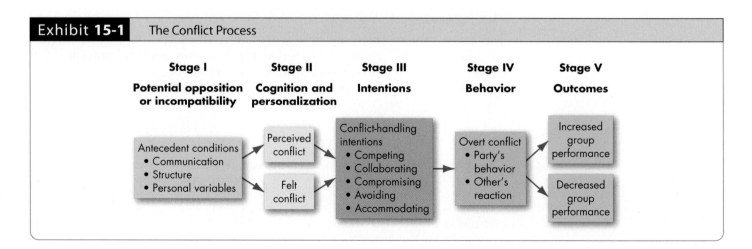

Exhibit 15-1   The Conflict Process

This statement is probably false. A popular myth in organizations is that poor communication is the primary source of conflicts. And certainly problems in the communication process do act to retard collaboration, stimulate misunderstandings, and create conflicts. But a review of the literature suggests that within organizations, structural factors and individual value differences are probably greater sources of conflict.[9]

Conflicts in organizations are frequently structurally derived. For instance, in the movie-making business, conflicts between directors and producers are often due to different goals. Directors want to create artistic films, regardless of costs. Producers want to make financially profitable movies by minimizing costs. When people have to work together, but are pursuing diverse goals, conflicts ensue.

Similarly, increased organizational size, routinization, work specialization, and zero-sum reward systems are all examples of structural factors that can lead to conflicts.

Many conflicts attributed to poor communication are, on closer examination, due to value differences. When managers incorrectly treat a value-based conflict as a communication problem, the conflict is rarely eliminated. Increased communication efforts are likely to crystallize and reinforce differences. "Before this conversation, I thought you *might* be closed-minded. Now I *know* you are!"

Lack of communication *can* be a source of conflict. But managers should first look to structural or value-based explanations because they are more prevalent in organizations. ■

Communication Susan had worked in supply-chain management at Bristol-Myers Squibb for 3 years. She enjoyed her work in large part because her boss, Tim McGuire, was a great guy to work for. Then Tim got promoted 6 months ago and Chuck Benson took his place. Susan says her job is a lot more frustrating now. "Tim and I were on the same wavelength. It's not that way with Chuck. He tells me something and I do it. Then he tells me I did it wrong. I think he means one thing but says something else. It's been like this since the day he arrived. I don't think a day goes by when he isn't yelling at me for something. You know, there are some people you just find it easy to communicate with. Well, Chuck isn't one of those!"

Susan's comments illustrate that communication can be a source of conflict.[10] They represent the opposing forces that arise from semantic difficulties, misunderstandings, and "noise" in the communication channels. Much of this discussion can be related back to our comments on communication in Chapter 11.

A review of the research suggests that differing word connotations, jargon, insufficient exchange of information, and noise in the communication channel are all barriers to communication and potential antecedent conditions to conflict. Evidence demonstrates that semantic difficulties arise as a result of differences in training, selective perception, and inadequate information about others. Research has further demonstrated a surprising finding: The potential for conflict increases when either too little or too much communication takes place. Apparently, an increase in communication is functional up to a point, whereupon it is possible to over communicate, with a resultant increase in the potential for conflict. Too much information as well as too little can lay the foundation for conflict.

functional conflict *Conflict that supports the goals of the group and improves its performance.*

dysfunctional conflict *Conflict that hinders group performance.*

task conflict *Conflicts over content and goals of the work.*

relationship conflict *Conflict based on interpersonal relationships.*

process conflict *Conflict over how work gets done.*

conflict process *Process with five stages: potential opposition or incompatibility, cognition and personalization, intentions, behavior, and outcomes.*

Hewlett-Packard manager Tom Alexander stood on a HP printer during a meeting of company engineers to make a point about incompatible goals. HP's goal was to develop a low-cost, lightweight printer to compete in the low-end market. The engineers' goal was to continue designing high-quality, high-cost printers. "Alexander's Stand" achieved goal compatibility, convincing engineers that customers don't need or want printers strong enough to withstand the weight of a man.

Furthermore, the channel chosen for communicating can have an influence on stimulating opposition. The filtering process that occurs as information is passed between members and the divergence of communications from formal or previously established channels offer potential opportunities for conflict to arise.

Structure   Charlotte and Teri both work at the Portland Furniture Mart—a large discount furniture retailer. Charlotte is a salesperson on the floor; Teri is the company credit manager. The two women have known each other for years and have much in common—they live within two blocks of each other, and their oldest daughters attend the same middle school and are best friends. In reality, if Charlotte and Teri had different jobs they might be best friends themselves, but these two women are consistently fighting battles with each other. Charlotte's job is to sell furniture and she does a heck of a job. But most of her sales are made on credit. Because Teri's job is to make sure the company minimizes credit losses, she regularly has to turn down the credit application of a customer with whom Charlotte has just closed a sale. It's nothing personal between Charlotte and Teri—the requirements of their jobs just bring them into conflict.

The conflicts between Charlotte and Teri are structural in nature. The term *structure* is used, in this context, to include variables such as size, degree of specialization in the tasks assigned to group members, jurisdictional clarity, member-goal compatibility, leadership styles, reward systems, and the degree of dependence between groups.

Research indicates that size and specialization act as forces to stimulate conflict. The larger the group and the more specialized its activities, the greater the likelihood of conflict. Tenure and conflict have been found to be inversely related. The potential for conflict tends to be greatest when group members are younger and when turnover is high.

The greater the ambiguity in precisely defining where responsibility for actions lies, the greater the potential for conflict to emerge. Such jurisdictional ambiguities increase intergroup fighting for control of resources and territory.

Groups within organizations have diverse goals. For instance, supply management is concerned with the timely acquisition of inputs at low prices, marketing's goals concentrate on disposing of outputs and increasing revenues, quality control's attention is focused on improving quality and ensuring that the organization's products meet standards, and production units seek efficiency of operations by maintaining a steady production flow. This diversity of goals among groups is a major source of conflict. When groups within an organization seek diverse ends, some of which—like sales and credit at Portland Furniture Mart—are inherently at odds, there are increased opportunities for conflict.

There is some indication that a close style of leadership—tight and continuous observation with general control of others' behaviors—increases conflict potential, but the evidence is not particularly strong. Too much reliance on participation may also stimulate conflict. Research tends to confirm that participation and conflict are highly correlated, apparently because participation encourages the promotion of differences. Reward systems, too, are found to create conflict when one member's gain is at another's expense. Finally, if a group is dependent on another group (in contrast to the two being mutually independent) or if interdependence allows one group to gain at another's expense, opposing forces are stimulated.[11]

Personal Variables   Did you ever meet someone to whom you took an immediate disliking? Most of the opinions they expressed, you disagreed with. Even insignificant characteristics—the sound of their voice, the smirk when they smiled, their personality—annoyed you. We've all met people like that. When you have to work with such individuals, there is often the potential for conflict.

Our last category of potential sources of conflict is personal variables, which include personality, emotions, and values. Evidence indicates that certain personality types—for example, individuals who are highly authoritarian and dogmatic—lead to potential conflict. Emotions can also cause conflict. For example, an employee who shows up to work irate from her hectic morning commute may carry that anger with her to her 9:00 A.M. meeting. The problem? Her anger can annoy her colleagues, which may lead to a tension-filled meeting.[12]

Finally, differing values can explain conflict. Value differences, for example, are the best explanation of diverse issues such as prejudice, disagreements over one's contribution to the group and the rewards one deserves, and assessments of whether this particular book is any good. That John dislikes African Americans and Dana believes John's position indicates his ignorance, that an employee thinks he is worth $55,000 a year but his boss believes him to be worth $50,000, and that Ann thinks this book is interesting to read while Jennifer views it as trash are all value judgments. And differences in value systems are important sources for creating the potential for conflict. It is also important to note that culture can be a source of differing values. For example, research indicates that individuals in Japan and in the United States view conflict differently. Compared to Japanese negotiators, Americans are more likely to see offers from their counterparts as unfair and to reject such offers.[13]

Stage II: Cognition and Personalization

If the conditions cited in Stage I negatively affect something that one party cares about, then the potential for opposition or incompatibility becomes actualized in the second stage.

As we noted in our definition of conflict, perception is required. Therefore, one or more of the parties must be aware of the existence of the antecedent conditions. However, because a conflict is **perceived** does not mean that it is personalized. In other words, "*A* may be aware that *B* and *A* are in serious disagreement . . . but it may not make *A* tense or anxious, and it may have no effect whatsoever on *A*'s affection toward *B*."[14] It is at the **felt** level, when individuals become emotionally involved, that parties experience anxiety, tension, frustration, or hostility.

Keep in mind two points. First, Stage II is important because it's where conflict issues tend to be defined. This is the place in the process where the parties decide what the conflict is about.[15] And, in turn, this "sense making" is critical because the way a conflict is defined goes a long way toward establishing the sort of outcomes that might settle it. For instance, if I define our salary disagreement as a zero-sum situation—that is, if you get the increase in pay you want, there will be just that amount less for me—I am going to be far less willing to compromise than if I frame the conflict as a potential win-win situation (that is, the dollars in the salary pool might be increased so that both of us could get the added pay we want). So the definition of a conflict is important, because it typically delineates the set of possible settlements. Our second point is that emotions play a major role in shaping perceptions.[16] For example, negative emotions have been found to produce oversimplification of issues, reductions in trust, and negative interpretations of the other party's behavior.[17] In contrast, positive feelings have been found to increase the tendency to see potential

perceived conflict   *Awareness by one or more parties of the existence of conditions that create opportunities for conflict to arise.*

felt conflict   *Emotional involvement in a conflict creating anxiety, tenseness, frustration, or hostility.*

relationships among the elements of a problem, to take a broader view of the situation, and to develop more innovative solutions.[18]

Stage III: Intentions

Intentions intervene between people's perceptions and emotions and their overt behavior. These intentions are decisions to act in a given way.[19]

Why are intentions separated out as a distinct stage? You have to infer the other's intent to know how to respond to that other's behavior. A lot of conflicts are escalated merely by one party attributing the wrong intentions to the other party. In addition, there is typically a great deal of slippage between intentions and behavior, so behavior does not always accurately reflect a person's intentions.

Exhibit 15-2 represents one author's effort to identify the primary conflict-handling intentions. Using two dimensions—*cooperativeness* (the degree to which one party attempts to satisfy the other party's concerns) and *assertiveness* (the degree to which one party attempts to satisfy his or her own concerns)—five conflict-handling intentions can be identified: *competing* (assertive and uncooperative), *collaborating* (assertive and cooperative), *avoiding* (unassertive and uncooperative), *accommodating* (unassertive and cooperative), and *compromising* (midrange on both assertiveness and cooperativeness).[20]

Competing   When one person seeks to satisfy his or her own interests, regardless of the impact on the other parties to the conflict, that person is **competing**. Examples include intending to achieve your goal at the sacrifice of the other's goal, attempting to convince another that your conclusion is correct and that his or hers is mistaken, and trying to make someone else accept blame for a problem.

Collaborating   When the parties to conflict each desire to fully satisfy the concerns of all parties, we have cooperation and the search for a mutually beneficial outcome. In **collaborating**, the intention of the parties is to solve the problem by clarifying differences rather than by accommodating various points of view. Examples include attempting to find a win-win solution that allows both parties' goals to be completely achieved and seeking a conclusion that incorporates the valid insights of both parties.

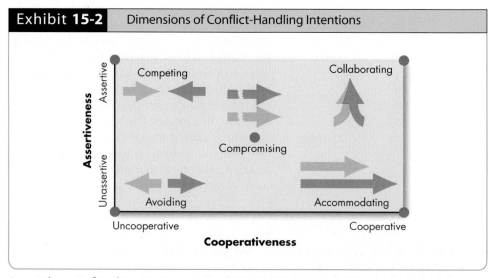

Exhibit **15-2**	Dimensions of Conflict-Handling Intentions

Source: K. Thomas, "Conflict and Negotiation Processes in Organizations," in M. D. Dunnette and L. M. Hough (eds.), *Handbook of Industrial and Organizational Psychology*, 2nd ed. vol. 3 (Palo Alto, CA: Consulting Psychologists Press, 1992), p. 668. With permission.

Avoiding   A person may recognize that a conflict exists and want to withdraw from it or suppress it. Examples of **avoiding** include trying to just ignore a conflict and avoiding others with whom you disagree.

Accommodating   When one party seeks to appease an opponent, that party may be willing to place the opponent's interests above his or her own. In other words, in order for the relationship to be maintained, one party is willing to be self-sacrificing. We refer to this intention as **accommodating**. Examples are a willingness to sacrifice your goal so that the other party's goal can be attained, supporting someone else's opinion despite your reservations about it, and forgiving someone for an infraction and allowing subsequent ones.

Compromising   When each party to the conflict seeks to give up something, sharing occurs, resulting in a compromised outcome. In **compromising**, there is no clear winner or loser. Rather, there is a willingness to ration the object of the conflict and accept a solution that provides incomplete satisfaction of both parties' concerns. The distinguishing characteristic of compromising, therefore, is that each party intends to give up something. Examples might be willingness to accept a raise of $2 an hour rather than $3, to acknowledge partial agreement with a specific viewpoint, and to take partial blame for an infraction.

   Intentions provide general guidelines for parties in a conflict situation. They define each party's purpose. Yet, people's intentions are not fixed. During the course of a conflict, they might change because of reconceptualization or because of an emotional reaction to the behavior of the other party. However, research indicates that people have an underlying disposition to handle conflicts in certain ways.[21] Specifically, individuals have preferences among the five conflict-handling intentions just described; these preferences tend to be relied on quite consistently, and a person's intentions can be predicted rather well from a combination of intellectual and personality characteristics. So it may be more appropriate to view the five conflict-handling intentions as relatively fixed rather than as a set of options from which individuals choose to fit an appropriate situation. That is, when confronting a conflict situation, some people want to win it all at any cost, some want to find an optimal solution, some want to run away, others want to be obliging, and still others want to "split the difference."

Stage IV: Behavior

When most people think of conflict situations, they tend to focus on Stage IV. Why? Because this is where conflicts become visible. The behavior stage includes the statements, actions, and reactions made by the conflicting parties. These conflict behaviors are usually overt attempts to implement each party's intentions. But these behaviors have a stimulus quality that is separate from intentions. As a result of miscalculations or unskilled enactments, overt behaviors sometimes deviate from original intentions.[22]

   It helps to think of Stage IV as a dynamic process of interaction. For example, you make a demand on me; I respond by arguing; you threaten me; I threaten you back; and so on. Exhibit 15-3 provides a way of visualizing conflict

intentions   *Decisions to act in a given way.*
competing   *A desire to satisfy one's interests, regardless of the impact on the other party to the conflict.*

collaborating   *A situation in which the parties to a conflict each desire to satisfy fully the concerns of all parties.*
avoiding   *The desire to withdraw from or suppress a conflict.*

accommodating   *The willingness of one party in a conflict to place the opponent's interests above his or her own.*
compromising   *A situation in which each party to a conflict is willing to give up something.*

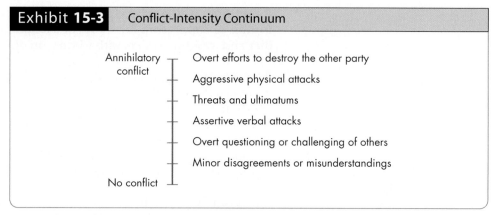

Exhibit 15-3   Conflict-Intensity Continuum

Annihilatory conflict — Overt efforts to destroy the other party

Aggressive physical attacks

Threats and ultimatums

Assertive verbal attacks

Overt questioning or challenging of others

Minor disagreements or misunderstandings

No conflict

Source: Based on S. P. Robbins, *Managing Organizational Conflict: A Nontraditional Approach* (Upper Saddle River, NJ: Prentice Hall, 1974), pp. 93–97; and F. Glasi, "The Process of Conflict Escalation and the Roles of Third Parties," in G. B. J. Bomers and R. Peterson (eds.), *Conflict Management and Industrial Relations* (Boston: Kluwer-Nijhoff, 1982), pp. 119–40.

behavior. All conflicts exist somewhere along this continuum. At the lower part of the continuum, we have conflicts characterized by subtle, indirect, and highly controlled forms of tension. An illustration might be a student questioning in class a point the instructor has just made. Conflict intensities escalate as they move upward along the continuum until they become highly destructive. Strikes, riots, and wars clearly fall in this upper range. For the most part, you should assume that conflicts that reach the upper ranges of the continuum are almost always dysfunctional. Functional conflicts are typically confined to the lower range of the continuum.

If a conflict is dysfunctional, what can the parties do to de-escalate it? Or, conversely, what options exist if conflict is too low and needs to be increased? This brings us to **conflict-management** techniques. Exhibit 15-4 lists the major resolution and stimulation techniques that allow managers to control conflict levels. Note that several of the resolution techniques were described earlier as conflict-handling intentions. This, of course, shouldn't be surprising. Under ideal conditions, a person's intentions should translate into comparable behaviors.

Stage V: Outcomes

The action–reaction interplay between the conflicting parties results in consequences. As our model (see Exhibit 15-1) demonstrates, these outcomes may be functional in that the conflict results in an improvement in the group's performance, or dysfunctional in that it hinders group performance.

Functional Outcomes   How might conflict act as a force to increase group performance? It is hard to visualize a situation in which open or violent aggression could be functional. But there are a number of instances in which it's possible to envision how low or moderate levels of conflict could improve the effectiveness of a group. Because people often find it difficult to think of instances in which conflict can be constructive, let's consider some examples and then review the research evidence. Note how all these examples focus on task and process conflicts and exclude the relationship variety.

Conflict is constructive when it improves the quality of decisions, stimulates creativity and innovation, encourages interest and curiosity among group members, provides the medium through which problems can be aired and tensions released, and fosters an environment of self-evaluation and change. The evidence suggests that conflict can improve the quality of decision making by allowing all points, particularly the ones that are unusual or held by a minority,

Exhibit **15-4**	Conflict-Management Techniques

Conflict-Resolution Techniques

Problem solving	Face-to-face meeting of the conflicting parties for the purpose of identifying the problem and resolving it through open discusssion.
Superordinate goals	Creating a shared goal that cannot be attained without the cooperation of each of the conflicting parties.
Expansion of resources	When a conflict is caused by the scarcity of a resource—say, money, promotion, opportunities, office space—expansion of the resource can create a win–win solution.
Avoidance	Withdrawal from, or suppression of, the conflict.
Smoothing	Playing down differences while emphasizing common interests between the conflicting parties.
Compromise	Each party to the conflict gives up something of value.
Authoritative command	Management uses its formal authority to resolve the conflict and then communicates its desires to the parties involved.
Altering the human variable	Using behavioral change techniques such as human relations training to alter attitudes and behaviors that cause conflict.
Altering the structural variables	Changing the formal organization structure and the interaction patterns of conflicting parties through job redesign, transfers, creation of coordinating positions, and the like.

Conflict-Stimulation Techniques

Communication	Using ambiguous or threatening messages to increase conflict levels.
Bringing in outsiders	Adding employees to a group whose backgrounds, values, attitudes, or managerial styles differ from those of present members.
Restructuring the organization	Realigning work groups, altering rules and regulations, increasing interdependence, and making similar structural changes to disrupt the status quo.
Appointing a devil's advocate	Designating a critic to purposely argue against the majority positions held by the group.

Source: Based on S. P. Robbins, *Managing Organizational Conflict: A Nontraditional Approach* (Upper Saddle River, NJ: Prentice Hall, 1974), pp. 59–89.

to be weighed in important decisions.[23] Conflict is an antidote for groupthink. It doesn't allow the group to passively "rubber-stamp" decisions that may be based on weak assumptions, inadequate consideration of relevant alternatives, or other debilities. Conflict challenges the status quo and therefore furthers the creation of new ideas, promotes reassessment of group goals and activities, and increases the probability that the group will respond to change.

For an example of a company that suffered because it had too little functional conflict, you don't have to look further than automobile behemoth General Motors.[24] Many of GM's problems, from the late 1960s to the late 1990s, can be traced to a lack of functional conflict. It hired and promoted individuals who were "yes-men," loyal to GM to the point of never questioning company actions. Managers were, for the most part, homogenous: conservative white males raised in the Midwestern United States who resisted change—they preferred looking back to past successes rather than forward to new challenges. They were almost sanctimonious in their belief that what had worked in the past would continue to work in the future. Moreover, by sheltering executives in the company's Detroit offices and encouraging them to socialize with others inside the GM ranks, the company further insulated managers from conflicting perspectives.

More recently, Yahoo! provides an illustration of a company that suffered because of too little functional conflict.[25] Begun in 1994, by 1999 Yahoo! had become one of the best-known brand names on the Internet. Then the implosion

conflict management   *The use of resolution and stimulation techniques to achieve the desired level of conflict.*

Terry Semel, a former executive at the Warner Brothers movie studio, brought expertise in handling conflict to his new job as CEO of Yahoo! Semel staged a revival at Yahoo! by replacing the firm's conflict-free culture with tight controls and functional conflict. He cut the number of business units from 44 to 5, eliminating many managers' pet projects. Semel then created a Product Council, composed of managers from different parts of the company, that serves as a rigorous sounding board for new projects. Through these moves, Semel brought focus and discipline to Yahoo! and boosted its profits.

of dot.com stocks hit. By the spring of 2001, Yahoo!'s advertising sales were plunging and the company's stock was down 92 percent from its peak. It was at this point that Yahoo!'s most critical problem became exposed: The company was too insulated and void of functional conflict. It couldn't respond to change. Managers and staff were too comfortable with each other to challenge the status quo. This kept new ideas from percolating upward and held dissent to a minimum. The source of the problem was the company's CEO, Tim Koogle. He set the tone of nonconfrontation. Only when Koogle was replaced in 2001, with a new CEO who openly challenged the company's conflict-free climate, did Yahoo! begin to successfully solve its problems.

Research studies in diverse settings confirm the functionality of conflict. Consider the following findings.

The comparison of six major decisions made during the administration of four different U.S. presidents found that conflict reduced the chance that groupthink would overpower policy decisions. The comparisons demonstrated that conformity among presidential advisors was related to poor decisions, whereas an atmosphere of constructive conflict and critical thinking surrounded the well-developed decisions.[26]

There is evidence indicating that conflict can also be positively related to productivity. For instance, it was demonstrated that, among established groups, performance tended to improve more when there was conflict among members than when there was fairly close agreement. The investigators observed that when groups analyzed decisions that had been made by the individual members of that group, the average improvement among the high-conflict groups was 73 percent greater than was that of those groups characterized by low-conflict conditions.[27] Others have found similar results: Groups composed of members with different interests tend to produce higher-quality solutions to a variety of problems than do homogeneous groups.[28]

The preceding leads us to predict that the increasing cultural diversity of the workforce should provide benefits to organizations. And that's what the evidence indicates. Research demonstrates that heterogeneity among group and organization members can increase creativity, improve the quality of decisions, and facilitate change by enhancing member flexibility.[29] For example, researchers compared decision-making groups composed of all-Caucasian individuals with groups that also contained members from Asian, Hispanic, and Black ethnic groups. The ethnically diverse groups produced more effective and more feasible ideas and the unique ideas they generated tended to be of higher quality than the unique ideas produced by the all-Caucasian group.

Similarly, studies of professionals—systems analysts and research and development scientists—support the constructive value of conflict. An investigation of 22 teams of systems analysts found that the more incompatible groups were likely to be more productive.[30] Research and development scientists have been found to be most productive when there is a certain amount of intellectual conflict.[31]

Dysfunctional Outcomes   The destructive consequences of conflict on a group's or organization's performance are generally well known. A reasonable summary might state: Uncontrolled opposition breeds discontent, which acts to dissolve common ties, and eventually leads to the destruction of the group. And, of course, there is a substantial body of literature to document how conflict—the dysfunctional varieties—can reduce group effectiveness.[32] Among the more undesirable consequences are a retarding of communication, reductions in group cohesiveness, and subordination of group goals to the primacy of infighting among members. At the extreme, conflict can bring group functioning to a halt and potentially threaten the group's survival.

The demise of an organization as a result of too much conflict isn't as unusual as it might first appear. For instance, one of New York's best-known law firms, Shea & Gould, closed down solely because the 80 partners just couldn't get along.[33] As one legal consultant familiar with the organization said: "This was a firm that had basic and principled differences among the partners that were basically irreconcilable." That same consultant also addressed the partners at their last meeting: "You don't have an economic problem," he said. "You have a personality problem. You hate each other!"

Creating Functional Conflict   In this section we ask: If managers accept the interactionist view toward conflict, what can they do to encourage functional conflict in their organizations?[34]

There seems to be general agreement that creating functional conflict is a tough job, particularly in large American corporations. As one consultant put it, "A high proportion of people who get to the top are conflict avoiders. They don't like hearing negatives; they don't like saying or thinking negative things. They frequently make it up the ladder in part because they don't irritate people on the way up." Another suggests that at least seven out of ten people in American business hush up when their opinions are at odds with those of their superiors, allowing bosses to make mistakes even when they know better.

Such anticonflict cultures may have been tolerable in the past but not in today's fiercely competitive global economy. Organizations that don't encourage and support dissent may find their survival threatened. Let's look at some approaches organizations are using to encourage their people to challenge the system and develop fresh ideas.

Hewlett-Packard rewards dissenters by recognizing go-against-the-grain types, or people who stay with the ideas they believe in even when those ideas are rejected by management. Herman Miller Inc., an office furniture manufacturer, has a formal system in which employees evaluate and criticize their bosses. IBM also has a formal system that encourages dissension. Employees can question their boss with impunity. If the disagreement can't be resolved, the system provides a third party for counsel. Royal Dutch Shell Group, General Electric, and Anheuser-Busch build devil's advocates into the decision process. For instance, when the policy committee at Anheuser-Busch considers a major move, such as getting into or out of a business or making a major capital expenditure, it often assigns teams to make the case for each side of the question. This process frequently results in decisions and alternatives that hadn't been considered previously.

One common ingredient in organizations that successfully create functional conflict is that they reward dissent and punish conflict avoiders. The real challenge for managers, however, is when they hear news that they don't want to hear. The news may make their blood boil or their hopes collapse, but they can't show it. They have to learn to take the bad news without flinching. No tirades, no tight-lipped sarcasm, no eyes rolling upward, no gritting of teeth. Rather, managers should ask calm, even-tempered questions: "Can you tell me more about what happened?" "What do you think we ought to do?" A sincere "Thank you for bringing this to my attention" will probably reduce the likelihood that managers will be cut off from similar communications in the future.

Having considered conflict—its nature, causes, and consequences—now we turn to negotiation. Negotiation and conflict are closely related because negotiation often resolves conflict.

Negotiation

Negotiation permeates the interactions of almost everyone in groups and organizations. There's the obvious: Labor bargains with management. There's the not so obvious: Managers negotiate with employees, peers, and bosses; salespeople negotiate with customers; purchasing agents negotiate with suppliers. And there's the subtle: An employee agrees to answer a colleague's phone for a few minutes in exchange for some past or future benefit. In today's loosely structured organizations, in which members are increasingly finding themselves having to work with colleagues over whom they have no direct authority and with whom they may not even share a common boss, negotiation skills become critical.

We'll define **negotiation** as a process in which two or more parties exchange goods or services and attempt to agree on the exchange rate for them.[35] Note that we'll use the terms *negotiation* and *bargaining* interchangeably. In this section, we'll contrast two bargaining strategies, provide a model of the negotiation process, ascertain the role of moods and personality traits on bargaining, review gender and cultural differences in negotiation, and take a brief look at third-party negotiations.

Bargaining Strategies

There are two general approaches to negotiation—*distributive bargaining* and *integrative bargaining*.[36] These are compared in Exhibit 15-5. As the exhibit shows, distributive and integrative bargaining differ in their goal and motivation, focus, interests, information sharing, and duration of relationship. We now define distributive and integrative bargaining and illustrate the differences between these two approaches.

Negotiation skills are critical in the buyer-seller relationship. At this open-air cheese market in Alkmaar, Netherlands, two purchasing agents for food buyers taste a sample of Edam cheese before they negotiate prices with the seller of the cheese.

Exhibit 15-5	Distributive Versus Integrative Bargaining	
Bargaining Characteristic	**Distributive Bargaining**	**Integrative Bargaining**
Goal	Get as much of the pie as possible	Expand the pie so that both parties are satisfied
Motivation	Win-Lose	Win-Win
Focus	Positions ("I can't go beyond this point on this issue.")	Interests ("Can you explain why this issue is so important to you?")
Interests	Opposed	Congruent
Information sharing	Low (sharing information will only allow other party to take advantage)	High (sharing information will allow each party to find ways to satisfy interests of each party)
Duration of relationship	Short term	Long term

Distributive Bargaining   You see a used car advertised for sale in the newspaper. It appears to be just what you've been looking for. You go out to see the car. It's great and you want it. The owner tells you the asking price. You don't want to pay that much. The two of you then negotiate over the price. The negotiating strategy you're engaging in is called **distributive bargaining**. Its most identifying feature is that it operates under zero-sum conditions. That is, any gain I make is at your expense, and vice versa. Referring back to the used-car example, every dollar you can get the seller to cut from the car's price is a dollar you save. Conversely, every dollar more the seller can get from you comes at your expense. So the essence of distributive bargaining is negotiating over who gets what share of a **fixed pie**. By fixed pie, we mean that the bargaining parties believe there is only a set amount of goods or services to be divvied up. Therefore, fixed pies are zero-sum games in that every dollar in one party's pocket is a dollar out of their counterpart's pocket. When parties believe the pie is fixed, they tend to bargain distributively.

Probably the most widely cited example of distributive bargaining is in labor-management negotiations over wages. Typically, labor's representatives come to the bargaining table determined to get as much money as possible out of management. Because every cent more that labor negotiates increases management's costs, each party bargains aggressively and treats the other as an opponent who must be defeated.

The essence of distributive bargaining is depicted in Exhibit 15-6. Parties *A* and *B* represent two negotiators. Each has a *target point* that defines what he or she would like to achieve. Each also has a *resistance point*, which marks the lowest outcome that is acceptable—the point below which they would break off negotiations rather than accept a less-favorable settlement. The area between these two points makes up each one's aspiration range. As long as there is some overlap between *A*'s and *B*'s aspiration ranges, there exists a settlement range in which each one's aspirations can be met.

When engaged in distributive bargaining, one's tactics focus on trying to get one's opponent to agree to a specific target point or to get as close to it as

negotiation   *A process in which two or more parties exchange goods or services and attempt to agree on the exchange rate for them.*

distributive bargaining   *Negotiation that seeks to divide up a fixed amount of resources; a win-lose situation.*

fixed pie   *The belief that there is only a set amount of goods or services to be divvied up between the parties.*

Exhibit 15-6	Staking Out the Bargaining Zone

possible. Examples of such tactics are persuading your opponent of the impossibility of getting to his or her target point and the advisability of accepting a settlement near yours; arguing that your target is fair, while your opponent's isn't; and attempting to get your opponent to feel emotionally generous toward you and thus accept an outcome close to your target point.

But what are some less obvious examples of distributive bargaining tactics? One routine you have likely heard of—perhaps from your favorite crime show—is the good cop, bad cop routine where one negotiator is friendly and accommodating and the other is as tough as nails. Research shows that negotiating teams that use this tactic when engaged in distributive bargaining achieve better settlements than a negotiation team that doesn't use the good cop, bad cop tactic.[37] But it appears that the good cop, bad cop routine works only when the positive negotiator follows the negative negotiator. Why? Because the positive negotiator *seems* much more accommodating and likeable after following the disagreeable negotiator. For example, let's say you're negotiating over a lease for office space with two people: Jim and Susan. When you ask for a lower rental rate, Jim reacts very negatively—accusing you of deception, making threats about leasing the space to another party, and in general appearing irritated and disrespectful. Jim leaves and Susan takes over. Susan apologizes for Jim's behavior. She appears to be understanding of your position and also seems supportive and cooperative. But she politely says they've made the best offer they possibly can. Do you think you'd accept Susan's terms? Judging from past research, you probably would, because the contrast between Susan's and Jim's behavior leads you to believe that you've done your best, and you form a liking for Susan and want to cooperate with her.

Another distributive bargaining tactic is revealing a deadline. Consider the following example. Erin is a human resources manager. She is negotiating salary with Ron, who is a highly sought after new hire. Because Ron knows the company needs him, he decides to play hardball and ask for an extraordinary salary and many benefits. Erin tells Ron that the company can't meet his requirements. Ron tells Erin he is going to have to think things over. Worried the company is going to lose Ron to a competitor, Erin decides to tell Ron that she is under time pressure and that she needs to reach an agreement with him immediately or she will have to offer the job to another candidate. Would you consider Erin to be a savvy negotiator? Well, she is. Why? Negotiators who reveal deadlines speed concessions from their negotiating counterparts, making them reconsider their position. And even though negotiators don't *think* this tactic works, in reality negotiators who reveal deadlines do better.[38]

Integrative Bargaining   A sales representative for a women's sportswear manufacturer has just closed a $15,000 order from a small clothing retailer. The sales rep calls in the order to her firm's credit department. She is told that the firm can't approve credit to this customer because of a past slow-payment

General Motors chairman Rick Wagoner (standing front left) and United Auto Workers president Ron Gettelfinger shook hands when they opened negotiations for a new contract expiring in 2007. Both General Motors management and the union are committed to integrative bargaining in finding mutually agreeable solutions to complex problems such as rising health-care costs and the funding of pension plans. This attempt at integrative bargaining contrasts with past negotiations that were essentially distributive in nature.

record. The next day, the sales rep and the firm's credit manager meet to discuss the problem. The sales rep doesn't want to lose the business. Neither does the credit manager, but he also doesn't want to get stuck with an uncollectible debt. The two openly review their options. After considerable discussion, they agree on a solution that meets both their needs: The credit manager will approve the sale, but the clothing store's owner will provide a bank guarantee that will ensure payment if the bill isn't paid within 60 days. This sales-credit negotiation is an example of **integrative bargaining**. In contrast to distributive bargaining, integrative bargaining operates under the assumption that there exists one or more settlements that can create a win-win solution.

In terms of intraorganizational behavior, all things being equal, integrative bargaining is preferable to distributive bargaining. Why? Because the former builds long-term relationships. It bonds negotiators and allows them to leave the bargaining table feeling that they have achieved a victory. Distributive bargaining, however, leaves one party a loser. It tends to build animosities and deepen divisions when people have to work together on an ongoing basis.

Why, then, don't we see more integrative bargaining in organizations? The answer lies in the conditions necessary for this type of negotiation to succeed. These include parties who are open with information and candid about their concerns, a sensitivity by both parties to the other's needs, the ability to trust one another, and a willingness by both parties to maintain flexibility.[39] Because these conditions often don't exist in organizations, it isn't surprising that negotiations often take on a win-at-any-cost dynamic.

There are some ways to achieve more integrative outcomes. For example, individuals who bargain in teams reach more integrative agreements than those who bargain individually. This happens because more ideas are generated when

integrative bargaining   *Negotiation that seeks one or more settlements that can create a win-win solution.*

more people are at the bargaining table. So, try bargaining in teams.[40] Another way to achieve higher joint-gain settlements is to put more issues on the table. The more negotiable issues that are introduced into a negotiation, the more opportunity there is for "logrolling" where issues are traded because of differences in preferences. This creates better outcomes for each side than if each issue were negotiated individually.[41]

Finally, you should realize that compromise may be your worst enemy in negotiating a win-win agreement. This is because compromising reduces the pressure to bargain integratively. After all, if you or your opponent caves in easily, it doesn't require anyone to be creative to reach a settlement. Thus, people end up settling for less than they could have obtained if they had been forced to consider the other party's interests, trade off issues, and be creative.[42] Think of the classic example where two sisters are arguing over who gets an orange. Unbeknownst to the other party, one sister wants the orange to drink the juice, whereas the other sister wants the orange peel to bake a cake. If one sister simply capitulates and gives the other sister the orange, then they never would have been forced to explore their reasons for wanting the orange, and thus they never would find the win-win solution: They could *each* have the orange because they want different parts of it!

The Negotiation Process

Exhibit 15-7 provides a simplified model of the negotiation process. It views negotiation as made up of five steps: (1) preparation and planning; (2) definition of ground rules; (3) clarification and justification; (4) bargaining and problem solving; and (5) closure and implementation.[43]

Preparation and Planning   Before you start negotiating, you need to do your homework. What's the nature of the conflict? What's the history leading up to this negotiation? Who's involved and what are their perceptions of the conflict?

What do you want from the negotiation? What are *your* goals? If you're a supply manager at Dell Computer, for instance, and your goal is to get a significant cost reduction from your supplier of keyboards, make sure that this goal stays paramount in your discussions and doesn't get overshadowed by other issues. It often helps to put your goals in writing and develop a range of outcomes—from "most hopeful" to "minimally acceptable"—to keep your attention focused.

You also want to prepare an assessment of what you think the other party's goals are. What are they likely to ask for? How entrenched are they likely to be in their position? What intangible or hidden interests may be important to them? What might they be willing to settle on? When you can anticipate your opponent's position, you are better equipped to counter arguments with the facts and figures that support your position.

The importance of sizing up the other party is illustrated by the experience of Keith Rosenbaum, a partner in a major Los Angeles law firm. "Once when we were negotiating to buy a business, we found that the owner was going through a nasty divorce. We were on good terms with the wife's attorney and we learned the seller's net worth. California is a community-property-law state, so we knew he had to pay her half of everything. We knew his time frame. We knew what he was willing to part with and what he was not. We knew a lot more about him than he would have wanted us to know. We were able to twist him a little bit, and get a better price."[44]

Once you've gathered your information, use it to develop a strategy. For example, expert chess players have a strategy. They know ahead of time how they will respond to any given situation. As part of your strategy, you should determine yours and the other side's *Best Alternative To a Negotiated Agreement* (**BATNA**).[45] Your BATNA determines the lowest value acceptable to

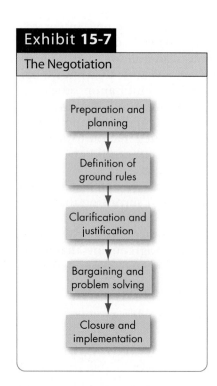

Exhibit 15-7

The Negotiation

Preparation and planning

↓

Definition of ground rules

↓

Clarification and justification

↓

Bargaining and problem solving

↓

Closure and implementation

you for a negotiated agreement. Any offer you receive that is higher than your BATNA is better than an impasse. Conversely, you shouldn't expect success in your negotiation effort unless you're able to make the other side an offer they find more attractive than their BATNA. If you go into your negotiation having a good idea of what the other party's BATNA is, even if you're not able to meet theirs, you might be able to get them to change it.

Definition of Ground Rules   Once you've done your planning and developed a strategy, you're ready to begin defining the ground rules and procedures with the other party over the negotiation itself. Who will do the negotiating? Where will it take place? What time constraints, if any, will apply? To what issues will negotiation be limited? Will there be a specific procedure to follow if an impasse is reached? During this phase, the parties will also exchange their initial proposals or demands.

Clarification and Justification   When initial positions have been exchanged, both you and the other party will explain, amplify, clarify, bolster, and justify your original demands. This needn't be confrontational. Rather, it's an opportunity for educating and informing each other on the issues, why they are important, and how each arrived at their initial demands. This is the point at which you might want to provide the other party with any documentation that helps support your position.

Bargaining and Problem Solving   The essence of the negotiation process is the actual give-and-take in trying to hash out an agreement. It is here where concessions will undoubtedly need to be made by both parties.

Closure and Implementation   The final step in the negotiation process is formalizing the agreement that has been worked out and developing any procedures that are necessary for implementation and monitoring. For major negotiations—which would include everything from labor-management negotiations to bargaining over lease terms to buying a piece of real estate to negotiating a job offer for a senior management position—this will require hammering out the specifics in a formal contract. For most cases, however, closure of the negotiation process is nothing more formal than a handshake.

Issues in Negotiation

We conclude our discussion of negotiation by reviewing four contemporary issues in negotiation: the role of mood and personality traits, gender differences in negotiating, the effect of cultural differences on negotiating styles, and the use of third parties to help resolve differences.

The Role of Mood and Personality Traits in Negotiation   You're probably not surprised to learn that mood matters in negotiation. Negotiators who are in positive moods negotiate better outcomes than those who are in average moods. Why? Negotiators who are upbeat or happy tend to trust the other party more and therefore reach more joint-gain settlements.[46] Let's assume Carlos, a

BATNA   *The best alternative to a negotiated agreement; the lowest acceptable value to an individual for a negotiated agreement.*

manager, is a very effective negotiator. One of the reasons Carlos is a good negotiator is because he opens negotiations by trying to put his counterparts in a good mood—he tells jokes, provides refreshments, or emphasizes the positive side of what's at stake. This technique makes his counterparts bargain more integratively because they communicate their priorities, they more accurately perceive others' interests, and they also think more creatively.

What about personality? Can you predict an opponent's negotiating tactics if you know something about his or her personality? It's tempting to answer "Yes" to this question. For instance, you might assume that high-risk takers would be more aggressive bargainers who make fewer concessions. Surprisingly, the evidence hasn't always supported this intuition.[47]

Assessments of the personality–negotiation relationship have been that personality traits have no significant direct effect on either the bargaining process or the negotiation outcomes. However, recent research has started to question the theory that personality and the negotiation process aren't connected. In fact, it appears that several of the Big Five traits are related to negotiation outcomes. For example, negotiators who are agreeable or extraverted are not very successful when it comes to distributive bargaining. Why? Because extraverts are outgoing and friendly, they tend to share more information than they should. And agreeable people are more interested in finding ways to cooperate rather than butt heads. These traits, while slightly helpful in integrative negotiations, are liabilities when interests are opposed.[48] So, the best distributive bargainer appears to be a disagreeable introvert—that is, someone who is interested in his own outcomes versus pleasing the other party and having a pleasant social exchange.

A big ego can also affect negotiations. For example, Samantha is an executive with a major clothing manufacturer. She is convinced that everything she touches turns to gold, and she cannot stand to look bad. An important contract with one of her company's suppliers just came up for negotiation. Excited, Samantha thinks she will take the reins during the negotiation process, but her boss tells her she is off the negotiating team. Is her boss smart to keep such a hardliner off the case? Absolutely. Why? Because a study found that individuals who are concerned with appearing competent and successful in negotiations (that is, saving face)—can have a negative affect on the outcome of the negotiation process. Individuals who were more concerned with saving face were less likely to reach agreements than those who were less concerned with coming out on top. This is because those who are overly competitive in negotiating negotiate to look good personally rather

Exhibit 15-8

than to attain the best agreement for all concerned.[49] So those who are able to check their egos at the door are able to negotiate better agreements—for themselves and for others, whether the bargaining situation is distributive or integrative.

Gender Differences in Negotiations   Do men and women negotiate differently? And does gender affect negotiation outcomes? The answer to the first question appears to be No.[50] The answer to the second is a qualified Yes.[51]

A popular stereotype held by many is that women are more cooperative and pleasant in negotiations than are men. The evidence doesn't support this belief. However, men have been found to negotiate better outcomes than women, although the difference is relatively small. It's been postulated that this difference might be due to men and women placing divergent values on outcomes. "It is possible that a few hundred dollars more in salary or the corner office is less important to women than forming and maintaining an interpersonal relationship."[52]

The belief that women are "nicer" than men in negotiations is probably due to confusing gender and the lower power typically held by women in most large organizations. The research indicates that low-power managers, regardless of gender, attempt to placate their opponents and to use softly persuasive tactics rather than direct confrontation and threats. In situations in which women and men have similar power bases, there shouldn't be any significant differences in their negotiation styles. It's interesting to note that when typical stereotypes are activated—that is, women are "nicer" and men are "tougher"—it becomes a self-fulfilling prophecy, reinforcing the stereotypical gender differences between male and female negotiators.[53] For example, Maria may set lower aspirations and give in more readily when negotiating because she thinks, even subconsciously, that's how women are expected to bargain. Similarly, Sunil may think he has to bargain aggressively because he believes that's how men are expected to negotiate.

The evidence suggests that women's attitudes toward negotiation and toward themselves as negotiators appear to be quite different from men's. Managerial women demonstrate less confidence in anticipation of negotiating and are less satisfied with their performance after the process is complete, even when their performance and the outcomes they achieve are similar to those for men.[54] This latter conclusion suggests that women may unduly penalize themselves by failing to engage in negotiations when such action would be in their best interests.

Cultural Differences in Negotiations   Negotiating styles clearly vary across national cultures.[55] The French like conflict. They frequently gain recognition and develop their reputations by thinking and acting against others. As a result, the French tend to take a long time in negotiating agreements and they aren't overly concerned about whether their opponents like or dislike them.[56] The Chinese also draw out negotiations but that's because they believe negotiations never end. Just when you think you've pinned down every detail and reached a final solution with a Chinese executive, that executive might smile and start the process all over again. The Chinese—and the Japanese, too—negotiate to develop a relationship and a commitment to work together rather than to tie up every loose end.[57] Compared to American negotiators, the Japanese communicate indirectly and adapt their behaviors to the situation.[58] Americans are known around the world for their impatience and their desire to be liked.[59] Astute negotiators from other countries often turn these characteristics to their advantage by dragging out negotiations and making friendship conditional on the final settlement. Exhibit 15-9

In negotiating the creation of a theme park in France, Walt Disney Company learned about cultural differences when it presented its plan to the French government. In France, a hierarchical country, decisions are made at the top. So the top leader in France, the late Prime Minister Francois Mitterand, was involved in the negotiations of Euro Disneyland. To navigate the levels of hierarchy, Disney hired local French people who were familiar with the rules of decision making to secure official approvals for its project.

Exhibit **15-9**	Why American Managers Might Have Trouble in Cross-Cultural Negotiations

- Italians, Germans, and French don't soften up executives with praise before they criticize. Americans do, and to many Europeans this seems manipulative.
- Israelis, accustomed to fast-paced meetings, have no patience for American small talk.
- British executives often complain that their U.S. counterparts chatter too much.
- Indian executives are used to interrupting one another. When Americans listen without asking for clarification or posing questions, Indians can feel the Americans aren't paying attention.
- Americans often mix their business and personal lives. They think nothing, for instance, about asking a colleague a question like, "How was your weekend?" In many cultures such a question is seen as intrusive because business and private lives are totally compartmentalized.

Source: Adapted from L. Khosla, "You Say Tomato," *Forbes,* May 21, 2001, p. 36.

offers some insights into why American managers might have trouble in cross-cultural negotiations.

The cultural context of the negotiation significantly influences the amount and type of preparation for bargaining, the relative emphasis on task versus interpersonal relationships, the tactics used, and even where the negotiation should be conducted. To further illustrate some of these differences, let's look at two studies that compare the influence of culture on business negotiations.

The first study compared North Americans, Arabs, and Russians.[60] Among the factors looked at were their negotiating style, how they responded to an opponent's arguments, their approach to making concessions, and how they handled negotiating deadlines. North Americans tried to persuade by relying on facts and appealing to logic. They countered opponents' arguments with objective facts. They made small concessions early in the negotiation to establish a relationship and usually reciprocated opponent's concessions. North Americans treated deadlines as very important. The Arabs tried to persuade by appealing to emotion. They countered opponent's arguments with subjective feelings. They made concessions throughout the bargaining process and almost always reciprocated opponents' concessions. Arabs approached deadlines very casually. The Russians based their arguments on asserted ideals. They made few, if any, concessions. Any concession offered by an opponent was viewed as a weakness and almost never reciprocated. Finally, the Russians tended to ignore deadlines.

The second study looked at verbal and nonverbal negotiation tactics exhibited by North Americans, Japanese, and Brazilians during half-hour bargaining sessions.[61] Some of the differences were particularly interesting. For instance, the Brazilians on average said "No" 83 times, compared to 5 times for the Japanese and 9 times for the North Americans. The Japanese displayed more than 5 periods of silence lasting longer than 10 seconds during the 30-minute sessions. North Americans averaged 3.5 such periods; the Brazilians had none. The Japanese and North Americans interrupted their opponent about the same number of times, but the Brazilians interrupted 2.5 to 3 times more often than the North Americans and the Japanese. Finally, the Japanese and the North Americans had no physical contact with their opponents during negotiations except for handshaking, but the Brazilians touched each other almost five times every half hour.

Now that you know more about the different types of bargaining strategies, the negotiation process in general, and contemporary issues in negotiation, do you think you could negotiate with the best of them? Take the self-assessment to learn about your negotiating style.

Negotiating Across Cultures

OBTAINING A FAVORABLE OUTCOME IN A NEGOTIAtion may in part depend on the cultural characteristics of your opponent. A study of negotiators in the United States, China, and Japan found that culture plays an important role in successful negotiation. The study found that, overall, negotiators who had both a self-serving "egoistic" orientation and a high goal level fared the best overall compared to negotiators with an otherserving "prosocial" orientation and low goal level. In other words, the strategy combining a self-serving negotiation position, where one is focused only on maximizing one's own outcomes, coupled with a strong desire to obtain the best outcomes, led to the most favorable negotiation results.

However, the degree to which this particular strategy resulted in better outcomes depended on the negotiating partner. The results showed that being self-serving and having a high negotiation goal level resulted in higher outcomes (in this case, profits) only when the negotiating opponent was other-serving. Negotiators from the United States are more likely to be self-serving and have high goal levels. In China and Japan, however, there is a greater likelihood that negotiators are other-serving and thus are more concerned with others' outcomes. Consequently, negotiators from the United States are likely to obtain better outcomes for themselves when negotiating with individuals from China and Japan because American negotiators tend to be more concerned with their own outcomes, sometimes at the expense of the other party.

Though this study suggests that being self-serving can be beneficial in some situations, negotiators should be wary of being too self-serving. Though American negotiators may benefit from a self-serving negotiation position and a high goal level when negotiating with individuals from China or Japan, being too self-serving may result in damaged relationships, leading to less favorable outcomes in the long run.

Source: Based on Y. Chen, E. A. Mannix, and T. Okumura, "The Importance of Who You Meet: Effects of Self- Versus Other-Concerns Among Negotiators in the United States, the People's Republic of China, and Japan," *Journal of Experimental Social Psychology,* January, 2003, pp. 1–15.

SELF ASSESSMENT LIBRARY

WHAT'S MY NEGOTIATING STYLE?

In the Self-Assessment Library (available on CD, online, and in print), take assessment II.C.6 (What's My Negotiating Style?) and answer the following questions.

1. *Are you surprised by your score?*
2. *Do you think your perception of your negotiating skills might hinder your ability to negotiate effectively? If yes, why? If no, why not?*
3. *Drawing from the material in the chapter, how might you improve your negotiating skills?*

Third-Party Negotiations To this point, we've discussed bargaining in terms of direct negotiations. Occasionally, however, individuals or group representatives reach a stalemate and are unable to resolve their differences through direct negotiations. In such cases, they may turn to a third party to help them find a solution. There are four basic third-party roles: mediator, arbitrator, conciliator, and consultant.[62]

An Effective Negotiation Experience

After Russ Berrie & Co. acquired the company that made Koosh Ball, it was Bernie Tenenbaum's job to improve sales and profit. The balls were made in Asia so he began by flying to Hong Kong and meeting with the manufacturer. But before the meeting, he contacted another firm in Asia to get a competitive price. They offered to make the balls for 3 cents less per ball. Tenenbaum now knew there was room for cost cutting with his primary manufacturer.

Upon arriving in Hong Kong, Tenenbaum and his executive team had a very elaborate dinner with the current manufacturer and his whole family to find out whether it was possible to get the price down. Tenenbaum says he had three goals at that dinner. "First, we want to have a good relationship. Especially in China, your word really matters and the honor you give your partner means everything. If we had walked in and said, 'I've second-sourced your product and we can make it for 3 cents less,' he might have walked away because we would've embarrassed him. Second, we wanted to let him know we were growing the business and there was an opportunity for him to make more products for us. Third, we had to ask for his help. We never told him we needed to lower his price; we asked, was there anything he could do to help us. He understood what we meant, and he came back with a price that was a penny below the second source."

Source: Based on "How to Treat Your Adversary With Respect—and Win," *INC.*, August 2003, p. 77.

A **mediator** is a neutral third party who facilitates a negotiated solution by using reasoning and persuasion, suggesting alternatives, and the like. Mediators are widely used in labor-management negotiations and in civil court disputes. The overall effectiveness of mediated negotiations is fairly impressive. The settlement rate is approximately 60 percent, with negotiator satisfaction at about 75 percent. But the situation is the key to whether or not mediation will succeed; the conflicting parties must be motivated to bargain and resolve their conflict. In addition, conflict intensity can't be too high; mediation is most effective under moderate levels of conflict. Finally, perceptions of the mediator are important; to be effective, the mediator must be perceived as neutral and noncoercive.

An **arbitrator** is a third party with the authority to dictate an agreement. Arbitration can be voluntary (requested) or compulsory (forced on the parties by law or contract).

The authority of the arbitrator varies according to the rules set by the negotiators. For instance, the arbitrator might be limited to choosing one of the negotiator's last offers or to suggesting an agreement point that is nonbinding, or free to choose and make any judgment he or she wishes.

The big plus of arbitration over mediation is that it always results in a settlement. Whether or not there is a negative side depends on how "heavy-handed" the arbitrator appears. If one party is left feeling overwhelmingly defeated, that party is certain to be dissatisfied and unlikely to graciously accept the arbitrator's decision. Therefore, the conflict may resurface at a later time.

A **conciliator** is a trusted third party who provides an informal communication link between the negotiator and the opponent. This role was made famous by Robert Duval in the first *Godfather* film. As Don Corleone's adopted son and a lawyer by training, Duval acted as an intermediary between the Corleone family and the other Mafioso families.

Conciliation is used extensively in international, labor, family, and community disputes. Comparing its effectiveness to mediation has proven difficult because the two overlap a great deal. In practice, conciliators typically act as more than mere communication conduits. They also engage in fact-finding, interpreting messages, and persuading disputants to develop agreements.

A **consultant** is a skilled and impartial third party who attempts to facilitate problem solving through communication and analysis, aided by a knowledge of conflict management. In contrast to the previous roles, the consultant's role is not to settle the issues, but, rather, to improve relations between the conflicting parties so that they can reach a settlement themselves. Instead of putting forward specific solutions, the consultant tries to help the parties learn to understand and work with each other. Therefore, this approach has a longer-term focus: to build new and positive perceptions and attitudes between the conflicting parties.

Summary and Implications for Managers

Many people automatically assume that conflict is related to lower group and organizational performance. This chapter has demonstrated that this assumption is frequently incorrect. Conflict can be either constructive or destructive to the functioning of a group or unit. As shown in Exhibit 15-10,

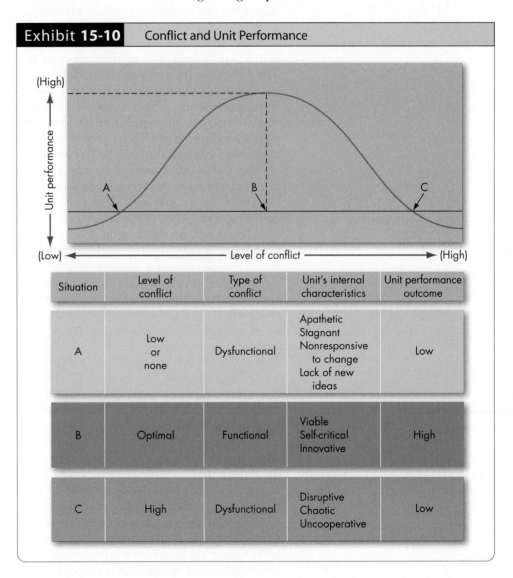

Exhibit **15-10**	Conflict and Unit Performance

Situation	Level of conflict	Type of conflict	Unit's internal characteristics	Unit performance outcome
A	Low or none	Dysfunctional	Apathetic Stagnant Nonresponsive to change Lack of new ideas	Low
B	Optimal	Functional	Viable Self-critical Innovative	High
C	High	Dysfunctional	Disruptive Chaotic Uncooperative	Low

mediator   *A neutral third party who facilitates a negotiated solution by using reasoning, persuasion, and suggestions for alternatives.*

arbitrator   *A third party to a negotiation who has the authority to dictate an agreement.*

conciliator   *A trusted third party who provides an informal communication link between the negotiator and the opponent.*

consultant   *An impartial third party, skilled in conflict management, who attempts to facilitate creative problem solving through communication and analysis.*

levels of conflict can be either too high or too low. Either extreme hinders performance. An optimal level is one at which there is enough conflict to prevent stagnation, stimulate creativity, allow tensions to be released, and initiate the seeds for change, yet not so much as to be disruptive or to deter coordination of activities.

Inadequate or excessive levels of conflict can hinder the effectiveness of a group or an organization, resulting in reduced satisfaction of group members, increased absence and turnover rates, and, eventually, lower productivity. However, when conflict is at an optimal level, complacency and apathy should be minimized, motivation should be enhanced through the creation of a challenging and questioning environment with a vitality that makes work interesting, and there should be the amount of turnover needed to rid the organization of misfits and poor performers.

What advice can we give managers faced with excessive conflict and the need to reduce it? Don't assume there's one conflict-handling intention that will always be best! You should select an intention appropriate for the situation. The following provides some guidelines:[63]

Use *competition* when quick, decisive action is vital (in emergencies); on important issues, where unpopular actions need implementing (in cost cutting, enforcing unpopular rules, discipline); on issues vital to the organization's welfare when you know you're right; and against people who take advantage of noncompetitive behavior.

Use *collaboration* to find an integrative solution when both sets of concerns are too important to be compromised; when your objective is to learn; to merge insights from people with different perspectives; to gain commitment by incorporating concerns into a consensus; and to work through feelings that have interfered with a relationship.

Use *avoidance* when an issue is trivial or more important issues are pressing; when you perceive no chance of satisfying your concerns; when potential disruption outweighs the benefits of resolution; to let people cool down and regain perspective; when gathering information supersedes immediate decision; when others can resolve the conflict more effectively; and when issues seem tangential or symptomatic of other issues.

Use *accommodation* when you find you're wrong and to allow a better position to be heard, to learn, and to show your reasonableness; when issues are more important to others than to yourself and to satisfy others and maintain cooperation; to build social credits for later issues; to minimize loss when you are outmatched and losing; when harmony and stability are especially important; and to allow employees to develop by learning from mistakes.

Use *compromise* when goals are important but not worth the effort of potential disruption of more assertive approaches; when opponents with equal power are committed to mutually exclusive goals; to achieve temporary settlements to complex issues; to arrive at expedient solutions under time pressure; and as a backup when collaboration or competition is unsuccessful.

Negotiation was shown to be an ongoing activity in groups and organizations. Distributive bargaining can resolve disputes but it often negatively affects one or more negotiators' satisfaction because it is focused on the short term and because it is confrontational. Integrative bargaining, in contrast, tends to provide outcomes that satisfy all parties and that build lasting relationships.

Point ◀▷ Counterpoint

Conflict Benefits Organizations

Let's briefly review how stimulating conflict can provide benefits to the organization.

Conflict is a means by which to bring about radical change. It's an effective device by which management can drastically change the existing power structure, current interaction patterns, and entrenched attitudes.

Conflict facilitates group cohesiveness. Whereas conflict increases hostility between groups, external threats tend to cause a group to pull together as a unit. Intergroup conflicts raise the extent to which members identify with their own group and increase feelings of solidarity.

Conflict improves group and organizational effectiveness. The stimulation of conflict initiates the search for new means and goals and provides the stimulus for innovation. The successful solution of a conflict leads to greater effectiveness, to more trust and openness, to greater attraction of members for each other, and to depersonalization of future conflicts.

Conflict brings about a slightly higher, more constructive level of tension. When the level of tension is very low, the parties are not sufficiently motivated to do something about a conflict.

Groups or organizations devoid of conflict are likely to suffer from apathy, stagnation, groupthink, and other debilitating diseases. In fact, more organizations probably fail because they have *too little* conflict, not because they have too much. Take a look at a list of large organizations that have failed or suffered serious financial setbacks over the past decade or two. You see names like Smith Corona, Western Union, Kmart, Montgomery Ward, Morrison Knudsen, Greyhound, and Digital Computer. The common thread through these companies is that they stagnated. Their managements became complacent and unable or unwilling to facilitate change. These organizations could have benefited from functional conflict.

It may be true that conflict is an inherent part of any group or organization. It may not be possible to eliminate it completely. However, just because conflicts exist is no reason to deify them. In general, conflicts are dysfunctional, and it is one of management's major responsibilities to keep conflict intensity as low as humanly possible. A few points will support this case.

The negative consequences from conflict can be devastating. The list of negatives associated with conflict is awesome. The most obvious are increased turnover, decreased employee satisfaction, inefficiencies between work units, sabotage, and labor grievances and strikes. One study estimated that managing conflict at work costs the average employer nearly 450 days of management time a year.[64] And there are also emotional costs. Think about the nervous tension that arises when people argue. Conflict also stimulates anger. And there is a clear link between anger and physical aggression. These emotions should be avoided, not cultivated.

Effective managers build teamwork. A good manager builds a coordinated team. Conflict works against such an objective. A successful work group is like a successful sports team; each member knows his or her role and supports his or her teammates. When a team works well, the whole becomes greater than the sum of the parts. Management creates teamwork by minimizing internal conflicts and facilitating internal coordination.

Managers who accept and stimulate conflict don't survive in organizations. The whole argument of the value of conflict may be moot as long as the majority of senior executives in organizations view conflict from the traditional view. In the traditional view, any conflict will be seen as bad. Since the evaluation of a manager's performance is made by higher-level executives, those managers who do not succeed in eliminating conflicts are likely to be appraised negatively. This, in turn, will reduce opportunities for advancement. Any manager who aspires to move up in such an environment will be wise to follow the traditional view and eliminate any outward signs of conflict. Failure to follow this advice might result in the premature departure of the manager.

Questions for Review

1. What are the disadvantages to conflict? What are its advantages?

2. What is the difference between functional and dysfunctional conflict? What determines functionality?

3. Under what conditions might conflict be beneficial to a group?

4. What are the components in the conflict process model? From your own experiences, give an example of how a conflict proceeded through the five stages.

5. How could a manager stimulate conflict in his or her department?

6. What defines the settlement range in distributive bargaining?

7. Why isn't integrative bargaining more widely practiced in organizations?

8. How do men and women differ, if at all, in their approaches to negotiation?

9. What problems might Americans have in negotiating with people from collectivist cultures like China and Japan?

10. What can you do to improve your negotiating effectiveness?

Questions for Critical Thinking

1. Do you think competition and conflict are different? Explain.

2. "Participation is an excellent method for identifying differences and resolving conflicts." Do you agree or disagree? Discuss.

3. From your own experience, describe a situation in which you were involved for which the conflict was dysfunctional. Describe another example, from your experience for which the conflict was functional. Now analyze how other parties in both conflicts might have interpreted the situation in terms of whether the conflicts were functional or dysfunctional.

4. Assume a Canadian had to negotiate a contract with someone from Spain. What problems might come up? What suggestions would you make to help facilitate a settlement?

5. Paul S. Pressler, CEO at The Gap Inc., wants to stimulate conflict inside his firm. But he wants to minimize conflict with outside parties—agents, contractors, unions, and so on. What does this say about conflict levels, functional versus dysfunctional conflict, and managing conflict?

Team Exercise

A NEGOTIATION ROLE PLAY

This role play is designed to help you develop your negotiating skills. The class is to break into pairs. One person will play the role of Alex, the department supervisor. The other person will play C.J., Alex's boss. Both participants should read The Situation, The Negotiation, and then their role only.

The Situation

Alex and C.J. work for Nike in Portland, Oregon. Alex supervises a research laboratory. C.J. is the manager of research and development. Alex and C.J. are former college runners who have worked for Nike for more than 6 years. C.J. has been Alex's boss for 2 years. One of Alex's employees has greatly impressed Alex. This employee is Lisa Roland. Lisa was hired 11 months ago. She is 24 years old and holds a master's degree in mechanical engineering. Her entry-level salary was $47,500 a year. She was told

by Alex that, in accordance with corporation policy, she would receive an initial performance evaluation at 6 months and a comprehensive review after 1 year. Based on her performance record, Lisa was told she could expect a salary adjustment at the time of the 1-year evaluation.

Alex's evaluation of Lisa after 6 months was very positive. Alex commented on the long hours Lisa was putting in, her cooperative spirit, the fact that others in the lab enjoyed working with her, and that she was making an immediate positive impact on the project she had been assigned. Now that Lisa's first anniversary is coming up, Alex has again reviewed Lisa's performance. Alex thinks Lisa may be the best new person the R&D group has ever hired. After only a year, Alex has ranked Lisa as the number-three performer in a department of 11.

Salaries in the department vary greatly. Alex, for instance, has a base salary of $76,000, plus eligibility for a bonus that might add another $7,000 to $12,000 a year. The salary range of the 11 department members is $38,400 to $66,350. The lowest salary is a recent hire with a bachelor's degree in physics. The two people that Alex has rated above Lisa earn base salaries of $59,200 and $66,350. They're both 27 years old and have been at Nike for 3 and 4 years, respectively. The median salary in Alex's department is $54,960.

Alex's Role

You want to give Lisa a big raise. Although she's young, she has proven to be an excellent addition to the department. You don't want to lose her. More importantly, she knows in general what other people in the department are earning and she thinks she's underpaid. The company typically gives 1-year raises of 5 percent, although 10 percent is not unusual and 20 to 30 percent increases have been approved on occasion. You'd like to get Lisa as large an increase as C.J. will approve.

C.J.'s Role

All your supervisors typically try to squeeze you for as much money as they can for their people. You understand this because you did the same thing when you were a supervisor, but your boss wants to keep a lid on costs. He wants you to keep raises for recent hires generally in the 5-to-8-percent range. In fact, he's sent a memo to all managers and supervisors saying this. He also said that managers will be evaluated on their ability to maintain budgetary control. However, your boss is also concerned with equity and paying people what they're worth. You feel assured that he will support any salary recommendation you make, as long as it can be justified. Your goal, consistent with cost reduction, is to keep salary increases as low as possible.

The Negotiation

Alex has a meeting scheduled with C.J. to discuss Lisa's performance review and salary adjustment. Take a couple of minutes to think through the facts in this exercise and to prepare a strategy. Then you have up to 15 minutes to conduct your negotiation. When your negotiation is complete, the class will compare the various strategies used and pair outcomes.

Ethical Dilemma

IS IT UNETHICAL TO LIE AND DECEIVE DURING NEGOTIATIONS?

In Chapter 11, we addressed lying in the context of communication. Here we return to the topic of lying but specifically as it relates to negotiation. We think this issue is important because, for many people, there is no such thing as lying when it comes to negotiating.

It's been said that the whole notion of negotiation is built on ethical quicksand: To succeed, you must deceive. Is this true? Apparently a lot of people think so. For instance, one study found that 28 percent of negotiators lied about a common-interest issue during negotiations, while another study found that 100 percent of negotiators either failed to reveal a problem or actively lied about it during negotiations if they were not directly asked about the issue. Why do you think these numbers are so high? The research on negotiation provides numerous examples of when lying gives the negotiator a strategic advantage.[65]

Is it possible for someone to maintain high ethical standards and, at the same time, deal with the daily need to negotiate with bosses, peers, staff, people from other organizations, friends, and even relatives?

We can probably agree that bald-faced lies during negotiation are wrong. At least most ethicists would probably agree. The universal dilemma surrounds the little lies—the omissions, evasions, and concealments that are often necessary to best an opponent.

During negotiations, when is a lie a *lie*? Is exaggerating benefits, downplaying negatives, ignoring flaws, or saying "I don't know" when in reality you do considered lying? Is declaring that "this is my final offer and nonnegotiable" (even when you're posturing) a lie? Is pretending to bend over backward to make meaningful concessions lying? Rather than being considered unethical practices, the use of these "lies" is considered by many as indicators that a negotiator is strong, smart, and savvy.

When is evasiveness and deception out of bounds? Is it naive to be completely honest and bare your soul during negotiations? Or are the rules of negotiations unique: Any tactic that will improve your chance of winning is acceptable?

Source: Based on M. E. Schweitzer, "Deception in Negotiations," in S. J. Hoch and H. C. Kunreuther (eds.), *Wharton on Making Decisions* (New York: Wiley, 2001), pp. 187–200; and M. Diener, "Fair Enough," *Entrepreneur*, January 2002, pp. 100–102.

Case Incident 1

SCHNEIDER NATIONAL

Schneider National is a Green Bay, Wisconsin-based transportation and logistics firm. Begun in 1935, the private company now operates 14,000 trucks and 40,000 trailers that haul freight 5 million miles per day. Revenues are approximately $2.4 billion a year.

The company has had only three leaders. The first was the founder; second was his son, Donald; and in August 2002, the first nonfamily member took the helm when Chris Lofgren was made CEO, replacing Schneider who was 67 years old. But it wasn't as if the company wasn't making preparations for executive leadership. Don Schneider told his board of directors in 1988 that their primary task was finding a successor. Lofgren joined the company in 1994 as a vice president and became chief operating officer in 2000. After being appointed COO, Lofgren began to lay the framework for the six-person executive group that today shares many of the company's strategic responsibilities.

Everyone who knows Don Schneider concedes that he's a tough act to follow. "Don is an icon," says another top Schneider executive. "He probably commands more respect in transportation and logistics than anybody in the industry." Says Lofgren, "Our approach has been to put together an executive team that has a set of skills, perspectives and experiences that, when you put that team together, is broader and bigger than Don Schneider." The idea, according to Lofgren, is to have individuals with product-line or functional focus, and, while maintaining their oversight of those areas, who develop a sense of responsibility for the financial performance of the whole company. "If you have people who aren't taking an enterprise solution, their only role is their function or their business, then ultimately it has to go to someone who's going to referee the points of tension," says Lofgren. And Lofgren has no intention of playing the referee role.

To mediate the points of conflict, the executive group has had to learn how to work together. They've even brought in outside counsel to help them better listen and understand one another and focus debate on critical issues. "Conflict between people or between groups of people is not positive. Conflict around business issues is the most wonderful, healthy thing," says Lofgren. "Any business without tension will fall to its lowest level of performance."

Questions

1. What view toward conflict does Lofgren support? Explain.

2. Explain why the transition in leadership from Don Schneider to Lofgren was relatively conflict-free.

3. How does the organization of the executive group create conflict? How does it reduce conflict?

4. How does Lofgren manage conflict?

Source: Based on D. Drickhamer, "Rolling On," *Industry Week*, December 1, 2002.

Case Incident 2

NEGOTIATION PUTS HOCKEY IN THE PENALTY BOX

Not every negotiation ends on a good note. Just ask National Hockey League (N.H.L.) Commissioner Gary Bettman, who, on February 16, 2005, cancelled all of the games remaining in the season following a 5-month lockout by the owners. Though professional sports such as hockey and baseball have had close calls with losing an entire season, Bettman's decision was a first: The whole schedule was lost. Said Bettman, "This is a sad, regrettable day."

On the other side of the dispute, Bob Goodenow, executive director of the N.H.L. Player's Association, similarly regretted the impasse. He said, "Yes, we apologize to the fans." Though the repercussions to the league and its players are obvious, canceling the season also had ramifications on a broader level, including lost revenues for local businesses and N.H.L. game merchandise sales.

So, why did Bettman cancel the season? The primary issue was a salary cap, but Goodenow said, "The players never asked for more money. They didn't want to be locked out. Gary owes the apology. He started the lockout. We've done an awful lot to try to get to a fair resolution." According to reports, negotiations began when the league attempted to lower the average salary from $1.8 million per year to $1.3 million per year—a 28 percent decrease. The league's reason? Although the N.H.L.'s total revenue had reached $2.1 billion a year, players were paid 75 percent of this revenue. According to the league, this high percentage kept the league from being profitable and directly contributed to the league's loss of $479 million over the past two seasons. The player's union then countered with an offer to reduce salaries by 24 percent rather than the 28 percent the league wanted. Bettman then tried an alternative solution: to persuade the union to accept a salary percentage of no more than 55 percent of league revenues. Instead of reducing pay to an average level, this proposal would link players' pay to the leagues' revenues, which could fluctuate up or down. The league's players opposed both ideas until Bettman and the N.H.L. team owners offered a salary cap that did not link payroll and revenue. At this point, negotiations looked promising.

However, neither party could agree on an amount. The owners offered a cap of $40 million per team and then increased it to $42.5 million. But the players wanted a cap of $52 million per team and then lowered their proposal to $49 million. Although the dollar difference in this round of negotiations amounted to only 6.5 million, neither side could agree, negotiations stopped, and the season was cancelled.

Said Goodenow, "Gary gave us a final offer, a take-it-or-leave-it offer. We made a counterproposal and events ground to a halt." A reporter asked both sides whether they would have accepted a compromise of around $45 million per team. Such a compromise may have saved the season. Bettman stated, "If they wanted $45 million, I'm not saying we would have gone there, but they sure should have told us." Goodenow, however, wouldn't speculate: "The what-ifs aren't for real."

So how did the two sides eventually get the players back on the ice? They agreed to a 6-year deal that set a salary cap of $39 million per team for the 2005-2006 season (remember the players wanted a cap of $49 million). Many players were unhappy with the terms of the deal but felt that fighting the salary cap was a waste of time that did nothing but alienate the fans. Many players spoke out against Goodenow, arguing that he put the players in a no-win situation. Less than a week after the lockout ended,

Goodenow resigned as executive director of the N.H.L. Player's Association. He denied that his resignation was in response to the players' complaints. The lack of an agreement in the N.H.L. negotiations was a loss to everyone – the league and businesses connected to the league, the owners, the players, and, of course, the fans.

Questions

1. How would you characterize the N.H.L. negotiation – as distributive or integrative? From what perspective (distributive or integrative) did the parties approach the negotiation? How might this approach have affected the outcome?

2. What factors do you believe led to the lack of a settlement in the N.H.L. negotiations? How might you have handled the negotiation if you were a representative of the league? Of the player's union?

3. Negotiating parties are often reluctant to reveal their BATNA (best alternative to a negotiated agreement) to the opposing party. Do you believe that parties in the N.H.L. negotiation were aware of each other's BATNA? How might this knowledge have affected the negotiation?

4. It appears that a point of compromise (a $45 million per team salary cap, for example) may have existed. What steps could both parties have taken to reach this point of compromise?

Source: Based on J. Lapointe, and R. Westhead, "League Cancels Hockey Season in Labor Battle," *The New York Times,* February 17, 2005, p. A.1

Endnotes

1. J. B. Stewart, "Partners: Eisner, Ovitz, and the Disney Wars," *The New Yorker,* January 10, 2005, pp. 46–57; and C. Eller and R. Verrier, "Ovitz, Eisner Can Win and Still Lose," *Los Angeles Times,* January 20, 2005 (http://www.latimes.com/business/custom/cotown/la-fi-eisner20jan20,1,2778081.story?coll=la-headlines-business-enter&ctrack=2&cset=true).

2. See, for instance, C. F. Fink, "Some Conceptual Difficulties in the Theory of Social Conflict," *Journal of Conflict Resolution,* December 1968, pp. 412–60; and E. Infante, "On the Definition of Interpersonal Conflict: Cluster Analysis Applied to the Study of Semantics," *Revista de Psicologia Social* 13, no. 3 (1998), pp. 485–93.

3. L. L. Putnam and M. S. Poole, "Conflict and Negotiation," in F. M. Jablin, L. L. Putnam, K. H. Roberts, and L. W. Porter (eds.), *Handbook of Organizational Communication: An Interdisciplinary Perspective* (Newbury Park, CA: Sage, 1987), pp. 549–99.

4. K. W. Thomas, "Conflict and Negotiation Processes in Organizations," in M. D. Dunnette and L. M. Hough (eds.), *Handbook of Industrial and Organizational Psychology,* 2nd ed., vol. 3 (Palo Alto, CA: Consulting Psychologists Press, 1992), pp. 651–717.

5. For a comprehensive review of the interactionist approach, see C. De Dreu and E. Van de Vliert (eds.), *Using Conflict in Organizations* (London: Sage Publications, 1997).

6. See K. A. Jehn, "A Multimethod Examination of the Benefits and Detriments of Intragroup Conflict," *Administrative Science Quarterly,* June 1995, pp. 256–82; K. A. Jehn, "A Qualitative Analysis of Conflict Types and Dimensions in Organizational Groups," *Administrative Science Quarterly,* September 1997, pp. 530–57; K. A. Jehn and E. A. Mannix, "The Dynamic Nature of Conflict: A Longitudinal Study of Intragroup Conflict and Group Performance," *Academy of Management Journal,* April 2001, pp. 238–51; K. A. Jehn and C. Bendersky, "Intragroup Conflict in Organizations: A Contingency Perspective on the Conflict-Outcome Relationship," in R. M. Kramer and B. M. Staw (eds.), *Research in Organizational Behavior,* vol. 25 (Oxford, UK: Elsevier, 2003), pp. 199–210; and C. K. W. De Dreu and L. R. Weingart, "Task Versus Relationship Conflict, Team Performance, and Team Member Satisfaction: A Meta-Analysis," *Journal of Applied Psychology,* August 2003, pp. 741–49.

7. J. Yang and K. W. Mossholder, "Decoupling Task and Relationship Conflict: The Role of Intragroup Emotional Processing," *Journal of Organizational Behavior* 25, no. 5 (August 2004), pp. 589–605.

8. See S. P. Robbins, *Managing Organizational Conflict: A Nontraditional Approach* (Upper Saddle River, NJ: Prentice Hall, 1974), pp. 31–55; and Walland Callister, "Conflict and Its Management," pp. 517–23.

9. Robbins, *Managing Organizational Conflict*.

10. R. S. Peterson and K. J. Behfar, "The Dynamic Relationship Between Performance Feedback, Trust, and Conflict in Groups: A Longitudinal Study," *Organizational Behavior & Human Decision Processes*, September–November 2003, pp. 102–12.

11. Jehn, "A Multimethod Examination of the Benefits and Detriments of Intragroup Conflict."

12. R. Friedman, C. Anderson, J. Brett, M. Olekalns, N. Goates, and C. C. Lisco, "The Positive and Negative Effects of Anger on Dispute Resolution: Evidence from Electronically Mediated Disputes," *Journal of Applied Psychology*, April 2004, pp. 369–76.

13. M. J. Gelfand, M. Higgins, L. H. Nishii, J. L. Raver, A. Dominguez, F. Murakami, S. Yamaguchi, M. Toyama, "Culture and Egocentric Perceptions of Fairness in Conflict and Negotiation," *Journal of Applied Psychology*, October 2002, pp. 833–45.

14. L. R. Pondy, "Organizational Conflict: Concepts and Models," *Administrative Science Quarterly*, September 1967, p. 302.

15. See, for instance, R. L. Pinkley, "Dimensions of Conflict Frame: Disputant Interpretations of Conflict," *Journal of Applied Psychology*, April 1990, pp. 117–26; and R. L. Pinkley and G. B. Northcraft, "Conflict Frames of Reference: Implications for Dispute Processes and Outcomes," *Academy of Management Journal*, February 1994, pp. 193–205.

16. R. Kumar, "Affect, Cognition and Decision Making in Negotiations: A Conceptual Integration," in M. A. Rahim (ed.), *Managing Conflict: An Integrative Approach* (New York: Praeger, 1989), pp. 185–94; for a more recent study, see A. M. Isen, A. A. Labroo, and P. Durlach, "An Influence of Product and Brand Name on Positive Affect: Implicit and Explicit Measures," *Motivation & Emotion*, March 2004, pp. 43–63.

17. Ibid.

18. P. J. D. Carnevale and A. M. Isen, "The Influence of Positive Affect and Visual Access on the Discovery of Integrative Solutions in Bilateral Negotiations," *Organizational Behavior and Human Decision Processes*, February 1986, pp. 1–13.

19. Thomas, "Conflict and Negotiation Processes in Organizations."

20. Ibid.

21. See R. J. Sternberg and L. J. Soriano, "Styles of Conflict Resolution," *Journal of Personality and Social Psychology*, July 1984, pp. 115–26; R. A. Baron, "Personality and Organizational Conflict: Effects of the Type A Behavior Pattern and Self-Monitoring," *Organizational Behavior and Human Decision Processes*, October 1989, pp. 281–96; R. J. Volkema and T. J. Bergmann, "Conflict Styles as Indicators of Behavioral Patterns in Interpersonal Conflicts," *Journal of Social Psychology*, February 1995, pp. 5–15; and J. A. Rhoades, J. Arnold, and C. Jay, "The Role of Affective Traits and Affective States in Disputants' Motivation and Behavior During Episodes of Organizational Conflict," *Journal of Organizational Behavior*, May 2001, pp. 329–45.

22. Thomas, "Conflict and Negotiation Processes in Organizations."

23. See, for instance, R. A. Cosier and C. R. Schwenk, "Agreement and Thinking Alike: Ingredients for Poor Decisions," *Academy of Management Executive*, February 1990, pp. 69–74; K. A. Jehn, "Enhancing Effectiveness: An Investigation of Advantages and Disadvantages of Value-Based Intragroup Conflict," *International Journal of Conflict Management*, July 1994, pp. 223–38; R. L. Priem, D. A. Harrison, and N. K. Muir, "Structured Conflict and Consensus Outcomes in Group Decision Making," *Journal of Management* 21, no. 4 (1995), pp. 691–710; and K. A. Jehn and

E. A. Mannix, "The Dynamic Nature of Conflict: A Longitudinal Study of Intragroup Conflict and Group Performance," *Academy of Management Journal*, April 2001, pp. 238–51.

24. See, for instance, C. J. Loomis, "Dinosaurs?" *Fortune*, May 3, 1993, pp. 36–42.

25. K. Swisher, "Yahoo! May Be Down, But Don't Count It Out," *The Wall Street Journal*, March 9, 2001, p. B1; and M. Mangalindan and S. L. Hwang, "Coterie of Early Hires Made Yahoo! A Hit But an Insular Place," *The Wall Street Journal*, March 9, 2001, p. A1.

26. I. L. Janis, *Victims of Groupthink* (Boston: Houghton Mifflin, 1972).

27. J. Hall and M. S. Williams, "A Comparison of Decision-Making Performances in Established and Ad-Hoc Groups," *Journal of Personality and Social Psychology*, February 1966, p. 217.

28. R. L. Hoffman, "Homogeneity of Member Personality and Its Effect on Group Problem-Solving," *Journal of Abnormal and Social Psychology*, January 1959, pp. 27–32; R. L. Hoffman and N. R. F. Maier, "Quality and Acceptance of Problem Solutions by Members of Homogeneous and Heterogeneous Groups," *Journal of Abnormal and Social Psychology*, March 1961, pp. 401–07; and P. Pitcher and A. D. Smith, "Top Management Team Heterogeneity: Personality, Power, and Proxies," *Organization Science*, January–February 2001, pp. 1–18.

29. See T. H. Cox and S. Blake, "Managing Cultural Diversity: Implications for Organizational Competitiveness," *Academy of Management Executive*, August 1991, pp. 45–56; T. H. Cox, S. A. Lobel, and P. L. McLeod, "Effects of Ethnic Group Cultural Differences on Cooperative Behavior on a Group Task," *Academy of Management Journal*, December 1991, pp. 827–47; P. L. McLeod and S. A. Lobel, "The Effects of Ethnic Diversity on Idea Generation in Small Groups," paper presented at the Annual Academy of Management Conference, Las Vegas, August 1992; C. Kirchmeyer and A. Cohen, "Multicultural Groups: Their Performance and Reactions with Constructive Conflict," *Group & Organization Management*, June 1992, pp. 153–70; D. E. Thompson and L. E. Gooler, "Capitalizing on the Benefits of Diversity through Workteams," in E. E. Kossek and S. A. Lobel (eds.), *Managing Diversity: Human Resource Strategies for Transforming the Workplace* (Cambridge, MA: Blackwell, 1996), pp. 392–437; L. H. Pelled, K. M. Eisenhardt, and K. R. Xin, "Exploring the Black Box: An Analysis of Work Group Diversity, Conflict, and Performance," *Administrative Science Quarterly*, March 1999, pp. 1–28; and D. van Knippenberg, C. K. W. De Dreu, and A. C. Homan, "Work Group Diversity and Group Performance: An Integrative Model and Research Agenda," *Journal of Applied Psychology*, December 2004, pp. 1008–22.

30. R. E. Hill, "Interpersonal Compatibility and Work Group Performance among Systems Analysts: An Empirical Study," *Proceedings of the Seventeenth Annual Midwest Academy of Management Conference*, Kent, OH, April 1974, pp. 97–110.

31. D. C. Pelz and F. Andrews, *Scientists in Organizations* (New York: Wiley, 1966).

32. For example, see J. A. Wall, Jr., and R. R. Callister, "Conflict and Its Management," pp. 523–26 for evidence supporting the argument that conflict is almost uniformly dysfunctional; see also P. J. Hinds, and D. E. Bailey, "Out of Sight, Out of Sync: Understanding Conflict in Distributed Teams," *Organization Science*, November–December 2003, pp. 615–32.

33. M. Geyelin and E. Felsenthal, "Irreconcilable Differences Force Shea & Gould Closure," *The Wall Street Journal*, January 31, 1994, p. B1.

34. This section is based on F. Sommerfield, "Paying the Troops to Buck the System," *Business Month*, May 1990, pp. 77–79; W. Kiechel III, "How to Escape the Echo Chamber," *Fortune*, June 18, 1990, pp. 129–30; E. Van de Vliert and C. De Dreu, "Optimizing Performance by Stimulating Conflict," *International Journal of Conflict Management*, July 1994, pp. 211–22; E. Van de Vliert, "Enhancing Performance by Conflict-Stimulating Intervention," in C. De Dreu and E. Van de Vliert (eds.), *Using Conflict in Organizations*, pp. 208–22; K. M. Eisenhardt, J. L. Kahwajy, and L. J. Bourgeois III, "How Management Teams Can Have a Good Fight," *Harvard Business Review*, July–August 1997, pp. 77–85; S. Wetlaufer, "Common Sense and Conflict," *Harvard Business Review*, January–February 2000, pp. 114–24; and G. A. Okhuysen and K. M. Eisenhardt, "Excel Through Group Process," in E. A. Locke (ed.), *Handbook of Principles of Organizational Behavior* (Malden, MA: Blackwell, 2004), pp. 216–18.

35. J. A. Wall, Jr., *Negotiation: Theory and Practice* (Glenview, IL: Scott, Foresman, 1985).

36. R. E. Walton and R. B. McKersie, *A Behavioral Theory of Labor Negotiations: An Analysis of a Social Interaction System* (New York: McGraw-Hill, 1965).

37. S. E. Brodt, M. Tuchinsky, "Working Together but in Opposition: An Examination of the 'Good Cop/Bad Cop' Negotiating Team Tactic," *Organizational Behavior & Human Decision Processes*, March 2000, pp. 155–77.

38. D. A. Moore, "Myopic Prediction, Self-Destructive Secrecy, and the Unexpected Benefits of Revealing Final Deadlines in Negotiation," *Organizational Behavior & Human Decision Processes*, July 2004, pp. 125–39.

39. Thomas, "Conflict and Negotiation Processes in Organizations."

40. P. M. Morgan and R. S. Tindale, "Group vs. Individual Performance in Mixed-Motive Situations: Exploring an Inconsistency," *Organizational Behavior & Human Decision Processes*, January 2002, pp. 44–65.

41. C. E. Naquin, "The Agony of Opportunity in Negotiation: Number of Negotiable Issues, Counterfactual Thinking, and Feelings of Satisfaction," *Organizational Behavior & Human Decision Processes*, May 2003, pp. 97–107.

42. C. K. W. De Dreu, L. R. Weingart, and S. Kwon, "Influence of Social Motives on Integrative Negotiation: A Meta-Analytic Review and Test of Two Theories," *Journal of Personality & Social Psychology*, May 2000. pp. 889–905.

43. This model is based on R. J. Lewicki, "Bargaining and Negotiation," *Exchange: The Organizational Behavior Teaching Journal* 6, no. 2 (1981), pp. 39–40.

44. J. Lee, "The Negotiators," *Forbes*, January 11, 1999, pp. 22–24.

45. M. H. Bazerman and M. A. Neale, *Negotiating Rationally* (New York: Free Press, 1992), pp. 67–68.

46. C. Anderson and L. L. Thompson, "Affect from the Top Down: How Powerful Individuals' Positive Affect Shapes Negotiations," *Organizational Behavior & Human Decision Processes*, November 2004, pp. 125–39.

47. J. A. Wall, Jr., and M. W. Blum, "Negotiations," *Journal of Management*, June 1991, pp. 278–82.

48. B. Barry and R. A. Friedman, "Bargainer Characteristics in Distributive and Integrative Negotiation," *Journal of Personality & Social Psychology*, February 1998, pp. 345–59.

49. J. B. White, R. Tynan, A. D. Galinsky, and L. Thompson, "Face Threat Sensitivity in Negotiation: Roadblock to Agreement and Joint Gain," *Organizational Behavior & Human Decision Processes*, July 2004, pp. 102–24.

50. C. Watson and L. R. Hoffman, "Managers as Negotiators: A Test of Power versus Gender as Predictors of Feelings, Behavior, and Outcomes," *Leadership Quarterly*, Spring 1996, pp. 63–85.

51. A. E. Walters, A. F. Stuhlmacher, and L. L. Meyer, "Gender and Negotiator Competitiveness: A Meta-Analysis," *Organizational Behavior and Human Decision Processes*, October 1998, pp. 1–29; and A. F. Stuhlmacher and A. E. Walters, "Gender Differences in Negotiation Outcome: A Meta-Analysis," *Personnel Psychology*, Autumn 1999, pp. 653–77.

52. Stuhlmacher and Walters, "Gender Differences in Negotiation Outcome," p. 655.

53. L. J. Kray, A. D. Galinsky, and L. Thompson, "Reversing the Gender Gap in Negotiations: An Exploration of Stereotype Regeneration," *Organizational Behavior & Human Decision Processes*, March 2002, pp. 386–409.

54. C. K. Stevens, A. G. Bavetta, and M. E. Gist, "Gender Differences in the Acquisition of Salary Negotiation Skills: The Role of Goals, Self-Efficacy, and Perceived Control," *Journal of Applied Psychology* 78, no. 5 (October 1993), pp. 723–35.

55. See N. J. Adler, *International Dimensions of Organizational Behavior*, 4th ed. (Cincinnati, OH: Southwestern, 2002), pp. 208–56; W. L. Adair, T. Okurmura, and J. M. Brett, "Negotiation Behavior When Cultures Collide: The United States and Japan," *Journal of Applied Psychology*, June 2001, pp. 371–85; M. J. Gelfand, M. Higgins, L. H. Nishii, J. L. Raver, A. Dominguez, F. Murakami, S. Yamaguchi, and M. Toyama, "Culture and Egocentric Perceptions of Fairness in Conflict and Negotiation," *Journal of Applied Psychology*, October 2002, pp. 833–45; and X. Lin and S. J. Miller, "Negotiation Approaches: Direct and Indirect Effect of National Culture," *International Marketing Review* 20, no. 3 (2003), pp. 286–303.

56. K. D. Schmidt, *Doing Business in France* (Menlo Park, CA: SRI International, 1987).

57. S. Lubman, "Round and Round," *The Wall Street Journal*, December 10, 1993, p. R3.

58. W. L. Adair, T. Okumura, and J. M. Brett, "Negotiation Behavior When Cultures Collide: The United States and Japan," *Journal of Applied Psychology*, June 2001, pp. 371–85.

59. P. R. Harris and R. T. Moran, *Managing Cultural Differences*, 5th ed. (Houston: Gulf Publishing, 1999), pp. 56–59.

60. E. S. Glenn, D. Witmeyer, and K. A. Stevenson, "Cultural Styles of Persuasion," *Journal of Intercultural Relations*, Fall 1977, pp. 52–66.

61. J. Graham, "The Influence of Culture on Business Negotiations," *Journal of International Business Studies*, Spring 1985, pp. 81–96.

62. Wall and Blum, "Negotiations," pp. 283–87.

63. K. W. Thomas, "Toward Multidimensional Values in Teaching: The Example of Conflict Behaviors," *Academy of Management Review*, July 1977, p. 487.

64. Q. Reade, "Workplace Conflict Is Time-Consuming Problem for Business," *PersonnelToday.com*. (http://www.personneltoday.co.uk) (September 30, 2004).

65. K. O'Connor and P. Carnevale, "A Nasty but Effective Negotiation Strategy: Misrepresentation of a Common-Value Issue," *Personality and Social Psychology Bulletin*, May 1997, pp. 504–15.

Every revolution evaporates and leaves behind only the slime of a new bureaucracy.

— Franz Kafka

Foundations of Organization Structure

After studying this chapter, you should be able to:

LEARNING OBJECTIVES

Reorganizing Vanderbilt University's Athletic Department

I t's rare for a month to go by without a sports scandal surfacing at one of the campuses that compete in big-time athletics. For instance, athletic departments admit to doctoring athletes' transcripts to help them gain admission or maintain eligibility; coaches are charged with recruiting violations; or alumni are found to be providing athletes with cars and illegal cash payments. Critics argue that football and basketball programs at major universities are out of control and that the separate and special status given to varsity sports' programs makes them ripe for abuse. Though these criticisms have been building for decades, few changes have been implemented to deal with them. Why? There's a lot of money and prestige involved, and university administrators seem willing to look the other way so as not to upset the system.

One exception is Gordon Gee, the chancellor at Vanderbilt University. In September 2003, he "declared war" on the culture surrounding college athletics.[1] "For too long, college athletics has been segregated from the core mission of the university," Gee said. "As a result, we have created a culture, both on this campus and nationally, that is disconnected from our students, faculty and other constituents, where responsibility is diffused, the potential abuse considerable and the costs—both

financial and academic—unsustainable." Gee then announced a major reorganization at Vanderbilt that included elimination of its athletic department. Although Vanderbilt would continue playing intercollegiate sports and maintain membership in the Southeastern Conference, Gee announced that the departments that control varsity and intramural athletics would be merged and placed under the university's central administration. The position of athletic director would be eliminated and a new Office of Student Athletics, Recreation, and Wellness would be created to oversee the university's athletic programs. Moreover, this new office would be under the direction of Vanderbilt's academic administrators. Gee intends to use this reorganization as a means to bring sports, academics, and student life together more successfully; integrate athletic programs more tightly into the university's academic mission; and curb many of

537

the ills of big-time college sports. One *Sports Illustrated* writer nominated Gee for 2004 *SI Sportsman of the Year*, noting, "As an alum, I'm glad Gee is running my school. And as a sports fan I'm glad there are people like Gee out there who have a vision of making intercollegiate sports a more respectable enterprise—and who aren't afraid to act." ■

ordon Gee is using a change in organization structure as a means to attempt to change the behavior of coaches, athletes, and other constituencies at Vanderbilt. And that's the theme of this chapter: Organization structures *can* shape attitudes and behavior. In the following pages, we define the key components that make up an organization's structure, present half a dozen or so structural design options from which managers can choose, identify the contingency factors that make certain structural designs preferable in varying situations, and conclude by considering the different effects that various organizational designs have on employee behavior.

What Is Organizational Structure?

An **organizational structure** defines how job tasks are formally divided, grouped, and coordinated. There are six key elements that managers need to address when they design their organization's structure. These are: work specialization, departmentalization, chain of command, span of control, centralization and decentralization, and formalization.[2] Exhibit 16-1 presents each of these elements as answers to an important structural question. The following sections describe these six elements of structure.

Work Specialization

Early in the twentieth century, Henry Ford became rich and famous by building automobiles on an assembly line. Every Ford worker was assigned a specific, repetitive task. For instance, one person would just put on the right-front wheel and someone else would install the right-front door. By breaking jobs up into small standardized tasks, which could be performed over and over again, Ford was able to produce cars at the rate of one every 10 seconds, while using employees who had relatively limited skills.

Exhibit 16-1	Key Design Questions and Answers for Designing the Proper Organizational Structure	
The Key Question		**The Answer Is Provided By**
1. To what degree are activities subdivided into separate jobs?		Work specialization
2. On what basis will jobs be grouped together?		Departmentalization
3. To whom do individuals and groups report?		Chain of command
4. How many individuals can a manager efficiently and effectively direct?		Span of control
5. Where does decision-making authority lie?		Centralization and decentralization
6. To what degree will there be rules and regulations to direct employees and managers?		Formalization

Ford demonstrated that work can be performed more efficiently if employees are allowed to specialize. Today we use the term **work specialization**, or *division of labor*, to describe the degree to which activities in the organization are subdivided into separate jobs. The essence of work specialization is that rather than an entire job being done by one individual, it is broken down into a number of steps, with each step being completed by a separate individual. In essence, individuals specialize in doing part of an activity rather than the entire activity.

By the late 1940s, most manufacturing jobs in industrialized countries were being done with high work specialization. Management saw this as a means to make the most efficient use of its employees' skills. In most organizations, some tasks require highly developed skills and others can be performed by untrained workers. If all workers were engaged in each step of, say, an organization's manufacturing process, all would have to have the skills necessary to perform both the most demanding and the least demanding jobs. The result would be that, except when performing the most skilled or highly complex tasks, employees would be working below their skill levels. And because skilled workers are paid more than unskilled workers and their wages tend to reflect their highest level of skill, it represents an inefficient use of organizational resources to pay highly skilled workers to do easy tasks.

Managers also saw other efficiencies that could be achieved through work specialization. Employee skills at performing a task successfully increase through repetition. Less time is spent in changing tasks, in putting away one's tools and equipment from a prior step in the work process, and in getting ready for another. Equally important, training for specialization is more efficient from the organization's perspective. It's easier and less costly to find and train workers to do specific and repetitive tasks. This is especially true of highly sophisticated and complex operations. For example, could Cessna produce one Citation jet a year if one person had to build the entire plane alone? Not likely! Finally, work specialization increases efficiency and productivity by encouraging the creation of special inventions and machinery.

For much of the first half of the twentieth century, managers viewed work specialization as an unending source of increased productivity. And they were probably right. Because specialization was not widely practiced, its introduction almost always generated higher productivity. But by the 1960s, there came increasing evidence that a good thing can be carried too far. The point had been reached in some jobs at which the human diseconomies from specialization—which surfaced as boredom, fatigue, stress, low productivity, poor quality, increased absenteeism, and high turnover—more than offset the economic advantages (see Exhibit 16-2). In such cases, productivity could be increased by enlarging, rather than narrowing, the scope of job activities. In addition, a number of companies found that by giving employees a variety of activities to do, allowing them to do a whole and complete job, and putting them into teams with interchangeable skills, they often achieved significantly higher output, with increased employee satisfaction.

Most managers today see work specialization as neither obsolete nor an unending source of increased productivity. Rather, managers recognize the economies it provides in certain types of jobs and the problems it creates when it's carried too far. You'll find, for example, high work specialization being used by McDonald's to efficiently make and sell hamburgers and fries, and by medical specialists in most health maintenance organizations. On the other hand,

organizational structure   *How job tasks are formally divided, grouped, and coordinated.*

work specialization   *The degree to which tasks in the organization are subdivided into separate jobs.*

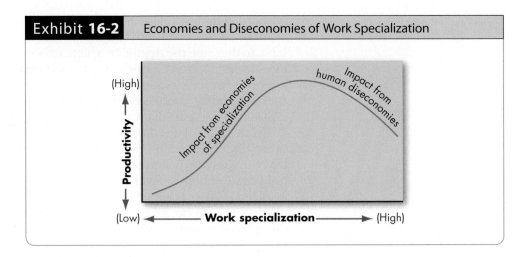

Exhibit 16-2   Economies and Diseconomies of Work Specialization

companies like Saturn Corporation have had success by broadening the scope of jobs and reducing specialization.

Departmentalization

Once you've divided jobs up through work specialization, you need to group these jobs together so that common tasks can be coordinated. The basis by which jobs are grouped together is called **departmentalization**.

One of the most popular ways to group activities is by *functions* performed. A manufacturing manager might organize a plant by separating engineering, accounting, manufacturing, personnel, and supply specialists into common departments. Of course, departmentalization by function can be used in all types of organizations. Only the functions change to reflect the organization's objectives and activities. A hospital might have departments devoted to research, patient care, accounting, and so forth. A professional football franchise might have departments entitled Player Personnel, Ticket Sales, and Travel and Accommodations. The major advantage to this type of grouping is obtaining efficiencies from putting like specialists together. Functional departmentalization seeks to achieve economies of scale by placing people with common skills and orientations into common units.

Jobs can also be departmentalized by the type of *product* the organization produces. Procter & Gamble, for instance, is organized along these lines. Each major product—such as Tide, Pampers, Charmin, and Pringles—is placed under the authority of an executive who has complete global responsibility for that product. The major advantage to this type of grouping is increased accountability for product performance, since all activities related to a specific product are under the direction of a single manager. If an organization's activities are service- rather than product-related, each service would be autonomously grouped. For instance, Automatic Data Processing has departments for each of its employer-provided services—payroll, retirement, expense management, taxes, and the like. Each offers a common array of services under the direction of a product or service manager.

Another way to departmentalize is on the basis of *geography* or territory. The sales function, for instance, may have western, southern, midwestern, and eastern regions. Each of these regions is, in effect, a department organized around geography. If an organization's customers are scattered over a large geographic area and have similar needs based on their location, then this form of departmentalization can be valuable.

At an Alcoa aluminum tubing plant in upstate New York, production is organized into five departments: casting; press; tubing; finishing; and inspecting,

Now, begin to see your scar fade
in as little as 8 weeks.

...roducing BAND-AID® Brand SCAR HEALING—the first treatment of its kind.
Our revolutionary wafer-thin strips are clinically proven to flatten and fade
red, raised—even older scars. So you can actually
do more than just wish that scar away.

*Dermatologist tested,
clinically proven.*

...formation, go to
...aid.com

Johnson & Johnson has a product
organization structure for the
manufacture and marketing of
health-care products for the
consumer, pharmaceutical, and
professional markets. Each of J&J's
200 operating units is highly
autonomous and has its own
finance, human resources, and other
functional staff. This decentralized
structure supports J&J's strategy of
growth through innovation, as each
unit is responsible for growing
profitable brands through
innovative products like J&J's new
Band-Aid brand Scar Healing strips.

packing, and shipping. This is an example of *process* departmentalization because each department specializes in one specific phase in the production of aluminum tubing. The metal is cast in huge furnaces; sent to the press department, where it is extruded into aluminum pipe; transferred to the tube mill, where it is stretched into various sizes and shapes of tubing; moved to finishing, where it is cut and cleaned; and finally, arrives in the inspecting, packing, and shipping department. Since each process requires different skills, this method offers a basis for the homogeneous categorizing of activities.

Process departmentalization can be used for processing customers as well as products. If you've ever been to a state motor vehicle office to get a driver's license, you probably went through several departments before receiving your license. In one state, applicants must go through three steps, each handled by a separate department: (1) validation by motor vehicle division; (2) processing by the licensing department; and (3) payment collection by the treasury department.

A final category of departmentalization is to use the particular type of *customer* the organization seeks to reach. Microsoft, for instance, is organized around four customer markets: consumers, large corporations, software developers, and small businesses. The assumption underlying customer departmentalization is that customers in each department have a common set of problems and needs that can best be met by having specialists for each.

Large organizations may use all of the forms of departmentalization that we've described. A major Japanese electronics firm, for instance, organizes each of its divisions along functional lines and its manufacturing units around processes; it departmentalizes sales around seven geographic regions and divides each sales region into four customer groupings. Across organizations of all sizes, one strong trend has developed over the past decade. Rigid, functional departmentalization is being increasingly complemented by teams that cross over traditional departmental lines. As we described in Chapter 10, as tasks have become more complex and more diverse skills are needed to accomplish those tasks, management has turned to cross-functional teams.

Chain of Command

Thirty-five years ago, the chain-of-command concept was a basic cornerstone in the design of organizations. As you'll see, it has far less importance today.[3] But contemporary managers should still consider its implications when they decide how best to structure their organizations. The **chain of command** is an unbroken line of authority that extends from the top of the organization to the lowest echelon and clarifies who reports to whom. It answers questions for employees such as "To whom do I go if I have a problem?" and "To whom am I responsible?"

You can't discuss the chain of command without discussing two complementary concepts: *authority* and *unity of command*. **Authority** refers to the rights inherent in a managerial position to give orders and expect the orders to be obeyed. To facilitate coordination, each managerial position is given a place in the chain of command, and each manager is given a degree of authority in order to meet his or her responsibilities. The **unity-of-command** principle helps preserve the concept of an unbroken line of authority. It states that a person

---

departmentalization   *The basis by which jobs are grouped together.*

chain of command   *The unbroken line of authority that extends from the top of the organization to the lowest echelon and clarifies who reports to whom.*

authority   *The rights inherent in a managerial position to give orders and to expect the orders to be obeyed.*

unity of command   *The idea that a subordinate should have only one superior to whom he or she is directly responsible.*

should have one and only one superior to whom that person is directly responsible. If the unity of command is broken, an employee might have to cope with conflicting demands or priorities from several superiors.

Times change and so do the basic tenets of organizational design. The concepts of chain of command, authority, and unity of command have substantially less relevance today because of advancements in information technology and the trend toward empowering employees. For instance, a low-level employee today can access information in seconds that 35 years ago was available only to top managers. Similarly, networked computers increasingly allow employees anywhere in an organization to communicate with anyone else without going through formal channels. Moreover, the concepts of authority and maintaining the chain of command are increasingly less relevant as operating employees are being empowered to make decisions that previously were reserved for management. Add to this the popularity of self-managed and cross-functional teams and the creation of new structural designs that include multiple bosses, and the unity-of-command concept takes on less relevance. There are, of course, still many organizations that find they can be most productive by enforcing the chain of command. There just seem to be fewer of them nowadays.

Span of Control

How many employees can a manager efficiently and effectively direct? This question of **span of control** is important because, to a large degree, it determines the number of levels and managers an organization has. All things being equal, the wider or larger the span, the more efficient the organization. An example can illustrate the validity of this statement.

Assume that we have two organizations, both of which have approximately 4,100 operative-level employees. As Exhibit 16-3 illustrates, if one has a uniform span of four and the other a span of eight, the wider span would have two fewer levels and approximately 800 fewer managers. If the average manager made $50,000 a year, the wider span would save $40 million a year in management salaries! Obviously, wider spans are more efficient in terms of cost. However, at some point wider spans reduce effectiveness. That is, when the span becomes too large, employee performance suffers because supervisors no longer have the time to provide the necessary leadership and support.

Exhibit **16-3**	Contrasting Spans of Control

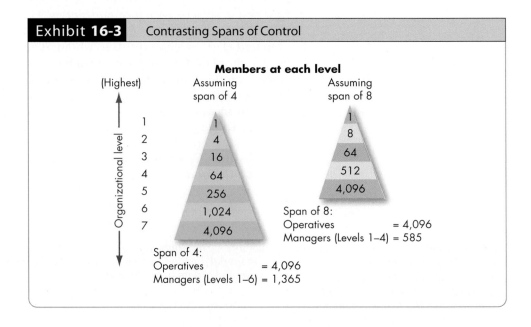

There Is No One Right Span of Control

Pat Harpell learned a lesson that many entrepreneurs fail to learn: Having too many people report to you can undermine your effectiveness.

Harpell runs Harpell Inc., a transactive marketing services company she founded in 1982 in Maynard, Massachusetts. As her firm grew, she added managers. Eventually she had 18 people reporting directly to her. It took her a few years but she finally recognized that she had to reduce the number of people over whom she had direct control. "I realized I was the bottleneck," Harpell says. "By limiting the number of people reporting to me, I was able to look beyond day to day and focus on building a unique brand and position for the company." Today, Harpell has only six people reporting directly to her and she has the time to focus on important issues. A study of entrepreneurs found that among two dozen popular management principles, span of control was the least appreciated. Only 23 percent of the respondents agreed that "span of control shouldn't be too large," and just 16 percent believed "top managers cannot deal with all problems personally."

Other organizations, of course, have problems with span of control being too small, leading to an excess of management layers. This is a particular problem in federal and state government. Small spans of control create inefficiency (a glut of supervisors) and also can lead to slow response times, slow decision making, rigidity toward change (entrenchment), and poor client/customer response. Recently, the state of Iowa, with 19,000 employees, achieved a higher span of control (1:12) by reducing the number of employees classified as supervisors. The goal was to save money and more efficiently allocate resources.

Source: Based on M. Henricks, "Span Control," *Entrepreneur*, January 2001, pp. 97–98; "Assessing Span of Control," State of Texas Human Resources. www.hr.state.tx.us/systems/fte/ChangingOrganizationalStructures.html (September 24, 2003); "Results Iowa." (www.resultsiowa.org/opscan.html) (2003).

Narrow or small spans have their advocates. By keeping the span of control to five or six employees, a manager can maintain close control.[4] But narrow spans have three major drawbacks. First, as already described, they're expensive because they add levels of management. Second, they make vertical communication in the organization more complex. The added levels of hierarchy slow down decision making and tend to isolate upper management. Third, narrow spans of control encourage overly tight supervision and discourage employee autonomy.

The trend in recent years has been toward wider spans of control.[5] They're consistent with recent efforts by companies to reduce costs, cut overhead, speed up decision making, increase flexibility, get closer to customers, and empower employees. However, to ensure that performance doesn't suffer because of these wider spans, organizations have been investing heavily in employee training. Managers recognize that they can handle a wider span when employees know their jobs inside and out or can turn to their coworkers when they have questions.

Centralization and Decentralization

In some organizations, top managers make all the decisions. Lower-level managers merely carry out top management's directives. At the other extreme, there are organizations in which decision making is pushed down to the managers who are closest to the action. The former organizations are highly centralized; the latter are decentralized.

The term **centralization** refers to the degree to which decision making is concentrated at a single point in the organization. The concept includes only formal authority—that is, the rights inherent in one's position. Typically, it's said that if top management makes the organization's key decisions with little or no input from

span of control   *The number of subordinates a manager can efficiently and effectively direct.*

centralization   *The degree to which decision making is concentrated at a single point in the organization.*

Exhibit 16-4

Source: S. Adams, *Dogbert's Big Book of Business*, DILBERT reprinted by permission of United Features Syndicate, Inc.

lower-level personnel, then the organization is centralized. In contrast, the more that lower-level personnel provide input or are actually given the discretion to make decisions, the more decentralization there is. An organization characterized by centralization is an inherently different structural animal from one that is decentralized. In a decentralized organization, action can be taken more quickly to solve problems, more people provide input into decisions, and employees are less likely to feel alienated from those who make the decisions that affect their work lives.

Consistent with recent management efforts to make organizations more flexible and responsive, there has been a marked trend toward decentralizing decision making. In large companies, lower-level managers are closer to "the action" and typically have more detailed knowledge about problems than do top managers. For instance, big retailers like Sears and JCPenney have given their store managers considerably more discretion in choosing what merchandise to stock. This allows those stores to compete more effectively against local merchants.

If you were a manager in a decentralized organization, would you be comfortable delegating important decisions and tasks to your subordinates? The Self-Assessment feature will help you assess how at ease you are with delegating.

HOW WILLING AM I TO DELEGATE?

In the Self-Assessment Library (available on CD, online, and in print), take assessment III.A.2 (How Willing Am I to Delegate?) and answer the following questions.

1. *Judging from the results, how willing are you to delegate?*
2. *If your delegation skills need improvement, why are you unwilling to delegate? If your delegation skills are superior, why are you willing to delegate?*
3. *How might you improve your delegation skills?*
4. *Why is the ability to delegate important?*

Formalization

Formalization refers to the degree to which jobs within the organization are standardized. If a job is highly formalized, then the job incumbent has a minimum amount of discretion over what is to be done, when it is to be done, and how it is to be done. Employees can be expected always to handle the same input in exactly the same way, resulting in a consistent and uniform output. There are explicit job descriptions, lots of organizational rules, and clearly defined procedures covering work processes in organizations in which there is high formalization. Where formalization is low, job behaviors are relatively nonprogrammed and employees have a great deal of freedom to exercise discretion in their work. Because an individual's discretion on the job is inversely related to the amount of behavior in that job that is preprogrammed by the organization, the greater the standardization, the less input the employee has into how the work is to be done. Standardization not only eliminates the possibility of employees engaging in alternative behaviors but it even removes the need for employees to consider alternatives.

The degree of formalization can vary widely between organizations and within organizations. Certain jobs, for instance, are well known to have little formalization. College book travelers—the representatives of publishers who call on professors to inform them of their company's new publications—have a great deal of freedom in their jobs. They have no standard sales "spiel," and the extent of rules and procedures governing their behavior may be little more than the requirement that they submit a weekly sales report and some suggestions on what to emphasize for the various new titles. At the other extreme, there are clerical and editorial positions in the same publishing houses for which employees are required to be at their desks by 8:00 A.M. or be docked a half-hour's pay and, once at that desk, to follow a set of precise procedures dictated by management.

Common Organizational Designs

We now turn to describing three of the more common organizational designs found in use: the *simple structure*, the *bureaucracy*, and the *matrix structure*.

The Simple Structure

What do a small retail store, an electronics firm run by a hard-driving entrepreneur, and an airline in the midst of a companywide pilot's strike have in common? They probably all use the **simple structure**.

The simple structure is said to be characterized most by what it is not rather than by what it is. The simple structure is not elaborate.[6] It has a low degree of departmentalization, wide spans of control, authority centralized in a single person, and little formalization. The simple structure is a "flat" organization; it usually has only two or three vertical levels, a loose body of employees, and one individual in whom the decision-making authority is centralized.

---

formalization *The degree to which jobs within the organization are standardized.*

simple structure *A structure characterized by a low degree of departmentalization, wide spans of control, authority centralized in a single person, and little formalization.*

| Exhibit **16-5** | A Simple Structure (Jack Gold's Men's Store) |

The simple structure is most widely practiced in small businesses in which the manager and the owner are one and the same. This, for example, is illustrated in Exhibit 16-5, an organization chart for a retail men's store. Jack Gold owns and manages this store. Although he employs five full-time salespeople, a cashier, and extra personnel for weekends and holidays, he "runs the show." But large companies, in times of crisis, can become simple structures for short periods. IBM, for instance, became a simple structure for more than a year back in the early 1990s.[7] When Louis Gerstner was hired as CEO in 1993, he immediately put the company into what he called "survival mode." "We had to cut $9 billion a year in expenses. We had to bring the company back, literally from the brink of death." So Gerstner implemented a highly centralized, personalized leadership and organizational style. Said Gerstner: "It was a benevolent dictatorship, with me as the dictator."

The strength of the simple structure lies in its simplicity. It's fast, flexible, and inexpensive to maintain, and accountability is clear. One major weakness is that it's difficult to maintain in anything other than small organizations. It becomes increasingly inadequate as an organization grows because its low formalization and high centralization tend to create information overload at the top. As size increases, decision making typically becomes slower and can eventually come to a standstill as the single executive tries to continue making all the decisions. This often proves to be the undoing of many small businesses. When an organization begins to employ 50 or 100 people, it's very difficult for the owner-manager to make all the choices. If the structure isn't changed and made more elaborate, the firm often loses momentum and can eventually fail. The simple structure's other weakness is that it's risky—everything depends on one person. One heart attack can literally destroy the organization's information and decision-making center.

The Bureaucracy

Standardization! That's the key concept that underlies all bureaucracies. Take a look at the bank where you keep your checking account, the department store where you buy your clothes, or the government offices that collect your taxes, enforce health regulations, or provide local fire protection. They all rely on standardized work processes for coordination and control.

The **bureaucracy** is characterized by highly routine operating tasks achieved through specialization, very formalized rules and regulations, tasks that are grouped into functional departments, centralized authority, narrow spans of control, and decision making that follows the chain of command. As the opening quote to this chapter attests, *bureaucracy* is a dirty word in many people's minds. However, it does have its advantages. The primary strength of the bureaucracy lies in its ability to perform standardized activities in a highly efficient manner. Putting like specialties together in functional departments

The U.S. Postal Service relies on standardized work processes for coordination and control. Postal workers follow formalized rules and regulations in performing their routine operating tasks. The bureaucracy of the postal system enables employees to perform standardized activities in a highly efficient way. For example, the mail sorters at the San Francisco Processing and Distribution Center can process more than 2.5 million pieces of mail a day during the busy Christmas holiday season.

results in economies of scale, minimum duplication of personnel and equipment, and employees who have the opportunity to talk "the same language" among their peers. Furthermore, bureaucracies can get by nicely with less talented—and, hence, less costly—middle- and lower-level managers. The pervasiveness of rules and regulations substitutes for managerial discretion. Standardized operations, coupled with high formalization, allow decision making to be centralized. There is little need, therefore, for innovative and experienced decision makers below the level of senior executives.

One of the major weaknesses of a bureaucracy is illustrated in the following dialogue among four executives in one company: "Ya know, nothing happens in this place until we *produce* something," said the production executive. "Wrong," commented the research and development manager, "nothing happens until we *design* something!" "What are you talking about?" asked the marketing executive. "Nothing happens here until we *sell* something!" Finally, the exasperated accounting manager responded, "It doesn't matter what you produce, design, or sell. No one knows what happens until we *tally up the results*!" This conversation points up the fact that specialization creates subunit conflicts. Functional unit goals can override the overall goals of the organization.

The other major weakness of a bureaucracy is something we've all experienced at one time or another when having to deal with people who work in these organizations: obsessive concern with following the rules. When cases arise that don't precisely fit the rules, there is no room for modification. The

bureaucracy   *A structure with highly routine operating tasks achieved through specialization, very formalized rules and regulations, tasks that are grouped into functional departments, centralized authority, narrow spans of control, and decision making that follows the chain of command.*

Structural Considerations in Multinationals

WHEN BRINGING OUT A BUSINESS INNOVATION IN any country, trudging through corporate bureaucracy can cause delays that result in a competitive disadvantage. This is especially true in China, one of the world's fastest-growing economies. Successful multinational corporations operating in China are realizing that the optimal structure is decentralized with a relatively high degree of managerial autonomy. Given that over 1.3 billion people live in China, the opportunity for businesses is tremendous, and as a result, competition is increasing. To take advantage of this opportunity, companies must be able to respond to changes before their competitors.

For example, Tyson Foods gives its vice president and head of the company's China operations, James Rice, the freedom to build the company's business overseas. While walking past a food vendor in Shanghai, Rice got the idea for cumin-flavored chicken strips. Without the need to obtain approval from upper management, Rice and his team immediately developed the recipe, tested it, and, after receiving a 90 percent customer-approval rating, began selling the product within 2 months of coming up with the idea.

Other companies that have implemented more formalized, bureaucratic structures have fared less well. One manager of a consumer electronics company who wanted to reduce the package size of a product to lower its cost and attract lower-income Chinese customers had to send the idea to his boss. His boss, the vice president of Asian operations, then sent the idea to the vice president of international operations, who in turn sent the idea to upper management in the United States. Although the idea was approved, the process took 5 months, during which a competitor introduced a similarly packaged product.

So, when it comes to innovating in a dynamic, fast-paced economy such as China, decentralization and autonomy can be major competitive advantages for multinational companies. To gain this competitive advantage, companies like Tyson are empowering their overseas managers to make their own decisions.

Source: Based on C. Hymowitz, "Executives in China Need Both Autonomy and Fast Access to Boss," *The Wall Street Journal,* May 10, 2005, p. B.1.

---

bureaucracy is efficient only as long as employees confront problems that they have previously encountered and for which programmed decision rules have already been established.

The Matrix Structure

Another popular organizational design option is the **matrix structure**. You'll find it being used in advertising agencies, aerospace firms, research and development laboratories, construction companies, hospitals, government agencies, universities, management consulting firms, and entertainment companies.[8] Essentially, the matrix combines two forms of departmentalization: functional and product.

The strength of functional departmentalization lies in putting like specialists together, which minimizes the number necessary while allowing the pooling and sharing of specialized resources across products. Its major disadvantage is the difficulty of coordinating the tasks of diverse functional specialists so that their activities are completed on time and within budget. Product departmentalization, on the other hand, has exactly the opposite benefits and disadvantages. It facilitates coordination among specialties to achieve on-time completion and to meet budget targets. Furthermore, it provides clear responsibility for all activities related to a product, but with duplication of activities and costs. The matrix attempts to gain the strengths of each, while avoiding their weaknesses.

The most obvious structural characteristic of the matrix is that it breaks the unity-of-command concept. Employees in the matrix have two bosses—their functional department managers and their product managers. Therefore, the matrix has a dual chain of command.

Exhibit 16-6 shows the matrix form as used in a college of business administration. The academic departments of accounting, decision and information systems, marketing, and so forth are functional units. In addition, specific programs (that is, products) are overlaid on the functions. In this way, members in a matrix structure have a dual assignment—to their functional department and to their product groups. For instance, a professor of accounting who is teaching an undergraduate course may report to the director of undergraduate programs as well as to the chairperson of the accounting department.

The strength of the matrix lies in its ability to facilitate coordination when the organization has a multiplicity of complex and interdependent activities. As an organization gets larger, its information-processing capacity can become overloaded. In a bureaucracy, complexity results in increased formalization. The direct and frequent contact between different specialties in the matrix can make for better communication and more flexibility. Information permeates the organization and more quickly reaches the people who need to take account of it. Furthermore, the matrix reduces "bureaupathologies"—the dual lines of authority reduce the tendencies of departmental members to become so busy protecting their little worlds that the organization's overall goals become secondary.

There is another advantage to the matrix. It facilitates the efficient allocation of specialists. When individuals with highly specialized skills are lodged in one functional department or product group, their talents are monopolized

| Exhibit **16-6** | Matrix Structure for a College of Business Administration |

Academic departments \ Programs	Undergraduate	Master's	Ph.D.	Research	Executive development	Community service
Accounting						
Finance						
Decision and information systems						
Management						
Marketing						

matrix structure *A structure that creates dual lines of authority and combines functional and product departmentalization.*

and underused. The matrix achieves the advantages of economies of scale by providing the organization with both the best resources and an effective way of ensuring their efficient deployment.

The major disadvantages of the matrix lie in the confusion it creates, its propensity to foster power struggles, and the stress it places on individuals.[9] When you dispense with the unity-of-command concept, ambiguity is significantly increased, and ambiguity often leads to conflict. For example, it's frequently unclear who reports to whom, and it is not unusual for product managers to fight over getting the best specialists assigned to their products. Confusion and ambiguity also create the seeds of power struggles. Bureaucracy reduces the potential for power grabs by defining the rules of the game. When those rules are "up for grabs," power struggles between functional and product managers result. For individuals who desire security and absence from ambiguity, this work climate can produce stress. Reporting to more than one boss introduces role conflict, and unclear expectations introduce role ambiguity. The comfort of bureaucracy's predictability is absent, replaced by insecurity and stress.

New Design Options

Over the past decade or two, senior managers in a number of organizations have been working to develop new structural options that can better help their firms to compete effectively. In this section, we'll describe three such structural designs: the *team structure*, the *virtual organization*, and the *boundaryless organization*.

The Team Structure

As described in Chapter 10, teams have become an extremely popular means around which to organize work activities. When management uses teams as its central coordination device, you have a horizontal organization or a **team structure**.[10] The primary characteristics of the team structure are that it breaks down departmental barriers and decentralizes decision making to the level of the work team. Team structures also require employees to be generalists as well as specialists.[11]

In smaller companies, the team structure can define the entire organization. For instance, Whole Foods Market, Inc., the largest natural-foods grocer in the United States, is structured entirely around teams.[12] Every one of Whole Foods' stores is an autonomous profit center composed of an average of 10 self-managed teams, each with a designated team leader. The team leaders in each store are a team; store leaders in each region are a team; and the company's six regional presidents are a team.

More often, particularly among larger organizations, the team structure complements what is typically a bureaucracy. This allows the organization to achieve the efficiency of bureaucracy's standardization while gaining the flexibility that teams provide. To improve productivity at the operating level, for instance, companies like DaimlerChrysler, Motorola, and Xerox have made extensive use of self-managed teams. On the other hand, when companies like Boeing need to design new products or coordinate major projects, they'll structure activities around cross-functional teams.

The Virtual Organization

Why own when you can rent? That question captures the essence of the **virtual organization** (also sometimes called the *network* or *modular* organization), typically a small, core organization that outsources major business functions.[13] In

Three doctors and a medical-device entrepreneur created a virtual organization called "1747" to conduct clinical trials for drugs that have been approved by the FDA but need self-reported results. 1747 uses e-mail and the Internet for coordinating patient screening, medication shipments, and patient responses. It has no office and only two employees, shown here, who work from home or their cars. As a virtual organization, 1747 provides a cost-saving alternative to traditional face-to-face clinical trials.

structural terms, the virtual organization is highly centralized, with little or no departmentalization.

The prototype of the virtual structure is today's movie-making organization. In Hollywood's golden era, movies were made by huge, vertically integrated corporations. Studios such as MGM, Warner Brothers, and 20th Century Fox owned large movie lots and employed thousands of full-time specialists—set designers, camera people, film editors, directors, and even actors. Nowadays, most movies are made by a collection of individuals and small companies who come together and make films project by project.[14] This structural form allows each project to be staffed with the talent most suited to its demands, rather than having to choose just from the people employed by the studio. It minimizes bureaucratic overhead because there is no lasting organization to maintain. And it lessens long-term risks and their costs because there is no long term—a team is assembled for a finite period and then disbanded.

Ancle Hsu and David Ji run a virtual organization. Their firm, California-based Apex Digital, is one of the world's largest producers of DVD players, yet the company neither owns a factory nor employs an engineer. They contract everything out to firms in China. With minimal investment, Apex has grown from nothing to annual sales of over $500 million in just 3 years. Similarly, Paul Newman's food products company, Newman's Own, sells about $190 million in food every year yet employs only 18 people. This is because it outsources almost everything—manufacturing, procurement, shipping, and quality control.

When large organizations use the virtual structure, they frequently use it to outsource manufacturing. Cisco, for instance, is essentially a research and development company that uses outside suppliers and independent manufacturers to

team structure   *The use of teams as the central device to coordinate work activities.*

virtual organization   *A small, core organization that outsources major business functions.*

assemble the Internet routers that its engineers design. National Steel Corp. contracts out its mail-room operations, and Procter & Gamble outsources its information-technology operation to Hewlett-Packard.

What's going on here? A quest for maximum flexibility. These virtual organizations have created networks of relationships that allow them to contract out manufacturing, distribution, marketing, or any other business function for which management feels that others can do better or more cheaply. The virtual organization stands in sharp contrast to the typical bureaucracy that has many vertical levels of management and where control is sought through ownership. In such organizations, research and development are done in-house, production occurs in company-owned plants, and sales and marketing are performed by the company's own employees. To support all this, management has to employ extra staff, including accountants, human resource specialists, and lawyers. The virtual organization, however, outsources many of these functions and concentrates on what it does best. For most U.S. firms, that means focusing on design or marketing.

Exhibit 16-7 shows a virtual organization in which management outsources all of the primary functions of the business. The core of the organization is a small group of executives whose job is to oversee directly any activities that are done in-house and to coordinate relationships with the other organizations that manufacture, distribute, and perform other crucial functions for the virtual organization. The dotted lines in Exhibit 16-7 represent the relationships typically maintained under contracts. In essence, managers in virtual structures spend most of their time coordinating and controlling external relations, typically by way of computer-network links.

The major advantage to the virtual organization is its flexibility. For instance, it allowed individuals with an innovative idea and little money, such as Ancle Hsu and David Ji, to successfully compete against the likes of Sony, Hitachi, and Sharp Electronics. The primary drawback to this structure is that it reduces management's control over key parts of its business.

The Boundaryless Organization

General Electric's former chairman, Jack Welch, coined the term **boundaryless organization** to describe his idea of what he wanted GE to become. Welch wanted to turn his company into a "family grocery store."[15] That is, in spite of its mon-

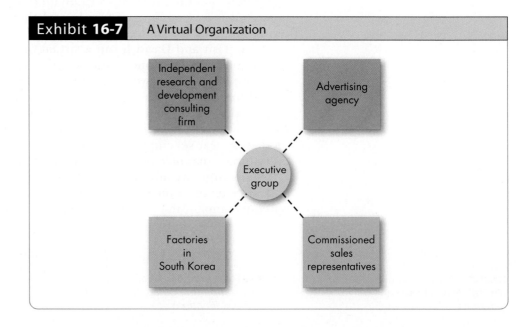

Exhibit **16-7**	A Virtual Organization

Networked computers are transforming hospitals from bureaucracies to boundaryless operations. At Indiana Heart Hospital in Indianapolis, 650 networked computers allow employees to share patient information. This information is entered in the computer when patients check in and digitally recorded on wristbands they wear during their stay. Digital records have eliminated nurses' stations, chart racks, and the medical-records department. Doctors use wireless laptop computers to check patient records anywhere, like this doctor working from his home.

strous size (2004 revenues were in excess of $135 billion), he wanted to eliminate *vertical* and *horizontal* boundaries within GE and break down *external* barriers between the company and its customers and suppliers. The boundaryless organization seeks to eliminate the chain of command, have limitless spans of control, and replace departments with empowered teams. And because it relies so heavily on information technology, some have turned to calling this structure the *T-form* (or technology-based) organization.[16] Although GE has not yet achieved this boundaryless state—and probably never will—it has made significant progress toward that end. So have other companies, such as Hewlett-Packard, AT&T, Motorola, and Oticon A/S. Let's take a look at what a boundaryless organization would look like and what some firms are doing to try to make it a reality.[17]

By removing vertical boundaries, management flattens the hierarchy. Status and rank are minimized. Cross-hierarchical teams (which include top executives, middle managers, supervisors, and operative employees), participative decision-making practices, and the use of 360-degree performance appraisals (in which peers and others above and below the employee evaluate performance) are examples of what GE is doing to break down vertical boundaries. At Oticon A/S, a $160-million-a-year Danish hearing aid manufacturer, all traces of hierarchy have disappeared. Everyone works at uniform mobile workstations. And project teams, not functions or departments, are used to coordinate work.

Functional departments create horizontal boundaries. And these boundaries stifle interaction between functions, product lines, and units. The way to reduce these barriers is to replace functional departments with cross-functional teams and to organize activities around processes. For instance, Xerox now develops new products through multidisciplinary teams that work in a single

boundaryless organization *An organization that seeks to eliminate the chain of command, have limitless spans of control, and replace departments with empowered teams.*

process instead of around narrow functional tasks. Similarly, some AT&T units are now doing annual budgets based not on functions or departments but on processes such as the maintenance of a worldwide telecommunications network. Another way management can cut through horizontal barriers is to use lateral transfers, rotating people into and out of different functional areas. This approach turns specialists into generalists.

When fully operational, the boundaryless organization also breaks down barriers to external constituencies (suppliers, customers, regulators, and so on) and barriers created by geography. Globalization, strategic alliances, customer-organization links, and telecommuting are all examples of practices that reduce external boundaries. Coca-Cola, for instance, sees itself as a global corporation, not as a U.S. or Atlanta company. Firms such as NEC Corp., Boeing, and Apple Computer each have strategic alliances or joint partnerships with dozens of companies. These alliances blur the distinction between one organization and another as employees work on joint projects. And some companies are allowing customers to perform functions that previously were done by management. For instance, some AT&T units are receiving bonuses based on customer evaluations of the teams that serve them. Finally, we suggest that telecommuting is blurring organizational boundaries. The security analyst with Merrill Lynch who does his job from his ranch in Montana or the software designer who works for a San Francisco company but does her job in Boulder, Colorado, are just two examples of the millions of workers who are now doing their jobs outside the physical boundaries of their employers' premises.

Why Do Structures Differ?

In the previous sections, we described a variety of organizational designs ranging from the highly structured and standardized bureaucracy to the loose and amorphous boundaryless organization. The other designs we discussed tend to exist somewhere between these two extremes.

Exhibit 16-8 reconceptualizes our previous discussions by presenting two extreme models of organizational design. One extreme we'll call the **mechanistic model**. It's generally synonymous with the bureaucracy in that it has extensive departmentalization, high formalization, a limited information network (mostly downward communication), and little participation by low-level members in decision making. At the other extreme is the **organic model**. This model looks a lot like the boundaryless organization. It's flat, uses cross-hierarchical and cross-functional teams, has low formalization, possesses a comprehensive information network (using lateral and upward communication as well as downward), and involves high participation in decision making.[18]

With these two models in mind, we're now prepared to address the question: Why are some organizations structured along more mechanistic lines whereas others follow organic characteristics? What are the forces that influence the design that is chosen? In the following pages, we present the major forces that have been identified as causes or determinants of an organization's structure.[19]

Strategy

An organization's structure is a means to help management achieve its objectives. Because objectives are derived from the organization's overall strategy, it's only logical that strategy and structure should be closely linked. More specifically, structure should follow strategy. If management makes a significant change in its organization's strategy, the structure will need to be modified to accommodate and support this change.[20]

Exhibit **16-8**	Mechanistic Versus Organic Models

The mechanistic model

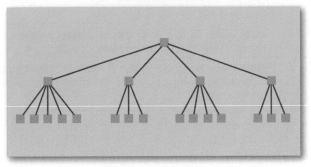

The organic model

- High specialization
- Rigid departmentalization
- Clear chain of command
- Narrow spans of control
- Centralization
- High formalization

- Cross-functional teams
- Cross-hierarchical teams
- Free flow of information
- Wide spans of control
- Decentralization
- Low formalization

Most current strategy frameworks focus on three strategy dimensions—innovation, cost minimization, and imitation—and the structural design that works best with each.[21]

To what degree does an organization introduce major new products or services? An **innovation strategy** does not mean a strategy merely for simple or cosmetic changes from previous offerings but rather one for meaningful and unique innovations. Obviously, not all firms pursue innovation. This strategy may appropriately characterize 3M Co. and Apple Computer, but it's not a strategy pursued by conservative retailer Marks & Spencer.

An organization that is pursuing a **cost-minimization strategy** tightly controls costs, refrains from incurring unnecessary innovation or marketing expenses, and cuts prices in selling a basic product. This would describe the strategy pursued by Wal-Mart or the makers of generic grocery products.

Organizations following an **imitation strategy** try to capitalize on the best of both of the previous strategies. They seek to minimize risk and maximize opportunity for profit. Their strategy is to move into new products or new markets only after viability has been proven by innovators. They take the successful ideas of innovators and copy them. Manufacturers of mass-marketed fashion goods that are rip-offs of designer styles follow the imitation strategy. This label probably also characterizes well-known firms such as IBM and Caterpillar. They essentially follow their smaller and more innovative competitors with superior products, but only after their competitors have demonstrated that the market is there.

Exhibit **16-9**	The Strategy-Structure Relationship
Strategy	**Structural Option**
Innovation	**Organic:** A loose structure; low specialization, low formalization, decentralized
Cost minimization	**Mechanistic:** Tight control; extensive work specialization, high formalization, high centralization
Imitation	**Mechanistic and organic:** Mix of loose with tight properties; tight controls over current activities and looser controls for new undertakings

Exhibit 16-9 describes the structural option that best matches each strategy. Innovators need the flexibility of the organic structure, whereas cost minimizers seek the efficiency and stability of the mechanistic structure. Imitators combine the two structures. They use a mechanistic structure in order to maintain tight controls and low costs in their current activities, while at the same time they create organic subunits in which to pursue new undertakings.

Organization Size

There is considerable evidence to support the idea that an organization's size significantly affects its structure.[22] For instance, large organizations—those that typically employ 2,000 or more people—tend to have more specialization, more departmentalization, more vertical levels, and more rules and regulations than do small organizations. However, the relationship isn't linear. Rather, size affects structure at a decreasing rate. The impact of size becomes less important as an organization expands. Why is this? Essentially, once an organization has around 2,000 employees, it's already fairly mechanistic. An additional 500 employees will not have much impact. On the other hand, adding 500 employees to an organization that has only 300 members is likely to result in a significant shift toward a more mechanistic structure.

Technology

The term **technology** refers to how an organization transfers its inputs into outputs. Every organization has at least one technology for converting financial, human, and physical resources into products or services. The Ford Motor Co., for instance, predominantly uses an assembly-line process to make its products. On the other hand, colleges may use a number of instruction technologies—the ever-popular formal lecture method, the case-analysis method, the experiential exercise method, the programmed learning method, and so forth. In this section we want to show that organizational structures adapt to their technology.

Numerous studies have been carried out on the technology-structure relationship.[23] The details of those studies are quite complex, so we'll go straight to "the bottom line" and attempt to summarize what we know.

The common theme that differentiates technologies is their *degree of routineness.* By this we mean that technologies tend toward either routine or nonroutine activities. The former are characterized by automated and standardized operations. Nonroutine activities are customized. They include varied operations such as furniture restoring, custom shoemaking, and genetic research.

Automobile manufacturers use the assembly-line process as the technology for mass production of cars. At the Volkswagen plant in Wolfsburg, Germany, the carmaker uses robotic equipment for routine activities, such as the welding robots shown here on the Golf V assembly line.

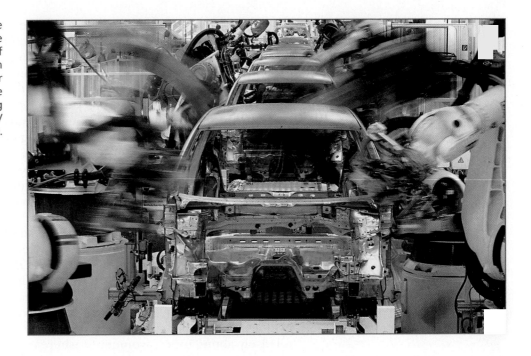

What relationships have been found between technology and structure? Although the relationship is not overwhelmingly strong, we find that routine tasks are associated with taller and more departmentalized structures. The relationship between technology and formalization, however, is stronger. Studies consistently show routineness to be associated with the presence of rule manuals, job descriptions, and other formalized documentation. Finally, an interesting relationship has been found between technology and centralization. It seems logical that routine technologies would be associated with a centralized structure, while nonroutine technologies, which rely more heavily on the knowledge of specialists, would be characterized by delegated decision authority. This position has met with some support. However, a more generalizable conclusion is that the technology-centralization relationship is moderated by the degree of formalization. Formal regulations and centralized decision making are both control mechanisms and management can substitute one for the other. Routine technologies should be associated with centralized control if there is a minimum of rules and regulations. However, if formalization is high, routine technology can be accompanied by decentralization. So, we would predict that routine technology would lead to centralization, but only if formalization is low.

Environment

An organization's **environment** is composed of institutions or forces outside the organization that potentially affect the organization's performance. These typically include suppliers, customers, competitors, government regulatory agencies, public pressure groups, and the like.

technology   *How an organization transfers its inputs into outputs.*

environment   *Institutions or forces outside the organization that potentially affect the organization's performance.*

Why should an organization's structure be affected by its environment? Because of environmental uncertainty. Some organizations face relatively static environments—few forces in their environment are changing. There are, for example, no new competitors, no new technological breakthroughs by current competitors, or little activity by public pressure groups to influence the organization. Other organizations face very dynamic environments—rapidly changing government regulations affecting their business, new competitors, difficulties in acquiring raw materials, continually changing product preferences by customers, and so on. Static environments create significantly less uncertainty for managers than do dynamic ones. And because uncertainty is a threat to an organization's effectiveness, management will try to minimize it. One way to reduce environmental uncertainty is through adjustments in the organization's structure.[24]

Recent research has helped clarify what is meant by environmental uncertainty. It's been found that there are three key dimensions to any organization's environment: capacity, volatility, and complexity.[25]

The *capacity* of an environment refers to the degree to which it can support growth. Rich and growing environments generate excess resources, which can buffer the organization in times of relative scarcity. Abundant capacity, for example, leaves room for an organization to make mistakes, while scarce capacity does not. In 2004, firms operating in the multimedia software business had relatively abundant environments, whereas those in the full-service brokerage business faced relative scarcity.

The degree of instability in an environment is captured in the *volatility* dimension. When there is a high degree of unpredictable change, the environment is dynamic. This makes it difficult for management to predict accurately the probabilities associated with various decision alternatives. At the other extreme is a stable environment. The accelerated changes in Eastern Europe

Myth or Science?

"Bureaucracy Is Dead"

This statement is false. Some bureaucratic characteristics are in decline. And bureaucracy is undoubtedly going through changes. But it's far from dead.

Bureaucracy is characterized by specialization, formalization, departmentalization, centralization, narrow spans of control, and adherence to a chain of command. Have these characteristics disappeared from today's modern organizations? No. In spite of the increased use of empowered teams and flattened structures, certain facts remain.[26] (1) Large size prevails. Organizations that succeed and survive tend to grow to large size, and bureaucracy is efficient with large size. Small organizations and their nonbureaucratic structures are more likely to fail, so over time, small organizations may come and go but large bureaucracies stay. Moreover, while the average business today has considerably fewer employees than those of 30 years ago, these smaller firms are increasingly part of a large, multilocation organization with the financial and technological resources to compete in a global marketplace. (2) Environmental turbulence can be largely managed. The impact of uncertainties in the environment on the organization is substantially reduced by management strategies

such as environmental scanning, strategic alliances, advertising, and lobbying. This allows organizations facing dynamic environments to maintain bureaucratic structures and still be efficient. (3) Bureaucracy's goal of standardization can be increasingly achieved through hiring people who have undergone extensive educational training. Rational discipline, rather than that imposed by rules and regulations, is internalized by hiring professionals with college and university training. They come preprogrammed. In addition, strong cultures help achieve standardization by substituting for high formalization. (4) Finally, technology maintains control. Networked computers allow management to closely monitor the actions of employees without centralization or narrow spans of control. Technology has merely replaced some previously bureaucratic characteristics, but without any loss of management control.

In spite of some changes, bureaucracy is alive and well in many venues. It continues to be a dominant structural form in manufacturing, service firms, hospitals, schools and colleges, the military, and voluntary associations. Why? Because it's still the most efficient way to organize large-scale activities. ■

Exhibit **16-10**	Three-Dimensional Model of the Environment

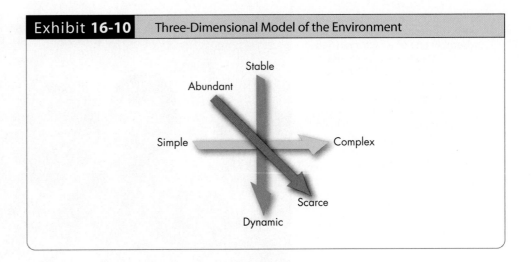

and the demise of the Cold War had dramatic effects on the U.S. defense industry in the 1990s. This moved the environment of major defense contractors like Lockheed Martin, General Dynamics, and Northrop Grumman from relatively stable to dynamic.

Finally, the environment needs to be assessed in terms of *complexity*—that is, the degree of heterogeneity and concentration among environmental elements. Simple environments are homogeneous and concentrated. This might describe the tobacco industry, since there are relatively few players. It's easy for firms in this industry to keep a close eye on the competition. In contrast, environments characterized by heterogeneity and dispersion are called complex. This is essentially the current environment for firms competing in the Internet-connection business. Every day there seems to be another "new kid on the block" with whom current Internet access providers have to deal.

Exhibit 16-10 summarizes our definition of the environment along its three dimensions. The arrows in this figure are meant to indicate movement toward higher uncertainty. So organizations that operate in environments characterized as scarce, dynamic, and complex face the greatest degree of uncertainty. Why? Because they have little room for error, high unpredictability, and a diverse set of elements in the environment to monitor constantly.

Given this three-dimensional definition of environment, we can offer some general conclusions. There is evidence that relates the degrees of environmental uncertainty to different structural arrangements. Specifically, the more scarce, dynamic, and complex the environment, the more organic a structure should be. The more abundant, stable, and simple the environment, the more the mechanistic structure will be preferred.

Organizational Designs and Employee Behavior

We opened this chapter by implying that an organization's structure can have significant effects on its members. In this section, we want to assess directly just what those effects might be.

A review of the evidence linking organizational structures to employee performance and satisfaction leads to a pretty clear conclusion—you can't generalize!

The tasks of these women making parts for pressure cookers on an assembly line at a factory in São Paulo, Brazil, are highly standardized. Individual differences influence how these women respond to their high work specialization. Many may enjoy the routine and repetitiveness of their specialized tasks because working closely with other employees gives them the chance to socialize on the job.

Not everyone prefers the freedom and flexibility of organic structures. Some people are most productive and satisfied when work tasks are standardized and ambiguity is minimized—that is, in mechanistic structures. So any discussion of the effect of organizational design on employee behavior has to address individual differences. To illustrate this point, let's consider employee preferences for work specialization, span of control, and centralization.[27]

The evidence generally indicates that *work specialization* contributes to higher employee productivity, but at the price of reduced job satisfaction. However, this statement ignores individual differences and the type of job tasks people do. As we noted previously, work specialization is not an unending source of higher productivity. Problems start to surface, and productivity begins to suffer, when the human diseconomies of doing repetitive and narrow tasks overtake the economies of specialization. As the workforce has become more highly educated and desirous of jobs that are intrinsically rewarding, the point at which productivity begins to decline seems to be reached more quickly than in decades past.

Although more people today are undoubtedly turned off by overly specialized jobs than were their parents or grandparents, it would be naive to ignore the reality that there is still a segment of the workforce that prefers the routine and repetitiveness of highly specialized jobs. Some individuals want work that makes minimal intellectual demands and provides the security of routine. For these people, high work specialization is a source of job satisfaction. The empirical question, of course, is whether this represents 2 percent of the workforce or 52 percent. Given that there is some self-selection operating in the choice of careers, we might conclude that negative behavioral outcomes from high specialization are most likely to surface in professional jobs occupied by individuals with high needs for personal growth and diversity.

A review of the research indicates that it is probably safe to say there is no evidence to support a relationship between *span of control* and employee performance. Although it is intuitively attractive to argue that large spans might lead to higher employee performance because they provide more distant supervision and more opportunity for personal initiative, the research fails to support this notion. At this point it's impossible to state that any particular span of control is best for producing high performance or high satisfaction among employees. Again, the reason is probably individual differences. That is, some people like to be left alone, while others prefer the security of a boss who is quickly available at all times. Consistent with several of the contingency theories of leadership discussed in Chapter 12, we would expect factors such as employees' experiences and abilities and the degree of structure in their tasks to explain when wide or narrow spans of control are likely to contribute to their performance and job satisfaction. However, there is some evidence indicating that a manager's job satisfaction increases as the number of employees supervised increases.

We find fairly strong evidence linking *centralization* and job satisfaction. In general, organizations that are less centralized have a greater amount of participative decision making. And the evidence suggests that participative decision making is positively related to job satisfaction. But, again, individual differences surface. The decentralization-satisfaction relationship is strongest with employees who have low self-esteem. Because individuals with low self-esteem have less confidence in their abilities, they place a higher value on shared decision making, which means that they're not held solely responsible for decision outcomes.

Our conclusion: To maximize employee performance and satisfaction, individual differences, such as experience, personality, and the work task, should be taken into account. In addition, national culture influences the preference for structure, so it, too, needs to be considered.[28] For instance, organizations that operate with people from high power distance cultures, such as those found in Greece, France, and most of Latin America, will find employees much more accepting of mechanistic structures than where employees come from low power distance countries. So you need to consider cultural differences along with individual differences when making predictions on how structure will affect employee performance and satisfaction.

One obvious insight needs to be made before we leave this topic: People don't select employers randomly. There is substantial evidence that individuals are attracted to, selected by, and stay with organizations that suit their personal characteristics.[29] Job candidates who prefer predictability, for instance, are likely to seek out and take employment in mechanistic structures, and those who want autonomy are more likely to end up in an organic structure. So the effect of structure on employee behavior is undoubtedly reduced when the selection process facilitates proper matching of individual characteristics with organizational characteristics.

Summary and Implications for Managers

The theme of this chapter has been that an organization's internal structure contributes to explaining and predicting behavior. That is, in addition to individual and group factors, the structural relationships in which people work has a bearing on employee attitudes and behavior.

What's the basis for the argument that structure has an impact on both attitudes and behavior? To the degree that an organization's structure reduces ambiguity for employees and clarifies concerns such as "What am I supposed to do?" "How am I supposed to do it?" "To whom do I report?" and "To whom do I go if I have a problem?" it shapes their attitudes and facilitates and motivates them to higher levels of performance.

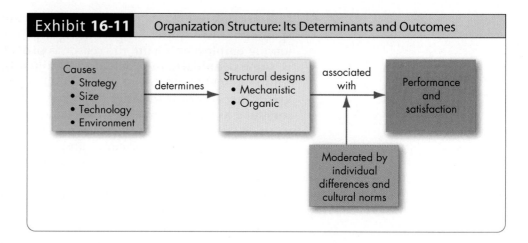

Exhibit 16-11   Organization Structure: Its Determinants and Outcomes

Of course, structure also constrains employees to the extent that it limits and controls what they do. For example, organizations structured around high levels of formalization and specialization, strict adherence to the chain of command, limited delegation of authority, and narrow spans of control give employees little autonomy. Controls in such organizations are tight, and behavior will tend to vary within a narrow range. In contrast, organizations that are structured around limited specialization, low formalization, wide spans of control, and the like provide employees greater freedom and, thus, will be characterized by greater behavioral diversity.

Exhibit 16-11 visually summarizes what we've discussed in this chapter. Strategy, size, technology, and environment determine the type of structure an organization will have. For simplicity's sake, we can classify structural designs around one of two models: mechanistic or organic. The specific effect of structural designs on performance and satisfaction is moderated by employees' individual preferences and cultural norms.

One last point: Managers need to be reminded that structural variables like work specialization, span of control, formalization, and centralization are objective characteristics that can be measured by organizational researchers. The findings and conclusions we've offered in this chapter, in fact, are directly a result of the work of these researchers. But employees don't objectively measure these structural characteristics. They observe things around them in an unscientific fashion and then form their own implicit models of what the organization's structure is like. How many people did they have to interview with before they were offered their jobs? How many people work in their departments and buildings? Is there an organization policy manual? If so, is it readily available and do people follow it closely? How are the organization and its top management described in newspapers and periodicals? Answers to questions such as these, when combined with an employee's past experiences and comments made by peers, lead members to form an overall subjective image of what their organization's structure is like. This image, though, may in no way resemble the organization's actual objective structural characteristics.

The importance of these **implicit models of organizational structure** should not be overlooked. As we noted in Chapter 5, people respond to their perceptions rather than objective reality. The research, for instance, on the relationship between many structural variables and subsequent levels of performance or job satisfaction is far from consistent. We explained some of this as being attributable to individual differences. However, an additional contributing cause to these inconsistent findings might be diverse perceptions of the objective characteristics. Researchers typically focus on actual levels of the various structural components, but these may be irrelevant if people interpret similar components differently. The bottom line, therefore, is to understand how employees interpret their organization's structure. That should prove a more meaningful predictor of their behavior than the objective characteristics themselves.

implicit models of organizational structure
Perceptions that people hold regarding structural variables formed by observing things around them in an unscientific fashion.

Technology Is Reshaping Organizations

In today's chaotic, uncertain, and high-tech world, there is essentially only one type of design that is going to survive. This is the electronically configured organic organization.[30]

We are undergoing a second Industrial Revolution and it will transform every aspect of people's lives. The changes that large corporations used to take a decade to implement now occur in 1 to 2 years. Companies that are successful will be designed to thrive on change. And the structure of those organizations will have common characteristics.

Ten years from now there will be nothing but electronic organizations. Brick-and-mortar organizations won't go away, but click-and-mortar will become the only means to survive. In addition, every organization will need to keep its finger on the pulse of its customers. Customer priorities will change very rapidly. What customers will pay a premium for will become a commodity so rapidly that those who lose touch with their customers will be candidates for extinction. Consumers are gaining the ability to compare the prices of hundreds of competitors' offerings rather than just two or three. This is going to dramatically drive down prices. If firms don't improve their productivity to match these drops in prices, they'll be out of business.

Technology allows firms to stay closer to the customer, to move jobs to where costs are lowest, and to make decisions much more rapidly. For instance, executives at Cisco Systems can monitor expenses, gross margins, the supply chain, and profitability in real time. There no longer need to be surprises. Every employee can make decisions that might have had to come from the top management ranks a few years ago. At the end of a quarter, individual product managers at Cisco can see exactly what the gross margins are on their products, measure whether they are below expectations, and determine the cause of any discrepancy. Quicker decision making at lower levels will translate into higher profit margins. So instead of the CEO or chief financial officer making 50 to 100 different decisions in a quarter, managers throughout the organization can make millions of decisions. Companies that don't adjust to create this capability will be noncompetitive.

There's an old saying that every generation thinks it has discovered sex. This seems to be the case with technology and how it's going to change the world completely.

Technology will transform the structure of organizations at a much slower rate than many believe.[31] For instance, it's useful to go back and ask if the railroads changed the world. There were definitely changes in how commerce and industry were arranged. But life remained the same, and the way people related to each other remained the same.

There are changes occurring that will influence the way businesses organize. But the changes have been, and will continue to be, gradual. They may accelerate some, but we're not going to see a revolution in the design of organizations. Take the case of globalization. It's significant but it is also evolutionary. Has the formation of the European Union abolished national borders in the largest continental society in the Western World? No. France is still France, and Germany is still Germany. Things have changed, but things have not changed.

The emphasis on speed has its limits. Brains don't speed up. The exchange of ideas doesn't really speed up, only the overhead that slowed down the exchange. When it comes down to the bulk of knowledge work, the twenty-first century works the same as the twentieth century: You can reach people around the clock, but they won't think any better or faster just because you've reached them faster. The give-and-take remains a limiting factor.

The virtual organization also has its limitations. When you farm out your data processing, manufacturing, and other functions, you make your capabilities available to your competitors. So virtualization of work diminishes competitive advantages. It leads to rapidly spreading commoditization of everything. Any function that an organization uses to achieve a competitive advantage cannot be outsourced.

Look back over the past 40 years. People haven't changed. And our fundamental organizations haven't changed. On the fringes, there is more looseness in the organization. But more hasn't changed than has. The changes we've seen have been slow and gradual. And that pace is likely to continue into the future.

Questions for Review

1. Why isn't work specialization an unending source of increased productivity?

2. In what ways can management departmentalize?

3. All things being equal, which is more efficient, a wide or a narrow span of control? Why?

4. What is a matrix structure? When would management use it?

5. Contrast the virtual organization with the boundaryless organization.

6. What type of structure works best with an innovation strategy? A cost-minimization strategy? An imitation strategy?

7. Summarize the size-structure relationship.

8. Define and give an example of what is meant by the term *technology*.

9. Summarize the environment-structure relationship.

10. Explain the importance of the statement: "Employees form implicit models of organizational structure."

Questions for Critical Thinking

1. How is the typical large corporation of today organized in contrast to how that same organization was probably organized in the 1960s?

2. Do you think most employees prefer high formalization? Support your position.

3. If you were an employee in a matrix structure, what pluses do you think the structure would provide? What about minuses?

4. What behavioral predictions would you make about people who worked in a "pure" boundaryless organization (if such a structure were ever to exist)?

5. Pfizer buys Warner-Lambert. Alcoa purchases Reynolds Metals. Nestlés S.A. merges with Ralston Purina. Each of these is a recent example of large companies combining with other large companies. Does this imply that small isn't necessarily beautiful? Are mechanistic forms winning the "survival-of-the-fittest" battle? What are the implications of this consolidation trend for organizational behavior?

Team Exercise

AUTHORITY FIGURES

Purpose
To learn about one's experiences with and feelings about authority.

Time
Approximately 75 minutes.

Procedure

1. Your instructor will separate class members into groups based on their birth order. Groups are formed consisting of "only children," "eldest," "middle," and "youngest," according to placement in families. Larger groups will be broken into smaller ones, with four or five members, to allow for freer conversation.

2. Each group member should talk about how he or she "typically reacts to the authority of others." Focus should be on specific situations that offer general information about how individuals deal with authority figures (for example, bosses, teachers, parents, or coaches). The group has 25 minutes to develop a written list of how the group generally deals with others' authority. Be sure to separate tendencies that group members share and those they do not.

3. Repeat Step 2, except this time discuss how group members "typically are as authority figures." Again make a list of shared characteristics.

4. Each group will share its general conclusions with the entire class.

5. Class discussion will focus on questions such as:
   (a) What patterned differences have surfaced between the groups?
   (b) What may account for these differences?
   (c) What hypotheses might explain the connection between how individuals react to the authority of others and how they are as authority figures?

Source: This exercise is adapted from W. A. Kahn, "An Exercise of Authority," *Organizational Behavior Teaching Review* XIV, no. 2 (1989–90), pp. 28–42. Reprinted with permission.

Ethical Dilemma

JUST FOLLOWING ORDERS

In 1996, Betty Vinson took a job as a midlevel accountant for $50,000 a year with a small long-distance company in Jackson, Mississippi. Within 5. years, that long-distance company had grown up to become telecom giant WorldCom.

Hardworking and diligent, Ms. Vinson was promoted to senior manager in WorldCom's corporate accounting division within 2 years. In her new job, she helped compile quarterly results, along with 10 employees who reported to her. Soon after she took the position, Vinson's bosses asked her to make false accounting entries. At first, she said no. But continued pressure led to her finally caving in. Her decision to make the false entries came after the company's chief financial officer assured her that he would assume all responsibility.

Over the course of six quarters, Ms. Vinson made illegal entries to bolster WorldCom's profits at the request of her superiors. At the end of 18 months, she had helped falsify at least $3.7 billion in profits. Of course, the whole scheme unraveled in 2002, in what became the largest fraud case in corporate history.

Ms. Vinson pleaded guilty to two criminal counts of conspiracy and securities fraud, charges that carry a maximum sentence of 15 years in prison. On August 5, 2005, Vinson was sentenced to 5 months in prison and 5 months house arrest. She was also sentenced to 3 years of probation.

What would you have done had you been in Ms. Vinson's job? Is "just following orders" an acceptable excuse for breaking the law? If your livelihood is on the line, do you say no to a powerful boss? What can organizations do to lessen the chance that employees might capitulate to unethical pressures imposed by their boss?

Source: Based on S. Pulliam, "A Staffer Ordered to Commit Fraud Balked, Then Caved," *The Wall Street Journal,* June 23, 2003, p. A1.

Case Incident 1

"I DETEST BUREAUCRACY"

Greg Strakosch, founder and CEO of interactive media company TechTarget, hates bureaucracy. So he's created a workplace where his 210 employees are free to come and go as they please. There are no set policies mandating working hours or detailing sick, personal, or vacation days. Employees are free to take as much vacation as they want and to work those hours when they're most productive—even if it's between midnight and 4 A.M. Need a day off to take your kid to camp? No problem. Strakosch says ideas like setting a specific number of sick days "strikes me as arbitrary and dumb." He trusts his employees to act responsibly.

Strakosch is quick to state that "this isn't a country club." A painstaking hiring process is designed to weed out all but the most autonomous. Managers set ambitious quarterly goals and employees are given plenty of independence to achieve them. But there is little tolerance for failure. In the most recent 12-month period, for instance, Strakosch fired 7 percent of his workforce for underachieving. And while hours are flexible, employees frequently put in at least 50 hours a week. Regardless of the number of hours they've worked, they are required to remain accessible via e-mail, cell phones, or instant messaging.

Strakosch's approach seems to be working. Sales in 2003 were expected to hit $35 million—up nearly 30 percent from 2002.

Questions

1. What type of organization is this?

2. Why does TechTarget's structure work?

3. How transferable is this structure to other organizations?

4. Would you want to work at TechTarget? Why or why not?

Source: P. J. Sauer, "Open-Door Management," *INC.,* June 2003, p. 44.

Case Incident 2

NO BOSSES AT W. L. GORE & ASSOCIATES

You've probably bought a garment made of W. L. Gore & Associates' flagship product, Gore-Tex, a fabric that blocks wind and water, yet is highly breathable thanks to Gore's patented technology. But you might not know that the company offers a host of other products, from heart patches and synthetic blood vessels to air pollution filters and fuel cells. In fact, W. L. Gore & Associates makes more than 1,000 products. Though its financial data are not publicly available, a spokesperson for the company said that Gore had double-digit revenue growth the past three years. With this type of performance and extensive product line, you might expect Gore to be structured like big companies such as General Electric, Microsoft, or 3M. But it's not, and it never was.

Wilbert L. Gore founded W. L. Gore & Associates in 1958. Gore believed that too much hierarchy and bureaucracy stifled creativity and adaptation, a view he formed during his 17-year career as a DuPont engineer. He stated once that "communication really happens in the car pool," meaning informal arenas allowed employees to share their ideas openly without fear of criticism from management. So Gore decided to eliminate the hierarchy found in most organizations. Instead, he instructed everyone to communicate openly, with little regard to status differences. In fact, Gore eliminated status differences altogether. At W. L. Gore & Associates, there are no job titles. Each employee works on projects collaboratively, while at the same time is given the freedom to develop new ideas. Ideas that are deemed worthy of pursuing by team members are then developed.

In addition to the lack of bureaucracy, Gore also kept his facilities staffed with a small number of employees to promote information sharing and foster teamwork. For example, he limited staffing at manufacturing plants to 200 employees, which is smaller than typical manufacturing firms. Gore believed the number was low enough for employees to get to know one another, allowing them to talk freely about their knowledge and ideas. The result of such a corporate structure has been tremendous growth and profit. Gore also has been an industry leader in innovation.

Gore's unique structure does take some getting used to, particularly for new employees. Diane Davidson recalls that the lack of a formal hierarchy was bewildering at first. As a sales executive in the apparel industry, Davidson was hired by Gore to promote its fabrics to designers such as Prada and Hugo Boss. States Davidson, "I came from a very traditional, male-dominated business—the men's shoe business. When I arrived at Gore, I didn't know who did what. I wondered how anything got done here. It was driving me crazy." Instead of a formal supervisor, Davidson was assigned to a "starting sponsor." As opposed to a traditional supervisor, the sponsor at Gore helps new hires learn the ropes—which primarily consist of getting to know one's team.

"Who's my boss." she repeatedly asked her sponsor. Her sponsor would reply, "Stop using the b-word."

Davidson eventually got used to Gore's structure. "Your team is your boss, because you don't want to let them down. Everyone's your boss, and no one's your boss," she explains. Not only are there no formal supervisors at Gore, but employees' job descriptions are conspicuously absent as well. Employees at Gore perform multiple tasks to create a new product. Davidson, for example, is involved in marketing, sales, and sponsorship—roles that typically are separated in other organizations. As John Morgan, an employee of Gore for more than 20 years, states, "You join a team and you're an idiot. It takes 18 months to build credibility. Early on, it's really frustrating. In hindsight, it makes sense. As a sponsor, I tell new hires, 'Your job for the first 6 months is to get to know the team,' but they have trouble believing it—and not contributing when other people are."

Questions

1. How would you characterize Gore's organizational structure using terms from this chapter? For example, is it mechanistic or organic? How might this structure influence Gore's strategy?

2. Considering what you know about individual differences such as personality, what types of employees might respond more or less favorably to Gore's lack of hierarchy?

3. What are some advantages and disadvantages of Gore's structure from a company perspective? What about from an employee perspective?

4. How might Gore's organizational design affect its relationships with external companies that are more hierarchical in nature?

Source: Based on A. Deutschman, "The Fabric of Creativity," *Fast Company,* December 2004, pp. 54–62.

Endnotes

1. This opening vignette is based on Mark Bechtel, "My Sportsman Choice: Gordon Gee," SI.com. (http://sportsillustrated. cnn.com/2004/magazine/specials/sportsman/2004/11/22/ bechtel.gee/) November 22, 2004; "Major Changes for Vanderbilt Athletics," *The New York Times*, September 10, 2003, p. C19; M. Cass, "Vanderbilt Realigns Management," *USA Today*, September 10, 2003, p. 7C; and "Vanderbilt University is Not Getting Rid of Sports," *The Chronicle of Higher Education*, September 19, 2003, p. A35.

2. See, for instance, R. L. Daft, *Organization Theory and Design*, 8th ed. (Cincinnati, OH: Southwestern, 2004).

3. C. Hymowitz, "Managers Suddenly Have to Answer to a Crowd of Bosses," *The Wall Street Journal*, August 12, 2003, p. B1.

4. See, for instance, L. Urwick, *The Elements of Administration* (New York: Harper & Row, 1944), pp. 52–53; and J. H. Gittell, "Supervisory Span, Relational Coordination, and Flight Departure Performance: A Reassessment of Postbureaucracy Theory," *Organization Science*, July–August 2001, pp. 468–83.

5. J. Child and R. G. McGrath, "Organizations Unfettered: Organizational Form in an Information-Intensive Economy," *Academy of Management Journal*, December 2001, pp. 1135–48.

6. H. Mintzberg, *Structure in Fives: Designing Effective Organizations* (Upper Saddle River, NJ: Prentice Hall, 1983), p. 157.

7. S. Lohr, "I.B.M. Chief Gerstner Recalls Difficult Days at Big Blue," *The New York Times*, July 31, 2000, p. C5.

8. K. Knight, "Matrix Organization: A Review," *Journal of Management Studies*, May 1976, pp. 111–30; L. R. Burns and D. R. Wholey, "Adoption and Abandonment of Matrix Management Programs: Effects of Organizational Characteristics and Interorganizational Networks," *Academy of Management Journal*, February 1993, pp. 106–38; and R. E. Anderson, "Matrix Redux," *Business Horizons*, November–December 1994, pp. 6–10.

9. See, for instance, S. M. Davis and P. R. Lawrence, "Problems of Matrix Organization," *Harvard Business Review*, May–June 1978, pp. 131–42; and T. Sy and S. Cote, "Emotional Intelligence: A Key Ability to Succeed in the Matrix Organization," *Journal of Management Development* 23, no. 5 (2004), pp. 437–55.

10. S. A. Mohrman, S. G. Cohen, and A. M. Mohrman, Jr., *Designing Team-Based Organizations* (San Francisco: Jossey-Bass, 1995); F. Ostroff, *The Horizontal Organization* (New York: Oxford University Press, 1999); and R. Forrester and A. B. Drexler, "A Model for Team-Based Organization Performance," *Academy of Management Executive*, August 1999, pp. 36–49.

11. M. Kaeter, "The Age of the Specialized Generalist," *Training*, December 1993, pp. 48–53.

12. C. Fishman, "Whole Foods Is All Teams," *Fast Company*, Greatest Hits, vol. 1, 1997, pp. 102–13.

13. See, for instance, R. E. Miles and C. C. Snow, "The New Network Firm: A Spherical Structure Built on Human Investment Philosophy," *Organizational Dynamics*, Spring 1995, pp. 5–18; D. Pescovitz, "The Company Where Everybody's a Temp," *The New York Times Magazine*, June 11, 2000, pp. 94–96; W. F. Cascio, "Managing a Virtual Workplace," *Academy of Management Executive*, August 2000, pp. 81–90; B. Hedberg, G. Dahlgren, J. Hansson, and N. Olve, *Virtual Organizations and Beyond* (New York: Wiley, 2001); M. A. Schilling and H. K. Steensma, "The Use of Modular Organizational Forms: An Industry-Level Analysis," *Academy of Management Journal*, December 2001, pp. 1149–68; K. R. T. Larsen and C. R. McInerney, "Preparing to Work in the Virtual Organization," *Information and Management*, May 2002, pp. 445–56; J. Gertner, "Newman's Own: Two Friends and a Canoe Paddle," *The New York Times*, November 16, 2003, p. 4BU; and Y. Shin, "A Person-Environment Fit Model for Virtual Organizations," *Journal of Management*, October 2004, pp. 725–43.

14. J. Bates, "Making Movies and Moving On," *Los Angeles Times*, January 19, 1998, p. A1.

15. "GE: Just Your Average Everyday $60 Billion Family Grocery Store," *Industry Week*, May 2, 1994, pp. 13–18.

16. H. C. Lucas Jr., *The T-Form Organization: Using Technology to Design Organizations for the 21st Century* (San Francisco: Jossey-Bass, 1996).

17. This section is based on D. D. Davis, "Form, Function and Strategy in Boundaryless Organizations," in A. Howard (ed.), *The Changing Nature of Work* (San Francisco: Jossey-Bass, 1995), pp. 112–38; P. Roberts, "We Are One Company, No Matter Where We Are. Time and Space Are Irrelevant," *Fast Company*, April–May 1998, pp. 122–28; R. L. Cross, A. Yan, and M. R. Louis, "Boundary Activities in 'Boundaryless' Organizations: A Case Study of a Transformation to a Team-Based Structure," *Human Relations*, June 2000, pp. 841–68; and R. Ashkenas, D. Ulrich, T. Jick, and S. Kerr, *The Boundaryless Organization: Breaking the Chains of Organizational Structure*, revised and updated (San Francisco: Jossey-Bass, 2002).

18. T. Burns and G. M. Stalker, *The Management of Innovation* (London: Tavistock, 1961); and J. A. Courtright, G. T. Fairhurst, and L. E. Rogers, "Interaction Patterns in Organic and Mechanistic Systems," *Academy of Management Journal*, December 1989, pp. 773–802.

19. This analysis is referred to as a contingency approach to organization design. See, for instance, J. M. Pennings, "Structural Contingency Theory: A Reappraisal," in B. M. Staw and L. L. Cummings (eds.), *Research in Organizational Behavior*, vol. 14 (Greenwich, CT: JAI Press, 1992), pp. 267–309; J. R. Hollenbeck, H. Moon, A. P. J. Ellis, B. J. West, D. R. Ilgen, L. Sheppard, C. O. L. H. Porter, and J. A. Wagner III, "Structural Contingency Theory and Individual Differences: Examination of External and Internal Person-Team Fit," *Journal of Applied Psychology*, June 2002, pp. 599–606; and H. Moon, J. R. Hollenbeck, S. E. Humphrey, D. R. Ilgen, B. West, A. P. J. Ellis, and C. O. L. H. Porter, "Asymmetric Adaptability: Dynamic Team Structures as One-Way Streets," *Academy of Management Journal*, October 2004, pp. 681–95.

20. The strategy-structure thesis was originally proposed in A. D. Chandler, Jr., *Strategy and Structure: Chapters in the History of the Industrial Enterprise* (Cambridge, MA: MIT Press, 1962). For an updated analysis, see T. L. Amburgey and T. Dacin, "As the Left Foot Follows the Right? The Dynamics of Strategic and Structural Change," *Academy of Management Journal*, December 1994, pp. 1427–52.

21. See R. E. Miles and C. C. Snow, *Organizational Strategy, Structure, and Process* (New York: McGraw-Hill, 1978); D. Miller, "The Structural and Environmental Correlates of Business Strategy," *Strategic Management Journal*, January–February

1987, pp. 55–76; D. C. Galunic and K. M. Eisenhardt, "Renewing the Strategy-Structure-Performance Paradigm," in B. M. Staw and L. L. Cummings (eds.), *Research in Organizational Behavior*, vol. 16 (Greenwich, CT: JAI Press, 1994), pp. 215–55; and I. C. Harris and T. W. Ruefli, "The Strategy/Structure Debate: An Examination of the Performance Implications," *Journal of Management Studies*, June 2000, pp. 587–603.

22. See, for instance, P. M. Blau and R. A. Schoenherr, *The Structure of Organizations* (New York: Basic Books, 1971); D. S. Pugh, "The Aston Program of Research: Retrospect and Prospect," in A. H. Van de Ven and W. F. Joyce (eds.), *Perspectives on Organization Design and Behavior* (New York: John Wiley, 1981), pp. 135–66; R. Z. Gooding and J. A. Wagner III, "A Meta-Analytic Review of the Relationship Between Size and Performance: The Productivity and Efficiency of Organizations and Their Subunits," *Administrative Science Quarterly*, December 1985, pp. 462–81; and A. C. Bluedorn, "Pilgrim's Progress: Trends and Convergence in Research on Organizational Size and Environments," *Journal of Management*, Summer 1993, pp. 163–92.

23. See J. Woodward, *Industrial Organization: Theory and Practice* (London: Oxford University Press, 1965); C. Perrow, "A Framework for the Comparative Analysis of Organizations," *American Sociological Review*, April 1967, pp. 194–208; J. D. Thompson, *Organizations in Action* (New York: McGraw-Hill, 1967); J. Hage and M. Aiken, "Routine Technology, Social Structure, and Organizational Goals," *Administrative Science Quarterly*, September 1969, pp. 366–77; C. C. Miller, W. H. Glick, Y. Wang, and G. P. Huber, "Understanding Technology-Structure Relationships: Theory Development and Meta-Analytic Theory Testing," *Academy of Management Journal*, June 1991, pp. 370–99; and K. H. Roberts and M. Grabowski, "Organizations, Technology, and Structuring," in S. R. Clegg, C. Hardy, and W. R. Nord (eds.), *Managing Organizations: Current Issues* (Thousand Oaks, CA: Sage, 1999), pp. 159–71.

24. See F. E. Emery and E. Trist, "The Causal Texture of Organizational Environments," *Human Relations*, February 1965, pp. 21–32; P. Lawrence and J. W. Lorsch, *Organization and Environment: Managing Differentiation and Integration* (Boston: Harvard Business School, Division of Research, 1967); M. Yasai-Ardekani, "Structural Adaptations to Environments," *Academy of Management Review*, January 1986, pp. 9–21; Bluedorn, "Pilgrim's Progress"; and M. Arndt, and B. Bigelow, "Presenting Structural Innovation in an Instituational Environment: Hospitals' Use of Impression Management," *Administrative Science Quarterly*, September 2000, pp. 494–522.

25. G. G. Dess and D. W. Beard, "Dimensions of Organizational Task Environments," *Administrative Science Quarterly*, March 1984, pp. 52–73; E. A. Gerloff, N. K. Muir, and W. D. Bodensteiner, "Three Components of Perceived Environmental Uncertainty: An Exploratory Analysis of the Effects of Aggregation," *Journal of Management*, December 1991, pp. 749–68; and O. Shenkar, N. Aranya, and T. Almor, "Construct Dimensions in the Contingency Model: An Analysis Comparing Metric and Non-Metric Multivariate Instruments," *Human Relations*, May 1995, pp. 559–80.

26. See S. P. Robbins, *Organization Theory: Structure, Design, and Applications*, 3rd ed. (Upper Saddle River, NJ: Prentice Hall, 1990), pp. 320–25; and B. Harrison, *Lean and Mean: The Changing Landscape of Corporate Power in the Age of Flexibility* (New York: Basic Books, 1994).

27. See, for instance, L. W. Porter and E. E. Lawler III, "Properties of Organization Structure in Relation to Job Attitudes and Job Behavior," *Psychological Bulletin*, July 1965, pp. 23–51; L. R. James and A. P. Jones, "Organization Structure: A Review of Structural Dimensions and Their Conceptual Relationships with Individual Attitudes and Behavior," *Organizational Behavior and Human Performance*, June 1976, pp. 74–113; D. R. Dalton, W. D. Todor, M. J. Spendolini, G. J. Fielding, and L. W. Porter, "Organization Structure and Performance: A Critical Review," *Academy of Management Review*, January 1980, pp. 49–64; W. Snizek and J. H. Bullard, "Perception of Bureaucracy and Changing Job Satisfaction: A Longitudinal Analysis," *Organizational Behavior and Human Performance*, October 1983, pp. 275–87; and D. B. Turban and T. L. Keon, "Organizational Attractiveness: An Interactionist Perspective," *Journal of Applied Psychology*, April 1994, pp. 184–93.

28. See, for example, P. R. Harris and R. T. Moran, *Managing Cultural Differences*, 5th ed. (Houston: Gulf Publishing, 1999).

29. See, for instance, B. Schneider, "The People Make the Place," *Personnel Psychology*, Autumn 1987, pp. 437–53; B. Schneider, H. W. Goldstein, and D. B. Smith, "The ASA Framework: An Update," *Personnel Psychology*, Winter 1995, pp. 747–73; J. Schaubroeck, D. C. Ganster, and J. R. Jones, "Organization and Occupation Influences in the Attraction-Selection-Attrition Process," *Journal of Applied Psychology*, December 1998, pp. 869–91; and B. Schneider, D. B. Smith, and M. C. Paul, "P-E Fit and the Attraction-Selection-Attrition Model of Organizational Functioning: Introduction and Overview" in M. Erez and U. Kleinbeck (eds.), *Work Motivation in the Context of a Globalizing Economy* (Mahwah, NJ: Lawrence Erlbaum Associates, 2001), pp. 231–46.

30. This argument was presented by J. Chambers, "Nothing Except E-Companies," *BusinessWeek*, August 28, 2000, pp. 210–12.

31. This argument was presented by A. Grove, "I'm a Little Skeptical . . . Brains Don't Speed Up," *BusinessWeek*, August 28, 2000, pp. 212–14.

Organizational Culture

After studying this chapter, you should be able to:

1 Describe institutionalization and its relationship to organizational culture.

2 Define the common characteristics making up organizational culture.

3 Identify the functional and dysfunctional effects of organizational culture on people and the organization.

4 Explain the factors determining an organization's culture.

5 List the factors that maintain an organization's culture.

6 Outline the various socialization alternatives available to management.

7 Clarify how culture is transmitted to employees.

8 Describe a customer-responsive culture.

9 Identify characteristics of a spiritual culture.

L E A R N I N G   O B J E C T I V E S

CHAPTER 17

Google's Organizational Culture

Google's founders Larry Page and Sergey Brin developed the idea for their company in their Stanford University dorm room. Today, Google is the world's largest search engine. Its 82 million users per month have access to more than 8 billion Web pages. More than 50 percent of Google's traffic occurs outside the United States. (By the way, *googol* is the mathematical term for a 1 followed by 100 zeros.)

Though growing rapidly, Google still maintains a small-company feel. At the Googleplex headquarters in Mountain View, California, "Googlers" eat in the Google café known as "Charlie's Place." Topics range from the trivial to the technical, and whether the discussion is about computer games or encryption or ad-serving software, it's not unusual to hear someone say, "That's a product I helped develop before I came to Google."

Google's culture is informal. Googlers work in high-density clusters, with three or four staffers sharing space with couches and dogs. There's little in the way of corporate hierarchy, and employees wear different hats. The international Webmaster who creates Google's holiday logos spent a week translating the entire site into Korean. The chief operations engineer is also a licensed neurosurgeon.

Google's hiring policy emphasizes ability over experience. The result is a staff that reflects the global audience the search engine serves. Google has offices around the globe and Google engineering centers are recruiting local talent in locations from Zurich to Bangalore. Dozens of languages are spoken by Google staffers, from Turkish to Telugu. When not at work, Googlers pursue interests from cross-country cycling to wine tasting, from flying to Frisbee™. Reza Behforooz, a Google software engineer, comments, "Google has an amazingly cool and passionate work environment—and a strong commitment to technical excellence so that we can build the best products to help people all around the globe."[1] ■

A strong organizational culture like Google's gives the company direction. It also provides direction to employees. It helps them to understand "the way things are done around here." A strong culture additionally provides stability to an organization. But, for some organizations, it can also be a major barrier to change. In this chapter, we show that every organization has a culture and, depending on its strength, it can have a significant influence on the attitudes and behaviors of organization members.

Institutionalization: A Forerunner of Culture

The idea of viewing organizations as cultures—where there is a system of shared meaning among members—is a relatively recent phenomenon. Until the mid-1980s, organizations were, for the most part, simply thought of as rational means by which to coordinate and control a group of people. They had vertical levels, departments, authority relationships, and so forth. But organizations are more. They have personalities too, just like individuals. They can be rigid or flexible, unfriendly or supportive, innovative or conservative. General Electric offices and people *are* different from the offices and people at General Mills. Harvard and MIT are in the same business—education—and separated only by the width of the Charles River, but each has a unique feeling and character beyond its structural characteristics. Organizational theorists now acknowledge this by recognizing the important role that culture plays in the lives of organization members. Interestingly, though, the origin of culture as an independent variable affecting an employee's attitudes and behavior can be traced back more than 50 years ago to the notion of **institutionalization**.[2]

When an organization becomes institutionalized, it takes on a life of its own, apart from its founders or any of its members. Ross Perot created Electronic Data Systems (EDS) in the early 1960s, but he left in 1987 to found a new company, Perot Systems. EDS has continued to thrive despite the departure of its founder. Sony, Gillette, McDonald's, and Disney are examples of organizations that have existed beyond the life of their founder or any one member.

In addition, when an organization becomes institutionalized, it becomes valued for itself, not merely for the goods or services it produces. It acquires immortality. If its original goals are no longer relevant, it doesn't go out of business. Rather, it redefines itself. A classic example is the March of Dimes. It was originally created to fund the battle against polio. When polio was essentially eradicated in the 1950s, the March of Dimes didn't close down. It merely redefined its objectives as funding research for reducing birth defects and lowering infant mortality.

Institutionalization operates to produce common understandings among members about what is appropriate and, fundamentally, meaningful behavior.[3] So when an organization takes on institutional permanence, acceptable modes of behavior become largely self-evident to its members. As we'll see, this is essentially the same thing that organizational culture does. So an understanding of what makes up an organization's culture and how it is created, sustained, and learned will enhance our ability to explain and predict the behavior of people at work.

What Is Organizational Culture?

A number of years back, an executive was asked what he thought *organizational culture* meant. He gave essentially the same answer that a Supreme Court Justice once gave in attempting to define pornography: "I can't define it, but I know it

Highly aggressive and competitive describes the culture of Ireland's Ryanair Airlines. Ryanair was founded in 1985 as the first low-cost airline in Europe to compete against well-established large airlines like British Airways and Aer Lingus. Ryanair's competitive culture has fueled the airline's rapid growth. Carrying 5,000 passengers on one route from Ireland to England during its first operating year, Ryanair now carries 35 million passengers on 235 routes across 20 European countries. Leading the airline's competitive charge is CEO Michael O'Leary, shown here, who frequently serves as Ryanair's spokesman in ads and promotions that focus on the airline's low fares.

when I see it." This executive's approach to defining organizational culture isn't acceptable for our purposes. We need a basic definition to provide a point of departure for our quest to better understand the phenomenon. In this section, we propose a specific definition and review several peripheral issues that revolve around this definition.

A Definition

There seems to be wide agreement that **organizational culture** refers to a system of shared meaning held by members that distinguishes the organization from other organizations.[4] This system of shared meaning is, on closer examination, a set of key characteristics that the organization values. The research suggests that there are seven primary characteristics that, in aggregate, capture the essence of an organization's culture.[5]

1. *Innovation and risk taking* The degree to which employees are encouraged to be innovative and take risks.
2. *Attention to detail* The degree to which employees are expected to exhibit precision, analysis, and attention to detail.
3. *Outcome orientation* The degree to which management focuses on results or outcomes rather than on the techniques and processes used to achieve those outcomes.
4. *People orientation* The degree to which management decisions take into consideration the effect of outcomes on people within the organization.

institutionalization   *A condition that occurs when an organization takes on a life of its own, apart from any of its members, and acquires immortality.*

organizational culture   *A system of shared meaning held by members that distinguishes the organization from other organizations.*

5. *Team orientation* The degree to which work activities are organized around teams rather than individuals.
6. *Aggressiveness* The degree to which people are aggressive and competitive rather than easygoing.
7. *Stability* The degree to which organizational activities emphasize maintaining the status quo in contrast to growth.

Each of these characteristics exists on a continuum from low to high. Appraising the organization on these seven characteristics, then, gives a composite picture of the organization's culture. This picture becomes the basis for feelings of shared understanding that members have about the organization, how things are done in it, and the way members are supposed to behave. Exhibit 17-1 demonstrates how these characteristics can be mixed to create highly diverse organizations.

Before you move on to the next section, take some time to think about the organizational culture that would suit you best. For example, do you thrive on taking risks? Would you want to work for a manager who cares more about the bottom line than her employees? Do you like working on a team, or would you rather accomplish a task on your own? The Self-Assessment feature on pg. 575 can give you some insight into the type of organization you might want to work for.

Exhibit 17-1   Contrasting Organizational Cultures

Organization A

This organization is a manufacturing firm. Managers are expected to fully document all decisions, and "good managers" are those who can provide detailed data to support their recommendations. Creative decisions that incur significant change or risk are not encouraged. Because managers of failed projects are openly criticized and penalized, managers try not to implement ideas that deviate much from the status quo. One lower-level manager quoted an often-used phrase in the company: "If it ain't broke, don't fix it."

There are extensive rules and regulations in this firm that employees are required to follow. Managers supervise employees closely to ensure there are no deviations. Management is concerned with high productivity, regardless of the impact on employee morale or turnover.

Work activities are designed around individuals. There are distinct departments and lines of authority, and employees are expected to minimize formal contact with other employees outside their functional area or line of command. Performance evaluations and rewards emphasize individual effort, although seniority tends to be the primary factor in the determination of pay raises and promotions.

Organization B

This organization is also a manufacturing firm. Here, however, management encourages and rewards risk taking and change. Decisions based on intuition are valued as much as those that are well rationalized. Management prides itself on its history of experimenting with new technologies and its success in regularly introducing innovative products. Managers or employees who have a good idea are encouraged to "run with it." And failures are treated as "learning experiences." The company prides itself on being market-driven and rapidly responsive to the changing needs of its customers.

There are few rules and regulations for employees to follow, and supervision is loose because management believes that its employees are hardworking and trustworthy. Management is concerned with high productivity, but believes that this comes through treating its people right. The company is proud of its reputation as being a good place to work.

Job activities are designed around work teams, and team members are encouraged to interact with people across functions and authority levels. Employees talk positively about the competition between teams. Individuals and teams have goals, and bonuses are based on achievement of these outcomes. Employees are given considerable autonomy in choosing the means by which the goals are attained.

In the Self-Assessment Library (available on CD, online, and in print), take assessment III.B.1 (What's the Right Organizational Culture for Me?) and answer the following questions.

1. *Judging from your results, do you fit better in a more formal and structured culture or in a more informal and unstructured culture?*
2. *Did your results surprise you? Why do you think you scored as you did?*
3. *How might your results affect your career path?*

Culture Is a Descriptive Term

Organizational culture is concerned with how employees perceive the characteristics of an organization's culture, not with whether or not they like them. That is, it's a descriptive term. This is important because it differentiates this concept from that of job satisfaction.

Research on organizational culture has sought to measure how employees see their organization: Does it encourage teamwork? Does it reward innovation? Does it stifle initiative? In contrast, job satisfaction seeks to measure affective responses to the work environment. It's concerned with how employees feel about the organization's expectations, reward practices, and the like. Although the two terms undoubtedly have overlapping characteristics, keep in mind that the term *organizational culture* is descriptive, while *job satisfaction* is evaluative.

Do Organizations Have Uniform Cultures?

Organizational culture represents a common perception held by the organization's members. This was made explicit when we defined culture as a system of *shared* meaning. We should expect, therefore, that individuals with different backgrounds or at different levels in the organization will tend to describe the organization's culture in similar terms.[6]

Acknowledgment that organizational culture has common properties does not mean, however, that there cannot be subcultures within any given culture. Most large organizations have a dominant culture and numerous sets of subcultures.[7] A **dominant culture** expresses the core values that are shared by a majority of the organization's members. When we talk about an organization's culture, we are referring to its dominant culture. It is this macro view of culture that gives an organization its distinct personality.[8] **Subcultures** tend to develop in large organizations to reflect common problems, situations, or experiences that members face. These subcultures are likely to be defined by department designations and geographical separation. The purchasing department, for example, can have a subculture that is uniquely shared by members of that department. It will include the **core values** of the dominant culture plus additional values unique to members of the purchasing department. Similarly, an office or unit of the organization that is physically separated from the organization's main operations may take on a different personality. Again, the core

---

dominant culture *A culture that expresses the core values that are shared by a majority of the organization's members.*

subcultures *Minicultures within an organization, typically defined by department designations and geographical separation.*

core values *The primary or dominant values that are accepted throughout the organization.*

values are essentially retained, but they are modified to reflect the separated unit's distinct situation.

If organizations had no dominant culture and were composed only of numerous subcultures, the value of organizational culture as an independent variable would be significantly lessened because there would be no uniform interpretation of what represented appropriate and inappropriate behavior. It is the "shared meaning" aspect of culture that makes it such a potent device for guiding and shaping behavior. That's what allows us to say, for example, that Microsoft's culture values aggressiveness and risk taking[9] and then to use that information to better understand the behavior of Microsoft executives and employees. But we cannot ignore the reality that many organizations also have subcultures that can influence the behavior of members.

Strong Versus Weak Cultures

It has become increasingly popular to differentiate between strong and weak cultures.[10] The argument here is that strong cultures have a greater impact on employee behavior and are more directly related to reduced turnover.

In a **strong culture**, the organization's core values are both intensely held and widely shared.[11] The more members who accept the core values and the greater their commitment to those values is, the stronger the culture is. Consistent with this definition, a strong culture will have a great influence on the behavior of its members because the high degree of sharedness and intensity creates an internal climate of high behavioral control. For example, Seattle-based Nordstrom has developed one of the strongest service cultures in the retailing industry. Nordstrom employees know in no uncertain terms what is expected of them and these expectations go a long way in shaping their behavior.

One specific result of a strong culture should be lower employee turnover. A strong culture demonstrates high agreement among members about what the organization stands for. Such unanimity of purpose builds cohesiveness, loyalty, and organizational commitment. These qualities, in turn, lessen employees' propensity to leave the organization.[12]

A strong culture of collaboration and knowledge sharing points all employees in the same direction at PaeTec Communications. Company founder and CEO Arunas Chesonis meets with employees every Friday morning to share information about the telecommunication firm's financing, acquisition plans, and profits. For Chesonis, sharing breaks down boundaries between coworkers and between employees and customers, enabling PaeTec to execute its mission of being the most customer- and employee-oriented business in each market it serves.

A Good Organizational Culture Knows No Boundaries

IN A STUDY OF 230 ORGANIZATIONS FROM DIFFERENT industries around the world, and from regions including North America, Asia, Europe, the Middle East, and Africa, having a strong and positive organizational culture was associated with increased organizational effectiveness.

The study, published in the journal *Organizational Dynamics*, found that the strong and positive aspects of organizational culture most critical to success across regions generally included

- empowering employees
- having a team orientation
- having a clear strategic direction and intent
- possessing a strong and recognizable vision

Though there were similarities when comparing regions in terms of organizational culture and effectiveness, there were some differences when researchers compared individual countries. An organizational culture that stresses empowerment, for example, appears to be more important for performance in countries such as the United States and Brazil and less important in countries such as Japan because of the former two countries' focus on the individual. Also, a focus on creating change within the organization appears to be a strong predictor of organizational effectiveness in South Africa but a relatively weak predictor in Jamaica, but it currently is unclear as to why this is the case.

Overall, the study confirms that having a strong, productive organizational culture is associated with increased sales growth, profitability, employee satisfaction, and overall organizational performance regardless of where the organization is physically located.

Source: Based on D. R. Denison, S. Haaland, and P. Goelzer, "Corporate Culture and Organizational Effectiveness: Is Asia Different from the Rest of the World?" *Organizational Dynamics*, February 2004, pp. 98–109.

Culture Versus Formalization

A strong organizational culture increases behavioral consistency. In this sense, we should recognize that a strong culture can act as a substitute for formalization.[13]

In the previous chapter, we discussed how formalization's rules and regulations act to regulate employee behavior. High formalization in an organization creates predictability, orderliness, and consistency. Our point here is that a strong culture achieves the same end without the need for written documentation. Therefore, we should view formalization and culture as two different roads to a common destination. The stronger an organization's culture, the less management need be concerned with developing formal rules and regulations to guide employee behavior. Those guides will be internalized in employees when they accept the organization's culture.

strong culture *Culture in which the core values are intensely held and widely shared.*

Organizational Culture Versus National Culture

Throughout this book we've argued that national differences—that is, national cultures—must be taken into account if accurate predictions are to be made about organizational behavior in different countries. But does national culture override an organization's culture? Is an IBM facility in Germany, for example, more likely to reflect German ethnic culture or IBM's corporate culture?

The research indicates that national culture has a greater impact on employees than does their organization's culture.[14] German employees at an IBM facility in Munich, therefore, will be influenced more by German culture than by IBM's culture. This means that as influential as organizational culture is in shaping employee behavior, national culture is even more influential. The preceding conclusion has to be qualified to reflect the self-selection that goes on at the hiring stage.[15] A British multinational corporation, for example, is likely to be less concerned with hiring the "typical Italian" for its Italian operations than in hiring an Italian who fits with the corporation's way of doing things. We should expect, therefore, that the employee selection process will be used by multinationals to find and hire job applicants who are a good fit with their organization's dominant culture, even if such applicants are somewhat atypical for members of their country.

What Do Cultures Do?

We've alluded to organizational culture's impact on behavior. We've also explicitly argued that a strong culture should be associated with reduced turnover. In this section, we will more carefully review the functions that culture performs and assess whether culture can be a liability for an organization.

Culture's Functions

Culture performs a number of functions within an organization. First, it has a boundary-defining role; that is, it creates distinctions between one organization and others. Second, it conveys a sense of identity for organization members. Third, culture facilitates the generation of commitment to something larger than one's individual self-interest. Fourth, it enhances the stability of the social system. Culture is the social glue that helps hold the organization together by providing appropriate standards for what employees should say and do. Finally, culture serves as a sense-making and control mechanism that guides and shapes the attitudes and behavior of employees. It is this last function that is of particular interest to us.[16] As the following quote makes clear, culture defines the rules of the game:

> Culture by definition is elusive, intangible, implicit, and taken for granted. But every organization develops a core set of assumptions, understandings, and implicit rules that govern day-to-day behavior in the workplace. . . . Until newcomers learn the rules, they are not accepted as full-fledged members of the organization. Transgressions of the rules on the part of high-level executives or front-line employees result in universal disapproval and powerful penalties. Conformity to the rules becomes the primary basis for reward and upward mobility.[17]

The role of culture in influencing employee behavior appears to be increasingly important in today's workplace.[18] As organizations have widened spans of control, flattened structures, introduced teams, reduced formalization, and empowered employees, the *shared meaning* provided by a strong culture ensures that everyone is pointed in the same direction.

As we show later in this chapter, who receives a job offer to join the organization, who is appraised as a high performer, and who gets the promotion are strongly influenced by the individual-organization "fit"—that is, whether the applicant or employee's attitudes and behavior are compatible with the culture. It's not a coincidence that employees at Disney theme parks appear to be almost universally attractive, clean, and wholesome looking, with bright smiles. That's the image Disney seeks. The company selects employees who will maintain that image. And once on the job, a strong culture, supported by formal rules and regulations, ensures that Disney theme-park employees will act in a relatively uniform and predictable way.

Culture as a Liability

We are treating culture in a nonjudgmental manner. We haven't said that it's good or bad, only that it exists. Many of its functions, as outlined, are valuable for both the organization and the employee. Culture enhances organizational commitment and increases the consistency of employee behavior. These are clearly benefits to an organization. From an employee's standpoint, culture is valuable because it reduces ambiguity. It tells employees how things are done and what's important. But we shouldn't ignore the potentially dysfunctional aspects of culture, especially a strong one, on an organization's effectiveness.

Barriers to Change   Culture is a liability when the shared values are not in agreement with those that will further the organization's effectiveness. This is most likely to occur when an organization's environment is dynamic.[19] When an environment is undergoing rapid change, an organization's entrenched culture may no longer be appropriate. So consistency of behavior is an asset to an organization when it faces a stable environment. It may, however, burden the organization and make it difficult to respond to changes in the environment. This helps to explain the challenges that executives at organizations like Mitsubishi, Eastman Kodak, Boeing, and the U.S. Federal Bureau of Investigation have had in recent years in adapting to upheavals in their environment.[20] These organizations have strong cultures that worked well for them in the past. But these strong cultures become barriers to change when "business as usual" is no longer effective.

Barriers to Diversity   Hiring new employees who, because of race, age, gender, disability, or other differences, are not like the majority of the organization's members creates a paradox.[21] Management wants new employees to accept the organization's core cultural values. Otherwise, these employees are unlikely to fit in or be accepted. But at the same time, management wants to openly acknowledge and demonstrate support for the differences that these employees bring to the workplace.

Strong cultures put considerable pressure on employees to conform. They limit the range of values and styles that are acceptable. In some instances, such as the widely publicized Texaco case (which was settled on behalf of 1,400 employees for $176 million) in which senior managers made disparaging remarks about minorities, a strong culture that condones prejudice can even undermine formal corporate diversity policies.[22] Organizations seek out and hire diverse individuals because of the alternative strengths these people bring to the workplace. Yet these diverse behaviors and strengths are likely to diminish in strong cultures as people attempt to fit in. Strong cultures, therefore, can be liabilities when they effectively eliminate the unique strengths that people of different backgrounds bring to the organization. Moreover, strong cultures can also be liabilities when they support institutional bias or become insensitive to people who are different.

Barriers to Acquisitions and Mergers   Historically, the key factors that management looked at in making acquisition or merger decisions were related to financial advantages or product synergy. In recent years, cultural compatibility has become the primary concern.[23] While a favorable financial statement or product line may be the initial attraction of an acquisition candidate, whether

"Success Breeds Success"

This statement is not always true. Generally speaking, success creates positive momentum. People like being associated with a successful team or organization, which allows winning teams and organizations to get the best new recruits. Microsoft's incredible success in the 1990s made it a highly desirable place to work. The company had its pick among the "best and the brightest" job applicants when filling job slots. Success led to further successes. Microsoft's experience echoes past results at other companies. In the 1960s, when General Motors controlled nearly 50 percent of the U.S. automobile market, GM was the employer most sought after by newly minted MBAs. In the early 1990s, Motorola was routinely described as one of the best-managed and successful companies in the United States, and it was able to attract the best and the brightest engineers and professionals.

But success often breeds failure, especially in organizations with strong cultures.[24] Organizations that have tremendous successes begin to believe in their own invulnerability. They often become arrogant. They lose their competitive edge. Their strong cultures reinforce past practices and make change difficult. "Why change? It worked in the past. If it ain't broke, don't fix it."

The corporate highway is littered with companies that let arrogance undermine previous successes. JCPenney and Sears once ruled the retail-department-store market. Their executives considered their markets immune to competition. Beginning in the mid-1970s, Wal-Mart did a pretty effective job of humbling JCPenney and Sears management. General Motors executives, safe and cloistered in their Detroit headquarters, ignored the aggressive efforts by Japanese auto firms to penetrate their markets. The result? GMs' market share has been in a free fall for three decades. Motorola may have been the high-tech darling of the early 1990s, when it dominated world markets for semiconductors and analog cellular phones, but the company became arrogant. It stumbled badly in the digital market, failed to listen to the needs of its customers, and overextended itself in Asia. In 2003, in an effort to rekindle what it had lost, Motorola's board ousted the company's long-term CEO and replaced him with the former president of Sun Microsystems.[25] ■

the acquisition actually works seems to have more to do with how well the two organizations' cultures match up.

Many acquisitions fail shortly after their consummation. A survey by consultants A.T. Kearney revealed that 58 percent of mergers failed to reach the value goals set by top managers.[26] The primary cause of failure is conflicting organizational cultures. As one expert commented, "Mergers have an unusually high failure rate, and it's always because of people issues." For instance, the 2001 $183 billion merger between America Online (AOL) and Time Warner was the largest in corporate history. The merger has been a disaster—only 2 years later, the stock had fallen an astounding 90 percent. Culture clash is commonly argued to be one of the causes of AOL Time Warner's problems. As one expert noted, "In some ways the merger of AOL and Time Warner was like the marriage of a teenager to a middle-aged banker. The cultures were vastly different. There were open collars and jeans at AOL. Time Warner was more buttoned-down."[27]

Creating and Sustaining Culture

An organization's culture doesn't pop out of thin air. Once established, it rarely fades away. What forces influence the creation of a culture? What reinforces and sustains these forces once they're in place? We answer both of these questions in this section.

How a Culture Begins

An organization's current customs, traditions, and general way of doing things are largely due to what it has done before and the degree of success it has had with those endeavors. This leads us to the ultimate source of an organization's culture: its founders.[28]

The founders of an organization traditionally have a major impact on that organization's early culture. They have a vision of what the organization should

The source of IKEA's culture is founder Ingvar Kamprad, who grew up in a poor farming area in Sweden where people worked hard and lived frugally. Kamprad combined the lessons he learned while growing up with his vision of creating a better everyday life for people by offering them affordable, functional, and well-designed furniture. He named his company IKEA by combining his initials with the first letters of Elmtaryd and Agunnaryd, the farm and village where he grew up. IKEA's success in expanding to 216 stores in 44 countries stems from Kamprad's vision and his continued influence as an active senior advisor to the company.

be. They are unconstrained by previous customs or ideologies. The small size that typically characterizes new organizations further facilitates the founders' imposition of their vision on all organizational members. Culture creation occurs in three ways.[29] First, founders hire and keep only employees who think and feel the same way they do. Second, they indoctrinate and socialize these employees to their way of thinking and feeling. And finally, the founders' own behavior acts as a role model that encourages employees to identify with them and thereby internalize their beliefs, values, and assumptions. When the organization succeeds, the founders' vision becomes seen as a primary determinant of that success. At this point, the founders' entire personality becomes embedded in the culture of the organization.

The culture at Hyundai, the giant Korean conglomerate, is largely a reflection of its founder Chung Ju Yung. Hyundai's fierce, competitive style and its disciplined, authoritarian nature are the same characteristics often used to describe Chung. Other contemporary examples of founders who have had an immeasurable impact on their organization's culture would include Bill Gates at Microsoft, Ingvar Kamprad at IKEA, Herb Kelleher at Southwest Airlines, Fred Smith at Federal Express, and Richard Branson at the Virgin Group.

Keeping a Culture Alive

Once a culture is in place, there are practices within the organization that act to maintain it by giving employees a set of similar experiences.[30] For example, many of the human resource practices we discuss in the next chapter reinforce the organization's culture. The selection process, performance evaluation criteria, training and development activities, and promotion procedures ensure that those hired fit in with the culture, reward those who support it, and penalize (and even expel) those who challenge it. Three forces play a particularly important part in sustaining a culture: selection practices, the actions of top management, and socialization methods. Let's take a closer look at each.

Selection   The explicit goal of the selection process is to identify and hire individuals who have the knowledge, skills, and abilities to perform the jobs within the organization successfully. Typically, more than one candidate will be identified who meets any given job's requirements. When that point is reached, it would be naive to ignore the fact that the final decision as to who is hired will be significantly influenced by the decision-maker's judgment of how well the candidates will fit into the organization. This attempt to ensure a proper match, whether purposely or inadvertently, results in the hiring of people who have values essentially consistent with those of the organization, or at least a good portion of those values.[31] In addition, the selection process provides information to applicants about the organization. Candidates learn about the organization and, if they perceive a conflict between their values and those of the organization, they can self-select themselves out of the applicant pool. Selection, therefore, becomes a two-way street, allowing employer or applicant to abrogate a marriage if there appears to be a mismatch. In this way, the selection process sustains an organization's culture by selecting out those individuals who might attack or undermine its core values.

For instance, W. L. Gore & Associates, the maker of Gore-Tex fabric used in outerwear, prides itself on its democratic culture and teamwork. There are no job titles at Gore, nor bosses nor chains of command. All work is done in teams. In Gore's selection process, teams of employees put job applicants through extensive interviews to ensure that candidates who can't deal with the level of uncertainty, flexibility, and teamwork that employees have to deal with in Gore plants are selected out.[32]

Top Management   The actions of top management also have a major impact on the organization's culture.[33] Through what they say and how they behave, senior executives establish norms that filter down through the organization as to whether risk taking is desirable; how much freedom managers should give their employees; what is appropriate dress; what actions will pay off in terms of pay raises, promotions, and other rewards; and the like.

For example, Robert A. Keirlin has been called "the cheapest CEO in America."[34] Keirlin is chairman and CEO of Fastenal Co., the largest specialty retailer of nuts and bolts in the United States, with 6,500 employees. He takes a salary of only $60,000 a year. He owns only three suits, each of which he bought used. He clips grocery coupons, drives a Toyota, and stays in low-priced motels when he travels on business. Does Keirlin need to pinch pennies? No. The market value of his stock in Fastenal is worth about $300 million. But the man prefers a modest personal lifestyle. And he prefers the same for his company. Keirlin argues that his behavior should send a message to all his employees: We don't waste things in this company. Keirlin sees himself as a role model for frugality, and employees at Fastenal have learned to follow his example.

Socialization   No matter how good a job the organization does in recruiting and selection, new employees are not fully indoctrinated in the organization's culture. Because they are unfamiliar with the organization's culture, new employees are potentially likely to disturb the beliefs and customs that are in place. The organization will, therefore, want to help new employees adapt to its culture. This adaptation process is called **socialization**.[35]

All Marines must go through boot camp, where they "prove" their commitment. Of course, at the same time, the Marine trainers are indoctrinating new recruits in the "Marine way." All new employees at Neumann Homes in Warrenville, Illinois, go through a 40-hour orientation program.[36] They're

Starbucks' international employees travel to Seattle headquarters to become immersed in the company's culture of caring for employees, customers, communities, and the environment. By socializing employees from other countries, Starbucks sustains its culture of treating others with respect, embracing diversity, and developing satisfied customers. Shown here are employees from Puerto Rico, Kuwait, China, and Australia learning about Starbuck's high coffee standards during a coffee-tasting session.

socialization   *The process that adapts employees to the organization's culture.*

introduced to the company's values and culture through a variety of activities—including a customer service lunch, an interactive departmental roundtable fair, and presentations made by groups of new hires to the CEO regarding the company's core values. For new incoming employees in the upper ranks, companies often put considerably more time and effort into the socialization process. At Limited Brands, newly hired vice presidents and regional directors go through an intensive 1-month program, called "onboarding," designed to immerse these executives in Limited Brands' culture.[37] During this month they have no direct responsibilities for tasks associated with their new positions. Instead, they spend all their work time meeting with other senior leaders and mentors, working the floors of retail stores, evaluating employee and customer habits, investigating the competition, and studying Limited Brands' past and current operations.

As we discuss socialization, keep in mind that the most critical socialization stage is at the time of entry into the organization. This is when the organization seeks to mold the outsider into an employee "in good standing." Employees who fail to learn the essential or pivotal role behaviors risk being labeled "nonconformists" or "rebels," which often leads to expulsion. But the organization will be socializing every employee, though maybe not as explicitly, throughout his or her entire career in the organization. This further contributes to sustaining the culture.

Socialization can be conceptualized as a process made up of three stages: prearrival, encounter, and metamorphosis.[38] The first stage encompasses all the learning that occurs before a new member joins the organization. In the second stage, the new employee sees what the organization is really like and confronts the possibility that expectations and reality may diverge. In the third stage, the relatively long-lasting changes take place. The new employee masters the skills required for the job, successfully performs the new roles, and makes the adjustments to the work group's values and norms.[39] This three-stage process has an impact on the new employee's work productivity, commitment to the organization's objectives, and eventual decision to stay with the organization. Exhibit 17-2 depicts this process.

The **prearrival stage** explicitly recognizes that each individual arrives with a set of values, attitudes, and expectations. These cover both the work to be done and the organization. For instance, in many jobs, particularly professional work, new members will have undergone a considerable degree of prior socialization in training and in school. One major purpose of a business school, for example, is to socialize business students to the attitudes and behaviors that business firms want. If business executives believe that successful employees value the profit ethic, are loyal, will work hard, and desire to achieve, they can hire individuals out of business schools who have been premolded in this pattern. Moreover, most people in business realize that no matter how well they

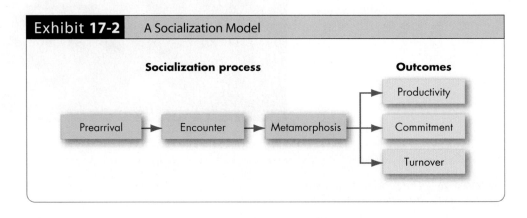

Exhibit 17-2   A Socialization Model

Socialization process   Outcomes

Prearrival → Encounter → Metamorphosis → Productivity
                                                          Commitment
                                                          Turnover

think they can socialize newcomers, the most important predictor of newcomers' future behavior is their past behavior. Research shows that what people know before they join the organization, and how proactive their personality is, are critical predictors of how well they adjust to a new culture.[40]

One way to capitalize on the importance of prehire characteristics in socialization is to select employees with the "right stuff," and to use the selection process to inform prospective employees about the organization as a whole. In addition, as noted previously, the selection process also acts to ensure the inclusion of the "right type"—those who will fit in. "Indeed, the ability of the individual to present the appropriate face during the selection process determines his ability to move into the organization in the first place. Thus, success depends on the degree to which the aspiring member has correctly anticipated the expectations and desires of those in the organization in charge of selection."[41]

On entry into the organization, the new member enters the **encounter stage**. Here the individual confronts the possible dichotomy between expectations—about the job, the coworkers, the boss, and the organization in general—and reality. If expectations prove to have been more or less accurate, the encounter stage merely provides a reaffirmation of the perceptions gained earlier. However, this is often not the case. Where expectations and reality differ, the new employee must undergo socialization that will detach her from her previous assumptions and replace them with another set that the organization deems desirable. At the extreme, a new member may become totally disillusioned with the actualities of the job and resign. Proper selection should significantly reduce the probability of the latter occurrence. Also, an employee's network of friends and coworkers can play a critical role in helping them "learn the ropes." Newcomers are more committed to the organization when their friendship networks are large and diverse. So, organizations can help newcomers socialize by encouraging friendship ties in organizations.[42]

Finally, the new member must work out any problems discovered during the encounter stage. This may mean going through changes—hence, we call this the **metamorphosis stage**. The options presented in Exhibit 17-3 are alternatives designed to bring about the desired metamorphosis. Note, for example, that the more management relies on socialization programs that are formal, collective, fixed, serial, and emphasize divestiture, the greater the likelihood that newcomers' differences and perspectives will be stripped away and replaced by standardized and predictable behaviors. Careful selection by management of newcomers' socialization experiences can—at the extreme—create conformists who maintain traditions and customs, or inventive and creative individualists who consider no organizational practice sacred.

We can say that metamorphosis and the entry socialization process is complete when new members have become comfortable with the organization and their job. They have internalized the norms of the organization and their work group, and understand and accept those norms. New members feel accepted by their peers as trusted and valued individuals. They are self-confident that they have the competence to complete the job successfully. They understand the system—not only their own tasks but the rules, procedures, and informally accepted practices as well.

prearrival stage   *The period of learning in the socialization process that occurs before a new employee joins the organization.*

encounter stage   *The stage in the socialization process in which a new employee sees what the organization is really like and confronts the possibility that expectations and reality may diverge.*

metamorphosis stage   *The stage in the socialization process in which a new employee changes and adjusts to the job, work group, and organization.*

Exhibit **17-3**   Entry Socialization Options

Formal vs. Informal The more a new employee is segregated from the ongoing work setting and differentiated in some way to make explicit his or her newcomer's role, the more formal socialization is. Specific orientation and training programs are examples. Informal socialization puts the new employee directly into the job, with little or no special attention.

Individual vs. Collective New members can be socialized individually. This describes how it's done in many professional offices. They can also be grouped together and processed through an identical set of experiences, as in military boot camp.

Fixed vs. Variable This refers to the time schedule in which newcomers make the transition from outsider to insider. A fixed schedule establishes standardized stages of transition. This characterizes rotational training programs. It also includes probationary periods, such as the 8- to 10-year "associate" status used by accounting and law firms before deciding on whether or not a candidate is made a partner. Variable schedules give no advance notice of their transition timetable. Variable schedules describe the typical promotion system, in which one is not advanced to the next stage until one is "ready."

Serial vs. Random Serial socialization is characterized by the use of role models who train and encourage the newcomer. Apprenticeship and mentoring programs are examples. In random socialization, role models are deliberately withheld. New employees are left on their own to figure things out.

Investiture vs. Divestiture Investiture socialization assumes that the newcomer's qualities and qualifications are the necessary ingredients for job success, so these qualities and qualifications are confirmed and supported. Divestiture socialization tries to strip away certain characteristics of the recruit. Fraternity and sorority "pledges" go through divestiture socialization to shape them into the proper role.

Source: Based on J. Van Maanen, "People Processing: Strategies of Organizational Socialization," *Organizational Dynamics,* Summer 1978, pp. 19–36; and E. H. Schein, "Organizational Culture," *American Psychologist,* February 1990, p. 116.

Finally, they know how they will be evaluated; that is, what criteria will be used to measure and appraise their work. They know what is expected of them and what constitutes a job "well done." As Exhibit 17-2 shows, successful metamorphosis should have a positive impact on new employees' productivity and their commitment to the organization and reduce their propensity to leave the organization.

Summary: How Cultures Form

Exhibit 17-4 summarizes how an organization's culture is established and sustained. The original culture is derived from the founder's philosophy. This, in turn, strongly influences the criteria used in hiring. The actions of the current top management set the general climate of what is acceptable behavior and what is not. How employees are to be socialized will depend both on the degree of success achieved in matching new employees' values to those of the organization's in the selection process and on top management's preference for socialization methods.

Exhibit **17-4**   How Organization Cultures Form

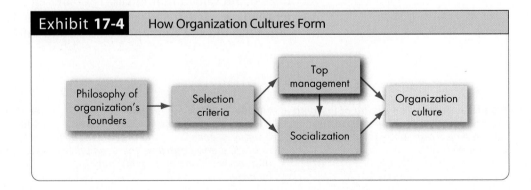

How Employees Learn Culture

Culture is transmitted to employees in a number of forms, the most potent being stories, rituals, material symbols, and language.

Stories

During the days when Henry Ford II was chairman of the Ford Motor Co., one would have been hard pressed to find a manager who hadn't heard the story about Mr. Ford reminding his executives, when they got too arrogant, that "it's my name that's on the building." The message was clear: Henry Ford II ran the company.

Nike has a number of senior executives who spend much of their time serving as corporate storytellers. And the stories they tell are meant to convey what Nike is about.[43] When they tell the story of how cofounder (and Oregon track coach) Bill Bowerman went to his workshop and poured rubber into his wife's waffle iron to create a better running shoe, they're talking about Nike's spirit of innovation. When new hires hear tales of Oregon running star Steve Prefontaine's battles to make running a professional sport and to attain better-performance equipment, they learn of Nike's commitment to helping athletes.

Stories such as these circulate through many organizations. They typically contain a narrative of events about the organization's founders, rule breaking, rags-to-riches successes, reductions in the workforce, relocation of employees, reactions to past mistakes, and organizational coping.[44] These stories anchor the present in the past and provide explanations and legitimacy for current practices.

Rituals

Rituals are repetitive sequences of activities that express and reinforce the key values of the organization—what goals are most important, which people are important, and which people are expendable.[45] One of the better-known corporate rituals is Wal-Mart's company chant. Begun by the company's founder, Sam Walton, as a way to motivate and unite his workforce, "Gimme a W, gimme an A, gimme an L, gimme a squiggle, give me an M, A, R, T!" has become a company ritual that bonds Wal-Mart workers and reinforces Sam Walton's belief in the importance of his employees to the company's success. Similar corporate chants are used by IBM, Ericsson, Novell, Deutsche Bank, and Pricewaterhouse-Coopers.[46]

Material Symbols

The headquarters of Alcoa doesn't look like your typical head-office operation. There are few individual offices, even for senior executives. It is essentially made up of cubicles, common areas, and meeting rooms. This informal corporate headquarters conveys to employees that Alcoa values openness,

rituals *Repetitive sequences of activities that express and reinforce the key values of the organization, which goals are most important, which people are important, and which are expendable.*

At Wal-Mart, culture is transmitted to employees through the daily ritual of the "Wal-Mart cheer." Shown here is the manager of a Wal-Mart store leading employees in the motivational chant that helps preserve a small-family spirit and work environment within the world's largest retailer.

equality, creativity, and flexibility. Some corporations provide their top executives with chauffeur-driven limousines and, when they travel by air, unlimited use of the corporate jet. Others may not get to ride in limousines or private jets but they might still get a car and air transportation paid for by the company. Only the car is a Chevrolet (with no driver) and the jet seat is in the economy section of a commercial airliner.

The layout of corporate headquarters, the types of automobiles top executives are given, and the presence or absence of corporate aircraft are a few examples of material symbols. Others include the size of offices, the elegance of furnishings, executive perks, and attire.[47] These material symbols convey to employees who is important, the degree of egalitarianism desired by top management, and the kinds of behavior (for example, risk taking, conservative, authoritarian, participative, individualistic, social) that are appropriate.

Language

Many organizations and units within organizations use language as a way to identify members of a culture or subculture. By learning this language, members attest to their acceptance of the culture and, in so doing, help to preserve it. The following are examples of terminology used by employees at Knight-Ridder Information, a California-based data redistributor: *accession number* (a number assigned to each individual record in a database); *KWIC* (a set of key-words-in-context); and *relational operator* (searching a database for names or key terms in some order). If you're a new employee at Boeing, you'll find yourself learning a whole unique vocabulary of acronyms, including: BOLD (Boeing online data), CATIA (computer-graphics-aided three-dimensional interactive application), MAIDS (manufacturing assembly and installation data system), POP (purchased outside production), and SLO (service level objectives).[48]

Organizations, over time, often develop unique terms to describe equipment, offices, key personnel, suppliers, customers, or products that relate to its business. New employees are frequently overwhelmed with acronyms and jargon that, after 6 months on the job, have become fully part of their language. Once assimilated, this terminology acts as a common denominator that unites members of a given culture or subculture.

Creating an Ethical Organizational Culture

The content and strength of a culture influence an organization's ethical climate and the ethical behavior of its members.[49] An organizational culture most likely to shape high ethical standards is one that's high in risk tolerance, low to moderate in aggressiveness, and focuses on means as well as outcomes. Managers in such a culture are supported for taking risks and innovating, are discouraged from engaging in unbridled competition, and will pay attention to *how* goals are achieved as well as to *what* goals are achieved.

A strong organizational culture will exert more influence on employees than a weak one. If the culture is strong and supports high ethical standards, it should have a very powerful and positive influence on employee behavior. Johnson & Johnson, for example, has a strong culture that has long stressed corporate obligations to customers, employees, the community, and shareholders, in that order. When poisoned Tylenol (a Johnson & Johnson product) was found on store shelves, employees at Johnson & Johnson across the United States independently pulled the product from these stores before management had even issued a statement concerning the tamperings. No one had to tell these individuals what was morally right; they knew what Johnson & Johnson would expect them to do. On the other hand, a strong culture that encourages pushing the limits can be a powerful force in shaping unethical behavior. For instance, Enron's aggressive culture, with unrelenting pressure on executives to rapidly expand earnings, encouraged ethical corner-cutting and eventually contributed to the company's collapse.[50]

What can management do to create a more ethical culture? We suggest a combination of the following practices:

- *Be a visible role model.* Employees will look to top-management behavior as a benchmark for defining appropriate behavior. When senior management is seen as taking the ethical high road, it provides a positive message for all employees.
- *Communicate ethical expectations.* Ethical ambiguities can be minimized by creating and disseminating an organizational code of ethics. It should state the organization's primary values and the ethical rules that employees are expected to follow.
- *Provide ethical training.* Set up seminars, workshops, and similar ethical training programs. Use these training sessions to reinforce the organization's standards of conduct, to clarify what practices are and are not permissible, and to address possible ethical dilemmas.
- *Visibly reward ethical acts and punish unethical ones.* Performance appraisals of managers should include a point-by-point evaluation of how his or her decisions measure up against the organization's code of ethics. Appraisals must include the means taken to achieve goals as well as the ends themselves. People who act ethically should be visibly rewarded for their behavior. Just as importantly, unethical acts should be conspicuously punished.
- *Provide protective mechanisms.* The organization needs to provide formal mechanisms so that employees can discuss ethical dilemmas and report unethical behavior without fear of reprimand. This might include creation of ethical counselors, ombudsmen, or ethical officers.

Creating a Customer-Responsive Culture

French retailers have a well-established reputation for indifference to customers.[51] Salespeople, for instance, routinely make it clear to customers that their phone conversations should not be interrupted. Just getting any help at all from a salesperson can be a challenge. And no one in France finds it particularly surprising that the owner of a Paris store should complain that he was unable to work on his books all morning because he kept being bothered *by customers*!

Most organizations today are trying very hard to be un-French-like. They are attempting to create a customer-responsive culture because they recognize that this is the path to customer loyalty and long-term profitability. Companies that have created such cultures—like Southwest Airlines, FedEx, Johnson & Johnson, Nordstrom, Olive Garden, Walt Disney theme parks, Enterprise Rent-A-Car, Whole Foods, and L.L. Bean—have built a strong and loyal customer base and have generally outperformed their competitors in revenue growth and financial performance. In this section, we will briefly identify the variables that shape customer-responsive cultures and offer some suggestions that management can follow for creating such cultures.

Key Variables Shaping Customer-Responsive Cultures

A review of the evidence finds that half-a-dozen variables are routinely evident in customer-responsive cultures.[52]

First is the type of employees themselves. Successful, service-oriented organizations hire employees who are outgoing and friendly. Second is low formalization. Service employees need to have the freedom to meet changing customer-service requirements. Rigid rules, procedures, and regulations make this difficult. Third is an extension of low formalization—it's the widespread use of empowerment. Empowered employees have the decision discretion to do what's necessary to please the customer. Fourth is good listening skills. Employees in customer-responsive cultures have the ability to listen to and understand messages sent by the customer. Fifth is role clarity. Service employees act as "boundary spanners" between the organization and its customers. They have to acquiesce to the demands of both their employer and the customer. This can create considerable role ambiguity and conflict, which reduces employees' job satisfaction and can hinder employee service performance. Successful customer-responsive cultures reduce employee uncertainty about the best way to perform their jobs and the importance of job activities. Finally, customer-responsive cultures have employees who exhibit organizational citizenship behavior. They are conscientious in their desire to please the customer. And they're willing to take the initiative, even when it's outside their normal job requirements, to satisfy a customer's needs.

In summary, customer-responsive cultures hire service-oriented employees with good listening skills and the willingness to go beyond the constraints of their job description to do what's necessary to please the customer. It then clarifies their roles, frees them up to meet changing customer needs by minimizing rules and regulations, and provides them with a wide range of decision discretion to do their job as they see fit.

Managerial Action

Based on the previously identified characteristics, we can suggest a number of actions that management can take if it wants to make its culture more customer-responsive. These actions are designed to create employees with the competence, ability, and willingness to solve customer problems as they arise.

Rackspace, a San Antonio-based company that manages the technology backend of Web sites, obsesses on its dedication to customers. To provide fanatical service, the company is organized around small teams that are empowered with full responsibility for specific customers. Team leader Joey Parsons, pictured here, recently won the Straightjacket Award, Rackspace's most coveted employee distinction.

Selection The place to start in building a customer-responsive culture is hiring service-contact people with the personality and attitudes consistent with a high service orientation. Southwest Air is a shining example of a company that has focused its hiring process on selecting out job candidates whose personalities aren't people-friendly. Job applicants go through an extensive interview process at Southwest in which company employees and executives carefully assess whether candidates have the outgoing and fun-loving personality that it wants in all its employees.

Studies show that friendliness, enthusiasm, and attentiveness in service employees positively affect customers' perceptions of service quality.[53] So managers should look for these qualities in applicants. In addition, job candidates should be screened so new hires have the patience, concern about others, and listening skills that are associated with customer-oriented employees.

Training and Socialization Organizations that are trying to become more customer-responsive don't always have the option of hiring all new employees. More typically, management is faced with the challenge of making its current employees more customer-focused. In such cases, the emphasis will be on training rather than hiring. This describes the dilemma that senior executives at companies such as General Motors, Shell, and J.P. Morgan Chase have faced in the past decade as they have attempted to move away from their product focus. The content of these training programs will vary widely but should focus on improving product knowledge, active listening, showing patience, and displaying emotions.

In addition, even new employees who have a customer-friendly attitude may need to understand management's expectations, so all new service-contact people should be socialized into the organization's goals and values. Lastly, even the most customer-focused employees can lose direction every once in a while. This should be addressed with regular training updates in which the organization's customer-focused values are restated and reinforced.

Structural Design Organization structures need to give employees more control. This can be achieved by reducing rules and regulations. Employees are better able to satisfy customers when they have some control over the service encounter. So management needs to allow employees to adjust their behavior to the changing needs and requests of customers. What customers *don't* want to hear are responses such as "I can't handle this. You need to talk to someone else"; or "I'm sorry but that's against our company policy." In addition, the use of cross-functional teams can often improve customer service because service delivery frequently requires a smooth, coordinated effort across different functions.

Empowerment Consistent with low formalization is empowering employees with the discretion to make day-to-day decisions about job-related activities. It's a necessary component of a customer-responsive culture because it allows service employees to make on-the-spot decisions to satisfy customers completely.[54] Enterprise Rent-A-Car, for instance, has found that high customer satisfaction doesn't require a problem-free experience. The "completely satisfied" customer was one who, when he or she had a problem, found that it was quickly and courteously resolved by an employee. By empowering their employees to make decisions on the spot, Enterprise improved its customer satisfaction ratings.[55]

Leadership Leaders convey the organization's culture through both what they say and what they do. Effective leaders in customer-responsive cultures deliver by conveying a customer-focused vision and demonstrating by their continual behavior that they are committed to customers. In almost every organization that has successfully created and maintained a strong customer-responsive culture, its chief executive officer has played a major role in championing the message. For instance, Taiwan microchip manufacturer United Microelectronics Corp. recently hired Jackson Hu as its new CEO specifically for his prior successes at changing a company's culture to focus employees on better understanding customer needs and improving customer service.[56]

Performance Evaluation   There is an impressive amount of evidence demonstrating that behavior-based performance evaluations are consistent with improved customer service.[57] Behavior-based evaluations appraise employees on the basis of how they behave or act—on criteria such as effort, commitment, teamwork, friendliness, and the ability to solve customer problems—rather than on the measurable outcomes they achieve. Why are behaviors superior to outcomes for improving service? Because it gives employees the incentive to engage in behaviors that are conducive to improved service quality and it gives employees more control over the conditions that affect their performance evaluations.[58]

In addition, a customer-responsive culture will be fostered by using evaluations that include input from customers. For instance, the performance evaluation of account managers at software company PeopleSoft is based on customer satisfaction and customers' ability to use the company's software.[59] Just the fact that employees know that part of their performance appraisal will include evaluations from customers is likely to make those employees more concerned with satisfying customer needs. Of course, this should only be used with employees who have direct contact with customers.

Reward Systems   Finally, if management wants employees to give good service, it has to reward good service. It needs to provide ongoing recognition to employees who have demonstrated extraordinary effort to please customers and who have been singled out by customers for "going the extra mile." And it needs to make pay and promotions contingent on outstanding customer service.

Spirituality and Organizational Culture

What do Southwest Airlines, Hewlett-Packard, The Men's Wearhouse, AES, Wetherill Associates, and Tom's of Maine have in common? They're among a growing number of organizations that have embraced workplace spirituality.

What Is Spirituality?

Workplace spirituality is *not* about organized religious practices. It's not about God or theology. **Workplace spirituality** recognizes that people have an inner life that nourishes and is nourished by meaningful work that takes place in the context of community.[60] Organizations that promote a spiritual culture recognize that people have both a mind and a spirit, seek to find meaning and purpose in their work, and desire to connect with other human beings and be part of a community.

Why Spirituality Now?

Historical models of management and organizational behavior had no room for spirituality. As we noted in our discussion of emotions in Chapter 8, the myth of rationality assumed that the well-run organization eliminated feelings. Similarly, concern about an employee's inner life had no role in the perfectly rational model. But just as we've now come to realize that the study of emotions improves our understanding of organizational behavior, an awareness of spirituality can help you to better understand employee behavior in the twenty-first century.

Exhibit **17-5**	Reasons for the Growing Interest in Spirituality

- As a counterbalance to the pressures and stress of a turbulent pace of life. Contemporary lifestyles—single-parent families, geographic mobility, the temporary nature of jobs, new technologies that create distance between people—underscore the lack of community many people feel and increases the need for involvement and connection.

- Formalized religion hasn't worked for many people and they continue to look for anchors to replace lack of faith and to fill a growing feeling of emptiness.

- Job demands have made the workplace dominant in many people's lives, yet they continue to question the meaning of work.

- The desire to integrate personal life values with one's professional life.

- An increasing number of people are finding that the pursuit of more material acquisitions leaves them unfulfilled.

Of course, employees have always had an inner life. So why has the search for meaning and purposefulness in work surfaced now? There are a number of reasons. We summarize them in Exhibit 17-5.

Characteristics of a Spiritual Organization

The concept of workplace spirituality draws on our previous discussions of topics such as values, ethics, motivation, leadership, and work/life balance. Spiritual organizations are concerned with helping people develop and reach their full potential. Similarly, organizations that are concerned with spirituality are more likely to directly address problems created by work/life conflicts. What differentiates spiritual organizations from their nonspiritual counterparts? Although research on this question is only preliminary, our review identified five cultural characteristics that tend to be evident in spiritual organizations.[61]

- *Strong Sense of Purpose* Spiritual organizations build their cultures around a meaningful purpose. Although profits may be important, they're not the primary values of the organization. People want to be inspired by a purpose that they believe is important and worthwhile.
- *Focus on Individual Development* Spiritual organizations recognize the worth and value of people. They aren't just providing jobs. They seek to create cultures in which employees can continually learn and grow.
- *Trust and Respect* Spiritual organizations are characterized by mutual trust, honesty, and openness. Managers aren't afraid to admit mistakes. The president of Wetherill Associates, a highly successful auto parts distribution firm, says: "We don't tell lies here, and everyone knows it. We are specific and honest about quality and suitability of the product for our customers' needs, even if we know they might not be able to detect any problem."[62]
- *Humanistic Work Practices* These practices embraced by spiritual organizations include flexible work schedules, group- and organization-based rewards, narrowing of pay and status differentials, guarantees of individual worker rights, employee empowerment, and job security. Hewlett-Packard, for instance, has handled temporary downturns through voluntary attrition and shortened workweeks (shared by all), and longer-term declines through early retirements and buyouts.

workplace spirituality   *The recognition that people have an inner life that nourishes and is nourished by meaningful work that takes place in the context of community.*

Footwear marketer The Timberland Company balances its business goals with a strong sense of purpose in creating positive change through community service. Timberland encourages employees to speak openly about the company's culture of giving and to form diverse employee groups involved in service projects. Timberland gives employees 40 hours a year of paid time off for volunteer work. In this photo, a Timberland employee participates in a project that gives men shoes and boots at a rescue mission.

- *Toleration of Employee Expression* The final characteristic that differentiates spiritually based organizations is that they don't stifle employee emotions. They allow people to be themselves—to express their moods and feelings without guilt or fear of reprimand. Employees at Southwest Air, for instance, are encouraged to express their sense of humor on the job, to act spontaneously, and to make their work fun.

Criticisms of Spirituality

Critics of the spirituality movement in organizations have focused on three issues. First is the question of scientific foundation. What really is workplace spirituality—is this just some new management buzzword? Second, are spiritual organizations legitimate? Specifically, do organizations have the right to impose spiritual values on their employees? Third is the question of economics. Are spirituality and profits compatible?

First, as you might imagine, there is very little research on workplace spirituality. We don't know whether the concept will have staying power. Do the cultural characteristics just identified really separate spiritual organizations? What is a nonspiritual organization, anyway? Do employees of so-called spiritual organizations perceive that they work in spiritual organizations? Although there is some research suggesting support for workplace spirituality (as we discuss later), before the concept of spirituality gains full credence, the questions we've just posed need to be answered.

On the second question, there is clearly the potential for an emphasis on spirituality to make some employees uneasy. Critics might argue that secular institutions, especially business firms, have no business imposing spiritual values on employees. This criticism is undoubtedly valid when spirituality is defined as bringing religion and God into the workplace.[63] However, the criticism seems less stinging when the goal is limited to helping employees find meaning in their work lives. If the concerns listed in Exhibit 17-5 truly characterize a growing segment of the workforce, then perhaps the time is right for organizations to help employees find meaning and purpose in their work and to use the workplace as a source of community.

Finally, the issue of whether spirituality and profits are compatible objectives is certainly relevant for managers and investors in business. The evidence, although limited, indicates that the two objectives may be very compatible. A recent research study by a major consulting firm found that companies that introduced spiritually based techniques improved productivity and significantly reduced turnover.[64] Another study found that organizations that provide their employees with opportunities for spiritual development outperformed those that didn't.[65] Other studies also report that spirituality in organizations was positively related to creativity, employee satisfaction, team performance, and organizational commitment.[66] And if you're looking for a single case to make the argument for spirituality, it's hard to beat Southwest Air. Southwest has one of the lowest employee turnover rates in the airline industry; it consistently has the lowest labor costs per miles flown of any major airline; it regularly outpaces its competitors for achieving on-time arrivals and fewest customer complaints; and it has proven itself to be the most consistently profitable airline in the United States.[67]

Summary and Implications for Managers

Exhibit 17-6 depicts organizational culture as an intervening variable. Employees form an overall subjective perception of the organization based on factors such as degree of risk tolerance, team emphasis, and support of people. This overall perception becomes, in effect, the organization's culture or personality. These favorable or unfavorable perceptions then affect employee performance and satisfaction, with the impact being greater for stronger cultures.

Just as people's personalities tend to be stable over time, so too do strong cultures. This makes strong cultures difficult for managers to change. When a culture becomes mismatched to its environment, management will want to change it. But as the Point/Counterpoint demonstrates, changing an organization's culture is a long and difficult process. The result, at least in the short term, is that managers should treat their organization's culture as relatively fixed.

One of the more important managerial implications of organizational culture relates to selection decisions. Hiring individuals whose values don't align with those of the organization is likely to lead to employees who lack motivation and commitment and who are dissatisfied with their jobs and the organization.[68] Not surprisingly, employee "misfits" have considerably higher turnover rates than individuals who perceive a good fit.[69]

| Exhibit **17-6** | How Organizational Cultures Have an Impact on Employee Performance and Satisfaction |

We should also not overlook the influence socialization has on employee performance. An employee's performance depends to a considerable degree on knowing what he should or should not do. Understanding the right way to do a job indicates proper socialization. Furthermore, the appraisal of an individual's performance includes how well the person fits into the organization. Can he or she get along with coworkers? Does he or she have acceptable work habits and demonstrate the right attitude? These qualities differ between jobs and organizations. For instance, on some jobs, employees will be evaluated more favorably if they are aggressive and outwardly indicate that they are ambitious. On another job, or on the same job in another organization, such an approach may be evaluated negatively. As a result, proper socialization becomes a significant factor in influencing both actual job performance and how it's perceived by others.

Organizational Cultures Can't Be Changed

An organization's culture is made up of relatively stable characteristics. It develops over many years and is rooted in deeply held values to which employees are strongly committed. In addition, there are a number of forces continually operating to maintain a given culture. These include written statements about the organization's mission and philosophy, the design of physical spaces and buildings, the dominant leadership style, hiring criteria, past promotion practices, entrenched rituals, popular stories about key people and events, the organization's historic performance evaluation criteria, and the organization's formal structure.

Selection and promotion policies are particularly important devices that work against cultural change. Employees chose the organization because they perceived their values to be a "good fit" with the organization. They become comfortable with that fit and will strongly resist efforts to disturb the equilibrium. The terrific difficulties that organizations like General Motors, AT&T, and the U.S. Postal Service have had in trying to reshape their cultures attest to this dilemma. These organizations historically tended to attract individuals who desired situations that were stable and highly structured. Those in control in organizations will also select senior managers who will continue the current culture. Even attempts to change a culture by going outside the organization to hire a new chief executive are unlikely to be effective. The evidence indicates that the culture is more likely to change the executive than the other way around.

Our argument should not be viewed as saying that culture can *never* be changed. In the unusual case in which an organization confronts a survival-threatening crisis, members of the organization will be responsive to efforts at cultural change. However, anything less than that is unlikely to be effective in bringing about cultural change.

Changing an organization's culture is extremely difficult, but cultures *can* be changed. The evidence suggests that cultural change is most likely to take place when most or all of the following conditions exist:

A dramatic crisis This is the shock that undermines the status quo and calls into question the relevance of the current culture. Examples are a surprising financial setback, the loss of a major customer, and a dramatic technological breakthrough by a competitor.

Turnover in leadership New top leadership, which can provide an alternative set of key values, may be perceived as more capable of responding to the crisis.

Young and small organizations. The younger the organization is, the less entrenched its culture will be. Similarly, it's easier for management to communicate its new values when the organization is small.

Weak culture The more widely held a culture is and the higher the agreement among members on its values, the more difficult it will be to change. Conversely, weak cultures are more amenable to change than strong ones.

If all or most of these conditions exist, the following management actions may lead to change: initiating new stories and rituals, selecting and promoting employees who espouse the new values, changing the reward system to support the new values, and undermining current subcultures through transfers, job rotation, and terminations.

Under the best of conditions, these actions won't result in an immediate or dramatic shift in the culture. In the final analysis, cultural change is a lengthy process—measured in years rather than in months. But cultures can be changed. The success that new leadership had in turning around the cultures at companies like Harley-Davidson, IBM, and Electronic Data Systems attests to this claim.

Questions for Review

1. What's the difference between job satisfaction and organizational culture?
2. What defines an organization's subcultures?
3. Can an employee survive in an organization if he or she rejects its core values? Explain.
4. Contrast organizational culture with national culture.
5. How can culture be a liability to an organization?
6. How does a strong culture affect an organization's efforts to improve diversity?
7. What benefits can socialization provide for the organization? For the new employee?
8. How is language related to organizational culture?
9. How can management create an ethical culture?
10. What criticisms have been targeted against bringing spirituality to the workplace?

Questions for Critical Thinking

1. Is socialization brainwashing? Explain.
2. If management sought a culture characterized as innovative and autonomous, what might its socialization program look like?
3. Can you identify a set of characteristics that describes your college's culture? Compare them with those of several of your peers. How closely do they agree?
4. Today's workforce is increasingly made up of part-time or contingent employees. Is organizational culture really important if the workforce is mostly temporaries?
5. "We should be opposed to the manipulation of individuals for organizational purposes, but a degree of social uniformity enables organizations to work better." Do you agree or disagree with this statement? What are its implications for organizational culture? Discuss.

Team Exercise

RATE YOUR CLASSROOM CULTURE

Listed here are 14 statements. Using the 5-item scale (from Strongly Agree to Strongly Disagree), respond to each statement by circling the number that best represents your opinion.

	Strongly Agree	Agree	Neutral	Disagree	Strongly Disagree
1. I feel comfortable challenging statements made by my instructor.	5	4	3	2	1
2. My instructor heavily penalizes assignments that are not turned in on time.	1	2	3	4	5
3. My instructor believes that "it's final results that count."	1	2	3	4	5
4. My instructor is sensitive to my personal needs and problems.	5	4	3	2	1
5. A large portion of my grade depends on how well I work with others in the class.	5	4	3	2	1

	Strongly Agree	Agree	Neutral	Disagree	Strongly Disagree
6. I often feel nervous and tense when I come to class.	1	2	3	4	5
7. My instructor seems to prefer stability over change.	1	2	3	4	5
8. My instructor encourages me to develop new and different ideas.	5	4	3	2	1
9. My instructor has little tolerance for sloppy thinking.	1	2	3	4	5
10. My instructor is more concerned with how I came to a conclusion than with the conclusion itself.	5	4	3	2	1
11. My instructor treats all students alike.	1	2	3	4	5
12. My instructor frowns on class members helping each other with assignments.	1	2	3	4	5
13. Aggressive and competitive people have a distinct advantage in this class.	1	2	3	4	5
14. My instructor encourages me to see the world differently.	5	4	3	2	1

Calculate your total score by adding up the numbers you circled. Your score will fall between 14 and 70.

A high score (49 or above) describes an open, risk-taking, supportive, humanistic, team-oriented, easy-going, growth-oriented culture. A low score (35 or below) describes a closed, structured, task-oriented, individualistic, tense, and stability-oriented culture. Note that differences count, so a score of 60 is a more open culture than one that scores 50. Also, realize that one culture isn't preferable over the other. The "right" culture depends on you and your preferences for a learning environment.

Form teams of five to seven members each. Compare your scores. How closely do they align? Discuss and resolve any discrepancies. Based on your team's analysis, what type of student do you think would perform best in this class?

Ethical Dilemma

IS INVOLUNTARY ETHICS TRAINING UNETHICAL?

A lot of companies rely on training as an essential part of their efforts to create an ethical culture. In some cases, this training is short in duration and requires little emotional investment by the employee. For instance, the training might only require reading a pamphlet describing the company's code of ethics, followed by an online quiz to ensure employee understanding. In contrast, some organizations' ethics training is quite lengthy, requiring employees to seriously address their values and principles and to share them with their coworkers. For example, the Boeing Company's training program, called "Questions of Integrity: The Ethics Challenge," is conducted within an employee's work group. Led by their supervisor, employees discuss more than four dozen ethical situations. Each includes four possible ways of dealing with the problem. After the supervisor discusses each situation, employees are asked to choose the best outcome by holding up cards marked A, B, C, or D. Then the supervisor indicates the "ethically correct" answer.

Most of the evidence indicates that for ethics training to be effective, it needs to be intensive and frequently reinforced. Some of the best programs require participants to spend several days a year, every year, engaged in discussions and exercises designed to clarify the organization's ethical expectations.

Is it unethical to ask employees to share their deepest personal values regarding right and wrong with their boss and coworkers? Should employees have the right not to participate in ethical training programs that might require them to publicly vocalize their ethical standards, religious principles, or other personal beliefs?

Case Incident 1

SOUTHWEST AIRLINES FACES NEW CHALLENGES

For 32 years, Southwest Airlines has used the same formula to maintain its position as the most profitable airline in the United States. It offers low fares, high-frequency flights, and good service; it flies only Boeing 737s; it doesn't offer connecting flights, reserved seating, or free meals; it often relies on less expensive, secondary airports; and it prides itself on having the hardest-working and most productive employees in the industry. The company believes its true competitive advantage is its workforce.

Most of the major airlines' cost per seat-mile is nearly 100 percent higher than Southwest's. The company gets this cost advantage by paying its pilots and flight attendants considerably less than the competition and having them fly more hours. It has made up for the lower pay with generous profit-sharing and stock-option plans. In addition, because of Southwest's rapid growth, it has provided its employees with something rare in the airline industry: job security. Because a large portion of a Southwest employees' compensation comes in the form of stock options, employees have worked harder and more flexibly than their peers at other airlines. For instance, pilots will often help ground crew move luggage and work extra hard to turn planes around fast. Of course, many Southwest employees originally joined the company and have stayed because of its spirit of fun. The company has always encouraged employees to work hard but to also have a good time. A sense of humor, for instance, has long been a basic criterion in the selection of new employees.

In the last couple of years, the environment has been changing for Southwest. First, it faces a number of new, upstart airlines in many of its markets. JetBlue, Frontier, AirTran, Song, and Ted are matching Southwest's low prices but offering benefits like reserved seating and free live-satellite TV. They're able to do this because they have newer, more fuel-efficient planes and young, lower-paid workforces. In many markets, Southwest's planes and service look dated. Second, the declining stock market of 2001–02 took much of the air out of Southwest's stock

(although it has revived somewhat, its stock is still trading at 1997 levels). The company's stock option plan no longer looks so attractive to employees. Third, Southwest has to deal with the reality that it is no longer the underdog. For decades, employees enjoyed the challenge of competing against United, American, Delta, and other major airlines. They loved the role of being the underdogs and having to work harder to survive. Southwest's employees are increasingly vocal and aggressive in demanding higher wages and shorter hours. In the past, workers were willing to go beyond the call of duty to help the airline thrive. It's harder for management to motivate employees now by portraying the airline as the underdog. Finally, as the company has grown and matured, management has become more remote from the rank and file. When the company had a few hundred employees, it was easy for management to communicate its messages. Now, with 35,000 workers, it's much tougher.

Southwest's managers realize that times have changed. Now they face the question of whether they need to make changes in their basic strategy and, if they do, what effect it will have on the company's culture. For instance, in the fall of 2003, the company was considering adding in-flight entertainment, although it would cost millions to install and many more millions to maintain; and purchasing smaller jets to maintain competitiveness in smaller markets. The operating costs of these smaller jets would be 15 to 25 percent higher than those of its current fleet.

Questions

1. What has sustained Southwest's culture?

2. Do you think upstart airlines can successfully duplicate this culture?

3. Now that the company is no longer the underdog, what can Southwest's management do to retain its high-productivity culture?

4. What does the case imply about sustaining culture in a changing environment?

Source: This case is based on S. B. Donnelly, "One Airline's Magic," *Time*, October 28, 2002, pp. 45–47; M. Trottman, "Inside Southwest Airlines, Storied Culture Feels Strains," *The Wall Street Journal*, July 11, 2003, p. A1; M. Trottman, "Southwest Air Considers Shift in its Approach," *The Wall Street Journal*, December 23, 2003, p. B1; and M. Maynard, "Low-Fare Airlines Decide Frills Maybe Aren't So Bad After All," *The New York Times*, January 7, 2004, p. C1.

Case Incident 2

WEGMANS

Amid corporate giants such as Microsoft, GM, and General Electric stands a relatively small grocery store that was named by *Fortune* magazine in 2005 as the best company to work for, primarily because of how well its employees are treated.

Typically, grocery stores are not thought of as great places to work. Hours are anything but 9 to 5, and the pay is low compared to other occupations. The result is an industry that sees high annual turnover rates. Employees at Wegmans, however, view working for a grocer a bit differently. Instead of viewing their job as a temporary setback on the way to a more illustrious career, many employees at Wegmans view working for the grocer as their career. And given Wegman's high profitability (it had sales in 2004 of $3.4 billion from 67 stores, giving it one of the highest profit-per-store ratios in the industry), it looks like the grocer will be around long enough to make such careers a reality for those who pursue them.

Why is Wegman's so effective? One reason is its culture. The chain began in 1930 when brothers John and Walter Wegman opened their first grocery store in Rochester, New York. One of its distinguishing features was a café that seated 300 customers. The store's immediate focus on fine foods quickly separated it from other grocers—a focus which is maintained by the company's employees, many of whom are hired based on their interest in food.

In 1950, Walter's son, Robert, became president and immediately added a generous amount of employee benefits such as profit sharing and medical coverage, completely paid for by the company. What was Robert's reason for offering such great benefits? "I was no different from them," he said, referring to the company's employees. Though the benefits are still generous at Wegmans, the rising cost of health care has forced it to have all employees contribute for coverage.

Now, Robert's son, Danny, is president of the company, and he has continued the Wegman's tradition of taking care of its employees. To date, Wegman's has paid more than $54 million in college scholarships for its employees, both full time and part time. In addition to benefits, employees receive pay that is well above the market average. As a result, annual turnover at Wegman's for full-time employees is a mere 6 percent, according to the Food Marketing Institute, when is it is 24 percent in the industry overall.

The culture that has developed at Wegman's is an important part of the company's success. Employees are proud to say they work at Wegman's. For example, Sara Goggins, a 19-year-old college student who works part time at Wegman's, recalls when Danny Wegman personally complimented her on a store display that she helped set up. "I love this place," she says. "If teaching doesn't work out, I would so totally work at Wegman's." And Kelly Schoeneck, a store manager, recounts that a few years ago, her supervisor asked her to analyze a frequent-shopper program that a competitor had recently adopted. Though she assumed that her supervisor would take credit for her findings, Schoeneck's supervisor had her present her findings directly to Robert Wegman.

Maintaining a culture of driven, happy, and loyal employees who are eager to help one another is not easy. Wegman's carefully selects each employee, and growth is often slow and meticulous, with only two new stores opened each year. When a new store is opened, employees from existing stores are brought in to the new store to maintain the culture. The existing employees are then able to transmit their knowledge and the store's values to new employees.

Managers especially are ingrained in the Wegman's culture. More than half started working at Wegman's when they were teenagers. Says Edward McLaughlin, director of Cornell's Food Industry Management Program, "When you're a 16-year-old kid, the last thing you want to do is wear a geeky shirt and work for a supermarket. But at Wegman's, it's a badge of honor. You are not a geeky cashier. You are part of the social fabric."

Employees at Wegman's are not selected based on intellectual ability or experience alone. "Just about everybody in the store has some genuine interest in food," states Jeff Burris, a supervisor at the Dulles, Virginia store. Those employees who do not express this interest may not fit in and are sometimes not hired. The result is a culture that "is bigger than Danny in the same way that Wal-Mart's became bigger than Sam [Walton]," says Darrell Rigby, a consultant at Bain & Co.

Questions

1. Would you characterize Wegman's culture as strong or weak? Why? How is the strength of the culture at Wegman's likely to affect its employees, particularly new hires?

2. Wegman's attempts to maintain its core cultural values by hiring individuals who are passionate about the food industry and by staffing new stores partly with existing employees. What are some advantages and disadvantages of trying to impose a similar culture throughout different areas of a company?

3. What is the primary source of Wegman's culture, and what are some ways that it has been able to sustain itself?

4. How might stories and rituals play a role in maintaining Wegman's corporate culture?

Source: Based on M. Boyle and E. F. Kratz, "The Wegman's Way," *Fortune,* January 24, 2005, pp. 62–66.

Endnotes

1. Source: "The Google Culture." (http://www.google.com/corporate/culture.html).

2. P. Selznick, "Foundations of the Theory of Organizations," *American Sociological Review*, February 1948, pp. 25–35.

3. See L. G. Zucker, "Organizations as Institutions," in S. B. Bacharach (ed.), *Research in the Sociology of Organizations* (Greenwich, CT: JAI Press, 1983), pp. 1–47; A. J. Richardson, "The Production of Institutional Behaviour: A Constructive Comment on the Use of Institutionalization Theory in Organizational Analysis," *Canadian Journal of Administrative Sciences*, December 1986, pp. 304–16; L. G. Zucker, *Institutional Patterns and Organizations: Culture and Environment* (Cambridge, MA: Ballinger, 1988); R. L. Jepperson, "Institutions, Institutional Effects, and Institutionalism," in W. W. Powell and P. J. DiMaggio (eds.), *The New Institutionalism in Organizational Analysis* (Chicago: University of Chicago Press, 1991), pp. 143–63; and T. B. Lawrence, M. K. Mauws, B. Dyck, and R. F. Kleysen, "The Politics of Organizational Learning: Integrating Power into the 4I Framework," *Academy of Management Review*, January 2005, pp. 180–91.

4. See, for example, H. S. Becker, "Culture: A Sociological View," *Yale Review*, Summer 1982, pp. 513–27; and E. H. Schein, *Organizational Culture and Leadership* (San Francisco: Jossey-Bass, 1985), p. 168.

5. This seven-item description is based on C. A. O'Reilly III, J. Chatman, and D. F. Caldwell, "People and Organizational Culture: A Profile Comparison Approach to Assessing Person-Organization Fit," *Academy of Management Journal*, September 1991, pp. 487–516; and J. A. Chatman and K. A. Jehn, "Assessing the Relationship between Industry Characteristics and Organizational Culture: How Different Can You Be?" *Academy of Management Journal*, June 1994, pp. 522–53. For a review of cultural dimensions, see N. M. Ashkanasy, C. P. M. Wilderom, and M. F. Peterson (eds.), *Handbook of Organizational Culture and Climate* (Thousand Oaks, CA: Sage, 2000), pp. 131–45.

6. The view that there will be consistency among perceptions of organizational culture has been called the "integration" perspective. For a review of this perspective and conflicting approaches, see D. Meyerson and J. Martin, "Cultural Change: An Integration of Three Different Views," *Journal of Management Studies*, November 1987, pp. 623–47; and P. J. Frost, L. F. Moore, M. R. Louis, C. C. Lundberg, and J. Martin (eds.), *Reframing Organizational Culture* (Newbury Park, CA: Sage Publications, 1991).

7. See J. M. Jermier, J. W. Slocum, Jr., L. W. Fry, and J. Gaines, "Organizational Subcultures in a Soft Bureaucracy: Resistance Behind the Myth and Facade of an Official Culture," *Organization Science*, May 1991, pp. 170–94; S. A. Sackmann, "Culture and Subcultures: An Analysis of Organizational Knowledge," *Administrative Science Quarterly*, March 1992, pp. 140–61; G. Hofstede, "Identifying Organizational Subcultures: An Empirical Approach," *Journal of Management Studies*, January 1998, pp. 1–12; and A. Boisner, and J. A. Chatman, "The Role of Subcultures in Agile Organizations" in R. S. Peterson, and E. A. Mannix (eds.), *Leading and Managing People in the Dynamic Organization* (Mahwah, NJ: Lawrence Erlbaum Associates, 2003), pp. 87–112.

8. T. A. Timmerman, "Do Organizations Have Personalities?" paper presented at the 1996 National Academy of Management Conference; Cincinnati, OH, August 1996.

9. S. Hamm, "No Letup—and No Apologies," *Business Week*, October 26, 1998, pp. 58–64; and C. Carlson, "Former Intel Exec Slams Microsoft Culture," eWeek.com, March 26, 2002.

10. See, for example, G. G. Gordon and N. DiTomaso, "Predicting Corporate Performance from Organizational Culture," *Journal of Management Studies*, November 1992, pp. 793–98; J. B. Sorensen, "The Strength of Corporate Culture and the Reliability of Firm Performance," *Administrative Science Quarterly*, March 2002, pp. 70–91; and J. Rosenthal and M. A. Masarech, "High-Performance Cultures: How Values Can Drive Business Results," *Journal of Organizational Excellence*, Spring 2003, pp. 3–18.

11. Y. Wiener, "Forms of Value Systems: A Focus on Organizational Effectiveness and Cultural Change and Maintenance," *Academy of Management Review*, October 1988, p. 536.

12. R. T. Mowday, L. W. Porter, and R. M. Steers, *Employee-Organization Linkages: The Psychology of Commitment, Absenteeism, and Turnover* (New York: Academic Press, 1982); and C. Vandenberghe, "Organizational Culture, Person-Culture Fit, and Turnover: A Replication in the Health Care Industry," *Journal of Organizational Behavior*, March 1999, pp. 175–84.

13. S. L. Dolan and S. Garcia, "Managing By Values: Cultural Redesign for Strategic Organizational Change at the Dawn of the Twenty-First Century," *Journal of Management Development* 21, no. 2 (2002), pp. 101–17.

14. See N. J. Adler, *International Dimensions of Organizational Behavior*, 4th ed. (Cincinnati, OH: Southwestern, 2002), pp. 67–69.

15. S. C. Schneider, "National vs. Corporate Culture: Implications for Human Resource Management," *Human Resource Management*, Summer 1988, p. 239.

16. See C. A. O'Reilly and J. A. Chatman, "Culture as Social Control: Corporations, Cults, and Commitment," in B. M. Staw and L. L. Cummings (eds.), *Research in Organizational Behavior*, vol. 18 (Greenwich, CT: JAI Press, 1996), pp. 157–200; see also M. Pinae Cunha, "The 'Best Place to Be': Managing Control and Employee Loyalty in a Knowledge-Intensive Company," *Journal of Applied Behavioral Science*, December 2002, pp. 481–95.

17. T. E. Deal and A. A. Kennedy, "Culture: A New Look Through Old Lenses," *Journal of Applied Behavioral Science*, November 1983, p. 501.

18. J. Case, "Corporate Culture," *INC.*, November 1996, pp. 42–53.

19. Sorensen, "The Strength of Corporate Culture and the Reliability of Firm Performance."

20. See, for instance, P. L. Moore, "She's Here to Fix the Xerox," *BusinessWeek*, August 6, 2001, pp. 47–48; and C. Ragavan, "FBI Inc.," *U.S. News & World Report*, June 18, 2001, pp. 15–21.

21. See C. Lindsay, "Paradoxes of Organizational Diversity: Living within the Paradoxes," in L. R. Jauch and J. L. Wall (eds.), *Proceedings of the 50th Academy of Management Conference* (San Francisco, 1990), pp. 374–78; T. Cox, Jr., *Cultural Diversity in Organizations: Theory, Research & Practice* (San Francisco: Berrett-Koehler, 1993), pp. 162–70; and L. Grensing-Pophal, "Hiring to Fit Your Corporate Culture," *HRMagazine*, August 1999, pp. 50–54.

22. K. Labich, "No More Crude at Texaco," *Fortune*, September 6, 1999, pp. 205–12; and "Rooting Out Racism," *BusinessWeek*, January 10, 2000, p. 66.

23. A. F. Buono and J. L. Bowditch, *The Human Side of Mergers and Acquisitions: Managing Collisions between People, Cultures, and Organizations* (San Francisco: Jossey-Bass, 1989); S. Cartwright and C. L. Cooper, "The Role of Culture Compatibility in Successful Organizational Marriages," *Academy of Management Executive*, May 1993, pp. 57–70; E. Krell, "Merging Corporate Cultures," *Training*, May 2001, pp. 68–78; and R. A. Weber and C. F. Camerer, "Cultural Conflict and Merger Failure: An Experimental Approach," *Management Science*, April 2003, pp. 400–12.

24. D. Miller, "What Happens After Success: The Perils of Excellence," *Journal of Management Studies*, May 1994, pp. 11–38.

25. "Motorola Is Poised to Fill Top Posts," *The Wall Street Journal*, December 16, 2003, p. A3.

26. P. Gumbel, "Return of the Urge to Merge," *Time Europe Magazine*. (http://www.time.com/time/europe/magazine/article/0,13005,901030721-464418,00.html) (July 13, 2003).

27. S. F. Gale, "Memo to AOL Time Warner: Why Mergers Fail—Case Studies," *Workforce* . (www.workforce.com) (February 2003; W. Bock, "Mergers, Bubbles, and Steve Case," *Wally Bock's Monday Memo*. (www.mondaymemo.net/030120feature.htm) (January 2003).

28. E. H. Schein, "The Role of the Founder in Creating Organizational Culture," *Organizational Dynamics*, Summer 1983, pp. 13–28.

29. E. H. Schein, "Leadership and Organizational Culture," in F. Hesselbein, M. Goldsmith, and R. Beckhard (eds.), *The Leader of the Future* (San Francisco: Jossey-Bass, 1996), pp. 61–62.

30. See, for example, J. R. Harrison and G. R. Carroll, "Keeping the Faith: A Model of Cultural Transmission in Formal Organizations," *Administrative Science Quarterly*, December 1991, pp. 552–82; see also G. George, R. G. Sleeth, and M. A. Siders, "Organizational Culture: Leader Roles, Behaviors, and Reinforcement Mechanisms," *Journal of Business & Psychology*, Summer 1999, pp. 545–60.

31. B. Schneider, "The People Make the Place," *Personnel Psychology*, Autumn 1987, pp. 437–53; D. E. Bowen, G. E. Ledford, Jr., and B. R. Nathan, "Hiring for the Organization, Not the Job," *Academy of Management Executive*, November 1991, pp. 35–51; B. Schneider, H. W. Goldstein, and D. B. Smith, "The ASA Framework: An Update," *Personnel Psychology*, Winter 1995, pp. 747–73; A. L. Kristof, "Person-Organization Fit: An Integrative Review of Its Conceptualizations, Measurement, and Implications," *Personnel Psychology*, Spring 1996, pp. 1–49; D. M. Cable and T. A. Judge, "Interviewers' Perceptions of Person-Organization Fit and Organizational Selection Decisions," *Journal of Applied Psychology*, August 1997, pp. 546–61; J. Schaubroeck, D. C. Ganster, and J. R. Jones, "Organization and Occupation Influences in the Attraction-Selection-Attrition Process," *Journal of Applied Psychology*, December 1998, pp. 869–91; G. Callaghan and P. Thompson, " 'We Recruit Attitude': The Selection and Shaping of Routine Call Centre Labour," *Journal of Management Studies*, March 2002, pp. 233–47; and M. L. Verquer, T. A. Beehr, and S. H. Wagner, "A Meta-Analysis of Relations Between Person-Organization Fit and Work Attitudes," *Journal of Vocational Behavior*, December 2003, pp. 473–89.

32. L. Grensing-Pophal, "Hiring to Fit Your Corporate Culture," *HRMagazine*, August 1999, pp. 50–54.

33. D. C. Hambrick and P. A. Mason, "Upper Echelons: The Organization as a Reflection of Its Top Managers," *Academy of Management Review*, April 1984, pp. 193–206; B. P. Niehoff, C. A. Enz, and R. A. Grover, "The Impact of Top-Management Actions on Employee Attitudes and Perceptions," *Group & Organization Studies*, September 1990, pp. 337–52; and H. M. Trice and J. M. Beyer, "Cultural Leadership in Organizations," *Organization Science*, May 1991, pp. 149–69.

34. J. S. Lublin, "Cheap Talk," *The Wall Street Journal*, April 11, 2002, p. B14.

35. See, for instance, J. P. Wanous, *Organizational Entry*, 2nd ed. (New York: Addison-Wesley, 1992); G. T. Chao, A. M. O'Leary-Kelly, S. Wolf, H. J. Klein, and P. D. Gardner, "Organizational Socialization: Its Content and Consequences," *Journal of Applied Psychology*, October 1994, pp. 730–43; B. E. Ashforth, A. M. Saks, and R. T. Lee, "Socialization and Newcomer Adjustment: The Role of Organizational Context," *Human Relations*, July 1998, pp. 897–926; D. A. Major, "Effective Newcomer Socialization into High-Performance Organizational Cultures," in N. M. Ashkanasy, C. P. M. Wilderom, and M. F. Peterson (eds.), *Handbook of Organizational Culture & Climate*, pp. 355–68; D. M. Cable and C. K. Parsons, "Socialization Tactics and Person-Organization Fit," *Personnel Psychology*, Spring 2001, pp. 1–23; and K. Rollag, "The Impact of Relative Tenure on Newcomer Socialization Dynamics," *Journal of Organizational Behavior*, November 2004, pp. 853–72.

36. J. Schettler, "Orientation ROI," *Training*, August 2002, p. 38.

37. K. Rhodes, "Breaking in the Top Dogs," *Training*, February 2000, pp. 67–74.

38. J. Van Maanen and E. H. Schein, "Career Development," in J. R. Hackman and J. L. Suttle (eds.), *Improving Life at Work* (Santa Monica, CA: Goodyear, 1977), pp. 58–62.

39. D. C. Feldman, "The Multiple Socialization of Organization Members," *Academy of Management Review*, April 1981, p. 310.

40. G. Chen and R. J. Klimoski, "The Impact of Expectations on Newcomer Performance in Teams as Mediated by Work Characteristics, Social Exchanges, and Empowerment," *Academy of Management Journal* 46 (2003), pp. 591–607; C. R. Wanberg and J. D. Kammeyer-Mueller, "Predictors and Outcomes of Proactivity in the Socialization Process," *Journal of Applied Psychology* 85 (2000), pp. 373–85; J. D. Kammeyer-Mueller and C. R. Wanberg, "Unwrapping the Organizational Entry Process: Disentangling Multiple Antecedents and Their Pathways to Adjustment," *Journal of Applied Psychology*, 88 (2003), pp. 779–94; E. W. Morrison, "Longitudinal Study of the Effects of Information Seeking on Newcomer Socialization," *Journal of Applied Psychology*, 78 (2003), pp. 173–83.

41. Van Maanen and Schein, "Career Development," p. 59.

42. E. W. Morrison, "Newcomers' Relationships: The Role of Social Network Ties During Socialization," *Academy of Management Journal* 45 (2002), pp. 1149–60.

43. E. Ransdell, "The Nike Story? Just Tell It!" *Fast Company*, January–February 2000, pp. 44–46.

44. D. M. Boje, "The Storytelling Organization: A Study of Story Performance in an Office-Supply Firm," *Administrative Science Quarterly*, March 1991, pp. 106–26; C. H. Deutsch, "The Parables of Corporate Culture," *The New York Times*, October 13, 1991, p. F25; and M. Ricketts and J. G. Seiling, "Language,

Metaphors, and Stories: Catalysts for Meaning Making in Organizations," *Organization Development Journal*, Winter 2003, pp. 33–43.

45. See K. Kamoche, "Rhetoric, Ritualism, and Totemism in Human Resource Management," *Human Relations*, April 1995, pp. 367–85.

46. V. Matthews, "Starting Every Day with a Shout and a Song," *Financial Times*, May 2, 2001, p. 11; and M. Gimein, "Sam Walton Made Us a Promise," *Fortune*, March 18, 2002, pp. 121–30.

47. A. Rafaeli and M. G. Pratt, "Tailored Meanings: On the Meaning and Impact of Organizational Dress," *Academy of Management Review*, January 1993, pp. 32–55; and J. M. Higgins and C. McAllaster, "Want Innovation? Then Use Cultural Artifacts That Support It," *Organizational Dynamics*, August 2002, pp. 74–84.

48. "DCACronyms," April 1997, Rev. D, published by The Boeing Co.

49. See B. Victor and J. B. Cullen, "The Organizational Bases of Ethical Work Climates," *Administrative Science Quarterly*, March 1988, pp. 101–25; L. K. Trevino, "A Cultural Perspective on Changing and Developing Organizational Ethics," in W. A. Pasmore and R. W. Woodman (eds.), *Research in Organizational Change and Development*, vol. 4 (Greenwich, CT: JAI Press, 1990); M. W. Dickson, D. B. Smith, M. W. Grojean, and M. Ehrhart, "An Organizational Climate Regarding Ethics: The Outcome of Leader Values and the Practices That Reflect Them," *Leadership Quarterly*, Summer 2001, pp. 197–217; and R. L. Dufresne, "An Action Learning Perspective on Effective Implementation of Academic Honor Codes," *Group & Organization Management*, April 2004, pp. 201–18.

50. J. A. Byrne, "The Environment was Ripe for Abuse," *Business Week*, February 25, 2002, pp. 118–20; and A. Raghavan, K. Kranhold, and A. Barrionuevo, "How Enron Bosses Created a Culture of Pushing Limits," *The Wall Street Journal*, August 26, 2002, p. A1.

51. S. Daley, "A Spy's Advice to French Retailers: Politeness Pays," *The New York Times*, December 26, 2000, p. A4.

52. Based on M. J. Bitner, B. H. Booms, and L. A. Mohr, "Critical Service Encounters: The Employee's Viewpoint," *Journal of Marketing*, October 1994, pp. 95–106; M. D. Hartline and O. C. Ferrell, "The Management of Customer-Contact Service Employees: An Empirical Investigation," *Journal of Marketing*, October 1996, pp. 52–70; M. L. Lengnick-Hall and Cynthia A. Lengnick-Hall, "Expanding Customer Orientation in the HR Function," *Human Resource Management*, Fall 1999, pp. 201–14; B. Schneider, D. E. Bowen, M. G. Ehrhart, and K. M. Holcombe, "The Climate for Service: Evolution of a Construct," in N. M. Ashkanasy, C. P. M. Wilderom, and M. F. Peterson (eds.), *Handbook of Organizational Culture and Climate* (Thousand Oaks, CA: Sage, 2000), pp. 21–36; M. D. Hartline, J. G. Maxham III, and D. O. McKee, "Corridors of Influence in the Dissemination of Customer-Oriented Strategy to Customer Contact Service Employees," *Journal of Marketing*, April 2000, pp. 35–50; L. A. Bettencourt, K. P. Gwinner, and M. L. Meuter, "A Comparison of Attitude, Personality, and Knowledge Predictors of Service-Oriented Organizational Citizenship Behaviors," *Journal of Applied Psychology*, February 2001, pp. 29–41; R. Peccei and P. Rosenthal, "Delivering Customer-Oriented Behaviour Through Empowerment: An Empirical Test of HRM Assumptions," *Journal of Management*,

September 2001, pp. 831–56; R. Batt, "Managing Customer Services: Human Resource Practices, Quit Rates, and Sales Growth," *Academy of Management Journal*, June 2002, pp. 587–97; S. D. Pugh, J. Dietz, J. W. Wiley, and S. M. Brooks, "Driving Service Effectiveness Through Employee-Customer Linkages," *Academy of Management Executive*, November 2002, pp. 73–84; and A. M. Sussking, K. M. Kacmar, and C. P. Borchgrevink, "Customer Service Providers' Attitudes Relating to Customer Service and Customer Satisfaction in the Customer-Service Exchange," *Journal of Applied Psychology*, February 2003, pp. 179–87.

53. D. E. Bowen and B. Schneider, "Boundary-Spanning-Role Employees and the Service Encounter: Some Guidelines for Future Management and Research," in J. Czepiel, M. R. Solomon, and C. F. Surprenant (eds.), *The Service Encounter* (New York: Lexington Books, 1985), pp. 127–47; W.-C. Tsai, "Determinants and Consequences of Employee Displayed Positive Emotions," *Journal of Management* 27, no. 4 (2001), pp. 497–512; and S. D. Pugh, "Service with a Smile: Emotional Contagion in the Service Encounter," *Academy of Management Journal*, October 2001, pp. 1018–27.

54. Hartline and Ferrell, "The Management of Customer-Contact Service Employees," p. 56; and R. C. Ford and C. P. Heaton, "Lessons from Hospitality That Can Serve Anyone," *Organizational Dynamics*, Summer 2001, pp. 41–42.

55. A. Taylor, "Driving Customer Satisfaction," *Harvard Business Review*, July 2002, pp. 24–25.

56. M. Clendenin, "UMC's New CEO Brings Customer Focus," *EBN*, July 21, 2003, p. 4.

57. See, for instance, E. Anderson and R. L. Oliver, "Perspectives on Behavior-Based Versus Outcome-Based Salesforce Control Systems," *Journal of Marketing*, October 1987, pp. 76–88; W. R. George, "Internal Marketing and Organizational Behavior: A Partnership in Developing Customer-Conscious Employees at Every Level," *Journal of Business Research*, January 1990, pp. 63–70; and K. K. Reardon and B. Enis, "Establishing a Company-Wide Customer Orientation Through Persuasive Internal Marketing," *Management Communication Quarterly*, February 1990, pp. 376–87.

58. Hartline and Ferrell, "The Management of Customer-Contact Service Employees," p. 57.

59. A. M. Webber and H. Row, "For Who Know How," *Fast Company*, October 1997, p. 130.

60. D. P. Ashmos and D. Duchon, "Spirituality at Work: A Conceptualization and Measure," *Journal of Management Inquiry*, June 2000, p. 139. For a comprehensive review of definitions of workplace spirituality, see R. A. Giacalone and C. L. Jurkiewicz, "Toward a Science of Workplace Spirituality," in R. A. Giacalone and C. L. Jurkiewicz (eds.), *Handbook of Workplace Spirituality and Organizational Performance* (Armonk, NY: M. E. Sharpe, 2003), pp. 6–13.

61. This section is based on C. Ichniowski, D. L. Kochan, C. Olson, and G. Strauss, "What Works at Work: Overview and Assessment," *Industrial Relations*, 1996, pp. 299–333; I. A. Mitroff and E. A. Denton, *A Spiritual Audit of Corporate America: A Hard Look at Spirituality, Religion, and Values in the Workplace* (San Francisco: Jossey-Bass, 1999); J. Milliman, J. Ferguson, D. Trickett, and B. Condemi, "Spirit and Community at Southwest Airlines: An Investigation of a Spiritual Values-Based Model," *Journal of Organizational Change Management*, vol. 12, no. 3, 1999,

pp. 221–33; E. H. Burack, "Spirituality in the Workplace," *Journal of Organizational Change Management*, vol. 12, no. 3, 1999, pp. 280–91; F. Wagner-Marsh and J. Conley, "The Fourth Wave: The Spiritually-Based Firm," *Journal of Organizational Change Management*, vol. 12, no. 3, 1999, pp. 292–302; and J. Pfeffer, "Business and the Spirit: Management Practices That Sustain Values," in R. A. Giacalone and C. L. Jurkiewicz (eds.), *Handbook of Workplace Spirituality and Organizational Performance*, pp. 32–41.

62. Cited in Wagner-Marsh and Conley, "The Fourth Wave," p. 295.

63. M. Conlin, "Religion in the Workplace: The Growing Presence of Spirituality in Corporate America," *Business Week*, November 1, 1999, pp. 151–58; and P. Paul, "A Holier Holiday Season," *American Demographics*, December 2001, pp. 41–45.

64. Cited in Conlin, "Religion in the Workplace," p. 153.

65. C. P. Neck and J. F. Milliman, "Thought Self-Leadership: Finding Spiritual Fulfillment in Organizational Life," *Journal of Managerial Psychology* 9, no. 8 (1994), p. 9; for a recent review, see J.-C. Garcia-Zamor, "Workplace Spirituality and Organizational Performance," *Public Administration Review*, May–June 2003, pp. 355–63.

66. D. W. McCormick, "Spirituality and Management," *Journal of Managerial Psychology* 9, no. 6 (1994), p. 5; E. Brandt, "Corporate Pioneers Explore Spiritual Peace," *HRMagazine* 41, no. 4 (1996), p. 82; P. Leigh, "The New Spirit at Work," *Training and Development* 51, no. 3 (1997), p. 26; P. H. Mirvis, "Soul Work in Organizations," *Organization Science* 8, no. 2 (1997), p. 193; and J. Milliman, A. Czaplewski, and J. Ferguson, "An Exploratory Empirical Assessment of the Relationship Between Spirituality and Employee Work Attitudes," paper presented at the National Academy of Management Meeting, Washington, D.C., August 2001.

67. Cited in Milliman et al., "Spirit and Community at Southwest Airlines."

68. J. A. Chatman, "Matching People and Organizations: Selection and Socialization in Public Accounting Firms," *Administrative Science Quarterly*, September 1991, pp. 459–84; B. Z. Posner, "Person-Organization Values Congruence: No Support for Individual Differences as a Moderating Influence," *Human Relations*, April 1992, pp. 351–61; and A. E. M. Van Vianen, "Person-Organization Fit: The Match Between Newcomers' and Recruiters Preferences for Organizational Cultures," *Personnel Psychology*, Spring 2000, pp. 113–49.

69. J. E. Sheridan, "Organizational Culture and Employee Retention," *Academy of Management Journal*, December 1992, pp. 1036–56; and Ibid. 68.

The only thing that differentiates Enron from our competitors is our people, our talent.

— former CEO Kenneth Lay

Human Resource Policies and Practices

After studying this chapter, you should be able to:

1 Assess the validity and usefulness of tests as selection devices.

2 Describe jobs for which interviews are effective selection devices.

3 Define four general skill categories.

4 Identify four types of employee training.

5 Explain the purposes of performance evaluation and who can conduct it.

CHAPTER 18

Wanted: Friendly and Outgoing People

As we learned in Chapter 4, a good part of an individual's personality is dictated by heredity. As a result, many companies that want friendly and outgoing employees are focusing on the hiring process to identify applicants with these traits. These companies have come to realize that it's a lot easier to hire people with the personalities they're looking for than to select only on the basis of technical skills, and then try to change personalities through training. One such company is Song, the low-cost startup from Delta Air Lines.[1]

Song hopes to differentiate itself from the competition through its efficiency and in-flight entertainment. It wants flight attendants with a sense of humor and a bit of craziness. So its hiring process emphasizes finding people with these characteristics. To get a job with Song, applicants need to excel at "auditions" in which they have to sing, dance, recite poetry, or otherwise humiliate themselves. One aspiring Song flight attendant was hired only after he belted out a 15-minute rendition of "Mustang Sally."

Although these auditions may seem silly, management takes them seriously. Song's president, John Selvaggio, sees them as a vital element in his strategy for making his airline profitable. What's more, Song doesn't have a specific performance appraisal system. Instead, managers try to "go out and talk" with employees as often as they can. Song also prides itself on its egalitarian culture. Frontline employees have Selvaggio's cell phone number, and managers often listen to employee's suggestions. For example, a Tampa-based flight attendant suggested that Song sell pink martinis and provide a portion of the proceeds to breast cancer research. The airline jumped on the suggestion.

Selvaggio hopes that, by hiring and encouraging a playful, open workforce, he can make the carrier so popular that its friendly employees will entice flyers to become return customers, and it won't have to spend much on advertising.

In late 2005 Delta announced it was merging Song into its main operations, but the company has vowed to keep the brand and to spread its customer focus to the rest of the airline. ■

T he message of this chapter is that human resource policies and practices—such as employee selection, training, and performance management—influence an organization's effectiveness.[2] We begin our discussion with the subject of hiring.

Selection Practices

The objective of effective selection is to match individual characteristics (ability, experience, and so on) with the requirements of the job.[3] When management fails to get a proper match, both employee performance and satisfaction suffer.

How the Selection Process Works

Exhibit 18-1 shows how the selection process works in most organizations. Having decided to apply for a job, applicants go through several stages—three are shown in the exhibit—during which they can be rejected at any time. In practice, some organizations forego some of these steps in the interests of time. A meat-packing plant may hire someone who walks in the door (there is not a long line of people who want to "thread" a pig's intestines for a living). But, most organizations follow a process that looks something like this. Let's go into a bit more detail for each of the stages.

Initial Selection

Initial selection devices are the first information applicants submit and are used for preliminary "rough cuts" to decide whether an applicant meets the basic qualifications for a job. Application forms (including letters of recommendation) are initial selection devices. We list background checks as either an initial selection device or a contingent selection device, depending on how the organization does it. Some organizations prefer to check into an applicant's background right away. Others wait until the applicant is about ready to be hired, contingent on everything checking out.

Application Forms   You've no doubt submitted your fair share of applications. By itself, the information submitted on an application form is not a very useful predictor of performance. However, it can be a good initial screen. For example, there's no sense in spending time interviewing an applicant for a registered nurse position if he or she doesn't have the proper credentials (education, certification, experience). More and more organizations encourage applicants to submit an application online. It takes only a few minutes, and the form can be forwarded to the people responsible for making the hiring decision. For example, Starbucks (www.starbucks.com) has a career center page, where you can search for available positions by location or job type and then apply online.

It's important that organizations be careful about the questions they ask on applications. It's pretty obvious that questions about race, gender, and nationality are disallowed. However, it might surprise you to learn that other questions also put companies in legal jeopardy. For example, it generally is not permissible to ask about prior arrest records or even convictions unless the answer is job-related.

Background Checks   More than 80 percent of employers conduct reference checks on applicants at some point in the hiring process. The reason is obvious: They want to know how an applicant did in past jobs and whether former employers would recommend hiring the person. The problem is that rarely

Exhibit **18-1**	Model of Selection Process in Organizations

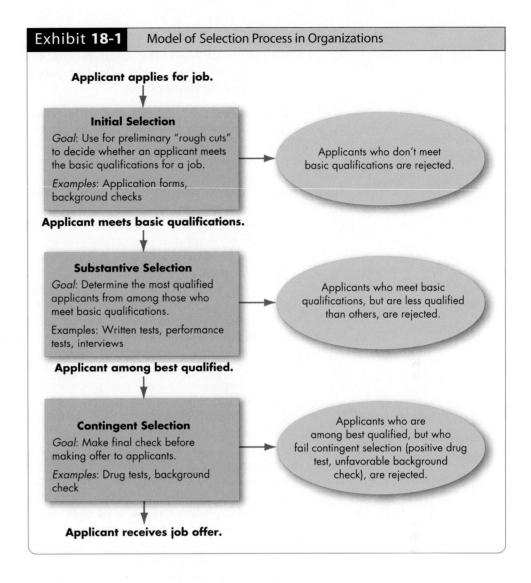

Applicant applies for job.

Initial Selection

Goal: Use for preliminary "rough cuts" to decide whether an applicant meets the basic qualifications for a job.

Examples: Application forms, background checks

Applicants who don't meet basic qualifications are rejected.

Applicant meets basic qualifications.

Substantive Selection

Goal: Determine the most qualified applicants from among those who meet basic qualifications.

Examples: Written tests, performance tests, interviews

Applicants who meet basic qualifications, but are less qualified than others, are rejected.

Applicant among best qualified.

Contingent Selection

Goal: Make final check before making offer to applicants.

Examples: Drug tests, background check

Applicants who are among best qualified, but who fail contingent selection (positive drug test, unfavorable background check), are rejected.

Applicant receives job offer.

do former employers provide useful information. In fact, nearly two-thirds of employers refuse to provide detailed reference information on applicants. Why? They are afraid of being sued for saying something bad about a former employee. Although this concern is often unfounded (employers are safe as long as they stick to documented facts), in our litigious society, most employers play it safe. The result is a paradox: Most employers want reference information, but few will give it out.

Letters of recommendation are another form of background check. These also aren't as useful as they may seem. Applicants self-select those who will write good letters, so almost all letters of recommendation are positive. In the end, readers of such letters either ignore them altogether or read "between the lines" to try to find hidden meaning there.

Finally, some employers do background checks on credit history or on criminal records. A bank hiring tellers, for example, would probably want to know about an applicant's criminal and credit histories. Because of the invasive nature of such checks, employers need to be sure there is a need for them. However, not checking can carry a legal cost. Manor Park Nursing Home in Texas failed to do a criminal background check of an employee who later sexually assaulted a resident of the nursing home. The jury awarded the plaintiff $1.1 million, concluding that the nursing home was negligent for failing to conduct a background check.[4]

Substantive Selection

If an applicant passes the initial screens, next are substantive selection methods. These are the heart of the selection process and include written tests, performance tests, and interviews.

Written Tests Long popular as selection devices, written tests ("paper-and-pencil" tests—though most are now available online) suffered a decline in use between the late 1960s and mid-1980s, especially in the United States. They were frequently characterized as discriminatory, and many organizations had not validated them as job-related. The past 20 years, however, have seen a resurgence in their use. It's been estimated that today more than 60 percent of all U.S. organizations and most of the Fortune 1000 use some type of employment test.[5] Managers have come to recognize that there are valid tests available and they can be helpful in predicting who will be successful on the job.[6] Applicants, however, tend to view written tests as less valid and fair than interviews or performance tests.[7]

Typical written tests include: (1) intelligence or cognitive ability tests; (2) personality tests; (3) integrity tests; and (4) interest inventories.

Tests of intellectual ability, spatial and mechanical ability, perceptual accuracy, and motor ability have proven to be valid predictors for many skilled, semi-skilled, and unskilled operative jobs in industrial organizations.[8] Intelligence tests have proven to be particularly good predictors for jobs that include cognitively complex tasks.[9] Many experts argue that intelligence tests are the *single best* selection measure across jobs. A recent review of the literature suggested that intelligence tests are at least as valid in European Economic Community (EEC) nations as in the United States.[10]

Even the NFL uses intelligence tests in making draft decisions. Eli Manning, the first player picked in the 2004 draft (now playing quarterback for the N.Y. Giants), scored very high on the cognitive ability test (close to genius level), whereas Ben Roethlisberger, the 11th player picked (playing quarterback for the Pittsburgh Steelers), scored only slightly above average. (Offensive tackles typically have the highest average scores on the intelligence tests the NFL uses.)

The use of personality tests has grown in the past decade. Japanese automakers, when staffing plants in the United States, have relied heavily on written tests to identify candidates who will be high performers.[11] Getting a job with Toyota can take up to three days of testing and interviewing. Organizations use numerous measures of the Big-Five traits in selection decisions. The traits that best predict job performance are conscientiousness and positive self-concept.[12] This makes sense in that conscientious people tend to be motivated and dependable and positive people are "can-do" oriented and persistent. Personality tests are relatively inexpensive and simple to use and administer.

As ethical problems have increased in organizations, integrity tests have gained in popularity. These are paper-and-pencil tests that measure factors such as dependability, carefulness, responsibility, and honesty. The evidence is impressive that these tests are powerful in predicting supervisory ratings of job performance and counterproductive employee behavior on the job, such as theft, discipline problems, and excessive absenteeism.[13]

You may wonder why applicants would respond truthfully to personality and integrity tests. After all, who would answer "strongly disagree" to the question "I always show up on time," even if they were generally late? Research shows that although applicants can "fake good" if they are motivated to do so, it doesn't appear that this fakery undermines the validity of personality and integrity tests.[14] Why? One speculation is that if faking does exist, those who "fake good" on selection tests also probably continue to present themselves in a desirable light once on the job. Thus, this sort of impression management not only helps get people hired but it helps them perform better on the job, at least unless taken to pathological degrees.

Performance-Simulation Tests   What better way to find out whether applicants can do a job successfully than by having them do it? That's precisely the logic of performance-simulation tests.

Although they are more complicated to develop and more difficult to administer than written tests, performance-simulation tests have increased in popularity during the past several decades. This appears to be due to the fact that they have higher "face validity" than do most written tests.

The two best-known performance-simulation tests are work samples and assessment centers. The former are suited to routine jobs, while the latter are relevant for the selection of managerial personnel.

Work sample tests are hands-on simulations of part or all of the job that must be performed by applicants. By carefully devising work samples based on specific job tasks, management determines the knowledge, skills, and abilities needed for each job. Then each work sample element is matched with a corresponding job performance element. Work samples are widely used in the hiring of skilled workers, such as welders, machinists, carpenters, and electricians. For instance, job candidates for production jobs at BMW's factory in South Carolina have 90 minutes to perform a variety of typical work tasks on a specially built simulated assembly line.[15] Work samples yield validities superior to written aptitude and personality tests.[16]

A more elaborate set of performance-simulation tests, specifically designed to evaluate a candidate's managerial potential, are administered in **assessment centers**. In these tests, line executives, supervisors, and/or trained psychologists evaluate candidates as they go through one to several days of exercises that simulate

Honda Manufacturing of Alabama uses work sample tests to assess job applicants' ability to perform jobs. Assessors watch applicants perform tasks such as spray-painting and caulking and then measure their ability to do the job, as well as their speed, accuracy, and ability to follow instructions.

work sample tests   *Creating a miniature replica of a job to evaluate the performance abilities of job candidates.*

assessment centers   *A set of performance-simulation tests designed to evaluate a candidate's managerial potential.*

real problems they would confront on the job.[17] Based on a list of descriptive dimensions the actual job incumbent has to meet, activities might include interviews, in-basket problem-solving exercises, leaderless group discussions, and business decision games. For instance, a candidate might be required to play the role of a manager who must decide how to respond to 10 memos in an in-basket within a 2-hour period. Assessment centers have consistently demonstrated results that predict later job performance in managerial positions.[18]

Interviews   In Korea, Japan, and many other Asian countries, employee interviews have not traditionally been part of the selection process. Decisions tend to be made almost entirely on the basis of exam scores, scholastic accomplishments, and letters of recommendation. This is not the case, however, throughout most of the rest of the world. In fact, of all the selection devices organizations around the globe use to differentiate candidates, the interview continues to be the most common.[19] Even companies in Asian countries have begun to rely on employee interviews as a screening device.[20]

Not only is the interview widely used, it also seems to carry a great deal of weight. That is, the results tend to have a disproportionate amount of influence on the selection decision. The candidate who performs poorly in the employment interview is likely to be cut from the applicant pool regardless of experience, test scores, or letters of recommendation. Conversely, "all too often, the person most polished in job-seeking techniques, particularly those used in the interview process, is the one hired, even though he or she may not be the best candidate for the position."[21]

These findings are important because of the unstructured manner in which the selection interview is frequently conducted.[22] The unstructured interview—short in duration, casual, and made up of random questions—is not a very effective selection device.[23] The data gathered from such interviews are typically biased and often only modestly related to future job performance. Still, managers are reluctant to use structured interviews in place of their favorite pet questions (such as "If you could be any animal, what would you be, and why?").[24]

Without structure, a number of biases can distort interview results. These biases include interviewers tending to favor applicants who share their atti-

Myth *or* Science?

"It's First Impressions That Count"

This statement is true. When we meet someone for the first time, we notice a number of things about that person—physical characteristics, clothes, firmness of handshake, gestures, tone of voice, and the like. We then use these impressions to fit the person into ready-made categories. And this early categorization, formed quickly and on the basis of minimal information, tends to hold greater weight than impressions and information received later.

The best evidence about first impressions comes from research on employment interviews. Findings clearly demonstrate that first impressions count. For instance, the primacy effect is potent. That is, the first information presented affects judgments more than information presented later.[25]

Research on applicant appearance confirms the power of first impressions.[26] Studies have looked at assessments made of appli-

cants before the actual interview—that brief period in which the applicant walks into an interview room, exchanges greetings with the interviewer, sits down, and engages in minor chit-chat. The evidence indicates that the way applicants walk, talk, dress, and look can have a great impact on the interviewer's evaluation of applicant qualifications. Facial attractiveness seems to be particularly influential. Applicants who are highly attractive are evaluated as more qualified for a variety of jobs than persons who are unattractive.

A final body of confirming research finds that interviewers' postinterview evaluations of applicants conform, to a substantial degree, to their preinterview impressions.[27] That is, those first impressions carry considerable weight in shaping the interviewers' final evaluations, assuming the interview elicits no highly negative information. ■

tudes, giving unduly high weight to negative information, and allowing the order in which applicants are interviewed to influence evaluations.[28] Using a standardized set of questions, providing interviewers with a uniform method of recording information, and standardizing the rating of the applicant's qualifications reduce the variability of results across applicants and greatly enhance the validity of the interview as a selection device. The effectiveness of the interview also improves when employers use behavioral structured interviews.[29] This interview technique requires applicants to describe how they handled specific problems and situations in previous jobs. It's built on the assumption that past behavior offers the best predictor of future behavior.

The evidence indicates that interviews are most valuable for assessing an applicant's applied mental skills, level of conscientiousness, and interpersonal skills.[30] When these qualities are related to job performance, the validity of the interview as a selection device increases and biases decrease.[31] For example, these qualities have demonstrated relevance for performance in upper managerial positions. This may explain why applicants for senior management positions typically undergo dozens of interviews with executive recruiters, board members, and other company executives before a final decision is made. It can also explain why organizations that design work around teams may similarly put applicants through an unusually large number of interviews.

In practice, most organizations use interviews for more than a "prediction-of-performance" device.[32] Companies as diverse as Southwest Airlines, Disney, Bank of America, Microsoft, Procter & Gamble, and Harrah's Entertainment use the interview to assess applicant–organization fit. So in addition to specific, job-relevant skills, organizations are looking at candidates' personality characteristics, personal values, and the like to find individuals who fit with the organization's culture and image.

Contingent Selection

Finally, if applicants pass the substantive selection methods, they are basically ready to be hired, contingent on a final check. One common contingent method is a drug test. For example, Publix grocery stores make a tentative offer to applicants contingent on their passing a drug test. This means Publix is ready to make an offer to the applicant as long as the person checks out to be drug-free.

Drug testing is controversial. Many applicants think it is unfair or invasive to test them without reasonable suspicion. Such individuals likely believe that drug use is a private matter and applicants should be tested on factors that directly bear on job performance, not lifestyle issues that may or may not be job-relevant. Drug tests typically screen out individuals who have used marijuana but not alcohol (for both legal and practical reasons—alcohol is legal and leaves the system in 24 hours).

Employers might counter this view with the argument that drug use and abuse are extremely costly, not just in terms of financial resources, but in terms of people's safety. Moreover, employers have the law on their side. The Supreme Court has concluded that drug tests are "minimally invasive" selection procedures that as a rule do not violate individuals' rights.

Drug tests are not cheap. If the first test (typically a urine test) turns up positive, then the result is reanalyzed to make sure. Contrary to popular claims, the tests generally are quite accurate and not easily faked. They tend to be quite precise, telling the employer what specific kind of drug appeared to be in the applicant's system. Despite the controversy over drug testing, it's probably here to stay.

Training and Development Programs

Competent employees don't remain competent forever. Skills deteriorate and can become obsolete and new skills need to be learned. That's why organizations spend billions of dollars each year on formal training. For instance, it was reported that U.S. corporations with 100 or more employees spent more than $51 billion on formal training in one recent year.[33] For example, IBM, Accenture, Intel, and Lockheed Martin alone each spend in excess of $300 million a year on employee training.[34]

Types of Training

Training can include everything from teaching employees basic reading skills to conducting advanced courses in executive leadership. Here we discuss four general skill categories—basic literacy and technical, interpersonal, and problem-solving skills. In addition, we briefly discuss ethics training.

Basic Literacy Skills   A recent report by the Organization of Economic Cooperation and Development found that 50 percent of the U.S. population reads below the eighth-grade level and about 90 million adults are functionally illiterate.[35] Moreover, statistics show that nearly 40 percent of the U.S. labor force and more than 50 percent of high school graduates don't possess the basic work skills needed to perform in today's workplace.[36] The National Institute of Learning estimates that this literacy problem costs corporate America about $60 billion a year in lost productivity.[37] This problem, of course, isn't unique to the United States. It's a worldwide problem—from the most developed countries to the least.[38] For many Third World countries, where few workers can read or have gone beyond the equivalent of the third grade, widespread illiteracy means there is almost no hope of competing in a global economy.

Organizations increasingly have to teach basic reading and math skills to their employees. For instance, jobs at Springfield, Massachusetts–based Smith and Wesson have become more complex.[39] Employees need improved math skills for understanding numerical control equipment, better reading and writing skills to interpret process sheets, and better oral communication skills for working in teams. A literacy audit showed that employees needed to have at least an eighth-grade reading level to do typical workplace tasks. Yet 30 percent of the company's 676 workers with no degree scored below eighth-grade levels in either reading or math. These employees were told that they wouldn't lose their jobs, but they had to take basic skill classes, paid for by the company and provided on company time. After the first round of classes, 70 percent of attendees brought their skills up to the target level. And these improved skills allowed employees to do a better job. They displayed greater ease in writing and reading charts, graphs, and bulletin boards, increased abilities to use fractions and decimals, better overall communication, and a significant increase in confidence.

Technical Skills   Most training is directed at upgrading and improving an employee's technical skills. Technical training has become increasingly important today for two reasons—new technology and new structural designs in the organization.

Jobs change as a result of new technologies and improved methods. For instance, many auto repair personnel have had to undergo extensive training to fix and maintain recent models with computer-monitored engines, electronic stabilizing systems, GPS, keyless entry, and other innovations. Similarly,

Medical personnel continually update their technical skills to provide patients with required treatment. Because of the increased risk of chemical warfare, paramedics and emergency room doctors are learning new technical skills for the treatment of antiterror medical emergencies. At Montefiore Hospital in Bronx, New York, medical emergency staff participate in a crisis medicine training program that uses a computer-controlled mannequin to simulate various chemical injuries.

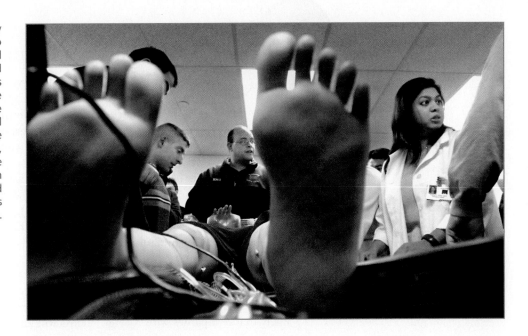

computer-controlled equipment has required millions of production employees to learn a whole new set of skills.[40]

In addition, technical training has become increasingly important because of changes in organization design. As organizations flatten their structures, expand their use of teams, and break down traditional departmental barriers, employees need mastery of a wider variety of tasks and increased knowledge of how their organization operates. For instance, the restructuring of jobs at Miller Brewing Co. around empowered teams has led management to introduce a comprehensive business literacy program to help employees better understand competition, the state of the beer industry, where the company's revenues come from, how costs are calculated, and where employees fit into the company's value chain.[41]

Interpersonal Skills   Almost all employees belong to a work unit, and their work performance depends to some degree on their ability to effectively interact with their coworkers and their boss. Some employees have excellent interpersonal skills, but others require training to improve theirs. This includes learning how to be a better listener, how to communicate ideas more clearly, and how to be a more effective team player.

Problem-Solving Skills   Managers, as well as many employees who perform nonroutine tasks, have to solve problems on their jobs. When people require these skills but are deficient in them, they can participate in problem-solving training. This can include activities to sharpen their logic, reasoning, and problem-defining skills, as well as their abilities to assess causation, develop and analyze alternatives, and select solutions. Problem-solving training has become a basic part of almost every organizational effort to introduce self-managed teams or implement quality-management programs.

What About Ethics Training?   A recent survey finds that about 75 percent of employees working in the 1,000 largest U.S. corporations receive ethics training.[42] This training may be included in a newly hired employee's orientation program, made part of an ongoing developmental training program, or provided to all employees as a periodic reinforcement of ethical principles.[43] But the jury is still out on whether you can actually teach ethics.[44]

Cultural Training

IN A GLOBAL ECONOMY, EMPLOYEE TRAINING IS NO longer limited to the specific tasks of the job. As more and more positions in the information technology and service industries move to India from the United States, many companies are training their Indian employees to improve their cultural skills when dealing with American clients.

For example, the Hyderabad offices of Sierra Atlantic, a California-based software company, trains its Indian employees in various aspects of American culture, including addressing colleagues as Mr. or Ms., learning how to interact with others during a conference call, and even how to sip wine. According to Lu Ellen Schafer, executive director at Global Savvy, a consulting firm based in California, "The training in American culture is not to make Indian software professionals less Indian. It is to make them more globally competent."

Some companies are benefiting from cultural training. Sierra Atlantic's offices in Hyderabad, for example, won a bid with an American firm over an Indian competitor because the Sierra employees were viewed as a better cultural fit. Such successes make it likely that companies with foreign clients will either adopt or continue to use cultural training.

Source: Based on S. Rai, "Indian Companies are Adding Western Flavor," *The New York Times,* August 19, 2003, p. W.1.

Critics argue that ethics are based on values, and value systems are fixed at an early age. By the time employers hire people, their ethical values have already been established. The critics also claim that ethics cannot be formally "taught," but must be learned by example.

Supporters of ethics training argue that values can be learned and changed after early childhood. And even if they couldn't, ethics training would be effective because it helps employees to recognize ethical dilemmas and become more aware of the ethical issues underlying their actions. Another argument is that ethics training reaffirms an organization's expectations that members will act ethically.

Training Methods

Training methods are most readily classified as formal or informal, and on-the-job or off-the-job.

Historically, training meant *formal training.* It's planned in advance and has a structured format. However, recent evidence indicates that 70 percent of workplace learning is made up of *informal training*—unstructured, unplanned, and easily adapted to situations and individuals—for teaching skills and keeping employees current.[45] In reality, most informal training is nothing other than employees helping each other out. They share information and solve work-related problems with one another. Perhaps the most important outcome of this realization is that many managers are now supportive of what used to be considered "idle chatter." At a Siemens plant in North Carolina, for instance, management now recognizes that people needn't be on the production line to be working.[46] Discussions around the water cooler or in the cafeteria weren't, as managers thought, about nonwork topics such as sports or politics. They largely focused on solving work-related problems. So now Siemens' management encourages such casual meetings.

On-the-job training includes job rotation, apprenticeships, understudy assignments, and formal mentoring programs. But the primary drawback of these on-

At Ito Yokado, the largest supermarket chain in Japan, week-long training for new employees includes role-playing exercises. The group of young men shown here is learning the proper techniques of guiding blind, disabled, and elderly people. This off-the-job training technique of role-playing is effective because employees become sensitive to the special needs of shoppers who require assistance.

the-job training methods is that they often disrupt the workplace. So organizations invest in *off-the-job training*. The $51 billion figure we cited earlier for training costs was largely spent on the formal off-the-job variety. What types of training might this include? The most popular continues to be live classroom lectures. But it also encompasses videotapes, public seminars, self-study programs, Internet courses, satellite-beamed television classes, and group activities that use role plays and case studies.

In recent years, the fastest-growing means for delivering training is probably computer-based or e-training.[47] Kinko's, for instance, has created an internal network that allows its 20,000 employees to take online courses covering everything from products to policies.[48] Cisco Systems provides a curriculum of training courses on its corporate intranet, organized by job titles, specific technologies, and products.[49] Although more than 5,000 companies now offer all or some of their employee training online, it's unclear how effective it actually is. On the positive side, e-training increases flexibility by allowing organizations to deliver materials anywhere and at any time. It also seems to be fast and efficient. On the other hand, it's expensive to design self-paced online materials, many employees miss the social interaction provided by a classroom environment, online learners are often more susceptible to distractions, and "clicking through" training is no assurance that employees have actually learned anything.[50]

Individualizing Formal Training to Fit the Employee's Learning Style

The way you process, internalize, and remember new and difficult material isn't necessarily the same way others do. This fact means that effective formal training should be individualized to reflect the learning style of the employee.[51]

Some examples of different learning styles are reading, watching, listening, and participating. Some people absorb information better when they read about it. They're the kind of people who can learn to use computers by sitting in their study and reading manuals. Some people learn best by observation. They watch others and then imitate the behaviors they've seen. Such people can watch someone use a computer for a while, then copy what they've done. Listeners rely heavily on their auditory senses to absorb information. They would prefer to learn how to use a computer, for instance, by listening to an audiotape. People who prefer a participating style learn by doing. They want to sit down, turn on the computer, and gain hands-on experience by practicing.

You can translate these styles into different learning methods. To maximize learning, readers should be given books or other reading material to review; watchers should get the opportunity to observe individuals modeling the new skills either in person or on video; listeners will benefit from hearing lectures or audiotapes; and participants will benefit most from experiential opportunities in which they can simulate and practice the new skills.

These different learning styles are obviously not mutually exclusive. In fact, good teachers recognize that their students learn differently and, therefore, provide multiple learning methods. They assign readings before class; give lectures; use visual aids to illustrate concepts; and have students participate in group projects, case analyses, role plays, and experiential learning exercises. If you know the preferred style of an employee, you can design a formal training program to take advantage of this preference. If you don't have that information, it's probably best to design the program to use a variety of learning styles. Overreliance on a single style places individuals who don't learn well from that style at a disadvantage.

Evaluating Effectiveness

Most training programs work rather well in that the majority of people who undergo training learn more than those who do not, react positively to the training experience, and after the training engage in the behaviors targeted by the program. Still, some factors make certain programs work better than others. For example, although lecture styles have a poor reputation, they are surprisingly effective training methods. On the other hand, conducting a needs assessment prior to training was relatively unimportant in predicting the success of a training program.[52]

The success of training also depends on the individual. If individuals are unmotivated to learn, they will benefit very little. What factors determine training motivation? Personality is important: Those with an internal locus of control, high conscientiousness, high cognitive ability, and high self-efficacy learn more in training programs. The training climate also is important: When trainees believe that there are opportunities on the job to apply their newly learned skills and enough resources to apply what they have learned, they are more motivated to learn and do better in training programs.[53]

Performance Evaluation

Would you study differently or exert a different level of effort for a college course graded on a pass–fail basis than for one that awarded letter grades from A to F? Students typically tell us they study harder when letter grades are at stake. In addition, when they take a course on a pass–fail basis, they tend to do just enough to ensure a passing grade.

This finding illustrates how performance evaluation systems influence behavior. Major determinants of your in-class behavior and out-of-class studying effort in college are the criteria and techniques your instructor uses to evaluate your performance. What applies in the college context also applies to employees at work. In this section, we show how the choice of a performance evaluation system and the way it's administered can be an important force influencing employee behavior.

Purposes of Performance Evaluation

Performance evaluation serves a number of purposes.[54] One purpose is to help management make general *human resource decisions*. Evaluations provide input into important decisions such as promotions, transfers, and terminations. Evaluations also *identify training and development needs*. They pinpoint employee skills and competencies that are currently inadequate but for which remedial programs can be developed. Performance evaluations can also serve as a *criterion against which management validates selection and development programs*. Management can identify newly hired employees who perform poorly. Similarly, the organization determines the effectiveness of training and development programs by assessing how well participants do on their performance evaluation. Evaluations also fulfill the purpose of *providing feedback to employees* on how the organization views their performance. Furthermore, performance evaluations are the *basis for reward allocations*. Decisions as to who gets merit pay increases and other rewards are frequently determined by performance evaluations.

Each of these functions of performance evaluation is valuable. Yet their importance to us depends on the perspective we're taking. Several are clearly relevant to human resource management decisions. But our interest is in organizational behavior. As a result, we shall be emphasizing performance evaluation as a mechanism for providing feedback and as a determinant of reward allocations.

What Do We Evaluate?

The criteria that management chooses to evaluate when appraising employee performance will have a major influence on what employees do. The three most popular sets of criteria are individual task outcomes, behaviors, and traits.

Individual Task Outcomes   If ends count, rather than means, then management should evaluate an employee's task outcomes. Using task outcomes, a plant manager could be judged on criteria such as quantity produced, scrap generated, and cost per unit of production. Similarly, a salesperson could be assessed on overall sales volume in the territory, dollar increase in sales, and number of new accounts established.

Behaviors   In many cases, it's difficult to identify specific outcomes that can be directly attributed to an employee's actions. This is particularly true of personnel in advisory or support positions and individuals whose work assignments are intrinsically part of a group effort. We may readily evaluate the group's performance but have difficulty distinguishing clearly the contribution of each group member. In such instances, it's not unusual for management to evaluate the employee's behavior. Using the previous examples, behaviors of a plant manager that could be used for performance evaluation purposes might include promptness in submitting monthly reports or the leadership style the manager exhibits. Pertinent salesperson behaviors could be the average number of contact calls made per day or sick days used per year.

Note that these behaviors needn't be limited to those directly related to individual productivity.[55] As we pointed out in our previous discussion on organizational citizenship behavior (see specifically Chapters 1 and 4), helping others, making suggestions for improvements, and volunteering for extra duties make work groups and organizations more effective. So including subjective or contextual factors in a performance evaluation—as long as they contribute to organizational effectiveness—may not only make sense, it may

Behavior is an important element in appraising the performance of resident aides in retirement homes. In addition to individual task outcomes, this aide at a retirement home in Pennsylvania is evaluated on behaviors such as helping others and building caring and trusting relationships with residents and their family members. These subjective factors contribute to the effectiveness of the retirement home and its reputation as a place where the elderly are treated with love and respect.

also improve coordination, teamwork, cooperation, and overall organizational performance.

Traits   The weakest set of criteria, yet one that is still widely used by organizations, is individual traits.[56] We say they're weaker than either task outcomes or behaviors because they're farthest removed from the actual performance of the job itself. Traits such as having a good attitude, showing confidence, being dependable, looking busy, or possessing a wealth of experience may or may not be highly correlated with positive task outcomes, but only the naive would ignore the reality that such traits are frequently used as criteria for assessing an employee's level of performance.

Who Should Do the Evaluating?

Who should evaluate an employee's performance? By tradition, the task has fallen to the manager, on the grounds that managers are held responsible for their employees' performance. But that logic may be flawed. Others may actually be able to do the job better.

With many of today's organizations using self-managed teams, telecommuting, and other organizing devices that distance bosses from their employees, an employee's immediate superior may not be the most reliable judge of that employee's performance. Thus, in more and more cases, peers and even subordinates are being asked to participate in the performance evaluation process. Also, increasingly, employees are participating in their own performance evaluation. For instance, a recent survey found that about half of executives and 53 percent of employees now have input into their performance evaluations.[57] As you might surmise, self-evaluations often suffer from overinflated assessment and self-serving bias. Moreover, self-evaluations are often low in agreement with superiors' ratings.[58] Because of these drawbacks, self-evaluations are probably better suited to developmental than evaluative purposes and should be combined with other sources of information to reduce rating errors.

In most situations, in fact, it is highly advisable to use multiple sources of ratings. Any individual performance rating may say as much about the rater as about the person being evaluated. By averaging across raters, we can obtain a more reliable, unbiased, and accurate performance evaluation.

The latest approach to performance evaluation is the use of 360-degree evaluations.[59] It provides for performance feedback from the full circle of daily contacts that an employee might have, ranging from mailroom personnel to customers to bosses to peers (see Exhibit 18-2). The number of appraisals can be as few as 3 or 4 or as many as 25, with most organizations collecting 5 to 10 per employee.

A recent survey shows that about 21 percent of U.S. organizations are using full 360-degree programs.[60] Some of them are Alcoa, Du Pont, Levi Strauss, Honeywell, UPS, Sprint, AT&T, and W.L. Gore & Associates. What's the appeal of 360-degree evaluations? They fit well into organizations that have introduced teams, employee involvement, and quality-management programs. By relying on feedback from coworkers, customers, and subordinates, these organizations are hoping to give everyone more of a sense of participation in the review process and gain more accurate readings on employee performance. On this latter point, 360-degree evaluations are consistent with evidence that employee performance varies across contexts and that people behave differently with different constituencies.[61] The use of multiple sources is more likely to capture this variety of behavior accurately.

The evidence on the effectiveness of 360-degree evaluations is mixed.[62] It provides employees with a wider perspective of their performance. But it also has the potential for being misused. For instance, to minimize costs, many organizations don't spend the time to train evaluators in giving constructive criticism. Some organizations allow employees to choose the peers and subordinates who evaluate them, which can artificially inflate feedback. Problems also arise from the difficulty of reconciling disagreements and contradictions between rater groups.

Exhibit **18-2**	360-Degree Evaluations

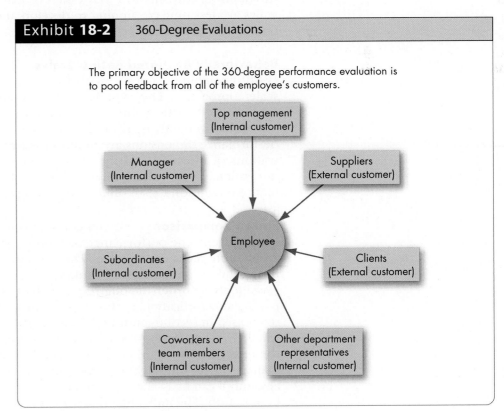

Source: Adapted from *Personnel Journal,* November 1994, p. 100.

Methods of Performance Evaluation

The previous sections explained *what* we evaluate and *who* should do the evaluating. Now we ask: *How* do we evaluate an employee's performance? That is, what are the specific techniques for evaluation?

Written Essays   Probably the simplest method of evaluation is to write a narrative describing an employee's strengths, weaknesses, past performance, potential, and suggestions for improvement. The written essay requires no complex forms or extensive training to complete. But in this method a good or bad appraisal may be determined as much by the evaluator's writing skill as by the employee's actual level of performance.

Critical Incidents   **Critical incidents** focus the evaluator's attention on the behaviors that are key in making the difference between executing a job effectively and executing it ineffectively. That is, the appraiser writes down anecdotes that describe what the employee did that was especially effective or ineffective. The key here is to cite only specific behaviors, not vaguely defined personality traits. A list of critical incidents provides a rich set of examples from which the employee can be shown the behaviors that are desirable and those that call for improvement.

Graphic Rating Scales   One of the oldest and most popular methods of evaluation is the use of **graphic rating scales**. In this method, a set of performance factors, such as quantity and quality of work, depth of knowledge, cooperation, attendance, and initiative, is listed. The evaluator then goes down the list and rates each on incremental scales. The scales may specify five points, so a factor such as *job knowledge* might be rated 1 ("poorly informed about work duties") to 5 ("has complete mastery of all phases of the job"). Although they don't provide the depth of information that essays or critical incidents do, graphic rating scales are less time-consuming to develop and administer. They also allow for quantitative analysis and comparison.

Behaviorally Anchored Rating Scales   **Behaviorally anchored rating scales** (BARS) combine major elements from the critical incident and graphic rating scale approaches: The appraiser rates the employees based on items along a continuum, but the points are examples of actual behavior on the given job rather than general descriptions or traits. Examples of job-related behavior and performance dimensions are found by asking participants to give specific illustrations of effective and ineffective behavior regarding each performance dimension. These behavioral examples are then translated into a set of performance dimensions, each dimension having varying levels of performance.

Forced Comparisons   Forced comparisons evaluate one individual's performance against the performance of another or others. It is a relative rather than an absolute measuring device. The two most popular comparisons are group order ranking and individual ranking.

The **group order ranking** requires the evaluator to place employees into a particular classification, such as top one-fifth or second one-fifth. This method is often used in recommending students to graduate schools. Evaluators are asked whether the student ranks in the top 5 percent of the class, the next 5 percent, the next 15 percent, and so forth. But in this type of performance appraisal, managers deal with all their subordinates. Therefore, if a rater has 20 employees, only 4 can be in the top fifth and, of course, 4 must also be relegated to the bottom fifth. The **individual ranking** approach rank-orders employees from best to worst. If the manager is required to appraise 30 employees, this approach assumes that the difference between the first and second employee is the same as that between the twenty-first and twenty-second. Even though some of the employees may be closely grouped, no ties are permitted. The result is a clear ordering of employees, from the highest performer down to the lowest.

One parallel to the use of forced ranking systems is a forced distribution in the giving of college grades. Why would universities do this?

As shown in Exhibit 18-3, the average GPA of a Princeton University undergraduate has gotten much higher over time.[63]

It's not just Princeton. For example, the average student GPA at Wheaton College was 2.75 in 1962. Now it's 3.40. At Pomona College, the average GPA was 3.06 in 1970. Now it's 3.43. About half the grades at Duke, Harvard, and Columbia are in the "A" range. At Harvard, 91 percent of seniors graduated with some sort of honors in 2001. These are just randomly selected examples. Almost all universities have seen considerable grade inflation, although, interestingly, it may be more severe at prestigious institutions.

In response to grade inflation, some colleges have instituted forced grade distributions whereby professors must give a certain percentage of students A's, B's, and C's. This is exactly what Princeton recently did; each department can now give A's to no more than 35 percent of its students. Natasha Gopaul, a senior at Princeton, commented, "You do feel you might be one of the ones they just cut off."

Exhibit **18-3**	Grade Inflation at Princeton University

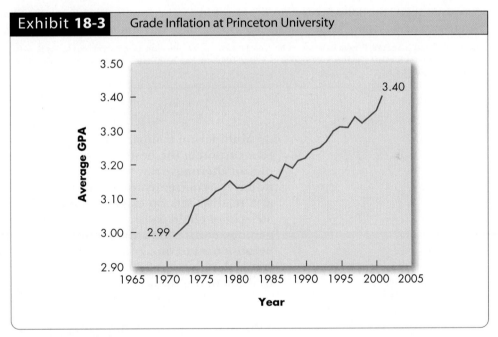

Source: http://www.gradeinflation.com

---

critical incidents   *Evaluating the behaviors that are key in making the difference between executing a job effectively and executing it ineffectively.*

graphic rating scales   *An evaluation method in which the evaluator rates performance factors on an incremental scale.*

behaviorally anchored rating scales (BARS)   *Scales that combine major elements from the critical incident and graphic rating scale approaches: The appraiser rates the employees based on items along a continuum, but the points are examples of actual behavior on the given job rather than general descriptions or traits.*

group order ranking   *An evaluation method that places employees into a particular classification, such as quartiles.*

individual ranking   *An evaluation method that rank-orders employees from best to worst.*

The Rise and Fall of Forced Ranking

As recently as 2002, it was one of the fastest-growing trends in performance evaluation. Companies like Ford, GE, Microsoft, Sun Microsystems, H&R Block, and Sprint were among the 33 percent of U.S. companies that were ranking their employees from best to worst and then using those rankings to determine pay, identify employees for firing, and make other human resource decisions.

Forced ranking, or what has derisively been called "rank and yank" by its critics, was created because many top executives had become frustrated by managers who rated all their employees "above average." In addition, executives wanted a system that would increase the organization's competitiveness—one that would reward the very best performers and encourage poor performers to leave.

For instance, all 18,000 of Ford Motor's managers underwent the forced ranking process. These managers were divided into groups of 30 to 50 and then rated. For each group, 10 percent had to get an A, 80 percent a B, and 10 percent a C. Anyone receiving a C was barred from a pay raise and two consecutive years of a C rating resulted in either a demotion or a termination.

The best-known "rank and yank" program is GE's "20-70-10 plan." The company forces the heads of each of its divisions to review all managers and professional employees and to identify their top 20 percent, middle 70 percent, and bottom 10 percent. GE then does everything possible to keep and reward its top performers and fires all bottom-group performers. The company's former CEO stated, "A company that bets its future on its people must remove the lower 10 percent, and keep removing it every year—always raising the bar of performance and increasing the quality of its leadership."

Forced ranking grew in popularity because it was seen as a means to continually improve an organization's workforce and to reward those who are most deserving. But many companies that adopted the system, like Hallmark Cards, have recently dropped it. They found it undermined employee morale and created a "zero-sum game" that discouraged cooperation and teamwork. In addition, several companies have been hit with age discrimination suits by older workers who claim the system has adversely impacted them. Ford, for example, overhauled its ranking system after it settled a $10.6 million lawsuit filed by older employees who felt the system was discriminatory.

Sources: Based on D. Stafford, "Forced Rankings Are No Cure," *Kansas City Star* (www.kansascity.com/mld/kansascity/business/10742914.htm?1c) (January 27, 2005); D. Jones, "More Firms Cut Workers Ranked at Bottom to Make Way for Talent," *USA Today*, May 30, 2001, p. 1B; and D. Sears and D. McDermott, "The Rise and Fall of Rank and Yank," *Information Strategy*, Spring 2003, p. 6.

Multiperson comparisons can be combined with one of the other methods to incorporate the best from both absolute and relative standards. For example, an alternative way for universities to deal with the problem of grade inflation is to require instructors to include not only an absolute letter grade but also relative data on class size and rank. So a prospective employer or graduate school could look at two students who each got an "A" in their physical geology courses and draw considerably different conclusions about each, because next to one grade it says "ranked 2nd out of 26," while the other says "ranked 14th out of 30." Obviously, the first student performed better, relatively, than did the second.

Suggestions for Improving Performance Evaluations

The performance evaluation process is a potential minefield of problems. For instance, evaluators can unconsciously inflate evaluations (positive leniency), understate performance (negative leniency), or allow the assessment of one characteristic to unduly influence the assessment of others (the halo error). Some appraisers bias their evaluations by unconsciously favoring people who have qualities and traits similar to their own (the similarity error). And, of course, some evaluators see the evaluation process as a political opportunity to overtly reward or punish employees they like or dislike. Although there are no protections that will *guarantee* accurate performance evaluations, the following suggestions can significantly help to make the process more objective and fair.

Use Multiple Evaluators   As the number of evaluators increases, the probability of attaining more accurate information increases. If rater error tends to follow a normal curve, an increase in the number of appraisers will tend to find the majority congregating about the middle. We often see multiple evaluators in competitions in such sports as diving and gymnastics. A set of evaluators judges a performance, the highest and lowest scores are dropped, and the final evaluation is made up of those remaining. The logic of multiple evaluators applies to organizations as well.

If an employee has had 10 supervisors, 9 having rated her excellent and 1 poor, we can safely discount the one poor evaluation. Therefore, by moving employees about within the organization so as to gain a number of evaluations or by using multiple assessors (as provided in 360-degree appraisals), we increase the probability of achieving more valid and reliable evaluations.

Evaluate Selectively   Appraisers should evaluate only in areas in which they have some expertise.[64] This precaution increases the interrater agreement and makes the evaluation a more valid process. It also recognizes that different organizational levels often have different orientations toward those being rated and observe them in different settings. In general, therefore, appraisers should be as close as possible, in terms of organizational level, to the individual being evaluated. Conversely, the more levels that separate the evaluator and the person being evaluated, the less opportunity the evaluator has to observe the individual's behavior and, not surprisingly, the greater the possibility for inaccuracies.

Train Evaluators   If you can't *find* good evaluators, the alternative is to *make* good evaluators. There is substantial evidence that training evaluators can make them more accurate raters.[65]

Common errors such as halo and leniency have been minimized or eliminated in workshops where managers practice observing and rating behaviors. These workshops typically run from 1 to 3 days, but allocating many hours to training may not always be necessary. One case has been cited in which both halo and leniency errors were decreased immediately after exposing evaluators to explanatory training sessions lasting only 5 minutes.[66] But the effects of training appear to diminish over time.[67] This suggests the need for regular refresher sessions.

Provide Employees with Due Process   The concept of *due process* can be applied to appraisals to increase the perception that employees are being treated fairly.[68] Three features characterize due process systems: (1) Individuals are provided with adequate notice of what is expected of them; (2) all evidence relevant to a proposed violation is aired in a fair hearing so the individuals affected can respond; and (3) the final decision is based on the evidence and free of bias.

There is considerable evidence that evaluation systems often violate employees' due process by providing them with infrequent and relatively general performance feedback, allowing them little input into the appraisal process, and knowingly introducing bias into performance ratings. However, when due process has been part of the evaluation system, employees report positive reactions to the appraisal process, perceive the evaluation results as more accurate, and express increased intent to remain with the organization.

Providing Performance Feedback

For many managers, few activities are more unpleasant than providing performance feedback to employees.[69] In fact, unless pressured by organizational policies and controls, managers are likely to ignore this responsibility.[70]

Why the reluctance to give performance feedback? There seem to be at least three reasons. First, managers are often uncomfortable discussing performance weaknesses directly with employees. Even though almost every employee could stand to improve in some areas, managers fear a confrontation when presenting negative feedback. This apprehension apparently applies even when people give negative feedback to a computer! Bill Gates reports that Microsoft conducted a project requiring users to rate their experience with a computer. "When we had the computer the users had worked with ask for an evaluation of its performance, the responses tended to be positive. But when we had a second computer ask the same people to evaluate their encounters with the first machine, the people were significantly more critical. Their reluctance to criticize the first computer 'to its face' suggested that they didn't want to hurt its feelings, even though they knew it was only a machine."[71]

Second, many employees tend to become defensive when their weaknesses are pointed out. Instead of accepting the feedback as constructive and a basis for improving performance, some employees challenge the evaluation by criticizing the manager or redirecting blame to someone else. A survey of 151 area managers in Philadelphia, for instance, found that 98 percent encountered some type of aggression after giving employees negative appraisals.[72]

Finally, employees tend to have an inflated assessment of their own performance. Statistically speaking, half of all employees must be below-average performers. But the evidence indicates that the average employee's estimate of his or her own performance level generally falls around the 75th percentile.[73] So even when managers are providing good news, employees are likely to perceive it as not good enough.

Many managers find it difficult to give performance feedback. The solution is training managers to give employees constructive information that will motivate them to improve their performance. During the review, managers should act like counselors in providing feedback that guides employee development rather than critical judges of task outcomes and behavior.

The solution to the performance feedback problem is not to ignore it, but to train managers to conduct constructive feedback sessions. An effective review—one in which the employee perceives the appraisal as fair, the manager as sincere, and the climate as constructive—can result in the employee's leaving the interview in an upbeat mood, informed about the performance areas needing improvement, and determined to correct the deficiencies.[74] In addition, the performance review should be designed more as a counseling activity than a judgment process. This can best be accomplished by allowing the review to evolve out of the employee's own self-evaluation.

Have you ever had to give colleagues or classmates feedback on their performance? Did you try to stay positive or did you find you took a negative approach? Maybe you would handle the situation differently next time. If you are curious about how good you are at giving performance feedback, see the Self-Assessment feature.

HOW GOOD AM I AT GIVING PERFORMANCE FEEDBACK?

In the Self-Assessment Library (available on CD, online, and in print), take assessment III.A.3 (How Good Am I at Giving Performance Feedback?) and answer the following questions.

1. *How did you score compared to your classmates? Did the results surprise you?*
2. *Do you think giving people feedback is easy or difficult? Is your opinion reflected in your scores?*
3. *How might you further develop your skills in providing feedback to people?*

International Human Resource Practices: Selected Issues

Many of the human resource policies and practices discussed in this chapter have to be modified to reflect societal differences.[75] To illustrate this point, let's briefly look at the universality of selection practices and the importance of performance evaluation in different cultures.

Selection

A recent study of 300 large organizations in 22 countries demonstrated that selection practices differ by nation.[76] A few common procedures were found. For instance, the use of educational qualifications in screening candidates seems to be a universal practice. For the most part, however, different countries tend to emphasize different selection techniques. Structured interviews, as a case in point, were popular in some countries and nonexistent in others. The authors of the study suggested that "certain cultures may find structured interviews antithetical to beliefs about how one should conduct an interpersonal interaction or the extent to which one should trust the judgment of the interviewer."[77]

This study, when combined with earlier research, tells us that there are no universal selection practices. Moreover, global firms that attempt to implement standardized worldwide selection practices can expect to face considerable resistance from local managers. Policies and practices need to be modified to reflect culture-based norms and social values, as well as legal and economic differences.

Performance Evaluation

We've looked at the role performance evaluation plays in motivating and affecting behavior. We must use caution, however, in generalizing across cultures. Why? Because many cultures are not particularly concerned with performance appraisal or, if they are, they don't look at it the same way as do managers in the United States or Canada.

Let's look at performance evaluation in the context of four cultural dimensions: individualism/collectivism, a person's relationship to the environment, time orientation, and focus of responsibility.

Individual-oriented cultures like the United States emphasize formal performance evaluation systems more than informal systems. They advocate, for instance, written evaluations performed at regular intervals, the results of which are shared with employees and used in the determination of rewards. On the other hand, the collectivist cultures that dominate Asia and much of Latin America are characterized by more informal systems—downplaying formal feedback and disconnecting reward allocations from performance ratings. Japanese technology giant Fujitsu, for instance, introduced a formal, performance-based evaluation system in Japan in the mid-1990s. But the company recently began to dismantle it, recognizing that it "had proved flawed and a poor fit with Japanese [collectivist] business culture."[78]

U.S. and Canadian organizations hold people responsible for their actions because people in these countries believe they can dominate their environment. In Middle Eastern countries, on the other hand, performance evaluations aren't likely to be widely used because managers in these countries tend to see people as subject to their environment.

Some countries, such as the United States, have a short-term time orientation. Performance evaluations are likely to be frequent in such a culture—at least once a year. In Japan, however, where people hold a long-term time frame, performance appraisals may occur only every 5 or 10 years.

Israel's culture values group activities much more than does the culture of the United States or Canada. So, whereas North American managers tradi-

In spite of ranking system failures at Ford and Fujitsu, Mitsubishi Motors abandoned its seniority system and replaced it with performance evaluations for Japanese managers, salaried personnel, and assembly workers at plants like the one shown here in Nagoya. Used to determine promotions and demotions, Mitsubishi ranks workers on behavior, achievement, and competency. Partly because of the cultural bias in Japan that favors older workers, Mitsubishi doesn't anticipate discrimination complaints.

tionally emphasize the individual in performance evaluations, their counterparts in Israel are much more likely to emphasize group contributions and performance.

Managing Diversity in Organizations

David Morris and his father, Saul, started Habitat International in 1981. Located in Rossville, Georgia, the company manufacturers a grasslike indoor-outdoor carpet. From the beginning, the Morrises hired refugees from Cambodia, Bosnia, and Laos, many of whom didn't speak English. But when a social-service worker suggested in 1984 that the company hire mentally challenged people, Saul balked. Hiring someone with a condition such as Down syndrome seemed too chancy. But David thought otherwise. He talked his dad into giving it a try.[79]

The first group of eight mentally disabled workers came in with their job coach from the social-services agency and went straight to work boxing mats. Two weeks later, says Saul, employees were coming to him and wondering why the company couldn't "hire more people like this, who care, do their work with pride, and smile?"

Today, 75 percent of Habitat's employees have some kind of disability. People with schizophrenia, for instance, are driving forklifts next to employees with autism or cerebral palsy. Meanwhile, the Morris father-son team is doing good things both for these people and for themselves. The disabled employees have enhanced self-esteem and are now self-sufficient enough to be off government aid, and the Morrises enjoy the benefits of a dedicated, hard-working labor force. "We have practically zero absenteeism and very little turnover," says David.

Habitat International illustrates the role of employee selection in increasing diversity. But effective diversity programs go well beyond merely hiring a diverse workforce. They also include managing work-life conflicts and providing diversity training. These seem to be common characteristics among major organizations that have developed reputations as diversity leaders—including Avon, McDonald's, Fannie Mae, PepsiCo, Coca-Cola, Xerox, and Safeway.[80]

Work-Life Conflicts

We introduced work-life balance in Chapter 1 and discussed the forces that are blurring the lines between work life and personal life. In this section we want to elaborate on this issue—specifically focusing on what organizations can do to help employees reduce conflicts.

Work-life conflicts grabbed management's attention in the 1980s, largely as a result of the growing number of women with dependent children entering the workforce. In response, most major organizations took actions to make their workplaces more family-friendly.[81] They introduced programs such as on-site child care, summer day camps, flextime, job sharing, leaves for school functions, telecommuting, and part-time employment. But organizations quickly realized that work-life conflicts were not experienced only by female employees with children. Male workers and women without children were also facing this problem. Heavy workloads and increased travel demands, for instance, were making it increasingly hard for a wide range of employees to meet both work and personal responsibilities. A Harvard study found that 82 percent of men between the ages of 20 and 39 said a "family-friendly" schedule was their most important job criterion.[82]

Through a global initiative called The Wellness Exchange, Goldman Sachs helps employees balance their work and family responsibilities. The investment banking firm offers 16 weeks' paid maternity leave and provides services such as back-up child care and a child-care resource and referral service. Goldman Sachs' flexible work schedules allow dads like Mark Diorio, who helps manage the firm's database team, to work at home Mondays and alternate Fridays to be there with his children.

Organizations are modifying their workplaces to accommodate the varied needs of a diverse workforce. This includes providing a wide range of scheduling options and benefits that allow employees more flexibility at work and permit them to better balance or integrate their work and personal lives. For instance, employees at the corporate office of retailer Eddie Bauer are provided with flexible scheduling, plus a full array of on-site services, including dry cleaning pick-up and delivery, an ATM machine, a gym with personal trainers, flu shots, Weight Watchers classes, and financial seminars.[83] Exhibit 18-4 lists some broader examples of initiatives that organizations provide to help their employees reduce work-life conflicts.

Recent research on work-life conflicts has provided new insights for managers into what works and when. For instance, evidence indicates that time pressures aren't the primary problem underlying work-life conflicts.[84] It's the psychological incursion of work into the family domain and vice versa. People are worrying about personal problems at work and thinking about work problems at home. So dad may physically make it home in time for dinner but his mind is elsewhere while he's at the dinner table. This suggests that organizations should spend less effort helping employees with time-management issues and more helping them clearly segment their lives. Keeping workloads reasonable, reducing work-related travel, and offering on-site quality child care are examples of practices that can help in this endeavor.

Also, not surprisingly, people have been found to differ in their preference for scheduling options and benefits.[85] Some people prefer organizational initiatives that better segment work from their personal lives. Others prefer initiatives that facilitate integration. For instance, flextime segments because it allows employees to schedule work hours that are less likely to conflict with personal responsibilities. On the other hand, on-site child care integrates by blurring the boundaries between work and family responsibilities. People who prefer segmentation are more likely to be satisfied and com-

Exhibit 18-4	Work-Life Initiatives	

Strategy	Program or Policy	Example
Time-based strategies	Flextime Job sharing Part-time work Leave for new parents Telecommuting Closing plants/offices for special occasions	At Mentor Graphics, 98 percent of employees use flextime IBM; gives parents three years of job-guaranteed leave following childbirth J. M. Smuckers shuts down plants in deer country for first day of hunting season
Information-based strategies	Intranet work/life Web site Relocation assistance Eldercare resources	Ernst & Young provides intranet work/life Web sites that include information on how to write flexible work arrangements proposals, finds a job share partner, etc.
Money-based strategies	Vouchers for child care Flexible benefits Adoption assistance Discounts for child-care tuition Leave with pay	At Lucent Technologies, employees with 6 months of service receive 52 weeks of childbirth leave at half pay
Direct services	On-site child care Emergency back-up care On-site health/beauty services Concierge services Takeout dinners	S. C. Johnson offers its employees subsidized concierge services for car maintenance, shopping, etc. AFLAC has two on-site child-care centers Genentech has an on-site hair salon Stratus Technologies provides on-site mammograms and skin-cancer testing Every major location of Johnson & Johnson has a fitness center
Culture-change strategies	Training for managers to help employees deal with work/life conflicts Tie manager pay to employee satisfaction Focus on employees' actual performance, not "face time"	Lucent, Marriott, Merck, Pfizer, Prudential, and Xerox, among others, tie manager pay to employee satisfaction

Source: Based on C. A. Thompson, "Managing the Work-Life Balance Act: An Introductory Exercise," *Journal of Management Education,* April 2002, p. 210; and R. Levering and M. Maskowitz, "The Best in the Worst of Times," *Fortune,* February 4, 2002, pp. 60–90.

mitted to their work when offered options such as flextime, job sharing, and part-time hours. People who prefer integration are more likely to respond positively to options such as on-site child care, gym facilities, and company-sponsored family picnics.

Diversity Training

The centerpiece of most diversity programs is training. For instance, a relatively recent survey found that 93 percent of companies with diversity initiatives used training as part of their programs.[86] Diversity training programs are generally intended to provide a vehicle for increasing awareness and examining stereotypes. Participants learn to value individual differences, increase their cross-cultural understanding, and confront stereotypes.[87]

Summary and Implications for Managers

An organization's human resource policies and practices represent important forces for shaping employee behavior and attitudes. In this chapter, we specifically discussed the influence of selection practices, training and development programs, and performance evaluation systems.

Selection Practices   An organization's selection practices will determine who gets hired. If properly designed, they will identify competent candidates and accurately match them to the job and the organization. The use of the proper selection devices will increase the probability that the right person will be chosen to fill a slot.

Although employee selection is far from a science, some organizations fail to design their selection systems so as to increase the likelihood that the right person–job fit will be achieved. When errors are made, the chosen candidate's performance may be less than satisfactory. Training may be necessary to improve the candidate's skills. At worst, the candidate will prove unacceptable and a replacement will need to be found. Similarly, when the selection process results in the hiring of less-qualified candidates or individuals who don't fit into the organization, those chosen are likely to feel anxious, tense, and uncomfortable. This, in turn, is likely to increase dissatisfaction with the job.

Training and Development Programs   Training programs can affect work behavior in two ways. The most obvious is by directly improving the skills necessary for the employee to successfully complete the job. An increase in ability improves the employee's potential to perform at a higher level. Of course, whether that potential becomes realized is largely an issue of motivation.

A second benefit of training is that it increases an employee's self-efficacy. As you'll remember from Chapter 6, self-efficacy is a person's expectation that he or she can successfully execute the behaviors required to produce an outcome.[88] For employees, those behaviors are work tasks and the outcome is effective job performance. Employees with high self-efficacy have strong expectations about their abilities to perform successfully in new situations. They're confident and expect to be successful. Training, then, is a means to positively affect self-efficacy because employees may be more willing to undertake job tasks and exert a high level of effort. Or in expectancy terms (see Chapter 6), individuals are more likely to perceive their effort as leading to performance.

Performance Evaluation   A major goal of performance evaluation is to assess an individual's performance contribution accurately as a basis for making reward allocation decisions. If the performance evaluation process emphasizes the wrong criteria or inaccurately appraises actual job performance, employees will be overrewarded or underrewarded. As demonstrated in Chapter 6, in our discussion of equity theory, this can lead to negative consequences such as reduced effort, increases in absenteeism, or a search for alternative job opportunities. In addition, the content of the performance evaluation has been found to influence employee performance and satisfaction.[89] Specifically, performance and satisfaction are increased when the evaluation is based on behavioral, results-oriented criteria, when career issues as well as performance issues are discussed, and when the employee has an opportunity to participate in the evaluation.

Point ◀▶ Counterpoint

Get Rid of the SAT and ACT as Tools to Select Students[90]

We should get rid of these big standardized tests to select students into college. There are many good reasons; let's just review a few.

First, these tests are not very valid. They correlate anywhere from .20 to .30 with grades in college. This means that on a 0–10 scale, where 0 = no correlation and 10 = perfect correlation, the correlation of test scores to grades is about 2–3. Not very impressive. Of course, this matches our common sense. Can you really expect to predict college success with a 4-hour test? It's much better to rely on the student's history of performance in high school as well as other measures of intellectual attainment and motivation.

Second, these tests unfairly discriminate against women and minorities. Women score lower than men on the math or quantitative part of the ACT, SAT, and GRE even though we know that women are as intelligent as men. African Americans score substantially lower than Caucasians on the tests; there is good evidence these tests are culturally biased against minorities. It is not fair to use biased tests as the predominant means of selecting people into colleges and universities.

Third, research by Stanford professor Claude Steele has shown that these sorts of tests activate what's called a "stereotype threat." What this means is that since minorities have learned they are *supposed* to score less well on these tests, they perform according to the stereotype. Why do they do this? Steele argues that the tests prompt a view that they are less intelligent, so minority students are upset and demoralized.

Finally, people can learn how to "game" these tests with courses like Kaplan and the Princeton Review. So, the people who end up getting into good colleges are those who can afford to take these courses.

The SAT and ACT exams were developed precisely because high school performance doesn't tell you that much about how a student will do in college. In the United States, there are dramatic differences between secondary schools, even within the same city. For example, in Florida's Miami-Dade County, 86 percent of students at Coral Reef Senior High achieved the minimum proficiency level in a statewide math test, compared to only 3 percent of students at Miami Douglas MacArthur Senior High. So, does a 3.0 GPA at Coral Reef mean the same thing as a 3.0 GPA at Douglas MacArthur? Of course not. And this is why high school grades are poor predictors of college success. It is impossible for universities to compare applicants across different high schools based on their GPA.

The SAT and ACT tests have been subject to massive validation efforts by some of the best industrial psychologists in the world. No, the validity isn't perfect, but it's better than anything else researchers have been able to identify, including high school achievement. The reason is that these tests are carefully developed and validated, and all applicants take the same basic test. So, we don't have the "apples and oranges" problem we do with high school grades. By the same token, the GRE also works well. The authors of an analysis of 1,753 independent samples of the GRE (on 82,659 graduate students) concluded, "The GRE is valid across disciplines for a variety of important criterion measures, and not just 1st-year graduate grade-point average, as is often assumed."

In terms of bias, the research shows that, although African Americans do score lower on the test, the test results predict college success as well for African Americans as they do for Caucasians. So, the tests aren't biased. Women do tend to score lower on the math part, but that is offset by the fact that they tend to score higher on the verbal part.

Finally, evidence indicates that test preparation courses do help somewhat. But the benefit is modest, and evidence suggests that the existence of such courses has done nothing to undermine the validity of the SAT, ACT, or GRE.

Questions for Review

1. What are the stages of the selection process? What methods are used at each stage?

2. What are the major types of tests companies use in hiring? How well do they work?

3. What are assessment centers? Why do you think they might be more effective for selecting managers than traditional written tests?

4. Contrast formal and informal training.

5. What's the relationship between learning styles and training effectiveness?

6. Why do organizations evaluate employees?

7. What problems, if any, can you see developing as a result of using 360-degree evaluations?

8. What are the advantages and disadvantages of the following performance evaluation methods: (a) written essays, (b) graphic rating scales, and (c) behaviorally anchored rating scales?

9. How can an organization's performance evaluation system affect employee behavior?

10. What is diversity training? Do you think it is effective?

Questions for Critical Thinking

1. How could the phrase "the best predictor of future behavior is past behavior" guide you in managing human resources?

2. Why do you think employers put so much emphasis on the interview as a selection device?

3. Describe a training program you might design to help employees develop their interpersonal skills. How would that program differ from one you designed to improve employee ethical behavior?

4. GE prides itself on continually raising the performance bar by annually letting go employees who perform in the lowest 10 percent. In contrast, Cleveland-based Lincoln Electric Co. prides itself on its no-layoff policy. Lincoln Electric has provided its employees with guaranteed employment since 1958. How can two successful companies have such different approaches to employment security? How can they both work? What implications can you derive from the success of these different practices?

5. "Programs to reduce work-life conflicts discriminate against single employees." Do you agree or disagree? Explain.

Team Exercise

EVALUATING PERFORMANCE AND PROVIDING FEEDBACK

Objective

To experience the assessment of performance and observe the providing of performance feedback.

Time

Approximately 30 minutes.

Procedure

A class leader is to be selected. The leader may be either a volunteer or someone chosen by your instructor. The class leader will preside over the class discussion and perform the role of manager in the evaluation review.

Your instructor will leave the room. The class leader is then to spend up to 15 minutes helping the class to evaluate your instructor. Your instructor understands that this is only a class exercise and is prepared to accept criticism (and, of course, any praise you may want to convey). Your instructor also recognizes that the leader's evaluation is actually a composite of many students' input. So be open and honest in your evalua-

tion and have confidence that your instructor will not be vindictive.

Research has identified seven performance dimensions to the college instructor's job: (1) instructor knowledge, (2) testing procedures, (3) student–teacher relations, (4) organizational skills, (5) communication skills, (6) subject relevance, and (7) utility of assignments. The discussion of your instructor's performance should focus on these seven dimensions. The leader may want to take notes for personal use but will not be required to give your instructor any written documentation.

When the 15-minute class discussion is complete, the leader will invite the instructor back into the room. The performance review will begin as soon as the instructor walks through the door, with the class leader becoming the manager and the instructor playing himself or herself.

When completed, class discussion will focus on performance evaluation criteria and how well your class leader did in providing performance feedback.

Ethical Dilemma

IS IT UNETHICAL TO "SHAPE" YOUR RESUME?

When does "putting a positive spin" on your accomplishments step over the line to become misrepresentation or lying? Does a resume have to be 100 percent truthful? Apparently, a lot of people don't think so. A recent survey of 2.6 million job applicants found that 44 percent of all resumes contained some lies.[91] To help clarify your ethical views on this issue, consider the following three situations.

Sean left a job for which his title was "credit clerk." When looking for a new job, he describes his previous title as "credit analyst." He thinks it sounds more impressive. Is this retitling of a former job wrong?

About 8 years ago, Emily took 9 months off between jobs to travel overseas. Afraid that people might consider her unstable or lacking in career motivation, she put down on her resume that she was engaged in "independent consulting activities" during the period. Was she wrong?

Michael is 50 years old with an impressive career record. He spent 5 years in college 30 years ago, but he never got a degree. He is being considered for a $175,000-a-year vice presidency at another firm. He knows that he has the ability and track record to do the job, but he won't get the interview if he admits to not having a college degree. He knows that the probability that anyone would check his college records, at this point in his career, is very low. Should he put on his resume that he completed his degree?

Case Incident 1

A UNIQUE TRAINING PROGRAM AT UPS

Mark Colvard, a United Parcel manager in San Ramon, California, recently faced a difficult decision. One of his drivers asked for 2 weeks off to help an ailing family member. But company rules said this driver wasn't eligible. If Colvard went by the book, the driver would probably take the days off anyway and be fired. On the other hand, Colvard was likely to be criticized by other drivers if he bent the rules. Colvard chose to give the driver the time off. Although he took some heat for the decision, he also kept a valuable employee.

Had Colvard been faced with this decision 6 months earlier, he says he would have gone the other way. What changed his thinking was a month he spent living in McAllen, Texas. It was part of a UPS management training experience called the Community Internship Program (CIP). During his month in McAllen, Colvard built housing for the poor, collected clothing for the Salvation Army, and worked in a drug rehab center. Colvard gives the program credit for helping him empathize with employees facing crises back home. And he says that CIP has made him a better manager. "My goal was to make the numbers, and in some cases that meant not looking at the individual but looking at the bottom line. After that one-month stay, I immediately started reaching out to people in a different way."

CIP was established by UPS in the late 1960s to help open the eyes of the company's predominantly white managers to the poverty and inequality in many cities. Today, the program takes 50 of the company's most promising executives each summer and brings them to cities around the country. There they deal with a variety of problems—from transportation to housing, education, and health care. The company's goal is to awaken these managers to the challenges that many of their employees face, bridging the cultural divide that separates a white manager from an African American driver or an upper-income suburbanite from a worker raised in the rural South.

Questions

1. Do you think individuals can learn empathy from something like a 1-month CIP experience? Explain why or why not.

2. How could UPS's CIP help the organization better manage work-life conflicts?

3. How could UPS's CIP help the organization improve its response to diversity?

4. What negatives, if any, can you envision resulting from CIP?

5. UPS has 2,400 managers. CIP includes only 50 each year. How can the program make a difference if it includes only 2 percent of all managers? Does this suggest that the program is more public relations than management training?

6. How can UPS justify the cost of a program like CIP if competitors like FedEx, DHL, and the U.S. Postal Service don't offer such programs? Does the program increase costs or reduce UPS profits?

Source: Based on L. Lavelle, "For UPS Managers, A School of Hard Knocks," *Business Week,* July 22, 2002.

Case Incident 2

JOB CANDIDATES WITHOUT STRONG SAT SCORES NEED NOT APPLY

Many high school students probably believe that once they get into college, their SAT scores are a thing of the past. However, many job seekers are now discovering that their would-be employers are asking for their SAT scores as part of the selection process. Donna Chan, a 23-year-old graduate of New York's Wagner College, learned that one of the minimum requirements for many of the entry-level financial services jobs she was seeking was a combined SAT score of 1300. How strong of a score is 1300? The maximum score on the old version of the SAT (the new version has added a writing section, in addition to the traditional math and verbal sections) was 1600. According to the College Board, the organization that administers the exam, the average combined math and verbal score of the freshman class of 2005 (the last class to take the old version of the SAT) was 1028. Donna Chan's score was "in the 1200s"—a good score to be sure, but not good enough to obtain any of the positions she was seeking, even though she obtained a 3.9 grade-point average in college. "I think it's asking a bit much," says Chan. "That's something high school kids have to worry about. After four years of working hard, I think you've paid your dues, and unless you're applying to Princeton Review or some math-related, analytical job, I don't see the relevance."

Apparently, however, some recruiters do see the relevance. Alan Sage, a vice president at systems-management software company Configuresoft Inc., states that SAT scores are a good predictor of success in his company and regularly has applicants submit their scores when applying for sales positions. He set the mark at a combined score of 1200—lower than what Donna Chan had to face, but well above average nonetheless. Says Sage, "In my experience, people with high SAT scores tend to do better." Sage himself scored between 1200 and 1300. He adds, however, that "We wouldn't exclude someone from an interview if he or she didn't score high."

Some do not believe there is a connection between high SAT scores and job performance. Seppy Basilli, vice president of Kaplan Inc., one of several companies that provides instruction on taking the SAT, believes that companies are misusing SAT scores. "It's such a maligned instrument," he says. "It's not designed to measure job performance, and the kind of person who performs well on the SATs is not necessarily the kind of person who will perform well sitting at her desk." Morgan Denny, who works as a headhunter in New York, shares a similar opinion. Though his clients typically want to consider only applicants with high SAT scores, Denny often shows his clients applicants who he believes are strong candidates for the position despite a lower score. "The SAT is an annoyance for us and an annoyance for our candidates," says Denny.

Some individuals, such as Kristin Carnahan, a spokesperson for the College Board, feel that companies should use other measures of cognitive ability to screen job applicants. Carnahan states that college grades, which are more recent indicators of performance than SAT scores, should be given greater weight. However, critics argue that grades are not "standardized" across different educational institutions, meaning that grades from different colleges cannot be compared like SAT scores can. Grade inflation also may make it more difficult for recruiters to assess the validity of an applicant's G.P.A. Because research in organizational behavior has shown that cognitive ability is a strong predictor of job performance—and the SAT is supposedly a measure of cognitive ability—many companies may continue to use the SAT as a benchmark for job applicants.

Questions

1. Is it fair for organizations to require minimum scores on standardized tests such as the SAT? Why or why not?

2. As a recruiter, in choosing between two individuals with different SAT scores, would it be difficult for you to give the job to the individual with the lower score? What additional factors might your choice depend on?

3. What are some other indicators of job performance, besides SAT scores, that you could use to screen potential job applicants? What are the advantages and disadvantages of each?

4. Say you worked at a company that uses SAT scores for hiring purposes. How would you handle diverse applicants, such as those from a foreign country who may not have taken the SAT?

Source: Based on K. J. Dunham, "Career Journal: More Employers Ask Job Seekers for SAT Scores," *The Wall Street Journal*, October 28, 2003, p. B.1.

Endnotes

1. M. Burke, "Funny Business," *Forbes,* June 9, 2003, p. 173; and D. Wolk, "Air Carrier Song: An Escape from 'Oppressive' Airline Jobs," *Workforce Management* (www.workforce.com/archive/article/23/92/75.php) (January, 2005).

2. See B. Becker and B. Gerhart, "The Impact of Human Resource Management on Organizational Performance: Progress and Prospects," *Academy of Management Journal,* August 1996, pp. 779–801; J. T. Delaney and M. A. Huselid, "The Impact of Human Resource Management Practices on the Perceptions of Organizational Performance," *Academy of Management Journal,* August 1996, pp. 949–69; M. A. Huselid, S. E. Jackson, and R. S. Schuler, "Technical and Strategic Human Resource Management Effectiveness as Determinants of Firm Performance," *Academy of Management Journal,* February 1997, pp. 171–88; and G. A. Gelade and M. Ivery, "The Impact of Human Resource Management and Work Climate on Organizational Performance," *Personnel Psychology,* Summer 2003, pp. 383–404; C. J. Collins, and K. D. Clark, "Strategic Human Resource Practices, Top Management Team Social Networks, and Firm Performance: The Role of Human Resource Practices in Creating Organizational Competitive Advantage," *Academy of Management Journal,* December 2003, pp. 740–51; and D. E. Bowen and C. Ostroff, "Understanding HRM–Firm Performance Linkages: The Role of the 'Strength' of the HRM System," *Academy of Management Review,* April 2004, pp. 203–21.

3. See, for instance, C. T. Dortch, "Job-Person Match," *Personnel Journal,* June 1989, pp. 49–57; and S. Rynes and B. Gerhart, "Interviewer Assessments of Applicant 'Fit': An Exploratory Investigation," *Personnel Psychology,* Spring 1990, pp. 13–34.

4. C. Lachnit, "The Cost of Not Doing Background Checks," *Workforce Management* (www.workforce.com/archive/feature/22/16/22/224149.php).

5. Cited in J. H. Prager, "Nasty or Nice: 56-Question Quiz," *The Wall Street Journal,* February 22, 2000, p. A-4; and H. Wessel, "Personality Tests Grow Popular," *Seattle Post-Intelligencer,* August 3, 2003, p. G1.

6. G. Nicholsen, "Screen and Glean: Good Screening and Background Checks Help Make the Right Match for Every Open Position," *Workforce,* October 2000, pp. 70–72.

7. J. P. Hausknecht, D. V. Day, S. C. Thomas, "Applicant Reactions to Selection Procedures: An Updated Model and Meta-Analysis," *Personnel Psychology,* September 2004, pp. 639–83.

8. E. E. Ghiselli, "The Validity of Aptitude Tests in Personnel Selection," *Personnel Psychology,* Winter 1973, p. 475.

9. R. J. Herrnstein and C. Murray, *The Bell Curve: Intelligence and Class Structure in American Life* (New York: Free Press, 1994); and M. J. Ree, J. A. Earles, and M. S. Teachout, "Predicting Job Performance: Not Much More Than g," *Journal of Applied Psychology,* August 1994, pp. 518–24.

10. J. F. Salgado, N. Anderson, S. Moscoso, C. Bertua, F. de Fruyt, Filip, and J. P. Rolland, "A Meta-Analytic Study of General Mental Ability Validity for Different Occupations in the European Community," *Journal of Applied Psychology,* December 2003, pp. 1068–81.

11. J. Flint, "Can You Tell Applesauce From Pickles?" *Forbes,* October 9, 1995, pp. 106–08.

12. M. R. Barrick, M. K. Mount, and T. A. Judge, "Personality and Performance at the Beginning of the New Millennium: What Do We Know and Where Do We Go Next?," *International Journal of Selection & Assessment,* March-June 2001, pp. 9-30; M. R. Barrick, G. L. Stewart, and M. Piotrowski, "Personality and Job Performance: Test of the Mediating Effects of Motivation Among Sales Representatives," *Journal of Applied Psychology,* February 2002, pp. 43-51; and C. J. Thoresen, J. C. Bradley, P. D. Bliese, and J. D. Thoresen, "The Big Five Personality Traits and Individual Job Performance and Growth Trajectories in Maintenance and Transitional Job Stages," *Journal of Applied Psychology,* October 2004, pp. 835-853.

13. D. S. Ones, C. Viswesvaran, and F. L. Schmidt, "Comprehensive Meta-Analysis of Integrity Test Validities: Findings and Implications for Personnel Selection and Theories of Job Performance," *Journal of Applied Psychology,* August 1993, pp. 679–703; P. R. Sackett and J. E. Wanek, "New Developments in the Use of Measures of Honesty, Integrity, Conscientiousness, Dependability, Trustworthiness, and Reliability for Personnel Selection," *Personnel Psychology,* Winter 1996, pp. 787–829; F. L. Schmidt and J. E. Hunter, "The Validity and Utility of Selection Methods in Personnel Psychology: Practical and Theoretical Implications of 85 Years of Research Findings," *Psychological Bulletin,* September 1998, pp. 262–74; and D. S. Ones, C. Viswesvaran, and F. L. Schmidt, "Personality and Absenteeism: A Meta-Analysis of Integrity Tests," *European Journal of Personality,* March–April 2003, Supplement 1, pp. S19–S38.

14. See D. B. Smith, P. J. Hanges, and M. W. Dickson, "Personnel Selection and the Five-Factor Model: Reexamining the Effects of Applicant's Frame of Reference," *Journal of Applied Psychology,* April 2001, pp. 304–15; R. Mueller-Hanson, E. D. Heggestad, and G. C. Thornton III, "Faking and Selection: Considering the Use of Personality from Select-In and Select-Out Perspectives," *Journal of Applied Psychology,* April 2003, pp. 348–55.

15. P. Carbonara, "Hire for Attitude, Train for Skill," *Fast Company,* Greatest Hits, vol. 1, 1997, p. 68.

16. J. J. Asher and J. A. Sciarrino, "Realistic Work Sample Tests: A Review," *Personnel Psychology,* Winter 1974, pp. 519–33; I. T. Robertson and R. S. Kandola, "Work Sample Tests: Validity, Adverse Impact and Applicant Reaction," *Journal of Occupational Psychology,* Spring 1982, pp. 171–82; and M. Callinan and I. T. Robertson, "Work Sample Testing," *International Journal of Selection & Assessment,* December 2000, pp. 248–60.

17. See, for instance, A. C. Spychalski, M. A. Quinones, B. B. Gaugler, and K. Pohley, "A Survey of Assessment Center Practices in Organizations in the United States, *Personnel Psychology,* Spring 1997, pp. 71–90; C. Woodruffe, *Development and Assessment Centres: Identifying and Assessing Competence* (London: Institute of Personnel and Development, 2000); and J. Schettler, "Building Bench Strength," *Training,* June 2002, pp. 55–58.

18. B. B. Gaugler, D. B. Rosenthal, G. C. Thornton, and C. Benson, "Meta-Analysis of Assessment Center Validity," *Journal of Applied Psychology,* August 1987, pp. 493–511; P. G. W. Jansen and B. A. M. Stoop, "The Dynamics of Assessment Center Validity: Results of a 7-Year Study," *Journal of Applied Psychology,* August 2001, pp. 741–53; and W. Arthur, Jr., E. A. Day, T. L.

McNelly, and P. S. Edens, "A Meta-Analysis of the Criterion-Related Validity of Assessment Center Dimensions," *Personnel Psychology*, Spring 2003, pp. 125–54.

19. R. A. Posthuma, F. P. Moregeson, and M. A. Campion, "Beyond Employment Interview Validity: A Comprehensive Narrative Review of Recent Research and Trend Over Time," *Personnel Psychology*, Spring 2002, p. 1; and S. L. Wilk and P. Cappelli, "Understanding the Determinants of Employer Use of Selection Methods," *Personnel Psychology*, Spring 2003, p. 111.

20. L. Yoo-Lim, "More Companies Rely on Employee Interviews," *Business Korea*, November 1994, pp. 22–23.

21. T. J. Hanson and J. C. Balestreri-Spero, "An Alternative to Interviews," *Personnel Journal*, June 1985, p. 114. See also T. W. Dougherty, D. B. Turban, and J. C. Callender, "Confirming First Impressions in the Employment Interview: A Field Study of Interviewer Behavior," *Journal of Applied Psychology*, October 1994, pp. 659–65.

22. K. I. van der Zee, A. B. Bakker, and P. Bakker, "Why are Structured Interviews So Rarely Used in Personnel Selection?" *Journal of Applied Psychology*, February 2002, pp. 176–84.

23. See M. A. McDaniel, D. L. Whetzel, F. L. Schmidt, and S. D. Maurer, "The Validity of Employment Interviews: A Comprehensive Review and Meta-Analysis," *Journal of Applied Psychology*, August 1994, pp. 599–616; J. M. Conway, R. A. Jako, and D. F. Goodman, "A Meta-Analysis of Interrater and Internal Consistency Reliability of Selection Interviews," *Journal of Applied Psychology*, October 1995, pp. 565–79; M. A. Campion, D. K. Palmer, and J. E. Campion, "A Review of Structure in the Selection Interview," *Personnel Psychology*, Autumn 1997, pp. 655–702; F. L. Schmidt and J. E. Hunter, "The Validity and Utility of Selection Methods in Personnel Psychology: Practical and Theoretical Implications of 85 Years of Research Findings," *Psychological Bulletin*, September 1998, pp. 262–74; A. I. Huffcutt and D. J. Woehr, "Further Analysis of Employment Interview Validity: A Quantitative Evaluation of Interviewer-Related Structuring Methods," *Journal of Organizational Behavior*, July 1999, pp. 549–60.

24. van der Zee, Bakker, and Bakker, "Why Are Structured Interviews so Rarely Used in Personnel Selection?"

25. R. E. Carlson, "Effect of Interview Information in Altering Valid Impressions," *Journal of Applied Psychology*, February 1971, pp. 66–72; M. London and M. D. Hakel, "Effects of Applicant Stereotypes, Order, and Information on Interview Impressions," *Journal of Applied Psychology*, April 1974, pp. 157–62; E. C. Webster, *The Employment Interview: A Social Judgment Process* (Ontario, Canada: S.I.P., 1982); and T. W. Dougherty, D. B. Turban, and J. C. Callender, "Confirming First Impressions in the Employment Interview: A Field Study of Interviewer Behavior," *Journal of Applied Psychology*, October 1994, pp. 659–65.

26. N. R. Bardack and F. T. McAndrew, "The Influence of Physical Attractiveness and Manner of Dress on Success in a Simulated Personnel Decision," *Journal of Social Psychology*, August 1985, pp. 777–78; R. Bull and N. Rumsey, *The Social Psychology of Facial Appearance* (London: Springer-Verlag, 1988); and L. M. Watkins, and L. Johnston, "Screening Job Applicants: The Impact of Physical Attractiveness and Application Quality," *International Journal of Selection & Assessment*, June 2000, pp. 76–84.

27. T. W. Dougherty, R. J. Ebert, and J. C. Callender, "Policy Capturing in the Employment Interview," *Journal of Applied*

Psychology, vol. 71, no. 1, February 1986, pp. 9–15; and T. M. Macan and R. L. Dipboye, "The Relationship of the Interviewers' Preinterview Impressions to Selection and Recruitment Outcomes," *Personnel Psychology*, Autumn 1990, pp. 745–69.

28. R. L. Dipboye, *Selection Interviews: Process Perspectives* (Cincinnati, OH: South-Western Publishing, 1992), pp. 42–44; and R. A. Posthuma, F. P. Moregeson, and M. A. Campion, "Beyond Employment Interview Validity," pp. 1–81.

29. J. F. Salgado and S. Moscoso, "Validity of the Structured Behavioral Interview," *Revista de Psicologla del Trabajo y las Organizaciones* 11 (1995), pp. 9–24; see also S. Moscoso, and J. F. Salgado, "Psychometric Properties of a Structured Behavioral Interview to Hire Private Security Personnel," *Journal of Business & Psychology*, Fall 2001, pp. 51–59.

30. A. I. Huffcutt, J. M. Conway, P. L. Roth, and N. J. Stone, "Identification and Meta-Analytic Assessment of Psychological Constructs Measured in Employment Interviews," *Journal of Applied Psychology*, October 2001, p. 910.

31. J. M. Sacco, C. R. Scheu, A. M. Ryan, and N. Schmitt, "An Investigation of Race and Sex Similarity Effects in Interviews: A Multilevel Approach to Relational Demography," *Journal of Applied Psychology*, October 2003, pp. 852–65.

32. See G. A. Adams, T. C. Elacqua, and S. M. Colarelli, "The Employment Interview as a Sociometric Selection Technique," *Journal of Group Psychotherapy*, Fall 1994, pp. 99–113; R. L. Dipboye, "Structured and Unstructured Selection Interviews: Beyond the Job-Fit Model," *Research in Personnel Human Resource Management* 12 (1994), pp. 79–123; B. Schneider, D. B. Smith, S. Taylor, and J. Fleenor, "Personality and Organizations: A Test of the Homogeneity of Personality Hypothesis," *Journal of Applied Psychology*, June 1998, pp. 462–70; and M. Burke, "Funny Business," *Forbes*, June 9, 2003, p. 173.

33. Cited in *Training*, October 2003, p. 21.

34. Cited in *Training*, March 2003, p. 20.

35. Cited in D. Baynton, "America's $60 Billion Problem," *Training*, May 2001, p. 51.

36. "Basic Skills Training Pays Off for Employers," *HRMagazine*, October 1999, p. 32.

37. Baynton, "America's $60 Billion Problem," p. 51.

38. A. Bernstein, "The Time Bomb in the Workforce: Illiteracy," *Business Week*, February 25, 2002, p. 122.

39. Baynton, "America's $60 Billion Problem," p. 52.

40. C. Ansberry, "A New Blue-Collar World," *The Wall Street Journal*, June 30, 2003, p. B1.

41. J. Barbarian, "Mark Spear: Director of Management and Organizational Development, Miller Brewing Co.," *Training*, October 2001, pp. 34–38.

42. G. R. Weaver, L. K. Trevino, and P. L. Cochran, "Corporate Ethics Practices in the Mid-1990's: An Empirical Study of the Fortune 1000," *Journal of Business Ethics*, February 1999, pp. 283–94.

43. M. B. Wood, *Business Ethics in Uncertain Times* (Upper Saddle River, NJ: Prentice Hall, 2004), p. 61.

44. See, for example, D. Seligman, "Oxymoron 101," *Forbes*, October 28, 2002, pp. 160–64; and R. B. Schmitt, "Companies Add Ethics Training; Will It Work?" *The Wall Street Journal*, November 4, 2002, p. B1.

45. K. Dobbs, "The U.S. Department of Labor Estimates that 70 Percent of Workplace Learning Occurs Informally," *Sales & Marketing Management*, November 2000, pp. 94–98.

46. S. J. Wells, "Forget the Formal Training. Try Chatting at the Water Cooler," *The New York Times*, May 10, 1998, p. BU-11.

47. See, for instance, K. G. Brown, "Using Computers to Deliver Training: Which Employees Learn and Why?" *Personnel Psychology*, Summer 2001, pp. 271–96; "The Delivery: How U.S. Organizations Use Classrooms and Computers in Training," *Training*, October 2001, pp. 66–72; and L. K. Long, and R. D. Smith, "The Role of Web-Based Distance Learning in HR Development," *Journal of Management Development* 23, no. 3 (2004), pp. 270–84.

48. "Web Smart 50: Kinko's," *Business Week*, November 24, 2003, p. 101.

49. A. Muoio, "Cisco's Quick Study," *Fast Company*, October 2000, pp. 287–95.

50. E. A. Ensher, T. R. Nielson, and E. Grant-Vallone, "Tales from the Hiring Line: Effects of the Internet and Technology on HR Processes," *Organizational Dynamics* 31, no. 3 (2002), pp. 232–33.

51. D. A. Kolb, "Management and the Learning Process," *California Management Review*, Spring 1976, pp. 21–31; and B. Filipczak, "Different Strokes: Learning Styles in the Classroom," *Training*, March 1995, pp. 43–48.

52. W. J. Arthur, Jr., W. Bennett, Jr., P. S. Edens, and S. T. Bell, "Effectiveness of Training in Organizations: A Meta-Analysis of Design and Evaluation Features," *Journal of Applied Psychology*, April 2003, pp. 234–45.

53. J. A. Colquitt, J. A. LePine, and R. A. Noe, "Toward an Integrative Theory of Training Motivation: A Meta-Analytic Path Analysis of 20 Years of Research," *Journal of Applied Psychology*, October 2000, pp. 678–707.

54. W. F. Cascio, *Applied Psychology in Human Resource Management*, 5th ed. (Upper Saddle River, NJ: Prentice Hall, 1998), p. 59.

55. See W. C. Borman and S. J. Motowidlo, "Expanding the Criterion Domain to Include Elements of Contextual Performance," in N. Schmitt and W. C. Borman (eds.), *Personnel Selection in Organizations* (San Francisco, CA: Jossey-Bass, 1993), pp. 71–98; W. H. Bommer, J. L. Johnson, G. A. Rich, P. M. Podsakoff, and S. B. MacKenzie, "On the Interchangeability of Objective and Subjective Measures of Employee Performance: A Meta-Analysis," *Personnel Psychology*, Autumn 1995, pp. 587–605; and S. E. Scullen, M. K. Mount, and T. A. Judge, "Evidence of the Construct Validity of Developmental Ratings of Managerial Performance," *Journal of Applied Psychology*, February 2003, pp. 50–66.

56. A. H. Locher and K. S. Teel, "Appraisal Trends," *Personnel Journal*, September 1988, pp. 139–45.

57. Cited in S. Armour, "Job Reviews Take on Added Significance in Down Times," *USA Today*, July 23, 2003, p. 4B.

58. See review in R. D. Bretz, Jr., G. T. Milkovich, and W. Read, "The Current State of Performance Appraisal Research and Practice: Concerns, Directions, and Implications," *Journal of Management*, June 1992, p. 326; and P. W. B. Atkins and R. E. Wood, "Self- Versus Others' Ratings as Predictors of Assessment Center Ratings: Validation Evidence for 360-Degree Feedback Programs," *Personnel Psychology*, Winter 2002, pp. 871–904.

59. See, for instance, W. W. Tornow and M. London (eds.), *Maximizing the Value of 360-Degree Feedback* (San Francisco, CA: Jossey-Bass, 1998); J. Ghorpade, "Managing Five Paradoxes of 360-Degree Feedback," *Academy of Management Executive*, February 2000, pp. 140–50; J. D. Facteau and S. B. Craig, "Are

Performance Appraisal Ratings from Different Rating Sources Compatible?" *Journal of Applied Psychology*, April 2001, pp. 215–27; J. F. Brett and L. E. Atwater, "360-Degree Feedback: Accuracy, Reactions, and Perceptions of Usefulness," *Journal of Applied Psychology*, October 2001, pp. 930–42; C. Wingrove, "Untangling the Myths of 360: Straight Talk for Successful Outcomes," *Compensation & Benefits Review*, November–December 2001, pp. 34–37; B. Pfau, I. Kay, K. M. Nowack, and J. Ghorpade, "Does 360-Degree Feedback Negatively Affect Company Performance?" *HR Magazine*, June 2002, pp. 54–59; F. Luthans and S. J. Peterson, "360 Degree Feedback with Systematic Coaching: Empirical Analysis Suggests a Winning Combination," *Human Resource Management*, Fall 2003, pp. 243–56; and B. I. J. M. van der Heijden, and A. H. J. Nijhof, "The Value of Subjectivity: Problems and Prospects for 360-Degree Appraisal Systems," *International Journal of Human Resource Management*, May 2004, pp. 493–511.

60. Cited in K. Clark, "Judgment Day," *U. S. News & World Report*, January 13, 2003, p. 31.

61. D. V. Day, "Leadership Development: A Review in Context," *Leadership Quarterly*, Winter 2000, pp. 587–89.

62. Atkins and Wood, "Self- Versus Others' Ratings as Predictors of Assessment Center Ratings"; and Pfau, Kay, Nowack, and Ghorpade, "Does 360-Degree Feedback Negatively Affect Company Performance?"

63. "Princeton Cracks Down on Grade Inflation," *USA Today*, (www.usatoday.com/news/education/2005-01-22-princeton-grade-inflation_x.htm (January 22, 2005).

64. See, for instance, J. W. Hedge and W. C. Borman, "Changing Conceptions and Practices in Performance Appraisal," in A. Howard (ed.), *The Changing Nature of Work* (San Francisco, CA: Jossey-Bass, 1995), pp. 453–59.

65. See, for instance, D. E. Smith, "Training Programs for Performance Appraisal: A Review," *Academy of Management Review*, January 1986, pp. 22–40; T. R. Athey and R. M. McIntyre, "Effect of Rater Training on Rater Accuracy: Levels-of-Processing Theory and Social Facilitation Theory Perspectives," *Journal of Applied Psychology*, November 1987, pp. 567–72; and D. J. Woehr, "Understanding Frame-of-Reference Training: The Impact of Training on the Recall of Performance Information," *Journal of Applied Psychology*, August 1994, pp. 525–34.

66. H. J. Bernardin, "The Effects of Rater Training on Leniency and Halo Errors in Student Rating of Instructors," *Journal of Applied Psychology*, June 1978, pp. 301–08.

67. Ibid.; and J. M. Ivancevich, "Longitudinal Study of the Effects of Rater Training on Psychometric Error in Ratings," *Journal of Applied Psychology*, October 1979, pp. 502–08.

68. M. S. Taylor, K. B. Tracy, M. K. Renard, J. K. Harrison, and S. J. Carroll, "Due Process in Performance Appraisal: A Quasi-Experiment in Procedural Justice," *Administrative Science Quarterly*, September 1995, pp. 495–523.

69. J. S. Lublin, "It's Shape-up Time for Performance Reviews," *The Wall Street Journal*, October 3, 1994, p. B1.

70. Much of this section is based on H. H. Meyer, "A Solution to the Performance Appraisal Feedback Enigma," *Academy of Management Executive*, February 1991, pp. 68–76.

71. B. Gates, *The Road Ahead* (New York: Viking, 1995), p. 86.

72. T. D. Schelhardt, "It's Time to Evaluate Your Work, and All Involved Are Groaning," *The Wall Street Journal*, November 19, 1996, p. A1.

73. R. J. Burke, "Why Performance Appraisal Systems Fail," *Personnel Administration,* June 1972, pp. 32–40.

74. B. R. Nathan, A. M. Mohrman, Jr., and J. Milliman, "Interpersonal Relations as a Context for the Effects of Appraisal Interviews on Performance and Satisfaction: A Longitudinal Study," *Academy of Management Journal,* June 1991, pp. 352–69. See also B. D. Cawley, L. M. Keeping, and P. E. Levy, "Participation in the Performance Appraisal Process and Employee Reactions: A Meta-Analytic Review of Field Investigations," *Journal of Applied Psychology,* August 1998, pp. 615–33; and P. E. Levy, and J. R. Williams, "The Social Context of Performance Appraisal: A Review and Framework for the Future," *Journal of Management* 30, no. 6 (2004), pp. 881–905.

75. See, for instance, M. Mendonca and R. N. Kanungo, "Managing Human Resources: The Issue of Cultural Fit," *Journal of Management Inquiry,* June 1994, pp. 189–205; N. Ramamoorthy and S. J. Carroll, "Individualism/Collectivism Orientations and Reactions toward Alternative Human Resource Management Practices," *Human Relations,* May 1998, pp. 571–88; and C. Fletcher and E. L. Perry, "Performance Appraisal and Feedback: A Consideration of National Culture and a Review of Contemporary Research and Future Trends," in N. Anderson, D. S. Ones, H. K. Sinangil, and C. Viswesvaran (eds.), *Handbook of Industrial, Work, & Organizational Psychology,* vol. 1 (Thousand Oaks, CA: Sage, 2001), pp. 127–44.

76. A. M. Ryan, L. McFarland, H. Baron, and R. Page, "An International Look at Selection Practices: Nation and Culture as Explanations for Variability in Practice," *Personnel Psychology,* Summer 1999, pp. 359–92.

77. Ibid., p. 386.

78. M. Tanikawa, "Fujitsu Decides to Backtrack on Performance-Based Pay," *The New York Times,* March 22, 2001, p. W1.

79. N. B. Henderson, "An Enabling Work Force," *Nation's Business,* June 1998, p. 93.

80. See J. Hickman, "50 Best Companies for Minorities," *Fortune,* June 28, 2004, pp. 136–42.

81. See, for instance, *Harvard Business Review on Work and Life Balance* (Boston: Harvard Business School Press, 2000); and R. Rapoport, L. Bailyn, J. K. Fletcher, and B. H. Pruitt, *Beyond Work-Family Balance* (San Francisco: Jossey-Bass, 2002).

82. "On the Daddy Track," *The Wall Street Journal,* May 11, 2000, p. A1.

83. K. Weiss, "Eddie Bauer Uses Time as an Employee Benefit," *Journal of Organizational Excellence,* Winter 2002, pp. 67–72.

84. S. D. Friedman and J. H. Greenhaus, *Work and Family—Allies or Enemies?* (New York: Oxford University Press, 2000).

85. N. P. Rothbard, T. L. Dumas, and K. W. Phillips, "The Long Arm of the Organization: Work-Family Policies and Employee Preferences for Segmentation," paper presented at the 61st Annual Academy of Management Meeting; Washington, DC, August 2001.

86. Cited in "Survey Shows 75% of Large Corporations Support Diversity Programs," *Fortune,* July 6, 1998, p. S14.

87. See, for example, J. K. Ford and S. Fisher, "The Role of Training in a Changing Workplace and Workforce: New Perspectives and Approaches," in E. E. Kossek and S. A. Lobel (eds.), *Managing Diversity* (Cambridge, MA: Blackwell Publishers, 1996), pp. 164–93; and J. Barbian, "Moving Toward Diversity," *Training,* February 2003, pp. 44–48.

88. A. Bandura, "Self-Efficacy: Towards a Unifying Theory of Behavioral Change," *Psychological Review,* March 1977, pp. 191–215; and P. C. Earley, "Self or Group? Cultural Effects of Training on Self-Efficacy and Performance," *Administrative Science Quarterly,* March 1994, pp. 89–117.

89. B. R. Nathan, A. M. Mohrman, Jr., and J. Milliman, "Interpersonal Relations as a Context for the Effects of Appraisal Interviews on Performance and Satisfaction: A Longitudinal Study;" and Cawley, Keeping, and Levy, "Participation in the Performance Appraisal Process and Employee Reactions."

90. See C. M. Steele, "Through the Back Door to Theory," *Psychological Inquiry* 13, no. 3–4 (2003), pp. 314–17; N. R. Kuncel, S. A. Hezlett, and D. S. Ones, "A Comprehensive Meta-Analysis of the Predictive Validity of the Graduate Record Examinations: Implications for Graduate Student Selection and Performance," *Psychological Bulletin,* January 2001, pp. 162–81; M. J. Cullen, C. M. Hardison, and P. R. Sackett, "Using SAT-Grade and Ability-Job Performance Relationships to Test Predictions Derived From Stereotype Threat Theory," *Journal of Applied Psychology,* April 2004, pp. 220–30.

91. Cited in J. Kluger, "Pumping Up Your Past," *Time,* June 10, 2002, p. 45.

*I cannot say whether things will get better if we change;
what I can say is they must change if they are to get better.*

— Georg Christoph Lichtenberg

Organizational Change and Stress Management

After studying this chapter, you should be able to:

1 Describe forces that act as stimulants to change.

2 Summarize sources of individual and organizational resistance to change.

3 Summarize Lewin's three-step change model.

4 Explain the values underlying most organizational development (OD) efforts.

5 Contrast continuous improvement processes and process reengineering.

6 Identify properties of innovative organizations.

7 List characteristics of a learning organization.

8 Describe potential sources of stress.

9 Explain individual difference variables that moderate the stress–outcome relationship.

LEARNING OBJECTIVES

Radical Change for the Sake of Innovation

On June 7, 1993, Samsung's chairman, Kun-Hee Lee (see photo), officially announced his "New Management" policy. His goal? To completely overhaul the Samsung organization. Instead of focusing on producing cheap products that were copycats of stuff designed by others, Lee challenged his staff to turn Samsung into a truly innovative company, applying cutting-edge technology.[1]

A decade later, Lee has achieved his goal. Today, South Korea–based Samsung is the world leader in memory chips, LCDs, monitors, and Braun tubes. And it has introduced a number of innovative products, including combined cell phone and handheld devices, flat-screen TVs, and ultrathin laptops.

Following his announcement, however, Lee faced a number of barriers in bringing about change at Samsung. Two were particularly thorny. One was a lack of concern for quality. The company's historical focus on production volume encouraged employees to emphasize quantity rather than quality. So defective products were seen as just a "necessary evil" that comes from high volume. The other was employees who were afraid to speak out. The hierarchical and deferential culture of Samsung discouraged employees from questioning authority or "thinking outside the box."

To overcome these barriers and to make his New Management a reality, Lee introduced a number of radical changes. To improve quality, he implemented a Line Stop system that allows any worker to shut down production if a defect is found; adopted a quality management program that establishes a goal of no more than 3.4 defects per million parts or procedures; and introduced a number of other advanced quality-control methods. To deal with his employees' complacency, Lee challenged them to "change everything except your spouses and children." To shake up Samsung's culture, employees in the field were empowered with much greater decision-making authority; senior managers were required to leave their offices and visit the field regularly; unnecessary or inconsistent regulations were eliminated; jobs were restructured so that engineers and designers from across the company were forced to work together on multiple projects; and breaking with the company's long-time tradition of lifetime employment, a number of senior managers were fired to make room for younger and more aggressive leaders.

While many of its major competitors—like Fujitsu, Hitachi, Matsushita, Toshiba, Ericsson, and Gateway—are losing money or barely staying profitable, Samsung continues to be solidly profitable. Although Samsung's profits dropped in 2005 due to a global oversupply of DRAM chips, the company's profits still exceeded expectations and the company expects a strong performance in 2006 and beyond. This success in highly competitive global markets is in no small part due to Lee's New Management and ongoing commitment to change. ■

This chapter is about change and stress. We describe environmental forces that are requiring managers to implement comprehensive change programs. We also consider why people and organizations often resist change and how this resistance can be overcome. We review various processes for managing organizational change. We also discuss contemporary change issues for today's managers. Then we move to the topic of stress. We elaborate on the sources and consequences of stress. Finally, we conclude this chapter with a discussion of what individuals and organizations can do to better manage stress levels.

Forces for Change

As recently as the late 1990s, music retailers Wherehouse Entertainment and Tower Records were rapidly growing and profitable companies. Young people were flocking to their superstores because they offered a wide selection and competitive prices. But the market changed and these chains suffered the consequences.[2] Downloading, legal and otherwise, cut hard into their CD sales; and growing competition from Amazon.com and discounters such as Wal-Mart and Target stole a sizeable part of their market share. In January 2003, Wherehouse filed for bankruptcy. Tower followed suit in February 2004.

More and more organizations today face a dynamic and changing environment. This, in turn, is requiring these organizations to adapt. "Change or die!" is the rallying cry among today's managers worldwide. Exhibit 19-1 summarizes six specific forces that are acting as stimulants for change.

In a number of places in this book, we've discussed the *changing nature of the workforce*. For instance, almost every organization is having to adjust to a multicultural environment. Human resource policies and practices have to change to reflect the needs of an aging labor force. And many companies are having to spend large amounts of money on training to upgrade reading, math, computer, and other skills of employees.

Technology is changing jobs and organizations. For instance, computers are now commonplace in almost every organization; and cell phones and handheld PDAs are seen as indispensable by a large segment of the population. Computer networks are also reshaping entire industries. The music business, as a case in point, is now struggling to cope with the economic consequences of widespread online music sharing. For the longer term, recent breakthroughs in deciphering the human genetic code offer the potential for pharmaceutical companies to produce drugs designed for specific individuals and create serious ethical dilemmas for insurance companies as to who is insurable and who isn't.

Exhibit **19-1**	Forces for Change

Force	Examples
Nature of the workforce	More cultural diversity Aging population Many new entrants with inadequate skills
Technology	Faster, cheaper, and more mobile computers Online music sharing Deciphering of the human genetic code
Economic shocks	Rise and fall of dot-com stocks 2000–02 stock market collapse Record low interest rates
Competition	Global competitors Mergers and consolidations Growth of e-commerce
Social trends	Internet chat rooms Retirement of baby boomers Rise in discount and "big box" retailers
World politics	Iraq–U.S. war Opening of markets in China War on terrorism following 9/11/01

We live in an "age of discontinuity." In the 1950s and 1960s, the past was a pretty good prologue to the future. Tomorrow was essentially an extended trend line from yesterday. That's no longer true. Beginning in the early 1970s, with the overnight quadrupling of world oil prices, *economic shocks* have continued to impose changes on organizations. In recent years, for instance, new dot-com businesses have been created, turned tens of thousands of investors into overnight millionaires, and then crashed. The stock market decline from 2000 to 2002 eroded approximately 40 percent of the average employee's retirement account, which may force many employees to postpone their anticipated retirement date. And record low interest rates have stimulated a rapid rise in home values, helped sustain consumer spending, and proven a spur to home builders and remodelers, furniture retailers, mortgage bankers, and other home-related businesses.

Competition is changing. The global economy means that competitors are as likely to come from across the ocean as from across town. Heightened competition also makes it necessary for established organizations to defend themselves against both traditional competitors who develop new products and services and small, entrepreneurial firms with innovative offerings. Successful organizations will be the ones that can change in response to the competition. They'll be fast on their feet, capable of developing new products rapidly and getting them to market quickly. They'll rely on short production runs, short product cycles, and an ongoing stream of new products. In other words, they'll be flexible. They will require an equally flexible and responsive workforce that can adapt to rapidly and even radically changing conditions.

Social trends don't remain static. For instance, in contrast to just 15 years ago, people are meeting and sharing information in Internet chat rooms; baby boomers have begun to retire; and consumers are increasingly doing their shopping at discount warehouses and "big box" retailers like Home Depot and Circuit City.

Throughout this book we have argued strongly for the importance of seeing OB in a global context. Business schools have been preaching a global perspective since the early 1980s, but no one—not even the strongest proponents of globalization—could have imagined how *world politics* would change in recent years. We've seen the breakup of the Soviet Union; the opening up of South

Africa and China; almost daily suicide bombings in the Middle East; and, of course, the rise of Muslim fundamentalism. The unilateral invasion of Iraq by the United States has led to an expensive postwar rebuilding and an increase in anti-American attitudes in much of the world. The attacks on New York and Washington on September 11, 2001 and the subsequent war on terrorism have led to changes in business practices related to the creation of backup systems, employee security, employee stereotyping and profiling, and post-terrorist-attack anxiety.

Managing Planned Change

A group of housekeeping employees who work for a small hotel confronted the owner: "It's very hard for most of us to maintain rigid 7-to-4 work hours," said their spokeswoman. "Each of us has significant family and personal responsibilities. And rigid hours don't work for us. We're going to begin looking for someplace else to work if you don't set up flexible work hours." The owner listened thoughtfully to the group's ultimatum and agreed to its request. The next day the owner introduced a flextime plan for these employees.

A major automobile manufacturer spent several billion dollars to install state-of-the-art robotics. One area that would receive the new equipment was quality control. Sophisticated computer-controlled equipment would be put in place to significantly improve the company's ability to find and correct defects. Because the new equipment would dramatically change the jobs of the people working in the quality-control area, and because management anticipated considerable employee resistance to the new equipment, executives were developing a program to help people become familiar with the equipment and to deal with any anxieties they might be feeling.

Both of the previous scenarios are examples of **change**. That is, both are concerned with making things different. However, only the second scenario describes a **planned change**. Many changes in organizations are like the one that occurred at the hotel—they just happen. Some organizations treat all change as an accidental occurrence. We're concerned with change activities that are proactive and purposeful. In this chapter, we address change as an intentional, goal-oriented activity.

What are the goals of planned change? Essentially there are two. First, it seeks to improve the ability of the organization to adapt to changes in its environment. Second, it seeks to change employee behavior.

If an organization is to survive, it must respond to changes in its environment. When competitors introduce new products or services, government agencies enact new laws, important sources of supplies go out of business, or similar environmental changes take place, the organization needs to adapt. Efforts to stimulate innovation, empower employees, and introduce work teams are examples of planned-change activities directed at responding to changes in the environment.

Because an organization's success or failure is essentially due to the things that its employees do or fail to do, planned change also is concerned with changing the behavior of individuals and groups within the organization. Later in this chapter, we review a number of techniques that organizations can use to get people to behave differently in the tasks they perform and in their interactions with others.

Who in organizations is responsible for managing change activities? The answer is **change agents**.[3] Change agents can be managers or nonmanagers, current employees of the organization, newly hired employees, or outside consultants. A contemporary example of a change agent is Lawrence Summers, president of Harvard University.[4] Since accepting the presidency in 2001, Summers has aggressively sought to shake up the complacent institution by, among other things, leading the battle to reshape the undergraduate curricu-

Toyota Motor Corporation is taking a proactive and purposeful stance to change by developing "partner robots" designed to function in the areas of personal assistance, care of the elderly, manufacturing, and mobility. With Japan's decreasing birthrates and rapidly aging population, Toyota recognizes the need to secure a stable labor force for the future so its people will be able to enjoy comfortable standards of living. The partner robot shown here has artificial lips that enable it to play the trumpet.

lum, proposing that the university be more directly engaged with problems in education and public health, and reorganizing to consolidate more power in the president's office. While his critics admit that he has "offended nearly everyone," he is successfully bringing about revolutionary changes at Harvard that many thought were not possible. One of the reasons Summers may be a change agent is that he came to Harvard from outside academia (prior to joining Harvard, he served in the Clinton administration). Research shows that organizations are more likely to embark on transformational change when headed by leaders from outside the traditional network.[5]

In some instances, internal management will hire the services of outside consultants to provide advice and assistance with major change efforts. Because they are from the outside, these individuals can offer an objective perspective often unavailable to insiders. Outside consultants, however, are disadvantaged because they usually have an inadequate understanding of the organization's history, culture, operating procedures, and personnel. Outside consultants also may be prone to initiating more drastic changes—which can be a benefit or a disadvantage—because they don't have to live with the repercussions after the change is implemented. In contrast, internal staff specialists or managers, when acting as change agents, may be more thoughtful (and possibly more cautious) because they have to live with the consequences of their actions.

Resistance to Change

One of the most well-documented findings from studies of individual and organizational behavior is that organizations and their members resist change. In a sense, this is positive. It provides a degree of stability and predictability to behavior. If there weren't some resistance, organizational behavior would take on the characteristics of chaotic randomness. Resistance to change can also be a source of functional conflict. For example, resistance to a reorganization plan or a change in a product line can stimulate a healthy debate over the merits of the idea and result in a better decision. But there is a definite downside to resistance to change. It hinders adaptation and progress.

Resistance to change doesn't necessarily surface in standardized ways. Resistance can be overt, implicit, immediate, or deferred. It's easiest for management to deal with resistance when it is overt and immediate. For instance, a change is proposed and employees quickly respond by voicing complaints, engaging in a work slowdown, threatening to go on strike, or the like. The greater challenge is managing resistance that is implicit or deferred. Implicit resistance efforts are more subtle—loss of loyalty to the organization, loss of motivation to work, increased errors or mistakes, increased absenteeism due to "sickness"—and hence are more difficult to recognize. Similarly, deferred actions cloud the link between the source of the resistance and the reaction to it. A change may produce what appears to be only a minimal reaction at the time it is initiated, but then resistance surfaces weeks, months, or even years later. Or a single change that in and of itself might have little impact becomes the straw that breaks the camel's back. Reactions to change can build up and then explode in some response that seems totally out of proportion to the change

change *Making things different.*

planned change *Change activities that are intentional and goal-oriented.*

change agents *Persons who act as catalysts and assume the responsibility for managing change activities.*

Exhibit **19-2**	Sources of Resistance to Change

Individual Sources

Habit—To copy with life's complexities, we rely on habits or programmed responses. But when confronted with change, this tendency to respond in our accustomed ways becomes a source of resistance.

Security—People with a high need for security are likely to resist change because it threatens their feelings of safety.

Economic factors—Changes in job tasks or established work routines can arouse economic fears if people are concerned that they won't be able to perform the new tasks or routines to their previous standards, especially when pay is closely tied to productivity.

Fear of the unknown—Change substitutes ambiguity and uncertainty for the unknown.

Selective information processing—Individuals are guilty of selectively processing information in order to keep their perceptions intact. They hear what they want to hear and they ignore information that challenges the world they've created.

Organizational Sources

Structural inertia—Organizations have built-in mechanisms—like their selection processes and formalized regulations—to produce stability. When an organization is confronted with change, this structural inertia acts as a counterbalance to sustain stability.

Limited focus of change—Organizations are made up of a number of interdependent subsystems. One can't be changed without affecting the others. So limited changes in subsystems tend to be nullified by the larger system.

Group inertia—Even if individuals want to change their behavior, group norms may act as a constraint.

Threat to expertise—Changes in organizational patterns may threaten the expertise of specialized groups.

Threat to established power relationships—Any redistribution of decision-making authority can threaten long-established power relationships within the organization.

Threat to established resource allocations—Groups in the organization that control sizable resources often see change as a threat. They tend to be content with the way things are.

action it follows. The resistance, of course, has merely been deferred and stock-piled. What surfaces is a response to an accumulation of previous changes.

Exhibit 19-2 summarizes major forces for resistance to change, categorized by individual and organizational sources. Individual sources of resistance reside in basic human characteristics such as perceptions, personalities, and needs. Organizational sources reside in the structural makeup of organizations themselves.

Before we move on to ways to overcome resistance to change, it's important to note that not all change is good. Research has shown that sometimes an emphasis on making speedy decisions can lead to bad decisions. Sometimes the line between resisting needed change and falling into a "speed trap" is a fine one indeed. What's more, sometimes in the "fog of change," those who are initiating change fail to realize the full magnitude of the effects they are causing or to estimate their true costs to the organization. Thus, although the perspective generally taken is that rapid, transformational change is good, this is not always the case. Some organizations, such as Baring Brothers Bank in the U.K., have collapsed for this reason.[6] Change agents need to carefully think through the full implications.

Overcoming Resistance to Change

Seven tactics have been suggested for use by change agents in dealing with resistance to change.[7] Let's review them briefly.

Education and Communication   Resistance can be reduced through communicating with employees to help them see the logic of a change. Communication can reduce resistance on two levels. First, it fights the effects of misinformation and poor communication: If employees receive the full facts and get any misunderstandings cleared up, resistance should subside. Second, communication can be helpful in "selling" the need for change. Indeed, research shows that the way the need for change is sold matters—change is more likely when the necessity of changing is packaged properly.[8]

Participation   It's difficult for individuals to resist a change decision in which they participated. Prior to making a change, those opposed can be brought into the decision process. Assuming that the participants have the expertise to make a meaningful contribution, their involvement can reduce resistance, obtain commitment, and increase the quality of the change decision. However, against these advantages are the negatives: potential for a poor solution and great consumption of time.

Building Support and Commitment   Change agents can offer a range of supportive efforts to reduce resistance. When employees' fear and anxiety are high, employee counseling and therapy, new-skills training, or a short paid leave of absence may facilitate adjustment. Research on middle managers has shown that when managers or employees have low emotional commitment to change, they favor the status quo and resist it.[9] So, firing up employees can also help them emotionally commit to the change rather than embrace the status quo.

Negotiation   Another way for the change agent to deal with potential resistance to change is to exchange something of value for a lessening of the resistance. For instance, if the resistance is centered in a few powerful individuals, a specific reward package can be negotiated that will meet their individual needs. Negotiation as a tactic may be necessary when resistance comes from a powerful source. Yet one cannot ignore its potentially high costs. In addition, there is the risk that, once a change agent negotiates with one party to avoid resistance, he or she is open to the possibility of being blackmailed by other individuals in positions of power.

Manipulation and Cooptation   *Manipulation* refers to covert influence attempts. Twisting and distorting facts to make them appear more attractive, withholding undesirable information, and creating false rumors to get employees to accept a change are all examples of manipulation. If corporate management threatens to close down a particular manufacturing plant if that plant's employees fail to accept an across-the-board pay cut, and if the threat is actually untrue, management is using manipulation. *Cooptation*, on the other hand, is a form of both manipulation and participation. It seeks to "buy off" the leaders of a resistance group by giving them a key role in the change decision. The leaders' advice is sought, not to seek a better decision, but to get their endorsement. Both manipulation and cooptation are relatively inexpensive and easy ways to gain the support of adversaries, but the tactics can backfire if the targets become aware that they are being tricked or used. Once discovered, the change agent's credibility may drop to zero.

Selecting People Who Accept Change   Research suggests that the ability to easily accept and adapt to change is related to personality. It appears that people who adjust best to change are those who are open to experience, take a positive attitude toward change, are willing to take risks, and are flexible in their behavior. One study of managers in the United States, Europe, and Asia found that those with a positive self-concept and high risk tolerance coped better with organizational change. The study authors suggested that organizations could facilitate the change process by selecting people who score high on these characteristics. Another study found that selecting people based on a resistance-to-change scale worked well in winnowing out those who tended to react emotionally to change or to be rigid.[10]

Coercion   Last on the list of tactics is coercion; that is, the application of direct threats or force on the resisters. If the corporate management mentioned in the previous discussion really is determined to close a manufacturing plant if employees don't acquiesce to a pay cut, then coercion would be the label attached to its change tactic. Other examples of coercion are threats of transfer, loss of promotions, negative performance evaluations, and a poor letter of recommendation. The advantages and drawbacks of coercion are approximately the same as those mentioned for manipulation and cooptation.

Before we move on to the next section, consider how you feel about change. Do you think you would respond well to a major change in your life? Or do you tend to prefer that your job, your course load, your personal life, and so on remain the same? The Self-Assessment feature will show you how comfortable you are with change.

| **HOW WELL DO I RESPOND TO TURBULENT CHANGE?** |

In the Self-Assessment Library (available on CD, online, and in print), take assessment III.C.1 (How Well Do I Respond to Turbulent Change?) and answer the following questions.

1. *How did you score? Are you surprised by your score?*
2. *During what time of your life have you experienced the most change? How did you deal with it? Would you handle these changes in the same way today? Why or why not?*
3. *Are there ways you might reduce your resistance to change?*

The Politics of Change

No discussion of resistance to change would be complete without a brief mention of the politics of change. Because change invariably threatens the status quo, it inherently implies political activity.[11]

Internal change agents typically are individuals high in the organization who have a lot to lose from change. They have, in fact, risen to their positions of authority by developing skills and behavioral patterns that are favored by the organization. Change is a threat to those skills and patterns. What if they are no longer the ones the organization values? Change creates the potential for others in the organization to gain power at their expense.

Politics suggests that the impetus for change is more likely to come from outside change agents, employees who are new to the organization (and have less invested in the status quo), or from managers slightly removed from the main power structure. Managers who have spent their entire careers with a single organization and eventually achieve a senior position in the hierarchy are often major impediments to change. Change, itself, is a very real threat to their status and position. Yet they may be expected to implement changes to demonstrate that they're not merely caretakers. By acting as change agents, they can symbolically convey to various constituencies—stockholders, suppliers, employees, customers—that they are on top of problems and adapting to a dynamic environment. Of course, as you might guess, when forced to introduce change, these long-time power holders tend to implement incremental changes. Radical change is too threatening.

Power struggles within the organization will determine, to a large degree, the speed and quantity of change. You should expect that long-time career executives will be sources of resistance. This, incidentally, explains why boards of directors that recognize the imperative for the rapid introduction of radical change in their organizations frequently turn to outside candidates for new leadership.[12]

Approaches to Managing Organizational Change

Now we turn to several approaches to managing change: Lewin's classic three-step model of the change process, Kotter's eight-step plan, action research, and organizational development.

Lewin's Three-Step Model

Kurt Lewin argued that successful change in organizations should follow three steps: **unfreezing** the status quo, **movement** to a desired end state, and **refreezing** the new change to make it permanent.[13] (See Exhibit 19-3) The value of this model can be seen in the following example when the management of a large oil company decided to reorganize its marketing function in the western United States.

The oil company had three divisional offices in the West, located in Seattle, San Francisco, and Los Angeles. The decision was made to consolidate the divisions into a single regional office to be located in San Francisco. The reorganization meant transferring over 150 employees, eliminating some duplicate managerial positions, and instituting a new hierarchy of command. As you might guess, a move of this magnitude was difficult to keep secret. The rumor of its occurrence preceded the announcement by several months. The decision itself was made unilaterally. It came from the executive offices in New York. The people affected had no say whatsoever in the choice. For those in Seattle or Los Angeles, who may have disliked the decision and its consequences—the problems inherent in transferring to another city, pulling youngsters out of school, making new friends, having new coworkers, undergoing the reassignment of responsibilities—their only recourse was to quit. In actuality, less than 10 percent did.

The status quo can be considered to be an equilibrium state. To move from this equilibrium—to overcome the pressures of both individual resistance and group conformity—unfreezing is necessary. It can be achieved in one of three ways. (See Exhibit 19-4.) The **driving forces**, which direct behavior away from the status quo, can be increased. The **restraining forces**, which

Exhibit **19-3**	Lewin's Three-Step Change Model

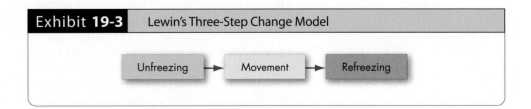

| Exhibit **19-4** | Unfreezing the Status Quo |

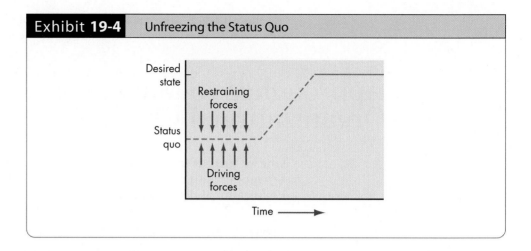

hinder movement from the existing equilibrium, can be decreased. A third alternative is to combine the first two approaches. Companies that have been successful in the past are likely to encounter restraining forces because people question the need for change.[14] Similarly, research shows that companies with strong cultures excel at incremental change but are overcome by restraining forces against radical change.[15]

The oil company's management could expect employee resistance to the consolidation. To deal with that resistance, management could use positive incentives to encourage employees to accept the change. For instance, increases in pay can be offered to those who accept the transfer. Very liberal moving expenses can be paid by the company. Management might offer low-cost mortgage funds to allow employees to buy new homes in San Francisco. Of course, management might also consider unfreezing acceptance of the status quo by removing restraining forces. Employees could be counseled individually. Each employee's concerns and apprehensions could be heard and specifically clarified. Assuming that most of the fears are unjustified, the counselor could assure the employees that there was nothing to fear and then demonstrate, through tangible evidence, that restraining forces are unwarranted. If resistance is extremely high, management may have to resort to both reducing resistance and increasing the attractiveness of the alternative if the unfreezing is to be successful.

Research on organizational change has shown that, to be effective, change has to happen quickly.[16] Organizations that build up to change do less well than those that get to and through the movement stage quickly.

Once the consolidation change has been implemented, if it is to be successful, the new situation needs to be refrozen so that it can be sustained over time. Unless this last step is taken, there is a very high chance that the change will be short-lived and that employees will attempt to revert to the previous equilibrium state. The objective of refreezing, then, is to stabilize the new situation by balancing the driving and restraining forces.

How could the oil company's management refreeze its consolidation change? By systematically replacing temporary forces with permanent ones. For instance, management might impose a permanent upward adjustment of salaries. The formal rules and regulations governing behavior of those affected by the change should also be revised to reinforce the new situation. Over time, of course, the work group's own norms will evolve to sustain the new equilibrium. But until that point is reached, management will have to rely on more formal mechanisms.

Kotter's Eight-Step Plan for Implementing Change

John Kotter of the Harvard Business School built on Lewin's three-step model to create a more detailed approach for implementing change.[17] Kotter began by listing common failures that managers make when trying to initiate change. These included the inability to create a sense of urgency about the need for change, failure to create a coalition for managing the change process, the absence of a vision for change and to effectively communicate that vision, not removing obstacles that could impede the achievement of the vision, failure to provide short-term and achievable goals, the tendency to declare victory too soon, and not anchoring the changes into the organization's culture.

Kotter then established eight sequential steps to overcome these problems. They're listed in Exhibit 19-5.

Notice how Exhibit 19-5 builds on Lewin's model. Kotter's first four steps essentially extrapolate on the "unfreezing" stage. Steps 5 through 7 represent "movement." And the final step works on "refreezing." So Kotter's contribution lies in providing managers and change agents with a more detailed guide for successfully implementing change.

Action Research

Action research refers to a change process based on the systematic collection of data and then selection of a change action based on what the analyzed data indicate.[18] Its importance lies in providing a scientific methodology for managing planned change. The process of action research consists of five steps: diagnosis, analysis, feedback, action, and evaluation. You'll note that these steps closely parallel the scientific method.

The change agent, often an outside consultant in action research, begins by gathering information about problems, concerns, and needed changes from members of the organization. This *diagnosis* is analogous to the physician's search to find specifically what ails a patient. In action research, the change

Exhibit **19-5**	Kotter's Eight-Step Plan for Implementing Change

1. Establish a sense of urgency by creating a compelling reason for why change is needed.
2. Form a coalition with enough power to lead the change.
3. Create a new vision to direct the change and strategies for achieving the vision.
4. Communicate the vision throughout the organization.
5. Empower others to act on the vision by removing barriers to change and encouraging risk taking and creative problem solving.
6. Plan for, create, and reward short-term "wins" that move the organization toward the new vision.
7. Consolidate improvements, reassess changes, and make necessary adjustments in the new programs.
8. Reinforce the changes by demonstrating the relationship between new behaviors and organizational success.

Source: Based on J. P. Kotter, *Leading Change* (Boston: Harvard Business School Press, 1996).

action research   *A change process based on systematic collection of data and then selection of a change action based on what the analyzed data indicate.*

agent asks questions, interviews employees, reviews records, and listens to the concerns of employees.

Diagnosis is followed by *analysis*. What problems do people key in on? What patterns do these problems seem to take? The change agent synthesizes this information into primary concerns, problem areas, and possible actions.

Action research includes extensive involvement of the change targets. That is, the people who will be involved in any change program must be actively involved in determining what the problem is and participating in creating the solution. So the third step—*feedback*—requires sharing with employees what has been found from steps one and two. The employees, with the help of the change agent, develop action plans for bringing about any needed change.

Now the *action* part of action research is set in motion. The employees and the change agent carry out the specific actions to correct the problems that have been identified.

The final step, consistent with the scientific underpinnings of action research, is *evaluation* of the action plan's effectiveness. Using the initial data gathered as a benchmark, any subsequent changes can be compared and evaluated.

Action research provides at least two specific benefits for an organization. First, it's problem-focused. The change agent objectively looks for problems, and the type of problem determines the type of change action. Although this may seem intuitively obvious, a lot of change activities aren't done this way. Rather, they're solution-centered. The change agent has a favorite solution—for example, implementing flextime, teams, or a process reengineering program—and then seeks out problems that the solution fits. Second, because action research so heavily involves employees in the process, resistance to change is reduced. In fact, once employees have actively participated in the feedback stage, the change process typically takes on a momentum of its own. The employees and groups that have been involved become an internal source of sustained pressure to bring about the change.

Organizational Development

No discussion of managing change would be complete without including organizational development. **Organizational development (OD)** is not an easily defined single concept. Rather, it's a term used to encompass a collection of planned-change interventions built on humanistic-democratic values that seek to improve organizational effectiveness and employee well-being.[19]

The OD paradigm values human and organizational growth, collaborative and participative processes, and a spirit of inquiry.[20] The change agent may be directive in OD; however, there is a strong emphasis on collaboration. The following briefly identifies the underlying values in most OD efforts.

1. *Respect for people* Individuals are perceived as being responsible, conscientious, and caring. They should be treated with dignity and respect.
2. *Trust and support* The effective and healthy organization is characterized by trust, authenticity, openness, and a supportive climate.
3. *Power equalization* Effective organizations deemphasize hierarchical authority and control.
4. *Confrontation* Problems shouldn't be swept under the rug. They should be openly confronted.
5. *Participation* The more that people who will be affected by a change are involved in the decisions surrounding that change, the more they will be committed to implementing those decisions.

What are some of the OD techniques or interventions for bringing about change? In the following pages, we present six interventions that change agents might consider using.

Sensitivity Training It can go by a variety of names—**sensitivity training**, laboratory training, encounter groups, or T-groups (training groups)—but all refer to a method of changing behavior through unstructured group interaction.[21] Members are brought together in a free and open environment in which participants discuss themselves and their interactive processes, loosely directed by a professional behavioral scientist. The group is process-oriented, which means that individuals learn through observing and participating rather than being told. The professional creates the opportunity for participants to express their ideas, beliefs, and attitudes and does not accept—in fact, overtly rejects—any leadership role.

The objectives of the T-groups are to provide the subjects with increased awareness of their own behavior and how others perceive them, greater sensitivity to the behavior of others, and increased understanding of group processes. Specific results sought include increased ability to empathize with others, improved listening skills, greater openness, increased tolerance of individual differences, and improved conflict-resolution skills.

Survey Feedback One tool for assessing attitudes held by organizational members, identifying discrepancies among member perceptions, and solving these differences is the **survey feedback** approach.[22]

Everyone in an organization can participate in survey feedback, but of key importance is the organizational family—the manager of any given unit and the employees who report directly to him or her. A questionnaire is usually completed by all members in the organization or unit. Organization members may be asked to suggest questions or may be interviewed to determine what issues are relevant. The questionnaire typically asks members for their perceptions and attitudes on a broad range of topics, including decision-making practices; communication effectiveness; coordination between units; and satisfaction with the organization, job, peers, and their immediate supervisor.

The data from this questionnaire are tabulated with data pertaining to an individual's specific "family" and to the entire organization and then distributed to employees. These data then become the springboard for identifying problems and clarifying issues that may be creating difficulties for people. Particular attention is given to the importance of encouraging discussion and ensuring that discussions focus on issues and ideas and not on attacking individuals.

Finally, group discussion in the survey feedback approach should result in members identifying possible implications of the questionnaire's findings. Are people listening? Are new ideas being generated? Can decision making, interpersonal relations, or job assignments be improved? Answers to questions like these, it is hoped, will result in the group agreeing on commitments to various actions that will remedy the problems that are identified.

Process Consultation No organization operates perfectly. Managers often sense that their unit's performance can be improved, but they're unable to identify what can be improved and how it can be improved. The purpose of

---

organizational development (OD) *A collection of planned change interventions, built on humanistic-democratic values, that seeks to improve organizational effectiveness and employee well-being.*

sensitivity training *Training groups that seek to change behavior through unstructured group interaction.*

survey feedback *The use of questionnaires to identify discrepancies among member perceptions; discussion follows and remedies are suggested.*

process consultation is for an outside consultant to assist a client, usually a manager, "to perceive, understand, and act upon process events" with which the manager must deal.[23] These might include work flow, informal relationships among unit members, and formal communication channels.

Process consultation (PC) is similar to sensitivity training in its assumption that organizational effectiveness can be improved by dealing with interpersonal problems and in its emphasis on involvement. But PC is more task-directed than is sensitivity training. Consultants in PC are there to "give the client 'insight' into what is going on around him, within him, and between him and other people."[24] They do not solve the organization's problems. Rather, the consultant is a guide or coach who advises on the process to help the client solve his or her own problems. The consultant works with the client in *jointly* diagnosing what processes need improvement. The emphasis is on "jointly" because the client develops a skill at analyzing processes within his or her unit that can be continually called on long after the consultant is gone. In addition, by having the client actively participate in both the diagnosis and the development of alternatives, there will be greater understanding of the process and the remedy and less resistance to the action plan chosen.

Team Building   As we've noted in numerous places throughout this book, organizations are increasingly relying on teams to accomplish work tasks. **Team building** uses high-interaction group activities to increase trust and openness among team members.[25] Team building can be applied within groups or at the intergroup level, at which activities are interdependent. For our discussion, we emphasize the intragroup level and leave intergroup development to the next section. As a result, our interest concerns applications to organizational families (command groups), as well as to committees, project teams, self-managed teams, and task groups. Team building is applicable where group activities are interdependent. The objective is to improve coordinative efforts of members, which will result in increasing the team's performance.

The activities considered in team building typically include goal setting, development of interpersonal relations among team members, role analysis to clarify each member's role and responsibilities, and team process analysis. Of course, team building may emphasize or exclude certain activities, depending on the purpose of the development effort and the specific problems with which the team is confronted. Basically, however, team building attempts to use high interaction among members to increase trust and openness.

It may be beneficial to begin by having members attempt to define the goals and priorities of the team. This will bring to the surface different perceptions of what the team's purpose may be. Following this, members can evaluate the team's performance—how effective is the team in structuring priorities and achieving its goals? This should identify potential problem areas. This self-critique discussion of means and ends can be done with members of the total team present or, when large size impinges on a free interchange of views, may initially take place in smaller groups followed by the sharing of their findings with the total team.

Team building can also address itself to clarifying each member's role on the team. Each role can be identified and clarified. Previous ambiguities can be brought to the surface. For some individuals, it may offer one of the few opportunities they have had to think through thoroughly what their job is all about and what specific tasks they are expected to carry out if the team is to optimize its effectiveness.

Intergroup Development   A major area of concern in OD is the dysfunctional conflict that exists between groups. As a result, this has been a subject to which change efforts have been directed.

To improve dysfunctional relationships between management and union employees, American Airlines CEO Gerard Arpey (right in photo) formed problem-solving teams to find new ways to compete on efficiency and service. A joint leadership team of senior managers and union officials meets monthly to discuss strategy and finances, another team communicates with employees through American's and union Web sites, and other teams of flight attendants and airport workers are trying to improve customer service. To resolve the problem of funding pensions, Arpey is shown here joining pilots and flight attendants in lobbying Congress for support of pension reform legislation.

Intergroup development seeks to change the attitudes, stereotypes, and perceptions that groups have of each other. For example, in one company, the engineers saw the accounting department as composed of shy and conservative types, and the human resources department as having a bunch of "ultra-liberals who are more concerned that some protected group of employees might get their feelings hurt than with the company making a profit." Such stereotypes can have an obvious negative impact on the coordination efforts between the departments.

Although there are several approaches for improving intergroup relations,[26] a popular method emphasizes problem solving.[27] In this method, each group meets independently to develop lists of its perception of itself, the other group, and how it believes the other group perceives it. The groups then share their lists, after which similarities and differences are discussed. Differences are clearly articulated, and the groups look for the causes of the disparities.

Are the groups' goals at odds? Were perceptions distorted? On what basis were stereotypes formulated? Have some differences been caused by misunderstandings of intentions? Have words and concepts been defined differently by each group? Answers to questions like these clarify the exact nature of the conflict. Once the causes of the difficulty have been identified, the groups can move to the integration phase—working to develop solutions that will improve relations between the groups. Subgroups, with members from each of the conflicting groups, can now be created for further diagnosis and to begin to formulate possible alternative actions that will improve relations.

process consultation *A consultant assisting a client to understand process events with which he or she must deal and to identify processes that need improvement.*

team building *High interaction among team members to increase trust and openness.*

intergroup development *OD efforts to change the attitudes, stereotypes, and perceptions that groups have of each other.*

Appreciative Inquiry   Most OD approaches are problem-centered. They identify a problem or set of problems, then look for a solution. **Appreciative inquiry** accentuates the positive.[28] Rather than looking for problems to fix, this approach seeks to identify the unique qualities and special strengths of an organization, which can then be built on to improve performance. That is, it focuses on an organization's successes rather than on its problems.

Advocates of appreciative inquiry (AI) argue that problem-solving approaches always ask people to look backward at yesterday's failures, to focus on shortcomings, and rarely result in new visions. Instead of creating a climate for positive change, action research and OD techniques such as survey feedback and process consultation end up placing blame and generating defensiveness. AI proponents claim it makes more sense to refine and enhance what the organization is already doing well. This allows the organization to change by playing to its strengths and competitive advantages.

The AI process essentially consists of four steps, often played out in a large-group meeting over a 2- or 3-day time period, and overseen by a trained change agent. The first step is one of *discovery*. The idea is to find out what people think are the strengths of the organization. For instance, employees are asked to recount times they felt the organization worked best or when they specifically felt most satisfied with their jobs. The second step is *dreaming*. The information from the discovery phase is used to speculate on possible futures for the organization. For instance, people are asked to envision the organization in 5 years and to describe what's different. The third step is *design*. Based on the dream articulation, participants focus on finding a common vision of how the organization will look and agree on its unique qualities. The fourth stage seeks to define the organization's *destiny*. In this final step, participants discuss how the organization is going to fulfill its dream. This typically includes the writing of action plans and development of implementation strategies.

AI has proven to be an effective change strategy in organizations such as GTE, Roadway Express, and the U.S. Navy. For instance, during a recent 3-day AI seminar with Roadway employees in North Carolina, workers were asked to recall ideal work experiences—when they were treated with respect, when trucks were loaded to capacity or arrived on time. Assembled into nine groups, the workers were then encouraged to devise money-saving ideas. A team of short-haul drivers came up with 12 cost-cutting and revenue-generating ideas, one alone that could generate $1 million in additional profits.[29]

Contemporary Change Issues for Today's Managers

In this section, we address four contemporary change issues. First, *how are changes in technology affecting the work lives of employees?* Second, *what can managers do to help their organizations become more innovative?* Third, *how do managers create organizations that continually learn and adapt?* And fourth, *is managing change culture-bound?*

Technology in the Workplace

Recent advances in technology are changing the workplace and affecting the work lives of employees. In this section, we'll look at two specific issues related to process technology and work. These are continuous improvement processes and process reengineering.

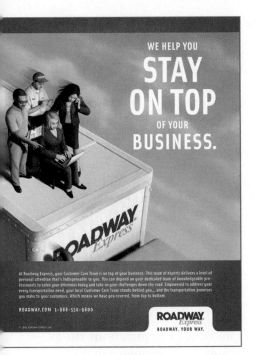

At Roadway Express, your Customer Care Team is on top of your business. This team of experts delivers a level of personal attention that's indispensable to you. You can depend on your dedicated team of knowledgeable professionals to solve your dilemmas today and take on your challenges down the road. Empowered to address your every transportation need, your local Customer Care Team stands behind you... and the transportation promises you make to your customers. Which means we have you covered, from top to bottom.

ROADWAY.COM 1-888-550-9800

ROADWAY. *Express* ROADWAY. YOUR WAY.

Roadway Express combines technology with teamwork to constantly improve the quality of its transportation services. Roadway's digital communication system links employees and customers with information about package delivery, eliminating wasted time in the communication process. To respond quickly to customer needs, Roadway formed Customer Care Teams consisting of pickup and delivery drivers, customer care specialists, account representatives, and inside sales representatives. The teams are empowered to make decisions that satisfy customers' requirements for on-time delivery, reliability, and shipment security.

Continuous Improvement Processes   In Chapter 1, we described quality management as seeking the constant attainment of customer satisfaction through the continuous improvement of all organizational processes. This search for continuous improvement recognizes that *good isn't good enough* and that even excellent performance can, and should, be improved upon. For instance, a 99.9 percent error-free performance sounds like a high standard of excellence. However it doesn't sound so great when you realize that this standard would result in the U.S. Post Office losing 2,000 pieces of mail an hour or two plane crashes a day at O'Hare Airport in Chicago![30] Quality management programs seek to achieve continuous process improvements so that variability is constantly reduced. When you eliminate variations, you increase the uniformity of the product or service. Increasing uniformity, in turn, results in lower costs and higher quality.

As tens of thousands of organizations introduce continuous process improvement, how will employees be affected? They will no longer be able to rest on their previous accomplishments and successes. So some people may experience increased stress from a work climate that no longer accepts complacency with the status quo. A race with no finish line can never be won—a situation that creates constant tension. This tension may be positive for the organization (remember *functional conflict* from Chapter 15?), but the pressures from an unrelenting search for process improvements can create stress in some employees.

Process Reengineering   We also introduced process reengineering in Chapter 1. Process reengineering is how you would do things if you could start all over from scratch. The term *reengineering* comes from the process of taking apart an electronic product and designing a better version. As applied to organizations, process reengineering means that management should start with a clean sheet of paper—rethinking and redesigning those processes by which the organization creates value and does work, ridding itself of operations that have become antiquated.[31] The three key elements of process reengineering are identifying an organization's distinctive competencies, assessing core processes, and reorganizing horizontally by process.

An organization's distinctive competencies define what it is that the organization does better than its competition. Why is identifying distinctive competencies so important? Because it guides decisions regarding what activities are crucial to the organization's success. Dell, for instance, differentiates itself from its competitors by emphasizing high-quality hardware, comprehensive service and technical support, and low prices.

Management also needs to assess the core processes that clearly add value to the organization's distinctive competencies. These are the processes that transform materials, capital, information, and labor into products and services that the customer values. When the organization is viewed as a series of processes, ranging from strategic planning to after-sales customer support, management can determine to what degree each adds value. This process-value analysis typically uncovers a whole lot of activities that add little or nothing of value and whose only justification is "we've always done it this way."

Process reengineering requires management to reorganize around horizontal processes. This means using cross-functional and self-managed teams. It

appreciative inquiry   *Seeking to identify the unique qualities and special strengths of an organization, which can then be built on to improve performance.*

means focusing on processes rather than functions. It also means cutting out unnecessary levels of middle management.

Process reengineering has been popular since the early 1990s. One of the main consequences has been that many people—especially support staff and middle managers—have lost their jobs. Those employees who keep their jobs after process reengineering have typically found that their jobs are no longer the same. These new jobs typically require a wider range of skills, including more interaction with customers and suppliers, greater challenge, increased responsibilities, and higher pay. However, the 3- to 5-year period it takes to implement process reengineering is usually tough on employees. They suffer from uncertainty and anxiety associated with taking on new tasks and having to discard long-established work practices and formal social networks.

Stimulating Innovation

How can an organization become more innovative? An excellent model is W. L. Gore, the $1.4-billion-a-year company best known as the maker of Gore-Tex fabric.[32] Gore has developed a reputation as one of America's most innovative companies by developing a stream of diverse products—including guitar strings, dental floss, medical devices, and fuel cells.

What's the secret of Gore's success? What can other organizations do to duplicate its track record for innovation? Although there is no guaranteed formula, certain characteristics surface again and again when researchers study innovative organizations. We've grouped them into structural, cultural, and human resource categories. Our message to change agents is that they should consider introducing these characteristics into their organization if they want to create an innovative climate. Before we look at these characteristics, however, let's clarify what we mean by innovation.

Definition   We said change refers to making things different. **Innovation** is a more specialized kind of change. Innovation is a new idea applied to initiating or improving a product, process, or service.[33] So all innovations involve change, but not all changes necessarily involve new ideas or lead to significant improvements. Innovations in organizations can range from small incremental improvements, such as Nabisco's extension of the Oreo product line to include double stuffs and chocolate-covered Oreos, up to radical breakthroughs, such as Toyota's battery-fueled Prius.

Sources of Innovation   *Structural variables* have been the most studied potential source of innovation.[34] A comprehensive review of the structure–innovation relationship leads to the following conclusions.[35] First, organic structures positively influence innovation. Because they're lower in vertical differentiation, formalization, and centralization, organic organizations facilitate the flexibility, adaptation, and cross-fertilization that make the adoption of innovations easier. Second, long tenure in management is associated with innovation. Managerial tenure apparently provides legitimacy and knowledge of how to accomplish tasks and obtain desired outcomes. Third, innovation is nurtured when there are slack resources. Having an abundance of resources allows an organization to afford to purchase innovations, bear the cost of instituting innovations, and absorb failures. Finally, interunit communication is high in innovative organizations.[36] These organizations are high users of committees, task forces, cross-functional teams, and other mechanisms that facilitate interaction across departmental lines.

Innovative organizations tend to have similar *cultures*. They encourage experimentation. They reward both successes and failures. They celebrate mistakes. Unfortunately, in too many organizations, people are rewarded for the

L'Oreal is an innovative organization that encourages experimentation. Innovation has transformed L'Oreal from a French firm to the world's largest marketer of cosmetics and hair-care products. CEO Lindsay Owen-Jones, who has led the firm for the past 20 years, says L'Oreal must be more innovative as it moves into new markets. In expanding to the U.S. ethnic-beauty market, researchers shown here test new cosmetics and hair-care products designed for African Americans at L'Oreal's ethnic-beauty institute in Chicago.

absence of failures rather than for the presence of successes. Such cultures extinguish risk taking and innovation. People will suggest and try new ideas only when they feel such behaviors exact no penalties. Managers in innovative organizations recognize that failures are a natural byproduct of venturing into the unknown. When Barry Bonds set the Major League Baseball record for home runs (73), he also had more strikeouts (93). And he is remembered (and paid $20 million a year) for the former, not the latter.

Within the *human resources* category, we find that innovative organizations actively promote the training and development of their members so that they keep current, offer high job security so employees don't fear getting fired for making mistakes, and encourage individuals to become champions of change. Once a new idea is developed, **idea champions** actively and enthusiastically promote the idea, build support, overcome resistance, and ensure that the innovation is implemented.[37] The evidence indicates that champions have common personality characteristics: extremely high self-confidence, persistence, energy, and a tendency to take risks. Idea champions also display characteristics associated with transformational leadership. They inspire and energize others with their vision of the potential of an innovation and through their strong personal conviction in their mission. They are also good at gaining the commitment of others to support their mission. In addition, idea champions have jobs that provide considerable decision-making discretion. This autonomy helps them introduce and implement innovations in organizations.[38]

innovation   *A new idea applied to initiating or improving a product, process, or service.*

idea champions   *Individuals who take an innovation and actively and enthusiastically promote the idea, build support, overcome resistance, and ensure that the idea is implemented.*

Summary   Given Gore's status as a premier product innovator, we would expect it to have most or all of the properties we've identified. And it does. The company has a highly organic structure. Its dozens of plants, for instance, are limited in size to only 200 people. And almost everything is done in teams. The culture strongly fosters experimentation. Employees are free to choose what projects they want to work on based on what they believe is most worthy of their time and most likely to contribute to the company's success. Also, all researchers are encouraged to spend 10 percent of their work time on developing their own ideas. Finally, Gore's human resources policies encourage employees to expand their skills and responsibilities, and to help others in the organization do the same.

Creating a Learning Organization

The learning organization has recently developed a groundswell of interest from managers and organization theorists looking for new ways to successfully respond to a world of interdependence and change.[39] In this section, we describe what a learning organization looks like and methods for managing learning.

What's a Learning Organization?   A **learning organization** is an organization that has developed the continuous capacity to adapt and change. Just as individuals learn, so too do organizations. "All organizations learn, whether they consciously choose to or not—it is a fundamental requirement for their sustained existence."[40] However, some organizations just do it better than others.

Most organizations engage in what has been called **single-loop learning**.[41] When errors are detected, the correction process relies on past routines and present policies. In contrast, learning organizations use **double-loop learning**. When an error is detected, it's corrected in ways that involve the modification of the organization's objectives, policies, and standard routines. Double-loop learning challenges deeply rooted assumptions and norms within an organization. In this way, it provides opportunities for radically different solutions to problems and dramatic jumps in improvement.

Exhibit 19-6 summarizes the five basic characteristics of a learning organization. It's an organization in which people put aside their old ways of thinking, learn to be open with each other, understand how their organization really works, form a plan or vision that everyone can agree on, and then work together to achieve that vision.[42]

Proponents of the learning organization envision it as a remedy for three fundamental problems inherent in traditional organizations: fragmentation, competition, and reactiveness.[43] First, *fragmentation* based on specialization creates "walls" and "chimneys" that separate different functions into inde-

Exhibit **19-6**   Characteristics of a Learning Organization

1. There exists a shared vision which everyone agrees on.

2. People discard their old ways of thinking and the standard routines they use for solving problems or doing their jobs.

3. Members think of all organizational processes, activities, functions, and interactions with the environment as part of a system of interrelationships.

4. People openly communicate with each other (across vertical and horizontal boundaries) without fear of criticism or punishment.

5. People sublimate their personal self-interest and fragmented departmental interests to work together to achieve the organization's shared vision.

Source: Based on P. M. Senge, *The Fifth Discipline*, (New York: Doubleday, 1990).

pendent and often warring fiefdoms. Second, an overemphasis on *competition* often undermines collaboration. Members of the management team compete with one another to show who is right, who knows more, or who is more persuasive. Divisions compete with one another when they ought to cooperate and share knowledge. Team project leaders compete to show who the best manager is. And third, *reactiveness* misdirects management's attention to problem solving rather than creation. The problem solver tries to make something go away, while a creator tries to bring something new into being. An emphasis on reactiveness pushes out innovation and continuous improvement and, in its place, encourages people to run around "putting out fires."

It may help to better understand what a learning organization is if you think of it as an *ideal* model that builds on a number of previous OB concepts. No company has successfully achieved all the characteristics described in Exhibit 19-6. As such, you should think of a learning organization as an ideal to strive toward rather than a realistic description of structured activity. Note, too, how learning organizations draw on previous OB concepts such as quality management, organizational culture, the boundaryless organization, functional conflict, and transformational leadership. For instance, the learning organization adopts quality management's commitment to continuous improvement. Learning organizations are also characterized by a specific culture that values risk taking, openness, and growth. It seeks "boundarylessness" through breaking down barriers created by hierarchical levels and fragmented departmentation. A learning organization supports the importance of disagreements, constructive criticism, and other forms of functional conflict. And transformational leadership is needed in a learning organization to implement the shared vision.

Managing Learning   How do you change an organization to make it into a continual learner? What can managers do to make their firms learning organizations?

- *Establish a strategy.* Management needs to make explicit its commitment to change, innovation, and continuous improvement.
- *Redesign the organization's structure.* The formal structure can be a serious impediment to learning. By flattening the structure, eliminating or combining departments, and increasing the use of cross-functional teams, interdependence is reinforced and boundaries between people are reduced.
- *Reshape the organization's culture.* As noted earlier, learning organizations are characterized by risk taking, openness, and growth. Management sets the tone for the organization's culture both by what it says (strategy) and what it does (behavior). Managers need to demonstrate by their actions that taking risks and admitting failures are desirable traits. That means rewarding people who take chances and make mistakes. And management needs to encourage functional conflict. "The key to unlocking real openness at work," says one expert on learning organizations, "is to teach people to give up having to be in agreement. We think agreement is so important. Who cares? You have to bring paradoxes, conflicts, and dilemmas out in the open, so collectively we can be more intelligent than we can be individually."[44]

---

learning organization   *An organization that has developed the continuous capacity to adapt and change.*

single-loop learning   *Correcting errors using past routines and present policies.*

double-loop learning   *Correcting errors by modifying the organization's objectives, policies, and standard routines.*

An excellent illustration of a learning organization is the U.S. Army.[45] This organization's environment has changed dramatically in the past several decades. Most significantly, the Soviet threat, which was a major justification for the army's military buildup following World War II, is largely gone. Now army soldiers are more likely to be peacekeeping in Iraq or helping to fight fires in the Pacific Northwest. In response to this new mission, the army's high command has redesigned its structure. Its formerly rigid, hierarchical, war-based command-and-control structure has been replaced with an adaptive and flexible structure to match its more varied objectives. In addition, everyone from PFCs to brigadier generals has gone through team training to make the army's culture more egalitarian. For instance, soldiers are now encouraged to question authority and have been given new skills that allow them to make decisions in the field. The "new army" is developing soldiers and officers who can adapt rapidly to different tasks and missions—fighting, peacekeeping, humanitarian rescue—and who can quickly improvise in complex and ambiguous situations.

Managing Change: It's Culture-Bound

A number of change issues we've discussed in this chapter are culture-bound. To illustrate, let's briefly look at five questions: (1) Do people believe change is possible? (2) If it's possible, how long will it take to bring it about? (3) Is resistance to change greater in some cultures than in others? (4) Does culture influence how change efforts will be implemented? (5) Do successful idea champions do things differently in different cultures?

Do people believe change is possible? Remember that cultures vary in terms of beliefs about their ability to control their environment. In cultures in which people believe that they can dominate their environment, individuals will take a proactive view of change. This, for example, would describe the United States and Canada. In many other countries, such as Iran and Saudi Arabia, people see themselves as subjugated to their environment and thus will tend to take a passive approach toward change.

Middle Eastern countries tend to take a passive approach toward change. In banking centers like Bahrain, a state on the Persian Gulf, culture dictates gender separation so banks continue to have special sections for women.

If change is possible, how long will it take to bring it about? A culture's time orientation can help us answer this question. Societies that focus on the long term, such as Japan, will demonstrate considerable patience while waiting for positive outcomes from change efforts. In societies with a short-term focus, such as the United States and Canada, people expect quick improvements and will seek change programs that promise fast results.

Is resistance to change greater in some cultures than in others? Resistance to change will be influenced by a society's reliance on tradition. Italians, as an example, focus on the past, whereas Americans emphasize the present. Italians, therefore, should generally be more resistant to change efforts than their American counterparts.

Does culture influence how change efforts will be implemented? Power distance can help with this issue. In high-power-distance cultures, such as Spain or Thailand, change efforts will tend to be autocratically implemented by top management. In contrast, low-power-distance cultures value democratic methods. We'd predict, therefore, a greater use of participation in countries such as Denmark and the Netherlands.

Finally, do successful idea champions do things differently in different cultures? The evidence indicates that the answer is Yes.[46] People in collectivist cultures, in contrast to individualistic cultures, prefer appeals for cross-functional support for innovation efforts; people in high-power-distance cultures prefer champions to work closely with those in authority to approve innovative activities before work is conducted on them; and the higher the uncertainty avoidance of a society, the more champions should work within the organization's rules and procedures to develop the innovation. These findings suggest that effective managers will alter their organization's championing strategies to reflect cultural values. So, for instance, although idea champions in Russia might succeed by ignoring budgetary limitations and working around confining procedures, champions in Austria, Denmark, Germany or other cultures high in uncertainty avoidance will be more effective by closely following budgets and procedures.

Work Stress and Its Management

Most of us are aware that employee stress is an increasing problem in organizations. Friends tells us they're stressed out from greater workloads and having to work longer hours because of downsizing at their company (see Exhibit 19-7). Parents talk about the lack of job stability in today's world and reminisce about a time when a job with a large company implied lifetime security. We read surveys in which employees complain about the stress created in trying to balance work and family responsibilities.[47] In this section we'll look at the causes and

Exhibit **19-7**	Too Much Work, Too Little Time

With companies downsizing workers, those who remain find their jobs are demanding increasing amounts of time and energy. A national sample of U.S. employees finds that they:

Feel overworked	54%
Are overwhelmed by workload	55%
Lack time for reflection	59%
Don't have time to complete tasks	56%
Must multitask too much	45%

Source: Business Week, July 16, 2001, p. 12.

consequences of stress, and then consider what individuals and organizations can do to reduce it.

What Is Stress?

Stress is a dynamic condition in which an individual is confronted with an opportunity, demand, or resource related to what the individual desires and for which the outcome is perceived to be both uncertain and important.[48] This is a complicated definition. Let's look at its components more closely.

Stress is not necessarily bad in and of itself. Although stress is typically discussed in a negative context, it also has a positive value.[49] It's an opportunity when it offers potential gain. Consider, for example, the superior performance that an athlete or stage performer gives in "clutch" situations. Such individuals often use stress positively to rise to the occasion and perform at or near their maximum. Similarly, many professionals see the pressures of heavy workloads and deadlines as positive challenges that enhance the quality of their work and the satisfaction they get from their job.

In short, some stress can be good, and some can be bad. Recently, researchers have argued that *challenge stress*, or stress associated with challenges in the work environment (such as having lots of projects, assignments, and responsibilities), operates quite differently from *hindrance stress*, or stress that keeps you from reaching your goals (red tape, office politics, confusion over job responsibilities). Although research on challenge and hindrance stress is just starting to accumulate, early evidence suggests that challenge stress has many fewer negative implications than hindrance stress.[50]

More typically, stress is associated with **demands** and **resources**. Demands are responsibilities, pressures, obligations, and even uncertainties that individu-

Exhibit 19-8

als face in the workplace. Resources are things within an individual's control that can be used to resolve the demands. This demands-resources model has received increasing support in the literature.[51] Let's discuss what it means.

When you take a test at school or you undergo your annual performance review at work, you feel stress because you confront opportunities and performance pressures. A good performance review may lead to a promotion, greater responsibilities, and a higher salary. But a poor review may prevent you from getting the promotion. An extremely poor review might even result in your being fired. In such a situation, to the extent you can apply resources to the demands—such as being prepared, placing the exam or review in perspective, or obtaining social support—you will feel less stress.

As another example, whereas the demand of working long hours leads to stress, this stress can be reduced by the resource of social support such as having friends or family to talk to. A recent study found this to be true of workers in a diverse set of countries (Australia, Canada, England, New Zealand, the United States, China, Taiwan, Argentina, Brazil, Colombia, Ecuador, Mexico, Peru, and Uruguay).[52]

Understanding Stress and Its Consequences

What causes stress? What are its consequences for individual employees? Why is it that the same set of conditions that creates stress for one person seems to have little or no effect on another person? Exhibit 19-9 provides a model that can help to answer questions such as these.[53]

Exhibit **19-9**	A Model of Stress

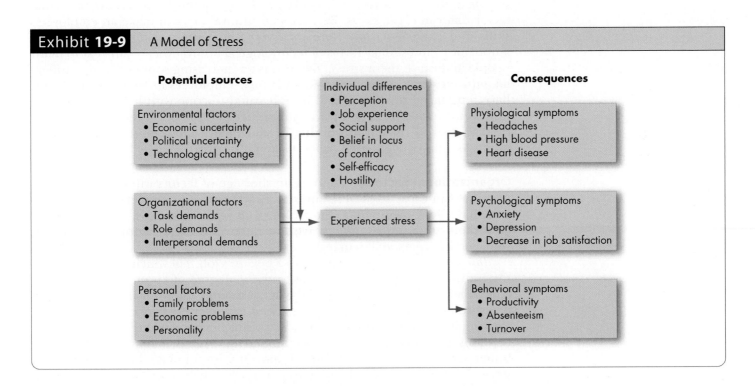

stress   *A dynamic condition in which an individual is confronted with an opportunity, demand, or resource related to what the individual desires and for which the outcome is perceived to be both uncertain and important.*

demands   *Responsibilities, pressures, obligations, and even uncertainties that individuals face in the workplace.*

resources   *Things within an individual's control that can be used to resolve demands.*

The model identifies three sets of factors—environmental, organizational, and personal—that act as *potential* sources of stress. Whether they become *actual* stress depends on individual differences such as job experience and personality. When stress is experienced by an individual, its symptoms can surface as physiological, psychological, and behavioral outcomes.

Potential Sources of Stress

As the model in Exhibit 19-9 shows, there are three categories of potential stressors: environmental, organizational, and personal. Let's take a look at each.[54]

Environmental Factors   Just as environmental uncertainty influences the design of an organization's structure, it also influences stress levels among employees in that organization. Changes in the business cycle create *economic uncertainties*. When the economy is contracting, for example, people become increasingly anxious about their job security. *Political uncertainties* don't tend to create stress among North Americans as they do for employees in countries like Haiti or Venezuela. The obvious reason is that the United States and Canada have stable political systems, in which change is typically implemented in an orderly manner. Yet political threats and changes, even in countries like the United States and Canada, can induce stress. For instance, the threats by Quebec to separate from Canada, or the difficulties of East Germany integrating with West Germany, lead to political uncertainty that becomes stressful to people in these countries.[55] *Technological change* is a third type of environmental factor that can cause stress. Because new innovations can make an employee's skills and experience obsolete in a very short time, computers, robotics, automation, and similar forms of technological innovation are a threat to many people and cause them stress. *Terrorism* is an increasing source of environmental-induced stress in the twenty-first century. Employees in Israel, for instance, have long faced this threat and have learned to cope with it. For Americans, however, the events of 9/11 and subsequent color-coded terror alerts have increased stress related to working in skyscrapers and attending large public events and have heightened concerns about security.

Organizational Factors   There is no shortage of factors within the organization that can cause stress. Pressures to avoid errors or complete tasks in a limited time, work overload, a demanding and insensitive boss, and unpleasant coworkers are a few examples. We've categorized these factors around task, role, and interpersonal demands.[56]

Task demands are factors related to a person's job. They include the design of the individual's job (autonomy, task variety, degree of automation), working conditions, and the physical work layout. Assembly lines, for instance, can put pressure on people when the line's speed is perceived as excessive. Similarly, working in an overcrowded room or in a visible location where noise and interruptions are constant can increase anxiety and stress.[57] Increasingly, as customer service becomes ever more important, emotional labor is a source of stress.[58] Imagine being a flight attendant for Southwest Airlines or a cashier at Starbucks. Do you think you could put on a happy face when you're having a bad day?

Role demands relate to pressures placed on a person as a function of the particular role he or she plays in the organization. Role conflicts create expectations that may be hard to reconcile or satisfy. Role overload is experienced when the employee is expected to do more than time permits. Role ambiguity is created when role expectations are not clearly understood and the employee is not sure what he or she is to do.

Terrorist attacks and subsequent terror alerts continue to escalate stress levels among employees. The terrorist bombing attack on London's bus and underground train system during the morning rush hour resulted in terror alerts for mass-transit commuters throughout the world. As an environmental-induced stress, terror attacks raise the anxiety and fear of millions of employees who rely on public transportation to get to work. Shown here are London commuters using the subway after the attack affecting the King's Cross station.

Interpersonal demands are pressures created by other employees. Lack of social support from colleagues and poor interpersonal relationships can cause stress, especially among employees with a high social need.

Personal Factors   The typical individual works about 40 to 50 hours a week. But the experiences and problems that people encounter in those other 120-plus nonwork hours each week can spill over to the job. Our final category, then, encompasses factors in the employee's personal life. Primarily, these factors are family issues, personal economic problems, and inherent personality characteristics.

National surveys consistently show that people hold *family* and personal relationships dear. Marital difficulties, the breaking off of a relationship, and discipline troubles with children are examples of relationship problems that create stress for employees that aren't left at the front door when they arrive at work.[59]

Economic problems created by individuals overextending their financial resources is another set of personal troubles that can create stress for employees and distract their attention from their work. Regardless of income level—people who make $80,000 a year seem to have as much trouble handling their finances as those who earn $18,000—some people are poor money managers or have wants that always seem to exceed their earning capacity.

Studies in three diverse organizations found that stress symptoms reported prior to beginning a job accounted for most of the variance in stress symptoms reported 9 months later.[60] This led the researchers to conclude that some people may have an inherent tendency to accentuate negative aspects of the world in general. If this is true, then a significant individual factor that influences stress is a person's basic disposition. That is, stress symptoms expressed on the job may actually originate in the person's *personality.*

Stressors Are Additive   A fact that tends to be overlooked when stressors are reviewed individually is that stress is an additive phenomenon.[61] Stress builds up. Each new and persistent stressor adds to an individual's stress level. So a single stressor may be relatively unimportant in and of itself, but if it's added to an already high level of stress, it can be "the straw that breaks the camel's back." If we want to appraise the total amount of stress an individual is under, we have to sum up his or her opportunity stresses, constraint stresses, and demand stresses.

Individual Differences

Some people thrive on stressful situations, while others are overwhelmed by them. What is it that differentiates people in terms of their ability to handle stress? What individual difference variables moderate the relationship between *potential* stressors and *experienced* stress? At least six variables—perception, job experience, social support, belief in locus of control, self-efficacy, and hostility—have been found to be relevant moderators.

In Chapter 5, we demonstrated that employees react in response to their perception of reality rather than to reality itself. *Perception*, therefore, will moderate the relationship between a potential stress condition and an employee's reaction to it. For example, one person's fear that he'll lose his job because his company is laying off personnel may be perceived by another as an opportunity to get a large severance allowance and start his own business. So stress potential doesn't lie in objective conditions; it lies in an employee's interpretation of those conditions.

The evidence indicates that *experience* on the job tends to be negatively related to work stress. Why? Two explanations have been offered.[62] First is the idea of selective withdrawal. Voluntary turnover is more probable among people who experience more stress. Therefore, people who remain with the organization longer are those with more stress-resistant traits or those who are more resistant to the stress characteristics of their organization. Second, people eventually develop coping mechanisms to deal with stress. Because this takes time, senior members of the organization are more likely to be fully adapted and should experience less stress.

There is increasing evidence that *social support*—that is, collegial relationships with coworkers or supervisors—can buffer the impact of stress.[63] The logic underlying this moderating variable is that social support acts as a palliative, mitigating the negative effects of even high-strain jobs.

Locus of control was introduced in Chapter 4 as a personality attribute. As you may recall, internal locus of control is an indicator of positive core self-evaluations because people who think they're in control of their life (internal locus of control) have a more positive self-view than those who think they're controlled by their environment (external locus of control). Evidence indicates that internals perceive their jobs to be less stressful than do externals, and internals cope better with job demands than do externals.[64] When internals and externals confront a similar stressful situation, the internals are likely to believe that they can have a significant effect on the results. They, therefore, act to take control of events. In contrast, externals are more likely to be passive and feel helpless.

Self-efficacy has also been found to influence stress outcomes. You'll remember from Chapter 6 that this term refers to an individual's belief that he or she is capable of performing a task. A recent study indicated that individuals with strong self-efficacy reacted less negatively to the strain created by long work hours and work overload than did those with low levels of self-efficacy.[65] That is, confidence in one's own abilities appears to decrease stress. As with an internal locus of control, strong efficacy confirms the power of self-beliefs in moderating the effect of a high-strain situation.

Some people's personality includes a high degree of hostility and anger. These people are chronically suspicious and mistrustful of others. Evidence indicates that this *hostility* significantly increases a person's stress and risk for heart disease.[66] More specifically, people who are quick to anger, maintain a

A collegial atmosphere reigns at Yahoo France, where employees and supervisors often gather for lunch at a café across the street from their Paris office. Yahoo France created a socially supportive work environment where open workstations encourage communication and help reduce the negative effects of high-stress jobs. Yahoo France, the first portal to offer quality service in the French language, strives to maintain its market leadership since France Telecom entered the market with competing portals.

persistently hostile outlook, and project a cynical mistrust of others are more likely to experience stress in situations.

Consequences of Stress

Stress shows itself in a number of ways. For instance, an individual who is experiencing a high level of stress may develop high blood pressure, ulcers, irritability, difficulty in making routine decisions, loss of appetite, accident-proneness, and the like. These can be subsumed under three general categories: physiological, psychological, and behavioral symptoms.[67]

Physiological Symptoms   Most of the early concern with stress was directed at physiological symptoms. This was predominantly due to the fact that the topic was researched by specialists in the health and medical sciences. This research led to the conclusion that stress could create changes in metabolism, increase heart and breathing rates, increase blood pressure, bring on headaches, and induce heart attacks.

The link between stress and particular physiological symptoms is not clear. Traditionally, researchers concluded that there were few, if any, consistent relationships.[68] This is attributed to the complexity of the symptoms and the difficulty of objectively measuring them. More recently, some evidence suggests that stress may have harmful physiological effects. For example, one recent study linked stressful job demands to increase susceptibility to upper respiratory illnesses and poor immune system functioning, especially for individuals who had low self-efficacy.[69]

Psychological Symptoms   Stress can cause dissatisfaction. Job-related stress can cause job-related dissatisfaction. Job dissatisfaction, in fact, is "the simplest and most obvious psychological effect" of stress.[70] But stress shows itself in other psychological states—for instance, tension, anxiety, irritability, boredom, and procrastination.

The evidence indicates that when people are placed in jobs that make multiple and conflicting demands or in which there is a lack of clarity about

Stress Levels Reach Record Highs

A few years back, many stress experts attributed all the talk about overstress in the workplace to people just being more aware of their stress. Not any more. The evidence that stress in the workplace is real and skyrocketing is too overwhelming to ignore. Consider some data.

- According to a recent study by the U.S. National Institute for Occupational Safety and Health, more than half the working people in the United States view job stress as a major problem in their lives. This is more than double the percentage reported in the early 1990s.
- The number of people who called in sick due to stress tripled between 1999 and 2002.
- In an annual survey released in 2002, 29 percent of respondents put themselves in the highest category of stress—extreme or quite a bit—the highest percentage in the poll's 6-year history.
- The American Institute of Stress estimates that stress and the ills it can cause—absenteeism, burnout, mental health problems—cost American business more than $300 billion a year.
- The European Community officially dubbed stress the second-biggest occupational health problem facing employers in Europe.

Source: Based on M. Lewis, "The Last Taboo," *Fortune,* October 28, 2002, pp. 137–44.

the incumbent's duties, authority, and responsibilities, both stress and dissatisfaction are increased.[71] Similarly, the less control people have over the pace of their work, the greater the stress and dissatisfaction. Although more research is needed to clarify the relationship, the evidence suggests that jobs that provide a low level of variety, significance, autonomy, feedback, and identity to incumbents create stress and reduce satisfaction and involvement in the job.[72]

Behavioral Symptoms   Behavior-related stress symptoms include changes in productivity, absence, and turnover, as well as changes in eating habits, increased smoking or consumption of alcohol, rapid speech, fidgeting, and sleep disorders.[73]

There has been a significant amount of research investigating the stress–performance relationship. The most widely studied pattern in the stress–performance literature is the inverted-U relationship.[74] This is shown in Exhibit 19-10

The logic underlying the inverted U is that low to moderate levels of stress stimulate the body and increase its ability to react. Individuals then often perform their tasks better, more intensely, or more rapidly. But too much stress

Exhibit **19-10**	Inverted-U Relationship Between Stress and Job Performance

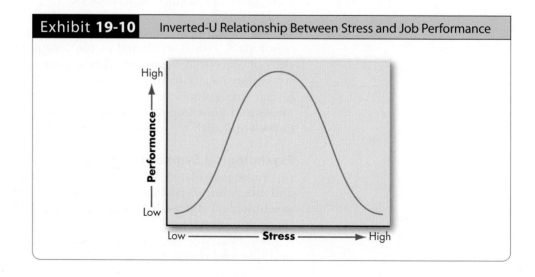

places unattainable demands on a person, which result in lower performance. This inverted-U pattern may also describe the reaction to stress over time as well as to changes in stress intensity. That is, even moderate levels of stress can have a negative influence on performance over the long term as the continued intensity of the stress wears down the individual and saps energy resources. An athlete may be able to use the positive effects of stress to obtain a higher performance during every Saturday's game in the fall season, or a sales executive may be able to psych herself up for her presentation at the annual national meeting. But moderate levels of stress experienced continually over long periods, as typified by the emergency room staff in a large urban hospital, can result in lower performance. This may explain why emergency room staffs at such hospitals are frequently rotated and why it is unusual to find individuals who have spent the bulk of their career in such an environment. In effect, to do so would expose the individual to the risk of "career burnout."

In spite of the popularity and intuitive appeal of the inverted-U model, it doesn't get a lot of empirical support.[75] At this time, managers should be careful in assuming that this model accurately depicts the stress–performance relationship.

Managing Stress

From the organization's standpoint, management may not be concerned when employees experience low to moderate levels of stress. The reason, as we showed earlier, is that such levels of stress may be functional and lead to higher employee performance. But high levels of stress, or even low levels sustained over long periods, can lead to reduced employee performance and, thus, require action by management.

Although a limited amount of stress may benefit an employee's performance, don't expect employees to see it that way. From the individual's standpoint, even low levels of stress are likely to be perceived as undesirable. It's not unlikely, therefore, for employees and management to have different notions of what constitutes an acceptable level of stress on the job. What management may consider to be "a positive stimulus that keeps the adrenalin running" is very likely to be seen as "excessive pressure" by the employee. Keep this in mind as we discuss individual and organizational approaches toward managing stress.[76]

Individual Approaches   An employee can take personal responsibility for reducing stress levels. Individual strategies that have proven effective include implementing time-management techniques, increasing physical exercise, relaxation training, and expanding the social support network.

Many people manage their time poorly. The well-organized employee, like the well-organized student, can often accomplish twice as much as the person who is poorly organized. So an understanding and utilization of basic *time-management* principles can help individuals better cope with tensions created by job demands.[77] A few of the more well-known time-management principles are: (1) making daily lists of activities to be accomplished; (2) prioritizing activities by importance and urgency; (3) scheduling activities according to the priorities set; and (4) knowing your daily cycle and handling the most demanding parts of your job during the high part of your cycle when you are most alert and productive.[78]

Noncompetitive physical exercise such as aerobics, walking, jogging, swimming, and riding a bicycle have long been recommended by physicians as a way to deal with excessive stress levels. These forms of *physical exercise* increase heart capacity, lower the at-rest heart rate, provide a mental diversion from work pressures, and offer a means to "let off steam."[79]

Individuals can teach themselves to reduce tension through *relaxation techniques* such as meditation, hypnosis, and biofeedback. The objective is to reach a state of deep relaxation, in which one feels physically relaxed, somewhat detached from the immediate environment, and detached from body sensations.[80] Deep relaxation for 15 or 20 minutes a day releases tension and provides a person with a pronounced sense of peacefulness. Importantly, significant changes in heart rate, blood pressure, and other physiological factors result from achieving the condition of deep relaxation.

As we noted earlier in this chapter, having friends, family, or work colleagues to talk to provides an outlet when stress levels become excessive. Expanding your *social support network*, therefore, can be a means for tension reduction. It provides you with someone to hear your problems and to offer a more objective perspective on the situation.

Organizational Approaches Several of the factors that cause stress—particularly task and role demands—are controlled by management. As such, they can be modified or changed. Strategies that management might want to consider include improved personnel selection and job placement, training, use of realistic goal setting, redesigning of jobs, increased employee involvement, improved organizational communication, offering employee sabbaticals, and establishment of corporate wellness programs.

Certain jobs are more stressful than others but, as we learned earlier in this chapter, individuals differ in their response to stressful situations. We know, for example, that individuals with little experience or an external locus of control tend to be more prone to stress. *Selection and placement* decisions should take these facts into consideration. Obviously, management shouldn't restrict hiring to only experienced individuals with an internal locus, but such individuals may adapt better to high-stress jobs and perform those jobs more effectively. Similarly, *training* can increase an individual's self-efficacy and thus lessen job strain.

We discussed *goal setting* in Chapter 6. Based on an extensive amount of research, we concluded that individuals perform better when they have specific and challenging goals and receive feedback on how well they are progressing toward these goals. The use of goals can reduce stress as well as provide motivation. Specific goals that are perceived as attainable clarify performance expectations. In addition, goal feedback reduces uncertainties about actual job performance. The result is less employee frustration, role ambiguity, and stress.

Redesigning jobs to give employees more responsibility, more meaningful work, more autonomy, and increased feedback can reduce stress because these factors give the employee greater control over work activities and lessen dependence on others. But as we noted in our discussion of work design, not all employees want enriched jobs. The right redesign, then, for employees with a low need for growth might be less responsibility and increased specialization. If individuals prefer structure and routine, reducing skill variety should also reduce uncertainties and stress levels.

Role stress is detrimental to a large extent because employees feel uncertain about goals, expectations, how they'll be evaluated, and the like. By giving these employees a voice in the decisions that directly affect their job performance, management can increase employee control and reduce this role stress. So managers should consider *increasing employee involvement* in decision making.[81]

Increasing formal *organizational communication* with employees reduces uncertainty by lessening role ambiguity and role conflict. Given the importance that perceptions play in moderating the stress–response relationship, management can also use effective communications as a means to shape employee per-

Coping with Stress: Cultural Differences

STRESS IS A COMMON COMPLAINT OF WORKERS worldwide. But how workers manage that stress, and whether they seek social support for relief, varies from one culture to the next. A recent study examined this issue.

The study compared the tendency to seek social support to relieve stress among some Asian groups (Koreans and Asian Americans) to that of European Americans. Given that Asians tend to be more collectivist than European Americans (who tend to be more individualist), two possibilities arise. One, a collectivist orientation might increase the likelihood that one would want to talk about stressful problems, in essence seeking social support. But two, because collectivists strive for group harmony, they may keep problems to themselves and fail to use social support as a means of coping with stress.

The study found support for the latter suggestion: Koreans, Asians, and Asian Americans reported using social support less often than European Americans because they were concerned about maintaining group harmony. What's the upshot? Collectivists experiencing stress may be limiting themselves in terms of coping mechanisms and may need to find other means of coping with work-related stress.

Source: Based on S. Taylor, D. K. Sherman, H. S. Kim, J. Jarcho, K. Takagi, and M. Dunagan, "Culture and Social Support: Who Seeks It and Why?" *Journal of Personality and Social Psychology*, September 2004, pp. 354–62.

ceptions. Remember that what employees categorize as demands, threats, or opportunities are merely an interpretation, and that interpretation can be affected by the symbols and actions communicated by management.

What some employees need is an occasional escape from the frenetic pace of their work. In recent years, companies such as Charles Schwab, Du Pont, L.L. Bean, Nike, and 3Com have begun to provide extended voluntary leaves.[82] These *sabbaticals*—ranging in length from a few weeks to several months—allow employees to travel, relax, or pursue personal projects that consume time beyond normal vacation weeks. Proponents argue that these sabbaticals can revive and rejuvenate workers who might be headed for burnout.

Our final suggestion is to offer organizationally supported **wellness programs**. These programs focus on the employee's total physical and mental condition.[83] For example, they typically provide workshops to help people quit smoking, control alcohol use, lose weight, eat better, and develop a regular exercise program. The assumption underlying most wellness programs is that employees need to take personal responsibility for their physical and mental health. The organization is merely a vehicle to facilitate this end.

wellness programs *Organizationally supported programs that focus on the employee's total physical and mental condition.*

BMC Software in Houston encourages employees to take personal responsibility for their mental and physical health. The company makes it easy for employees to keep physically fit and reduce stress by providing basketball courts in the gym, a swimming pool, putting green, horseshoe pits, a beach volleyball court, and massage therapists. BMC stocks kitchens throughout its offices with healthy snacks like free fruit and popcorn.

Organizations can expect a payoff from their investment in wellness programs. And most of those firms that have introduced wellness programs have found significant benefits. For instance, a study of eight Canadian organizations found that every dollar spent on their comprehensive wellness programs generated a return of $1.64, and for high-risk employees, like smokers, the return was nearly $4.00.[84]

Summary and Implications for Managers

The need for change has been implied throughout this text. "A casual reflection on change should indicate that it encompasses almost all of our concepts in the organizational behavior literature."[85] For instance, think about attitudes, motivation, work teams, communication, leadership, organizational structures, human resource practices, and organizational cultures. Change was an integral part in the discussion of each.

If environments were perfectly static, if employees' skills and abilities were always up-to-date and incapable of deteriorating, and if tomorrow were always exactly the same as today, organizational change would have little or no relevance to managers. But the real world is turbulent, requiring organizations and their members to undergo dynamic change if they are to perform at competitive levels.

Managers are the primary change agents in most organizations. By the decisions they make and their role-modeling behaviors, they shape the organization's change culture. For instance, management decisions related to structural design, cultural factors, and human resource policies largely determine the level of innovation within the organization. Similarly, management decisions, policies, and practices will determine the degree to which the organization learns and adapts to changing environmental factors.

We found that the existence of work stress, in and of itself, need not imply lower performance. The evidence indicates that stress can be either a positive or a negative influence on employee performance. For many people, low to moderate amounts of stress enable them to perform their jobs better by increasing their work intensity, alertness, and ability to react. However, a high level of stress, or even a moderate amount sustained over a long period, eventually takes its toll, and performance declines. The impact of stress on satisfaction is far more straightforward. Job-related tension tends to decrease general job satisfaction.[86] Even though low to moderate levels of stress may improve job performance, employees find stress dissatisfying.

Point / Counterpoint

Managing Change Is an Episodic Activity

Organizational change is an episodic activity. That is, it starts at some point, proceeds through a series of steps, and culminates in some outcome that those involved hope is an improvement over the starting point. It has a beginning, a middle, and an end.

Lewin's three-step model represents a classic illustration of this perspective. Change is seen as a break in the organization's equilibrium. The status quo has been disturbed, and change is necessary to establish a new equilibrium state. The objective of refreezing is to stabilize the new situation by balancing the driving and restraining forces.

Some experts have argued that organizational change should be thought of as balancing a system made up of five interacting variables within the organization—people, tasks, technology, structure, and strategy. A change in any one variable has repercussions on one or more of the others. This perspective is episodic in that it treats organizational change as essentially an effort to sustain equilibrium. A change in one variable begins a chain of events that, if properly managed, requires adjustments in the other variables to achieve a new state of equilibrium.

Another way to conceptualize the episodic view of looking at change is to think of managing change as analogous to captaining a ship. The organization is like a large ship traveling across the calm Mediterranean Sea to a specific port. The ship's captain has made this exact trip hundreds of times before with the same crew. Every once in a while, however, a storm will appear, and the crew has to respond. The captain will make the appropriate adjustments—that is, implement changes—and, having maneuvered through the storm, will return the ship to calm waters. Like this ship's voyage, managing an organization should be seen as a journey with a beginning and an end, and implementing change as a response to a break in the status quo and needed only occasionally.

The episodic approach may be the dominant paradigm for handling organizational change, but it has become obsolete. It applies to a world of certainty and predictability. The episodic approach was developed in the 1950s and 1960s, and it reflects the environment of those times. It treats change as the occasional disturbance in an otherwise peaceful world. However, it bears little resemblance to today's environment of constant and chaotic change.[87]

If you want to understand what it's like to manage change in today's organizations, think of it as equivalent to permanent white-water rafting.[88] The organization is not a large ship, but more akin to a 40-foot raft. Rather than sailing a calm sea, this raft must traverse a raging river made up of an uninterrupted flow of permanent white-water rapids. To make things worse, the raft is manned by 10 people who have never worked together or traveled the river before, much of the trip is in the dark, the river is dotted by unexpected turns and obstacles, the exact destination is not clear, and at irregular intervals the raft needs to pull to shore, where some new crew members are added and others leave. Change is a natural state and managing change is a continual process. That is, managers never get the luxury of escaping the white-water rapids.

The stability and predictability characterized by the episodic perspective no longer captures the world we live in. Disruptions in the status quo are not occasional, temporary, and followed by a return to an equilibrium state. There is, in fact, no equilibrium state. Managers today face constant change, bordering on chaos. They're being forced to play a game they've never played before, governed by rules that are created as the game progresses.

Questions for Review

1. What is meant by the phrase "we live in an age of discontinuity"?

2. "Resistance to change is an irrational response." Do you agree or disagree? Explain.

3. Why is participation considered such an effective technique for lessening resistance to change?

4. Why does change so frequently become a political issue in organizations?

5. How does Kotter's eight-step plan deal with resistance to change?

6. In an organization that has a history of "following the leader," what changes can be made to foster innovation?

7. "Learning organizations attack fragmentation, competitiveness, and reactiveness." Explain this statement.

8. How is change culture-bound?

9. How are opportunities, demands, and resources related to stress? Give an example of each.

10. What can organizations do to reduce employee stress?

Questions for Critical Thinking

1. How have changes in the workforce during the past 25 years affected organizational policies?

2. "Managing today is easier than at the turn of the twentieth century because the years of real change took place between the Civil War and World War I." Do you agree or disagree? Discuss.

3. Are all managers change agents? Discuss.

4. Discuss the link between learning theories discussed in Chapter 2 and the issue of organizational change.

5. Do you think the workplace today is more stressful than it was in the 1990s? Support your position.

Team Exercise

POWER AND THE CHANGING ENVIRONMENT

Objectives

1. To describe the forces for change influencing power differentials in organizational and interpersonal relationships.

2. To understand the effect of technological, legal/political, economic, and social changes on the power of individuals within an organization.

The Situation

Your organization manufactures golf carts and sells them to country clubs, golf courses, and consumers. Your team is faced with the task of assessing how environmental changes will affect individuals' organizational power. Read each of the five scenarios and then, for each, identify the five members in the organization whose power will increase most in light of the environmental condition(s).

(m) = male	(f) = female
Advertising expert (m)	Accountant-CPA (m)
Chief financial officer (f)	General manager (m)
Securities analyst (m)	Marketing manager (f)
Operations manager (f)	Computer programmer (f)
Industrial engineer (m)	Chemist (m)
Product designer (m)	In-house counsel (m)
Public relations expert (m)	Human resource manager (f)
Corporate trainer (m)	

1. New computer-aided manufacturing technologies are being introduced in the workplace during the upcoming 2 to 18 months.

2. New federal emission standards are being legislated by the government.

3. Sales are way down; the industry appears to be shrinking.

4. The company is planning to go international in the next 12 to 18 months.

5. The U.S. Equal Employment Opportunity Commission is applying pressure to balance the male–female population in the organization's upper hierarchy by threatening to publicize the predominance of men in upper management.

The Procedure

1. Divide the class into teams of three to four students each.

2. Teams should read each scenario and identify the five members whose power will increase most in light of the external environmental condition described.

3. Teams should then address the question: Assuming that the five environmental changes are taking place at once, which five members of the organization will now have the most power?

4. After 20 to 30 minutes, representatives of each team will be selected to present and justify their conclusions to the entire class. Discussion will begin with scenario 1 and proceed through to scenario 5 and the "all at once" scenario.

Source: Adapted from J. E. Barbuto Jr., "Power and the Changing Environment," *Journal of Management Education*, April 2000, pp. 288–96.

Ethical Dilemma

INCREASING EMPLOYEE PRODUCTIVITY AND STRESS

Ellen West supervises a staff of 15 people handling back-office functions for a regional brokerage firm in St. Louis. With company revenues down, Ellen's boss has put increasing pressure on her to improve her department's productivity.

The quickest way for Ellen to increase productivity in her department is to lay off two or three employees and fill the gap by asking the rest of the staff to work harder and put in more time on the job. Since all her employees are on salary, they are not paid for overtime. So if Ellen let three people go and asked her remaining staff to each put in an additional 10 hours a week on the job, she could effectively handle the same workload with 20 percent fewer employees.

As Ellen considered this idea, she had mixed feelings. Reducing her staff and asking people to work more hours would please her boss and increase job security for those people remaining. On the other hand, she was fearful that she was taking advantage of a weak labor market. Her employees knew that jobs were scarce and they would be hard put to find comparable positions elsewhere in the securities industry. They were unlikely to openly complain about working longer hours for fear that they, too, would be let go. But was it fair to increase the department's productivity on the backs of already hardworking employees? Was it ethical to ask her employees to put in 10 hours more a week, for no additional money, because the current weak labor market worked to her advantage? If you were Ellen West, what would you do?

Case Incident 1

GE'S WORK-OUT

General Electric established its Work-Out process in the early 1990s. It continues to be a mainstay in GE's efforts to initiate change. In the interim years, the Work-Out process has also been adopted by such diverse organizations as General Motors, Home Depot, Frito-Lay, L.L. Bean, Sears, IBM, and the World Bank.

The impetus for the Work-Out was the belief by GE's CEO that the company's culture was too bureaucratic and slow to respond to change. He wanted to create a vehicle that would effectively engage and empower GE workers.

Essentially, Work-Out brings together employees and managers from many different functions and levels within an organization for an informal 3-day meeting to discuss and solve problems that have been identified by employees or senior management. Set into small teams, people are encouraged to challenge prevailing assumptions about "the way we have always done things" and develop recommendations for significant improvements in organizational processes. The Work-Out teams then present their recommendations to a senior manager in a public gathering called a Town Meeting.

At the Town Meeting, the manager in charge oversees a discussion about the recommendation and then is required to make a yes-or-no decision on the spot. Only in unusual circumstances can a recommendation be tabled for further study. Recommendations that are accepted are assigned to managers who have volunteered to carry them out. Typically, a recommendation will move from inception to implementation in 90 days or less. The logic behind the Work-Out is to identify problems, stimulate diverse input, and provide a mechanism for speedy decision and action.

More recently, GE CEO Jeffrey Immelt has extended the Work-Out concept to build capabilities in anticipating future technologies and engage in long-range planning. GE wants all its managers to be adept at the kind of strategic thinking that most companies entrust only to senior management. For example, GE is offering managers new classes focused on learning how to create new lines of business.

Questions

1. What type of change process would you call this? Explain.

2. Why should it work?

3. What negative consequences do you think might result from this process?

4. Why do you think new GE CEO Jeff Immelt has revised the Work-Out concept?

Source: Based on D. Ulrich, S. Kerr, and R. Ashkenas, *The GE Work-Out* (New York: McGraw-Hill, 2002); and A. Kleiner, "GE's Next Workout," *strategy + business*, Winter 2004, pp. 1–5.

Case Incident 2

INNOVATING INNOVATION

Executives at Procter and Gamble (P&G) are quite happy these days. At the end of 2004, sales growth was up almost 27 percent and the company's stock price had nearly doubled. P&G's annual report to its stockholders stated that, "P&G exceeded all it financial goals in fiscal 2004." For a $51 billion consumer products company with 300 different brands, exceeding its goals is no small feat.

Many at P&G might point to chief technology officer Gil Cloyd as one of the sources of this success. Cloyd, who was the recipient of *Industry Week's* 2004 Technology Leader of the Year award, is changing how P&G approaches research and development (R&D). Given the enormous variety of products that P&G offers, including toilet paper, laundry detergents, personal care products, and pet food, the ability to sustain a competitive level of innovation is a tremendous challenge. Says Cloyd, "One of the challenges we have is serving the needs of a very diverse consumer population, but yet be able to do that quickly and very cost effectively. In the consumer products world we estimate that the required pace of innovation has doubled in the last three years. That means we have less time to benefit from any innovation that we bring into the marketplace." Cloyd's approach is simple yet complex: innovate innovation.

What is innovating innovation? As Cloyd explains, "What we've done is refine our thinking on how we conduct and evaluate research and development. We've made some changes. For example, historically, we tended to put the evaluation emphasis on technical product performance, patents, and other indicators of internal R&D efforts. Now there is more emphasis on perceived customer value." Cloyd describes P&G's innovation process as holistic, meaning it touches every department of an organization. Holistic innovation includes first setting appropriate financial goals and then implementing an innovation program for all aspects of the product—from its manufacturing technology to those aspects that the customer experiences directly, such as the product's packaging and appearance.

One of Cloyd's major goals at P&G is to acquire 50 percent of its product ideas from sources external to the organization. Cloyd is not there yet, but he likes his progress. Currently, P&G obtains 35 percent of its product ideas externally, and this number is up from 20 per-

cent in 2002 and 10 percent in 2000. Cloyd describes this goal as the "Connect + Develop (C+D) initiative." The C+D initiative is responsible for many of P&G's recent product successes. For example, C+D resulted in the Swiffer Wet Jet and Duster, Olay Daily Facials, and Crest Whitestrips. According to Henry Chesbrough, author of the book *Open Innovation*, C+D is successful because "Not all the smart people work for you," and "External ideas can help create value, but it takes internal R&D to claim a portion of that value for you."

Though P&G is enjoying enormous success due in part to its innovation program, Cloyd is not resting on his laurels. He emphasizes learning as a critical element to continued innovation success. One area that he is exploring is computer modeling and simulation. Previously, manufacturing was the main user of computer modeling. Now, Cloyd is using it in the product design process. Explains Cloyd, "A computational model helps us more quickly to understand what's going on. The simulation capabilities are also allowing us to interact with consumers much more quickly on design options. For example, Internet panels can engage consumers in as little as 24 hours. Digital technology is very important in helping us learn faster. Not only will it accelerate innovation, but the approach will greatly enhance the creativity of our people." By continually looking for new ways to design, produce, and market products, Cloyd and P&G are indeed "innovating innovation."

Questions

1. This book covered the notion of "idea champions." What characteristics of Gil Cloyd make him an idea champion?

2. Would you consider P&G to be a "learning organization?" What aspects of P&G lead you to your answer?

3. Although Cloyd is a major reason for P&G's innovation success, what are some structural features of P&G that might contribute to its ability to innovate so well?

4. The benefits of technological innovations for companies are often short-lived due to other companies adopting the same technology soon after. What factors do you believe contribute to P&G's ability to continually innovate at such a competitive level?

Source: Based on J. Teresko, "P&G's Secret: Innovating Innovation," *Industry Week*, December 2004, pp. 26–34.

Endnotes

1. Based on "New Management," http://www.samsung.com; W. J. Holstein, "Samsung's Golden Touch," *Fortune*, April 1, 2002, pp. 89–94; H. W. Choi, "Samsung Remakes Itself by Revamping Its Image," *The Wall Street Journal*, November 17, 2003, p. C3; and "Yun Jong Yong: Samsung," *Business Week*, January 12, 2004, p. 65.

2. L. Lee, "Taps for Music Retailers?" *Business Week*, June 23, 2003; and J. Scott, "Big Music Retailer Is Seeking Bankruptcy Protection," *The New York Times*, February 10, 2004, p. D1.

3. See, for instance, K. H. Hammonds, "Practical Radicals," *Fast Company*, September 2000, pp. 162–74; and P. C. Judge, "Change Agents," *Fast Company*, November 2000, pp. 216–26.

4. J. Taub, "Harvard Radical," *The New York Times Magazine*, August 24, 2003, pp. 28–45+.

5. M. S. Kraatz and J. H. Moore, "Executive Migration and Institutional Change," *Academy of Management Journal*, February 2002, pp. 120–43.

6. M. T. Hannan, L. Pólos, and G. R. Carroll, "The Fog of Change: Opacity and Asperity in Organizations," *Administrative Science Quarterly*, September 2003. pp. 399–432.

7. J. P. Kotter and L. A. Schlesinger, "Choosing Strategies for Change," *Harvard Business Review*, March–April 1979, pp. 106–14.

8. J. E. Dutton, S. J. Ashford, R. M. O'Neill, and K. A. Lawrence, "Moves that Matter: Issue Selling and Organizational Change," *Academy of Management Journal*, August 2001, pp. 716–36.

9. Q. N. Huy, "Emotional Balancing of Organizational Continuity and Radical Change: The Contribution of Middle Managers," *Administrative Science Quarterly*, March 2002, pp. 31–69.

10. J. A. LePine, J. A. Colquitt, and A. Erez, "Adaptability to Changing Task Contexts: Effects of General Cognitive Ability, Conscientiousness, and Openness to Experience," *Personnel Psychology*, Fall, 2000, pp. 563–93; T. A. Judge, C. J. Thoresen, V. Pucik, and T. M. Welbourne, "Managerial Coping with Organizational Change: A Dispositional Perspective," *Journal of Applied Psychology*, February 1999, pp. 107–22; and S. Oreg, "Resistance to Change: Developing an Individual Differences Measure," *Journal of Applied Psychology*, August 2003, pp. 680–93.

11. See J. Pfeffer, *Managing with Power: Politics and Influence in Organizations* (Boston: Harvard Business School Press, 1992), pp. 7, and 318–20; D. Knights and D. McCabe, "When 'Life Is but a Dream': Obliterating Politics Through Business Process Reengineering?" *Human Relations*, June 1998, pp. 761–98; and E. Porter, "Politics, Change and Reflective Practitioners," *Organization Development Journal*, Fall 2002, pp. 18–29.

12. See, for instance, W. Ocasio, "Political Dynamics and the Circulation of Power: CEO Succession in U.S. Industrial Corporations, 1960–1990," *Administrative Science Quarterly*, June 1994, pp. 285–312.

13. K. Lewin, *Field Theory in Social Science* (New York: Harper & Row, 1951).

14. P. G. Audia, E. A. Locke, and K. G. Smith, "The Paradox of Success: An Archival and a Laboratory Study of Strategic Persistence Following Radical Environmental Change," *Academy of Management Journal*, October 2000, pp. 837–53.

15. J. B. Sorensen, "The Strength of Corporate Culture and the Reliability of Firm Performance," *Administrative Science Quarterly*, March 2002, pp. 70–91.

16. J. Amis, T. Slack, and C. R. Hinings, "The Pace, Sequence, and Linearity of Radical Change," *Academy of Management Journal*, February 2004, pp. 15–39; and E. Autio, H. J. Sapienza, and J. G. Almeida, "Effects of Age at Entry, Knowledge Intensity, and Imitability on International Growth," *Academy of Management Journal*, October 2000, pp. 909–24.

17. J. P. Kotter, "Leading Changes: Why Transformation Efforts Fail," *Harvard Business Review*, March–April 1995, pp. 59–67; and J. P. Kotter, *Leading Change* (Harvard Business School Press, 1996).

18. See, for example, A. B. Shani and W. A. Pasmore, "Organization Inquiry: Towards a New Model of the Action Research Process," in D. D. Warrick (ed.), *Contemporary Organization Development: Current Thinking and Applications* (Glenview, IL: Scott, Foresman, 1985), pp. 438–48; and C. Eden and C. Huxham, "Action Research for the Study of Organizations," in S. R. Clegg, C. Hardy, and W. R. Nord (eds.), *Handbook of Organization Studies* (London: Sage, 1996).

19. For a sampling of various OD definitions, see N. Nicholson (ed.), *Encyclopedic Dictionary of Organizational Behavior* (Malden, MA: Blackwell, 1998), pp. 359–61; G. Farias and H. Johnson, "Organizational Development and Change Management," *Journal of Applied Behavioral Science*, September 2000, pp. 376–79; and H. K. Sinangil and F. Avallone, "Organizational Development and Change," in N. Anderson, D. S. Ones, H. K. Sinangil, and C. Viswesvaran (eds.), *Handbook of Industrial, Work and Organizational Psychology*, vol. 2 (Thousand Oaks, CA: Sage, 2001), pp. 332–35.

20. See, for instance, W. A. Pasmore and M. R. Fagans, "Participation, Individual Development, and Organizational Change: A Review and Synthesis," *Journal of Management*, June 1992, pp. 375–97; T. G. Cummings and C .G. Worley, *Organization Development and Change*, 7th ed. (Cincinnati: Southwestern, 2001); and R. Lines, "Influence of Participation in Strategic Change: Resistance, Organizational Commitment and Change Goal Achievement," *Journal of Change Management*, September 2004, pp. 193–215.

21. S. Highhouse, "A History of the T-Group and Its Early Application in Management Development," *Group Dynamics: Theory, Research, & Practice*, December 2002, pp. 277–90.

22. J. E. Edwards and M. D. Thomas, "The Organizational Survey Process: General Steps and Practical Considerations," in P. Rosenfeld, J. E. Edwards, and M. D. Thomas (eds.), *Improving Organizational Surveys: New Directions, Methods, and Applications* (Newbury Park, CA: Sage, 1993), pp. 3–28.

23. E. H. Schein, *Process Consultation: Its Role in Organizational Development*, 2nd ed. (Reading, MA: Addison-Wesley, 1988), p. 9. See also E. H. Schein, *Process Consultation Revisited: Building Helpful Relationships* (Reading, MA: Addison-Wesley, 1999).

24. Ibid.

25. W. Dyer, *Team Building: Issues and Alternatives* (Reading, MA: Addison-Wesley, 1994).

26. See, for example, E. H. Neilsen, "Understanding and Managing Intergroup Conflict," in J. W. Lorsch and P. R.

Lawrence (eds.), *Managing Group and Intergroup Relations* (Homewood, IL: Irwin-Dorsey, 1972), pp. 329–43.

27. R. R. Blake, J. S. Mouton, and R. L. Sloma, "The Union–Management Intergroup Laboratory: Strategy for Resolving Intergroup Conflict," *Journal of Applied Behavioral Science*, no. 1 (1965), pp. 25–57.

28. See, for example, G. R. Bushe, "Advances in Appreciative Inquiry as an Organization Development Intervention," *Organizational Development Journal*, Summer 1999, pp. 61–68; D. L. Cooperrider and D. Whitney, *Collaborating for Change: Appreciative Inquiry* (San Francisco: Berrett-Koehler, 2000); R. Fry, F. Barrett, J. Seiling, and D. Whitney (eds.), *Appreciative Inquiry & Organizational Transformation: Reports From the Field* (Westport, CT: Quorum, 2002); J. K. Barge and C. Oliver, "Working With Appreciation in Managerial Practice," *Academy of Management Review*, January 2003, pp. 124–42; and D. van der Haar, and D. M. Hosking, "Evaluating Appreciative Inquiry: A Relational Constructionist Perspective," *Human Relations*, August 2004, pp. 1017–36.

29. J. Gordon, "Meet the Freight Fairy," *Forbes*, January 20, 2003, p. 65.

30. See, for example, H. S. Gitlow, *Quality Management Systems: A Practical Guide for Improvement* (Boca Raton, FL: CRC Press, 2001); and J. W. Cortada, *The Quality Yearbook 2001* (New York: McGraw-Hill, 2001).

31. M. Hammer and J. Champy, *Reengineering the Corporation: A Manifesto for Business Revolution* (New York: Harper-Business, 1993).

32. D. Anfuso, "Core Values Shape W. L. Gore's Innovative Culture," *Workforce*, March 1999, pp. 48–51; and A. Harrington, "Who's Afraid of a New Product?" *Fortune*, November 10, 2003, pp. 189–92.

33. See, for instance, A. Van de Ven, "Central Problems in the Management of Innovation," *Management Science* 32 (1986), pp. 590–607; and R. M. Kanter, "When a Thousand Flowers Bloom: Structural, Collective and Social Conditions for Innovation in Organizations," in B. M. Staw and L. L. Cummings (eds.), *Research in Organizational Behavior*, vol. 10 (Greenwich, CT: JAI Press, 1988), pp. 169–211.

34. F. Damanpour, "Organizational Innovation: A Meta-Analysis of Effects of Determinants and Moderators," *Academy of Management Journal*, September 1991, p. 557.

35. Ibid., pp. 555–90.

36. See also P. R. Monge, M. D. Cozzens, and N. S. Contractor, "Communication and Motivational Predictors of the Dynamics of Organizational Innovation," *Organization Science*, May 1992, pp. 250–74.

37. J. M. Howell and C. A. Higgins, "Champions of Change," *Business Quarterly*, Spring 1990, pp. 31–32; and D. L. Day, "Raising Radicals: Different Processes for Championing Innovative Corporate Ventures," *Organization Science*, May 1994, pp. 148–72.

38. Howell and Higgins, "Champions of Change."

39. See, for example, the special edition on organizational learning in *Organizational Dynamics*, Autumn 1998; P. Senge, *The Dance of Change: The Challenges to Sustaining Momentum in Learning Organizations* (New York: Doubleday/Currency, 1999); A. M. Webber, "Will Companies Ever Learn?" *Fast Company*, October 2000, pp. 275–82; R. Snell, "Moral Foundations of the Learning Organization," *Human Relations*, March 2001, pp.

319–42; M. M. Brown and J. L. Brudney, "Learning Organizations in the Public Sector? A Study of Police Agencies Employing Information and Technology to Advance Knowledge," *Public Administration Review*, January/February 2003, pp. 30–43; and T. B. Lawrence, M. K. Mauws, B. Dyck, and R. F. Kleysen, "The Politics of Organizational Learning: Integrating Power Into the 4I Framework," *Academy of Management Review*, January 2005, pp. 180–91.

40. D. H. Kim, "The Link Between Individual and Organizational Learning," *Sloan Management Review*, Fall 1993, p. 37.

41. C. Argyris and D. A. Schon, *Organizational Learning* (Reading, MA: Addison-Wesley, 1978).

42. B. Dumaine, "Mr. Learning Organization," *Fortune*, October 17, 1994, p. 148.

43. F. Kofman and P. M. Senge, "Communities of Commitment: The Heart of Learning Organizations," *Organizational Dynamics*, Autumn 1993, pp. 5–23.

44. Dumaine, "Mr. Learning Organization," p. 154.

45. L. Smith, "New Ideas from the Army (Really)," *Fortune*, September 19, 1994, pp. 203–12; and L. Baird, P. Holland, and S. Deacon, "Imbedding More Learning into the Performance Fast Enough to Make a Difference," *Organizational Dynamics*, Spring 1999, pp. 19–32.

46. See S. Shane, S. Venkataraman, and I. MacMillan, "Cultural Differences in Innovation Championing Strategies," *Journal of Management* 21, no. 5 (1995), pp. 931–52.

47. See, for instance, K. Slobogin, "Many U.S. Employees Feel Overworked, Stressed, Study Says," www.cnn.com (May 16, 2001); and S. Armour, "Rising Job Stress Could Affect Bottom Line," *USA Today*, July 29, 2003, p. 1B.

48. Adapted from R. S. Schuler, "Definition and Conceptualization of Stress in Organizations," *Organizational Behavior and Human Performance*, April 1980, p. 189. For an updated review of definitions, see C. L. Cooper, P. J. Dewe, and M. P. O'Driscoll, *Organizational Stress: A Review and Critique of Theory, Research, and Applications* (Thousand Oaks, CA: Sage, 2002).

49. See, for instance, M. A. Cavanaugh, W. R. Boswell, M. V. Roehling, and J. W. Boudreau, "An Empirical Examination of Self-Reported Work Stress Among U.S. Managers," *Journal of Applied Psychology*, February 2000, pp. 65–74.

50. J. A. LePine, M. A. LePine, and C. L. Jackson, "Challenge and Hindrance Stress: Relationships With Exhaustion, Motivation to Learn, and Learning Performance," *Journal of Applied Psychology*, October 2004, pp. 883–91; and M. A. Cavanaugh, W. R. Boswell, M. V. Roehling, and J. W. Boudreau, "An Empirical Examination of Self-reported Work Stress Among U.S. Managers," *Journal of Applied Psychology*, February 2000, pp. 65–74.

51. E. Demerouti, A. B. Bakker, F. Nachreiner, and W. B. Schaufeli, "The Job Demands-Resources Model of Burnout," *Journal of Applied Psychology*, June 2001, pp. 499–512; N. W. Van Yperen and O. Janssen, "Fatigued and Dissatisfied or Fatigued but Satisfied? Goal Orientations and Responses to High Job Demands," *Academy of Management Journal*, December 2002, pp. 1161–71; and N. W. Van Yperen and M. Hagedoorn, "Do High Job Demands Increase Intrinsic Motivation or Fatigue or Both? The Role of Job Control and Job Social Support," *Academy of Management Journal*, June 2003, pp. 339–48.

52. P. E. Spector et al., "A Cross-National Comparative Study of Work-Family Stressors, Working Hours, and Well-Being:

China and Latin America Versus the Anglo World," *Personnel Psychology*, Spring 2004, pp. 119–42.

53. This model is based on D. F. Parker and T. A. DeCotiis, "Organizational Determinants of Job Stress," *Organizational Behavior and Human Performance*, October 1983, p. 166, S. Parasuraman and J. A. Alutto, "Sources and Outcomes of Stress in Organizational Settings: Toward the Development of a Structural Model," *Academy of Management Journal*, June 1984, p. 333; and R. L. Kahn and P. Byosiere, "Stress in Organizations," p. 592.

54. This section is adapted from C. L. Cooper and R. Payne, *Stress at Work* (London: Wiley, 1978); Parasuraman and Alutto, "Sources and Outcomes of Stress in Organizational Settings," pp 330–50; and P. M. Hart and C. L. Cooper, "Occupational Stress: Toward a More Integrated Framework," in N. Anderson, D. S. Ones, H. K. Sinangil, and C. Viswesvaran (eds.), *Handbook of Industrial, Work and Organizational Psychology*, vol. 2, pp. (London: Sage, 93–114).

55. H. Garst, M. Frese, and P. C. M. Molenaar, "The Temporal Factor of Change in Stressor-Strain Relationships: A Growth Curve Model on a Longitudinal Study in East Germany," *Journal of Applied Psychology*, June 2000, pp. 417–38.

56. See, for example, D. R. Frew and N. S. Bruning, "Perceived Organizational Characteristics and Personality Measures as Predictors of Stress/Strain in the Work Place," *Journal of Management*, Winter 1987, pp. 633–46; and M. L. Fox, D. J. Dwyer, and D. C. Ganster, "Effects of Stressful Job Demands and Control of Physiological and Attitudinal Outcomes in a Hospital Setting," *Academy of Management Journal*, April 1993, pp. 289–318.

57. G. W. Evans and D. Johnson, "Stress and Open-Office Noise," *Journal of Applied Psychology*, October 2000, pp. 779–83.

58. T. M. Glomb, J. D. Kammeyer-Mueller, and M. Rotundo, "Emotional Labor Demands and Compensating Wage Differentials," *Journal of Applied Psychology*, August 2004. pp. 700–14; A. A. Grandey, "When 'The Show Must Go On': Surface Acting and Deep Acting as Determinants of Emotional Exhaustion and Peer-Rated Service Delivery," *Academy of Management Journal*, February 2003, pp. 86–96.

59. V. S. Major, K. J. Klein, and M. G. Ehrhart, "Work Time, Work Interference with Family, and Psychological Distress," *Journal of Applied Psychology*, June 2002, pp. 427–36; see also P. E. Spector, C. L. Cooper, S. Poelmans, T. D. Allen, M. O'Driscoll, J. I. Sanchez, O. L. Siu, P. Dewe, P. Hart, L. Lu, L. F. R. De Moreas, G. M. Ostrognay, K. Sparks, P. Wong, and S. Yu, "A Cross-National Comparative Study of Work-Family Stressors, Working Hours, and Well-Being: China and Latin America Versus the Anglo World," *Personnel Psychology*, Spring 2004, pp. 119–42.

60. D. L. Nelson and C. Sutton, "Chronic Work Stress and Coping: A Longitudinal Study and Suggested New Directions," *Academy of Management Journal*, December 1990, pp. 859–69.

61. H. Selye, *The Stress of Life*, rev. ed. (New York: McGraw-Hill, 1956).

62. S. J. Motowidlo, J. S. Packard, and M. R. Manning, "Occupational Stress: Its Causes and Consequences for Job Performance," *Journal of Applied Psychology*, November 1987, pp. 619–20.

63. See, for instance, R. C. Cummings, "Job Stress and the Buffering Effect of Supervisory Support," *Group & Organization Studies*, March 1990, pp. 92–104; M. R. Manning, C. N. Jackson, and M. R. Fusilier, "Occupational Stress, Social Support, and the Cost of Health Care," *Academy of Management Journal*, June 1996, pp. 738–50; P. D. Bliese and T. W. Britt, "Social Support, Group Consensus and Stressor-Strain Relationships: Social Context Matters," *Journal of Organizational Behavior*, June 2001, pp. 425–36; and C. L. Stamper and M. C. Johlke, "The Impact of Perceived Organizational Support on the Relationship Between Boundary Spanner Role Stress and Work Outcomes," *Journal of Management* 29, no. 4 (2003), pp. 569–88.

64. P. E. Spector et al., "Locus of Control and Well-Being at Work: How Generalizable Are Western Findings?" *Academy of Management Journal*, April 2002, pp. 453–66.

65. S. M. Jex, P. D. Bliese, S. Buzzell, and J. Primeau, ", The Impact of Self-Efficacy on Stressor-Strain Relations: Coping Style as an Explanatory Mechanism," *Journal of Applied Psychology*, June 2001, pp. 401–09; and J. Schaubroeck, S. S. K. Lam, and J. L. Xie, "Collective Efficacy versus Self-Efficacy in Coping Responses to Stressors and Control: A Cross-Cultural Study," *Journal of Applied Psychology*, August 2000, pp. 512–25.

66. R. Williams, *The Trusting Heart: Great News About Type A Behavior* (New York: Times Books, 1989).

67. Schuler, "Definition and Conceptualization of Stress," pp. 200–05; and Kahn and Byosiere, "Stress in Organizations," pp. 604–10.

68. See T. A. Beehr and J. E. Newman, "Job Stress, Employee Health, and Organizational Effectiveness: A Facet Analysis, Model, and Literature Review," *Personnel Psychology*, Winter 1978, pp. 665–99; and B. D. Steffy and J. W. Jones, "Workplace Stress and Indicators of Coronary-Disease Risk," *Academy of Management Journal*, September 1988, pp. 686–98.

69. J. Schaubroeck, J. R. Jones, and J. L. Xie, "Individual Differences in Utilizing Control to Cope with Job Demands: Effects on Susceptibility to Infectious Disease," *Journal of Applied Psychology*, April 2001, pp. 265–78.

70. Steffy and Jones, "Workplace Stress and Indicators of Coronary-Disease Risk," p. 687.

71. C. L. Cooper and J. Marshall, "Occupational Sources of Stress: A Review of the Literature Relating to Coronary Heart Disease and Mental Ill Health," *Journal of Occupational Psychology* 49, no. 1 (1976), pp. 11–28.

72. J. R. Hackman and G. R. Oldham, "Development of the Job Diagnostic Survey," *Journal of Applied Psychology*, April 1975, pp. 159–70.

73. E. M. de Croon, J. K. Sluiter, R. W. B. Blonk, J. P. J. Broersen, and M. H. W. Frings-Dresen, "Stressful Work, Psychological Job Strain, and Turnover: A 2-Year Prospective Cohort Study of Truck Drivers," *Journal of Applied Psychology*, June 2004, pp. 442–54; and R. Cropanzano, D. E. Rupp, and Z. S. Byrne, "The Relationship of Emotional Exhaustion to Work Attitudes, Job Performance, and Organizational Citizenship Behaviors," *Journal of Applied Psychology*, February 2003. pp. 160–69.

74. See, for instance, J. M. Ivancevich and M. T. Matteson, *Stress and Work* (Glenview, IL: Scott, Foresman, 1981); R. D. Allen, M. A. Hitt, and C. R. Greer, "Occupational Stress and Perceived Organizational Effectiveness in Formal Groups: An Examination of Stress Level and Stress Type," *Personnel Psychology*, Summer 1982, pp. 359–70; and S. Zivnuska, C. Kiewitz, W. A. Hochwarter, P. L. Perrewe, and K. L. Zellars, "What Is Too Much or Too Little? The Curvilinear Effects of Job Tension on Turnover Intent, Value Attainment, and Job

Satisfaction," *Journal of Applied Social Psychology*, July 2002, pp. 1344–60.

75. S. E. Sullivan and R. S. Bhagat, "Organizational Stress, Job Satisfaction and Job Performance: Where Do We Go From Here?" *Journal of Management*, June 1992, pp. 361–64; and M. Westman and D. Eden, "The Inverted-U Relationship between Stress and Performance: A Field Study," *Work & Stress*, Spring 1996, pp. 165–73; and L. A. Muse, S. G. Harris, and H. S. Field, "Has the Inverted-U Theory of Stress and Job Performance Had a Fair Test?" *Human Performance* 16, no. 4 (2003), pp. 349–364.

76. The following discussion has been influenced by J. E. Newman and T. A. Beehr, "Personal and Organizational Strategies for Handling Job Stress," *Personnel Psychology*, Spring 1979, pp. 1–38; J. M. Ivancevich and M. T. Matteson, "Organizational Level Stress Management Interventions: A Review and Recommendations," *Journal of Organizational Behavior Management*, Fall–Winter 1986, pp. 229–48; M. T. Matteson and J. M. Ivancevich, "Individual Stress Management Interventions: Evaluation of Techniques," *Journal of Management Psychology*, January 1987, pp. 24–30; J. M. Ivancevich, M. T. Matteson, S. M. Freedman, and J. S. Phillips, "Worksite Stress Management Interventions," *American Psychologist*, February 1990, pp. 252–61; and R. Schwarzer, "Manage Stress at Work Through Preventive and Proactive Coping," in E. A. Locke (ed.), *Handbook of Principles of Organizational Behavior* (Malden, MA: Blackwell, 2004), pp. 342–55.

77. T. H. Macan, "Time Management: Test of a Process Model," *Journal of Applied Psychology*, June 1994, pp. 381–91; and B. J. C. Claessens, W. Van Eerde, C. G. Rutte, and R. A. Roe, "Planning Behavior and Perceived Control of Time at Work," *Journal of Organizational Behavior*, December 2004, pp. 937–50.

78. See, for example, G. Lawrence-Ell, *The Invisible Clock: A Practical Revolution in Finding Time for Everyone and Everything* (Seaside Park, NJ: Kingsland Hall, 2002); and B. Tracy, *Time Power* (New York: AMACOM, 2004).

79. J. Kiely and G. Hodgson, "Stress in the Prison Service: The Benefits of Exercise Programs," *Human Relations*, June 1990, pp. 551–72.

80. E. J. Forbes and R. J. Pekala, "Psychophysiological Effects of Several Stress Management Techniques," *Psychological Reports*, February 1993, pp. 19–27; and M. Der Hovanesian, "Zen and the Art of Corporate Productivity," *Business Week*, July 28, 2003, p. 56.

81. S. E. Jackson, "Participation in Decision Making as a Strategy for Reducing Job-Related Strain," *Journal of Applied Psychology*, February 1983, pp. 3–19.

82. S. Greengard, "It's About Time," *Industry Week*, February 7, 2000, pp. 47–50; and S. Nayyar, "Gimme a Break," *American Demographics*, June 2002, p. 6.

83. See, for instance, B. Leonard, "Health Care Costs Increase Interest in Wellness Programs," *HRMagazine*, September 2001, pp. 35–36; and "Healthy, Happy and Productive," *Training*, February 2003, p. 16.

84. D. Brown, "Wellness Programs Bring Healthy Bottom Line," *Canadian HR Reporter*, December 17, 2001, p. 1+.

85. P. S. Goodman and L. B. Kurke, "Studies of Change in Organizations: A Status Report," in P. S. Goodman (ed.), *Change in Organizations* (San Francisco: Jossey-Bass, 1982), p. 1.

86. Kahn and Byosiere, "Stress in Organizations," pp. 605–08.

87. For contrasting views on episodic and continuous change, see K. E. Weick and R. E. Quinn, "Organizational Change and Development," in J. T. Spence, J. M. Darley, and D. J. Foss (eds.), *Annual Review of Psychology*, vol. 50 (Palo Alto, CA: Annual Reviews, 1999), pp. 361–86.

88. This perspective is based on P. B. Vaill, *Managing as a Performing Art: New Ideas for a World of Chaotic Change* (San Francisco: Jossey-Bass, 1989).

Appendix A
Research in Organizational Behavior

For every complex problem, there is a solution
that is simple, neat, and wrong.

—H.L. Mencken

A number of years ago, a friend of mine was all excited because he had read about the findings from a research study that finally, once and for all, resolved the question of what it takes to make it to the top in a large corporation. I doubted there was any simple answer to this question but, not wanting to dampen his enthusiasm, I asked him to tell me of what he had read. The answer, according to my friend, was *participation in college athletics*. To say I was skeptical of his claim is a gross understatement, so I asked him to tell me more.

The study encompassed 1,700 successful senior executives at the 500 largest U.S. corporations. The researchers found that half of these executives had played varsity-level college sports.[1] My friend, who happens to be good with statistics, informed me that since fewer than 2 percent of all college students participate in intercollegiate athletics, the probability of this finding occurring by mere chance is less than 1 in 10 million! He concluded his analysis by telling me that, based on this research, I should encourage my management students to get into shape and to make one of the varsity teams.

My friend was somewhat perturbed when I suggested that his conclusions were likely to be flawed. These executives were all males who attended college in the 1940s and 1950s. Would his advice be meaningful to females in the twenty-first century? These executives also weren't your typical college students. For the most part, they had attended elite private colleges such as Princeton and Amherst, where a large proportion of the student body participates in intercollegiate sports. And these "jocks" hadn't necessarily played football or basketball; many had participated in golf, tennis, baseball, cross-country running, crew, rugby, and similar minor sports. Moreover, maybe the researchers had confused the direction of causality. That is, maybe individuals with the motivation and ability to make it to the top of a large corporation are drawn to competitive activities like college athletics.

My friend was guilty of misusing research data. Of course, he is not alone. We are all continually bombarded with reports of experiments that link certain substances to cancer in mice and surveys that show changing attitudes toward sex among college students, for example. Many of these studies are carefully designed, with great caution taken to note the implications and limitations of the findings. But some studies are poorly designed, making their conclusions at best suspect, and at worst meaningless.

Rather than attempting to make you a researcher, the purpose of this appendix is to increase your awareness as a consumer of behavioral research. A knowledge of research methods will allow you to appreciate more fully the care in data collection that underlies the information and conclusions presented in this text. Moreover, an understanding of research methods will make you a more skilled evaluator of the OB studies you will encounter in business and professional journals. So an appreciation of behavioral research is important because (1) it's the foundation on which the theories in this text are built, and (2) it will benefit you in future years when you read reports of research and attempt to assess their value.

Purposes of Research

Research is concerned with the systematic gathering of information. Its purpose is to help us in our search for the truth. Although we will never find ultimate truth—in our case, that would be to know precisely how any person or group would behave in any organizational context—ongoing research adds to our body of OB knowledge by supporting some theories, contradicting others, and suggesting new theories to replace those that fail to gain support.

Research Terminology

Researchers have their own vocabulary for communicating among themselves and with outsiders. The following briefly defines some of the more popular terms you're likely to encounter in behavioral science studies.[2]

Variable

A *variable* is any general characteristic that can be measured and that changes in amplitude, intensity, or both. Some examples of OB variables found in this textbook are job satisfaction, employee productivity, work stress, ability, personality, and group norms.

Hypothesis

A tentative explanation of the relationship between two or more variables is called a *hypothesis*. My friend's statement that participation in college athletics leads to a top executive position in a large corporation is an example of a hypothesis. Until confirmed by empirical research, a hypothesis remains only a tentative explanation.

Dependent Variable

A *dependent variable* is a response that is affected by an independent variable. In terms of the hypothesis, it is the variable that the researcher is interested in explaining. Referring back to our opening example, the dependent variable in my friend's hypothesis was executive succession. In organizational behavior research, the most popular dependent variables are productivity, absenteeism, turnover, job satisfaction, and organizational commitment.[3]

Independent Variable

An *independent variable* is the presumed cause of some change in the dependent variable. Participating in varsity athletics was the independent variable in my friend's hypothesis. Popular independent variables studied by OB researchers include intelligence, personality, job satisfaction, experience, motivation, reinforcement patterns, leadership style, reward allocations, selection methods, and organization design.

You may have noticed we said that job satisfaction is frequently used by OB researchers as both a dependent and an independent variable. This is not an error. It merely reflects that the label given to a variable depends on its place in the hypothesis. In the statement "Increases in job satisfaction lead to reduced turnover," job satisfaction is an independent variable. However, in the statement "Increases in money lead to higher job satisfaction," job satisfaction becomes a dependent variable.

Moderating Variable

A *moderating variable* abates the effect of the independent variable on the dependent variable. It might also be thought of as the contingency variable: If X (independent variable), then Y (dependent variable) will occur, but only under conditions Z (moderating variable). To translate this into a real-life example, we might say that if we increase the amount of direct supervision in the work area (X), then there will be a change in worker productivity (Y), but this effect will be moderated by the complexity of the tasks being performed (Z).

Causality

A hypothesis, by definition, implies a relationship. That is, it implies a presumed cause and effect. This direction of cause and effect is called *causality*. Changes in the independent variable are assumed to cause changes

in the dependent variable. However, in behavioral research, it's possible to make an incorrect assumption of causality when relationships are found. For example, early behavioral scientists found a relationship between employee satisfaction and productivity. They concluded that a happy worker was a productive worker. Follow-up research has supported the relationship, but disconfirmed the direction of the arrow. The evidence more correctly suggests that high productivity leads to satisfaction rather than the other way around.

Correlation Coefficient

It's one thing to know that there is a relationship between two or more variables. It's another to know the *strength* of that relationship. The term *correlation coefficient* is used to indicate that strength, and is expressed as a number between -1.00 (a perfect negative relationship) and $+1.00$ (a perfect positive correlation).

When two variables vary directly with one another, the correlation will be expressed as a positive number. When they vary inversely—that is, one increases as the other decreases—the correlation will be expressed as a negative number. If the two variables vary independently of each other, we say that the correlation between them is zero.

For example, a researcher might survey a group of employees to determine the satisfaction of each with his or her job. Then, using company absenteeism reports, the researcher could correlate the job satisfaction scores against individual attendance records to determine whether employees who are more satisfied with their jobs have better attendance records than their counterparts who indicated lower job satisfaction. Let's suppose the researcher found a correlation coefficient of $+0.50$ between satisfaction and attendance. Would that be a strong association? There is, unfortunately, no precise numerical cutoff separating strong and weak relationships. A standard statistical test would need to be applied to determine whether the relationship was a significant one.

A final point needs to be made before we move on: A correlation coefficient measures only the strength of association between two variables. A high value does *not* imply causality. The length of women's skirts and stock market prices, for instance, have long been noted to be highly correlated, but one should be careful not to infer that a causal relationship between the two exists. In this instance, the high correlation is more happenstance than predictive.

Theory

The final term we introduce in this section is *theory*. Theory describes a set of systematically interrelated concepts or hypotheses that purports to explain and predict phenomena. In OB, theories are also frequently referred to as *models*. We use the two terms interchangeably.

There are no shortages of theories in OB. For instance, we have theories to describe what motivates people, the most effective leadership styles, the best way to resolve conflicts, and how people acquire power. In some cases, we have half a dozen or more separate theories that purport to explain and predict a given phenomenon. In such cases, is one right and the others wrong? No! They tend to reflect science at work—researchers testing previous theories, modifying them, and, when appropriate, proposing new models that may prove to have higher explanatory and predictive powers. Multiple theories attempting to explain common phenomena merely attest that OB is an active discipline, still growing and evolving.

Evaluating Research

As a potential consumer of behavioral research, you should follow the dictum of *caveat emptor*—let the buyer beware! In evaluating any research study, you need to ask three questions.[4]

Is it valid? Is the study actually measuring what it claims to be measuring? A number of psychological tests have been discarded by employers in recent years because they have not been found to be valid measures of the applicants' ability to do a given job successfully. But the validity issue is relevant to all research studies. So, if you find a study that links cohesive work teams with higher productivity, you want to know how each of these variables was measured and whether it is actually measuring what it is supposed to be measuring.

Is it reliable? Reliability refers to consistency of measurement. If you were to have your height measured every day with a wooden yardstick, you'd get highly reliable results. On the other hand, if you were measured each day by an elastic tape measure, there would probably be considerable disparity between your height measurements from one day to the next. Your height, of course, doesn't change from day to day. The variability is due to the unreliability of the measuring device. So if a company asked a group of its employees to complete a reliable job satisfaction questionnaire, and then repeat the questionnaire six months later, we'd expect the results to be very similar—provided nothing changed in the interim that might significantly affect employee satisfaction.

Is it generalizable? Are the results of the research study generalizable to groups of individuals other than those who participated in the original study? Be aware, for example, of the limitations that might exist in research that uses college students as subjects. Are the findings in such studies generalizable to full-time employees in real jobs? Similarly, how generalizable to the overall work population are the results from a study that assesses job stress among 10 nuclear power plant engineers in the hamlet of Mahone Bay, Nova Scotia?

Research Design

Doing research is an exercise in trade-offs. Richness of information typically comes with reduced generalizability. The more a researcher seeks to control for confounding variables, the less realistic his or her results are likely to be. High precision, generalizability, and control almost always translate into higher costs. When researchers make choices about whom they'll study, where their research will be done, the methods they'll use to collect data, and so on, they must make some concessions. Good research designs are not perfect, but they do carefully reflect the questions being addressed. Keep these facts in mind as we review the strengths and weaknesses of five popular research designs: case studies, field surveys, laboratory experiments, field experiments, and aggregate quantitative reviews.

Case Study

You pick up a copy of Soichiro Honda's autobiography. In it he describes his impoverished childhood; his decisions to open a small garage, assemble motorcycles, and eventually build automobiles; and how this led to the creation of one of the largest and most successful corporations in the world. Or you're in a business class and the instructor distributes a 50-page handout covering two companies: Wal-Mart and Kmart. The handout details the two firms' histories; describes their corporate strategies, management philosophies, and merchandising plans; and includes copies of their recent balance sheets and income statements. The instructor asks the class members to read the handout, analyze the data, and determine why Wal-Mart has been so much more successful than Kmart in recent years.

Soichiro Honda's autobiography and the Wal-Mart and Kmart handouts are case studies. Drawn from real-life situations, case studies present an in-depth analysis of one setting. They are thorough descriptions, rich in details about an individual, a group, or an organization. The primary source of information in case studies is obtained through observation, occasionally backed up by interviews and a review of records and documents.

Case studies have their drawbacks. They're open to the perceptual bias and subjective interpretations of the observer. The reader of a case is captive to what the observer/case writer chooses to include and exclude. Cases also trade off generalizability for depth of information and richness of detail. Because it's always dangerous to generalize from a sample of one, case studies make it difficult to prove or reject a hypothesis. On the other hand, you can't ignore the in-depth analysis that cases often provide. They are an excellent device for initial exploratory research and for evaluating real-life problems in organizations.

Field Survey

A lengthy questionnaire was created to assess the use of ethics policies, formal ethics structures, formalized activities such as ethics training, and executive involvement in ethics programs among billion-dollar corporations. The public affairs or corporate communications office of all *Fortune* 500 industrial firms and 500 service corporations were contacted to get the name and address of the "officer most responsible for dealing with ethics and conduct issues" in each firm. The questionnaire, with a cover letter explaining the nature of the study, was mailed to these 1,000 officers. Of the total, 254 returned a completed questionnaire, for a response rate just above 25 percent. The results of the survey found, among other things, that 77 percent had formal codes of ethics and 54 percent had a single officer specifically assigned to deal with ethics and conduct issues.[5]

The preceding study illustrates a typical field survey. A sample of respondents (in this case, 1,000 corporate officers in the largest U.S. publicly held corporations) was selected to represent a larger group that was under examination (billion-dollar U.S. business firms). The respondents were then surveyed using a questionnaire or interviewed to collect data on particular characteristics (the content and structure of ethics programs and practices) of interest to the researchers. The standardization of response items allows for data to be easily quantified, analyzed, and summarized, and for the researchers to make inferences from the representative sample about the larger population.

The field survey provides economies for doing research. It's less costly to sample a population than to obtain data from every member of that population. (There are, for instance, more than 5,000 U.S. business firms with sales in excess of a billion dollars; and since some of these are privately held and don't release financial data to the public, they are excluded from the *Fortune* list). Moreover, as the ethics study illustrates, field surveys provide an efficient way to find out how people feel about issues or how they say they behave. These data can then be easily quantified.

But the field survey has a number of potential weaknesses. First, mailed questionnaires rarely obtain 100 percent returns. Low response rates call into question whether conclusions based on respondents' answers are generalizable to nonrespondents. Second, the format is better at tapping respondents' attitudes and perceptions than behaviors. Third, responses can suffer from social desirability; that is, people saying what they think

the researcher wants to hear. Fourth, since field surveys are designed to focus on specific issues, they're a relatively poor means of acquiring depth of information. Finally, the quality of the generalizations is largely a factor of the population chosen. Responses from executives at *Fortune* 500 firms, for instance, tell us nothing about small- or medium-sized firms or not-for-profit organizations. In summary, even a well-designed field survey trades off depth of information for breadth, generalizability, and economic efficiencies.

Laboratory Experiment

The following study is a classic example of the laboratory experiment. A researcher, Stanley Milgram, wondered how far individuals would go in following commands. If subjects were placed in the role of a teacher in a learning experiment and told by an experimenter to administer a shock to a learner each time that learner made a mistake, would the subjects follow the commands of the experimenter? Would their willingness to comply decrease as the intensity of the shock was increased?

To test these hypotheses, Milgram hired a set of subjects. Each was led to believe that the experiment was to investigate the effect of punishment on memory. Their job was to act as teachers and administer punishment whenever the learner made a mistake on the learning test.

Punishment was administered by an electric shock. The subject sat in front of a shock generator with 30 levels of shock—beginning at zero and progressing in 15-volt increments to a high of 450 volts. The demarcations of these positions ranged from "Slight Shock" at 15 volts to "Danger: Severe Shock" at 450 volts. To increase the realism of the experiment, the subjects received a sample shock of 45 volts and saw the learner—a pleasant, mild-mannered man about 50 years old—strapped into an "electric chair" in an adjacent room. Of course, the learner was an actor, and the electric shocks were phony, but the subjects didn't know this.

Taking his seat in front of the shock generator, the subject was directed to begin at the lowest shock level and to increase the shock intensity to the next level each time the learner made a mistake or failed to respond.

When the test began, the shock intensity rose rapidly because the learner made many errors. The subject got verbal feedback from the learner: At 75 volts, the learner began to grunt and moan; at 150 volts, he demanded to be released from the experiment; at 180 volts, he cried out that he could no longer stand the pain; and at 300 volts, he insisted that he be let out, yelled about his heart condition, screamed, and then failed to respond to further questions.

Most subjects protested and, fearful they might kill the learner if the increased shocks were to bring on a heart attack, insisted they could not go on with their job. Hesitations or protests by the subject were met by the experimenter's statement, "You have no choice, you must go on! Your job is to punish the learner's mistakes." Of course, the subjects did have a choice. All they had to do was stand up and walk out.

The majority of the subjects dissented. But dissension isn't synonymous with disobedience. Sixty-two percent of the subjects increased the shock level to the maximum of 450 volts. The average level of shock administered by the remaining 38 percent was nearly 370 volts.[6]

In a laboratory experiment such as that conducted by Milgram, an artificial environment is created by the researcher. Then the researcher manipulates an independent variable under controlled conditions. Finally, since all other things are held equal, the researcher is able to conclude that any change in the dependent variable is due to the manipulation or change imposed on the independent variable. Note that, because of the controlled conditions, the researcher is able to imply causation between the independent and dependent variables.

The laboratory experiment trades off realism and generalizability for precision and control. It provides a high degree of control over variables and precise measurement of those variables. But findings from laboratory studies are often difficult to generalize to the real world of work. This is because the artificial laboratory rarely duplicates the intricacies and nuances of real organizations. In addition, many laboratory experiments deal with phenomena that cannot be reproduced or applied to real-life situations.

Field Experiment

The following is an example of a field experiment. The management of a large company is interested in determining the impact that a four-day workweek would have on employee absenteeism. To be more specific, management wants to know if employees working four 10-hour days have lower absence rates than similar employees working the traditional five-day week of 8 hours each day. Because the company is large, it has a number of manufacturing plants that employ essentially similar workforces. Two of these are chosen for the experiment, both located in the greater Cleveland area. Obviously, it would not be appropriate to compare two similar-sized plants if one is in rural Mississippi and the other is in urban Copenhagen because factors such as national culture, transportation, and weather might be more likely to explain any differences found than changes in the number of days worked per week.

In one plant, the experiment was put into place—workers began the four-day week. At the other plant, which became the control group, no changes were made in the employees' five-day week. Absence data

were gathered from the company's records at both locations for a period of 18 months. This extended time period lessened the possibility that any results would be distorted by the mere novelty of changes being implemented in the experimental plant. After 18 months, management found that absenteeism had dropped by 40 percent at the experimental plant, and by only 6 percent in the control plant. Because of the design of this study, management believed that the larger drop in absences at the experimental plant was due to the introduction of the compressed workweek.

The field experiment is similar to the laboratory experiment, except it is conducted in a real organization. The natural setting is more realistic than the laboratory setting, and this enhances validity but hinders control. In addition, unless control groups are maintained, there can be a loss of control if extraneous forces intervene—for example, an employee strike, a major layoff, or a corporate restructuring. Maybe the greatest concern with field studies has to do with organizational selection bias. Not all organizations are going to allow outside researchers to come in and study their employees and operations. This is especially true of organizations that have serious problems. Therefore, since most published studies in OB are done by outside researchers, the selection bias might work toward the publication of studies conducted almost exclusively at successful and well-managed organizations.

Our general conclusion is that, of the four research designs we've discussed to this point, the field experiment typically provides the most valid and generalizable findings and, except for its high cost, trades off the least to get the most.[7]

Aggregate Quantitative Reviews

What's the overall effect of organizational behavior modification (OB Mod) on task performance? There have been a number of field experiments that have sought to throw light on this question. Unfortunately, the wide range of effects from these various studies makes it hard to generalize.

To try to reconcile these diverse findings, two researchers reviewed all the empirical studies they could find on the impact of OB Mod on task performance over a 20-year period.[8] After discarding reports that had inadequate information, had nonquantitative data, or didn't meet all conditions associated with principles of behavioral modification, the researchers narrowed their set to 19 studies that included data on 2,818 individuals. Using an aggregating technique called *meta-analysis*, the researchers were able to synthesize the studies quantitatively and to conclude that the average person's task performance will rise from the 50th percentile to the 67th percentile after an OB Mod intervention.

The OB Mod–task performance review done by these researchers illustrates the use of meta-analysis, a quantitative form of literature review that enables researchers to look at validity findings from a comprehensive set of individual studies, and then apply a formula to them to determine if they consistently produced similar results.[9] If results prove to be consistent, it allows researchers to conclude more confidently that validity is generalizable. Meta-analysis is a means for overcoming the potentially imprecise interpretations of qualitative reviews and to synthesize variations in quantitative studies. In addition, the technique enables researchers to identify potential moderating variables between an independent and a dependent variable.

In the past 25 years, there's been a surge in the popularity of this research method. Why? It appears to offer a more objective means for doing traditional literature reviews. Although the use of meta-analysis requires researchers to make a number of judgment calls, which can introduce a considerable amount of subjectivity into the process, there is no arguing that meta-analysis reviews have now become widespread in the OB literature.

Ethics in Research

Researchers are not always tactful or candid with subjects when they do their studies. For instance, questions in field surveys may be perceived as embarrassing by respondents or as an invasion of privacy. Also, researchers in laboratory studies have been known to deceive participants about the true purpose of their experiment "because they felt deception was necessary to get honest responses."[10]

The "learning experiments" conducted by Stanley Milgram, which were conducted more than 30 years ago, have been widely criticized by psychologists on ethical grounds. He lied to subjects, telling them his study was investigating learning, when, in fact, he was concerned with obedience. The shock machine he used was a fake. Even the "learner" was an accomplice of Milgram's who had been trained to act as if he were hurt and in pain. Yet ethical lapses continue. For instance, in 2001, a professor of organizational behavior at Columbia University sent out a common letter on university letterhead to 240 New York City restaurants in which he detailed how he had eaten at this restaurant with his wife in celebration of their wedding anniversary, how he had gotten food poisoning, and that he had spent the night in his bathroom throwing up.[11] The letter closed with: "Although it is not my intention to file any reports with the Better Business Bureau or the Department of Health, I want you to understand what I went through in anticipation that you will respond accordingly. I await your response." The fictitious letter was part of the professor's study to determine how restaurants responded to complaints. But it created culinary chaos among many of the restaurant owners, managers, and chefs as they reviewed menus and produce deliveries for possibly spoiled food, and questioned kitchen workers about possible lapses. A follow-up letter of apology from the university for "an egregious error in judgment by a junior faculty member" did little to offset the distress it created for those affected.

Professional associations like the American Psychological Association, the American Sociological Association, and the Academy of Management have published formal guidelines for the conduct of research. Yet the ethical debate continues. On one side are those who argue that strict ethical controls can damage the scientific validity of an experiment and cripple future research. Deception, for example, is often necessary to avoid contaminating results. Moreover, proponents of minimizing ethical controls note that few subjects have been appreciably harmed by deceptive experiments. Even in Milgram's highly manipulative experiment, only 1.3 percent of the subjects reported negative feelings about their experience. The other side of this debate focuses on the rights of participants. Those favoring strict ethical controls argue that no procedure should ever be emotionally or physically distressing to subjects, and that, as professionals, researchers are obliged to be completely honest with their subjects and to protect the subjects' privacy at all costs.

Summary

The subject of organizational behavior is composed of a large number of theories that are research based. Research studies, when cumulatively integrated, become theories, and theories are proposed and followed by research studies designed to validate them. The concepts that make up OB, therefore, are only as valid as the research that supports them.

The topics and issues in this book are for the most part research-derived. They represent the result of systematic information gathering rather than merely hunch, intuition, or opinion. This doesn't mean, of course, that we have all the answers to OB issues. Many require far more corroborating evidence. The generalizability of others is limited by the research methods used. But new information is being created and published at an accelerated rate. To keep up with the latest findings, we strongly encourage you to regularly review the latest research in organizational behavior. The more academic work can be found in journals such as the *Academy of Management Journal, Academy of Management Review, Administrative Science Quarterly, Human Relations, Journal of Applied Psychology, Journal of Management, Journal of Organizational Behavior*, and *Leadership Quarterly*. For more practical interpretations of OB research findings, you may want to read the *Academy of Management Executive, California Management Review, Harvard Business Review, Organizational Dynamics,* and the *Sloan Management Review.*

Endnotes

1. J. A. Byrne, "Executive Sweat," *Forbes,* May 20, 1985, pp. 198–200.

2. See D. P. Schwab, *Research Methods for Organizational Behavior* (Mahwah, NJ: Lawrence Erlbaum Associates, 1999); and S. G. Rogelberg (ed.), *Blackwell Handbook of Research Methods in Industrial and Organizational Psychology* (Malden, MA: Blackwell, 2002).

3. B. M. Staw and G. R. Oldham, "Reconsidering Our Dependent Variables: A Critique and Empirical Study," *Academy of Management Journal,* December 1978, pp. 539–59; and B. M. Staw, "Organizational Behavior: A Review and Reformulation of the Field's Outcome Variables," in M. R. Rosenzweig and L. W. Porter (eds.), *Annual Review of Psychology,* vol. 35 (Palo Alto, CA: Annual Reviews, 1984), pp. 627–66.

4. R. S. Blackburn, "Experimental Design in Organizational Settings," in J. W. Lorsch (ed.), *Handbook of Organizational Behavior* (Upper Saddle River, NJ: Prentice Hall, 1987), pp. 127–28; and F. L. Schmidt, C. Viswesvaran, D. S. Ones, "Reliability Is Not Validity and Validity Is Not Reliability," *Personnel Psychology,* Winter 2000, pp. 901–12.

5. G. R. Weaver, L. K. Trevino, and P. L. Cochran, "Corporate Ethics Practices in the Mid-1990's: An Empirical Study of the Fortune 1000," *Journal of Business Ethics,* February 1999, pp. 283–94.

6. S. Milgram, *Obedience to Authority* (New York: Harper & Row, 1974). For a critique of this research, see T. Blass, "Understanding Behavior in the Milgram Obedience Experiment: The Role of Personality, Situations, and Their Interactions," *Journal of Personality and Social Psychology,* March 1991, pp. 398–413.

7. See, for example, W. N. Kaghan, A. L. Strauss, S. R. Barley, M. Y. Brannen, and R. J. Thomas, "The Practice and Uses of Field Research in the 21st Century Organization," *Journal of Management Inquiry,* March 1999, pp. 67–81.

8. A. D. Stajkovic and F. Luthans, "A Meta-Analysis of the Effects of Organizational Behavior Modification on Task Performance, 1975–1995," *Academy of Management Journal,* October 1997, pp. 1122–49.

9. See, for example, K. Zakzanis, "The Reliability of Meta Analytic Review," *Psychological Reports,* August 1998, pp. 215–22; C. Ostroff and D. A. Harrison, "Meta-Analysis, Level of Analysis, and Best Estimates of Population Correlations: Cautions for Interpreting Meta-Analytic Results in Organizational Behavior," *Journal of Applied Psychology,* April 1999, pp. 260–70; R. Rosenthal and M. R. DiMatteo, "Meta-Analysis: Recent Developments in Quantitative Methods for Literature Reviews," in S. T. Fiske, D. L. Schacter, and C. Zahn-Wacher (eds.), *Annual Review of Psychology,* vol. 52 (Palo Alto, CA: Annual Reviews, 2001), pp. 59–82; and F. L. Schmidt and J. E. Hunter, "Meta-Analysis," in N. Anderson, D. S. Ones, H. K. Sinangil, and C. Viswesvaran (eds.), *Handbook of Industrial, Work & Organizational Psychology,* vol. 1 (Thousand Oaks, CA: Sage, 2001), pp. 51–70.

10. For more on ethical issues in research, see T. L. Beauchamp, R. R. Faden, R. J. Wallace, Jr., and L. Walters (eds.), *Ethical Issues in Social Science Research* (Baltimore, MD: Johns Hopkins University Press, 1982); and J. G. Adair, "Ethics of Psychological Research: New Policies, Continuing Issues, New Concerns," *Canadian Psychology,* February 2001, pp. 25–37.

11. J. Kifner, "Scholar Sets Off Gastronomic False Alarm," *New York Times,* September 8, 2001, p. A1.

Case 1 Arnold Schwarzenegger: Leader of California?

The governor of California, Arnold Schwarzenegger, or "Arnold" as the state's residents like to call him, is arguably playing the biggest role of his career. Elected in the October 2003 recall election that featured a hodgepodge of 135 candidates, including celebrities Gary Coleman, Larry Flint, and Mary "Mary Carey" Cook, Schwarzenegger replaced incumbent Gray Davis as the governor of the most populous state in the country by raking in 48.1 percent of the popular vote. Californians, weary of Gray Davis's lack of progress, decided to put their trust in a man best known for his roles in action movies such as the *The Terminator* and *Total Recall.*

Schwarzenegger's ascent to the governor's seat is impressive when one considers his background. Born in the small town of Thal, Austria, on July 30, 1947, Schwarzenegger was the product of a modest and harsh upbringing. His parents strictly disciplined him—treatment that he says "would be called child abuse" today. Schwarzenegger explains, "My hair was pulled. I was hit with belts. So was the kid next door, and so was the kid next door. It was just the way it was. Many of the children I've seen were broken by their parents, which was the German-Austrian mentality. Break the will. They didn't want to create an individual . . . It was all about conforming. I was the one who did not conform and whose will could not be broken. Therefore I became a rebel. Every time I got hit, and every time someone said, 'You can't do this,' I said, 'This is not going to be for much longer, because I'm going to move out of here. I want to be rich. I want to be somebody.' "

Determined to leave Austria, Schwarzenegger began to search for a way out, a way to become "somebody." He found that way out through bodybuilding. As a child, he idolized bodybuilder Reg Park, a former Mr. Universe. Though his parents objected, Schwarzenegger pursued bodybuilding so vehemently that at one point he was able to bench-press 520 pounds (for comparison, physical fitness experts typically say that it is good to be able to bench press one's own body weight).

At age 19, Schwarzenegger was crowned Mr. Universe. He continued to win championships, and, in 1970, he even defeated his idol, Reg Park, for the Mr. Universe title. Schwarzenegger now says that bodybuilding was instrumental to his success as an actor and as a politician. "I know it from my bodybuilding— that I can see my goals very clearly . . . It takes the confidence to ignore critics and naysayers," he states.

Having accomplished his goal of becoming Mr. Universe, Schwarzenegger set his sights on America to pursue acting and moved to the United States at age 21. Although he attended acting school, his odd last name and thick accent at first kept him from acquiring roles. He eventually landed a small role in the film *Hercules in New York* and continued to appear in other films such as *Stay Hungry* and *Pumping Iron.* In 1982, however, Schwarzenegger made his mark in the film *Conan the Barbarian*, which grossed more than $100 million worldwide. His on-screen charisma, massive physique, and uniqueness compared to American actors made him a standout. Since moving to the United States, Schwarzenegger has made 33 movies and has become one of the most highly paid actors in the world. For *Terminator 3*, Schwarzenegger earned an astounding $33 million—a record sum at the time.

After succeeding as a bodybuilder and an actor, Schwarzenegger began eyeing a bigger prize: the California governor's seat. During his acting career, Schwarzenegger had formed a strong network of powerful friends and advisors, including investor Warren Buffet, economist Milton Friedman, and Israeli Prime Minister Benjamin Netanyahu. As the recall election neared, Schwarzenegger consulted with his network of allies. Buffet told Schwarzenegger that California needed strong leadership, and Friedman gave him advice on how to improve California's dismal economy. All of this advice gave Schwarzenegger the vision he needed to propel himself to the rank of governor. Running as a moderate Republican, he sought to unite Democrats and Republicans, pass a balanced budget, reduce government spending, and resuscitate the business community. Once he accomplished these goals, Schwarzenegger would confidently state to the rest of the world that California was *back*. Schwarzenegger's vision came at a perfect time: Governor Davis witnessed the rise and fall of the tech boom. When the tech bubble burst, revenue plummeted. In 2001 and 2002, state revenue from the income tax fell 27 percent, yet spending remained the same. Although Davis was not solely responsible for the resulting Californian debt, Californians were eager to place blame.

Hungry for someone to take the reigns from Gray Davis and steer California away from its troubles, many Californians embraced Schwarzenegger as he campaigned across the state. His name recognition and charismatic personality made him a leading candidate. Schwarzenegger's style is vastly different from other politicians. His wit, honesty, and lack of concern for political correctness struck a chord with voters. (As he told one interviewer at *Fortune* magazine following the election, "I love smart women. I have no patience for bimbos.") It was perhaps this larger-than-life persona that led him to "terminate" Gray Davis in the recall election.

Following the election, Schwarzenegger immediately began making policy for California. Within only a few days of his swearing in, Schwarzenegger had a viable economic recovery plan. To the praise of the state's residents, he repealed the car-tax increase, which would have raised almost $4 billion in revenue but was hated by Californians. He continued his strong push for reform, passing propositions that made a $15 billion bond offering possible and that paved the way for a balanced budget. In April 2004, he persuaded the state's legislature to pass a bill overhauling workers' compensation, a victory for businesses trying to reduce costs but a defeat for workers.

A testament to his approachable personality was the fact that he broke tradition by actually going from his office on the first floor to the upstairs offices of the legislators to meet with them. Schwarzenegger's chief of staff, Pat Clarey, can't remember the previous four governors doing that. All in all, the newly elected "governator," using his charisma and network of powerful friends, inched closer each day to his vision.

Even the Republican party took notice. Though more moderate than the Republican Party would like, Schwarzenegger knew that his popularity and charisma were an asset to the Republican convention during President George W. Bush's 2004 reelection campaign. While the Republican party convention organizers were debating whether to invite the moderate Schwarzenegger to speak, Schwarzenegger told the *New York Times*, "If they're smart, they'll have me obviously in prime time." Schwarzenegger got his wish. Two days after the interview, he was invited to speak during his requested time. Republican operatives weren't disappointed with quips such as "This is like winning an Oscar. As if I would know! Speaking of acting, one of my movies was called *True Lies*. And that's what the Democrats should have called their convention." Schwarzenegger's speech at the convention electrified the crowd, further solidifying his role as a charismatic leader.

Not everything has been rosy. One of his major goals was to pass a $103 billion budget plan that he believed would be a tremendous step toward economic recovery. He set an optimistic timeline of passing the budget by June 30, 2004. Schwarzenegger worked tirelessly, negotiating budget reductions with state-affiliated organizations such as universities, prisons, and the teacher's union. However, negotiations began to fall apart when he made conflicting promises to the opposing parties on state and local budget linkages. Instead of victoriously passing his budget on time, the state legislature recessed for the July 4th weekend, leaving Schwarzenegger and his budget on hold.

Not to be dissuaded, Schwarzenegger began campaigning to the public to garner support for his budget. He even went so far as to call opponents "girlie men" at a public rally—an incident that infuriated his critics. Though eventually he was able to pass a revised version of his original budget, Schwarzenegger continued to attempt to fix California's financial crisis through various cost-cutting initiatives. He took on the California teachers' union, trying to persuade it to revamp entirely the way it hires, pays, and fires teachers. During this time, his approval rating fell to 55 percent. Though still high, his approval rating was down from a staggering 65 percent. Many of his ideas are abhorrent to the teachers' union. For example, Schwarzenegger wants to tie teachers' pay to test scores. Many teachers feel that this undermines their ability to teach what they think are important topics and will result in a narrow curriculum.

Some believe Arnold Schwarzenegger is a powerful politician, but he says that he really doesn't like the word *power* because it tends to have a negative connotation. Schwarzenegger says, "Power is basically influence. That's the way I see it. It's being able to have the influence to make changes to improve things." Schwarzenegger has a clear vision of how he wants to improve things; the question is not only whether he can create beneficial policies but also whether he has the ability and support to implement those policies. Although he realizes that his charisma helped him to become governor, Schwarzenegger also knows the importance of vision to a leader. As he puts it, "There is no one, and when I say no one, I mean no one, who will back me off my vision. I will go over burning coals for that."

Questions for Discussion

1. What words would you use to describe Arnold Schwarzenegger's personality? Do any of these fit into the Big Five taxonomy of personality? How might these personality traits influence Schwarzenegger's leadership skills? How might these traits have helped Schwarzenegger get to where he is now?

2. Based on the case, as governor of California, what types of power is Schwarzenegger likely to have? What types of influence tactics does Schwarzenegger appear to use?

3. How would you describe Schwarzenegger's leadership style using the leadership theories covered in this textbook? What details of the case lead you to these conclusions? Is Schwarzenegger's leadership style likely to be effective? Why or why not?

4. Applying concepts from goal-setting theory, explain how goals have influenced Schwarzenegger's progression to the governor's seat. What aspects of the case suggest that Schwarzenegger is committed to the goals that he has set for himself?

5. Are there any "dark sides" to Schwarzenegger's charisma and leadership skills? What might these be, and how might they affect his relationships with others and his ability to govern?

6. How might Schwarzenegger's personality and leadership style help or hinder his ability to effectively negotiate with other parties such as the teachers' union?

Source: Based on B. Morris, A. Gil, P. Neering, and O. Ryan, "Arnold Power," *Fortune,* August 9, 2004, 77–87; and R. Grover and A. Bernstein, "Arnold Gets Strict with the Teachers," *Business Week,* May 2, 2005, 84–85.

Case 2 What Customers Don't Know Won't Hurt Them, or Will It?

Sitting at her desk at the car rental shop where she worked, Elena couldn't believe what she was hearing. Gripping the phone tightly, Elena listened as the head manager of the company's legal department told her that a car that she had recently rented to a customer had blown a tire while the customer was driving on a nearby highway. Although the customer, Jim Reynolds, tried to maintain control of the vehicle, he crashed into another car, seriously injuring himself and the other driver. Apparently, the tire had noticeable structural damage that caused it to blow. Elena stared at her desk in shock as the legal department manager asked whether she was aware of the tire's condition before renting the car to Mr. Reynolds.

"I . . . I'm sorry, what did you say?" asked Elena.

"I asked whether you were aware that the tire was damaged before renting the car to Mr. Reynolds," repeated the manager.

Elena paused, thinking back to when she had rented the car to Mr. Reynolds. Unfortunately, she knew the answer to the manager's question, but she did not know whether she wanted to answer it. Her mind raced with worried thoughts about how she let herself get into this position, and then she remembered when her supervisor first told her to lie to a customer.

Elena had started working for the rental car company 2 years ago. Fresh out of college, she was intrigued by the possibilities of joining a company and moving up the ranks into management. She worked hard, sometimes putting in 50 or more hours a week. And she was good at her job, too. Customers would frequently tell her supervisor of Elena's great service and courtesy. Within no time, the supervisor began telling her that she was a strong candidate for management and would probably be running her own rental office within the next year.

Intrigued with becoming a manager, Elena began to work even harder. She was the first one at the office each morning and the last one to leave. Things were going well, until one particularly busy day, when the rental office had more business than it could handle. The office typically had a few vehicles left for walk-in customers, but on this day the lot was empty except for one SUV, which a couple had reserved for their vacation. The couple's reservation was for 1 P.M., and it was now 12 noon. Proactive as usual, Elena decided to go check the SUV to make sure it was ready for the couple. As she got up from her desk, the door to the rental office flew open, and a man rushed toward the counter.

"Do you have anything to rent?" he quickly asked. "I don't have a reservation, but I really need a car right now for the rest of the week."

Elena apologized and explained that the only vehicle they had at the moment was reserved, but that he could wait at the office until another car was returned. In fact, she said, they expected to have two vehicles returned around 3 P.M.

"That's not good enough," the man replied. "I need a car now."

"Again, I do apologize sir, but it wouldn't be fair to those with a reservation to rent the only car that is available," said Elena.

With a frown, the man turned to leave. As he did, Elena's supervisor, who had been listening to the conversation, chimed in. "So you really need a car, huh?" he asked the man.

The man whirled around. "Yes, I do."

"I'll rent it to you for $150 a day," said Elena's supervisor. One hundred and fifty dollars a day was much more than the rental company's usual fee.

The man paused for a moment and then said, "Fine, I'll take it."

As he left with the only vehicle left on the lot, a stunned Elena asked her supervisor why he had rented the SUV when he knew that it was reserved—and at such a high price.

"That guy would have paid anything, and he ended up paying twice as much as we would have gotten out of it," her supervisor said, laughing. Look, if you're going to be a manager, you need to know how to make money. Always take the best deal you can get."

"Even if it means losing another customer?" Elena asked. "What are we going to tell the couple who had a reservation for that SUV?"

"*You're* going to tell them that it broke down unexpectedly and it's at the shop. If you want to be a manager, start acting like one."

Soon after, the couple with the reservation walked into the rental office. Elena didn't want to lie to them, but she also didn't want to jeopardize her chances of obtaining a management position. She also figured that the couple would be more understanding if she told them that the SUV had broken down than if she told them that she had rented it to another customer. So, Elena followed her manager's advice and lied to the couple.

In the months that followed, Elena encountered several more instances where her supervisor asked her to lie to customers because her office had reserved too many vehicles. Pretty soon, it became second nature, as she found herself lying to customers without pressure from her supervisor. To date, however, her lies hadn't caused any serious harm to anyone, at least as far as she knew. That track record changed, however, the day Jim Reynolds rented a car from her.

The day was routine in that the rental office was very busy. There were only two vehicles on the lot—a compact car and a new luxury sedan. Mr. Reynolds had reserved the less expensive compact car. However, when checking the car over before Mr. Reynolds arrived, Elena noticed a large lump on the outside well of the passenger-side front tire. From her training, she knew that this lump could be dangerous. But Elena also knew that she would have to give Mr. Reynolds the luxury sedan for the same price as the compact car if she decided not to rent him the compact car. She thought about what her supervisor had told her and knew that he probably would be upset if she didn't get a high rate out of their new luxury sedan. Besides, she reasoned, the car will be fine and Mr. Reynolds would have it for only a day. So, Elena went through the routine. With a smile and a handshake, she rented the compact car to Mr. Reynolds, who didn't notice the tire because it was on the passenger side, and Elena didn't walk Mr. Reynolds around the car—a routine practice at the rental company.

Fast-forward one day and Elena's world had completely changed. Now, Elena was on the phone with the manager of the company's legal department, wondering how she ever thought it would be safe to rent the car to Mr. Reynolds. She could admit that she knew about the tire and decided to rent the car anyway, or she could lie and say that the tire looked fine when she rented the car. If she told the truth, becoming a manager would probably be out of the question, at least for a long while. Anger welled up inside her. She had worked hard to get where she was. She regretted not having told her supervisor that she wasn't going to lie to customers, even if it meant getting a better rate. But that moment had passed. She could tell the legal department manager that her supervisor had told her to lie to customers, but she knew that her manager would deny it. Either way, the options weren't too appealing.

"Hello? . . . hello?" asked the legal department manager.

Elena returned to the conversation. "Sorry, I lost you for a moment," she said. "Yeah . . . about Mr. Reynolds . . . "

Questions for Discussion

1. Using concepts from reinforcement theory, explain why Elena might be motivated to lie to customers. With reinforcement theory in mind, do you think that Elena will confess to the legal representative? Why or why not?

2. How might the rental office's climate influence Elena's behavior? What factors contribute to the current climate? What steps could you take to improve the ethics at this office?

3. Do you blame Elena for her behavior or do you attribute her behavior to external factors? How do concepts from attribution theory fit in?

4. Consider Elena's personality. Would you predict that escalation of commitment will occur (and she will lie to the legal representative), or will she decide to come clean? Explain your answer.

5. Do you think Elena would make a good leader some day? Why or why not? What factors might this depend on?

6. What emotions might Elena be experiencing? How might Elena's emotions affect her decision to tell the legal department manager about the incident with Mr. Reynolds?

Case 3   Are Five Heads Better Than One?

Evan, Conner, Alexis, Derek, and Judy had been team members for only one week, but they felt that they were already working well together. Upper management at their company, Advert, a medium-sized marketing firm, picked the five employees for a special project: the development of a commercial promoting the launch of a client's 60-inch plasma flat-screen television. The project was especially critical because the television company was one of Advert's most important clients, and the firm's revenues had been slipping lately due to a few poor ad campaigns. Needless to say, upper management at Advert wanted the team to hit a home run with the project.

Upper management didn't have any trouble picking the five employees. All were bright, talented individuals who came up with creative ideas. More important, reasoned the top managers, the employees were similar on a number of characteristics. Evan, Conner, Alexis, Derek, and Judy were around the same age, had worked for the company for about the same amount of time, and because they all tended to be sociable, friendly, and valued getting along with others, their personalities seemed to mesh as well.

To give the team creative room, management allowed them as much autonomy as possible. It gave the team the freedom to see the project through from start to finish—coming up with their own ideas, hiring someone to film the commercial once the idea was in place, creating and maintaining a budget, and presenting the final commercial to the client. Advert's top managers had already met with and assured the client that it was in good hands with this team.

Excited to begin working, the team decided to meet in person to discuss ideas for the commercial. Conner, who was used to leading others in his previous work groups, took the head seat at the group's table. Immediately, he told the group his idea for the commercial.

"I've been thinking about this a lot since I was first told about the project," he said. "I know our client well, and I think they want us to do something out of the box—something that will grab people's attention."

Conner proceeded to explain his idea for the commercial, which centered on a college student "loser" trying to get a date. After one particular attractive female turns him down, and she and her friends ridicule him, the student returns sullenly to his dorm, plunks down on an old sofa, and turns on his small, black-and-white "loser" television. But in the next shot, the student is setting up a 60-inch plasma television in his dorm room, door ajar. While he's doing this, the group of attractive females walks by. In the final shot, the student is in his dorm room watching his new television, with the group of attractive females around him.

Following his explanation, Conner leaned back in his seat and folded his arms across his chest. Grinning proudly, he asked, "Well, what do you think?"

Alexis was the first to speak up. "Um, I don't know." She paused. "I think it's a pretty good start." Hesitantly, she added, "The only thing that I worry about is that our client won't like it. They pride themselves on being more sophisticated than their competitors. To them, this television is both an electronics device and a work of art." But then Alexis quickly added, "But I don't know, maybe you're right that we need to do something different."

Conner, with a slight frown on his face, asked the other group members, "What do the rest of you think?"

Evan responded, "Yeah, I think it's a pretty good idea."

"Judy?" asked Conner.

"I agree. It has potential."

"Well, everyone else seems to agree with me. What do you think Derek?" Conner asked, with the other three members staring at Derek.

Derek paused for a moment. He had his own ideas as well, and because he had worked with the client, perhaps more than any of the other team members, he wasn't sure about Conner's idea. Derek had pictured a commercial that placed the television in a stylish, contemporary Manhattan apartment, with a couple in their 30s enjoying a classic movie, a bottle of red wine on the coffee table.

Feeling the heat from his teammates' gazes, reluctantly Derek said, "Yeah, that sounds good."

"Great, it's settled then," beamed Conner. "We'll have this commercial to them in no time if we stay at this pace."

So the team fleshed out the commercial over the next month. Everyone got along, and the feeling of camaraderie strengthened. Once on board with Conner's idea, the team members became more confident that they would be successful, so much so that they made the commercial even racier than the original idea. The attractive girls would be dressed provocatively, and instead of watching the television, the student and the girls would be laughing and drinking, with the television on in the background. There were a few hesitations here and there as members expressed other ideas, but each team member, enjoying the group's solidarity, decided that it would be better to keep the team in good spirits rather than risk losing the team's morale.

The team quickly decided on a company to shoot the commercial and approved the actors. In a short time, they had completed their commercial. The next step was to present the commercial to their client. Conner took it upon himself to alert management that the team was ready to present the commercial.

"Impressive. Your team is a month ahead of the deadline," said one of the top managers. "We have a lot riding on this, so I hope that it's good. I presume everything went well then?"

Conner nodded. "Yes, very well. No problems or disagreements at all. I think we worked really well together."

On the day of the presentation, the team waited anxiously in a meeting room for their client to arrive. Advert's top managers took their seats in the meeting room. Soon after, three of the client's managers, dressed in professional attire, walked into the meeting room and sat down quietly. After welcoming the clients to the presentation, Conner and his teammates began the presentation, with Conner leading the way. He explained that the idea had come to the team almost instantly, and that given that everyone thought it was a good idea, he was sure that their company would feel the same. Then he dimmed the lights, pressed play, and let the commercial run.

It did not take long for the team to realize that the commercial was not having the effect they had wanted on their clients or their managers. The clients exchanged several sideways glances with one another, and the managers shifted nervously in their seats. After what seemed like an eternity, the commercial ended and the lights came back on. An awkward silence filled the room. The clients began murmuring among themselves.

"That was, um, interesting," said one of the clients, finally.

Conner replied that he thought the idea was "out of the box," and that, therefore, audiences would easily remember it.

"Oh, they'll remember it all right," smirked one of the clients. She then turned to Advert's top managers and stated, "This is not at all what we were looking for. The commercial doesn't fit our needs and doesn't portray the image that we are trying to obtain. Given that you told us that we would be in good hands with this team, my colleagues and I fear that your company will not be able to meet our goals. We appreciate the time that this took, but we will likely employ another advertising firm to film our commercial." With that, she and her colleagues left the room.

After a thorough lecturing from Advert's top managers, the team was disbanded. One month later, Derek was at home watching television when a commercial came on. Classical music played in the background as the camera swept through a modern home. The camera slowly rose up behind a tan leather sofa seating a couple enjoying a bottle of wine and watching a new 60-inch plasma television. In the bottom corner of the screen, in small writing, was the name of one of Advert's competitors. Apparently, Advert's former clients got what they were looking for in the end, but from a competitor. Derek shook his head and vowed to speak up next time he had an idea.

Questions for Discussion

1. What factors contributed to the poor performance of the Advert team? As a manager, what could you have done to help the team perform better?

2. According to the case, the Advert team was given a relatively high degree of autonomy. How might this autonomy have contributed to the presence of groupthink?

3. Teams can be either homogeneous or heterogeneous. How would you characterize the Advert team, and how did this affect the team's creativity and performance?

4. What are some group decision-making techniques that could have helped reduce conformity pressures and groupthink among the Advert team?

5. What different forms of communication could have been employed to improve the sharing of ideas among the Advert team? How might this have affected its performance and satisfaction?

6. How would you describe Conner's leadership style? Why do you think his style wasn't effective? In what situations might Conner be an effective leader?

Case 4   Wal-Mart's World

Just how does Wal-Mart, the world's largest retailer, maintain its corporate culture across all of its 4,000 stores? How does this giant, with sales a staggering $288 billion in fiscal year 2004, promote and preserve its image as a small-town store where the customer is king? Part of the answer lies in Wal-Mart's legendary Saturday Morning Meeting.

The Saturday Meeting started with Wal-Mart founder Sam Walton, who thought it unfair that he could take off on the weekends while his employees worked. So, in 1962, Sam Walton began arriving at his store, Walton's Five & Dime, in Bentonville, Arkansas, each Saturday between two and three in the morning. There, he would scrutinize the previous week's records to determine which merchandise was selling and which was not, as well as how sales were faring. However, Mr. Walton didn't stop there. When his store's "associates" (Walton called all his workers associates to emphasize that they were his colleagues as well as his employees) arrived, he would hold a quick morning meeting to openly share the store's information with them. He would also ask for their opinions on matters such as what items he should put on sale and how he should display certain products. Such meetings served not only to use the store's employees in multiple ways but also to convey to his employees that he valued their input and wanted them to learn the business.

Even as Wal-Mart grew into a multibillion-dollar company, the Saturday Morning Meeting continued. Ever since, Wal-Mart has held them at the home office in Bentonville. Each Saturday morning, some 600 managers, many of whom live in Bentonville and make weekly trips to their respective territories, pack the 400-seat auditorium, waiting for their fearless leader to arrive. First, it was Sam Walton. Then, it was CEO David Glass. Now, at 7:00 A.M. sharp, current CEO Lee Scott heads the meeting. As usual, Scott starts off the meeting by leading the crowd in a Wal-Mart cheer: "Give me a W! Give me an A! Give me an L! Give me a Squiggly! . . . "

Though Saturday Morning Meeting topics typically include the company's financial performance, merchandising, and areas of improvement, the meeting is, above all else, a means to keep the company and its employees as close-knit as possible. Such solidarity is imperative to Wal-Mart's strategy of quick market response. When new ideas or problems surface, managers are comfortable sharing them with others. Decisions are made quickly, and action is taken.

For example, while discussing merchandising mistakes during a meeting, Paul Busby, regional vice president for the Northeastern United States, was concerned about a particular item that Wal-Mart was not carrying. "I went into a Kmart near one of my stores to look around and found an item that made me wonder why we don't have it." With a Kmart bag next to him, Busby pulls out a poker table cover and chip set that Kmart is selling for $9.99. "We should really have this product because it's a much better value than ours."

In response to Busby's concern, Scott McCall, the divisional merchandise manager for toys, replied, "We've got a pretty nice poker set in our stores, but I'll check with our sources and get back to you."

A mere 10 minutes passed before McCall asked for the microphone again. With cheers from the crowd, McCall stated, "Paul, I just wanted you to know that I've arranged for those Kmart poker sets to be acquired and be on the trucks rolling out to all the stores next week." Examples such as this illustrate the trust that Sam Walton had in his staff to make decisions. Instead of going through layers of red tape, Wal-Mart's managers can have their ideas implemented quickly. Of course, not all decisions are beneficial; however, those that are can result in immediate gains.

Such quick responses are difficult, if not impossible, for other large companies to execute. As former CEO David Glass explains, "The Saturday Morning Meeting was always a decision-making meeting to take corrective action, and the rule of thumb was that by noon we wanted all the corrections made in the stores." Glass clarifies, "Noon on Saturday." Glass further explains that since no other companies could even come close to the speed at which Wal-Mart executes strategy and change, Wal-Mart developed and sustains a competitive advantage. Wal-Mart's vast distribution network and purchasing power allow it to move products efficiently and sell them at a low price. For example, following the devastation of hurricane Katrina, Wal-Mart, rather than FEMA (Federal Emergency Management Agency), was one of the first organizations to distribute food and other goods to hurricane victims.

The Saturday Morning Meeting serves other purposes as well. Perhaps due to Wal-Mart's culture of retail fanaticism and continuous improvement of efficiency, the culture of Wal-Mart has been described as "neurotic." According to one Wal-Mart insider, "Mechanisms like these meetings keep that neurotic tension alive even at this enormous scale."

In fact, the Saturday Morning Meeting is not the only meeting Wal-Mart uses to maintain company culture. On Friday there is a merchandising meeting, where regional vice presidents get together to discuss what products are selling well. And not all meetings are for managers. Consistent with Sam Walton's emphasis on employee involvement, every Wal-Mart store has a 15-minute shift-change meeting three times a day. During these meetings, managers go over the store's performance numbers as well as ask their associates whether they have specific ideas that might improve sales. Managers send what they think are good ideas up to the regional vice president, who then proposes the ideas at the Saturday-morning meeting. The Wal-Mart greeter was one such idea, which a rank-and-file employee suggested. The greeter helped to put a friendly face on what might be viewed as a large, impersonal organization. Such structure helps to ensure that Wal-Mart's upper managers, who oftentimes are responsible for 100 or more stores, keep in touch with the daily happenings of their business.

One other aspect of Wal-Mart's culture is its frugality, a characteristic of Sam Walton that has endured even through Wal-Mart's tremendous growth and financial success. Walton began his strict focus on keeping costs low early on to gain an advantage over competitors such as Sears and Kmart. Walton was known to make executives sleep eight to a room on company trips. He himself drove a modest old pick-up truck and flew coach whenever he traveled. Amazingly, these characteristics have remained ingrained in Wal-Mart's culture. The current CEO, Lee Scott, drives a Volkswagen Beetle and has also shared hotel rooms to reduce costs.

But maintaining Wal-Mart's culture has not always been easy. In the late 1980s and early 1990s, attendance at the Saturday Morning Meetings grew tremendously, which made it impossible for everyone to speak. David Glass, CEO during that time, recalls complaints of boredom. So some of Wal-Mart's suppliers (who often attend the Saturday Morning Meetings), eager to impress and ingratiate themselves with the top brass, began bringing in entertainers such as singer Garth Brooks and former football player Joe Montana. However, the meetings began to lose focus. As Glass recalls of the entertainment, "You had to be careful how you did that because it becomes more fun to do that than fix the problems." By the late 1990s, the company began inviting guests who had more educational value, such as Bill Clinton and CEOs Jack Welch and Warren Buffet. These speakers were able to share their success stories with Wal-Mart's managers, giving them new ideas on how to conduct business and run the organization.

Perhaps the biggest obstacle to Wal-Mart is the increased public scrutiny that comes with being the world's largest company. In the past, the company had more tolerance for employee mistakes. It would strongly reprimand an employee who made an offhand sexist remark, for example, but if the employee altered his or her behavior, then the company let the employee stay. Today, however, Wal-Mart adheres to a stricter policy. As Mr. Scott explains, Wal-Mart is "not mean but less kind. Today, when you find somebody doing something wrong, you not only have to let them go, you have to document it so it is covered and people understand. That is a bit of a culture change. It's a company that operates in a different context than when Sam Walton was alive and when David Glass ran the company. Management cannot allow extraneous issues to bleed over. My role has to be, besides focusing on driving sales, to eliminate the constant barrage of negatives that causes people to wonder if Wal-Mart will be allowed to grow."

Indeed, Wal-Mart frequently finds itself in the news, though lately in stories that paint the company in a negative light. Controversies over Wal-Mart's anti-union position, its hiring and promotion practices (such as outsourcing the cleaning of its stores to illegal immigrants and working them seven days a week), and its treatment of employees (including accusations of discrimination and underpayment of employees) all make it increasingly difficult for Wal-Mart to maintain the image of a friendly, affordable retailer that Sam Walton had in mind when he founded the company. On this topic, Scott says, "Over the last couple of years I've been spending much of the time talking about all the negative publicity we've been getting, not from the standpoint that we hate the press, but by asking our people what we are doing that allows people to perpetuate these kinds of negative discussions about Wal-Mart."

If Wal-Mart is to enjoy continued success, it will have to find solutions to the above problems and the negative publicity that results. Perhaps the company should go back to its Walton roots? Or maybe it should alter its culture and market position to match its growth. For a company that has over 4,000 stores operating in the United States, Mexico, Canada, South America, Korea, China, and Europe; 1.5 million employees; and over 100,000 different products for sale, sustaining or changing the company's culture is a tremendous challenge. Thus far, however, Wal-Mart appears to be handling the challenge well.

Questions for Discussion

1. According to the textbook, there are seven primary characteristics that capture the essence of an organization's culture. How would you describe Wal-Mart's culture using these seven characteristics?

2. Based on this case, would you characterize Wal-Mart's culture as strong or weak? Why? How might Wal-Mart's culture contribute to its long-term performance?

3. As an upper manager of Wal-Mart, what steps could you take to either maintain or enhance the culture of Wal-Mart?

4. What are some aspects of Wal-Mart's culture that have persevered, but yet may be disadvantageous in today's economy?

5. How might Wal-Mart's negative press affect employee morale, job satisfaction, and organizational commitment? As a manager, what steps would you take to improve employee attitudes?

6. Characterize Wal-Mart's organizational structure. Is it mechanistic or organic? Does it have a high degree of centralization or decentralization? How might Wal-Mart's structure affect its employees in terms of their productivity and job attitudes?

Source: Based on D. Garbato, "Wal-Mart's Scott Concedes Size Impacts Corporate Culture," *Retail Merchandiser*, October 2004, p. 12; B. Schlender, "Wal-Mart's $288 Billion Meeting," *Fortune*, April 18, 2005, 90–99; and "Wal Around the World," *The Economist*, December 8, 2001, pp. 55–57.

Management guru Jim Collins calls him the "Beethoven of business," Wall Street loves him, and Bill Gates was once his nemesis. Who is this powerful man? It's Steve Jobs, cofounder and current chief executive officer of Apple Computer. But despite its trailblazing start, Apple has suffered in recent years, losing sales and market share to big companies such as IBM and Microsoft. The slide even caused many analysts to question whether Apple had anything innovative left to offer. But Jobs, in characteristic fashion, has once again cornered a market, thanks to a small device—with big musical power—called the iPod.

Although Apple competed with computer giant Microsoft during the early 1980s, it soon found itself on the fringes of the computer industry because its computer, the Mac, wasn't compatible with many software programs that businesses needed. Personal computers (PCs), along with Microsoft's Windows operating system, began to dominate, sending the Mac to niche markets. By 1986, Apple's board of directors forced Steve Jobs out of the company. By the late 1990s, even the most fanatic Apple users were turning to different products because of the Mac's compatibility issues and Microsoft's ever-increasing dominance. Apple's share in the computer industry continued to decline, bottoming out at a mere 2 percent in the mid-1990s.

Apple knew it had to improve its operating system, so it bought the computer company. Next in 1997, which, as circumstances would have it, Jobs himself was running. Along with Next came Jobs, who eventually returned to the forefront of Apple. Jobs's plan was simple: Rather than focus on hardware, Apple should focus on software. Create the right software, he reasoned, and the hardware sales would follow.

So, Jobs began making moves that at first seemed risky but in the end paid off. One of the first things he did was to partner with his former rival, Bill Gates. Gates agreed to supply Apple with its popular Office and Internet Explorer programs as well as buy $150 million of Apple stock. Though this deal was good for Microsoft, it was even better for Apple, whose future was now tied to the more successful Microsoft in that Microsoft now had an interest in maintaining Apple's survival. Apple was no longer a competitor in a strict sense.

Because developing software is a costly undertaking, Jobs tried to keep the company afloat by offering computer hardware, which was simply a means to get into the software business. He pushed the company's managers for innovative thinking, which led to the introduction of the iMac in 1998. The iMac immediately stood out from its competitors for its odd, colorful styling, but compatibility issues with some widely used programs still remained. Though the iMac was not the innovative success that Jobs had hoped for, it bought him time to continue developing software.

During this time, Apple developed a new operating system that Jobs thought would revolutionize the computer industry: Mac OS X. The system was based on the operating system Unix and was superior to Windows in several areas, including stability and security. Now that he had the operating system, Jobs needed exciting software to go along with it. Knowing that he already had a deal with Microsoft, Jobs headed to Adobe Systems to ask them to develop a video editing program for his new operating system. Jobs recalled, "They said flat-out no. We were shocked, because they had been a big supporter in the early days of the Mac. But we said, 'Okay, if nobody wants to help us, we're just going to have to do this ourselves.' "

Adobe's rejection may have been a blessing in disguise for Apple. Jobs quickened the pace on software development, and in less than a year released two video editing programs, one for professionals and one for consumers. The software helped keep the buzz alive for Apple's innovative reputation. Feeling confident, Jobs knew that Apple needed to develop more software applications if it were to thrive, but he still hadn't noticed a phenomenon taking place on the Internet: the birth of online music.

In 2000, music lovers the world over, particularly young adults and teenagers, were downloading MP3s (digital music files) by the thousands from what were then illegal online music services, Napster being the company most in the news at that time. Online music delivery was an exciting product for consumers in that they could easily pick and choose what songs to buy and create their own music libraries on their computers. It was also a controversial issue in that there was no way (yet) to compensate artists and their record companies for the sales.

But for Jobs, the opportunity to deliver music to online consumers in a legitimate, user-friendly way was right up his alley. "I felt like a dope," he said. "I thought we had missed it. We had to work hard to catch up." He set out to develop the best "customer experience" possible.

So, Apple began to install CD-ROM burners as a standard feature on all of its computers, hoping that it hadn't missed an opportunity. The burners allowed users to save electronic files, such as digital music files, onto a CD. The addition of burners as a standard feature was a crucial first step in marketing digital music because it offered a way to play digital music on devices other than a computer.

But Apple still needed to offer software that allowed users to manage their digital music files. Microsoft already sold several computer programs of this sort. For Apple, developing software that could easily manage and navigate through thousands of songs and allow a user to call up a song on a whim was no easy task. Jobs didn't have the answer himself, but he found it in a company called SoundStep. Jeff Robbin, the founder of SoundStep, teamed with several engineers and developed the program iTunes in just over three months. Not only was iTunes Apple's answer to comparable Windows jukeboxes but many consumers found it a superior program with great search and sorting capabilities.

Jobs then hit on his big, Apple-saving idea: Develop a small, portable device, like the Sony Walkman, that could hold a user's entire digital music library. Jobs turned to Robbin again. In November 2001—a mere nine months later— Robbin and his team had developed the iPod, which is basically a small, handheld computer the size of a deck of cards (now, some are even smaller) with a simple interface for navigating through one's digital library and a set of earphones for easy listening. Music could be taken from a user's existing CD collection and "ripped" to the iPod via the user's computer, or online music filesharing services such as Napster could be used to download songs onto the iPod.

Though Jobs believed that the iPod would be a success, he kept at his goal of developing the best "customer experience" possible. Napster, as well as other online music file-sharing services, was in the midst of lawsuits, leaving the door open for more legitimate, licensed services to emerge. By April 2003, Apple debuted its online iTunes Music store, allowing customers to legitimately buy songs for 99 cents that they could then download and store on their Mac computers and iPods. Major recording companies, such as Sony and Universal, agreed to sell their songs on iTunes, and the result was a tremendous success. As Eddy Cue, vice president for applications at Apple recalled, "We had hoped to sell a million songs in the first six months, but we did that in the first six days." While the iTunes store was busy selling digital music, Robbin and his team developed a Windows version of the iTunes store, further broadening Apple's market.

To say that Apple has done well with the iPod is an understatement. By January 2005, the company had sold more than 10 million iPods and 250 million songs. As a result, its stock price hit a record high of almost $80 per share in February 2005, and analysts estimated that Apple would earn $13 billion in revenues in 2005.

Jobs credits Apple's success to maintaining its core values of innovation and a continuous focus on the consumer. "The great thing is that Apple's DNA hasn't changed. The place where Apple has been standing for the last two decades is exactly where computer technology and the consumer electronics markets are converging. So it's not like we're having to cross the river to go somewhere else; the other side of the river is coming to us." Jobs further stated, "At Apple we come at everything asking, 'How easy is this going to be for the user? How great is it going to be for the user?' "

Though it appears that Apple is on a roll, its competitors are beginning to catch up. Not only has Microsoft entered the online music market but companies such as Wal-Mart and Napster (Napster is now on legal footing) are trying to capture some of the market share. As of the latest look, Wal-Mart was offering songs at 88 cents each, undercutting Apple's iTunes. Indeed, Apple's first-mover advantage will erode as competitors mimic Apple's product. Because they can copy Apple's online music store instead of creating it from scratch, start-up costs are lower for new entrants. What, then, will be the next move for Steve Jobs and Apple?

Questions for Discussion

1. Using the three-component model of creativity, describe what makes Steve Jobs, and by extension, Apple Computer, successful. Based on the case, which components does Jobs seem to possess in the highest degree? What aspects of the case led you to this conclusion?

2. What leadership theories are most applicable to Steve Jobs and why? How can these theories explain Jobs's recent successes?

3. Based on the case's description of Jobs, what can you infer about his personality? In other words, how would you describe his personality using terms from the book?

4. Are situational factors solely responsible for Apple's success, or is it due to the traits and leadership skills of Steve Jobs? If both contribute, which do you believe is more important and why?

5. Using Lewin's Three-Step Model of organizational change, explain Apple's development of and success with the iPod.

6. Would you characterize Apple as a learning organization? Why or why not? As a manager, what could you do to ensure that Apple continues to be innovative?

Source: Based on B. Schendler, "How Big Can Apple Get?" *Fortune*, February 21, 2005, 66–73.

Case 6 GM and the UAW: A One-Sided Negotiation?

From 1947 through 1977, General Motors (GM) dominated the automobile industry, capturing an average of 45 percent of the auto market. Of the "Big Three" U.S. automakers (GM, Ford, and Chrysler), GM ranked first in sales in every year during this time frame and ranked first in profits for 16 of the 20 years. Needless to say, GM sat comfortably atop the automobile industry.

Now, decades later, GM's share of the U.S. automobile market is down to 25.4 percent, its lowest level since it competed with Henry Ford's Model T. Rumors of bankruptcy abound. In March of 2005, GM lowered its earnings forecast, which sent its stock price to its worst one-day fall since October 19, 1987 when the stock market crashed. Following this, GM announced that it had lost a staggering 1 billion dollars during its first quarter alone. Finally, adding insult to injury, GM disclosed that its sales were plummeting, and for this its stock earned Standard & Poor's grade of junk-bond status. What once was the world's largest and most profitable auto manufacturer is now puttering along in the slow lane.

So who or what is responsible for GM's decline? Though there are numerous factors that are hurting the company, one major factor has been the United Auto Workers (UAW) union and its long relationship with GM over the years.

The relationship first took shape during the Depression, when demand for cars overall fell sharply and almost half of all autoworkers lost their jobs as a result. Those autoworkers that did keep their jobs received greatly reduced pay because the major auto companies could barely afford to stay in business. However, GM, through the leadership of Alfred Sloan, remained competitive and profitable. But working conditions paled in comparison to today's standards. It was not typical for companies, including GM, to provide benefits such as health insurance, and pension plans were unheard of.

All of this began to change for GM in 1936, when two major players in the UAW, Walter and Victor Reuther, staged a sit-down strike at one of GM's primary plants, Fisher Body Plant No. 1, in GM's hometown of Flint, Michigan. Though the governor at the time, Frank Murphy, instructed over 4,000 guardsmen to maintain peace at the strike, he did not give them the authority to evict the strikers, forcing Sloan to negotiate with the UAW (though Sloan later stated that "we would not negotiate with the union while its agents forcibly held possession of our properties . . . we finally felt obliged to do so"). As a result of the strike, GM formally recognized the UAW as a legal organization in 1937. Shortly after, in 1941, Ford formally recognized the UAW, giving the union even greater power.

What followed was a relationship that endured over the years, giving the UAW and its members some of the best benefits in the country. Indeed, the UAW was a powerful negotiator. Victor Reuther, believing strongly that all workers should have health insurance, tried first to bargain with the federal government. After several failed attempts, he turned to Sloan at GM. Although Sloan initially viewed Reuther's request for health insurance and pension plans as "extravagant beyond reason," one of Reuther's proposals eventually persuaded him. Previously, GM and the UAW engaged in contract renegotiations each year, which made it difficult for GM's managers and workers to plan ahead because they were unsure what the costs would be for the following year. Reuther, capitalizing on this problem, offered to agree to longer contracts. As Sloan later stated, "Longer intervals gave the corporation more assurance that it could meet its long-range production schedules." What was the catch to the UAW's concession? In return for longer contracts, the UAW insisted that each and every contract be better for the UAW than the one before it. Sloan agreed to the terms of the negotiation, setting the stage for health insurance, pension plans, and other employee benefits.

During the economic boom following World War II, demand soared, leaving the auto industry rich with profit. As Reuther stated to the auto industry during these times, "It's a growing market—we have nothing to fight over." So, at first, contract renegotiations went smoothly and costs of employee benefits stayed at a minimum. But little by little, the UAW negotiated better benefits for its members. In 1943, GM allowed workers to purchase health insurance; however, GM did not incur any of the cost because workers put their money into a pool. Five years later, the union successfully negotiated two powerful benefits. The first, an "escalator clause," stipulated that GM give raises based on the cost of living. The second, the "improvement factor," rewarded workers for increasing efficiency. As a plant increased in efficiency, and lowered costs as a result, workers at the plant received raises. Then, in 1950, GM agreed to pay 50 percent of all its workers' health care premiums, including workers' families, and it also agreed to develop and pay for a pension plan. Three years later, GM extended these benefits to its retired workers.

Business was still booming in 1959, when the UAW persuaded GM to guarantee workers' wages—even for those workers the company had laid off. Thus, workers could be assured that they would receive no less than what GM had promised to pay them, even during economic hardship. The UAW continued to push GM to further sweeten its benefits—per their original deal—and in 1961, GM agreed to pay 100 percent of all health care premiums, again for workers and their families. Three years later, GM extended this benefit to its retirees.

GM's market share around that time peaked at 50.7 percent, but in 1966, the same year that Alfred Sloan died, a little-known company called Datsun exported a car to the United States, marking the entry of Japanese automakers in the U.S. market. During this time, Japan's influence was minimal, and GM continued to agree to increase benefits to its workers. In 1970, for instance, the UAW persuaded GM to provide full retirement benefits after 30 years of service. In addition, GM agreed to extend health insurance benefits to cover mental and pre-and postnatal conditions. As UAW negotiator Douglas Fraser recalls, "We had a lot of arguments over mental health. I don't believe we had any arguments over full premiums."

From GM's standpoint, the concessions it made over the years may be relatively minor when considered in isolation, but their cumulative impact is now taking its toll. As the company has lost market share to increased competition from both domestic and foreign producers, particularly Japanese producers, more and more workers have retired, leaving GM with huge expenses. GM anticipates health care costs to top $5.6 billion in 2005 alone, and it is estimated that GM's long-term health care liabilities are $77 billion. To fund its pension plans, GM has long-term liabilities of $89 billion—a tremendous amount when one considers that GM's revenues in 2004 were $193 billion.

And costs continue to soar as baby boomers retire in droves, leaving younger workers to support retirees and causing large discrepancies in the number of current and retired workers. GM now employs 150,000 people, yet it funds health care for 1.1 million people. And because of the ever-increasing benefits packages that the UAW negotiated with GM over the years, GM's health care plan is far better than what the average U.S. company provides. While average U.S. citizens pay 32 percent of their medical costs, GM workers and members of the UAW pay only 7 percent. In fact, GM now spends more than double on health care what it spends on steel to produce its automobiles. As one former GM investor quipped, "When you invest in GM, you are not investing in a car company. You are investing in a money-management firm and an HMO."

All of these rising costs have caused GM considerable financial problems. Although some analysts suggest that GM should streamline operations, Thomas Kowaleski, a spokesperson for GM, said, regarding the enormous cost of benefits, "We cannot be profitable at 20 percent market share because legacy costs won't go away." Even closing a plant is no longer under GM's discretion—the UAW must approve it. To make matters worse, even if GM halts production at a given plant, it still has to pay its workers 95 percent of their regular wages, even though GM's wages are 60 percent more than the industry average.

All in all, GM may have negotiated itself into a stranglehold with the UAW. But there are two sides to consider. On the one hand, offering great employee benefits is a goal that all organizations should have, as workers should receive the best treatment possible and companies want to attract the best workers possible. On the other hand, if the UAW continues to press GM for improvements, and GM concedes, the company may no longer exist to provide those benefits.

Questions for Discussion

1. How would you characterize the type of conflict that exits between GM and the UAW using the various conflict-handling interventions described in Chapter 15?

2. Based on the case, would you conclude that GM and the UAW have engaged in distributive or integrative bargaining? Which type would be better for the two parties in the long term, and why?

3. What types of power does the UAW hold over GM? How has this power influenced its ability to negotiate with GM?

4. Based on the case, what decision-making errors with the union might have led GM to its current financial position? What can GM do to eliminate these errors in the future?

5. Although benefits such as a "guaranteed wage" likely are appealing to workers, how might such benefits affect employee motivation? How might they affect job satisfaction and organizational commitment? Could this be a case where management engages in the "folly of rewarding A, while hoping for B?"

6. As a manager of a large company such as GM that operates in a highly competitive environment, how would you attempt to strike an appropriate balance between employee treatment and company profitability?

Source: Based on R. Lowenstein, "What Went Wrong at GM," *Smart Money,* July 2005, 78–82.

Alex and Stephanie have a few things in common. Both are students at their state's university, and both work full-time at a local supermarket to make ends meet and help pay for college. Though the pay isn't great, it's a steady job that allows them some flexibility, which helps when scheduling classes. Both students joined the supermarket two years ago, and, given their similar situations, became friends quickly.

Although Stephanie seems to enjoy her job, arriving and leaving work each day with a smile on her face, Alex often grumbles and complains about his work. Much of the time, Alex complains about his boss, Dan, who oversees the produce department. Stephanie works for Jonathan, a 10-year veteran who everyone generally admires for his friendly demeanor and relaxed management style.

Most employees want to work for Jonathan, as he often assigns his employees different duties each week so workers don't get bored. Stephanie, for instance, can be working at the checkout counter one week, stocking shelves the next, and the store's culinary center the following week.

The culinary center is a new service that the store is test-marketing. Employees show customers how to create exciting recipes from start to finish. It is Stephanie's favorite place in the store to work. She is also responsible for taking customers around the store to locate ingredients for a culinary center recipe, many of the ingredients being some of the store's finest. And she enjoys allowing customers to sample what she cooks. So far, the culinary center is a success, and many of the store's more expensive ingredients are becoming difficult to keep in stock. To help with this issue, Jonathan encourages his employees to notify him immediately when an item is running low and even empowers employees to reorder items from vendors. By doing this, Stephanie has quickly grasped how the supermarket operates.

Alex's supervisor, in contrast, prefers most of his employees to work in the same area each day—Alex is one of those employees. Dan believes that the best way to master a job is to do it over and over again. This means that Alex has to stock the same produce areas each day. As boxes of produce are delivered to the store's supply room, Alex unloads their contents onto the shelves. Alex also must constantly reorganize the produce already on the shelves to make them look as orderly as possible. Most of the time, though, he doesn't feel inclined to do either task.

After a particularly boring morning of restocking apples (the store had apples on sale that day), Alex met Stephanie for lunch in the break room. After sitting down, Alex reached into his lunchbox and pulled out an apple, a look of disgust on his face. "Ugh . . . If I have to look at another apple, I'm going to be sick."

"Bad day again?" asked Stephanie as Alex stuffed the apple back into his lunchbox.

"I stocked apples all morning—what do you think?" Alex retorted.

"Why don't you tell Dan you want to do something else?" Stephanie inquired. "I see that he lets Denise work in other areas." Stephanie leaned closer. "I've even heard that she gets paid more than you. Is that true?" she whispered.

"Apparently, she gets paid $2.00 more an hour, but I do the same things that she does. Oh, that's right. One thing I don't do is tell Dan what a cool shirt he has on or how awesome his car is. They're both pathetic if you ask me," frowned Alex.

"Two dollars more an hour, but she's been here for only 3 months!" Stephanie exclaimed. "And I know that you work just as hard as she does. No wonder you're so irritated all the time."

"I don't even care any more. What's the point? If I stock more apples, or something meaningless like that, what does it get me—another sticker that says 'good job'? Oooh, that's really great. Thanks a bunch Dan!" replied Alex, punctuating his last sentence with a sarcastic thumbs-up. "Anyway, enough about my day. How's yours going?"

"Pretty good, actually. Jonathan and I met earlier today, and we both set a goal for me to sell 10 bottles of truffle oil next week."

"Wow. That stuff is pretty expensive, isn't it?" asked Alex.

"Thirty-five dollars for four ounces," replied Stephanie. "It'll be tough, but I found a pretty good recipe that I'll be making for customers who stop by the culinary center." She paused, then said, "I think I'll be able to do it. I've made quite a few similar recipes before, and even though this one is more difficult, it shouldn't be too bad. Besides, if I sell the oil Jonathan said that he'll give me a $75 bonus. So I'm definitely going to give it a shot. The nice thing is that I'll be able to do this on my own, without someone breathing down my neck."

"Well that's certainly more than I'll be making this week," said Alex. "This job is okay, but I'd probably leave if I could. It's too risky right now to just quit. If I can't find something, then I'll be in trouble when that next tuition bill comes around."

"Look on the bright side. At least you make more than Jean. She's been here for 7 years, still working in the deli," replied Stephanie.

"That's true," sighed Alex as he returned to his lunch. He looked up at the clock. They had been at lunch for a half hour already. Dan was quite the stickler about keeping lunch to a minimum. Although store policy allowed employees 45 minutes for lunch, Dan often pushed his employees to keep it to 30 minutes. As Alex quickened his chewing, Dan strolled into the break room and opened the refrigerator, his back to Alex and Stephanie.

Wheeling around with a soda in hand, Dan commented, "Bit of a long lunch, hey Alex?"

Alex could feel the blood rising to his face. "It's been exactly a half hour, and I'm almost finished," he said.

"Well, we're running low on apples again. So quit lying around and get back to work." Dan walked toward the door, stopped, and turned around. "I thought that college students were supposed to be smarter than this. At the very least I would hope that they could tell time." He added, "I guess the university must have glossed over your application." And with that, Dan left.

"What a jerk," said Stephanie after Dan was out of earshot.

"What else is new," said Alex. "I'd guess I'd better get back to work." Alex got up and returned what was left of his lunch to the refrigerator. When he opened the door, he noticed a sandwich labeled with a post-it note that read "Dan's." After glancing quickly to the door, he casually swept the sandwich onto the floor. Stephanie turned around at the sound.

"Oops," smirked Alex. He paused, staring down at the sandwich. "Five-second rule!" he said as he picked up the sandwich, being sure to smear the underside of it on the floor. After putting it neatly back on the shelf, Alex turned to Stephanie. "Well Steph, have a good one. I think maybe I'll take my time on those apples."

Questions for Discussion

1. How can expectancy theory be used to explain the differences in motivation between Alex and Stephanie? What specifics from the case apply to expectancy theory?

2. Alex states that he is underpaid for the work he does. What motivational theory does this apply to, and how would it explain Alex's behavior?

3. Using concepts from organizational justice, explain why Alex knocks his boss's lunch to the floor. What should Alex's boss do to improve the fairness of his treatment?

4. Using concepts from the emotions and moods chapter, explain why Alex retaliates toward his supervisor. Was his behavior driven purely by emotion, or did cognition also play a role? How so?

5. Compare and contrast Alex and Stephanie in terms of each person's level of work stress. How might stress affect their attitudes and behaviors within their work environment?

6. Discuss Alex and Stephanie in terms of each person's job attitudes (for example, job satisfaction, organizational commitment). What factors might be responsible for any differences?

Case 8   The Big Promotion

Devon and Isabella arrived outside their boss's office at the same time and took a seat. Both exchanged a cordial "hello," but they didn't say much else as they waited outside. Fidgeting nervously in their seats, the two knew that only one of them was going to receive what would be the biggest promotion of their careers.

Devon and Isabella worked for a large software company and each was responsible for managing one of the company's largest divisions. Both had been in their current position for years, hoping that a spot at the company's corporate headquarters would open up. That time had arrived a month earlier when one of the company's senior executives retired. Such positions did not open frequently, so Devon and Isabella knew that this was a tremendous opportunity.

For the past month, they had prepared for their meeting with the company's CEO, Paul McAllister. Although Paul already knew Devon and Isabella well, he wanted to meet with them at the same time to see how they handled the pressure of being interviewed in front of each other.

After waiting for what seemed like an eternity, Devon and Isabella looked up simultaneously as Paul opened the door to his office.

"Isabella. Devon. Good to see you. Come on in," said Paul.

Devon and Isabella entered Paul's office and took the chairs ready for them at the front of his desk.

Paul broke the silence by saying, "Well, you both know why you are here, so there's no need to waste time. I already know your resumes backwards and forwards, and I've gathered as much information as possible from those who know you best, so now it comes down to hearing it, 'straight from the horses' mouths. I'm going to ask you both one question only, and it's the same question for both of you. Let me flip a coin to see who will respond first." He flipped the coin. "Devon, you're up."

Devon sat up with confidence, eyeing Paul.

Paul began. "To function effectively in an executive position requires strong leadership skills. Both of you have gained valuable experience as managers of your respective divisions, making decisions that have resulted in strong performances from those divisions. But you have also, as managers, followed directives that this corporate office has handed down. As an executive, this will change. You will no longer take directives—you will give them. In short, you will be responsible for guiding the future of this company, and its success will depend greatly on you. So my question to you both is: How do you plan to succeed as a leader if you are offered this position?"

"Well Paul," responded Devon, "That is an excellent question. I believe that, to be a successful leader, one must be able to exert influence. When you get down to it, that is what leadership is all about—the ability to influence others. I have demonstrated that I have this ability since I joined the ranks of management." Devon paused, collecting his thoughts. "It is my opinion that leadership boils down to what actions you take with your employees. For me, leadership is all about rewarding and punishing appropriately. I try to make my employees' jobs less complicated by stating exactly what they need to do, assigning particular tasks, setting appropriate goals, and ensuring that my subordinates have the resources they need."

Paul listened carefully as Devon continued. "Basically, I am an organizer. When employees accomplish a given task or goal, I reward them appropriately for their work. When employees fail to accomplish an assignment, an appropriate response from me is needed. If it is clear that the employee did not try to accomplish the task, then punishment is necessary, and this punishment could range from a verbal reprimand to termination, depending, of course, on the circumstances. If the employee did not have the necessary skills or resources to complete a task, then my job is to provide those skills and resources. By rewarding and punishing employees based on their performance, I am able not only to influence employee behavior to match the goals of the organization but also to send a clear message as to what I expect."

Devon added, "I also want to note that a strong sense of fairness guides all of my decisions—I reward and punish justly. As a result, my employees are satisfied with their work and perform at high levels. So, I will bring my ability to influence behavior with me if I am offered this position, and in doing so will be able to shape the future of our company."

"Thank you Devon," responded Paul. "Isabella, how would you answer this question?"

"Well Paul," said Isabella, "I think you'll find that my perspective on leadership is different from Devon's. Although I certainly agree with Devon that giving clear guidance to employees, setting appropriate goals, and rewarding employees for accomplishing tasks is a fundamental leadership quality, I believe that it takes more than that to be a successful leader. You see, I do not believe that just anyone can be a leader. To be a leader requires a certain 'something' that not all people possess."

"And you believe that you possess that certain something?" interrupted Paul.

Isabella grinned. "I think you'll find that my record suggests that I do, in fact. You see, successful leadership is about motivating people beyond the formal requirements of their jobs. It is not enough in today's global economy to simply ensure that employees are completing their tasks. To survive, and moreover, grow, leaders must challenge employees to look ahead, to contribute ideas, and to make sacrifices for the good of the company. My job as a leader of this company is to create a vision of where we will be 5, 10, and 15 years from now. I see us creating new technologies, as well as merging existing technologies, to give our company the competitive advantage it needs to sustain growth in the long term. By sharing this vision with my employees, we will all be able to pursue the same goals."

Isabella continued, "I inspire my subordinates to see the company as their own, rather than as a means to a paycheck. I consider employee input and the different needs of each worker, and I challenge each and every one of them to think outside the box and develop innovative solutions to the problems facing us. The end result is, in my opinion, a highly motivated workforce with a common goal—to make sure our company is the industry leader."

Paul nodded, thinking about both answers. He had scrutinized each person's record carefully, and both were qualified for the job. However, the two candidates differed in important ways. Devon had built a strong reputation for being a traditional, straightforward leader, motivating his employees well, setting appropriate goals, and ensuring that employees accomplished tasks on time—even ahead of schedule. However, Devon was not known for developing the most creative solutions, and he lacked the vision that Paul knew was an important competency to have as an executive.

Isabella, in contrast, had built a reputation as being a visionary leader. Though her ideas were a bit unconventional at times, in many cases they were directly responsible for getting the company out of a jam. In addition, her magnetic personality made her a favorite among employees. However, Isabella often revealed a somewhat egotistical personality, and Paul was unsure whether this egoism would be amplified if she were in a more authoritative position.

Paul had to make a tough decision. He thought about his company's future. Things were relatively stable now, and business was good, but he knew that stability was not always certain.

"I would like to thank you both for coming today. You're making this a tough decision for me," said Paul. "I need to think about this a bit more, but I'll be getting back to you soon." He paused, then added, "You'll have my answer tomorrow morning."

Questions for Discussion

1. Using terms from the text, how would you describe Devon's leadership style? How would you describe Isabella's leadership style?

2. Whose leadership style do you believe would be more effective, Isabella's or Devon's? Why? What, if any, situational factors might their effectiveness depend on?

3. If you were Paul, who would you hire and why?

4. What are some potential downsides to each candidate's leadership style?

5. Whose employees do you think are likely to be more motivated, Devon's or Isabella's? Whose employees are likely to have higher job satisfaction, trust in leadership, and organizational commitment? Why?

6. Based on their leadership styles, in what type of organizational structure would Devon be most effective? What about Isabella? Why?

Illustration Credits

Indexes

Organization Index

Glindex A COMBINED GLOSSARY/SUBJECT INDEX

SINGLE PC LICENSE AGREEMENT AND LIMITED WARRANTY

READ THIS LICENSE CAREFULLY BEFORE USING THIS PACKAGE. BY USING THIS PACKAGE, YOU ARE AGREEING TO THE TERMS AND CONDITIONS OF THIS LICENSE. IF YOU DO NOT AGREE, DO NOT USE THE PACKAGE. PROMPTLY RETURN THE UNUSED PACKAGE AND ALL ACCOMPANYING ITEMS TO THE PLACE YOU OBTAINED THEM. *THESE TERMS APPLY TO ALL LICENSED SOFTWARE ON THE DISK EXCEPT THAT THE TERMS FOR USE OF ANY SHAREWARE OR FREEWARE ON THE DISKETTES ARE AS SET FORTH IN THE ELECTRONIC LICENSE LOCATED ON THE DISK:*

1.   **GRANT OF LICENSE and OWNERSHIP:**   The enclosed computer programs <<and data>> ("Software") are licensed, not sold, to you by Pearson Education, Inc. publishing as Prentice Hall, Inc. ("We" or the "Company") and in consideration of your purchase or adoption of the accompanying Company textbooks and/or other materials, and your agreement to these terms. We reserve any rights not granted to you. You own only the disk(s) but we and/or our licensors own the Software itself.   This license allows you to use and display your copy of the Software on a single computer (i.e., with a single CPU) at a single location for academic use only, so long as you comply with the terms of this Agreement. You may make one copy for back up, or transfer your copy to another CPU, provided that the Software is usable on only one computer.

2.   **RESTRICTIONS:**   You may not transfer or distribute the Software or documentation to anyone else. Except for backup, you may not copy the documentation or the Software. You may not network the Software or otherwise use it on more than one computer or computer terminal at the same time. You may not reverse engineer, disassemble, decompile, modify, adapt, translate, or create derivative works based on the Software or the Documentation. You may be held legally responsible for any copying or copyright infringement that is caused by your failure to abide by the terms of these restrictions.

3.   **TERMINATION:**   This license is effective until terminated. This license will terminate automatically without notice from the Company if you fail to comply with any provisions or limitations of this license. Upon termination, you shall destroy the Documentation and all copies of the Software. All provisions of this Agreement as to limitation and disclaimer of warranties, limitation of liability, remedies or damages, and our ownership rights shall survive termination.

4.   **LIMITED WARRANTY AND DISCLAIMER OF WARRANTY:**   Company warrants that for a period of 60 days from the date you purchase this SOFTWARE (or purchase or adopt the accompanying textbook), the Software, when properly installed and used in accordance with the Documentation, will operate in substantial conformity with the description of the Software set forth in the Documentation, and that for a period of 30 days the disk(s) on which the Software is delivered shall be free from defects in materials and workmanship under normal use. The Company does not warrant that the Software will meet your requirements or that the operation of the Software will be uninterrupted or error-free. Your only remedy and the Company's only obligation under these limited warranties is, at the Company's option, return of the disk for a refund of any amounts paid for it by you or replacement of the disk. THIS LIMITED WARRANTY IS THE ONLY WARRANTY PROVIDED BY THE COMPANY AND ITS LICENSORS, AND THE COMPANY AND ITS LICENSORS DISCLAIM ALL OTHER WARRANTIES, EXPRESS OR IMPLIED, INCLUDING WITHOUT LIMITATION, THE IMPLIED WARRANTIES OF MERCHANTABILITY AND FITNESS FOR A PARTICULAR PURPOSE. THE COMPANY DOES NOT WARRANT, GUARANTEE OR MAKE ANY REPRESENTATION REGARDING THE ACCURACY, RELIABILITY, CURRENTNESS, USE, OR RESULTS OF USE, OF THE SOFTWARE.

5.   **LIMITATION OF REMEDIES AND DAMAGES:**   IN NO EVENT, SHALL THE COMPANY OR ITS EMPLOYEES, AGENTS, LICENSORS, OR CONTRACTORS BE LIABLE FOR ANY INCIDENTAL, INDIRECT, SPECIAL, OR CONSEQUENTIAL DAMAGES ARISING OUT OF OR IN CONNECTION WITH THIS LICENSE OR THE SOFTWARE, INCLUDING FOR LOSS OF USE, LOSS OF DATA, LOSS OF INCOME OR PROFIT, OR OTHER LOSSES, SUSTAINED AS A RESULT OF INJURY TO ANY PERSON, OR LOSS OF OR DAMAGE TO PROPERTY, OR CLAIMS OF THIRD PARTIES, EVEN IF THE COMPANY OR AN AUTHORIZED REPRESENTATIVE OF THE COMPANY HAS BEEN ADVISED OF THE POSSIBILITY OF SUCH DAMAGES. IN NO EVENT SHALL THE LIABILITY OF THE COMPANY FOR DAMAGES WITH RESPECT TO THE SOFTWARE EXCEED THE AMOUNTS ACTUALLY PAID BY YOU, IF ANY, FOR THE SOFTWARE OR THE ACCOMPANYING TEXTBOOK. BECAUSE SOME JURISDICTIONS DO NOT ALLOW THE LIMITATION OF LIABILITY IN CERTAIN CIRCUMSTANCES, THE ABOVE LIMITATIONS MAY NOT ALWAYS APPLY TO YOU.

6.   **GENERAL:**   THIS AGREEMENT SHALL BE CONSTRUED IN ACCORDANCE WITH THE LAWS OF THE UNITED STATES OF AMERICA AND THE STATE OF NEW YORK, APPLICABLE TO CONTRACTS MADE IN NEW YORK, AND SHALL BENEFIT THE COMPANY, ITS AFFILIATES AND ASSIGNEES. THIS AGREEMENT IS THE COMPLETE AND EXCLUSIVE STATEMENT OF THE AGREEMENT BETWEEN YOU AND THE COMPANY AND SUPERSEDES ALL PROPOSALS OR PRIOR AGREEMENTS, ORAL, OR WRITTEN, AND ANY OTHER COMMUNICATIONS BETWEEN YOU AND THE COMPANY OR ANY REPRESENTATIVE OF THE COMPANY RELATING TO THE SUBJECT MATTER OF THIS AGREEMENT. If you are a U.S. Government user, this Software is licensed with "restricted rights" as set forth in subparagraphs (a)-(d) of the Commercial Computer-Restricted Rights clause at FAR 52.227-19 or in subparagraphs (c)(1)(ii) of the Rights in Technical Data and Computer Software clause at DFARS 252.227-7013, and similar clauses, as applicable.

Should you have any questions concerning this agreement or if you wish to contact the Company for any reason, please contact: Pearson Product Support at http://247.prenhall.com or by calling Pearson Customer Service at 1-800-282-0693.